ESSENTIAL READINGS IN

WORLD
POLITICS

5TH EDITION

THE NORTON SERIES IN WORLD POLITICS
Jack L. Snyder, General Editor

Essentials of International Relations, Sixth Edition
Karen A. Mingst and Ivan M. Arreguín-Toft

From Voting to Violence: Democratization and Nationalist Conflict
Jack L. Snyder

Prosperity and Violence: The Political Economy of Development
Robert H. Bates

Triangulating Peace: Democracy, Interdependence, and International Organizations
Bruce Russett and John Oneal

The Tragedy of Great Power Politics
John J. Mearsheimer

The Justice Cascade: How Human Rights Prosecutions Are Changing World Politics
Kathryn Sikkink

Lenses of Analysis (website)
Richard Harknett

ESSENTIAL READINGS IN

WORLD POLITICS

5TH EDITION

Karen A. Mingst and Jack L. Snyder

W. W. NORTON & COMPANY

New York · London

W. W. Norton & Company has been independent since its founding in 1923, when William Warder Norton and Mary D. Herter Norton first published lectures delivered at the People's Institute, the adult education division of New York City's Cooper Union. The firm soon expanded its program beyond the Institute, publishing books by celebrated academics from America and abroad. By midcentury, the two major pillars of Norton's publishing program—trade books and college texts—were firmly established. In the 1950s, the Norton family transferred control of the company to its employees, and today—with a staff of four hundred and a comparable number of trade, college, and professional titles published each year—W. W. Norton & Company stands as the largest and oldest publishing house owned wholly by its employees.

The text of this book is composed in 10.5/13 Adobe Garamond Pro
with the display set in Neutraface 2 Text.
Book design by Guenet Abraham.

Composition and project management by the Westchester Book Group
Project supervisor: Lyndee Stalter

Manufacturing by Courier—Westford, MA
Editor: Lisa Camner McKay
Associate Director of Production, College: Benjamin Reynolds
Associate Editor: Jake Schindel
Editorial Assistant: Sarah Wolf

ISBN 13: 978-0-393-92196-0

W. W. Norton & Company, Inc., 500 Fifth Avenue, New York, N.Y. 10110-0017
www.wwnorton.com

W. W. Norton & Company Ltd., Castle House, 75/76 Wells Street, London W1T 3QT

1 2 3 4 5 6 7 8 9 0

CONTENTS

4. THE INTERNATIONAL SYSTEM 98

5. THE STATE 173

PREFACE

This reader is a quintessential collaborative effort between the two co-editors. For each of the editions, the co-editors suggested articles for inclusion, traced the sources, and rejected or accepted them, defending choices to skeptical colleagues. This interaction was completed in a flurry of emails and conversations. The final product reflects the fact that while the co-editors are both international relations scholars, they read very different literatures. This book represents a product of that collaborative process and is all the better for the differences.

The articles have been selected to meet several criteria. First, the collection is designed to augment and amplify the core text, *Essentials of International Relations,* Sixth Edition, by Karen Mingst and Ivan Arreguín-Toft. The chapters in this book follow those in the text. Second, the selections are purposefully eclectic; that is, key theoretical articles are paired with contemporary pieces found in the literature. When possible, articles have been chosen to reflect diverse theoretical perspectives and policy viewpoints. Finally, the articles are intended to be both readable and engaging to undergraduates. The co-editors struggled to maintain the integrity of the challenging pieces while making them accessible to undergraduates at a variety of colleges and universities.

Special thanks go to those individuals who provided reviews of this book and offered suggestions and reflections based on teaching experience. Our product benefited greatly from these evaluations, although had we included all the suggestions, the book would have been thousands of pages! Jake Schindel, associate editor at W. W. Norton, guided part of the process, compiling thorough evaluations from users of earlier editions and providing suggestions. Lisa Camner McKay has kept us "on task" and offered excellent suggestions as the book took final shape. Their professionalism and understanding made this process much more rewarding. We also thank W. W. Norton's copyediting and production staff for their careful work on this book.

GUIDE TO THIS READER

Many of the selections included here are reprinted in their entirety. A number have been excerpted from longer works. A * * * indicates that word(s) or sentence(s) are omitted. A ■ ■ ■ indicates that paragraph(s) or section(s) are omitted. Brackets indicate text added by the editors for purposes of clarification. Complete bibliographic citations are included at the bottom of the first page of each selection. Readers who desire to delve deeper into the source material are encouraged to pursue these citations as well as those cited in the readings.

1 APPROACHES TO INTERNATIONAL RELATIONS

In *Essentials of International Relations*, Sixth Edition, Karen A. Mingst and Ivan M. Arreguín-Toft introduce theories and approaches used to study international relations. The readings in this section of *Essential Readings in World Politics* complement that introduction. Jack Snyder provides an overview of rival critical theories and suggests how theories guide decision makers at times.

Both historical analysis and philosophical discourse contribute to the study of international relations. In his history of the Peloponnesian War, Thucydides (460 BCE–c. 395 BCE) presents a classic realist/idealist dilemma in the Melian dialogue. The leaders of Melos ponder the fate of the island, deciding whether to fight their antagonists, the Athenians, or to rely on the gods and the enemy of Athens, the Lacedaemonians (also known as Spartans), for their safety.

Jack Snyder

ONE WORLD, RIVAL THEORIES

The U.S. government has endured several painful rounds of scrutiny as it tries to figure out what went wrong on Sept. 11, 2001. The intelligence community faces radical restructuring; the military has made a sharp pivot to face a new enemy; and a vast new federal agency has blossomed to coordinate homeland security. But did September 11 signal a failure of theory on par with the failures of intelligence and policy? Familiar theories about how the world works still dominate academic debate. Instead of radical change, academia has adjusted existing theories to meet new realities. Has this approach succeeded? Does international relations theory still have something to tell policymakers?

Six years ago, political scientist Stephen M. Walt published a much-cited survey of the field in these pages ("One World, Many Theories," Spring 1998). He sketched out three dominant approaches: realism, liberalism, and an updated form of idealism called "constructivism." Walt argued that these theories shape both public discourse and policy analysis. Realism focuses on the shifting distribution of power among states. Liberalism highlights the rising number of democracies and the turbulence of democratic transitions. Idealism illuminates the changing norms of sovereignty, human rights, and international justice, as well as the increased potency of religious ideas in politics.

The influence of these intellectual constructs extends far beyond university classrooms and tenure committees. Policymakers and public commentators invoke elements of all these theories when articulating solutions to global security dilemmas.

From *Foreign Policy* (Nov./Dec. 2004): 53–62.

President George W. Bush promises to fight terror by spreading liberal democracy to the Middle East and claims that skeptics "who call themselves 'realists' . . . have lost contact with a fundamental reality" that "America is always more secure when freedom is on the march." Striking a more eclectic tone, National Security Advisor Condoleezza Rice, a former Stanford University political science professor, explains that the new Bush doctrine is an amalgam of pragmatic realism and Wilsonian liberal theory. During the recent presidential campaign, Sen. John Kerry sounded remarkably similar: "Our foreign policy has achieved greatness," he said, "only when it has combined realism and idealism."

International relations theory also shapes and informs the thinking of the public intellectuals who translate and disseminate academic ideas. During the summer of 2004, for example, two influential framers of neoconservative thought, columnist Charles Krauthammer and political scientist Francis Fukuyama, collided over the implications of these conceptual paradigms for U.S. policy in Iraq. Backing the Bush administration's Middle East policy, Krauthammer argued for an assertive amalgam of liberalism and realism, which he called "democratic realism." Fukuyama claimed that Krauthammer's faith in the use of force and the feasibility of democratic change in Iraq blinds him to the war's lack of legitimacy, a failing that "hurts both the realist part of our agenda, by diminishing our actual power, and the idealist portion of it, by undercutting our appeal as the embodiment of certain ideas and values."

Indeed, when realism, liberalism, and idealism enter the policymaking arena and public debate,

Figure 1.1. From Theory to Practice

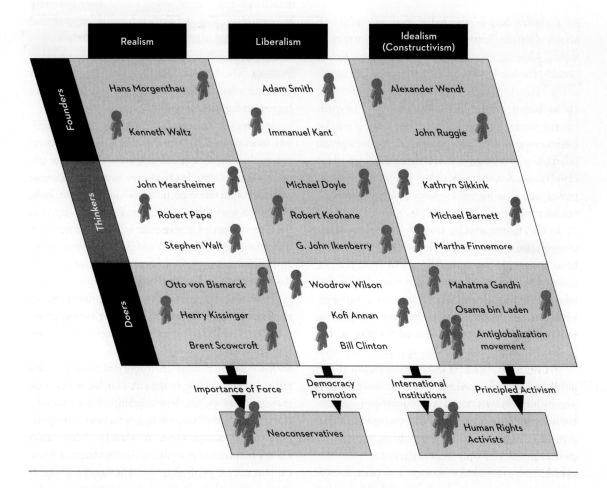

they can sometimes become intellectual window dressing for simplistic worldviews. Properly understood, however, their policy implications are subtle and multifaceted. Realism instills a pragmatic appreciation of the role of power but also warns that states will suffer if they overreach. Liberalism highlights the cooperative potential of mature democracies, especially when working together through effective institutions, but it also notes democracies' tendency to crusade against tyrannies and the propensity of emerging democracies to collapse into violent ethnic turmoil.

Idealism stresses that a consensus on values must underpin any stable political order, yet it also recognizes that forging such a consensus often requires an ideological struggle with the potential for conflict.

Each theory offers a filter for looking at a complicated picture. As such, they help explain the assumptions behind political rhetoric about foreign policy. Even more important, the theories act as a powerful check on each other. Deployed effectively, they reveal the weaknesses in arguments that can lead to misguided policies.

Is Realism Still Realistic?

At realism's core is the belief that international affairs is a struggle for power among self-interested states. Although some of realism's leading lights, notably the late University of Chicago political scientist Hans J. Morgenthau, are deeply pessimistic about human nature, it is not a theory of despair. Clearsighted states can mitigate the causes of war by finding ways to reduce the danger they pose to each other. Nor is realism necessarily amoral; its advocates emphasize that a ruthless pragmatism about power can actually yield a more peaceful world, if not an ideal one.

In liberal democracies, realism is the theory that everyone loves to hate. Developed largely by European émigrés at the end of World War II, realism claimed to be an antidote to the naive belief that international institutions and law alone can preserve peace, a misconception that this new generation of scholars believed had paved the way to war. In recent decades, the realist approach has been most fully articulated by U.S. theorists, but it still has broad appeal outside the United States as well. The influential writer and editor Josef Joffe articulately comments on Germany's strong realist traditions. (Mindful of the overwhelming importance of U.S. power to Europe's development, Joffe once called the United States "Europe's pacifier.") China's current foreign policy is grounded in realist ideas that date back millennia. As China modernizes its economy and enters international institutions such as the World Trade Organization, it behaves in a way that realists understand well: developing its military slowly but surely as its economic power grows, and avoiding a confrontation with superior U.S. forces.

Realism gets some things right about the post-9/11 world. The continued centrality of military strength and the persistence of conflict, even in this age of global economic interdependence, does not surprise realists. The theory's most obvious success is its ability to explain the United States' forceful military response to the September 11 terrorist attacks. When a state grows vastly more powerful than any opponent, realists expect that it will eventually use that power to expand its sphere of domination, whether for security, wealth, or other motives. The United States employed its military power in what some deemed an imperial fashion in large part because it could.

It is harder for the normally state-centric realists to explain why the world's only superpower announced a war against al Qaeda, a nonstate terrorist organization. How can realist theory account for the importance of powerful and violent individuals in a world of states? Realists point out that the central battles in the "war on terror" have been fought against two states (Afghanistan and Iraq), and that states, not the United Nations or Human Rights Watch, have led the fight against terrorism.

Even if realists acknowledge the importance of nonstate actors as a challenge to their assumptions, the theory still has important things to say about the behavior and motivations of these groups. The realist scholar Robert A. Pape, for example, has argued that suicide terrorism can be a rational, realistic strategy for the leadership of national liberation movements seeking to expel democratic powers that occupy their homelands. Other scholars apply standard theories of conflict in anarchy to explain ethnic conflict in collapsed states. Insights from political realism—a profound and wide-ranging intellectual tradition rooted in the enduring philosophy of Thucydides, Niccolò Machiavelli, and Thomas Hobbes—are hardly rendered obsolete because some nonstate groups are now able to resort to violence.

Post-9/11 developments seem to undercut one of realism's core concepts: the balance of power. Standard realist doctrine predicts that weaker states will ally to protect themselves from stronger ones and thereby form and reform a balance of power. So, when Germany unified in the late 19th century and became Europe's leading military and industrial power, Russia and France (and later,

Britain) soon aligned to counter its power. Yet no combination of states or other powers can challenge the United States militarily, and no balancing coalition is imminent. Realists are scrambling to find a way to fill this hole in the center of their theory. Some theorists speculate that the United States' geographic distance and its relatively benign intentions have tempered the balancing instinct. Second-tier powers tend to worry more about their immediate neighbors and even see the United States as a helpful source of stability in regions such as East Asia. Other scholars insist that armed resistance by U.S. foes in Iraq, Afghanistan, and elsewhere, and foot-dragging by its formal allies actually constitute the beginnings of balancing against U.S. hegemony. The United States' strained relations with Europe offer ambiguous evidence: French and German opposition to recent U.S. policies could be seen as classic balancing, but they do not resist U.S. dominance militarily. Instead, these states have tried to undermine U.S. moral legitimacy and constrain the superpower in a web of multilateral institutions and treaty regimes—not what standard realist theory predicts.

These conceptual difficulties notwithstanding, realism is alive, well, and creatively reassessing how its root principles relate to the post-9/11 world. Despite changing configurations of power, realists remain steadfast in stressing that policy must be based on positions of real strength, not on either empty bravado or hopeful illusions about a world without conflict. In the run-up to the recent Iraq war, several prominent realists signed a public letter criticizing what they perceived as an exercise in American hubris. And in the continuing aftermath of that war, many prominent thinkers called for a return to realism. A group of scholars and public intellectuals (myself included) even formed the Coalition for a Realistic Foreign Policy, which calls for a more modest and prudent approach. Its statement of principles argues that "the move toward empire must be halted immediately." The coalition, though politically diverse, is largely inspired by realist theory. Its membership of seemingly odd bedfellows—including former Democratic Sen. Gary Hart and Scott McConnell, the executive editor of the *American Conservative* magazine—illustrates the power of international relations theory to cut through often ephemeral political labels and carry debate to the underlying assumptions.

The Divided House of Liberalism

The liberal school of international relations theory, whose most famous proponents were German philosopher Immanuel Kant and U.S. President Woodrow Wilson, contends that realism has a stunted vision that cannot account for progress in relations between nations. Liberals foresee a slow but inexorable journey away from the anarchic world the realists envision, as trade and finance forge ties between nations, and democratic norms spread. Because elected leaders are accountable to the people (who bear the burdens of war), liberals expect that democracies will not attack each other and will regard each other's regimes as legitimate and nonthreatening. Many liberals also believe that the rule of law and transparency of democratic processes make it easier to sustain international cooperation, especially when these practices are enshrined in multilateral institutions.

Liberalism has such a powerful presence that the entire U.S. political spectrum, from neoconservatives to human rights advocates, assumes it as largely self-evident. Outside the United States, as well, the liberal view that only elected governments are legitimate and politically reliable has taken hold. So it is no surprise that liberal themes are constantly invoked as a response to today's security dilemmas. But the last several years have also produced a fierce tug-of-war between disparate strains of liberal thought. Supporters and critics of the Bush administration, in particular, have emphasized very different elements of the liberal canon.

For its part, the Bush administration highlights democracy promotion while largely turning its back on the international institutions that most liberal theorists champion. The U.S. National Security Strategy of September 2002, famous for its support of preventive war, also dwells on the need to promote democracy as a means of fighting terrorism and promoting peace. The Millennium Challenge program allocates part of U.S. foreign aid according to how well countries improve their performance on several measures of democratization and the rule of law. The White House's steadfast support for promoting democracy in the Middle East—even with turmoil in Iraq and rising anti-Americanism in the Arab world—demonstrates liberalism's emotional and rhetorical power.

In many respects, liberalism's claim to be a wise policy guide has plenty of hard data behind it. During the last two decades, the proposition that democratic institutions and values help states cooperate with each other is among the most intensively studied in all of international relations, and it has held up reasonably well. Indeed, the belief that democracies never fight wars against each other is the closest thing we have to an iron law in social science.

But the theory has some very important corollaries, which the Bush administration glosses over as it draws upon the democracy-promotion element of liberal thought. Columbia University political scientist Michael W. Doyle's articles on democratic peace warned that, though democracies never fight each other, they are prone to launch messianic struggles against warlike authoritarian regimes to "make the world safe for democracy." It was precisely American democracy's tendency to oscillate between self-righteous crusading and jaded isolationism that prompted early Cold War realists' call for a more calculated, prudent foreign policy.

Countries transitioning to democracy, with weak political institutions, are more likely than other states to get into international and civil wars. In the last 15 years, wars or large-scale civil violence followed experiments with mass electoral democracy in countries including Armenia, Burundi, Ethiopia, Indonesia, Russia, and the former Yugoslavia. In part, this violence is caused by ethnic groups' competing demands for national self-determination, often a problem in new, multiethnic democracies. More fundamental, emerging democracies often have nascent political institutions that cannot channel popular demands in constructive directions or credibly enforce compromises among rival groups. In this setting, democratic accountability works imperfectly, and nationalist politicians can hijack public debate. The violence that is vexing the experiment with democracy in Iraq is just the latest chapter in a turbulent story that began with the French Revolution.

Contemporary liberal theory also points out that the rising democratic tide creates the presumption that all nations ought to enjoy the benefits of self-determination. Those left out may undertake violent campaigns to secure democratic rights. Some of these movements direct their struggles against democratic or semidemocratic states that they consider occupying powers—such as in Algeria in the 1950s, or Chechnya, Palestine, and the Tamil region of Sri Lanka today. Violence may also be directed at democratic supporters of oppressive regimes, much like the U.S. backing of the governments of Saudi Arabia and Egypt. Democratic regimes make attractive targets for terrorist violence by national liberation movements precisely because they are accountable to a cost-conscious electorate.

Nor is it clear to contemporary liberal scholars that nascent democracy and economic liberalism can always cohabitate. Free trade and the multifaceted globalization that advanced democracies promote often buffet transitional societies. World markets' penetration of societies that run on patronage and protectionism can disrupt social relations and spur strife between potential winners and

Figure 1.2. The Leading Brands

Theories:	Realism	Liberalism	Idealism (Constructivism)
Core Beliefs	Self-interested states compete for power and security	Spread of democracy, global economic ties, and international organizations will strengthen peace	International politics is shaped by persuasive ideas, collective values, culture, and social identities
Key Actors in International Relations	States, which behave similarly regardless of their type of government	States, international institutions, and commercial interests	Promoters of new ideas, transnational activist networks, and nongovernmental organizations
Main Instruments	Military power and state diplomacy	International institutions and global commerce	Ideas and values
Theory's Intellectual Blind Spots	Doesn't account for progress and change in international relations or understanding that legitimacy can be a source of military power	Fails to understand that democratic regimes survive only if they safeguard military power and security; some liberals forget that transitions to democracy are sometimes violent	Does not explain which power structures and social conditions allow for changes in values
What the Theory Explains about the Post-9/11 World	Why the United States responded aggressively to terrorist attacks; the inability of international institutions to restrain military superiority	Why spreading democracy has become such an integral part of current U.S. international security strategy	The increasing role of polemics about values; the importance of transnational political networks (whether terrorists or human rights advocates)
What the Theory Fails to Explain about the Post-9/11 World	The failure of smaller powers to militarily balance the United States; the importance of non-state actors such as al Qaeda; the intense U.S. focus on democratization	Why the United States has failed to work with other democracies through international organizations	Why human rights abuses continue, despite intense activism for humanitarian norms and efforts for international justice

losers. In other cases, universal free trade can make separatism look attractive, as small regions such as Aceh in Indonesia can lay claim to lucrative natural resources. So far, the trade-fueled boom in China has created incentives for improved relations with the advanced democracies, but it has also set the stage for a possible showdown between the relatively wealthy coastal entrepreneurs and the still impoverished rural masses.

While aggressively advocating the virtues of democracy, the Bush administration has shown little patience for these complexities in liberal thought—or for liberalism's emphasis on the importance of international institutions. Far from trying to assure other powers that the United States would adhere to a constitutional order, Bush "unsigned" the International Criminal Court statute, rejected the Kyoto environmental agreement, dictated take-it-or-leave-it arms control changes to Russia, and invaded Iraq despite opposition at the United Nations and among close allies.

Recent liberal theory offers a thoughtful challenge to the administration's policy choices. Shortly before September 11, political scientist G. John Ikenberry studied attempts to establish international order by the victors of hegemonic struggles in 1815, 1919, 1945, and 1989. He argued that even the most powerful victor needed to gain the willing cooperation of the vanquished and other weak states by offering a mutually attractive bargain, codified in an international constitutional order. Democratic victors, he found, have the best chance of creating a working constitutional order, such as the Bretton Woods system after World War II, because their transparency and legalism make their promises credible.

Does the Bush administration's resistance to institution building refute Ikenberry's version of liberal theory? Some realists say it does, and that recent events demonstrate that international institutions cannot constrain a hegemonic power if its preferences change. But international institutions can nonetheless help coordinate outcomes that are in the long-term mutual interest of both the hegemon and the weaker states. Ikenberry did not contend that hegemonic democracies are immune from mistakes. States can act in defiance of the incentives established by their position in the international system, but they will suffer the consequences and probably learn to correct course. In response to Bush's unilateralist stance, Ikenberry wrote that the incentives for the United States to take the lead in establishing a multilateral constitutional order remain powerful. Sooner or later, the pendulum will swing back.

Idealism's New Clothing

Idealism, the belief that foreign policy is and should be guided by ethical and legal standards, also has a long pedigree. Before World War II forced the United States to acknowledge a less pristine reality, Secretary of State Henry Stimson denigrated espionage on the grounds that "gentlemen do not read each other's mail." During the Cold War, such naive idealism acquired a bad name in the Kissingerian corridors of power and among hardheaded academics. Recently, a new version of idealism—called

constructivism by its scholarly adherents—returned to a prominent place in debates on international relations theory. Constructivism, which holds that social reality is created through debate about values, often echoes the themes that human rights and international justice activists sound. Recent events seem to vindicate the theory's resurgence; a theory that emphasizes the role of ideologies, identities, persuasion, and transnational networks is highly relevant to understanding the post-9/11 world.

The most prominent voices in the development of constructivist theory have been American, but Europe's role is significant. European philosophical currents helped establish constructivist theory, and the *European Journal of International Relations* is one of the principal outlets for constructivist work. Perhaps most important, Europe's increasingly legalistic approach to international relations, reflected in the process of forming the European Union out of a collection of sovereign states, provides fertile soil for idealist and constructivist conceptions of international politics.

Whereas realists dwell on the balance of power and liberals on the power of international trade and democracy, constructivists believe that debates about ideas are the fundamental building blocks of international life. Individuals and groups become powerful if they can convince others to adopt their ideas. People's understanding of their interests depends on the ideas they hold. Constructivists find absurd the idea of some identifiable and immutable "national interest," which some realists cherish. Especially in liberal societies, there is overlap between constructivist and liberal approaches, but the two are distinct. Constructivists contend that their theory is deeper than realism and liberalism because it explains the origins of the forces that drive those competing theories.

For constructivists, international change results from the work of intellectual entrepreneurs who proselytize new ideas and "name and shame" actors whose behavior deviates from accepted standards. Consequently, constructivists often study the role of transnational activist networks—such as Human Rights Watch or the International Campaign to Ban Landmines—in promoting change. Such groups typically uncover and publicize information about violations of legal or moral standards at least rhetorically supported by powerful democracies, including "disappearances" during the Argentine military's rule in the late 1970s, concentration camps in Bosnia, and the huge number of civilian deaths from land mines. This publicity is then used to press governments to adopt specific remedies, such as the establishment of a war crimes tribunal or the adoption of a landmine treaty. These movements often make pragmatic arguments as well as idealistic ones, but their distinctive power comes from the ability to highlight deviations from deeply held norms of appropriate behavior.

Progressive causes receive the most attention from constructivist scholars, but the theory also helps explain the dynamics of illiberal transnational forces, such as Arab nationalism or Islamist extremism. Professor Michael N. Barnett's 1998 book *Dialogues in Arab Politics: Negotiations in Regional Order* examines how the divergence between state borders and transnational Arab political identities requires vulnerable leaders to contend for legitimacy with radicals throughout the Arab world—a dynamic that often holds moderates hostage to opportunists who take extreme stances.

Constructivist thought can also yield broader insights about the ideas and values in the current international order. In his 2001 book, *Revolutions in Sovereignty: How Ideas Shaped Modern International Relations*, political scientist Daniel Philpott demonstrates how the religious ideas of the Protestant Reformation helped break down the medieval political order and provided a conceptual basis for the modern system of secular sovereign states. After September 11, Philpott focused on the challenge to the secular international order posed by political Islam. "The attacks and the broader resurgence of public religion," he says, ought to lead international relations scholars to "direct far more energy to understanding the impetuses behind movements across the globe that are reorienting purposes and policies." He notes that both liberal human rights movements and radical Islamic movements have transnational structures and principled motivations that challenge the traditional supremacy of self-interested states in international politics. Because constructivists believe that ideas and values helped shape the modern state system, they expect intellectual constructs to be decisive in transforming it—for good or ill.

When it comes to offering advice, however, constructivism points in two seemingly incompatible directions. The insight that political orders arise from shared understanding highlights the need for dialogue across cultures about the appropriate rules of the game. This prescription dovetails with liberalism's emphasis on establishing an agreed international constitutional order. And, yet, the notion of cross-cultural dialogue sits awkwardly with many idealists' view that they already know right and wrong. For these idealists, the essential task is to shame rights abusers and cajole powerful actors into promoting proper values and holding perpetrators accountable to international (generally Western) standards. As with realism and liberalism, constructivism can be many things to many people.

Stumped by Change

None of the three theoretical traditions has a strong ability to explain change—a significant weakness in such turbulent times. Realists failed to predict the end of the Cold War, for example. Even after it happened, they tended to assume that the new system would become multipolar ("back to the future," as the scholar John J. Mearsheimer put it). Likewise, the liberal theory of democratic peace is stronger on what happens after states become democratic than in predicting the timing of democratic transitions, let alone prescribing how to make transitions happen peacefully. Constructivists are good at describing changes in norms and ideas, but they are weak on the material and institutional circumstances necessary to support the emergence of consensus about new values and ideas.

With such uncertain guidance from the theoretical realm, it is no wonder that policymakers, activists, and public commentators fall prey to simplistic or wishful thinking about how to effect change by, say, invading Iraq or setting up an International Criminal Court. In lieu of a good theory of change, the most prudent course is to use the insights of each of the three theoretical traditions as a check on the irrational exuberance of the others. Realists should have to explain whether policies based on calculations of power have sufficient legitimacy to last. Liberals should consider whether nascent democratic institutions can fend off powerful interests that oppose them, or how international institutions can bind a hegemonic power inclined to go its own way. Idealists should be asked about the strategic, institutional, or material conditions in which a set of ideas is likely to take hold.

Theories of international relations claim to explain the way international politics works, but each of the currently prevailing theories falls well short of that goal. One of the principal contributions that international relations theory can make is not predicting the future but providing the vocabulary and conceptual framework to ask hard questions of those who think that changing the world is easy.

Thucydides
MELIAN DIALOGUE

adapted by Suresht Bald

It was the sixteenth year of the Peloponnesian War, but for the last six years the two great feuding empires headed by Athens and Sparta (Lacedaemon) had avoided open hostile action against each other. Ten years into the war they had signed a treaty of peace and friendship; however, this treaty did not dissipate the distrust that existed between them. Each feared the other's hegemonic designs on the Peloponnese and sought to increase its power to thwart the other's ambitions. Without openly attacking the other, each used persuasion, coercion, and subversion to strengthen itself and weaken its rival. This struggle for hegemony by Athens and Sparta was felt most acutely by small, hitherto "independent" states who were now being forced to take sides in the bipolar Greek world of the fifth century B.C. One such state was Melos.

Despite being one of the few island colonies of Sparta, Melos had remained neutral in the struggle between Sparta and Athens. Its neutrality, however, was unacceptable to the Athenians, who, accompanied by overwhelming military and naval power, arrived in Melos to pressure it into submission. After strategically positioning their powerful fleet, the Athenian generals sent envoys to Melos to negotiate the island's surrender.

The commissioners of Melos agreed to meet the envoys in private. They were afraid the Athenians, known for their rhetorical skills, might sway the people if allowed a public forum. The envoys came with an offer that if the Melians submitted

From Thucydides, *Complete Writings: The Peloponnesian War*, trans. Richard Crawley (New York: Modern Library, 1951), adapted by Suresht Bald, Willamette University.

and became part of the Athenian empire, their people and their possessions would not be harmed. The Melians argued that by the law of nations they had the right to remain neutral, and no nation had the right to attack without provocation. Having been a free state for seven hundred years they were not ready to give up that freedom. Thucydides captures the exchange between the Melian commissioners and the Athenian envoys:

MELIANS: . . . All we can reasonably expect from this negotiation is war, if we prove to have right on our side and refuse to submit, and in the contrary case, slavery.

ATHENIANS: . . . We shall not trouble you with specious pretenses—either of how we have a right to our empire because we overthrew the Mede, or are now attacking you because of the wrong that you have done us—and make a long speech that would not be believed; and in return we hope that you, instead of thinking to influence us by saying that you did not join the Lacedaemonians, although their colonists, or that you have done us no wrong, will aim at what is feasible, . . . since you know as well as we do that right, as the world goes, is only in question between equals in power, while the strong do what they can and the weak suffer what they want. (331)

The Melians pointed out that it was in the interest of all states to respect the laws of nations: "you should not destroy what is our common protection, the privilege of being allowed in danger to invoke what is fair and right. . . ." (331) They reminded the Athenians that a day might come when the Athenians themselves would need such protection.

But the Athenians were not persuaded. To them, Melos' submission was in the interest of their empire, and Melos.

MELIANS: And how pray, could it turn out as good for us to serve as for you to rule?
ATHENIANS: Because you would have the advantage of submitting before suffering the worst, and we should gain by not destroying you.
MELIANS: So you would not consent to our being neutral, friends instead of enemies, but allies of neither side.
ATHENIANS: No; for your hostility cannot so much hurt us as your friendship will be an argument to our subjects of our weakness, and your enmity of our power. (332)

When the Melians asked if that was their "idea of equity," the Athenians responded,

> As far as right goes . . . one has as much of it as the other, and if any maintain their independence it is because they are strong, and that if we do not molest them it is because we are afraid. . . . (332)

By subjugating the Melians the Athenians hoped not only to extend their empire but also to improve their image and thus their security. To allow the weaker Melians to remain free, according to the Athenians, would reflect negatively on Athenian power.

Aware of their weak position the Melians hoped that the justice of their cause would gain them the support of the gods, "and what we want in power will be made up by the alliance with the Lacedaemonians, who are bound, if only for very shame, to come to the aid of their kindred."

ATHENIANS: . . . Of the gods we believe, and of men we know, that by a necessary law of their nature they rule wherever they can. And it is not as if we were the first to make this law, or

to act upon it when made: we found it existing before us, and will leave it to exist for ever after us; all we do is to make use of it, knowing that you and everybody else having the same power as we have, would do the same as we do. Thus, as far as the gods are concerned we have no fear and no reason to fear that we shall be at a disadvantage. But . . . your notion about the Lacedaemonians, which leads you to believe that shame will make them help you, here we bless your simplicity but do not envy your folly. The Lacedaemonians . . . are conspicuous in considering what is agreeable honourable, and what is expedient just. . . . Your strongest arguments depend upon hope and the future, and your actual resources are too scanty as compared to those arrayed against you, for you to come out victorious. You will therefore show great blindness of judgment, unless, after allowing us to retire you can find some counsel more prudent than this. (334–36)

The envoys then left the conference, giving the Melians the opportunity to deliberate on the Athenian offer and decide the best course for them to follow.

The Melians decided to stand by the position they had taken at the conference with the Athenian envoys. They refused to submit, placing their faith in the gods and the Lacedaemonians. Though they asked the Athenians to accept their neutrality and leave Melos, the Athenians started preparations for war.

In the war that ensued the Melians were soundly defeated. The Athenians showed no mercy, killing all the adult males and selling the women and children as slaves. Subsequently, they sent out five hundred colonists to settle in Melos, which became an Athenian colony.

■   ■   ■

2 HISTORICAL CONTEXT

Core ideas about international relations, introduced in Chapter 1 and elaborated in Chapter 3 of *Essentials of International Relations*, Sixth Edition, have emerged as responses to historic diplomatic challenges. The three selections in this chapter provide insight into key events and trends that spawned many of the ideas that still shape debates about contemporary international politics.

The post–World War I peace process led to a clear statement of the liberal perspective. U.S. President Woodrow Wilson's "Fourteen Points," in an address to Congress in January 1918, summarizes some of the key ideas of liberal theory. Wilson blames power politics, secret diplomacy, and autocratic leaders for the devastating world war. He suggests that with the spread of democracy and the creation of a "league of nations," aggression would be stopped.

The Cold War provides a historical setting for the realist perspective. George F. Kennan, then director of the State Department's Policy Planning Staff, published his famous "X" article in *Foreign Affairs* in 1947. He assesses Soviet conduct and provides the intellectual justification for Cold War containment policy. Using realist logic, he suggests that counterpressure must be applied to prevent Soviet expansion.

At the end of the Cold War in 1989, Francis Fukuyama published a controversial essay, "The End of History." Twenty-five years later, he reprises the argument of a broad universal consensus for liberal democracy with no rival ideology. But here he worries about the future should there continue to be a decline in the middle class, one of the hallmarks of liberal democracy.

Woodrow Wilson
THE FOURTEEN POINTS

It will be our wish and purpose that the processes of peace, when they are begun, shall be absolutely open and that they shall involve and permit henceforth no secret understandings of any kind. The day of conquest and aggrandizement is gone by; so is also the day of secret covenants entered into in the interest of particular governments and likely at some unlooked-for moment to upset the peace of the world. It is this happy fact, now clear to the view of every public man whose thoughts do not still linger in an age that is dead and gone, which makes it possible for every nation whose purposes are consistent with justice and the peace of the world to avow now or at any other time the objects it has in view.

We entered this war because violations of right had occurred which touched us to the quick and made the life of our own people impossible unless they were corrected and the world secured once and for all against their recurrence. What we demand in this war, therefore, is nothing peculiar to ourselves. It is that the world be made fit and safe to live in; and particularly that it be made safe for every peace-loving nation which, like our own, wishes to live its own life, determine its own institutions, be assured of justice and fair dealing by the other people of the world as against force and selfish aggression. All the peoples of the world are in effect partners in this interest, and for our own part we see very clearly that unless justice be done to others it will not be done to us. The program of the world's peace, therefore, is our program; and that program, the only possible program, as we see it, is this:

From Woodrow Wilson's address to the U.S. Congress, January 8, 1918.

I. Open covenants of peace, openly arrived at, after which there shall be no private international understandings of any kind but diplomacy shall proceed always frankly and in the public view.

II. Absolute freedom of navigation upon the seas, outside territorial waters, alike in peace and in war, except as the seas may be closed in whole or in part by international action for the enforcement of international covenants.

III. The removal, so far as possible, of all economic barriers and the establishment of an equality of trade conditions among all the nations consenting to the peace and associating themselves for its maintenance.

IV. Adequate guarantees given and taken that national armaments will be reduced to the lowest point consistent with domestic safety.

V. A free, open-minded, and absolutely impartial adjustment of all colonial claims, based upon a strict observance of the principle that in determining all such questions of sovereignty the interests of the populations concerned must have equal weight with the equitable claims of the government whose title is to be determined.

VI. The evacuation of all Russian territory and such a settlement of all questions affecting Russia as will secure the best and freest cooperation of the other nations of the world in obtaining for her an unhampered and unembarrassed opportunity for the independent determination of her own political development and national policy and assure her of a sincere welcome into the society of free nations under institutions of her own choosing; and, more than a welcome, assistance also of every kind that she may need and may herself desire. The treatment accorded Russia by her sister nations in the months to come will be the acid test of their good will, of their comprehension of her needs as distinguished from their own interests, and of their intelligent and unselfish sympathy.

VII. Belgium, the whole world will agree, must be evacuated and restored, without any attempt to limit the sovereignty which she enjoys in common with all other free nations. No other single act will serve as this will serve to restore confidence among the nations in the laws which they have themselves set and determined for the government of their relations with one another. Without this healing act the whole structure and validity of international law is forever impaired.

VIII. All French territory should be freed and the invaded portions restored, and the wrong done to France by Prussia in 1871 in the matter of Alsace-Lorraine, which has unsettled the peace of the world for nearly fifty years, should be righted, in order that peace may once more be made secure in the interest of all.

IX. A readjustment of the frontiers of Italy should be effected along clearly recognizable lines of nationality.

X. The peoples of Austria-Hungary, whose place among the nations we wish to see safeguarded and assured, should be accorded the freest opportunity of autonomous development.

XI. Rumania, Serbia, and Montenegro should be evacuated; occupied territories restored; Serbia accorded free and secure access to the sea; and the relations of the several Balkan states to one another determined by friendly counsel along historically established lines of allegiance and nationality; and international guarantees of the political and economic independence and territorial integrity of the several Balkan states should be entered into.

XII. The Turkish portions of the present Ottoman Empire should be assured a secure sovereignty, but the other nationalities which are now under Turkish rule should be assured an undoubted security of life and an absolutely unmolested opportunity of autonomous development, and the Dardanelles should be permanently opened as a free passage to the ships and commerce of all nations under international guarantees.

XIII. An independent Polish state should be erected which should include the territories inhabited by indisputably Polish populations, which should be assured a free and secure access to the sea, and whose political and economic independence and territorial integrity should be guaranteed by international covenant.

XIV. A general association of nations must be formed under specific covenants for the purpose of affording mutual guarantees of political independence and territorial integrity to great and small states alike.

In regard to these essential rectifications of wrong and assertions of right we feel ourselves to be intimate partners of all the governments and peoples associated together against the imperialists. We cannot be separated in interest or divided in purpose. We stand together until the end.

For such arrangements and covenants we are willing to fight and to continue to fight until they are achieved; but only because we wish the right to prevail and desire a just and stable peace such as can be secured only by removing the chief provocations to war, which this program does remove. We have no jealousy of German greatness, and there is nothing in this program that impairs it. We grudge her no achievement or distinction of learning or of pacific enterprise such as have made her record very bright and very enviable. We do not wish to injure her or to block in any way her legitimate influence or power. We do not wish to fight her either with arms or with hostile arrangements of trade if she is willing to associate herself with us and the other peace-loving nations of the world in covenants of justice and law and fair dealing. We wish her only to accept a place of equality among the peoples of the world—the new world in which we now live—instead of a place of mastery.

Neither do we presume to suggest to her any alteration or modification of her institutions. But it is necessary, we must frankly say, and necessary as a preliminary to any intelligent dealings with her on our part, that we should know whom her spokesmen speak for when they speak to us, whether for the Reichstag majority or for the military party and the men whose creed is imperial domination.

We have spoken now, surely, in terms too concrete to admit of any further doubt or question. An evident principle runs through the whole program I have outlined. It is the principle of justice to all peoples and nationalities, and their right to live on equal terms of liberty and safety with one another, whether they be strong or weak. Unless this principle be made its foundation no part of the structure of international justice can stand. The people of the United States could act upon no other principle; and to the vindication of this principle they are ready to devote their lives, their honor, and everything that they possess. The moral climax of this the culminating and final war for human liberty has come, and they are ready to put their own strength, their own highest purpose, their own integrity and devotion to the test.

George F. Kennan ("X")

THE SOURCES OF SOVIET CONDUCT

I

The political personality of Soviet power as we know it today is the product of ideology and circumstances: ideology inherited by the present Soviet leaders from the movement in which they had their political origin, and circumstances of the power which they now have exercised for nearly three decades in Russia. There can be few tasks of psychological analysis more difficult than to try to trace the interaction of these two forces and the relative role of each in the determination of official Soviet conduct. Yet the attempt must be made if that conduct is to be understood and effectively countered.

It is difficult to summarize the set of ideological concepts with which the Soviet leaders came into power. Marxian ideology, in its Russian-Communist projection, has always been in process of subtle evolution. The materials on which it bases itself are extensive and complex. But the outstanding features of Communist thought as it existed in 1916 may perhaps be summarized as follows: (*a*) that the central factor in the life of man, the fact which determines the character of public life and the "physiognomy of society," is the system by which material goods are produced and exchanged; (*b*) that the capitalist system of production is a nefarious one which inevitably leads to the exploitation of the working class by the capital-owning class and is incapable of developing adequately the economic resources of society or of distributing

fairly the material goods produced by human labor; (*c*) that capitalism contains the seeds of its own destruction and must, in view of the inability of the capital-owning class to adjust itself to economic change, result eventually and inescapably in a revolutionary transfer of power to the working class; and (*d*) that imperialism, the final phase of capitalism, leads directly to war and revolution.

■   ■   ■

Now it must be noted that through all the years of preparation for revolution, the attention of these men, as indeed of Marx himself, had been centered less on the future form which Socialism[1] would take than on the necessary overthrow of rival power which, in their view, had to precede the introduction of Socialism. Their views, therefore, on the positive program to be put into effect, once power was attained, were for the most part nebulous, visionary and impractical. Beyond the nationalization of industry and the expropriation of large private capital holdings there was no agreed program. The treatment of the peasantry, which according to the Marxist formulation was not of the proletariat, had always been a vague spot in the pattern of Communist thought; and it remained an object of controversy and vacillation for the first ten years of Communist power.

The circumstances of the immediate post-Revolution period—the existence in Russia of civil war and foreign intervention, together with the obvious fact that the Communists represented only a tiny minority of the Russian people—made

From *Foreign Affairs* 25, no. 4 (July 1947): 566–582.

the establishment of dictatorial power a necessity. The experiment with "war Communism" and the abrupt attempt to eliminate private production and trade had unfortunate economic consequences and caused further bitterness against the new revolutionary regime. While the temporary relaxation of the effort to communize Russia, represented by the New Economic Policy, alleviated some of this economic distress and thereby served its purpose, it also made it evident that the "capitalistic sector of society" was still prepared to profit at once from any relaxation of governmental pressure, and would, if permitted to continue to exist, always constitute a powerful opposing element to the Soviet regime and a serious rival for influence in the country. Somewhat the same situation prevailed with respect to the individual peasant who, in his own small way, was also a private producer.

Lenin, had he lived, might have proved a great enough man to reconcile these conflicting forces to the ultimate benefit of Russian society, though this is questionable. But be that as it may, Stalin, and those whom he led in the struggle for succession to Lenin's position of leadership, were not the men to tolerate rival political forces in the sphere of power which they coveted. Their sense of insecurity was too great. Their particular brand of fanaticism, unmodified by any of the Anglo-Saxon traditions of compromise, was too fierce and too jealous to envisage any permanent sharing of power. From the Russian-Asiatic world out of which they had emerged they carried with them a skepticism as to the possibilities of permanent and peaceful coexistence of rival forces. Easily persuaded of their own doctrinaire "rightness," they insisted on the submission or destruction of all competing power. Outside of the Communist Party, Russian society was to have no rigidity. There were to be no forms of collective human activity or association which would not be dominated by the Party. No other force in Russian society was to be permitted to achieve vitality or integrity. Only the Party was to have structure. All else was to be an amorphous mass.

And within the Party the same principle was to apply. The mass of Party members might go through the motions of election, deliberation, decision and action; but in these motions they were to be animated not by their own individual wills but by the awesome breath of the Party leadership and the overbrooding presence of "the world."

Let it be stressed again that subjectively these men probably did not seek absolutism for its own sake. They doubtless believed—and found it easy to believe—that they alone knew what was good for society and that they would accomplish that good once their power was secure and unchallengeable. But in seeking that security of their own rule they were prepared to recognize no restrictions, either of God or man, on the character of their methods. And until such time as that security might be achieved, they placed far down on their scale of operational priorities the comforts and happiness of the peoples entrusted to their care.

Now the outstanding circumstance concerning the Soviet regime is that down to the present day this process of political consolidation has never been completed and the men in the Kremlin have continued to be predominantly absorbed with the struggle to secure and make absolute the power which they seized in November 1917. They have endeavored to secure it primarily against forces at home, within Soviet society itself. But they have also endeavored to secure it against the outside world. For ideology, as we have seen, taught them that the outside world was hostile and that it was their duty eventually to overthrow the political forces beyond their borders. The powerful hands of Russian history and tradition reached up to sustain them in this feeling. Finally, their own aggressive intransigence with respect to the outside world began to find its own reaction; and they were soon forced, to use another Gibbonesque phrase [from Edward Gibbon, *The Decline and Fall of the Roman Empire*], "to chastise the contumacy" which they themselves had provoked. It is an undeniable privilege of every man to prove himself right in the thesis that the world is his enemy; for if he reiterates it frequently enough and makes it the background of his conduct he is bound eventually to be right.

Now it lies in the nature of the mental world of the Soviet leaders, as well as in the character of their ideology, that no opposition to them can be officially recognized as having any merit or justification whatsoever. Such opposition can flow, in theory, only from the hostile and incorrigible forces of dying capitalism. As long as remnants of capitalism were officially recognized as existing in Russia, it was possible to place on them, as an internal element, part of the blame for the maintenance of a dictatorial form of society. But as these remnants were liquidated, little by little, this justification fell away; and when it was indicated officially that they had been finally destroyed, it disappeared altogether. And this fact created one of the most basic of the compulsions which came to act upon the Soviet regime: since capitalism no longer existed in Russia and since it could not be admitted that there could be serious or widespread opposition to the Kremlin springing spontaneously from the liberated masses under its authority, it became necessary to justify the retention of the dictatorship by stressing the menace of capitalism abroad.

■   ■   ■

Now the maintenance of this pattern of Soviet power, namely, the pursuit of unlimited authority domestically, accompanied by the cultivation of the semi-myth of implacable foreign hostility, has gone far to shape the actual machinery of Soviet power as we know it today. Internal organs of administration which did not serve this purpose withered on the vine. Organs which did serve this purpose became vastly swollen. The security of Soviet power came to rest on the iron discipline of the Party, on the severity and ubiquity of the secret police, and on the uncompromising economic monopolism of the state. The "organs of suppression," in which the Soviet leaders had sought security from rival forces, became in large measure the masters of those whom they were designed to serve. Today the major part of the structure of Soviet power is committed to the perfection of the dictatorship and to the maintenance of the concept of Russia as in a state of siege, with the enemy lowering beyond the walls. And the millions of human beings who form that part of the structure of power must defend at all costs this concept of Russia's position, for without it they are themselves superfluous.

As things stand today, the rulers can no longer dream of parting with these organs of suppression. The quest for absolute power, pursued now for nearly three decades with a ruthlessness unparalleled (in scope at least) in modern times, has again produced internally, as it did externally, its own reaction. The excesses of the police apparatus have fanned the potential opposition to the regime into something far greater and more dangerous than it could have been before those excesses began.

But least of all can the rulers dispense with the fiction by which the maintenance of dictatorial power has been defended. For this fiction has been canonized in Soviet philosophy by the excesses already committed in its name; and it is now anchored in the Soviet structure of thought by bonds far greater than those of mere ideology.

II

So much for the historical background. What does it spell in terms of the political personality of Soviet power as we know it today?

Of the original ideology, nothing has been officially junked. Belief is maintained in the basic badness of capitalism, in the inevitability of its destruction, in the obligation of the proletariat to assist in that destruction and to take power into its own hands. But stress has come to be laid primarily on those concepts which relate most specifically to the Soviet regime itself: to its position as the sole truly Socialist regime in a dark and misguided world, and to the relationships of power within it.

The first of these concepts is that of the innate antagonism between capitalism and Socialism. We have seen how deeply that concept has become imbedded in foundations of Soviet power. It has profound implications for Russia's conduct as a member of international society. It means that there can never be on Moscow's side any sincere assumption of a community of aims between the Soviet Union and powers which are regarded as capitalism. It must invariably be assumed in Moscow that the aims of the capitalist world are antagonistic to the Soviet regime and, therefore, to the interests of the peoples it controls. If the Soviet Government occasionally sets its signature to documents which would indicate the contrary, this is to be regarded as a tactical maneuver permissible in dealing with the enemy (who is without honor) and should be taken in the spirit of *caveat emptor* [let the buyer beware]. Basically, the antagonism remains. It is postulated. And from it flow many of the phenomena which we find disturbing in the Kremlin's conduct of foreign policy: the secretiveness, the lack of frankness, the duplicity, the war suspiciousness, and the basic unfriendliness of purpose. These phenomena are there to stay, for the foreseeable future. There can be variations of degree and of emphasis. When there is something the Russians want from us, one or the other of these features of their policy may be thrust temporarily into the background; and when that happens there will always be Americans who will leap forward with gleeful announcements that "the Russians have changed," and some who will even try to take credit for having brought about such "changes." But we should not be misled by tactical maneuvers. These characteristics of Soviet policy, like the postulate from which they flow, are basic to the internal nature of Soviet power, and will be with us, whether in the foreground or the background, until the internal nature of Soviet power is changed.

This means that we are going to continue for a long time to find the Russians difficult to deal with. It does not mean that they should be considered as embarked upon a do-or-die program to overthrow our society by a given date. The theory of the inevitability of the eventual fall of capitalism has the fortunate connotation that there is no hurry about it. * * *

■   ■   ■

* * * [T]he Kremlin is under no ideological compulsion to accomplish its purposes in a hurry. Like the Church, it is dealing in ideological concepts which are of long-term validity, and it can afford to be patient. It has no right to risk the existing achievements of the revolution for the sake of vain baubles of the future. The very teachings of Lenin himself require great caution and flexibility in the pursuit of Communist purposes. Again, these precepts are fortified by the lessons of Russian history: of centuries of obscure battles between nomadic forces over the stretches of a vast unfortified plain. Here caution, circumspection, flexibility and deception are the valuable qualities; and their value finds natural appreciation in the Russian or the oriental mind. Thus the Kremlin has no compunction about retreating in the face of superior force. And being under the compulsion of no timetable, it does not get panicky under the necessity for such retreat. Its political action is a fluid stream which moves constantly, wherever it is permitted to move, toward a given goal. Its main concern is to make sure that it has filled every nook and cranny available to it in the basin of world power. But if it finds unassailable barriers in its path, it accepts these philosophically and accommodates itself to them. The main thing is that there should always be pressure, increasing constant pressure, toward the desired goal. There is no trace of any feeling in Soviet psychology that the goal must be reached at any given time.

These considerations make Soviet diplomacy at once easier and more difficult to deal with than the diplomacy of individual aggressive leaders like Napoleon and Hitler. On the one hand it is more sensitive to contrary force, more ready to yield on individual sectors of the diplomatic front when that force is felt to be too strong, and thus more rational in the logic and rhetoric of power. On the other hand it cannot be easily defeated or discouraged by a single victory on the part of its opponents. And the patient persistence by which it is animated means that it can be effectively countered not by sporadic acts which represent the momentary whims of democratic opinion but only by intelligent long-range policies on the part of Russia's adversaries—policies no less steady in their purpose, and no less variegated and resourceful in their application, than those of the Soviet Union itself.

In these circumstances it is clear that the main element of any United States policy toward the Soviet Union must be that of a long-term, patient but firm and vigilant containment of Russian expansive tendencies. It is important to note, however, that such a policy has nothing to do with outward histrionics: with threats or blustering or superfluous gestures of outward "toughness." While the Kremlin is basically flexible in its reaction to political realities, it is by no means unamenable to considerations of prestige. Like almost any other government, it can be placed by tactless and threatening gestures in a position where it cannot afford to yield even though this might be dictated by its sense of realism. The Russian leaders are keen judges of human psychology, and as such they are highly conscious that loss of temper and of self-control is never a source of strength in political affairs. They are quick to exploit such evidences of weakness. For these reasons, it is a *sine qua non* of successful dealing with Russia that the foreign government in question should remain at all times cool and collected and that its demands on Russian policy should be put forward in such a manner as to leave the way open for a compliance not too detrimental to Russian prestige.

III

In the light of the above, it will be clearly seen that the Soviet pressure against the free institutions of the Western world is something that can be contained by the adroit and vigilant application of counter-force at a series of constantly shifting geographical and political points, corresponding to the shifts and maneuvers of Soviet policy, but which cannot be charmed or talked out of existence. * * *

■ ■ ■

IV

■ ■ ■

But in actuality the possibilities for American policy are by no means limited to holding the line and hoping for the best. It is entirely possible for the United States to influence by its actions the internal developments, both within Russia and throughout the international Communist movement, by which Russian policy is largely determined. This is not only a question of the modest measure of informational activity which this government can conduct in the Soviet Union and elsewhere, although that, too, is important. It is rather a question of the degree to which the United States can create among the peoples of the world generally the impression of a country which knows what it wants, which is coping successfully with the problems of its internal life and with the responsibilities of a World Power, and which has a spiritual vitality capable of holding its own among the major ideological currents of the time. To the extent that such an impression can be created and maintained, the aims of Russian Communism must appear sterile and quixotic, the hopes and enthusiasm of Moscow's supporters must wane, and added strain must be imposed on the Kremlin's foreign policies. For the palsied decrepitude of the capitalist world is the keystone of Communist philosophy. Even the failure of the United States to experience the early economic depression which the ravens of the Red Square have been predicting with such complacent confidence since hostilities ceased would have deep and important repercussions throughout the Communist world.

By the same token, exhibitions of indecision, disunity and internal disintegration within this country have an exhilarating effect on the whole Communist movement. * * *

* * * [T]he United States has it in its power to increase enormously the strains under which Soviet policy must operate, to force upon the Kremlin a far greater degree of moderation and circumspection than it has had to observe in recent years, and in this way to promote tendencies which must eventually find their outlet in either the break-up or the gradual mellowing of Soviet power. For no mystical, Messianic movement—and particularly not that of the Kremlin—can face frustration indefinitely without eventually adjusting itself in one way or another to the logic of that state of affairs.

■　■　■

NOTE

1. Here and elsewhere in this paper "Socialism" refers to Marxist or Leninist Communism. * * *

Francis Fukuyama

THE FUTURE OF HISTORY

Can Liberal Democracy Survive the Decline of the Middle Class?

Something strange is going on in the world today. The global financial crisis that began in 2008 and the ongoing crisis of the euro are both products of the model of lightly regulated financial capitalism that emerged over the past three decades. Yet despite widespread anger at Wall Street bailouts, there has been no great upsurge of left-wing American populism in response. It is conceivable that the Occupy Wall Street movement will gain traction, but the most dynamic recent populist movement to date has been the right-wing Tea Party, whose main target is the regulatory state that seeks to protect ordinary people from financial speculators. Something similar is true in Europe as well, where the left is anemic and right-wing populist parties are on the move.

There are several reasons for this lack of left-wing mobilization, but chief among them is a failure in the realm of ideas. For the past generation, the ideological high ground on economic issues has been held by a libertarian right. The left has not been able to make a plausible case for an agenda other than a return to an unaffordable form of old-fashioned social democracy. This absence of a plausible progressive counter-narrative is unhealthy, because competition is good for intellectual debate just as it is for economic activity. And serious intellectual debate is urgently needed, since the current form of globalized capitalism is

From *Foreign Affairs* 91, no. 1 (Jan/Feb. 2012).

eroding the middle-class social base on which liberal democracy rests.

The Democratic Wave

Social forces and conditions do not simply "determine" ideologies, as Karl Marx once maintained, but ideas do not become powerful unless they speak to the concerns of large numbers of ordinary people. Liberal democracy is the default ideology around much of the world today in part because it responds to and is facilitated by certain socioeconomic structures. Changes in those structures may have ideological consequences, just as ideological changes may have socioeconomic consequences.

Almost all the powerful ideas that shaped human societies up until the past 300 years were religious in nature, with the important exception of Confucianism in China. The first major secular ideology to have a lasting worldwide effect was liberalism, a doctrine associated with the rise of first a commercial and then an industrial middle class in certain parts of Europe in the seventeenth century. (By "middle class," I mean people who are neither at the top nor at the bottom of their societies in terms of income, who have received at least a secondary education, and who own either real property, durable goods, or their own businesses.)

As enunciated by classic thinkers such as Locke, Montesquieu, and Mill, liberalism holds that the legitimacy of state authority derives from the state's ability to protect the individual rights of its citizens and that state power needs to be limited by the adherence to law. One of the fundamental rights to be protected is that of private property; England's

Glorious Revolution of 1688–89 was critical to the development of modern liberalism because it first established the constitutional principle that the state could not legitimately tax its citizens without their consent.

At first, liberalism did not necessarily imply democracy. The Whigs who supported the constitutional settlement of 1689 tended to be the wealthiest property owners in England; the parliament of that period represented less than ten percent of the whole population. Many classic liberals, including Mill, were highly skeptical of the virtues of democracy: they believed that responsible political participation required education and a stake in society—that is, property ownership. Up through the end of the nineteenth century, the franchise was limited by property and educational requirements in virtually all parts of Europe. Andrew Jackson's election as U.S. president in 1828 and his subsequent abolition of property requirements for voting, at least for white males, thus marked an important early victory for a more robust democratic principle.

In Europe, the exclusion of the vast majority of the population from political power and the rise of an industrial working class paved the way for Marxism. The *Communist Manifesto* was published in 1848, the same year that revolutions spread to all the major European countries save the United Kingdom. And so began a century of competition for the leadership of the democratic movement between communists, who were willing to jettison procedural democracy (multiparty elections) in favor of what they believed was substantive democracy (economic redistribution), and liberal democrats, who believed in expanding political participation while maintaining a rule of law protecting individual rights, including property rights.

At stake was the allegiance of the new industrial working class. Early Marxists believed they would win by sheer force of numbers: as the franchise was expanded in the late nineteenth century,

parties such as the United Kingdom's Labour and Germany's Social Democrats grew by leaps and bounds and threatened the hegemony of both conservatives and traditional liberals. The rise of the working class was fiercely resisted, often by nondemocratic means; the communists and many socialists, in turn, abandoned formal democracy in favor of a direct seizure of power.

Throughout the first half of the twentieth century, there was a strong consensus on the progressive left that some form of socialism—government control of the commanding heights of the economy in order to ensure an egalitarian distribution of wealth—was unavoidable for all advanced countries. Even a conservative economist such as Joseph Schumpeter could write in his 1942 book, *Capitalism, Socialism, and Democracy,* that socialism would emerge victorious because capitalist society was culturally self-undermining. Socialism was believed to represent the will and interests of the vast majority of people in modern societies.

Yet even as the great ideological conflicts of the twentieth century played themselves out on a political and military level, critical changes were happening on a social level that undermined the Marxist scenario. First, the real living standards of the industrial working class kept rising, to the point where many workers or their children were able to join the middle class. Second, the relative size of the working class stopped growing and actually began to decline, particularly in the second half of the twentieth century, when services began to displace manufacturing in what were labeled "postindustrial" economies. Finally, a new group of poor or disadvantaged people emerged below the industrial working class—a heterogeneous mixture of racial and ethnic minorities, recent immigrants, and socially excluded groups, such as women, gays, and the disabled. As a result of these changes, in most industrialized societies, the old working class has become just another domestic interest group, one using the political power of trade unions to protect the hard-won gains of an earlier era.

Economic class, moreover, turned out not to be a great banner under which to mobilize populations in advanced industrial countries for political action. The Second International got a rude wake-up call in 1914, when the working classes of Europe abandoned calls for class warfare and lined up behind conservative leaders preaching nationalist slogans, a pattern that persists to the present day. Many Marxists tried to explain this, according to the scholar Ernest Gellner, by what he dubbed the "wrong address theory":

> Just as extreme Shi'ite Muslims hold that Archangel Gabriel made a mistake, delivering the Message to Mohamed when it was intended for Ali, so Marxists basically like to think that the spirit of history or human consciousness made a terrible boob. The awakening message was intended for classes, but by some terrible postal error was delivered to nations.

Gellner went on to argue that religion serves a function similar to nationalism in the contemporary Middle East: it mobilizes people effectively because it has a spiritual and emotional content that class consciousness does not. Just as European nationalism was driven by the shift of Europeans from the countryside to cities in the late nineteenth century, so, too, Islamism is a reaction to the urbanization and displacement taking place in contemporary Middle Eastern societies. Marx's letter will never be delivered to the address marked "class."

Marx believed that the middle class, or at least the capital-owning slice of it that he called the bourgeoisie, would always remain a small and privileged minority in modern societies. What happened instead was that the bourgeoisie and the middle class more generally ended up constituting the vast majority of the populations of most advanced countries, posing problems for socialism. From the days of Aristotle, thinkers have believed that stable democracy rests on a broad middle class and that societies with extremes of wealth and poverty are susceptible either to oligarchic domination or populist revolution. When much of the developed world succeeded in creating middle-class societies, the appeal of Marxism vanished. The only places where leftist radicalism persists as a powerful force are in highly unequal areas of the world, such as parts of Latin America, Nepal, and the impoverished regions of eastern India.

What the political scientist Samuel Huntington labeled the "third wave" of global democratization, which began in southern Europe in the 1970s and culminated in the fall of communism in Eastern Europe in 1989, increased the number of electoral democracies around the world from around 45 in 1970 to more than 120 by the late 1990s. Economic growth has led to the emergence of new middle classes in countries such as Brazil, India, Indonesia, South Africa, and Turkey. As the economist Moisés Naím has pointed out, these middle classes are relatively well educated, own property, and are technologically connected to the outside world. They are demanding of their governments and mobilize easily as a result of their access to technology. It should not be surprising that the chief instigators of the Arab Spring uprisings were well-educated Tunisians and Egyptians whose expectations for jobs and political participation were stymied by the dictatorships under which they lived.

Middle-class people do not necessarily support democracy in principle: like everyone else, they are self-interested actors who want to protect their property and position. In countries such as China and Thailand, many middle-class people feel threatened by the redistributive demands of the poor and hence have lined up in support of authoritarian governments that protect their class interests. Nor is it the case that democracies necessarily meet the expectations of their own middle classes, and when they do not, the middle classes can become restive.

The Least Bad Alternative?

There is today a broad global consensus about the legitimacy, at least in principle, of liberal democracy. In the words of the economist Amartya Sen, "While democracy is not yet universally practiced, nor indeed uniformly accepted, in the general climate of world opinion, democratic governance has now achieved the status of being taken to be generally right." It is most broadly accepted in countries that have reached a level of material prosperity sufficient to allow a majority of their citizens to think of themselves as middle class, which is why there tends to be a correlation between high levels of development and stable democracy.

Some societies, such as Iran and Saudi Arabia, reject liberal democracy in favor of a form of Islamic theocracy. Yet these regimes are developmental dead ends, kept alive only because they sit atop vast pools of oil. There was at one time a large Arab exception to the third wave, but the Arab Spring has shown that Arab publics can be mobilized against dictatorship just as readily as those in Eastern Europe and Latin America were. This does not of course mean that the path to a well-functioning democracy will be easy or straightforward in Tunisia, Egypt, or Libya, but it does suggest that the desire for political freedom and participation is not a cultural peculiarity of Europeans and Americans.

The single most serious challenge to liberal democracy in the world today comes from China, which has combined authoritarian government with a partially marketized economy. China is heir to a long and proud tradition of high-quality bureaucratic government, one that stretches back over two millennia. Its leaders have managed a hugely complex transition from a centralized, Soviet-style planned economy to a dynamic open one and have done so with remarkable competence—more competence, frankly, than U.S. leaders have shown in the management of their own macroeconomic

policy recently. Many people currently admire the Chinese system not just for its economic record but also because it can make large, complex decisions quickly, compared with the agonizing policy paralysis that has struck both the United States and Europe in the past few years. Especially since the recent financial crisis, the Chinese themselves have begun touting the "China model" as an alternative to liberal democracy.

This model is unlikely to ever become a serious alternative to liberal democracy in regions outside East Asia, however. In the first place, the model is culturally specific: the Chinese government is built around a long tradition of meritocratic recruitment, civil service examinations, a high emphasis on education, and deference to technocratic authority. Few developing countries can hope to emulate this model; those that have, such as Singapore and South Korea (at least in an earlier period), were already within the Chinese cultural zone. The Chinese themselves are skeptical about whether their model can be exported; the so-called Beijing consensus is a Western invention, not a Chinese one.

It is also unclear whether the model can be sustained. Neither export-driven growth nor the top-down approach to decision-making will continue to yield good results forever. The fact that the Chinese government would not permit open discussion of the disastrous high-speed rail accident last summer and could not bring the Railway Ministry responsible for it to heel suggests that there are other time bombs hidden behind the facade of efficient decision-making.

Finally, China faces a great moral vulnerability down the road. The Chinese government does not force its officials to respect the basic dignity of its citizens. Every week, there are new protests about land seizures, environmental violations, or gross corruption on the part of some official. While the country is growing rapidly, these abuses can be swept under the carpet. But rapid growth will not continue forever, and the government will have to pay a price in pent-up anger. The regime no longer has any guiding ideal around which it is organized; it is run by a Communist Party supposedly committed to equality that presides over a society marked by dramatic and growing inequality.

So the stability of the Chinese system can in no way be taken for granted. The Chinese government argues that its citizens are culturally different and will always prefer benevolent, growth-promoting dictatorship to a messy democracy that threatens social stability. But it is unlikely that a spreading middle class will behave all that differently in China from the way it has behaved in other parts of the world. Other authoritarian regimes may be trying to emulate China's success, but there is little chance that much of the world will look like today's China 50 years down the road.

Democracy's Future

There is a broad correlation among economic growth, social change, and the hegemony of liberal democratic ideology in the world today. And at the moment, no plausible rival ideology looms. But some very troubling economic and social trends, if they continue, will both threaten the stability of contemporary liberal democracies and dethrone democratic ideology as it is now understood.

The sociologist Barrington Moore once flatly asserted, "No bourgeois, no democracy." The Marxists didn't get their communist Utopia because mature capitalism generated middle-class societies, not working-class ones. But what if the further development of technology and globalization undermines the middle class and makes it impossible for more than a minority of citizens in an advanced society to achieve middle-class status?

There are already abundant signs that such a phase of development has begun. Median incomes in the United States have been stagnating in real terms since the 1970s. The economic impact of this stagnation has been softened to some extent by the fact that most U.S. households have shifted to two income earners in the past generation. Moreover, as the economist Raghuram Rajan has persuasively argued, since Americans are reluctant to engage in straightforward redistribution, the United States has instead attempted a highly dangerous and inefficient form of redistribution over the past generation by subsidizing mortgages for low-income households. This trend, facilitated by a flood of liquidity pouring in from China and other countries, gave many ordinary Americans the illusion that their standards of living were rising steadily during the past decade. In this respect, the bursting of the housing bubble in 2008–9 was nothing more than a cruel reversion to the mean. Americans may today benefit from cheap cell phones, inexpensive clothing, and Facebook, but they increasingly cannot afford their own homes, or health insurance, or comfortable pensions when they retire.

A more troubling phenomenon, identified by the venture capitalist Peter Thiel and the economist Tyler Cowen, is that the benefits of the most recent waves of technological innovation have accrued disproportionately to the most talented and well-educated members of society. This phenomenon helped cause the massive growth of inequality in the United States over the past generation. In 1974, the top one percent of families took home nine percent of GDP; by 2007, that share had increased to 23.5 percent.

Trade and tax policies may have accelerated this trend, but the real villain here is technology. In earlier phases of industrialization—the ages of textiles, coal, steel, and the internal combustion engine—the benefits of technological changes almost always flowed down in significant ways to the rest of society in terms of employment. But this is not a law of nature. We are today living in what the scholar Shoshana Zuboff has labeled "the age of the smart machine," in which technology is increasingly able to substitute for more and higher human functions. Every great advance for Silicon Valley likely means a loss of low-skill jobs elsewhere in the economy, a trend that is unlikely to end anytime soon.

Inequality has always existed, as a result of natural differences in talent and character. But today's technological world vastly magnifies those differences. In a nineteenth-century agrarian society, people with strong math skills did not have that many opportunities to capitalize on their talent. Today, they can become financial wizards or software engineers and take home ever-larger proportions of the national wealth.

The other factor undermining middle-class incomes in developed countries is globalization. With the lowering of transportation and communications costs and the entry into the global work force of hundreds of millions of new workers in developing countries, the kind of work done by the old middle class in the developed world can now be performed much more cheaply elsewhere. Under an economic model that prioritizes the maximization of aggregate income, it is inevitable that jobs will be outsourced.

Smarter ideas and policies could have contained the damage. Germany has succeeded in protecting a significant part of its manufacturing base and industrial labor force even as its companies have remained globally competitive. The United States and the United Kingdom, on the other hand, happily embraced the transition to the postindustrial service economy. Free trade became less a theory than an ideology: when members of the U.S. Congress tried to retaliate with trade sanctions against China for keeping its currency undervalued, they were indignantly charged with protectionism, as if the playing field were already level. There was a lot of happy talk about the wonders of the knowledge economy, and how dirty, dangerous manufacturing jobs would inevitably be replaced by highly educated workers doing creative and interesting things. This was a gauzy veil placed over the hard facts of deindustrialization. It overlooked the fact that the benefits of the new order accrued disproportionately to a very small number of people in finance and high technology, interests that dominated the media and the general political conversation.

The Absent Left

One of the most puzzling features of the world in the aftermath of the financial crisis is that so far, populism has taken primarily a right-wing form, not a left-wing one.

In the United States, for example, although the Tea Party is anti-elitist in its rhetoric, its members vote for conservative politicians who serve the interests of precisely those financiers and corporate elites they claim to despise. There are many explanations for this phenomenon. They include a deeply embedded belief in equality of opportunity rather than equality of outcome and the fact that cultural issues, such as abortion and gun rights, crosscut economic ones.

But the deeper reason a broad-based populist left has failed to materialize is an intellectual one. It has been several decades since anyone on the left has been able to articulate, first, a coherent analysis of what happens to the structure of advanced societies as they undergo economic change and, second, a realistic agenda that has any hope of protecting a middle-class society.

The main trends in left-wing thought in the last two generations have been, frankly, disastrous as either conceptual frameworks or tools for mobilization. Marxism died many years ago, and the few old believers still around are ready for nursing homes. The academic left replaced it with postmodernism, multiculturalism, feminism, critical theory, and a host of other fragmented intellectual trends that are more cultural than economic in focus. Postmodernism begins with a denial of the possibility of any master narrative of history or society, undercutting its own authority as a voice for the majority of citizens who feel betrayed by their elites. Multiculturalism validates the victimhood of virtually every out-group. It is impossible to generate a mass progressive movement on the basis of such a motley coalition: most of the working- and lower-middle-class citizens victimized by the system are culturally conservative and would be embarrassed to be seen in the presence of allies like this.

Whatever the theoretical justifications underlying the left's agenda, its biggest problem is a lack of credibility. Over the past two generations, the mainstream left has followed a social democratic program that centers on the state provision of a variety of services, such as pensions, health care, and education. That model is now exhausted: welfare states have become big, bureaucratic, and inflexible; they are often captured by the very organizations that administer them, through public-sector unions; and, most important, they are fiscally unsustainable given the aging of populations virtually everywhere in the developed world. Thus, when existing social democratic parties come to power, they no longer aspire to be more than custodians of a welfare state that was created decades ago; none has a new, exciting agenda around which to rally the masses.

An Ideology of the Future

Imagine, for a moment, an obscure scribbler today in a garret somewhere trying to outline an ideology of the future that could provide a realistic path toward a world with healthy middle-class societies and robust democracies. What would that ideology look like?

It would have to have at least two components, political and economic. Politically, the new ideology would need to reassert the supremacy of democratic politics over economics and legitimize anew government as an expression of the public interest. But the agenda it put forward to protect middle-class life could not simply rely on the existing mechanisms of the welfare state. The ideology would need to somehow redesign the public sector, freeing it from its dependence on existing stakeholders and using new, technology-empowered approaches to delivering services. It would have to argue

forthrightly for more redistribution and present a realistic route to ending interest groups' domination of politics.

Economically, the ideology could not begin with a denunciation of capitalism as such, as if old-fashioned socialism were still a viable alternative. It is more the variety of capitalism that is at stake and the degree to which governments should help societies adjust to change. Globalization need be seen not as an inexorable fact of life but rather as a challenge and an opportunity that must be carefully controlled politically. The new ideology would not see markets as an end in themselves: instead, it would value global trade and investment to the extent that they contributed to a flourishing middle class, not just to greater aggregate national wealth.

It is not possible to get to that point, however, without providing a serious and sustained critique of much of the edifice of modern neoclassical economics, beginning with fundamental assumptions such as the sovereignty of individual preferences and that aggregate income is an accurate measure of national well-being. This critique would have to note that people's incomes do not necessarily represent their true contributions to society. It would have to go further, however, and recognize that even if labor markets were efficient, the natural distribution of talents is not necessarily fair and that individuals are not sovereign entities but beings heavily shaped by their surrounding societies.

Most of these ideas have been around in bits and pieces for some time; the scribbler would have to put them into a coherent package. He or she would also have to avoid the "wrong address" problem. The critique of globalization, that is, would have to be tied to nationalism as a strategy for mobilization in a way that defined national interest in a more sophisticated way than, for example, the "Buy American" campaigns of unions in the United States. The product would be a synthesis of ideas from both the left and the right, detached from the agenda of the marginalized groups that constitute the existing progressive movement. The ideology would be populist; the message would begin with a critique of the elites that allowed the benefit of the many to be sacrificed to that of the few and a critique of the money politics, especially in Washington, that overwhelmingly benefits the wealthy.

The dangers inherent in such a movement are obvious: a pullback by the United States, in particular, from its advocacy of a more open global system could set off protectionist responses elsewhere. In many respects, the Reagan-Thatcher revolution succeeded just as its proponents hoped, bringing about an increasingly competitive, globalized, friction-free world. Along the way, it generated tremendous wealth and created rising middle classes all over the developing world, and the spread of democracy in their wake. It is possible that the developed world is on the cusp of a series of technological breakthroughs that will not only increase productivity but also provide meaningful employment to large numbers of middle-class people.

But that is more a matter of faith than a reflection of the empirical reality of the last 30 years, which points in the opposite direction. Indeed, there are a lot of reasons to think that inequality will continue to worsen. The current concentration of wealth in the United States has already become self-reinforcing: as the economist Simon Johnson has argued, the financial sector has used its lobbying clout to avoid more onerous forms of regulation. Schools for the well-off are better than ever; those for everyone else continue to deteriorate. Elites in all societies use their superior access to the political system to protect their interests, absent a countervailing democratic mobilization to rectify the situation. American elites are no exception to the rule.

That mobilization will not happen, however, as long as the middle classes of the developed world remain enthralled by the narrative of the past generation: that their interests will be best served by ever-freer markets and smaller states. The alternative narrative is out there, waiting to be born.

3 CONTENDING PERSPECTIVES

Over the past century, the most prominent perspectives for understanding the basic nature of international politics have been realism, liberalism, radicalism, and constructivism. These viewpoints have vied for influence both in public debates and in academic arguments.

The readings in this chapter constitute some of the most concise and important statements of these theoretical traditions. Hans J. Morgenthau, the leading figure in the field of international relations in the period after World War II, presents a realist view of power politics. His influential book, *Politics among Nations* (1948), excerpted here, played a central role in intellectually preparing Americans to exercise global power in the Cold War period and to reconcile power politics with the idealistic ethics that had often dominated American discussions about foreign relations.

In *The Tragedy of Great Power Politics* (2001), John J. Mearsheimer offers a contemporary interpretation of international politics that he calls "offensive realism." The chapter reprinted here describes clearly and concisely international anarchy and its implications. States operate in a self-help system; to ensure their survival in that system, states must strive to become as powerful as possible. This competitive striving for security makes conflict the enduring and dominant feature of international relations, in Mearsheimer's view.

Michael W. Doyle advances the liberal theory of the democratic peace. His 1986 article in the *American Political Science Review* points out that no two democracies had ever fought a war against each other. This sparked an ongoing debate among academics and public commentators on why this was the case, and whether it meant that the United States and other democracies should place efforts to promote the further spreading of democracy at the head of their foreign policy agendas.

Whereas realists like Mearsheimer argue that the condition of anarchy necessarily causes insecurity and fear among states, social constructivists such as Alexander Wendt insist that behavior in anarchy depends on the ideas, cultures, and identities that people and their states bring to the anarchical situation. The excerpt here is drawn from the seminal piece in that debate, which has spawned influential research on such topics as the taboo against using nuclear weapons, changing norms of humanitarian military intervention, and the rise of powerful transnational human rights networks.

Hans J. Morgenthau

A REALIST THEORY OF INTERNATIONAL POLITICS

This book purports to present a theory of international politics. The test by which such a theory must be judged is not *a priori* and abstract but empirical and pragmatic. The theory, in other words, must be judged not by some preconceived abstract principle or concept unrelated to reality, but by its purpose: to bring order and meaning to a mass of phenomena which without it would remain disconnected and unintelligible. It must meet a dual test, an empirical and a logical one: Do the facts as they actually are lend themselves to the interpretation the theory has put upon them, and do the conclusions at which the theory arrives follow with logical necessity from its premises? In short, is the theory consistent with the facts and within itself?

The issue this theory raises concerns the nature of all politics. The history of modern political thought is the story of a contest between two schools that differ fundamentally in their conceptions of the nature of man, society, and politics. One believes that a rational and moral political order, derived from universally valid abstract principles, can be achieved here and now. It assumes the essential goodness and infinite malleability of human nature, and blames the failure of the social order to measure up to the rational standards on lack of knowledge and understanding, obsolescent social institutions, or the depravity of certain isolated individuals or groups. It trusts in education, reform, and the sporadic use of force to remedy these defects.

The other school believes that the world, imperfect as it is from the rational point of view, is the result of forces inherent in human nature. To improve the world one must work with those forces, not against them. This being inherently a world of opposing interests and of conflict among them, moral principles can never be fully realized, but must at best be approximated through the ever temporary balancing of interests and the ever precarious settlement of conflicts. This school, then, sees in a system of checks and balances a universal principle for all pluralist societies. It appeals to historic precedent rather than to abstract principles, and aims at the realization of the lesser evil rather than of the absolute good.

■ ■ ■

* * * Principles of Political Realism

Political realism believes that politics, like society in general, is governed by objective laws that have their roots in human nature. In order to improve society it is first necessary to understand the laws by which society lives. The operation of these laws

From Hans J. Morganthau, *Politics among Nations: The Struggle for Power and Peace* (1948; reprint, New York: Knopf, 1960), Chaps. 1 and 3. The author's notes have been omitted.

being impervious to our preferences, men will challenge them only at the risk of failure.

Realism, believing as it does in the objectivity of the laws of politics, must also believe in the possibility of developing a rational theory that reflects, however imperfectly and one-sidedly, these objective laws. It believes also, then, in the possibility of distinguishing in politics between truth and opinion—between what is true objectively and rationally, supported by evidence and illuminated by reason, and what is only a subjective judgment, divorced from the facts as they are and informed by prejudice and wishful thinking.

■　　■　　■

For realism, theory consists in ascertaining facts and giving them meaning through reason. It assumes that the character of a foreign policy can be ascertained only through the examination of the political acts performed and of the foreseeable consequences of these acts. Thus, we can find out what statesmen have actually done, and from the foreseeable consequences of their acts we can surmise what their objectives might have been.

Yet examination of the facts is not enough. To give meaning to the factual raw material of foreign policy, we must approach political reality with a kind of rational outline, a map that suggests to us the possible meanings of foreign policy. In other words, we put ourselves in the position of a statesman who must meet a certain problem of foreign policy under certain circumstances, and we ask ourselves what the rational alternatives are from which a statesman may choose who must meet this problem under these circumstances (presuming always that he acts in a rational manner), and which of these rational alternatives this particular statesman, acting under these circumstances, is likely to choose. It is the testing of this rational hypothesis against the actual facts and their consequences that gives meaning to the facts of international politics and makes a theory of politics possible.

The main signpost that helps political realism to find its way through the landscape of international politics is the concept of interest defined in terms of power. This concept provides the link between reason trying to understand international politics and the facts to be understood. * * *

We assume that statesmen think and act in terms of interest defined as power, and the evidence of history bears that assumption out. That assumption allows us to retrace and anticipate, as it were, the steps a statesman—past, present, or future—has taken or will take on the political scene. We look over his shoulder when he writes his dispatches; we listen in on his conversation with other statesmen; we read and anticipate his very thoughts. Thinking in terms of interest defined as power, we think as he does, and as disinterested observers we understand his thoughts and actions perhaps better than he, the actor on the political scene, does himself.

■　　■　　■

Political realism is aware of the moral significance of political action. It is also aware of the ineluctable tension between the moral command and the requirements of successful political action. And it is unwilling to gloss over and obliterate that tension and thus to obfuscate both the moral and the political issue by making it appear as though the stark facts of politics were morally more satisfying than they actually are, and the moral law less exacting than it actually is.

Realism maintains that universal moral principles cannot be applied to the actions of states in their abstract universal formulation, but that they must be filtered through the concrete circumstances of time and place. The individual may say for himself: *"Fiat justitia, pereat mundus* (Let justice be done, even if the world perish)," but the state has no right to say so in the name of those who are in its care. Both individual and state must judge political action by universal moral principles, such as that of liberty. Yet while the individual has a moral right to sacrifice himself in defense of such a moral principle, the state has no right to let its moral disapprobation of the infringement of liberty get in the way of successful political action, itself inspired by the moral principle of national survival. There can be no political morality without prudence; that is, without consideration of the political consequences of seemingly moral action. Realism, then, considers prudence—the weighing of the consequences of alternative political actions—to be the supreme virtue in politics. Ethics in the abstract judges action by its conformity with the moral law; political ethics judges action by its political consequences. * * *

POLITICAL POWER

What Is Political Power?

■ ■ ■

International politics, like all politics, is a struggle for power. Whatever the ultimate aims of international politics, power is always the immediate aim. Statesmen and peoples may ultimately seek freedom, security, prosperity, or power itself. They may define their goals in terms of a religious, philosophic, economic, or social ideal. They may hope that this ideal will materialize through its own inner force, through divine intervention, or through the natural development of human affairs. They may also try to further its realization through nonpolitical means, such as technical co-operation with other nations or international organizations. But whenever they strive to realize their goal by means of international politics, they do so by striving for power. The Crusaders wanted to free the holy places from domination by the Infidels; Woodrow Wilson wanted to make the world safe for democracy; the Nazis wanted to open Eastern Europe to German colonization, to dominate Europe, and to conquer the world. Since they all chose power to achieve these ends, they were actors on the scene of international politics.

■ ■ ■

* * * When we speak of power, we mean man's control over the minds and actions of other men. By political power we refer to the mutual relations of control among the holders of public authority and between the latter and the people at large.

Political power, however, must be distinguished from force in the sense of the actual exercise of physical violence. The threat of physical violence in the form of police action, imprisonment, capital punishment, or war is an intrinsic element of politics. When violence becomes an actuality, it signifies the abdication of political power in favor of military or pseudo-military power. In international politics in particular, armed strength as a threat or a potentiality is the most important material factor making for the political power of a nation. If it becomes an actuality in war, it signifies the substitution of military for political power. The actual exercise of physical violence substitutes for the psychological relation between two minds, which is of the essence of political power, the physical relation between two bodies, one of which is strong enough to dominate the other's movements. It is for this reason that in the exercise of physical violence the psychological element of the political relationship is lost, and that we must distinguish between military and political power.

Political power is a psychological relation between those who exercise it and those over whom it is exercised. It gives the former control over certain actions of the latter through the influence which the former exert over the latter's minds. That influence derives from three sources: the expectation of benefits, the fear of disadvantages, the respect or love for men or institutions. It may be exerted through orders, threats, persuasion, the authority or charisma of a man or of an office, or a combination of any of these.

While it is generally recognized that the interplay of these factors, in ever changing combinations, forms the basis of all domestic politics, the importance of these factors for international politics is less obvious, but no less real. There has been a tendency to reduce political power to the actual application of force or at least to equate it with successful threats of force and with persuasion, to the neglect of charisma. That neglect * * * accounts in good measure for the neglect of prestige as an independent element in international politics. * * *

∎   ∎   ∎

An economic, financial, territorial, or military policy undertaken for its own sake is subject to evaluation in its own terms. Is it economically or financially advantageous? * * *

When, however, the objectives of these policies serve to increase the power of the nation pursuing them with regard to other nations, these policies and their objectives must be judged primarily from the point of view of their contribution to national power. An economic policy that cannot be justified in purely economic terms might nevertheless be undertaken in view of the political policy pursued. The insecure and unprofitable character of a loan to a foreign nation may be a valid argument against it on purely financial grounds. But the argument is irrelevant if the loan, however unwise it may be from a banker's point of view, serves the political policies of the nation. It may of course be that the economic or financial losses involved in such policies will weaken the nation in its international position to such an extent as to outweigh the political advantages to be expected. On these grounds such policies might be rejected. In such a case, what decides the issue is not purely economic and financial considerations but a comparison of the political changes and risks involved; that is, the probable effect of these policies upon the power of the nation.

The Depreciation of Political Power

The aspiration for power being the distinguishing element of international politics, as of all politics, international politics is of necessity power politics. While this fact is generally recognized in the practice of international affairs, it is frequently denied in the pronouncements of scholars, publicists, and even statesmen. Since the end of the Napoleonic Wars, ever larger groups in the Western world have been persuaded that the struggle for power on the international scene is a temporary phenomenon, a historical accident that is bound to disappear once the peculiar historic conditions that have given rise to it have been eliminated. * * * During the nineteenth century, liberals everywhere shared the conviction that power politics and war were residues of an obsolete system of government, and that with the victory of democracy and constitutional government over absolutism and autocracy international harmony and permanent peace would win out over power politics and war. Of this liberal school of thought, Woodrow Wilson was the most eloquent and most influential spokesman.

In recent times, the conviction that the struggle for power can be eliminated from the international scene has been connected with the great attempts at organizing the world, such as the League of Nations and the United Nations. * * *

* * * [In fact,] the struggle for power is universal in time and space and is an undeniable fact of experience. It cannot be denied that throughout historic time, regardless of social, economic, and political conditions, states have met each other in contests for power. Even though anthropologists have shown that certain primitive peoples seem to be free from the desire for power, nobody has yet shown how their state of mind and the conditions under which they live can be recreated on a world-wide scale so as to eliminate the struggle for power from the international scene.[1] It would be useless and even self-destructive to free one or the other of the peoples of the earth from the desire for power while leaving it extant in others. If the desire for power cannot be abolished everywhere in the world, those who might be cured would simply fall victims to the power of others.

The position taken here might be criticized on the ground that conclusions drawn from the past are unconvincing, and that to draw such conclusions has always been the main stock in trade of the enemies of progress and reform. Though it is true that certain social arrangements and institutions have always existed in the past, it does not necessarily follow that they must always exist in the future. The situation is, however, different when we deal not with social arrangements and institutions created by man, but with those elemental biopsychological drives by which in turn society is created. The drives to live, to propagate, and to dominate are common to all men.[2] Their relative strength is dependent upon social conditions that may favor one drive and tend to repress another, or that may withhold social approval from certain manifestations of these drives while they encourage others. Thus, to take examples only from the sphere of power, most societies condemn killing as a means of attaining power within society, but all societies encourage the killing of enemies in that struggle for power which is called war. * * *

NOTES

1. For an illuminating discussion of this problem, see Malcolm Sharp, "Aggression: A Study of Values and Law," *Ethics*, Vol. 57, No. 4, Part II (July 1947).
2. Zoologists have tried to show that the drive to dominate is found even in animals, such as chickens and monkeys, who create social hierarchies on the basis of the will and the ability to dominate. See, e.g., Warder Allee, *Animal Life and Social Growth* (Baltimore: The Williams and Wilkins Company, 1932), and *The Social Life of Animals* (New York: W. W. Norton and Company, Inc., 1938).

John J. Mearsheimer
ANARCHY AND THE STRUGGLE FOR POWER

Great powers, I argue, are always searching for opportunities to gain power over their rivals, with hegemony as their final goal. This perspective does not allow for status quo powers, except for the unusual state that achieves preponderance. Instead, the system is populated with great powers that have revisionist intentions at their core.[1] This chapter presents a theory that explains this competition for power. Specifically, I attempt to show that there is a compelling logic behind my claim that great powers seek to maximize their share of world power. I do not, however, test offensive realism against the historical record in this chapter. That important task is reserved for later chapters.

Why States Pursue Power

My explanation for why great powers vie with each other for power and strive for hegemony is derived from five assumptions about the international system. None of these assumptions alone mandates that states behave competitively. Taken together, however, they depict a world in which states have considerable reason to think and sometimes behave aggressively. In particular, the system encourages states to look for opportunities to maximize their power vis-à-vis other states.

How important is it that these assumptions be realistic? Some social scientists argue that the assumptions that underpin a theory need not

From *The Tragedy of Great Power Politics* (New York: Norton, 2001): 29–54. Some of the author's notes have been edited.

conform to reality. Indeed, the economist Milton Friedman maintains that the best theories "will be found to have assumptions that are wildly inaccurate descriptive representations of reality, and, in general, the more significant the theory, the more unrealistic the assumptions."[2] According to this view, the explanatory power of a theory is all that matters. If unrealistic assumptions lead to a theory that tells us a lot about how the world works, it is of no importance whether the underlying assumptions are realistic or not.

I reject this view. Although I agree that explanatory power is the ultimate criterion for assessing theories, I also believe that a theory based on unrealistic or false assumptions will not explain much about how the world works.[3] Sound theories are based on sound assumptions. Accordingly, each of these five assumptions is a reasonably accurate representation of an important aspect of life in the international system.

Bedrock Assumptions

The first assumption is that the international system is anarchic, which does not mean that it is chaotic or riven by disorder. It is easy to draw that conclusion, since realism depicts a world characterized by security competition and war. By itself, however, the realist notion of anarchy has nothing to do with conflict; it is an ordering principle, which says that the system comprises independent states that have no central authority above them.[4] Sovereignty, in other words, inheres in states because there is no higher ruling body in the international system.[5] There is no "government over governments."[6]

The second assumption is that great powers inherently possess some offensive military capability, which gives them the wherewithal to hurt and possibly destroy each other. States are potentially dangerous to each other, although some states have more military might than others and are therefore more dangerous. A state's military power is usually identified with the particular weaponry at its disposal, although even if there were no weapons, the individuals in those states could still use their feet and hands to attack the population of another state. After all, for every neck, there are two hands to choke it.

The third assumption is that states can never be certain about other states' intentions. Specifically, no state can be sure that another state will not use its offensive military capability to attack the first state. This is not to say that states necessarily have hostile intentions. Indeed, all of the states in the system may be reliably benign, but it is impossible to be sure of that judgment because intentions are impossible to divine with 100 percent certainty.[7] There are many possible causes of aggression, and no state can be sure that another state is not motivated by one of them.[8] Furthermore, intentions can change quickly, so a state's intentions can be benign one day and hostile the next. Uncertainty about intentions is unavoidable, which means that states can never be sure that other states do not have offensive intentions to go along with their offensive capabilities.

The fourth assumption is that survival is the primary goal of great powers. Specifically, states seek to maintain their territorial integrity and the autonomy of their domestic political order. Survival dominates other motives because, once a state is conquered, it is unlikely to be in a position to pursue other aims. Soviet leader Josef Stalin put the point well during a war scare in 1927: "We can and must build socialism in the [Soviet Union]. But in order to do so we first of all have to exist."[9]

States can and do pursue other goals, of course, but security is their most important objective.

The fifth assumption is that great powers are rational actors. They are aware of their external environment and they think strategically about how to survive in it. In particular, they consider the preferences of other states and how their own behavior is likely to affect the behavior of those other states, and how the behavior of those other states is likely to affect their own strategy for survival. Moreover, states pay attention to the long term as well as the immediate consequences of their actions.

As emphasized, none of these assumptions alone dictates that great powers as a general rule *should* behave aggressively toward each other. There is surely the possibility that some state might have hostile intentions, but the only assumption dealing with a specific motive that is common to all states says that their principal objective is to survive, which by itself is a rather harmless goal. Nevertheless, when the five assumptions are married together, they create powerful incentives for great powers to think and act offensively with regard to each other. In particular, three general patterns of behavior result: fear, self-help, and power maximization.

State Behavior

Great powers fear each other. They regard each other with suspicion, and they worry that war might be in the offing. They anticipate danger. There is little room for trust among states. For sure, the level of fear varies across time and space, but it cannot be reduced to a trivial level. From the perspective of any one great power, all other great powers are potential enemies. This point is illustrated by the reaction of the United Kingdom and France to German reunification at the end of the Cold War. Despite the fact that these three states had been close allies for almost forty-five years, both the United Kingdom and France immediately began worrying about the potential dangers of a united Germany.[10]

The basis of this fear is that in a world where great powers have the capability to attack each other and might have the motive to do so, any state bent on survival must be at least suspicious of other states and reluctant to trust them. Add to this the "911" problem—the absence of a central authority to which a threatened state can turn for help—and states have even greater incentive to fear each other. Moreover, there is no mechanism, other than the possible self-interest of third parties, for punishing an aggressor. Because it is sometimes difficult to deter potential aggressors, states have ample reason not to trust other states and to be prepared for war with them.

The possible consequences of falling victim to aggression further amplify the importance of fear as a motivating force in world politics. Great powers do not compete with each other as if international politics were merely an economic marketplace. Political competition among states is a much more dangerous business than mere economic intercourse; the former can lead to war, and war often means mass killing on the battlefield as well as mass murder of civilians. In extreme cases, war can even lead to the destruction of states. The horrible consequences of war sometimes cause states to view each other not just as competitors, but as potentially deadly enemies. Political antagonism, in short, tends to be intense, because the stakes are great.

States in the international system also aim to guarantee their own survival. Because other states are potential threats, and because there is no higher authority to come to their rescue when they dial 911, states cannot depend on others for their own security. Each state tends to see itself as vulnerable and alone, and therefore it aims to provide for its own survival. In international politics, God helps those who help themselves. This emphasis on self-help does not preclude states from forming alliances.[11] But alliances are only temporary marriages of convenience: today's alliance partner might be tomorrow's enemy, and today's enemy might be tomorrow's alliance partner. For example, the United States fought with China and the Soviet Union against Germany and Japan in World War II, but soon thereafter flip-flopped enemies and partners and allied with West Germany and Japan against China and the Soviet Union during the Cold War.

States operating in a self-help world almost always act according to their own self-interest and do not subordinate their interests to the interests of other states, or to the interests of the so-called international community. The reason is simple: it pays to be selfish in a self-help world. This is true in the short term as well as in the long term, because if a state loses in the short run, it might not be around for the long haul.

Apprehensive about the ultimate intentions of other states, and aware that they operate in a self-help system, states quickly understand that the best way to ensure their survival is to be the most powerful state in the system. The stronger a state is relative to its potential rivals, the less likely it is that any of those rivals will attack it and threaten its survival. Weaker states will be reluctant to pick fights with more powerful states because the weaker states are likely to suffer military defeat. Indeed, the bigger the gap in power between any two states, the less likely it is that the weaker will attack the stronger. Neither Canada nor Mexico, for example, would countenance attacking the United States, which is far more powerful than its neighbors. The ideal situation is to be the hegemon in the system. As Immanuel Kant said, "It is the desire of every state, or of its ruler, to arrive at a condition of perpetual peace by conquering the whole world, if that were possible."[12] Survival would then be almost guaranteed.[13]

Consequently, states pay close attention to how power is distributed among them, and they make a special effort to maximize their share of world power. Specifically, they look for opportunities to alter the balance of power by acquiring additional increments of power at the expense of potential rivals. States employ a variety of means—economic, diplomatic, and military—to shift the balance of power in their favor, even if doing so makes other states suspicious or even hostile. Because one state's gain in power is another state's loss, great powers tend to have a zero-sum mentality when dealing with each other. The trick, of course, is to be the winner in this competition and to dominate the other states in the system. Thus, the claim that states maximize relative power is tantamount to arguing that states are disposed to think offensively toward other states, even though their ultimate motive is simply to survive. In short, great powers have aggressive intentions.[14]

Even when a great power achieves a distinct military advantage over its rivals, it continues looking for chances to gain more power. The pursuit of power stops only when hegemony is achieved. The idea that a great power might feel secure without dominating the system, provided it has an "appropriate amount" of power, is not persuasive, for two reasons.[15] First, it is difficult to assess how much relative power one state must have over its rivals before it is secure. Is twice as much power an appropriate threshold? Or is three times as much power the magic number? The root of the problem is that power calculations alone do not determine which side wins a war. Clever strategies, for example, sometimes allow less powerful states to defeat more powerful foes.

Second, determining how much power is enough becomes even more complicated when great powers contemplate how power will be distributed among them ten or twenty years down the road. The capabilities of individual states vary over time, sometimes markedly, and it is often difficult to predict the direction and scope of change in the balance of power. Remember, few in the West anticipated the collapse of the Soviet Union before it happened. In fact, during the first half of the Cold War, many in the West feared that the Soviet economy would eventually generate greater wealth than the American economy, which would cause a marked power shift against the United States and its allies. What the future holds for China and Russia and what the balance of power will look like in 2020 is difficult to foresee.

Given the difficulty of determining how much power is enough for today and tomorrow, great powers recognize that the best way to ensure their security is to achieve hegemony now, thus eliminating any possibility of a challenge by another great power. Only a misguided state would pass up an opportunity to be the hegemon in the system because it thought it already had sufficient power to survive.[16] But even if a great power does not have the wherewithal to achieve hegemony (and that is usually the case), it will still act offensively to amass as much power as it can, because states are almost always better off with more rather than less power. In short, states do not become status quo powers until they completely dominate the system.

All states are influenced by this logic, which means that not only do they look for opportunities to take advantage of one another, they also work to ensure that other states do not take advantage of them. After all, rival states are driven by the same logic, and most states are likely to recognize their own motives at play in the actions of other states. In short, states ultimately pay attention to defense as well as offense. They think about conquest themselves, and they work to check aggressor states from gaining power at their expense. This inexorably leads to a world of constant security competition, where states are willing to lie, cheat, and use brute force if it helps them gain advantage over their rivals. Peace, if one defines that concept as a state of tranquility or mutual concord, is not likely to break out in this world.

The "security dilemma," which is one of the most well-known concepts in the international relations literature, reflects the basic logic of offensive realism. The essence of the dilemma is that the measures a state takes to increase its own security usually decrease the security of other states. Thus, it is difficult for a state to increase its own chances of survival without threatening the survival of other states. John Herz first introduced the security dilemma in a 1950 article in the journal *World Politics*.[17] After discussing the anarchic nature of international politics, he writes, "Striving to attain security from . . . attack, [states] are driven to acquire more and more power in order to escape the impact of the power of others. This, in turn, renders the others more insecure and compels them to prepare for the worst. Since none can ever feel entirely secure in such a world of competing units, power competition ensues, and the vicious circle of security and power accumulation is on."[18] The implication of Herz's analysis is clear: the best way for a state to survive in anarchy is to take advantage of other states and gain power at their expense. The best defense is a good offense. Since this message is widely understood, ceaseless security competition ensues. Unfortunately, little can be done to ameliorate the security dilemma as long as states operate in anarchy.

It should be apparent from this discussion that saying that states are power maximizers is tantamount to saying that they care about relative power, not absolute power. There is an important distinction here, because states concerned about relative power behave differently than do states interested in absolute power.[19] States that maximize relative power are concerned primarily with the distribution of material capabilities. In particular, they try to gain as large a power advantage as possible over potential rivals, because power is the best means to survival in a dangerous world. Thus, states motivated by relative power concerns are likely to forgo large gains in their own power, if such gains give rival states even greater power, for smaller national gains that nevertheless provide them with a power advantage over their rivals.[20] States that maximize absolute power, on the other hand, care only about the size of their own gains, not those of other states. They are not motivated by balance-of-power logic but instead are concerned with amassing power without regard to how much power other states control. They would jump at the opportunity for large gains, even if a rival gained more in the deal. Power, according to this logic, is not a means to an end (survival), but an end in itself.[21]

Calculated Aggression

There is obviously little room for status quo powers in a world where states are inclined to look for opportunities to gain more power. Nevertheless, great powers cannot always act on their offensive intentions, because behavior is influenced not only by what states want, but also by their capacity to realize these desires. Every state might want to be king of the hill, but not every state has the wherewithal to compete for that lofty position, much less achieve it. Much depends on how military might is distributed among the great powers. A great power that has a marked power advantage over its rivals is likely to behave more aggressively, because it has the capability as well as the incentive to do so.

By contrast, great powers facing powerful opponents will be less inclined to consider offensive action and more concerned with defending the existing balance of power from threats by their more powerful opponents. Let there be an opportunity for those weaker states to revise the balance in their own favor, however, and they will take advantage of it. Stalin put the point well at the end of World War II: "Everyone imposes his own system as far as his army can reach. It cannot be otherwise."[22] States might also have the capability to gain advantage over a rival power but nevertheless decide that the perceived costs of offense are too high and do not justify the expected benefits.

In short, great powers are not mindless aggressors so bent on gaining power that they charge headlong into losing wars or pursue Pyrrhic victories. On the contrary, before great powers take offensive actions, they think carefully about the balance of power and about how other states will react to their moves. They weigh the costs and risks of offense against the likely benefits. If the benefits do not outweigh the risks, they sit tight and wait for a more propitious moment. Nor do states start arms races that are unlikely to improve their overall position. As discussed at greater length in Chapter 3, states sometimes limit defense spending either because spending more would bring no strategic advantage or because spending more would weaken the economy and undermine the state's power in the long run.[23] To paraphrase Clint Eastwood, a state has to know its limitations to survive in the international system.

Nevertheless, great powers miscalculate from time to time because they invariably make important decisions on the basis of imperfect information. States hardly ever have complete information about any situation they confront. There are two dimensions to this problem. Potential adversaries have incentives to misrepresent their own strength or weakness, and to conceal their true aims.[24] For example, a weaker state trying to deter a stronger state is likely to exaggerate its own power to discourage the potential aggressor from attacking. On the other hand, a state bent on aggression is likely to emphasize its peaceful goals while exaggerating its military weakness, so that the potential victim does not build up its own arms and thus leaves itself vulnerable to attack. Probably no national leader was better at practicing this kind of deception than Adolf Hitler.

But even if disinformation was not a problem, great powers are often unsure about how their own military forces, as well as the adversary's, will perform on the battlefield. For example, it is sometimes difficult to determine in advance how new weapons and untested combat units will perform in the face of enemy fire. Peacetime maneuvers and war games are helpful but imperfect indicators of what is likely to happen in actual combat. Fighting wars is a complicated business in which it is often difficult to predict outcomes. Remember that although the United States and its allies scored a stunning and remarkably easy victory against Iraq in early 1991, most experts at the time believed that Iraq's military would be a formidable foe and put up stubborn resistance before finally succumbing to American military might.[25]

Great powers are also sometimes unsure about the resolve of opposing states as well as allies. For example, Germany believed that if it went to war against France and Russia in the summer of 1914, the United Kingdom would probably stay out of the fight. Saddam Hussein expected the United States to stand aside when he invaded Kuwait in August 1990. Both aggressors guessed wrong, but each had good reason to think that its initial judgment was correct. In the 1930s, Adolf Hitler believed that his great-power rivals would be easy to exploit and isolate because each had little interest in fighting Germany and instead was determined to get someone else to assume that burden. He guessed right. In short, great powers constantly find themselves confronting situations in which they have to make important decisions with incomplete information. Not surprisingly, they sometimes make faulty judgments and end up doing themselves serious harm.

Some defensive realists go so far as to suggest that the constraints of the international system are so powerful that offense rarely succeeds, and that aggressive great powers invariably end up being punished.[26] As noted, they emphasize that 1) threatened states balance against aggressors and ultimately crush them, and 2) there is an offense-defense balance that is usually heavily tilted toward the defense, thus making conquest especially difficult. Great powers, therefore, should be content with the existing balance of power and not try to change it by force. After all, it makes little sense for a state to initiate a war that it is likely to lose; that would be self-defeating behavior. It is better to concentrate instead on preserving the balance of power.[27] Moreover, because aggressors seldom succeed, states should understand that security is abundant, and thus there is no good strategic reason for wanting more power in the first place. In a world where conquest seldom pays, states should have relatively benign intentions toward each other. If they do not, these defensive realists argue, the reason is probably poisonous domestic politics, not smart calculations about how to guarantee one's security in an anarchic world.

There is no question that systemic factors constrain aggression, especially balancing by threatened states. But defensive realists exaggerate those restraining forces.[28] Indeed, the historical record provides little support for their claim that offense rarely succeeds. One study estimates that there were 63 wars between 1815 and 1980, and the initiator won 39 times, which translates into about a 60 percent success rate.[29] Turning to specific cases, Otto von Bismarck unified Germany by winning military victories against Denmark in 1864, Austria in 1866, and France in 1870, and the United States as we know it today was created in good part by conquest in the nineteenth century. Conquest certainly paid big dividends in these cases. Nazi Germany won wars against Poland in 1939 and France in 1940, but lost to the Soviet Union between 1941 and 1945. Conquest ultimately did not pay for the Third Reich, but if Hitler had restrained himself after the fall of France and had not invaded the Soviet Union, conquest probably would have paid handsomely for the Nazis. In short, the historical record shows that offense sometimes succeeds and sometimes does not. The trick for a sophisticated power maximizer is to figure out when to raise and when to fold.[30]

Hegemony's Limits

Great powers, as I have emphasized, strive to gain power over their rivals and hopefully become hegemons. Once a state achieves that exalted position, it becomes a status quo power. More needs to be said, however, about the meaning of hegemony.

A hegemon is a state that is so powerful that it dominates all the other states in the system.[31] No other state has the military wherewithal to put up a serious fight against it. In essence, a hegemon is the only great power in the system. A state that is substantially more powerful than the other great powers in the system is not a hegemon, because it faces, by definition, other great powers. The United Kingdom in the mid-nineteenth century, for example, is sometimes called a hegemon. But it was not a hegemon, because there were four other great powers in Europe at the time—Austria, France, Prussia, and Russia—and the United Kingdom did not dominate them in any meaningful way. In fact, during that period, the United Kingdom considered France to be a serious threat to the balance of power. Europe in the nineteenth century was multipolar, not unipolar.

Hegemony means domination of the system, which is usually interpreted to mean the entire world. It is possible, however, to apply the concept of a system more narrowly and use it to describe particular regions, such as Europe, Northeast Asia, and the Western Hemisphere. Thus, one can distinguish between *global hegemons*, which dominate the world, and *regional hegemons*, which dominate distinct geographical areas. The United States has been a regional hegemon in the Western Hemisphere for at least the past one hundred years. No other state in the Americas has sufficient military might to challenge it, which is why the United States is widely recognized as the only great power in its region.

My argument, which I develop at length in subsequent chapters, is that except for the unlikely event wherein one state achieves clear-cut nuclear superiority, it is virtually impossible for any state to achieve global hegemony. The principal impediment to world domination is the difficulty of projecting power across the world's oceans onto the territory of a rival great power. The United States, for example, is the most powerful state on the planet today. But it does not dominate Europe and Northeast Asia the way it does the Western Hemisphere, and it has no intention of trying to conquer and control those distant regions, mainly because of the stopping power of water. Indeed, there is reason to think that the American military commitment to Europe and Northeast Asia might wither away over the next decade. In short, there has never been a global hegemon, and there is not likely to be one anytime soon.

The best outcome a great power can hope for is to be a regional hegemon and possibly control another region that is nearby and accessible over land. The United States is the only regional hegemon in modern history, although other states have fought major wars in pursuit of regional hegemony: imperial Japan in Northeast Asia, and Napoleonic France, Wilhelmine Germany, and Nazi Germany in Europe. But none succeeded. The Soviet Union, which is located in Europe and Northeast Asia, threatened to dominate both of those regions during the Cold War. The Soviet Union might also have attempted to conquer the oil-rich Persian Gulf region, with which it shared a border. But even if Moscow had been able to dominate Europe, Northeast Asia, and the Persian Gulf, which it never came close to doing, it still would have been unable to conquer the Western Hemisphere and become a true global hegemon.

States that achieve regional hegemony seek to prevent great powers in other regions from duplicating their feat. Regional hegemons, in other words, do not want peers. Thus the United States, for example, played a key role in preventing imperial Japan, Wilhelmine Germany, Nazi Germany, and the Soviet Union from gaining regional supremacy. Regional hegemons attempt to check aspiring hegemons in other regions because they fear that a rival great power that dominates its own region will be an especially powerful foe that is essentially free to cause trouble in the fearful great power's backyard. Regional hegemons prefer that there be at least two great powers located together in other regions, because their proximity will force them to concentrate their attention on each other rather than on the distant hegemon.

Furthermore, if a potential hegemon emerges among them, the other great powers in that region might be able to contain it by themselves, allowing the distant hegemon to remain safely on the sidelines. Of course, if the local great powers were unable to do the job, the distant hegemon would take the appropriate measures to deal with the threatening state. The United States, as noted, has assumed that burden on four separate occasions in the twentieth century, which is why it is commonly referred to as an "offshore balancer."

In sum, the ideal situation for any great power is to be the only regional hegemon in the world. That state would be a status quo power, and it would go to considerable lengths to preserve the existing distribution of power. The United States is in that enviable position today; it dominates the Western Hemisphere and there is no hegemon in any other area of the world. But if a regional hegemon is confronted with a peer competitor, it would no longer be a status quo power. Indeed, it would go to considerable lengths to weaken and maybe even destroy its distant rival. Of course, both regional hegemons would be motivated by that logic, which would make for a fierce security competition between them.

Power and Fear

That great powers fear each other is a central aspect of life in the international system. But as noted, the level of fear varies from case to case. For example, the Soviet Union worried much less about Germany in 1930 than it did in 1939. How much states fear each other matters greatly, because the amount of fear between them largely determines the severity of their security competition, as well as the probability that they will fight a war. The more profound the fear is, the more intense is the security competition, and the more likely is war. The logic is straightforward: a scared state will look especially hard for ways to enhance its security, and it will be disposed to pursue risky policies to achieve that end. Therefore, it is important to understand what causes states to fear each other more or less intensely.

Fear among great powers derives from the fact that they invariably have some offensive military capability that they can use against each other, and the fact that one can never be certain that other states do not intend to use that power against oneself. Moreover, because states operate in an anarchic system, there is no night watchman to whom they can turn for help if another great power attacks them. Although anarchy and uncertainty about other states' intentions create an irreducible level of fear among states that leads to power-maximizing behavior, they cannot account for why sometimes that level of fear is greater than at other times. The reason is that anarchy and the difficulty of discerning state intentions are constant facts of life, and constants cannot explain variation. The capability that states have to threaten each other, however, varies from case to case, and it is the key factor that drives fear levels up and down. Specifically, the more power a state possesses, the more fear it generates among its rivals. Germany, for example, was much more powerful at the end of the 1930s than it was at the decade's beginning, which is why the Soviets became increasingly fearful of Germany over the course of that decade.

This discussion of how power affects fear prompts the question, What is power? It is important to distinguish between potential and actual power. A state's potential power is based on the size of its population and the level of its wealth. These two assets are the main building blocks of military power. Wealthy rivals with large populations can usually build formidable military forces. A state's actual power is embedded mainly in its army and the air and naval forces that directly support it.

Armies are the central ingredient of military power, because they are the principal instrument for conquering and controlling territory—the paramount political objective in a world of territorial states. In short, the key component of military might, even in the nuclear age, is land power.

Power considerations affect the intensity of fear among states in three main ways. First, rival states that possess nuclear forces that can survive a nuclear attack and retaliate against it are likely to fear each other less than if these same states had no nuclear weapons. During the Cold War, for example, the level of fear between the superpowers probably would have been substantially greater if nuclear weapons had not been invented. The logic here is simple: because nuclear weapons can inflict devastating destruction on a rival state in a short period of time, nuclear-armed rivals are going to be reluctant to fight with each other, which means that each side will have less reason to fear the other than would otherwise be the case. But as the Cold War demonstrates, this does not mean that war between nuclear powers is no longer thinkable; they still have reason to fear each other.

Second, when great powers are separated by large bodies of water, they usually do not have much offensive capability against each other, regardless of the relative size of their armies. Large bodies of water are formidable obstacles that cause significant power-projection problems for attacking armies. For example, the stopping power of water explains in good part why the United Kingdom and the United States (since becoming a great power in 1898) have never been invaded by another great power. It also explains why the United States has never tried to conquer territory in Europe or Northeast Asia, and why the United Kingdom has never attempted to dominate the European continent. Great powers located on the same landmass are in a much better position to attack and conquer each other. That is especially true of states that share a common border. Therefore, great powers separated by water are likely to fear each other less than great powers that can get at each other over land.

Third, the distribution of power among the states in the system also markedly affects the levels of fear.[32] The key issue is whether power is distributed more or less evenly among the great powers or whether there are sharp power asymmetries. The configuration of power that generates the most fear is a multipolar system that contains a potential hegemon—what I call "unbalanced multipolarity."

A potential hegemon is more than just the most powerful state in the system. It is a great power with so much actual military capability and so much potential power that it stands a good chance of dominating and controlling all of the other great powers in its region of the world. A potential hegemon need not have the wherewithal to fight all of its rivals at once, but it must have excellent prospects of defeating each opponent alone, and good prospects of defeating some of them in tandem. The key relationship, however, is the power gap between the potential hegemon and the second most powerful state in the system: there must be a marked gap between them. To qualify as a potential hegemon, a state must have—by some reasonably large margin—the most formidable army as well as the most latent power among all the states located in its region.

Bipolarity is the power configuration that produces the least amount of fear among the great powers, although not a negligible amount by any means. Fear tends to be less acute in bipolarity, because there is usually a rough balance of power between the two major states in the system. Multipolar systems without a potential hegemon, what I call "balanced multipolarity," are still likely to have power asymmetries among their members, although these asymmetries will not be as pronounced as the gaps created by the presence of an aspiring hegemon. Therefore, balanced multipolarity is likely to generate less fear than unbalanced multipolarity, but more fear than bipolarity.

This discussion of how the level of fear between great powers varies with changes in the distribution of power, not with assessments about each other's intentions, raises a related point. When a state surveys its environment to determine which states pose a threat to its survival, it focuses mainly on the offensive *capabilities* of potential rivals, not their intentions. As emphasized earlier, intentions are ultimately unknowable, so states worried about their survival must make worst-case assumptions about their rivals' intentions. Capabilities, however, not only can be measured but also determine whether or not a rival state is a serious threat. In short, great powers balance against capabilities, not intentions.[33]

Great powers obviously balance against states with formidable military forces, because that offensive military capability is the tangible threat to their survival. But great powers also pay careful attention to how much latent power rival states control, because rich and populous states usually can and do build powerful armies. Thus, great powers tend to fear states with large populations and rapidly expanding economies, even if these states have not yet translated their wealth into military might.

The Hierarchy of State Goals

Survival is the number one goal of great powers, according to my theory. In practice, however, states pursue non-security goals as well. For example, great powers invariably seek greater economic prosperity to enhance the welfare of their citizenry. They sometimes seek to promote a particular ideology abroad, as happened during the Cold War when the United States tried to spread democracy around the world and the Soviet Union tried to sell communism. National unification is another goal that sometimes motivates states, as it did with

Prussia and Italy in the nineteenth century and Germany after the Cold War. Great powers also occasionally try to foster human rights around the globe. States might pursue any of these, as well as a number of other non-security goals.

Offensive realism certainly recognizes that great powers might pursue these non-security goals, but it has little to say about them, save for one important point: states can pursue them as long as the requisite behavior does not conflict with balance-of-power logic, which is often the case.[34] Indeed, the pursuit of these non-security goals sometimes complements the hunt for relative power. For example, Nazi Germany expanded into eastern Europe for both ideological and realist reasons, and the superpowers competed with each other during the Cold War for similar reasons. Furthermore, greater economic prosperity invariably means greater wealth, which has significant implications for security, because wealth is the foundation of military power. Wealthy states can afford powerful military forces, which enhance a state's prospects for survival. As the political economist Jacob Viner noted more than fifty years ago, "there is a long-run harmony" between wealth and power.[35] National unification is another goal that usually complements the pursuit of power. For example, the unified German state that emerged in 1871 was more powerful than the Prussian state it replaced.

Sometimes the pursuit of non-security goals has hardly any effect on the balance of power, one way or the other. Human rights interventions usually fit this description, because they tend to be small-scale operations that cost little and do not detract from a great power's prospects for survival. For better or for worse, states are rarely willing to expend blood and treasure to protect foreign populations from gross abuses, including genocide. For instance, despite claims that American foreign policy is infused with moralism, Somalia (1992–93) is the only instance during the past one hundred years in which U.S. soldiers were killed in action on a humanitarian mission. And in that case, the loss of a mere eighteen soldiers in an infamous firefight in October 1993 so traumatized American policymakers that they immediately pulled all U.S. troops out of Somalia and then refused to intervene in Rwanda in the spring of 1994, when ethnic Hutu went on a genocidal rampage against their Tutsi neighbors.[36] Stopping that genocide would have been relatively easy and it would have had virtually no effect on the position of the United States in the balance of power.[37] Yet nothing was done. In short, although realism does not prescribe human rights interventions, it does not necessarily proscribe them.

But sometimes the pursuit of non-security goals conflicts with balance-of-power logic, in which case states usually act according to the dictates of realism. For example, despite the U.S. commitment to spreading democracy across the globe, it helped overthrow democratically elected governments and embraced a number of authoritarian regimes during the Cold War, when American policymakers felt that these actions would help contain the Soviet Union.[38] In World War II, the liberal democracies put aside their antipathy for communism and formed an alliance with the Soviet Union against Nazi Germany. "I can't take communism," Franklin Roosevelt emphasized, but to defeat Hitler "I would hold hands with the Devil."[39] In the same way, Stalin repeatedly demonstrated that when his ideological preferences clashed with power considerations, the latter won out. To take the most blatant example of his realism, the Soviet Union formed a non-aggression pact with Nazi Germany in August 1939—the infamous Molotov-Ribbentrop Pact—in hopes that the agreement would at least temporarily satisfy Hitler's territorial ambitions in eastern Europe and turn the Wehrmacht toward France and the United Kingdom.[40] When great powers confront a serious threat, in short, they pay little attention to ideology as they search for alliance partners.[41]

Security also trumps wealth when those two goals conflict, because "defence," as Adam Smith wrote in *The Wealth of Nations,* "is of much more importance than opulence."[42] Smith provides a good illustration of how states behave when forced to choose between wealth and relative power. In 1651, England put into effect the famous Navigation Act, protectionist legislation designed to damage Holland's commerce and ultimately cripple the Dutch economy. The legislation mandated that all goods imported into England be carried either in English ships or ships owned by the country that originally produced the goods. Since the Dutch produced few goods themselves, this measure would badly damage their shipping, the central ingredient in their economic success. Of course, the Navigation Act would hurt England's economy as well, mainly because it would rob England of the benefits of free trade. "The act of navigation," Smith wrote, "is not favorable to foreign commerce, or to the growth of that opulence that can arise from it." Nevertheless, Smith considered the legislation "the wisest of all the commercial regulations of England" because it did more damage to the Dutch economy than to the English economy, and in the mid-seventeenth century Holland was "the only naval power which could endanger the security of England."[43]

Creating World Order

The claim is sometimes made that great powers can transcend realist logic by working together to build an international order that fosters peace and justice. World peace, it would appear, can only enhance a state's prosperity and security. America's political leaders paid considerable lip service to this line of argument over the course of the twentieth century. President Clinton, for example, told an audience at the United Nations in September 1993 that "at the birth of this organization 48 years ago . . . a generation of gifted leaders from many nations stepped forward to organize the world's efforts on behalf of security and prosperity. . . .

Now history has granted to us a moment of even greater opportunity. . . . Let us resolve that we will dream larger. . . . Let us ensure that the world we pass to our children is healthier, safer and more abundant than the one we inhabit today."[44]

This rhetoric notwithstanding, great powers do not work together to promote world order for its own sake. Instead, each seeks to maximize its own share of world power, which is likely to clash with the goal of creating and sustaining stable international orders.[45] This is not to say that great powers never aim to prevent wars and keep the peace. On the contrary, they work hard to deter wars in which they would be the likely victim. In such cases, however, state behavior is driven largely by narrow calculations about relative power, not by a commitment to build a world order independent of a state's own interests. The United States, for example, devoted enormous resources to deterring the Soviet Union from starting a war in Europe during the Cold War, not because of some deep-seated commitment to promoting peace around the world, but because American leaders feared that a Soviet victory would lead to a dangerous shift in the balance of power.[46]

The particular international order that obtains at any time is mainly a by-product of the self-interested behavior of the system's great powers. The configuration of the system, in other words, is the unintended consequence of great-power security competition, not the result of states acting together to organize peace. The establishment of the Cold War order in Europe illustrates this point. Neither the Soviet Union nor the United States intended to establish it, nor did they work together to create it. In fact, each superpower worked hard in the early years of the Cold War to gain power at the expense of the other, while preventing the other from doing likewise.[47] The system that emerged in Europe in the aftermath of World War II was the unplanned consequence of intense security competition between the superpowers.

Although that intense superpower rivalry ended along with the Cold War in 1990, Russia and the

United States have not worked together to create the present order in Europe. The United States, for example, has rejected out of hand various Russian proposals to make the Organization for Security and Cooperation in Europe the central organizing pillar of European security (replacing the U.S.-dominated NATO). Furthermore, Russia was deeply opposed to NATO expansion, which it viewed as a serious threat to Russian security. Recognizing that Russia's weakness would preclude any retaliation, however, the United States ignored Russia's concerns and pushed NATO to accept the Czech Republic, Hungary, and Poland as new members. Russia has also opposed U.S. policy in the Balkans over the past decade, especially NATO's 1999 war against Yugoslavia. Again, the United States has paid little attention to Russia's concerns and has taken the steps it deems necessary to bring peace to that volatile region. Finally, it is worth noting that although Russia is dead set against allowing the United States to deploy ballistic missile defenses, it is highly likely that Washington will deploy such a system if it is judged to be technologically feasible.

For sure, great-power rivalry will sometimes produce a stable international order, as happened during the Cold War. Nevertheless, the great powers will continue looking for opportunities to increase their share of world power, and if a favorable situation arises, they will move to undermine that stable order. Consider how hard the United States worked during the late 1980s to weaken the Soviet Union and bring down the stable order that had emerged in Europe during the latter part of the Cold War.[48] Of course, the states that stand to lose power will work to deter aggression and preserve the existing order. But their motives will be selfish, revolving around balance-of-power logic, not some commitment to world peace.

Great powers cannot commit themselves to the pursuit of a peaceful world order for two reasons. First, states are unlikely to agree on a general formula for bolstering peace. Certainly, international relations scholars have never reached a consensus on what the blueprint should look like. In fact, it seems there are about as many theories on the causes of war and peace as there are scholars studying the subject. But more important, policymakers are unable to agree on how to create a stable world. For example, at the Paris Peace Conference after World War I, important differences over how to create stability in Europe divided Georges Clemenceau, David Lloyd George, and Woodrow Wilson.[49] In particular, Clemenceau was determined to impose harsher terms on Germany over the Rhineland than was either Lloyd George or Wilson, while Lloyd George stood out as the hard-liner on German reparations. The Treaty of Versailles, not surprisingly, did little to promote European stability.

Furthermore, consider American thinking on how to achieve stability in Europe in the early days of the Cold War.[50] The key elements for a stable and durable system were in place by the early 1950s. They included the division of Germany, the positioning of American ground forces in Western Europe to deter a Soviet attack, and ensuring that West Germany would not seek to develop nuclear weapons. Officials in the Truman administration, however, disagreed about whether a divided Germany would be a source of peace or war. For example, George Kennan and Paul Nitze, who held important positions in the State Department, believed that a divided Germany would be a source of instability, whereas Secretary of State Dean Acheson disagreed with them. In the 1950s, President Eisenhower sought to end the American commitment to defend Western Europe and to provide West Germany with its own nuclear deterrent. This policy, which was never fully adopted, nevertheless caused significant instability in Europe, as it led directly to the Berlin crises of 1958–59 and 1961.[51]

Second, great powers cannot put aside power considerations and work to promote international peace because they cannot be sure that their efforts will succeed. If their attempt fails, they are likely to pay a steep price for having neglected the balance of power, because if an aggressor appears at the door there will be no answer when they dial 911. That is a risk few states are willing to run. Therefore, prudence dictates that they behave according to realist logic. This line of reasoning accounts for why collective security schemes, which call for states to put aside narrow concerns about the balance of power and instead act in accordance with the broader interests of the international community, invariably die at birth.[52]

Cooperation among States

One might conclude from the preceding discussion that my theory does not allow for any cooperation among the great powers. But this conclusion would be wrong. States can cooperate, although cooperation is sometimes difficult to achieve and always difficult to sustain. Two factors inhibit cooperation: considerations about relative gains and concern about cheating.[53] Ultimately, great powers live in a fundamentally competitive world where they view each other as real, or at least potential, enemies, and they therefore look to gain power at each other's expense.

Any two states contemplating cooperation must consider how profits or gains will be distributed between them. They can think about the division in terms of either absolute or relative gains (recall the distinction made earlier between pursuing either absolute power or relative power; the concept here is the same). With absolute gains, each side is concerned with maximizing its own profits and cares little about how much the other side gains or loses in the deal. Each side cares about the other only to the extent that the other side's behavior affects its own prospects for achieving maximum profits. With relative gains, on the other hand, each side considers not only its own individual gain, but also how well it fares compared to the other side.

Because great powers care deeply about the balance of power, their thinking focuses on relative gains when they consider cooperating with other states. For sure, each state tries to maximize its absolute gains; still, it is more important for a state to make sure that it does no worse, and perhaps better, than the other state in any agreement. Cooperation is more difficult to achieve, however, when states are attuned to relative gains rather than absolute gains.[54] This is because states concerned about absolute gains have to make sure that if the pie is expanding, they are getting at least some portion of the increase, whereas states that worry about relative gains must pay careful attention to how the pie is divided, which complicates cooperative efforts.

Concerns about cheating also hinder cooperation. Great powers are often reluctant to enter into cooperative agreements for fear that the other side will cheat on the agreement and gain a significant advantage. This concern is especially acute in the military realm, causing a "special peril of defection," because the nature of military weaponry allows for rapid shifts in the balance of power.[55] Such a development could create a window of opportunity for the state that cheats to inflict a decisive defeat on its victim.

These barriers to cooperation notwithstanding, great powers do cooperate in a realist world. Balance-of-power logic often causes great powers to form alliances and cooperate against common enemies. The United Kingdom, France, and Russia, for example, were allies against Germany before and during World War I. States sometimes cooperate to gang up on a third state, as Germany and the Soviet Union did against Poland in 1939.[56] More recently, Serbia and Croatia agreed to conquer and divide Bosnia between them, although the United States and its European allies prevented them from executing their agreement.[57] Rivals as well as allies cooperate. After all, deals can be struck that roughly reflect the distribution of power and satisfy concerns about cheating. The various arms control agreements signed by the superpowers during the Cold War illustrate this point.

The bottom line, however, is that cooperation takes place in a world that is competitive at its core—one where states have powerful incentives to take advantage of other states. This point is graphically highlighted by the state of European politics in the forty years before World War I. The great powers cooperated frequently during this period, but that did not stop them from going to war on August 1, 1914.[58] The United States and the Soviet Union also cooperated considerably during World War II, but that cooperation did not prevent the outbreak of the Cold War shortly after Germany and Japan were defeated. Perhaps most amazingly, there was significant economic and military cooperation between Nazi Germany and the Soviet Union during the two years before the Wehrmacht attacked the Red Army.[59] No amount of cooperation can eliminate the dominating logic of security competition. Genuine peace, or a world in which states do not compete for power, is not likely as long as the state system remains anarchic.

Conclusion

In sum, my argument is that the structure of the international system, not the particular characteristics of individual great powers, causes them to think and act offensively and to seek hegemony.[60] I do not adopt Morgenthau's claim that states invariably behave aggressively because they have a will to power hardwired into them. Instead, I assume that the principal motive behind great-power behavior is survival. In anarchy, however, the desire to survive encourages states to behave aggressively. Nor does my theory classify states as more or less aggressive on the basis of their economic or political systems. Offensive realism makes only a handful of assumptions about great powers, and these assumptions apply equally to all great powers. Except for differences in how much power each state controls, the theory treats all states alike.

I have now laid out the logic explaining why states seek to gain as much power as possible over their rivals. * * *

NOTES

1. Most realist scholars allow in their theories for status quo powers that are not hegemons. At least some states, they argue, are likely to be satisfied with the balance of power and thus have no incentive to change it. See Randall L. Schweller, "Neorealism's Status-Quo Bias: What Security Dilemma?" *Security Studies* 5, No. 3 (Spring 1996, special issue on "Realism: Restatements and Renewal," ed. Benjamin Frankel), pp. 98–101; and Arnold Wolfers, *Discord and Collaboration: Essays on International Politics* (Baltimore, MD: Johns Hopkins University Press, 1962), pp. 84–86, 91–92, 125–26.

2. Milton Friedman, *Essays in Positive Economics* (Chicago: University of Chicago Press, 1953), p. 14. Also see Kenneth N. Waltz, *Theory of International Politics* (Reading, MA: Addison-Wesley, 1979), pp. 5–6, 91, 119.

3. Terry Moe makes a helpful distinction between assumptions that are simply useful simplifications of reality (i.e., realistic in themselves but with unnecessary details omitted), and assumptions that are clearly contrary to reality (i.e., that directly violate well-established truths). See Moe, "On the Scientific Status of Rational Models," *American Journal of Political Science* 23, No. 1 (February 1979), pp. 215–43.

4. The concept of anarchy and its consequences for international politics was first articulated by G. Lowes Dickinson, *The European Anarchy* (New York: Macmillan, 1916). For a more recent and more elaborate discussion of anarchy, see Waltz, *Theory of International Politics*, pp. 88–93. Also see Robert J. Art and Robert Jervis, eds., *International Politics: Anarchy, Force, Imperialism* (Boston: Little, Brown, 1973), pt. 1; and Helen Milner, "The Assumption of

Anarchy in International Relations Theory: A Critique," *Review of International Studies* 17, No. 1 (January 1991), pp. 67–85.

5. Although the focus in this study is on the state system, realist logic can be applied to other kinds of anarchic systems. After all, it is the absence of central authority, not any special characteristic of states, that causes them to compete for power.

6. Inis L. Claude, Jr., *Swords into Plowshares: The Problems and Progress of International Organization*, 4th ed. (New York: Random House, 1971), p. 14.

7. The claim that states might have benign intentions is simply a starting assumption. I argue subsequently that when you combine the theory's five assumptions, states are put in a position in which they are strongly disposed to having hostile intentions toward each other.

8. My theory ultimately argues that great powers behave offensively toward each other because that is the best way for them to guarantee their security in an anarchic world. The assumption here, however, is that there are many reasons besides security for why a state might behave aggressively toward another state. In fact, it is uncertainty about whether those non-security causes of war are at play, or might come into play, that pushes great powers to worry about their survival and thus act offensively. Security concerns alone cannot cause great powers to act aggressively. The possibility that at least one state might be motivated by non-security calculations is a necessary condition for offensive realism, as well as for any other structural theory of international politics that predicts security competition.

9. Quoted in Jon Jacobson, *When the Soviet Union Entered World Politics* (Berkeley: University of California Press, 1994), p. 271.

10. See Elizabeth Pond, *Beyond the Wall: Germany's Road to Unification* (Washington, DC: Brookings Institution Press, 1993), chap. 12; Margaret Thatcher, *The Downing Street Years* (New York: HarperCollins, 1993), chaps. 25–26; and Philip Zelikow and Condoleezza Rice, *Germany Unified and Europe Transformed: A Study in Statecraft* (Cambridge, MA: Harvard University Press, 1995), chap. 4.

11. Frederick Schuman introduced the concept of self-help in *International Politics: An Introduction to the Western State System* (New York: McGraw-Hill, 1933), pp. 199–202, 514, although Waltz made the concept famous in *Theory of International Politics*, chap. 6. On realism and alliances, see Stephen M. Walt, *The Origins of Alliances* (Ithaca, NY: Cornell University Press, 1987).

12. Quoted in Martin Wight, *Power Politics* (London: Royal Institute of International Affairs, 1946), p. 40.

13. If one state achieves hegemony, the system ceases to be anarchic and becomes hierarchic. Offensive realism, which assumes international anarchy, has little to say about politics under hierarchy. But as discussed later, it is highly unlikely that any state will become a global hegemon, although regional hegemony is feasible. Thus, realism is likely to provide important insights about world politics for the foreseeable future, save for what goes on inside in a region that is dominated by a hegemon.

14. Although great powers always have aggressive intentions, they are not always *aggressors*, mainly because sometimes they do not have the capability to behave aggressively. I use the term "aggressor" throughout this book to denote great powers that have the material wherewithal to act on their aggressive intentions.

15. Kenneth Waltz maintains that great powers should not pursue hegemony but instead should aim to control an "appropriate" amount of world power. See Waltz, "The Origins of War in Neorealist Theory," in Robert I. Rotberg and Theodore K. Rabb, eds., *The Origin and Prevention of Major Wars* (Cambridge: Cambridge University Press, 1989), p. 40.

16. The following hypothetical example illustrates this point. Assume that American policy-makers were forced to choose between two different power balances in the Western Hemisphere. The first is the present distribution of power, whereby the United States is a hegemon that no state in the region would dare challenge militarily. In the second scenario, China replaces Canada and Germany takes the place of Mexico. Even though the United States would have a significant military advantage over both China

and Germany, it is difficult to imagine any American strategist opting for this scenario over U.S. hegemony in the Western Hemisphere.

17. John H. Herz, "Idealist Internationalism and the Security Dilemma," *World Politics* 2, No. 2 (January 1950), pp. 157–80. Although Dickinson did not use the term "security dilemma," its logic is clearly articulated in *European Anarchy*, pp. 20, 88.

18. Herz, "Idealist Internationalism," p. 157.

19. See Joseph M. Grieco, "Anarchy and the Limits of Cooperation: A Realist Critique of the Newest Liberal Institutionalism," *International Organization* 42, No. 3 (Summer 1988), pp. 485–507; Stephen D. Krasner, "Global Communications and National Power: Life on the Pareto Frontier," *World Politics* 43, No. 3 (April 1991), pp. 336–66; and Robert Powell, "Absolute and Relative Gains in International Relations Theory," *American Political Science Review* 85, No. 4 (December 1991), pp. 1303–20.

20. See Michael Mastanduno, "Do Relative Gains Matter? America's Response to Japanese Industrial Policy," *International Security* 16, No. 1 (Summer 1991), pp. 73–113.

21. Waltz maintains that in Hans Morgenthau's theory, states seek power as an end in itself; thus, they are concerned with absolute power, not relative power. See Waltz, "Origins of War," pp. 40–41; and Waltz, *Theory of International Politics*, pp. 126–27.

22. Quoted in Marc Trachtenberg, *A Constructed Peace: The Making of the European Settlement, 1945–1963* (Princeton, NJ: Princeton University Press, 1999), p. 36.

23. In short, the key issue for evaluating offensive realism is not whether a state is constantly trying to conquer other countries or going all out in terms of defense spending, but whether or not great powers routinely pass up promising opportunities to gain power over rivals.

24. See Richard K. Betts, *Surprise Attack: Lessons for Defense Planning* (Washington, DC: Brookings Institution Press, 1982); James D. Fearon, "Rationalist Explanations for War," *International Organization* 49, No. 3 (Summer 1995), pp. 390–401; Robert Jervis,

The Logic of Images in International Relations (Princeton, NJ: Princeton University Press, 1970); and Stephen Van Evera, *Causes of War: Power and the Roots of Conflict* (Ithaca, NY: Cornell University Press, 1999), pp. 45–51, 83, 137–42.

25. See Joel Achenbach, "The Experts in Retreat: After-the-Fact Explanations for the Gloomy Predictions," *Washington Post*, February 28, 1991; and Jacob Weisberg, "Gulfballs: How the Experts Blew It, Big-Time," *New Republic*, March 25, 1991.

26. Jack Snyder and Stephen Van Evera make this argument in its boldest form. See Jack Snyder, *Myths of Empire: Domestic Politics and International Ambition* (Ithaca, NY: Cornell University Press, 1991), esp. pp. 1, 307–8; and Van Evera, *Causes of War*, esp. pp. 6, 9.

27. Relatedly, some defensive realists interpret the security dilemma to say that the offensive measures a state takes to enhance its own security force rival states to respond in kind, leaving all states no better off than if they had done nothing, and possibly even worse off. See Charles L. Glaser, "The Security Dilemma Revisited," *World Politics* 50, No. 1 (October 1997), pp. 171–201.

28. Although threatened states sometimes balance efficiently against aggressors, they often do not, thereby creating opportunities for successful offense. Snyder appears to be aware of this problem, as he adds the important qualifier "at least in the long run" to his claim that "states typically form balancing alliances to resist aggressors." *Myths of Empire*, p. 11.

29. John Arquilla, *Dubious Battles: Aggression, Defeat, and the International System* (Washington, DC: Crane Russak, 1992), p. 2. Also see Bruce Bueno de Mesquita, *The War Trap* (New Haven, CT: Yale University Press, 1981), pp. 21–22; and Kevin Wang and James Ray, "Beginners and Winners: The Fate of Initiators of Interstate Wars Involving Great Powers since 1495," *International Studies Quarterly* 38, No. 1 (March 1994), pp. 139–54.

30. Although Snyder and Van Evera maintain that conquest rarely pays, both concede in subtle but important ways that aggression sometimes succeeds. Snyder, for example, distinguishes between expansion

(successful offense) and overexpansion (unsuccessful offense), which is the behavior that he wants to explain. See, for example, his discussion of Japanese expansion between 1868 and 1945 in *Myths of Empire*, pp. 114–16. Van Evera allows for variation in the offense-defense balance, to include a few periods where conquest is feasible. See *Causes of War*, chap. 6. Of course, allowing for successful aggression contradicts their central claim that offense hardly ever succeeds.

31. See Robert Gilpin, *War and Change in World Politics* (Cambridge: Cambridge University Press, 1981), p. 29; and William C. Wohlforth, *The Elusive Balance: Power and Perceptions during the Cold War* (Ithaca, NY: Cornell University Press, 1993), pp. 12–14.

32. In subsequent chapters, the power-projection problems associated with large bodies of water are taken into account when measuring the distribution of power (see Chapter 4). Those two factors are treated separately here, however, simply to highlight the profound influence that oceans have on the behavior of great powers.

33. For an opposing view, see David M. Edelstein, "Choosing Friends and Enemies: Perceptions of Intentions in International Relations," Ph.D. diss., University of Chicago, August 2000; Andrew Kydd, "Why Security Seekers Do Not Fight Each Other," *Security Studies* 7, No. 1 (Autumn 1997), pp. 114–54; and Walt, *Origins of Alliances*.

34. See note 8 in this chapter.

35. Jacob Viner, "Power versus Plenty as Objectives of Foreign Policy in the Seventeenth and Eighteenth Centuries," *World Politics* I, No. 1 (October 1948), p. 10.

36. See Mark Bowden, *Black Hawk Down: A Story of Modern War* (London: Penguin, 1999); Alison Des Forges, *"Leave None to Tell the Story": Genocide in Rwanda* (New York: Human Rights Watch, 1999), pp. 623–25; and Gerard Prunier, *The Rwanda Crisis: History of a Genocide* (New York: Columbia University Press, 1995), pp. 274–75.

37. See Scott R. Feil, *Preventing Genocide: How the Early Use of Force Might Have Succeeded in Rwanda* (New York: Carnegie Corporation, 1998); and John Mueller, "The Banality of 'Ethnic War,'" *International Security* 25, No. 1 (Summer 2000), pp. 58–62. For a less sanguine view of how many lives would have been saved had the United States intervened in Rwanda, see Alan J. Kuperman, "Rwanda in Retrospect," *Foreign Affairs* 79, No. 1 (January–February 2000), pp. 94–118.

38. See David F. Schmitz, *Thank God They're on Our Side: The United States and Right-Wing Dictatorships, 1921–1965* (Chapel Hill: University of North Carolina Press, 1999), chaps. 4–6; Gaddis Smith, *The Last Years of the Monroe Doctrine, 1945–1993* (New York: Hill and Wang, 1994); Tony Smith, *America's Mission: The United States and the Worldwide Struggle for Democracy in the Twentieth Century* (Princeton, NJ: Princeton University Press, 1994); and Stephen Van Evera, "Why Europe Matters, Why the Third World Doesn't: American Grand Strategy after the Cold War," *Journal of Strategic Studies* 13, No. 2 (June 1990), pp. 25–30.

39. Quoted in John M. Carroll and George C. Herring, eds., *Modern American Diplomacy*, rev. ed. (Wilmington, DE: Scholarly Resources, 1996), p. 122.

40. Nikita Khrushchev makes a similar point about Stalin's policy toward Chinese nationalist leader Chiang Kai-shek during World War II.

41. See Walt, *Origins of Alliances*, pp. 5, 266–68.

42. Adam Smith, *An Inquiry into the Nature and Causes of the Wealth of Nations,* ed. Edwin Cannan (Chicago: University of Chicago Press, 1976), Vol. 1, p. 487. All the quotes in this paragraph are from pp. 484–87 of that book.

43. For an overview of the Anglo-Dutch rivalry, see Jack S. Levy, "The Rise and Decline of the Anglo-Dutch Rivalry, 1609–1689," in William R. Thompson, ed., *Great Power Rivalries* (Columbia: University of South Carolina Press, 1999), pp. 172–200; and Paul M. Kennedy, *The Rise and Fall of British Naval Mastery* (London: Allen Lane, 1976), chap. 2.

44. William J. Clinton, "Address by the President to the 48th Session of the United Nations General Assembly," United Nations, New York, September 27, 1993.

Also see George Bush, "Toward a New World Order: Address by the President to a Joint Session of Congress," September 11, 1990.

45. Bradley Thayer examined whether the victorious powers were able to create and maintain stable security orders in the aftermath of the Napoleonic Wars, World War I, and World War II, or whether they competed among themselves for power, as realism would predict. Thayer concludes that the rhetoric of the triumphant powers notwithstanding, they remained firmly committed to gaining power at each other's expense. See Bradley A. Thayer, "Creating Stability in New World Orders," Ph.D. diss., University of Chicago, August 1996.

46. See Melvyn P. Leffler, *A Preponderance of Power: National Security, the Truman Administration, and the Cold War* (Stanford, CA: Stanford University Press, 1992).

47. For a discussion of American efforts to undermine Soviet control of Eastern Europe, see Peter Grose, *Operation Rollback: America's Secret War behind the Iron Curtain* (Boston: Houghton Mifflin, 2000); Walter L. Hixson, *Parting the Curtain: Propaganda, Culture, and the Cold War, 1945–1961* (New York: St. Martin's, 1997); and Gregory Mitrovich, *Undermining the Kremlin: America's Strategy to Subvert the Soviet Bloc, 1947–1956* (Ithaca, NY: Cornell University Press, 2000).

48. For a synoptic discussion of U.S. policy toward the Soviet Union in the late 1980s that cites most of the key sources on the subject, see Randall L. Schweller and William C. Wohlforth, "Power Test: Evaluating Realism in Response to the End of the Cold War," *Security Studies* 9, No. 3 (Spring 2000), pp. 91–97.

49. The editors of a major book on the Treaty of Versailles write, "The resulting reappraisal, as documented in this book, constitutes a new synthesis of peace conference scholarship. The findings call attention to divergent peace aims within the American and Allied camps and underscore the degree to which the negotiators themselves considered the Versailles Treaty a work in progress." Manfred F. Boemeke, Gerald D. Feldman, and Elisabeth Glaser, eds., *The*

Treaty of Versailles: A Reassessment after 75 Years (Cambridge: Cambridge University Press, 1998), p. 1.

50. This paragraph draws heavily on Trachtenberg, *Constructed Peace*; and Marc Trachtenberg, *History and Strategy* (Princeton, NJ: Princeton University Press, 1991), chaps. 4–5. Also see G. John Ikenberry, "Rethinking the Origins of American Hegemony," *Political Science Quarterly* 104, No. 3 (Autumn 1989), pp. 375–400.

51. The failure of American policymakers during the early Cold War to understand where the security competition in Europe was leading is summarized by Trachtenberg, "The predictions that were made pointed as a rule in the opposite direction: that Germany could not be kept down forever; that the Federal Republic would ultimately . . . want nuclear forces of her own; that U.S. troops could not be expected to remain in . . . Europe. . . . Yet all these predictions—every single one—turned out to be wrong." Trachtenberg, *History and Strategy*, pp. 231–32. Also see Trachtenberg, *Constructed Peace*, pp. vii–viii.

52. For more discussion of the pitfalls of collective security, see John J. Mearsheimer, "The False Promise of International Institutions," *International Security* 19, No. 3 (Winter 1994–95), pp. 26–37.

53. See Grieco, "Anarchy and the Limits of Cooperation," pp. 498, 500.

54. For evidence of relative gains considerations thwarting cooperation among states, see Paul W. Schroeder, *The Transformation of European Politics, 1763–1848* (Oxford: Clarendon, 1994), chap. 3.

55. Charles Lipson, "International Cooperation in Economic and Security Affairs," *World Politics* 37, No. 1 (October 1984), p. 14.

56. See Randall L. Schweller, "Bandwagoning for Profit: Bringing the Revisionist State Back In," *International Security* 19, No. 1 (Summer 1994), pp. 72–107. See also the works cited in note 59 in this chapter.

57. See Misha Glenny, *The Fall of Yugoslavia: The Third Balkan War*, 3d rev. ed. (New York: Penguin, 1996), p. 149; Philip Sherwell and Alina Petric, "Tudjman Tapes Reveal Plans to Divide Bosnia and Hide War

Crimes," *Sunday Telegraph* (London), June 18, 2000; Laura Silber and Allan Little, *Yugoslavia: Death of a Nation*, rev. ed. (New York: Penguin, 1997), pp. 131–32, 213; and Warren Zimmerman, *Origins of a Catastrophe: Yugoslavia and Its Destroyers— America's Last Ambassador Tells What Happened and Why* (New York: Times Books, 1996), pp. 116–17.

58. See John Maynard Keynes, *The Economic Consequences of the Peace* (New York: Penguin, 1988), chap. 2; and J. M. Roberts, *Europe, 1880–1945* (London: Longman, 1970), pp. 239–41.

59. For information on the Molotov-Ribbentrop Pact of August 1939 and the ensuing cooperation between those states, see Alan Bullock, *Hitler and Stalin: Parallel Lives* (London: HarperCollins, 1991), chaps. 14–15; I.C.B. Dear, ed., *The Oxford Companion to World War II* (Oxford: Oxford University Press, 1995), pp. 780–82; Anthony Read and David Fisher, *The Deadly Embrace: Hitler, Stalin, and the Nazi-Soviet Pact, 1939–1941* (New York: Norton, 1988); Geoffrey Roberts, *The Unholy Alliance: Stalin's Pact with Hitler* (Bloomington: Indiana University Press, 1989), chaps. 8–10; and Adam B. Ulam, *Expansion and Coexistence: Soviet Foreign Policy, 1917–1973*, 2d ed. (New York: Holt, Rinehart, and Winston, 1974), chap. 6.

60. Waltz maintains that structural theories can explain international outcomes—i.e., whether war is more likely in bipolar or multipolar systems—but that they cannot explain the foreign policy behavior of particular states. A separate theory of foreign policy, he argues, is needed for that task. See *Theory of International Politics*, pp. 71–72, 121–23.

Michael W. Doyle
LIBERALISM AND WORLD POLITICS

Promoting freedom will produce peace, we have often been told. In a speech before the British Parliament in June of 1982, President Reagan proclaimed that governments founded on a respect for individual liberty exercise "restraint" and "peaceful intentions" in their foreign policy. He then announced a "crusade for freedom" and a "campaign for democratic development" (Reagan, June 9, 1982).

In making these claims the president joined a long list of liberal theorists (and propagandists) and echoed an old argument: the aggressive instincts of authoritarian leaders and totalitarian ruling parties make for war. Liberal states, founded on such individual rights as equality before the law, free speech and other civil liberties, private property, and elected representation are fundamentally against war this argument asserts. When the citizens who bear the burdens of war elect their governments, wars become impossible. Furthermore, citizens appreciate that the benefits of trade can be enjoyed only under conditions of peace. Thus the very existence of liberal states, such as the U.S., Japan, and our European allies, makes for peace.

Building on a growing literature in international political science, I reexamine the liberal claim President Reagan reiterated for us. I look at three distinct theoretical traditions of liberalism, attributable to three theorists: Schumpeter, a brilliant explicator of the liberal pacifism the president invoked; Machiavelli, a classical republican whose glory is an imperialism we often practice; and Kant.

Despite the contradictions of liberal pacifism and liberal imperialism, I find, with Kant and other liberal republicans, that liberalism does leave a coherent legacy on foreign affairs. Liberal states are different. They are indeed peaceful, yet they are also prone to make war, as the U.S. and our "freedom fighters" are now doing, not so covertly, against Nicaragua. Liberal states have created a separate peace, as Kant argued they would, and have also discovered liberal reasons for aggression, as he feared they might. I conclude by arguing that the differences among liberal pacifism, liberal imperialism, and Kant's liberal internationalism are not arbitrary but rooted in differing conceptions of the citizen and the state.

Liberal Pacifism

There is no canonical description of liberalism. What we tend to call *liberal* resembles a family portrait of principles and institutions, recognizable by certain characteristics—for example, individual freedom, political participation, private property, and equality of opportunity—that most liberal states share, although none has perfected them all. Joseph Schumpeter clearly fits within this family when he considers the international effects of capitalism and democracy.

Schumpeter's "Sociology of Imperialisms," published in 1919, made a coherent and sustained argument concerning the pacifying (in the sense

From *American Political Science Review* 80, no. 4 (Dec. 1986): 1151–1169. The author's notes have been omitted.

of nonaggressive) effects of liberal institutions and principles (Schumpeter, 1955; see also Doyle, 1986, pp. 155–59). Unlike some of the earlier liberal theorists who focused on a single feature such as trade (Montesquieu, 1949, vol. I, bk. 20, chap. 1) or failed to examine critically the arguments they were advancing, Schumpeter saw the interaction of capitalism and democracy as the foundation of liberal pacifism, and he tested his arguments in a sociology of historical imperialisms.

He defines *imperialism* as "an objectless disposition on the part of a state to unlimited forcible expansion" (Schumpeter, 1955, p. 6). Excluding imperialisms that were mere "catchwords" and those that were "object-ful" (e.g., defensive imperialism), he traces the roots of objectless imperialism to three sources, each an atavism. Modern imperialism, according to Schumpeter, resulted from the combined impact of a "war machine," warlike instincts, and export monopolism.

Once necessary, the war machine later developed a life of its own and took control of a state's foreign policy: "Created by the wars that required it, the machine now created the wars it required" (Schumpeter, 1955, p. 25). Thus, Schumpeter tells us that the army of ancient Egypt, created to drive the Hyksos out of Egypt, took over the state and pursued militaristic imperialism. Like the later armies of the courts of absolutist Europe, it fought wars for the sake of glory and booty, for the sake of warriors and monarchs—wars *gratia* warriors.

A warlike disposition, elsewhere called "instinctual elements of bloody primitivism," is the natural ideology of a war machine. It also exists independently; the Persians, says Schumpeter (1955, pp. 25–32), were a warrior nation from the outset.

Under modern capitalism, export monopolists, the third source of modern imperialism, push for imperialist expansion as a way to expand their closed markets. The absolute monarchies were the last clear-cut imperialisms. Nineteenth-century imperialisms merely represent the vestiges of the imperialisms created by Louis XIV and Catherine the Great. Thus, the export monopolists are an atavism of the absolute monarchies, for they depend completely on the tariffs imposed by the monarchs and their militaristic successors for revenue (Schumpeter, 1955, p. 82–83). Without tariffs, monopolies would be eliminated by foreign competition.

Modern (nineteenth century) imperialism, therefore, rests on an atavistic war machine, militaristic attitudes left over from the days of monarchical wars, and export monopolism, which is nothing more than the economic residue of monarchical finance. In the modern era, imperialists gratify their private interests. From the national perspective, their imperialistic wars are objectless.

Schumpeter's theme now emerges. Capitalism and democracy are forces for peace. Indeed, they are antithetical to imperialism. For Schumpeter, the further development of capitalism and democracy means that imperialism will inevitably disappear. He maintains that capitalism produces an unwarlike disposition; its populace is "democratized, individualized, rationalized" (Schumpeter, 1955, p. 68). The people's energies are daily absorbed in production. The disciplines of industry and the market train people in "economic rationalism"; the instability of industrial life necessitates calculation. Capitalism also "individualizes"; "subjective opportunities" replace the "immutable factors" of traditional, hierarchical society. Rational individuals demand democratic governance.

Democratic capitalism leads to peace. As evidence, Schumpeter claims that throughout the capitalist world an opposition has arisen to "war, expansion, cabinet diplomacy"; that contemporary capitalism is associated with peace parties; and that the industrial worker of capitalism is "vigorously anti-imperialist." In addition, he points out that the capitalist world has developed means of preventing war, such as the Hague Court and that the least feudal, most capitalist society—the United States—has demonstrated the least imperialistic tendencies (Schumpeter, 1955, pp. 95–96). An example of the lack of imperialistic tendencies in the U.S., Schumpeter thought, was our leaving over half of Mexico unconquered in the war of 1846–48.

Schumpeter's explanation for liberal pacifism is quite simple: Only war profiteers and military aristocrats gain from wars. No democracy would pursue a minority interest and tolerate the high costs of imperialism. When free trade prevails, "no class" gains from forcible expansion because

> foreign raw materials and food stuffs are as accessible to each nation as though they were in its own territory. Where the cultural backwardness of a region makes normal economic intercourse dependent on colonization it does not matter, assuming free trade, which of the "civilized" nations undertakes the task of colonization. (Schumpeter, 1955, pp. 75–76)

Schumpeter's arguments are difficult to evaluate. In partial tests of quasi-Schumpeterian propositions, Michael Haas (1974, pp. 464–65) discovered a cluster that associates democracy, development, and sustained modernization with peaceful conditions. However, M. Small and J. D. Singer (1976) have discovered that there is no clearly negative correlation between democracy and war in the period 1816–1965—the period that would be central to Schumpeter's argument (see also Wilkenfeld, 1968, Wright, 1942, p. 841).

* * * A recent study by R. J. Rummel (1983) of "libertarianism" and international violence is the closest test Schumpeterian pacifism has received. "Free" states (those enjoying political and economic freedom) were shown to have considerably less conflict at or above the level of economic sanctions than "nonfree" states. The free states, the partly free states (including the democratic socialist countries such as Sweden), and the nonfree states accounted for 24%, 26%, and 61%, respectively, of the international violence during the period examined.

These effects are impressive but not conclusive for the Schumpeterian thesis. The data are limited, in this test, to the period 1976 to 1980. It includes, for example, the Russo-Afghan War, the Vietnamese invasion of Cambodia, China's invasion of Vietnam, and Tanzania's invasion of Uganda but just misses the U.S., quasi-covert intervention in Angola (1975) and our not so covert war against Nicaragua (1981–). More importantly, it excludes the cold war period, with its numerous interventions, and the long history of colonial wars (the Boer War, the Spanish-American War, the Mexican Intervention, etc.) that marked the history of liberal, including democratic capitalist, states (Doyle, 1983b; Chan, 1984; Weede, 1984).

The discrepancy between the warlike history of liberal states and Schumpeter's pacifistic expectations highlights three extreme assumptions. First, his "materialistic monism" leaves little room for noneconomic objectives, whether espoused by states or individuals. Neither glory, nor prestige, nor ideological justification, nor the pure power of ruling shapes policy. These nonmaterial goals leave little room for positive-sum gains, such as the comparative advantages of trade. Second, and relatedly, the same is true for his states. The political life of individuals seems to have been homogenized at the same time as the individuals were "rationalized, individualized, and democratized." Citizens—capitalists and workers, rural and urban—seek material welfare. Schumpeter seems to presume that ruling makes no difference. He also presumes that no one is prepared to take those measures (such as stirring up foreign quarrels to preserve a domestic ruling coalition) that enhance one's political power, despite deterimental effects on mass welfare. Third, like domestic politics, world politics are homogenized. Materially monistic and democratically capitalist, all states evolve toward free trade and liberty together. Countries differently constituted seem to disappear from Schumpeter's analysis. "Civilized" nations govern "culturally backward" *regions*. These assumptions are not shared by Machiavelli's theory of liberalism.

Liberal Imperialism

Machiavelli argues, not only that republics are not pacifistic, but that they are the best form of state for imperial expansion. Establishing a republic fit for imperial expansion is, moreover, the best way to guarantee the survival of a state.

Machiavelli's republic is a classical mixed republic. It is not a democracy—which he thought would quickly degenerate into a tyranny—but is characterized by social equality, popular liberty, and political participation (Machiavelli, 1950, bk. 1, chap. 2, p. 112; see also Huliung, 1983, chap. 2; Mansfield, 1970; Pocock, 1975, pp. 198–99; Skinner, 1981, chap. 3). The consuls serve as "kings," the senate as an aristocracy managing the state, and the people in the assembly as the source of strength.

Liberty results from "disunion"—the competition and necessity for compromise required by the division of powers among senate, consuls, and tribunes (the last representing the common people). Liberty also results from the popular veto. The powerful few threaten the rest with tyranny, Machiavelli says, because they seek to dominate. The mass demands not to be dominated, and their veto thus preserves the liberties of the state (Machiavelli, 1950, bk. 1, chap. 5, p. 122). However, since the people and the rulers have different social characters, the people need to be "managed" by the few to avoid having their recklessness overturn or their fecklessness undermine the ability of the state to expand (Machiavelli, 1950, bk. 1, chap. 53, pp. 249–50). Thus the senate and the consuls plan expansion, consult oracles, and employ religion to manage the resources that the energy of the people supplies.

Strength, and then imperial expansion, results from the way liberty encourages increased population and property, which grow when the citizens know their lives and goods are secure from arbitrary seizure. Free citizens equip large armies and provide soldiers who fight for public glory and the common good because these are, in fact, their own (Machiavelli, 1950, bk. 2, chap. 2, pp. 287–90). If you seek the honor of having your state expand, Machiavelli advises, you should organize it as a free and popular republic like Rome, rather than as an aristocratic republic like Sparta or Venice. Expansion thus calls for a free republic.

"Necessity"—political survival—calls for expansion. If a stable aristocratic republic is forced by foreign conflict "to extend her territory, in such a case we shall see her foundations give way and herself quickly brought to ruin"; if, on the other hand, domestic security prevails, "the continued tranquility would enervate her, or provoke internal disensions, which together, or either of them separately, will apt to prove her ruin" (Machiavelli, 1950, bk. 1, chap. 6, p. 129). Machiavelli therefore believes it is necessary to take the constitution of Rome, rather than that of Sparta or Venice, as our model.

Hence, this belief leads to liberal imperialism. We are lovers of glory, Machiavelli announces. We seek to rule or, at least, to avoid being oppressed. In either case, we want more for ourselves and our states than just material welfare (materialistic monism). Because other states with similar aims thereby threaten us, we prepare ourselves for expansion. Because our fellow citizens threaten us if we do not allow them either to satisfy their ambition or to release their political energies through imperial expansion, we expand.

There is considerable historical evidence for liberal imperialism. Machiavelli's (Polybius's) Rome and Thucydides' Athens both were imperial republics in the Machiavellian sense (Thucydides, 1954, bk. 6). The historical record of numerous U.S. interventions in the postwar period supports Machiavelli's argument (* * * Barnet, 1968, chap. 11), but the current record of liberal pacifism, weak as it is, calls some of his insights into question. To the extent that the modern populace actually controls (and thus unbalances) the mixed republic, its diffidence may outweigh elite ("senatorial") aggressiveness.

We can conclude either that (1) liberal pacifism has at least taken over with the further development of capitalist democracy, as Schumpeter predicted it would or that (2) the mixed record of liberalism—pacifism and imperialism—indicates that some liberal states are Schumpeterian democracies while others are Machiavellian republics. Before we accept either conclusion, however, we must consider a third apparent regularity of modern world politics.

Liberal Internationalism

Modern liberalism carries with it two legacies. They do not affect liberal states separately, according to whether they are pacifistic or imperialistic, but simultaneously.

The first of these legacies is the pacification of foreign relations among liberal states. * * *

Beginning in the eighteenth century and slowly growing since then, a zone of peace, which Kant called the "pacific federation" or "pacific union," has begun to be established among liberal societies. More than 40 liberal states currently make up the union. Most are in Europe and North America, but they can be found on every continent, as Appendix 1 indicates.

Here the predictions of liberal pacifists (and President Reagan) are borne out: liberal states do exercise peaceful restraint, and a separate peace exists among them. This separate peace provides a solid foundation for the United States' crucial alliances with the liberal powers, e.g., the North Atlantic Treaty Organization and our Japanese alliance. This foundation appears to be impervious to the quarrels with our allies that bedeviled the Carter and Reagan administrations. It also offers the promise of a continuing peace among liberal states, and as the number of liberal states increases, it announces the possibility of global peace this side of the grave or world conquest.

Of course, the probability of the outbreak of war in any given year between any two given states is low. The occurrence of a war between any two adjacent states, considered over a long period of time, would be more probable. The apparent absence of war between liberal states, whether adjacent or not, for almost 200 years thus may have significance. Similar claims cannot be made for feudal, fascist, communist, authoritarian, or totalitarian forms of rule (Doyle, 1983a, p. 222), nor for pluralistic or merely similar societies. More significant perhaps is that when states are forced to decide on which side of an impending world war they will fight, liberal states all wind up on the same side despite the complexity of the paths that take them there. These characteristics do not prove that the peace among liberals is statistically significant nor that liberalism is the sole valid explanation for the peace. They do suggest that we consider the possibility that liberals have indeed established a separate peace—but only among themselves.

Liberalism also carries with it a second legacy: international "imprudence" (Hume, 1963, pp. 346–47). Peaceful restraint only seems to work in liberals' relations with other liberals. Liberal states have fought numerous wars with nonliberal states. (For a list of international wars since 1816 see Appendix 2.)

Many of these wars have been defensive and thus prudent by necessity. Liberal states have been attacked and threatened by nonliberal states that do not exercise any special restraint in their dealings with the liberal states. Authoritarian rulers both stimulate and respond to an international political environment in which conflicts of prestige, interest, and pure fear of what other states might do all lead states toward war. War and conquest have thus characterized the careers of many authoritarian rulers and ruling parties, from Louis XIV and Napoleon to Mussolini's fascists, Hitler's Nazis, and Stalin's communists.

Yet we cannot simply blame warfare on the authoritarians or totalitarians, as many of our more enthusiastic politicians would have us do. Most wars arise out of calculations and miscalculations of interest, misunderstandings, and mutual suspicions, such as those that characterized the origins of World War I. However, aggression by the liberal state has also characterized a large number of wars. Both France and Britain fought expansionist colonial wars throughout the nineteenth century. The United States fought a similar war with Mexico from 1846 to 1848, waged a war of annihilation against the American Indians, and intervened militarily against sovereign states many times before and after World War II. Liberal states invade weak nonliberal states and display striking distrust in dealings with powerful nonliberal states (Doyle, 1983b).

Neither realist (statist) nor Marxist theory accounts well for these two legacies. While they can account for aspects of certain periods of international stability (* * * Russett, 1985), neither the logic of the balance of power nor the logic of international hegemony explains the separate peace maintained for more than 150 years among states sharing one particular form of governance—liberal principles and institutions. Balance-of-power theory expects—indeed is premised upon—flexible arrangements of geostrategic rivalry that include preventive war. Hegemonies wax and wane, but the liberal peace holds. Marxist "ultra-imperialists" expect a form of peaceful rivalry among capitalists, but only liberal capitalists maintain peace. Leninists expect liberal capitalists to be aggressive toward nonliberal states, but they also (and especially) expect them to be imperialistic toward fellow liberal capitalists.

Kant's theory of liberal internationalism helps us understand these two legacies. * * * *Perpetual Peace*, written in 1795 (Kant, 1970, pp. 93–130), helps us understand the interactive nature of international relations. Kant tries to teach us methodologically that we can study neither the systemic relations of states nor the varieties of state behavior in isolation from each other. Substantively, he anticipates for us the ever-widening pacification of a liberal pacific union, explains this pacification,

and at the same time suggests why liberal states are not pacific in their relations with nonliberal states. Kant argues that perpetual peace will be guaranteed by the ever-widening acceptance of three "definitive articles" of peace. When all nations have accepted the definitive articles in a metaphorical "treaty" of perpetual peace he asks them to sign, perpetual peace will have been established.

The First Definitive Article requires the civil constitution of the state to be republican. By *republican* Kant means a political society that has solved the problem of combining moral autonomy, individualism, and social order. A private property and market-oriented economy partially addressed that dilemma in the private sphere. The public, or political, sphere was more troubling. His answer was a republic that preserved juridical freedom—the legal equality of citizens as subjects—on the basis of a representative government with a separation of powers. Juridical freedom is preserved because the morally autonomous individual is by means of representation a self-legislator making laws that apply to all citizens equally, including himself or herself. Tyranny is avoided because the individual is subject to laws he or she does not also administer (Kant, *PP* [*Perpetual Peace*], pp. 99–102 * * *).

Liberal republics will progressively establish peace among themselves by means of the pacific federation, or union (*foedus pacificum*), described in Kant's Second Definitive Article. The pacific union will establish peace within a federation of free states and securely maintain the rights of each state. The world will not have achieved the "perpetual peace" that provides the ultimate guarantor of republican freedom until "a late stage and after many unsuccessful attempts" (Kant, *UH* [*The Idea for a Universal History with a Cosmopolitan Purpose*], p. 47). At that time, all nations will have learned the lessons of peace through right conceptions of the appropriate constitution, great and sad experience, and good will. Only then will individuals enjoy perfect republican rights or the full guarantee of a global and just peace. In the meantime, the "pacific federation" of liberal republics—"an enduring and gradually expanding federation likely to prevent war"—brings within it more and more republics—despite republican collapses, backsliding, and disastrous wars—creating an ever-expanding separate peace (Kant, *PP*, p. 105). Kant emphasizes that

> it can be shown that this idea of federalism, extending gradually to encompass all states and thus leading to perpetual peace, is practicable and has objective reality. For if by good fortune one powerful and enlightened nation can form a republic (which is by nature inclined to seek peace), this will provide a focal point for federal association among other states. These will join up with the first one, thus securing the freedom of each state in accordance with the idea of international right, and the whole will gradually spread further and further by a series of alliances of this kind. (Kant, *PP*, p. 104)

The pacific union is not a single peace treaty ending one war, a world state, nor a state of nations. Kant finds the first insufficient. The second and third are impossible or potentially tyrannical. National sovereignty precludes reliable subservience to a state of nations; a world state destroys the civic freedom on which the development of human capacities rests (Kant, *UH*, p. 50). Although Kant obliquely refers to various classical interstate confederations and modern diplomatic congresses, he develops no systematic organizational embodiment of this treaty and presumably does not find institutionalization necessary (Riley, 1983, chap. 5; Schwarz, 1962, p. 77). He appears to have in mind a mutual nonaggression pact, perhaps a collective security agreement, and the cosmopolitan law set forth in the Third Definitive Article.

The Third Definitive Article establishes a cosmopolitan law to operate in conjunction with the pacific union. The cosmopolitan law "shall be limited to conditions of universal hospitality." In this Kant calls for the recognition of the "right of a foreigner not to be treated with hostility when he arrives on someone else's territory." This "does not extend beyond those conditions which make it possible for them [foreigners] to attempt to enter into relations [commerce] with the native inhabitants" (Kant, *PP*, p. 106). Hospitality does not require extending to foreigners either the right to citizenship or the right to settlement, unless the foreign visitors would perish if they were expelled. Foreign conquest and plunder also find no justification under this right. Hospitality does appear to include the right of access and the obligation of maintaining the opportunity for citizens to exchange goods and ideas without imposing the obligation to trade (a voluntary act in all cases under liberal constitutions).

Perpetual peace, for Kant, is an epistemology, a condition for ethical action, and, most importantly, an explanation of how the "mechanical process of nature visibly exhibits the purposive plan of producing concord among men, even against their will and indeed by means of their very discord" (Kant, *PP*, p. 108; *UH*, pp. 44–45). Understanding history requires an epistemological foundation, for without a teleology, such as the promise of perpetual peace, the complexity of history would overwhelm human understanding (Kant, *UH*, pp. 51–53). Perpetual peace, however, is not merely a heuristic device with which to interpret history. It is guaranteed, Kant explains in the "First Addition" to *Perpetual Peace* ("On the Guarantee of Perpetual Peace"), to result from men fulfilling their ethical duty or, failing that, from a hidden plan. Peace is an ethical duty because it is only under conditions of peace that all men can treat each other as ends, rather than means to an end (Kant, *UH*, p. 50; Murphy, 1970, chap. 3). * * *

In the end, however, our guarantee of perpetual peace does not rest on ethical conduct. * * *

The guarantee thus rests, Kant argues, not on the probable behavior of moral angels, but on that of "devils, so long as they possess understanding" (*PP*, p. 112). In explaining the sources of each of the three definitive articles of the perpetual peace, Kant then tells us how we (as free and intelligent devils) could be motivated by fear, force, and calculated advantage to undertake a course of action whose outcome we could reasonably anticipate to be perpetual peace. Yet while it is possible to conceive of the Kantian road to peace in these terms, Kant himself recognizes and argues that social evolution also makes the conditions of moral behavior less onerous and hence more likely (*CF* [*The Contest of Faculties*], pp. 187–89; Kelly, 1969, pp. 106–13). In tracing the effects of both political and moral development, he builds an account of why liberal states do maintain peace among themselves and of how it will (by implication, has) come about that the pacific union will expand. He also explains how these republics would engage in wars with nonrepublics and therefore suffer the "sad experience" of wars that an ethical policy might have avoided.

■ ■ ■

Kant shows how republics, once established, lead to peaceful relations. He argues that once the aggressive interests of absolutist monarchies are tamed and the habit of respect for individual rights engrained by republican government, wars would appear as the disaster to the people's welfare that he and the other liberals thought them to be. The fundamental reason is this:

> If, as is inevitability the case under this constitution, the consent of the citizens is required to decide whether or not war should be declared, it is very natural that they will have a great hesitation in embarking on so dangerous an enterprise. For this would mean calling down on themselves all the miseries of war, such as doing the fighting themselves, supplying the costs of the war from their own resources, painfully making good the ensuing devastation, and, as the crowning evil, having to take upon themselves a burden of debts which will embitter peace itself and which can never be paid off on account of the constant threat of new wars. But under a constitution where the subject is not a citizen, and which is therefore not republican, it is the simplest thing in the world to go to war. For the head of state is not a fellow citizen, but the owner of the state, and war will not force him to make the slightest sacrifice so far as his banquets, hunts, pleasure palaces and court festivals are concerned. He can thus decide on war, without any significant reason, as a kind of amusement, and unconcernedly leave it to the diplomatic corps (who are always ready for such proposes) to justify the war for the sake of propriety. (Kant, *PP*, p. 100).

Yet these domestic republican restraints do not end war. If they did, liberal states would not be warlike, which is far from the case. They do introduce republican caution—Kant's "hesitation"—in place of monarchical caprice. Liberal wars are only fought for popular, liberal purposes. The historical liberal legacy is laden with popular wars fought to promote freedom, to protect private property, or to support liberal allies against nonliberal enemies. Kant's position is ambiguous. He regards these wars as unjust and warns liberals of their susceptibility to them (Kant, *PP*, p. 106). At the same time, Kant argues that each nation "can and ought to" demand that its neighboring nations enter into the pacific union of liberal states (*PP*, p. 102). * * *

■ ■ ■

* * * As republics emerge (the first source) and as culture progresses, an understanding of the legitimate rights of all citizens and of all republics

comes into play; and this, now that caution characterizes policy, sets up the moral foundations for the liberal peace. Correspondingly, international law highlights the importance of Kantian publicity. Domestically, publicity helps ensure that the officials of republics act according to the principles they profess to hold just and according to the interests of the electors they claim to represent. Internationally, free speech and the effective communication of accurate conceptions of the political life of foreign peoples is essential to establishing and preserving the understanding on which the guarantee of respect depends. Domestically just republics, which rest on consent, then presume foreign republics also to be consensual, just, and therefore deserving of accommodation. * * * Because nonliberal governments are in a state of aggression with their own people, their foreign relations become for liberal governments deeply suspect. In short, fellow liberals benefit from a presumption of amity; nonliberals suffer from a presumption of enmity. Both presumptions may be accurate; each, however, may also be self-confirming.

Lastly, cosmopolitan law adds material incentives to moral commitments. The cosmopolitan right to hospitality permits the "spirit of commerce" sooner or later to take hold of every nation, thus impelling states to promote peace and to try to avert war. Liberal economic theory holds that these cosmopolitan ties derive from a cooperative international division of labor and free trade according to comparative advantage. Each economy is said to be better off than it would have been under autarky; each thus acquires an incentive to avoid policies that would lead the other to break these economic ties. Because keeping open markets rests upon the assumption that the next set of transactions will also be determined by prices rather than coercion, a sense of mutual security is vital to avoid security-motivated searches for economic autarky. Thus, avoiding a challenge to another liberal state's security or even enhancing each other's security by means of alliance naturally follows economic interdependence.

A further cosmopolitan source of liberal peace is the international market's removal of difficult decisions of production and distribution from the direct sphere of state policy. A foreign state thus does not appear directly responsible for these outcomes, and states can stand aside from, and to some degree above, these contentious market rivalries and be ready to step in to resolve crises. The interdependence of commerce and the international contacts of state officials help create crosscutting transnational ties that serve as lobbies for mutual accommodation. According to modern liberal scholars, international financiers and transnational and transgovernmental organizations create interests in favor of accommodation. Moreover, their variety has ensured that no single conflict sours an entire relationship by setting off a spiral of reciprocated retaliation * * *. Conversely, a sense of suspicion, such as that characterizing relations between liberal and nonliberal governments, can lead to restrictions on the range of contacts between societies, and this can increase the prospect that a single conflict will determine an entire relationship.

No single constitutional, international, or cosmopolitan source is alone sufficient, but together (and only together) they plausibly connect the characteristics of liberal polities and economies with sustained liberal peace. Alliances founded on mutual strategic interest among liberal and nonliberal states have been broken; economic ties between liberal and nonliberal states have proven fragile; but the political bonds of liberal rights and interests have proven a remarkably firm foundation for mutual nonaggression. A separate peace exists among liberal states.

In their relations with nonliberal states, however, liberal states have not escaped from the insecurity caused by anarchy in the world political system considered as a whole. Moreover, the very constitutional restraint, international respect for individual rights, and shared commercial interests that establish grounds for peace among liberal states establish grounds for additional conflict in relations between liberal and nonliberal societies.

Conclusion

Kant's liberal internationalism, Machiavelli's liberal imperialism, and Schumpeter's liberal pacifism rest on fundamentally different views of the nature of the human being, the state, and international relations. Schumpeter's humans are rationalized, individualized, and democratized. They are also homogenized, pursuing material interests "monistically." Because their material interests lie in peaceful trade, they and the democratic state that these fellow citizens control are pacifistic. Machiavelli's citizens are splendidly diverse in their goals but fundamentally unequal in them as well, seeking to rule or fearing being dominated. Extending the rule of the dominant elite or avoiding the political collapse of their state, each calls for imperial expansion.

Kant's citizens, too, are diverse in their goals and individualized and rationalized, but most importantly, they are capable of appreciating the moral equality of all individuals and of treating other individuals as ends rather than as means. The Kantian state thus is governed publicly according to law, as a republic. Kant's is the state that solves the problem of governing individualized equals, whether they are the "rational devils" he says we often find ourselves to be or the ethical agents we can and should become. Republics tell us that

> in order to organize a group of rational beings who together require universal laws for their survival, but of whom each separate individual is secretly inclined to exempt himself from them, the constitution must be so designed so that, although the citizens are opposed to one another in their private attitudes, these opposing views may inhibit one another in such a way that the public conduct of the citizens will be the same as if they did not have such evil attitudes. (Kant, *PP*, p. 113)

Unlike Machiavelli's republics, Kant's republics are capable of achieving peace among themselves because they exercise democratic caution and are capable of appreciating the international rights of foreign republics. These international rights of republics derive from the representation of foreign individuals, who are our moral equals. Unlike Schumpeter's capitalist democracies, Kant's republics—including our own—remain in a state of war with nonrepublics. Liberal republics see themselves as threatened by aggression from nonrepublics that are not constrained by representation. Even though wars often cost more than the economic return they generate, liberal republics also are prepared to protect and promote—sometimes forcibly—democracy, private property, and the rights of individuals overseas against nonrepublics, which, because they do not authentically represent the rights of individuals, have no rights to noninterference. These wars may liberate oppressed individuals overseas; they also can generate enormous suffering.

■ ■ ■

Perpetual peace, Kant says, is the end point of the hard journey his republics will take. The promise of perpetual peace, the violent lessons of war, and the experience of a partial peace are proof of the need for and the possibility of world peace. They are also the grounds for moral citizens and statesmen to assume the duty of striving for peace.

Appendix 1. Liberal Regimes and the Pacific Union, 1700–1982

PERIOD	PERIOD	PERIOD
18th Century	Argentina, 1880–	Ireland, 1920–
Swiss Cantons[a]	Chile, 1891–	Mexico, 1928–
French Republie, 1790–1795	Total = 13	Lebanon, 1944–
United States,[a] 1776–		Total = 29
Total = 3	**1900–1945**	
	Switzerland	**1945–[b]**
1800–1850	United States	Switzerland
Swiss Confederation	Great Britain	United States
United States	Sweden	Great Britain
France, 1830–1849	Canada	Sweden
Belgium, 1830–	Greece, –1911; 1928–1936	Canada
1800–1850 (cont.)	Italy, –1922	Australia
Great Britain, 1832–	Belgium, –1940	New Zealand
Netherlands, 1848–	Netherlands, –1940	Finland
Piedmont, 1848–	Argentina, –1943	Ireland
Denmark, 1849–	France, –1940	Mexico
Total = 8	Chile, –1924; 1932–	Uruguay, –1973
	Australia, 1901	Chile, –1973
1850–1900	Norway, 1905–1940	Lebanon, –1975
Switzerland	New Zealand, 1907–	Costa Rica, –1948; 1953–
United States	Colombia, 1910–1949	Iceland, 1944–
Belgium	Denmark, 1914–1940	France, 1945–
Great Britain	Poland, 1917–1935	Denmark, 1945
Netherlands	Latvia, 1922–1934	Norway, 1945
Piedmont, –1861	Germany, 1918–1932	Austria, 1945–
Italy, 1861–	Austria, 1918–1934	Brazil, 1945–1954; 1955–1964
Denmark, –1866	Estonia, 1919–1934	Belgium, 1946–
Sweden, 1864–	Finland, 1919–	Luxembourg, 1946–
Greece, 1864–	Uruguay, 1919–	Netherlands, 1946–
Canada, 1867–	Costa Rica, 1919–	Italy, 1946–
France, 1871–	Czechosovakia, 1920–1939	Philippines, 1946–1972

(continued)

PERIOD	PERIOD	PERIOD
1945–(cont.)	Turkey, 1950–1960;	Senegal, 1963–
India, 1947–1975; 1977–	1966–1971	Malaysia, 1963–
Sri Lanka, 1948–1961;	Japan, 1951–	Botswana, 1966–
1963–1971; 1978–	Bolivia, 1956–1969; 1982–	Singapore, 1965–
Ecuador, 1948–1963; 1979–	Colombia, 1958–	Portugal, 1976–
Israel, 1949–	Venezuela, 1959–	Spain, 1978–
West Germany, 1949–	Nigeria, 1961–1964;	Dominican Republic, 1978–
Greece, 1950–1967; 1975–	1979–1984	Honduras, 1981–
Peru, 1950–1962; 1963–	Jamaica, 1962–	Papua New Guinea, 1982–
1968; 1980–	Trinidad and Tobago, 1962–	Total = 50
El Salvador, 1950–1961		

Note: I have drawn up this approximate list of "Liberal Regimes" according to the four institutions Kant described as essential: market and private property economies; politics that are externally sovereign; citizens who possess juridical rights; and "republican" (whether republican or parliamentary monarchy), representative government. This latter includes the requirement that the legislative branch have an effective role in public policy and be formally and competitively (either inter- or intra-party) elected. Furthermore, I have taken into account whether male suffrage is wide (i.e., 30%) or, as Kant (*MM* [*The Metaphysics of Morals*], p. 139) would have had it, open by "achievement" to inhabitants of the national or metropolitan territory (e.g., to poll-tax payers or householders). This list of liberal regimes is thus more inclusive than a list of democratic regimes, or polyarchies (Powell, 1982, p. 5). Other conditions taken into account here are that female suffrage is granted within a generation of its being demanded by an extensive female suffrage movement and that representative government is internally sovereign (e.g., including, and especially over military and foreign affairs) as well as stable (in existence for at least three years). Sources for these data are Banks and Overstreet (1983), Gastil (1985), *The Europa Yearbook, 1985* (1985), Langer (1968), U.K. Foreign and Commonwealth Office (1980), and U.S. Department of State (1981). Finally, these lists exclude ancient and medieval "republics," since none appears to fit Kant's commitment to liberal individualism (Holmes, 1979).

[a]There are domestic variations within these liberal regimes: Switzerland was liberal only in certain cantons; the United States was liberal only north of the Mason-Dixon line until 1865, when it became liberal throughout.

[b]Selected list, excludes liberal regimes with populations less than one million. These include all states categorized as "free" by Gastil and those "partly free" (four-fifths or more free) states with a more pronounced capitalist orientation.

Appendix 2. International Wars Listed Chronologically

British-Maharattan (1817–1818)

Greek (1821–1828)

Franco-Spanish (1823)

First Anglo-Burmese (1823–1826)

Javanese (1825–1830)

Russo-Persian (1826–1828)

Russo-Turkish (1828–1829)

First Polish (1831)

First Syrian (1831–1832)

Texas (1835–1836)

(continued)

Appendix 2. International Wars Listed Chronologically (Continued)

First British-Afghan (1838–1842)
Second Syrian (1839–1940)
Franco-Algerian (1839–1847)
Peruvian-Bolivian (1841)
First British-Sikh (1845–1846)
Mexican-American (1846–1848)
Austro-Sardinian (1848–1849)
First Schleswig-Holstein (1848–1849)
Hungarian (1848–1849)
Second British-Sikh (1848–1849)
Roman Republic (1849)
La Plata (1851–1852)
First Turco-Montenegran (1852–1853)
Crimean (1853–1856)
Anglo-Persian (1856–1857)
Sepoy (1857–1859)
Second Turco-Montenegran (1858–1859)
Italian Unification (1859)
Spanish-Moroccan (1859–1860)
Italo-Roman (1860)
Italo-Sicilian (1860–1861)
Franco-Mexican (1862–1867)
Ecuadorian-Colombian (1863)
Second Polish (1863–1864)
Spanish-Santo Dominican (1863–1865)
Second Schleswig-Holstein (1864)
Lopez (1864–1870)
Spanish-Chilean (1865–1866)
Seven Weeks (1866)
Ten Years (1868–1878)
Franco-Prussian (1870–1871)
Dutch-Achinese (1873–1878)

Balkan (1875–1877)
Russo-Turkish (1877–1878)
Bosnian (1878)
Second British-Afghan (1878–1880)
Pacific (1879–1883)
British-Zulu (1879)
Franco-Indochinese (1882–1884)
Mahdist (1882–1885)
Sino-French (1884–1885)
Central American (1885)
Serbo-Bulgarian (1885)
Sino-Japanese (1894–1895)
Franco-Madagascan (1894–1895)
Cuban (1895–1898)
Italo-Ethiopian (1895–1896)
First Philippine (1896–1898)
Greco-Turkish (1897)
Spanish-American (1898)
Second Philippine (1899–1902)·
Boer (1899–1902)
Boxer Rebellion (1900)
Ilinden (1903)
Vietnamese-Cambodian (1975–)
Timor (1975–)
Saharan (1975–)
Ogaden (1976–)
Russo-Japanese (1904–1905)
Central American (1906)
Central American (1907)
Spanish-Moroccan (1909–1910)
Italo-Turkish (1911–1912)
First Balkan (1912–1913)

(continued)

Appendix 2. International Wars Listed Chronologically (Continued)

Second Balkan (1913)

World War I (1914–1918)

Russian Nationalities (1917–1921)

Russo-Polish (1919–1920)

Hungarian-Allies (1919)

Greco-Turkish (1919–1922)

Riffian (1921–1926)

Druze (1925–1927)

Sino-Soviet (1929)

Manchurian (1931–1933)

Chaco (1932–1935)

Italo-Ethiopian (1935–1936)

Sino-Japanese (1937–1941)

Changkufeng (1938)

Nomohan (1939)

World War II (1939–1945)

Russo-Finnish (1939–1940)

Franco-Thai (1940–1941)

Indonesian (1945–1946)

Indochinese (1945–1954)

Madagascan (1947–1948)

First Kashmir (1947–1949)

Palestine (1948–1949)

Hyderabad (1948)

Korean (1950–1953)

Algerian (1954–1962)

Russo-Hungarian (1956)

Sinai (1956)

Tibetan (1956–1959)

Sino-Indian (1962)

Vietnamese (1965–1975)

Second Kashmir (1965)

Six Day (1967)

Israeli-Egyptian (1969–1970)

Football (1969)

Bangladesh (1971)

Philippine-MNLF (1972–)

Yom Kippur (1973)

Turco-Cypriot (1974)

Ethiopian-Eritrean (1974–)

Ugandan-Tanzanian (1978–1979)

Sino-Vietnamese (1979)

Russo-Afghan (1979–)

Iran-Iraqi (1980–)

Note: This table is taken from Melvin Small and J. David Singer (1982, pp. 79–80). This is a partial list of international wars fought between 1816 and 1980. In Appendices A and B, Small and Singer identify a total of 575 wars during this period, but approxi Note: This table is taken from Melvin Small and J. David Singer (1982, pp. 79–80). This is a partial list of international wars fought between 1816 and 1980. In Appendices A and B, Small and Singer identify a total of 575 wars during this period, but approximately 159 of them appear to be largely domestic, or civil wars. mately 159 of them appear to be largely domestic, or civil wars.

This list excludes covert interventions, some of which have been directed by liberal regimes against other liberal regimes—for example, the United States' effort to destabilize the Chilean election and Allende's government. Nonetheless, it is significant that such interventions are not pursued publicly as acknowledged policy. The covert destabilization campaign against Chile is recounted by the Senate Select Committee to Study Governmental Operations with Respect to Intelligence Activities (1975, *Covert Action in Chile, 1963–73*).

Following the argument of this article, this list also excludes civil wars. Civil wars differ from international wars, not in the ferocity of combat, but in the issues that engender them. Two nations that could abide one another as independent neighbors separated by a border might well be the fiercest of enemies if forced to live together in one state, jointly deciding how to raise and spend taxes, choose leaders, and legislate fundamental questions of value. Notwithstanding these differences, no civil wars that I recall upset the argument of liberal pacification.

REFERENCES

Banks, Arthur, and William Overstreet, eds. 1983. *A Political Handbook of the World; 1982–1983*. New York: McGraw Hill.

Barnet, Richard. 1968. *Intervention and Revolution*. Cleveland: World Publishing Co.

Chan, Steve. 1984. Mirror, Mirror on the Wall . . . : Are Freer Countries More Pacific? *Journal of Conflict Resolution*, 28:617–48.

Doyle, Michael W. 1983a. Kant, Liberal Legacies, and Foreign Affairs: Part 1. *Philosophy and Public Affairs*, 12:205–35.

Doyle, Michael W. 1983b. Kant, Liberal Legacies, and Foreign Affairs: Part 2. *Philosophy and Public Affairs*, 12:323–53.

Doyle, Michael W. 1986. *Empires*. Ithaca: Cornell University Press.

The Europa Yearbook for 1985. 1985. 2 vols. London: Europa Publications.

Gastil, Raymond. 1985. The Comparative Survey of Freedom 1985. *Freedom at Issue*, 82:3–16.

Haas, Michael. 1974. *International Conflict*. New York: Bobbs-Merrill.

Holmes, Stephen. 1979. Aristippus in and out of Athens. *American Political Science Review*, 73:113–28.

Huliung, Mark. 1983. *Citizen Machiavelli*. Princeton: Princeton University Press.

Hume, David. 1963. Of the Balance of Power. *Essays: Moral, Political, and Literary*. Oxford: Oxford University Press.

Kant, Immanuel. 1970. *Kant's Political Writings*. Hans Reiss, ed. H. B. Nisbet, trans. Cambridge: Cambridge University Press.

Kelly, George A. 1969. *Idealism, Politics, and History*. Cambridge: Cambridge University Press.

Langer, William L., ed. 1968. *The Encyclopedia of World History*. Boston: Houghton Mifflin.

Machiavelli, Niccolo. 1950. *The Prince and the Discourses*. Max Lerner, ed. Luigi Ricci and Christian Detmold, trans. New York: Modern Library.

Mansfield, Harvey C. 1970. Machiavelli's New Regime. *Italian Quarterly*, 13:63–95.

Montesquieu, Charles de. 1949. *Spirit of the Laws*. New York: Hafner. (Originally published in 1748.)

Murphy, Jeffrie. 1970. *Kant: The Philosophy of Right*. New York: St. Martins.

Pocock, J. G. A. 1975. *The Machiavellian Moment*. Princeton: Princeton University Press.

Powell, G. Bingham. 1982. *Contemporary Democracies*. Cambridge, MA: Harvard University Press.

Reagan, Ronald. June 9, 1982. Address to Parliament. *New York Times*.

Riley, Patrick. 1983. *Kant's Political Philosophy*. Totowa, NJ: Rowman and Littlefield.

Rummel, Rudolph J. 1983. Libertarianism and International Violence. *Journal of Conflict Resolution*, 27:27–71.

Russett, Bruce. 1985. The Mysterious Case of Vanishing Hegemony. *International Organization*, 39:207–31.

Schumpeter, Joseph. 1955. The Sociology of Imperialism. In *Imperialism and Social Classes*. Cleveland: World Publishing Co. (Essay originally published in 1919.)

Schwarz, Wolfgang. 1962. Kant's Philosophy of Law and International Peace. *Philosophy and Phenomenonological Research*, 23:71–80.

Skinner, Quentin. 1981. *Machiavelli*. New York: Hill and Wang.

Small, Melvin, and J. David Singer. 1976. The War-Proneness of Democratic Regimes. *The Jerusalem Journal of International Relations*, 1(4):50–69.

Small, Melvin, and J. David Singer. 1982. *Resort to Arms*. Beverly Hills: Sage Publications.

Thucydides. 1954. *The Peloponnesian War*. Rex Warner, ed. and trans. Baltimore: Penguin.

U.K. Foreign and Commonwealth Office. 1980. *A Yearbook of the Commonwealth 1980*. London: HMSO.

U.S. Congress. Senate. Select Committee to Study Governmental Operations with Respect to Intelligence Activities. 1975. *Covert Action in Chile, 1963–74*. 94th Cong., 1st sess., Washington, D.C.: U.S. Government Printing Office.

U.S. Department of State. 1981. *Country Reports on Human Rights Practices.* Washington, D.C.: U.S. Government Printing Office.

Weede, Erich. 1984. Democracy and War Involvement. *Journal of Conflict Resolution*, 28:649–64.

Wilkenfeld, Jonathan. 1968. Domestic and Foreign Conflict Behavior of Nations. *Journal of Peace Research*, 5:56–69.

Wright, Quincy. 1942. *A Study of History.* Chicago: Chicago University Press.

Alexander Wendt

ANARCHY IS WHAT STATES MAKE OF IT
The Social Construction of Power Politics

The debate between realists and liberals has reemerged as an axis of contention in international relations theory.[1] Revolving in the past around competing theories of human nature, the debate is more concerned today with the extent to which state action is influenced by "structure" (anarchy and the distribution of power) versus "process" (interaction and learning) and institutions. Does the absence of centralized political authority force states to play competitive power politics? Can international regimes overcome this logic, and under what conditions? What in anarchy is given and immutable, and what is amenable to change?

■ ■ ■

* * * I argue that self-help and power politics do not follow either logically or causally from anarchy and that if today we find ourselves in a self-help world, this is due to process, not structure. There is no "logic" of anarchy apart from the practices that create and instantiate one structure of identities and interests rather than another; structure has no existence or causal powers apart from process. Self-help and power politics are institutions, not essential features of anarchy. *Anarchy is what states make of it.*

■ ■ ■

From *International Organization* 46, no. 2 (Spring 1992): 391–425. Some of the author's notes have been omitted.

Anarchy and Power Politics

Classical realists such as Thomas Hobbes, Reinhold Niebuhr, and Hans Morgenthau attributed egoism and power politics primarily to human nature, whereas structural realists or neorealists emphasize anarchy. The difference stems in part from different interpretations of anarchy's causal powers. Kenneth Waltz's work is important for both. In *Man, the State, and War,* he defines anarchy as a condition of possibility for or "permissive" cause of war, arguing that "wars occur because there is nothing to prevent them."[2] It is the human nature or domestic politics of predator states, however, that provide the initial impetus or "efficient" cause of conflict which forces other states to respond in kind.[3] Waltz is not entirely consistent about this, since he slips without justification from the permissive causal claim that in anarchy war is always possible to the active causal claim that "war may at any moment occur."[4] But despite Waltz's concluding call for third-image theory, the efficient causes that initialize anarchic systems are from the first and second images. This is reversed in Waltz's *Theory of International Politics,* in which first- and second-image theories are spurned as "reductionist," and the logic of anarchy seems by itself to constitute self-help and power politics as necessary features of world politics.[5]

This is unfortunate, since whatever one may think of first- and second-image theories, they have the virtue of implying that practices determine the character of anarchy. In the permissive view, only if human or domestic factors cause A to attack B will B have to defend itself. Anarchies may contain dynamics that lead to competitive power politics, but they also may not, and we can argue about when particular structures of identity and interest will emerge. In neorealism, however, the role of practice in shaping the character of anarchy is substantially reduced, and so there is less about which to argue: self-help and competitive power politics are simply given exogenously by the structure of the state system.

I will not here contest the neorealist description of the contemporary state system as a competitive, self-help world;[6] I will only dispute its explanation. I develop my argument in three stages. First, I disentangle the concepts of self-help and anarchy by showing that self-interested conceptions of security are not a constitutive property of anarchy. Second, I show how self-help and competitive power politics may be produced causally by processes of interaction between states in which anarchy plays only a permissive role. In both of these stages of my argument, I self-consciously bracket the first- and second-image determinants of state identity, not because they are unimportant (they are indeed important), but because like Waltz's objective, mine is to clarify the "logic" of anarchy. Third, I reintroduce first- and second-image determinants to assess their effects on identity-formation in different kinds of anarchies.

Anarchy, Self-Help, and Intersubjective Knowledge

Waltz defines political structure on three dimensions: ordering principles (in this case, anarchy), principles of differentiation (which here drop out), and the distribution of capabilities.[7] By itself, this definition predicts little about state behavior. It does not predict whether two states will be friends or foes, will recognize each other's sovereignty, will have dynastic ties, will be revisionist or status quo powers, and so on. These factors, which are fundamentally intersubjective, affect states' security interests and thus the character of their interaction under anarchy. In an important revision of Waltz's theory, Stephen Walt implies as much when he argues that the "balance of threats," rather than the balance of power, determines state action, threats being socially constructed.[8] Put more generally, without assumptions about the structure of identities and interests in the system, Waltz's definition of structure cannot predict the content or dynamics of anarchy. Self-help is one such intersubjective structure and, as such, does the decisive explanatory work in the theory. The question is whether self-help is a logical or contingent feature of anarchy. In this section, I develop the concept of a "structure of identity and interest" and show that no particular one follows logically from anarchy.

A fundamental principle of constructivist social theory is that people act toward objects, including other actors, on the basis of the meanings that the objects have for them.[9] States act differently toward enemies than they do toward friends because enemies are threatening and friends are not. Anarchy and the distribution of power are insufficient to tell us which is which. U.S. military power has a different significance for Canada than for Cuba, despite their similar "structural" positions, just as British missiles have a different significance for the United States than do Soviet missiles. The distribution of power may always affect states' calculations, but how it does so depends on the intersubjective understandings and expectations, on the "distribution of knowledge," that constitute their conceptions of self and other.[10] If society "forgets" what a university is, the powers and practices of professor and student cease to exist; if the United States and Soviet Union decide that they are no longer enemies, "the cold war is over." It is collective meanings that constitute the structures which organize our actions.

Actors acquire identities—relatively stable, role-specific understandings and expectations about self—by participating in such collective meanings.[11] Identities are inherently relational: "Identity, with its appropriate attachments of psychological reality, is always identity within a specific, socially constructed world," Peter Berger argues.[12] Each person has many identities linked to institutional roles, such as brother, son, teacher, and citizen. Similarly, a state may have multiple identities as "sovereign," "leader of the free world," "imperial power," and so on.[13] The commitment to and the salience of particular identities vary, but each identity is an inherently social definition of the actor grounded in the theories which actors collectively hold about themselves and one another and which constitute the structure of the social world.

Identities are the basis of interests. Actors do not have a "portfolio" of interests that they carry around independent of social context; instead, they define their interests in the process of defining situations.[14] As Nelson Foote puts it: "Motivation . . . refer[s] to the degree to which a human being, as a participant in the ongoing social process in which he necessarily finds himself, defines a problematic situation as calling for the performance of a particular act, with more or less anticipated consummations and consequences, and thereby his organism releases the energy appropriate to performing it."[15] Sometimes situations are unprecedented in our experience, and in these cases we have to construct their meaning, and thus our interests, by analogy or invent them de novo. More often they have routine qualities in which we assign meanings on the basis of institutionally defined roles. When we say that professors have an "interest" in teaching, research, or going on leave, we are saying that to function in the role identity of "professor," they have to define certain situations as calling for certain actions. This does not mean that they will necessarily do so (expectations and competence do not equal performance), but if they do not, they will not get tenure. The

absence or failure of roles makes defining situations and interests more difficult, and identity confusion may result. This seems to be happening today in the United States and the former Soviet Union: without the cold war's mutual attributions of threat and hostility to define their identities, these states seem unsure of what their "interests" should be.

An institution is a relatively stable set or "structure" of identities and interests. Such structures are often codified in formal rules and norms, but these have motivational force only in virtue of actors' socialization to and participation in collective knowledge. Institutions are fundamentally cognitive entities that do not exist apart from actors' ideas about how the world works.[16] This does not mean that institutions are not real or objective, that they are "nothing but" beliefs. As collective knowledge, they are experienced as having an existence "over and above the individuals who happen to embody them at the moment."[17] In this way, institutions come to confront individuals as more or less coercive social facts, but they are still a function of what actors collectively "know." Identities and such collective cognitions do not exist apart from each other; they are "mutually constitutive."[18] On this view, institutionalization is a process of internalizing new identities and interests, not something occurring outside them and affecting only behavior; socialization is a cognitive process, not just a behavioral one. Conceived in this way, institutions may be cooperative or conflictual, a point sometimes lost in scholarship on international regimes, which tends to equate institutions with cooperation. There are important differences between conflictual and cooperative institutions to be sure, but all relatively stable self-other relations—even those of "enemies"—are defined intersubjectively.

Self-help is an institution, one of various structures of identity and interest that may exist under anarchy. Processes of identity-formation under anarchy are concerned first and foremost with preservation or "security" of the self. Concepts of security therefore differ in the extent to which and the manner in which the self is identified cognitively with the other,[19] and, I want to suggest, it is upon this cognitive variation that the meaning of anarchy and the distribution of power depends. Let me illustrate with a standard continuum of security systems.[20]

At one end is the "competitive" security system, in which states identify negatively with each other's security so that ego's gain is seen as alter's loss. Negative identification under anarchy constitutes system of "realist" power politics: risk-averse actors that infer intentions from capabilities and worry about relative gains and losses. At the limit—in the Hobbesian war of all against all—collective action is nearly impossible in such a system because each actor must constantly fear being stabbed in the back.

In the middle is the "individualistic" security system, in which states are indifferent to the relationship between their own and others' security. This constitutes "neoliberal" systems: states are still self-regarding about their security but are concerned primarily with absolute gains rather than relative gains. One's position in the distribution of power is less important, and collective action is more possible (though still subject to free riding because states continue to be "egoists").

Competitive and individualistic systems are both "self-help" forms of anarchy in the sense that states do not positively identify the security of self with that of others but instead treat security as the individual responsibility of each. Given the lack of a positive cognitive identification on the basis of which to build security regimes, power politics within such systems will necessarily consist of efforts to manipulate others to satisfy self-regarding interests.

This contrasts with the "cooperative" security system, in which states identify positively with one another so that the security of each is perceived as the responsibility of all. This is not self-help in any interesting sense, since the "self" in

terms of which interests are defined is the community; national interests are international interests.[21] In practice, of course, the extent to which states' identification with the community varies, from the limited form found in "concerts" to the full-blown form seen in "collective security" arrangements.[22] Depending on how well developed the collective self is, it will produce security practices that are in varying degrees altruistic or prosocial. This makes collective action less dependent on the presence of active threats and less prone to free riding.[23] Moreover, it restructures efforts to advance one's objectives, or "power politics," in terms of shared norms rather than relative power.[24]

On this view, the tendency in international relations scholarship to view power and institutions as two opposing explanations of foreign policy is therefore misleading, since anarchy and the distribution of power only have meaning for state action in virtue of the understandings and expectations that constitute institutional identities and interests. Self-help is one such institution, constituting one kind of anarchy but not the only kind. Waltz's three-part definition of structure therefore seems underspecified. In order to go from structure to action, we need to add a fourth: the intersubjectively constituted structure of identities and interests in the system.

This has an important implication for the way in which we conceive of states in the state of nature before their first encounter with each other. Because states do not have conceptions of self and other, and thus security interests, apart from or prior to interaction, we assume too much about the state of nature if we concur with Waltz that, in virtue of anarchy, "international political systems, like economic markets, are formed by the coaction of self-regarding units."[25] We also assume too much if we argue that, in virtue of anarchy, states in the state of nature necessarily face a "stag hunt" or "security dilemma."[26] These claims presuppose a history of interaction in which actors have acquired "selfish" identities and interests; before interaction (and still in abstraction from first- and second-image factors) they would have no experience upon which to base such definitions of self and other. To assume otherwise is to attribute to states in the state of nature qualities that they can only possess in society.[27] Self-help is an institution, not a constitutive feature of anarchy.

What, then, *is* a constitutive feature of the state of nature before interaction? Two things are left if we strip away those properties of the self which presuppose interaction with others. The first is the material substrate of agency, including its intrinsic capabilities. For human beings, this is the body; for states, it is an organizational apparatus of governance. In effect, I am suggesting for rhetorical purposes that the raw material out of which members of the state system are constituted is created by domestic society before states enter the constitutive process of international society,[28] although this process implies neither stable territoriality nor sovereignty, which are internationally negotiated terms of individuality (as discussed further below). The second is a desire to preserve this material substrate, to survive. This does not entail "self-regardingness," however, since actors do not have a self prior to interaction with an other; how they view the meaning and requirements of this survival therefore depends on the processes by which conceptions of self evolve.

This may all seem very arcane, but there is an important issue at stake: are the foreign policy identities and interests of states exogenous or endogenous to the state system? The former is the answer of an individualistic or undersocialized systemic theory for which rationalism is appropriate; the latter is the answer of a fully socialized systemic theory. Waltz seems to offer the latter and proposes two mechanisms, competition and socialization, by which structure conditions state action.[29] The content of his argument about this conditioning, however, presupposes a self-help system that is not itself a constitutive feature of anarchy. As James Morrow points out, Waltz's two mechanisms condition behavior, not identity and interest.[30] This explains how Waltz can be accused of both "individualism" and "structuralism."[31] He is the former with respect to systemic constitutions of identity and interest, the latter with respect to systemic determinations of behavior.

Anarchy and the Social Construction of Power Politics

If self-help is not a constitutive feature of anarchy, it must emerge causally from processes in which anarchy plays only a permissive role.[32] This reflects a second principle of constructivism: that the meanings in terms of which action is organized arise out of interaction.[33] This being said, however, the situation facing states as they encounter one another for the first time may be such that only self-regarding conceptions of identity can survive; if so, even if these conceptions are socially constructed, neorealists may be right in holding identities and interests constant and thus in privileging one particular meaning of anarchic structure over process. In this case, rationalists would be right to argue for a weak, behavioral conception of the difference that institutions make, and realists would be right to argue that any international institutions which are created will be inherently unstable, since without the power to transform identities and interests they will be "continuing objects of choice" by exogenously constituted actors constrained only by the transaction costs of behavioral change.[34] Even in a permissive causal role, in other words, anarchy may decisively restrict interaction and therefore restrict viable forms of systemic theory. I address these causal issues first by showing how self-regarding ideas about security might develop and then by examining the conditions under which a key efficient cause—predation—may dispose states in this direction rather than others.

Conceptions of self and interest tend to "mirror" the practices of significant others over time. This principle of identity-formation is captured by the symbolic interactionist notion of the "looking-glass self," which asserts that the self is a reflection of an actor's socialization.

Consider two actors—ego and alter—encountering each other for the first time.[35] Each wants to survive and has certain material capabilities, but neither actor has biological or domestic imperatives for power, glory, or conquest (still bracketed), and there is no history of security or insecurity between the two. What should they do? Realists would probably argue that each should act on the basis of worst-case assumptions about the other's intentions, justifying such an attitude as prudent in view of the possibility of death from making a mistake. Such a possibility always exists, even in civil society; however, society would be impossible if people made decisions purely on the basis of worst-case possibilities. Instead, most decisions are and should be made on the basis of probabilities, and these are produced by interaction, by what actors *do*.

In the beginning is ego's gesture, which may consist, for example, of an advance, a retreat, a brandishing of arms, a laying down of arms, or an attack.[36] For ego, this gesture represents the basis on which it is prepared to respond to alter. This basis is unknown to alter, however, and so it must make an inference or "attribution" about ego's intentions and, in particular, given that this is anarchy, about whether ego is a threat.[37] The content of this inference will largely depend on two considerations. The first is the gesture's and ego's physical qualities, which are in part contrived by ego and which include the direction of movement, noise, numbers, and immediate consequences of the gesture.[38] The second consideration concerns what alter would intend by such qualities were it to make such a gesture itself. Alter may make an attributional "error" in its inference about ego's intent, but there is also no reason for it to assume a priori—before the gesture—that ego is threatening, since it is only through a process of signaling and interpreting that the costs and probabilities of being wrong can be determined.[39] Social threats are constructed, not natural.

Consider an example. Would we assume, a priori, that we were about to be attacked if we are ever contacted by members of an alien civilization? I think not. We would be highly alert, of course, but whether we placed our military forces on alert or launched an attack would depend on how we interpreted the import of their first gesture for our security—if only to avoid making an immediate enemy out of what may be a dangerous adversary. The possibility of error, in other words, does not force us to act on the assumption that the aliens are threatening: action depends on the probabilities we assign, and these are in key part a function of what the aliens do; prior to their gesture, we have no systemic basis for assigning probabilities. If their first gesture is to appear with a thousand spaceships and destroy New York, we will define the situation as threatening and respond accordingly. But if they appear with one spaceship, saying what seems to be "we come in peace," we will feel "reassured" and will probably respond with a gesture intended to reassure them, even if this gesture is not necessarily interpreted by them as such.[40]

This process of signaling, interpreting, and responding completes a "social act" and begins the process of creating intersubjective meanings. It advances the same way. The first social act creates expectations on both sides about each other's future behavior: potentially mistaken and certainly tentative, but expectations nonetheless. Based on this tentative knowledge, ego makes a new gesture, again signifying the basis on which it will respond to alter, and again alter responds, adding to the pool of knowledge each has about the other, and so on over time. The mechanism here is reinforcement; interaction rewards actors for holding certain ideas about each other and discourages them from holding others. If repeated long enough, these "reciprocal typifications" will create relatively stable concepts of self and other regarding the issue at stake in the interaction.[41]

It is through reciprocal interaction, in other words, that we create and instantiate the relatively enduring social structures in terms of which we define our identities and interests. Jeff Coulter sums up the ontological dependence of structure on process this way: "The parameters of social organization themselves are reproduced only in and through the orientations and practices of members engaged in social interactions over time. . . . Social configurations are not 'objective' like mountains or forests, but neither are they 'subjective' like dreams or flights of speculative fancy. They are, as most social scientists concede at the theoretical level, intersubjective constructions."[42]

The simple overall model of identity- and interest-formation proposed in Figure 3.1 applies to competitive institutions no less than to cooperative ones. Self-help security systems evolve from cycles of interaction in which each party acts in ways that the other feels are threatening to the self, creating expectations that the other is not to be trusted. Competitive or egoistic identities are caused by such insecurity; if the other is threatening, the self is forced to "mirror" such behavior in its conception of the self's relationship to that other.[43] Being treated as an object for the gratification of others precludes the positive identification with others necessary for collective security; conversely, being treated by others in ways that are empathic with respect to the security of the self permits such identification.[44]

Competitive systems of interaction are prone to security "dilemmas," in which the efforts of actors to enhance their security unilaterally threatens the security of the others, perpetuating distrust and

Figure 3.1. The Codetermination of Institutions and Process

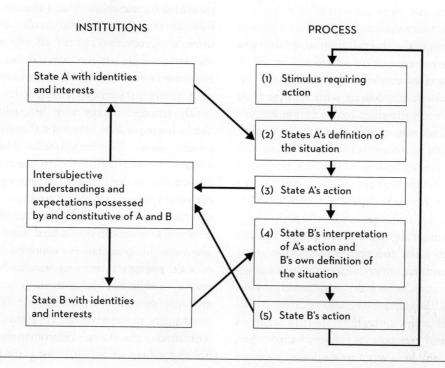

alienation. The forms of identity and interest that constitute such dilemmas, however, are themselves ongoing effects of, not exogenous to, the interaction; identities are produced in and through "situated activity."[45] We do not *begin* our relationship with the aliens in a security dilemma; security dilemmas are not given by anarchy or nature. Of course, once institutionalized such a dilemma may be hard to change (I return to this below), but the point remains: identities and interests are constituted by collective meanings that are always in process. As Sheldon Stryker emphasizes, "The social process is one of constructing and reconstructing self and social relationships."[46] If states find themselves in a self-help system, this is because their practices made it that way. Changing the practices will change the intersubjective knowledge that constitutes the system.

Predator States and Anarchy as Permissive Cause

The mirror theory of identity-formation is a crude account of how the process of creating identities and interests might work, but it does not tell us why a system of states—such as, arguably, our own—would have ended up with self-regarding and not collective identities. In this section, I examine an efficient cause, predation, which, in conjunction with anarchy as a permissive cause, may generate a self-help system. In so doing, however, I show the key role that the structure of identities and interests plays in mediating anarchy's explanatory role.

The predator argument is straightforward and compelling. For whatever reasons—biology, domestic politics, or systemic victimization— some states may become predisposed toward aggression. The aggressive behavior of these predators or "bad apples" forces other states to engage in competitive power politics, to meet fire with fire, since failure to do so may degrade or destroy them.

One predator will best a hundred pacifists because anarchy provides no guarantees. This argument is powerful in part because it is so weak: rather than making the strong assumption that all states are inherently power-seeking (a purely reductionist theory of power politics), it assumes that just one is power-seeking and that the others have to follow suit because anarchy permits the one to exploit them.

In making this argument, it is important to reiterate that the possibility of predation does not in itself force states to anticipate it a priori with competitive power politics of their own. The possibility of predation does not mean that "war may at any moment occur"; it may in fact be extremely unlikely. Once a predator emerges, however, it may condition identity- and interest-formation in the following manner.

In an anarchy of two, if ego is predatory, alter must either define its security in self-help terms or pay the price. This follows directly from the above argument, in which conceptions of self mirror treatment by the other. In an anarchy of many, however, the effect of predation also depends on the level of collective identity already attained in the system. If predation occurs right after the first encounter in the state of nature, it will force others with whom it comes in contact to defend themselves, first individually and then collectively *if* they come to perceive a common threat. The emergence of such a defensive alliance will be seriously inhibited if the structure of identities and interests has already evolved into a Hobbesian world of maximum insecurity, since potential allies will strongly distrust each other and face intense collective action problems; such insecure allies are also more likely to fall out amongst themselves once the predator is removed. If collective security identity is high, however, the emergence of a predator may do much less damage. If the predator attacks any member of the collective, the latter will come to the victim's defense on the principle of "all for one, one for all," even if the predator is not presently a threat to other members of the collective. If the predator is not strong enough to withstand the collective, it will be defeated and collective security will obtain. But if it is strong enough, the logic of the two-actor case (now predator and collective) will activate, and balance-of-power politics will reestablish itself.

The timing of the emergence of predation relative to the history of identity-formation in the community is therefore crucial to anarchy's explanatory role as a permissive cause. Predation will always lead victims to defend themselves, but whether defense will be collective or not depends on the history of interaction within the potential collective as much as on the ambitions of the predator. Will the disappearance of the Soviet threat renew old insecurities among the members of the North Atlantic Treaty Organization? Perhaps, but not if they have reasons independent of that threat for identifying their security with one another. Identities and interests are relationship-specific, not intrinsic attributes of a "portfolio"; states may be competitive in some relationships and solidary in others. "Mature" anarchies are less likely than "immature" ones to be reduced by predation to a Hobbesian condition, and maturity, which is a proxy for structures of identity and interest, is a function of process.[47]

The source of predation also matters. If it stems from unit-level causes that are immune to systemic impacts (causes such as human nature or domestic politics taken in isolation), then it functions in a manner analogous to a "genetic trait" in the constructed world of the state system. Even if successful, this trait does not select for other predators in an evolutionary sense so much as it teaches other states to respond in kind, but since traits cannot be unlearned, the other states will continue competitive behavior until the predator is either destroyed or transformed from within. However, in the more likely event that predation stems at least in part from prior systemic interaction—perhaps as a result of being victimized in the past

(one thinks here of Nazi Germany or the Soviet Union)—then it is more a response to a learned identity and, as such, might be transformed by future social interaction in the form of appeasement, reassurances that security needs will be met, systemic effects on domestic politics, and so on. In this case, in other words, there is more hope that process can transform a bad apple into a good one.

The role of predation in generating a self-help system, then, is consistent with a systematic focus on process. Even if the source of predation is entirely exogenous to the system, it is what states *do* that determines the quality of their interactions under anarchy. In this respect, it is not surprising that it is classical realists rather than structural realists who emphasize this sort of argument. The former's emphasis on unit-level causes of power politics leads more easily to a permissive view of anarchy's explanatory role (and therefore to a processual view of international relations) than does the latter's emphasis on anarchy as a "structural cause";[48] neorealists do not need predation because the system is given as self-help.

This raises anew the question of exactly how much and what kind of role human nature and domestic politics play in world politics. The greater and more destructive this role, the more significant predation will be, and the less amenable anarchy will be to formation of collective identities. Classical realists, of course, assumed that human nature was possessed by an inherent lust for power or glory. My argument suggests that assumptions such as this were made for a reason: an unchanging Hobbesian man provides the powerful efficient cause necessary for a relentless pessimism about world politics that anarchic structure alone, or even structure plus intermittent predation, cannot supply. One can be skeptical of such an essentialist assumption, as I am, but it does produce determinate results at the expense of systemic theory. A concern with systemic process over structure suggests that perhaps it is time to revisit the debate over the relative importance of first-, second-, and third-image theories of state identity-formation.[49]

Assuming for now that systemic theories of identity-formation in world politics are worth pursuing, let me conclude by suggesting that the realist-rationalist alliance "reifies" self-help in the sense of treating it as something separate from the practices by which it is produced and sustained. Peter Berger and Thomas Luckmann define reification as follows: "[It] is the apprehension of the products of human activity *as if* they were something else than human products—such as facts of nature, results of cosmic laws, or manifestations of divine will. Reification implies that man is capable of forgetting his own authorship of the human world, and further, that the dialectic between man, the producer, and his products is lost to consciousness. The reified world is . . . experienced by man as a strange facticity, an *opus alienum* over which he has no control rather than as the *opus proprium* of his own productive activity."[50] By denying or bracketing states' collective authorship of their identities and interests, in other words, the realist-rationalist alliance denies or brackets the fact that competitive power politics help create the very "problem of order" they are supposed to solve—that realism is a self-fulfilling prophecy. Far from being exogenously given, the intersubjective knowledge that constitutes competitive identities and interests is constructed every day by processes of "social will formation."[51] It is what states have made of themselves.

Institutional Transformations of Power Politics

Let us assume that processes of identity- and interest-formation have created a world in which states do not recognize rights to territory or existence—a war of all against all. In this world, anarchy has a "realist" meaning for state action: be insecure and concerned with relative power. Anarchy has this meaning only in virtue of collective, insecurity-producing practices, but if those practices are relatively stable, they do constitute a system that may resist change. The fact that worlds of power politics are socially constructed, in other words, does not guarantee they are malleable, for at least two reasons.

The first reason is that once constituted, any social system confronts each of its members as an objective social fact that reinforces certain behaviors and discourages others. Self-help systems, for example, tend to reward competition and punish altruism. The possibility of change depends on whether the exigencies of such competition leave room for actions that deviate from the prescribed script. If they do not, the system will be reproduced and deviant actors will not.[52]

The second reason is that systemic change may also be inhibited by actors' interests in maintaining relatively stable role identities. Such interests are rooted not only in the desire to minimize uncertainty and anxiety, manifested in efforts to confirm existing beliefs about the social world, but also in the desire to avoid the expected costs of breaking commitments made to others—notably domestic constituencies and foreign allies in the case of states—as part of past practices. The level of resistance that these commitments induce will depend on the "salience" of particular role identities to the actor.[53] The United States, for example, is more likely to resist threats to its identity as "leader of anticommunist crusades" than to its identity as "promoter of human rights." But for almost any role identity, practices and information that challenge it are likely to create cognitive dissonance and even perceptions of threat, and these may cause resistance to transformations of the self and thus to social change.[54]

For both systemic and "psychological" reasons, then, intersubjective understandings and expectations may have a self-perpetuating quality, constituting path-dependencies that new ideas about self and other must transcend. This does not change the fact that through practice agents are continuously producing and reproducing identities and interests, continuously "choosing now the preferences [they] will have later."[55] But it does mean that choices may not be experienced with meaningful degrees of freedom. This could be a constructivist justification for the realist position that only simple learning is possible in self-help systems. The realist might concede that such systems are socially constructed and still argue that after the corresponding identities and interests have become institutionalized, they are almost impossible to transform.

In the remainder of this article, I examine three institutional transformations of identity and security interest through which states might escape a Hobbesian world of their own making. In so doing, I seek to clarify what it means to say that "institutions transform identities and interests," emphasizing that the key to such transformations is relatively stable practice.

Sovereignty, Recognition, and Security

In a Hobbesian state of nature, states are individuated by the domestic processes that constitute them as states and by their material capacity to deter threats from other states. In this world, even if free momentarily from the predations of others, state security does not have any basis in social recognition—in intersubjective understandings or norms that a state has a right to its existence, territory, and subjects. Security is a matter of national power, nothing more.

The principle of sovereignty transforms this situation by providing a social basis for the individuality and security of states. Sovereignty is an institution, and so it exists only in virtue of certain intersubjective understandings and expectations; there is no sovereignty without an other.

These understandings and expectations not only constitute a particular kind of state—the "sovereign" state—but also constitute a particular form of community, since identities are relational. The essence of this community is a mutual recognition of one another's right to exercise exclusive political authority within territorial limits. These reciprocal "permissions"[56] constitute a spatially rather than functionally differentiated world—a world in which fields of practice constitute and are organized around "domestic" and "international" spaces rather than around the performance of particular activities.[57] The location of the boundaries between these spaces is of course sometimes contested, war being one practice through which states negotiate the terms of their individuality. But this does not change the fact that it is only in virtue of mutual recognition that states have "territorial property rights."[58] This recognition functions as a form of "social closure" that disempowers nonstate actors and empowers and helps stabilize interaction among states.[59]

Sovereignty norms are now so taken for granted, so natural, that it is easy to overlook the extent to which they are both presupposed by and an ongoing artifact of practice. When states tax "their" "citizens" and not others, when they "protect" their markets against foreign "imports," when they kill thousands of Iraqis in one kind of war and then refuse to "intervene" to kill even one person in another kind, a "civil" war, and when they fight a global war against a regime that sought to destroy the institution of sovereignty and then give Germany back to the Germans, they are acting against the background of, and thereby reproducing, shared norms about what it means to be a sovereign state.

If states stopped acting on those norms, their identity as "sovereigns" (if not necessarily as "states") would disappear. The sovereign state is an ongoing accomplishment of practice, not a once-and-for-all creation of norms that somehow exist apart from practice.[60] Thus, saying that "the institution of sovereignty transforms identities" is shorthand for saying that "regular practices produce mutually constituting sovereign identities (agents) and their associated institutional norms (structures)." Practice is the core of constructivist resolutions of the agent-structure problem. This ongoing process may not be politically problematic in particular historical contexts and, indeed, once a community of mutual recognition is constituted, its members—even the disadvantaged ones[61]—may have a vested interest in reproducing it. In fact, this is part of what having an identity means. But this identity and institution remain dependent on what actors do: removing those practices will remove their intersubjective conditions of existence.

This may tell us something about how institutions of sovereign states are reproduced through social interaction, but it does not tell us why such a structure of identity and interest would arise in the first place. Two conditions would seem necessary for this to happen: (1) the density and regularity of interactions must be sufficiently high and (2) actors must be dissatisfied with preexisting forms of identity and interaction. Given these conditions, a norm of mutual recognition is relatively undemanding in terms of social trust, having the form of an assurance game in which a player will acknowledge the sovereignty of the others as long as they will in turn acknowledge that player's own sovereignty. Articulating international legal principles such as those embodied in the Peace of Augsburg (1555) and the Peace of Westphalia (1648) may also help by establishing explicit criteria for determining violations of the nascent social consensus.[62] But whether such a consensus holds depends on what states do. If they treat each other as if they were sovereign, then over time they will institutionalize that mode of subjectivity; if they do not, then that mode will not become the norm.

Practices of sovereignty will transform understandings of security and power politics in at least three ways. First, states will come to define their (and our) security in terms of preserving their "property rights" over particular territories. We now see this as natural, but the preservation of territorial frontiers is not, in fact, equivalent to the survival of the state or its people. Indeed, some states would probably be more secure if they would relinquish certain territories—the "Soviet Union" of some minority republics, "Yugoslavia" of Croatia and Slovenia, Israel of the West Bank, and so on. The fact that sovereignty practices have historically been oriented toward producing distinct territorial spaces, in other words, affects states' conceptualization of what they must "secure" to function in that identity, a process that may help account for the "hardening" of territorial boundaries over the centuries.[63]

Second, to the extent that states successfully internalize sovereignty norms, they will be more respectful toward the territorial rights of others.[64] This restraint is *not* primarily because of the costs of violating sovereignty norms, although when violators do get punished (as in the Gulf War) it reminds everyone of what these costs can be, but because part of what it means to be a "sovereign" state is that one does not violate the territorial rights of others without "just cause." A clear example of such an institutional effect, convincingly argued by David Strang, is the markedly different treatment that weak states receive within and outside communities of mutual recognition.[65] What keeps the United States from conquering the Bahamas, or Nigeria from seizing Togo, or Australia from occupying Vanuatu? Clearly, power is not the issue, and in these cases even the cost of sanctions would probably be negligible. One might argue that great powers simply have no "interest" in these conquests, and this might be so, but this lack of interest can only be understood in terms of their recognition of weak states' sovereignty. I have no interest in exploiting my friends, not because of the relative costs and benefits of such action but because they are my friends. The absence of recognition, in turn, helps explain the Western states' practices of territorial conquest, enslavement, and genocide against Native American and African peoples. It is in *that* world that only power matters, not the world of today.

Finally, to the extent that their ongoing socialization teaches states that their sovereignty depends on recognition by other states, they can afford to rely more on the institutional fabric of international society and less on individual national means—especially military power—to protect their security. The intersubjective understandings embodied in the institution of sovereignty, in other words, may redefine the meaning of others' power for the security of the self. In policy terms, this means that states can be less worried about short-term survival and relative power and can thus shift their resources accordingly. Ironically, it is the great powers, the states with the greatest national means, that may have the hardest time learning this lesson; small powers do not have the luxury of relying on national means and may therefore learn faster that collective recognition is a cornerstone of security.

None of this is to say that power becomes irrelevant in a community of sovereign states. Sometimes states *are* threatened by others that do not recognize their existence or particular territorial claims, that resent the externalities from their economic policies, and so on. But most of the time, these threats are played out within the terms of the sovereignty game. The fates of Napoleon and Hitler show what happens when they are not.

Cooperation among Egoists and Transformations of Identity

We began this section with a Hobbesian state of nature. Cooperation for joint gain is extremely difficult in this context, since trust is lacking, time horizons are short, and relative power concerns are high. Life is "nasty, brutish, and short." Sovereignty transforms this system into a Lockean world of (mostly) mutually recognized property rights and (mostly) egoistic rather than competitive conceptions of security, reducing the fear that what states already have will be seized at any moment by potential collaborators, thereby enabling them to contemplate more direct forms of cooperation. A necessary condition for such cooperation is that outcomes be positively interdependent in the sense that potential gains exist which cannot be realized by unilateral action. States such as Brazil and Botswana may recognize each other's sovereignty, but they need further incentives to engage in joint action. One important source of incentives is the growing "dynamic density" of interaction among states in a world with new communications technology, nuclear weapons, externalities from industrial development, and so on.[66] Unfortunately, growing dynamic density does not ensure that states will in fact realize joint gains; interdependence also entails vulnerability and the risk of being "the sucker," which if exploited will become a source of conflict rather than cooperation.

This is the rationale for the familiar assumption that egoistic states will often find themselves facing prisoners' dilemma, a game in which the dominant strategy, if played only once, is to defect. As Michael Taylor and Robert Axelrod have shown, however, given iteration and a sufficient shadow of the future, egoists using a tit-for-tat strategy can escape this result and build cooperative institutions.[67] The story they tell about this process on the surface seems quite similar to George Herbert Mead's constructivist analysis of interaction, part of which is also told in terms of "games."[68] Cooperation is a gesture indicating ego's willingness to cooperate; if alter defects, ego does likewise, signaling its unwillingness to be exploited; over time and through reciprocal play, each learns to form relatively stable expectations about the other's behavior, and through these, habits of cooperation (or defection) form. Despite similar concerns with communication, learning, and habit-formation, however, there is an important difference between the game-theoretic and constructivist analysis of interaction that bears on how we conceptualize the causal powers of institutions.

In the traditional game-theoretic analysis of cooperation, even an iterated one, the structure of the game—of identities and interests—is exogenous to interaction and, as such, does not change.[69] A "black box" is put around identity- and interest-formation, and analysis focuses instead on the relationship between expectations and behavior. The norms that evolve from interaction are treated as rules and behavioral regularities which are external to the actors and which resist change because of the transaction costs of creating new ones. The game-theoretic analysis of cooperation among egoists is at base behavioral.

A constructivist analysis of cooperation, in contrast, would concentrate on how the expectations produced by behavior affect identities and interests. The process of creating institutions is one of internalizing new understandings of self and other, of acquiring new role identities, not just of creating external constraints on the behavior of exogenously constituted actors.[70] Even if not intended as such, in other words, the process by which egoists learn to cooperate is at the same time a process of reconstructing their interests in terms of shared commitments to social norms. Over time, this will tend to transform a positive interdependence of *outcomes* into a positive interdependence of *utilities* or collective interest organized around the norms in question. These norms will resist change because they are tied to actors' commitments to their identities and interests, not merely because of transaction costs. A constructivist analysis of "the cooperation problem," in other words, is at base cognitive rather than behavioral, since it treats the intersubjective knowledge that defines the structure of identities and interests, of the "game," as endogenous to and instantiated by interaction itself.

The debate over the future of collective security in Western Europe may illustrate the significance of this difference. A weak liberal or rationalist analysis would assume that the European states' "portfolio" of interests has not fundamentally changed and that the emergence of new factors, such as the collapse of the Soviet threat and the rise of Germany, would alter their cost-benefit ratios for pursuing current arrangements, thereby causing existing institutions to break down. The European states formed collaborative institutions for good, exogenously constituted egoistic reasons, and the same reasons may lead them to reject those institutions; the game of European power politics has not changed. A strong liberal or constructivist analysis of this problem would suggest that four decades of cooperation may have transformed a positive interdependence of outcomes into a collective "European identity" in terms of which states increasingly define their "self"-interests.[71] Even if egoistic reasons were its starting point, the process of cooperating tends to redefine those reasons by reconstituting identities and interests in terms of new intersubjective understandings and commitments. Changes in the distribution of power during the late twentieth century are undoubtedly a challenge to these new understandings, but it is not as if West European states have some inherent, exogenously given interest in abandoning collective security if the price is right. Their identities and security interests are continuously in process, and if collective identities become "embedded," they will be as resistant to change as egoistic ones.[72] Through participation in new forms of social knowledge, in other words, the European states of 1990 might no longer be the states of 1950.

Critical Strategic Theory and Collective Security

The transformation of identity and interest through an "evolution of cooperation" faces two important constraints. The first is that the process is incremental and slow. Actors' objectives in such a process are typically to realize joint gains within what they take to be a relatively stable context, and they are therefore unlikely to engage in substantial reflection about how to change the parameters of that context (including the structure of identities and interests) and unlikely to pursue policies specifically designed to bring about such changes. Learning to cooperate may change those parameters, but this occurs as an unintended consequence of policies pursued for other reasons rather than as a result of intentional efforts to transcend existing institutions.

A second, more fundamental, constraint is that the evolution of cooperation story presupposes that actors do not identify negatively with one another. Actors must be concerned primarily with absolute gains; to the extent that antipathy and distrust lead them to define their security in relativistic terms, it will be hard to accept the vulnerabilities that attend cooperation.[73] This is important because it is precisely the "central balance" in the state system that seems to be so often afflicted with such competitive thinking, and realists can therefore argue that the possibility of cooperation within one "pole" (for example, the West) is parasitic on the dominance of competition between poles (the East–West conflict). Relations between the poles may be amenable to some positive reciprocity in areas such as arms control, but the atmosphere of distrust leaves little room for such cooperation and its transformative consequences.[74] The conditions of negative identification that make an "evolution of cooperation" most needed work precisely against such a logic.

This seemingly intractable situation may nevertheless be amenable to quite a different logic of transformation, one driven more by self-conscious efforts to change structures of identity and interest than by unintended consequences. Such voluntarism may seem to contradict the spirit of constructivism, since would-be revolutionaries are presumably themselves effects of socialization to structures of identity and interest. How can they

think about changing that to which they owe their identity? The possibility lies in the distinction between the social determination of the self and the personal determination of choice, between what Mead called the "me" and the "I."[75] The "me" is that part of subjectivity which is defined in terms of others; the character and behavioral expectations of a person's role identity as "professor," or of the United States as "leader of the alliance," for example, are socially constituted. Roles are not played in mechanical fashion according to precise scripts, however, but are "taken" and adapted in idiosyncratic ways by each actor.[76] Even in the most constrained situations, role performance involves a choice by the actor. The "I" is the part of subjectivity in which this appropriation and reaction to roles and its corresponding existential freedom lie.

The fact that roles are "taken" means that, in principle, actors always have a capacity for "character planning"—for engaging in critical self-reflection and choices designed to bring about changes in their lives.[77] But when or under what conditions can this creative capacity be exercised? Clearly, much of the time it cannot: if actors were constantly reinventing their identities, social order would be impossible, and the relative stability of identities and interests in the real world is indicative of our propensity for habitual rather than creative action. The exceptional, conscious choosing to transform or transcend roles has at least two preconditions. First, there must be a reason to think of oneself in novel terms. This would most likely stem from the presence of new social situations that cannot be managed in terms of preexisting self-conceptions. Second, the expected costs of intentional role change—the sanctions imposed by others with whom one interacted in previous roles—cannot be greater than its rewards.

When these conditions are present, actors can engage in self-reflection and practice specifically designed to transform their identities and interests and thus to "change the games" in which they are embedded. Such "critical" strategic theory and practice has not received the attention it merits from students of world politics (another legacy of exogenously given interests perhaps), particularly given that one of the most important phenomena in contemporary world politics, Mikhail Gorbachev's policy of "New Thinking," is arguably precisely that.[78] Let me therefore use this policy as an example of how states might transform a competitive security system into a cooperative one, dividing the transformative process into four stages.

The first stage in intentional transformation is the breakdown of consensus about identity commitments. In the Soviet case, identity commitments centered on the Leninist theory of imperialism, with its belief that relations between capitalist and socialist states are inherently conflictual, and on the alliance patterns that this belief engendered. In the 1980s, the consensus within the Soviet Union over the Leninist theory broke down for a variety of reasons, principal among which seem to have been the state's inability to meet the economic-technological-military challenge from the West, the government's decline of political legitimacy at home, and the reassurance from the West that it did not intend to invade the Soviet Union, a reassurance that reduced the external costs of role change.[79] These factors paved the way for a radical leadership transition and for a subsequent "unfreezing of conflict schemas" concerning relations with the West.[80]

The breakdown of consensus makes possible a second stage of critical examination of old ideas about self and other and, by extension, of the structures of interaction by which the ideas have been sustained. In periods of relatively stable role identities, ideas and structures may become reified and thus treated as things that exist independently of social action. If so, the second stage is one of denaturalization, of identifying the practices that reproduce seemingly inevitable ideas about self and other; to that extent, it is a form of "critical" rather than "problem-solving" theory.[81] The result of such a critique should be an identification of new "possible selves" and aspirations.[82] New Thinking embodies such critical theorizing. Gorbachev wants to free the Soviet Union from the coercive social logic of the cold war and engage the West in far-reaching cooperation. Toward this end, he has rejected the Leninist belief in the inherent conflict of interest between socialist and capitalist states and, perhaps more important, has recognized the crucial role that Soviet aggressive practices played in sustaining that conflict.

Such rethinking paves the way for a third stage of new practice. In most cases, it is not enough to rethink one's own ideas about self and other, since old identities have been sustained by systems of interaction with *other* actors, the practices of which remain a social fact for the transformative agent. In order to change the self, then, it is often necessary to change the identities and interests of the others that help sustain those systems of interaction. The vehicle for inducing such change is one's own practice and, in particular, the practice of "altercasting"—a technique of interactor control in which ego uses tactics of self-presentation and stage management in an attempt to frame alter's definitions of social situations in ways that create the role which ego desires alter to play.[83] In effect, in altercasting ego tries to induce alter to take on a new identity (and thereby enlist alter in ego's effort to change itself) by treating alter *as if* it already had that identity. The logic of this follows directly from the mirror theory of identity-formation, in which alter's identity is a reflection of ego's practices; change those practices and ego begins to change alter's conception of itself.

What these practices should consist of depends on the logic by which the preexisting identities were sustained. Competitive security systems are sustained by practices that create insecurity and distrust. In this case, transformative practices should attempt to teach other states that one's own state can be trusted and should not be viewed as a threat to their security. The fastest way to do this is to make unilateral initiatives and self-binding commitments of sufficient significance that another state is faced with "an offer it cannot refuse."[84] Gorbachev has tried to do this by withdrawing from Afghanistan and Eastern Europe, implementing asymmetric cuts in nuclear and conventional forces, calling for "defensive defense," and so on. In addition, he has skillfully cast the West in the role of being morally required to give aid and comfort to the Soviet Union, has emphasized the bonds of common fate between the Soviet Union and the West, and has indicated that further progress in East–West relations is contingent upon the West assuming the identity being projected onto it. These actions are all dimensions of altercasting, the intention of which is to take away the Western "excuse" for distrusting the Soviet Union, which, in Gorbachev's view, has helped sustain competitive identities in the past.

Yet by themselves such practices cannot transform a competitive security system, since if they are not reciprocated by alter, they will expose ego to a "sucker" payoff and quickly wither on the vine. In order for critical strategic practice to transform competitive identities, it must be "rewarded" by alter, which will encourage more such practice by ego, and so on.[85] Over time, this will institutionalize a positive rather than a negative identification between the security of self and other and will thereby provide a firm intersubjective basis for what were initially tentative commitments to new identities and interests.[86]

Notwithstanding today's rhetoric about the end of the cold war, skeptics may still doubt whether Gorbachev (or some future leader) will succeed in building an intersubjective basis for a new Soviet (or Russian) role identity. There are important domestic, bureaucratic, and cognitive-ideological sources of resistance in both East and West to such a change, not the least of which is the shakiness of the democratic forces' domestic position. But if my argument about the role of intersubjective knowledge in creating competitive structures of identity and interest is right, then at least New Thinking shows a greater appreciation—conscious or not—for the deep structure of power politics than we are accustomed to in international relations practice.

Conclusion

All theories of international relations are based on social theories of the relationship between agency, process, and social structure. Social theories do not determine the content of our international theorizing, but they do structure the questions we ask about world politics and our approaches to answering those questions. The substantive issue at stake in debates about social theory is what kind of foundation offers the most fruitful set of questions and research strategies for explaining the revolutionary changes that seem to be occurring in the late twentieth century international system. Put simply, what should systemic theories of international relations look like? How should they conceptualize the relationship between structure and process? Should they be based exclusively on "microeconomic" analogies in which identities and interests are exogenously given by structure and process is reduced to interactions within those parameters? Or should they also be based on "sociological" and "social psychological" analogies in which identities and interests and therefore the meaning of structure are endogenous to process? Should a behavioral-individualism or a cognitive-constructivism be the basis for systemic theories of world politics?

This article notwithstanding, this question is ultimately an empirical one in two respects. First, its answer depends in part on how important interaction among states is for the constitution of their identities and interests. On the one hand, it may be that domestic or genetic factors, which I have systematically bracketed, are in fact much more important determinants of states' identities and interests than are systemic factors. To the extent that this is true, the individualism of a rationalist approach and the inherent privileging of structure over process in this approach become more substantively appropriate for systemic theory (if not for first- and second-image theory), since identities and interests are *in fact* largely exogenous to interaction among states. On the other hand, if the bracketed factors are relatively unimportant or if the importance of the international system varies historically (perhaps with the level of dynamic density and interdependence in the system), then such a framework would not be appropriate as an exclusive foundation for general systemic theory.

Second, the answer to the question about what systemic theories should look like also depends on how easily state identities and interests can change as a result of systemic interaction. Even if interaction is initially important in constructing identities and interests, once institutionalized its logic may make transformation extremely difficult. If the meaning of structure for state action changes so slowly that it becomes a de facto parameter within which process takes place, then it may again be substantively appropriate to adopt the rationalist assumption that identities and interests are given (although again, this may vary historically).

We cannot address these empirical issues, however, unless we have a framework for doing systemic research that makes state identity and interest an issue for both theoretical and empirical inquiry. Let me emphasize that this is *not* to say we should never treat identities and interests as given. The framing of problems and research strategies should be question-driven rather than method-driven, and if we are not interested in identity- and interest-formation, we may find the assumptions of a rationalist discourse perfectly reasonable. Nothing in this article, in other words, should be taken as an attack on rationalism per se. By the same token, however, we should not let this legitimate analytical stance become a de facto

ontological stance with respect to the content of third-image theory, at least not until after we have determined that systemic interaction does not play an important role in processes of state identity- and interest-formation. We should not choose our philosophical anthropologies and social theories prematurely. By arguing that we cannot derive a self-help structure of identity and interest from the principle of anarchy alone—by arguing that anarchy is what states make of it—this article has challenged one important justification for ignoring processes of identity- and interest-formation in world politics. As such, it helps set the stage for inquiry into the empirical issues raised above and thus for a debate about whether communitarian or individualist assumptions are a better foundation for systemic theory.

I have tried to indicate by crude example what such a research agenda might look like. Its objective should be to assess the causal relationship between practice and interaction (as independent variable) and the cognitive structures at the level of individual states and of systems of states which constitute identities and interests (as dependent variable)—that is, the relationship between what actors *do* and what they *are*. We may have some a priori notion that state actors and systemic structures are "mutually constitutive," but this tells us little in the absence of an understanding of how the mechanics of dyadic, triadic, and *n*-actor interaction shape and are in turn shaped by "stocks of knowledge" that collectively constitute identities and interests and, more broadly, constitute the structures of international life. Particularly important in this respect is the role of practice in shaping attitudes toward the "givenness" of these structures. How and why do actors reify social structures, and under what conditions do they denaturalize such reifications?

The state-centrism of this agenda may strike some, particularly postmodernists, as "depressingly familiar."[87] The significance of states relative to multinational corporations, new social movements, transnationals, and intergovernmental organizations is clearly declining, and "postmodern" forms of world politics merit more research attention than they have received. But I also believe, with realists, that in the medium run sovereign states will remain the dominant political actors in the international system. Any transition to new structures of global political authority and identity—to "postinternational" politics—will be mediated by and path-dependent on the particular institutional resolution of the tension between unity and diversity, or particularism and universality, that is the sovereign state.[88] In such a world there should continue to be a place for theories of anarchic interstate politics, alongside other forms of international theory; to that extent, I am a statist and a realist. I have argued in this article, however, that statism need not be bound by realist ideas about what "state" must mean. State identities and interests can be collectively transformed within an anarchic context by many factors—individual, domestic, systemic, or transnational—and as such are an important dependent variable. Such a reconstruction of state-centric international theory is necessary if we are to theorize adequately about the emerging forms of transnational political identity that sovereign states will help bring into being. To that extent, I hope that statism, like the state, can be historically progressive.

■　■　■

NOTES

1. See, for example, Joseph Grieco, "Anarchy and the Limits of Cooperation: A Realist Critique of the Newest Liberal Institutionalism," *International Organization* 42 (Summer 1988), pp. 485–507; Joseph Nye, "Neorealism and Neoliberalism," *World Politics* 40 (January 1988), pp. 235–51; Robert Keohane, "Neoliberal Institutionalism: A Perspective on World Politics," in his collection of essays entitled *International Institutions and State Power* (Boulder, Colo.: Westview Press, 1989), pp. 1–20; John Mearsheimer, "Back to the Future: Instability in Europe after the Cold War," *International Security* 13 (Summer 1990), pp. 5–56.

2. Kenneth Waltz, *Man, the State, and War* (New York: Columbia University Press, 1959), p. 232.

3. Ibid., pp. 169–70.

4. Ibid., p. 232. This point is made by Hidemi Suganami in "Bringing Order to the Causes of War Debates," *Millennium* 19 (Spring 1990), p. 34, fn. 11.

5. Kenneth Waltz, *Theory of International Politics* (Boston: Addison-Wesley, 1979).

6. The neorealist description is not unproblematic. For a powerful critique, see David Lumsdaine, [*Moral Vision in International Politics:*] *The Foreign Aid Regime, 1949–1989* (Princeton, N.J.: Princeton University Press, [1993]).

7. Waltz, *Theory of International Politics*, pp. 79–101.

8. Stephen Walt, *The Origins of Alliances* (Ithaca, N.Y.: Cornell University Press, 1987).

9. See, for example, Herbert Blumer, "The Methodological Position of Symbolic Interactionism," in his *Symbolic Interactionism: Perspective and Method* (Englewood Cliffs, N.J.: Prentice-Hall, 1969), p. 2. Throughout this article, I assume that a theoretically productive analogy can be made between individuals and states.

10. The phrase "distribution of knowledge" is Barry Barnes's, as discussed in his work *The Nature of Power* (Cambridge: Polity Press, 1988); see also Peter Berger and Thomas Luckmann, *The Social Construction of Reality* (New York: Anchor Books, 1966).

11. For an excellent short statement of how collective meanings constitute identities, see Peter Berger, "Identity as a Problem in the Sociology of Knowledge," *European Journal of Sociology,* vol. 7, no. 1, 1966, pp. 32–40.

12. Berger, "Identity as a Problem in the Sociology of Knowledge," p. 111.

13. While not normally cast in such terms, foreign policy scholarship on national role conceptions could be

adapted to such identity language. See Kal Holsti, "National Role Conceptions in the Study of Foreign Policy," *International Studies Quarterly* 14 (September 1970), pp. 233–309; and Stephen Walker, ed., *Role Theory and Foreign Policy Analysis* (Durham, N.C.: Duke University Press, 1987). For an important effort to do so, see Stephen Walker, "Symbolic Interactionism and International Politics: Role Theory's Contribution to International Organization," in C. Shih and Martha Cottam, eds., *Contending Dramas: A Cognitive Approach to Post-War International Organizational Processes* (New York: Praeger, [1992]).

14. On the "portfolio" conception of interests, see Barry Hindess, *Political Choice and Social Structure* (Aldershot, U.K.: Edward Elgar, 1989), pp. 2–3. The "definition of the situation" is a central concept in interactionist theory.

15. Nelson Foote, "Identification as the Basis for a Theory of Motivation," *American Sociological Review* 16 (February 1951), p. 15. Such strongly sociological conceptions of interest have been criticized, with some justice, for being "oversocialized"; see Dennis Wrong, "The Oversocialized Conception of Man in Modern Sociology," *American Sociological Review* 26 (April 1961), pp. 183–93. For useful correctives, which focus on the activation of presocial but nondetermining human needs within social contexts, see Turner, *A Theory of Social Interaction,* pp. 23–69; and Viktor Gecas, "The Self-Concept as a Basis for a Theory of Motivation," in Judith Howard and Peter Callero, eds., *The Self-Society Dynamic* (Cambridge: Cambridge University Press, 1991), pp. 171–87.

16. In neo-Durkheimian parlance, institutions are "social representations." See Serge Moscovici, "The Phenomenon of Social Representations," in Rob Farr and Serge Moscovici, eds., *Social Representations* (Cambridge: Cambridge University Press, 1984), pp. 3–69.

17. Berger and Luckmann, *The Social Construction of Reality,* p. 58.

18. See Giddens, *Central Problems in Social Theory;* and Alexander Wendt and Raymond Duvall, "Institutions and International Order," in Ernst-Otto Czempiel and James Rosenau, eds., *Global Changes and Theoretical Challenges* (Lexington, Mass.: Lexington Books, 1989), pp. 51–74.

19. Proponents of choice theory might put this in terms of "interdependent utilities."

20. Security systems might also vary in the extent to which there is a functional differentiation or a hierarchical relationship between patron and client, with the patron playing a hegemonic role within its sphere of influence in defining the security interests of its clients. I do not examine this dimension here; for preliminary discussion, see Alexander Wendt, "The States System and Global Militarization," Ph.D. diss., University of Minnesota, Minneapolis, 1989; and Alexander Wendt and Michael Barnett, "The International System and Third World Militarization," unpublished manuscript, 1991.

21. This amounts to an "internationalization of the state." For a discussion of this subject, see Raymond Duvall and Alexander Wendt, "The International Capital Regime and the Internationalization of the State," unpublished manuscript, 1987. See also R. B. J. Walker, "Sovereignty, Identity, Community: Reflections on the Horizons of Contemporary Political Practice," in R. B. J. Walker and Saul Mendlovitz, eds., *Contending Sovereignties* (Boulder, Colo.: Lynne Rienner, 1990), pp. 159–85.

22. On the spectrum of cooperative security arrangements, see Charles Kupchan and Clifford Kupchan, "Concerts, Collective Security, and the Future of Europe," *International Security* 16 (Summer 1991), pp. 114–61; and Richard Smoke, "A Theory of Mutual Security," in Richard Smoke and Andrei Kortunov, eds., *Mutual Security* (New York: St. Martin's Press, 1991), pp. 59–111. These may be usefully set alongside Christopher Jencks' "Varieties of Altruism," in Jane Mansbridge, ed., *Beyond Self-Interest* (Chicago: University of Chicago Press, 1990), pp. 53–67.

23. On the role of collective identity in reducing collective action problems, see Bruce Fireman and William Gamson, "Utilitarian Logic in the Resource Mobilization Perspective," in Mayer Zald and John McCarthy, eds., *The Dynamics of Social Movements*

(Cambridge, Mass.: Winthrop, 1979), pp. 8–44; Robyn Dawes et al., "Cooperation for the Benefit of Us—Not Me, or My Conscience," in Mansbridge, *Beyond Self-Interest,* pp. 97–110; and Craig Calhoun, "The Problem of Identity in Collective Action," in Joan Huber, ed., *Macro-Micro Linkages in Sociology* (Beverly Hills, Calif.: Sage, 1991), pp. 51–75.

24. See Thomas Risse-Kappen, "Are Democratic Alliances Special?" unpublished manuscript, Yale University, New Haven, Conn., 1991.

25. Waltz, *Theory of International Politics,* p. 91.

26. See Waltz, *Man, the State, and War;* and Robert Jervis, "Cooperation Under the Security Dilemma," *World Politics* 30 (January 1978), pp. 167–214.

27. My argument here parallels Rousseau's critique of Hobbes. For an excellent critique of realist appropriations of Rousseau, see Michael Williams, "Rousseau, Realism, and Realpolitik," *Millennium* 18 (Summer 1989), pp. 188–204. Williams argues that far from being a fundamental starting point in the state of nature, for Rousseau the stag hunt represented a stage in man's fall. On p. 190, Williams cites Rousseau's description of man prior to leaving the state of nature: "Man only knows himself; he does not see his own well-being to be identified with or contrary to that of anyone else; he neither hates anything nor loves anything; but limited to no more than physical instinct, he is no one, he is an animal." For another critique of Hobbes on the state of nature that parallels my constructivist reading of anarchy, see Charles Landesman, "Reflections on Hobbes: Anarchy and Human Nature," in Peter Caws, ed., *The Causes of Quarrel* (Boston: Beacon, 1989), pp. 139–48.

28. Empirically, this suggestion is problematic, since the process of decolonization and the subsequent support of many Third World states by international society point to ways in which even the raw material of "empirical statehood" is constituted by the society of states. See Robert Jackson and Carl Rosberg, "Why Africa's Weak States Persist: The Empirical and the Juridical in Statehood," *World Politics* 35 (October 1982), pp. 1–24.

29. Waltz, *Theory of International Politics,* pp. 74–77.

30. See James Morrow, "Social Choice and System Structure in World Politics," *World Politics* 41 (October 1988), p. 89. Waltz's behavioral treatment of socialization may be usefully contrasted with the more cognitive approach taken by Ikenberry and the Kupchans in the following articles: G. John Ikenberry and Charles Kupchan, "Socialization and Hegemonic Power," *International Organization* 44 (Summer 1989), pp. 283–316; and Kupchan and Kupchan, "Concerts, Collective Security, and the Future of Europe." Their approach is close to my own, but they define socialization as an elite strategy to induce value change in others, rather than as a ubiquitous feature of interaction in terms of which all identities and interests get produced and reproduced.

31. Regarding individualism, see Richard Ashley, "The Poverty of Neorealism," *International Organization* 38 (Spring 1984), pp. 225–86; Wendt, "The Agent-Structure Problem in International Relations Theory"; and David Dessler, "What's at Stake in the Agent-Structure Debate?" *International Organization* 43 (Summer 1989), pp. 441–74. Regarding structuralism, see R. B. J. Walker, "Realism, Change, and International Political Theory," *International Studies Quarterly* 31 (March 1987), pp. 65–86; and Martin Hollis and Steven Smith, *Explaining and Understanding International Relations* (Oxford: Clarendon Press, 1989).

32. The importance of the distinction between constitutive and causal explanations is not sufficiently appreciated in constructivist discourse. See Wendt, "The Agent-Structure Problem in International Relations Theory," pp. 362–65; Wendt, "The States System and Global Militarization," pp. 110–13; and Wendt, "Bridging the Theory/Meta-Theory Gap in International Relations," *Review of International Studies* 17 (October 1991), p. 390.

33. See Blumer, "The Methodological Position of Symbolic Interactionism," pp. 2–4.

34. See Robert Grafstein, "Rational Choice: Theory and Institutions," in Kristen Monroe, ed., *The Economic Approach to Politics* (New York: Harper Collins, 1991), pp. 263–64. A good example of the promise and limits of transaction cost approaches to

institutional analysis is offered by Robert Keohane in his *After Hegemony* (Princeton, N.J.: Princeton University Press, 1984).

35. This situation is not entirely metaphorical in world politics, since throughout history states have "discovered" each other, generating an instant anarchy as it were.

36. Mead's analysis of gestures remains definitive. See Mead's *Mind, Self, and Society.* See also the discussion of the role of signaling in the "mechanics of interaction" in Turner's *A Theory of Social Interaction,* pp. 74–79 and 92–115.

37. On the role of attribution processes in the interactionist account of identity-formation, see Sheldon Stryker and Avi Gottlieb, "Attribution Theory and Symbolic Interactionism," in John Harvey et al., eds., *New Directions in Attribution Research,* vol. 3 (Hillsdale, N.J.: Lawrence Erlbaum, 1981), pp. 425–58; and Kathleen Crittenden, "Sociological Aspects of Attribution," *Annual Review of Sociology,* vol. 9, 1983, pp. 425–46. On attributional processes in international relations, see Shawn Rosenberg and Gary Wolfsfeld, "International Conflict and the Problem of Attribution," *Journal of Conflict Resolution* 21 (March 1977), pp. 75–103.

38. On the "stagecraft" involved in "presentations of self," see Erving Goffman, *The Presentation of Self in Everyday Life* (New York: Doubleday, 1959). On the role of appearance in definitions of the situation, see Gregory Stone, "Appearance and the Self," in Arnold Rose, ed., *Human Behavior and Social Processes* (Boston: Houghton Mifflin, 1962), pp. 86–118.

39. This discussion of the role of possibilities and probabilities in threat perception owes much to Stewart Johnson's comments on an earlier draft of my article.

40. On the role of "reassurance" in threat situations, see Richard Ned Lebow and Janice Gross Stein, "Beyond Deterrence," *Journal of Social Issues,* vol. 43, no. 4, 1987, pp. 5–72.

41. On "reciprocal typifications," see Berger and Luckmann, *The Social Construction of Reality,* pp. 54–58.

42. Jeff Coulter, "Remarks on the Conceptualization of Social Structure," *Philosophy of the Social Sciences* 12 (March 1982), pp. 42–43.

43. The following articles by Noel Kaplowitz have made an important contribution to such thinking in international relations: "Psychopolitical Dimensions of International Relations: The Reciprocal Effects of Conflict Strategies," *International Studies Quarterly* 28 (December 1984), pp. 373–406; and "National Self-Images, Perception of Enemies, and Conflict Strategies: Psychopolitical Dimensions of International Relations," *Political Psychology* 11 (March 1990), pp. 39–82.

44. These arguments are common in theories of narcissism and altruism. See Heinz Kohut, *Self-Psychology and the Humanities* (New York: Norton, 1985); and Martin Hoffmann, "Empathy, Its Limitations, and Its Role in a Comprehensive Moral Theory," in William Kurtines and Jacob Gewirtz, eds., *Morality, Moral Behavior, and Moral Development* (New York: Wiley, 1984), pp. 283–302.

45. See C. Norman Alexander and Mary Glenn Wiley, "Situated Activity and Identity Formation," in Morris Rosenberg and Ralph Turner, eds., *Social Psychology: Sociological Perspectives* (New York: Basic Books, 1981), pp. 269–89.

46. Sheldon Stryker, "The Vitalization of Symbolic Interactionism," *Social Psychology Quarterly* 50 (March 1987), p. 93.

47. On the "maturity" of anarchies, see Barry Buzan, *People, States, and Fear* (Chapel Hill: University of North Carolina Press, 1983).

48. A similar intuition may lie behind Ashley's effort to reappropriate classical realist discourse for critical international relations theory. See Richard Ashley, "Political Realism and Human Interests," *International Studies Quarterly* 38 (June 1981), pp. 204–36.

49. Waltz has himself helped open up such a debate with his recognition that systemic factors condition but do not determine state actions. See Kenneth Waltz, "Reflections on *Theory of International Politics:* A Response to My Critics," in Robert Keohane, ed., *Neorealism and Its Critics* (New York: Columbia University Press, 1986), pp. 322–45. The growing literature on the observation that "democracies do not fight each other" is relevant to this question, as

are two other studies that break important ground toward a "reductionist" theory of state identity: William Bloom's *Personal Identity, National Identity and International Relations* (Cambridge: Cambridge University Press, 1990) and Lumsdaine's *Ideals and Interests.*

50. See Berger and Luckmann, *The Social Construction of Reality,* p. 89. See also Douglas Maynard and Thomas Wilson, "On the Reification of Social Structure," in Scott McNall and Gary Howe, eds., *Current Perspectives in Social Theory,* vol. 1 (Greenwich, Conn.: JAI Press, 1980), pp. 287–322.

51. See Richard Ashley, "Social Will and International Anarchy," in Hayward Alker and Richard Ashley, eds., *After Realism,* work in progress, Massachusetts Institute of Technology, Cambridge, and Arizona State University, Tempe, 1992.

52. See Ralph Turner, "Role-Taking: Process Versus Conformity," in Rose, *Human Behavior and Social Processes,* pp. 20–40; and Judith Howard, "From Changing Selves toward Changing Society," in Howard and Callero, *The Self-Society Dynamic,* pp. 209–37.

53. On the relationship between commitment and identity, see Foote, "Identification as the Basis for a Theory of Motivation"; Howard Becker, "Notes on the Concept of Commitment," *American Journal of Sociology* 66 (July 1960), pp. 32–40; and Stryker, *Symbolic Interactionism.* On role salience, see Stryker, ibid.

54. On threats to identity and the types of resistance that they may create, see Glynis Breakwell, *Coping with Threatened Identities* (London: Methuen, 1986); and Terrell Northrup, "The Dynamic of Identity in Personal and Social Conflict," in Louis Kreisberg et al., eds., *Intractable Conflicts and Their Transformation* (Syracuse, N.Y.: Syracuse University Press, 1989), pp. 55–82. For a broad overview of resistance to change, see Timur Kuran, "The Tenacious Past: Theories of Personal and Collective Conservatism," *Journal of Economic Behavior and Organization* 10 (September 1988), pp. 143–71.

55. James March, "Bounded Rationality, Ambiguity, and the Engineering of Choice," *Bell Journal of Economics* 9 (Autumn 1978), p. 600.

56. Haskell Fain, *Normative Politics and the Community of Nations* (Philadelphia: Temple University Press, 1987).

57. This is the intersubjective basis for the principle of functional nondifferentiation among states, which "drops out" of Waltz's definition of structure because the latter has no explicit intersubjective basis. In international relations scholarship, the social production of territorial space has been emphasized primarily by poststructuralists. See, for example, Richard Ashley, "The Geopolitics of Geopolitical Space: Toward a Critical Social Theory of International Politics," *Alternatives* 12 (October 1987), pp. 403–34; and Simon Dalby, *Creating the Second Cold War* (London: Pinter, 1990). But the idea of space as both product and constituent of practice is also prominent in structurationist discourse. See Giddens, *Central Problems in Social Theory;* and Derek Gregory and John Urry, eds., *Social Relations and Spatial Structures* (London: Macmillan, 1985).

58. See John Ruggie, "Continuity and Transformation in the World Polity: Toward a Neorealist Synthesis," *World Politics* 35 (January 1983), pp. 261–85.

59. For a definition and discussion of "social closure," see Raymond Murphy, *Social Closure* (Oxford: Clarendon Press, 1988).

60. See Richard Ashley, "Untying the Sovereign State: A Double Reading of the Anarchy Problematique," *Millennium* 17 (Summer 1988), pp. 227–62.

61. See, for example, Mohammed Ayoob, "The Third World in the System of States: Acute Schizophrenia or Growing Pains?" *International Studies Quarterly* 33 (March 1989), pp. 67–80.

62. See William Coplin, "International Law and Assumptions about the State System," *World Politics* 17 (July 1965), pp. 615–34.

63. See Anthony Smith, "States and Homelands: The Social and Geopolitical Implications of National Territory," *Millennium* 10 (Autumn 1981), pp. 187–202.

64. This assumes that there are no other, competing, principles that organize political space and identity in the international system and coexist with traditional notions of sovereignty; in fact, of course, there are.

On "spheres of influence" and "informal empires," see Jan Triska, ed., *Dominant Powers and Subordinate States* (Durham, N.C.: Duke University Press, 1986); and Ronald Robinson, "The Excentric Idea of Imperialism, With or Without Empire," in Wolfgang Mommsen and Jurgen Osterhammel, eds., *Imperialism and After: Continuities and Discontinuities* (London: Allen & Unwin, 1986), pp. 267–89. On Arab conceptions of sovereignty, see Michael Barnett, "Sovereignty, Institutions, and Identity: From Pan-Arabism to the Arab State System," unpublished manuscript, University of Wisconsin, Madison, 1991.

65. David Strang, "Anomaly and Commonplace in European Expansion: Realist and Institutional Accounts," *International Organization* 45 (Spring 1991), pp. 143–62.

66. On "dynamic density," see Ruggie, "Continuity and Transformation in the World Polity"; and Waltz, "Reflections on *Theory of International Politics*." The role of interdependence in conditioning the speed and depth of social learning is much greater than the attention to which I have paid it. On the consequences of interdependence under anarchy, see Helen Milner, "The Assumption of Anarchy in International Relations Theory: A Critique," *Review of International Studies* 17 (January 1991), pp. 67–85.

67. See Michael Taylor, *Anarchy and Cooperation* (New York: Wiley, 1976); and Robert Axelrod, *The Evolution of Cooperation* (New York: Basic Books, 1984).

68. Mead, *Mind, Self, and Society.*

69. Strictly speaking, this is not true, since in iterated games the addition of future benefits to current ones changes the payoff structure of the game at T1, in this case from prisoners' dilemma to an assurance game. This transformation of interest takes place entirely within the actor, however, and as such is not a function of interaction with the other.

70. In fairness to Axelrod, he does point out that internalization of norms is a real possibility that may increase the resilience of institutions. My point is that this important idea cannot be derived from an approach to theory that takes identities and interests as exogenously given.

71. On "European identity," see Barry Buzan et al., eds., *The European Security Order Recast* (London: Pinter, 1990), pp. 45–63.

72. On "embeddedness," see John Ruggie, "International Regimes, Transactions, and Change: Embedded Liberalism in a Postwar Economic Order," in Krasner, *International Regimes,* pp. 195–232.

73. See Grieco, "Anarchy and the Limits of Cooperation."

74. On the difficulties of creating cooperative security regimes given competitive interests, see Robert Jervis, "Security Regimes," in Krasner, *International Regimes,* pp. 173–94; and Charles Lipson, "International Cooperation in Economic and Security Affairs," *World Politics* 37 (October 1984), pp. 1–23.

75. See Mead, *Mind, Self, and Society.*

76. Turner, "Role-Taking."

77. On "character planning," see Jon Elster, *Sour Grapes: Studies in the Subversion of Rationality* (Cambridge: Cambridge University Press, 1983), p. 117.

78. For useful overviews of New Thinking, see Mikhail Gorbachev, *Perestroika: New Thinking for Our Country and the World* (New York: Harper & Row, 1987); and Allen Lynch, *Gorbachev's International Outlook: Intellectual Origins and Political Consequences* (New York: Institute for East–West Security Studies, 1989).

79. For useful overviews of these factors, see Jack Snyder, "The Gorbachev Revolution: A Waning of Soviet Expansionism?" *World Politics* 12 (Winter 1987–88), pp. 93–121; and Stephen Meyer, "The Sources and Prospects of Gorbachev's New Political Thinking on Security," *International Security* 13 (Fall 1988), pp. 124–63.

80. See Daniel Bar-Tal et al., "Conflict Termination: An Epistemological Analysis of International Cases," *Political Psychology* 10 (June 1989), pp. 233–55.

81. See Robert Cox, "Social Forces, States and World Orders: Beyond International Relations Theory," in Keohane, *Neorealism and Its Critics,* pp. 204–55. See also Brian Fay, *Critical Social Science* (Ithaca, N.Y.: Cornell University Press, 1987).

82. Hazel Markus and Paula Nurius, "Possible Selves," *American Psychologist* 41 (September 1986), pp. 954–69.

83. See Goffman, *The Presentation of Self in Everyday Life*; Eugene Weinstein and Paul Deutschberger, "Some Dimensions of Altercasting," *Sociometry* 26 (December 1963), pp. 454–66; and Walter Earle, "International Relations and the Psychology of Control: Alternative Control Strategies and Their Consequences," *Political Psychology* 7 (June 1986), pp. 369–75.

84. See Volker Boge and Peter Wilke, "Peace Movements and Unilateral Disarmament: Old Concepts in a New Light," *Arms Control* 7 (September 1986), pp. 156–70; Zeev Maoz and Daniel Felsenthal, "Self-Binding Commitments, the Inducement of Trust, Social Choice, and the Theory of International Cooperation," *International Studies Quarterly* 31 (June 1987), pp. 177–200; and V. Sakamoto, "Unilateral Initiative as an Alternative Strategy," *World Futures,* vol. 24, nos. 1–4, 1987, pp. 107–34.

85. On rewards, see Thomas Milburn and Daniel Christie, "Rewarding in International Politics," *Political Psychology* 10 (December 1989), pp. 625–45.

86. The importance of reciprocity in completing the process of structural transformation makes the logic in this stage similar to that in the "evolution of cooperation." The difference is one of prerequisites and objective: in the former, ego's tentative redefinition of self enables it to try and change alter by acting "as if" both were already playing a new game; in the latter, ego acts only on the basis of given interests and prior experience, with transformation emerging only as an unintended consequence.

87. Yale Ferguson and Richard Mansbach, "Between Celebration and Despair: Constructive Suggestions for Future International Theory," *International Studies Quarterly* 35 (December 1991), p. 375.

88. For excellent discussions of this tension, see Walker, "Sovereignty, Identity, Community"; and R. B. J. Walker, "Security, Sovereignty, and the Challenge of World Politics," *Alternatives* 15 (Winter 1990), pp. 3–27. On institutional path dependencies, see Stephen Krasner, "Sovereignty: An Institutional Perspective," *Comparative Political Studies* 21 (April 1988), pp. 66–94.

4 THE INTERNATIONAL SYSTEM

The different theoretical traditions offer different conceptions of the international system. Realist Hans J. Morgenthau writes in *Politics among Nations* (4th ed., 1967) that the international system is characterized by competition among states, each seeking to enhance its power. As a consequence of the competition, a balance of power tends to emerge. In this selection, Morgenthau discusses what states can do to stabilize the balance.

What are the characteristics of the contemporary international system? John Ikenberry, Michael Mastanduno, and William C. Wohlforth argue that the United States emerged from the 1990s as the unrivaled global power in a unipolar international system. What, they ask, are the policy and theoretical implications of unipolarity? Are constraints on the United States really removed with unipolarity? What are the implications for balance of power or power transition theories? The authors suggest the need to rethink not only balance of power and alliances but also the logic of international economic cooperation and the relationship between power and legitimacy in light of unipolarity.

Randall L. Schweller and Xiaoyu Pu envision a period after unipolarity when rising states may contest the authority of the United States as hegemonic leader. With China as the likely contender, the authors discuss whether China has stronger incentives to challenge the rules of the U.S.-led international order, to support the U.S.-led system, or to try to gain opportunistically from that system without contributing to its maintenance.

Coming from a constructivist framework, Martha Finnemore focuses on the social rather than the material structure of unipolarity. She elucidates the social limits and possible pitfalls to the unipole's power: the difficulty of maintaining legitimacy and controlling the rules, and the danger of falling into the trap of hypocrisy. Taking the U.S. intervention in Kosovo as her example, Finnemore admits, "being a unipole isn't all it's cracked up to be."

Hans J. Morgenthau

THE BALANCE OF POWER[1]

The aspiration for power on the part of several nations, each trying either to maintain or overthrow the status quo, leads of necessity to a configuration that is called the balance of power and to policies that aim at preserving it. We say "of necessity" advisedly. For here again we are confronted with the basic misconception that has impeded the understanding of international politics and has made us the prey of illusions. This misconception asserts that men have a choice between power politics and its necessary outgrowth, the balance of power, on the other hand, and a different, better kind of international relations on the other. It insists that a foreign policy based on the balance of power is one among several possible foreign policies and that only stupid and evil men will choose the former and reject the latter.

It will be shown * * * that the international balance of power is only a particular manifestation of a general social principle to which all societies composed of a number of autonomous units owe the autonomy of their component parts; that the balance of power and policies aiming at its preservation are not only inevitable but are an essential stabilizing factor in a society of sovereign nations; and that the instability of the international balance of power is due not to the faultiness of the principle but to the particular conditions under which the principle must operate in a society of sovereign nations.

From Hans J. Morgenthau, *Politics among Nations: The Struggle for Power and Peace*, 4th ed. (New York: Knopf, 1967), Chaps. 11, 12, 14. Some of the author's notes have been omitted.

Social Equilibrium

Balance of Power as Universal Concept

The concept of "equilibrium" as a synonym for "balance" is commonly employed in many sciences—physics, biology, economics, sociology, and political science. It signifies stability within a system composed of a number of autonomous forces. Whenever the equilibrium is disturbed either by an outside force or by a change in one or the other elements composing the system, the system shows a tendency to re-establish either the original or a new equilibrium. Thus equilibrium exists in the human body. While the human body changes in the process of growth, the equilibrium persists as long as the changes occurring in the different organs of the body do not disturb the body's stability. This is especially so if the quantitative and qualitative changes in the different organs are proportionate to each other. When, however, the body suffers a wound or loss of one of its organs through outside interference, or experiences a malignant growth or a pathological transformation of one of its organs, the equilibrium is disturbed, and the body tries to overcome the disturbance by reestablishing the equilibrium either on the same or a different level from the one that obtained before the disturbance occurred.[2]

The same concept of equilibrium is used in a social science, such as economics, with reference to the relations between the different elements of the economic system, e.g., between savings and investments, exports and imports, supply and demand, costs and prices. Contemporary capitalism itself has been described as a system of "countervailing power."[3] It also applies to society as a whole. Thus we search for a proper balance between different geographical regions, such as the East and the West, the North and the South; between different kinds of activities, such as agriculture and industry, heavy and light industries, big and small businesses, producers and consumers, management and labor, between different functional groups, such as city and country, the old, the middle-aged, and the young, the economic and the political sphere, the middle classes and the upper and lower classes.

Two assumptions are at the foundation of all such equilibriums: first, that the elements to be balanced are necessary for society or are entitled to exist and, second, that without a state of equilibrium among them one element will gain ascendancy over the others, encroach upon their interests and rights, and may ultimately destroy them. Consequently, it is the purpose of all such equilibriums to maintain the stability of the system without destroying the multiplicity of the elements composing it. If the goal were stability alone, it could be achieved by allowing one element to destroy or overwhelm the others and take their place. Since the goal is stability plus the preservation of all the elements of the system, the equilibrium must aim at preventing any element from gaining ascendancy over the others. The means employed to maintain the equilibrium consist in allowing the different elements to pursue their opposing tendencies up to the point where the tendency of one is not so strong as to overcome the tendency of the others, but strong enough to prevent the others from overcoming its own. * * *

■ ■ ■

DIFFERENT METHODS OF THE BALANCE OF POWER

The balancing process can be carried on either by diminishing the weight of the heavier scale or by increasing the weight of the lighter one.

Divide and Rule

The former method has found its classic manifestation, aside from the imposition of onerous conditions in peace treaties and the incitement to treason and revolution, in the maxim "divide and rule." It has been resorted to by nations who tried to make or keep their competitors weak by dividing them or keeping them divided. The most consistent and important policies of this kind in modern times are the policy of France with respect to Germany and the policy of the Soviet Union with respect to the rest of Europe. From the seventeenth century to the end of the Second World War, it has been an unvarying principle of French foreign policy either to favor the division of the German Empire into a number of small independent states or to prevent the coalescence of such states into one unified nation. * * * Similarly, the Soviet Union from the twenties to the present has consistently opposed all plans for the unification of

Europe, on the assumption that the pooling of the divided strength of the European nations into a "Western bloc" would give the enemies of the Soviet Union such power as to threaten the latter's security.

The other method of balancing the power of several nations consists in adding to the strength of the weaker nation. This method can be carried out by two different means: Either B can increase its power sufficiently to offset, if not surpass, the power of A, and vice versa; or B can pool its power with the power of all the other nations that pursue identical policies with regard to A, in which case A will pool its power with all the nations pursuing identical policies with respect to B. The former alternative is exemplified by the policy of compensations and the armament race as well as by disarmament; the latter, by the policy of alliances.

Compensations

Compensations of a territorial nature were a common device in the eighteenth and nineteenth centuries for maintaining a balance of power which had been, or was to be, disturbed by the territorial acquisitions of one nation. The Treaty of Utrecht of 1713, which terminated the War of the Spanish Succession, recognized for the first time expressly the principle of the balance of power by way of territorial compensations. It provided for the division of most of the Spanish possessions, European and colonial, between the Hapsburgs and the Bourbons *"ad conservandum in Europa equilibrium,"* as the treaty put it.

■　■　■

In the latter part of the nineteenth and the beginning of the twentieth century, the principle of compensations was again deliberately applied to the distribution of colonial territories and the delimitation of colonial or semicolonial spheres of influence. Africa, in particular, was during that period the object of numerous treaties delimiting spheres of influence for the major colonial powers. Thus the competition between France, Great Britain, and Italy for the domination of Ethiopia was provisionally resolved * * * by the treaty of 1906, which divided the country into three spheres of influence for the purpose of establishing in that region a balance of power among the nations concerned. * * *

Even where the principle of compensations is not deliberately applied, however, * * * it is nowhere absent from political arrangements, territorial or other, made within a balance-of-power system. For, given such a system, no nation will agree to concede political advantages to another nation without the expectation, which may or may not be well founded, of receiving proportionate advantages in return. The bargaining of diplomatic negotiations, issuing in political compromise, is but the principle of compensations in its most general form, and as such it is organically connected with the balance of power.

Armaments

The principal means, however, by which a nation endeavors with the power at its disposal to maintain or re-establish the balance of power are armaments. The armaments race in which Nation A tries to keep up with, and then to outdo, the armaments of Nation B, and vice versa, is the typical instrumentality of an unstable, dynamic balance of power. The necessary corollary of the armaments race is a constantly increasing burden of military preparations devouring an ever greater portion of the national budget and making for ever deepening fears, suspicions, and insecurity. The situation preceding the First World War, with the naval competition between Germany and Great Britain and the rivalry of the French and German armies, illustrates this point.

It is in recognition of situations such as these that, since the end of the Napoleonic Wars, repeated attempts have been made to create a stable balance of power, if not to establish permanent peace, by means of the proportionate disarmament of competing nations. The technique of stabilizing the balance of power by means of a proportionate reduction of armaments is somewhat similar to the technique of territorial compensations. For both techniques require a quantitative evaluation of the influence that the arrangement is likely to exert on the respective power of the individual nations. The difficulties in making such a quantitative evaluation—in correlating, for instance, the military strength of the French army of 1932 with the military power represented by the industrial potential of Germany—have greatly contributed to the failure of most attempts at creating a stable balance of power by means of disarmament. The only outstanding success of this kind was the Washington Naval Treaty of 1922, in which Great Britain, the United States, Japan, France, and Italy agreed to a proportionate reduction and limitation of naval armanents. Yet it must be noted that this treaty was part of an over-all political and territorial settlement in the Pacific which sought to stabilize the power relations in that region on the foundation of Anglo-American predominance.

Alliances

The historically most important manifestation of the balance of power, however, is to be found not in the equilibrium of two isolated nations but in the relations between one nation or alliance of nations and another alliance.

■　■　■

Alliances are a necessary function of the balance of power operating within a multiple-state system. Nations A and B, competing with each other, have three choices in order to maintain and improve their relative power positions. They can increase their own power, they can add to their own power the power of other nations, or they can withhold the power of other nations from the adversary. When they make the first choice, they embark upon an armaments race. When they choose the second and third alternatives, they pursue a policy of alliances.

Whether or not a nation shall pursue a policy of alliances is, then, a matter not of principle but of expediency. A nation will shun alliances if it believes that it is strong enough to hold its own unaided or that the burden of the commitments resulting from the alliance is likely to outweigh the advantages to be expected. It is for one or the other or both of these reasons that, throughout the better part of their history, Great Britain and the United States have refrained from entering into peacetime alliances with other nations.

■　■　■

The "Holder" of the Balance

Whenever the balance of power is to be realized by means of an alliance—and this has been generally so throughout the history of the Western world—two possible variations of this pattern have to be distinguished. To use the metaphor of the balance, the system may consist of two scales, in each of which are to be found the nation or nations identified with the same policy of the status quo or of imperialism. The continental nations of Europe have generally operated the balance of power in this way.

The system may, however, consist of two scales plus a third element, the "holder" of the balance or the "balancer." The balancer is not permanently identified with the policies of either nation or group of nations. Its only objective within the system is the maintenance of the balance, regardless of the concrete policies the balance will serve. In consequence, the holder of the balance will throw its weight at one time in this scale, at another time in the other scale, guided only by one consideration—the relative position of the scales. Thus it will put its weight always in the scale that seems to be higher than the other because it is lighter. The balancer may become in a relatively short span of history consecutively the friend and foe of all major powers, provided they all consecutively threaten the balance by approaching predominance over the others and are in turn threatened by others about to gain such predominance. To paraphrase a statement of Palmerston: while the holder of the balance has no permanent friends, it has no permanent enemies either; it has only the permanent interest of maintaining the balance of power itself.

The balancer is in a position of "splendid isolation." It is isolated by its own choice; for, while the two scales of the balance must vie with each other to add its weight to theirs in order to gain the overweight necessary for success, it must refuse to enter into permanent ties with either side. The holder of the balance waits in the middle in watchful detachment to see which scale is likely to sink. Its isolation is "splendid"; for, since its support or lack of support is the decisive factor in the struggle for power, its foreign policy, if cleverly managed, is able to extract the highest price from those whom it supports. But since this support, regardless of the price paid for it, is always uncertain and shifts from one side to the other in accordance with the movements of the balance, its policies are resented and subject to condemnation on moral grounds. Thus it has been said of the outstanding balancer in modern times, Great Britain, that it lets others fight its wars, that it keeps Europe divided in order to dominate the continent, and that the fickleness of its policies is such as to make alliances with Great Britain impossible. "Perfidious Albion" has become a byword in the mouths of those who either were unable to gain Great Britain's support, however hard they tried, or else lost it after they had paid what seemed to them too high a price.

The holder of the balance occupies the key position in the balance-of-power system, since its position determines the outcome of the struggle for power. It has, therefore, been called the "arbiter" of the system, deciding who will win and who will lose. By making it impossible for any nation or combination of nations to gain predominance over the others, it preserves its own independence as well as the independence of all the other nations, and is thus a most powerful factor in international politics.

The holder of the balance can use this power in three different ways. It can make its joining one or the other nation or alliance dependent upon certain conditions favorable to the maintenance or restoration of the balance. It can make its support of the peace settlement dependent upon similar conditions. It can, finally, in either situation see to it that the objectives of its own national policy, apart from the maintenance of the balance of power, are realized in the process of balancing the power of others.

■　■　■

EVALUATION OF THE BALANCE OF POWER

■ ■ ■

The Unreality of the Balance of Power

[The] uncertainty of all power calculations not only makes the balance of power incapable of practical application but leads also to its very negation in practice. Since no nation can be sure that its calculation of the distribution of power at any particular moment in history is correct, it must at least make sure that, whatever errors it may commit, they will not put the nation at a disadvantage in the contest for power. In other words, the nation must try to have at least a margin of safety which will allow it to make erroneous calculations and still maintain the balance of power. To that effect, all nations actively engaged in the struggle for power must actually aim not at a balance—that is, equality—of power, but at superiority of power in their own behalf. And since no nation can foresee how large its miscalculations will turn out to be, all nations must ultimately seek the maximum of power obtainable under the circumstances. Only thus can they hope to attain the maximum margin of safety commensurate with the maximum of errors they might commit. The limitless aspiration for power, potentially always present * * * in the power drives of nations, finds in the balance of power a mighty incentive to transform itself into an actuality.

Since the desire to attain a maximum of power is universal, all nations must always be afraid that their own miscalculations and the power increases of other nations might add up to an inferiority for themselves which they must at all costs try to avoid. Hence all nations who have gained an apparent edge over their competitors tend to consolidate that advantage and use it for changing the distribution of power permanently in their favor. This can be done through diplomatic pressure by bringing the full weight of that advantage to bear upon the other nations, compelling them to make the concessions that will consolidate the temporary advantage into a permanent superiority. It can also be done by war. Since in a balance-of-power system all nations live in constant fear lest their rivals deprive them, at the first opportune moment, of their power position, all nations have a vital interest in anticipating such a development and doing unto the others what they do not want the others to do unto them. * * *

NOTES

1. The term "balance of power" is used in the text with four different meanings: (1) as a policy aimed at a certain state of affairs, (2) as an actual state of affairs, (3) as an approximately equal distribution of power, (4) as any distribution of power. Whenever the term is used without qualification, it refers to an actual state of affairs in which power is distributed among several nations with approximate equality. * * *

2. Cf., for instance, the impressive analogy between the equilibrium in the human body and in society in Walter B. Cannon, *The Wisdom of the Body* (New York: W. W. Norton and Company, 1932), pp. 293,

294: "At the outset it is noteworthy that the body politic itself exhibits some indications of crude automatic stabilizing processes. In the previous chapter I expressed the postulate that a certain degree of constancy in a complex system is itself evidence that agencies are acting or are ready to act to maintain that constancy. And moreover, that when a system remains steady it does so because any tendency towards change is met by increased effectiveness of the factor or factors which resist the change. Many familiar facts prove that these statements are to some degree true for society even in its present unstabilized condition. A display of conservatism excites a radical revolt and that in turn is followed by a return to conservatism. Loose government and its consequences bring the reformers into power, but their tight reins soon provoke restiveness and the desire for release. The noble enthusiasms and sacrifices of war are succeeded by moral apathy and orgies of self-indulgence. Hardly any strong tendency in a nation continues to the stage of disaster; before that extreme is reached corrective forces arise which check the tendency and they commonly prevail to such an excessive degree as themselves to cause a reaction. A study of the nature of these social swings and their reversal might lead to valuable understanding and possibly to means of more narrowly limiting the disturbances. At this point, however, we merely note that the disturbances are roughly limited, and that this limitation suggests, perhaps, the early stages of social homeostasis." (Reprinted by permission of the publisher. Copyright 1932, 1939, by Walter B. Cannon.)

3. John K. Galbraith, *American Capitalism, the Concept of Countervailing Power* (Boston: Houghton Mifflin, 1952).

G. John Ikenberry, Michael Mastanduno,
and William C. Wohlforth

UNIPOLARITY, STATE BEHAVIOR, AND SYSTEMIC CONSEQUENCES

American primacy in the global distribution of capabilities is one of the most salient features of the contemporary international system. The end of the cold war did not return the world to multipolarity. Instead the United States—already materially preeminent—became more so. We currently live in a one superpower world, a circumstance unprecedented in the modern era. No other great power has enjoyed such advantages in material capabilities—military, economic, technological, and geographical. Other states rival the United States in one area or another, but the multifaceted character of American power places it in a category of its own. The sudden collapse of the Soviet Union and its empire, slower economic growth in Japan and Western Europe during the 1990s, and America's outsized military spending have all enhanced these disparities. While in most historical eras the distribution of capabilities among major states has tended to be multipolar or bipolar—with several major states of roughly equal size and capability—the United States emerged from the 1990s as an unrivaled global power. It became a "unipolar" state.

Not surprisingly, this extraordinary imbalance has triggered global debate. Governments, including that of the United States, are struggling to respond to this peculiar international environment. What is the character of domination in a unipolar distribution? If world politics is always a mixture of force and consent, does

unipolarity remove restraints and alter the mix in favor of force? Is a unipolar world likely to be built around rules and institutions or based more on the unilateral exercise of unipolar power? To what extent and in what ways can a unipolar state translate its formidable capabilities into meaningful political influence? These questions have been asked in the context of a global debate over the projection of power by the Bush administration. To what extent has America's foreign policy after 2001 been a reflection simply of the idiosyncratic and provocative strategies of the Bush administration itself, rather than a manifestation of the deeper structural features of the global system of power? These concerns over how a unipolar world operates—and how the unipolar state itself behaves—are the not-so-hidden subtext of world politics at the turn of the twenty-first century.

Classic questions of international relations theory are at stake in the debate over unipolarity. The most obvious question concerns balance of power theory, which predicts that states will respond to concentrated power by counterbalancing.[1] Some are puzzled by what they see as the absence of a balancing response to American unipolar power, whereas others argue, to the contrary, that incipient or specific types of balancing behavior are in fact occurring.[2] A related debate concerns power transition theory, which focuses on the specific forms of conflict that are generated between rising and declining hegemonic states.[3] The abrupt shift in the distribution of capabilities that followed the

From *World Politics* 61, no. 1 (Jan. 2009): 1–27.

end of the cold war and the rise of China after the cold war raise questions about the character of conflict between dominant and challenger states as they move along trajectories of rise and decline. A unipolar distribution also raises issues that scholars grappled with during the cold war, namely, about the structure and dynamics of different types of polar systems. Here the questions concern the ways in which the features of polarity affect the durability and war proneness of the state system.[4] Likewise, scholarly debates about threat perception, the impact of regime characteristics on foreign policy, the propensity of dominant states to provide collective goods, and the ability of a state to translate preponderant capabilities into effective influence are also at stake in the debate over unipolarity.[5]

This [essay introduces] systematic inquiry into the logic and dynamics of unipolarity. Its starting point is the distinctive distribution of capabilities among states in the contemporary global system. The central question driving our inquiry is straightforward: to what extent—and how—does this distribution of capabilities matter for patterns of international politics?

In their initial efforts to make sense of an American-dominated international system, scholars and observers have invoked a wide array of grand terms such as empire, hegemony, unipolarity, imperium, and "uni-multipolarity."[6] Scholars are searching for a conceptual language to depict and place in historical and comparative perspective the distinctive political formation that has emerged after the cold war. But this multiplicity of terms obscures more than it reveals. In this project unipolarity refers narrowly to the underlying material distribution of capabilities and not to the political patterns or relationships depicted by terms such as empire, imperium, and hegemony. What makes the global system unipolar is the distinctive distribution of material resources. An important research question is whether and in what ways this particular distribution of capabilities affects patterns of international politics to create outcomes that are different from what one might expect under conditions of bipolarity or multipolarity.

Setting up the inquiry in this manner requires a basic distinction between power as material resources and power as influence. Power resources refer to the distribution of material capabilities among states. The global system today—seen in comparative historical perspective—has concentrated power capabilities unprecedented in the modern era. But this observation should not prejudge questions about the extent and character of influence or about the logic of political relationships within the global system. Nor should this observation prejudge the question of whether the global system is coercive, consensual, legitimate, or illegitimate. Describing the system as unipolar leaves unanswered the Weberian questions about the logic and character of the global political system that is organized around unipolarity.[7]

In [this essay] we develop a framework for analyzing unipolarity[,] highlight the arguments of * * * hypotheses[,] and explore the impact of unipolarity on the behavior of the dominant state, on the reactions of other states, and on the properties of the international system. Collectively, we find that unipolarity does have a profound impact on international politics. International relations under conditions of unipolarity force us to rethink conventional and received understandings about the operation of the balance of power, the meaning of alliance partnerships, the logic of international economic cooperation, the relationship between power and legitimacy, and the behavior of satisfied and revisionist states. A unipolar distribution of capabilities will eventually give way to other distributions. The argument advanced here is not that unipolarity will last indefinitely but rather that as long as it does last, it will constitute a critical factor in understanding patterns of foreign policy and world politics.

Definition and Measurement

Scholars use the term unipolarity to distinguish a system with one extremely capable state from systems with two or more great powers (bi-, tri-, and multipolarity). Unipolarity should also be distinguished from hegemony and empire, terms that refer to political relationships and degrees of influence rather than to distributions of material capability. The adjective unipolar describes something that has a single pole. International relations scholars have long defined a pole as a state that (1) commands an especially large share of the resources or capabilities states can use to achieve their ends and that (2) excels in all the component elements of state capability, conventionally defined as size of population and territory, resource endowment, economic capacity, military might, and organizational-institutional "competence."[8]

A unipolar system is one whose structure is defined by the fact of only one state meeting these criteria. The underpinnings of the concept are familiar to international relations scholars. They flow from the massive literature on polarity, especially from Waltz's seminal treatment. The core contention is that polarity structures the horizon of states' probable actions and reactions, narrowing the range of choice and providing subtle incentives and disincentives for certain types of behavior. An appreciation of polarity yields important insights about patterns of behavior in international politics over the long term. Even for those scholars most persuaded of its analytical utility, polarity is at best a necessary part of an explanation rather than a sufficient explanation.[9] The distribution of capabilities may be a place to begin an explanation, but it is rarely enough to complete one.

Polarity is a theoretical construct; real international systems only approximate various polar ideal types. The polarity concept implies a threshold value of the distribution of capabilities. The more unambiguously the poles in a real international system pass the threshold, the more confident analysts can be that the properties attributed to a given system structure in theory will obtain in practice. The more unambiguously the capabilities of the great powers in a multipolar system clearly stand apart from all other states and are comparable to each other, the more relevant are the insights from the theoretical literature on multipolarity. Waltz often discussed the logic of a bipolar system as if it were a two-actor system. The more dominant the superpowers were in reality, the more confidence analysts could have that those logical deductions actually applied. In reality, the cold war international system was never "perfectly" bipolar. Analysts used to speak of loose versus tight bipolarity and debated whether the Soviet Union had the full complement of capabilities to measure up as a pole.

How do we know whether or to what degree an international system has passed the unipolar threshold? Using the conventional definition of a pole, an international system can be said to be unipolar if it contains one state whose overall share of capabilities places it unambiguously in a class by itself compared to all other states. This reflects the fact that poles are defined not on an absolute scale but relative to each other and to other states. In addition, preponderance must characterize all the relevant categories of state capabilities.[10] To determine polarity, one has to examine the distribution of capabilities and identify the states whose shares of overall resources obviously place them into their own class.

There will doubtless be times in which polarity cannot be determined, but now does not appear to be one of them. Scholars largely agree that there were four or more states that qualified as poles before 1945; that by 1950 or so only two measured up; and that by the 1990s one of these two poles was gone. They largely agree, further, that no other power—not Japan, China, India, or Russia, not any European country and not the EU—has increased its overall portfolio of capabilities sufficiently to transform its standing.[11] This leaves a single pole.

There is widespread agreement, moreover, that any plausible index aggregating the relevant dimensions of state capabilities would place the United States in a separate class by a large margin.[12] The most widely used measures of capability are GDP and military spending. As of 2006 the United States accounted for roughly one-quarter of global GDP and nearly 50 percent of GDP among the conventionally defined great powers (see Table 4.1). This surpasses the relative economic size of any leading state in modern history, with the sole exception of the United States itself in the early cold war years, when World War II had temporarily depressed every other major economy. By virtue of the size and wealth of the United States economy, its massive military capabilities represented only about 4 percent of its GDP in 2006 (Table 4.2), compared with the nearly 10 percent it averaged over the peak years of the cold war—1950–70—as well as with the burdens borne by most of the major powers of the past.[13]

The United States now likely spends more on defense than the rest of the world combined (Table 4.2). Military research and development (R&D) may best capture the scale of the long-term investments that now give the United States its dramatic qualitative edge over other states. As Table 4.2 shows, in 2004 U.S. military expenditures on R&D were more than six times greater than those of Germany, Japan, France, and Britain combined. By some estimates over half of the military R&D expenditures in the world are American, a disparity that has been sustained for decades: over the past thirty years, for example, the United States invested more than three times what the EU countries combined invested in military R&D. Hence, on any composite index featuring these two indicators the United States obviously looks like a unipole.

That perception is reinforced by a snapshot of science and technology indicators for the major powers (see Table 4.3).

These vast commitments do not make the United States omnipotent, but they do facilitate a preeminence in military capabilities vis-à-vis all other major powers that is unique in the post-seventeenth-century experience. While other powers can contest U.S. forces operating in or very near their homelands, especially over issues that involve credible nuclear deterrence, the United States is and will long remain the only state capable of projecting major military power globally.[14] This dominant position is enabled by what Barry Posen calls "command of the commons"—that is, unassilable military dominance over the sea, air, and space. The result is an international system that contains only one state with the capability to organize major politico-military action any-where in the system.[15] No other state or even combination of states is capable of mounting and deploying a major expeditionary force outside its own region, except with the assistance of the United States.

Conventional measures thus suggest that the concentration of military and overall economic potential in the United States distinguishes the current international system from its predecessors over the past four centuries (see Figure 4.1). As historian Paul Kennedy observed: "Nothing has ever existed like this disparity of power; nothing, . . . I have returned to all of the comparative defense spending and military personnel statistics over the past 500 years that I compiled in *The Rise and Fall of the Great Powers*, and no other nation comes close."[16]

The bottom line is that if we adopt conventional definitions of polarity and standard measures of capabilities, then the current international system is as unambiguously unipolar as past systems were multipolar and bipolar.

Table 4.1. Economic Indicators for the Major Powers, 2006[a]

	GDP Current Prices ($ Billion)	% Great Power GDP, Current Prices	% World GDP, Current Prices	% World GDP, PPP	GDP per Capita, Current Prices	Public Debt (% GDP)	Productivity ($ GDP per Hour Worked)
United States	13,245	46.1	27.5	22.5	44,190	64.7	48.3
China	2,630	9.2	5.5	9.7	2,001	22.1	n.a.
Japan	4,367	15.2	9.1	7.4	34,188	176.2	34.4
Germany	2,897	10.1	6	4.6	35,204	66.8	44
Russia	979	3.4	2	3.1	6,856	8	n.a.
France	2,232	7.8	4.6	3.4	35,404	64.7	49
Britain	2,374	8.3	4.9	3.5	39,213	42.2	40.1

[a]% World GDP, PPP is World Bank estimate for 2005; differences between PPP and market exchange rate measures are discussed in Brooks and Wohlforth (n. 10), chap. 2. Data for United States public debt are from 2005. Productivity estimates are from 2005.

Sources: *International Monetary Fund, World Economic Outlook Database, April 2007,* at http://www.imf.org/external/pubs/ft/weo/2007/01/data/index.aspx (accessed November 7, 2007); World Bank, *2005 International Comparison Program, Preliminary Results,* at http://siteresources.worldbank.org/ICPINT/Resources/ICPre-portprelim.pdf (accessed December 12, 2007); Central Intelligence Agency, *CIA World Factbook,* at https://www.cia.gov/library/publications/the-world-factbook/ (accessed November 8, 2007); Organization for Economic Development and Cooperation, *OECD Employment Outlook 2007, Statistical Annex,* at http://www.oecd.org/document/26/0,3343,en_2649_33927 _38551002_1_1_1,00.html (accessed November 8, 2007); Organization for Economic Development and Cooperation, *OECD Compendium of Productivity Indicators 2006.*

Table 4.2. Defense Expenditures for the Major Powers, 2006[a]

	Defense Expenditures ($ Billion)	% Great Power Defense Expenditures	% World Defense Expenditures	Defense Expenditures % of GDP	Defense R&D Expenditures ($ Billion)
United States	528.6	65.6	46	4.1	75.5
China	49.5	6.1	4	2	n.a.
Japan	43.9	5.4	4	1	1.1
Germany	36.9	4.6	3	1.4	1.1
Russia	34.7	4.3	3	4.1	n.a.
France	53	6.6	5	2.5	3.9
Britain	59.2	7.3	5	2.7	4.4

[a]Defense expenditures as % GDP are 2005 estimates; R&D expenditures are for 2004.

Sources: Stockholm International Peace Research Institute, "The 15 Major Spending Countries in 2006," at http://www.sipri.org/contents/milap/milex/mex_data_index.html (accessed November 8, 2007); Stockholm International Peace Research Institute Military Expenditures Database, at http://www.sipri.org/contents/milap/milex/mex_database1.html (accessed November 8, 2007); Organization for Economic Development and Cooperation, *OECD Main Science and Technology Indicators* 2006, no. 2 (Paris: OECD, 2006), 49.

Unipolarity and Its Consequences

* * * [T]he effects of unipolarity are potentially widespread. For purposes of analytical clarity it is possible to consider these effects in three ways, in terms of (1) the behavior of the unipole, (2) the actions of other states, and (3) the properties of the international system itself.

Behavior of the Unipole

The specific characteristics and dynamics of any unipolar system will obviously depend on how the unipolar state behaves. But the unipole's behavior might be affected by incentives and constraints associated with its structural position in the international system. Indeed, even the unipole's domestic politics and institutions—the immediate well-springs of its behavior on the international scene—might themselves change profoundly under the influence of its position of primacy in the international system. * * * [H]ypotheses concerning four general behavioral patterns [follow].

UNIPOLARITY AND REVISIONISM: IS THE UNIPOLE A SATISFIED STATE?

The stability of any international system depends significantly on the degree to which the major powers are satisfied with the status quo.[17] In *War and Change in World Politics*, Robert Gilpin argued that leading states "will attempt to change the international system if the expected benefits exceed the expected costs."[18] In the quarter century since

Table 4.3 *Science and Technology Indicators for the Major Powers, 2003-6*

	High Tech Production ($ Millions) (2003)[a]	% World High Tech Production (2003)	Gross Domestic Expenditure R&D ($ Million PPP) (2006)	# of Triadic Patent Families (2005)[b]	Science and Engineering Doctoral Degrees (2003)[c]	PCs per 1000 People (2004)	Internet Access per 1000 People (2005)	Secure Internet Servers[e] per Million People (2006)
United States	1,351,048.7	39	343,747.5	16,368	26,891	762.2	630.1[d]	869.2
China	423,825.9	12	115,196.9	433	8,153	40.9	85.1	0.4
Japan	376,250.1	11	130,745.4	15,239	7,581	541.6	667.5	331.9
Germany	146,494	4	62,493.2	6,266	10,796	545.3	454.7	348.6
Russia	n.a.	n.a.	16,668.7	49	10,409	104.3	152.3	3.2
France	136,665.7	4	40,392	2,463	6,890	495.7	429.6	96.5
Britain	116,200.2	3	35,171.10	1,588	8,810	599.8	473.5	561.5

[a]In 1997 dollars.

[b]Triadic patents families represent attempt to receive patents for an invention in the United States, Europe, and Japan.

[c]The data for China are from 2001; the data for France are from 2002; and the data for Russia are from 2000.

[d]Data are from 2005, with the exception of the U.S. data, which are from 2004.

[e]Secure Internet servers use encryption technology in Internet transactions; see www.netcraft.com.

Sources: World Bank, *World Development Indicators 2007,* at http://go.worldbank.org/3JU2HA60D0 (accessed November 8, 2007); Organization for Economic Development and Cooperation, *OECD Main Science and Technology Indicators,* 2007, vol. 1, at http://www.oecd.org/document/33/0,3343,en_2694_344551_1901082_1_1_1,00.html (accessed November 8, 2007); National Science Board, "Science and Engineering Indicators 2006, Volume 2," at http://nsf.gov/statistics/seind06/pdf/colume2.pdf (accessed November 8, 2007).

interest in bearing those costs because it benefits disproportionately from promoting systemwide outcomes that reflect its values and interests.

During the cold war the United States took on the responsibilities that Kindleberger argued were needed to promote international economic stability, such as serving as an open market of last resort and allowing the use of its currency for exchange and reserve purposes. International economic stability among the Western powers reinforced their security alliance against the Soviet Union. The United States also bore a disproportionate share of the direct costs of Western alliance security. The Soviet Union, on its side of the international divide, ultimately shouldered disproportionate alliance costs as well.[24] Waltz took the argument a step further, arguing that in the bipolar system the United States and the Soviet Union may have been adversaries but, as the two dominant powers, shared a mutual interest in system stability, an interest that prompted them to cooperate in providing public goods such as nuclear nonproliferation.[25] Hedley Bull makes a similar point in his classic study of the international system as a society of states.[26]

How might the shift from a bipolar to a unipolar system affect the inclination of the now singularly dominant state to provide international public goods? Two hypotheses arise, with contradictory behavioral expectations. First, we might expect a unipole to take on an even greater responsibility for the provision of international public goods. The capabilities of a unipole relative to other major states are greater than those of either dominant power in a bipolar structure. The unipole's incentive should be stronger as well, since it now has the opportunity to influence international outcomes globally, not just in its particular subsystem. We should expect the unipole to try to "lock in" a durable international order that reflects its interests and values.[27]

A second hypothesis, however, suggests the opposite. We should expect a unipolar power to underproduce public goods despite its preponderant capabilities. The fact that it is unthreatened by peer competitors and relatively unconstrained by other states creates incentives for the unipole to pursue more parochial interests even at the expense of a stable international order. The fact that it is extraordinarily powerful means that the unipole will be more inclined to force adjustment costs on others, rather than bear disproportionate burdens itself.

* * * Michael Mastanduno's analysis of the global political economy ["System Maker and Privilege Taker: U.S. Power and the International Political Economy," pp. 121–154] shows that the dominant state will be both system maker and privilege taker—it will seek simultaneously to provide public goods and to exploit its advantageous structural position for parochial gain. It enlists the cooperation of other states and seeks, with varying degrees of success, to force adjustment burdens upon them. Jervis suggests that because the unipole has wide discretion in determining the nature and the extent of the goods provided, its efforts are likely to be perceived by less powerful states as hypocritical attempts to mask the actual pursuit of private goods.

UNIPOLARITY AND CONTROL OVER OUTCOMES

It has long been an axiom of social science that resources (or capabilities as defined herein) do not translate automatically into power (control over outcomes or over the behavior of other actors).[28] Yet most observers regard it as similarly axiomatic that there is some positive relationship between a state's relative capability to help or harm others and its ability to get them to do what it wants. Even if the relationship is complex, more capabilities relative to others ought to translate generally into more power and influence. By this commonsense logic, a unipole should be expected to have more influence than either of the two great powers in a bipolar system.

* * * Some articles in the *World Politics* 2009 special issue on unipolarity argue that the shift

from bipolarity to unipolarity may not be an unambiguous benefit for the unipole's ability to wield influence. On the contrary, a unipolar state may face the paradoxical situation of being simultaneously more capable and more constrained. Two distinct theoretical logics suggest that a unipole might enjoy less power to shape the international system than a superpower in bipolarity. First is the logic of balancing, alliance, and opposition, [as] discussed * * * by Stephen Walt and Michael Mastanduno. The increased concentration of capabilities in the unipole may elicit increased opposition from other states—in the form of either traditional counterbalancing or subtler soft balancing. Even if such resistance falls short of offering a real counterweight, it may materially hamstring the unipole's ability to exercise influence. As Walt ["Alliances in a Unipolar World," pp. 86–120] argues, the structural shift to unipolarity removed one of the major motivations for the middle-ranked great powers to defer to the United States. Mastanduno offers a similar argument: the collapse of a unifying central threat signifies that in this post–cold war era the United States has less control over adjustment struggles with its principal economic partners, because it can no longer leverage their security dependence to dictate international economic outcomes. Globalization reinforces this U.S. predicament by expanding the number of relevant players in the world economy and by offering them alternatives to economic reliance on the United States. While under bipolarity the propensity of other middle powers to defer to the United States was structurally favored, under unipolarity the opposite may obtain. Even if observable balancing behavior reminiscent of bipolarity or multipolarity never occurs, a structurally induced tendency of the middle-ranked great powers to withhold cooperation may sap the unipole's effective power.

Second is a social logic of legitimacy, analyzed by Martha Finnemore ["Legitimacy, Hypocrisy, and the Social Structure of Unipolarity: Why Being a Unipole Isn't All It's Cracked Up to Be,"

pp. 58–85]. To use capabilities effectively, she argues, a unipole must seek to legitimate its role. But any system of legitimation imposes limits on the unipole's ability to translate capabilities into power. Finnemore stresses that the legitimation strategy followed by the United States after World War II—institutionalization—imposes especially severe constraints on the use of its material capabilities in pursuit of power. The rules, norms, and institutions that constitute the current international order are thus especially resistant to the unilateral use of superior capabilities to drive outcomes. Hence, for reasons Finnemore spells out in detail, the shift from bipolarity to unipolarity may well have diminished the effective utility of the preponderant capabilities of the United States.

UNIPOLARITY AND DOMESTIC POLITICS

The impact of domestic politics on foreign policy is of long-standing interest in the study of politics. In his classic appraisal of the United States, Tocqueville concluded that the U.S. political system was "decidedly inferior" to other types in the conduct of foreign policy, with a tendency to "obey impulse rather than prudence" and to "abandon a mature design for the gratification of a momentary passion."[29] During the cold war Theodore Lowi, Stephen Krasner, and others reinforced the idea that American political institutions create disadvantages in external policy.[30] More recent literature has reversed the presumption and argues that democracy offers distinctive advantages in foreign policy, including legitimacy, transparency, the ability to mobilize the public for war fighting efforts, and the potential to use competition among branches of government to gain advantage in diplomacy and negotiations.[31]

Political scientists have placed greater emphasis on the impact of regime type on foreign policy than on how changes in the relative international position of a country affect the role domestic politics play in its foreign policy.[32] Nonetheless, conventional wisdom during the cold war suggested that the bipolar structure had a double disciplining effect on the conduct of U.S. foreign policy. The external threat disciplined American society, leading interest groups and the public generally to defer to central decision makers on the definition of national interest and how best to achieve it. Domestic politics stopped at the "water's edge" because the international stakes were so high. The cold war constrained American decision makers as well, forcing them to exercise caution in the international arena and to assure that public opinion or interest groups did not capture or derail foreign policy for parochial reasons.

Under unipolarity, the double disciplining effect is no longer operative, with neither publics nor central decision makers as constrained as in a bipolar context. The consequent impact of domestic politics on foreign policy will depend in part on which party is more inclined to take the initiative: central decision makers or societal actors. One hypothesis is that under unipolarity the line between domestic and foreign policy will blur and domestic politics will no longer stop at the water's edge. With less at stake in foreign policy, it is harder for leaders to discipline societal actors and easier for societal actors to capture aspects of the foreign policy agenda to suit their parochial needs. The likely results are a less coherent foreign policy and a tendency for the state to underperform in the international arena, missing opportunities to exercise influence commensurate with its preponderant capabilities. A second hypothesis is that central decision makers will exploit the lack of constraint to manipulate a public—one that no longer has clear guiding principles in foreign policy—to respond to a wide array of possible threats and opportunities. As Jervis suggests, for the unipole threats may be nowhere—or everywhere.

* * * Jack Snyder, Robert Shapiro, and Yaeli Bloch-Elkon ["Free Hand Abroad, Divide and Rule at Home," pp. 155–187] [take] up the impact of domestic politics under unipolarity. They find that the Bush administration has taken advantage of the structural discretion offered by unipolarity to conduct a far more active and risky foreign policy than would be possible under the constraints of bipolarity. Developments in American politics such as political polarization have not only encouraged this effort by leaders but have also enabled interest groups to tie their particular domestic concerns to the more activist foreign policy agenda, and they have encouraged opportunistic leaders to use foreign policy as a salient issue in domestic political debate.

Unipolarity and the Behavior of Secondary States

Unipolarity may present secondary states with dramatically different incentives and constraints than would bipolar or multipolar settings. * * * [T]hree general behavioral patterns * * * may be shaped by the unipolar stucture: strategies of resistance to or insulation from the unipole's overweening capabilities, alliances and alignments, and the use of international institutions.

BALANCING AND OTHER FORMS OF RESISTANCE

The proposition that great concentrations of capabilities generate countervailing tendencies toward balance is among the oldest and best known in international relations.[33] Applying this balancing proposition to a unipolar system is complex, however, for even as unipolarity increases the incentives for counterbalancing it also raises the costs. Walt and Finnemore each analyze the interplay between these incentives. They agree on the basic proposition that the current unipolar order pushes secondary states away from traditional hard counterbalancing—formal military alliances and/or military buildups meant to create a global counterweight to the unipole—and toward other, often subtler strategies, such as soft balancing, hiding, binding, delegitimation, or norm entrapment. These analyses lead to the general expectation that a shift from a multipolar or bipolar to a unipolar structure would increase the relative salience of such subtler balancing/resistance strategies.

Walt argues that standard neorealist balance of power theory predicts the absence of counterbalancing under unipolarity. Yet he contends that the core causal mechanisms of balance-of-threat theory remain operative in a unipolar setting. Walt develops a modification of the theory that highlights the role of soft balancing and other subtler strategies of resistance as vehicles to overcome the particular challenges unipolarity presents to counterbalancing. He contends that balancing dynamics remain latent within a unipolar structure and can be brought forth if the unipole acts in a particularly threatening manner.

Finnemore develops a contrasting theoretical architecture for explaining secondary state behavior. For her, both the absence of balancing and the presence of other patterns of resistance can be explained only by reference to the social, as opposed to the material, structure of international politics. In particular, secondary state strategies that have the effect of reining in the unipole cannot be understood as the result of standard security-maximizing incentives. Rather, they are partially the outgrowth of the secondary states' internalization of the norms and rules of the institutional order. If the unipole acts in accordance with those rules, the tendency of other states to resist or withhold cooperation will be muted. Finnemore establishes three social mechanisms that constrain the unipole: legitimation, institutionalization, and incentives for hypocrisy. Each of these entails a logic of resistance to actions by the unipole that violate certain socially defined boundaries.

ALLIANCES AND ALIGNMENT

Scholars have long recognized that the dynamics of alliance and alignment transcend the imperative of counterhegemonic balancing.[34] Aggregating capabilities against a potentially dominant state is thus only one of the many purposes alliances serve. States may also choose to ally with a dominant power either to shield themselves from its capabilities or to seek to influence its policies. In addition, secondary states may ally with each other for purposes not directly connected to resistance to the dominant state, such as influencing each other's domestic or foreign policies or coordinating policies on regional or functional issues.

Larger patterns of such alliance behavior may be systematically related to the international system's structure. Scholars contend that in classic multipolar systems, especially those with no clear hegemon in sight, a large proportion of alliance behavior was unconnected to systemic balancing imperatives.[35] Under bipolarity, the proportion of alliance dynamics that was an outgrowth of systemic balancing increased, yet the rivalry between the two superpowers also created opportunities for secondary states to use alliance choices as leverage, playing each superpower off against the other. Walt argues that in a unipolar system nearly all significant alliance behavior will in one way or another be a reaction to the unipole—to contain, influence, or exploit it. As a result, independent alliances focused on other threats will be relatively rare, compared to bipolar or multipolar systems. Walt also contends that under unipolarity leverage opportunities dramatically decline compared to bipolarity, and he specifies the conditions under which secondary states will tend to opt for alignments with the unipole, neutrality, or resistance.

USE OF INTERNATIONAL INSTITUTIONS

Although their relative power affords opportunities to go it alone, dominant states find a variety of reasons to use international institutions. Institutions may be helpful in coalition building. They facilitate the exercise of power by creating patterns of behavior that reflect the interests and values of the dominant state. Institutions can conceal or soften the exercise of power, and they can lock in a hegemonic order and enable it to persist "after hegemony."[36]

Weaker states in a unipolar structure similarly have incentives to utilize institutions. Two types of motivation are relevant. First, weaker states may engage a unipole by enlisting its participation in new or modified institutional arrangements in order to constrain or tie it down. Since a unipolar state may be powerful enough to follow its own rules, possibly to the detriment of weaker states, those states may appeal within an institutional context to the unipole's concern for its reputation as a member of the international community or to its need for cooperating partners, in order to persuade it to engage in rule-based order even if it cannot simply determine the rules unilaterally. The dispute between the United States and some of its allies over U.S. participation in the International Criminal Court reflects the attempt by weaker states to tie the unipole down and the unipole's effort in turn to remain a free agent in the event it cannot define the institutional rules. Second, weaker states may create or strengthen international institutions that exclude the unipolar state. These institutions might be designed or intended to foster a common identity (for example, the European Union, the East Asian Economic Caucus), build capacity to withstand influence attempts by the unipole (for example, the European common currency), or create the potential to act independently of the unipole or at cross-purposes with it (for example, Shanghai Cooperation Organization, European Rapid Reaction Force).

In bipolarity, weaker states tend to participate in institutional arrangements defined and dominated by one or the other of the major players. The nonaligned movement during the cold war was distinctive precisely because it sought—though not necessarily with success—to institutionalize a path independent of either superpower. Under conditions of unipolarity, we can hypothesize that

weaker states, lacking the capacity to balance the unipole, will turn to a variety of institutional initiatives intended to constrain the unipolar state or to enhance their own autonomy in the face of its power. The use of international institutions by weaker states is highlighted in the articles by Walt and Finnemore [discussed earlier].

Systemic Properties: How Peaceful Is Unipolarity, and Will It Endure?

The classical systems theorists were preoccupied with two dependent variables: peacefulness and stability.[37] Scholars today have reason to be less optimistic that deterministic laws of stability or peacefulness can be derived from the structural characteristics of any international system.[38] Nonetheless, the questions of whether some types of international systems are more prone to conflict than others and whether some types are more likely to endure than others remain critical and take on added significance in the context of the more novel international system of unipolarity.

UNIPOLARITY AND GREAT POWER CONFLICT

Two major theoretical traditions deal with causes of war in ways that may relate to system structure: neorealism and power transition theory. Applying these in the context of unipolarity yields the general proposition that military conflicts involving the unipole and other major powers (that is, great power wars) are less likely in unipolar systems than in either bipolar or multipolar systems. According to neorealist theory, bipolarity is less war prone than multipolarity because each superpower knows that only the other can threaten it, realizes that it cannot pass the buck to third parties, and recognizes it can balance accretions to the other's capabilities by internal rather than external means. Bipolarity blocks or at least complicates three common paths to war in neorealism: uncertainty, free riding, and fear of allied defection. The first and second operated during the 1930s and the third operated prior to World War I. By the same logic, unipolarity is even less war prone: none of these causal mechanisms is relevant to a unipole's interactions with other great powers. Power transition and hegemonic theories predict that major war involving the leading state and a challenger becomes more likely as their relative capabilities approach parity.[39] Under unipolarity, parity is beyond the reach of a would-be challenger, so this mechanism does not operate. In any event, many scholars question whether these traditional theories of war remain relevant in a world in which the declining benefits of conquest, nuclear deterrence among most major powers, the spread of democracy, and changing collective norms and ideas reduce the probability of major war among great powers to a historically low level.[40] The absence of major conflicts among the great powers may thus be overdetermined or have little to do with unipolarity.

[William] Wohlforth ["Unipolarity, Status Competition, and Great Power War," pp. 28–57] develops an alternative theoretical framework for assessing the consequences of unipolarity for great power conflict, one that focuses on status or prestige seeking as opposed to security as the core preference for major states. From a diverse theoretical literature he derives a single hypothesis on the relationship between unipolar capability distributions and great power conflict. He tests it in the current international system and historically, and he derives further implications for relationships between the unipole and secondary states. He supplies theoretical reasons and initial empirical support for the proposition that unipolarity itself helps to explain low levels of militarized interactions among great powers since 1991. The same logic and evidence, however, suggest that the route back to bipolarity or multipolarity may be more prone to great power conflict than many scholars now suppose.

THE DURABILITY OF A UNIPOLAR SYSTEM

The current unipolar system has already lasted longer than some scholars were anticipating at the end of the cold war.[41] How much longer it will persist before transforming itself into the more "normal" systemic pattern of multipolarity or perhaps into to a new bipolarity remains to be seen. Durability will depend primarily on developments in the capabilities and behavior of the unipole and other major powers. Because the unipole is such a disproportionately powerful actor in this system, the evolution of its own capabilities and behavior is likely to carry the greatest weight. Other actors are more likely to react to the unipole than to trigger system-transforming processes on their own.

The evolution of relative *capabilities* is obviously a crucial variable, and there is no clear theoretical presumption. One hypothesis is that unipolarity is self-reinforcing. The unipole is so far ahead militarily that it finds it relatively easy to maintain and even widen its capability lead over that of would-be peers—especially if, as some scholars argue, the contemporary U.S. defense industry benefits from increasing returns to scale.[42] Given massive investments in the military requirements of unipolar status over many years, other states face formidable barriers to entry—technological, economic, and domestic political—in any effort to become peer competitors.

The contrary hypothesis can be drawn from Gilpin's work, which highlights the tendency of dominant powers to plant the seeds of their own demise. Dominant states may not maintain or widen their capability lead because they fall prey to overextension abroad and/or the corrupting influences of affluence at home.[43] Similarly, the very success of their order may inadvertently encourage or develop challengers to their dominant role within it.[44] The U.S.-centered system promotes openness and globalization; the diffusion of the benefits of these processes strengthens states on the periphery that can outpace the United States economically and eventually translate their economic strength into political influence and military capacity.

The *behavior* of the unipole matters as well, again with potentially divergent effects. A unipole may discourage peer competition by reassuring states already inclined toward the status quo and by providing the benefits of system integration to those with ambivalent intentions.[45] Through its behavior, the unipole may encourage would-be challengers to accept subordinate but beneficial roles. Alternatively, and because it has the capability and discretion to act as a revisionist state itself, the unipole's behavior might heighten the insecurity of other states and prompt them to contemplate individual or collective challenges to its dominance.

The impact of developments across capabilities and behavior may be reinforcing or contradictory. A unipole might successfully reassure other states while simultaneously maintaining its capability lead over them. It might alarm other states while dissipating its relative advantages. Or its behavior might point in one direction while its capabilities point in another.

Conclusion

One of the oldest insights in the study of international relations is that power, in the form of material capabilities, has a decisive impact on relations among states. Thucydides famously recorded the frank and brutal observation that "the strong do what they can and the weak suffer what they must." In a world of states, power disparities generate both security and insecurity and have an impact on what states want and what they can get. Few scholars embrace theories of world politics that rely exclusively on the structural circumstances created by

material capabilities of states and its distribution within the international system. But it is also widely agreed that one ignores such factors at one's explanatory peril.

For most of modern world history, the distribution of material capabilities has been best characterized as multipolar or bipolar. The contemporary structure is extraordinary and has the potential to endure beyond a historical "moment." One of the great theoretical challenges in the study of international relations is to identify the extent to which and the various ways in which a unipolar distribution of power influences how states act and generates patterns of conflict and cooperation. In broad terms, the articles in this issue are concerned with how a unipolar international order differs in its character and functioning from a bipolar or multipolar order. In more operational terms, we are interested in how the shift from the cold war bipolar system to the current American-centered unipolar system matters for the behavior of states and the character of international rule and order.

There are obvious limitations on our ability to validate hypotheses or subject theoretical claims to rigorous empirical tests. Precisely because a unipolar distribution of power has not appeared routinely in earlier eras, we do not possess multiple historical cases for systematic comparisons. It is equally difficult to draw inferences about the impact of unipolarity because we are still living through it. In effect, we are in the midst of a historical cycle. Patterns of foreign policy and international outcomes will be better discerned after unipolarity has given way to bipolarity or multipolarity. What this [essay] does accomplish, however, is to lay out the questions, categories, and hypotheses that should continue to guide inquiry and to offer initial empirical determinations of our claims. The set of hypotheses we develop collectively in three categories—the behavior of the unipole, the reactions of secondary states, and the overall functioning of the international system—constitutes a rich agenda for future theoretical and empirical research. Three aspects of that agenda strike us as sufficiently salient to merit emphasis in closing.

First, scholarship needs to untangle and clarify three related but distinct manifestations of unipolarity that easily become confused in the process of making causal arguments. One is the unipolar distribution of power as an ideal type across time, the second is unipolarity in the particular international circumstances of the early twenty-first century (for example, including the existence of nuclear weapons and a security community among some of the leading powers), and the third is American unipolarity, or unipolarity with the United States as the dominant state with its particular institutional and ideological features. In making causal claims, it is exceedingly difficult to determine how deeply rooted cause and effect are in the distribution of power. Do the foreign policy patterns of the Bush administration follow in a relatively straightforward way from conditions of unipolarity or are they much more circumstantial? Would other states—were they to emerge as a unipolar power—act in a similar way, or is behavior more contingent on the character of the state or the peculiarities of its leaders? [There are] various answers to these questions of causation, but [scholars] tend to agree that there remains considerable contingency in a unipolar system. Constraints and opportunities—as well as threats and interests—do shift when the global system moves from bipolarity to unipolarity, but the linkages between the structure of power and the actions of states are not straightforward. Future research will want to specify these linkages and the way in which circumstance modifies and mediates the structural impact of unipolarity.

A second research agenda concerns the nature and character of constraints on the unipolar state. One of the defining features of unipolarity is that the power of the leading state is not balanced by other major states. Yet in the absence of this classic mechanism of power constraint it remains unclear what, if anything, in fact disciplines and restrains unipolar power. Finnemore looks closely at the role of legitimacy as a constraint on state power and provides some evidence that this so-called soft mechanism of constraint does matter. It is plausible to expect that a unipolar state, any unipolar state, would prefer to lead and operate in an international order that is seen as normatively acceptable—that is, legitimate—to other states. Legitimate domination is more desirable than coercive domination. But questions remain about how powerful this incentive is for the leaders of a dominant state and how costly it actually becomes to the unipole, in the short and longer term, when its behavior and the system associated with its power are perceived by others as less legitimate.

A third research area concerns how unipolarity affects the logic of hegemonic behavior. As noted earlier, there are two lines of argument regarding how a unipolar state might act in regard to the provisioning of public goods, rules, and institutions. One suggests that the leading state has a clear incentive to commit itself to leadership in the establishment and management of a cooperative, rule-based system. It receives a flow of material rewards and enjoys reduced costs of enforcement according to this logic. But the theoretical and policy-relevant question is whether the shift from cold war bipolarity to unipolarity has altered hegemonic leadership incentives. One possibility is that the decline in a shared security threat makes it harder to strike bargains: the leading state's offerings of security are less needed by other states and it is less dependent on the frontline support of weaker and secondary states. Another possibility is that unipolarity increases the incentives for free riding by subordinate states while at the same time reducing the willingness of the lead state to bear the disproportionate costs of public goods provision. Hegemonic leadership may also hinge on judgments about the overall life cycle of unipolarity. If a unipolar state assumes that its dominance is semipermanent, it may be willing to suffer lost legitimacy or the costs of enforcement—costs that are seen as less consequential than the freedom of action that is achieved by reducing its hegemonic responsibilities. But if the leading state judges that its unipolar position will decline in the years ahead, the value of rules and institutions may increase to the extent those rules and institutions are "sticky" and can help protect the leading state's interests and lock in its preferred international order during the days when it inevitably becomes relatively less capable.

The hypotheses and findings * * * ultimately take us back to basic questions in the study of international relations. The surprising onset of unipolarity encourages us to revisit questions about how the international structure of capabilities shapes, encourages, and constrains state behavior. In attempting to make sense of this new type of global structure, we are forced to grapple with the enduring issue of how the powerful and the weak make their way in a changing international environment.

NOTES

1. See Jack S. Levy, "Balances and Balancing: Concepts, Propositions and Research Design," in John A. Vasquez and Colin Elman, eds., *Realism and the Balancing of Power: A New Debate* (Saddle River, N.J.: Prentice-Hall, 2003).

2. G. John Ikenberry, ed., *America Unrivaled: The Future of the Balance of Power* (Ithaca, N.Y.: Cornell University Press, 2002); and T. V. Paul, James J. Wirtz, and Michel Fortman, eds., *Balance of Power: Theory and Practice in the 21st Century* (Stanford, Calif.: Stanford University Press, 2004). On incipient balancing, see Kenneth Waltz, "Structural Realism after the Cold War," *International Security* 24 (Summer 2000); Christopher Layne, "The Unipolar Illusion: Why New Great Powers Will Arise," *International Security* 17 (Spring 1993); Robert Pape, "Soft Balancing against the United States," *International Security* 30 (Summer 2005); and Keir Lieber and Gerard Alexander,

"Waiting for Balancing: Why the World Is Not Pushing Back," *International Security* 30 (Summer 2005).

3. Robert Gilpin, *War and Change in World Politics* (New York: Cambridge University Press, 1981); A. F. K. Organski, *World Politics* (New York: Alfred A. Knopf, 1958); and A. F. K. Organski and Jacek Kugler, *The War Ledger* (Chicago: University of Chicago Press, 1980).

4. See Karl W. Deutsch and J. David Singer, "Multipolar Power Systems and International Stability," *World Politics* 16 (April 1964); Richard N. Rosecrance, "Bipolarity, Mutilpolarity and the Future," *Journal of Conflict Resolution* 10 (September 1966); Kenneth N. Waltz, "The Stability of a Bipolar World," *Daedalus* 93 (Summer 1964); and Morton A. Kaplan, *System and Process in International Politics* (New York: John Wiley, 1957).

5. For example, Stephen Walt, *Taming American Power: The Global Responses to American Primacy* (New York: Norton, 2006); Robert Jervis, "The Remaking of a Unipolar World," *Washington Quarterly* 29 (Summer 2006).

6. A huge literature has emerged—or returned—depicting America as an empire. See, for example, Charles Maier, *Among Empires: American Ascendancy and Its Predecessors* (Cambridge: Harvard University Press, 2006); Niall Ferguson, *Colossus: The Price of America's Empire* (New York: Penguin, 2004); Chalmers Johnson, *The Sorrows of Empire: Militarism, Secrecy, and the End of the Republic* (New York: Metropolitan Books, 2004). On hegemony, see G. John Ikenberry, *After Victory: Institutions, Strategic Restraint, and the Rebuilding of Order after Major War* (Princeton: Princeton University Press, 2001). On imperium, see Peter Katzenstein, *A World of Regions: Asia and Europe in the American Imperium* (Ithaca, N.Y.: Cornell University Press, 2006). On uni-multipolarity, see Samuel Huntington, "The Lonely Superpower," *Foreign Affairs* 78 (March–April 1999).

7. In this way, we are following a basic distinction made in the power theory literature. See, in particular, David A. Baldwin, *Paradoxes of Power* (New York: Basil Blackwell, 1989).

8. Kenneth Waltz, *Theory of International Politics* (Reading, Mass.: Addison-Wesley 1979), 131.

9. For a comprehensive critical review of the polarity literature, see Barry Buzan, *The United States and the Great Powers: World Politics in the Twenty-first Century* (Cambridge: Polity Press, 2004).

10. [William] Wohlforth, "The Stability of a Unipolar World," *International Security* 21 (Summer 1999); idem, "U.S. Strategy in a Unipolar World," in Ikenberry (n. 2); Stephen G. Brooks and William Wohlforth, *World Out of Balance: International Relations and the Challenge of American Primacy* (Princeton: Princeton University Press, 2008).

11. Some scholars argue that bipolarity or multipolarity might characterize international politics in certain regional settings. See, for example, Robert Ross, "The Geography of the Peace: East Asia in the Twenty-first Century," *International Security* 23 (Spring 1999); and Andrew Moravcsik, "The Quiet Superpower," *Newsweek*, June 17 2002.

12. See, for example, Ethan B. Kapstein, "Does Unipolarity Have a Future?" in Kapstein and Michael Mastanduno, eds., *Unipolar Politics: Realism and State Strategies after the Cold War* (New York: Columbia University Press, 1999); Birthe Hansen, *Unipolarity and the Middle East* (New York: St. Martin's, 2000); Wohlforth (n. 10, 1999, 2002); Brooks and Wohlforth (n. 10); William E. Odom and Robert Dujarric, *America's Inadvertent Empire* (New Haven: Yale University Press, 2004); and Arvind Virmani, "Global Power from the 18th to the 21st Century: Power Potential (VIP2), Strategic Assets and Actual Power (VIP)," Working Paper no. 175 (New Delhi: Indian Council for Research on International Economic Relations, 2005). The most comprehensive contrarian view is Michael Mann, whose main arguments are that the United States is weaker economically that it seems (a claim mainly about the future) and that U.S. military capability is comparatively ineffective at achieving favorable outcomes (a claim about utility); Mann, *Incoherent Empire* (London: Verso, 2003).

13. Calculated from *Budget of the United States Government Fiscal Year 2005: Historical Tables* (Washington, D.C.: United States Government Printing Office, 2005).

14. Sustained U.S. investment in nuclear capabilities, against the backdrop of Russian decline and Chinese stasis, have even led some to question the existence of stable deterrence between these countries. See Keir A. Lieber and Daryl G. Press, "The End of MAD? The Nuclear Dimension of U.S. Primacy," *International Security* 30 (Spring 2006).

15. David Wilkinson, "Unipolarity without Hegemony," *International Studies Review* 1 (Spring 1999); Hansen (n. 12); Stuart Kaufman, Richard Little, and William Wohlforth, eds., *The Balance of Power in World History* (London: Palgrave Macmillan, 2007); and Posen, "Command of the Commons: The Military Foundations of U.S. Hegemony," *International Security* 28 (Fall 2003).

16. "The Eagle Has Landed: The New U.S. Global Military Position," *Financial Times Weekend*, February 1, 2002.

17. E. H. Carr, *The Twenty Years' Crisis* (London: Macmillan and Company, 1939); Organski [and Kugler] (n. 3); Randall L. Schweller, "Bandwagoning for Profit: Bringing the Revisionist State Back In," *International Security* 19 (Summer 1994); and Robert Powell, "Stability and the Distribution of Power," *World Politics* 48 (January 1996).

18. Gilpin (n. 3), chap. 2.

19. See, for example, Ronald L. Tammen, Jacek Kugler, Douglas Lemke, Carole Alsharabati, Brian Efird, Alan C. Stam III, and A. F. K. Organski, *Power Transitions: Strategies for the 21st Century* (New York: Chatham House, 2000); Jonathan M. DiCicco and Jack S. Levy, "Power Shifts and Problem Shifts," *Journal of Conflict Resolution* 43 (December 1999); and Jason Davidson, *The Origins of Revisionist and Status-quo States* (New York: Palgrave Macmillan, 2006).

20. Josef Joffe, "Bismarck or Britain? Toward an American Grand Strategy after Unipolarity," *International Security* 19 (Spring 1995); and Michael Mastanduno, "Preserving the Unipolar Moment: Realist Theories and U.S. Grand Strategy after the Cold War," *International Security* 21 (Spring 1997).

21. See Robert O. Keohane, *After Hegemony: Cooperation and Discord in the World Political Economy* (Princeton: Princeton University Press, 1984), and the literature discussed therein.

22. Kenneth Oye, ed., *Cooperation under Anarchy* (Princeton: Princeton University Press, 1986).

23. This literature is vast, and its claims have been subject to considerable critical scrutiny. Key statements include Charles P. Kindleberger, *The World in Depression, 1929–1939* (Berkeley: University of California Press, 1973); Robert O. Keohane, "The Theory of Hegemonic Stability and Changes in International Economic Regimes," in Alexander L. George, Ole R. Holsti, and Randolph M. Siverson, *Change in the International System* (Boulder, Colo.: Westview Press, 1980); Stephen D. Krasner, "State Power and the Structure of International Trade," *World Politics* 28 (April 1976); Bruce Russett, "The Mysterious Case of Vanishing Hegemony," *International Organization* 39 (Spring 1985); Duncan Snidal, "The Limits of Hegemonic Stability Theory," *International Organization* 39 (Autumn 1985); David A. Lake, "Leadership, Hegemony and the International Economy: Naked Emperor or Tattered Monarch with Potential?" *International Studies Quarterly* 37 (December 1993); and Joanne Gowa, "Rational Hegemons, Excludable Goods, and Small Groups: An Epitaph for Hegemonic Stability Theory?" *World Politics* 41 (April 1989).

24. See Valerie Bunce, "The Empire Strikes Back: The Evolution of the Eastern Bloc from Soviet Asset to Liability," *International Organization* 39 (Winter 1985); and Randall Stone, *Satellites and Commissars: Strategy and Conflict in the Politics of Soviet-Bloc Trade* (Princeton: Princeton University Press, 1996).

25. Waltz (n. 8).

26. Hedley Bull, *The Anarchical Society: A Study of Order in World Politics* (New York: Columbia University Press, 1977).

27. Ikenberry (n. 6).

28. Robert Dahl, "The Concept of Power," *Behavioral Science* 2 (July 1957); Baldwin (n. 7).

29. Alexis de Tocqueville, *Democracy in America*, trans. Henry Reeve (Cambridge: Sever and Francis, 1863), 1: 299–300.

30. Theodore Lowi, "Making Democracy Safe for the World," in G. John Ikenberry, ed., *American Foreign Policy: Theoretical Essays* (New York: Harper Collins 1989); and Stephen Krasner, "United States Commercial and Monetary Policy: Unravelling the Paradox of Internal Weakness and External Strength," in Peter Katzenstein, ed., *Between Power and Plenty* (Madison: University of Wisconsin Press, 1978).

31. For example, David Lake, "Powerful Pacifists: Democratic States and War," *American Political Science Review* 86 (March 1992); Dan Reiter and Allan C. Stam, *Democracies at War* (Princeton: Princeton University Press, 2002); and Robert Pastor, "The President vs. Congress," in Robert Art and Seyom Brown, eds., *U.S. Foreign Policy: The Search for a New Role* (New York: Macmillan, 1993).

32. See Otto Hintze, "Military Organization and the Organization of States," in Felix Gilbert, ed., *The Historical Essays of Otto Hintze* (New York: Oxford University Press, 1975); and Peter Alexis Gourevitch, "The Second Image Reversed," *International Organization* 32 (Autumn 1978).

33. See the reviews and discussion in Jack S. Levy, "Balances and Balancing: Concepts, Propositions, and Research Design," in John A. Vasquez and Colin Elman, eds., *Realism and the Balancing of Power: A New Debate* (Englewood Cliffs, N.J.: Prentice-Hall, 2003); and Jack S. Levy and William R. Thompson, "Hegemonic Threats and Great-Power Balancing in Europe, 1495–1999," *Security Studies* 14 (January–March 2005).

34. See, for example, Glen H. Snyder, *Alliance Politics* (Ithaca, N.Y.: Cornell University Press, 1997); Stephen M. Walt, "Alliances in Theory and Practice: What Lies Ahead?" *Journal of International Affairs* 43 (Summer–Fall 1989); idem, "Why Alliances Endure or Collapse," *Survival* 39 (Spring 1997); and Paul W. Schroeder, "Historical Reality versus Neorealist Theory," *International Security* 19 (Winter 1994).

35. See Schroeder (n. 34); and R. Harrison Wagner, "What Was Bipolarity?" *International Organization* 47 (Winter 1993).

36. Keohane (n. 21); Ikenberry (n. 6).

37. See the discussion in Jervis, *System Effects: Complexity in Political and Social Life* (Princeton: Princeton University Press 1997), chap. 3; and idem, "Unipolarity: A Structural Perspective," [*World Politics* 61, no. 1 (January 2009)].

38. See Robert Powell, *In the Shadow of Power: States and Strategies in International Politics* (Princeton: Princeton University Press, 1999); and Alexander Wendt, *Social Theory of International Politics* (Cambridge: Cambridge University Press, 1999).

39. See Gilpin (n. 3); Tammen et al. (n. 19); and * * * DiCiccio [and Levy] (n. 19).

40. Robert Jervis, *American Foreign Policy in a New Era* (London: Routledge, 2005), 31.

41. See Christopher Layne, "The Unipolar Illusion: Why New Great Powers Will Arise," *International Security* 14 (Spring 1993); Kenneth N. Waltz, "The Emerging Structure of International Politics," *International Security* 18 (Fall 1993); and idem, "Structural Realism after the Cold War," in Ikenberry (n. 2). See also the retrospective in Christopher Layne, "The Unipolar Illusion Revisited," *International Security* 31 (Winter 2006).

42. See Jonathan Caverley, "United States Hegemony and the New Economics of Defense," *Security Studies* 16 (October 2007).

43. Gilpin (n. 3).

44. Ibid., 75.

45. Michael Mastanduno, "Preserving the Unipolar Moment: Realist Theories and U.S. Grand Strategy after the Cold War," in Kapstein and Mastanduno (n. 12).

Randall L. Schweller and Xiaoyu Pu

AFTER UNIPOLARITY

China's Visions of International Order
in an Era of U.S. Decline

The post–Cold War era was a brief and uncertain period. As Condoleezza Rice observes, "We knew better where we had been than where we were going."[1] Whereas the sudden peace that broke out in the late 1980s had been unexpected, the exuberant idealism that followed was all too predictable. Realism was pronounced dead, and the future of international politics became legalized, cosmopolitanized, and network globalized.[2]

Since the terrorist attacks of September 11, 2001, the world does not appear so easily transformed, or history so easily escaped.[3] Even unipolarity, which seemed strangely durable only a few years ago, appears today as a "passing moment"— one that most realists predicted.[4] Although the United States remains the lone superpower, it is no longer a hyperpower towering over potential contenders. The rest of the world is catching up.[5] If a great transformation is coming, it is not one that heralds a radically altered world politics based on legalism, constitutionalism, or global civic activism. Rather, it is a structural transformation from unipolarity to multipolarity that most realists believe promises a return to the familiar history of great powers struggling for power and prestige.[6] This prediction is grounded in the proposition that multipolar systems arise from traditional "hard" balancing in the system's core and are inherently conflictual. We disagree. A return to multipolarity tells us that several great powers will emerge to join the United States as poles within the international system. That is all. It does not tell us how multipolarity will arrive (whether by means of traditional balancing behavior or as an unintended consequence of inwardly focused states growing at different rates) or what the specific content of international politics will be on the other side of the transition from unipolarity to multipolarity (whether emerging powers will accept or resist the inherited Western order). These issues largely depend on what roles the emerging powers, especially China, decide to play. They may choose to be (1) supporters, who assume their fair share of the responsibilities associated with co-managing an evolving but essentially unchanged global order, (2) spoilers, who seek to destroy the existing order and replace it with something entirely different, or (3) shirkers, who want the privileges of power but are unwilling to pay for them by contributing to global governance.[7]

History tells us that dramatic structural changes rarely unfold smoothly or peacefully. Realists as far back as Thucydides have noted the danger of situations in which states undergo rapid rises and declines in relative power, where one state aspires to hegemonic status and another seeks to maintain it. Indeed, history's most destructive and influential armed conflicts have been titanic struggles called hegemonic wars: systemwide military contests of unlimited means between coalitions led by a declining leader and a rising challenger. The fundamental issue at stake in hegemonic wars is the maintenance or acquisition

From *International Security*, 36, no. 1 (Summer 2011): 41–72.

of prestige, defined as the reputation for power that serves as the everyday currency of international politics. Prestige decides who will order and govern the international system, the nature of that order (its social purpose), and how that order will be provided (whether by means of coercive or legitimate authority).[8]

The main causal driver of Robert Gilpin's theory of hegemonic war and international change is the law of uneven rates of growth among states, which redistributes power in the international system. Hegemonic wars concentrate power in the hands of one victorious state, in whose interests a new international order is established. For a time, roughly twenty-five years, there is little disjuncture between actual power and prestige, and so the international order remains stable and legitimate. Over time, however, the law of uneven growth diffuses power throughout the system. As the hegemon's competitors grow more powerful, their dissatisfaction with the status quo, ambitions, and demands for prestige and influence grow as well. Prestige, however, tends to be sticky: reputations for power, divisions of territory, and the institutional architecture of the international order do not move in lockstep with changes in power. When a large enough disjuncture arises, the system enters a state of disequilibrium.[9] Eventually, serious international crises ensue, as spectacular growth in the economic and military capabilities of rising powers triggers "intense competition among countries for resources and markets, military power, political influence, and prestige."[10] Dramatic shifts in power also engender security dilemmas. Whatever their true intentions, rapidly growing states often appear as threats to their neighbors, as well as to the hegemon and its allies.[11]

Prior to military confrontation or even the threat of such conflict, we argue that the rising challenger must delegitimize the hegemon's global authority and order.[12] This delegitimation phase, which appears years before the critical inflection point of a power transition, creates the conditions for the emergence of a revisionist counterhegemonic coalition. During this phase, the revisionist power voices its dissatisfaction with the established order and forges the social purpose that will become the foundation of its demand for a new world order. This phase occurs within the larger cyclical pattern of (1) a stable order, (2) the deconcentration and delegitimation of the hegemon's power (3) arms buildups and the formation of alliances, (4) a resolution of the international crisis, often through hegemonic war, and (5) system renewal.[13] Is contemporary international politics following this conventional pattern and, if so, where are we in the cycle?

The nuclear age makes power transition by means of a deliberately waged hegemonic war unthinkable. In this crucial sense, the hegemonic-war cycle has been permanently broken. That said, we argue that the transition from unipolarity to some form of global balance will conform to the early phases of this cyclical pattern. Where it goes from there is anyone's guess. The key issue is whether international order will be preserved by peaceful adjustment or undone by military balancing or mismanagement and incompetence. In our view, the latter outcome is most probable.

Leaving these questions aside for the moment, we argue that the current international system is entering a deconcentration/delegitimation phase. Delegitimation involves two components: a delegitimating rhetoric (the discourse of resistance) and cost-imposing strategies that fall short of full-fledged balancing behavior (the practice of resistance). The discourse and practice of delegitimation are mutually sustaining and necessary for the next phase of balancing behavior. Unipolarity, however, represents an unprecedented historical anomaly that makes delegitimation strategies more necessary and complex than ever before. In multipolar and bipolar systems, balancing is the primary mechanism to preserve the status quo. Under unipolarity, in contrast, balancing becomes the very definition of revisionism: the goal of restoring a global balance of power requires the overthrow of the existing unipolar structure. Hence, concentrated power within the unipole is not the only obstacle that states seeking a balance must overcome; they must also overcome the revisionist label attached to any state seeking to restore global equilibrium.[14]

The article is laid out as follows. First, we explain why emerging powers will initially attempt to undermine the legitimacy of the hegemon— through cost-imposing measures short of hard balancing—to pave the way for global contestation. The next two sections explore various forms of resistance to hegemonic domination: the discourse and practices of resistance and the strategies of everyday and rightful resistance. We then focus on China as the most viable contender for a hegemonic challenge, exploring its ambitions and blueprints for a new world order.[15] These blueprints or visions are associated with various state strategies and scenarios about how the transition from unipolarity to a restored global balance of power— whether bipolar, multipolar, or nonpolar—will develop. We then discuss what we believe to be the most likely alternative future. As inwardly focused emerging powers grow at faster rates than those of the established powers, a global balance will be restored as an unintended consequence of the law of uneven growth among states. The predominant behavior within this new multipolar system will not be balancing but rather shirking: emerging powers will attempt to free ride on U.S. contributions to global governance.

Balancing as Revisionist Behavior under Unipolarity

International relations scholars have virtually ignored a crucial obstacle under unipolarity to balancing behavior: unipolarity is the only system in which balancing is a revisionist, rather than a status quo, policy. This ideational hurdle and the huge power disparity inherent in unipolarity have been the main obstacles to balancing behavior.[16] Any state or coalition of states seeking to restore a balance is, by definition, revisionist: it seeks to overthrow the established order of unbalanced power and replace it with a balance of power system. The goal is a change of system, not a change within the system, and so achieving this goal will alter the very structure of international politics from unipolarity to bipolarity or multipolarity. Because balancing under unipolarity is a revisionist process, any state intent on restoring system equilibrium will be labeled an aggressor.

This reality implies that balancing under unipolarity must be preceded by a delegitimation phase. States must first come to see hegemony as so incompetent and so dangerous that its rule must be overturned. Otherwise, the risks and high costs of attempting to restore a global balance will be prohibitive. The delegitimation phase that we have in mind is most associated with George Modelski's theory of long cycles.[17] For Modelski and his followers, Karen Rasler and William Thompson, delegitimation succeeds a "world power" phase: delegitimation "is a response to the erosion of the phase of leadership, order, and peak concentration found in the world power/execution period."[18] That is, delegitimation occurs after the hegemon (or unipole) has begun its relative decline. In Modelski's scheme, delegitimation is followed by a "deconcentration/coalition building" phase, in which power becomes even more diffuse and balance of power alliances start to form.[19] This is essentially what we argue, but there are some differences having to do with timing and the fact that the current system is the first truly unipolar, not just hegemonic, structure.[20]

In our view, unipolarity requires both delegitimation and deconcentration to move in lockstep. Delegitimation provides the rationale (embodied in a discourse of resistance) for internal and external balancing practices, while deconcentration, by dispersing power more evenly throughout the system, lowers the barriers to both the discourse and practice of resistance to hegemonic rule. Thus, delegitimation affects the will to pursue costly balancing strategies, while deconcentration affects the ability to do so. The two phases occur simultaneously because, as mentioned, balancing under unipolarity is not a conservative policy as it is under bipolarity or multipolarity but rather an extremely revisionist one. Therefore, any state that openly espouses a desire to restore a balance of power will be targeted by the hegemon as a threat not only to its primacy but also to its established order and the interests of allies that support that order. Given these risks, delegitimation and deconcentration of power within the system must occur together.

The Discourse and Practice of Resistance under Unipolarity

The interplay of great power politics in a unipolar setting is an example of the more general phenomenon of relations of domination and resistance. James Scott observes that "most of the political life of subordinate groups is to be found neither in overt collective defiance of powerholders nor in complete hegemonic compliance, but in the vast territory between these two polar opposites."[21] Unipolar systems, by definition, have yet to undergo a significant deconcentration of power. Secondary states, therefore, do not have the capabilities to balance against the unipole. This does not mean that they must obey the hegemon's every wish. Rather, they practice the arts of resistance, for relations of resistance always coexist with relations of domination.[22]

What types of resistance occur in a delegitimation phase? Scott points out that "subordinate classes throughout most of history have rarely been afforded the luxury of open, organized, political activity. [S]uch activity was dangerous, if not suicidal."[23] The purpose of competing ideologies (the conservative ideologies of the rulers and the "deviant" ones espoused by the weak) "is not just to convince but to control; better stated, they aim to control by convincing."[24] The complex relationship between thought and action is key to understanding how delegitimation of hegemonic authority works.

Dreams inform consciousness, infusing the words, symbolic language, deviant ideologies, and discourses with shared values and pathways for action, which will be taken if and when the power situation changes. As such, the dreams, intentions, symbols, ideas, and language of subordinate actors not only presage future rebellions (blows against the established order) but are necessary precursors for them.[25] Acts and thoughts of resistance engage in regular conversation; taken together, they pose an alternative or imagined world, a vision of what could be, and the ways and means to achieve this goal. It all begins, however, with symbolic sanctions: "The rich, while they may be relatively immune to material sanctions, cannot escape symbolic sanctions: slander, gossip, character assassination."[26] It is this type of process to which we are referring when we say "delegitimation."

In addition to their competing visions of global order (the discourse of resistance), subordinate actors may adopt "cost-imposing" strategies (the practice of resistance) vis-à-vis the unipolar power that fall short of balancing against it.[27] States (weak ones included) and even nonstates can impose costs on a unipolar power in a variety of ways, ranging from the mere withdrawal of goodwill to actual attacks on its soil. In the current world, cost-imposing strategies include engaging in diplomatic friction or foot-dragging;[28] denying U.S. military forces access to bases;[29] launching terrorist attacks against the United States; aiding, abetting, and harboring terrorist groups; voting against the United States in international institutions; preventing or reversing the forward-basing of U.S. military forces; pursuing protectionism and other coercive economic policies; engaging in conventional uses of force such as blockades against U.S. allies;[30] making threats against pivotal states that affect regional and international security;[31] and proliferating weapons of mass destruction among anti-Western states or groups. Therefore, in the delegitimation and deconcentration phase, the discourse of resistance and the practice of resistance are mutually sustaining.

Everyday and Rightful Resistance to U.S. Hegemony

In addition to the discourse and practice of resistance, subordinate states may practice everyday resistance and rightful resistance, which share the principle that such states apply various "weapons of the weak" to contest the hegemon without openly defying it through violence.[32] These strategies appear in the early stages of a power transition and are, therefore, consistent with the concept of "shaping strategies," whereby rising powers in a unipolar system attempt to shape the environment without directly confronting the hegemon.[33]

The concept of everyday resistance identifies the prosaic but constant struggle between dominant and subordinate actors that occurs across different social contexts.[34] In international politics, the concept of hegemony refers not only to concentrated material capabilities and processes of physical domination but also to ideological control by means of the hegemon's virtual monopoly on the production of social, cultural, and symbolic capital. Through these nonmaterial mechanisms of social domination and reproduction, the hegemon ensures that the arbitrariness of the social order is either ignored or posited as natural, thereby justifying the legitimacy of existing social

structures.[35] It is the pervasiveness of ideological hegemony that normally guarantees international stability without resort to coercion or violence by the dominant power.

Everyday resistance assumes that weak actors resent the hegemonic order and criticize its legitimacy and the hegemon's authority to rule. Consistent with the discourse of resistance, everyday resistance counters this ideological hegemony and its associated notion of the inevitability of the existing structure with a revolutionary consciousness. This process often starts out with uncoordinated and spontaneous dissident speeches and other petty displays of rebellion. Over time, however, these low-level forms of resistance aggregate to a point where they form a coherent ideological movement that puts in danger the existing structures of power and order.

The notion of everyday resistance, however, does not capture key aspects of the arts of resistance. Here we add the concept of rightful resistance. Consistent with the practice of resistance, rightful resistance assumes that weak actors (1) partially and temporarily accept the legitimacy of the hegemon, and (2) take advantage of opportunities and authorized channels within the order to make relative gains and to contest particular behaviors of the hegemon.[36] The strategy of rightful resistance can have opposite goals. It can strengthen the state's position for the purpose of working within the established order or for the purpose of waging a hegemonic bid to overturn that order when doing so becomes a viable option. Accordingly, the strategy works for both limited-aims revisionists—those who believe that the order is essentially legitimate but want prestige commensurate with their power or have other grievances that can be satisfied without fundamental changes to the existing order—and unlimited-aims revisionists—those who seek the overthrow of the existing order, which they consider illegitimate and intolerable.

A rising power may employ a strategy of rightful resistance to improve its position within the established order.[37] Such a state does not seek to overthrow the order but merely to gain recognition of its rights and prestige within the system and to garner a better position for itself as a power broker at various international bargaining tables. Here, the grievance is not over the essential rules of the game but over representation and the application of the rules, that is, the hypocrisy, pitfalls, injustices, and corruption behind the existing manifestation of that order. The U.S. civil rights and women's movements, for example, did not seek to fundamentally challenge democracy but to make its ideals a reality for disenfranchised groups.[38]

As an unintended consequence, the strategy of rightful resistance may also deepen the legitimacy of the existing order. Because the strategy dictates that emerging powers follow established rules, norms, and practices of international politics and act through authorized channels, even "rightful resistors" that initially seek the order's overthrow may inadvertently become socialized by it. That is, a revisionist state that employs this strategy runs the risk of gradually entrapping itself—of becoming enmeshed and bound by the web of multilateral institutions that define the established liberal order.[39] This outcome is most likely under conditions of thick and deeply entrenched international institutionalization and when the rising challenger becomes so wildly successful under the existing order (e.g., China's unprecedented economic growth rate of 10 percent over the past two decades) that it becomes too costly for it to maintain its revisionist aims, that is, for it not to undergo a fundamental change of its identity and goals.

Alternatively, the strategy of rightful resistance may have the short-term goal of steadily increasing the emerging power's economic and military capabilities so that someday it can fulfill its long-term goal of overthrowing the established order. Here, rightful resistance positions the state to make wholesale changes to the system later on, when its enhanced capabilities enable a direct challenge. This begs the question: Why would an increasingly powerful state that is growing faster than its established competitors want to overthrow the very system under which it is benefiting (given its unmatched growth rate) more than any other state? This core question can be leveled at all hegemonic theories that posit revisionist powers as the primary agents of change. The answer is essentially that the rising power believes, rightly or wrongly, that it could do even better under an international order of its own design—an order that it governs and that reflects its interests and desires, institutional architecture, and idiosyncratic norms and rules.[40]

In summary, a strategy of rightful resistance does not provide reliable information about the rising state's intentions. Behaviors associated with this strategy are consistent with both the intention of strengthening the legitimacy of the existing order and of significantly revising or overthrowing it at a later date. And because intentions can change, there is no guarantee that they will remain consistent over time.[41] Indeed, the rising power may not know or have the ability to accurately predict its future goals. That noted, the built-in flexibility of rightful resistance makes it an effective hedging strategy, which, given the rising power's uncertainty about its future intentions, may be the reason why the ascending power selects this strategy in the first place.

Chinese Arts of Resistance: Rising and Contesting within the Order

If China continues modernizing its economy at a rapid pace, it will someday become the wealthiest great power and, as such, the most likely peer competitor to the United States. China's leadership and intellectuals have not yet directly and openly challenged the dominant ideology of *Pax Americana*, but they have started thinking beyond the existing order. At this early stage of development, Chinese ideas about alternative world orders remain inchoate and contested within China itself. Accordingly, these visions have not yet gained traction within or beyond China. We suspect, however, that they will develop into a more appealing and consequential alternative ideology as they become more coherent and as China increases its power and prestige. In the meantime, however, China has found more subtle ways to resist U.S. unipolarity—resistance that may be likened to "prudent opposition newspaper editors under strict censorship," wherein subordinate actors must "find ways of getting their message across, while staying somehow within the law. This requires an experimental spirit and a capacity to test and exploit all the loopholes, ambiguities, silences, and lapses available to them."[42]

Chinese resistance operates along two dimensions: the ways by which China exploits the current order and its thinking beyond that order. To cope with the existing order, China pragmatically accommodates U.S. hegemony, on the one hand, while it contests the legitimacy of U.S. hegemony, on the other. This type of resistance is similar to rightful resistance in a domestic context, in which weak actors partially accept the legitimacy of the hegemon but seize opportunities to grow and contest perceived injustice. Thus, China has worked within the current international system to expand its economy and increase its visibility and status as a global political player, while avoiding actions that directly challenge U.S. hegemony. Relying on existing institutionalized channels to contest U.S. hegemony, China seeks to increase its political influence and prestige through active participation in, not confrontation with, the existing order. Specific tactics include (1) denouncing U.S. unilateralism and promoting the concept (if not always the practice) of multilateralism; (2) participating in and creating new international organizations; (3) pursuing a proactive "soft power" diplomacy in the developing world;[43] (4) voting against the United States in international institutions; and (5) setting the agenda within international and regional organizations. In the short term, China seeks a gradual modification of *Pax Americana*, not a direct challenge to it.

There are several reasons why China's grand strategy incorporates accommodation with the United States. First, China's ability to grow requires a stable relationship with the United States. Contemporary Chinese leaders view the first two decades of the twenty-first century as "a period of important strategic opportunities."[44] Second, since the end of the Cold War, the United States has generally pursued engagement with China, not containment of it.[45] Third, Chinese strategists have a realistic estimate of their country's relative strength. It "would be foolhardy," Wang Jisi, dean of Peking University's School of International Studies, proclaims, "for Beijing to challenge directly the international order and the institutions favored by the Western world—and, indeed, such a challenge is unlikely."[46] Predicting continued U.S. domination during this era, Chinese leaders believe that they must accommodate the United States while relentlessly building China's own strength. At the end of this period, China will be in a better position to defend and advance its interests.[47]

Although China cannot balance the economic and military power of the United States, it can challenge the legitimacy of the U.S.-led order and pose problems for U.S. interests, especially in East Asia.[48] China has been contesting the current order in several ways.

First, an integral part of China's diplomacy in recent years has been the call for multilateralism, which has not only expanded China's political influence in Asian regional affairs but helped build its global image. Before the mid-1990s, China was skeptical about the value of participating in regional multilateral organizations, preferring instead to deal with its neighbors and other major powers bilaterally. Since the mid-1990s, however, China has actively participated in most regional multilateral institutions, such as Asia-Pacific Economic Cooperation, the Association of Southeast Asian Nations plus Three (ASEAN plus China, Japan, and South Korea), and ASEAN plus One (ASEAN plus China), becoming an entrepreneurial agent for Asian regional cooperation.[49]

Second, China has used international institutions to project power, particularly with regard to agenda setting, through a gradualist reform strategy.[50] Thus, when China makes concessions to join a major international institution such as the World Trade Organization (WTO), it seeks not short-term economic gains but a seat at the bargaining table to influence the rules of the game.[51] As a Chinese ambassador reportedly thundered during China's negotiations to enter the WTO, "We know we have to play the game your way now, but in ten years we will set the rules!"[52] China has taken a similarly gradualist approach in its response to the financial crisis that began in 2008. At the Group of Twenty summit held in November 2008, for instance, Chinese President Hu Jintao made proposals to gradually reform international financial institutions, including changing representation mechanisms and encouraging regional financial cooperation along with diversification of the international currency regime.[53]

Third, China is increasingly using its financial power to gain political and diplomatic influence, most importantly, as a "hedge" against the excesses of U.S. hegemony.[54] Beijing is particularly worried that its huge dollar-denominated foreign exchange reserves—the largest in the world, valued at nearly $2 trillion, with more than half of those holdings estimated to be made up of U.S. Treasuries and other dollar-denominated bonds—could lose significant value in coming years. Thus, in yet another indication that China is growing increasingly concerned about holding huge dollar reserves, Zhou Xiaochuan, the head of its central bank, called for the eventual creation of a new currency reserve system controlled by the International Monetary Fund.[55] The March 2009

proposal, though impractical, signaled Chinese dissatisfaction with the existing international monetary order and served as a trial balloon to elicit responses from like-minded emerging powers such as Brazil and Russia. For the United States, the danger is real. If the Chinese lose their appetite for Treasuries—because of fears that large U.S. government deficits will lead to inflation and erode the purchasing power of their dollar-denominated financial assets—borrowing costs in the United States will soar, making it more costly for Washington to carry out economic stimulus packages and for Americans to pay off their mortgages. Although the dollar's status will remain uncontested in the near future, China is taking steps to lay the groundwork for a possible long-term challenge by, among other things, gradually enhancing the international status of the Chinese currency (the renminbi).[56] Within East Asia, for instance, the Chiang Mai Initiative—a $120 billion multilateral currency swap arrangement among the ten ASEAN countries, China, Japan, and South Korea—is a regional reserve (an insurance pool of liquidity) that supplements the lending facilities of the International Monetary Fund, strengthening the region's capacity to safeguard against increased risks and challenges in the global economy.[57]

Fourth, China continues to expand its influence in defining legitimate norms in international affairs.[58] According to some Chinese scholars, a rising power such as China must not only increase its material capabilities but grow "socially" within the existing international society. This expansion requires international recognition of China's status and normative preferences as legitimate.[59] In the security domain, for example, China zealously defends its definition of legitimate war through multilateral institutions such as the United Nations. As Guo Shuyong, an international relations expert at Shanghai Jiao Tong University, points out, "Legitimacy plays an indispensable important role in the structuring and socializing of international political behavior, and the ability to wage legitimate wars constitutes an important part of a nation's soft national power."[60] In recent years, China has become more active in UN peacekeeping operations, partly because the nature of these operations has changed in such a way that China's normative concerns have been addressed.[61] With respect to human rights, the influence of the European Union and the United States has been declining in recent years, while Chinese and Russian positions on human rights have garnered increasingly more votes in the UN General Assembly. The success of China and Russia in this regard reflects not only their commitment to a strict definition of state sovereignty but also their enhanced diplomatic skill and influence within the United Nations.[62]

Fifth, China has gained influence and prestige in Africa, Central Asia, Latin America, and the Middle East through its soft power diplomacy.[63] Soft power can become a source of zero-sum U.S.-China competition because social goods associated with soft power—such as political influence, leadership, and prestige—can spark highly charged competitions with important long-term strategic implications.[64] The Chinese view the term "soft power" broadly to include anything outside the traditional security domain, such as popular culture, foreign aid, and economic cooperation.[65] China's soft-power diplomacy has several ingredients. First, China has increasingly promoted its language and traditional culture, which has bolstered its central status in Asian civilization. Second, China's economic miracle and its gradualist reforms and political authoritarianism provide an attractive developmental model for many poor, nondemocratic countries.[66] Third, China's flexible economic diplomacy attracts many developing countries, mainly because its aid, in contrast to that of Western donors, is typically offered without political preconditions.

In this section, we outlined several of China's short-term strategies to contest U.S. hegemony within the established order. Some Chinese strategists, however, are starting to think about the long term, when China overtakes the United States as the global hegemon and must establish its own social and material structures for global governance. The next section explores these competing visions of a future Chinese-led global order.

Thinking beyond the Order

Hegemonic orders rest on both material and ideational bases, and weak actors, though unable to confront the hegemon directly, can still delegitimize the ideational foundation of hegemony through everyday resistance and visions of alternative orders. The United States has successfully shaped world politics with some big ideas such as "capitalism is better than socialism" and "democracy is better than dictatorship."[67] Recently, however, the emerging non-Western powers have let it be known that they do not share the United States' views on these issues.[68] As Bruce Jentleson and Steven Weber argue, "Outside the United States, people no longer believe that the alternative to Washington-led order is chaos. . . . [T]he rest of the world has no fear about experimenting with alternatives."[69] This section analyzes Chinese visions of the current and future international order. Pluralistic in their views on the outside world, Chinese strategists have been passionately debating how Beijing should proceed.[70] Rather than presenting one particular Chinese idea,[71] therefore, we present diverse Chinese perspectives, showing consensus where it exists and general trends in Chinese thinking.[72] We categorize these visions of global order into three ideal types: a new Chinese order, a modified liberal order, and a negotiated order, each challenging U.S. hegemony in different ways.[73] These visions of a future order map on to three potential strategies. China might (1) embrace delegitimation, functioning as a spoiler with a competing view for how the world should be structured; (2) emerge as a supporter of the existing system, working within the existing rules of the game and contributing its fair share to global governance; or (3) continue to shirk some of its international commitments and responsibilities, focusing on internal development and consolidation, contributing selectively to global governance, and seeking to implement its vision of global order gradually.[74]

We analyze these visions against four dimensions of U.S. hegemonic ideology (U.S. hegemony, capitalism, democracy, and Western culture).[75] The overall trend is consistent with our earlier discussion of delegitimation and deconcentration in the international system. China's increasing material power—particularly its rapid economic growth—has boosted its ideational self-confidence. Accordingly, Chinese intellectuals are increasingly questioning the inevitability of what they regard as Western ideational dominance.[76]

Moreover, the influence of these three Chinese visions of international order has been shifting in lockstep with China's growth in power. When China was relatively weak in the 1980s and 1990s, its strategy stressed integration within the Western-led order. As China's power and capabilities have increased, its strategists have gradually shifted the debate toward visions of a negotiated order, and an embryonic vision of a new Chinese order has emerged. Given the relatively early stage of China's rise, such rhetoric is a relatively new phenomenon and has yet to lead to fundamental change in China's foreign policy. This is not surprising, as Chinese leaders understand that unrealistic goals could be deeply destabilizing at home and abroad.[77]

A NEW CHINESE ORDER: THE SPOILER STRATEGY IN A POWER TRANSITION

An ambitious and controversial idea within China, the vision of a new Chinese order suggests that (1) Chinese traditional philosophy provides a better framework than the current order to deal with world problems; (2) U.S. hegemony is losing international legitimacy; (3) Chinese political and economic systems are gaining legitimacy and provide the basis for a better social model for the world; and (4) China should build a global *datong* (Great Harmony) society, in which emphasis is given to social welfare and collective goods.

This vision aims to undermine the legitimacy of U.S. hegemony in a comprehensive sense. It is a vision and strategy consistent with the traditional realist story of power transitions. China may or may not be pursuing this spoiler strategy now.[78] But, as we have argued, prior to a traditional hegemonic bid to overthrow the current order, China must successfully challenge the ideational foundations of the existing liberal order and offer an appealing blueprint for a new one. What are the elements of this potential Chinese challenge and new world order?

First, the vision of a new Chinese order fundamentally disputes the notion that Western ideas and culture are superior to those of the rest of the world. In recent years, China's leaders and some of its intellectuals have rekindled an interest in the philosophy and history of traditional Chinese order. Contemporary philosopher Zhao Tingyang argues that traditional Chinese ideas provide a better philosophical framework for solving global problems, asserting that the Chinese theory of Tianxia (literally, "all under Heaven") is simply "the best philosophy for world governance."[79] Compared with the Westphalian international system, the traditional Chinese notion of global order has some distinctive features, such as a holistic and inclusive view—as opposed to the dualistic and exclusive one offered by the West—with a foundation in benign hierarchical relationships similar to that between fathers and sons in the Confucian family.[80]

Second, the U.S. "empire," according to Zhao, is a comprehensive and contradictory ruling model in global politics. The United States, he believes, often fights wars in the name of peace, damages freedom in the name of freedom, and rejects ethics in the name of ethical reasons.[81] Zhao argues that the key feature of Western empires (including that of the United States) is "dominance" for the purpose of maximizing the interests of their peoples; they offer no "order" to maximize the interests of all people.[82] Consequently, Western imperial orders always rest on dubious and unsustainable legitimacy claims.[83] Here, it is useful to note that rising powers often portray their visions of order in terms of universal solutions to world problems. In history, some leaders of rising powers have truly believed this rhetoric, whereas others have cynically made such proclamations for self-serving purposes. The Tianxia world view claims to offer a posthegemonic order but, when articulated, it often gives the impression that China seeks to impose its views on the world.[84] It is not surprising, therefore, that Tianxia philosophy appears to its detractors within and outside China as ideational preparation for a new hegemonic, not a posthegemonic, world order.[85]

Third, the vision of a new Chinese order raises doubts about the inevitability of democratic liberalism. Zhao argues that contemporary democracy is increasingly commercialized and, therefore, does not serve the interests or values of the masses.[86] Peking University professor Pan Wei argues that "democratization" is a myth, and claims that China should instead develop its political institutions along Chinese traditions and build an effective non-Western bureaucracy and legal system.[87] According to Yan Xuetong, dean of the Institute of Modern International Relations at Tsinghua University and chief editor of the *Chinese Journal of International Politics*, if China wants to supplant the United States as a global leader, it must "present to the world a better social role model."[88] It is unclear whether China is promoting a "Beijing Consensus" to counterbalance the influence of the so-called Washington Consensus. What is clear, however, is that the Chinese developmental model has gained popularity in many parts of the developing world.

Fourth, in terms of economic ideas (capitalism vs. socialism), the vision of a Chinese world order might or might not challenge the fundamentals of capitalism. It does, however, have a collectivist mind-set, which emphasizes social justice and collective welfare, and seems to be rooted in the Chinese Confucian tradition of seeking a *datong* society.[89]

Related to the discourse of a new Chinese world order, many scholars in China who argue that China is an "intellectual colony" of the United States have been seeking to develop a distinct "Chinese school" of international relations theory.[90] The trouble, they argue, with Chinese intellectuals learning about international politics from their American counterparts is that Western theories cannot be expected to emphasize, much less solve, the problem of "American domination."[91] To be sure, China's scholars of world affairs have good intellectual reasons to explore a "Chinese school," and their efforts will have political implications with respect to legitimating and delegitimating particular social orders.[92] As Jack Snyder points out, "Having a distinctively Chinese school of thought about international politics—especially one that portrays China as a benign dominant power because of its wise cultural traditions—will help to establish China's intellectual independence and will legitimate China's challenge to the liberal democratic states for international leadership."[93]

A MODIFIED LIBERAL ORDER: THE SUPPORTER STRATEGY IN A CONCERT SYSTEM

The second vision posits the continuation of the current liberal order, which has nurtured China's historically unprecedented economic growth. It is a future of peaceful evolution, not system transformation. The U.S. unipolar distribution of power gives way to either a U.S.–China bipolar system or a multipolar "great power concert" system, but it is still an international order dominated and run by the major states, which establish a relatively stable system of cooperation and managed competition. All of these major states are status quo oriented, value global and regional political stability, are willing to make strategic bargains and compromises with one another, abide by great power norms of restraint and accommodation, and continue to move along a trajectory toward greater integration into a "one world" global political economy. Over the course of several decades, the major powers develop rules and institutions for joint management of the global system. The United States and the other democratic states retain their alliance partnerships, but more encompassing institutions emerge, bringing all the great powers together within regional and global governance structures. It is a world without grand ideological divides and conflicts, where all states are deeply integrated within a unitary global system governed by the rule of law and centrally organized international institutions that place strict limits on the returns to power.

By furthering China's miraculous growth and liberal socialization, this transition from the current unipolar system to a future bipolar or multipolar one, in which the great powers (old and new) find ways to build an architecture for joint management of the system, suggests a peaceful path to the ultimate demise of U.S. hegemony. For China to become a stakeholder within the future system, several implications follow. First, the vision of a modified liberal order assumes that democracy and human rights, as originated in the West, are universally valid norms. From this perspective, China must continue to develop its internal politics to become a more respected and "normal" country within international society.[94]

Second, China has been a hugely successful player under the existing order, which states consider legitimate because it benefits not just the United States but all countries willing to invest in the system and abide by its rules. Because the Western-led order has provided China with unparalleled opportunities to become a stronger, safer, and more respected country, China should largely pursue a grand strategy of "bandwagoning" and "transcendency," participating in international regimes and forming a largely accommodative relationship with the United States and the community of Western nations.[95] This vision also acknowledges the positive effects that U.S. provision of global public goods has had on China, as well as the deep economic interdependence between China and the United States. While Western strategists debate how to manage the rise of China, some Chinese scholars worry about the damaging effects that a rapidly declining America would have on China and the world.[96] The United States would still protect its core areas of hegemony (finance and security), while sharing responsibilities in less crucial areas with emerging powers. The most realistic and prudent goal for China, therefore, is not to challenge the core areas of U.S. hegemony but to increase China's power and prestige in less crucial areas.[97] In this way, a rising China can become not just a stakeholder but an indispensable pillar of the "one world" capitalist system.[98]

A third implication is that democratic liberalism is universally valid and that China should eventually become democratic. The vision of a modified liberal order accepts the notion that democracy is not only a universally valid norm but also one that could be helpful in overcoming many political problems.[99] Yu Keping, a leading Chinese intellectual and prominent figure in China's official think tank, published a widely read essay, emphasizing that "democracy is a good thing."[100] The question for China is not whether it will become democratic but when and how such a transition will happen.

Fourth, liberal economic ideas such as trade, a market economy, and economic globalization are keys to China's success. The vision of a modified liberal order holds that China's rapid growth is largely the result of domestic market-driven reforms and the embrace of economic globalization.[101] According to Shi Yinghong, professor of international relations at Renmin University in Beijing, China's "peaceful rise" is an extraordinary example of Richard Rosecrance's thesis about the rise of trading states in the contemporary world.[102]

A NEGOTIATED ORDER: THE SHIRKER STRATEGY IN A POWER DIFFUSION PROCESS

The stark dichotomy of China either confronting the existing order or becoming a full-fledged member of it perhaps simplifies a complex reality.[103] Between these two extremes, we posit a third vision of a negotiated order during a messy transition out of unipolarity—one more consistent with a power diffusion process of system change than with one based on the transition of power.[104] Change brought about by a power diffusion process would generate an international system in which states do not have the capacities to shape and direct the system. No state or group of states would be in control. Moreover, polarity would become less meaningful as a predictor of state behavior and system dynamics than it has been in the past—so much so that it might be more accurate to say that unipolarity will be replaced not by bi- or multipolarity but by nonpolarity.[105]

Both power transition theory and power diffusion theory posit that concentrated power will disperse over time. The theories disagree, however, about the likely consequences of this inevitable process of power deconcentration. Power transition theory sees it triggering large-scale war and system change, whereas power diffusion theory predicts peace and more system continuity than change. This is because power diffusion theory challenges the core logics and expectations of power transition theory. Most basically, power diffusion theory does not expect rising powers to become dissatisfied challengers. Far from aiming to overthrow the international order, rising powers are not eager to manage the existing international order. They would prefer, instead, that the declining hegemon pay the costs of order, while they free ride. If tensions arise among the unipole and the rising polar powers, it will be over this issue, namely, that the declining hegemon expects these powers to assume the role of supporters, while they attempt to shirk some of their responsibilities and obligations. Frustrated by the free-riding behavior of its peer competitors and seeking to stem the tide of decline, the hegemon will ultimately retrench from its global commitments, leaving no state or group of states to manage the international system.

While the power diffusion model predicts shirking behavior, it does not expect the coming poles to be spoilers. After all, the rising powers are doing far better than everyone else under the current order. Why would they seek its overthrow? Why would they choose an enormously costly global war of uncertain outcome to destroy an order that has demonstrably worked for them, only to replace it with an untested order that they have to pay the costs to manage? The traditional notion of prestige (as the reputation for power that serves as the everyday currency of international politics) matters most when powerful states have serious material conflicts of interests, disagreements over international norms and rules, and expectations that they will settle their differences by fighting. Conflicts and expectations of this kind are largely absent today and are unlikely to arise in the future.

The diffusion of power occurs spontaneously as a result of differential growth rates among nations.[106] This process occurs peacefully because the restored global balance arises without traditional balancing behavior in the system's core. In a world in which (1) security is plentiful, (2) territory is devalued, and (3) a robust liberal consensus exists, the rising great powers will behave more akin to rational egoists driven to maximize their absolute gains than defensive or offensive positionalists, who seek to avoid relative losses or make relative gains. Rational egoists driven to maximize absolute gains are inward-looking actors unconcerned with the fate of others or the larger system in which they are embedded. If global order persists, it will do so without an orderer. It is also worth noting that complex adaptive systems often succumb to precipitous and unexpected change, and so the restored global balance of power may not arise gradually and predictably as the next phase in a smooth cycle.[107] Instead, U.S. power and the American global order may simply collapse.

For China, the vision of a negotiated order supports a hedging strategy of avoiding direct confrontation with the United States but preparing favorable conditions for China to shape an emerging world order in the long term. It is a strategy that appears most consistent with what China is currently doing.[108] First, this approach neither rejects Western culture nor ignores the potential values of traditional Chinese ideas. Instead, it champions an order of "peaceful coexistence with differences," in which the Chinese worldview is recognized by the United States and the rest of the world as being different but legitimate.[109] This vision refrains from posing Chinese ideas as a universally applicable alternative model that directly confronts Western ideas.

Second, the vision of a negotiated order does not reject the legitimacy of U.S. hegemony.[110] Instead, it critiques the current order on its own terms. For instance, China is using the notion of democracy against the United States to contest its hegemonic behavior. Despite the promotion of liberal democracy having long been the capstone of U.S. foreign policy, Chinese intellectuals have critiqued the contradictions of U.S. liberal democracy at home and abroad. In domestic politics, the U.S. government has applied checks and balances to protect democracy and the rule of law, whereas in international politics it seeks to preserve its dominant status so that it can act without constraints.[111] In a supposedly "democratic" world

order, Chinese intellectuals ask, how can the United States assume the roles of police, prosecutor, and judge?[112]

Third, although the vision of a negotiated order does not reject liberal democracy, it demands that the practices and meanings of Chinese democracy be adjusted to fit the specific cultural context. Given the pressure of global constitutive norms of democracy, many Chinese leaders and scholars have increasingly come to use the term "democracy" to describe the goal of China's political development. In their view, no matter what kind of political arrangements define China's future, the overall system must be called a "democracy."[113]

Finally, the vision of a negotiated order takes a flexible and pragmatic approach to economic policymaking. On the relationship between the state and markets, for instance, Chinese Premier Wen Jiabao argues that the combination of both "the invisible hand" and "the visible hand" explains China's economic success.[114]

A core prediction of this "power diffusion" future is that China, like other emerging great powers, will attempt to shirk its newfound global responsibilities and obligations. Given the speed and size of its economic miracle, China can be expected to experience growing pains as it transforms from a regional to a global player. It may even be wary of assuming this new role. After all, Chinese officials have much to fear: their nation is heading to either superpower status or economic and social implosion. China's potential is great, but its domestic pitfalls are many. For instance, China is a rapidly aging society with demographic trends accelerated by China's coercive attempt to limit population growth. The biggest question hanging over China, of course, is its political stability, especially during a global recession that may turn into a global depression. The bottom line is that China is strong abroad but fragile at home.[115] Thus, China maybe reluctant to take on major international responsibilities with respect to the global economic, climate change, and security crises. Instead, it may choose to focus inward, negotiating favorable international deals, while shouldering less global burdens than others (including the United States) will want and expect it to bear.

Under this scenario, the United States will encourage China to play a larger global role and will not view China's increased global influence as a threat to U.S. hegemony or interests. To the contrary, the United States will gladly offer China more prestige. In return, however, Washington will expect Beijing to shoulder greater international responsibilities and obligations. This "prestige at a price" trade-off is, in our view, key to understanding the relationship of a rising power and a declining hegemon. Surprisingly, it is a trade-off that has gone unrecognized by power transition theory. Instead, the theory expects all rising powers to seek prestige commensurate with their relative growth in capabilities, and it is this unmet demand for prestige that triggers hegemonic wars.

Do rising challengers to hegemony invariably demand increased prestige, as power transition theory claims? Consider the last hegemonic leadership transition. During the 1930s, a declining Britain—one gravely imperiled by threats in Europe and elsewhere and too weak to both defend its interests and manage the international system—grudgingly decided that it was time for the United States to become the global leader. As the British persistently grumbled, however, the United States demanded unparalleled prestige but was unwilling to pay the price of increased global responsibilities and obligations associated with an exalted position in the international pecking order.

Roughly the same problem exists today and, if this scenario plays out, will persist in the future. The United States complains that China wants enhanced prestige but not the responsibilities that global leaders are obligated to perform. While some Western observers argue that China must be coerced into taking appropriate actions when global crises arise, it is useful to recall that the United States accepted leadership of the system commensurate with its actual power only after Japan attacked Pearl Harbor in 1941, and in the aftermath of World War II, when it emerged as the only victor willing and able to construct a liberal international order. In fact, most rising powers throughout history have been less than eager to assume the responsibilities associated with system management.

Thus, during the global financial crisis of 2008, it was widely expected that China would play a larger role on the world stage. Yet, as David Shambaugh pointed out, "China doesn't want to lead the world—it doesn't even want to be seen as a leader of the developing world."[116] Little surprise, then, that Chinese leaders said "no thanks" to the development of a G-2—a group of two advocated by Zbigniew Brzezinski that would have elevated China to the status of the United States' co-managing partner on issues such as trade and currency reform, climate change, food safety, peace and stability in East Asia, the proliferation of weapons of mass destruction, and perhaps even the Israeli-Palestinian conflict.[117]

Chinese strategists have begun to explore seriously the geopolitical implications of the financial crisis of 2008, particularly the boost it has given China's international status and the appeal of its economic model with respect to the developing world. As Wu Xinbo, a professor at Fudan University in Shanghai, opines:

In the post-Cold War era, the U.S. model used to be hailed as the only way to economic prosperity. Now, the Chinese model seems to provide an alternative. To be sure, the Chinese model is not perfect and is actually confronted with many challenges such as a widening income gap, serious environment pollution, and rampant corruption. Yet, the record of tiding over two financial crises (the 1998–1999 Asian financial crisis and the 2008–2009 global financial crisis) and securing three decades of a high economic growth rate testifies to its strength. Unlike Washington, Beijing does not like to boast of its model and impose it on others, but the increased appeal of the Chinese experience will certainly enhance Beijing's international status and augment its influence among developing countries.[118]

For the moment, China's political elites and bureaucracies—ill-prepared for the country's sudden high profile in global affairs—remain resistant to changing its global status and obligations, emphasizing instead that China remains a developing country and, therefore, need not take on new and unwanted responsibilities. At the UN General Assembly in September 2010, for instance, Premier Wen Jiabo urged the international audience to recognize "the real China," which is not a superpower but a mere "developing country" whose further progress is constrained by a shortage of resources, energy, and complex environmental issues.[119]

In sum, the lack of U.S.-Chinese cooperation stems neither from the failure of Washington to acknowledge how much China matters nor U.S. unwillingness to grant China more status and prestige. Rather it derives from China's tendency to shirk its contributions to global governance at this stage of its development as well as mismatched interests, values, and capabilities within the U.S.-Chinese relationship.[120]

Conclusion

The current unipolar order is unprecedented and therefore a condition rife with uncertainty and ambiguity. For all the real and imagined dangers posed by U.S. hegemony, however, a balance of power has yet to emerge. We have argued that a key reason for this missing balance is that this type of behavior under unipolarity means, by definition, the overthrow of the current system—tantamount

to the goal of an unlimited-aims revisionist power. For active and intense balancing campaigns to commence, therefore, peer competitors to U.S. power and prestige must first undermine the legitimacy of the American order. Otherwise, they risk being portrayed as dangerous threats to international order. Moreover, without the requisite power to balance against the United States, the other major powers have little choice but to employ "weapons of the weak": dissident rhetoric and cost-imposing strategies short of actual balancing behavior. These antihegemonic discursive and diplomatic strategies lay the groundwork for the more formidable revisionist project of dislodging the United States from its preeminent position.

As evidence that we are in a delegitimation phase, we have described the recent arts of resistance by China, the United States' most viable peer competitor. A skeptic might say that these delegitimating discourses and their accompanying low-level, cost-imposing policies are simply empty posturing—just hollow posing and, as such, not intended to be acted out in earnest. China makes these public statements either to gain political leverage with the United States on various issues of vital concern to them or to impress their domestic audiences or both. These domestic audiences want to see some defiance by their country's leaders of what they perceive as U.S. global imperialism.[121] Perhaps. But larger forces may be at work here; and historical evidence suggests that deviant discourses and practices presage rebellions or, at the least, are preconditions for them.

Another explanation for this anti-American rhetoric is that emerging non-Western powers, unable to balance against or control the exercise of U.S. power, can only voice their displeasure with U.S. foreign policies. Harsh speeches serve as a harmless catharsis that substitutes for aggressive action. Once again, there may be some truth to this "safety valve" hypothesis, but social psychological experiments have yielded little support for it. Instead, subjects who were unjustly harmed experienced little or no reduction in their level of frustration and anger through forms of aggressive expression that left the source of anger untouched. Thus, speeches and other acts of anger that fall short of actual direct injury to the frustrating agent are not alternatives to eventual outbursts but rather preparations for them.[122]

Whatever the calculations behind China's current delegitimating activities, for a balance to emerge against the United States, its rule must be "exposed" as dangerous to the wealth and security of the other great powers. A similar situation existed in the nineteenth century under *Pax Britannica*. At that time, Friedrich List implored the other countries of Europe to form a continental alliance and pool their naval power to counterbalance British supremacy in naval and manufacturing power:

> It has always been felt that the ultimate aim of politics must be the equalization of the nations. That which people call the European balance of power has always been nothing else than the endeavors of the less powerful to impose a check on the encroachments of the more powerful. . . . That the idea of this Continental system will ever recur, that the necessity of realizing it will the more forcibly impress itself on the Continental nations in a proportion as the preponderance of England in industry, wealth, and power further increases, is already very clear, and will continually become more evident. . . . An effective Continental system can only originate from the free union of the Continental powers, and succeed only in the case it has for its object (and also effect) an equal participation in the advantages which result from it.[123]

As List understood, the strength of a revisionist challenge, whether from a single dissatisfied state or a coalition of such powers, is not discerned from the challenger's current capability to destroy the existing status quo. Rather, the challenge derives its strength from the indispensable need to restore a balance of power.[124] This will not be easy, however. The culture of hegemony attempts to eliminate alternatives to it by transforming everything that is not inevitable into the improbable. Under unipolarity, the structure of power and prestige come to be taken for granted to the point where dramatic displays of hegemonic power and coercion become unnecessary.[125]

While the consensus opinion is that U.S. power is eroding, the legitimacy of the United States' international order and authority to rule have not, to this point, been seriously undermined. Any challenger that seeks to restore global balance-of-power dynamics, therefore, must put forward an alternative idea of order that appeals to other powerful states. Delegitimizing U.S. unipolarity and proposing a viable new order are prerequisite exercises for traditional balancing behavior to commence.

NOTES

1. Condoleezza Rice, "Rethinking the National Interest: American Realism for a New World," *Foreign Affairs*, Vol. 87, No. 4 (July/August 2008), p. 2.

2. Judith L. Goldstein, Miles Kahler, Robert O. Keohane, and Anne-Marie Slaughter, eds., *Legalization and World Politics* (Cambridge, Mass.: MIT Press, 2001); Anne-Marie Slaughter, "The Real New World Order," *Foreign Affairs*, Vol. 76, No. 5 (September/October 1997), pp. 183–197; Anne-Marie Slaughter, "America's Edge: Power in the Networked Century," *Foreign Affairs*, Vol. 88, No. 1 (January/February 2009), pp. 94–113; Luis Cabrera, *Political Theory of Global Justice: A Cosmopolitan Case for the World State* (London: Routledge, 2004); Kwame Anthony Appiah, *Cosmopolitanism: Ethics in a World of Strangers* (New York: W.W. Norton, 2007); David Held, *Democracy and the Global Order: From the Modern State to Cosmopolitan Governance* (Stanford, Calif.: Stanford University Press, 1996); and Daniele Archibugi and David Held, eds., *Cosmopolitan Democracy: An Agenda for a New World Order* (London: Polity, 1999).

3. George H.W. Bush and Brent Scowcroft, *A World Transformed* (New York: Alfred A. Knopf, 1998); and Robert Kagan, *The Return of History and the End of Dreams* (New York: Alfred A. Knopf, 2008).

4. Christopher Layne, "The Unipolar Illusion: Why New Great Powers Will Rise," *International Security*, Vol. 17, No. 4 (Spring 1993), pp. 5–51; John J. Mearsheimer, "Back to the Future: Instability in Europe after the Cold War," *International Security*, Vol. 15, No. 1 (Summer 1990), pp. 5–56; Kenneth N. Waltz, "The Emerging Structure of International Politics," *International Security*, Vol. 18, No. 2 (Fall 1993), pp. 44–79; and Kenneth N. Waltz, "Structural Realism after the Cold War," *International Security*, Vol. 25, No. 1 (Summer 2000), pp. 5–41.

5. Fareed Zakaria, *The Post-American World* (New York: W.W. Norton, 2008); National Intelligence Council, *Global Trends 2025: A Transformed World* (Washington, D.C.: U.S. Government Printing Office, November 2008); and Christopher Layne, "The Unipolar Illusion Revisited: The Coming End of the United States' Unipolar Moment," *International Security*, Vol. 31, No. 2 (Fall 2006), pp. 7–41.

6. See, for example, John J. Mearsheimer, *The Tragedy of Great Power Politics* (New York: W.W. Norton, 2001), chap. 10.

7. See David A. Lake, "Beneath the Commerce of Nations: A Theory of International Economic Structures," *International Studies Quarterly*, Vol. 28, No. 2 (June 1984), pp. 143–170.

8. Robert Gilpin, *War and Change in World Politics* (New York: Cambridge University Press, 1983), pp. 197–209.

9. The foregoing discussion follows Robert Gilpin's theory of hegemonic war and international change in ibid. Gilpin's theory is related to but not the same as power transition theory. The classic statements of power transition are A.F.K. Organski, *World Politics* (New York: Alfred A. Knopf, 1958); and A.F.K. Organski and Jacek Kugler, *The War Ledger* (Chicago: University of Chicago Press, 1980). See also Ronald L. Tammen, Jacek Kugler, Douglas Lemke, Allan C. Stam III, Mark Abdollahian, Carole Alsharabati, Brian Efird, and A.F.K. Organski, *Power Transitions: Strategies for the 21st Century* (New York: Chatham House, 2000); Jonathan M. DiCicco and Jack S. Levy, "The Power Transition Research Program: A Lakatosian Analysis," in Colin Elman and Miriam Fendius Elman, eds., *Progress in International Relations Theory: Appraising the Field* (Cambridge, Mass.: MIT Press, 2003), pp. 109–157; Jacek Kugler and Douglas Lemke, eds., *Parity and War: Evaluations and Extensions of The War Ledger* (Ann Arbor; University of Michigan Press, 1996); Woosang Kim and James D. Morrow, "When Do Power Shifts Lead to War?" *American Journal of Political Science*, Vol. 36, No. 4 (November 1992), pp. 896–922; and Douglas Lemke and William Reed, "Regime Types and Status Quo Evaluations: Power Transition Theory and the Democratic Peace," *International Interactions*, Vol. 22, No. 2 (October 1996), pp. 143–164.

10. Nazli Choucri and Robert C. North, *Nations in Conflict: National Growth and International Violence* (San Francisco, Calif.: W.H. Freeman, 1975), p. 28.

11. Without considering international legitimacy, realist theory should assume that the hegemon and rising powers are equally threatening to each other. Kenneth N. Waltz himself emphasizes that the hegemon can appear more threatening than the rising power. See Waltz, *Realism and International Politics* (New York: Routledge, 2008), p. xiii. The legitimacy gap between the hegemon and rising power often accounts for why the latter appears more threatening than the former. Currently, the legitimacy of U.S. hegemony is widely recognized, whereas the status of a potential peer competitor is unconsolidated and uncertain.

12. For the strategy of delegitimation, see Stephen M. Walt, *Taming American Power: The Global Response to U.S. Primacy* (New York: W.W. Norton, 2005), pp. 160–178.

13. For similar cyclical patterns of international politics, see George Modelski, "The Long Cycle of Global Politics and the Nation-State," *Comparative Studies in Society and History*, Vol. 20, No. 2 (April 1978), pp.

214–235; and George Modelski and William R. Thompson, *Leading Sectors and World Powers: The Coevolution of Global Economics and Politics* (Columbia: University of South Carolina Press, 1996).

14. There are many ways to measure "revisionism" in international relations. Some scholars argue that the hegemon itself can be revisionist if it breaks the rules of its own global order or does not follow prevailing international norms, or both. See Robert Jervis, "The Remaking of a Unipolar World," *Washington Quarterly*, Vol. 29, No. 3 (Summer 2006), pp. 7–19; and Ian Hurd, "Breaking and Making Norms: American Revisionism and Crises of Legitimacy," *International Politics*, Vol. 44, Nos. 2–3 (March 2007), pp. 194–213. For more on the distinctions between revisionist and status quo states and their associated behaviors, see Alastair Iain Johnston, "Is China a Status Quo Power?" *International Security*, Vol. 27, No. 4 (Spring 2003), p. 56; Randall L. Schwelter, *Deadly Imbalances: Tripolarity and Hitler's Strategy of World Conquest* (New York: Columbia University Press, 1998); and Jason W. Davidson, *The Origins of Revisionist and Status-quo States* (New York: Palgrave, 2006).

15. For many observers, the Georgia conflict indicates that Russia is taking a more confrontational approach to the U.S.-led order. In contrast, China's "peaceful rise" or "peaceful development" strategy emphasizes accommodation with the West. For analysis of the Russian challenge, see Stephen Sestanovich, "What Has Moscow Done? Rebuilding U.S.-Russian Relations," *Foreign Affairs,* Vol. 87, No. 6 (November–December 2008), pp. 12–28. Of course, Russia is a great power in decline, having been reduced to little more than a petro-state. China, on the other hand, though not yet a peer competitor of the United States, is a comprehensive rising power with a complete portfolio of great power capabilities.

16. For the most comprehensive analysis of the structural hurdles to balancing under unipolarity, see Stephen G. Brooks and William C. Wohlforth, *World Out of Balance: International Relations and the Challenge of American Primacy* (Princeton, N.J.: Princeton University Press, 2010). Compared with other systems, unipolarity is the most dangerous structural condition for China's rise, which partly explains why China has pursued a reassurance strategy since the end of the Cold War. See Jia Qingguo, "Danji Shijie yu Zhongguo de Heping Fazhan [Unipolarity and China's peaceful development]," *International Politics Quarterly* (Beijing), No. 4 (November 2007), pp. 51–64. For an overview of China's grand strategy, see Avery Goldstein, *Rising to the Challenge: China's Grand Strategy and International Security* (Stanford, Calif.: Stanford University Press, 2005).

17. See, for example, George Modelski, *Long Cycles in World Politics* (Seattle; University of Washington Press, 1987); and George Modelski, ed., *Exploring long Cycles* (Boulder, Colo.: Lynne Rienner, 1987).

18. Karen Rasler and William R. Thompson, "Global War and the Political Economy of Structural Change," in Manus I. Midlarsky, ed., *Handbook of War Studies*, Vol. 2 (Ann Arbor: University of Michigan Press, 2000), p. 315.

19. Modelski, *Long Cycles in World Politics.*

20. In terms of timing, our notion of a delegitimation/deconcentration phase is closer to that of the "challenge" phase offered by Brian M. Pollins and Kevin P. Murrin: " 'Challenge' is a time in which rising new powers begin to take issue with the existing order. This is followed by a period of jockeying among contenders, a period we label 'Balancing,' to reflect the important alliance dynamics of this time." Pollins and Murrin, "Where Hobbes Meets Hobson: Core Conflict and Colonialism, 1495–1985," *International Studies Quarterly*, Vol. 43, No. 3 (September 1999), p. 433.

21. James C. Scott, *Domination and the Arts of Resistance: Hidden Transcripts* (New Haven, Conn.: Yale University Press, 1990), p. 138.

22. As Scott puts it, "Relations of dominations are, at the same time, relations of resistance." Ibid., p. 45.

23. James C. Scott, *Weapons of the Weak: Everyday Forms of Peasant Resistance* (New Haven, Conn.: Yale University Press, 1985), p. xv.

24. Ibid., p. 23.

25. Scott writes, "It is possible and common for human actors to conceive of a line of action, that is, at the moment, either impractical or impossible. Thus a person may dream of a revenge or a millennial kingdom of justice that may never occur. On the other hand, as circumstances change, it may become possible to act on those dreams." Ibid., p. 38.

26. Ibid., p. 25.

27. What we are calling "cost-imposing" strategies others have called "soft balancing." See Michael E. Brown, Owen R. Coté Jr., Sean M. Lynn-Jones, and Steven E. Miller, eds., *Primacy and Its Discontents: American Power and International Stability* (Cambridge, Mass.: MIT Press, 2009).

28. For example, Israel said that it would dismantle its settlements in the occupied territories but did so very slowly while expanding others without notifying the United States.

29. An example is Turkey's refusal to give the United States access to its bases prior to the invasion of Iraq in 2003.

30. A Chinese blockade of Taiwan's trade through the destruction of ports or shipping would be an example of this behavior.

31. Robert S. Chose, Emily B. Hill, and Paul Kennedy, "Pivotal States and U.S. Strategy," *Foreign Affairs*, Vol. 75, No. 1 (January/February 1996), pp. 33–51.

32. Scott, *Weapons of the Weak;* and Kevin J. O'Brien and Lianjiang Li, *Rightful Resistance in Rural China* (New York: Cambridge University Press, 2006). See also Martha Finnemore, "Legitimacy, Hypocrisy, and the Social Structure of Unipolarity: Why Being a Unipole Isn't All It's Cracked Up to Be," *World Politics*, Vol. 61, No. 1 (January 2009), pp. 58–85. In domestic and transnational contexts, nonviolent resistance is a forceful alternative to violence that can pose effective challenges to opponents; indeed, nonviolent resistance is sometimes more effective than violent resistance. See Maria J. Stephan and Erica Chenoweth, "Why Civil Resistance Works: The Strategic Logic of Nonviolent Conflict," *International Security*, Vol. 33, No. 1 (Summer 2008), pp. 7–44.

33. See David Edelstein and M. Taylor Fravel, "Life on the Great Power Frontier: Capabilities, Influence, and Trajectory in China's Rise," unpublished manuscript, Georgetown University and Massachusetts Institute of Technology, 2010. This is also similar to the notion of "reformist revisionist" proposed in Barry Buzan, "China in International Society: Is 'Peaceful Rise' Possible?" *Chinese Journal of International Politics*, Vol. 3, No. 1 (Spring 2010), p. 14.

34. Contrary to standard notions of hegemony and false consciousness, (1) most subordinate actors (whether classes, racial minorities, or weak states) can "penetrate and demystify the prevailing ideology"; (2) inevitability is not seen as implying legitimacy; and (3) hegemonic ideologies inherently beget contestation, because they "represent an idealization which creates the contradictions that permit it to be criticized in its own terms." Scott, *Weapons of the Weak*, pp. 317–318.

35. See Pierre Bourdieu, *Outline of a Theory of Practice* (New York: Cambridge University Press, 1977); and Pierre Bourdieu, *Language and Symbolic Power* (Cambridge, Mass.: Harvard University Press, 1991).

36. For these two assumptions, see O'Brien and Li, *Rightful Resistance in Rural China*, pp. 2, 15–24.

37. Imperial Germany's demand for its rightful "place in the sun" is an example of this type of grievance. Germany did not seek an overthrow of the rules of the system, but a modification of the division of territory that reflected Germany's dramatic gains in economic and military capabilities relative to the more established powers.

38. See Kevin J. O'Brien, "Rightful Resistance," *World Politics*, Vol. 49, No. 1 (October 1996), pp. 48–51.

39. This is consistent with the arguments made in G. John Ikenberry, *After Victory: Institutions, Strategic Restraint, and the Rebuilding of Order after Major Wars* (Princeton, N.J.: Princeton University Press, 2001).

40. Rising powers often fantasize about world order, and in this sense contemporary China is not a unique case. See, for instance, Liu Mingfu, *Zhongguo Meng: Hou Meiguo Shidai de DaGuo Siwei yu Zhanlile Dingwei* [China's dream: Major power thinking and

strategic posture in a post-American era] (Beijing: China Friendship Publishing Company, 2010). It should be noted that Liu's book is controversial in China.

41. Although our argument about the indeterminacy of China's intentions contradicts Iain Johnston's claim that China is presently a status quo power, Johnston admits that although he detects a "decline in the level and scope of revisionist interest in China's overall diplomacy," this "trend [could] reverse in the future." Johnston, "Is China a Status Quo Power?" p. 56.

42. Scott, *Domination and the Arts of Resistance*, p. 138.

43. Joseph S. Nye Jr., *Bound to Lead: The Changing Nature of American Power* (New York: Basic Books, 1991); and Joseph S. Nye Jr., *Soft Power: The Means to Success in World Politics* (New York: PublicAffairs, 2004).

44. Jiang Zemin's report to the Sixteenth Congress of the Chinese Communist Party, quoted in Pan Zhongqi, "Change of International Security Order and China's Period of Important Strategic Opportunities," in Shanghai Institute for International Studies, ed., *China and Asia's Security* (Singapore: Marshall Cavendish International, 2005), p. 79.

45. Thomas J. Christensen, "Fostering Stability or Creating a Monster? The Rise of China and U.S. Policy toward East Asia," *International Security*, Vol. 31, No. 1 (Summer 2006), pp. 81–126; and Thomas J. Christensen, "Shaping the Choices of a Rising China: Recent Lessons for the Obama Administration," *Washington Quarterly*, Vol. 32, No. 3 (July 2009), pp. 89–104.

46. Wang Jisi, "China's Search for Stability with America," *Foreign Affairs*, Vol. 84, No. 5 (September/October 2005), p. 44.

47. See David M. Lampton, *The Three Faces of Chinese Power: Might, Money, and Minds* (Berkeley: University of California Press, 2008), p. 2.

48. China does not need to match U.S. military power to pose problems and achieve its own limited political objectives. See Thomas J. Christensen, "Posing Problems without Catching Up: China's Rise and Challenges for U.S. Security Policy," *International Security*, Vol. 25, No. 4 (Spring 2001), pp. 5–40.

49. David Shambaugh, "China Engages Asia: Reshaping the Regional Order," *International Security*, Vol. 29, No. 3 (Winter 2004/05), pp. 64–99.

50. According to Chinese strategist Yan Xuetong, the priority of China's diplomacy is to increase the capability of agenda setting in international institutions, not to satisfy the demands of the U.S.-led international community. See "Xuyan" [preface], in Yan Xuetong and Sun Xuefeng, *Zhongguo Jueqi Jiqi Zhanlue* [The rise of China and its strategy] (Beijing: Peking University Press, 2005), p. 5.

51. Chinese leaders emphasize that WTO membership was primarily a political issue rather than a purely economic issue. See Li Peng, *Li Peng Waishi Riji* [Foreign affairs diary of Li Peng] (Beijing: Xinhua, 2008), p. 806.

52. Quoted in C. Fred Bergsten, "A Partnership of Equals: How Washington Should Respond to China's Economic Challenge," *Foreign Affairs*, Vol. 87, No. 4 (July/August 2008), pp. 57–69, at p. 65.

53. For China's proposals during the Group of Twenty summit on the international financial crisis, see "Hu Urges Revamp of Finance System," *China Daily*, November 17, 2008.

54. Daniel W. Drezner, "U.S. Debt to China: Implications and Repercussions," testimony before the U.S.-China Economic and Security Review Commission, 111th Cong., 2d sess., February 25, 2010; and Daniel W. Drezner, "Bad Debts: Assessing China's Financial Influence in Great Power Politics," *International Security*, Vol. 32, No. 2 (Fall 2009), pp. 7–45.

55. More specifically, Zhou Xiaochuan proposed that the dollar be replaced as the world's reserve currency by special drawing rights. See Jamil Anderlini, "China Calls for New Reserve Currency," *Financial Times*, March 24, 2009.

56. See Paul Krugman, "China's Dollar Trap," *New York Times*, April 2, 2009; and Yu Yongding, "Zhongguo Shenxian Meiyuan Xianjing" [China is deeply trapped by U.S. dollars], *Di Yi Caijin Ribao*, May 31, 2010. Whether China can succeed in challenging the dominant status of the U.S. dollar is debatable. For a systematic examination of the dollar's status, see Eric

Helleiner and Jonathan Kirshner, eds., *The Future of the Dollar* (Ithaca, N.Y.: Cornell University Press, 2009); and Stephen S. Cohen and J. Bradford DeLong, *The End of Influence: What Happens When Other Countries Have the Money* (New York: Basic Books, 2010).

57. For the impracticalities of the proposal, see Barry Eichengreen, "The Dollar Dilemma: The World's Top Currency Faces Competition," *Foreign Affairs*, Vol. 88, No. 5 (September/October 2009), pp. 61–63. For the Chiang Mai Initiative, see Drezner, "U.S. Debt to China."

58. Most of the literature focuses on how China is "socialized" or "integrated" into the existing international society. See, for example, Alastair Iain Johnston, *Social States: China in International Institutions, 1980–2000* (Princeton, N.J.: Princeton University Press, 2007). In contrast, the other side of the story—how China might influence the evolution of norms in international institutions—has been relatively undertheorized, probably because this is a relatively new face of China's foreign policy. "Socialization," however, is typically understood as a two-way process: people are not only the targets of socialization but are also active agents who influence the content and outcomes of the process. See Kent L. Sandstrom, Daniel D. Martin, and Gary Alan Fine, *Symbols, Selves, and Social Reality: A Symbolic Interactionist Approach to Social Psychology and Sociology* (Los Angeles, Calif.: Roxbury, 2002), pp. 65–66.

59. Guo Shuyong, *Daguo Cheugzhang de Luoji: Xifang Daguo Jueqi de Guojizhengzhi Shehuixue fenxi* [The logic of the great power growth: A study of the rise of Western powers from the perspective of international political sociology] (Beijing: Peking University Press, 2006).

60. For the discussion of legitimate wars and the rise of China, see Guo Shuyong, "Legitimacy, War, and the Rise of China: An International Political Sociology Perspective," *Korean Journal of Defense Analysis*, Vol. 19, No. 1 (Spring 2007), pp. 47–77, at p. 47.

61. Stefan Stähle, "China's Shifting Attitude towards United Nations Peacekeeping Operations," *China Quarterly*, Vol. 195 (September 2008), pp. 631–655.

62. Richard Gowan and Franziska Brantner, "A Global Force for Human Rights? An Audit of European Power at the UN," Policy Paper (London: European Council on Foreign Relations, 2008), http://ecfr.3cdn.net/3a4f39da1b34463d16_tom6b928f.pdf.

63. Soft power "rests on the ability to shape the preference of others," according to Joseph Nye. "It is leading by example and attracting others to do what you want." Nye, *Soft Power*, pp. 5–6.

64. It is not necessarily true that every dimension of China's soft power diplomacy will become part of a zero-sum game with the United States. In some situations, China's increasing soft power might create opportunities for U.S.-Chinese cooperation. See Christensen, "Fostering Stability or Creating a Monster?" pp. 81–84. Moreover, China confronts significant barriers in its promotion of soft power. See Yanzhong Huang and Sheng Ding, "The Dragon's Underbelly: An Analysis of China's Soft Power," *East Asia*, Vol. 23, No. 4 (Winter 2006), pp. 22–44.

65. Joshua Kurlantzick, *Charm Offensive: How China's Soft Power Is Transforming the World* (New Haven, Conn.: Yale University Press, 2007), p. 6.

66. "Even if the People's Republic had done nothing in the world, the power of the Chinese example would have presented a major challenge to promoters of democracy," writes Mark Leonard. Leonard, *What Does China Think?* (New York: PublicAffairs, 2008), p. 124.

67. Bruce W. Jentleson and Steven Weber, "America's Hard Sell," *Foreign Policy*, No. 169 (November/December 2008), pp. 43–49, at p. 43.

68. See Stewart Patrick, "Irresponsible Stakeholders? The Difficulty of Integrating Rising Powers," *Foreign Affairs*, Vol. 89, No. 6 (November/December 2010), pp. 44–53.

69. Jentleson and Weber, "America's Hard Sell," pp. 46–47.

70. Thomas J. Christensen, Alastair Iain Johnston, and Robert S. Ross, "Conclusions and Future Directions," in Johnston and Ross, eds., *New Directions in the Study of China's Foreign Policy* (Stanford, Calif.: Stanford University Press, 2006), p. 380.

71. William A. Callahan's analysis of emerging Chinese visions of world order is insightful but limited, focusing on only one particular Chinese scholar, Zhao Tingyang. Although Zhao's philosophical thinking informs debates among some Chinese international relations experts, Zhao is also heavily criticized in China. See Callahan, "Chinese Visions of World Order: Post-hegemonic or a New Hegemony?" *International Studies Review*, Vol. 10, No. 4 (December 2008), pp. 749–61.

72. Chinese visions of international order partly depend on the uncertain prospect of its domestic politics, of which there is a parallel debate (e.g., democracy vs. resilient authoritarianism). For overviews of this debate, see Daniel C. Lynch, "Envisioning China's Political Future: Elite Responses to Democracy as a Global Constitutive Norm," *International Studies Quarterly*, Vol. 51, No. 3 (September 2007), pp. 701–22; and David Shambaugh, *China's Communist Party: Atrophy and Adaptation* (Berkeley: University of California Press, 2008), chap. 8.

73. We do not claim that any particular Chinese vision is accurate or unrealistic. Instead, we present what the Chinese think the future international order would look like from their perspective. Whether these Chinese visions are logically coherent (or historically accurate) is not our major concern here.

74. Beijing's strategies may shift as China continues to grow. The various strategies during different rising periods (early period vs. late period of rising) have been identified by several scholars. See Edelstein and Fravel, "Life on the Great Power Frontier"; Yan and Sun, *Zhougguo Jueqi Jiqi Zhanlue*, pp. 13–15; and Sheena Chestnut and Alastair Iain Johnston, "Is China Rising?" in Eva Paus, Penelope B. Prime, and Jon Western, eds., *Global Giant: Is China Changing the Rules of the Game?* (New York: Palgrave Macmillan 2009), pp. 237–260.

75. The four dimensions are adapted from Jentleson and Weber, "America's Hard Sell."

76. A similar trend is also occurring in China's thinking about its domestic political future. See Lynch, "Envisioning China's Political Future," p. 718.

77. Yong Deng, *China's Struggle for Status: The Realignment of International Relations* (New York: Cambridge University Press, 2008), pp. 53–54.

78. Again, we emphasize that Chinese revisionist alternatives to the current order are still embryonic and contested at this point. For example, Zhao Tingyang's Tianxia philosophy and Liu Mingfu's book, *China's Dream*, are controversial and hotly debated in China. Some argue, however, that China is already pursuing a spoiler strategy and that China's challenge is increasingly an ideational one. See, for example, Edward Friedman, "Appeasing a Rising Authoritarian China: Implications for Democracy and Peace," paper presented at the annual meeting of the International Studies Association, New York, New York, February 15, 2009; and Stefan Halper, *The Beijing Consensus: How China's Authoritarian Model Will Dominate the Twenty-first Century* (New York: Basic Books, 2010). For a counterargument, see Edward S. Steinfeld, *Playing Our Game: Why China's Rise Doesn't Threaten the West* (New York: Oxford University Press, 2010).

79. Tingyang Zhao, "Rethinking Empire from a Chinese Concept 'All-under-Heaven' (Tianxia)," *Social Identities*, Vol. 12, No. 1 (January 2006), pp. 29–41. For a comprehensive view of Zhao's Tianxia philosophy, see Zhao Tingyang, *Tianxia tixi: Shijie zhidu zhexue daolun* [The Tianxia system: A philosophy for the world institution] (Nanjing, China: Jiangsu jiaoyu chubanshe, 2005).

80. Victoria Tin-bor Hui argues that an interpretation of Chinese history as a benign Confucian order is historically inaccurate. See Hui, "How China Was Ruled," *American Interest*, Vol. 3, No. 4 (March–April 2008), pp. 53–65. In contrast, Zhao Tingyang argues that the contemporary "reconstruction" of traditional Chinese ideas is key, not the historical accuracy of those ideas. See Zhao, "Tianxia Tixi de Yige Jianyao Biaoshu" [An introduction of Tianxia (all-under-heaven) system], *World Economics and Politics*, October 2008, p. 85. Some Chinese scholars view the hierarchic nature of this alternative world as highly problematic. See Yaqing Qin, "Why Is There

No Chinese International Relations Theory?" *International Relations of the Asia-Pacific*, Vol. 7, No. 3 (September 2007), p. 330.

81. Zhao Tingyang, "Tianxia gainian yu shijie zhidu" [The Tianxia concept and the world system], in Qin Yaqing, ed., *Zhongguo Xuezhe Kan Shijie: Guoji Zhixue Juan* [Chinese scholars' views of the world: International order] (Beijing: New World Press, 2006), p. 6.

82. Ibid., p. 8.

83. Ibid.

84. Xiang Lanxing, "Jieyan Jueqi, Shenyan Hexle" [Stop talking "rise," be cautious about talking "harmony"], *Lianhe Zaobao*, March 26, 2006. See also Callahan, "Chinese Visions of World Order."

85. Callahan, "Chinese Visions of World Order."

86. Zhao, "Tianxia gainian yu shijie zhidu," pp. 30–31.

87. Pan Wei, "Toward a Consultative Rule of Law Regime in China," *Journal of Contemporary China*, Vol. 12, No. 34 (2003), pp. 3–43.

88. Yan Xuetong, "Xun Zi's Thoughts on International Politics and Their Implications," *Chinese Journal of International Politics*, Vol. 2, No. 1 (Summer 2008), p. 159.

89. For an overview, see Shiping Hua, "A Perfect World," *Wilson Quarterly*, Vol. 29, No. 4 (Autumn 2005), pp. 62–67.

90. Not all Chinese scholars, however, share this vision of building a Chinese school.

91. Ren Xiao, "Toward a Chinese School of International Relations?" in Wang Gungwu and Zheng Yongnian, eds., *China and the New International Order* (London: Routledge, 2008), pp. 296–297.

92. Yaqing Qin, "Guanxi benwei yu guocheng jiangou: Jiang Zhongguo linian zhiru guoji guanxi lilun" [Relationality and processual construction: Bringing Chinese ideas into international relations theory] *Zhongguo Shehui Kexue* [Social Sciences in China], No. 4 (2009), pp. 5–20; and Yaqing Qin, "International Society as a Process: Institutions, Identities, and China's Peaceful Rise," *Chinese Journal of International Politics*, Vol. 3, No. 2 (Summer 2010), pp. 129–153.

93. Jack L. Snyder, "Some Good and Bad Reasons for a Distinctively Chinese Approach to International Relations Theory," paper presented at the annual meeting of the American Political Science Association, Boston, Massachusetts, August 28–31, 2008, p. 6.

94. Yinghong Shi, "Fengwu Changyi Fangyanliang: Zhongguo Yinyou De Waijiao Zhexue he Shiji Dazhanlue" [To have a long vision: Diplomatic philosophy on external affairs and secular grand strategy for China in the 21st century], *Journal of HIT* (Social Science edition), Vol. 3, No. 2 (June 2001), p. 15.

95. Ibid., pp. 13–20.

96. Wang Yiwei, "Zhongguo Fuxin Bushi Fengxiang Meiguo Baquan" [China's rise is not to share the American hegemony], *Huanqiu Shibao*, January 17, 2008, http://column.huanqiu.com/wangyiwei/2008-01/48528.html.

97. Ibid.

98. Wang Yiwei, "China's Rise: An Unlikely Pillar of U.S. Hegemony," *Harvard International Review*, Vol. 29, No. 1 (Spring 2007), pp. 60–63.

99. Shi, "Fengwu Changyi Fangyanliang," p. 15.

100. For an English translation of this essay, see Yu Keping, *Democracy Is a Good Tiling: Essays on Politics, Society, and Culture in Contemporary China* (Washington, D.C.: Brookings Institution Press, 2008).

101. For a detailed documentation of this approach, see Steinfeld, *Playing Our Game.*

102. Yinghong Shi, "Zhongmei Guanxi Jiben Toushi He Zhanlue Fengxi" [U.S.-China relations: Basic perspectives and strategic analysis], *Forum of World Economy and Politics*, No. 4 (2007), p. 11. See also Richard Rosecrance, "Power and International Relations: The Rise of China and Its Effects," *International Studies Perspectives*, Vol. 7, No. 1 (February 2006), pp. 31–35.

103. Naazneen Barma, Ely Ratner, and Steven Weber, "Chinese Ways," *Foreign Affairs*, Vol. 87, No. 3 (May/June 2008), p. 166.

104. The existing international relations literature conceptualizes negotiated orders in a liberal political sense, such as in terms of "constitutional contracts" or "legislative bargaining." See Oran R.

Young, "Regime Dynamics: The Rise and Fall of International Regimes," *International Organization*, Vol. 36, No. 2 (Spring 1982), especially p. 283. We use this term in a broader sense, meaning the process of how actors with diverse preferences build and maintain an order through constant interactions and negotiations. This is closer to a sociological understanding of the term. See Gary Alan Fine, "Negotiated Orders and Organizational Cultures," *Annual Review of Sociology*, Vol. 10 (August 1984), p. 241. Chinese scholar Yaqing Qin expresses a similar idea to describe the ideational interaction between China and the West. See Yaqing Qin, "Yanjiu Shejie yu Xueshu Zhuanxin" [Research design for academic innovation], *World Economics and Politics*, No. 8 (2008), p. 76.

105. For the discussion of a nonpolar world or a world in which polarity is less important, see Richard N. Haass, "The Age of Nonpolarity," *Foreign Affairs*, Vol. 87, No. 3 (May/June 2008), pp. 44–56. For a discussion of power diffusion, see Randall L. Schweller, "Entropy and the Trajectory of World Politics: Why Polarity Has Become Less Meaningful," *Cambridge Review of International Affairs*, Vol. 23, No. 1 (March 2010), pp. 145–163; and Chen Yugang, Quanqiu Jingrong Weiji, and Melguo Shuailuo, "You Guoji Zhixu De Bianpinghua" (Global financial crisis, the United States' decline, and the flattening of international order], *World Economics and Politics*, No. 5 (2009), pp. 28–34.

106. Growth rates differ for many reasons: for example, innovation tends to cluster; the diffusion of technology benefits secondary and late movers (imitation costs are much lower than innovation costs); hegemons overpay for defense and become addicted to consumption, resulting in massive debt that eventually crowds out research and development spending; the ratio of retirees to workers; and so on.

107. Niall Ferguson, "Complexity and Collapse: Empires on the Edge of Chaos," *Foreign Affairs*, Vol. 89, No. 2 (March/April 2010), pp. 18–32; and Randall L. Schweller, "The Future Is Uncertain and the End Is Always Near," *Cambridge Review of International Affairs*.

108. This vision and strategy are related to the "rightful resistance" approach.

109. Ren Xiao, "Women Ruhe Duidai Chayi: Dui Hexie Shijie zhi neihai De Yige Tantao" [How we should deal with differences: An inquiry into the meaning of a harmonious world], *Foreign Affairs Review* (Beijing), No. 97 (August 2007), pp. 37–39.

110. Wang, "China's Search for Stability with America." See also Wang Jisi, "America in Asia: How Much Does China Care?" *Global Asia*, Vol. 2, No. 2 (Fall 2007), pp. 27–28.

111. Wang Jisi, "Meiguo Baquan de Luoji" [The logic of American hegemony], in Qin, *Zhongguo Xuezhe Kan Shijie*, p. 95.

112. Ren Xiao, "'Meilijian Diguo' Lun de Xingqi Yu Meiguo De DaZhanlue" [The rise of "the American empire" proposition and America's grand strategy], in Qin, *Zhongguo Xuezhe Kan Shijie*, p. 150.

113. For a summary of such an orientation, see Lynch, "Envisioning China's Political Future," pp. 701–22.

114. "Transcript of Interview with Chinese Premier Wen Jiabao," *CNN.com/asia*, September 28, 2008, http://edition.cnn.com/2008/WORLD/asiapcf/09/29/chinese.premier.transcript/.

115. Susan L. Shirk, *China: Fragile Superpower: How China's Internal Politics Could Derail Its Peaceful Rise* (New York: Oxford University Press, 2007); and Wang Jisi, "Inside China," *Global Asia*, Vol. 5, No. 2 (Summer 2010), pp. 8–9.

116. Quoted in Melinda Liu, "Analyze This: On the Eve of Obama's Visit, China Reveals an Identity Crisis," *Newsweek*, November 14, 2009, http://www.newsweek.com/2009/11/13/analyze-this.html.

117. Elizabeth C. Economy and Adam Segal, "The G-2 Mirage: Why the United States and China Are Not Ready to Upgrade Ties," *Foreign Affairs*, Vol. 88, No. 3 (May/June 2009), pp. 14–23; and Jian Junbo, "China Says 'No Thanks' to G2," *Asian Times*, May 29, 2009, http://www.atimes.com/atimes/China/KE29Ad01.html.

118. Wu Xinbo, "Understanding the Geopolitical Implications of the Global Financial Crisis," *Washington Quarterly*, Vol. 33, No. 4 (October 2010), p. 159.

119. Wu Jiao and Zhang Yuwen, "China Will Focus on Peaceful Development: Wen," *China Daily*, September 24, 2010, http://www.chinadaily.com.cn/chlna/2010WenUN/2010-09/24/content_11340567.htm.

120. These mismatches within the relationship center on Washington's and Beijing's dramatically different views on sovereignty, sanctions, and the use of force. See Economy and Segal, "The G-2 Mirage," p. 16.

121. For a response to this type of criticism that involves the "infrapolitics" of subordinate groups, see Scott, *Domination and the Arts of Resistance*, chap. 7.

122. Leonard Berkowitz, *Aggression: A Social Psychological Analysis* (New York: McGraw-Hill, 1962), pp. 204–27.

123. Friedrich List, *The National System of Political Economy*, trans. S.S. Lloyd (Roseville, Calif.: Dry Bones, 2000), pp. 98, 110.

124. "The proximate task of politics," writes List, "always consists in clearly perceiving in what respect the alliance and equalization of the different interests is at the moment most pressing, and to strive that until this equalization is attained all other questions may be suspended and kept in the background." Ibid., p. 98.

125. Zygmunt Bauman, *Socialism: The Active Utopia* (New York: Holmes and Meier, 1976), p. 123.

Martha Finnemore

LEGITIMACY, HYPOCRISY, AND THE SOCIAL STRUCTURE OF UNIPOLARITY
Why Being a Unipole Isn't All It's Cracked Up to Be

One would think that unipoles have it made. After all, unipolarity is a condition of minimal constraint. Unipoles should be able to do pretty much what they want in the world since, by definition, no other state has the power to stop them. In fact, however, the United States, arguably the closest thing to a unipole we have seen in centuries, has been frustrated in many of its policies since it achieved that status at the end of the Cold War. Much of this frustration surely stems from nonstructural causes—domestic politics, leaders' poor choices, bad luck. But some sources of this frustration may be embedded in the logic of contemporary unipolarity itself.

Scholarship on polarity and system structures created by various distributions of power has focused almost exclusively on material power; the structure of world politics, however, is social as much as it is material.[1] Material distributions of power alone tell us little about the kind of politics states will construct for themselves.[2] This is particularly true in a unipolar system, where material constraints are small. Much is determined by social factors, notably the identity of the unipole and the social fabric of the system it inhabits. One would expect a U.S. unipolar system to look

different from a Nazi unipolar system or a Soviet one; the purposes to which those three states would use preponderant power are very different. Similarly, one would expect a U.S. unipolar system in the twenty-first century to look very different from, say, the Roman world, or the Holy Roman Empire (if either of those counts as a unipolar system). Social structures of norms concerning sovereignty, liberalism, self-determination, and border rigidity (among other things) have changed over time and create vastly different political dynamics among these systems.[3] Generalizing about the social structure of unipolarity seems risky, perhaps impossible, when so much depends on the particulars of unipole identity and social context, but in the spirit of this project, I will try.

Even a very thin notion of social structure suggests some reasons why contemporary unipolar power may be inherently limited (or self-limiting) and why unipoles often cannot get their way.[4] Power is only a means to other, usually social, ends. States, including unipoles, want power as a means of deterring attacks, amassing wealth, imposing preferred political arrangements, or creating some other array of effects on the behavior of others. Even states with extraordinary material power must figure out how to use

From *World Politics* 61, no. 1 (Jan. 2009), 58–85.

it. They must figure out what they want and what kinds of policies will produce those results. Creating desired social outcomes, even with great material power, is not simple, as the U.S. is discovering. By better understanding the social nature of power and the social structures through which it works its effects, we might identify some contingently generalizable propositions about unipolar politics and, specifically, about social-structural reasons why great material powers may not get their way.[5]

In this article I explore three social mechanisms that limit unipolar power and shape its possible uses. The first involves legitimation. To exercise power effectively, unipoles must legitimate it and in the act of legitimating their power, unipoles must diffuse it. They must recognize the power of others over them since legitimation lies in the hands of others. Of course, unipoles can always exercise their power without regard to legitimacy. If one simply wants to destroy or kill, the legitimacy of bombs or bullets is not going to change their physical effects on buildings or bodies. However, simple killing and destruction are rarely the chief goal of political leaders using power. Power is usually the means to some other end in social life, some more nuanced form of social control or influence. Using power as more than a sledgehammer requires legitimation, and legitimation makes the unipole dependent, at least to some extent, on others.

The second involves the institutionalization of unipolar power. In the contemporary world powerful Western states, including the U.S., have relied on rational-legal authorities—law, rules, institutions—to do at least some of the legitimation work. Unipoles can create these institutions and tailor them to suit their own preferences. Indeed, the U.S. expended a great deal of energy doing exactly this kind of rational-legal institution building in the era after WWII.[6] Constructing institutions involves more than simple credible commitments and self-binding by the unipole,

however. Laws, rules, and institutions have a legitimacy of their own in contemporary politics that derives from their particular rational-legal, impersonal character.[7] Once in place these laws, rules, and institutions have powers and internal logics that unipoles find difficult to control.[8] This, too, contributes to the diffusion of power away from unipole control.

These social structures of legitimation and institutionalization do more than simply diffuse power away from the unipole. They can trap and punish as well. Unipoles often feel the constraints of the legitimation structures and institutions that they, themselves, have created and one common behavioral manifestation of these constraints is hypocrisy. Actors inconvenienced by social rules often resort to hypocrisy proclaiming adherence to rules while busily violating them. Such hypocrisy obviously undermines trust and credible commitments but the damage runs deeper: hypocrisy undermines respect and deference both for the unipole and for the values on which it has legitimized its power. Hypocrisy is not an entirely negative phenomenon for unipoles, or any state, however. While unrestrained hypocrisy by unipoles undermines the legitimacy of their power, judicious use of hypocrisy can, like good manners, provide crucial strategies for melding ideals and interests. Indeed, honoring social ideals or principles in the breach can have long-lasting political effects as decades of U.S. hypocrisy about democratization and human rights suggests.

These three mechanisms almost certainly do not exhaust the social constraints on unipolar power, but they do seem logically entailed in any modern unipolar order. Short of such sweeping social changes as the delegitimation of all rational-legal forms of authority or the establishment of some new globally accepted religion, it is hard to see how a unipole could exercise power effectively without dealing with these social dynamics. Each mechanism and its effects are, in turn, discussed below.

The Legitimacy of Power and the Power of Legitimacy

Legitimacy is, by its nature, a social and relational phenomenon. One's position or power cannot be legitimate in a vacuum. The concept only has meaning in a particular social context. Actors, even unipoles, cannot create legitimacy unilaterally. Legitimacy can only be given by others. It is conferred either by peers, as when great powers accept or reject the actions of another power, or by those upon whom power is exercised. Reasons to confer legitimacy have varied throughout history. Tradition, blood, and claims of divine right have all provided reasons to confer legitimacy, although in contemporary politics conformity with international norms and law is more influential in determining which actors and actions will be accepted as legitimate.[9]

Recognizing the legitimacy of power does not mean these others necessarily like the powerful or their policies, but it implies at least tacit acceptance of the social structure in which power is exercised. One may not like the inequalities of global capitalism but still believe that markets are the only realistic or likely way to organize successful economic growth. One may not like the P5 vetoes of the Security Council but still understand that the United Nations cannot exist without this concession to power asymmetries. We can see the importance of legitimacy by thinking about its absence. Active rejection of social structures and the withdrawal of recognition of their legitimacy create a crisis. In domestic politics, regimes suffering legitimacy crises face resistance, whether passive or active and armed. Internationally, systems suffering legitimacy crises tend to be violent and noncooperative. Post-Reformation Europe might be an example of such a system. Without at least tacit acceptance of power's legitimacy, the wheels of international social life get derailed. Material force alone remains to impose order, and order creation or maintenance by that means is difficult, even under unipolarity. Successful and stable orders require the grease of some legitimation structure to persist and prosper.[10]

The social and relational character of legitimacy thus strongly colors the nature of any unipolar order and the kinds of orders a unipole can construct. Yes, unipoles can impose their will, but only to an extent. The willingness of others to recognize the legitimacy of a unipole's actions and defer to its wishes or judgment shapes the character of the order that will emerge. Unipolar power without any underlying legitimacy will have a very particular character. The unipole's policies will meet with resistance, either active or passive, at every turn. Cooperation will be induced only through material quid pro quo payoffs. Trust will be thin to nonexistent. This is obviously an expensive system to run and few unipoles have tried to do so.

More often unipoles attempt to articulate some set of values and shared interests that induce acquiescence or support from others, thereby legitimating their power and policies. In part this invocation of values may be strategic; acceptance by or overt support from others makes exercise of power by the unipole cheaper and more effective. Smart leaders know how to "sell" their policies. Wrapping policies in shared values or interests smoothes the path to policy success by reassuring skeptics.[11] Rhetoric about shared interests in prosperity and economic growth accompanies efforts to push free trade deals on unwilling partners and publics. Rhetoric about shared love of human rights and democracy accompanies pushes for political reforms in other states.

In their examination of debates leading up to the 2003 Iraq war in this issue of *World Politics*, Jack Snyder, Robert Shapiro, and Yaeli Bloch-Elkon provide an example of unipolar attempts to create legitimacy through strategic use of rhetoric. They show how "evocative and evasive rhetoric" allowed proponents of the war to imply links between the 9/11 attacks, weapons of mass destruction, and Saddam Hussein's regime. Potentially unpopular or controversial policies were rationalized by situating them in a larger strategic vision built on more widely held values, as when the authors of the 2002 National Security Strategy memorandum wove together the global war on terror, the promotion of American democratic values abroad, and the struggle against authoritarian regimes to create a justification for preventive war.[12] Indeed, as Ronald Krebs and Patrick Jackson argue, rhetorical "sales pitches" of this kind can be highly coercive. Examining the same case (the selling of the Iraq war), Krebs and Jennifer Lobasz show how the administration's "war-on-terror" discourse, which cast the U.S. as a blameless victim (attacked for "who we are" rather than anything we did), was designed in such a way as to leave opponents with very few arguments they could use to rally effective opposition in Congress.[13]

Usually this articulation of values is not simply a strategic ploy. Decision makers and publics in the unipole actually hold these values and believe their own rhetoric to some significant degree. Unipole states, like all states, are social creatures. They are composed of domestic societies that cohere around some set of national beliefs. Their leaders are products of those societies and often share those beliefs. Even where leaders may be skeptical, they likely became leaders by virtue of their abilities to rally publics around shared goals and to construct foreign and domestic policies that reflect domestic values. Even authoritarian (and certainly totalitarian) regimes articulate shared goals and function only because of the web of social ties that knit people together. Certainly all recent and contemporary strong states that could be candidates for unipoles—the U.S., China, Russia, Germany, and Britain—do.[14]

Thus unipole states, like all states, find naked self-aggrandizement or even the prescriptions of Machiavellian *virtú* difficult to pursue.[15] Unipoles and the people who lead them pursue a variety of goals derived from many different values. Even "national interest" as most people and states conceive of it involves some broader vision of social good beyond mere self-aggrandizement. Americans like to see democracy spread around the world in part for instrumental reasons—they believe a world of democracies is a safer, more prosperous world for Americans—and also for normative ones—they believe in the virtues of democracy for all. Likewise, Americans like to see markets open in part for instrumental reasons—they believe a world of markets will make Americans richer—and also for normative ones—they believe that markets are the ticket out of poverty.

Much of unipolar politics is thus likely to revolve around the degree to which policies promoting the unipole's goals are accepted or resisted by others. Other states and foreign publics may need to be persuaded, but often influential domestic constituencies must also be brought on board. Channels for such persuasion are many and varied, as is evident from past U.S. diplomatic efforts to sell its policies under bipolarity. The shift from laissez-faire to what John Ruggie terms the "embedded liberal compromise" as the basis for the U.S.-led economic order after WWII required extensive diplomatic effort to persuade other states and New York's financial elite to go along. The tools of influence used to accomplish this were sometimes material but also intellectual and ideological. It was the "shared social purposes" of these economic arrangements that gave them legitimacy among both state and societal actors cross-nationally.[16]

A unipole's policies are thus circumscribed on two fronts. The policies must reflect values held at home, making them legitimate domestically. At the same time, in order to induce acquiescence or support from abroad, they must appeal to the leaders and publics of other states. Constructing policies across these two spheres—domestic and international—may be more or less difficult, depending on circumstances, but the range of choices satisfying both constituencies is unlikely to be large. Widespread disaffection on either front is likely to create significant legitimacy costs to leaders, either as electoral or stability threats domestically or as decreased cooperation and increased resistance internationally.

Creating legitimacy for its policies is thus essential for the unipole but it is also difficult, dangerous, and prone to unforeseen consequences. Domestically, the need to cement winning coalitions in place has polarized U.S. politics, creating incentives to exploit wedge issues and ideological narratives. As Snyder, Shapiro, and Bloch-Elkon describe, neoconservatives, particularly after 9/11, used these tools to great effect to generate support for the Bush administration's policies. Such ideologically-driven persuasion efforts entail risks, however. Constructing coherent ideological narratives often involves sidelining inconvenient facts, what Snyder and his coauthors call "fact bulldozing." This is more than just highlighting some facts at the expense of others. It may (or may not) begin with that aim, but it can also involve changing the facts people believe to be true, as when large numbers of people came to believe that weapons of mass destruction were indeed found in Iraq. Thus, to the degree that these persuasion efforts are successful, if their ideology does not allow them to entertain contrary facts, policymakers and publics may make decisions based on bad information. This kind of self-delusion would seem unlikely to result in smart policy. To the extent that ideological narratives become entrenched, these delusions may extend to future generations of policymakers and make them victims of blowback. Even if successors come to terms with the facts, they may be entrapped by the powerful legitimating rhetoric constructed by their predecessors.[17]

Internationally, this need to construct legitimate policies also creates important opportunities for opponents and potential challengers to a unipole. As Stephen Walt notes in this issue, opportunities for conventional material balancing are limited under our current unipolar situation and, by definition,

one would expect this to be so in most, if not all, unipolar systems. What is a challenger to do? With material balancing options limited, one obvious opening for rival states is to undermine the legitimacy of unipolar power. A creative rival who cannot match or balance a unipole's military or economic strength can easily find strategies to undercut the credibility and integrity of the unipole and to concoct alternative values or political visions that other states may find more attractive. Thus, even as a unipole struggles to construct political programs that will attract both domestic and international support with an ideology or values that have wide appeal, others may be trying to paint those same programs as self-aggrandizing or selfish.

Attacks on legitimacy are important "weapons of the weak."[18] Even actors with limited or no material capability can mount damaging attacks on the credibility, reputation, and legitimacy of the powerful. The tools to mount such attacks are not hard to come by in contemporary politics. Information and the ability to disseminate it strategically are the most potent weapons for delegitimating power in all kinds of situations, domestic and international. Even non-state actors like nongovernmental organizations (NGOs) and activist networks whose material capabilities are negligible in the terms used in this article have been able to challenge the legitimacy of policies of powerful states and the legitimacy of the states themselves. The International Campaign to Ban Landmines (ICBL) is one prominent example. Civil society groups and like-minded states were able to attract signatures from more than 120 governments to ban these devices in 1997 despite opposition from the unipole (U.S.) government. The fact that the ICBL received the Nobel Peace Prize for its efforts is suggestive of its success at delegitimating unipole policies on this issue. If legitimacy were irrelevant, the U.S. would have ignored this challenge; it did not. The Pentagon has begun phasing out these weapons and replacing them with newer, more expensive devices meant to conform to the treaty requirements. Indeed, that the U.S. began touting the *superiority* of its new mine policy (promulgated in February 2004) over the ICBL's Ottawa treaty requirements highlights the power of this transnational civil society network to set standards for legitimate behavior in this area.[19] Similar cases of NGO pressure on environmental protection (including climate change), human rights, weapons taboos, and democratization amply suggest that this ability to change what is "legitimate" is a common and consequential way to challenge unipoles.[20] The fact that these challenges are mounted on two fronts—international pressure from foreign governments, international organizations, and NGO activists on the one hand, and domestic pressure from the unipole's own citizens who support the activists' views on the other— makes these challenges doubly difficult to manage.

State actors, too, can use these weapons to attack the unipole's policies and do so regularly. Among states, attempts to delegitimate the policies of others are a staple of foreign policy-making and may be employed more often in states that have fewer material capabilities with which to achieve their goals against a unipole. France may be unable to balance effectively against U.S. material power in contemporary politics, but it can (and has) raised questions about U.S. leadership and the legitimacy of U.S. policies, especially U.S. inclinations toward unilateralism. Exploiting multilateralism's legitimacy as a form of action, French attempts since the late 1990s to label the U.S. a "hyperpower" and to promote a more multilateral, even multipolar, vision of world politics are clearly designed to constrain the U.S. by undermining the legitimacy of any U.S. action that does not receive widespread international support and meet international standards for "multilateralism."[21]

Countering such attacks on legitimacy is neither easy nor costless. It requires constant management of the transnational conversation surrounding the unipole's behavior and continuing demonstrations of the unipole's commitment to the values or vision that legitimate its power. To simply dismiss or ignore these attacks is dangerous; it smacks of contempt. It says to others, "You are not even worth my time and attention." A unipole need not cater to the wishes of the less powerful to avoid conveying contempt. It can argue, justify, and respectfully disagree—but all of these take time, attention, and diplomacy. Dismissal is very different than disagreement, however. Peers disagree and argue; subordinates and servants are dismissed. By treating the less powerful with contempt the unipole communicates that it does not care about their views and, ultimately, does not care about the legitimacy of its own power. To dismiss or ignore the views of the less capable is a form of self-delegitimation. Contempt is thus a self-defeating strategy for unipoles; by thumbing its metaphorical nose at others, the unipole undercuts the legitimacy needed to create a wide range of policy outcomes.[22]

Social control is never absolute and material power alone cannot create it. Effective and long-lasting social control requires some amount of recognition, deference, and, preferably, acceptance on the part of those over whom power is exercised. Other parties, not the unipole, thus hold important keys to the establishment of effective and stable order under unipolarity. Paradoxically, then, preponderant power can only be converted into social control if it is diffused. To exercise power to maximum effect, unipoles must give up some of that power to secure legitimacy for their policies.

Institutionalizing Power: Rational-Legal Authority and Its Effects on Unipolar Power

In contemporary politics, the legitimation strategy of choice for most exercises of power is to institutionalize it—to vest power in rational-legal authorities such as organizations, rules, and law. A unipole can create these and shape them to its liking. Indeed, the U.S. expended a great deal of energy doing exactly this in the era after WWII. But as with legitimacy, institutionalization of power in rational-legal authorities diffuses it. Once in place, these laws, rules, and institutions have a power and internal logic of their own that unipoles find difficult to control.[23] This is true in several senses.

First, institutionalizing power as rational-legal authority changes it. Power and authority are not the same. Much like legitimacy, authority is both social and relational. Indeed, authority is the concept that joins legitimacy to power. Authority is, according to Max Weber, domination legitimated.[24] A more practical definition might be that authority is the ability of one actor to induce deference from another.[25] Unlike power, authority cannot be seized or taken. One cannot be an authority in a vacuum nor can one plausibly create or claim authority unilaterally. Authority must be conferred or recognized by others. Consequently, institutionalizing power in authority structures necessarily involves some diffusion of that power. If others cease to recognize or defer to the authorities a unipole constructs, crisis, and perhaps eventual collapse of authority, would ensue, leaving little but material coercion to the unipole.

Transformation of power into authority is not the only consequential change under institutionalization. The fact that authority has a rational-legal character also matters. Unlike traditional and what Weber called "charismatic" types of authority, which are vested in leaders, rational-legal authority is invested in legalities, procedures, rules, and bureaucracies and thus rendered impersonal. Part of what makes such authority attractive, ergo legitimate, in the modern world is that the impersonal nature of these rules creates an odd sense of equality. Even substantively unequal rules may take on an egalitarian cast when they are promulgated in impersonal form, since it suggests that the same rules apply to everyone. Laws of war and rules of trade are legitimated in part because everyone plays by the same rules, even the powerful, even the unipole. This is what makes such rules potentially attractive and legitimate to others. However, such rules also diminish the unipole's discretion, and by implication, its power. Of course, there are a great many ways in which impersonal rules can create unequal outcomes, and often inequality occurs by the design of the unipole. Unipoles, after all, write many of the system's impersonal rules. It is no accident that current systemic rules demand open markets and free trade; they are rules that benefit strong economies like the U.S. My point is that unequal outcomes created by impersonal rule are more legitimate in contemporary politics than inequality created by a particularized or ad hoc decree of the powerful. It is more legitimate to say, "Only countries that have stabilized their economies may borrow from the International Monetary Fund (IMF)," than to say, "Only countries the U.S. likes may borrow from the IMF."

Living according to general, impersonal rules circumscribes unipole behavior in several ways, however. Unipoles have difficulty claiming they are exempt from the rules they expect others to be bound by. The U.S. has difficulty demanding human rights protections and respect for due process from other states when it does not abide consistently by these same rules. Impersonal rules may require short-term sacrifices of interests. This might be worthwhile for long-term gains but institutionalization makes it harder for unipoles to have their cake and eat it; institutionalization decreases room for unipole opportunism. For example, by institutionalizing power in the World Trade Organization's (WTO) Dispute Settlement Body, the U.S. implicitly agreed to lose sometimes (often this has occurred at inconvenient times, such as during the steel tariff flap that preceded the 2004 elections).[26] Not accepting decisions against itself would undermine the institution that the U.S. helped create. Locked-in rules and institutions also may not keep up with changes in unipole interests. Unipoles may construct one set of impersonal rules and institutions that serve long-term interests as calculated at time t1 but find these less useful at time t2 if interests have changed. Both of these effects of institutions have been extensively studied.[27]

Less well studied is another feature of rational-legal authority: the expansionary dynamic built into all bureaucracies and formal organizations. This, too, can dilute unipole control. Like other large public bureaucracies, international organizations are usually created with broad mandates derived from very general shared goals and principles. The UN is charged with securing world peace; the IMF is supposed to stabilize member economies and promote economic growth; and the World Bank pursues "a world free from poverty." These institutions are legitimated by broad aspirations and principles. At the same time, such breadth sits uneasily with the much narrower actual mandates and capabilities of the organizations, which are given few resources and are hamstrung by restrictions. Over time, broad mandates tend to put pressure on the constrained structures. Efforts by staff, constituents, and interested states to ensure that these organizations actually do their job have, over time, expanded the size and scope of most international institutions far beyond the intention of their creators. The IMF and the World Bank now intrude into minute details of borrowers' societies and economies in ways explicitly rejected by states at the founding of these organizations.[28] The UN's peace-building apparatus now reconstitutes entire states—from their laws and constitution to their economy and security apparatus.[29] These sweeping powers were not envisioned when the UN was created. Unipoles can usually stop such expansion if they strongly object, but to the extent international organizations (IO) can persuade other states and publics of the value of their activities, objections by the unipole are costly. More fundamentally, IOs are often able to persuade unipoles of the utility and rightness of an expanded scope of action. International organizations can set agendas for unipoles and reshape goals and the sense of what is possible or desirable. They can appeal directly to publics in unipole states for support, creating domestic constituencies for their actions and domestic costs for opposing or damaging them. For example, Americans generally like the UN and would prefer to act with it in Iraq and elsewhere, as recent polling consistently showed.[30] NGOs have also mobilized around IO agendas such as the Millennium Development Goals or Jubilee 2000, and have proven powerful at creating costs and benefits that induce even powerful states to pursue them.[31]

Loss of control over the institutions it creates is thus not simply a problem of poor oversight on the part of the U.S. or any other modern unipole. It is not simply a principal-agent problem or a case of IOs run amok. Institutionalizing power in rational-legal authorities changes the social structure of the system in fundamental ways. It creates alternatives to the unipole and, indeed, to states as sources of authoritative rule-making and judgment. It creates non-state actors that not only make rules that bind the powerful, but that also become influential actors in their own right with some degree of autonomy from their creators. Sometimes IOs exercise this power in a purely regulative way, making rules to coordinate interstate cooperation, but often they do much more. To carry out their mandates, these international organizations must and do exercise power that is both generative and transformative of world politics. As authorities, IOs can construct new goals for actors, such as poverty alleviation, good governance, and human rights protection, which become accepted by publics and leaders even in strong states—including unipoles. They can constitute new actors, such as election monitors and weapons inspectors, which become consequential in politics even among powerful states. Understanding unipolar politics requires some understanding of the influence and internal logic of the institutions in which power has been vested and their often unforeseen transformative and generative potential in the international system.

Ideals, Interests, and Hypocrisy

Social structures of legitimation, including international organizations, law, and rules, do more than simply diffuse power away from the unipole. They can trap and punish as well. Unipoles often feel the constraints of the legitimation structures they, themselves, have created. One common behavioral manifestation of these constraints is hypocrisy. Actors inconvenienced by social rules often resort to hypocrisy: they proclaim adherence to rules or values while violating them in pursuit of other goals.

Why is hypocrisy a problem in the international realm? After all, hypocrisy is usually associated with public masking of private immorality while international politics is claimed by many to be a realm in which morality has little role.[32] If true, no one should care much about hypocrisy; but accusations of hypocrisy are not meaningless in international politics and actors do not treat them as inconsequential. Charges of hypocrisy are often leveled at state leaders by both their own publics and by other states, and leaders respond to the accusations. Even a seemingly technical area like trade politics has been rife with such charges as continued protection and subsidy of U.S. farmers sits uneasily with the drumbeat of U.S. calls for other countries to liberalize.[33] So what is the problem, exactly?

Hypocrisy is a double-edged sword in politics. It is both dangerous and essential. On the one hand, unrestrained hypocrisy undermines the legitimacy of power; it undermines the willingness of others to accept or defer to the actions of the powerful. There are several ways to think about this. One might be to define hypocrisy simply as saying one thing while doing another. This minimizes the moral or normative component of hypocrisy in that it eschews judgments about the virtue of the various things we are saying or doing.

What matters is not the virtue of what we say or the venality of what we do, but rather the fact that the two are inconsistent. This approach has the advantage of reducing morality to things international relations (IR) scholars know how to study—promise-keeping and trust—both of which are valued primarily because they serve self-interest. This would probably be the most common approach to hypocrisy in IR, drawing as it does from microeconomics and economic notions of interest.[34]

Seen as such, hypocrisy is a problem for at least two reasons. First, it interferes with credible commitments and entails reputation costs. Saying one thing and doing another shows that the state in question is not trustworthy. If a unipole proclaims x but does y (or says that it is not bound by x), others will not trust future proclamations or commitments. A second problem might be that hypocrisy is a symptom of difficulties in foregoing short-term gains for long-term interests. Over the long term a state wants outcome x, but in the short term opportunities for benefits from y are tempting, so a state proclaims x but does y. Political institutions sometimes structure incentives that encourage such myopia, as when electoral systems encourage leaders to heavily discount the future because those leaders will not have to deal with costs incurred after their terms are over. Both of these problems, credibility and myopia, are well understood in IR but both minimize the problem posed by hypocrisy. Hypocrisy produces bad (or at least suboptimal) outcomes that punish the hypocrite as much as anyone else. Hypocrisy is stupid from this perspective, but it is not immoral or evil.

Promise-breaking and short-sightedness are certainly common and consequential, but they by no means exhaust the damage hypocrisy can do. When foreign leaders and publics react to hypocrisy, they usually bring a much richer fund of moral condemnation. Hypocrisy is more than mere inconsistency of deeds with words. Hypocrisy involves deeds that are inconsistent with particular kinds of words—proclamations of moral value and virtue. States often make such proclamations as a means of legitimating their policies and power. Unipoles, which aspire to lead, perhaps do this more than other states because they need legitimacy more than most. Certainly the United States, with its notions of "American exceptionalism," has a long history of moralistic justifications for its power and policies. International institutions, often created by unipoles and extensions of unipolar power, are also prone to such proclamations. The UN, the World Bank, and the IMF all work hard to legitimate themselves with claims for the moral virtue of what they do—pursuing peace, defending human rights, alleviating poverty. When their actions do not match their rhetoric, states and IOs may get off lightly and be seen only as incompetent. But when others doubt the intent and sincerity of these actors, accusations escalate from mere incompetence to deceit and hypocrisy.

Failure to conform to the values and norms that legitimate power and policies is not only counterproductive for particular policies: it is also perceived by others as providing information about character and identity. We despise and condemn hypocrites because they try to deceive us: they pretend to be better than they are. Hypocrisy leads others to question the authenticity of an actor's (in this case, a unipole's) moral commitments but also its moral constitution and character. Actors want reputations for more than just promise-keeping. They may seek reputations for virtue, generosity, piety, resolve, lawfulness, and a host of other values. A unipole might cultivate such a reputation simply because it is useful. Such a reputation enhances trust, increases deference, and makes the unipole's position more legitimate, more secure, and more powerful. However, if reputations are perceived to be cultivated only for utility, those reputations are weak and of limited value. Reputations must be perceived as heartfelt to convince others of their weight. Sincerity is the antidote to hypocrisy.[35]

Demonstrating the sincerity necessary to legitimate power often requires the powerful to sacrifice and pay for the promotion or protection of shared values. Power legitimated by its service to and love of democracy must be used to promote and protect democracy, even when democracy is inconvenient or costly. Installation of authoritarian or nonrepresentative governments that happen to be friendly or accommodating by an actor that proclaims its love of democracy, smacks of hypocrisy. Power legitimated by its love of human rights must be brought to bear on violators of those rights, even when those violators may be strategic allies. Failure to do so raises doubts about the sincerity of the powerful and spawns reluctance to defer to policies of that state.

Thus, hypocrisy has three elements. First, the actor's actions are at odds with its proclaimed values. Second, alternative actions are available. Third, the actor is likely trying to deceive others about the mismatch between its actions and values (obviously, to admit up front that one's values are empty rhetoric would be to forfeit any respect or legitimacy associated with invoking those values).[36] Observers will differ in their judgment about whether all of these elements apply in a given case. What looks like deceit or a break with values to one observer may not appear so to others. What constitutes a viable alternative may similarly be a matter of dispute. Like many things in social life, acts of hypocrisy vary in both degree and kind. The price paid by the accused hypocrite will thus vary as well. It could range from public criticism and difficult-to-measure reductions in respect and deference to more concrete withdrawal of support, such as refusal to endorse or contribute resources to an actor's proposed policy. To illustrate, it is worth considering three recent cases in which the contemporary unipole, the U.S., has been charged with hypocrisy and the ways in which such charges may (or may not) have hampered its leadership abilities.

Iraq Sanctions and the "Oil for Food" Program

Marc Lynch's analysis of the Iraq sanctions regime illustrates several aspects of the dangers hypocrisy poses for unipoles. Following Iraq's invasion of Kuwait in 1990, the UN, at U.S. urging, imposed economic sanctions to pressure the Iraqi regime to withdraw and, following the 1991 U.S.-led military action, to disarm and comply with UN resolutions. Widespread publicity about the humanitarian costs of the sanctions quickly came to threaten their legitimacy, however. The UN's own inspection team reported in 1991 that the Iraqi people faced a humanitarian "catastrophe," including epidemic and famine.[37] The Oil for Food program, proposed by the U.S., was supposed to restore the sanctions' legitimacy. Authorized by UN resolution 986 in April 1995 and subsequently administered by the UN, the program allowed Iraq to sell limited amounts of oil (such sales having been banned under the sanctions) provided that the revenues were used to purchase humanitarian goods such as food and medicines.

The moral character of the critique of the sanctions (that they caused suffering of innocents) invited, perhaps required, a policy response billed as moral and humanitarian. The "Oil for Food" program was thus trumpeted as a moral action: it was designed to alleviate suffering caused by U.S. and UN policies. Once implemented, though, a policy justified on moral grounds is scrutinized by others for moral effects. The media, NGOs, and activists monitored implementation of the program and were not shy about publicizing its failures. Reports of widespread civilian suffering, rising infant mortality, and increasing civilian death rates sparked opposition to the policy in the publics of the lead sanctioning states. Denunciation of the program by its UN coordinator, Denis Halliday, followed by his resignation, fueled the criticism both outside the UN and within it.[38]

The failure of Oil for Food to deliver humanitarian outcomes, compounded by the rampant (and much publicized) corruption that riddled the program, destroyed the legitimacy of the policy. Violations of the sanctions regime for private enrichment were not understood as "promise breaking" or credible commitment problems; they were not mere inconsistencies between the words and deeds of sanctioning governments. Rather, humanitarian suffering compounded by widespread profiteering and corruption of the sanctions program by Western businesses, with varying degrees of complicity by their governments and UN officials, became a moral issue in part because the program had been sold in those terms. Returning to the three criteria, while failure of the program to reduce suffering might (or might not) have been excused as incompetence, the profiteering and corruption were clearly at odds with the santioners' proclaimed virtuous values. Alternative actions (sanctions without corruption) were possible, and a variety of actors, including governments, were trying to cover up their self-serving actions. Exposure of this kind of hypocrisy made the motives of the sanctioners suspect and made it difficult for the U.S. in particular to create legitimacy for any policy on Iraq.[39]

Intervention in Kosovo

Reactions to the U.S.-led intervention in Kosovo also illustrate the ways in which the three elements of hypocrisy (mismatched words and actions, available alternative actions, and attempts to dissemble or deceive) can corrode legitimacy of a unipole's action. In 1999, at U.S. urging, NATO launched airstrikes against Serb targets in Kosovo. The goal was to stop violent repression of ethnic Albanians and force the Serbian government back to the negotiating table. Again, the intervention was justified as a humanitarian action: military force was needed to protect civilians from violence at the hands of the Milosevic regime (whose record of atrocities no one disputed). Accusations of hypocrisy came on two grounds. First, while sympathetic to its moral aims, most observers viewed the action as plainly contrary to international law. The UN Security Council did not authorize NATO's use of force, as the charter requires. The U.S. could have simply stated that the charter and the law in this situation were flawed and moral concerns trumped law. Moral concerns, not legality, could have been called upon to legitimate the intervention policy in this case. Instead, the U.S. tried to have it both ways—to make the intervention both virtuous and legal. For example, Secretary of State Albright claimed that "NATO will, in all cases, act in accordance with the principles of the UN [c]harter."[40] President Clinton, himself, framed the Kosovo action not only as consistent with the UN charter but also as an exemplar of UN effectiveness.[41] The charter's explicit prohibition against unauthorized uses of force was swept under the rug. So one potential hypocrisy problem involved an attempt to misrepresent the legality of the intervention by minimizing the profound legal issues it raised. As a result, U.S. professions to value international law and the UN were questioned.[42]

A second potential hypocrisy problem (and a much-criticized aspect of the intervention) involved the execution of the intervention and whether it was actually designed with the well-being of Kosovar Albanians as its foremost goal. Most conspicuously, NATO's use of high altitude bombing against Serb positions appeared to many observers as designed to minimize casualties to NATO pilots rather than Kosovar civilians. At such high altitudes, the accuracy of NATO bombs was diminished. Suspicions about humanitarian motives deepened when it was discovered that the U.S. and Britain had used cluster bombs in their attacks on the city of Nis. Cluster bombs, by their nature, are indiscriminate in their effects and so may violate laws of war when used in civilian areas.[43] Again, the problem here was that

the intervention was justified as a humanitarian action. Consequently, the U.S. action invited judgment on those terms. Civilian casualties, by themselves, need not have compromised the mission's legitimacy. It was the fact that alternative actions were available (more precise bombing from lower altitudes, different weapons) that raised questions about U.S. sincerity as a humanitarian actor.[44]

Democracy Promotion and Palestinian Elections

Democracy promotion provides another example of the dynamics of hypocrisy at work. Claims to spread democracy have figured prominently in the U.S.'s efforts to legitimate its power and win support for what might otherwise be viewed as illegitimate interference in the domestic affairs of other states. Spreading democracy can be risky though. If you let people vote, you might not like the results, and if you take action against the victors when you promoted freedom to choose, you look hypocritical. This has happened more than once in recent decades. U.S. action to topple elected governments in Iran (1953), Guatemala (1954), Chile (1973), and Nicaragua (1980s) come to mind.

Democracy promotion took on new force after the end of the Cold War, however, and has been a particular hallmark of the George W. Bush administration. Following 9/11, democracy promotion in the Middle East was central to the U.S.'s security strategy in that region. It provided one rationale for the Iraq war and was also a prominent (and not always welcome) demand by the U.S. in its dealings with nondemocratic states.[45] When Palestinians held their first presidential elections in January 2005, the United States applauded and held them up as exemplars to neighboring states.[46] But when Palestinians later held internationally monitored legislative elections (in 2006) and Hamas won 74 of the 132 seats (as compared to Fatah's 45), the U.S. faced a dilemma. Hamas is viewed as a terrorist organization by the administration (indeed, it is formally listed as such by the U.S. Department of State), yet it had been freely chosen by Palestinian voters despite U.S. efforts to bolster support for Fatah.[47] To reject the election outcome outright would undercut a centerpiece of the administration's policy in the region (democracy promotion). On the other hand, to accept Hamas jeopardized another of the administration's central values, fighting terrorism. The resulting policy tried to square this circle by cutting off direct aid to the Palestinian Authority while leaving in tact funding for humanitarian projects run through NGOs and international organizations.[48]

Reactions to U.S. policy in this case varied among audiences, but focusing on the three elements of hypocrisy helps pinpoint the nature of disagreement. The second criterion, availability of an alternative policy, is perhaps the most interesting here because it reveals a central and common aspect of our judgments about hypocrisy. In this case, the U.S. had made two conflicting proclamations of values. On the one hand, it wanted to spread democracy and support elections. On the other hand, it abhorred terrorism and judged Hamas to be a terrorist organization. In this view, Hamas' electoral victory presented a "tragic choice" in which the U.S. was forced to choose between two deeply held values. From the administration's perspective there was no "nonhypocritical" alternative: whatever the U.S. did would betray a core value.

Variation in judgments about U.S. hypocrisy hinged on the degree to which observers shared the U.S.'s core values and recognized the conflict between them. Palestinians, not surprisingly, saw no value conflict, ergo, great hypocrisy.[49] They saw a clear alternative: support the legitimately elected Hamas government. Europeans were more sympathetic. They shared both U.S. values and were caught in a similar dilemma but were quicker to publicly recognize the irony (if not hypocrisy) of their position.[50] Some U.S. domestic actors also recognized the dilemma, but saw alternatives to the full cut off of aid, and were correspondingly critical of U.S. policy.[51]

Judgments about hypocrisy thus can and should vary, and costs to the potential hypocrite will vary accordingly. Hypocrisy involves proclaiming some virtue then engaging in blameworthy behavior contrary to public proclamations. If the behavior is unmitigated vice—gratuitous torture (cruelty) or private enrichment at public expense (greed or venality)—then charges of hypocrisy are easy to make and appropriately damaging. But what about cases in which apparently blameworthy behavior is, in another light, justified by a different virtue? What happens when proclaimed virtues demand conflicting action? What about cases in which, for example, we torture prisoners and violate their human rights in an effort to secure the country against future terrorist attacks? If protecting the country and respecting individual rights come into conflict, we do not really want leaders to say, "We don't care about rights" or "We don't care about security." We want them to continue to value both and proclaim those values publicly, even if they cannot or will not reconcile them.

Hypocrisy provides one means to do this. It allows actors to espouse, often loudly, some dearly held value but to carry out policies that are not entirely consistent with that value and may even undercut it. We often condemn such action as hypocrisy and it may well be so. Such action may be motivated by duplicitous impulses, but when it is prompted at least in part by value conflict, some sympathy may be in order. The alternatives to this type of hypocrisy are often much less attractive. Denying that value conflicts exist and imposing some kind of ideology of certitude that allows no room for doubt or debate is hardly a promising solution. Certainly this has been tried. Ideological purists tend not to produce happy politics, however. Maintaining such purity in practice requires a great deal of repression and violence. Such fervent ideological commitment also tends to breed its own forms of hypocrisy since purity is hard to maintain in lived lives. Another alternative to hypocrisy is constant exposure of hypocrisy to public scrutiny—anti-hypocrisy. This is more attractive and, indeed, can be a very useful device for keeping hypocrites on several sides of a public debate in check and somewhat honest. But exposing all policies as hypocrisies all the time breeds cynicism and antipathy to politics. It undermines public trust and social capital in a host of ways, delegitimating the political system overall.[52] Hypocrisy, it seems, is something we cannot live with but cannot live without.

Effective leadership often requires hypocrisy of this kind, hypocrisy that balances conflicting values. Forging common goals and policies that will receive broad acquiescence or even allegiance is what leaders do, but that requires compromise and a delicate balancing of conflicting values. To the extent that unipoles seek to lead rather than dictate and coerce, this type of hypocrisy must be central to their policies. Indeed, in the case of unipoles, this type of hypocrisy is often expected and even appreciated by foreign leaders and publics as necessary for the maintenance of international order and stability. If the United States truly pursued its democracy-promotion agenda with single-minded commitment, many would perceive it as tyrannical or reckless and unfit to continue to lead the rest of the world.[53] Elections are means to peaceful, humane, self-determining policies; they are not ends in themselves. Elections that trigger wars, civil wars, and mass violence may be self-defeating. Promoting elections without regard to context or consequences would hardly be a moral or virtuous policy.

Double talk is the bread and butter of any politician or political leader. Saying one thing while doing another, at least sometimes, is essential in public life and no polity could survive without a great deal of such inconsistency. There are simply too many values conflicting in too many places to maintain consistency. Balancing inconsistent

values need not be a vice at all. Indeed, it is an essential skill. Labels for inconsistency between values and policy are not always pejorative. Hypocrisy has a number of close relatives that most of us like. Compromise, an important virtue in politics (especially liberal politics), sits uneasily close to it. Diplomacy, an essential component of a peaceful system, all but demands hypocrisy—and in large doses. Leadership, too, demands a significant divorce of rhetoric and policy to succeed. Unipoles, and sovereign states more generally, are not unusual in being organized hypocrisies. Virtually all politics, from the local PTA to the international system, organizes hypocrisy in important ways to survive and function. Organizing hypocrisy is a central social task for all social organizations and a crucial one for political organizations.[54]

Hypocrisy thus pervades international politics. It is a problem for any actor seeking to legitimate power domestically or internationally. Its effects are compounded, however, in the case of unipoles. Unipoles aspire to lead other states and, perhaps, establish an institutionalized international order. They therefore make more and more sweeping claims about the public-interest character of their policies. The assertiveness and intrusiveness of their policies into the lives of others makes their actions "public" and of public concern in unique ways. Consequently, they need legitimacy more than other states and are more vulnerable to charges of hypocrisy than others. This is probably a good thing. Great power deserves great scrutiny.

It suggests, however, that successful unipoles need strategies for managing inevitable hypocrisy—strategies that involve some combination of social strength (i.e., deep legitimacy) and sympathy among potential accusers with the values conflict that prompts unipole hypocrisy. If the unipole (or any actor) has great legitimacy and others believe deeply in the value claims that legitimate its power, they may simply overlook or excuse a certain amount of hypocrisy, even of a venal kind. Many countries for many years have accepted U.S. and

European protectionism in agriculture because they valued deeply the larger free-trade system supported by them.[55] "Good," or legitimate, unipoles get some slack. Others may tolerate hypocrisy if they can be persuaded that it flows from a trade-off among shared values, not just from convenience or opportunism of the unipole. Agreement to violate one value, sovereignty, to promote others, security and justice, by toppling a sitting government member of the UN was easy to come by in the case of Afghanistan after September 11, 2001. Other states were convinced that this was a necessary value trade-off. Conversely, side agreements protecting U.S. troops from International Criminal Court prosecution look self-serving since other troops receive no such protection.

Conclusion

The strength of a unipolar system depends heavily, not just on the unipole's material capabilities, but also on the social system in which unipolarity is embedded. Unipoles can shape that system at least to some degree. They can portray themselves as champions of universal values that appeal to other states and other publics. They can invest in the building of norms or institutions in which they believe and from which they will benefit. The U.S. was remarkably effective at this in the years following WWII. Within its own sphere of influence under bipolarity, the U.S. was a vocal (if not always consistent) proponent of freedom, democracy, and human rights. It built an extended institutional architecture designed to shape global politics in ways that both served its interests and propagated its values. So successful was the U.S. at legitimating and institutionalizing its power, that by the time the Berlin Wall fell, other models of political and economic organization had largely disappeared. The U.S.-favored liberal model of free markets and democracy became the model of choice for states around the world not through overt U.S. coercion, but in significant part because states and publics had accepted it as the best (ergo most legitimate) way to run a country.

Constructing a social system that legitimates preferred values can grease the wheels of unipolar power by inducing cooperation or at least acquiescence from others, but legitimacy's assistance comes at a price. The process by which a unipole's power is legitimated fundamentally alters the social fabric of politics. Successful legitimation persuades people that the unipole will serve some set of values. Those persuaded may include publics in the unipolar state, foreign states and publics, and even decision makers in the unipole itself. Legitimacy can thus constrain unipoles, creating resistance to policies deemed illegitimate. Voters may punish leaders at the next election; allies may withhold support for favored policies. But legitimacy can also have a more profound effect—it can change what unipoles want. To the extent that unipole leaders and publics are sincere, they will conform to legitimacy standards because they believe in them. Institutionalizing power similarly changes the political playing field. It creates new authoritative actors (intergovernmental organizations) that make rules, create programs, and make decisions based on the values they embody—values given to them in no small part by the unipole.

Legitimacy is invaluable to unipoles. Creating a robust international order is all but impossible without it and unipoles will bend over backward to secure it since great power demands great legitimacy. At the same time, service to the values that legitimate its power and institutions may be inconvenient for unipoles; examples of hypocritical behavior are never hard to find among the powerful. Hypocrisy varies in degree and kind, however, and the price a unipole pays for it will vary accordingly. Simple opportunism will be appropriately condemned by those who judge a unipole's actions, but other kinds of hypocrisy may provoke more mixed reactions. Like any social system, the one constructed by a unipole is bound to contain contradictions. Tragic choices created by conflict among widely shared values will be unavoidable and may evoke some sympathy. Balancing these contradictions and maintaining the legitimacy of its power requires at least as much attention from a unipole as building armies or bank accounts.

NOTES

1. The contributions to Paul, Wirtz, and Fortmann are representative of the materialist orientation of this literature. Only one contribution to this volume, Michael Bartletta and Harold Trinkunas, "Regime Type and Regional Security in Latin America: Toward a 'Balance of Identity' Theory," grapples in depth with nonmaterial factors. T. V. Paul, James J. Wirtz, and Michel Fortmann, eds., *Balance of Power: Theory and Practice in the 21st Century* (Stanford: Stanford University Press, 2004). Ikenberry similarly contains only one essay that explores nonmaterial factors explicitly. See Thomas Risse, "U.S. Power in a Liberal Security Community," in G. John Ikenberry, ed., *America Unrivaled: The Future of the Balance of Power* (Ithaca, N.Y.: Cornell University Press, 2002). The materialist orientation of the project of which this essay is a part draws on this tradition. See articles by Wohlforth and by Ikenberry, Mastanduno, and Wohlforth, in this issue.

2. The type of system states construct may not reflect the material distribution of power at all. After 1815, the European great powers consciously constructed a multipolar system under material conditions that might be variously categorized as hegemony or bipolarity, depending on how one measures, but are not multipolar by any material measure. See Martha Finnemore, *The Purpose of Intervention: Changing Beliefs about the Use of Force* (Ithaca, N.Y.: Cornell University Press, 2003), chap. 4, for an extended discussion.

3. See inter alia Hedley Bull and Adam Watson, eds., *The Expansion of International Society* (Oxford: Clarendon Press, 1984); Gerrit W. Gong, *The Standard of 'Civilisation' in International Society* (Oxford: Clarendon Press, 1984); Christian Reus-Smit, *The Moral Purpose of the State: Culture, Social Identity, and Institutional Rationality in International Relations* (Princeton: Princeton University Press, 1999); idem, *American Power and World Order* (Cambridge: Polity Press, 2004); Robert H. Jackson, *The Global Covenant: Human Conduct in a World of State* (New York: Oxford University Press, 2000); Stephen D. Krasner, *Sovereignty: Organized Hypocrisy* (Princeton: Princeton University Press, 1999); John G. Ruggie, "Territoriality and Beyond: Problematizing Modernity in International Relations," *International Organization* 46 (Winter 1993), 139–74; and Mlada Bukovansky, *Legitimacy and Power Politics: The American and French Revolutions in International Political Culture* (Princeton: Princeton University Press, 2002).

4. For a related conclusion derived from a somewhat different theoretical perspective and reasons, see Joseph P. Nye, Jr., *The Paradox of American Power: Why the World's Only Superpower Can't Go It Alone* (London: Oxford University Press, 2002).

5. For a fuller exploration of the nature of power in world politics see Michael Barnett and Raymond Duvall, "Power in International Politics," *International Organization* 59 (January 2005), 39–75; and Michael Barnett and Raymond Duvall, eds., *Power in Global Governance* (New York: Cambridge University Press, 2005).

6. G. John Ikenberry, *After Victory: Institutions, Strategic Restraint, and the Rebuilding of Order after Major Wars* (Princeton: Princeton University Press, 2001), esp. chap. 3.

7. Max Weber, *Economy and Society*, ed. Guenther Roth and Claus Wittich (Berkeley: University of California Press, 1978), chap. 3, esp. 212–15.

8. Michael Barnett and Martha Finnemore, *Rules for the World: International Organizations in Global Politics* (Ithaca, N.Y.: Cornell University Press, 2004); and Darren G. Hawkins, David A. Lake, Daniel L. Nielson, and Michael J. Tierney, eds., *Delegation and Agency in International Organizations* (New York: Cambridge University Press, 2006).

9. Ian Hurd, *After Anarchy: Legitimacy and Power at the United Nations* (Princeton: Princeton University Press, 2007); and idem, "Legitimacy and Authority

in International Politics," *International Organization* 53 (April 1999), 379–408.

10. Ibid.; Reus-Smit (fn. 3, 1999); and Thomas M. Franck, *The Power of Legitimacy among Nations* (New York: Oxford University Press, 1990).

11. Ian Hurd, "The Strategic Use of Liberal Internationalism: Libya and the UN Sanctions, 1992–2003," *International Organization* 59 (July 2005), 495–526; and Bruce W. Jentleson and Christopher A. Whytock, "Who 'Won' Libya?: The Force-Diplomacy Debate and its Implications for Theory and Policy," *International Security* 30, (Winter 2005). For more on the intertwined relationship of legitimacy and effectiveness in power projection, see Erik Voeten, "The Political Origins of the Legitimacy of the United Nations Security Council," *International Organization* 59 (July 2005) 527–57; and Martha Finnemore, "Fights about Rules: The Role of Efficacy and Power in Changing Multilateralism," *Review of International Studies* 3, supplement S1 (December 2005), 187–206.

12. Snyder, Shapiro, and Bloch-Elkon in this issue.

13. Ronald Krebs and Patrick T. Jackson, "Twisting Arms/Twisting Tongues," *European Journal of International Relations* 13 (March 2007), 35–66; and Krebs and Jennifer Lobasz, "Fixing the Meaning of 9/11: Hegemony, Coercion, and the Road to War in Iraq," *Security Studies* 16, (July 2007), 409–51.

14. Note that, like rhetoric, social ties can be very coercive. Social (and nonmaterial) forms of coercion include shame, blame, fear, and ridicule as well as notions about duty and honor.

15. Machiavelli understood very well how difficult his prescriptions were to follow. That is why a book of instruction was required for princes.

16. John G. Ruggie, "International Regimes, Transactions, and Change: Embedded Liberalism in the Postwar Economic Order," in Stephen D. Krasner, ed., *International Regimes* (Ithaca, N.Y.: Cornell University Press, 1983), 195–231; and Harold James, *International Monetary Cooperation since Bretton Woods* (New York: Oxford University Press, 1996).

17. Snyder, Shapiro, and Bloch-Elkon in this issue. On blowback, see Jack Snyder, *Myths of Empire: Domestic Politics and International Ambition* (Ithaca, N.Y.: Cornell University Press, 1991), 39–49. Terms in quotation marks are from Snyder 1991. Note that in making these arguments about the power of ideology and persuasion to create political effects, Snyder, Shapiro, and Bloch-Elkon, too, are departing from the materialist orientation of this project.

18. James C. Scott, *Weapons of the Weak: Everyday Forms of Peasant Resistance* (New Haven: Yale University Press, 1985). See also the discussion of "delegitimation" in Stephen Walt, *Taming American Power: The Global Response to U.S. Primacy* (New York: Norton, 2005).

19. The U.S. Department of Defense has spent hundreds of millions of dollars since 1998 and has requested hundreds of millions more for the development and procurement of landmine alternatives (including Spider and Intelligent Munitions Systems). See Department of the Army, *Descriptive Summaries of Statistics: Research, Development, Test, and Evaluation; Army Appropriations, Budget Activities 4 and 5* (Washington, D.C.: Department of the Army, 2008). On the 2004 landmines policy, see U.S. Department of State, "U.S. Landmine Policy," at http://www.state.gov/t/pm/wra/c11735.htm (accessed March 1, 2008). On U.S. claims of its superiority to the Ottawa standards, see U.S. Department of State, "U.S. Bans Nondetectable Landmines," January 3, 2005, www.state.gov/r/pa/prs/ps/2005/40193.htm (accessed March 1, 2008).

20. Margaret Keck and Kathryn Sikkink, *Activists Beyond Borders* (Ithaca, N.Y.: Cornell University Press, 1998); Thomas Risse, Stephen Ropp and Kathryn Sikkink, eds., *The Power of Human Rights: International Norms and Domestic Change* (New York: Cambridge University Press, 1999); Thomas Risse-Kappen, ed., *Bringing Transnational Relations Back In: Non-State Actors, Domestic Structures and International Institutions* (New York: Cambridge University Press, 1995); Paul Wapner, "Politics Beyond the State: Environmental Activism and World Civic Politics," *World Politics* 47 (April 1995), 311–40; Richard Price, "Reversing the Gunsights: Transnational Civil Society Targets

Landmines," *International Organization* 52 (Summer 1998), 613–44; Sanjeev Khagram, *Dams and Development: Transnational Struggles for Water and Power* (Ithaca, N.Y.: Cornell University Press, 2004); and idem, James V. Riker, and Kathryn Sikkink, eds., *Restructuring World Politics: Transnational Social Movements, Networks, and Norms* (Minneapolis: University of Minnesota Press, 2002).

21. See, for example, statements by Foreign Minister Hubert Vedrine and President Jacques Chirac in Craig R. Whitney, "France Presses for a Power Independent of the U.S.," *New York Times*, November 7, 1999, A9.

22. I am indebted to Steve Walt for bringing this issue of contempt to my attention.

23. Ikenberry (fn. 6); and Barnett and Finnemore (fn. 8), chap. 2. The causes and consequences of modernity's fascination with rational-legal authority have been central to a number of strands of sociology. See, for example, the work of Max Weber, Michael Mann, Immanuel Wallerstein, and John Meyer.

24. Weber (fn. 7), esp. 212–15.

25. Barnett and Finnemore (fn. 8), 5.

26. See, for example, "Bush Ditches Steel Import Duties," *BBC News*, December 4, 2003, http://news.bbc.co.uk/1/hi/business/3291537.stm; and "Steel Tariffs Spark International Trade Battle," *NewsHour*, November 17, 2003, http:/www.pbs.org/newshour/extra/features/july-dec03/steel_11-17.html (accessed February 27, 2008).

27. Krasner's discussion of "institutional lag" in the *International Regimes* volume was an early and particularly clear statement of this problem. Stephen Krasner, "Regimes and the Limits of Realism: Regimes as Autonomous Variables" in Krasner (fn. 16).

28. Sidney Dell, "On Being Grandmotherly: The Evolution of IMF Conditionality," *Essays in International Finance* 144 (Princeton: International Finance Section, Department of Economics, Princeton University, 1981); Harold James, "From Grandmotherliness to Governance: The Evolution of IMF Conditionality," *Finance and Development* 35 (December 1998), available online at http://www.imf.org/external/pubs/ft

/fandd/1998/12/james.htm (accessed February 27, 2008); and idem (fn. 16), esp. 78–84 and 322–35.

29. Chuck Call and Michael Barnett, "Looking for a Few Good Cops: Peacekeeping, Peacebuilding, and CIVPOL," *International Peacekeeping* 6 (Winter 1999), 43–68.

30. See, for example, polls showing that in January 2003 Americans thought it was "necessary" to get UN approval for an invasion of Iraq by a margin of more than 2:1 (67 percent to 29 percent) and that in June/July 2003, seven in ten Americans said that the U.S. should be willing to put the entire Iraq operation under the UN, with joint decision making, if other countries were willing to contribute troops. Program on International Policy Attitudes (PIPA), "PIPA-Knowledge Networks Poll: Americans On Iraq and the UN Inspections," January 21–16, 2003, question 12, http://www.pipa.org/OnlineReports/Iraq/IraqUN Insp1_Jan03/IraqUNInsp1%20Jan03%20quaire.pdf (accessed February 28, 2008); and Program on International Policy Attitudes, "Public Favors Putting Iraq Operations Under UN if Other Countries Will Contribute Troops," July 11–20, 2003, http://www.pipa.org/OnlineReports/Iraq/Iraq_Jul03/Iraq%20Jul03%20pr.pdf (accessed February 28, 2008).

31. For an empirical exploration of the mechanisms by which IO expansion may be fueled by broad mandates and normative claims, see Barnett and Finnemore (fn. 8).

32. Variants on this position permeate realist thinking going back to Thucydides. For overviews see Steven Forde, "Classical Realism," and Jack Donnelly, "Twentieth Century Realism," both in Terry Nardin and David Mapel, eds., *Traditions of International Ethics* (New York: Cambridge University Press, 1992), 62–84 and 85–111.

33. Mlada Bukovansky, "Yes, Minister: The Politics of Hypocrisy in the World Trade Organization" (paper presented at the International Studies Association Annual Convention, San Diego, Calif., March 22–25, 2006).

34. See, for example, Oliver Williamson, "Credible Commitments: Using Hostages to Support

Exchange," *American Economic Review* 73 (September 1983); idem, *The Economic Institutions of Capitalism: Firms, Markets, and Relational Contracting* (New York: Free Press, 1985); Diego Gambetta, ed., *Trust: Making and Breaking Cooperative Relations* (Oxford: Basil Blackwell, 1988); and Oliver Williamson, "Calculative, Trust, and Economic Organization," *Journal of Law and Economics* 36 (April 1993). The IR literature drawing on these economic notions is extensive. See, for example, Brett Ashley Leeds, "Domestic Political Institutions, Credible Commitments, and International Cooperation," *American Journal of Political Science* 43 (October 1999), 979–1002; James D. Fearon, "Rationalist Explanations for War," *International Organization* 49, (Summer 1995), 379–414; Lisa Martin, *Democratic Commitments: Legislatures and International Cooperation* (Princeton: Princeton University Press, 2000); Beth A. Simmons, "International Law and State Behavior: Commitment and Compliance in International Monetary Affairs," *American Political Science Review* 94 (December 2000), 819–35; and Jon Pevehouse, "Democratization, Credible Commitments, and International Organizations," in Daniel Drezner, ed., *Locating the Proper Authorities* (Ann Arbor: University of Michigan Press, 2002), 25–48. Note that even this very thin notion of hypocrisy (as promise breaking) cannot be analyzed without attention to social structure. *Pacta sunt servanda* is a social norm that is obtained only in some social contexts and often must be painstakingly constructed among actors.

35. Sincerity is not a perfect antidote. In individuals sincerity does not completely solve problems of rationalization and self-deceit. Hypocrites know their action to be wrong, but often deal with this discomfort, not by changing behavior but shifting their beliefs. Judith Shklar, *Ordinary Vices* (Cambridge: Harvard University Press, 1984), 58. In collectivities, like states, the practice of reformulating goals or values to fit behavior is at least as common. Nils Brunsson, *The Organization of Hypocrisy: Talk, Decisions, and Actions in Organizations,* trans. Nancy Adler, (New York: Wiley, 1989); and Catherine

Weaver, *Hypocrisy Trap: The Rhetoric, Reality and Reform of the World Bank* (Princeton: Princeton University Press, 2008).

36. Suzanne Dovi offers a more detailed list of criteria for discerning what she calls "political hypocrisy" in "Making the World Safe for Hypocrisy" *Polity* 34 (Autumn 2001), 16.

37. United Nations, "Report on Humanitarian Needs in Iraq in the Immediate Post-crisis Environment by a Mission to the Area Led by the Under Secretary General for Administration and Management, 10–17 March 1991," also known as the Ahtisaari Report, March 20, 1991, http://www.un.org/Depts/oip/back ground/reports/s22366.pdf (accessed February 28, 2008).

38. Middle East UN Official Blasts Iraq Sanctions," *BBC News*, September 30, 1998, http://news.bbc.co.uk/1 /hi/world/middle_east/183499.stm (accessed February 28, 2008).

39. Marc Lynch, "Lie to Me: Sanctions on Iraq, Moral Argument and the International Politics of Hypocrisy," in Richard Price, ed., *Moral Limit and Possibility* (New York: Cambridge University Press, 2008); and Sarah Graham-Brown, *Sanctioning Saddam: The Politics of Intervention in Iraq* (London: IB Tauris, 1999).

40. Madeleine Albright, "NATO: Preparing for the Washington Summit," *U.S. Department of State Dispatch* (December 1998), statement prepared for the North Atlantic Council, Brussels, Belgium, http://findarticles.com/p/articles/mi_m1584/is_11_9 /ai_53706253 (accessed February 28, 2008).

41. "In the last year alone, we have seen abundant evidence of the ways in which the United Nations benefits America and the world. The United Nations is the primary multilateral forum to press for international human rights and lead governments to improve their relations with their neighbors and their own people. As we saw during the Kosovo conflict, and more recently with regard to East Timor, the perpetrators of ethnic cleansing and mass murder can find no refuge in the United Nations and no source of comfort in its charter." See William J. Clinton,

"United Nations Day, 1999: A Proclamation by the President of the United States," October 24, 1999, available at http://clinton6.nara.gov/1999/10/1999-10-24-proclamation-on-united-nations-day.html. Similarly, National Security Advisor Sandy Berger stated within a single interview that UNSC Resolution 1199 gave the U.S. "all the international authority that we need here to act" but at the same time argued that "NATO cannot be a hostage to the United Nations" and had the authority to act in Kosovo without it. See his interview with Margaret Warner, *NewsHour*, October 2, 1998, http://www.pbs.org/newshour/bb/europe/july-dec98/berger_10-2.html (accessed February 28, 2008).

42. Dovi (fn. 36).

43. Human Rights Watch, *Civilian Deaths in the NATO Air Campaign*, February 7, 2000, http://www.hrw.org/reports/2000/nato/index.htm (accessed February 28, 2008).

44. Dovi (fn. 36).

45. For democracy as a rationale for the Iraq war, see Bush's radio address of March 1, 2003, http://www.whitehouse.gov/news/releases/2003/03/20030301.html (accessed February 28, 2008).

46. See, for example, Condoleezza Rice, "Remarks at the American University in Cairo," June 20, 2005, http://www.state.gov/secretary/rm/2005/48328.htm (accessed February 28, 2008).

47. Steven Erlanger, "U.S. Spent $1.9 Million to Aid Fatah in Palestinian Elections," *New York Times*, January 23, 2006, A11.

48. Paul Morro, "U.S. Foreign Aid to the Palestinians," *Congressional Research Service*, October 9, 2007, http://italy.usembassy.gov/pdf/other/RS22370.pdf (accessed February 28, 2008). See also "Overview of EU Relations with the Palestinians," on the European Commission Technical Assistance Office for the West Bank and the Gaza Strip's Web site at http://www.delwbg.cec.eu.int/en/eu_and_palestine/overview.htm#1 (accessed February 28, 2008).

49. "It would come as no surprise to us if this letter were to be met with dismissal, in keeping with this administration's policy of not dealing with 'terrorists,' despite the fact that we entered the democratic process and held a unilateral ceasefire of our own for over two years. But how do you think the Arab and Muslim worlds react to this American hypocrisy?" Open letter from Hamas Senior Political Advisor to Rice, December 2007, http://www.prospectsforpeace.com/Resources/Ahmad_Yousef_Letter_to_Condoleezza_Rice.pdf (accessed February 28, 2008).

50. See, for example, comments by Italy's foreign minister, Massimo D'Alema, recognizing the contradiction in EU policy, acknowledging that Mahmud Abbas had been correct in his fears about the election outcome, and expressing concern about "a certain 'democratic fundamentalism' that equates elections with democracy without regard to context. "Italian Foreign Minister Comments on Israel, U.S., Iraq, Iran," *BBC Monitoring Europe*, May 22, 2006.

51. See, for example, the *New York Times* February 15, 2006, editorial in which it recognizes that the U.S. "cannot possibly give political recognition or financial aid to such a government" but condemns the administration's policy as "deliberate destabilization." "Set aside the hypocrisy such a course would represent on the part of the two countries that have shouted the loudest about the need for Arab democracy, and consider the probable impact of such an approach on the Palestinians." The *Times* called for less provocative policies. See "The Right Way to Pressure Hamas," *New York Times*, February 15, 2006, http://www.nytimes.com/2006/02/15/opinion/15wed1.html (accessed February 28, 2008).

52. Shklar (fn. 35) has a nice discussion of hypocrites and antihypocrites in chap. 2.

53. I am grateful to Amir Stepak for bringing this point to my attention.

54. Nils Brunsson (fn. 35); and Krasner (fn. 3). Note that hypocrisy in organizations is somewhat different from our common notions about hypocrisy in individuals. For a more extended discussion of Brunsson's original concept and Krasner's use of it, see Michael Lipson "Peacekeeping: Organized Hypocrisy?" *European Journal of International Relations* 13 (March 2007), 5–34.

55. Bukovansky (fn. 33).

5 THE STATE

S tates are key actors in international relations and how they act depends, in part, on domestic political considerations, as explained in Chapter 5 of *Essentials of International Relations*. In a widely-cited article, Robert D. Putnam explains the entanglements between international and domestic factors during negotiations, using the metaphor and the language of the two-level game. Negotiators consider not only what the other state wants, but also what the domestic constituencies in each will accept. This approach connects the disciplines of international relations and comparative politics.

One of the key instruments states use to try to influence the policies and politics of other states is sanctions, including economic sanctions. In their article, Abel Escribà-Folch and Joseph Wright investigate whether sanctions are effective for promoting democratization. Differentiating among different types of authoritarian state systems, the authors use multiple research strategies to find that sanctions are most effective in changing personalistic dictators, but less effective in one-party regimes or military dictatorships.

The penetration of a state's domestic authority by other states challenges one of the basic rules of the system of states, that of state sovereignty. Political scientist Stephen D. Krasner discusses the principles of sovereignty, which have long been bent by hypocritical and flexible practices. In the contemporary world, Krasner says, pragmatic adaptation to the realities of failed states requires new options, including sharing the state's sovereignty with outside powers and de facto trusteeship in which the international community holds ultimate authority in the state.

Religion is posing a different kind of challenge to states. In the aftermath of the Arab Spring, Olivier Roy argues that the role of Islam in politics is being redefined across the region. Confronted by social and economic realities, states are being forced to operate in a democratic arena, although that democratization may be neither secular nor liberal. That optimistic assessment about the democratization process contrasts with the views of political scientist Samuel P. Huntington, who argued twenty years ago in an article included here and elaborated in the book *The Clash of Civilizations and the Remaking of the World Order* (1996) that the future international system will be characterized by a clash between Western and Islamic civilizations.

Robert D. Putnam

DIPLOMACY AND DOMESTIC POLITICS
The Logic of Two-Level Games

Introduction: The Entanglements of Domestic and International Politics

Domestic politics and international relations are often somehow entangled, but our theories have not yet sorted out the puzzling tangle. It is fruitless to debate whether domestic politics really determine international relations, or the reverse. The answer to that question is clearly "Both, sometimes." The more interesting questions are "When?" and "How?" This article offers a theoretical approach to this issue, but I begin with a story that illustrates the puzzle.

One illuminating example of how diplomacy and domestic politics can become entangled culminated at the Bonn summit conference of 1978.[1] In the mid-1970s, a coordinated program of global reflation, led by the "locomotive" economies of the United States, Germany, and Japan, had been proposed to foster Western recovery from the first oil shock.[2] This proposal had received a powerful boost from the incoming Carter administration and was warmly supported by the weaker countries, as well as the Organization for Economic Co-operation and Development (OECD) and many private economists, who argued that it would overcome international payments imbalances and speed growth all around. On the other hand, the Germans and the Japanese protested that prudent and successful economic managers should not be asked to bail out spendthrifts. Meanwhile, Jimmy Carter's ambitious National Energy Program remained deadlocked in Congress, while Helmut Schmidt led a chorus of complaints about the Americans' uncontrolled appetite for imported oil and their apparent unconcern about the falling dollar. All sides conceded that the world economy was in serious trouble, but it was not clear which was more to blame, tight-fisted German and Japanese fiscal policies or slack-jawed U.S. energy and monetary policies.

At the Bonn summit, however, a comprehensive package deal was approved, the clearest case yet of a summit that left all participants happier than when they arrived. Helmut Schmidt agreed to additional fiscal stimulus, amounting to 1 percent of GNP, Jimmy Carter committed himself to decontrol domestic oil prices by the end of 1980, and Takeo Fukuda pledged new efforts to reach a 7 percent growth rate. Secondary elements in the Bonn accord included French and British acquiescence in the Tokyo Round trade negotiations; Japanese undertakings to foster import growth and restrain exports; and a generic American promise to fight inflation. All in all, the Bonn summit produced a balanced agreement of unparalleled breadth and specificity.

From *International Organization* 42, no. 3 (Summer 1988), 427–460. Some of the author's notes have been omitted.

More remarkably, virtually all parts of the package were actually implemented.

Most observers at the time welcomed the policies agreed to at Bonn, although in retrospect there has been much debate about the economic wisdom of this package deal. However, my concern here is not whether the deal was wise economically, but how it became possible politically. My research suggests, first, that the key governments at Bonn adopted policies different from those that they would have pursued in the absence of international negotiations, but second, that agreement was possible only because a powerful minority within each government actually favored on domestic grounds the policy being demanded internationally.

Within Germany, a political process catalyzed by foreign pressures was surreptitiously orchestrated by expansionists inside the Schmidt government. Contrary to the public mythology, the Bonn deal was not forced on a reluctant or "altruistic" Germany. In fact, officials in the Chancellor's Office and the Economics Ministry, as well as in the Social Democratic party and the trade unions, had argued privately in early 1978 that further stimulus was domestically desirable, particularly in view of the approaching 1980 elections. However, they had little hope of overcoming the opposition of the Finance Ministry, the Free Democratic party (part of the government coalition), and the business and banking community, especially the leadership of the Bundesbank. Publicly, Helmut Schmidt posed as reluctant to the end. Only his closest advisors suspected the truth: that the chancellor "let himself be pushed" into a policy that he privately favored, but would have found costly and perhaps impossible to enact without the summit's package deal.

Analogously, in Japan a coalition of business interests, the Ministry of Trade and Industry (MITI), the Economic Planning Agency, and some expansion-minded politicians within the Liberal Democratic Party pushed for additional domestic stimulus, using U.S. pressure as one of their prime arguments against the stubborn resistance of the Ministry of Finance (MOF). Without internal divisions in Tokyo, it is unlikely that the foreign demands would have been met, but without the external pressure, it is even more unlikely that the expansionists could have overridden the powerful MOF. "Seventy percent foreign pressure, 30 percent internal politics," was the disgruntled judgment of one MOF insider. "Fifty-fifty," guessed an official from MITI.[3]

In the American case, too, internal politicking reinforced, and was reinforced by, the international pressure. During the summit preparations American negotiators occasionally invited their foreign counterparts to put more pressure on the Americans to reduce oil imports. Key economic officials within the administration favored a tougher energy policy, but they were opposed by the president's closest political aides, even after the summit. Moreover, congressional opponents continued to stymie oil price decontrol, as they had under both Nixon and Ford. Finally, in April 1979, the president decided on gradual administrative decontrol, bringing U.S. prices up to world levels by October 1981. His domestic advisors thus won a postponement of this politically costly move until after the 1980 presidential election, but in the end, virtually every one of the pledges made at Bonn was fulfilled. Both proponents and opponents of decontrol agree that the summit commitment was at the center of the administration's heated intramural debate during the winter of 1978–79 and instrumental in the final decision.[4]

In short, the Bonn accord represented genuine international policy coordination. Significant policy changes were pledged and implemented by the key participants. Moreover—although this counterfactual claim is necessarily harder to establish—those policy changes would very probably not have been pursued (certainly not the same scale and within the same time frame) in the absence of the international agreement. Within each country, one faction supported the policy shift being demanded of its country internationally, but that faction was initially outnumbered. Thus, international pressure was a necessary condition for these policy shifts. On the other hand, without domestic resonance, international forces would not have sufficed to produce the accord, no matter how balanced and intellectually persuasive the overall package. In the end, each leader believed that what he was doing was in his nation's interest—and probably in his own political interest, too, even though not all his aides agreed.[5] Yet without the summit accord he probably would not (or could not) have changed policies so easily. In that sense, the Bonn deal successfully meshed domestic and international pressures.

Neither a purely domestic nor a purely international analysis could account for this episode. Interpretations cast in terms either of domestic causes and international effects ("Second Image"[6]) or of international causes and domestic effects ("Second Image Reversed"[7]) would represent merely "partial equilibrium" analyses and would miss an important part of the story, namely, how the domestic politics of several countries became entangled via an international negotiation. The events of 1978 illustrate that we must aim instead for "general equilibrium" theories that account simultaneously for the interaction of domestic and international factors. This article suggests a conceptual framework for understanding how diplomacy and domestic politics interact.

Domestic-International Entanglements: The State of the Art

Much of the existing literature on relations between domestic and international affairs consists either of ad hoc lists of countless "domestic influences" on foreign policy or of generic observations that national and international affairs are somehow "linked."[8] James Rosenau was one of the first scholars to call attention to this area, but his elaborate taxonomy of "linkage politics" generated little cumulative research, except for a flurry of work correlating domestic and international "conflict behavior."[9]

A second stream of relevant theorizing began with the work by Karl Deutsch and Ernst Haas on regional integration.[10] Haas, in particular, emphasized the impact of parties and interest groups on the process of European integration, and his notion of "spillover" recognized the feedback between domestic and international developments. However, the central dependent variable in this work was the hypothesized evolution of new supranational institutions, rather than specific policy developments, and when European integration stalled, so did this literature. The intellectual heirs of this tradition, such as Joseph Nye and Robert Keohane, emphasized interdependence and transnationalism, but the role of domestic factors slipped more and more out of focus, particularly as the concept of international regimes came to dominate the subfield.[11]

The "bureaucratic politics" school of foreign policy analysis initiated another promising attack on the problem of domestic–international interaction. As Graham Allison noted, "Applied to relations between nations, the bureaucratic politics model directs attention to intra-national games, the overlap of which constitutes international relations."[12] Nevertheless, the nature of this "overlap" remained unclarified, and the theoretical contribution of this literature did not evolve much beyond the principle that bureaucratic interests matter in foreign policymaking.

More recently, the most sophisticated work on the domestic determinants of foreign policy has focused on "structural" factors, particularly "state strength." The landmark works of Peter Katzenstein and Stephen Krasner, for example, showed the importance of domestic factors in foreign economic policy. Katzenstein captured the essence of the problem: "The main purpose of all strategies of foreign economic policy is to make domestic policies compatible with the international political economy."[13] Both authors stressed the crucial point that central decision-makers ("the state") must be concerned simultaneously with domestic and international pressures.

■   ■   ■

Some work in the "state-centric" genre represents a unitary-actor model run amok. "The central proposition of this paper," notes one recent study, "is that the state derives its interests from and advocates policies consistent with the international system at all times and under all circumstances."[14] In fact, on nearly all important issues "central decision-makers" disagree about what the national interest and the international context demand. Even if we arbitrarily exclude the legislature from "the state" (as much of this literature does), it is wrong to assume that the executive is unified in its views. Certainly this was true in *none* of the states involved in the 1978 negotiations. * * *

Thus, the state-centric literature is an uncertain foundation for theorizing about how domestic and international politics interact. More interesting are recent works about the impact of the international economy on domestic politics and domestic economic policy, such as those by Alt, Evans, Gourevitch, and Katzenstein.[15] These case studies, representing diverse methodological approaches, display a theoretical sophistication on the international-to-domestic causal connection far greater than is characteristic of comparable studies on the domestic-to-international half of the loop. Nevertheless, these works do not purport to account for instances of reciprocal causation, nor do they examine cases in which the domestic politics of several countries became entangled internationally.

In short, we need to move beyond the mere observation that domestic factors influence international affairs and vice versa, and beyond simple catalogs of instances of such influence, to seek theories that integrate both spheres, accounting for the areas of entanglement between them.

Two-Level Games: A Metaphor for Domestic-International Interactions

Over two decades ago Richard E. Walton and Robert B. McKersie offered a "behavioral theory" of social negotiations that is strikingly applicable to international conflict and cooperation.[16] They pointed out, as all experienced negotiators know, that the unitary-actor assumption is often radically misleading. As Robert Strauss said of the Tokyo Round trade negotiations: "During my tenure as Special Trade Representative, I spent as much time negotiating with domestic constituents (both industry and labor) and members of the U.S. Congress as I did negotiating with our foreign trading partners."[17]

The politics of many international negotiations can usefully be conceived as a two-level game. At the national level, domestic groups pursue their interests by pressuring the government to adopt favorable policies, and politicians seek power by constructing coalitions among those groups. At the international level, national governments seek to maximize their own ability to satisfy domestic pressures, while minimizing the adverse consequences of foreign developments. Neither of the two games can be ignored by central decision-makers, so long as their countries remain interdependent, yet sovereign.

Each national political leader appears at both game boards. Across the international table sit his foreign counterparts, and at his elbows sit diplomats and other international advisors. Around the domestic table behind him sit party and parliamentary figures, spokespersons for domestic agencies, representatives of key interest groups, and the leader's own political advisors. The unusual complexity of this two-level game is that moves that are rational for a player at one board (such as raising energy prices, conceding territory, or limiting auto imports) may be impolitic for that same player at the other board. Nevertheless, there are powerful incentives for consistency between the two games. Players (and kibitzers) will tolerate some differences in rhetoric between the two games, but in the end either energy prices rise or they don't.

The political complexities for the players in this two-level game are staggering. Any key player at the international table who is dissatisfied with the outcome may upset the game board, and conversely, any leader who fails to satisfy his fellow players at the domestic table risks being evicted from his seat. On occasion, however, clever players will spot a move on one board that will trigger realignments on other boards, enabling them to achieve otherwise unattainable objectives. This "two-table" metaphor captures the dynamics of the 1978 negotiations better than any model based on unitary national actors.

* * * Probably the most interesting empirically based theorizing about the connection between domestic and international bargaining is that of Glenn Snyder and Paul Diesing. Though working in the neo-realist tradition with its conventional assumption of unitary actors, they found that, in fully half of the crises they studied, top decision-makers were *not* unified. They concluded that prediction of international outcomes is significantly improved by understanding internal bargaining, especially with respect to minimally acceptable compromises.[18]

Metaphors are not theories, but I am comforted by Max Black's observation that "perhaps every science must start with metaphor and end with algebra; and perhaps without the metaphor there would never have been any algebra."[19] Formal analysis of any game requires well-defined rules, choices, payoffs, players, and information, and even then, many simple two-person, mixed-motive games have no determinate solution. Deriving analytic solutions for two-level games will be a difficult challenge. In what follows I hope to motivate further work on that problem.

Towards a Theory of Ratification: The Importance of "Win-Sets"

Consider the following stylized scenario that might apply to any two-level game. Negotiators representing two organizations meet to reach an agreement between them, subject to the constraint that any tentative agreement must be ratified by their respective organizations. The negotiators might be heads of government representing nations, for example, or labor and management representatives, or party leaders in a multiparty coalition, or a finance minister negotiating with an IMF team, or leaders of a House-Senate conference committee, or ethnic-group leaders in a consociational democracy. For the moment, we shall presume that each side is represented by a single leader or "chief negotiator," and that this individual has no independent policy preferences, but seeks simply to achieve an agreement that will be attractive to his constituents.[20]

It is convenient analytically to decompose the process into two stages:

1. bargaining between the negotiators, leading to a tentative agreement; call that Level I.

2. separate discussions within each group of constituents about whether to ratify the agreement; call that Level II.

This sequential decomposition into a negotiation phase and a ratification phase is useful for purposes of exposition, although it is not descriptively accurate. In practice, expectational effects will be quite important. There are likely to be prior consultations and bargaining at Level II to hammer out an initial position for the Level I negotiations. Conversely, the need for Level II ratification is certain to affect the Level I bargaining. In fact, expectations of rejection at Level II may abort negotiations at Level I without any formal action at Level II. For example, even though both the American and Iranian governments seem to have favored an arms-for-hostages deal, negotiations collapsed as soon as they became public and thus liable to de facto "ratification." In many negotiations, the two-level process may be iterative, as the negotiators try out possible agreements and probe their constituents' views. In more complicated cases, as we shall see later, the constituents' views may themselves evolve in the course of the negotiations. Nevertheless, the requirement that any Level I agreement must, in the end, be ratified at Level II imposes a crucial theoretical link between the two levels.

"Ratification" may entail a formal voting procedure at Level II, such as the constitutionally required two-thirds vote of the U.S. Senate for ratifying treaties, but I use the term generically to refer to any decision-process at Level II that is required to endorse or implement a Level I agreement, whether formally or informally. It is sometimes convenient to think of ratification as a parliamentary function, but that is not essential. The actors at Level II may represent bureaucratic agencies, interest groups, social classes, or even "public opinion." For example, if labor unions in a debtor country withhold necessary cooperation from an austerity program that the government has negotiated with the IMF, Level II ratification of the agreement may be said to have failed; ex ante expectations about that prospect will surely influence the Level I negotiations between the government and the IMF.

Domestic ratification of international agreements might seem peculiar to democracies. As the German Finance Minister recently observed, "The limit of expanded cooperation lies in the fact that we are democracies, and we need to secure electoral majorities at home."[21] However, ratification need not be "democratic" in any normal sense. For example, in 1930 the Meiji Constitution was interpreted as giving a special role to the Japanese military in the ratification of the London Naval Treaty;[22] and during the ratification of any agreement between Catholics and Protestants in Northern Ireland, presumably the IRA would throw its power onto the scales. We need only stipulate that, for purposes of counting "votes" in the ratification process, different forms of political power can be reduced to some common denominator.

The only formal constraint on the ratification process is that since the identical agreement must be ratified by both sides, a preliminary Level I agreement cannot be amended at Level II without reopening the Level I negotiations. In other words, final ratification must be simply "voted" up or down; any modification to the Level I agreement counts as a rejection, unless that modification is approved by all other parties to the agreement.[23] Congresswoman Lynn Martin captured the logic of ratification when explaining her support for the 1986 tax reform bill as it emerged from the conference committee: "As worried as I am about what this bill does, I am even more worried about the current code. The choice today is not between this bill and a perfect bill; the choice is between this bill and the death of tax reform."[24]

Given this set of arrangements, we may define the "win-set" for a given Level II constituency as the set of all possible Level I agreements that would "win"—that is, gain the necessary majority among the constituents—when simply voted up or down.[25] For two quite different reasons, the contours of the Level II win-sets are very important for understanding Level I agreements.

First, larger win-sets make Level I agreement more likely, *ceterls paribus.*[26] By definition, any successful agreement must fall within the Level II win-sets of each of the parties to the accord. Thus, agreement is possible only if those win-sets overlap, and the larger each win-set, the more likely they are to overlap. Conversely, the smaller the win-sets, the greater the risk that the negotiations will break down. For example, during the prolonged pre-war Anglo-Argentine negotiations over the Falklands/Malvinas, several tentative agreements were rejected in one capital or the other for domestic political reasons; when it became clear that the initial British and Argentine win-sets did not overlap at all, war became virtually inevitable.[27]

■   ■   ■

The second reason why win-set size is important is that the relative size of the respective Level II win-sets will affect the distribution of the Joint gains from the international bargain. The larger the perceived win-set of a negotiator, the more he can be "pushed around" by the other Level I negotiators. Conversely, a small domestic win-set can be a bargaining advantage: "I'd like to accept your proposal, but I could never get it accepted at home." Lamenting the domestic constraints under which one must operate is (in the words of one experienced British diplomat) "the natural thing to say at the beginning of a tough negotiation."[28]

This general principle was, of course, first noted by Thomas Schelling nearly thirty years ago:

> The power of a negotiator often rests on a manifest inability to make concessions and meet demands. . . . When the United States Government negotiates with other governments . . . if the executive branch negotiates under legislative authority, with its position constrained by law, . . . then the executive branch has a firm

position that is visible to its negotiating partners. . . . [Of course, strategies such as this] run the risk of establishing an immovable position that goes beyond the ability of the other to concede, and thereby provoke the likelihood of stalemate or breakdown.[29]

Writing from a strategist's point of view, Schelling stressed ways in which win-sets may be manipulated, but even when the win-set itself is beyond the negotiator's control, he may exploit its leverage. A Third World leader whose domestic position is relatively weak (Argentina's Alfonsin?) should be able to drive a better bargain with his international creditors, other things being equal, than one whose domestic standing is more solid (Mexico's de la Madrid?).[30] The difficulties of winning congressional ratification are often exploited by American negotiators. During the negotiation of the Panama Canal Treaty, for example, "the Secretary of State warned the Panamanians several times . . . that the new treaty would have to be acceptable to at least sixty-seven senators," and "Carter, in a personal letter to Torrijos, warned that further concessions by the United States would seriously threaten chances for Senate ratification."[31] Precisely to forestall such tactics, opponents may demand that a negotiator ensure himself "negotiating room" at Level II before opening the Level I negotiations.

■   ■   ■

Determinants of the Win-Set

It is important to understand what circumstances affect win-set size. Three sets of factors are especially important:

- Level II preferences and coalitions
- Level II institutions
- Level I negotiators' strategies

Let us consider each in turn.

1. *The size of the win-set depends on the distribution of power, preferences, and possible coalitions among Level II constituents.*

Any testable two-level theory of international negotiation must be rooted in a theory of domestic politics, that is, a theory about the power and preferences of the major actors at Level II. This is not the occasion for even a cursory evaluation of the relevant alternatives, except to note that the two-level conceptual framework could in principle be married to such diverse perspectives as Marxism, interest group pluralism, bureaucratic politics, and neo-corporatism. For example, arms negotiations might be interpreted in terms of a bureaucratic politics model of Level II politicking, while class analysis or neo-corporatism might be appropriate for analyzing international macroeconomic coordination.

Abstracting from the details of Level II politics, however, it is possible to sketch certain principles that govern the size of the win-sets. For example, the lower the cost of "no-agreement" to constituents, the smaller the win-set,[32] Recall that ratification pits the proposed agreement, *not* against an array of other (possibly attractive) alternatives, but only against "no-agreement."[33] No-agreement often represents the status quo, although in some cases no-agreement may in fact lead to a worsening situation; that might be a reasonable description of the failed ratification of the Versailles Treaty.

Some constituents may face low costs from no-agreement, and others high costs, and the former will be more skeptical of Level I agreements than the latter. * * * The size of the win-set (and thus the negotiating room of the Level I negotiator) depends on the relative size of the "isolationist" forces (who oppose international cooperation in general) and the "internationalists" (who offer "all-purpose" support). All-purpose support for international agreements is probably greater in smaller, more dependent countries with more open economies, as compared to more self-sufficient countries, like the United States, for most of whose citizens the costs of no-agreement are generally lower. *Ceteris paribus*, more self-sufficient states with smaller win-sets should make fewer international agreements and drive harder bargains in those that they do make.

In some cases, evaluation of no-agreement may be the *only* significant disagreement among the Level II constituents, because their interests are relatively homogeneous. For example, if oil imports are to be limited by an agreement among the consuming nations—the sort of accord sought at the Tokyo summit of 1979, for example—then presumably every constituent would prefer to maximize his nation's share of the available supply, although some constituents may be more reluctant than others to push too hard, for fear of losing the agreement entirely. * * * Other international examples in which domestic interests are relatively homogeneous except for the evaluation or no-agreement might include the SALT talks, the Panama Canal Treaty negotiations, and the Arab-Israeli conflict. A negotiator is unlikely to face criticism at home that a proposed agreement reduces the opponents' arms too much, offers too little compensation for foreign concessions, or contains too few security guarantees for the other side, although in each case opinions may differ on how much to risk a negotiating deadlock in order to achieve these objectives.

The distinctive nature of such "homogeneous" issues is thrown into sharp relief by contrasting them to cases in which constituents' preferences are more heterogeneous, so that any Level I agreement bears unevenly on them. Thus, an internationally coordinated reflation may encounter domestic opposition *both* from those who think it goes too far (bankers, for example) *and* from those who think it does not go far enough (unions, for example). In 1919, some Americans opposed the Versailles Treaty because it was too harsh on the defeated powers and others because it was too lenient.[34] Such patterns are even more common, as we shall shortly see, where the negotiation involves multiple issues, such as an arms agreement that involves tradeoffs between seaborne and airborne weapons, or a labor agreement that involves tradeoffs between take-home pay and pensions. (Walton and McKersie term these "factional" conflicts, because the negotiator is caught between contending factions within his own organization.)

The problems facing Level I negotiators dealing with a *homogeneous* (or "boundary") conflict are quite different from those facing negotiators dealing with a *heterogeneous* (or "factional") conflict. In the former case, the more the negotiator can win at Level I—the higher his national oil allocation, the deeper the cuts in Soviet throw-weight, the lower the rent he promises for the Canal, and so on—the better his odds of winning ratification. In such cases, the negotiator may use the implicit threat from his own hawks to maximize his gains (or minimize his losses) at Level I, as Carter and Vance did in dealing with the Panamanians. Glancing over his shoulder at Level II, the negotiator's main problem in a homogeneous conflict is to manage the discrepancy between his constituents' expectations and the negotiable outcome. Neither negotiator is likely to find much sympathy for the enemy's demands among his own constituents, nor much support for his constituents' positions in the enemy camp. The effect of domestic division, embodied in hard-line opposition from hawks, is to raise the risk of involuntary defection and thus to impede agreement at Level I. The common belief that domestic politics is inimical to international cooperation no doubt derives from such cases.

The task of a negotiator grappling instead with a heterogeneous conflict is more complicated, but potentially more interesting. Seeking to maximize the chances of ratification, he cannot follow a simple "the more, the better" rule of thumb; imposing more severe reparations on the Germans in 1919 would have gained some votes at Level II but lost others, as would hastening the decontrol of domestic oil prices in 1978. In some cases, these lines of cleavage within the Level II constituencies will cut across the Level I division, and the Level I negotiator may find silent allies at his opponent's domestic table. German labor unions might welcome foreign pressure on their own government to adopt a more expansive fiscal policy, and Italian bankers might welcome international demands for a more austere Italian monetary policy. Thus transnational alignments may emerge, tacit or explicit, in which domestic interests pressure their respective governments to adopt mutually supportive policies. This is, of course, my interpretation of the 1978 Bonn summit accord.

In such cases, domestic divisions may actually improve the prospects for international cooperation. * * *

Thus far we have implicitly assumed that all eligible constituents will participate in the ratification process. In fact, however, participation rates vary across groups and across issues, and this variation often has implications for the size of the winset. For example, when the costs and/or benefits of a proposed agreement are relatively concentrated, it is reasonable to expect that those constituents whose interests are most affected will exert special influence on the ratification process.[35] One reason why Level II games are more important for trade negotiations than in monetary matters is that the "abstention rate" is higher on international monetary issues than on trade issues.[36]

The composition of the active Level II constituency (and hence the character of the win-set) also varies with the politicization of the issue. Politicization often activates groups who are less worried about the costs of no-agreement, thus reducing the effective win-set. For example, politicization of the Panama Canal issue seems to have reduced the negotiating flexibility on both sides of the diplomatic table.[37] This is one reason why most professional diplomats emphasize the value of secrecy to successful negotiations. However, Woodrow Wilson's transcontinental tour in 1919 reflected the opposite calculation, namely, that by expanding the active constituency he could ensure ratification of the Versailles Treaty, although in the end this strategy proved fruitless.[38]

Another important restriction of our discussion thus far has been the assumption that the negotiations involve only one issue. Relaxing this assumption has powerful consequences for the play at both levels.[39] Various groups at Level II are likely to have quite different preferences on the several issues involved in a multi-issue negotiation. As a general rule, the group with the greatest interest in a specific issue is also likely to hold the most extreme position on that issue. In the Law of the Sea negotiations, for example, the Defense Department felt most strongly about sea-lanes, the Department of the Interior about sea-bed mining rights, and so on.[40] If each group is allowed to fix the Level I negotiating position for "its" issue, the resulting package is almost sure to be "non-negotiable" (that is, nonratifiable in opposing capitals).[41]

Thus, the chief negotiator is faced with tradeoffs across different issues: how much to yield on mining rights in order to get sea-lane protection, how much to yield on citrus exports to get a better deal on beef, and so on. * * * The central point is simple: the possibility of package deals opens up a rich array of strategic alternatives for negotiators in a two-level game.

One kind of issue linkage is absolutely crucial to understanding how domestic and international politics can become entangled.[42] Suppose that a majority of constituents at Level II oppose a given policy (say, oil price decontrol), but that some members of that majority would be willing to switch their vote on that issue in return for more jobs (say, in export industries). If bargaining is limited to Level II, that tradeoff is not technically feasible, but if the chief negotiator can broker an international deal that delivers more jobs (say, via faster growth abroad), he can, in effect, overturn the initial outcome at the domestic table. Such a transnational issue linkage was a crucial element in the 1978 Bonn accord.

Note that this strategy works not by changing the preferences of any domestic constituents, but rather by creating a policy option (such as faster export growth) that was previously beyond domestic control. Hence, I refer to this type of issue linkage at Level I that alters the feasible outcomes at Level II as *synergistic linkage*. For example, "in the Tokyo Round . . . nations used negotiation to achieve internal reform in situations where constituency pressures would otherwise prevent action without the pressure (and tradeoff benefits) that an external partner could provide."[43] Economic interdependence multiplies the opportunities for altering domestic coalitions (and thus policy outcomes) by expanding the set of feasible alternatives in this way—in effect, creating political entanglements across national boundaries. Thus, we should expect synergistic linkage (which is, by definition, explicable only in terms of two-level analysis) to become more frequent as interdependence grows.

2. *The size of the win-set depends on the Level II political institutions.*

Ratification procedures clearly affect the size of the win-set. For example, if a two-thirds vote is required for ratification, the win-set will almost certainly be smaller than if only a simple majority is required. As one experienced observer has written: "Under the Constitution, thirty-four of the one hundred senators can block ratification of any treaty. This is an unhappy and unique feature of our democracy. Because of the effective veto power of a small group, many worthy agreements have been rejected, and many treaties are never considered for ratification."[44] As noted earlier, the U.S. separation of powers imposes a tighter constraint on the American win-set than is true in many other countries. This increases the bargaining power of American negotiators, but it also reduces the scope for international cooperation. It raises the odds for involuntary defection and makes potential partners warier about dealing with the Americans.

■   ■   ■

Not all significant ratification practices are formalized; for example, the Japanese propensity for seeking the broadest possible domestic consensus before acting constricts the Japanese win-set, as contrasted with majoritarian political cultures. Other domestic political practices, too, can affect the size of the win-set. Strong discipline within the governing party, for example, increases the win-set by widening the range of agreements for which the Level I negotiator can expect to receive backing. For example, in the 1986 House-Senate conference committee on tax reform, the final bill was closer to the Senate version, despite (or rather, *because of*) Congressman Rostenkowski's greater control of his delegation, which increased the House win-set. Conversely, a weakening of party discipline across the major Western nations would, *ceteris paribus*, reduce the scope for international cooperation.

The recent discussion of "state strength" and "state autonomy" is relevant here. The greater the autonomy of central decision-makers from their Level II constituents, the larger their win-set and thus the greater the likelihood of achieving international agreement. For example, central bank insulation from domestic political pressures in effect increases the win-set and thus the odds for international monetary cooperation; recent proposals for an enhanced role for central bankers in international policy coordination rest on this point.[45] However, two-level analysis also implies that, *ceteris paribus*, the stronger a state is in terms of autonomy from domestic pressures, the weaker its relative bargaining position internationally. For example, diplomats representing an entrenched dictatorship are less able than representatives of a democracy to claim credibly that domestic pressures preclude some disadvantageous deal.[46] This is yet another facet of the disconcerting ambiguity of the notion of "state strength."

For simplicity of exposition, my argument is phrased throughout in terms of only two levels. However, many institutional arrangements require several levels of ratification, thus multiplying the complexity (but perhaps also the importance) of win-set analysis. Consider, for example, negotiations between the United States and the European Community over agricultural trade. According to the Treaty of Rome, modifications of the Common Agricultural Policy require unanimous ratification by the Council of Ministers, representing each of the member states. In turn, each of those governments must, in effect, win ratification for its decision within its own national arena, and in coalition governments, that process might also require ratification within each of the parties. Similarly, on the American side, ratification would (informally, at least) necessitate support from most, if not all, of the major agricultural organizations, and within those organizations, further ratification by key interests and regions might be required. At each stage, cleavage patterns, issue linkages, ratification procedures, side-payments, negotiator strategies, and so on would need to be considered. At some point in this analytic regress the complexity of further decomposition would outweigh the advantages, but the example illustrates the need for careful thought about the logic of multiple-level games.

3. *The size of the win-set depends on the strategies of the Level I negotiators.*

Each Level I negotiator has an unequivocal interest in maximizing the other side's win-set, but with respect to his own win-set, his motives are mixed. The larger his win-set, the more easily he can conclude an agreement, but also the weaker his bargaining position vis-à-vis the other negotiator. This fact often poses a tactical dilemma. For example, one effective way to demonstrate commitment to a given position in Level I bargaining is to rally support from one's constituents (for example, holding a strike vote, talking about a "missile gap," or denouncing "unfair trading practices" abroad). On the other hand, such tactics may have irreversible effects on constituents' attitudes, hampering subsequent ratification of a compromise agreement.[47] Conversely, preliminary consultations at home, aimed at "softening up" one's constituents in anticipation of a ratification struggle, can undercut a negotiator's ability to project an implacable image abroad.

Nevertheless, disregarding these dilemmas for the moment and assuming that a negotiator wishes to expand his win-set in order to encourage ratification of an agreement, he may exploit both conventional side-payments and generic "good will," The use of side-payments to attract marginal supporters is, of course, quite familiar in game theory, as well as in practical politics. For example, the Carter White House offered many inducements (such as public works projects) to help persuade wavering Senators to ratify the Panama Canal Treaty.[48] In a two-level game the side-payments may come from unrelated domestic sources, as in this case, or they may be received as part of the international negotiation.

The role of side-payments in international negotiations is well known. However, the two-level approach emphasizes that the value of an international side-payment should be calculated in terms of its marginal contribution to the likelihood of ratification, rather than in terms of its overall value to the recipient nation. What counts at Level II is not total national costs and benefits, but their *incidence, relative to existing coalitions and proto-coalitioins.* An across-the-board trade concession (or still worse, a concession on a product of interest to a committed free-trade congressman) is less effective than a concession (even one of lesser intrinsic value) that tips the balance with a swing voter. Conversely, trade retaliation should be targeted, neither at free-traders nor at confirmed protectionists, but at the uncommitted.

An experienced negotiator familiar with the respective domestic tables should be able to maximize the cost-effectiveness (to him and his constituents) of the concessions that he must make to ensure ratification abroad, as well as the cost-effectiveness of his own demands and threats, by targeting his initiatives with an eye to their Level II incidence, both at home and abroad. In this endeavor Level I negotiators are often in collusion, since each has an interest in helping the other to get the final deal ratified. In effect, they are moving jointly towards points of tangency between their respective political indifference curves. The empirical frequency of such targeting in trade negotiations and trade wars, as well as in other international negotiations, would be a crucial test of the relative merits of conventional unitary-actor analysis and the two-level approach proposed here.[49]

In addition to the use of specific side-payments, a chief negotiator whose political standing at home is high can more easily win ratification of his foreign initiatives. Although generic good will cannot guarantee ratification, as Woodrow Wilson discovered, it is useful in expanding the win-set and thus fostering Level I agreement, for it constitutes a kind of "all-purpose glue" for his supporting coalition. * * *

Note that each Level I negotiator has a strong interest in the popularity of his opposite number, since Party A's popularity increases the size of his win-set, and thus increases both the odds of success and the relative bargaining leverage of Party B. Thus, negotiators should normally be expected to try to reinforce one another's standing with their respective constituents.

Partly for this reason and partly because of media attention, participation on the world stage normally gives a head of government a special advantage vis-à-vis his or her domestic opposition. Thus, although international policy coordination is hampered by high transaction costs, heads of government may also reap what we might term "transaction benefits." Indeed, the recent evolution of

Western summitry, which has placed greater emphasis on publicity than on substance, seems designed to appropriate these "transaction benefits" without actually seeking the sort of agreements that might entail transaction costs.[50]

Higher status negotiators are likely to dispose of more side-payments and more "good will" at home, and hence foreigners prefer to negotiate with a head of government than with a lower official. In purely distributive terms, a nation might have a bargaining advantage if its chief negotiator were a mere clerk. Diplomats are acting rationally, not merely symbolically, when they refuse to negotiate with a counterpart of inferior rank. America's negotiating partners have reason for concern whenever the American president is domestically weakened.

Uncertainty and Bargaining Tactics

Level I negotiators are often badly misinformed about Level II politics, particularly on the opposing side. In 1978, the Bonn negotiators were usually wrong in their assessments of domestic politics abroad; for example, most American officials did not appreciate the complex domestic game that Chancellor Schmidt was playing over the issue of German reflation. Similarly, Snyder and Diesing report that "decision makers in our cases only occasionally attempted such assessments, and when they tried they did pretty miserably. . . . Governments generally do not do well in analyzing each other's internal politics in crises [and, I would add, in normal times], and indeed it is inherently difficult."[51] Relaxing the assumption of perfect information to allow for uncertainty has many implications for our understanding of two-level games. Let me illustrate a few of these implications.

Uncertainty about the size of a win-set can be both a bargaining device and a stumbling block in two-level negotiation. In purely distributive Level I bargaining, negotiators have an incentive to understate their own win-sets. Since each negotiator is likely to know more about his own Level II than his opponent does, the claim has some plausibility. * * *

On the other hand, uncertainty about the opponent's win-set increases one's concern about the risk of involuntary defection. Deals can only be struck if each negotiator is convinced that the proposed deal lies within his opposite number's win-set and thus will be ratified. Uncertainty about party A's ratification lowers the expected value of the agreement to party B, and thus party B will demand more generous side-payments from party A than would be needed under conditions of certainty. In fact, party B has an incentive to feign doubt about party A's ability to deliver, precisely in order to extract a more generous offer.[52]

Thus, a utility-maximizing negotiator must seek to convince his opposite number that his own win-set is "kinky," that is, that the proposed deal is certain to be ratified, but that a deal slightly more favorable to the opponent is unlikely to be ratified. * * *

The analysis of two-level games offers many illustrations of Zartman's observation that all negotiation involves "the controlled exchange of partial information."[53]

Restructuring and Reverberation

Formally speaking, game-theoretic analysis requires that the structure of issues and payoffs be specified in advance. In reality, however, much of what happens in any bargaining situation involves attempts by the players to restructure the game and to alter one another's perceptions of the costs of no-agreement and the benefits of proposed agreements. Such tactics are more difficult in two-level games than in conventional negotiations, because it is harder to reach constituents on the other side with persuasive messages. Nevertheless, governments do seek to expand one another's winsets. Much ambassadorial activity—wooing opinion leaders, establishing contact with opposition parties, offering foreign aid to a friendly, but unstable government, and so on—has precisely this function. When Japanese officials visit Capitol Hill, or British diplomats lobby Irish-American leaders, they are seeking to relax domestic constraints that might otherwise prevent the administration from cooperating with their governments.

■　■　■

In some instances, perhaps even unintentionally, international pressures "reverberate" within domestic politics, tipping the domestic balance and thus influencing the international negotiations. Exactly this kind of reverberation characterized the 1978 summit negotiations. Dieter Hiss, the German sherpa and one of those who believed that a stimulus program was in Germany's own interest, later wrote that summits change national policy

> only insofar as they mobilize and/or change public opinion and the attitude of political groups. . . . Often that is enough, if the balance of opinion is shifted, providing a bare majority for the previously stymied actions of a strong minority. . . . No country violates its own interests, but certainly the definition of its interests can change through a summit with its possible tradeoffs and give-and-take.[54]

From the point of view of orthodox social-choice theory, reverberation is problematic, for it implies a certain interconnectedness among the utility functions of independent actors, albeit across different levels of the game. Two rationales may be offered to explain reverberation among utility-maximizing egoists. First, in a complex, interdependent, but often unfriendly world, offending foreigners may be costly in the long run. "To get along, go along" may be a rational maxim. This rationale is likely to be more common the more dependent (or interdependent) a nation, and it is likely to be more persuasive to Level II actors who are more exposed internationally, such as multinational corporations and international banks.

A second rationale takes into account cognitive factors and uncertainty. It would be a mistake for political scientists to mimic most economists' disregard for the suasive element in negotiations.[55] Given the pervasive uncertainty that surrounds many international issues, messages from abroad can change minds, move the undecided, and hearten those in the domestic minority. * * *

Suasive reverberation is more likely among countries with close relations and is probably more frequent in economic than in political–military negotiations. Communiqués from the Western summits are often cited by participants to domestic audiences as a way of legitimizing their policies. After one such statement by Chancellor Schmidt, one of his aides privately characterized the argument as "not intellectually valid, but politically useful." Conversely, it is widely believed by summit participants that a declaration contrary to a government's current policy could be used profitably by its opponents. Recent congressional proposals to ensure greater domestic publicity for international commentary on national economic policies (including hitherto confidential IMF recommendations) turn on the idea that reverberation might increase international cooperation.[56]

Reverberation as discussed thus far implies that international pressure expands the domestic win-set and facilitates agreement. However, reverberation can also be negative, in the sense that foreign pressure may create a domestic backlash. Negative reverberation is probably less common empirically than positive reverberation, simply because foreigners are likely to forgo public pressure if it is recognized to be counterproductive. Cognitive balance theory suggests that international pressure is more likely to reverberate negatively if its source is generally viewed by domestic audiences as an adversary rather than an ally. Nevertheless, predicting the precise effect of foreign pressure is admittedly difficult, although empirically, reverberation seems to occur frequently in two-level games.

The phenomenon of reverberation (along with synergistic issue linkage of the sort described earlier) precludes one attractive short-cut to modeling two-level games. If national preferences were exogenous from the point of view of international relations, then the domestic political game could be molded separately, and the "outputs" from that game could be used as the "inputs" to the international game.[57] The division of labor between comparative politics and international relations could continue, though a few curious observers might wish to keep track of the play on both tables. But if international pressures reverberate within domestic politics, or if issues can be linked synergistically, then domestic outcomes are not exogenous, and the two levels cannot be modeled independently.

The Role of the Chief Negotiator

In the stylized model of two-level negotiations outlined here, the chief negotiator is the only formal link between Level I and Level II. Thus far, I have assumed that the chief negotiator has no independent policy views, but acts merely as an honest broker, or rather as an agent on behalf of his constituents. That assumption powerfully simplifies the analysis of two-level games. However, as principal-agent theory reminds us, this assumption is unrealistic.[58] Empirically, the preferences of the chief negotiator may well diverge from those of his constituents. Two-level negotiations are costly and risky for the chief negotiator, and they often interfere with his other priorities, so it is reasonable to ask what is in it for him.

The motives of the chief negotiator include:

1. Enhancing his standing in the Level II game by increasing his political resources or by minimizing potential losses. * * *
2. Shifting the balance of power at Level II in favor of domestic policies that he prefers for exogenous reasons. International negotiations sometimes enable government leaders to do what they privately wish to do, but are powerless to do domestically. * * *
3. To pursue his own conception of the national interest in the international context. * * *

It is reasonable to presume, at least in the international case of two-level bargaining, that the chief negotiator will normally give primacy to his domestic calculus, if a choice must be made, not least because his own incumbency often depends on his standing at Level II. Hence, he is more likely to present an international agreement for ratification, the less of his own political capital he expects to have to invest to win approval, and the greater the likely political returns from a ratified agreement.

This expanded conception of the role of the chief negotiator implies that he has, in effect, a veto over possible agreements. Even if a proposed deal lies within his Level II win-set, that deal is unlikely to be struck if he opposes it.[59] Since this proviso applies on both sides of the Level I table, the actual international bargaining set may be narrower—perhaps much narrower—than the overlap between the Level II win-sets. Empirically, this additional constraint is often crucial to the outcome of two-level games. One momentous example is the fate of the Versailles Treaty. The best evidence suggests, first, that perhaps 80 percent of the American public *and* of the Senate in 1919 favored ratification of the treaty, if certain reservations were attached, and second, that those reservations were acceptable to the other key signatories, especially Britain and France. In effect, it was Wilson himself who vetoed this otherwise ratifiable package, telling the dismayed French Ambassador, "I shall consent to nothing."[60]

Yet another constraint on successful two-level negotiation derives from the leader's existing domestic coalition. Any political entrepreneur has a fixed investment in a particular pattern of policy positions and a particular supporting coalition. If a proposed international deal threatens that investment, or if ratification would require him to construct a different coalition, the chief negotiator will be reluctant to endorse it, even if (judged abstractly) it could be ratified. Politicians may be willing to risk a few of their normal supporters in the cause of ratifying an international agreement, but the greater the potential loss, the greater their reluctance.

In effect, the fixed costs of coalition-building thus imply this constraint on the win-set: How great a realignment of prevailing coalitions at Level II would be required to ratify a particular proposal? For example, a trade deal may expand export opportunities for Silicon Valley, but harm Aliquippa. This is fine for a chief negotiator (for example, Reagan?) who can easily add Northern California yuppies to his support coalition and who has no hope of winning Aliquippa steelworkers anyhow. But a different chief negotiator with a different support coalition (for example, Mondale?) might find it costly or even impossible to convert the gains from the same agreement into politically usable form. * * *

Relaxing the assumption that the chief negotiator is merely an honest broker, negotiating on behalf of his constituents, opens the possibility that the constituents may be more eager for an agreement (or more worried about "no-agreement") than he is. Empirical instances are not hard to find: in early 1987, European publics were readier to accept Gorbachev's "double-zero" arms control proposal than European leaders, just as in the early 1970s the American public (or at least the politically active public) was more eager for a negotiated end to the Vietnam War than was the Nixon administration.

As a rule, the negotiator retains a veto over any proposed agreement in such cases. However, if the negotiator's own domestic standing (or indeed, his incumbency) would be threatened if he were to reject an agreement that falls within his Level II win-set, and if this is known to all parties, then the other side at Level I gains considerable leverage. Domestic U.S. discontent about the Vietnam War clearly affected the agreement reached at the Paris talks.[61] Conversely, if the constituents are (believed to be) hard-line, then a leader's domestic weakness becomes a diplomatic asset. * * *

My emphasis on the special responsibility of central executives is a point of affinity between the two-level game model and the "state-centric" literature, even though the underlying logic is different. In this "Janus" model of domestic-international interactions, transnational politics are less prominent than in some theories of interdependence.[62] However, to disregard "cross-table" alliances at Level II is a considerable simplification, and it is more misleading, the lower the political visibility of the issue, and the more frequent the negotiations between the governments involved.[63] Empirically, for example, two-level games in the European Community are influenced by many direct ties among Level II participants, such as national agricultural spokesmen. In some cases, the same multinational actor may actually appear at more than one Level II table. In negotiations over mining concessions in some less-developed countries, for example, the same multinational corporation may be consulted privately by both the home and host governments. In subsequent work on the two-level model, the strategic implications of direct communication between Level II players should be explored.

Conclusion

The most portentous development in the fields of comparative politics and international relations in recent years is the dawning recognition among practitioners in each field of the need to take into account entanglements between the two. Empirical illustrations of reciprocal influence between domestic and international affairs abound. What we need now are concepts and theories that will help us organize and extend our empirical observations.

Analysis in terms of two-level games offers a promising response to this challenge. Unlike state-centric theories, the two-level approach recognizes the inevitability of domestic conflict about what the "national interest" requires. Unlike the "Second Image" or the "Second Image Reversed," the two-level approach recognizes that central decision-makers strive to reconcile domestic and international imperatives simultaneously. As we have seen, statesmen in this predicament face distinctive strategic opportunities and strategic dilemmas.

This theoretical approach highlights several significant features of the links between diplomacy and domestic politics, including:

- the important distinction between voluntary and involuntary defection from international agreements;
- the contrast between issues on which domestic interests are homogeneous, simply pitting hawks against doves, and issues on which domestic interests are more heterogeneous, so that domestic cleavage may actually foster international cooperation;
- the possibility of synergistic issue linkage, in which strategic moves at one game-table facilitate unexpected coalitions at the second table;
- the paradoxical fact that institutional arrangements which strengthen decision-makers at home may weaken their international bargaining position, and vice versa;
- the importance of targeting international threats, offers, and side-payments with an eye towards their domestic incidence at home and abroad;

- the strategic uses of uncertainty about domestic politics, and the special utility of "kinky win-sets";
- the potential reverberation of international pressures within the domestic arena;
- the divergences of interest between a national leader and those on whose behalf he is negotiating, and in particular, the international implications of his fixed investments in domestic politics.

Two-level games seem a ubiquitous feature of social life, from Western economic summitry to diplomacy in the Balkans and from coalition politics in Sri Lanka to legislative maneuvering on Capitol Hill. Far-ranging empirical research is needed now to test and deepen our understanding of how such games are played.

NOTES

1. The following account is drawn from Robert D. Putnam and C. Randall Henning, "The Bonn Summit of 1978: How Does International Economic Policy Coordination Actually Work?" *Brookings Discussion Papers in International Economics,* no. 53 (Washington, D.C: Brookings Institution, October 1986), and Robert D. Putnam and Nicholas Bayne, *Hanging Together: Cooperation and Conflict in the Seven-Power Summits*, rev. ed. (Cambridge, Mass.: Harvard University Press, 1987), pp. 62–94.

2. Among interdependent economies, most economists believe, policies can often be more effective if they are internationally coordinated. For relevant citations, see Putnam and Bayne, *Hanging Together*, p. 24.

3. For a comprehensive account of the Japanese story, see I. M. Destler and Hisao Mlisuyu, "Locomotives on Different Tracks; Macroeconomic Diplomacy, 1977–1979," in I. M. Destler and Hideo Sato, eds., *Coping with U.S.-Japanese Economic Conflicts* (Lexington, Mass.: Heath, 1982).

4. For an excellent account of U.S. energy policy during this period, see G. John Ikenberry, "Market Solutions for State Problems: The International and Domestic Politics of American Oil Decontrol," *International Organization* 42 (Winter 1988).

5. It is not clear whether Jimmy Carter fully understood the domestic implications of his Bonn pledge at the time. See Putnam and Henning, "The Bonn Summit," and Ikenberry, "Market Solutions for State Problems."

6. Kenneth N. Waltz, *Man, the State, and War: A Theoretical Analysis* (New York: Columbia University Press, 1959).

7. Peter Gourevitch, "The Second Image Reversed: The International Sources of Domestic Politics," *International Organization* 32 (Autumn 1978), pp. 881–911.

8. I am indebted to Stephen Haggard for enlightening discussions about domestic influences on international relations.

9. James Rosenau, "Toward the Study of National-International Linkages," in his *Linkage Politics: Essays on the Convergence of National and International Systems* (New York: Free Press, 1969), as well as his "Theorizing Across Systems: Linkage Politics Revisited," in Jonathan Wilkenfeld, ed., *Conflict Behavior and Linkage Politics* (New York: David McKay, 1973), especially p. 49.

10. Karl W. Deutsch et al., *Political Community in the North Atlantic Area: International Organization in the Light of Historical Experience* (Princeton: Princeton University Press, 1957) and Ernst B. Haas, *The Uniting of Europe: Political, Social, and Economic Forces, 1950–1957* (Stanford, Calif.: Stanford University Press, 1958).

11. Robert O. Keohane and Joseph S. Nye, *Power and Interdependence* (Boston: Little, Brown, 1977). On the regime literature, including its neglect of domestic factors, see Stephan Haggard and Beth Simmons, "Theories of International Regimes," *International Organization* 41 (Summer 1987), pp. 491–517.

12. Graham T. Allison, *Essence of Decision: Explaining the Cuban Missile Crisis* (Boston: Little, Brown, 1971), p. 149.

13. Peter J. Katzenstein, ed., *Between Power and Plenty: Foreign Economic Policies of Advanced Industrial States* (Madison: University of Wisconsin Press, 1978), p. 4. See also Katzenstein, "International Relations and Domestic Structures: Foreign Economic Policies of Advanced Industrial States," *International Organization* 30 (Winter 1976), pp. 1–45; Stephen D. Krasner, "United States Commercial and Monetary Policy: Unravelling the Paradox of External Strength and Internal Weakness," in Katzenstein, *Between Power and Plenty*, pp. 51–87; and Krasner, *Defending the National Interest: Raw Materials Investments and U.S. Foreign Policy* (Princeton: Princeton University Press, 1978).

14. David A. Lake, "The State as Conduit: The International Sources of National Political Action," presented at the 1984 annual meeting of the American Political Science Association, p. 13.

15. James E. Ali, "Crude Politics: Oil and the Political Economy of Unemployment in Britain and Norway, 1970–1985," *British Journal of Political Science* 17 (April 1987), pp. 149–99; Peter B. Evans, *Dependent Development: The Alliance of Multinational, State, and Local Capital in Brazil* (Princeton: Princeton University Press, 1979); Peter Gourevitch, *Politics in Hard Times: Comparative Responses to International Economic Crises* (Ithaca, N.Y.: Cornell University Press, 1986); Peter J. Katzenstein, *Small States in World Markets: Industrial Policy in Europe* (Ithaca, N.Y.: Cornell University Press, 1985).

16. Richard E. Walton and Robert B. McKersie, *A Behavioral Theory of Labor Negotiations: An Analysis of a Social Interaction System* (New York: McGraw-Hill, 1965).

17. Robert S. Strauss, "Foreword," in Joan E. Twiggs, *The Tokyo Round of Multilateral Trade Negotiations: A Case Study in Building Domestic Support for Diplomacy* (Washington, D.C.: Georgetown University Institute for the Study of Diplomacy, 1987), p. vii. Former Secretary of Labor John Dunlop is said to have remarked that "bilateral negotiations usually require three agreements—one across the table and

one on each side of the table," as cited in Howard Raiffa, *The Art and Science of Negotiation* (Cambridge, Mass.: Harvard University Press, 1982), p. 166.

18. Glenn H. Snyder and Paul Diesing, *Conflict Among Nations: Bargaining, Decision Making, and System Structure in International Crises* (Princeton: Princeton University Press, 1977), pp. 510–25.

19. Max Black, *Models and Metaphors* (Ithaca, N.Y.: Cornell University Press, 1962), p. 242, as cited in Duncan Snidal, "The Game Theory of International Politics," *World Politics* 38 (October 1985), p. 36n.

20. To avoid unnecessary complexity, my argument throughout is phrased in terms of a single chief negotiator, although in many cases some of his responsibilities may be delegated to aides. Later in this article I relax the assumption that the negotiator has no independent preferences.

21. Gerhardt Stoltenberg, *Wall Street Journal Europe*, 2 October 1986, as cited in C. Randall Henning, *Macroeconomic Diplomacy in the 1980s: Domestic Politics and International Conflict Among the United States, Japan, and Europe*, Atlantic Paper No. 65 (New York: Croom Helm, for the Atlantic Institute for International Affairs, 1987), p. 1.

22. Ito Takashi, "Conflicts and Coalition in Japan, 1930: Political Groups and the London Naval Disarmament Conference," in Sven Groennings et al., eds, *The Study of Coalition Behavior* (New York: Holt, Rinehart, & Winston, 1970); Kobayashi Tatsuo, "The London Naval Treaty, 1930," in James W. Morley, ed., *Japan Erupts: The London Naval Conference and the Manchurian Incident, 1928–1932* (New York: Columbia University Press, 1984), pp. 11–117. I am indebted to William Jarosz for this example.

23. This stipulation is, in fact, characteristic of most real-world ratification procedures, such as House and Senate action on conference committee reports, although it is somewhat violated by the occasional practice of appending "reservations" to the ratification of treaties.

24. *New York Times*, 26 September 1986.

25. For the conception of win-set, see Kenneth A. Shepsle and Barry R. Weingast, "The Institutional Foundations of Committee Power," *American Political Science Review* 81 (March 1987), pp, 85–104. I am indebted to Professor Shepsle for much help on this topic.

26. To avoid tedium, I do not repeat the "other things being equal" proviso in each of the propositions that follow. Under some circumstances an expanded win-set might actually make practicable some outcome that could trigger a dilemma of collective action. See Vincent P. Crawford, "A Theory of Disagreement in Bargaining." *Econometrica* 50 (May 1982), pp. 607–37.

27. The Sunday Times Insight Team, *The Falklands War* (London: Sphere, 1982); Max Hastings and Simon Jenkins, *The Battle for the Falklands* (New York: Norton, 1984); Alejandro Dabai and Luis Lorenzano, *Argentina: The Malvinas and the End of Military Rule* (London: Verso, 1984). I am indebted to Louise Richardson for these citations.

28. Geoffrey W. Harrison, in John C. Campbell, ed., *Successful Negotiation: Trieste 1954* (Princeton: Princeton University Press, 1976), p. 62.

29. Thomas C. Schelling, *The Strategy of Conflict* (Cambridge, Mass.: Harvard University Press, 1960), pp. 19–28.

30. I am grateful to Lara Putnam for this example. For supporting evidence, see Robert R. Kaufman, "Democratic and Authoritarian Responses to the Debt Issue: Argentina, Brazil, Mexico," *International Organization* 39 (Summer 1985), pp. 473–503.

31. W. Mark Habeeb and I. William Zartman, *The Panama Canal Negotiations* (Washington, D.C: Johns Hopkins Foreign Policy Institute, 1986), pp. 40, 42.

32. Thomas Romer and Howard Rosenthal, "Political Resource Allocation, Controlled Agendas, and the Status Quo," *Public Choice* 33 (no. 4, 1978), pp. 27–44.

33. In more formal treatments, the no-agreement outcome is called the "reversion point." A given constituent's evaluation of no-agreement corresponds to what Raiffa terms a seller's "walk-away price," that is, the price below which ho would prefer "no deal." (Raiffa, *Art and Science of Negotiation*.) No-agreement

is equivalent to what Snyder and Diesing term "breakdown," or the expected cost of war. (Snyder and Diesing, *Conflict Among Nations.*)

34. Thomas A. Bailey, *Woodrow Wilson and the Great Betrayal* (New York: Macmillan, 1945), pp. 16–37.

35. See James Q. Wilson, *Political Organization* (New York: Basic Books, 1975) on how the politics of an issue are affected by whether the costs and the benefits are concentrated or diffuse.

36. Another factor fostering abstention is the greater complexity and opacity of monetary issues; as Gilbert R. Winham ("Complexity in International Negotiation," in Daniel Druckman, ed., *Negotiations: A Social-Psychological Perspective* [Beverly Hills: Sage, 1977], p. 363) observes, "complexity can strengthen the hand of a negotiator vis-à-vis the organization he represents."

37. Habeeb and Zariman, *Panama Canal Negotiations.*

38. Bailey, *Wilson and the Great Betrayal.*

39. I am grateful to Ernst B. Haas and Robert O. Keohane for helpful advice on this point.

40. Ann L. Hollick, *U.S. Foreign Policy and the Law of the Sea* (Princeton: Princeton University Press, 1981), especially pp. 208–37, and James K. Sebenius, *Negotiating the Law of the Sea* (Cambridge, Mass.: Harvard University Press, 1984), especially pp. 74–78.

41. Raiffa, *Art and Science of Negotiation*, p. 175.

42. I am grateful to Henry Brady for clarifying this point for me.

43. Gilbert R. Winham, "The Relevance of Clausewitz to a Theory of International Negotiation," prepared for delivery at the 1987 annual meeting of the American Political Science Association.

44. Jimmy Carter, *Keeping Faith: Memoirs of a President* (New York: Bantam Books, 1982), p. 225.

45. Michael Artis and Sylvia Ostry, *International Economic Policy Coordination*, Chatham House Papers: 30 (London: Routledge & Kegan Paul, 1986) pp. 75–76. Of course, whether this is desirable in terms of democratic values is quite another matter.

46. Schelling, *Strategy of Conflict*, p. 28.

47. Walton and McKersie, *A Behavioral Theory of Labor Negotiations*, p. 345.

48. Carter, *Keeping Faith*, p. 172. See also Raiffa, *Art and Science of Negotiation*, p. 183.

49. The strategic significance of targeting at Level II is illustrated in John Conybeare, "Trade Wars: A Comparative Study of Anglo-Hanse, Franco-Italian, and Hawley-Smoot Conflicts," *World Politics* 38 (October 1985), p. 157. Retaliation in the Anglo-Hanse trade wars did not have the intended deterrent effect, because it was not (and perhaps could not have been) targeted at the crucial members of the opposing Level II coalition. Compare Snyder and Diesing, *Conflict Among Nations*, p. 552: "If one faces a coercive opponent, but the opponent's majority coalition includes a few wavering members inclined to compromise, a compromise proposal that suits their views may cause their defection and the formation of a different majority coalition. Or if the opponent's strategy is accommodative, based on a tenuous soft-line coalition, one knows that care is required in implementing one's own coercive strategy to avoid the opposite kind of shift in the other state."

50. Transaction benefits may be enhanced if a substantive agreement is reached, although sometimes leaders can benefit domestically by loudly rejecting a proffered international deal.

51. Snyder and Diesing, *Conflict Among Nations*, pp. 516, 522–23. Analogous misperceptions in Anglo-American diplomacy are the focus of Richard E. Neustadt, *Alliance Politics* (New York: Columbia University Press, 1970).

52. I am grateful to Robert O. Keohane for pointing out the impact of uncertainty on the expected value of proposals.

53. William Zartman, *The 50% Solution* (Garden City, N.J.: Anchor Books, 1976), p. 14. The present analysis assumes that constituents are myopic about the other side's Level II, an assumption that is not unrealistic empirically. However, a fully informed constituent would consider the preferences of key players on the other side, for if the current proposal lies well within the other side's win-set, then it would be rational for the constituent to vote against it, hoping for a second-round proposal that was more favorable to him and still ratifiable abroad; this might be a

reasonable interpretation of Senator Lodge's position in 1919 (Bailey, *Wilson and the Great Betrayal*). Consideration of such strategic voting at Level II is beyond the scope of this article.

54. Dieter Hiss, "Weitwirtschaftsgipfel: Betrachtungen eines Insiders [World Economic Summit: Observations of an Insider]," in Joachim Frohn and Reiner Staeglin, eds., *Empirische Wirtschaftsforschung* (Berlin: Duncker and Humblot, 1980), pp. 286–87.

55. On cognitive and communications explanations of international cooperation, see, for example, Ernst B. Haas, "Why Collaborate? Issue-Linkage and International Regimes," *World Politics* 32 (April 1980), pp 357–405; Richard N. Cooper, "International Cooperation in Public Health as a Prologue to Macroeconomic Cooperation," *Brookings Discussion Papers in International Economics* 44 (Washington, D.C.: Brookings Institution, 1986); and Zartman, *50% Solution*, especially Part 4.

56. Henning, *Macroeconomic Diplomacy in the 1980s*, pp. 62–63.

57. This is the approach used to analyze the Anglo-Chinese negotiations over Hong Kong in Bruce Bueno de Mesquita, David Newman, and Alvin Rabushka, *Forecasting Political Events: The Future of Hong Kong* (New Haven: Yale University Press, 1985).

58. For overviews of this literature, see Terry M. Moe, "The New Economics of Organization," *American Journal of Political Science* 28 (November 1984), pp. 739–77; John W. Prati and Richard J. Zeckhauser, eds., *Principals and Agents: The Structure of Business* (Boston, Mass.: Harvard Business School Press, 1985); and Barry M. Mitnick, "The Theory of Agency and Organizational Analysis," prepared for delivery at the 1986 annual meeting of the American Political Science Association. This literature is only indirectly relevant to our concerns here, for it has not yet adequately addressed the problems posed by multiple principals (or constituents, in our terms). For one highly formal approach to the problem of multiple principals, see R. Douglas Bernheim and Michael D. Whinston, "Common Agency," *Econometrica* 54 (July 1986), pp. 923–42.

59. This power of the chief negotiator is analogous to what Shepsle and Weingast term the "penultimate" or "ex post veto" power of the members of a Senate-House conference committee. (Shepsle and Weingast, "Institutional Foundations of Committee Power.")

60. Bailey, *Wilson and the Great Betrayal*, quotation at p. 15.

61. I. William Zartman, "Reality, Image, and Detail: The Paris Negotiations, 1969–1973," in Zartman, *50% Solution*, pp. 372–98.

62. Samuel P. Huntington, "Transnational Organizations in World Politics," *World Politics* 25 (April 1973), pp. 333–68; Keohane and Nye, *Power and Interdependence*; Neustadt, *Alliance Politics*.

63. Barbara Crane, "Policy Coordination by Major Western Powers in Bargaining with the Third World: Debt Relief and the Common Fund," *International Organization* 38 (Summer 1984), pp. 399–428.

Abel Escribà-Folch and Joseph Wright

DEALING WITH TYRANNY
International Sanctions and the Survival of Authoritarian Rulers

During his inaugural address in 2005, US President George W. Bush proclaimed that "it is the policy of the United States to seek and support the growth of democratic movements and institutions in every nation and culture, with the ultimate goal of ending tyranny in our world."[1] The general goal of ending tyranny has been shared by many of Western advanced democracies since the end of the Second World War. Yet there is little consensus over the most effective means to promote regime change and democratization.

Democratic governments have long tried to influence political regimes and institutional development in foreign countries. One way is full military intervention and invasion. The victorious allies imposed a democratic constitution on Japan after the Second World War; and the United States is currently still struggling to consolidate the new institutional system in Iraq after the 2003 invasion. Developed democracies have also provided domestic opposition movements with financial and strategic support. For example, South African exiles and their supporters created the Anti-Apartheid Movement in London in 1959 to mobilize international support for the African National Congress and the Pan Africanist Congress. American trade unions helped finance Solidarity, the union that headed the anti-communist opposition in Poland; at the same time, international agencies refused to grant Poland any economic aid until it legalized

Solidarity. Examples abound at the state level as well. The US administration had been both training and funding Iraqi anti-Hussein groups such as the Iraqi National Accord[2] and the Iraqi National Congress[3] prior to the 2003 invasion. In Europe, the Friedrich Ebert Foundation "provided financial and other support for Socialist politicians during dictatorships in Spain and Portugal" (Pinto-Duschinsky 1991:55).

Economic sanctions, however, are probably the most common foreign policy tool democracies use to bring about policy or institutional changes in authoritarian regimes. Askari, Forrer, Teegen, and Yang (2003) report that while there were only 12 cases of sanctions between 1914 and 1945, the number increased to over 50 during the 1990s. Most of the targets of these economic sanctions were authoritarian regimes. Further, Kaempfer, Lowenberg, and Mertens (2004) find that in 2001, 85% of US unilateral sanctions targets were countries rated as "not free" or "partly free" by Freedom House. Understanding whether and how international sanctions can effectively destabilize authoritarian rulers also has implications for current policy debates. For example, during the 2008 US presidential election campaign, candidates of both parties have discussed large-scale international sanctions against Iran as a way to deter Iranian nuclear weapons capacity and diminish Iranian influence in the Middle East. Recently, the United Nations has discussed the extension of sanctions against the Mugabe regime in Zimbabwe in the

From *International Studies Quarterly* 54, no.2 (June 2010), 335–359.

aftermath of the most recent fraudulent election and political repression.

Despite their continued use as a tool of foreign policy, there is little consensus as to whether sanctions can be effective in destabilizing authoritarian rulers (Van Bergeijk 1989; Haas 1997; Mueller and Mueller 1999; Nurnberger 2003). In fact, some of the most recent empirical studies on sanctions effectiveness find evidence that while sanctions may be effective against democracies, they are unlikely to succeed when imposed against authoritarian leaders (Nooruddin 2002; Marinov 2005; Lektzian and Souva 2007). Notable cases of sanctions failure include Iraq, Libya, and Cuba. This paper addresses the question of whether and how sanctions destabilize authoritarian rulers. We argue that the effect of sanctions on leadership stability is conditioned by the type of authoritarian rule in the target country. Specifically, personalist rulers are vulnerable to international sanctions because they are the most sensitive to the loss of external revenue to fund their patronage networks. Because leaders in these regimes typically have weak institutions such as the military and party system, they are the least capable of substituting cooptation or repression for patronage when sanctions decrease the resources available for political payoffs. Although personalist rulers can and do increase repression in response to sanctions, this is a risky and potentially counterproductive strategy that can further destabilize the regime.

The next section reviews the literature on autocratic stability, discussing the chief strategies dictators use to stay in power: repression and buying loyalty. The third section discusses the potential effect of international sanctions on dictators' survival and the mediating effect of authoritarian regime type in the target country. This section also provides descriptive data to show how sanctions affect patronage spending and repression in different types of authoritarian regimes. The fourth section presents the data and methodology used to test the main hypotheses linking sanctions to authoritarian stability, and the next section reports the results of the empirical tests. The final section summarizes the main findings.

Authoritarian Survival Strategies

The early literature on nondemocratic regimes focuses on repression as the main instrument to retain power, concentrating on the coercive capabilities and strategies of regimes (Friedrich and Brzezinski 1961; Arendt 1962). However, few dictators can survive using only sticks. Subsequent studies of authoritarianism analyze the trade-offs among different survival strategies dictators face once in power and the various political threats they confront (Tullock 1987). The focus turned from repression to buying loyalty and the combination of these two strategies (Wintrobe 1990, 1998; Gershenson and Grossman 2001; Gandhi and Przeworski 2006).

Central to this literature is the contention that rulers can decrease the probability of being deposed by co-opting potentially threatening political groups (Bertocchi and Spagat 2001). Most dictators do not rule in isolation, but build supporting coalitions whose loyalty is largely dependent on obtaining patronage resources or policy concessions from the dictator. As Brough and Kimenyi (1986:46) emphasized, "to keep the coalition intact, it is necessary for the dictator to distribute benefits to the coalition." Some scholars focus on the size of this coalition and the type of benefits they provide (Bueno de Mesquita, Smith, Siverson, and Morrow 2003), while others concentrate on the threats dictators face and the institutions they use to appease them (Gandhi and Przeworski 2007). The availability of natural resources and other non-tax revenue also figures prominently in theories of authoritarian survival precisely because these resources influence the capacity of the dictator to deliver rents, to co-opt opposition groups, and to pay for repression (Brautigam 2000; Ross 2001; Smith 2004; Ulfelder 2007; Morrison 2009).[4]

Accounts of authoritarian rule that focus on the stabilizing effects of economic growth or the institutional structure of the regime all consider the relationship between the ruler and the elites in the dictator's coalition. For example, some scholars argue that economic decline increases the risk of a coup because the incumbent loses the backing of his support coalition, members of which may back an alternative (O'Kane 1981, 1993; Johnson, Slater, and McGowan 1984; Londregan and Poole 1990; Galetovic and Sanhueza 2000). The economic payoff to the coalition that supports the incumbent regime is central to these arguments.

Institutionalists contend that legislatures and parties (Gandhi and Przeworski 2007) or the type of authoritarian system (Geddes 1999, 2003) structure the incentives facing the political actors and, hence, shape the vulnerability of the ruler and the regime itself. Distinguishing among different types of authoritarian regimes, Geddes (2003:26) argued that in military regimes, "because most officers value the unity and capacity of the military institution more than they value holding office, they cling less tightly to power than do office holders in other forms of authoritarianism." Conversely, in single-party regimes all factions within the regime have incentives to cooperate with the aim of remaining in office. Furthermore, party organizations provide party members with a durable framework wherein to resolve differences, bargain, and advance in influence. As a result, dominant party systems generate and maintain a cohesive leadership cadre (Brownlee 2004). As Smith (2005:431) suggests,

> During "routine" periods, strong parties provide a means for incorporated groups to present their political and policy preferences to the regime . . . During periods of crisis, the crucial task of

party institutions is to provide a credible guarantee to in-groups that their long-term interests will be best served by remaining loyal to the regime.

In personalist regimes, however, rival factions will remain loyal only if the pay-off from supporting the ruler exceeds the expected benefits of a risky plot, since "in contrast to single-party regimes, the leader's faction in a personalist regime may actually increase benefits to itself by excluding the rival faction from participation" (Geddes 2004:14). Similarly, Jackson and Rosberg (1984:424) argued that under personal rule, "the system favors the ruler and his allies and clients: its essential activity involves gaining access to a personal regime's patronage or displacing the ruler and perhaps his regime and installing another."

Scholars of authoritarian duration and survival have thus long noted the distinct mechanisms dictators use to stay in power. In the next section, we use these insights to examine how sanctions might affect the survival strategies of dictators, with careful attention to how these strategies and capacities differ across distinct authoritarian regime types.

Sanctions, Patronage, and Repression

Recent empirical research on sanctions suggests that the success of sanctions varies by the target country regime type (Nooruddin 2002; Marinov 2005; Lektzian and Souva 2007). The findings in these studies suggest that sanctions are unlikely to be effective when the target regime is a nondemocracy. However, researchers have yet to distinguish empirically among different types of authoritarian rule. We explore how international sanctions affect the alternative logics of intra-elite relations and survival strategies discussed in the previous section. We agree that "the effect of significant economic punishment is conditional on the target's regime type," as Lektzian and Souva (2007:841) argue, but take this analysis one step further by exploring how the effect of sanctions on dictatorial leaders' duration in power is mediated by different types of authoritarian regimes (for example, personalist, military, and single-party systems). In doing so, we build on earlier research which shows that authoritarian regime types mediate the effect of economic growth and contentious collective action on the likelihood of regime breakdown (Geddes 2003; Ulfelder 2005) and differ considerably in their propensity to initiate interstate conflict (Lai and Slater 2006; Weeks 2008).

Economists have studied the effect of sanctions on dictators' survival strategies by introducing sanctions or foreign pressure into political economy models of authoritarian rule. Kaempfer et al. (2004), for example, show that if sanctions increase the capacity of the opposition, this will reduce the repressive capacity of the dictator and possibly destabilize the regime. However, when sanctions do little to benefit the opposition, sanctions strengthen the rule of the dictator. Gershenson and Grossman's (2001) model suggests that a dictator's optimal response to increasing foreign pressure (such as international sanctions) is to increase both repression and cooptation to stay in power.

Much of the sanctions literature makes the strong assumption that dictators are able to capture the rents associated with economic sanctions and that the subsequent increase in resources available to payoff political supporters stabilizes their rule (Gershenson and Grossman 2001; Kaempfer et al. 2004; Lektzian and Souva 2007). However, this assumption may not apply equally to all types of regimes. Some dictators may not have the capacity to capture the rents associated with international sanctions or the increase in rents may not be sufficient to compensate the losses inflicted on other revenue streams,

such as foreign aid, non-tax revenue, or taxes on international trade. While we concur with the premise that more costly sanctions should increase the likelihood of success (Dashti-Gibson, Davis, and Radcliff 1997; Lektzian and Souva 2007), we argue that key to modeling sanctions effectiveness lies in understanding the relative capacity of authoritarian rulers to vary their level of cooptation and repression in response to international sanctions. If sanctions decrease government revenue and the resources available for rents, this will leave dictators less able to co-opt potential opposition forces and reward supporters. Unable to successfully co-opt the potential challengers, these dictators will resort to increasing the level of repression in the short term, especially if the consequences of losing power are particularly bad.

Cooptation with Rents

Kaempfer and Lowenberg (1988:792) argued that "the sanctions which are most likely to precipitate the desired political change in the target country are those which concentrate income losses on groups benefiting from the target government's policy." Similarly, Kirshner (1997) claims that for sanctions to be effective they should focus their pressure on either the central government or the core groups whose support is essential for the regime to remain in power. Hence, it is instructive to examine the sources of political support in different types of authoritarian regimes.

The durability of rulers in personalist regimes "depends largely on bargains among cliques with no claim to grass roots, so ruling elites are freer to ignore popular challenges" (Ulfelder 2005:314). Neo-patrimonial regimes are typically sustained by extensive patronage networks and are thus dependent on the availability of resources to buy the loyalty of their supporting elites (Bratton and van de Walle 1994). Further, the main revenue streams funding such networks—namely, non-tax revenue, taxes on international trade, and foreign aid—are principally external and do not require citizen cooperation (Lieberman 2002; Wright 2008).[5]

This dependence on external rents and trade taxes makes personalist rulers vulnerable to economic sanctions, especially to those aimed at curtailing governments' revenues, like trade or financial sanctions (Kirshner 1997). A reduction in rents used to payoff political supporters may thus cause divisions within the elite (Olson 1979). For example, when the United States was discussing possible sanctions against Amin's regime in Uganda, Ullman (1978) argued that sanctions would be effective in undermining Amin's regime precisely because of Uganda's dependence on coffee exports for obtaining foreign exchange. This foreign exchange was crucial to Amin's strategy of providing private goods to his core group of supporters such as the army and civil servants.[6] The initial commercial boycott and subsequent trade ban contributed to weaken Amin's regime. Similarly, in the Dominican Republic, sugar exports were the main source of the Trujillo family's resources used to buy the support of core supporters, including the armed forces. In addition to other coercive measures approved by the OAS,[7] the United States restricted Dominican sugar imports in an attempt to bring about a peaceful regime change.[8] Sanctions "signaled the weakness of the regime, constrained its resources and maneuverability, undermined its support, and emboldened opponents" (Kirshner 1997:59). Similarly, van de Walle points out that restrictions on aid flows in Africa during the early 1990s brought about regime instability: "with fewer resources at their disposal and an increasingly decrepit state apparatus, leaders found it harder to sustain critical clientelist networks, with the result that the old political aristocracy was more likely to fractionalize" (van de Walle 2001:240). Such were the cases of Hastings K. Banda in Malawi, and Mobutu Sese Seko in former Zaire.

While almost all authoritarian leaders use some form of patronage to buy support, personalist leaders may be the most sensitive to the loss of external revenue to buy support because these leaders lack strong institutions to help them rule: they typically have weak militaries and either weak or non-existent parties and legislative institutions (Wright 2008). Even with a weakened military, they may be reluctant to activate (and adequately supply) the military for fear the soldiers will organize against the leader. Thus, pursuing widespread repression when external resources available for patronage spending fall short can be a risky strategy for surviving in power. Further, because personalist leaders lack strong political institutions, they cannot make credible inter-temporal promises to their supporters. Dominant party regimes can and do make good on promises to distribute patronage in the future—particularly around election time (Magaloni 2006; Pepinsky 2007; Blaydes 2008).[9] Because of the long history of state patronage and large margin of electoral victories for dominant parties, supporters expect the party to remain in power at least in the near- to mid-term, if not indefinitely, and thus believe party promises of future support.[10] Likewise, policy concessions are less credible when dictators cannot rely on strong institutions to ensure political supporters that their demands will be met.[11] Hence, personalist rulers should have more difficulty substituting the promise of future rents or policy concessions for political rents in the current period when sanctions curtail patronage resources.

If sanctions can decrease the resources available for political payoffs, the elites' expected benefits of supporting the incumbent leader decrease, making elite defection more likely. In short, if the incumbent ruler is not able to capture sanction rents due to limited state capacity (or if these rents do not compensate the loss inflicted by the imposition of sanctions), a reduction in the flow of benefits can decrease the elites' utility from supporting the ruler and increase their expected utility from defection.

Leaders in single-party and military regimes also depend on patronage,[12] but they may not be as sensitive to the loss of external resources to fund it. In single-party systems, loyalty is mobilized through limited access to the decision-making process, policy concessions, and public goods. Large sectors of the population can be integrated in what Kasza (1995a:218) calls "administered mass organizations" that are "formal organizations structured and managed by the state's ruling apparatus to shape mass social action for the purpose of implementing public policy." These organizations extend state control in many different ways, including material dependency, consumption of time, organization of support, offices and honors, and self-directed local administration (Kasza 1995a,b). With larger coalitions, dominant single-party regimes are also more likely to rely on public goods provision to retain the support of their coalition (Bueno de Mesquita et al. 2003). Military regimes, on the other hand, have the greatest capacity to use repression in response to sanction-induced decreases in patronage resources (Davenport 2007). Thus, dominant single-party rulers may be better positioned to substitute policy concessions for patronage, while increasing repression when patronage resources diminish may be a much less risky strategy for leaders in military regimes.

Using government consumption as a measure of the level of cooptation and rent delivery suggests that personalist regimes are the most "patronage-intensive." Government consumption as a share of the GDP under personalist systems and monarchies is 6% higher, on average, than single-party regimes and 15% higher than military regimes.[13] So, contrary to the argument that small coalition dictators should be the most vulnerable to sanctions, we argue that if sanctions are well directed toward reducing elites' access to rents (Dashti-Gibson et al. 1997), international sanctions are most likely to undermine authoritarian rule in personalist (and monarchic) dictatorships.

In this line, Falk (1992:33) argues that "the maximum impact of human rights pressures, absent enforcement mechanisms, is to isolate a target government, perhaps denying it some of the benefits of trade and aid."

Single-party and military regimes and rulers may not be as sensitive to a small reduction in their supportive coalitions and their external rents as personalist ones. Descriptive data on revenue composition show that, once under sanctions, single-party and military regimes are better able to shift fiscal pressure from one stream to another, a capacity that may stem from their greater control over the territory and the population. Figure 5.1 shows aid receipts, non-tax revenue, and various streams of tax revenue for different types of regimes, under sanction and not under sanction. The imposition of sanctions in personalist regimes translates into sharp reductions of aid receipts and revenues from taxes on international trade and non-tax revenues, which constitute their main sources of revenues.[14] Besides, it is apparent that personalist rulers cannot generate new revenue streams due to their limited state capacity. Conversely, single-party and military regimes increase both their tax and non-tax revenues when targeted by sanctions. Non-tax revenue increases despite the loss of foreign aid. The increase in tax revenue in single-party and military regimes appears to come from increased taxes on goods and services, which are less likely to be affected by sanction-induced economic decline than taxes on income and profits.

In Figure 5.2, we use different categories of government spending (a proxy for cooptation) to examine how different types of regimes respond to sanctions. Expenditures on goods and services (including wages and salaries for government employees) and on subsidies and transfers (including pension and welfare programs for individuals and subsidies to firms) proxy for short-term expenditures useful as political payoffs, while capital expenditures capture spending on longer-term goals such as economic development. Two patterns

Figure 5.1. Revenue Composition (as a % of GDP), by Regime Type and Economic Sanctions

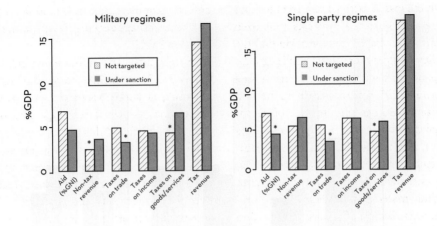

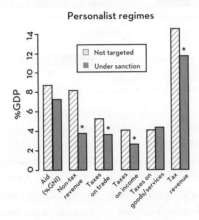

Note: *Difference in means is statistically different from zero at the .01 level.

emerge. First, all rulers reduce capital expenditures, as leaders under sanctions shift resources from long-term development and investment programs to current spending and consumption.[15] Yet, consistent with the expectation that sanctions shift spending the most in personalist regimes, we observe the largest decrease in capital expenditures in personalist regimes (falling from 8.29% to 3.27%). This may occur because as sanctions reduce the revenues available to personalist rulers, they reallocate resources to minimize the cuts in other categories of spending, particularly subsidies and transfers.[16] Second, spending on both goods/services and subsidies/transfers decreases in personalist regimes under sanctions, again consistent with the expectation that sanctions limit the patronage capacity of rulers in these regimes.

However, rulers in both single-party and military regimes under sanctions increase spending on goods/services and subsidies/transfers, suggesting that sanctions may increase their need to co-opt. The higher degree of inclusiveness in single-party

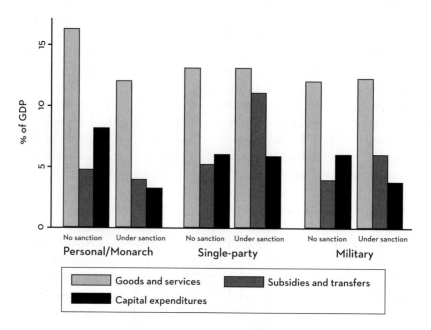

Figure 5.2. Cooptation, Sanctions, and Regime Type: Government Expenditures (% of the GDP)

Notes: The decrease in goods/services and capital spending in personalist regimes is statistically different from zero at the .01 level. The increase in spending on subsidies in single-party and military regimes is statistically different from zero. Finally, the decrease in capital expenditures in military regimes is statistically significant.

regimes may explain why sanctions lead them to concentrate spending increases on subsidies and transfers, which predominantly benefit supporting social sectors, such as the urban classes and business elites. Expenditures on goods and services show a similar pattern, increasing under sanctions in both single-party and military regimes. These descriptive data suggest that leaders in these two types of regimes prioritize cooptation over investment when under sanctions.

Repression

Figures 5.1 and 5.2 suggest that personalist rulers suffer the most revenue loss under sanctions, and thus cannot increase expenditures on goods and services and subsidies and transfers. If sanctions decrease a personalist dictator's resources available to payoff political supporters, these leaders may face difficulties in maintaining their loyalty payments, leaving them to increase repression. Yet, increasing repression may be counterproductive for a number of reasons. First, because most of the population is already excluded from the political process, the perception that repression may extend to a member of the already narrow supporting coalition can sharply increase (Gershenson and Grossman 2001). Second, personalist rulers are also the least likely to have complete control over the army and are thus less able to mobilize the military to systematically repress opponents for fear that this military mobilization may itself threaten the ruler (Geddes 2008).[17] Finally, some argue that high levels of repression may trigger a "backlash" so that dissidents react strongly to extremely harsh coercion (Francisco 1995; Rasler 1996).[18]

Personalist rulers are also the most likely to face particularly bad outcomes once they exit from power. In personalist regimes, the dictator rarely cedes power peacefully and is most often displaced via a coup. In contrast, leaders in military regimes can often return to the barracks if they can successfully negotiate a transition to a civilian government. Leaders of dominant single-party regimes rarely lose power in a coup and often win power in a subsequent election even after they step down from the executive. Thus, personalist dictators are more likely to endure a particularly nasty fate once they leave power—relative to leaders in other types of regimes. A brief look at the data bears this out. Conditional on having exited, only 19% of personalist rulers live in their home country unpunished, while over 50% of single-party and military rulers meet the same (good) fate. Given this disparity, it is unsurprising that personalist rulers are also more likely than rulers in other regime types to face punishment, exile, or assassination when exiting.[19] Thus, even though mobilizing the military to pursue repression is a risky option for personalist rulers with little room to maneuver due to the loss of revenue and rent resources, they nonetheless have a strong incentive to pursue this option to stay in power, as exiting carries many of its own risks.

In Figure 5.3 we examine the average repression levels for different types of regimes, under and not under sanctions. To measure repression, we use Hafner-Burton and Tsutsui's (2007) index of state repression, which combines information from different existing political terror scales. The scale ranges from 1 to 4 where 5 is the maximum level of repression.[20] While Wood (2008) finds that sanctions generally increase repression, especially in nondemocracies, our descriptive data indicate that the largest increases

in repression in response to international pressures are found among personalist regimes, which, when under sanctions, reach repression levels similar to those found in military regimes. Given the marked decrease in the availability of patronage rents and, consequently, in their capacity to reward loyalty, these data suggest that personalist rulers increase repression to retain power. Increasing repression, unlike building institutions that facilitate cooptation, can be an immediate response to the loss of patronage resources because, as Wintrobe (1998:47) notes, "repression is variable in the short as well as the long-run." Second, military regimes are the most "repression-intensive" of all regime types. Their coercive capacity makes them better-equipped to deal with potential sudden increases in opposition due to international coercion and poor economic performance. Moreover, if economic sanctions exacerbate protest, the military may renew its resolve to retain power with the aim of preserving public order (Ulfelder 2005). Single-party regimes increase the degree of their repressiveness as well, but less so than personalist regimes. Given the increases in redistributive spending, this data suggests that single-party regimes are less likely to rely on repression. Their levels of repression are on average the lowest, regardless of whether they are targeted by sanctions.[21]

To summarize, single-party and military regimes conform to the expectation that dictators under sanctions should increase both cooptation and repression (Gershenson and Grossman 2001; Kaempfer et al. 2004). Evidence from the descriptive data suggests that rulers in these regimes are unlikely to be destabilized by sanctions because they can adequately compensate for any sanction-induced political costs by diverting resources to repression and further cooptation. If these regimes can still collect revenue from alternative sources and increase expenditures and repression, the imposition of sanctions

Figure 5.3. Averaged Repression, by Authoritarian Regime Type and Sanctions

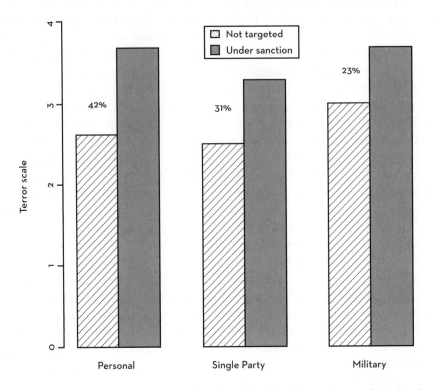

Note: Numbers listed are the percent increase in repression level, under sanctions. The difference in means for each regime type is statistically different from zero at the .0001 level.

may be ineffective in de-stabilizing these dictators. In personalist regimes, however, international sanctions are associated with a decrease in patronage rents. Further, if sanctions force rulers in these regimes to increase repression, mobilizing the military may backfire because they typically do not fully control the army. Consequently, we expect economic sanctions to be effective in destabilizing authoritarian rulers only in personalist regimes.

Hypothesis: *Sanctions are more likely to destabilize leaders in personalist regimes than other types of regimes.*

Data and Methods

Data on sanction episodes are taken from Marinov's (2005) replication data set, which updates the Hufbauer, Schott, and Elliott's (1990) data set in country-year format.[22] The variable *Sanction* can take two values: 1 if a country has been targeted by economic sanctions in a given year, 0 if not. We lag the sanctions variable 1 year. Moreover, we correct those instances for which lagged sanctions variable takes value 0 and it is just capturing the absence of a sanction on the previous leader, but then in the next current year the new leader is targeted by a sanction.

The classification of authoritarian regime types is based on the typology developed by Geddes (1999, 2003) and which has been recently extended and updated by Wright (2008). We have recoded the data into three basic categories for our baseline models. First, we group the monarchic and personalist regimes into a category named "personalist." Recent work on political institutions in authoritarian regimes shows that monarchies as well as personalist regimes share a common pool of socioeconomic determinants (Wright 2008). The second category is "single party" and includes pure single-party regimes and single-party hybrid regimes.[23] The third category includes military and military/personalist regimes. This categorization developed by Geddes captures the main distinctions between different types of regimes and has been used extensively in previous research (Milner and Kubota 2005; Lai and Slater 2006; Davenport 2007; Weeks 2008).

We control for the log GDP per capita, its annual growth rate, and the log of a country's population. These variables are taken from Maddison's (2006) data set, which has the most extensive time series economic data for authoritarian countries, particularly for years before 1990. *Growth* is the moving average of growth in the previous two years.[24] We also control for the possibility that sanctions are the result of a conflict or that they are applied to support foreign military intervention (Pape 1997). Hence, we include a dummy "foreign war" which indicates whether the country is a belligerent in an inter-state war. This variable is from the Correlates of War project.

Regarding institutions and regime history, we include a series of dummy variables that summarize the current institutions of the authoritarian regime as well as the previous regime existing in the country.[25] The variable *Previous Democracy*, which is intended to gauge the potential strength of the pro-democratic civil opposition, takes a value of 1 if the preceding regime was democratic and 0 otherwise. Similarly, the variable *Previous*

Colony is coded 1 if the country was under colonial administration prior to the current regime, 0 otherwise. This variable controls for the possibility that many leaders who became, heads of government after their anti-colonial activism might deter other elite members—particularly in the military—from challenging their position. Further, when state structure was still weak after independence, the process of elite substitution and government stability may have been extremely dependent on loyalty to the new ruler. We also include an index of religious fractionalization to control for the possibility that more diverse countries prove more unstable.[26] Finally, we include the yearly proportion of authoritarian regimes existing within the same geographical region to control for potential international trends in democratization and potential inter-regime cooperation. The aim of including this variable is to test whether ruler change and liberalization can be the result of a diffusion process, especially at the regional level (Gleditsch and Ward 2006). A dummy for the *Cold War* years takes a value of 1 for all the years between 1946 and 1990 and 0 otherwise.

It is also possible that sanctions' effect on the resources available for patronage may vary when the targeted country produces highly valued resources with concentrated supply sources and inelastic demand, such as oil.[27] This may be the main reason why sanctions failed to destabilize Hussein's regime in Iraq. Even in the event of sanctions, the inelasticity of demand for oil gives oil-importing countries a strong incentive to defect from a coalition imposing coercive restrictions.[28] We control for the presence of oil resources using Humphreys' (2005) measure of per capita oil reserves in a given year multiplied by the oil price index for that year.[29]

We use a binary dependent variable, *Ruler Exit*, which indicates whether a dictator loses power in a given year. This variable is coded 1 if the incumbent ruler is replaced that year, and 0 if the dictator remains in power in a given year. Leaders who died in power from natural causes are right-censored, and hence coded 0. In the second part of the analysis, we disaggregate *Ruler Exit* by establishing whether the ruler was replaced through regular or irregular means (Goemans et al. 2009). We use logistic regression to analyze the likelihood of autocratic failure, and multinomial logit to analyze the type of failure—whether the mode of exit was regular or irregular. To control for time dependence in the duration models, we include polynomial transformations of the duration of the leader-spell up to time t.[30] We report standard errors clustered on leader.

Because the coding of regime types and sanctions are by country-year, we use this as the unit of analysis. For some highly unstable countries, there are multiple leader-failures in a given year; however, we do not have data on sanctions directed at each specific leader in those years. Thus, using leader-year as the unit of analysis results in adding multiple failure observations to the data for a particular year, inflating the number of failure outcomes relative to the number of non-failure outcomes. Thus, our estimation of the country-data provides a more conservative estimate than analysis of leader-year data. When we analyze the leader-year data, the results are much stronger than those reported below. Henceforth, we discuss leader failure, but in reality our analysis addresses the probability of leader failure within a given year.

Empirical Analysis
Autocratic Survival and Foreign Pressure

The conditional nature of our hypotheses requires the use of interaction models. Therefore, we multiply the dummies created for each type of authoritarian regime by *Sanctions*. Table 5.1 reports the results of the duration models. The estimates reveal that the effect of international sanctions varies by the target country's authoritarian regime type.

In column 1, we report the baseline model without any interactions. The coefficient of the *Sanctions* dummy is small, negative, and indistinguishable from 0. This result is consistent with Lektzian and Souva's (2007) finding that economic sanctions are unlikely to be effective when targeting nondemocratic regimes. However, once we include the interaction between *Sanctions* and regime type, the results reveal why sanctions appear to be ineffective in the first column. In columns 2–7, the coefficient for sanctions[31] is positive and statistically significant, suggesting that sanctions destabilize rulers most dependent on patronage rents, namely, personalist autocrats. This result is consistent with our main hypothesis. In single-party and military regimes, the effect of sanctions is measured by adding the coefficients for the respective interaction term to the coefficient for *Sanctions*. For example, in column 2, the effect of sanctions in military regimes is given by: $-1.33 + 0.759 = -0.571$. This coefficient is statistically different from 0 at the 0.10 level, suggesting that sanctions have some positive effect on leadership survival in military regimes. The effect is much weaker and not significant for single-party regimes.

The effect of sanctions on personalist dictators' survival is stronger after introducing the interaction with oil rents (columns 3 and 5–8), and also after interacting regime type with past economic performance (columns 4–7).[32] The effect of sanctions in single-party regimes remains negligible, while the impact of sanctions on military leaders' duration is positive and significant in columns 4 and 8. In column 6, we exclude monarchies to ensure that the results are not driven by grouping monarchies with personalist regimes. In column 7, we include "triple-threat" regimes in the single-party category. Again, this does not alter the main result.

Finally, in column 8, we include an interaction of the regime type variables with the Cold War dummy as some regimes were receiving support from superpowers during the period 1945–1990,

Table 5.1. *The Effect of Sanctions on Autocratic Survival (Logistic Regression)*

INDEPENDENT VARIABLES	(1)	(2)	(3)	(4)	(5)	(6)	(7)	(8)
Sanction$_{t-1}$	−0.133 (0.222)	0.759† (0.432)	0.969* (0.454)	0.941* (0.440)	1.10* (0.459)	1.06* (0.472)	1.08* (0.462)	1.19** (0.460)
Sanction$_{t-1}$*Single party		−0.878 (0.536)	−1.02† (0.529)	−1.09† (0.548)	−1.19 (0.541)	−1.14 (0.549)	−1.13 (0.532)	−1.26* (0.538)
Sanction$_{t-1}$*Military		−1.33* (0.546)	−1.47** (0.567)	−1.57** (0.561)	−1.66** (0.575)	−1.60** (0.583)	−1.63** (0.570)	−1.81** (0.590)
Single party	0.188 (0.179)	0.278 (0.188)	0.286 (0.188)	0.350† (0.192)	0.352† (0.192)	0.144 (0.208)	0.295 (0.188)	0.927 (0.568)
Military	1.11** (0.231)	1.30** (0.247)	1.32** (0.249)	1.39** (0.259)	1.40** (0.260)	1.26** (0.262)	1.38** (0.256)	2.38** (0.675)
Log oil rents (pc)	−0.007 (0.043)	−0.011 (0.046)	0.012 (0.047)	−0.016 (0.044)	0.004 (0.046)	0.029 (0.054)	−0.0001 (0.045)	0.007 (0.047)
Sanction$_{t-1}$*Log oil rents						−0.170 (0.111)	−0.081 (0.108)	−0.141 (0.114)
Log(GDP pc)	−0.137 (0.109)	−0.142 (0.112)	−0.128 (0.116)	−0.125 (0.114)	−0.112 (0.112)	−0.061 (0.123)	−0.111 (0.114)	−0.137 (0.117)
Economic growth$_{t-1,t-2}$	−0.494 (1.38)	−0.324 (1.40)	−0.533 (1.39)	3.41 (2.33)	3.06 (2.33)	3.07 (2.45)	3.16 (2.30)	−0.728 (1.42)
Growth*Single party				−5.53† (3.21)	−5.32† (3.19)	−5.58† (3.27)	−4.94 (3.17)	
Growth*Military				−6.13† (3.24)	−5.83† (3.25)	−6.15† (3.36)	−5.70† (3.21)	
Log(population)	0.036 (0.054)	0.035 (0.056)	0.032 (0.056)	0.041 (0.056)	0.038 (0.056)	0.031 (0.057)	0.027 (0.055)	0.034 (0.056)
Dictatorships in region	−0.726† (0.372)	−0.738† (0.384)	−0.725† (0.386)	−0.648† (0.388)	−0.642† (0.390)	−0.518 (0.418)	−0.665† (0.376)	−0.695† (0.392)
Previous democracy	−0.421† (0.249)	−0.423† (0.249)	−0.413† (0.250)	−0.417† (0.250)	−0.409 (0.251)	−0.466† (0.251)	−0.406 (0.248)	−0.353 (0.251)
Previous colony	−0.546** (0.183)	−0.577** (0.184)	−0.586** (0.184)	−0.594** (0.185)	−0.600** (0.185)	−0.564** (0.191)	−0.534** (0.182)	−0.605** (0.185)
Religious diversity	0.029 (0.348)	0.044 (0.350)	0.016 (0.353)	0.031 (0.352)	0.008 (0.355)	−0.208 (0.355)	0.047 (0.355)	0.026 (0.352)
Cold War	0.245 (0.264)	0.279 (0.265)	0.268 (0.266)	0.260 (0.265)	0.251 (0.266)	0.164 (0.274)	0.282 (0.257)	0.885† (0.486)
Cold War*Single party								−0.702 (0.591)
Cold War*Military								−1.17† (0.713)
Foreign War	0.302 (0.399)	0.173 (0.420)	0.262 (0.401)	0.158 (0.422)	0.238 (0.404)	0.259 (0.409)	0.157 (0.391)	0.247 (0.402)
Time	−0.167** (0.047)	−0.162** (0.047)	−0.157† (0.047)	−0.155† (0.047)	−0.152** (0.047)	−0.200** (0.062)	−0.166** (0.046)	−0.157** (0.047)
Time^2	0.006* (0.002)	0.006† (0.002)	0.005* (0.002)	0.005* (0.002)	0.005* (0.002)	0.010* (0.004)	0.006* (0.002)	0.005* (0.002)
Time^3	−0.000† (0.000)	−0.000† (0.000)	−0.000 (0.000)	−0.000 (0.000)	−0.000 (0.000)	−0.000† (0.000)	−0.000† (0.000)	−0.000† (0.000)
Log likelihood	−716.585	−713.473	−712.830	−711.639	−711.152	−664.459	−736.201	−711.112
Observations	2,807	2,807	2,807	2,807	2,807	2,466	2,949	2,807
Sample	Baseline	Baseline	Baseline	Baseline	Baseline	No monarchies	Include triple-threat in single-party category	Baseline

Note: Dependent variable is Ruler Exit. Standard errors are clustered on leader. †$p < .10$; *$p < .05$; **$p < .01$.

which helped stabilize their rule, especially, anti-communist military regimes. The results are in line with this expectation. Personalist regimes are shown to have been particularly unstable during the Cold War years. The inclusion of this interaction makes our main result stronger: the sanctions dummy gets significant at the maximum level, while the negative effect of sanctions on military leaders' likelihood of exit becomes significant at the 0.10 level.[33]

Table 5.2 reports the probabilities of leader exit estimated from the results in the second, fifth, and eighth models in Table 5.1. In all models, the likelihood that a personalist ruler will lose power more than doubles when economic sanctions are in place. In single-party regimes, sanctions decrease the likelihood of leader exit by <1%—a small and statistically insignificant difference. Sanctions decrease the likelihood of leadership turnover in military regimes by between 7% (models 2 and 5) and 13% (model 8). This difference is not statistically significant in model 2, but it is in models 5 and 8. This suggests that sanctions help stabilize military leaders, perhaps because these leaders have greater repressive capacity than other regimes or are better able to generate a "rally around the flag" effect.

In columns 1, 2, and 4, when we do not interact sanctions with oil, we find that oil rents reduce the risk of being unseated (although not significantly), a result consistent with the empirical literature on oil and autocratic stability (Brough and Kimenyi 1986; Ross 2001; Smith 2004; Gandhi and Przeworski 2006; Escribà-Folch 2007; Ulfelder 2007; Morrison 2009). One interpretation of this finding is that oil rents provide autocrats with abundant patronage resources with which they can buy support. The interaction between sanctions and oil rents in columns 3 and 5–8 are all negative but not statistically significant.[34]

The control variables yield results in line with our expectations and the existing literature.[35] Good economic performance lowers the risk of autocratic turnover although not significantly; and, as models 4–7 show, growth affects regimes in different ways. The positive effect on duration is only found in single party and, especially, in military regimes. This result is in line with Geddes' (2004) previous findings, according to which military regimes were shown to be more sensitive to economic downturns. The international context, captured by the regional proportion of authoritarian regimes, stabilizes dictators. Consistent with Geddes' (1999, 2003) research, we find that leaders in military regimes are more likely to fail, all else being equal, than leaders in other regime types. Last, dictators in regimes that were previously democracies or colonies are more stable. This finding suggests that past institutions affect the stability of autocratic leaders.

Further Tests

To check the robustness of these findings, we test two different types of models: a Cox proportional hazards model and a fixed-effects model. The Cox model assumes that the effect of a change in a particular covariate remains constant over time. However, violations of this proportionality assumption may bias parameter estimates, so we checked for the possibility of non-proportionality among the individual covariates and in a global test. Both tests indicated the presence of non-proportionality. Following Box-Steffensmeier, Reiter, and Zorn (2003), we include interactions between non-proportional covariates[36] and the logged square-root of time.[37] In column 2, we test a fixed-effects logit model with the aim of controlling not only for political-economic factors but also for the country-specific likelihood of ruler stability. This is the strategy pursued by Marinov (2005). In the fixed-effects model, we dropped variables that do not vary much over time. Finally, we test a model that adds controls for foreign aid dependency and trade to alleviate concerns that the main result for personalist

Table 5.2. The Predicted Effect of Sanctions on the Autocrat's Likelihood of Losing Power

Pr(y = RulerExit), Sanctions = x, OtherVars = mean/ median	Personalist/ Monarch	Single-Party	Military
Column 2			
Not targeted	4.27%	6.07%	19.20%
Targeted by sanctions	9.29%	5.62%	12.19%
Difference	5.0%* (0.036)	−0.4% (0.017)	−7.0% (0.039)
Column 5			
Not targeted	4.28%	6.01%	19.06%
Targeted by sanctions	10.78%	5.31%	11.74%
Difference	6.2%* (0.035)	−0.7% (0.017)	−7.5%* (0.041)
Column 8			
Not targeted	4.19%	8.47%	36.80%
Targeted by sanctions	11.13%	7.57%	23.49%
Difference	7.01%* (0.038)	−0.9% (0.022)	−13.33%* (0.078)

Notes: Probabilities obtained from results in columns 2, 5 and 8, Table 5.1. Standard errors are given in parentheses. The control variables are held constant at their sample mean/median, except for oil rents, growth, and the time variables, which are set to the mean within each regime type. *$p < .10$ [two-tailed test].

regimes is driven by the higher dependency on foreign economic resources in these regimes. Table 5.3 reports the results of these models, revealing similar patterns as those reported in Table 5.1. None of these results are dependent on the inclusion or exclusion of the interaction between regime type and growth.

Modeling Selection

As Marinov (2005) emphasizes and Nooruddin (2002) shows, selection bias may arise in the study of sanctions for two reasons. First, senders may systematically target some regimes because they are more vulnerable to foreign pressure or because some regimes may be more repressive. Second, selection bias can occur if rulers self-select into sanctions or conflict episodes. The first mechanism is likely to depend on observable factors like political-economic conditions observed by the sender (and, consequently, by researchers). In the second case, though, self-selection may be unobservable to researchers because autocrats select on factors that only targeted rulers can actually observe, such as the resolve of the leader.

Table 5.3. *The Effect of Sanctions on Autocrats' Stability*

Model	Cox PH	Fixed-Effects	Logit
Independent Variables	(1)	(2)	(3)
Sanction$_{t-1}$	1.29** (0.447)	1.23* (0.573)	1.03* (0.463)
Sanction$_{t-1}$*Single party	−1.15* (0.516)	−0.782 (0.681)	−0.275 (0.575)
Sanction$_{t-1}$*Military	−1.91** (0.535)	−1.40* (0.666)	−1.59** (0.584)
Single party	0.532** (0.217)	0.419 (0.337)	0.362 (0.243)
Military	1.59** (0.278)	1.49** (0.346)	1.59** (0.315)
Log oil rents (pc)	−0.344** (0.079)	−0.012 (0.131)	−0.035 (0.063)
Sanction$_{t-1}$*Log oil rents	0.394 (0.144)	−0.128 (0.145)	−0.052 (0.121)
Log(GDP pc)	1.16** (0.148)	1.50** (0.435)	−0.187 (0.171)
Economic growth$_{t-1,t-2}$	3.56† (2.10)	3.30 (3.16)	2.38 (3.18)
Growth*Single party	−4.48 (2.95)	−8.04† (4.22)	−3.11 (4.22)
Growth*Military	−8.34** (3.09)	−9.06* (4.53)	−5.05 (4.04)
Log(population)	−0.050 (0.062)	−0.425 (0.534)	0.0007 (0.089)
Dictatorships in region	−0.779* (0.322)	−1.94* (0.930)	−1.05* (0.526)
Previous democracy	−1.06** (0.330)		−0.557† (0.300)
Previous colony	−0.457* (0.205)		−0.427 (0.272)
Religious diversity	−0.161 (0.383)		−0.066 (0.440)
Cold War	0.198 (0.257)	0.240 (0.389)	0.422 (0.314)
Foreign War	0.456 (0.322)	0.361 (0.445)	0.241 (0.560)
Log (sqrt(Time))*LogGDP	−1.84** (0.126)		
Log (sqrt(Time))*PrevDem	0.966* (0.450)		
Log (sqrt(Time))*Oil rents	0.543** (0.084)		
Log (sqrt(Time))*OilRents*Sanction	−0.889* (0.366)		
Trade % GDP			−0.001 (0.003)
Aid per capita			−0.005 (0.004)
Log likelihood	−1181.809	−512.524	−509.044
Observations	2,805	2,079	1,961

Notes: Dependent variable is Ruler Exit. Standard errors are given in parentheses. Time polynomials are included in columns 2 and 3 but not reported to save space. †$p < .10$; *$p < .05$; **$p < .01$.

One way of dealing with selection is to estimate a two-stage Heckman model, which has the advantage of controlling for both observable factors that senders use to target dictators and the unobservable factors influencing leaders' self-selection into conflicts. We use a probit model in the first stage to estimate the probability of being under sanctions or not under sanctions.[38] The second-stage estimates the duration model and includes the inverse Mill's ratios computed from the first-stage regressions. Then, for each value ($j \in [Sanctions, NoSanctions]$) of the dependent variable in the first stage, we estimate the second-stage equation including the respective Mill's ratios. The coefficients obtained through this method are unbiased and allow us to calculate the predicted probability of losing power of each first-stage outcome ($\hat{p}(y_j = RulerExit)$) for the whole sample and for each of the sanction settings of interest. Table 5.4 reports the mean values of the predicted probabilities of ruler exit using all observations and dividing the sample into personal and non-personal rulers. We also show the differences in means and the t-statistics from one-sided tests.

The probabilities in Table 5.4 confirm the findings from our naive models. The baseline sample mirrors the sample we have used throughout; in the expanded sample, we drop a number of variables in the selection equation (see the Appendix) to substantially increase the sample size. This does not affect the main results. Sanctions have little effect on rulers' duration when no interaction with the type of regime is considered; although the mean difference is significant in the model using the baseline sample, the difference is quite small—less than 1%. In personalist regimes, sanctions have a strong and positive effect of leaders' probability of losing power (over 4%). We have grouped rulers governing single-party and military regimes as their patterns were quite similar and to increase the number of observations. The selection-corrected results suggest that sanctions in these regimes are counterproductive, as they lengthen dictators' tenure.

Autocratic Modes of Exit

So far, we have argued that sanctions weaken authoritarian regimes and alter the calculus of the elite within the regime by reducing the amount of patronage rents available to the ruler. Personalist rulers are most susceptible to this type of pressure because they are the most dependent on patronage resources to stay in power. Sanctions may also cause social unrest if domestic opposition mobilizes against the regime in response to sanction-induced economic scarcity. Social unrest and economic insecurity may also trigger military intervention against the ruler, particularly if the ruler needs patronage resources to keep the army in the barracks. On the other hand, as Bratton and van de Walle contend, personalist rulers "resist political openings for as long as possible and seek to manage the process of transition only after it has been forced on them" (1997:83). This was the case of Hastings K. Banda (Malawi), who under donors' pressure and financial sanctions decided to hold a referendum on his regime and presidency in June 1993. Sixty-four percent voted in favor of multi-partyism. Thus, it is plausible that sanctions might affect personalist rulers' stability by increasing the likelihood of both a regular as well as an irregular transfer of power. This proposition parallels our earlier hypothesis that sanctions destabilize personalist dictators because these regimes are most dependent on patronage rents to stay in power. To test this proposition, we use the variable *Exit Mode*, from the *Archigos* database (Goemans et al. 2009). This variable indicates whether the leader lost office as a result of (i) an irregular transfer (like a coup, a putsch, a revolt, or an assassination); (ii) a regular transfer (such as a resignation, pact transitions, regulated

Table 5.4. Selection-Corrected Probabilities of Ruler Exit

	$\hat{p}(y_j = \text{RulerExit})$			
	Not targeted	Under sanctions	Difference	t-Test
Baseline sample ($N = 2,742$)				
All Observations	8.4%	7.9%	−0.004	2.25*
Personalist/Monarchy	5.1%	9.3%	0.042	16.67**
Single party/Military	10.3%	7.1%	−0.031	12.24**
Expanded sample ($N = 3,590$)				
All Observations	8.19%	8.17%	−0.0002	0.123
Personalist/Monarchy	4.9%	9.7%	0.048	20.20**
Single party/Military	9.9%	7.3%	0.026	10.68**

Notes: Mean predicted probability of event reported in each cell of the first two columns. Expanded sample includes 'triple-threat' regimes in the single-party category. *$p < .05$; **$p < .01$.)

successions, and so on); or (iii) whether the leader was deposed by a foreign state or died while still in office. We use a model similar to those in Table 5.1 to test whether sanctions affect the type of exit, again mediated by regime type. Because the dependent variable takes multiple discrete values, we estimate multinomial logistic regressions, with duration polynomials to control for time dependence and standard errors clustered on leader.

Table 5.5 reports the results of two models, the first with the interaction between regime type and economic growth and the second with the interaction between regime type and the Cold War dummy. The general pattern we have seen up to this point persists: the coefficients for *Sanction* are positive, while the coefficients for the interaction between *Sanction* and regime type are negative.[39] The size of the coefficients for *Sanction* is larger (and significant) for regular than irregular types of exit.[40]

Table 5.6 summarizes the predicted probabilities of each mode of exit using the results from model 1 of Table 5.5. In personalist regimes, sanctions increase the likelihood of regular exit by more than 3% while increasing the likelihood of irregular exit by 3%. The sanction-induced absolute increase in the risk of irregular exit is much higher because the overall level of risk of irregular removal, regardless of sanctions, is much higher as well. Sanctions have almost no effect on the stability of single-party leaders. Military dictators, however, are less likely to exit (particularly an irregular exit) when under sanctions, though this difference is not statistically different from 0. Increased cooptation may allow military rulers to reduce the risk of elite splits that might be conducive to a peaceful transfer of power to civilians, and military rulers' relatively high capacity for repression may reduce the likelihood of irregular exits. Overall, the pattern in Table 5.6 is consistent with the

Table 5.5. Dictators' Mode of Exit and Economic Sanctions (Multinomial Logit)

INDEPENDENT VARIABLES	PR (Y = RegularExit)		PR (Y = IrregularExit)	
	(1)	(2)	(1)	(2)
Sanction$_{t-1}$	2.51** (0.879)	2.36** (0.874)	0.739 (0.527)	0.844 (0.534)
Sanction$_{t-1}$*Single party	−3.01** (0.935)	−2.82** (0.921)	−0.561 (0.661)	−0.638 (0.660)
Sanction$_{t-1}$*Military	−3.04** (1.00)	−2.96** (1.00)	−1.20† (0.664)	−1.36* (0.693)
Single party	1.87** (0.441)	2.36* (1.16)	−0.251 (0.253)	0.413 (0.732)
Military	2.54** (0.514)	3.83** (1.32)	1.20** (0.296)	1.94* (0.768)
Log oil rents (pc)	−0.058 (0.076)	−0.059 (0.079)	0.080 (0.065)	0.084 (0.066)
Sanction$_{t-1}$*Log oil rents	−0.097 (0.181)	−0.141 (0.192)	−0.097 (0.142)	−0.121 (0.143)
Log(GDP pc)	0.318† (0.175)	0.322† (0.179)	−0.558** (0.156)	−0.563** (0.158)
Economic growth$_{t-1, t-2}$	8.73** (3.05)	−1.85 (1.99)	2.30 (2.68)	0.002 (1.83)
Growth*Single party	−12.26** (3.82)		−4.69 (4.48)	
Growth*Military	−13.58* (5.37)		−3.09 (3.69)	
Log(population)	0.231** (0.084)	0.227** (0.083)	−0.192* (0.076)	−0.196* (0.077)
Dictatorships in region	−0.696 (0.603)	−0.837 (0.606)	−0.915† (0.490)	−0.953* (0.485)
Previous democracy	−1.10** (0.430)	−0.987* (0.435)	0.082 (0.301)	0.123 (0.302)
Previous colony	−0.904** (0.352)	−0.899** (0.348)	−0.370 (0.227)	−0.374† (0.228)
Religious diversity	−0.057 (0.635)	−0.053 (0.632)	−0.104 (0.445)	−0.093 (0.439)
Cold War	0.202 (0.415)	1.13 (1.12)	0.394 (0.345)	0.885† (0.522)
Cold War*Single party		−0.838 (1.17)		−0.785 (0.758)
Cold War*Military		−1.79 (1.39)		−0.860 (0.802)
Foreign War	−0.478 (0.858)	−0.433 (0.877)	0.681 (0.425)	0.695† (0.421)
Time	−0.230* (0.104)	−0.231* (0.104)	−0.164** (0.056)	−0.169** (0.056)
Time^2	0.013† (0.007)	0.013† (0.007)	0.007* (0.002)	0.007* (0.002)
Time^3	−0.0002† (0.000)	−0.000† (0.000)	−0.000† (0.000)	−0.000* (0.000)
Log likelihood	−817.712		−818.410	
Observations	2,807		2,807	

Notes: Standard errors are given in parentheses. Errors are clustered on leader. $^\dagger p < .10$; $^* p < .05$; $^{**} p < .01$.

Table 5.6. Predicted Probabilities of Regular and Irregular Exit by Regime Type and Sanction

Sanction[†]	$\hat{p}$ $(y_j =$ (RegularExit)			$\hat{p}$ $(y_j =$ (IrregularExit)		
	Personalist	Single Party	Military	Personalist	Single Party	Military
Model 1						
Not targeted	0.3%	2.6%	6.2%	3.3%	2.4%	11.2%
Under sanctions	4.0%	1.6%	4.3%	6.3%	2.9%	7.7%
Difference	3.7%[*]	−1.0%	−1.9%	2.9%	0.4%	−3.5%
	(0.031)	(0.008)	(0.028)	(0.027)	(0.012)	(0.030)

Notes: Mean predicted probability of event reported in each cell. Standard errors are given in parentheses. The control variables are held constant at their sample mean/median, except for oil rents, growth, and the time variables, which are set to the mean within each regime type. *$p < .10$ [two-tailed test].

proposition that sanctions are most likely to destabilize a personalist ruler by increasing the risk of both a regular and an irregular transfer of power.

The effect of some of the control variables change when we disaggregate the dependent variable into regular and irregular exits from power. For instance, development (GDP per capita) and population increase the likelihood of regular changes but they reduce the probability of putsches, coups, revolutions, and assassinations. Single-party regimes are more likely than personalist to have regular exit, but no more or less likely to suffer irregular exit. One of the functions of single-party systems is to regulate leadership succession and access to power in order to facilitate cooperation among those already in power. This explains why regular changes are more frequent in single-party regimes than irregular exits. However, military dictators still face the highest risk of being replaced through both types of exits, again consistent with Geddes' (1999, 2003) findings for regime duration.

Concluding Remarks

Sanctions are one of the most widely used mechanisms of international pressure, and are often viewed as a potentially effective means to achieve foreign policy goals. While the imposition of sanctions by governments and international organizations against authoritarian regimes has increased over time, we still know little about whether and how sanctions affect the stability of authoritarian rulers. This article is an attempt to fill this gap in our understanding of international economic coercion by thinking about how sanctions affect the economic resources necessary for dictators to stay in power. Our main contribution is to disaggregate authoritarian leaders to understand how sanctions affect stability in different types of regimes.

Our theoretical argument emphasizes that sanctions can reduce a dictator's ability to obtain patronage rents from external sources.

Authoritarian regimes under sanctions suffer significant losses in revenue from foreign aid, taxes on international trade, and other forms of non-tax revenue. The detrimental effect of sanctions on sources of patronage is particularly acute in personalist dictatorships, which we argue have limited state capacity to compensate for this loss by increasing revenue collection from alternative streams. Further, personalist rulers are less capable of substituting cooptation for patronage. Personalist regimes typically have weak institutions, making cooptation less effective and promises of future rents less credible. Responding to a sanction-induced loss of patronage resources with repression may be counterproductive in these regimes because repression can increase the perception of threat on the part of elites in the supporting coalition, precisely when the benefits of such support are shrinking. Finally, because personalist rulers are the least likely to have full control over the army, mobilizing the military in response to domestic opposition entails substantial risks that the military will intervene against the incumbent.

In contrast, single-party and military regimes are able to increase their revenues even when targeted by sanctions, by shifting fiscal pressure from one stream to an alternative one (specifically, taxes on goods and services). This allows them to maintain cooptation while they increase repression to thwart the domestic opposition that reduced economic performance and international support may generate. Single-party regimes typically have strong parties and credible institutions which make cooptation more feasible, while military rulers can most effectively use repression. Departing from these facts, we hypothesized that sanctions would be effective in destabilizing personalist dictators, but would have little effect or possibly be counterproductive in single-party and military dictatorships.

Our results are generally consistent with the main hypothesis. We find that sanctions increase autocrats' likelihood of losing power in personalist regimes, but that sanctions are either ineffective or counterproductive in single-party and military regimes.[41] We also show that sanctions are less destabilizing in oil-producing countries, perhaps because demand for oil is highly inelastic in most sanction-sending countries, making them reluctant to disrupt energy supplies. When we examine the modes by which authoritarian leaders are deposed, we find that sanctions increase the likelihood of both irregular and regular exits from power in personalist regimes.

While the recent empirical literature on sanctions effectiveness suggests that sanctions are unlikely to destabilize dictators (Nooruddin 2002; Marinov 2005; Lektzian and Souva 2007), we offer a more nuanced account. We show that sanctions can destabilize some, but not all dictators. Our findings point toward two conclusions. First, if sanctions are to be effective in destabilizing dictators, they should strike at revenue sources the dictator needs to stay in power. This suggestion is consistent with Kirshner's (1997) contention that we should look at how sanctions affect the central government's grip on power in the targeted country and its key support groups. Second, if sending countries want sanctions against dictators to be more than expressions of disapproval, senders should consider how the targeted dictator is likely to respond. Here our contribution is more novel. Our results suggest that many dictators, even when they incur a sanction-induced reduction in patronage resources, can compensate for this loss by increasing revenues from other streams or by substituting cooptation for patronage. In personalist regimes, however, when sanctions deplete the resources available for patronage, dictators cannot adequately adjust and are thus likely to face destabilizing pressure.

Appendix: Selection Equations for Sanctions

Independent Variables	(1)	(2)
Log(oil rents)	0.044† (0.023)	
% Trade with democracies	−2.09** (0.189)	
Log(GDP pc)	0.250** (0.054)	0.240** (0.044)
Log(population)		0.295** (0.024)
Single party	0.244** (0.088)	0.468** (0.073)
Military	0.550** (0.110)	0.416** (0.097)
Cold War	−0.065 (0.172)	−0.682** (0.128)
Previous colony	−0.879** (0.095)	−0.251** (0.083)
Foreign war	0.926** (0.164)	0.435** (0.131)
Civil war	0.445** (0.103)	0.501** (0.088)
Democracies in the world	5.28** (0.753)	0.761 (0.524)
Sub-Saharan Africa	0.923** (0.316)	0.357 (0.220)
North Africa	1.63** (0.327)	0.677** (0.220)
Middle East	0.065 (0.337)	0.289 (0.214)
Central Asia	−0.114 (0.366)	0.113 (0.292)
Central America/Caribbean	1.06** (0.323)	0.955** (0.224)
East Asia	1.00** (0.320)	0.360 (0.224)
South America	0.840** (0.326)	0.163 (0.221)
Central/East Europe	0.501 (0.319)	0.413† (0.212)
Log likelihood	−996.879	−1359.72
Observations	2,742	3,590

Notes: Dependent variable is Sanction. Standard errors are given in parentheses. $^\dagger p < .10$; $^* p < .05$; $^{**} p < .01$.

NOTES

1. http://www.whitehouse.gov/inaugural/ (accessed June 2008).
2. Funded by the Central Intelligence Agency, British intelligence, and the Saudis, the INA staged a failed coup attempt in 1996.
3. The INC had received millions of dollars in American aid for military training.
4. Most of the work on authoritarian breakdowns focuses on regimes and not leaders as the unit of analysis.
5. For example, between 1960 and 2000 the average foreign aid per capita has been $33 for personalist and monarchic regimes, $23 for single-party systems,

and just $13 for military regimes. If we include mixed cases according to the pure type they most seem to resemble, personalist regimes (monarchies plus personalist regimes) have received on average $33 in aid per capita; single party (pure types plus personalist/single-party hybrids and single party/military) received $30, and military regimes (military plus military/personalist) just $20.

6. Numberger (1982) estimates that by 1977 coffee exports accounted for 97% of Uganda's foreign export earnings; those exports were controlled by the government-owned Coffee Marketing Board. Coffee purchases by the United States, United Kingdom, France, Japan, and West Germany accounted for 73% of Uganda's total export income.

7. Particularly, the suspension of arms sales in August 1960. These measures were extended in January 1961 to include oil, spare parts, and trucks.

8. In 1960, when Congress voted to reassign part of the Cuban sugar quota to existing sugar exporting countries, the Eisenhower administration ignored these provisions for the Dominican Republic. To compromise with Trujillo supporters in Congress, the Eisenhower administration subsequently reassigned some of the Cuban quota to the Dominican Republic, but imposed an entrance fee to limit the benefits to Dominican sellers. Facing less opposition in Congress, the Kennedy administration reduced the Dominican Republic's sugar quota to pre-1960 levels (Schreiber 1973).

9. This may be one reason dominant party regimes are relatively resistant to economic shocks (Haggard and Kaufman 1995: chapter 7; Geddes 1999), and typically only lose power once the state (and hence the party) contract their control over large portions of the economy (Greene 2010).

10. Magaloni (2006) shows that older voters who experienced decades of PRI rule under a growing economy were much more likely than younger voters to support the PRI in the wake of the 1994 *peso* crisis, in part, because the older voters expected PRI rule to continue and had been long-time recipients of PRI patronage.

11. See Gandhi and Przeworski (2006) on authoritarian institutions and policy concessions.

12. Even militaries can be quite adept at buying the support of key elite or the mass public with patronage. For example, Hunter argues the Brazilian military's attempt to ensure electoral victory after 1974 meant "transforming ARENA into a 'gigantic patronage machine'" (1907:103).

13. To obtain these figures, we regress logged government consumption as a share of GDI' on regime type, log(GDP per capita), and oil and gas rents per capita.

14. Data on revenue composition are taken from the World Bank's *World Development Indicators*. Aid figures are expressed as a percentage of GNI.

15. Public investment may also constitute a method of distributing rents, potentially increasing corruption (Robinson and Torvik 2005).

16. In fact, it seems that personalist regimes try to minimize the cuts in the subsidies category, as it is the only one for which the t-test is not significant when we compare the averages under economic sanctions and not under sanctions. The very limited existing data on military expenditures (as a percentage of the GNI, from WDI) indicates that personalist rulers cut spending on this category when targeted by sanctions as well, while single-party and military regimes increase them.

17. In Romania in December 1989, for example, the military sided with opposition protests that were triggered by President Ceaucescu's order to fire on anti-regime demonstrators in Timisoara. In response, Ceaucescu and his wife fled the capital, Bucharest, in a helicopter. Faking an engine failure, the pilot landed and the couple was captured by the armed forces. On December 25, the two were condemned to death by a military court on a range of charges, included genocide. Both were executed by firing squad.

18. India's economic sanctions against Nepal as a response to King Birendra's arms purchases from China in the late 1980s had a similar effect. The

embargo hurt the population, and student riots rapidly spread. After violent clashes with the security forces a large pro-democratic demonstration in the capital led the King to legalize political parties and a new transitional government was appointed. See a previous version of Marinov (2005).

19. These data are from Goemans, Gleditsch, and Chiozza (2009).

20. While we cannot make a causal argument with the descriptive data, we lag the measure of sanctions 1 year to mitigate against the possibility that the data simply show that repression causes sanctions.

21. This point echoes Davenport's (2007) findings on repression.

22. The main results hold if we use a measure of economic sanctions from the TIES data set ("Threat and imposition of Sanctions" Cliff Morgan, Valentin Krustev, Navin Bapat: http://www.unc.edu/bapat/TIES.htm). Marinov's updated sanctions variable and the TIES variable for sanctions are correlated at 0.41.

23. These include single party/military, single party/personalist, and single party/military/personalist. See Geddes (2003) for details on the distinctions between different hybrid types.

24. See Gasiorowski (1995).

25. The variables described in this paragraph are updated from Przeworski, Alvarez, Antonio Chelbub, and Limongi's (2000) ACLP.

26. Using ethnic fractionalization indices in lieu of religious fractionalization resulted in the same findings.

27. In contrast, it was relatively easy for the United States to reassign sugar quotas to Brazil and Mexico when sugar imports from Trujillo's Dominican Republic and Cuba were restricted in 1960 and 1961.

28. For example, the reliance of oil importing countries on Libyan oil exports may have pre-empted the imposition of comprehensive sanctions (including an oil embargo) against Muammar al-Gaddafi's regime in the mid 1990s after it refused to extradite the two agents allegedly involved in the Lockerbie airplane terrorist attack. Even while under international sanctions in the 1990s, Hussein's regime in Iraq was able to continue selling oil to countries such as Egypt, Turkey, Jordan, and Syria. The US Government Accountability Office (GAO) report revealed that Iraq Illicitly exported 30,000–40,000 barrels per day through the Persian Gulf in May 2002 with the cooperation of Iran (GAO 2002). At the same time, 180,000–250,000 barrels per day were exported through Syria, and a further 40,000–80,000 barrels per day through Turkey. According to the Independent Inquiry Committee (IIC) into the UN Oil-for-Food Programme (OFFP), Hussein's regime earned over $11 billion from illicit oil sales from 1990 to 2003. An estimated $1.8 billion was earned from kickbacks and surcharges on OFFP contracts and sales. These rents accrued directly to Hussein's regime (unlike income from legal exports, which was controlled by the UN), enabling him to pay off his supporters and hold onto power until the 2003 Invasion (*The Economist*, July 7, 2001, 45–46).

29. We log per capita oil revenue to mute the influence of outliers. We also use the log of Ross' data on oil and gas rents in a robustness test (Ross 2008), with similar results.

30. See Carter and Signorino (2007). Using cubic splines, as suggested by Beck, Katz, and Tucker (1998) yields similar results.

31. The reference category is *personalist* regimes, so the coefficient for *Sanctions* reflects the effect of sanctions in these regimes.

32. The inclusion of this interaction is theoretically motivated. Thus, Geddes argues that "some kinds of authoritarianism are more dependent on economic performance than others" (2004:4). Economic crises tend to cause division within the regime ruling elite over how to respond to it. Military regimes are particularly vulnerable to factionalism as military officers place a higher value on the unity, hierarchy, discipline, and corporate interests of the military than on retaining power. Disagreements among officers will prompt the military to go back to the

barracks in order to preserve the unity and discipline of the armed forces.

33. The coefficient for military rulers is in this case: $1.19 - 1.81 = -0.620$.

34. These results hold when we use an alternative measure of oil rents (Ross 2008).

35. We also tested models that excluded all the control variables listed in the lower panel of Table 5.1. These tests yielded even stronger results for our hypotheses than those reported in Table 5.1. We also tested models where we add controls for civil war and neighboring democracy. This latter control measures the percentage of neighboring countries with capital cities within 2,000 km of the target country that are democracies.

36. The chi-square values and (*p*-values) of the offending covariates are: $Log(GDPpc) = 26.68$ (0.000); $LogOilRents = 13.30$ (0.0003); $LogOilRents*Sanction = 13.48$ (0.0002); $PreviousDemocracy = 5.80$ (0.016). For the global test, $\chi^2 = 49.96$ (0.0001). We use the Brelow method for ties and report coefficients (not hazard ratios) with standard errors clustered on leader.

37. The main results remain if we exclude all of these interaction terms except $Log(sqrt(Time))*LogGDP(pc)$.

38. Results from the first-stage models are available in the Appendix. In a second specification aimed at maximizing sample size, we suppress some of the controls with less observations. The results of the first-stage equations suggest that personalist regimes are the least likely to be targeted by sanctions. To square this fact with the main finding of our analysis that sanctions are the most effective at destabilizing personalist rulers, it is important to note that not all sanctions are aimed at destabilizing the target country leader. Many sanctions may be symbolic, aimed at pleasing a domestic constituency in the sending country (Rowe 2001; Hufbauer, Schott, Elliott, and Oegg 2007). Other sanctions may have a much more narrow goal such as reducing the military capacity of the target country (Hufbauer et al. 2007).

39. The results remain if we exclude monarchies or include "triple-threat" regimes in single-party category.

40. When both interactions (between regime type and growth and Cold War) are added, the sanctions dummy reaches statistical significance in predicting irregular exits as well at the 0.10 level. These results are available from the authors.

41. In unreported results, we find that military rulers are sensitive to arms imports, while rulers in other types of regimes generally are not (single-party rulers are in some specifications). While this finding merits further research, initially we interpret it to suggest that even though economic sanctions generally are ineffective in destabilizing military rulers, cutting military aid and exports may be effective in these cases. We thank an anonymous reviewer for raising this point.

REFERENCES

Arendt, Hannah. (1962) *The Origins of Totalitarianism.* New York: Meridian.

Askari, Hossen G., John Forrer, Hildy Teegen, and Jiawen Yang. (2003) *Economic Sanctions: Explaining their Philosophy and Efficacy.* Westport, CT: Praeger.

Beck, Nathaniel, Jonathan Katz, and Richard Tucker. (1998) Taking Time Seriously. Time-Series-Cross-Section Analysis with a Binary Dependent Variable. *American Journal of Political Science* 42 (4): 1260–1288.

Bertocchi, Graziella, and Michael Spagat. (2001) The Politics of Co-optation. *Journal of Comparative Economics* 29 (4): 591–607.

Blaydes, Lisa. (2008) Electoral Budget Cycles under Authoritarianism: Economic Opportunism in Mubarak's Egypt. Unpublished manuscript, Palo Alto, CA, Stanford University.

Box-Steffensmeier, Janet M., Dan Reiter, and Christopher Zorn. (2003) Nonproportional Hazards and Event History Analysis in International Relations. *Journal of Conflict Resolution* 47 (1): 33–53.

Bratton, Michael, and Nicolas van de Walle. (1994) Patrimonial Regimes and Political Transitions in Africa. *World Politics* 46 (4): 453–489.

Bratton, Michael, and Nicolas van de Walle. (1997) *Democratic Experiments in Africa. Regime Transitions in Comparative Perspective.* New York: Cambridge University Press.

Brautigam, Deborah. (2000) *Aid, Dependence, and Governance.* Stockholm: Almqvist and Wiksell.

Brough, Wayne T., and Mwangi S. Kimenvi. (1986) On the Inefficient Extraction of Rents by Dictators. *Public Choice* 48 (1): 37–48.

Brownlee, Jason. (2004) Ruling Parties and Durable Authoritarianism. Paper presented at the American Political Science Association's annual meeting, Chicago, IL, September 2–5.

Bueno de Mesquita, Bruce, Alastair Smith, Randolph Siverson, and James Morrow. (2003) *Logic of Political Survival.* Cambridge, MA: MIT Press.

Carter, David, and Curt Signorino. (2007) Back to the Future: Modeling Time Dependence in Binary Data. Paper presented at the American Political Science Association's annual meeting, Chicago, IL, August 30 - September 2.

Dashti-Gidson, Jaleh, Patricia Davis, and Benjamin Radcliff. (1997) On the Determinants of the Success of Economic Sanctions: An Empirical Analysis. *American Journal of Political Science* 41 (2): 608–618.

Davenport, Christian. (2007) State Repression and the Tyrannical Peace. *Journal of Peace Research* 44 (4): 485–504.

Escribà-Folch, Adel. (2007) La Economía Política de la Supervivencia de los Diciadores. *Revista Española de Ciencia Politica* 16: 109–132.

Falk, Richard A. (1992) Theoretical Foundations of Human Rights. In *Human Rights in the World Community: Issues and Action*, edited by Richard Pierre Claude and Burns H. Weston.

Philadelphia, PA: University of Pennsylvania Press.

Feierabend, Rosalind, Ivo Feieradend, and Ted R. Gurr. (1972) *Anger, Violence, and Politics.* Englewood Cliffs, NJ: Prentice-Hall.

Francisco, Ronald A. (1995) The Relationship between Coercion and Protest: An Empirical Evaluation in Three Coercive States, *Journal of Conflict Resolution* 39 (2): 263–282.

Friedrich, Carl J., and Zbigniew E. Brzezinski. (1961) *Totalitarian Dictatorship and Autocracy.* New York: Praeger.

Galetovic, Alexander, and Ricardo Sanhueza. (2000) Citizens, Autocrats, and Plotters: A Model and New Evidence on Coups d'État. *Economics and Politics* 12 (2): 183–204.

Gandhi, Jennifer, and Adam Przeworski. (2006) Cooperation, Cooptation, and Rebellion under Dictatorships. *Economics and Politics* 18 (1): 1–26.

Gandhi, Jennifer, and Adam Przeworski. (2007) Authoritarian Institutions and the Survival of Autocrats. *Comparative Political Studies* 40 (11): 1279–1301.

GAO. (2002) *U.N. Confronts Significant Challenges in Implementing Sanctions against Iraq.* Washington, DC: GAO-02-625.

Gasiorowski, Mark. (1995) Economic Crisis and Political Regime Change: An Event History Analysis. *American Political Science Review* 89 (4): 882–887.

Geddes, Barbara. (1999) Authoritarian Breakdown: Empirical Test of a Game Theoretic Argument. Paper presented at the American Political Science Association's annual meeting, Atlanta, GA, September 2–5.

Geddes, Barbara. (2003) *Paradigms and Sand Castles.* Ann Arbor: University of Michigan Press.

Geddes, Barbara. (2004) Authoritarian Breakdown. Unpublished manuscript, Department of Political Science, UCLA.

Geddes, Barbara. (2008) Party Creation as an Autocratic Survival Strategy. Paper presented at

"Dictatorships: Their Governance and Social Consequences" Conference at Princeton University, April 25–26.

Gershenson, Dmitriy, and Herschel I. Grossman. (2001) Cooption and Repression in the Soviet Union. *Economics and Politics* 13 (1): 31–47.

Gleditsch, Kristian S., and Michael D. Ward. (2006) Diffusion and the International Context of Democratization. *International Organization* 60 (4): 911–933.

Goemans, Hein, Kristian S. Gleditsch, and Giacomo Chiozza. (2009) Introducing *Archigos*: A Data Set of Political Leaders, 1875–2003. *Journal of Peace Research* 46 (2): 269–283.

Greene, Kenneth F. (2010) The Political Economy of Authoritarian Single-Party Dominance. *Comparative Political Studies* 43 (9): 1–27.

Haas, Richard N. (1997) Sanctioning Madness. *Foreign Affairs* 76 (6): 74–85.

Hafner-Burton, Emilie M., and Kiyoteru Tsutsui. (2007) Justice Lost! The Failure of International Human Rights Law to Matter Where Needed Most. *Journal of Peace Research* 44 (4): 407–425.

Haggard, Stephen, and Robert R. Kaufman. (1995) *The Political Economy of Democratic Transitions.* Princeton, NJ: Princeton University Press.

Hufbauer, Gary C., Jeffrey J. Schott, and Kimberley A. Elliott. (1990) *Economic Sanctions Reconsidered: History and Current Policy.* Washington, DC: Peterson Institute for International Economics.

Hufbauer, Gary C., Jeffrey J. Schott, Kimberley A. Elliott, and Barbara Oegg. (2007) *Economic Sanctions Reconsidered*, 3rd edition. Washington, DC: Peterson Institute for International Economics.

Humphreys, Macartan. (2005) Natural Resources, Conflict and Conflict Resolution. *Journal of Conflict Resolution* 49 (4): 508–537.

Hunter, Wendy. (1997) *Eroding Military Influence in Brazil: Politicians against Soldiers.* Chapel Hill: University of North Carolina Press.

Jackson, Robert H., and Carl G. Rosberg. (1984) Personal Rule: Theory and Practice in Africa. *Comparative Politics* 16 (4): 421–442.

Johnson, Thomas H., Robert O. Slater, and Pat McGowan. (1984) Explaining African Military Coups d'État, 1960–1982. *American Political Science Review* 78 (3): 622–640.

Kaempfer, William H., and Anton D. Lowenberg. (1988) The Theory of International Economic Sanctions: A Public Choice Approach. *American Economic Review* 78 (4): 786–793.

Kaempfer, William H., Anton D. Lowenberg, and William Mertens. (2004) International Economic Sanctions against a Dictator. *Economics and Politics* 16 (1): 29–51.

Kasza, Gregory J. (1995a) *The Conscription Society: Administered Mass Organizations.* New Haven, CT: Yale University Press.

Kasza, Gregory J. (1995b) Weapons of the Strong: Organization and Terror. In *Politics, Society, and Democracy. Comparative Studies*, edited by H. E. Chebabi and Alfred Stepan. Boulder, CO: Westview.

Kirshner, Jonathan. (1997) The Microfoundations of Economic Sanctions. *Security Studies* 6 (3): 32–64.

Lai, Brian, and Dan Slater. (2006) Institutions of the Offensive: Domestic Sources of Dispute Initiation in Authoritarian Regimes, 1950–1992. *American Journal of Political Science* 50 (1): 113–126.

Lektzian, David, and Mark Souva. (2007) An Institutional Theory of Sanctions Onset and Success. *Journal of Conflict Resolution* 51 (6): 848–871.

Lieberman, Evan S. (2002) Taxation Data as Indicators of State-Society Relations: Possibilities and Pitfalls in Cross-National Research. *Studies in Comparative International Development* 36 (4): 89–115.

Londregan, John B., and Keith T. Poole. (1990) Poverty, the Coup Trap, and the Seizure of Executive Power. *World Politics* 42 (2): 151–183.

Maddison, Angus. (2006) World Population, GDP and Per Capita GDP, 1-2003 AD. Available at http://www.ggdc.net/maddison/. (Accessed April 30, 2010.)

Magaloni, Beatriz, (2006) *Voting for Autocracy.* New York: Cambridge University Press.

Marinov, Nikolay. (2005) Do Sanctions Destabilize Country Leaders? *American Journal of Political Science* 49 (3): 564–576.

Milner, Helen, and Keiko Kubota. (2005) Why the Move to Free Trade? Democracy and Trade Policy in the Developing Countries. *International Organization* 59 (1): 107–143.

Morrison, Kevin M. (2009) Oil, Nontax Revenue, and the Redistributional Foundations of Regime Stability. *International Organization* 63 (1): 107–138.

Mueller, John, and Karl Mueller. (1999) Sanctions of Mass Destruction. *Foreign Affairs* 78 (3): 43–53.

Nooruddin, Irfan. (2002) Modeling Selection Bias in Studies of Sanctions Efficacy. *International Interactions* 28 (1): 59–75.

Nurnberger, Ralph. (1982) The United States and Idi Amin: Congress to the Rescue. *African Studies Review* 25 (1): 49–65.

Nurnberger, Ralph. (2003) Why Sanctions (Almost) Never Work. *The International Economy* 17 (4): 71–72.

O'Kane, Rosemary H. T. (1981) A Probabilistic Approach to the Causes of Coups d'État, *British Journal of Political Science* 11 (3): 287–308.

O'Kane, Rosemary H. T. (1993) Coups d'État in Africa: A Political Economy Approach. *Journal of Peace Research* 30 (3): 251–270.

Olson, Robert S. (1979) Economic Coercion in World Politics: With a Focus on North-South Relations. *World Politics* 31 (4): 471–494.

Pape, Robert A. (1997) Why Economic Sanctions Do Not Work. *International Security* 22 (2): 90–136.

Pepinsky, Thomas B. (2007) Autocracy, Elections, and Fiscal Policy in Malaysia. *Studies in Comparative International Development* 42 (1–2): 136–163.

Pinto-Duschinsky, Michael. (1991) Foreign Political Aid: The German Political Foundations and Their US Counterparts. *International Affairs* 67 (1): 33–63.

Przeworski, Adam, Michael Alvarez, Jose Antonio Cheibub, and Fernando Limongi. (2000) *Democracy and Development*. Cambridge: Cambridge University Press.

Rasler, Karen. (1996) Concessions, Repression, and Political Protest in the Iranian Revolution. *American Sociological Review* 61 (1): 132–152.

Robinson, James, and Ragnar Torvik. (2005) White Elephants. *Journal of Public Economics* 89 (2–3): 197–210.

Ross, Michael. (2001) Does Oil Hinder Democracy? *World Politics* 53 (3): 325–361.

Ross, Michael. (2008) Oil, Islam, and Women. *American Political Science Review* 102 (1): 107–123.

Rowe, David M. (2001) *Manipulating the Market: Understanding Economic Sanctions, Institutional Change, and the Political Unity of White Rhodesia*. Ann Arbor: The University of Michigan Press.

Schreiber, Anna P. (1973) Economic Coercion as an Instrument of Foreign Policy: US Economic Measures against Cuba and the Dominican Republic. *World Politics* 25 (3): 387–413.

Smith, Benjamin. (2004) Oil Wealth and Regime Survival in the Developing World: 1960–1999. *American Journal of Political Science* 48 (2): 232–246.

Smith, Benjamin. (2005) Life of the Party: The Origins of Regime Breakdown and Persistence under Single-Party Rule. *World Politics* 57 (3): 421–451.

The Economist. (2001) Smart Exit; Sanctions on Iraq. July 7, 45–46.

Tullock, Gordon. (1987) *Autocracy*, Boston, MA: Kluwer Academic Publishers.

Ulfelder, Jay. (2005) Contentious Collective Action and the Breakdown of Authoritarian Regimes. *International Political Science Review* 26 (3): 311–334.

Ulfelder, Jay. (2007) Natural-Resource Wealth and the Survival of Autocracy. *Comparative Political Studies* 40 (8): 995–1018.

Ullman, Richard H. (1978) Human Rights and Economic Power: The United States versus Idi Amin. *Foreign Affairs* 50 (3): 529–543.

Van Bergeijk, Peter A. G. (1989) Success and Failure in Economic Sanctions. *Kyklos* 42 (3): 385–404.

Van de Walle, Nicolas. (2001) *African Economies and the Politics of Permanent Crisis, 1979–1999*. Cambridge: Cambridge University Press.

Weeks, Jessica L. (2008) Autocratic Audience Costs: Regime Type and Signaling Resolve. *International Organization* 62 (1): 35–64.

Wintrobe, Ronald. (1990) The Tinpot and the Totalitarian: An Economic Theory of Dictatorship. *American Political Science Review* 83 (4): 849–872.

Wintrobe, Ronald. (1998) *The Political Economy of Dictatorship*. Cambridge: Cambridge University Press.

Wood, Reed M. (2008). "A Hand upon the Throat of the Nation": Economic Sanctions and State Repression, 1976–2001. *International Studies Quarterly* 52 (3): 489–513.

Wright, Joseph. (2008) Do Authoritarian Institutions Constrain? How Legislatures Affect Economic Growth and Investment. *American Journal of Political Science* 52 (2): 322–343.

Stephen D. Krasner

SHARING SOVEREIGNTY
New Institutions for Collapsed and Failing States

Conventional sovereignty assumes a world of autonomous, internationally recognized, and well-governed states. Although frequently violated in practice, the fundamental rules of conventional sovereignty—recognition of juridically independent territorial entities and nonintervention in the internal affairs of other states—have rarely been challenged in principle. But these rules no longer work, and their inadequacies have had deleterious consequences for the strong as well as the weak. The policy tools that powerful and well-governed states have available to "fix" badly governed or collapsed states—principally governance assistance and transitional administration (whether formally authorized by the United Nations or engaged in by a coalition of the willing led by the United States)—are inadequate. In the future, better domestic governance in badly governed, failed, and occupied polities will require the transcendence of accepted rules, including the creation of shared sovereignty in specific areas. In some cases, decent governance may require some new form of trusteeship, almost certainly de facto rather than de jure.[1]

Many countries suffer under failed, weak, incompetent, or abusive national authority structures. The best that people living in such countries can hope for is marginal improvement in their material well-being; limited access to social

services, including health care and education; and a moderate degree of individual physical security. At worst they will confront endemic violence, exploitative political leaders, falling life expectancy, declining per capita income, and even state-sponsored genocide. In the Democratic Republic of Congo (formerly Zaire), for example, civil wars that have persisted for more than two decades have resulted in millions of deaths. In Zimbabwe the policies of President Robert Mugabe, who was determined to stay in office regardless of the consequences for his country's citizens, led to an economic debacle that began in 2000 with falling per capita income, inflation above 500 percent, and the threat of mass starvation. In Colombia much of the territory is controlled by the Revolutionary Armed Forces of Colombia (FARC), a Marxist rebel group that derives most of its income from drug trafficking. In Rwanda more than 700,000 people were slaughtered in a matter of weeks in 1994 as a result of a government-organized genocide.

The consequences of failed and inadequate governance have not been limited to the societies directly affected. Poorly governed societies can generate conflicts that spill across international borders. Transnational criminal and terrorist networks can operate in territories not controlled by the internationally recognized government. Humanitarian disasters not only prick the conscience of political leaders in advanced democratic societies but also leave them with no policy options that are appealing to voters.

From *International Security* 29, no. 2 (Fall 2004): 85–120. Some of the author's notes have been omitted.

Challenges related to creating better governance also arise where national authority structures have collapsed because of external invasion and occupation rather than internal conflict. The availability of weapons of mass destruction and the presence of transnational terrorism have created a historically unprecedented situation in which polities with very limited material capability can threaten the security of much more powerful states. These polities can be conquered and occupied with relative ease, leaving the occupying power with the more challenging task of establishing an acceptable domestic governing structure. Contemporary Afghanistan and Iraq are the obvious cases in point.

Left to their own devices, collapsed and badly governed states will not fix themselves because they have limited administrative capacity, not least with regard to maintaining internal security.[2] Occupying powers cannot escape choices about what new governance structures will be created and sustained. To reduce international threats and improve the prospects for individuals in such polities, alternative institutional arrangements supported by external actors, such as de facto trusteeships and shared sovereignty, should be added to the list of policy options.

The current menu of policy instruments for dealing with collapsed and failing states is paltry, consisting primarily of transitional administration and foreign assistance to improve governance, both of which assume that in more or less short order, targeted states can function effectively on their own. Nation-building or state-building efforts are almost always described in terms of empowering local authorities to assume the responsibilities of conventional sovereignty. The role of external actors is understood to be limited with regard to time, if not scope, in the case of transitional administration exercising full executive authority. Even as the rules of conventional sovereignty are de facto violated if not de jure challenged, and it is evident that in many cases effective autonomous

national government is far in the future, the language of diplomacy, the media, and the street portrays nothing other than a world of fully sovereign states.

The next section of this article describes the basic elements that constitute the conventional understanding of sovereignty and provides a taxonomy of alternative institutional forms. It is followed by a discussion of the ways in which conventional sovereignty has failed in some states, threatening the well-being of their own citizens and others. The inadequacy of the current repertoire of policy options for dealing with collapsed, occupied, and badly governed states—governance assistance and transitional administration—is then assessed. The possibilities for new institutional forms—notably shared sovereignty and some de facto form of trusteeship—are examined. Included is a discussion of why such arrangements might be accepted by political leaders in target as well as intervening states.

Conventional Sovereignty and Some Alternatives

Conventional sovereignty has three elements: international legal sovereignty, Westphalian/Vattelian sovereignty, and domestic sovereignty.[3] The basic rule of international legal sovereignty is to recognize juridically independent territorial entities. These entities then have the right to freely decide which agreements or treaties they will enter into. In practice, this rule has been widely but not universally honored. Some entities that are not juridically independent have been recognized (e.g., Byelorussia and the Ukraine during the Cold War), and some entities that are juridically independent have not been recognized (e.g., the People's Republic of China from 1949 to the 1970s).

The fundamental rule of Westphalian/Vattelian sovereignty is to refrain from intervening in the internal affairs of other states. Each state has the right to determine its own domestic authority structures. In practice, Westphalian/Vatellian sovereignty has frequently been violated.

Domestic sovereignty does not involve a norm or a rule, but is rather a description of the nature of domestic authority structures and the extent to which they are able to control activities within a state's boundaries. Ideally, authority structures would ensure a society that is peaceful, protects human rights, has a consultative mechanism, and honors a rule of law based on a shared understanding of justice.

In the ideal sovereign state system, international legal sovereignty, Westphalian/Vatellian sovereignty, and domestic sovereignty are mutually supportive. Recognized authorities within territorial entities regulate behavior, enjoy independence from outside interference, and enter into mutually beneficial contractual relations (treaties) with other recognized entities. This is the conventional world of international politics in which state-to-state relations are what count. One of the most striking aspects of the contemporary world is the extent to which domestic sovereignty has faltered so badly in states that still enjoy international legal, and sometimes even Westphalian/Vatellian, sovereignty. Somalia, for instance, is still an internationally recognized entity, even though it has barely any national institutions; and external actors have not, in recent years, tried to do much about Somalia's domestic sovereignty, or the lack thereof.

Conventional sovereignty was not always the hegemonic structure for ordering political life. Obviously, the basic rules of medieval Europe or the pre-nineteenth-century Sinocentric world were very different. But even in the nineteenth century, by which time conventional sovereignty had become a well-recognized structure, there were also legitimated and accepted alternatives. Protectorates were one alternative to conventional sovereignty; the rulers of a protectorate relinquished control over foreign policy to a more powerful state but retained authority over domestic affairs. For instance, in 1899 the ruler of Kuwait signed an agreement that gave Britain control of most elements of his country's foreign policy because he needed external support against threats from both Iraq and members of his own family.[4] In nineteenth-century China the major powers established treaty ports where British, French, German, and Japanese authorities regulated commerce and exercised extraterritorial authority over their own citizens and sometimes Chinese as well.[5] Within the British Empire, Australia, Canada, and South Africa became dominions that enjoyed almost complete control over their domestic affairs, recognized the British ruler as the head of state, but to some extent deferred to Britain in matters of foreign policy. Finally, colonization was a legitimated practice in the nineteenth century that allowed powerful states to assume international legal sovereignty and regulate the domestic authority structures of far-flung territories.

Conventional sovereignty is currently the only fully legitimated institutional form, but unfortunately, it does not always work. Honoring Westphalian/Vatellian sovereignty (and sometimes international legal sovereignty as well) makes it impossible to secure decent and effective domestic sovereignty, because the autochthonous political incentives facing political leaders in many failed, failing, or occupied states are perverse. These leaders are better able to enhance their own power and wealth by making exclusionist ethnic appeals or undermining even the limited legal routinized administrative capacity that might otherwise be available.

To secure decent domestic governance in failed, failing, and occupied states, new institutional forms are needed that compromise Westphalian/Vatellian sovereignty for an indefinite period. Shared sovereignty, arrangements under which individuals chosen by international organizations, powerful states, or ad hoc entities would

Table 5.7. Alternative Institutional Arrangements

	International Legal Sovereignty		Westphalian/Vatellian Sovereignty			Duration of Rule Violation		
	NO	YES	NONE	SOME	FULL	SHORT	MEDIUM	LONG
Conventional sovereignty		X			X	n/a	n/a	n/a
Colony	X		X					X
Transitional administration with full foreign executive authority	X		X			X		
Trusteeship	X		X or	X		X	X	
Shared sovereignty		X		X				X
Nineteenth-century protectorate	X			X				X

share authority with nationals over some aspects of domestic sovereignty, would be a useful addition to the policy repertoire. Ideally, shared sovereignty would be legitimated by a contract between national authorities and an external agent. In other cases, external interveners may conclude that the most attractive option would be the establishment of a de facto trusteeship or protectorate. Under such an arrangement, the Westphalian/Vatellian sovereignty of the target polity would be violated, executive authority would be vested primarily with external actors, and international legal sovereignty would be suspended. There will not, however, be any effort to formalize through an international convention or treaty a general set of principles for such an option.[6] (For a summary of these different institutional possibilities, see Table 5.7.)

Failures of Conventional Sovereignty

Failed, inadequate, incompetent, or abusive national authority structures have sabotaged the economic well-being, violated the basic human rights, and undermined the physical security of their countries' populations. In some cases, state authority has collapsed altogether for an extended period, although such instances are rare. Afghanistan in the early 1990s before the Taliban consolidated power, Liberia for much of the 1990s, and the Democratic Republic of Congo and Sierra Leone in the late 1990s are just a few of the examples. Governance challenges have also arisen in Afghanistan and Iraq, where authority structures collapsed as a result of external invasion rather than internal conflict. The occupying powers, most obviously the United States, were then confronted with the challenge of fashioning decent governance structures in both countries.

In some parts of the world, disorder (including civil war) has become endemic. For the period 1955 to 1998, the State Failure Task Force identified 136 occurrences of state failure in countries with populations larger than 500,000. The task force operationalized state failure as one of four kinds of internal political crisis: revolutionary war, ethnic war, "adverse regime change," or genocide. In 1955 fewer than 6 percent of the countries were in failure. In the early 1990s the figure had risen to almost 30 percent, falling to about 20 percent in 1998, the last year of the study. Adverse regime change was the most common form of state failure, followed by ethnic war, revolutionary war, and genocide. The task force identified partial democracy, trade closure, and low levels of economic well-being as indicated by high infant mortality rates as the primary causes of state failure. James Fearon and David Laitin show that internal strife is more likely in countries suffering from poverty, recent decolonization, high population, and mountainous terrain. These conditions allow even relatively small guerrilla bands to operate successfully because recognized governments do not have the administrative competence to engage in effective rural policing and counterinsurgency operations.[7]

States that experience failure or poor governance more generally are beset by many problems. In such states, infrastructure deteriorates; corruption is widespread; borders are unregulated; gross domestic product is declining or stagnant; crime is rampant; and the national currency is not widely accepted. Armed groups operate within the state's boundaries but outside the control of the government. The writ of the central government, the entity that exercises the prerogatives of international legal sovereignty (e.g., signing treaties and sending delegates to international meetings), may

not extend to the whole country; in some cases, it may not extend beyond the capital. Authority may be exercised by local entities in other parts of the country, or by no one at all.

Political leaders operating in an environment in which material and institutional resources are limited have often chosen policies that make a bad situation even worse. For some leaders, disorder and uncertainty are more attractive than order and stability because they are better able to extract resources from a disorderly society. Decisions affecting the distribution of wealth are based on personal connections rather than bureaucratic regulations or the rule of law. Leaders create multiple armed units that they can play off against each other. They find it more advantageous to take a bigger piece of a shrinking pie than a smaller piece of a growing pie.

The largest number of poorly governed states is found on the continent of Africa. Since the mid-1950s about a third of African states have been in failure.[8] In constant 1995 U.S. dollars, gross domestic product per capita for all of sub-Saharan Africa fell from $660 in 1980 to $587 in 1990 to $563 in 2000. Out of the sub-Saharan states for which data are available from the World Bank, eighteen had increases in their per capita gross domestic product from 1990 to 2000, seven had decreases of less than 5 percent, and seventeen experienced decreases of more than 5 percent. With the exception of the former Soviet Union, no other area of the world fared so badly with regard to economic performance.[9]

■　■　■

Thus, for many countries domestic sovereignty is not working, and the situation is not improving in any substantive way. Although the number and percentage of countries suffering from civil war declined during the 1990s, the per capita gross national income in current U.S. dollars of the least developed countries continued to drop, falling by

9 percent from 1990 to 2000, a period of robust growth for the world as a whole.

Why Sovereignty Failures Matter

In the contemporary world, powerful states have not been able to ignore governance failures. Polities where domestic authority has collapsed or been inadequate have threatened the economic and security interests of these states. Humanitarian crises have engaged electorates in advanced democracies and created no-win situations for political leaders who are damned if they intervene and damned if they do not. And, most obviously, when a state has been invaded, the occupiers have been confronted with the problem of establishing effective domestic sovereignty.

The availability of weapons of mass destruction, the ease of movement across borders, and the emergence of terrorist networks have attenuated the relationship between the underlying capabilities of actors and the ability to kill large numbers of people. In the past, state and nonstate actors with limited resources could not threaten the security of states with substantial resources. The killing power of a nation's military depended on the underlying wealth of the country. Nonstate actors such as anarchist groups in the nineteenth century could throw bombs that might kill fifty or even several hundred people, but not more. This is no longer true. States with limited means can procure chemical and biological weapons. Nuclear weapons demand more resources, but they are not out of reach of even a dismally poor country such as North Korea. Weapons of mass destruction can be delivered in myriad ways, not only by missiles but also by commercial ships, trucks, planes, and even envelopes. Failed or weak states may provide terrorists with territory in which they can operate freely.

Moreover, political leaders who have effective control within their borders but limited resources to defend or deter an invasion present a tempting target if they adopt policies that threaten the core security interests of powerful states. For instance, throughout his rule Saddam Hussein sought and sometimes used weapons of mass destruction, and even when faced with invasion, failed to fully cooperate with UN inspectors. In Afghanistan the Taliban supported al-Qa'ida, which had already demonstrated that it could strike core targets in the United States. Neither Iraq nor Afghanistan could defend itself against, or deter, a U.S. attack. When the threat is high and invasion is easy, powerful states are likely to use military force to bring down a menacing regime. When, however, the old regime has collapsed, the occupiers confront the challenge of creating effective and decent domestic sovereignty.

Sovereignty failures may also present problems in the area of transnational criminality. Drug trafficking is difficult to control under any circumstances, but such activities are more likely to flourish where domestic sovereignty is inadequate. About 95 percent of illicit drug production takes place in areas of civil strife. Colombia, where the FARC controls a large part of the territory, has been one of the major sources of such drugs for the United States. In the late 1990s Afghanistan cultivated 75 percent of the world's opium poppies, and despite a ban by the Taliban at the end of its rule, production revived after the regime was overthrown because the new government in Kabul had only limited control over much of the country. Transnational trafficking in persons is more likely, although not limited to, countries where domestic authority and control are weak or ineffective. A 2004 State Department report lists ten countries—Bangladesh, Burma, Cuba, Ecuador, Equatorial Guinea, Guyana, North Korea, Sierra Leone, Sudan, and Venezuela—that have not met minimum efforts to control trafficking in persons. Most of the ten are failed or badly governed states.[10] In addition, it is more difficult to trace and punish the perpetrators of transnational financial fraud in countries where the police and judiciary do not function well.

Finally, gross violations of human rights present unpleasant political choices for democratic leaders in powerful states. There have been a number of humanitarian catastrophes in recent years, with the killings in Rwanda in the mid-1990s being one of the most appalling and most widely reported. Millions of people have died in other countries as well at the hands of their own government or rival political groups. These and other humanitarian disasters have engaged attentive elites. The Canadian ministry of foreign affairs, for instance, organized the International Commission on Intervention and State Sovereignty in 2000 in response to UN Secretary-General Kofi Annan's appeal for a new consensus on the right of humanitarian intervention. The commission, composed of twelve eminent persons, produced a widely circulated report entitled *The Responsibility to Protect.* The report defends the principle of humanitarian intervention when governments abuse or fail to protect their own citizens. Samantha Power's book, *A Problem from Hell: America and the Age of Genocide,* which describes the failure of the United States to act either to prevent or to mitigate a number of genocides throughout the twentieth century, won a Pulitzer Prize in 2003.[11]

■ ■ ■

Humanitarian crises, then, present decisionmakers in democratic countries with a no-win situation. If they fail to intervene and a humanitarian disaster occurs, they may lose the votes of citizens who are attentive to and care about the fate of particular countries, regions, ethnic groups, or principled issues in general. On the other hand, if a political leader does intervene, the costs in terms of soldiers killed will be readily apparent, but the number of lives saved can never be demonstrated with certainty.

The Existing Institutional Repertoire: Governance Assistance and Transitional Administration

Political leaders in powerful and weak states have been reluctant to challenge the conventional norms of sovereignty. The policy options currently available to repair occupied or badly governed states—governance assistance and transitional administration—are consistent with these norms. They have made some limited contribution to improving governance in badly run and collapsed states, but policymakers would be better served if they had a wider repertoire of policy choices.

Governance Assistance

For the last decade international organizations, the United States, and other donor countries have devoted substantial resources to promoting better governance. U.S. foreign aid has been given to train judges, rewrite criminal codes, increase fiscal transparency, professionalize the police, encourage an open media, strengthen political parties, and monitor elections. In 2004 President George W. Bush's administration launched a new foreign aid initiative, the Millennium Challenge Account (MCA), which, if fully funded, will increase U.S. foreign assistance by 50 percent and provide these resources to a relatively small number of poor countries that have demonstrated good governance in the areas of promoting economic freedom, governing justly, and investing in people.[12]

Since the 1950s, international financial institutions have been involved in questions of policy and sometimes institutional reform in borrowing countries. The conditions attached to lending by the World Bank and the International Monetary Fund (IMF) have covered a wide range of issues such as aggregate credit expansion, subsidies, number of government employees, indexation of salaries, tariffs, tax rates, and institution building. International financial institutions have placed their own personnel in key bureaus.[13] In the mid-1990s the managing director of the IMF and the president of the World Bank committed themselves to a more aggressive attack on corruption in developing states.[14] In 1997 the World Bank subtitled its world development report *The State in a Changing World.* The report declares that the "clamor for greater government effectiveness has reached crisis proportions in many developing countries where the state has failed to deliver even such fundamental public goods as property rights, roads, and basic health and education."[15] Further, it lists basic tasks for the state, including establishing a foundation of law, protecting the environment, and shielding the vulnerable; chastises governments for spending too much on rich and middle-class students in universities while neglecting primary education; and urges these governments to manage ethnic and social differences. Finally, and most ambitiously, the 1991 Agreement Establishing the European Bank for Reconstruction and Development explicitly includes a commitment to democracy as a condition of membership.

Foreign assistance to improve governance in weak states does not usually contradict the rules of conventional sovereignty. Governments contract with external agencies (e.g., countries, multilateral organizations, and nongovernmental organizations [NGOs]) to provide training in various areas. Such contracting is a manifestation of international legal sovereignty and is consistent with Westphalian/Vatellian sovereignty, so long as the influence of external actors on domestic authority structures is limited to specific policies or improvements in the capabilities of government employees. When bargaining power is highly asymmetric, as may be the case in some conditionality agreements between international financial institutions and borrowing countries, Westphalian/Vatellian sovereignty can

be compromised. External actors can influence not just policies but also institutional arrangements in target states. The borrowing country is better off with the agreement, conditions or no, than it would have been without it; otherwise it would not have signed. Nevertheless, political leaders may accept undesired and intrusive engagement from external actors because the alternative is loss of access to international capital markets.

The effectiveness of governance assistance will always be limited. Some leaders will find the exploitation of their own populations more advantageous than the introduction of reforms. The leverage of external actors will usually be constrained. International financial institutions are in the business of lending money; they cannot put too stringent restrictions on their loans lest their customers disappear. Many IMF agreements are renegotiated, sometimes several times. Small social democratic countries in Europe have been committed, because of the views of their electorates, to assisting the poor; they will be loath to allow their funding levels to drop below the generally recognized target of 0.7 percent of national income. The wealthier countries also routinely provide humanitarian assistance, regardless of the quality of governance in a particular country.

Moreover, those providing governance assistance are likely to adopt formulas that reflect their own domestic experience and that may be ill suited to the environments of particular target countries. The United States, for instance, has emphasized elections and independent legislatures. Interest groups have been regarded as independent of the state, whereas in European social democratic countries, they are legitimated by and sometimes created by the state.

Transitional Administration

Transitional administration is the one recognized alternative to conventional sovereignty that exists in the present international environment, but it is explicitly not meant as a challenge to the basic norms of sovereignty. The scope of transitional administration or peacekeeping and peacebuilding operations has ranged from the full assertion of executive authority by the UN for some period of time, East Timor being an example, to more modest efforts involving monitoring the implementation of peace agreements, as was the case in Guatemala in the 1990s. Transitional administration, usually authorized by the UN Security Council, has always been seen as a temporary, transitional measure designed to create the conditions under which conventional sovereignty can be restored. The U.S. occupation of Iraq has followed the same script, albeit without any UN endorsement of the occupation itself, although the Security Council did validate the restoration of international legal sovereignty in June 2004. Westphalian/Vatellian sovereignty and sometimes international legal sovereignty are violated in the short term so that they can be restored in the longer term; at least that is the standard explanation.

The record of peacebuilding efforts since World War II has been mixed. One recent study identified 124 cases of peacebuilding by the international community. Of these, 43 percent were judged to be successful based on the absence of hostilities. If progress toward democracy is added as a measure of success, only 35 percent were successful.[16]

More extensive peacekeeping operations, those that might accurately be called "transitional administration" because they involve the assertion of wide-ranging or full executive authority by the UN (or the United States), are difficult: the demands are high; advance planning, which must prejudge outcomes, is complicated, especially for the UN; and resources—economic, institutional, and military—are often limited. UN missions have run monetary systems, enforced laws, appointed officials, created central banks, decided property claims, regulated businesses, and operated public utilities. The resources to undertake these tasks have rarely been adequate. Each operation has been ad hoc; no cadres of bureaucrats, police, soldiers, or judges permanently committed to transitional administration exist; and there is a tension between devolving authority to local actors and having international actors assume responsibility for all governmental functions because, at least at the outset, this latter course is seen as being more efficient.[17]

Transitional administration is particularly problematic in situations where local actors disagree about basic objectives among themselves and with external actors. Under these circumstances, as opposed to situations in which local actors agree on goals but need external monitoring to provide reassurances about the behavior of their compatriots, the inherently temporary character of transitional administration increases the difficulty of creating stable institutions. If indigenous groups disagree about the distribution of power and the constitutional structure of the new state, then the optimal strategy for their political leaders is to strengthen their own position in anticipation of the departure of external actors. They do so by maximizing support among their followers rather than backing effective national institutions. Alternatively, local leaders who become dependent on external actors during a transitional administration, but who lack support within their own country, do not have an incentive to invest in the development of new institutional arrangements that would allow their external benefactors to leave at an earlier date.[18]

Multiple external actors with varying interests and little reason to coordinate their activities have exacerbated the problems associated with transitional administration. The bureaucratic and financial interests of international organizations are not necessarily complementary. NGOs need to raise money and make a mark. The command structures for security and civilian activities have been separated. The permanent members of the Security Council, to whom UN peacekeeping authorities are ultimately responsible, have not always had the same interests.[19]

■ ■ ■

Transitional administration has been most effective when the level of violence in a country has been low, where there has been involvement by major powers, and where the contending parties within the country have reached a mutually acceptable agreement. The key role for the transitional administration is then to monitor the implementation of the agreement. For instance, in Namibia the contact group, comprising Canada, France, Germany, Great Britain, and the United States, was involved in UN discussions about the constitutional structure for an independent Namibia beginning in 1978. All of the major contending parties consented to the UN Transition Assistance Group (UNTAG) that was sent in 1989, allowing the lightly armed mission to play a neutral role between South Africa and Namibia. The strength of the major potential spoilers, hard-line whites, was undermined by the collapse of apartheid in South Africa. The major responsibility of UNTAG was to supervise the elections for the government that assumed power when Namibia secured international legal sovereignty.[20]

There were also successful missions in Central America in the 1990s. In both Guatemala and Nicaragua, government and rebel groups had reached a mutually acceptable settlement. Peacekeeping missions contributed to stability by supervising elections, helping to demobilize combatants, and training police.[21]

In sum, transitional administration has worked best for the easiest cases, those where the key actors have already reached a mutually acceptable agreement. In these situations, the transitional administration plays a monitoring role. It can be truly neutral among the contending parties. The mission does not have to be heavily armed. Transitional administration, however, is much more difficult in

cases such as Bosnia, Kosovo, Afghanistan, and Iraq—that is, where local leaders have not reached agreement on what the ultimate outcome for their polity should be and where they must think about positioning themselves to win support from parochial constituencies when transitional administration, along with its large foreign military force, comes to an end.

New Institutional Options: De Facto Trusteeships and Shared Sovereignty

Given the limitations of governance assistance and transitional administration, other options for dealing with countries where international legal sovereignty and Westphalian/Vatellian sovereignty are inconsistent with effective and responsible domestic sovereignty need to be explored. At least two such arrangements would add to the available tool kit of policy options. The first would be to revive the idea of trusteeship or protectorate, probably de facto rather than de jure. The second would be to explore possibilities for shared sovereignty in which national rulers would use their international legal sovereignty to legitimate institutions within their states in which authority was shared between internal and external actors.

De Facto Trusteeships

In a prescient article published in 1993, Gerald Helman and Steven Ratner argued that in extreme cases of state failure, the establishment of trusteeships under the auspices of the UN Security Council would be necessary. By the end of the 1990s, such suggestions had become more common. Analysts have noted that de facto trusteeships have become a fact of international life. In a monograph published in 2002, Richard Caplan argues, "An idea that once enjoyed limited academic currency at best—international trusteeship for failed states and contested territories—has become a reality in all but name." Martin Indyk, an assistant secretary of state during President Bill Clinton's administration, has argued that the most attractive path to permanent peace in the Middle East would be to establish a protectorate in Palestine, legitimated by the United Nations and with the United States playing a key role in security and other areas. Even if final status talks were completed, the trusteeship would remain in place until a responsible Palestinian government was established.[22]

Despite these recent observations, developing an alternative to conventional sovereignty, one that explicitly recognizes that international legal sovereignty will be withdrawn and that external actors will control many aspects of domestic sovereignty for an indefinite period of time, will not be easy. To date there has been no effort, for instance, to produce a treaty or convention that would define and embody in international law a new form of trusteeship. Just the opposite. The rhetorical commitment of all significant actors, including the United States, has been to restore authority to local actors at the soonest possible moment, a stance exemplified by the decision to give what U.S. officials insisted was full sovereignty to Iraq in June 2004.[23]

Codifying a general set of principles and rules for some new kind of trusteeship or protectorate would involve deciding who would appoint the authority and oversee its activities: the UN Security Council? A regional organization such as the European Union? A coalition of the willing? A single state? A treaty or convention would have to define the possible scope of authority of the governing entity: all activities of the state including security and international affairs? Only matters related to the provision of public goods such as roads, but not those related to the private sphere such as marriage? Given that there would be no fixed date for ending a trusteeship or protectorate, how would the appropriate moment for transferring authority to local actors be determined? What intermediate steps would be taken? Could a trusteeship, for instance, be granted international legal recognition and sovereignty, while some aspects of domestic governance remained under the control of the trustee or conservator?

The most substantial barrier to a general international treaty codifying a new form of trusteeship or protectorate is that it will not receive support from either the powerful, who would have to implement it, or the weak, who might be subject to it. There is widespread sentiment for the proposition that Westphalian/Vatellian sovereignty is not absolute and can be breached in cases of massive human rights violations. UN Secretary-General Annan expressed this view in 1999 to widespread international acclaim.[24] But arguing that Westphalian/Vatellian sovereignty is not absolute is quite different from codifying an explicit alternative that would deprive states of their international legal sovereignty as well as control over their domestic affairs.

An explicit and legitimated alternative to sovereignty would require, at minimum, agreement among the major powers. An arrangement supported by leading states that are not members of the OECD such as Brazil, China, India, Indonesia, Nigeria, and South Africa would be even better. Best of all would be an agreement endorsed by the Security Council and the General Assembly. There is no indication, however, that such widespread support would be given. None of the actors has a clear interest in doing so. The major powers, those with the capacity to create a trusteeship, want to be able to pick and choose not only where they intervene but also the policies they would follow. The endorsement of a new institutional arrangement would provide a new choice on the menu, but this option might make it difficult to engage in ad hoc arrangements better suited to specific circumstances. For states in the third world, any successor to the mandate system of the League of Nations, or the trusteeship system of the UN, would smell if not look too much like colonialism.[25]

Shared Sovereignty

Shared sovereignty would involve the engagement of external actors in some of the domestic authority structures of the target state for an indefinite period of time. Such arrangements would be legitimated by agreements signed by recognized national authorities. National actors would use their international legal sovereignty to enter into agreements that would compromise their Westphalian/Vatellian sovereignty with the goal of improving domestic sovereignty. One core element of sovereignty—voluntary agreements—would be preserved, while another core element—the principle of autonomy—would be violated.

National leaders could establish shared sovereignty through either treaties or unilateral commitments. To be effective, such arrangements would have to create self-enforcing equilibria involving either domestic players alone or some combination of domestic and international actors. Political elites in the target state would have to believe that they would be worse off if the shared sovereignty arrangement were violated.

For policy purposes, it would be best to refer to shared sovereignty as "partnerships." This would more easily let policymakers engage in organized hypocrisy, that is, saying one thing and doing another. Shared sovereignty or partnerships would allow political leaders to embrace sovereignty, because these arrangements would be legitimated by the target state's international legal sovereignty, even though they violate the core principle of Westphalian/Vatellian sovereignty: autonomy. Organized hypocrisy is not surprising in an environment such as the international system where there are competing norms (e.g., human rights vs. Westphalian/Vatellian sovereignty), power differentials that

allow strong actors to pursue policies that are inconsistent with recognized rules, and exceptional complexity that makes it impossible to write any set of rules that could provide optimal outcomes under all conditions. Shared sovereignty or partnerships would make no claim to being an explicit alternative to conventional sovereignty. It would allow actors to obfuscate the fact that their behavior would be inconsistent with their principles.

HISTORICAL EXAMPLES OF SHARED SOVEREIGNTY

Shared sovereignty agreements have been used in the past. There are several late nineteenth-century shared sovereignty arrangements in which external actors assumed control over part of the revenue-generating stream of a state that had defaulted on its debt. The state wanted renewed access to international capital markets. The lenders wanted assurance that they would be repaid. Direct control over the collection of specific taxes provided greater confidence than other available measures.

For example, a shared sovereignty arrangement between external lenders and the Porte (the government of the Ottoman Empire) was constructed for some parts of the revenue system of the empire during the latter part of the nineteenth century. The empire entered international capital markets in the 1850s to fund military expenditures associated with the Crimean War. By 1875, after receiving more than a dozen new loans, the empire was unable to service its foreign debt. To again secure access to international capital markets, the Ottomans agreed in 1881 to create, through government decree, the Council of the Public Debt. The members of the council—two from France; one each from Austria, Germany, Italy, and the Ottoman Empire itself; and one from Britain and the Netherlands together—were selected by foreign creditors. Until the debt was liquidated, the Porte gave control of several major sources of revenue to the council and authorized it to take initiatives that would increase economic activity. The council promoted, for instance, the export of salt (the tax on which it controlled) to India and introduced new technologies for the silk and wine industries. It increased the confidence of foreign investors in the empire's railways by collecting revenues that the government had promised to foreign companies. In the decade before World War I, the council controlled about one-quarter of the empire's revenue. It was disbanded after the war.[26]

Unlike classic gunboat diplomacy, where the governments of foreign creditors took over control of customs houses to secure repayment of loans, in the case of the Ottoman Council of the Public Debt, the norm of international legal sovereignty was honored, at least in form. The council was established by an edict issued by the Ottoman Empire at the behest of foreign creditors. International legal sovereignty was honored; Westphalian/Vatellian sovereignty was ignored. This arrangement was durable because if the empire had revoked its decree, it would have lost access to international capital markets.

The relationship of the Soviet Union to the satellite states of Eastern Europe during the Cold War is another example of shared sovereignty. For more than forty years, Soviet penetration of domestic regimes, close oversight of officials, and policy direction from Moscow kept communist regimes in power. During the 1950s the Polish secret police, for instance, reported directly to Moscow. The militaries of the satellites were integrated into the Soviet command structure and unable to operate independently. The communist regimes that Moscow had put in place and sustained by violating Westphalian/Vatellian sovereignty dutifully signed off on the security arrangements that their overlord preferred. Except in a few instances, such as the invasion of Czechoslovakia in 1968, Soviet behavior was consistent with international legal sovereignty. The implicit and sometimes explicit use of force, however, was necessary to support these regimes because many of the citizens of the satellite states were alienated from their rulers.

The shared sovereignty arrangements established by the United States after World War II were more successful. Germany is the prime example. The Western allies wanted to internationally legitimate the Federal Republic of Germany (FRG or West Germany) but at the same time constrain its freedom of action. The Bonn agreements, signed in 1952 by the FRG, France, the United Kingdom, and the United States and revised in Paris in 1954, gave West Germany full authority over its internal and external affairs but with key exceptions in the security area. Not only did the FRG renounce its right to produce chemical, biological, and nuclear weapons; it also signed a status of forces agreement that gave the allies expansive powers. These included exclusive jurisdiction over the members of their armed forces and the right to patrol public areas including roads, railways, and restaurants. Allied forces could take any measures necessary to ensure order and discipline.[27] West Germany's military was fully integrated into NATO. Article 5(2) of the Convention on Relations gave the Western powers the right to declare a state of emergency until FRG officials obtained adequate powers enabling them to take effective action to protect the security of the foreign forces.[28] Without a clear definition of these adequate powers, the Western allies formally retained the right to resume their occupation of the Federal Republic until 1990, when the 1990 Treaty on the Final Settlement with Respect to Germany terminated the Bonn agreements.

The United States succeeded in the West German case because most Germans supported democracy, a market economy, and constraints on the FRG's security policies. Obviously the strength of this support reflected many factors, including the long-term economic success of the West relative to the Soviet bloc. Shared sovereignty arrangements for security in the FRG contributed to effective domestic governance by taking a potentially explosive issue off the table both within and, more important, without West Germany. Security dilemmas that might have strengthened undemocratic forces in the FRG never occurred because the Bonn government did not have exclusive control of the country's defense.

■   ■   ■

INCENTIVES FOR SHARED SOVEREIGNTY

Shared sovereignty arrangements can work only if they create a self-enforcing equilibrium, which might include external as well as domestic players. There are at least four circumstances that might make shared sovereignty arrangements attractive for political decision-makers, those who hold international legal sovereignty, in target states: avarice, postconflict occupation, desperation, and elections.

NATURAL RESOURCES AND AVARICE   Rulers salivate at the wealth and power that natural resources, most notably oil, can bring them. Their bargaining position, however, depends on the acceptance of the precepts of conventional sovereignty: the state owns the oil and has the right to sign contracts and set rules governing its exploitation. Neither companies, nor consuming states, nor international organizations have challenged the property rights of the state. No one, at least no one in a position of authority, has suggested, for instance, that oil in badly governed states ought to be declared part of the common heritage of mankind and placed under the control of perhaps the World Bank.

For poorly governed countries, however, natural resources, especially oil, have been a curse that has feathered the nests of rulers and undermined democracy and economic growth. Oil concentrates resources in the hands of the state. The road to wealth and power for any ambitious individual leads through the offices of the central government, not through individual enterprise or productive economic activity. With oil wealth, the state can buy off dissenters and build military machines that can be used to repress those who cannot be bought off.[29]

Shared sovereignty arrangements for extractive industries would offer an alternative to conventional practices that would provide better governance in oil-abundant states, more benefits for their people, and fewer incentives for corruption and conflict. Such arrangements would depend on the willingness of wealthier democratic states to constrain the options available to political leaders in poorly governed resource-rich states. Conventional sovereignty would not be challenged in principle but would be compromised in practice. Political leaders in host countries would then be confronted with a choice between nothing and something, although much less than they might have at their private disposal under conventional practices.

A shared sovereignty arrangement for natural resources could work in the following way. An agreement between the host country and, say, the World Bank would create a trust. The trust would be domiciled in an advanced industrialized country with effective rule of law. All funds generated by the natural resources project would be placed in an international escrow account controlled by the trust. All disbursements from the account would have to be approved by a majority of the directors of the trust. Half of the board of directors of the trust would be appointed by the host government, the other half by the World Bank; the bank could name directors from any country but would not designate its own employees. Directors would have to believe that their success depended on the success of the trust.

The trust agreement would stipulate that a large part of these funds would be used for social welfare programs, although specific allocations for, say, health care or education would be left to the host government. The trust would refuse to dispense funds that did not conform with these commitments. The trust might even be charged with implementing programs using the resources of the escrow account if the government failed to act expeditiously.

The laws of the advanced democracy in which the trust was incorporated would hold accountable the directors of the trust. Legislation enacted by the country in which the trust was domiciled would back the firms' responsibility to pay revenues into the escrow account, and only the escrow account.

No doubt the leaders of oil-rich or other natural resource–rich countries would cringe at such arrangements. They would have much more difficulty putting billions of dollars in foreign bank accounts, as did Sani Abacha, the late Nigerian military dictator. It would be hard to spend half a billion dollars on a European vacation as did some members of the Saudi royal family in 2002. But if the major democracies passed legislation requiring that any imported oil be governed by a trust arrangement, avarice might induce political leaders in resource-rich countries to accept shared sovereignty, because without shared sovereignty they would get nothing.[30]

POSTCONFLICT OCCUPATION Postconflict occupation might also be conducive to creating shared sovereignty arrangements. When there is military intervention and occupation, local leaders have limited choice. In Afghanistan, Bosnia, East Timor, Iraq, and Kosovo, the local leaders have been dependent to some extent on external actors. They have had to accept the presence of nonnationals. Foreigners have been running many of the ministries in Bosnia. In Kosovo joint implementation for administrative structures has been the norm: there are twenty administrative departments and four independent agencies, all of which are codirected by a Kosovar and a senior UNMIK staff person.[31] In Afghanistan and Iraq, security has been provided in part by foreign forces.

Shared sovereignty contracts would make such arrangements permanent, not transitional. The presence of external actors would not be the result of a unilateral decision by an external administrator but rather of a contract between external and domestic actors who would be granted international legal sovereignty. Because the contract would have no termination date, local actors could no longer assume that they could simply wait for the foreigners to leave. Some local leaders might still decide that acting as a spoiler might maximize their interests, but others would see cooperation as more likely to enhance their long-term prospects.

Such arrangements could be successful in the long run only if they were supported by a winning coalition in the host country. Unlike oil trusts, external enforcement mechanisms would be difficult to create. External actors might bolster domestic agents committed to shared sovereignty or threaten to impose sanctions or cut foreign assistance if the agreement were violated, but there could not be an ironclad guarantee of success.

Still, shared sovereignty arrangements would be more promising than constitution writing, which has been the center of attention in recent occupations. The problem with relying on a constitution or any other legal commitments made under pressure at a particular moment in time is that once the occupying power leaves, the incentives for domestic actors to honor their earlier commitments can radically change. Shared sovereignty, in contrast, could generate a self-enforcing equilibrium if it provided benefits to a large enough group of domestic actors.

Monetary policy is one area where shared sovereignty might work in a postconflict or even a more benign environment. Controlling inflation can be a daunting problem. A few countries, East Timor being one example, have simply resorted to using the U.S. dollar. Others have tried to engineer credible commitments through domestic institutions, such as independent central banks. Appointment of the governors of the central bank by both government and external actors could enhance the credibility of such arrangements. In this regard, the IMF might be the right partner. Nonnational governors could be of any nationality. They would not be IMF employees. The fund would sign a contract with the host country setting up shared sovereignty on a permanent basis or until both parties agreed to end the arrangement. If the national government unilaterally abrogated the arrangement, it would be a clear signal to external actors that the government was abandoning the path of monetary responsibility. If the central bank were successful in constraining inflation, the arrangement would generate support from domestic actors. Like oil trusts, one major attraction of such an agreement is that it would not be costly for the IMF or any other external actor.

Commercial courts might be another area where shared sovereignty could be productive. Again, the opportunities in this area would not be limited to postconflict situations. In a state where the rule of law has been sketchy, the international legal sovereign would conclude a contract with an external entity—for instance, a regional organization such as the EU or the Organization of American States—to establish a separate commercial court system. The judges in these courts would be appointed by both the national government and its external partner. The expectation would be that local business interests would find this court system attractive. It would provide a venue in which they could resolve disagreements more effectively than would be the case within existing national institutions. The presence of such a court system might even attract higher levels of foreign investment. Like oil trusts and central banks, such an arrangement would not involve substantial costs for the external actor. The national government, or even to some extent the litigants, could fund commercial courts.

DESPERATION   Aside from the avarice associated with natural resources and the pressures arising from occupation, desperation for external resources might also motivate national authorities to enter into shared sovereignty arrangements. For countries that have spiraled into the abyss because of civil war or misgovernance, and that do not have easily exploited natural resources, foreign assistance might be a major potential source of revenue. The bargaining leverage of political leaders under such circumstances would be limited. The ability of external actors to negotiate shared sovereignty arrangements would be high.

As in the case of occupation, the most promising spheres for shared sovereignty, such as monetary policy and commercial courts, would not require substantial resources from external actors but would generate adequate domestic support. In collapsed or near-collapsed states, however, external actors would have to provide resources at least for some period of time. This would open additional possibilities for shared sovereignty for activities funded by external donors. A committee composed of national officials and individuals appointed by the education ministries of major donor countries might make, for instance, decisions about educational curriculum. A system of health care facilities administered by external aid workers or NGOs could be created separate from the national ministry of health. Because donors are not likely to be willing to provide aid on a quasi-permanent basis, however, such arrangements could be sustained only if a large enough domestic coalition were willing to support them even after foreign funding had been withdrawn.

ELECTIONS   Finally, in badly governed illiberal democracies, elections might provide an incentive for shared sovereignty contracts. Political candidates might make such policies part of their electoral platform. Illiberal democracies are polities that hold competitive elections but are deficient with regard to rule of law, an active civil society, and a free press. In illiberal democracies, government does not work very well. Public officials are disconnected from the citizenry. Individuals or parties might change, but policies remain more or less the same. Voters become cynical, and even potentially progressive political candidates have no way to make their campaign pledges credible. Shared sovereignty contracts could be an appealing political strategy for a dissident candidate. Such a political platform could win votes by signaling to the electorate that a politician would make a decisive break with the past by engaging external actors in domestic decisionmaking processes.

The long-term credibility of a shared sovereignty arrangement concluded by a successful dissident candidate in an illiberal democracy would depend both on the extent to which such practices have been internationally legitimated and on their effectiveness. The more common shared sovereignty agreements are, the easier it would be for any one leader to defend his actions against opponents who might claim that he had compromised the state's sovereignty. The greater the improvement in governance associated with shared sovereignty arrangements, the greater the likelihood that they would be honored over the long term.

Thus some form of de facto protectorate and, more promising, shared sovereignty are policy tools that could be added to the meager selection of options currently available to deal with bad governance or to create effective institutions following military occupations. Legitimacy for shared sovereignty would be provided by the agreement of those exercising the target state's international legal sovereignty.

Conclusion

During the twentieth century, the norms of international legal sovereignty and Westphalian/Vattelian sovereignty became universally accepted. It has often been tacitly assumed that these norms would be accompanied by effective domestic sovereignty, that is, by governance structures that exercised competent and ideally constructive control over their countries' populations and territory. This assumption has proven false. Poor, even malevolent, governance is a widespread problem. Badly governed states have become a threat to the interests of much more powerful actors: weapons of mass destruction have broken the connection between resources and the ability to do grievous harm; genocides leave political leaders in democratic polities with uncomfortable choices; and transnational disease and crime are persistent challenges.

The policy tools available to external actors—governance assistance and transitional administration—are inadequate, even when foreign powers have militarily occupied a country. Governance assistance can have positive results in occupied or badly governed states, but the available evidence suggests that the impact is weak. Transitional administration, which aims to restore conventional sovereignty in a relatively short time frame, can be effective only if indigenous political leaders believe that they will be better off allying with external actors not only while these actors are present but also after they leave.

The menu of options to deal with failing and collapsed states could be expanded in at least two ways. First, major states or regional or international organizations could assume some form of de facto trusteeship or protectorate responsibility for specific countries, even if there is no general international convention defining such arrangements. In a trusteeship, international actors would assume control over local functions for an indefinite period of time. They might also eliminate the international legal sovereignty of the entity or control treaty-making powers in whole or in part (e.g., in specific areas such as security or trade). There would be no assumption of a withdrawal in the short or medium term.

Second, domestic sovereignty in collapsed or poorly governed states could be improved through shared sovereignty contracts. These contracts would create joint authority structures in specific areas. They would not involve a direct assault on sovereignty norms because they would be formally consistent with international legal sovereignty, even though they would violate Westphalian/Vattelian sovereignty. Natural resources trusts, whose directors were appointed by national and nonnational entities, would be one possibility; central banks whose boards of governors comprised citizens and noncitizens would be another.

Political leaders in target states might accept such arrangements to secure external resources, either payments for raw materials' exploitation or foreign assistance, to encourage the departure of occupying forces or to attract voters. To be durable, shared sovereignty institutions either would require external enforcement, something that would be possible for natural resources trusts, or would have to create adequate domestic support, which would depend on the results delivered.

For external signatories—international organizations, regional organizations, and states—the most attractive shared sovereignty arrangements would be ones that did not require any significant commitment of resources over the long term. Natural resources trusts and central bank administration would meet this condition. In cases of states recovering from collapse, or something near to it, where foreign aid is the incentive for national leaders to accept shared sovereignty, resources commitments by external actors would be unavoidable for the short and medium terms. Over the longer term, though, shared sovereignty institutions could survive only if the services they provided were funded from internal sources of revenue.

De facto trusteeships or protectorates and shared sovereignty hardly exhaust the possibilities for improving domestic sovereignty in poorly governed states. Leaders in some polities have already used private firms to carry out some activities that have traditionally been in the hands of state officials. Indonesia, for instance, used a Swiss firm to collect its customs for more than eleven years. Other governments have hired private military companies (PMCs). Perhaps with stronger accountability mechanisms enforced by advanced industrial states, such as the ability to prosecute PMCs and their employees for abuses, the results might be more consistently salutary.

There is no panacea for domestic sovereignty failures. Even with the best of intentions and substantial resources, external actors cannot quickly eliminate the causes of these failures: poverty, weak indigenous institutions, insecurity, and the raw materials curse. But the instruments currently available to policy-makers to deal with places such as Congo, Liberia, and Iraq are woefully inadequate. De facto trusteeships, and especially shared sovereignty, would offer political leaders a better chance of bringing peace and prosperity to the populations of badly governed states and reduce the threat that such polities present to the wider international community.

NOTES

1. For a discussion of the requirements for successful international engagement that complements many of the points made in this article, see James D. Fearon and David D. Laitin, "Neotrusteeship and the Problem of Weak States," *International Security*, Vol. 28, No. 4 (Spring 2004), pp. 5–43.

2. See ibid., especially pp. 36–37.

3. Although the principle of nonintervention is traditionally associated with the Peace of Westphalia of 1648, the doctrine was not explicitly articulated until a century later by the Swiss jurist Emmerich de Vattel in his *The Law of Nations or Principles of the Law of Nature Applied to the Conduct and Affairs of Nations and Sovereigns*, originally published in French in 1758.

4. Mary Ann Tetreault, "Autonomy, Necessity, and the Small State: Ruling Kuwait in the Twentieth Century," *International Organization*, Vol. 45, No. 4 (Autumn 1991), pp. 565–591.

5. In Shanghai, for instance, the British established a municipal council that regulated the activities of Chinese living within Shanghai as well as non-Chinese. See Jean Chesneaux, Marianne Bastid, and Marie-Claire Bergere, *China from the Opium Wars to the 1911 Revolution* (Hassocks, Sussex, U.K.: Harvester, 1977), pp. 61–68.

6. For two very similar analyses, see Robert O. Keohane, "Political Authority after Intervention: Gradations in Sovereignty," in J.L. Holzgrefe and Keohane, eds., *Humanitarian Intervention: Ethical, Legal, and Political Dilemmas* (Cambridge: Cambridge University Press, 2003), pp. 276–277; and Gerald B. Helman and Steven R. Ratner, "Saving Failed States," *Foreign Policy*, No. 89 (Winter 1993), pp. 3–21. Keohane argues that there should be gradations of sovereignty. Helman and Ratner suggest that there are three forms of what they call "guardianship": governance assistance, the delegation of government authority, and trusteeship. They also suggest the term "conservatorship" as an alternative to trusteeship.

7. James D. Fearon and David D. Laitin, "Ethnicity, Insurgency, and Civil War," *American Political Science Review*, Vol. 97, No. 1 (March 2003), pp. 1–17; and Fearon and Laitin, "Neotrusteeship and the Problem of Weak States," pp. 36–37.

8. Goldstone et al., *State Failure Task Force Report*, p. 21.

9. These figures are derived from data found at World Bank, *WDI Online*, http://devdata.worldbank.org /dataonline/.

10. U.S. Department of State, *Trafficking in Persons Report* (Washington, D.C.: U.S. Department of State, June 2004), http://www.state.gov/documents/organi zation/33614.pdf.

11. International Commission on Intervention and State Sovereignty, *The Responsibility to Protect* (Ottawa: International Development Research Centre, 2001), http://www.dfait-maeci.gc.ca/icissciise/pdf/Commis sion-Report.pdf. See also Gareth Evans and Mohamed Sahnoun, "The Responsibility to Protect," *Foreign Affairs*, Vol. 81, No. 6 (November/December 2002), pp. 99–110.

12. For the White House description of the MCA, see http://www.whitehouse.gov/infocus/developingna tions/millenium.html. For a list of the first set of countries to receive funding from the MCA, see MCA, press release, "The Millennium Challenge Corporation Names MCA Eligible Countries," May 6, 2004, http://www.usaid.gov/mca/Documents/PR _Eligible.pdf. For a discussion of the World Bank's governance assistance programs, see http://www .worldbank.org/wbi/governance/about.html. See also Arthur A. Goldsmith, "Foreign Aid and Statehood in Africa," *International Organization*, Vol. 55, No. 1 (Winter 2000), pp. 135–136.

13. International Monetary Fund, Fiscal Affairs Department, *Fund-Supported Programs, Fiscal Policy, and Income Distribution*, Occasional Paper No. 46 (Washington, D.C.: International Monetary Fund, 1986), p. 40; and Robin Broad, *Unequal Alliance: The World Bank, the International Monetary Fund, and the Philippines* (Berkeley: University of California Press, 1988), pp. 51–53, Table 12.

14. Paul Lewis, "Global Lenders Use Leverage to Combat Corruption," *New York Times*, late ed., August 11, 1997, p. 4; and James C. McKinley Jr., "Kenyan Who Charged 4 Officials with Graft Is Suspended," *New York Times*, late ed., July 31, 1998, p. 4.

15. World Bank, *World Development Report, 1997: The State in a Changing World* (Washington, D.C.: World Bank, 1997), p. 2.

16. Michael W. Doyle and Nicholas Sambanis, "International Peacebuilding: A Theoretical and Quantitative Analysis," *American Political Science Review*, Vol. 94, No. 4 (December 2000), pp. 779–802. For a second study with a different database but comparable findings, see George Downs and Stephen John Stedman, "Evaluating Issues in Peace Implementation," in Stedman, Donald Rothchild, and Elizabeth M. Cousens, eds., *Ending Civil Wars: The Implementation of Peace Agreements* (Boulder, Colo.: Lynne Rienner, 2002), pp. 50–52.

17. Richard Caplan, *A New Trusteeship? The International Administration of War-torn Territories* (London: International Institute for Strategic Studies, 2002), pp. 8–9, 50–51; United Nations, *Report of the Panel on United Nations Peace Operations* (Brahimi report) (New York: United Nations, 2000), pp. 7, 14. In June 2003 Secretary of Defense Donald Rumsfeld discussed the possibility of a standing international peacekeeping force under the leadership of the United States. Ester Schrader, "U.S. Looks at Organizing Global Peacekeeping Force," *Los Angeles Times*, June 27, 2003, p. A1.

18. Fearon and Laitin, "Neotrusteeship and the Problem of Weak States," p. 37. See also David M. Edelstein, "Occupational Hazards: Why Military Occupations Succeed or Fail," *International Security*, Vol. 29, No. 1 (Summer 2004), pp. 49–81.

19. Michael Ignatieff points to the possibly negative consequences of competition among NGOs. Ignatieff, "State Failure and Nation-Building," p. 27.

20. For Namibia, see Downs and Stedman, "Evaluating Issues in Peace Implementation," pp. 59–61; and Roland Paris, *At War's End? Building Peace after Civil Conflict* (Cambridge: Cambridge University Press, 2004), chap. 8.

21. Downs and Stedman, "Evaluating Issues in Peace Implementation," pp. 62–63; and Paris, *At War's End*, chap. 7.

22. Helman and Ratner, "Saving Failed States," pp. 3–21; Caplan, *A New Trusteeship?* p. 7; Ignatieff, "State Failure and Nation-Building," p. 308; and Martin Indyk, "A Trusteeship for Palestine?" *Foreign Affairs*, Vol. 82, No. 3 (May/June 2003), pp. 51–66.

23. At least one way to interpret the strategy of U.S. decisionmakers is to understand the June transfer as one that gives Iraq international legal sovereignty. With this international legal sovereignty, the new Iraqi government will be able to legitimate agreements with external agents. Given the dependence of the new government on the United States for security and revenue, such agreements will allow the United States to continue to pursue its core interests.

24. Kofi Annan, "The Legitimacy to Intervene: International Action to Uphold Human Rights Requires a New Understanding of State and Individual Sovereignty," *Financial Times*, December 31, 1999.

25. Fearon and Laitin have suggested that "neotrusteeship" is the most appropriate term for arrangements that could cope with the postconflict security problems afflicting states suffering from weak administrative capacity, poverty, and rough terrain. Because such states are unlikely to be able to conduct effective policing and counterinsurgency operations on their own, maintaining security will require the engagement of external actors for an extended period of time. The authors do not, however, argue that neotrusteeship would involve a loss of international legal sovereignty. See Fearon and Laitin, "Neotrusteeship and the Problem of Weak States," especially pp. 24–41.

26. Donald C. Blaisdell, *European Financial Control in the Ottoman Empire: A Study of the Establishment, Activities, and Significance of the Administration of the Ottoman Public Debt* (New York: Columbia University Press, 1929), pp. 90–120, 124–130; Herbert Feis, *Europe, the World's Banker, 1870–1914: An Account of European Foreign Investment and the Connection of World Finance with Diplomacy before World War I* (New York: W. W. Norton, 1965), pp. 332–341; Bernard Lewis, *The Middle East: A Brief History of the Last 2,000 Years* (New York: Scribner, 1995), pp. 298–299; and Roger Owen, *The Middle East in the World Economy, 1800–1914* (Cambridge: Cambridge University Press, 1981), p. 101.

27. "Revised NATO SOFA Supplementary Agreement," articles 19, 22, 28. The full text of the agreement is available at http://www.oxc.army.mil/others/Gca/files%5Cgermany.doc.

28. "Convention on Relations between the Three Powers and the Federal Republic of Germany," *American*

Journal of International Law, Vol. 49, No. 3 (July 1955), pp. 57–69. For a detailed examination of the retained rights of the Western powers, see Joseph W. Bishop Jr., "The 'Contractual Agreements' with the Federal Republic of Germany," *American Journal of International Law*, Vol. 49, No. 2 (April 1955), pp. 125–147. For a general analysis of Germany's situation after World War II, see Peter J. Katzenstein, *Policy and Politics in West Germany: The Growth of a Semisovereign State* (Philadelphia: Temple University Press, 1987).

29. Michael Lewin Ross, "Does Oil Hinder Democracy?" *World Politics*, Vol. 53, No. 3 (April 2001), pp. 325–361.

30. This proposal assumes that oil could be exploited only by companies domiciled in advanced democratic polities interested in supporting good governance and that these countries cooperate with each other. Absent these conditions, the host country could play one oil company off against another and avoid the constraints that would come with a shared sovereignty trust.

31. Caplan, *A New Trusteeship?* p. 39.

Olivier Roy

THE TRANSFORMATION OF THE ARAB WORLD

The "Arab Spring" at first had nothing about it that was specifically "Arab" or "Muslim." The demonstrators were calling for dignity, elections, democracy, good governance, and human rights. Unlike any Arab revolutionary movements of the past sixty years, they were concerned with individual citizenship and not with some holistic entity such as "the people," the Muslim *umma*, or the Arab nation. The demonstrators referred to no Middle Eastern geopolitical conflicts, burned no U.S. or Israeli flags, offered no chants in favor of the main (that is to say, Islamist) opposition patties, and expressed no wish for the establishment of an Islamic state or the implementation of *shari'a*. Moreover, despite the Western media's frantic quest to put a face on events by talking up some of the protests' astonishingly young and modern spokespersons, the demonstrators produced no charismatic leaders. In short, the Arab Spring belied the "Arab predicament": It simply would not follow the script which holds that the centrality of the Arab-Israeli conflict is fostering an ever-growing Islamization within Arab societies, a search for charismatic leaders, and an identification with supranational causes.

But the demonstrators did not take power—indeed, they did not even try. Instead, they merely wanted to establish a new political scene. Predictably, the Egyptian and Tunisian elections brought ballot-box triumphs for Islamist parties. With deep roots in society, enjoying a legitimacy conferred by decades of political opposition, and defending

conservative and religious values shared by most of the populace, Egypt's Muslim Brotherhood and Tunisia's Ennahda party were able to attract votes from well beyond their respective hardcore bases because they looked like credible parties of government. More surprising was the strong showing of the Salafist al-Nur Party in Egypt. Even allowing for Salafism's rise in that country, the sudden transformation of an apolitical and informal school of thought into a successful political movement shows that no single Islamist party can claim a monopoly over the expression of Islam in the political sphere.

In any case, the actors who have taken to the electoral stage and benefited from the Arab Spring, whether familiar like the Islamists of the Muslim Brotherhood or newcomers like the Salafists, are not known for their attachment to democracy. Even if they have given up talk of the "Islamic revolution," they still put religion at the heart of their agenda. Islamists and Salafists alike deplore secularization, the influence of Western values, and the excesses of individualism. Everywhere, they seek to affirm the centrality of religion to national identity, and they are conservative in all areas except the economy. And in Egypt, as commonly happens with parties that are swept into power by landslide margins, they are tempted to think that they can dispense with the grubby business of having to form alliances and hand out government posts equitably. And why should Islamists, with no democratic culture to speak of, behave like good democrats who believe in pluralism?

From *Journal of Democracy* 23, No.3 (July 2012), 5–18.

Once the election results came in, the Western media's enthusiasm faded, and headlines celebrating a democracy-friendly Arab Spring gave way to coverage worrying about the onset of a neoauthoritarian "Arab Winter." Iran, Saudi Arabia, and the Taliban were casting long shadows over Tunis and Cairo. Was there any obstacle to Islamization in the last other than the Egyptian army, whose aversion to democracy is well known? Was the Arab Middle East hopelessly trapped, with no better choices than "secular" dictatorship or "Islamic" totalitarianism?

The answer to that last question is no. Something irreversible did happen in the Arab Spring. Whatever ups and downs may follow, we are witnessing the beginning of a process by which democratization is becoming rooted in Arab societies. Democratization is very much a process in this case—not a program of government implemented by deep-dyed democrats. Comparisons with other world regions (such as Latin America) are difficult, since the Middle East is the only place where the dominant opposition consists of strongly centralized and ideological parties with a religious agenda. A possible comparison might be with the Spanish and Portuguese communist parties of the late 1970s: Like the Islamists of Egypt and Tunisia, they too benefited from a democratization process that they did not trigger. Yet the Iberian communists never achieved the control over elected parliaments that Islamists now enjoy in Cairo and Tunis. Whatever their own agendas, the communist parties had no choice but to negotiate.

The Islamist parties may have more power and freedom to maneuver, but they too will find themselves being pushed to adjust to the democratization process. The pushing will be done by the constraints and dynamics characteristic of the social, religious, political, and geostrategic fields in which these parties must operate. They may accept the demands of the democratization process more willingly (Ennahda) or less willingly (the Egyptian Muslim Brotherhood), but accept them they will, or they will find themselves sidelined. This is not a question of who has or does not have a hidden agenda, or of whether Islam and democracy can or cannot be reconciled.

In order to grasp what is happening in the Middle East, we must set aside a number of deep-rooted prejudices. First among them is the assumption that democracy presupposes secularization: The democratization movement in the Arab world came precisely after thirty years of what has been called the "return of the sacred," an obvious process of re-Islamization of everyday life, coupled with the rise of Islamist parties. The second is the idea that a democrat must also, by definition, be a liberal. There was no flowering of "liberal Islam" preceding the spread of democratic ideas in the Middle East. There are a few reformist religious thinkers who are lauded here and there in the West, but none has ever had much popular appeal in any Arab country. Conversely, many staunch secularists, in Tunisia for instance, are not democrats. They would like to repress Islamists much as the Algerian secularist intellectuals known as *les éradicateurs* did during their own country's civil war in the 1990s. Moreover, fundamentalist religious actors such as the Islamists of Tunisia or even the Salafists of Egypt, could become reluctant agents of a form of specifically *political* secularization that should in no way be confused with a secularization of society.

The history of the West does not contradict these theses. Religious tolerance was not the fruit of liberalism and the Enlightenment. Rather, it was the product of grudging truces in savage wars of religion, from the Peace of Augsburg in 1555 to the Treaty of Westphalia in 1648. Politics played a bigger role than philosophy or theology. The greatest Western religious reformer, Martin Luther, was far from a model of democracy, tolerance, or liberalism (to say nothing of his anti-Semitism). The link between Protestantism and democratization is not a matter of theological propositions, but of complex political and social processes. The Founding Fathers of the United States were not secularists; for them, the separation of church and state was a way of protecting religion from government, not the reverse. The French Third Republic was established in 1871 by a predominantly conservative, Catholic, and monarchist parliament that had just crushed the Paris Commune. Christian democracy developed in Europe not because the Catholic Church wanted to promote secular values, but because that was the only way for it to maintain political influence, Finally, let us not forget that populist movements in Europe today align themselves with Christian democracy in calling for the continent's Christian identity to be inscribed in the EU constitution, but few would see this expression of "identity politics" as an omen of Europe's re-Christianization. All the talk of "Islamic identity" in the wake of the Arab Spring does not mean that mosques will henceforth become more crowded. Religious identity and faith are two different (and possibly opposed) concepts in politics. Identity might be a way to bury faith beneath secular politics.

The Islamists as well as the Salafists are entering into a political space formatted by certain constraints. These constraints will not only limit their supposed "hidden agenda" of establishing an Islamic state, but will push them toward a more open and democratic way of governance, because therein lies their only chance to remain at the center of political life. Thus the Islamists, and even the Salafists, will become reluctant agents of democratization.

A World of Change

The first of these constraints has to do with demographics. As Philippe Fargues has shown, there has been a dramatic decline in fertility across the Arab world.[1] In Tunisia, it has been below the French rate since the year 2000. Women have entered universities and the job market. Young people obtain more schooling than their parents

did and marry later. Husbands and wives are more often closer to each other in age and level of education. They have fewer children, with nuclear families replacing extended households. Mobile phones, satellite television, and the Internet have allowed the newer generations to associate, connect, and debate on a "peer-to-peer" basis rather than through a top-down, authoritarian system of knowledge transmission. The young feel less strongly bound to patriarchal customs and institutions that have been unable to cope with the challenges facing contemporary Middle Eastern societies.

Flowing from these changes in demographics have been changes in political culture. The young are more individualistic and less prone to feel the pull of holistic ideologies, whether Islamist or nationalist. Along with the decline of the patriarchal model has gone a drop in the appeal of charismatic leaders. The failure of political Islam that I pointed to twenty years ago is now obvious.[2] This does not mean that Islamist parties are absent from the political playing field—quite the contrary. But their utopian conception of an "Islamic state" has lost credibility. Islamist ideology is now finding itself challenged both by calls for democracy that reject any monopoly claim on power by a single party or ideology, and by neofundamentalist Salafists who declare that only a strict personal return to the true tenets of religious practice can serve as the basis of an "Islamic society." Even among the Muslim Brothers, young members reject blind obedience to the leadership. The new generation calls for debate, freedom, democracy, and good governance.

The appeal of democracy is not a consequence of the export of the concept of Western democracy, as fancied by supporters of the U.S. military intervention in Iraq. It is the political consequence of social and cultural changes in Arab societies (though these changes, of course, are part of the globalization process). It is precisely because the Arab Spring is a succession of indigenous upheavals, centered on particular nation-states and delinked from Western encroachments, that democracy is seen as both acceptable and desirable. This is why the ritual denunciations of imperialism—including the usual condemnations decrying Zionism as the source of all the Arab world's troubles—were so remarkably absent from the demonstrations. This also explains why al-Qaeda is out of the picture: The uprooted global jihadist is no longer a model for young activists and fails to find many takers when he seeks to enlist local militants for the global cause (al-Qaeda has been expelled from Iraq by local fighters). The only exceptions are places on the geographic fringes of the Arab world such as Somalia, Yemen, and the Sahel. Al-Qaeda, in short, is yesterday's news, part and parcel of the old anti-imperialist political culture that the Arab Middle East is now leaving behind.

Of course, the social changes are not completely linear and are not necessarily giving rise to a "democratic mind." Their effect is felt earliest, most widely, and most intensely in the big cities and among educated young people with access to the Internet. Others may feel excluded, including villagers in the Egyptian countryside, jobless urbanites in southern Tunisia, shopkeepers and merchants who fear that political tumult will hurt business, conservative milieus upset by what they see as sexual promiscuity among the demonstrators, and so on.

In a word, the Arab Spring masked large reservoirs of underlying conservatism in Arab societies. But even some of the more conservative corners of society are becoming part of the process of individualization. A remarkable field study shows how villagers in Egypt ignored the Muslim Brothers during recent elections because the Brotherhood came across as too monolithic and centralized.[3] These conservative religious voters preferred the Salafists on the grounds of what was seen as their greater *political* openness. The Salafist al-Nur Party's recent (albeit passing) endorsement of the presidential candidacy of former Muslim Brother Abdel Moneim Abul Futuh (who counts as a liberal in the Egyptian context) suggests that these villagers may have been onto something.

Change is affecting religion, too. The Salafists, like neofundamentalists the world over, are recasting religion as a code and a set of clear-cut norms disconnected from tradition and culture. They are thus best understood not as part of a traditionalist backlash, but as bearers of an attempt to adapt Islam to modernity and globalization.[4] Of course, this adaptation should not be thought of in terms of theology (the prepositional content of this or that religion), but rather in terms of religiosity (the way the adherent experiences his or her faith). The wave of re-Islamization hides a very important fact: It has contributed to the diversification and the individualization of the religious field.

Islam as a theological corpus has not changed, but *religiosity* has. And this religiosity, liberal or not, is compatible with democratization because it delinks personal faith from traditions, collective identity, and external authority. The usual religious authorities (*ulama* and Islamist leaders) have largely lost their legitimacy amid the rise of self-appointed and often self-taught religious entrepreneurs. Young "born-again" Muslims have found their own way by surfing the Internet or joining local peer groups. They have criticized the cultural Islam of their parents and have tried to construct their own brand of Islam, one that feels more like a matter of conviction and less like an inherited habit. Religion has become more and more a matter of personal choice, whether that choice be the strict Salafist approach to Islam or some sort of syncretism, to say nothing of conversion to another religion.[5]

Fundamentalism and Secularism: The Secret Sharers

This individualization and diversification have had the unexpected consequence of disconnecting religion from daily politics, of bringing religion back into the private sphere and excluding it from that of government management. Fundamentalism, by disconnecting religion from culture and by defining a faith community through believing and not just belonging, is in fact contributing to the secularization of society.[6]

One of the things this means is that an apparent rejection of secularization and democracy may nevertheless express "democracy-compatible" patterns: individualization, refusal of blind obedience, separation of faith from collective identity, and a certain distance from day-to-day politics. In such a context, any endeavor to restore traditional norms through laws and regulations will fail. After all, you cannot change a society by decree. In Saudi Arabia, the official imposition of *shari'a* on the rapidly increasing number of "emancipated" women among the middle and upper classes is leading to unbearable tensions. In Iran, all indicators suggest that society has become more modern and secular under the mullahs. Although a law adopted after 1979 allows girls as young as nine to be taken as brides, the average age at which Iranian women marry has continued to rise and now stands at about 25. In short, even when *shari'a* is theoretically implemented, we are not seeing a return to a traditional society.

As we have seen, the Islamists enjoy no religious monopoly in the public sphere. There are other movements, such as the Sufis and the Salafists. This diversification is the consequence of thirty years of "re-Islamization." Religion's centrality in everyday life, coupled with the individualization of religiosity, has given birth to a variety of religious movements. Some have had the encouragement of regimes eager to dilute the Muslim Brotherhood's appeal. Together, their presence contributes to a willy-nilly democratization of the religious field. An unexpected result of the Arab Spring has been that Cairo's al-Azhar Mosque, one of Egypt's most important religious institutions, has found a new legitimacy. The imam there, Sheikh Ahmed el-Tayeb, a conformist appointee of former president Hosni Mubarak, has suddenly become an advocate of human rights, liberty, and the separation of religious institutions from the state. In Tunisia, Ennahda reached power only to discover that it does not control and indeed does not even know the hundreds of young imams who have taken over mosques abandoned by discredited clerics who had held their jobs courtesy of the old Ben Ali regime.

In Egypt, the Muslim Brothers have been upset to learn that their six decades of steady religious and social activism have not been enough to stop Salafist newcomers from successfully challenging the Brotherhood's primacy. As a further twist, the Egyptian Salafists have been challenging the Brothers from the left by allying themselves with Brotherhood dissidents. (In Tunisia, the Salafists have lined up on Ennahda's right by opposing democracy and demanding immediate implementation of *shari'a*.) Among other things, this is a sign that 2011 was not 1979 all over again—unlike the Ayatollah Khomeini's Islamic Republic of Iran, Egypt and Tunisia are not places where some single source (the Muslim Brotherhood or Ennahda) can assert a right "to say what Islam says." The religious arena, too, has become pluralistic and open to democratic pressure, even if, for the faithful, there are some elements that remain nonnegotiable.

That said, there is no agreement among religious political actors over what is and is not negotiable beyond the centrality of Islam. Should there be a body that determines whether laws are sufficiently conformable to Islam? If so, who ought to be nominated to it and by whom? Should *hudud* (corporal punishment) be applied in cases where religious laws have been violated? Is conversion to Christianity possible for a Muslim? It is on the question of the definition of religious liberty that we can expect the most vigorous debates. If the Muslim Brotherhood presents itself as the protector of the rights of the minority Coptic Christians in Egypt to practice their religion, is it ready to make religious freedom an *individual* human right (abandoning the concept of apostasy in the process) rather than merely the collective right of a particular historic minority? The debate has already started. Abdel Moneim Abul Futuh, the Brotherhood dissident turned presidential candidate and surprising recipient of Salafist support, has declared that "nobody should interfere if a Christian decides to convert to Islam or a Muslim decides to leave Islam and become a Christian."[7]

Whenever the implementation of Islamic religious norms comes up for discussion, there is an internal debate in the institutions concerned. Democratization has affected the community of believers, too. The Salafists will certainly try to raise the stakes over *shari'a* and make the Muslim Brotherhood face up to the contradictions of its position. But they have also leapt into the political realm, forming parties of their own despite having previously challenged the very idea of political parties in the name of Islam. In their case, this is the compliment that vice pays to virtue: The Salafists know that without a parliamentary presence, they would lose their influence.

All the same, the Salafists have no program other than imposing *shari'a*, and thus are anything but a party of government, as the most realistic among them well know. The Muslim Brotherhood and the Salafists are fated to be rivals, and so one cannot rule out the possibility of their entering into unexpected alliances with other political forces.

The Failure of Political Islam

Islamists have changed, or at least they have understood that the world has changed. Even where they have taken control, as in Iran or Gaza, they have been unable to establish a successful model of an Islamic state. The gains that they have made in the wake of the Arab political openings are premised upon previous successes won by "others" (in Egypt and Tunisia, democratic secularists). In earlier cases, the "others" have been nationalists. In Gaza, it was Palestinian nationalism, not political Islam, that brought Hamas (the local wing of the Muslim Brotherhood) to power. Much the same is true for Lebanon's Hezbollah, which has built its success on its opposition to Israel and its ability to position itself as the champion of the country's large but traditionally underprivileged Shia community.

When Islamists went to jail, they rubbed elbows with secularists and human-rights advocates (such as Egypt's Saad Eddin Ibrahim). When they went into exile, it was more often to Europe than to Mecca. The Islamists came to understand the need to make alliances and to take into account other views. They tried to engage the West, but were too often rebuked. Calls for holy war and violent confrontation are the trademarks of countries or groups that are not friendly to these Islamists, and even consider them to be traitors: Iran or al-Qaeda. Implementation of *shari'a* is the official policy of regimes and movements with which they cannot identify, such as Saudi Arabia or the Taliban. Charitable work aside, the Islamists social agenda has slowly faded away as their constituents have become ever more bourgeois and entrepreneurial. The aging of their leadership has put them at odds with the new generation of believers. There is a cultural gap between the Islamists and the younger generation that is less about Islam per se than about what it means for a person to be a believer.

All these changes are pointing toward the rise of what Asef Bayat calls "post-Islamism."[8] This does not mean that the Islamists have disappeared, but that their Utopian ambitions have proved to be no match for existing social, political, and even geostrategic realities. There is, for instance, no blueprint of an "Islamic economy." Islamists are fairly status quo–friendly when it comes to economic affairs, content to run charities in poor neighborhoods but opposing strikes and approving the rescinding of land reform in Egypt. The wave of religious revival that has swept the Muslim world did not swell their ranks, but contributed on the contrary to the diversification of the religious field, transforming the Islamists into one set of religious actors among others.

Have the Islamists become "democrats"? They have long favored elections, recognizing that support for armed struggle serves jihadists like al-Qaeda on the one hand and repressive secular governments on the other, especially when the latter are eager to curry Western favor by posturing as the only bulwark against the "Islamist threat." Ennahda's leader Rachid al Ghannouchi has explicitly rejected the concept of an "Islamic state," and cites Turkey's Justice and Development Party (AKP) as a model of a post-Islamist religious-minded and conservative party.

Still, most Islamists are uneasy about sharing power with non-Islamic parties and turning their "brotherhood" organizations into modern political parties. They may, as in Morocco and Tunisia, give up formal support for *shari'a*, but they cannot define a concrete ruling program that goes beyond banning alcohol, promoting the veil, or pursuing other petty forms of "*shari'a*-fication." After the Arab Spring, which began outside Islamist ranks and took Islamist leaders by surprise, the Islamists must choose among options. Option 1 is the Turkish model as represented by the AKP. This would mean turning the "brotherhood" into a true modern political party; trying to attract voters from beyond a hard core of devout Muslims; recasting religious norms into vaguer conservative values (family, property, honesty, the work ethic); adopting a neoliberal approach to the economy; and endorsing the constitution, parliament, and regular elections.

Option 2 would be to ally themselves with "counterrevolutionary" forces (as in Egypt, for instance) out of fear that real democracy will prove too unpredictable and too hard to control. This choice would have large downsides, as Islamists would find themselves losing their remaining legitimacy, and might wind up becoming tools of the army. A modified form of this option would see Islamists siding with Salafists in a focus on certain high-profile issues (the veil and family law) while leaving other social and economic matters aside. Rather than ideological debate, it will most likely be the course of events itself that shapes what the Islamists do.

They are certainty neither secularists nor liberals, but they can be democrats. The convictions of political actors often play less of a role in shaping their policies than the constraints to which they are subject. The Islamists are entering an entirely new political space. Egypt and Tunisia did not have revolutions that replaced dictatorships with regimes that resembled their predecessors. There have been elections and there is a parliament. Political parties have been formed and, whatever the disappointments and fears of the secular left, it will be difficult simply to close down this new space, because what brought it into being in the first place—a savvy, connected young generation and a spirit of protest—is still there. And experience has shown that in the Middle East, when people are offered the opportunity to take part in free elections, they show up, even if threatened (as in Afghanistan and Iraq). Islamist movements throughout the region are constrained to operate in a democratic arena that they did not create and that has legitimacy in the eyes of the people.

Wary Voters

The Islamists must also listen to their voters, who will not follow them blindly. The "Islamic" electorate in Egypt or Tunisia today is not revolutionary; it is conservative. It wants order. It wants leaders who will kick-start the economy and affirm conventional religious values. It is not ready to plunge into reviving the caliphate or creating an Islamic republic. Ennahda and the Muslim Brotherhood know all this. They know that they need to attract voters because they have neither the desire nor the means to seize power by force. What is more, the protest movements in Egypt and Tunisia were not shaped by an all-encompassing ideology (as was the case in Iran in 1979) but by the ideals of democracy, pluralism, and good governance.

Iran's November 1979 election was held in the name of the Islamic Republic. The message was clear: This was an ideological revolution (even if there was disagreement about its complexion between the red of the Marxist-Leninists and the green of the Islamists). There is nothing of the kind in either Egypt or Tunisia. There is no revolutionary or ideological dynamic. It is significant, in this regard, that nowhere has the cult of the charismatic strongman reappeared. Instead, there are political patties and a new culture of debate that has influenced even the Islamists.

To impose an Islamist form of authoritarianism, the Islamists would need either control of the police and army or their own paramilitary forces, none of which they have. In Egypt and Tunisia, the army remains outside Islamist control (in Egypt, it may be outside anyone's control), and is not identified with the former regime the way the Imperial Iranian Army was in 1979. Then too, neither Egypt nor Tunisia enjoys oil rents large enough to pay for placating the poor and sustaining loyal militias.[9] Elections will really matter, and their results can be expected to swing back and forth for the next decade or more. Although Islamists tend to adopt a populist profile (talking a lot about matters of "national identity," blaming Westernized elites), they may find themselves being outbid along these lines by demagogues who, if not "holier than thou," are nonetheless "more populist than thou" and better at making populist appeals.

There is one further set of constraints on both the Islamists and the Salafists, and these are geostrategic. Neither group has reached office on a platform of *jihad* or special support for the Palestinians. Unlike the Nasserite and Baathist revolutions or even Anwar Sadat's 1974 counter-revolution (when he opened Egypt's economy and swapped the Soviet for the U.S. embrace), the Arab Spring and Winter have not turned on international questions. Neither the Brotherhood nor the Salafists have ever articulated a coherent supranational agenda of mobilizing the *umma,* instead leaving attempts to politicize the concept of a transnational Islamic community in the bloody hands of al-Qaeda. The various branches of the Muslim Brothers (whether in Egypt, Jordan, Kuwait, or Syria) as well as the Islamists of the Maghreb have always had their own national agendas and organizations; despite their ideological proximity, they have never been able to devise a regional common strategy. And recent events show how differently they may react: The Jordanian and Tunisian Islamists are far more open in their alliances and in their embrace of democracy than the Egyptians. The national and domestic scene is where the real action is. If supranational dynamics do make themselves felt, moreover, they will only push the Islamists to change their domestic agenda in the direction of more democracy and moderation.

The Israeli-Palestinian conflict surely retains emotional significance, but no one is ready to endanger geopolitical stability and economic development for the sake of the Palestinian cause. The Islamists dislike Israel, and in this respect they are in step with Arab public opinion, but they are not willing to go to war. They have accepted the existing geostrategic constraints. The invitation that Tunisia's new and democratically elected government extended to Hamas leader Ismail Haniyeh in January 2012 is in line with the one that Tunisia extended to the Palestine Liberation Organization after the Israelis took Beirut in 1982, and is evidence of continuity, rather than rupture. The care that Egypt's Muslim Brotherhood has taken to open a dialogue with Western diplomats is another sign that it is accepting strategic realities. The Brotherhood wants to remodel the relationship between Egypt and Israel, but through negotiations, not confrontation, Economic constraints such as the lack of oil rents and the need to maintain tourism also drive the new governments to want at least to appear moderate. There are projects to make tourism *halal* with gender-segregated beaches and alcohol-free resorts, but these seem like pipe dreams: Why should wealthy Saudis abandon Marbella or Beirut for a *halal* Sharm el-Sheikh that is just miles away from their own puritanically run five-star hotels?

The major conflict that is taking shape is not a clash between an Islamist-led Muslim world and the West. Rather, it is the one that pits the conservative Sunni Arab world (whether secular, Islamist, Wahhabi, or Salafist) against the "Shia crescent" of which Iran is the keystone. In the background is Saudi Arabia's discreet de facto alliance with Israel against the common Iranian threat. The crisis and fighting now raging in Syria are forcing regional actors to make unappetizing choices. Hezbollah is siding with Tehran and its client, the Assad regime in Syria. Hamas, though allied with Syria and Hezbollah, has reluctantly left Damascus for Cairo, returning to the fold of its old family, the Sunni Muslim Brothers. Turkey, having been evicted from the European dream, has turned from its dashed hopes of full EU membership to the task of carving out a new regional role for itself at the head of a Sunni alliance. The AKP leaders are well acquainted with the Arab Islamist leaders, and a new axis is taking shape, bringing together similar conservative Sunni parties. The Turkish connection is also a factor of moderation for the Islamist parties.

Of course this emerging Sunni axis antagonizes local minorities (Alevis in Turkey, Alawites in Syria), and accentuates tensions with the Shias in the Gulf (no support for the Bahraini demonstrators), in Saudi Arabia, Lebanon, and Iraq. Yet the isolation of Iran is also a step in favor of stabilization and moderation. An Israeli military strike against Iran's nuclear facilities will certainly trigger demonstrations in Casablanca, Cairo, and Tunis, But the Arab street will probably not mobilize against newly elected Arab governments, which will keep a lower profile than expected. Saudi Arabia, which cannot stand the concept of an Arab Spring, grows ever more estranged from the Islamist parties. The Saudis have played the Salafists against the Brothers, at least indirectly, but Saudis will not be able to find staunch and lasting allies among either Tunisia's hard-line Salafists or Egypt's milder variety.

The bottom line is that, for the first time since the early 1950s, the geostrategic situation of the Middle East neither dictates domestic agendas nor spurs the radicalization of domestic politics—both good omens for the process of democratization.

And What of Islam?

Whatever political ups and down lie ahead, whatever the diversity of national cases, and however intricate becomes the predictable fragmentation of both "democrats" and "Islamists" into various trends and parties, the main issue will be to redefine the role of Islam in politics. The growing de facto autonomy of the religious arena from political and ideological control does not mean that secularism is necessarily gaining ground in terms of culture and society. Yet certainly a new form of *political* secularism is emerging. Once it takes hold, religion will not dictate what politics should be, but will itself be reduced to politics.

What is at stake is the reformulation of religion's place in the public sphere. There is broad agreement that constitutions should announce the "Muslim" identity of society and the state. Yet there is similar agreement on the proposition that *shari'a* is not an autonomous and complete system of law that can replace "secular" law. Instead, *shari'a* is becoming a loose and somewhat hazily defined "reference point" (except in the realm of personal law, which means that issues of women's rights will be at the core of the debate). As we saw, modern forms of religiosity tend to stress individual faith and choices over any sense of conformity to institutional Islam. Whatever descriptive truth was left in the old saying "Islam admits no separation between *din* and *dunya*" (that is, between religion and the world) has been definitively emptied out by the Arab Spring.

What we are seeing is not so much a secularization as a deconstruction of Islam. Is Islam a matter of cultural identity, meaning that one might even be an "atheist Muslim"? Is it a faith that can be shared only by born-again believers (Salafists) in the confines of self-conscious faith communities? Or is it a "horizon of meaning," where references to *shari'a* are more virtual than real? The recasting of religious norms into "values" helps also to promote an interfaith coalition of religious conservatives that could unite around some specific causes: opposition to same-sex marriage, for instance. It is interesting to see how, in Western Europe, secular populists stress the continent's Christian identity, while many Muslim conservatives try to forge an alliance with believers of other faiths to defend shared values. In doing so, many of them tend to adopt Protestant evangelical concerns, fighting abortion and Darwinism even though these issues have never been prominent in traditional Islamic debates.[10]

In this sense, the modern neofundamentalists are trying to recast Islam into a Western-compatible kind of religious conservatism. This has become obvious in Turkey. In 2004, when the AKP's Prime Minister Recep Tayyip Erdoğan unsuccessfully tried to promote a legal ban on adultery, the crime was defined not in terms of *shari'a*, but rather by reference to the modern Western family (a monogamous marriage of a man and a woman with equal rights and duties). Interestingly, this made the traditional practice of polygamy, not

infrequent among old-line AKP local cadres, a crime. As episodes such as these reveal, Islam is becoming part of the recasting of a religious global marketplace disconnected from local cultures.[11]

Instead of the secularization of society, we might do better to speak of the "autonomization" of politics from religion and of religion from politics, due to the diversification of the religious field and the inability to reconstruct religion as a political ideology. When religion is everywhere, it is nowhere. That was the underlying meaning that I took away from what Egyptian parliament speaker and Muslim Brother Saad al-Katatni said to a Salafist deputy who wanted to perform the Muslim prayer call while the house was in session: "We are all Muslims; if you want to pray there is a mosque in parliament, but parliament is not a mosque."[12] The paradox of re-Islamization is that it leads to political secularization and opens the door to debate about what Islam means. This could lead to the reopening of theological debate, but that would be a consequence and not a cause of the democratization of Muslim societies.

NOTES

1. Philippe Fargues, *Générations arabes: L'Alchimie du nombre* (Paris: Fayard, 2000).

2. Olivier Roy, *The Failure of Political Islam*, trans. Carol Volk (Cambridge: Harvard University Press, 1994).

3. Yasmine Moataz Ahmed, "Who Do Egypt's Villagers Vote For? And Why?" *Egypt Independent*, 10 April 2012.

4. Olivier Roy, *Globalized Islam: The Search for a New Ummah* (New York: Columbia University Press, 2004).

5. In Morocco and Algeria, there have been enough Christian conversions for a Protestant evangelical church to have sprung up among former Muslims. See Nadia Marzouki, "Conversion as Statelessness: A Study of Contemporary Algerian Conversions to

Evangelical Christianity," *Middle East Law and Governance* 4, no. 1 (2012): 69–105.

6. Olivier Roy, *Holy Ignorance: When Religion and Culture Part Ways*, trans. Ros Schwartz (New York: Columbia University Press, 2010).

7. Noha El-Hennawy, "Islamist Presidential Candidate Declares Conversion Permissible," *Egypt Independent*, 16 May 2011.

8. Asef Bayat, "The Coming of a Post-Islamist Society," *Critique: Critical Middle East Studies* 9 (Fall 1996): 43–52.

9. There is a clear negative connection between the Arab Spring and oil rents. Governments without piles of petrodollars to spend must earn support the old-fashioned way—at the voting booth.

10. The works of the Turkish anti-Darwinist Adnan Oktar, who writes under the pen name Harun Yahya, have been widely distributed in the West since 2007. His *Atlas of Creation*, which he sent unsolicited to thousands of Western scholars and institutions, presents all the arguments and some iconography familiar from anti-Darwinist literature in the United States.

11. Olivier Roy, *Holy Ignorance*.

12. Ed Husain, "Egypt's Piety Contest," *The Arab Street*, 7 February 2012, http://blogs.cfr.org/husain/2012/02/07/egypts-piety-conlest.

Samuel P. Huntington

THE CLASH OF CIVILIZATIONS?

The Next Pattern of Conflict

World politics is entering a new phase, and intellectuals have not hesitated to proliferate visions of what it will be—the end of history, the return of traditional rivalries between nation states, and the decline of the nation state from the conflicting pulls of tribalism and globalism, among others. Each of these visions catches aspects of the emerging reality. Yet they all miss a crucial, indeed a central, aspect of what global politics is likely to be in the coming years.

It is my hypothesis that the fundamental source of conflict in this new world will not be primarily ideological or primarily economic. The great divisions among humankind and the dominating source of conflict will be cultural. Nation states will remain the most powerful actors in world affairs, but the principal conflicts of global politics will occur between nations and groups of different civilizations. The clash of civilizations will dominate global politics. The fault lines between civilizations will be the battle lines of the future.

Conflict between civilizations will be the latest phase in the evolution of conflict in the modern world. For a century and a half after the emergence of the modern international system with the Peace of Westphalia, the conflicts of the Western world were largely among princes—emperors, absolute monarchs and constitutional monarchs attempting to expand their bureaucracies, their armies, their mercantilist economic strength and,

From *Foreign Affairs* 72, no. 3 (Summer 1993): 22–49.

most important, the territory they ruled. In the process they created nation states, and beginning with the French Revolution the principal lines of conflict were between nations rather than princes. * * * [A]s a result of the Russian Revolution and the reaction against it, the conflict of nations yielded to the conflict of ideologies, first among communism, fascism-Nazism and liberal democracy, and then between communism and liberal democracy. During the Cold War, this latter conflict became embodied in the struggle between the two superpowers, neither of which was a nation state in the classical European sense and each of which defined its identity in terms of its ideology.

* * * With the end of the Cold War, international politics moves out of its Western phase, and its centerpiece becomes the interaction between the West and non-Western civilizations and among non-Western civilizations. In the politics of civilizations, the peoples and governments of non-Western civilizations no longer remain the objects of history as targets of Western colonialism but join the West as movers and shapers of history.

The Nature of Civilizations

During the Cold War the world was divided into the First, Second and Third Worlds. Those divisions are no longer relevant. It is far more meaningful now to group countries not in terms of their political or economic systems or in terms of their level of economic development but rather in terms of their culture and civilization.

What do we mean when we talk of a civilization? A civilization is a cultural entity. Villages, regions, ethnic groups, nationalities, religious groups, all have distinct cultures at different levels of cultural heterogeneity. The culture of a village in southern Italy may be different from that of a village in northern Italy, but both will share in a common Italian culture that distinguishes them from German villages. European communities, in turn, will share cultural features that distinguish them from Arab or Chinese communities. Arabs, Chinese and Westerners, however, are not part of any broader cultural entity. They constitute civilizations. A civilization is thus the highest cultural grouping of people and the broadest level of cultural identity people have short of that which distinguishes humans from other species. It is defined both by common objective elements, such as language, history, religion, customs, institutions, and by the subjective self-identification of people. * * *

* * * Civilizations are nonetheless meaningful entities, and while the lines between them are seldom sharp, they are real. Civilizations are dynamic; they rise and fall; they divide and merge. And, as any student of history knows, civilizations disappear and are buried in the sands of time.

Westerners tend to think of nation states as the principal actors in global affairs. They have been that, however, for only a few centuries. The broader reaches of human history have been the history of civilizations. In *A Study of History*, Arnold Toynbee identified 21 major civilizations; only six of them exist in the contemporary world.

Why Civilizations Will Clash

Civilization identity will be increasingly important in the future, and the world will be shaped in large measure by the interactions among seven or eight major civilizations. These include Western, Confucian, Japanese, Islamic, Hindu, Slavic-Orthodox, Latin American and possibly African civilization. The most important conflicts of the future will occur along the cultural fault lines separating these civilizations from one another.

Why will this be the case?

First, differences among civilizations are not only real; they are basic. Civilizations are differentiated from each other by history, language, culture, tradition and, most important, religion. The people of different civilizations have different views on the relations between God and man, the individual and the group, the citizen and the state, parents and children, husband and wife, as well as differing views of the relative importance of rights and responsibilities, liberty and authority, equality and hierarchy. These differences are the product of centuries. They will not soon disappear. * * *

Second, the world is becoming a smaller place. The interactions between peoples of different civilizations are increasing; these increasing interactions intensify civilization consciousness and awareness of differences between civilizations and commonalities within civilizations. * * *

Third, the processes of economic modernization and social change throughout the world are separating people from longstanding local identities. They also weaken the nation state as a source of identity. In much of the world religion has moved in to fill this gap, often in the form of movements that are labeled "fundamentalist." Such movements are found in Western Christianity, Judaism, Buddhism and Hinduism, as well as in Islam. * * * The "unsecularization of the world," George Weigel has remarked, "is one of the dominant social facts of life in the late twentieth century." * * *

Fourth, the growth of civilization-consciousness is enhanced by the dual role of the West. On the one hand, the West is at a peak of power. At the same time, however, and perhaps as a result, a return to the roots phenomenon is occurring among non-Western civilizations. Increasingly one hears references to trends toward a turning inward and "Asianization" in Japan, the end of the Nehru legacy and the "Hinduization" of India, the failure of Western ideas of socialism and nationalism and hence "re-Islamization" of the Middle East, and now a debate over Westernization versus Russianization in Boris Yeltsin's country. A West at the peak of its power confronts non-Wests that increasingly have the desire, the will and the resources to shape the world in non-Western ways.

■   ■   ■

Fifth, cultural characteristics and differences are less mutable and hence less easily compromised and resolved than political and economic ones. In the former Soviet Union, communists can become democrats, the rich can become poor and the poor rich, but Russians cannot become Estonians and Azeris cannot become Armenians. * * * Even more than ethnicity, religion discriminates sharply and exclusively among people. A person can be half-French and half-Arab and simultaneously even a citizen of two countries. It is more difficult to be half-Catholic and half-Muslim.

Finally, economic regionalism is increasing. * * * On the one hand, successful economic regionalism will reinforce civilization-consciousness. On the other hand, economic regionalism may succeed only when it is rooted in a common civilization. The European Community rests on the shared foundation of European culture and Western Christianity. The success of the North American Free Trade Area depends on the convergence now underway of Mexican, Canadian and American cultures. Japan, in contrast, faces difficulties in creating a comparable economic entity in East Asia because Japan is a society and civilization unique to itself. * * *

■   ■   ■

As people define their identity in ethnic and religious terms, they are likely to see an "us" versus "them" relation existing between themselves and people of different ethnicity or religion. The end

of ideologically defined states in Eastern Europe and the former Soviet Union permits traditional ethnic identities and animosities to come to the fore. Differences in culture and religion create differences over policy issues, ranging from human rights to immigration to trade and commerce to the environment. * * * Most important, the efforts of the West to promote its values of democracy and liberalism as universal values, to maintain its military predominance and to advance its economic interests engender countering responses from other civilizations. * * *

The clash of civilizations thus occurs at two levels. At the micro-level, adjacent groups along the fault lines between civilizations struggle, often violently, over the control of territory and each other. At the macro-level, states from different civilizations compete for relative military and economic power, struggle over the control of international institutions and third parties, and competitively promote their particular political and religious values.

The Fault Lines between Civilizations

The fault lines between civilizations are replacing the political and ideological boundaries of the Cold War as the flash points for crisis and bloodshed. The Cold War began when the Iron Curtain divided Europe politically and ideologically. The Cold War ended with the end of the Iron Curtain. As the ideological division of Europe has disappeared, the cultural division of Europe between Western Christianity, on the one hand, and Orthodox Christianity and Islam, on the other, has reemerged. The most significant dividing line in Europe, as William Wallace has suggested, may well be the eastern boundary of Western Christianity in the year 1500. This line runs along what are now the boundaries between Finland and

Russia and between the Baltic states and Russia, cuts through Belarus and Ukraine separating the more Catholic western Ukraine from Orthodox eastern Ukraine, swings westward separating Transylvania from the rest of Romania, and then goes through Yugoslavia almost exactly along the line now separating Croatia and Slovenia from the rest of Yugoslavia. In the Balkans this line, of course, coincides with the historic boundary between the Hapsburg and Ottoman empires. The peoples to the north and west of this line are Protestant or Catholic; they shared the common experiences of European history—feudalism, the Renaissance, the Reformation, the Enlightenment, the French Revolution, the Industrial Revolution; they are generally economically better off than the peoples to the east; and they may now look forward to increasing involvement in a common European economy and to the consolidation of democratic political systems. The peoples to the east and south of this line are Orthodox or Muslim; they historically belonged to the Ottoman or Tsarist empires and were only lightly touched by the shaping events in the rest of Europe; they are generally less advanced economically; they seem much less likely to develop stable democratic political systems. The Velvet Curtain of culture has replaced the Iron Curtain of ideology as the most significant dividing line in Europe. As the events in Yugoslavia show, it is not only a line of difference; it is also at times a line of bloody conflict.

Conflict along the fault line between Western and Islamic civilizations has been going on for 1,300 years. * * *

■   ■   ■

This centuries-old military interaction between the West and Islam is unlikely to decline. It could become more virulent. The Gulf War left some Arabs feeling proud that Saddam Hussein had attacked Israel and stood up to the West. It also left many feeling humiliated and resentful of the West's military presence in the Persian Gulf, the West's overwhelming military dominance, and their apparent inability to shape their own destiny. Many Arab countries, in addition to the oil exporters, are reaching levels of economic and social development where autocratic forms of government become inappropriate and efforts to introduce democracy become stronger. Some openings in Arab political systems have already occurred. The principal beneficiaries of these openings have been Islamist movements. * * *

Those relations are also complicated by demography. The spectacular population growth in Arab countries, particularly in North Africa, has led to increased migration to Western Europe. The movement within Western Europe toward minimizing internal boundaries has sharpened political sensitivities with respect to this development. * * *

■   ■   ■

Historically, the other great antagonistic interaction of Arab Islamic civilization has been with the pagan, animist, and now increasingly Christian black peoples to the south. In the past, this antagonism was epitomized in the image of Arab slave dealers and black slaves. It has been reflected in the on-going civil war in the Sudan between Arabs and blacks, the fighting in Chad between Libyan-supported insurgents and the government, the tensions between Orthodox Christians and Muslims in the Horn of Africa, and the political conflicts, recurring riots and communal violence between Muslims and Christians in Nigeria. The modernization of Africa and the spread of Christianity are likely to enhance the probability of violence along this fault line. Symptomatic of the intensification of this conflict was the Pope John Paul II's speech in Khartoum in February 1993 attacking the actions of the Sudan's Islamist government against the Christian minority there.

On the northern border of Islam, conflict has increasingly erupted between Orthodox and

Muslim peoples, including the carnage of Bosnia and Sarajevo, the simmering violence between Serb and Albanian, the tenuous relations between Bulgarians and their Turkish minority, the violence between Ossetians and Ingush, the unremitting slaughter of each other by Armenians and Azeris, the tense relations between Russians and Muslims in Central Asia. * * *

The conflict of civilizations is deeply rooted elsewhere in Asia. The historic clash between Muslim and Hindu in the subcontinent manifests itself now not only in the rivalry between Pakistan and India but also in intensifying religious strife within India between increasingly militant Hindu groups and India's substantial Muslim minority. The destruction of the Ayodhya mosque in December 1992 brought to the fore the issue of whether India will remain a secular democratic state or become a Hindu one. * * *

■   ■   ■

Groups or states belonging to one civilization that become involved in war with people from a different civilization naturally try to rally support from other members of their own civilization. * * *

■   ■   ■

Civilization rallying to date has been limited, but it has been growing, and it clearly has the potential to spread much further. As the conflicts in the Persian Gulf, the Caucasus and Bosnia continued, the positions of nations and the cleavages between them increasingly were along civilizational lines. Populist politicians, religious leaders and the media have found it a potent means of arousing mass support and of pressuring hesitant governments. In the coming years, the local conflicts most likely to escalate into major wars will be those, as in Bosnia and the Caucasus, along the fault lines between civilizations. The next world war, if there is one, will be a war between civilizations.

The West versus the Rest

The West is now at an extraordinary peak of power in relation to other civilizations. Its superpower opponent has disappeared from the map. Military conflict among Western states is unthinkable, and Western military power is unrivaled. Apart from Japan, the West faces no economic challenge. It dominates international political and security institutions and with Japan international economic institutions. Global political and security issues are effectively settled by a directorate of the United States, Britain and France, world economic issues by a directorate of the United States, Germany and Japan, all of which maintain extraordinarily close relations with each other to the exclusion of lesser and largely non-Western countries. Decisions made at the U.N. Security Council or in the International Monetary Fund that reflect the interests of the West are presented to the world as reflecting the desires of the world community. The very phrase "the world community" has become the euphemistic collective noun (replacing "the Free World") to give global legitimacy to actions reflecting the interests of the United States and other Western powers.[1] * * *

■   ■   ■

* * * V. S. Naipaul has argued that Western civilization is the "universal civilization" that "fits all men." At a superficial level much of Western culture has indeed permeated the rest of the world. At a more basic level, however, Western concepts differ fundamentally from those prevalent in other civilizations. Western ideas of individualism, liberalism, constitutionalism, human rights, equality, liberty, the rule of law, democracy, free markets, the separation of church and state often have little resonance in Islamic, Confucian, Japanese, Hindu, Buddhist or Orthodox cultures. Western efforts to propagate such ideas produce instead a reaction against "human rights imperialism" and a reaffirmation of

indigenous values, as can be seen in the support for religious fundamentalism by the younger generation in non-Western cultures. The very notion that there could be a "universal civilization" is a Western idea, directly at odds with the particularism of most Asian societies and their emphasis on what distinguishes one people from another. Indeed, the author of a review of 100 comparative studies of values in different societies concluded that "the values that are most important in the West are least important worldwide."[2] In the political realm, of course, these differences are most manifest in the efforts of the United States and other Western powers to induce other peoples to adopt Western ideas concerning democracy and human rights. Modern democratic government originated in the West. When it has developed in non-Western societies it has usually been the product of Western colonialism or imposition.

The central axis of world politics in the future is likely to be, in Kishore Mahbubani's phrase, the conflict between "the West and the Rest" and the responses of non-Western civilizations to Western power and values.[3] Those responses generally take one or a combination of three forms. At one extreme, non-Western states can, like Burma and North Korea, attempt to pursue a course of isolation, to insulate their societies from penetration or "corruption" by the West, and, in effect, to opt out of participation in the Western-dominated global community. The costs of this course, however, are high, and few states have pursued it exclusively. A second alternative, the equivalent of "bandwagoning" in international relations theory, is to attempt to join the West and accept its values and institutions. The third alternative is to attempt to "balance" the West by developing economic and military power and cooperating with other non-Western societies against the West, while preserving indigenous values and institutions; in short, to modernize but not to Westernize.

■   ■   ■

Implications for the West

This article does not argue that civilization identities will replace all other identities, that nation states will disappear, that each civilization will become a single coherent political entity, that groups within a civilization will not conflict with and even fight each other. This paper does set forth the hypotheses that differences between civilizations are real and important; civilization-consciousness is increasing; conflict between civilizations will supplant ideological and other forms of conflict as the dominant global form of conflict; international relations, historically a game played out within Western civilization, will increasingly be de-Westernized and become a game in which non-Western civilizations are actors and not simply objects; successful political, security and economic international institutions are more likely to develop within civilizations than across civilizations; conflicts between groups in different civilizations will be more frequent, more sustained and more violent than conflicts between groups in the same civilization; violent conflicts between groups in different civilizations are the most likely and most dangerous source of escalation that could lead to global wars; the paramount axis of world politics will be the relations between "the West and the Rest"; the elites in some torn non-Western countries will try to make their countries part of the West, but in most cases face major obstacles to accomplishing this; a central focus of conflict for the immediate future will be between the West and several Islamic-Confucian states.

This is not to advocate the desirability of conflicts between civilizations. It is to set forth descriptive hypotheses as to what the future may be like. If these are plausible hypotheses, however, it is necessary to consider their implications for Western policy. These implications should be divided between short-term advantage and long-term accommodation. In the short term it is clearly in the interest of the West to promote greater cooperation and unity within its own civilization, particularly between its European and North American components; to incorporate into the West societies in Eastern Europe, and Latin America whose cultures are close to those of the West; to promote and maintain cooperative relations with Russia and Japan; to prevent escalation of local inter-civilization conflicts into major inter-civilization wars; to limit the expansion of the military strength of Confucian and Islamic states; to moderate the reduction of Western military capabilities and maintain military superiority in East and Southwest Asia; to exploit differences and conflicts among Confucian and Islamic states; to support in other civilizations groups sympathetic to Western values and interests; to strengthen international institutions that reflect and legitimate Western interests and values and to promote the involvement of non-Western states in those institutions.

In the longer term other measures would be called for. Western civilization is both Western and modern. Non-Western civilizations have attempted to become modern without becoming Western. To date only Japan has fully succeeded in this quest. Non-Western civilizations will continue to attempt to acquire the wealth, technology, skills, machines and weapons that are part of being modern. They will also attempt to reconcile this modernity with their traditional culture and values. Their economic and military strength relative to the West will increase. Hence the West will increasingly have to accommodate these non-Western modern civilizations whose power approaches that of the West but whose values and interests differ significantly from those of the West. This will require the West to maintain the economic and military power necessary to protect its interests in relation to these civilizations. It will also, however, require the West to develop a more profound understanding of the basic religious and philosophical assumptions underlying other civilizations and the ways in which people in those civilizations see their interests. It will require an effort to identify elements of commonality between Western and other civilizations. For the relevant future, there will be no universal civilization, but instead a world of different civilizations, each of which will have to learn to coexist with the others.

NOTES

1. Almost invariably Western leaders claim they are acting on behalf of "the world community." One minor lapse occurred during the run-up to the Gulf War. In an interview on "Good Morning America," Dec. 21, 1990, British Prime Minister John Major referred to the actions "the West" was taking against Saddam Hussein. He quickly corrected himself and subsequently referred to "the world community." He was, however, right when he erred.

2. Harry C. Triandis, *The New York Times*, Dec. 25, 1990, p. 41, and "Cross-Cultural Studies of Individualism and Collectivism," Nebraska Symposium on Motivation, vol. 37, 1989, pp. 41–133.

3. Kishore Mahbubani, "The West and the Rest," *The National Interest*, Summer 1992, pp. 3–13.

6

THE INDIVIDUAL

Individual psychology is also important in shaping international relations. Individuals include not only foreign policy elites—the leaders who move the world—but also the diplomats, warriors, activists, and voters whose attitudes and perceptions animate the politics of international issues. In a now-classic piece originally published in 1968, Robert Jervis articulates hypotheses on the origins of misperceptions. Drawing heavily on psychology, he suggests strategies for decision makers to mitigate the effects of misperception.

Can individual-level characteristics—personality traits, emotions—be imputed to the state? In his article "We Will Not Swallow This Bitter Fruit," Todd Hall draws on "folk theory" to claim that emotion drives policy. Using the 1995–96 Taiwan Strait Crisis, he shows how the People's Republic of China exhibited a diplomacy of anger, hence assigning to the collective what is considered an individual behavior.

Robert Jervis

HYPOTHESES ON MISPERCEPTION

In determining how he will behave, an actor must try to predict how others will act and how their actions will affect his values. The actor must therefore develop an image of others and of their intentions. This image may, however, turn out to be an inaccurate one; the actor may, for a number of reasons, misperceive both others' actions and their intentions. * * * I wish to discuss the types of misperceptions of other states' intentions which states tend to make. * * *

■   ■   ■

Theories—Necessary and Dangerous

* * * The evidence from both psychology and history overwhelmingly supports the view (which may be labeled Hypothesis 1) that decision-makers tend to fit incoming information into their existing theories and images. Indeed, their theories and images play a large part in determining what they notice. In other words, actors tend to perceive what they expect. Furthermore (Hypothesis 1a), a theory will have greater impact on an actor's interpretation of data (a) the greater the ambiguity of the data and (b) the higher the degree of confidence with which the actor holds the theory.[1]

■   ■   ■

From *World Politics* 20, no. 3 (Apr. 1968): 454–479. Some of the author's notes have been omitted.

* * * Hypothesis 2: scholars and decision-makers are apt to err by being too wedded to the established view and too closed to new information, as opposed to being too willing to alter their theories. Another way of making this point is to argue that actors tend to establish their theories and expectations prematurely. In politics, of course, this is often necessary because of the need for action. But experimental evidence indicates that the same tendency also occurs on the unconscious level. * * *

However, when we apply these and other findings to politics and discuss kinds of misperception, we should not quickly apply the label of cognitive distortion. We should proceed cautiously for two related reasons. The first is that the evidence available to decision-makers almost always permits several interpretations. It should be noted that there are cases of visual perception in which different stimuli can produce exactly the same pattern on an observer's retina. Thus, for an observer using one eye the same pattern would be produced by a sphere the size of a golf ball which was quite close to the observer, by a baseball-sized sphere that was further away, or by a basketball-sized sphere still further away. Without other clues, the observer cannot possibly determine which of these stimuli he is presented with, and we would not want to call his incorrect perceptions examples of distortion. Such cases, relatively rare in visual perception, are frequent in international relations. The evidence available to decision-makers is almost always very ambiguous since accurate clues to others' intentions are surrounded by noise[2] and deception. In most cases, no matter how long, deeply, and "objectively" the evidence is analyzed, people can differ in their interpretations, and there are no general rules to indicate who is correct.

The second reason to avoid the label of cognitive distortion is that the distinction between perception and judgment, obscure enough in individual psychology, is almost absent in the making of inferences in international politics. Decision-makers who reject information that contradicts their views—or who develop complex interpretations of it—often do so consciously and explicitly. Since the evidence available contains contradictory information, to make any inferences requires that much information be ignored or given interpretations that will seem tortuous to those who hold a different position.

Indeed, if we consider only the evidence available to a decision-maker at the time of decision, the view later proved incorrect may be supported by as much evidence as the correct one—or even by more. Scholars have often been too unsympathetic with the people who were proved wrong. On closer examination, it is frequently difficult to point to differences between those who were right and those who were wrong with respect to their openness to new information and willingness to modify their views. Winston Churchill, for example, did not open-mindedly view each Nazi action to see if the explanations provided by the appeasers accounted for the data better than his own beliefs. Instead, like Chamberlain, he fitted each bit of ambiguous information into his own hypotheses. That he was correct should not lead us to overlook the fact that his methods of analysis and use of theory to produce cognitive consistency did not basically differ from those of the appeasers.

A consideration of the importance of expectations in influencing perception also indicates that the widespread belief in the prevalence of "wishful thinking" may be incorrect, or at least may be based on inadequate data. The psychological literature on the interaction between affect and perception is immense and cannot be treated here, but it should be noted that phenomena that at first were considered strong evidence for the impact of affect on perception often can be better treated as demonstrating the influence of expectations.[3] Thus, in international relations, cases like the United States' misestimation of the political climate in Cuba in April 1961, which may seem at first glance to have been instances of wishful thinking, may instead be more adequately explained by the theories held by the decision-makers (e.g., Communist governments are unpopular). Of course, desires may have an impact on perception by influencing expectations, but since so many other factors affect expectations, the net influence of desires may not be great.

There is evidence from both psychology[4] and international relations that when expectations and desires clash, expectations seem to be more important. The United States would like to believe that North Vietnam is about to negotiate or that the USSR is ready to give up what the United States believes is its goal of world domination, but ambiguous evidence is seen to confirm the opposite conclusion, which conforms to the United States' expectations. Actors are apt to be especially sensitive to evidence of grave danger if they think they can take action to protect themselves against the menace once it has been detected.

Safeguards

Can anything then be said to scholars and decision-makers other than "Avoid being either too open or too closed, but be especially aware of the latter danger"? Although decision-makers will always be faced with ambiguous and confusing evidence and will be forced to make inferences about others which will often be inaccurate, a number of safeguards may be suggested which could enable them to minimize their errors. First, and most obvious, decision-makers should be aware that they do not make "unbiased" interpretations of each new bit of incoming information, but rather are inevitably heavily influenced by the theories they expect to be verified. They should know that what may appear to them as a self-evident and unambiguous inference often seems so only because of their preexisting beliefs. To someone with a different theory the same data may appear to be unimportant or to support another explanation. Thus many events provide less independent support for the decision-makers' images than they may at first realize. Knowledge of this should lead decision-makers to examine more closely evidence that others believe contradicts their views.

Second, decision-makers should see if their attitudes contain consistent or supporting beliefs that are not logically linked. These may be examples of true psycho-logic. While it is not logically surprising nor is it evidence of psychological pressures to find that people who believe that Russia is aggressive are very suspicious of any Soviet move, other kinds of consistency are more suspect. For example, most people who feel that it is important for the United States to win the war in Vietnam also feel that a meaningful victory is possible. And most people who feel defeat would neither endanger U.S. national security nor be costly in terms of other values also feel that we cannot win. Although there are important logical linkages between the two parts of each of these views (especially through theories of guerrilla warfare), they do not seem strong enough to explain the degree to which the opinions are correlated. Similarly, in Finland in the winter of 1939, those who felt that grave consequences would follow Finnish agreement to give Russia a military base also believed that the Soviets would withdraw their demand if Finland stood firm. And those who felt that concessions would not lead to loss of major values also believed that Russia would fight if need be.[5] In this country, those who favored a nuclear test ban tended to argue that fallout was very harmful, that only limited improvements in technology would flow from further testing, and that a test ban would increase the chances for peace and security. Those who opposed the test ban were apt to disagree on all three points. This does not mean, of course, that the people holding such sets of supporting views were necessarily wrong in any one element. The Finns who wanted to make concessions to the USSR were probably correct in both parts of their argument. But decision-makers should be suspicious if they hold a position in which elements that are not logically connected support the same conclusion. This condition is psychologically comfortable and makes decisions easier to reach (since competing values do not have to be balanced off against each other). The chances are thus considerable that at least part of the reason why a person holds some of these views is related to psychology and not to the substance of the evidence.

Decision-makers should also be aware that actors who suddenly find themselves having an important shared interest with other actors have a tendency to overestimate the degree of common interest involved. This tendency is especially strong for those actors (e.g., the United States, at least before 1950) whose beliefs about international relations and morality imply that they can cooperate only with "good" states and that with those states there will be no major conflicts. On the other hand, states that have either a tradition of limited cooperation with others (e.g., Britain) or a strongly held theory that differentiates occasional from permanent allies[6] (e.g., the Soviet Union) find it easier to resist this tendency and need not devote special efforts to combating its danger.

A third safeguard for decision-makers would be to make their assumptions, beliefs, and the predictions that follow from them as explicit as possible. An actor should try to determine, before events occur, what evidence would count for and against his theories. By knowing what to expect he would know what to be surprised by, and surprise could indicate to that actor that his beliefs needed reevaluation.[7]

A fourth safeguard is more complex. The decision-maker should try to prevent individuals and organizations from letting their main task, political future, and identity become tied to specific theories and images of other actors.[8] If this occurs, subgoals originally sought for their contribution to higher ends will take on value of their own, and information indicating possible alternative routes to the original goals will not be carefully considered. For example, the U.S. Forest Service was unable to carry out its original purpose as effectively when it began to see its distinctive competence not in promoting the best use of lands and forests but rather in preventing all types of forest fires.[9]

Organizations that claim to be unbiased may not realize the extent to which their definition of their role has become involved with certain beliefs about the world. Allen Dulles is a victim of this lack of understanding when he says, "I grant that we are all creatures of prejudice, including CIA officials, but by entrusting intelligence coordination to our central intelligence service, which is excluded from policy-making and is married to no particular military hardware, we can avoid, to the greatest possible extent, the bending of facts obtained through intelligence to suit a particular occupational viewpoint."[10] This statement overlooks the fact that the CIA has developed a certain view of international relations and of the cold war which maximizes the importance of its information-gathering, espionage, and subversive activities. Since the CIA would lose its unique place in the government if it were decided that the "back alleys" of world politics were no longer vital to U.S. security, it is not surprising that the organization interprets information in a way that stresses the continued need for its techniques.

Fifth, decision-makers should realize the validity and implications of Roberta Wohlstetter's argument that "a willingness to play with material from different angles and in the context of unpopular as well as popular hypotheses is an essential ingredient of a good detective, whether the end is the solution of a crime or an intelligence estimate."[11] However, it is often difficult, psychologically and politically, for any one person to do this. Since a decision-maker usually cannot get "unbiased" treatments of data, he should instead seek to structure conflicting biases into the decision-making process. The decision-maker, in other words, should have devil's advocates around. Just as, as Neustadt points out,[12] the decision-maker will want to create conflicts among his subordinates in order to make appropriate choices, so he will also want to ensure that incoming information is examined from many different perspectives with many different hypotheses in mind. To some extent this kind of examination will be done automatically through the divergence of goals, training, experience, and information that exists in any large organization. But in many cases this divergence will not be sufficient. The views of those analyzing the data will still be too homogeneous, and the decision-maker will have to go out of his way not only to cultivate but to create differing viewpoints.

While all that would be needed would be to have some people examining the data trying to validate unpopular hypotheses, it would probably be more effective if they actually believed and had a stake in the views they were trying to support. If in 1941 someone had had the task of proving the view that Japan would attack Pearl Harbor, the government might have been less surprised by the attack. And only a person who was out to show that Russia would take objectively great risks would have been apt to note that several ships with especially large hatches going to Cuba were riding high in the water, indicating the presence of a bulky but light cargo that was not likely to be anything other than strategic missiles. And many people who doubt the wisdom of the administration's Vietnam policy would be somewhat reassured if there were people in the government who searched the statements and actions of both sides in an effort to prove that North Vietnam was willing to negotiate and that the official interpretation of such moves as the Communist activities during the Têt truce of 1967 was incorrect.

Of course all these safeguards involve costs. They would divert resources from other tasks and would increase internal dissension. Determining whether these costs would be worth the gains would depend on a detailed analysis of how the suggested safeguards might be implemented. Even if they were adopted by a government, of course, they would not eliminate the chance of misperception. However, the safeguards would make it more likely that national decision-makers would make conscious choices about the way data were interpreted rather than merely assuming that they can be seen in only one way and can mean only one thing. Statesmen would thus be reminded of alternative images of others just as they are constantly reminded of alternative policies.

These safeguards are partly based on Hypothesis 3: actors can more easily assimilate into their established image of another actor information contradicting that image if the information is transmitted and considered bit by bit than if it comes all at once. In the former case, each piece of discrepant data can be coped with as it arrives and each of the conflicts with the prevailing view will be small enough to go unnoticed, to be dismissed as unimportant, or to necessitate at most a slight modification of the image (e.g., addition of exceptions to the rule). When the information arrives in a block, the contradiction between it and the prevailing view is apt to be much clearer and the probability of major cognitive reorganization will be higher.

Sources of Concepts

An actor's perceptual thresholds—and thus the images that ambiguous information is apt to produce—are influenced by what he has experienced and learned about.[13] If one actor is to perceive that another fits in a given category he must first have, or develop, a concept for that category. We can usefully distinguish three levels at which a concept can be present or absent. First, the concept can be completely missing. The actor's cognitive structure may not include anything corresponding to the phenomenon he is encountering. This situation can occur not only in science fiction, but also in a world of rapid change or in the meeting of two dissimilar systems. Thus China's image of the Western world was extremely inaccurate in the mid-nineteenth century, her learning was very slow, and her responses were woefully inadequate. The West was spared a similar struggle only because it had the power to reshape the system it encountered. Once the actor clearly sees one instance of the new phenomenon, he is apt to recognize it much more quickly in the future.[14] Second, the actor can know about a concept but not believe that it reflects an actual phenomenon. Thus Communist and Western decision-makers are each aware of the other's explanation of how his system functions, but do not think that the concept corresponds to reality. Communist elites, furthermore, deny that anything *could* correspond to the democracies' description of themselves. Third, the actor may hold a concept, but not believe that another actor fills it at the present moment. Thus the British and French statesmen of the 1930s held a concept of states with unlimited ambitions. They realized that Napoleons were possible, but they did not think Hitler belonged in that category. Hypothesis 4 distinguishes these three cases: misperception is most difficult to correct in the case of a missing concept and least difficult to correct in the case of a recognized but presumably unfilled concept. All other things being equal (e.g., the degree to which the concept is central to the actor's cognitive structure), the first case requires more cognitive reorganization than does the second, and the second requires more reorganization than the third.

However, this hypothesis does not mean that learning will necessarily be slowest in the first case, for if the phenomena are totally new the actor may make such grossly inappropriate responses that he will quickly acquire information clearly indicating that he is faced with something he does not understand. And the sooner the actor realizes that things are not—or may not be—what they seem, the sooner he is apt to correct his image.[15]

Three main sources contribute to decision-makers' concepts of international relations and of other states and influence the level of their perceptual thresholds for various phenomena. First, an actor's beliefs about his own domestic political system are apt to be important. In some cases, like that of the USSR, the decision-makers' concepts are tied to an ideology that explicitly provides a frame of reference for viewing foreign affairs. Even where this is not the case, experience with his own system will partly determine what the actor is familiar with and what he is apt to perceive in others. Louis Hartz claims, "It is the absence of the experience of social revolution which is at the heart of the whole American dilemma. . . . In a whole series of specific ways it enters into our difficulty of communication with the rest of the world. We find it difficult to understand Europe's 'social question'. . . . We are not familiar with the deeper social struggles of Asia and hence tend to interpret even reactionary regimes as 'democratic.'"[16] Similarly, George Kennan argues that in World War I the Allied Powers, and especially America, could not understand the bitterness and violence of others' internal conflicts: ". . . The inability of the Allied statesmen to picture to themselves the passions of the Russian civil war [was partly caused by the fact that] we represent . . . a society in which the manifestations of evil have been carefully buried and sublimated in the social behavior of people, as in their very consciousness. For this reason, probably, despite our widely traveled and outwardly cosmopolitan lives, the mainsprings of political behavior in such a country as Russia tend to remain concealed from our vision."[17]

Second, concepts will be supplied by the actor's previous experiences. An experiment from another field illustrates this. Dearborn and Simon presented business executives from various divisions (e.g., sales, accounting, production) with the same hypothetical data and asked them for an analysis and recommendations from the standpoint of what would be best for the company as a whole. The executives' views heavily reflected their departmental perspectives.[18] William W. Kaufmann shows how the perceptions of Ambassador Joseph Kennedy were affected by his past: "As befitted a former chairman of the Securities Exchange and Maritime Commissions, his primary interest lay in economic matters. . . . The revolutionary character of the Nazi regime was not a phenomenon that he could easily grasp. . . . It was far simpler, and more in accord with his own premises, to explain German aggressiveness in economic terms. The Third Reich was dissatisfied, authoritarian, and expansive largely because her economy was unsound."[19] Similarly it has been argued that Chamberlain was slow to recognize Hitler's intentions partly because of the limiting nature of his personal background and business experiences. The impact of training and experience seems to be demonstrated when the background of the appeasers is compared to that of their opponents. One difference stands out: "A substantially higher percentage of the anti-appeasers (irrespective of class origins) had the kind of knowledge which comes from close acquaintance, mainly professional, with foreign affairs."[20] Since members of the diplomatic corps are responsible for meeting threats to the nation's security before these grow to major proportions and since they have learned about cases in which aggressive states were not recognized as such until very late, they may be prone to interpret ambiguous data as showing that others are aggressive. It should be stressed that we cannot say that the professionals of the 1930s were more apt to make accurate judgments of other states. Rather, they may have been more sensitive to the chance that others were aggressive. They would then rarely take an aggressor for a status-quo power, but would more often make the opposite error. Thus in the years before World War I the permanent officials in the British Foreign Office overestimated German aggressiveness.[21]

A parallel demonstration in psychology of the impact of training on perception is presented by an experiment in which ambiguous pictures were shown to both advanced and beginning police-administration students. The advanced group perceived more violence in the pictures than did the beginners. The probable explanation is that "the law enforcer may come to accept crime as a familiar personal experience, one which he himself is not surprised to encounter. The acceptance of crime as a familiar experience in turn increases the ability or readiness to perceive violence where clues to it are potentially available."[22] This experiment lends weight to the view that the British diplomats' sensitivity to aggressive states was not totally a product of personnel selection procedures.

A third source of concepts, which frequently will be the most directly relevant to a decision-maker's perception of international relations, is international history. As Henry Kissinger points out, one reason why statesmen were so slow to recognize the threat posed by Napoleon was that previous events had accustomed them only to actors who wanted to modify the existing system, not overthrow it.[23] The other side of the coin is even more striking: historical traumas can heavily influence future perceptions. They can either establish a state's image of the other state involved or can be used as analogies. An example of the former case is provided by the fact that for at least ten years after the Franco-Prussian War most of Europe's statesmen felt that Bismarck had aggressive plans when in fact his main goal was to protect the status quo. Of course the evidence was ambiguous. The post-1871 Bismarckian maneuvers, which were designed to keep peace, looked not unlike the pre-1871 maneuvers designed to set the stage for war. But that the post-1871 maneuvers were seen as indicating aggressive plans is largely attributable to the impact of Bismarck's earlier actions on the statesmen's image of him.

A state's previous unfortunate experience with a type of danger can sensitize it to other examples of that danger. While this sensitivity may lead the state to avoid the mistake it committed in the past, it may also lead it mistakenly to believe that the present situation is like the past one. Santayana's maxim could be turned around: "Those who remember the past are condemned to make the opposite mistakes." As Paul Kecskemeti shows, both defenders and critics of the unconditional surrender plan of the Second World War thought in terms of the conditions of World War I.[24] Annette Baker Fox found that the Scandinavian countries' neutrality policies in World War II were strongly influenced by their experiences in the previous war, even though vital aspects of the two situations were different. Thus "Norway's success [during the First World War] in remaining non-belligerent though pro-Allied gave the Norwegians confidence that their country could again stay out of war."[25] And the lesson drawn from the unfortunate results of this policy was an important factor in Norway's decision to join NATO.

The application of the Munich analogy to various contemporary events has been much commented on, and I do not wish to argue the substantive points at stake. But it seems clear that the probabilities that any state is facing an aggressor who has to be met by force are not altered by the career of Hitler and the history of the 1930s. Similarly the probability of an aggressor's announcing his plans is not increased (if anything, it is decreased) by the fact that Hitler wrote *Mein Kampf*. Yet decision-makers are more sensitive to these possibilities, and thus more apt to perceive ambiguous evidence as indicating they apply to a given case, than they would have been had there been no Nazi Germany.

Historical analogies often precede, rather than follow, a careful analysis of a situation (e.g., Truman's initial reaction to the news of the invasion of South Korea was to think of the Japanese invasion of Manchuria). Noting this precedence, however, does not show us which of many analogies will come to a decision-maker's mind. Truman could have thought of nineteenth-century European wars that were of no interest to the United States. Several factors having nothing to do with the event under consideration influence what analogies a decision-maker is apt to make. One factor is the number of cases similar to the analogy with which the decision-maker is familiar. Another is the importance of the past event to the political system of which the decision-maker is a part. The more times such an event occurred and the greater its consequences were, the more a decision-maker will be sensitive to the particular danger involved and the more he will be apt to see ambiguous stimuli as indicating another instance of this kind of event. A third factor is the degree of the decision-maker's personal involvement in the past case—in time, energy, ego, and position. The last-mentioned variable will affect not only the event's impact on the decision-maker's cognitive structure, but also the way he perceives the event and the lesson he draws. Someone who was involved in getting troops into South Korea after the attack will remember the Korean War differently from someone who was involved in considering the possible use of nuclear weapons or in deciding what messages should be sent to the Chinese. Greater personal involvement will usually give the event greater impact, especially if the decision-maker's own views were validated by the event. One need not accept a total application of learning theory to nations to believe that "nothing fails like success."[26] It also seems likely that if many critics argued at the time that the decision-maker was wrong, he will be even more apt to see

other situations in terms of the original event. For example, because Anthony Eden left the government on account of his views and was later shown to have been correct, he probably was more apt to see as Hitlers other leaders with whom he had conflicts (e.g., Nasser). A fourth factor is the degree to which the analogy is compatible with the rest of his belief system. A fifth is the absence of alternative concepts and analogies. Individuals and states vary in the amount of direct or indirect political experience they have had which can provide different ways of interpreting data. Decision-makers who are aware of multiple possibilities of states' intentions may be less likely to seize on an analogy prematurely. The perception of citizens of nations like the United States which have relatively little history of international politics may be more apt to be heavily influenced by the few major international events that have been important to their country.

The first three factors indicate that an event is more apt to shape present perceptions if it occurred in the recent rather than the remote past. If it occurred recently, the statesman will then know about it at first hand even if he was not involved in the making of policy at the time. Thus if generals are prepared to fight the last war, diplomats may be prepared to avoid the last war. Part of the Anglo-French reaction to Hitler can be explained by the prevailing beliefs that the First World War was to a large extent caused by misunderstandings and could have been avoided by farsighted and nonbelligerent diplomacy. And part of the Western perception of Russia and China can be explained by the view that appeasement was an inappropriate response to Hitler.[27]

The Evoked Set

The way people perceive data is influenced not only by their cognitive structure and theories about other actors but also by what they are concerned with at the time they receive the information. Information is evaluated in light of the small part of the person's memory that is presently active—the "evoked set." My perceptions of the dark streets I pass walking home from the movies will be different if the film I saw had dealt with spies than if it had been a comedy. If I am working on aiding a country's education system and I hear someone talk about the need for economic development in that state, I am apt to think he is concerned with education, whereas if I had been working on, say, trying to achieve political stability in that country, I would have placed his remarks in that framework.[28]

Thus Hypothesis 5 states that when messages are sent from a different background of concerns and information than is possessed by the receiver, misunderstanding is likely. Person A and person B will read the same message quite differently if A has seen several related messages that B does not know about. This difference will be compounded if, as is frequently the case, A and B each assume that the other has the same background he does. This means that misperception can occur even when deception is neither intended nor expected. Thus Roberta Wohlstetter found not only that different parts of the United States government had different perceptions of data about Japan's intentions and messages partly because they saw the incoming information in very different contexts, but also that officers in the field misunderstood warnings from Washington: "Washington advised General Short [in Pearl Harbor] on November 27 to expect 'hostile action' at any moment, by which it meant 'attack on American possessions from without,' but General Short understood this phrase to mean 'sabotage.'"[29] Washington did not realize the extent to which Pearl Harbor considered the danger of sabotage to be primary, and furthermore it incorrectly believed that General Short had received the intercepts of the secret Japanese diplomatic messages available in Washington which indicated that surprise attack was a distinct possibility.

Another implication of this hypothesis is that if important information is known to only part of the government of state A and part of the government of state B, international messages may be misunderstood by those parts of the receiver's government that do not match, in the information they have, the part of the sender's government that dispatched the message.[30]

Two additional hypotheses can be drawn from the problems of those sending messages. Hypothesis 6 states that when people spend a great deal of time drawing up a plan or making a decision, they tend to think that the message about it they wish to convey will be clear to the receiver.[31] Since they are aware of what is to them the important pattern in their actions, they often feel that the pattern will be equally obvious to others, and they overlook the degree to which the message is apparent to them only because they know what to look for. Those who have not participated in the endless meetings may not understand what information the sender is trying to convey. George Quester has shown how the German and, to a lesser extent, the British desire to maintain target limits on bombing in the first eighteen months of World War II was undermined partly by the fact that each side knew the limits it was seeking and its own reasons for any apparent "exceptions" (e.g., the German attack on Rotterdam) and incorrectly felt that these limits and reasons were equally clear to the other side.[32]

Hypothesis 7 holds that actors often do not realize that actions intended to project a given image may not have the desired effect because the actions themselves do not turn out as planned. Thus even without appreciable impact of different cognitive structures and backgrounds, an action may convey an unwanted message. For example, a country's representatives may not follow instructions and so may give others impressions contrary to those the home government wished to convey. The efforts of Washington and Berlin to settle their dispute over Samoa in the late 1880s were complicated by the provocative behavior of their agents on the spot. These agents not only increased the intensity of the local conflict, but led the decision-makers to become more suspicious of the other state because they tended to assume that their agents were obeying instructions and that the actions of the other side represented official policy. In such cases both sides will believe that the other is reading hostility into a policy of theirs which is friendly. Similarly, Quester's study shows that the attempt to limit bombing referred to above failed partly because neither side was able to bomb as accurately as it thought it could and thus did not realize the physical effects of its actions.[33]

Further Hypotheses from the Perspective of the Perceiver

From the perspective of the perceiver several other hypotheses seem to hold. Hypothesis 8 is that there is an overall tendency for decision-makers to see other states as more hostile than they are.[34] There seem to be more cases of statesmen incorrectly believing others are planning major acts against their interest than of statesmen being lulled by a potential aggressor. There are many reasons for this which are too complex to be treated here (e.g., some parts of the bureaucracy feel it is their responsibility to be suspicious of all other states; decision-makers often feel they are "playing it safe" to believe and act as though the other state were hostile in questionable cases; and often, when people do not feel they are a threat to others, they find it difficult to believe that others may see them as a threat). It should be noted, however, that decision-makers whose perceptions are described by this hypothesis would not necessarily further their own values by trying to correct for this tendency. The values of possible outcomes as well as their probabilities must be considered, and it may be that the probability of an unnecessary arms-tension cycle arising out of misperceptions, multiplied by the costs of such a cycle, may seem less to decision-makers than the probability of incorrectly believing another state is friendly, multiplied by the costs of this eventuality.

Hypothesis 9 states that actors tend to see the behavior of others as more centralized, disciplined, and coordinated than it is. This hypothesis holds true in related ways. Frequently, too many complex events are squeezed into a perceived pattern. Actors are hesitant to admit or even see that particular incidents cannot be explained by their theories.[35] Those events not caused by factors that are important parts of the perceiver's image are often seen as though they were. Further, actors see others as more internally united than they in fact are and generally overestimate the degree to which others are following a coherent policy. The degree to which the other side's policies are the product of internal bargaining,[36] internal misunderstandings, or subordinates' not following instructions is underestimated. This is the case partly because actors tend to be unfamiliar with the details of another state's policy-making processes. Seeing only the finished product, they find it simpler to try to construct a rational explanation for the policies, even though they know that such an analysis could not explain their own policies.[37]

Familiarity also accounts for Hypothesis 10: because a state gets most of its information about the other state's policies from the other's foreign office, it tends to take the foreign office's position for the stand of the other government as a whole. In many cases this perception will be an accurate one, but when the other government is divided or when the other foreign office is acting without specific authorization, misperception may result. For example, part of the reason why in 1918 Allied governments incorrectly thought "that the Japanese were preparing to take action [in Siberia], if need be, with agreement with the British and French alone, disregarding the absence of American consent,"[38] was that Allied ambassadors had talked mostly with Foreign Minister Motono, who was among the minority of the Japanese favoring this policy. Similarly, America's NATO allies may have gained an inaccurate picture of the degree to which the American government was committed to the MLF because they had greatest contact with parts of the government that strongly favored the MLF. And states that tried to get information about Nazi foreign policy from German diplomats were often misled because these officials were generally ignorant of or out of sympathy with Hitler's plans. The Germans and the Japanese sometimes purposely misinformed their own ambassadors in order to deceive their enemies more effectively.

Hypothesis 11 states that actors tend to overestimate the degree to which others are acting in response to what they themselves do when the others behave in accordance with the actor's desires; but when the behavior of the other is undesired, it is usually seen as derived from internal forces. If the *effect* of another's action is to injure or threaten the first side, the first side is apt to believe that such was the other's *purpose.* An example of the first part of the hypothesis is provided by Kennan's account of the activities of official and unofficial American representatives who protested to the new Bolshevik government against several of its actions. When the Soviets changed their position, these representatives felt it was largely because of their influence.[39] This sort of interpretation can be explained not only by the fact that it is gratifying to the individual making it, but also, taking the other side of the coin mentioned in Hypothesis 9, by the fact that the actor is most familiar with his own input into the other's decision and has less knowledge of other influences. The second part of Hypothesis 11 is illustrated by the tendency of actors to believe that the hostile behavior of others is to be explained by the other side's motives and not by its reaction to the first side. Thus Chamberlain did not see that Hitler's behavior was related in part to his belief that the British were weak. More common is the failure to see that the other side is reacting out of fear of the first side, which can lead to self-fulfilling prophecies and spirals of misperception and hostility.

This difficulty is often compounded by an implication of Hypothesis 12: when actors have intentions that they do not try to conceal from others, they tend to assume that others accurately perceive these intentions. Only rarely do they believe that others may be reacting to a much less favorable image of themselves than they think they are projecting.[40]

For state A to understand how state B perceives A's policy is often difficult because such understanding may involve a conflict with A's image of itself. Raymond Sontag argues that Anglo-German relations before World War I deteriorated partly because "the British did not like to think of themselves as selfish, or unwilling to tolerate 'legitimate' German expansion. The Germans did not like to think of themselves as aggressive, or unwilling to recognize 'legitimate' British vested interest."[41]

Hypothesis 13 suggests that if it is hard for an actor to believe that the other can see him as a menace, it is often even harder for him to see that issues important to him are not important to others. While he may know that another actor is on an opposing team, it may be more difficult for him to realize that the other is playing an entirely different game. This is especially true when the game he is playing seems vital to him.[42]

The final hypothesis, Hypothesis 14, is as follows: actors tend to overlook the fact that evidence consistent with their theories may also be consistent with other views. When choosing between two theories we have to pay attention only to data that cannot be accounted for by one of the theories. But it is common to find people claiming as proof of their theories data that could also support alternative views. This phenomenon is related to the point made earlier that any single bit of information can be interpreted only within a framework of hypotheses and theories. And while it is true that "we may without a vicious circularity accept some datum as a fact because it conforms to the very law for which it counts as another confirming instance, and reject an allegation of fact because it is already excluded by law,"[43] we should be careful lest we forget that a piece of information seems in many cases to confirm a certain hypothesis only because we already believe that hypothesis to be correct and that the information can with as much validity support a different hypothesis. For example, one of the reasons why the German attack on Norway took both that country and England by surprise, even though they had detected German ships moving toward Norway, was that they expected not an attack but an attempt by the Germans to break through the British blockade and reach the Atlantic. The initial course of the ships was consistent with either plan, but the British and Norwegians took this course to mean that their predictions were being borne out.[44] This is not to imply that the interpretation made was foolish, but only that the decision-makers should have been aware that the evidence was also consistent with an invasion and should have had a bit less confidence in their views.

The longer the ships would have to travel the same route whether they were going to one or another of two destinations, the more information would be needed to determine their plans. Taken as a metaphor, this incident applies generally to the treatment of evidence. Thus as long as Hitler made demands for control only of ethnically German areas, his actions could be explained either by the hypothesis that he had unlimited ambitions or by the hypothesis that he wanted to unite all the Germans. But actions against non-Germans (e.g., the takeover of Czechoslovakia in March 1938) could not be accounted for by the latter hypothesis. And it was this action that convinced the appeasers that Hitler had to be stopped. It is interesting to speculate on what the British reaction would have been had Hitler left Czechoslovakia

alone for a while and instead made demands on Poland similar to those he eventually made in the summer of 1939. The two paths would then still not have diverged, and further misperception could have occurred.

NOTES

1. Floyd Allport, *Theories of Perception and the Concept of Structure* (New York 1955), 382; Ole Holsti, "Cognitive Dynamics and Images of the Enemy," in David Finlay, Ole Holsti, and Richard Fagen, *Enemies in Politics* (Chicago 1967), 70.

2. For a use of this concept in political communication, see Roberta Wohlstetter, *Pearl Harbor* (Stanford 1962).

3. See, for example, Donald Campbell, "Systematic Error on the Part of Human Links in Communications Systems," *Information and Control*, I (1958), 346–50; and Leo Postman, "The Experimental Analysis of Motivational Factors in Perception," in Judson S. Brown, ed., *Current Theory and Research in Motivation* (Lincoln, Neb., 1953), 59–108.

4. Dale Wyatt and Donald Campbell, "A Study of Interviewer Bias as Related to Interviewer's Expectations and Own Opinions," *International Journal of Opinion and Attitude Research*, IV (Spring 1950), 77–83.

5. Max Jacobson, *The Diplomacy of the Winter War* (Cambridge, Mass., 1961), 136–39.

6. Raymond Aron, *Peace and War* (Garden City 1966), 29.

7. Cf. Kuhn, *The Structure of Scientific Revolution*, 65. A fairly high degree of knowledge is needed before one can state precise expectations. One indication of the lack of international relations theory is that most of us are not sure what "naturally" flows from our theories and what constitutes either "puzzles" to be further explored with the paradigm or "anomalies" that cast doubt on the basic theories.

8. See Philip Selznick, *Leadership in Administration* (Evanston 1957).

9. Ashley Schiff, *Fire and Water: Scientific Heresy in the Forest Service* (Cambridge, Mass., 1962). Despite its title, this book is a fascinating and valuable study.

10. *The Craft of Intelligence* (New York 1963), 53.

11. P. 302. See Beveridge, 93, for a discussion of the idea that the scientist should keep in mind as many hypotheses as possible when conducting and analyzing experiments.

12. *Presidential Power* (New York 1960).

13. Most psychologists argue that this influence also holds for perception of shapes. For data showing that people in different societies differ in respect to their predisposition to experience certain optical illusions and for a convincing argument that this difference can be explained by the societies' different physical environments, which have led their people to develop different patterns of drawing inferences from ambiguous visual cues, see Marshall Segall, Donald Campbell, and Melville Herskovits, *The Influence of Culture on Visual Perceptions* (Indianapolis 1966).

14. Thus when Bruner and Postman's subjects first were presented with incongruous playing cards (i.e., cards in which symbols and colors of the suits were not matching, producing red spades or black diamonds), long exposure times were necessary for correct identification. But once a subject correctly perceived the card and added this type of card to his repertoire of categories, he was able to identify other incongruous cards much more quickly. For an analogous example—in this case, changes in the analysis of aerial reconnaissance photographs of an enemy's secret weapons-testing facilities produced by the belief that a previously unknown object may be present—see David Irving, *The Mare's Nest* (Boston 1964), 66–67, 274–75.

15. Bruner and Postman, 220.

16. *The Liberal Tradition in America* (New York 1955), 306.

17. *Russia and the West Under Lenin and Stalin* (New York 1962), 142–43.

18. DeWitt Dearborn and Herbert Simon, "Selective Perception: A Note on the Departmental Identification of Executives," *Sociometry*, XXI (June 1958), 140–44.

19. "Two American Ambassadors: Bullitt and Kennedy," in Craig and Gilbert, 358–59.

20. Donald Lammer, *Explaining Munich* (Stanford 1966), 15.

21. George Monger, *The End of Isolation* (London 1963). I am also indebted to Frederick Collignon for his unpublished manuscript and several conversations on this point.

22. Hans Toch and Richard Schulte, "Readiness to Perceive Violence as a Result of Police Training," *British Journal of Psychology*, LII (November 1961), 392 (original italics omitted). It should be stressed that one cannot say whether or not the advanced police students perceived the pictures "accurately." The point is that their training predisposed them to see violence in ambiguous situations. Whether on balance they would make fewer perceptual errors and better decisions is very hard to determine. For an experiment showing that training can lead people to "recognize" an expected stimulus even when that stimulus is in fact not shown, see Israel Goldiamond and William F. Hawkins, "Vexierversuch: The Log Relationship between Word-Frequency and Recognition Obtained in the Absence of Stimulus Words," *Journal of Experimental Psychology*, LVI (December 1958), 457–63.

23. *A World Restored* (New York 1964), 2–3.

24. *Strategic Surrender* (New York 1964), 215–41.

25. *The Power of Small States* (Chicago 1959), 81.

26. William Inge, *Outspoken Essays*, First Series (London 1923), 88.

27. Of course, analogies themselves are not "unmoved movers." The interpretation of past events is not automatic and is informed by general views of international relations and complex judgments. And just as beliefs about the past influence the present, views about the present influence interpretations of history. It is difficult to determine the degree to which the United States' interpretation of the reasons it went to war in 1917 influenced American foreign policy in the 1920s and 1930s and how much the isolationism of that period influenced the histories of the war.

28. For some psychological experiments on this subject, see Jerome Bruner and A. Leigh Minturn, "Perceptual Identification and Perceptual Organization"

Journal of General Psychology, LIII (July 1955), 22–28; Seymour Feshbach and Robert Singer, "The Effects of Fear Arousal and Suppression of Fear upon Social Perception," *Journal of Abnormal and Social Psychology*, LV (November 1957), 283–88; and Elsa Sippoal, "A Group Study of Some Effects of Preparatory Sets," *Psychology Monographs*, XLVI, No. 210 (1935), 27–28. For a general discussion of the importance of the perceiver's evoked set, see Postman, 87.

29. Pp. 73–74.

30. For example, Roger Hilsman points out, "Those who knew of the peripheral reconnaissance flights that probed Soviet air defenses during the Eisenhower administration and the U-2 flights over the Soviet Union itself . . . were better able to understand some of the things the Soviets were saying and doing than people who did not know of these activities" (*To Move a Nation* [Garden City 1967], 66). But it is also possible that those who knew about the U-2 flights at times misinterpreted Soviet messages by incorrectly believing that the sender was influenced by, or at least knew of, these flights.

31. I am grateful to Thomas Schelling for discussion on this point.

32. *Deterrence before Hiroshima* (New York 1966), 105–22.

33. *Ibid.*

34. For a slightly different formulation of this view, see Holsti, 27.

35. The Soviets consciously hold an extreme version of this view and seem to believe that nothing is accidental. See the discussion in Nathan Leites, *A Study of Bolshevism* (Glencoe 1953), 67–73.

36. A. W. Marshall criticizes Western explanations of Soviet military posture for failing to take this into account. See his "Problems of Estimating Military Power," a paper presented at the 1966 Annual Meeting of the American Political Science Association, 16.

37. It has also been noted that in labor-management disputes both sides may be apt to believe incorrectly that the other is controlled from above, either from the international union office or from the company's central headquarters (Robert Blake, Herbert Shepard,

and Jane Mouton, *Managing Intergroup Conflict in Industry* [Houston 1964], 182). It has been further noted that both Democratic and Republican members of the House tend to see the other party as the one that is more disciplined and united (Charles Clapp, *The Congressman* [Washington 1963], 17–19).

38. George Kennan, *Russia Leaves the War* (New York 1967), 484.

39. *Ibid.*, 404, 408, 500.

40. Herbert Butterfield notes that these assumptions can contribute to the spiral of "Hobbesian fear. . . . You yourself may vividly feel the terrible fear that you have of the other party, but you cannot enter into the other man's counter-fear, or even understand why he should be particularly nervous. For you know that you yourself mean him no harm, and that you want nothing from him save guarantees for your own safety; and it is never possible for you to realize or remember properly that since he cannot see the inside of your mind, he can never have the same assurance of your intentions that you have" (*History and Human Conflict* [London 1951], 20).

41. *European Diplomatic History 1871–1932* (New York 1933), 125. It takes great mental effort to realize that actions which seem only the natural consequence of defending your vital interests can look to others as though you are refusing them any chance of increasing their influence. In rebutting the famous Crowe "balance of power" memorandum of 1907, which justified a policy of "containing" Germany on the grounds that she was a threat to British national security, Sanderson, a former permanent undersecretary in the Foreign Office, wrote, "It has sometimes seemed to me that to a foreigner reading our press the British Empire must appear in the light of some huge giant sprawling all over the globe, with gouty fingers and toes stretching in every direction, which cannot be approached without eliciting a scream" (quoted in Monger, 315). But few other Englishmen could be convinced that others might see them this way.

42. George Kennan makes clear that in 1918 this kind of difficulty was partly responsible for the inability of either the Allies or the new Bolshevik government to

understand the motivations of the other side: "There is . . . nothing in nature more egocentrical than the embattled democracy. . . . It . . . tends to attach to its own cause an absolute value which distorts its own vision of everything else. . . . It will readily be seen that people who have got themselves into this frame of mind have little understanding for the issues of any contest other than the one in which they are involved. The idea of people wasting time and substance on any *other* issue seems to them preposterous" (*Russia and the West*, 11–12).

43. Kaplan, 89.

44. Johan Jorgen Holst, "Surprise, Signals, and Reaction: The Attack on Norway," *Cooperation and Conflict*, No. 1 (1966), 34. The Germans made a similar mistake in November 1942 when they interpreted the presence of an Allied convoy in the Mediterranean as confirming their belief that Malta would be resupplied. They thus were taken by surprise when landings took place in North Africa (William Langer, *Our Vichy Gamble* [New York 1966], 365).

Todd H. Hall

WE WILL NOT SWALLOW THIS BITTER FRUIT

Theorizing a Diplomacy of Anger

"Angry China"—these were the words emblazoned over the image of a snarling dragon on a 2008 cover of the *Economist*.[1] What does it mean to say a state is angry? This type of language is not limited to journalists. Policy makers and academics also frequently use such terms to describe states and yet, despite its preponderance, this language lacks a theoretical basis in the field of international relations. One standard approach is dismissal: to truly comprehend state behavior we need to cut through the emotional rhetoric to get at "what is really going on," the interplay of hard signals and the coercive application of force. The other is less an articulated approach as much as a folk theory: "angry states" are the product of undiluted emotional responses.

The motivation behind this paper is that neither answer is satisfying. The standard approach ignores the effects that displays of anger may have on the perceptions, choices, and behaviors of state actors. Conversely, the folk theory papers over the complexity of what it means for a state to display emotion. This paper offers a third conceptual path, presenting a theoretical account of the diplomacy of anger.

Specifically, the diplomacy of anger is a course of action policy makers choose, but comprehending that choice requires placing it within a context of implicit, shared understandings and emotional dynamics. The diplomacy of anger has its own

logic and trajectory—it consists of a vehement and overt state-level display of anger in response to a perceived violation. Although the diplomacy of anger threatens precipitous escalation in the face of further violations, it can be ameliorated by reconciliatory gestures and will subside over time, absent new provocations. What is more, the diplomacy of anger can also exercise a reciprocal influence on the emotional dispositions of those that practice it. While the diplomacy of anger is not necessarily more effective than standard forms of coercion, it does differ in its effects. The diplomacy of anger can contribute to constructing particular issues as sensitive and volatile, and thus possibly outside the realm of standard cost-benefit calculations.

This paper argues the diplomacy of anger is an important addition to IR's theoretical toolbox for explaining state behavior. To explore its analytical traction, I look to a concrete case within recent history: the 1995–96 Taiwan Strait Crisis. The crisis began in May of 1995 when the Bill Clinton administration bowed to congressional pressure and approved a visit by Taiwanese president Lee Teng-hui to his alma mater, Cornell University. For the government of the People's Republic of China PRC, which was engaged in an international campaign to isolate Taiwan, this constituted a deliberate violation of prior understandings with the United States. Adding insult to injury, when Lee did visit Cornell several weeks later, he used it as a platform to make a political speech showcasing "the

From *Security Studies* 20, no.4 (2011), 521–555.

Taiwan experience" and appealing for more international space. The PRC subsequently responded with rhetorical attacks and large-scale military exercises, escalating into what one observer termed "one of the most frightening" crises of recent times.[2]

There are several reasons for looking to this case as a means to probe the explanatory power of the theoretical approach offered here. First, it is neither a minor nor trivial instance with little at stake, where policy makers would conceivably have the leeway to act frivolously. This case involves displays of military force between two nuclear-armed powers. Second, the crisis was not one single event, but instead had several phases with significant variation to be explained. Third, and perhaps most importantly, there already exist scholarly analyses of this case from the standard perspective of coercive diplomacy.[3] These provide a bar with which to measure the relative analytical utility of the theory presented here. Finally, albeit far from the only state to engage in displays of anger, as pertains to the issue of Taiwan, the PRC has arguably resorted to this type of behavior on multiple occasions.[4] Examining how the PRC acted in this instance can serve to shed light on more general patterns in PRC behavior.

This paper proceeds in five parts. First, I outline two major existing explanations for PRC behavior during the 1995–96 Taiwan Strait Crisis: the standard coercion approach and the folk theory. The standard coercion approach, as noted above, already is represented in several scholarly analyses of the conflict. The folk theory—which claims that emotion was driving policy—has fewer published scholarly advocates, but nevertheless is prominently featured in journalistic accounts, informal comments, and even in scholarly feedback to this piece in its earlier iterations. Second, I offer a theoretical basis for understanding the diplomacy of anger, importantly drawing upon the work of Erving Goffman and Robert Jervis. I develop a theory of the diplomacy of anger that locates it at an important point of intersection between strategic

behavior and social logics as well as state policy and individual emotion. Third, I apply this theory to the 1995–96 Taiwan Strait Crisis in order to test its relative explanatory power.[5] Finally, I explore how the approach here can be expanded to new avenues of inquiry.

Coercion and the 1995–96 Taiwan Strait Crisis

Coercion, in its most basic definition, is the use of threats of force to shape the behavior of a target.[6] Beyond that, there are multiple typologies of coercion, possibly the most famous being those of Thomas Schelling and Alexander George. Schelling subdivides coercion into compellence (the threat of punishment should an actor not carry out an action) and deterrence (the threat of punishment should an actor carry out an action).[7] George distinguishes between deterrence (defined similarly as above), blackmail (the use of threats to force a target to "give up something of value"), and coercive diplomacy (the threat of force in order to "stop or reverse an action.")[8] What differentiates each of these types of coercion is the content of the communicated threat. In all cases, coercion succeeds through making the perceived cost of noncompliance for a target greater than the benefits to be gained from defiance. Conversely, a target can successfully resist if the perceived costs to the coercing party of carrying out the threat outweigh, or are made to outweigh, its benefits. If neither side acquiesces, conflict ensues as the threat is realized. This has been the dominant lens of analysis for IR scholars approaching the Taiwan Strait Crisis.

For instance, Robert Ross writes in his impressively researched piece that the crisis "reflected the interaction of Chinese coercive diplomacy and U.S. deterrence diplomacy."[9] Ross breaks the crisis into two periods. In the first period, the PRC launched diplomatic salvos, military exercises, and missiles in response to Lee's visit, seeking to curb Lee's behavior and force the United States not only to make a strong statement regarding Taiwan in the form of a "fourth communiqué,"[10] but also to welcome PRC president Jiang Zemin for a full state visit with honors. This period, according to Ross, "ended with China's failure to achieve its objectives."[11] The United States did refrain from harsh criticism of PRC military behavior; offered private assurances that future visits from high-level Taiwanese officials would be unofficial, seldom, and only decided case-by-case; and confidentially pledged the "United States opposed Taiwan independence, did not support a two-China policy, or a policy of one-China and one-Taiwan, and did not support Taiwan membership in the UN."[12] The United States, however, "stood firm" and did not offer any formal, public statements regarding Taiwan, nor did it provide Jiang with a full state visit, forcing the PRC to settle for an informal summit in New York. What is more, lee continued with his "provocations"—the Taiwan military engaged in exercises of its own, and Lee pushed for Taiwanese membership in the UN.

Consequently, Ross argues the PRC decided that stronger measures were required in the second period. It continued escalating its military measures, engaging in large exercises before the Taiwanese legislative elections in December 1995, and preparing for even larger ones in prelude to Taiwan's first presidential elections in March 1996, in which Lee was a candidate. The United States, seeing these actions, did not fear a PRC invasion of Taiwan, but nevertheless "had to react" because the PRC had "ignored U.S. warnings" and "challenged U.S. credibility."[13] The United States therefore deployed two carrier groups into the waters surrounding Taiwan. The PRC persisted in carrying out several missile tests in zones near Taiwan, but ceased its military displays following Lee's election, thus ending the crisis. According to Ross, "because China and the United States pursued two different types of strategic objectives, each was able to achieve its purpose."[14] The PRC changed Taiwanese perceptions of the cost of independence, and the United States was moved to limit and constrain further developments in that direction. For Ross, this is coercive diplomacy because it aimed to alter existing trajectories of behavior by threatening force. The United States, for its part, "succeeded in maintaining its preconfrontation reputation, leaving the credibility of U.S. deterrence intact."[15]

Wallace Thies and Patrick Bratton also view the crisis through the lens of coercion, framing PRC efforts as aimed at compellence, but come to very different conclusions. Thies and Bratton divide the crisis into three rounds. In the first round (June 1995–August 1995), they claim the PRC began with an attempt at compellence but eventually retreated, sending "the message that if Washington held firm, China would drop its sanctions and threats."[16] Subsequently, in the second round (September 1995–November 1995) the PRC pursued a strategy of reconciliation with the United States so that it could continue to apply pressure to Taiwan. The third round (December 1995–March 1996), according to Thies and Bratton, was characterized by ambiguous and contradictory unofficial PRC threats toward the United States coupled with escalating military action. As the tensions in the strait increased, the United States sent carriers to deter greater conflict and possibly to prove that Clinton was not appeasing the PRC.[17] Thies and Bratton conclude the PRC was "largely unsuccessful" at coercion, not just failing to compel concessions from Taiwan or the United States but instead driving them closer together.[18]

This paper argues that the standard understandings of coercion applied to this crisis, as illustrated above, render an incomplete explanation. Disregarding the fact authors harboring virtually identical theoretical commitments came to entirely opposite conclusions, these analyses still face a number of difficulties by virtue of using existing theories of coercion as their analytical lens.

First, the approaches used by the authors do not offer a clean analytic fit. By focusing on the compellent aspects of PRC actions, they are forced to downplay or recast the deterrent and punitive elements of PRC behavior. For example, although Thies and Bratton claim PRC threats aimed at compellence "were confusing,"[19] there was a clear deterrent theme in PRC statements running throughout the crisis. In the words of one commentary from the *People's Daily*, "If Taiwan declares independence, China will not idly stand by, the word of the Chinese people is definite. Taiwan is a powder keg . . . Advice for the American government, advice for people like Lee Teng-hui, advice for all who are heating up this powder keg of Taiwan independence for their short-term interests: caution, caution!"[20] In the colorful language of the Liberation Army Daily describing People's Liberation Army (PLA) soldiers, "their iron oath resounds through the seas and heavens . . . there is no way to permit one inch of territory to separate from the homeland."[21] More practically, the PRC repeatedly made known it would not rule out the use of force should Taiwan declare independence.[22]

PRC behavior was also punitive. Using military exercises, the PRC struck back at Lee by seeking to harm both the Taiwanese economy and his electoral support. One could argue the PRC was seeking to ratchet up the costs for Lee in a "turning of the screw" approach.[23] But this misses how the exercises were declared at short notice for maximum impact as opposed to being made contingent on specific demands. The PRC also retaliated against the United States by cancelling meetings, allowing factories producing pirated goods to reopen, rounding up dissidents (including an American citizen), allegedly transferring weapons and technology to Pakistan, and being uncooperative in the sharing of counter-narcotics intelligence.[24] The PRC could have first threatened these actions in succession, but instead it simply acted.[25]

Proponents of the coercive approach might counter that one could simply expand the analysis to include these other facets. Additionally, deterrence and compellence/coercive diplomacy are ideal types; it is natural that these might bleed into one another in the real world.[26] Nevertheless, it is uncertain whether describing PRC behavior as a trifurcated deterrent/compellent/punitive strategy would add analytical clarity. When it is not obvious where one category ends and the other begins, it becomes particularly difficult to allocate ratios of intention and priority among them. More significantly, the fact that PRC behavior does not fit nicely into any one specific existing category raises the question of whether or not these categories are simply being superimposed upon a phenomenon driven by a different logic.

This is compounded by the fact that the empirical record contains several puzzles for the coercive approach. First, there is the odd lull in PRC attempts at coercion toward the United States in the fall of 1995. In the immediate aftermath of the Lee visit, the PRC launched a ferocious verbal barrage coupled with various sanctions and military exercises. But several months later it acquiesced regarding many of its apparent demands on the United States. Ross, Thies, and Bratton all classify this as a coercive failure, but argue the PRC backed down in order to repair relations with the United States in advance of further plans for saber-rattling in the direction of Taiwan in the winter of 1995. Yet deteriorating relations with the United States did not stop the PRC that following spring from engaging in its largest display of force toward Taiwan in decades. In March of 1996 the PRC leadership demonstrated the lengths to which it was willing to go by engaging in massive exercises and launching missiles into the sea around Taiwan. If it was willing to take such measures in 1996, why did it apparently back down so readily in the fall of 1995?

Second, the PRC communication strategy toward the United States, particularly in the period just following Lee's visit, was not what one would expect from the standard perspective of coercive diplomacy, even if one filters out the massive amount of emotionally laden flourishes of rhetoric. The basic coercion model involves articulating threats of costs for noncompliance. The PRC side, however, used a very different rhetorical frame. In the summer and fall of 1995, the PRC repeatedly emphasized that the United States needed to, in the words of one PRC foreign ministry speaker, "take full responsibility, adopt earnest measures, and thoroughly dispel the horrible effects [of its actions] . . . What polices the United States will take towards China, what direction [the United States] wants Sino-American relations to go, we are waiting to see."[27] The message was a clear one: the United States had damaged the Sino-American relationship and therefore bore the responsibility of taking acts to repair it. Instead of making clear threats to escalate should certain demands—such as for a "fourth communiqué"—not be met, the PRC portrayed itself as an aggrieved party deserving of compensation. To quote PRC Premier Li Peng, "the actions of the United States have enormously hurt the feelings of the entire Chinese people . . . The United States should acknowledge its own mistake . . . [and] should take real moves. . . ."[28] Robert Suettinger, former director for Asian affairs on the National Security Council (NSC), described PRC behavior in this period as an "effort to really milk this for all it was worth."[29] This all suggests less a "tightening of the screw" than a PRC attempt to extract concessions by depicting itself as an injured party requiring recompense—hardly the standard model of coercive threats.

Lastly, there is the issue of the U.S. response in 1995. If the United States saw itself as a target of coercion—or even if it saw Taiwan as the target of an escalating series of coercive threats—why in 1995 did it not react more strongly against PRC displays of force? Quite simply, from a coercive perspective, it would have made sense for the

United States to signal to the PRC early on that the cost-benefit balance of attempting coercion was not in its favor. Yet throughout 1995, the United States remained relatively muted in its response to PRC actions. Commenting on the first round of missile exercises in 1995, the State Department simply stated it does "not believe that this test contributes to peace and stability in the area."[30] Two weeks later, as a new round of exercises was announced, it reiterated the same formulation.[31] When the PRC held large military exercises in October, simulating an amphibious invasion, the official us; response was that "it is not unusual for a country to have military exercises."[32] Finally, when Joseph Nye, the assistant secretary of defense for International Security Affairs, was in Beijing in November, he remained purposefully vague, stating only "'we don't know and you don't know' exactly how the United States would respond to action against Taiwan."[33] This relative silence is difficult to explain.[34]

In short, while one can impose the conceptual framework of coercion upon the Taiwan Crisis, it remains an unwieldy and incomplete explanatory tool. This is not to say the coercion approach would not have greater analytical purchase in other situations; rather, there may be something going on in this case the coercion approach is ill equipped to capture. One can of course seek to explain away problems as complexities of the "real world" and the "noise" generated by all-too-human policy makers, but such post-hoc attempts run the risk of what George himself calls "pseudo-explanations" with "a circular character."[35]

Anger and the 1995–96 Taiwan Strait Crisis

The alternative existing explanation for PRC behavior is best termed a "folk theory," given that it lacks a clear theoretical grounding despite being

ubiquitous in journalistic accounts and even frequently lurking in academic ones. This folk theory
suggests the PRC was acting out of anger. For
instance, a simple search of news reports at the
time returns hundreds of news articles describing
the PRC with words such as "angry" or "furious."[36]
Numerous scholars and analysts have also used
similar terms.[37] According to this view the Taiwan
Crisis was a situation where, in the words of one
scholar, "China's emotion exploded."[38] This folk
theory, of course, is not limited to the Taiwan crisis. As Wendt writes, "in both academic and lay
discourse we often refer casually to states 'as if'
they have emotions and are therefore conscious.
States are routinely characterized as angry, greedy,
guilty, humiliated, and so on."[39] In the case of the
Taiwan Crisis, however, the image of anger—as I
shall argue in more detail below—was particularly
salient within PRC official discourse and behavior.

The trouble with the folk theory, however, is
that it attributes an emotional reaction—anger—
to a state. As Janice Stein notes, "This is a difficult
argument, because it attributes to the collective
what is an embodied individual experience."[40]
But more than simply postulating collective emotional experience—itself a difficult, but theorized
phenomena[41]—the folk theory is suggesting the
state is a collective emotional actor. While states
obviously are not "organisms" capable of emotional
feeling,[42] the reductionist alternative of equating
states displaying emotion with states composed of
emotional individuals erases the gulf between collections of individuals and institutionalized collective action. State behavior is the product of
complex, institutionalized decision-making processes—it is neither crowd behavior nor spontaneous mass action.

Within international relations there has been a
growing interest in the relationship of emotions to
outcomes on the international stage. Scholars such
as Jonathan Mercer and Rose McDermott, for
instance, have explored the ways in which affective dynamics undergird beliefs and rational

decision making.[43] Ross goes even further by
advocating a Deleuzian view of affect and its relationship to identity, whereby "affect is not a property of an individual but a capacity of a body that
brings it into some specific social relation, such as
a nation or political movement."[44] Others, such as
Karin Fierke, Paul Suarette, or Oded Löwenheim
and Gadi Heimann, have focused on particular
emotional dynamics—such as trauma, humiliation, or the desire for revenge—as a source of
motivation in international relations.[45]

Yet, postulating the influence of emotional
motivations on policy makers does not solve the
theoretical issue of what it means for states to display emotional reactions overtly such as anger. In
fact, Löwenheim and Heimann's piece on the role
of revenge in motivating Israeli behavior during
the Second Lebanon War of July 2006 is very
instructive in this regard. Löwenheim and Heimann note that although there is considerable evidence that Israel was driven by a desire for
vengeance, the actual official discourse reflected "a
material and utilitarian logic . . . revenge remained
implicit."[46] When they asked a former Israeli cabinet member why this was the case, he replied,
"Israeli leaders probably engage in auto-suggestive
processes that allow them to claim that their acts
are not led by emotions . . . from the fear of being
criticized for such "primitive" motivations."[47]
What this illustrates is the disjuncture between
emotions as a source of policy-maker motivation,
and the state-level decision to make the explicit
expression of emotion part of a foreign policy
strategy. What is more, it also shows the ways in
which the social perceptions attached to particular
emotions rendered them acceptable (or not) for
expression on the international stage.

The folk theory glosses these differences; current work in international relations has yet to fully
engage the phenomenon of overt state-level displays
of emotion. Moving beyond to a story of why complex institutional actors like states would engage in
behavior that explicitly projects anger—and what

that would even entail—requires theorizing complex reciprocal relations both between individual emotion and state-level decision making and behavior as well as between strategic action and social understandings of emotions. I now turn to that undertaking.

Theorizing the Diplomacy of Anger

Anger is not simply a subjective, felt response; it also has a social existence in the form of the meanings we attach to it and the expectations we have for when and how it will be expressed.[48] In this latter sense it is "a socially constituted syndrome or transitory social role" linked to an actor aggressively responding to a violation or insult.[49] Anger as a "socially constituted syndrome" is associated with a cluster of action tendencies and internal states. Actors in a state of anger are seen as less rational, more prone to aggressive behavior, and likely to lash out at the source of the obstruction or violation. Anger communicates the danger of escalation in the face of provocations and encourages—even demands—acts of reconciliation by the target to ameliorate the episode. Anger, however, is temporary, an immediate response to a specific situation whose intensity, without further stimulation, will dissipate with the passage of time.

Anger also has an important moral component—it is not simply that others are behaving against an actor's wishes, but that others ought not to be behaving in such a manner, that their conduct is unjust, unfair, or wrong. Importantly, not showing anger in the face of blatant affronts can signal acquiescence to the violation.[50] Anger consequently serves the social function of rectifying a wrong that has occurred by seeking satisfaction from the responsible party—whether through exacting retribution, eliciting compensation, or receiving apology and revalidation of the norms

that were broken.[51] In short, anger is not just something we subjectively feel, it is also socially significant.[52]

Because states are collective, institutional actors, one cannot claim that they feel angry—again, they do not have a coherent body capable of feeling anything. One can, however, say that they act out the "transitory social role" of being angry. What this means is that state actors—ranging from top leaders, policymakers, officials, and diplomats, to low-ranking soldiers—can collectively project an image of anger through their discourse, symbolic gestures, and concrete actions. This is the diplomacy of anger. It is not simply one or two individuals showing anger—it is, in the words of Erving Goffman, a "team performance" of anger.[53] The term "performance" is taken from the world of theater, but Goffman employs it to characterize a more expansive field of social behavior, namely the myriad ways in which social actors seek to shape the impressions formed of them by others. Calling behavior a performance is not meant to imply that those engaged in a performance are necessarily disingenuous or faking it.[54] Rather, even social actors behaving in earnest at some level need to coordinate their words, gestures, and actions in order to maintain a particular definition of a situation and their role in it—this is especially true for collective actors.

But why would state actors want to adopt the language and behaviors associated with anger? One possible answer is that the various officials that make up the state are motivated by feelings of anger. As Jacques Hymans notes, "states are not gigantic calculating machines; they are hierarchically organized groups of emotional people."[55] Yet at the same time, policy makers are not—for the most part—cognitive three-year-olds who display their emotions' whims on their sleeves. Simply taking the case of the PRC, there is significant variation in the degree to which PRC officials respond with angry rhetoric and behavior depending on the context, all suggesting something much more calculated.[56] In the words of the former PRC Foreign Minister, Li Zhaoxing, "having emotions does not mean doing things emotionally."[57] State action is by necessity of its collective nature deliberative, coordinated, and intentional; this means that emotional motivations must compete with entrenched institutionalized interests and concerns. Moreover, as the example of the Second Lebanon War cited above illustrates, even in those instances where emotional motivations may be at work, this does not mean a state will explicitly project an emotion in its behavior.

None of this is to slight the significance of emotional reactions as a source of motivation, but given the complexity and variation of state behavior it is difficult to assume that these are the only—let alone the most significant—factors in play when it comes to state-level performances of anger. I argue that equally important are concerns about the image a state is projecting on the international stage, or in the words of Goffman, "impression management."[58] Robert Jervis, who adopted Goffman's theoretical framework for international relations, illustrates well such concerns in his works on images.[59] As Jervis has noted, "One important instrument of statecraft is the ability to affect others' images of the state and therefore their beliefs about how it will behave."[60] The impressions other actors form of a state can, in turn, shape how they view and treat it, meaning that images have strategic value.[61]

The strategic value of the diplomacy of anger lies in the image state actors convey to others about what they will or will not tolerate, where the red lines of acceptable behavior are drawn, and what is the strength of their commitments. There are different issues in the world. Some concern straightforward interests, where bargaining and coercion are standard practice. Others are normative issues, issues of principle in which actors are emotionally invested and will not accept a breach. Displays of anger convey to their target that the latter is in play.[62] By projecting the image of anger,

state actors communicate that a violation has occurred concerning a normative, emotionally salient issue about which they care. The intensity of the display corresponds to the depth of their investment.

Yet, displaying anger has its risks. If a target remains defiant and engages in further provocations, the logic of anger requires steep escalation. This can cause damage to the relationship with the target and possibly end in outright conflict. Conversely, abandoning an initiated episode of anger can signal impotence. In some cases, once anger has been endorsed as an official response, as I shall discuss further below, it may even be difficult to reign back in.

Consequently, state actors will engage in the diplomacy of anger when they view the imperative of defending particular norms as outweighing the danger of harming their relationship with the targets and sparking greater conflict. Anger becomes a possible reaction when a violation occurs; the decision by state actors to overtly project an image of anger on the international stage may be encouraged by their own feelings, but it still involves weighing the necessity of opposing the violation against the risks. Such strategic considerations, however, only exist by virtue of the fact that anger constitutes a meaningful social role not only for individuals, but also for states.

Nevertheless, the strategic element does not mean that displays of anger on the international stage are nothing more than hollow kabuki, whereby all emotion is cynically feigned. Instead, there exist crucial reciprocal effects between the choice to make anger the public face of a state's foreign policy and the emotional attitudes of the officials tasked with executing that policy. For one, those who may indeed feel anger are allowed, even encouraged, to express it openly. Anger becomes not just sanctioned, but promoted as an emotional response toward particular actors. Second, the indignant discourse that state actors adopt as part of their display can work to elicit further outrage by pointing out and playing up in poignant terms the ways in which a state has been unjustly wronged. In short, angry rhetoric may generate emotional echoes. Finally, officials may generate in themselves emotional states for the purpose of being able to appear sincere in front of their interlocutors when representing their state. This last point highlights the fact that diplomacy involves emotional labor. This is illustrated in the anecdote Zou Jianhua, a former spokesman for the PRC Foreign Ministry, tells of a foreign ministry official who received a cell phone call from an American journalist about U.S. arms sales to Taiwan while shopping at a supermarket. The official on the spot worked himself into such a "vehement and impassioned" attack that, according to Zou, other customers mistook him for a "lunatic."[63] While IR scholars have hypothesized officials may feel certain emotions as a function of their position or group identity, relatively little has been done on the ways in which they might also cultivate emotions as part of performing their roles.[64] Sociologists have long been interested in the ways certain forms of work involve the fostering of particular emotional displays, even internal states.[65] Psychologists have also pointed to the ways in which enacting particular emotions can actually generate corresponding feelings.[66] Consequently, situationally mandated display can create and feed into actual feeling. Real emotion can be produced in the process of executing policy.

To sum up, the diplomacy of anger constitutes a point of intersection both between the social logics of anger and strategic concerns as well as between official policy and individual emotion. On the one hand, it is unlikely, given the collective and institutionalized nature of state decision making and behavior, that strategic considerations do not play a role in the choice by state actors to display anger conceitedly on the international stage. On the other hand, these choices are informed by the social logic of anger and stand in a reciprocally reinforcing relationship with actual emotions.

What Makes the Diplomacy of Anger Special?

The diplomacy of anger differs from standard notions of coercion in a number of ways. For one, it has a distinct expressive idiom. Most noticeably, this involves declarations of anger as well as rhetoric painting the situation in emotionally laden terms.[67] Its discourse also includes a particular framing of the conflict as a wrongdoing requiring rectification, for which the target bears responsibility. Demands are consequently made in reference to restoring norms or rectifying the violation. Coupled with this discourse are also gestures meant to convey displeasure—ranging from facial expressions and tone of voice to symbolic gestures like walking out of a meeting, terminating communication, or engaging in petty harassment. All these constitute the expressive component of the diplomacy of anger—while not necessarily costly, it serves to project an image.

But the diplomacy of anger also can involve substantive, more costly actions that enhance and reinforce the saliency of expressive gestures.[68] These are concrete acts meant to demonstrate anger through shows of force or harming the target's interests. These should be aggressive displays, belligerent and reactive, executed with the goal of striking back at the target. Ceasing cooperation, engaging in military exercises, and other forms of saber-rattling all would fall under this category.

One might object that stripped of accompanying rhetoric, these substantive actions are simply forms of coercion. Stripped of accompanying rhetoric, however, actions can take any number of meanings. As Jervis notes, "actions are not automatically less ambiguous than words . . . without an accompanying message it may be impossible for the perceiving actor to determine what image the other is trying to project."[69] Consider the case of a visible PRC display of force, the 2007 antisatellite test. Official PRC silence at the time led to wide-spread confusion and speculation, prompting some China experts to suggest that it was the product of "the left hand not knowing what the right hand was doing."[70] Lacking a clear message, it elicited debate over whether or not there was even any strategy behind it. Accompanying rhetoric is therefore important in determining the meaning of actions and not so easily dismissed.

That said, there is another way to differentiate substantive actions deployed according to standard models of coercion versus those that are part of the diplomacy of anger: sequencing. The standard logic of coercion and the logic of anger follow different trajectories. Standard coercion involves making a demand, waiting for a response, and, should the target not comply, engaging in a threatened substantive action. Anger, in contrast, involves an immediate "lashing out." It results in a strong initial punitive and aggressive display, which—absent further provocations—de-escalates over time and can be assuaged further by efforts of the target to reaffirm norms and rebuild the relationship. Targets of coercion can stop preannounced substantive action with compliance; targets of anger are expected first to suffer through before being allowed the opportunity for reconciliation. Additional provocation of an angry actor, however, can produce rapid escalation—not simply tit for tat—with the possibility that things might spiral out of control.

These differences are reflected further in the ways in which other states are likely to react to being the targets of the diplomacy of anger. It is not simply that targets will recognize the behavior of the state in question as "angry" or "emotional," but that they will choose their responses according to this logic. In other words, targets will see themselves as having the option of waiting for the episode to subside by avoiding additional provocations, making conciliatory gestures that would speed the process of reconciliation, or further agitating the situation with defiant responses. Conciliatory gestures should not be confused with payoffs. Given the moral nature of anger, they must include elements of reaffirming the norms that were broken and repairing relationships. Coercion is generally theorized as aimed at behavior and lacks this normative component.

Whether or not targets actually engage in conciliatory action or continue with further provocations depends on several factors. First, targets may see little need for reconciliation if they do not value the relationship with the target and welcome conflict. Second, targets may also refrain from conciliatory gestures if they view the anger as unjustified and disagree about the norms in question. Finally, targets may see little need for reconciliation if they believe that the anger is not intense enough to warrant concern.

A last significant point is that while the diplomacy of anger is not necessarily more effective than standard forms of coercion, it does have distinct effects. This is due to its ability to both mobilize and project an emotional image. Schelling has written on the benefits of appearing irrational and impervious to costs.[71] The diplomacy of anger threatens a similar dynamic, presenting the target with the possibility of rapid and disproportionate escalation in response to further violations. The diplomacy of anger can also work to constitute particular issues as "emotional" and "explosive." By rallying a large scale, collective display of anger through the reciprocal emotional dynamics described above, state actors can reinforce the message that a specific issue is beyond the conventional realm of politics and subject to nonnegotiable emotional commitments. Once unleashed, such reciprocal dynamics may even take on a trajectory of their own, such that state actors find it difficult to reverse course.[72] Mobilized emotion may not be easy simply to switch off. Even after an episode has subsided, targets may be left with the impression that a particular issue remains a source of emotional volatility. The diplomacy of anger thus works to frame issues as involving emotional factors outside standard cost-benefit calculations of interest.

Reexamining the Taiwan Strait Crisis of 1995–96

The purpose of this section is to examine the explanatory traction gained by looking at the Taiwan Strait Crisis of 1995–96 through the lens of the diplomacy of anger. One cannot, of course, expect to make any definitive statements about the validity of a theory on the basis of one case. One can, however, probe its ability to explain observable behavior in a case vis-à-vis existing accounts—here the coercive diplomacy approaches of Ross, Theis, and Bratton—in order to "determine whether more intensive and laborious testing is warranted."[73] The claim of this paper is that the standard notions of coercive diplomacy are insufficient to capture the ways in which displays of anger function in international relations. Specifically, the theory of the diplomacy of anger suggests important differences for (1) the overt messages states communicate, (2) the particular sequencing of aggressive substantive actions, (3) the perceptions and responses of a state's targets, and (4) the subsequent effects of an interaction. In what follows, I review the available evidence from the crisis—in the form of declarations by policy makers, official PRC press statements, scholarly analyses, and interviews—in order to evaluate the analytical traction gained by taking the diplomacy of anger as a category of its own.

The Initial Response—Expressive and Substantive

"On May 22, the American government, ignoring the Chinese side's firm opposition and numerous solemn conveyances, announced permission for Lee Teng-Hui to make a so-called private visit to the United States . . . Toward this the Chinese government and people express enormous indignation (*fenkai*), and moreover convey strong protest to the U.S. government."[74] Such read the front page of the *People's Daily* on 23 May 1995. Anything that would raise the international status of Taiwan as an official government was an anathema to PRC leaders, and a visit by Lee to Cornell fell squarely into that category.[75] Despite what the PRC government perceived as previous assurances to the contrary, the Clinton administration had bowed to congressional pressure to permit the Lee visit. The PRC Foreign Ministry declared, "Regarding such a major issue of principle, the U.S. government contradicted itself, ate its own words, is there any international believability left to speak of!"[76]

This message—replete with the language of indignation and anger—was soon repeated through multiple channels, PRC Foreign Minister Qian Qichen summoned the American ambassador to "express extreme indignation (*fenkai*) and strong condemnation toward the abominable U.S. government actions that had violated Chinese sovereignty and have done great damage to the cause of peaceful unification."[77] Qian added, "the development of the situation has forced U.S. to have no choice but to strongly respond, the U.S. side bears the entire responsibility for this."[78] The Foreign Affairs Committees of the People's National Congress and the People's Political Consultative Committee echoed his comments. The former announced that its members "felt tremendous shock and indignation (*fenkai*)"; the latter expressed "extreme indignation (*fenkai*) and strong condemnation."[79] The spokesperson for the Taiwan Affairs Office also expressed "extreme righteous anger (*yifen*)."[80] A further opinion piece in the *People's Daily* noted that such actions "cannot but make people indignant (*fenkai*)."[81]

These words were supplemented quickly with an escalating series of actions. The first was to postpone the visit of Defense Minister Chi Haotian and cut short the visits of State Council Member Li Chaogui and Air Force Commander Yu Zhenwu.[82] Shortly thereafter, the PRC announced that it was suspending all talks regarding nuclear cooperation and the Missile Technology Control Regime.[83]

Moreover, it deferred plans for visits by the U.S. Deputy Assistant Secretary for Political and Military Affairs and the head of the U.S. Arms Control and Disarmament Agency.[84] Arms control was an issue of importance to the U.S. government, particularly given past PRC military sales and sensitive technology transfers to countries such as Pakistan and Iran—by stopping all talks, the PRC government was striking back at something which mattered to the United States.

All the same, the U.S. government made a conciliatory effort to convince its PRC counterparts that Lee's visit did not represent anything more than a private visit, U.S. Secretary of State Warren Christopher sent a letter to Qian, explaining that Clinton had chosen to allow the visit in order to prevent Congress from taking stronger measures and, furthermore, stating that the visit was purely private—no White House representatives would meet with Lee.[85] Shortly before Lee was to make his speech at Cornell, Clinton invited the Chinese ambassador Li Daoyu to the White House where he personally explained that the goal of Lee's visit was not to create "one China, one Taiwan," and reaffirmed a "one China" policy.[86] Suettinger nevertheless describes Li during his meeting with Clinton as "angry and insolent, clenching his fist and pumping his legs to augment his brusque talking points."[87] This was a small foretaste of what was to come.

Lee arrived on 7 June, marking the first time that a Taiwanese president had ever visited the continental United States. Even if he was not given "presidential treatment" by the U.S. government, Lee nonetheless enjoyed an impressive degree of celebrity, traveling in limousine motorcades, being received by flag waving supporters, meeting with senators, congressmen, and local officials, and attracting significant international media coverage. Although all this probably would have been sufficient to elicit a harsh response from the PRC government, it was Lee's speech at Cornell that both PRC officials and members of the

Clinton administration would later cite as the most flagrant provocation.[88] While Lee touched upon the possibility of reunification, he was clearly pushing the agenda of attaining international recognition for Taiwan. In his concluding remarks, Lee stated, "The people of the Republic of China on Taiwan are determined to play a peaceful and constructive role among the family of nations. . . . We say to friends in this country and around the world: We are here to stay."[89]

Following Lee's speech, the expressive displays of anger toward both Lee and the United States by PRC policy makers and the official press in the form of accusations, name calling, and expressions of indignation are too numerous to reprint here in full. According to one scholar, within the two months after the Cornell speech, official PRC newspapers had published more than four hundred personal attacks on Lee.[90] A typical example is the language of an editorial published in the *People's Daily*:

> At the instigation of the American government, he enacted the farce of "alumni diplomacy," and moreover played up "two Chinas," "one China, one Taiwan," carelessly laying bare his real intentions of "faking reunification, actually seeking independence" . . . If Lee Teng-hui dares fly in the face of the will of the people, continue down along this dangerous road, then he will bring disgrace and ruin upon himself, become a traitor of the Chinese people for all time.[91]

The United States was also the target of countless rhetorical assaults. For instance, one editorial stated, "Towards the American government's mistaken decision, the Chinese government expressed strong protest, the Chinese people, including Taiwanese compatriots, expressed extreme, righteous indignation (*fenkai*), and world opinion ceaselessly condemned America's perfidious behavior."[92] There was a common pattern to the more than a dozen editorials attacking the United States carried by the *People's Daily* and *People's Liberation Army Daily* in the immediate aftermath of the visa decision: harsh and often emotionally laden language (*bianyici*), pointed accusations, and warnings of explosive danger.[93] Added to this was the blame the PRC assigned to the United States for what it perceived as a violation of past agreements about the unofficiality of U.S. relations with Taiwan. Indeed, *People's Daily* commentaries and articles mentioned the three communiqués, and the alleged violation thereof, literally over a hundred times in the aftermath of Lee's visit; for the "one China" principle, the number of references was even higher.[94]

PRC officials augmented their signals with the announcement of further retaliatory measures. On 16 June, the PRC ambassador in Washington was recalled to Beijing "to report."[95] Soon afterwards, the PRC also declined to receive the new U.S. ambassador scheduled to rotate in, and for the first time since diplomatic relations were established between the United States and the PRC, neither country had ambassador-level representation in the other's capital.[96] The State Department additionally confirmed that the PRC had canceled previously scheduled mid- and lower-level meetings, but expressed hope that PRC officials would respond to a proposal of high-level meetings.[97] The PRC Foreign Ministry quickly rejected the offer in no uncertain terms, explaining, "The United States still maintains its mistaken position and has not yet done anything to mitigate the odious results caused by Lee Teng-hui's visit . . . The United States wants to simply rely on a few empty statements or do some kind of posturing, intending to act like this is something big, this is absolutely unacceptable."[98] In other words, on the government-to-government level, the PRC was giving the United States the silent treatment. Even private channels and "old friends of China" hit a wall—an unofficial delegation led by Henry Kissinger in the beginning of July "was treated to the full display of Beijing's anger over the Lee visit, including a finger wagging lecture by Li Peng."[99]

The first concrete action taken by the PRC government toward Taiwan was to postpone indefinitely the upcoming round of cross-strait talks. A representative of the PRC's Taiwan Affairs Office declared that Lee had "wantonly poisoned the atmosphere between the two sides of the strait, damaged cross-strait development, obstructed Chinese unification, evoked the extreme righteous anger (*yifen*) and the strong condemnation of Chinese both in China and abroad . . . under these circumstances, the second round of Wang-Koo talks cannot proceed as planned."[100]

During the last week of June, the PLA began its first set of exercises in the Taiwan Strait area. These maneuvers caused the Taiwanese stock market to drop and prompted the Taiwanese government to make an appeal for its citizens not to panic.[101] Little more than two weeks later the PRC announced that it would "conduct a training for launching a surface-to-surface guided missile into the open sea on the East China Sea"—a location to the northeast of Taiwan.[102] True to its word, a week later the PLA fired off six missiles at the ocean. While none of these missiles struck Taiwan, the Taiwanese stock market and currency did take significant hits, with the former dropping 139.7 points and the latter losing eight percent of its value.[103] In concert with this, the official PRC press ran a slew of articles officially denouncing Lee Teng-hui and the "Taiwanese separatists." A special editorial series focused specifically on Lee's speech at Cornell, bearing titles like "A Confession Encouraging Separatism" and "Lee Teng-hui Is the Wrongdoer Responsible for Damaging Cross-Strait Relations."[104]

In considering the rationale of the PRC government for its behavior, there is evidence important officials were angered by the U.S. decision. An officially sanctioned biography of PRC President Jiang Zemin states that "Jiang was personally offended by what he felt was deception on the part of the American president . . . China had been insulted, and Jiang was irate."[105] Qian Qichen, the

PRC foreign minister at the time, also evidently felt betrayed. As he wrote in his memoirs, "Only a month before, the U.S Secretary of State had personally made a promise to me, stating that the U.S. would not allow Lee Teng-Hui to visit the United States . . . the foreign minister of a super power made a promise, and suddenly goes back on his word, this cannot but not make a person feel shocked and furious (qifen)."[106] What is more, in the first weeks of June Jiang allegedly had received "more than 100 letters a day" from the People's Liberation Army and People's Aimed Police ranks demanding an angry reaction."[107]

That said, PRC officials also saw themselves in the strategic position of having to send a message to the United States and Taiwan, or in other words engage in "impression management." As Qian writes in his memoirs, "Facing the diplomatic challenge from the American side, the Chinese government could not but adopt a series of forceful retaliatory measures to erase the illusion that after the United States had done a little posturing the Chinese side would swallow this bitter fruit, to make the United States truly realize the gravity of the problem."[108] Similarly, Jiang stated, "The United States brazenly fabricates 'two Chinas,' 'one China, one Taiwan' . . . we of course have to respond forcefully."[109]

The result was the PRC government engaged in a coordinated campaign of emotionally laden rhetoric, retaliatory symbolic gestures, and aggressive shows of force. The case that the overt message was one of anger is quite straightforward.[110] PRC official statements were replete with words like indignation and anger, as well as other negative, emotionally laden terms,[111] of which the above is but a small sample. This rhetoric was deployed in private as well as public settings; used in leadership statements, government events, and the official press; and repeated at multiple levels. More importantly, there was an implicit logic threaded throughout PRC statements: the United States and Taiwan had violated the norms of the relationship, forcing the PRC to take action; measures were needed on the part of the transgressors to restore the relationship and reaffirm those norms; and further provocations would be "playing with fire," the consequences would be the responsibility of the transgressors. This last element added to the "passionate" flavor of the statements by suggesting that the PRC response was out of its own control.

In analyzing substantive actions, it is necessary not only to point out that they were aggressive and punitive, but to look at how they were timed and coordinated with the PRC's overt message. Once the Lee visit occurred, the PRC immediately began a process of retaliation, culminating in the missile launches. The PRC did not present its targets a list of measures it would sequentially take should certain demands not be met, as the standard coercion model would expect; rather, the PRC launched a series of punitive actions on short (or in some cases no) notice. A standard coercive approach would suggest that the threat of missile tests or military exercises should be made in advance, with the threat's realization made dependent on the actions of its target. Instead the PRC made known it would engage in displays of force only after Lee had visited Cornell and, from the PRC perspective, significant damage had already been done.[112] Moreover, the announcements of the exercises would appear to have been timed for absolute effect, seeking to shock Taiwan and harm it economically. The extent to which this was coordinated with the rhetorical assault is captured in the phrase si ping liu dan (four critiques, six bombs) used to describe the combination of accusatory essays and missiles.[113] Only after the PRC had taken a number of these measures did it signal a willingness to consider ending its high-level silent treatment of the U.S. government.

The Targets React

The argument of this paper is not simply that states overtly project an image of anger, but that this also shapes the perceptions and reactions of its targets. There would appear to be significant evidence that the U.S. side did view the PRC as showing anger. That numerous journalists and academics described the PRC behavior as angry or furious has already been noted above. More importantly, this perception appears to have been shared by U.S. policy makers. According to Secretary of State Warren Christopher "Beijing erupted"; he explicitly characterized the PRC reaction as "enraged."[114] Assistant Secretary Winston Lord later similarly stated, "the Chinese went ballistic after [Lee's] speech."[115] Secretary of Defense William Perry wrote that the visit "outraged many in China."[116] Richard Bock, of the American Institute in Taiwan, also called the PRC reaction "outraged."[117] In the words of Ambassador Stapleton Roy, who was in the PRC at the time, "The Chinese were angry because we had reversed ourselves on an important issue."[118]

The concrete response of the United States was to adopt a strategy of moderate conciliation, seeking to repair the relationship by reaffirming the prior norms concerning Taiwan. In July, Christopher gave a public speech in which he reiterated that the United States was not seeking to promote "two Chinas" or "one China, one Taiwan" and restated a U.S. commitment to the three communiqués.[119] Shortly thereafter, Christopher met with Qian and delivered a letter from Clinton. The letter explained that Lee's visit was purely personal, reaffirmed the "one China" policy, and stated that no change in policy had taken place.[120] It additionally contained a statement of U.S. policy later known as "Clinton's three noes": no support for Taiwan independence, no support for Taiwan membership in the United Nations, and no support for "two Chinas" or "one China, one Taiwan."[121] Christopher expressed the U.S. desire to establish a "constructive, equal partnership" with China and offered the possibility of a visit by Jiang to Washington, D.C.[122] Although Qian viewed the position of the United States on future visits

by Taiwanese leaders as still unresolved, he agreed to allow Undersecretary of State Peter Tarnoff to visit Beijing.[123]

Tarnoff arrived in Beijing in late August. According to Qian, Tarnoff did not just reaffirm that the United States would abide by the three communiqués, but also made the further assurance that all future visits by Taiwanese leaders would be of an unofficial purpose, would avoid any trappings of an official character, and would be extremely seldom, only reviewed on a case-by-case basis.[124] Qian states that this "answered and resolved the Chinese side's most serious concerns."[125] In response, the PRC announced that its ambassador would be returning to the United States and, moreover, that it would accept the new U.S. ambassador.[126]

Nevertheless, the PRC sought to "milk" the situation for further concessions.[127] Over the following two months the PRC continued to unsuccessfully press for a fourth communiqué that would cement a U.S. position against allowing the Taiwanese leadership to visit and furthermore sought a formal, summit-level meeting between Jiang and Clinton.[128] While neither of these were forthcoming, the PRC did, however, express its satisfaction that the United States had "understood the gravity and sensitivity of the problem of Taiwanese leaders visiting the United States."[129] The two sides eventually agreed on a "working meeting" between the two leaders when Jiang was in New York to visit the United Nations.[130] During the meeting, Clinton reiterated the mantra of abiding by the three communiqués, restated his "three noes" and also repeated the promise that all further visits by Taiwanese leaders would be "unofficial, private, and rare."[131]

Under these circumstances, the relationship continued to improve. In November, Assistant Secretary of Defense Joseph Nye arrived in Beijing, reportedly viewing his trip as one of "relationship repair."[132] Jiang and Vice President Albert Gore, during their meeting at an Asia-Pacific Economic

Conference (APEC), exchanged platitudes about improving US-PRC relations.[133] In fact, after the meeting Jiang stated that the relationship was "back on track."[134]

The question is how to explain this U.S. response. The decision to allow the Lee visit, in the words of Assistant Secretary Winston Lord, "a public flip flop . . . [an] awkward reversal of policy."[135] According to Robert Suettinger, the director for Asian affairs on the NSC at the time, "There was a broad recognition . . . we [the US] had screwed up, that we needed to take some step that would put the relationship back on a healthier course."[136] As a result, he states, "statements were made, and the letter was written, and the invitations were made, and so forth—as an effort to sort of assuage anger in reaction to what we thought was perhaps a decision that maybe should not have been made."[137] The United States did not simply see the PRC as angry, they saw themselves as bearing some degree of responsibility for the violation of longstanding norms regarding Taiwan, and therefore took actions to assuage anger. These actions on their face were primarily aimed at reaffirming the norms of the relationship, and the PRC—although trying to gainer further concessions—was eventually willing to accept those gestures.

What is more, as noted in an earlier section, the United States had only a muted reaction to PRC military exercises at the time. The reason that Ross gives—himself coming from the perspective of coercive diplomacy—is that U.S. officials "believed that as the 'offended party,' Beijing needed to vent its anger."[138] Suettinger confirms that "looking at this as an opportunity for the PLA to sort of vent its rage, we didn't really consider those military exercises and tests as anything that was severely over the top."[139] Crucially, the U.S. side did not see these military actions as a set of escalating coercive measures, but rather as a display that would abate—as one would expect from an angry actor. In the words of National Security Advisor Anthony Lake, "it was seen as something that would blow over."[140]

In short, a specific logic of interaction was at work. The U.S. side saw the appropriate response to PRC behavior as moderate conciliatory gestures with the assumption that the episode would eventually subside. Significantly, the U.S. side also implicitly accepted that it needed to take moves to repair a damaged relationship in part due to its own behavior. This suggests a situation much different from one in which an actor is responding to coercive threats. The perceptions, the reactions, and even the explicit justifications given by actors—such as Suettinger, who was closely involved in the U.S. decision-making process—all fit with a response one would expect to a diplomacy of anger.

Under other circumstances, the incident may have indeed "blown over." The problem was, however, that Taiwan was not making similar moves—lee was not interested in placating the PRC for that meant restricting Taiwan's international space and autonomy. Lee indeed noted that "Peking is angry," but conciliatory behavior toward the PRC would not win political points for Lee, who had little gain for his political agenda by placating the PRC leadership.[141] The Taiwanese government continued to push for further foreign presidential visits, called for admission to the UN, and engaged in military parades and counter-exercises of its own. In response to the missile exercises of July, Lee made two defiant speeches, one defending his speech at Cornell, the other advocating the buildup of Taiwan's military forces, claiming that separation was a fact, and further declaring that Taiwan would make every effort to participate in international organizations and activities.[142] Lee subsequently called PRC military exercises "useless and stupid."[143]

Having committed itself early on to the image of anger, not responding would indicate that the PRC would "swallow such bitter fruit." Consequently, the logic of provocation and angry reaction continued to play out between the PRC and

Taiwan, PRC military gestures escalated in tandem with its outraged rhetoric, claiming for instance that Lee's "self deceptive vain desire makes one's hair stand on end with anger."[144] Large-scale military displays in August and October were followed again by further exercises in November, this time in the lead-up to Taiwanese legislative elections.

The Episode Plays Itself Out

So while U.S.-PRC relations were apparently on the mend toward the end of 1995, PRC behavior toward Taiwan continued within the idiom of anger that had been triggered in June of that year. For every perceived affront on the part of Taiwan, the PRC responded with even more outraged rhetoric and military posturing. Most significantly, in March of 1996 Taiwan was holding its first presidential elections, representative of a further "provocative" step toward democratizing the island. This was particularly so since Lee was expected to win and the question was mainly whether or not he would garner an outright majority.[145]

In the month before the presidential elections, the PRC launched a new wave of displays of outrage against Lee. In one publicized meeting, for example, PRC leaders stated that Lee Teng-Hui had "betrayed the nation's interest, is producing national separatism, hurting the great cause of the unification of the motherland, has incited the great indignation (*fenkai*) of all Chinese people."[146] At the same time the PLA began to concentrate a massive force of troops and equipment across the strait from Taiwan.[147] The U.S. government took notice and conveyed to the PRC that "the United States had a clear interest in protecting peace across the Taiwan Strait," but also softened the message with an assurance that no further Taiwanese officials would be permitted to visit that year.[148] As the tensions showed no signs of abating, the Clinton administration began reviewing "combat scenarios that escalated up to nuclear war."[149] Concerned, U.S.

officials scheduled for PRC Vice Foreign Minister Liu Huaqiu to come to Washington in order to establish a dialogue.

On 5 March, just two days before Liu was scheduled to arrive in Washington, the PRC press announced a further round of military exercises including missile tests targeting zones just outside of two important Taiwanese harbors.[150] At the same time, an intensified wave of angry, anti-independence, anti-Lee commentaries appeared in the official PRC press. On 8 March, the PLA fired three missiles into the preannounced target zones. In Taiwan, stock prices fell and the Taiwanese Central Bank had to intervene to maintain the value of the currency as Taiwanese bought gold and U.S. dollars.[151] In Washington, U.S. officials met with Vice Minister Liu Hauqiu to condemn the exercises. In response, Liu reportedly "laid out a full menu of Chinese recriminations over the visa issue, over the sale of F-16s to Taiwan, over sanctions, and over American churlishness with regard to providing the technology that China needed for its development."[152]

Following the meeting with Liu, U.S. officials decided a response was necessary. On the one hand, the U.S. officials viewed the PRC behavior as "reckless and provocative."[153] According to Clinton, "China had gone too far."[154] On the other hand, Lord testified before Congress that "we have not concluded that there is any imminent threat to Taiwan."[155] While there were rumors that the PRC might engage in action against Taiwanese-held offshore islands, intelligence did not indicate anything signaling preparation for a large-scale attack.[156] Additionally, as the elections grew closer, the Taiwanese side had also begun making, according to Lord, "a lot of conciliatory statements . . . about reaffirming that the leaders are against independence, that they're for unification, albeit gradually, et cetera."[157] Consequently, the speaker for the Defense Department announced that "everybody expects that there will be a peaceful [sic]—these are military exercises, which will end when they're scheduled to end—they will not lead to military action—they're exercises—and that China and Taiwan will return to their policies of peaceful reunification."[158]

Nevertheless, the Clinton administration still had concerns that miscalculations or provocations by either side might result in escalation.[159] U.S. officials thus met secretly with Taiwanese representatives "urging Taiwan . . . not to provoke Beijing."[160] As Lord later stated, "We were urging Taiwan to cool it."[161] They also made clear that "this cross-Strait confrontation was in significant measure traceable to the Cornell episode, and . . . that the Administration would not look kindly on another effort by Taiwan to take unilateral action."[162] At the same time, they wanted to prevent the PRC from doing, in the words of Perry, "something stupid" and demonstrate U.S. interest in preserving regional peace and stability.[163] The result was that the administration elected to send two full carrier groups, those of the USS *Independence.* and USS *Nimitz*, into the waters near Taiwan.[164] The objective was, according to Christopher, "to calm the situation."[165] The administration decided against sending the carriers into the strait as this, Perry stated, "would be unnecessarily provocative."[166]

In the U.S. response one can again observe a particular logic—one that saw the PRC behavior as likely to subside, but still needing precautionary measures to contain the danger of escalation from further provocations. The US side thus sought not only to demonstrate its commitments in the region, but also to deter any further exacerbation of the situation, either through PRC or Taiwanese actions. Concurrently, the U.S. side itself made sure to avoid behaviors that might overly provoke the PRC and actively reiterated that it was "not going to change our policy on One China."[167]

Still, the accusatory and emotionally laden rhetoric against Taiwan, and Lee in particular, showed no signs of ebbing in the days leading up to the election.[168] The PLA supplemented this with live fire exercises in areas in the strait across from Taiwan and launched yet another missile into the target box southwest of Taiwan.[169] Although the PRC government declared on 15 March that its missile exercises had officially concluded, it simultaneously announced new, large-scale military exercises overlapping exactly with the week of the Taiwanese presidential election.[170] As this latter round of exercises began, the USS *Independence* maintained its distance in the seas east of Taiwan as the USS *Nimitz* rushed from the Persian Gulf to arrive in the western Pacific by 23 March.

Despite everything, on 23 March the Taiwanese presidential election took place as scheduled; Lee won the race with a clear majority. This large majority was arguably a consequence of the PRC eliciting the indignation of the Taiwanese electorate. Nevertheless, the PRC official press gave the results slightly positive spin, pointing out that the vote for the pro-independence DDP' candidate was "surpassed" by the combined percentage of votes given to the anti-independence candidates.[171] When the PRC government announced the successful completion of its military exercises, it lauded them as demonstrating that "the Chinese armed forces are resolved and able to safeguard the unity of the motherland and defend state sovereignty and territorial integrity."[172]

As expected, the tensions did abate following the elections. On 25 March, Lord stated, "China cools anti-Taiwan rhetoric . . . initial comments out of Taiwan indicate a desire to cool things down . . . clearly both sides in the first 48 hours or so have made moderate statements."[173] That day, the U.S. Defense Department also made known that the *Independence* would be returning to Japan.[174] In his subsequent inaugural speech, Lee announced that Taiwan "ha[d] absolutely no need for, and [could not] possibly choose, the path of so-called Taiwan independence," declared that "both sides should pursue eventual national unification," and stated that he was willing "to undertake a journey of peace to mainland China."[175]

To sum up, in this round as well, the PRC did not give its targets the option of taking steps that would avert a missile test as one would expect from the standard model of coercive threat. Instead, they were declared at short notice for maximum effect and accompanied with a message seeped in a rhetoric of anger, vague danger, and denunciations. Some have claimed that the objective of the last round of missile tests was to coerce Taiwanese into not voting for Lee. Certainly, the PRC leadership would have liked to damage Lee politically as much as possible, but it was evident to virtually all involved that Lee would be elected.[176] Nevertheless, to have "stood idly by" would have signaled acquiescence—to various audiences, including the Taiwanese people—particularly given the backdrop of the prior year. Once the elections were over, however, the PRC display subsided as the space opened for conciliatory gestures.

The After Effects

Following the crisis, there were no further visas for Taiwanese leaders to make "personal visits" to the United States. Moreover, the Clinton administration later acceded to PRC demands to publicize "Clinton's three noes." On the other hand, the U.S. military began to pay more attention to the PRC as a serious threat and cooperation with the Taiwanese military increased.[177] Significant from the perspective of this paper, however, is the effect the crisis had on perceptions.

Ambassador Stapleton Roy later stated, "What the Chinese response in 1995 did is it restored understanding in the Clinton administration about the sensitivity of this issue."[178] Lord similarly described the PRC behavior as sending "a signal about the sensitivity of [the Taiwan] issue."[179] On the PRC side, numerous scholars and analysts have also claimed this crisis played a key role in communicating to the United States the "sensitivity"

(*minganxing*) of the Taiwan issue.[180] Sensitivity implies something more than simply importance; it suggests a degree of volatility, even emotional precariousness.

This description points to the ways in which PRC behavior helped contribute to framing Taiwan as an emotional issue. For as Andrew Nathan and Robert Ross observe, "China's interest in Taiwan is often viewed as emotional and nationalistic."[181] This belief that the fate of Taiwan constitutes an emotional issue to the PRC and thus one that is extremely volatile—both for the external actors and the Chinese leadership—is shared by a number of important "China hands" and foreign policy actors. Robert Sutter, a China expert and former U.S. intelligence official, describes Taiwan's status as "a deeply emotional and nationalistic issue for Chinese leaders and citizens."[182] Similarly, Susan Shirk, the former deputy assistant secretary of state responsible for U.S.-PRC relations, writes that "No matter how reasonable Chinese foreign policy becomes, the Taiwan issue remains an emotional blind spot."[183]

Importantly, this view is evident in National Security Advisor Lake's discussion of the crisis afterwards:

> I don't think either Perry or Christopher or I really thought that the Chinese were not going to react. And of course it is always very difficult to tell how much a reaction is real and how much of it is posturing. But certainly in my subsequent talks with the Chinese I was more and more impressed with how visceral their view of Taiwan is as opposed to all other issues . . . You could just tell from their expressions. You could tell because on almost every issue that I would address with them, they would read their talking points. But on Taiwan, they almost didn't have to read them and the voice would rise and you could see the emotion in them.[184]

Consequently, when asked how he judged PRC intentions regarding Taiwan, Lake answered, "you just remember that they are emotional about this issue. And so let's not do this purely in games of rational actor models . . . That is why I think Taiwan is a dangerous issue."[185] Lake would take the lead on U.S. policy toward the PRC following the crisis.[186]

Lake's comments reflect something not captured by standard coercive accounts—the ways in which emotions are projected and received within international relations. On the one hand, it is unlikely that PRC officials would be long in their jobs if they engaged in unsanctioned shows of emotion. On the other, it is also unlikely that he was deceived by brilliant actors. Rather, as I argue above, what we are observing are the reciprocally enforcing effects of state policy and individual emotional dynamics through endorsement, encouragement, and emotional labor. In this manner, the PRC projected the image that the Taiwan issue was emotional and volatile, and provocations were to be avoided.

In fact, the U.S. officials would appear to have been acting with exactly such an image in mind when tensions reignited in 1999. Specifically, in that year Lee Teng-hui initiated a new round of cross-strait conflict by claiming that PRC-Taiwan relations were "nation-to-nation, or at least as special state-to-state ties, rather than internal ties within 'one China.'"[187] Over the succeeding weeks, PRC officials angrily denounced Lee as a "troublemaker," "national separatist," "traitor," and "reactionary."[188] The PRC then suspended cross-strait exchanges and cancelled the Association for Relations Across the Taiwan Straits (ARATS) Chair Wang Daohan's visit to Taiwan. On the military front, PRC fighters became more aggressive in the Taiwan Strait and the PLA test-fired a new missile.[189]

This time, the U.S. government responded by quickly reaffirming its commitment to the "one China" policy and several days later went on to characterize Lee's remarks as "unhelpful"—the same language used to describe PRC missile tests in 1995.[190] Behind the scenes, it sent the American Institute in Taiwan (AIT) Chair Richard Bush to Taiwan to meet with Lee and emphasize the U.S. commitment to the "one China" principle; simultaneously, NSC Senior Director Kenneth Lieberthal and Assistant Secretary of State Stanley Roth were dispatched to Beijing to state the same.[191] On 18 July, Clinton took the additional measure of telephoning Jiang to restress that the United States stood by its "one China" policy.[192] The United States then put such pressure on Lee not to make further provocative moves that in 2000 the latter was reportedly referring to Clinton administration representatives as "Beijing's running dogs."[193]

Future Research

An officially endorsed account of the crisis by a PRC scholar states, "Facing the vehement anger and condemnation (*qianglie fennu be qianze*) of the Chinese government and people, the American policymakers realized the graveness of the issue."[194] The goal of this paper has been to offer a theoretical way to make sense of such a claim. The diplomacy of anger differs from standard notions of coercive diplomacy in its expressive and substantive manifestations, the ways in which it shapes target expectations and responses, and its effects on subsequent perceptions. In each of these areas the 1995–96 Taiwan Crisis demonstrated dynamics that one would not be able to explain fully with standard approaches to coercion, but are explicable as the product of the diplomacy of anger. The diplomacy of anger combines a punitive response with demands for conciliatory action, while simultaneously sending a warning against further provocations—and thus provides the logic for the trifurcated punitive/compellent/deterrent combination of PRC behavior. None of this is to say that there are not occasions where standard theories of coercive diplomacy are sufficient; but, as the 1995–96 Taiwan Crisis demonstrates, there are instances where the complex dynamics of state-level displays of emotion require additional theoretical tools.

Indeed, the concept of the diplomacy of anger by no means needs to be limited to analyzing PRC behavior. For example, past episodes in the relations between Russia and the Ukraine—strained under the shadow of disputes regarding natural gas, Ukrainian relations with the EU, and other issues—also possibly fit the mold.[195] Ukrainian officials harassed Russian military personnel and ousted Russian diplomats; in return Russian officials made accusations against Ukrainian soldiers and also expelled Ukrainian diplomats.[196] Both sides hurled accusations and denunciations. Similarly, relations between Colombia and Venezuela went through periods of angry tensions, including blowing up bridges on the border, cutting diplomatic relations, and exchanging personal insults—prompting the Secretary General of the Organization of American States to ask both sides to "cool their passions" (*calmar el espíritu*).[197] These tensions only ended when a new Colombian president, Juan Manuel Santos, came into office with a more conciliatory stance.

Moving forward, however, the framework offered here can also conceivably be expanded to include other forms of state-level emotional displays as well. States do not simply project images of anger, they arguably also show remorse (such as in the case of German-Israeli relations), sympathy (international responses to the United States following 9/11), even hatred (Iranian behavior toward Israel). All these examples challenge us to reconsider the ways in which individual-level emotion interacts with state policy and the social logics of emotions shape the image actors states seek to project.

NOTES

1. *Economist*, 3–5 May 2008.
2. Andrew Nathan, "Forward," in *Across the Taiwan Strait: Mainland China, Taiwan, and the 1995–1996 Crisis*, ed. Suisheng Zhao (London: Routledge, 1999), viii.
3. See Robert S. Ross, "The 1995–96 Strait Confrontation: Coercion, Credibility, and the Use of Force," *International Security* 25, No. 2 (Fall 2000): 112–18; Wallace Thies and Patrick Bratton, "When Governments Collide in the Taiwan Strait," *Journal of Strategic Studies* 27, No. 4 (December 2004): 556–84; and Suisheng Zhao, "Military Coercion and Peaceful Offence: Beijing's Strategy of National Reunification with Taiwan," *Pacific Affairs* 72, No. 4 (Winter 1999–2000): 495–512. Zhao does not, however, theorize coercion.
4. The most recent instance being the PRC reaction to U.S. approval of arms sales to Taiwan in January 2010, see Helen Cooper, "China Angered as U.S. Approves Arms Sales to Taiwan," *New York Times*, 30 January 2010, 5; and John Pomfret, "U.S. Sells Arms to Taiwanese; and China Warns of Reprisals Beijing 'Strongly Indignant' About Sales," *Washington Post*, 30 January, 2010, A08.
5. Note, all sources with cited Chinese titles are the author's translation. Sources taken from the *Renmin Ribao People's Daily* and *Jiefangjun Bao [Liberation Army Daily]* are cited as *RMRB* and *JFJB* with date and page number, respectively. Chinese scholars Interviewed for this piece, as is practice, will not be cited by name.
6. Thomas Schelling, *Arms and Influence* (New Haven: Yale University Press, 1966), 1–7; Alexander George, "Coercive Diplomacy: Definition and Characteristics," In *The Limits of Coercive Diplomacy*, ed. Alexander L. George and William E. Simmons (Boulder, CO: Westview Press, 1994), 7–8; Daniel Byman and Matthew Waxman, *The Dynamics of Coercion: American Foreign Policy and the Limits of Military Might* (New York: Cambridge University Press, 2002), 1–10; and Robert Art, "Introduction," in *The United States and Coercive Diplomacy*, ed. Robert Art and Patrick Cronin (Washington, DC: United States Institute of Peace Press, 2003), 7–10.
7. Schelling, *Arms and Influence*, 69–78.
8. George, "Coercive Diplomacy," 1–2. George views compellence as too broad a term and thus provides two alternative categories.

9. Ross, "The 1995–1996 Strait Confrontation," 88.

10. The existing "three communiqués" from 1972, 1979, and 1982 are joint statements by the United States and the PRC that form a basis of official understanding regarding Taiwan.

11. Ibid., 91.

12. Ibid., 96.

13. Ibid., 109.

14. Ibid., 90.

15. Ibid.

16. Thies and Bratton, "When Governments Collide," 566.

17. Ibid., 576.

18. Ibid., 576.

19. Ibid., 571.

20. *RMRB*, 10 June 1995, 3.

21. *JFJB*, 21 March 1996, 1.

22. *RMRB*, 9 August 1995, 4; 19 September 1995, 1; and 17 March 1996, 3.

23. Alexander I., George, "Theory and Practice," in *The Limits of Coercive Diplomacy*, eds., Alexander L. George and William E. Simmons (Boulder, CO: Westview Press, 1994), 18.

24. David Shambaugh, 'The United States and China: A New Cold War?" *Current History* 94, no. 593 (September 1995): 241.

25. Importantly, the fact some of these actions would not have been known to the PRC public highlights that PRC behavior was also not simply for public consumption.

26. Byman and Waxman, *The Dynamics of Coercion*, 7–8; Robert Art, "Coercive Diplomacy: What Do We Know?" in *The United States and Coercive Diplomacy*, eds., Robert Art and Patrick Cronin (Washington, DC: United States Institute of Peace Press, 2003), 382–83.

27. *RMRB*, 21 June 1995, 1. See also *RMRB*, 6 June 1995, 4; 10 June 1995, 3; 12 June 1995, 6; 13 June 1995, 6; and 18 June 1995, 1.

28. *RMRB*, 5 July 1995, 4.

29. Robert Suettinger, interview by author, December 2008.

30. *Federal News Service*, "State Department Regular Briefing," 24 July 1995.

31. *Federal News Service*, "State Department Regular Briefing," 11 August 1995.

32. *Federal News Service*, "State Department Regular Briefing," 19 October 1995.

33. R. Jeffrey Smith, "China Plans Maneuvers Off Taiwan; Big Military Exercise Is Meant to Intimidate, U.S. Officials Say," *Washington Post*, 5 February 1996, A01, quoted in Robert Suettinger, *Beyond Tiananmen: Tim Politics of U.S.-China Relations, 1989–2000* (Washington, DC: Brookings Institution Press, 2003), 244.

34. Ross explains it in terms of a U.S. desire to let the PRC "vent" and let Lee Teng Hui suffer the "consequences" of his actions, although this suggests the U.S. side thought things would blow over as opposed to escalate. It is not clear from the perspective of coercion why the U.S. side would believe this. See Ross, "The 1995–1996 Strait Confrontation," 104.

35. George, "Theory and Practice," 20–21.

36. A Lexis-Nexis news search for the terms "Taiwan, China, and Lee," and "angry, anger, fury, furious, Ire, outrage, or enrage" for the period 21 May 1995 to 1 September 1995 returns over five-hundred hits.

37. June Dryer, "A History of Cross-Strait Interchange," in *Crisis in the Taiwan Strait*, eds., Chuck Downs and James Lilley (Washington, DC, National Defense University Press, 1997), 34; Richard D. Fischer, "China's Missiles Over the Taiwan Strait: A Political and Military Assessment," in *Crisis in the Taiwan Strait*, 169; James Garver, *Pace Off* (Seattle; University of Washington Press, 1997), 72; Shelly Rigger, *Politics in Taiwan* (New York: Routedge, 1999), 175; Andrew Scobell, *China's Use of Military Force* (New York: Cambridge University Press, 2003), 241; Robert Suettinger, *Beyond Tiananmen*, 220; Thies and Bratton "When Governments Collide," 565; Nancy Tucker, *Strait Talk* (Cambridge: Harvard University Press, 2009), 217; Suisheng Zhao, "Changing Leadership Perceptions," in *Across the Taiwan Straits*, ed. Suisheng Zhao (London: Routledge, 1999), 120.

38. Arthur S. Ding, "The Lessons of the 1995–1996 Military Taiwan Straight Crisis," in *The Lessons of History:*

The Chinese People's liberation Army at 75, eds., Laurie Burkitt, Andrew Scobell, and Larry M. Wortzel (Carlisle, PA: Strategic Studies Institute, 2003), 379.

39. Alexander Wendt, "The State as Person in International Theory," *Review of International Studies* 30, no. 2 (2004): 313.

40. Janice Stein, "Psychological Dimensions of International Decision Making and Collective Behavior," (unpublished manuscript, Toronto, 2011), 24.

41. See, for instance, Andrew A. G. Ross, "Coming in from the Cold: Constructivism and Emotions," *European Journal of International Relations* 12, No. 2 (June 2006): 197–222; Janice Stein, "Psychological Dimensions of International Decision Making and Collective Behavior"; and Roger D. Petersen, *Understanding Ethnic Violence* (Cambridge: Cambridge University Press, 2002).

42. Alexander Wendt, "The State as Person in International Theory," 314.

43. Jonathan Mercer, "Human Nature and the First Image: Emotion in International Politics," *Journal of International Relations and Development* 9 (September 2006): 288–303; Mercer, "Emotional Beliefs," *International Organization* 64, no. 1 (Winter (2010): 1–31; and Rose McDermott, The Feeling of Rationality," *Perspectives on Politics* 2, no. 4 (December 2004): 691–706.

44. Andrew A. G. Ross, "Coming in from the Cold: Constructivism and Emotions."

45. Karin Fierke, "Whereof We Can Speak, Thereof We Must Not Be Silent: Trauma, Political Solipsism and War," *Review of International Studies* 30, no. 4 (2004): 471–91; Paul Saurette, "You Dissin Me? Humiliation and Post 9/11 Global Politics," *Review of International Studies* 32, no. 3 (July 2006): 495–522; and Oded Löwenheim and Gadi Heimann, "Revenge in International Politics," *Security Studies* 17, no. 4 (October 2008): 685–724.

46. Löwenheim and Heimann, "Revenge in International Politics," 702.

47. Ibid., 708.

48. For general reviews of anger and its associated behaviors, see James R. Averill, *Anger and Aggression: An Essay on Emotion* (New York: Springer Verlag, 1982),

318–25; Richard S. Lazarus, *Emotion and Adaptation* (New York, NY: Oxford University Press, 1991), 217–27; and Scott Schieman, "Anger," in *Handbook of the Sociology of Emotions*, ed. Jon Stets and Jonathan Turner (New York: Springer, 2007), 494–95.

49. Averill, *Anger and Aggression*, 318.

50. Schieman, "Anger," 508–9.

51. Averill, *Anger and Aggression*, 320–21.

52. This understanding of anger is one that it is not limited to "the West." Chinese sources also provide very similar characterizations. See Feng Jiangping, *Cuozbe xinlixue* (Psychology of Frustration) (Shanxi: Shanxi Jiaoyu Chubanshe, 1991), 93–98; Meng Zhaolan, *Qingxu xinlixue* [Emotional Psychology]. (Beijing: Beijing Daxue Chubanshe, 2005), 160–61, 194–97; Meng Zhaolan, *Reniei qingxu* [Human Emotions] (Shanghai Renmin Chubanshe,1989), 268–69, 321–23; Liu Fang, *Qingxu guantixue* [Emotional Management Studies] (Beijing: Zhongguo Wuzi Chubanshe, 1999), 238–40; and Luo Zheng, *Qingxu kongzhi de lilan yu fangfa* (Emotion Control: Theory and Methods] (Beijing: Guangming Ribao Chubanshe, 1989), 33–35.

53. Erving Goffman, *The Presentation of Self in Everyday Life* (Garden City, NY: Doubleday, 1959), 77–105.

54. Ibid., 16–19.

55. Jacques Hymans, "The Arrival of Psychological Constructivism," *International Theory* 2, no. 3 (November 2010): 462.

56. See for instance the work of Downs and Saunders on variations in PRC behavior toward Japan concerning the disputed Senkaku/Diaoyu Islands. Erica Downs and Phillip Saunders, "Legitimacy and the Limits of Nationalism," *International Security* 23, no. 3 (Winter 1998–1999): 114–46.

57. Zou Jianhua, *Waijiaobu Fayamen Jiemi* [The Speaker of the Foreign Ministry Reveals Secrets] (Beijing: Shijie Zhishi Chubanshe, 2005), 39.

58. Erving Goffman, *The Presentation of Self in Everyday Life*, 208.

59. Robert Jervis, *The Logic of Images in International Relations* (New York, NY: Columbia University Press, 1989 [1970]), xvi.

60. Ibid., xiv.

61. Robert Jervis, *The Logic of Images*, xvi.

62. Averill, *Anger and Aggression*, 320–21.

63. Zou Jianhua, *Waijiaobu Fayanren Jiemi*, 17.

64. Löwenheim and Heimann, "Revenge in International Politics"; and Saurette, "You Dissin Me?"

65. Adie Hochschild, "Emotion Work, Feeling Rules, and Social Structure," *American Journal of Sociology* 85, no. 3 (November 1979): 551–75; and Kathryn Lively, "Emotions in the Workplace," in *Handbook of the Sociology of Emotions*, eds., Jan Stets and Jonathan Turner (New York: Springer, 2007), 560–90.

66. Paul Ekman, *Emotions Revealed* (New York: Times Books, 2003).

67. Relevant to the PRC, words in the anger "family" used in diplomatic language include *fennu, fenkai, yifen*, and *jilie buman*. *Fenkai* and *yifen* are both frequently translated as "Indignation" or "righteous indignation" and like *fennu* (anger), carry moral and ethical connotations, suggesting outrage at a perceived Injustice. *Jilie buman* can be translated as "extreme dissatisfaction." Examples of terms that also give a derogatory feel (*bianyici*) are words such as *gongran* (brazenly) and *dasi* (wantonly). For more on anger words, see Feng Sihai and Huang Xiting, "Qingxu Xingrongci Ciyi de Mohu Fuzhi" [Fuzzy Evaluation Statistics for Emotional Adjective Semantics] *Xinii Xuebao* 36, no. 6 (2004): 704–11.

68. This is similar to Jervis's distinction between signals and indices, although less stringent in the sense that Jervis requires indices to be seen as non-manipulable indicators of sincerity. See Jervis, *Logic of Images*, 18–40.

69. Ibid., 19.

70. See Bill Gates and Martin Klieber, "China's Space Odyssey," *Foreign Affairs* (May/June 2007): 2–6.

71. Schelling, *Arms and Influence*, 36–43.

72. Neta Crawford, "The Passion of World Politics," *International Security* 24, no. 4 (Spring 2000): 155. This parallels, and adds an emotionally reinforcing dynamic, to existing arguments about audience costs. See James Fearon, "Domestic Political Audiences and the Escalation of International Disputes," *American Political Science Review* 88, no. 3 (September 1994); and Jessica Weeks, "Autocratic Audience Costs," *International Organization* 62, no. 1 (Winter 2008): 35–64.

73. Alexander L. George and Andrew Bennett, *Case Studies and Theory Development in the Social Sciences* (Cambridge: MIT Press, 2005), 75.

74. *RMRB*, 23 May 1995, 1.

75. Chen Qimao, "The Taiwan Strait Crisis," in *Across the Taiwan Strait*, ed. Suisheng Zhao (London: Routledge, 1999): 140–41.

76. *RMRB*, 23 May 1995, 1.

77. *RMRB*, 24 May 1995, 1.

78. Ibid.

79. *RMRB*, 25 May 1995, 1.

80. *RMRB*, 27 May 1995, 1.

81. *RMRB*, 26 May 1995, 6.

82. Liu Liandi, *Zhong-mei guanxi de guiji* [The Trajectory of Sino-U.S. Relations] (Beijing: Shishi Chubanshe, 2001), 69.

83. Ibid., 70.

84. *RMRB*, 29 May 1995, 1.

85. Qian Qichen, *Waijiao Shiji* [Ten Diplomatic Episodes] (Beijing: Shijie Zhishi Chubanshe, 2003), 265.

86. Tao Wenzhao, *Zhong-mei guanxi shi* [History of U.S.-- China Relations] (Shanghai: Shanghai Renmin Chubanshe, 2004), 266.

87. Suettinger, *Beyond Tiananmen*, 221.

88. See for example Alan Romberg, *Rein in at the Brink of the Precipice* (Washington, DC: Stimson Center, 2004), 166; and Jiang Dinnming, *Taiwan yi Jiu wa* [Taiwan 1995] (Beijing: Jiu Zhou Tushu Chubanshe, 1996), 482–84.

89. Ibid., 509–23.

90. Zhao, "Changing Leadership Perceptions," 113.

91. Jiang, *Taiwan yi jiu jiu wu*, 484.

92. *RMRB*, 18 June 1995, 1.

93. See *RMRB*, 26 May 1995, 6; 30 May 1995, 6; 8 June 1995, 4; 9 June 1995, 6; 10 June 1995, 3; 11 June 1995, 2; 12 June 1995, 6; 13 June 1995, 6; 16 June 1995, 6; 18 June 1995, 1; 20 June 1995, 6; 26 June 1995, 7; *JFJB*, 25 May 1995, 4; 8 June 1995, 4; 10 June 1995, 4; and 16 June 1995, 3.

94. A cursory count for the period between June and October finds the three communiqués mentioned 125 times: for the "one China principle" that number is 185.

95. Liu, *Zhong-mei guanxi de guiji*, 72.

96. Garver, *Face Off*, 73.

97. *Federal News Service*, "State Department Regular Briefing," 21 June 1995.

98. *RMRB*, 23-June 1995, 1.

99. Suettinger, *Beyond Tiananmen*, 231.

100. *RMRB*, 17 June 1995, 1.

101. Ibid.

102. *Xinhua News Agency*, "pla Announces Missile-Launch Training on East China Sea," 18 July 1995 (Item No. 071813).

103. Jiang, *Taiwan yi jiu jiu wu*. 336.

104. RMRB, 24 July 1995, 1; and 27 July 1995, 1.

105. Robert Kuhn, *The Man Who Changed China* (New York: Crown, 2004), 267–68.

106. Qian Qichen, *Waijiao Shiji* [Ten Diplomatic Episodes] (Beijing: Shijie Zhishi Chubanshe, 2003), 305–6.

107. *South China Morning Post*, 17 July 1995, 1. See also Robert Kuhn, *The Man Who Changed China*, 268.

108. Qian, *Waijiao Shiji*, 308.

109. Wang Yongqin, Zhongguo Jie [The China Knot] (Beijing: Xinhua Chubanshe, 2003), 192.

110. Chinese scholars also describe PRC behavior in these terms. See for instance, Su Ge, *Meiguo Dui Hua Zhengce yu Taiwan Wenii* [U.S. policy Toward China and the Taiwan Issue] (Beijing: Shijie Zhishi Chubanshe, 1998), 743; and Su Yan, *Taiwan Wenii yu Zhongmei Guauxi* [The Taiwan Issue and U.S.--China Relations] (Beijing: Beijing University Press: 2009), 259.

111. Such as "gongran" (brazenly), "cubao" (crudely), and "dasi" (wantonly).

112. Michael Swaine, "Chinese Decision Making Regarding Taiwan, 1979–2000," in *The Making of Chinese Foreign and Security Policy in the Era of Reform, 1978–2000*, ed. David M. Lampton (Stanford: Stanford University Press, 2001), 322–24.

113. Yu Keli and Jia Yaobin, *Haixia Liang'an Guanxi* [Cross-Strait Relations] (Wuhan: Changliang Chubanshe, 2010), 355.

114. Warren Christopher, *Chances of a Lifetime* (New York: Scribner, 2001), 244, 287.

115. Assistant Secretary of State Winston Lord, interview by author, September 2009.

116. Ashton Carter and William Perry, *Preventive Defense* (Washington, DC: Brookings Institution Press, 1999), 94.

117. "Interview with J. Richard Bock," *The Foreign Affairs Oral History Collection*, http://memory.loc .gov/cgi-bin/query/r?ammem/mfdip:@field(DOCID ±mfdip2004boc01), accessed August 2011.

118. Ambassador Stapleton Roy, former U.S. Ambassador to the PRC, interview by author, February 2009.

119. *Federal News Service*, "National Press Club Luncheon Speaker Secretary of State Warren Christopher," 28 July 1995.

120. Romberg, *Rein in at the Brink*, 170.

121. Suettinger, *Beyond Tiananmen*.

122. Qian, *Waijiao Shiji*, 312.

123. Ibid.

124. Qian, *Waijiao Shiji*, 313.

125. Ibid.

126. Tao, *Zhong-mei guanxi shi*, 268.

127. Suettinger, interview by author, December 2008.

128. Ross, "The 1995–1996 Strait Confrontation," 97–99.

129. *RMRB*, 29 September 1995, 6.

130. Xiong Zhiyong, *Bainian zhong-mei guanxi* [One Hundred Years of Sino U.S. Relations] (Beijing: Shijle Zhishi Chubanshe, 2006), 360.

131. John Harris "Clinton, Jiang Confer; Thaw in Relations Seen; Differences With China Remain, U.S. Aides Say," *Washington Post*, 24 October 1995, A01; and Xiong, *Bainian zbong-mei guanxi*, 361.

132. Suettinger, *Beyond Tiananmen*, 243-44; and Ross, "The 1995–1996 Strait Confrontation," 103.

133. China Pleased With Gore Meeting; Relations 'Back on Track,'" *Associated Press*, 18 November 1995; and RMRB, 19 November 1995, 1.

134. "China Pleased With Gore Meeting," *Associated Press*, 18 November 1995.

135. "Interview with Winston Lord," *The Foreign Affairs Oral History Collection*, http://memory.loc.gov/cgi

-bin/query?ammem/mfdip:@field%28DOCID
fdip20041or02%29, accessed August 2011.

136. Robert Suettinger, former director for Asian affairs
on the National Security Council, interview by
author, December 2008.

137. Interview by author.

138. Ross, "The 1995–1996 Strait Confrontation," 104.

139. Suettinger, interview by author, December 2008.

140. Anthony Lake, interview by author, September 2009.

141. Government Information Office, *Lee Teng-hui's
Selected Addresses and Messages 1996*, (Taipei:
Government Information Office, 1997), 29.

142. Jiang, *Taiwan yi hu hu wu*, 530–33.

143. "Relations with China," *BBC Summary of World
Broadcasts*, 20 November 1995.

144. *RMRB*, 29 September 1995, 11.

145. Hung-mao Tien, "Taiwan in 1995: Electoral Politics
and Cross-Strait Relations," *Asian Survey* 36, no. 1
(1996): 39; and Shelly Rigger, *Politics in Taiwan*
(New York: Routedge, 1999), 174.

146. *RMRB*, 31 January 1996, 1.

147. Garver, *Face Off*, 99–100.

148. Mann, *About Face*, 335; and Fisher, "China's
Missiles Over the Taiwan Strait," 183.

149. Suettinger, *Beyond Tiananmen*, 251.

150. *Xinhua News Agency*, "pla to Conduct Missile
Launching Trainings in Hast, South China Seas," 5
March 1996 (Item No. 0305024).

151. Peter Montagnon and Laura Tyson. "Chinese Cloud
Over Taiwan Stocks—Emerging Markets," *Financial Times*, 11 March 1996, 28.

152. Patrick Tyler, *A Great Wall: Six Presidents and China*
(New York: PublicAffairs, 1999), 32.

153. *Federal News Service*, "State Department Regular
Briefing," 8 March 1996.

154. Bill Clinton, *In My Life* (New York: Random
House, 2005), 703.

155. *Federal News Service*, "House International Relations Committee, Subcommittee on Asia and the
Pacific Hearing," 14 March 1996.

156. Suettinger, *Beyond Tiananmen*, 258; and *Federal
News Service*, "The U.S., China, and Taiwan,"
25-March 1996.

157. *Federal News Service*, "The U.S., China, and
Taiwan," 25 March 1996.

158. *Federal News Service*, "Defense Department Regular
Briefing," 19 March 1996.

159. "Interview with Winston Lord," *The Foreign Affairs
Oral History Collection*.

160. Suettinger, *Beyond Tiananmen*, 257.

161. "Interview with Winston Lord," *The Foreign Affairs
Oral History Collection*.

162. "Interview with Howard H. Lange," *The Foreign
Affairs Oral History Collection*, http://memory.loc
.gov/cgi-bin/query/r?ammem/mfdipblb:@field
%28DOCID±@lit%28mfdipbib001389%29%29,
accessed August 2011.

163. Suettinger, *Beyond Tiananmen*, 255.

164. Mann, *About Face*, 336–37; and Suettinger, *Beyond
Tiananmen*, 255.

165. Christopher, *In the Stream of History*, 426.

166. Carter and Perry, *Preventative Defense*, 98.

167. "Interview with Winston Lord," *The Foreign Affairs
Oral History Collection*.

168. See, for example, *RMRB*, 18 March 1996, 4; 20
March 1996, 5; 21 March 1996, 4; 23 March 1996,
4; and JFJB, 16 March 1996, 4; 21 March 1996, 1;
23 March 1996, 4.

169. Office of Naval Intelligence, Chinese Exercise Strait
961, 8 25 March 1996.

170. *Xinhua News Agency*, "PLA's Missile Launching
Trainings End," 15 March 1996 (Item No.
0315145); *Xinhua News Agency*, "PLA to Conduct
Joint Ground, Naval, Air Exercises in Taiwan
Straits," 15 March 1996 (Item No. 0315144).

171. *Xinhua News Agency*, "PLA Military Exercises in
Taiwan Straits Successful," 25 March 1996 (Item
No. 0325097).

172. Ibid.

173. *Federal News Service*, "The U.S., China, and
Taiwan," 25 March 1996.

174. *Japanese Economic News Wire*, "Independence Sailing Back to Yokosuka From Taiwan," 27 March
1996.

175. "Inaugural Address by Lee Teng-hui," http://www
.taiwan-panorama.com/en/print.php

?id=199668506016E.TXT&table=2, accessed August 2011.

176. Ji You, "Taiwan in the Political Calculations of the Chinese Leadership," *The China Journal*, 36 (July 1996): 123.

177. Ross, "The 1995–1996 Strait Confrontation," 117.

178. Roy, interview by author, February 2009.

179. "Interview with Winston Lord," *The Foreign Affairs Oral History Collection*.

180. Chen Chao, "Lengzhan hou mei-tal junshi guanxi de fazhan jiqi yingxiang" (Post-Cold War Development of US-Taiwan Military Relations and their Influence] *Shijie jingli yu zhengzhi luntan*, no. 2 (2003): 83; Ma Wanyi, "Lengzhan hou mei-tai guanxi de yanbian" [Evolution of Post-Cold War U.S.-Taiwan Relations] *Dangdai yatai: tathal guancha*, no. 10 (1999): 64; and Wu Xinbo, "Fanying yu tiaozheng: 1996 nian taihal weiji yu meiguo dui tai zhengce" [Response and Adjustment: 1996 Taiwan Strait Crisis and U.S. Policy Toward Taiwan] *Fudan xuebao (shebui kexue ban)*, no. 2 (2004): 57.

181. Andrew J. Nathan and Robert S. Ross, *The Great Wall and the Empty Fortress* (New York: W. W. Norton, 1997), 206.

182. Robert G. Sutter, *Chinese Foreign Relations* (New York: Rowan and Littlefield, 2008), 201.

183. Susan L. Shirk, *China, Fragile Superpower* (New York: Oxford University Press, 2007), 265.

184. Lake, Interview by author, September 2009.

185. Ibid.

186. Suettinger, *Beyond Tiananmen*, 263.

187. Xu Xuejiang, *Weixian De Yi Bu* [A Dangerous Step] (Beijing, Xinhua Chubanshe, 1999), 70.

188. Guowuyuan Taiwan Shiwu Bangongshï, *Zhongguo Taiwan Wenii*, 131.

189. Suettinger, *Beyond Tiananmen*, 383–84.

190. *Federal News Service*, "State Department Regular Briefing," 12 July 1999; and *Federal News Service*, "State Department Regular Briefing," 15 July 1999.

191. Richard Bush, "United States Policy Towards Taiwan," in B*reaking the China-Taiwan Impasse*, ed. Donald Zagoria (Westport: Praeger Publishers, 2003), 16.

192. Liu, *Zhong-mei guanxi de guiji*, 263.

193. Sheng Lijun, *China and Taiwan* (New York: Palgrave, 2002), 47.

194. Su, *Meiguo Dui Hua Zhengce yu Taiwan Wenii*, 743.

195. Steven Pifer, *Crisis Between Ukraine and Russia* (Washington, DC: Council on Foreign Relations, 2009).

196. "Crimea Tense as Ukraine and Russia Swap Barbs," *New York Times*, 28 August 2008, 4; and "Ukraine, Russia Expel Diplomats," *UPI*, 30 July 2009.

197. *VOA News*, "Chávez rompe relaciones con Colombia," ["Chávez breaks relations with Colombia"], 22 July 2010.

INTERGOVERNMENTAL ORGANIZATIONS, INTERNATIONAL LAW, AND NONGOVERNMENTAL ORGANIZATIONS

7

International organizations such as the United Nations (UN) are major actors in international relations. One of the key tasks of the UN, regional organizations, and ad hoc state coalitions is peacekeeping in countries that are at risk of war. Virginia Page Fortna, in an excerpt from her book *Does Peacekeeping Work? Shaping Belligerents' Choices after Civil War* (2008), poses two seemingly simple questions: Does peacekeeping work, and if so, how? Drawing on both statistical data and case studies, she finds not only that peacekeepers deploy to the most complicated cases, but also that the risk of war resuming is reduced by 55 percent or more when peacekeepers are deployed. While Fortna shows that peacekeeping does work under certain conditions, Samantha Power, in a selection from *The Atlantic*, explains why neither the United Nations and its bureaucracy nor the United States did more to stop the 1994 genocide in Rwanda. According to Power, both American politicians and UN bureaucrats are to blame.

What explains how international institutions facilitate cooperation more generally? Robert O. Keohane, in his highly regarded book *After Hegemony: Cooperation and Discord in the World Political Economy* (1984), lays out the theory of liberal institutionalism to explain how such institutions make cooperation possible despite the absence of a sovereign enforcement power standing above states. He explains that international institutions (or "international regimes") establish rules around which expectations converge. Rules reduce the costs of transactions, facilitate bargaining across different issue areas, and provide information that reduces the risk of cheating. By way of contrast, John J. Mearsheimer, the quintessential realist, is skeptical about the impact of international institutions. In his excerpt, he delineates the flaws of liberal institutionalist theory, arguing that international institutions exert no independent influence of their own because they simply reflect the underlying power and interests of states.

While the debate over the independence of international institutions continues, so, too, is there debate over international law. Does international law offer states a fixed standard to judge state behavior? Or is it a resource used by states to interpret and justify their behavior and that of others? Ian Hurd tackles this question using the law of humanitarian intervention. In a carefully reasoned argument, he makes the case that humanitarian intervention is both legal and illegal depending on the sources of the law. "The law may be incoherent," he concludes.

In addition to intergovernmental organizations (IGOs) and international law, research on nongovernmental organizations (NGOs), social movements, and transnational advocacy networks has expanded since the 1990s. Using a constructivist approach, Margaret E. Keck and Kathryn Sikkink, in an excerpt from their award-winning book *Activists beyond Borders: Advocacy Networks in International Politics* (1998), show how such networks develop by "building new links among actors in civil societies, states, and international organizations."

Virginia Page Fortna

FROM *DOES PEACEKEEPING WORK?*

Peacekeeping and the Peacekept * * *

The Questions

In countries wracked by civil war, the international community is frequently called upon to deploy monitors and troops to try to keep the peace. The United Nations, regional organizations, and sometimes ad hoc groups of states have sent peacekeepers to high-profile trouble-spots such as Rwanda and Bosnia and to lesser-known conflicts in places like the Central African Republic, Namibia, and Papua New Guinea. How effective are these international interventions? Does peacekeeping work? Does it actually keep the peace in the aftermath of civil war? And if so, how? How do peacekeepers change things on the ground, from the perspective of the "peacekept," such that war is less likely to resume? These are the questions that motivate this [project].

As a tool for maintaining peace, international peacekeeping was only rarely used in internal conflicts during the Cold War, but the number, size, and scope of missions deployed in the aftermath of civil wars has exploded since 1989. Early optimism about the potential of the UN and regional organizations to help settle internal conflicts after the fall of the Berlin Wall was soon tempered by the initial failure of the mission in Bosnia and the scapegoating of the UN mission in Somalia.[1] The United States in particular became disillusioned with peacekeeping, objecting to anything more than a minimal international response in war-torn countries (most notoriously in Rwanda). Even in Afghanistan and Iraq, where vital interests are now at stake, the United States has been reluctant to countenance widespread multilateral peacekeeping missions. But the demand for peacekeeping continues apace. In recent years, the UN has taken up an unprecedented number of large, complex peacekeeping missions, in places such as the Congo, Liberia, Haiti, and Sudan.

Through these ups and downs, scholars and practitioners of peacekeeping have debated the merits of the new wave of more "robust" and complex forms of peacekeeping and peace enforcement developed after the Cold War, and even the effectiveness of more traditional forms of peacekeeping.[2] However, this debate is hampered by shortcomings in our knowledge about peacekeeping. Despite a now vast literature on the topic, very little rigorous testing of the effectiveness of peacekeeping has taken place. We do not have a very good idea of whether it really works. Nor do we have an adequate sense of how exactly peacekeeping helps to keep the peace.

Casual observers and many policymakers opposed to a greater peacekeeping role for the international community can point to the dramatic failures that dominate news coverage of peacekeeping, but rarely acknowledge the success stories that make less exciting news. Meanwhile, most analysts

From Virginia Page Fortna, *Does Peacekeeping Work? Shaping Belligerents' Choices after Civil War* (Princeton and Oxford: Princeton University Press, 2008), Chaps. 1, 7. Some of the author's notes have been omitted.

of peacekeeping draw lessons from a literature that compares cases and missions, but with few exceptions, examines only cases in which peacekeepers are deployed, not cases in which belligerents are left to their own devices. This literature therefore cannot tell us whether peace is more likely to last when peacekeepers are present than when they are absent. Surprisingly little empirical work has addressed this question. Moreover, the few studies that do address it, at least in passing, come to contradictory findings. Some find that peacekeeping makes peace last longer, some find that it does not, and some find that only some kinds of peacekeeping are effective.[3] A closer look is clearly needed.

The literature on peacekeeping is also surprisingly underdeveloped theoretically. Causal arguments about peacekeeping are therefore often misinformed. Opponents of intervention dismiss peacekeeping as irrelevant, or worse, counterproductive.[4] Proponents, on the other hand, simply list the functions of peacekeeping (monitoring, interposition, electoral oversight, etc.), describing its practices with little discussion of how exactly the presence of peacekeepers might influence the prospects for peace. Little theoretical work has been done to specify what peacekeepers do to help belligerents maintain a cease-fire, or how peacekeepers might shape the choices made by the peacekept about war and peace.

Further, most existing studies of peacekeeping focus almost exclusively on the perspective of the peacekeepers or the international community. In discussions of mandates, equipment and personnel, relations among national contingents or between the field and headquarters, and so on, it is easy to lose track of the fundamental fact that it is the belligerents themselves who ultimately make decisions about maintaining peace or resuming the fight. Only by considering the perspective of the peacekept—their incentives, the information available to them, and their decision making—can we understand whether and how peacekeeping makes a difference.

In short, our current understanding of peacekeeping suffers from three gaps: we know too little about whether or how much peacekeepers contribute empirically to lasting peace, we lack a solid understanding of the causal mechanisms through which peacekeepers affect the stability of peace, and we know too little about the perspective of the peacekept on these matters. This project aims to rectify these shortcomings. [Discussion] draws on theories of cooperation and bargaining in international relations to develop the causal mechanisms through which peacekeepers might affect the decisions belligerents make about maintaining peace or returning to war. It assesses the empirical effects of peacekeeping by comparing (both quantitatively and qualitatively) civil conflicts in which peacekeeping was used to conflicts in which peacekeepers were not deployed. And it evaluates the causal mechanisms of peacekeeping by drawing on the perspective of the belligerents themselves.

Two simple questions drive this study: does peacekeeping work? And if so, how? Answering these questions is not so simple, however. To know whether peace lasts longer when international personnel are present than when belligerents are left to their own devices, we need to compare both types of cases. But we also need to know something about where peacekeepers tend to be deployed. Unlike treatments in a controlled laboratory experiment, peacekeeping is not "applied" to war-torn states at random. If the international community follows the common policy prescriptions to send peacekeepers when there is strong "political will" for peace and where the chances for success are high (that is, to the easy cases), then a simple comparison of how long peace lasts with and without peacekeeping would misleadingly suggest a very strong effect for peacekeeping. If, on the other hand, peacekeepers are sent where they are most needed—where peace is otherwise hardest to keep, then a simple comparison would lead us to conclude, again incorrectly, that peacekeeping is useless or even counterproductive.[5] To address whether and how peacekeeping works, I must first answer the question of why peacekeepers deploy to some cases and not others. The first empirical step in this project must therefore be to examine where peacekeepers go. The [project] therefore addresses three questions: Where do peacekeepers go? Do they make peace more likely to last? Through what causal mechanisms do they operate?

This project aims to have a direct impact on the policy debates over peacekeeping. It furthers our understanding of why some conflicts draw in international peacekeepers while others do not. It goes on to provide clear evidence that this policy tool is indeed extremely effective at maintaining peace, substantially reducing the risk of another war. And it spells out how peacekeeping works, so that more effective strategies for maintaining peace can be developed by the international community.

■   ■   ■

Conclusion and Implications

[The project] asks three empirical questions: Where do peacekeepers go? Does peacekeeping work? And if so, how does it work? This [discussion] summarizes the answers to these questions, drawing out implications for our understanding of the problem of recidivism after civil wars, and especially for policymakers trying to reduce it.

The first question is important for evaluating the other two, but it is also interesting in its own right. While existing studies of this question have focused on choices made by the international community, I argue that choices made by the belligerents themselves are as important, at least for the consent-based missions that make up the bulk of peacekeeping. Not surprisingly, peacekeeping is a matter of both supply and demand. That peacekeeping is unlikely in civil wars within or next door to the permanent five members of the Security Council is testament to a supply-side effect.

But the fact that peacekeeping is generally more likely when rebels are relatively strong (but not strong enough to win outright) reflects dynamics on the demand side. The case studies illustrate this point well. Whether or not consent-based peacekeeping happened in Bangladesh, Mozambique, and Sierra Leone was the result of choices made by the belligerents, and particularly by the relative bargaining strength of rebels and the government.

For the purposes of the rest of the analysis, the most important answer to the question of where peacekeepers go, is that they are much more likely to deploy when the danger of war recurring is particularly high. That is, peacekeepers select into the hardest cases. This finding flies in the face of policy admonitions that peacekeepers should only go where the chances of "success" are relatively good. A policy of sending peacekeepers only to the easy cases would help international organizations avoid embarrassment, but would ensure that peacekeeping was less useful than it could be. If peacekeepers only went where peace is likely to last in any case, they would render themselves irrelevant. Fortunately, however, this policy advice has apparently been ignored. As both the quantitative and qualitative evidence * * * makes clear, the higher the risk of recidivism in a particular case, the more likely peacekeepers are to deploy. In particular, peacekeeping is most likely when neither side has won outright, where mistrust is high, and where refugee flows threaten regional peace. Chapter VI consent-based peacekeeping is more likely where rebel groups are relatively strong and in countries with lower living standards. Chapter VII enforcement missions are more likely in less democratic states and where the war involves multiple fighting factions. In short, peacekeepers are most likely to be sent where they are most needed, where the job of maintaining peace is most difficult.

The answer to the question of whether peacekeeping works is a clear and resounding yes. To see this, it is crucial to control for the fact that peacekeepers select into the difficult cases. But once this selection is accounted for, the statistical evidence is overwhelming. [Even analyzing] the data in many different ways, * * * the conclusion is always the same; the risk of war resuming is much lower when peacekeepers are present than when belligerents are left to their own devices. Estimates of the size of this effect depend on how conservative one wants to be. If one sets up a particularly difficult test, in which peacekeepers are only given credit for keeping peace while they are actually deployed, not for peace that lasts after they leave, peacekeepers reduce the risk of another war by 55%–60%, all else equal. If peacekeepers are given credit for cases in which peace survives even after they go home (which, after all, is their main goal) estimates of the beneficial effects of peacekeeping are much more dramatic, suggesting that the risk of recidivism falls by at least 75%–85% relative to nonpeacekeeping cases. The evidence from interviews with rebel and government decision makers also supports this general conclusion that peacekeeping works. The belligerents themselves view peacekeeping as an important and effective tool that has helped them maintain peace.

Several other findings emerge from the analysis of peacekeeping's effects. One of the most important for peacekeeping policy is that Chapter VI consent-based missions are empirically just as effective as the militarily more robust Chapter VII enforcement missions. Much of the discussion within policy circles in the last several years has been about the importance of beefing up the mandates of peacekeeping missions. There are certainly cases in which an enforcement mandate may be necessary. More robust military capabilities can help peacekeepers protect themselves and others if peace begins to falter. And if the aim is to deter aggression militarily, then a Chapter VII mandate is needed. But it is not enough. Only enforcement missions that prove their willingness to fight, as missions that intervene to create a cease-fire by force have done, can deter effectively. Otherwise, a Chapter VII mandate does not a credible deterrent

make. Thus, UNAMSIL's [United Nations Mission in Sierra Leone] Chapter VII mandate meant little until British intervention and a robust force posture convinced the RUF [Revolutionary Unified Front (Sierra Leone)] that the international community was serious about enforcing peace.

However, the findings of this study show that peacekeeping is worthwhile even under consent-based mandates. Large and relatively well armed troop deployments are not necessarily essential for peacekeeping to work; even small, unarmed or very lightly armed missions significantly reduce the likelihood that peace will break down. Given that consent-based missions are typically much less expensive, and that it may be easier to find countries willing and able to contribute troops for them, this is an important finding. Robust Chapter VII–mandated peacekeeping may be the safest option, but the international community should not shy away from smaller, less robust Chapter VI peacekeeping if that is all that is possible politically. In other words, we should not conclude that the mission's mandate does not matter, but rather that even peacekeeping missions with limited mandates and constrained military power can be extremely effective. This is because many of the mechanisms through which peacekeepers have an effect are political and economic in nature and do not depend on robust mandates or strong military force (more on this below).

Among consent-based operations, multidimensional missions are most effective. The dearth of cases in each category makes it harder to reach strong conclusions about the relative effects of different types of Chapter VI missions, so this finding should be treated with some caution. But the available evidence suggests that the civilian aspects of peacekeeping that go into multidimensional missions—election monitoring, human rights training, police reform, and so on—do contribute to its general effectiveness. More of the causal mechanisms through which peacekeeping operates, particularly those relating to political exclusion, are at play in these multidimensional missions than in other types of peacekeeping.

Peacekeeping is not a cure-all. Beyond the task of maintaining peace, the international community increasingly aims to foster democracy in the war-torn societies in which it intervenes. While stable peace may be a requisite for the growth of democracy, and as we have seen here, peacekeeping promotes stable peace, outside intervention may in other ways undermine or crowd out democratization. So, while peacekeeping is clearly effective at maintaining peace, it has not necessarily left significantly more democratic societies in its wake.[6] Nonetheless, if the aim is simply to keep the peace, to keep civil war from recurring, then peacekeeping is an extremely effective policy tool.

While the answers to the first two questions addressed in this [project] can be summarized quickly—peacekeepers go where peace is hardest to keep, and yes, peacekeeping works to keep peace—the answer to the third question, how does peacekeeping work, is a bit more complicated. Peacekeeping works along multiple causal pathways. To understand the causal mechanisms of peacekeeping, we must consider the reasons belligerents who have recently been fighting each other might return to war. This work identified four analytically distinct, but in practice overlapping pathways: aggression, fear and mistrust, accident or the actions of rogue groups within either side, and political exclusion. I hypothesized particular ways that the presence of peacekeepers might block these potential causal pathways; that is, ways peacekeepers might (1) change the incentives for aggression relative to maintaining peace, (2) alleviate fear and mistrust so as to reduce security dilemmas, (3) prevent or control accidents or "involuntary defection" by hard-liners, and (4) dissuade either side (and particularly the government) from excluding the other from the political process.

An empirical evaluation of the specific causal mechanisms through which peacekeepers might achieve these results requires paying attention to the perspective of the peacekept. The peacekeeping literature tends to be a bit narcissistic. It pays attention mostly to the peacekeepers, to their functions, the particulars of mandates, troop deployments, command and control, relationships between headquarters and the field, "best practices," and so, while largely ignoring the peacekept. But it is the peacekept who must choose between war and peace. Only if peacekeepers change something for the peacekept can they have a causal impact on this choice. This project has tried to rectify this shortcoming in the literature by examining how the belligerents themselves viewed the situation they faced, and particularly how they thought the presence or absence of peacekeepers mattered in their case.

The evidence from interviews with the peacekept (or not peacekept in the Bangladeshi case) indicates a number of ways in which the presence of peacekeepers can shape belligerents' choices. In large enforcement missions, this shift can entail military deterrence, although, as stressed above, to be effective, a deterrent force must establish the credibility that all deterrence entails. Where peacekeeping will depend on military deterrence, the international community must expect to have to prove its credibility on the ground. Enforcement missions may actually have to fight to convince the peacekept that peacekeepers are willing to use force. Smaller missions and consent-based peacekeeping might serve as a trip wire for more robust intervention, but again, would-be spoilers must believe that the international community really will respond with a large-scale intervention. The conditions under which peacekeeping has a strong military effect are therefore fairly narrow. But many of the ways in which peacekeeping changes belligerents' incentives are nonmilitary in nature.

Peacekeepers can have a causal impact by changing economic incentives. For rank-and-file soldiers, this generally entails the material benefits of going through a demobilization, disarmament, and reintegration (DDR) process. For leaders, it can entail the general boost to the economy that a peacekeeping mission brings, a boost that political elites are often in a position to capitalize on. Or it may entail more direct forms of co-option. The Mozambique case provides examples of both. Co-option can happen without peacekeepers, of course. But as the CHT [Chittagons Hill Tracts] examples show, if one side buys off the other, as the Bangladeshi government did the PCJSS [Parbatya Chattagram Jana Samhati Saniti (Chittagong Hill Tracts United Peoples' Party)] by granting control of local budgets (and the opportunities for corruption that go with it), this leaves the co-opted open to charges of selling out. Co-option done by a peacekeeping mission, as a more neutral and acceptable body, is less likely to strengthen hard-liners at the expense of moderates than is co-option among the belligerents themselves.

Because altering economic incentives can be crucial to maintaining stable peace, contraband financing for rebels is not only a powerful factor in civil war recidivism, it also reduces peacekeepers' leverage. As shown * * *, peacekeeping still helps when parties have independent and illegal sources of funding, but its effect is diminished. Co-option will be more expensive, perhaps prohibitively so, in these cases. Alternatively, as was the case in Sierra Leone, attempts to alter economic incentives may work in conjunction with military deterrence when contraband financing is an issue.

Beyond economics, peacekeepers can influence the incentives of the peacekept by influencing perceptions of the parties' legitimacy, both internationally and domestically. In many civil wars, recognition as a legitimate political actor is itself a valuable and sought-after good, as well as one that may translate into international economic or other aid. Internally, pronouncements by peacekeepers about who is or is not cooperating with a peace process may affect parties' electoral prospects.

In short, while peacekeeping may deter aggression through military means in some cases, its effects on the incentives facing belligerents are largely economic and political. There are policy implications of this for peacekeepers. Peacekeeping strategy should focus at least as much on identifying the points of economic and political influence in a particular case that will provide the most leverage over belligerents' decision making as on beefing up the mission's military strength. Similarly, the allocation of scarce resources (money, personnel, etc.) should be directed at least as much to making peace profitable and politically viable for the peacekept as to the creation of militarily effective peacekeeping forces. Where possible, an attempt should be made to control or eliminate contraband sources of funding for belligerents.[7]

By alleviating fear and mistrust, peacekeeping also increases the chances that belligerents will maintain peace. It does this, in part, by helping erstwhile deadly enemies to communicate with one another. Thus, as the inevitable problems and glitches in the peace process arise, peacekeeping missions should emphasize ongoing mediation. They can also support peace by monitoring each side's compliance with a cease-fire. It is here, perhaps, that the military nature of peacekeeping is most important. Peacekeeping missions should include military personnel, not because they can fight (in fact, unarmed military observers may be most effective in some cases), but because they have the expertise to monitor demobilization and disarmament, and because they can garner the respect of the soldiers they monitor and the commanders they work with.

Peacekeepers also alleviate fear and mistrust, to some degree, merely by existing. To the extent that agreeing to peacekeeping allows the parties to signal their intentions to each other, it is less what peacekeepers actually do than whether the parties have asked for them or not that makes a difference. But for this signaling mechanism to work, it has to be credible, and to be credible, it has to be costly. Specifically, it has to be costly for a party that intends to resume fighting. Peacekeeping missions should thus be designed to be as intrusive as possible as a way of testing the credibility of this signal. Peacekeeping, particularly UN peacekeeping, traditionally proceeded on an assumption of good faith on the part of the belligerents. Lessons learned, usually the hard way, during the 1990s have tempered this assumption, with more attention now paid to the possibility of spoilers. But the signaling function of peacekeeping should be used proactively. Peacekeeping strategy should focus on identifying and insisting on things that those intending to go back to war or renege on a political deal would object to, but that those committed to peace would not necessarily mind. And because intentions can shift over time, peacekeepers should be intrusive not just when they first deploy, but over the life of the mission. This is not to say that they should go out of their way to antagonize the parties to the conflict, but rather that missions should be designed so as to maximize the clarity of the signal that consent and ongoing cooperation with peacekeeping provides to the other side.

Peacekeeping can make the resumption of war less likely by preventing hard-liners or rogue factions from inciting violence, and by helping to prevent or control accidents from sparking renewed conflict. Peacekeepers should work with moderates on each side to identify hard-liners within their own group who might pose a threat to peace. Peacekeeping strategy should determine whether these would-be spoiler splinter groups can be deterred militarily (something even relatively weak peacekeeping forces may be capable of), and how they can be weakened politically. By facilitating communication, peacekeeping can nip accidental conflagrations in the bud. This provides another reason peacekeepers should spend time and energy on continuing mediation between the parties, both among leaders and among local commanders, dealing with problems on the spot.

Providing security or basic law and order can help accidents from starting in the first place, so peacekeeping missions should continue to invest in policing, perhaps especially in identity conflicts where the actions of the general population might provide sparks for the fire. Similarly, providing security in particularly tense phases of the peace process (such as disarmament) or in particularly contested territory (diamond-mining areas, for example) can forestall problems that could easily escalate. Finally, peacekeeping missions should establish a formal mechanism for handling disputes over compliance. This gives both sides an alternative to, on the one hand, doing nothing in the face of perceived violations by their antagonists, and on the other, responding in kind and risking escalation. These dispute resolution mechanisms can appear irrelevant. Their formal findings may not tell either side anything it does not already know. But often it is not their role in providing information to the various parties that is important, but rather their existence as a political mechanism that allows the parties to save face by taking nonescalatory action in response to alleged violations.

Last, but certainly not least, peacekeepers can make peace more likely to endure by preventing either side from shutting the other out of a political process in a way that makes the political loser choose war. In most cases this entails pressuring the government, which can use the trappings of state power to influence political outcomes, not to abuse its position. There is a stark contrast in this regard between the Chittagong Hill Tracts conflict, where the absence of peacekeepers has given the Bangladeshi government a relatively free hand to disregard key elements of the peace deal, and Mozambique and Sierra Leone, where considerable pressure was brought to bear on the government to be inclusive. Beyond general political pressure (with international aid and legitimacy providing leverage), peacekeepers can minimize abuse by monitoring security forces and by monitoring or running electoral processes. They can help military groups (especially rebels) transform themselves into viable political parties, sometimes with the expenditure of relatively small amounts of money or other resources. (In some cases, computers and new suits can go a long way.) After some conflicts, peacekeepers may temporarily take over the entire administration of the country to prevent either side from dominating the political process during the most dangerous phases of the transition to peace. Again, peacekeeping strategy should be formed with an eye toward these mechanisms.

In short, peacekeeping intervenes in the most difficult cases, dramatically increases the chances that peace will last, and does so by altering the incentives of the peacekept, by alleviating their fear and mistrust of each other, by preventing and controlling accidents and misbehavior by hard-line factions, and by encouraging political inclusion.

Beyond its answers to these questions about peacekeeping and its effects, this study also makes both theoretical and empirical contributions. It builds on a theory of international cooperation developed for interstate conflict, extending it to the realm of internal warfare.[8] It provides further support for the notion that while cooperation is often extremely difficult, perhaps nowhere more so than among deadly enemies who have just fought a war, deliberate efforts by the belligerents themselves and by outsiders can often overcome the obstacles to peace.

It also helps us to understand the more general issue of recurrent civil war. Interstate war has, thankfully, become relatively rare since the end of the Cold War. This has left internal conflicts as arguably the greatest security problem facing the world as a whole.[9] Countries that have been torn apart by civil war face a significant recidivism problem—those who have had a civil war are especially likely to have another. The empirical findings of this study help us understand the nature of that problem. They point to particular factors (such as military outcomes, or contraband financing for rebels) that make civil wars particularly likely to recur. But they also show that this "conflict trap" is not inevitable.[10] The conclusions of this project are therefore fundamentally optimistic. The problem of maintaining peace in the aftermath of civil war is a serious one, but it is not a hopeless one.

Parties to civil war, together with the international community, can use the tool of peacekeeping to reduce dramatically the risk of another war.

Peacekeeping is not free. It costs money and personnel on the part of the international community and the countries that contribute troops. It also entails political costs for the peacekept, not least of which is the infringement on a country's sovereignty. Policymakers may decide peacekeeping is not worth these costs in a particular instance. But relative to the cost of recurrent warfare, peacekeeping is an extremely good investment. Peacekeeping is not a panacea, nor a silver bullet. It cannot guarantee that peace will last. But contrary to the views of many who think only of well-publicized failures, peacekeeping is an extremely effective tool for maintaining peace—a tool that the findings of this study will, I hope, make even more useful.

NOTES

1. Note that the U.S. led and UN missions in Somalia (UNITAF [Unified Task Force on Somalia] and UNOSOM [UN Operation in Somalia], respectively) were not peacekeeping missions as defined here, but rather humanitarian assistance missions (see definitions below). This distinction was lost, however, in the debates over the merits of peacekeeping after the fiasco in Mogadishu.

2. On this debate see, for example, Tharoor 1995–96 and Luttwak 1999.

3. See Hartzell, Hoddie, and Rothchild 2001; Dubey 2002; and Doyle and Sambanis 2000, respectively. See also Doyle and Sambanis 2006; Gilligan and Sergenti 2007. For studies of the effects of international involvement on peace after interstate (as opposed to civil) wars, see Diehl, Reifschneider, and Hensel 1996; and Fortna 2004.

4. Luttwak 1999; Weinstein 2005.

5. Peacekeeping is thus endogenous to processes that affect the duration of peace. The selection of peacekeeping must be accounted for before we can assess its effects.

6. See Fortna 2008.

7. The Kimberly Process Certification Scheme to combat the trafficking of "blood diamonds" from conflict zones is an important step in this direction.

8. Fortna 2003, 2004.

9. Other threats, such as terrorism or the proliferation of nuclear weapons, may be of greater concern to particular countries at particular moments. Civil wars may also be on the decline, but continue to pose a significant threat to the lives and livelihoods of millions.

10. See Collier et al. 2003.

REFERENCES

Collier, Paul, V. L. Elliot, Håvard Hegre, Anke Hoeffler, Marta Reynal-Querol, and Nicholas Sambanis. 2003. *Breaking the Conflict Trap: Civil War and Development Policy.* Washington, DC: World Bank and Oxford University Press.

Diehl, Paul F., Jennifer Reifschneider, and Paul R. Hensel. 1996. United Nations Intervention and Recurring Conflict. *International Organization* 50 (4): 683–700.

Doyle, Michael W., and Nicholas Sambanis. 2000. International Peacebuilding: A Theoretical and Quantitative Analysis. *American Political Science Review* 94 (4): 779–801.

———. 2006. *Making War and Building Peace: United Nations Peace Operations.* Princeton: Princeton University Press.

Dubey, Amitabh. 2002. Domestic Institutions and the Duration of Civil War Settlements. Paper presented at Annual Meeting of the International Studies Association, New Orleans.

Fortna, Virginia Page. 2003. Scraps of Paper? Agreements and the Durability of Peace. *International Organization* 57 (2): 337–72

Fortna, Virginia Page. 2004. *Peace Time: Cease-Fire Agreements and the Durability of Peace.* Princeton: Princeton University Press.

Fortna, Virginia Page. 2008. Peacekeeping and Democratization. In *From War to Democracy: Dilemmas of Peacebuilding,* edited by A. Jarstad and T. Sisk. Cambridge: Cambridge University Press.

Gilligan, Michael J., and Ernest J. Sergenti. 2007. Does Peacekeeping Keep Peace? Using Matching to Improve Causal Inference. Unpublished paper, New York University and Harvard University.

Hartzell, Caroline, Mathew Hoddie, and Donald Rothchild. 2001. Stabilizing the Peace after Civil War. *International Organization* 55 (1): 183–208.

Luttwak, Edward N. 1999. Give War a Chance. *Foreign Affairs* 78 (4): 36–44.

Tharoor, Shashi. 1995–96. Should UN Peacekeeping Go 'Back to Basics'? *Survival* 37 (4): 52–64.

Weinstein, Jeremy M. 2005. Autonomous Recovery and International Intervention in Comparative Perspective. Unpublished paper. Center for Global Development, Washington, DC.

———. 2007. *Inside Rebellion: The Politics of Insurgent Violence.* New York: Cambridge University Press.

Samantha Power

BYSTANDERS TO GENOCIDE
Why the United States Let the Rwandan Tragedy Happen

I. People Sitting in Offices

In the course of a hundred days in 1994 the Hutu government of Rwanda and its extremist allies very nearly succeeded in exterminating the country's Tutsi minority. Using firearms, machetes, and a variety of garden implements, Hutu militiamen, soldiers, and ordinary citizens murdered some 800,000 Tutsi and politically moderate Hutu. It was the fastest, most efficient killing spree of the twentieth century.

A few years later, in a series in *The New Yorker,* Philip Gourevitch recounted in horrific detail the story of the genocide and the world's failure to stop it. President Bill Clinton, a famously avid reader, expressed shock. He sent copies of Gourevitch's articles to his second-term national-security adviser, Sandy Berger. The articles bore confused, angry, searching queries in the margins. "Is what he's saying true?" Clinton wrote with a thick black felt-tip pen beside heavily underlined paragraphs. "How did this happen?" he asked, adding, "I want to get to the bottom of this." The President's urgency and outrage were oddly timed. As the terror in Rwanda had unfolded, Clinton had shown virtually no interest in stopping the genocide, and his Administration had stood by as the death toll rose into the hundreds of thousands.

Why did the United States not do more for the Rwandans at the time of the killings? Did the President really not know about the genocide, as his marginalia suggested? Who were the people in his Administration who made the life-and-death decisions that dictated U.S. policy? Why did they decide (or decide not to decide) as they did? Were any voices inside or outside the U.S. government demanding that the United States do more? If so, why weren't they heeded? And most crucial, what could the United States have done to save lives?

So far people have explained the U.S. failure to respond to the Rwandan genocide by claiming that the United States didn't know what was happening, that it knew but didn't care, or that regardless of what it knew there was nothing useful to be done. The account that follows is based on a three-year investigation involving sixty interviews with senior, mid-level, and junior State Department, Defense Department, and National Security Council officials who helped to shape or inform U.S. policy. It also reflects dozens of interviews with Rwandan, European, and United Nations officials and with peacekeepers, journalists, and nongovernmental workers in Rwanda. Thanks to the National Security Archive (www.nsarchive.org), a nonprofit organization that uses the Freedom of Information Act to secure the release of classified U.S. documents, this account also draws on hundreds of pages of newly available government records. This material provides a clearer picture than was previously possible of the interplay among people, motives, and events. It reveals that the U.S. government knew enough

From *The Atlantic* (Sept. 2001), 84–108.

about the genocide early on to save lives, but passed up countless opportunities to intervene.

In March of 1998, on a visit to Rwanda, President Clinton issued what would later be known as the "Clinton apology," which was actually a carefully hedged acknowledgment. He spoke to the crowd assembled on the tarmac at Kigali Airport: "We come here today partly in recognition of the fact that we in the United States and the world community did not do as much as we could have and should have done to try to limit what occurred" in Rwanda.

This implied that the United States had done a good deal but not quite enough. In reality the United States did much more than fail to send troops. It led a successful effort to remove most of the UN peacekeepers who were already in Rwanda. It aggressively worked to block the subsequent authorization of UN reinforcements. It refused to use its technology to jam radio broadcasts that were a crucial instrument in the coordination and perpetuation of the genocide. And even as, on average, 8,000 Rwandans were being butchered each day, U.S. officials shunned the term "genocide," for fear of being obliged to act. The United States in fact did virtually nothing "to try to limit what occurred." Indeed, staying out of Rwanda was an explicit U.S. policy objective.

With the grace of one grown practiced at public remorse, the President gripped the lectern with both hands and looked across the dais at the Rwandan officials and survivors who surrounded him. Making eye contact and shaking his head, he explained, "It may seem strange to you here, especially the many of you who lost members of your family, but all over the world there were people like me sitting in offices, day after day after day, who *did not fully appreciate* [pause] the depth [pause] and the speed [pause] with which you were being engulfed by this *unimaginable* terror."

Clinton chose his words with characteristic care. It was true that although top U.S. officials could not help knowing the basic facts—thousands of Rwandans were dying every day—that were being reported in the morning papers, many did not "fully appreciate" the meaning. In the first three weeks of the genocide the most influential American policymakers portrayed (and, they insist, perceived) the deaths not as astrocities or the components and symptoms of genocide but as wartime "casualties"— the deaths of combatants or those caught between them in a civil war.

Yet this formulation avoids the critical issue of whether Clinton and his close advisers might reasonably have been expected to "fully appreciate" the true dimensions and nature of the massacres. During the first three days of the killings U.S. diplomats in Rwanda reported back to Washington that well-armed extremists were intent on eliminating the Tutsi. And the American press spoke of the door-to-door hunting of unarmed civilians. By the end of the second week informed nongovernmental groups had already begun to call on the Administration to use the term "genocide," causing diplomats and lawyers at the State Department to begin debating the word's applicability soon thereafter. In order not to appreciate that genocide or something close to it was under way, U.S. officials had to ignore public reports and internal intelligence and debate.

The story of U.S. policy during the genocide in Rwanda is not a story of willful complicity with evil. U.S. officials did not sit around and conspire to allow genocide to happen. But whatever their convictions about "never again," many of them did sit around, and they most certainly did allow genocide to happen. In examining how and why the United States failed Rwanda, we see that without strong leadership the system will incline toward risk-averse policy choices. We also see that with the possibility of deploying U.S. troops to Rwanda taken off the table early on—and with crises elsewhere in the world unfolding—the slaughter never received the top-level attention it deserved. Domestic political forces that might have pressed for action were absent. And most U.S. officials opposed to American involvement in Rwanda were firmly convinced that they were doing all they could—and, most important, all they *should*—in light of competing American interests and a highly circumscribed understanding of what was "possible" for the United States to do.

One of the most thoughtful analyses of how the American system can remain predicated on the noblest of values while allowing the vilest of crimes was offered in 1971 by a brilliant and earnest young foreign-service officer who had just resigned from the National Security Council to protest the 1970 U.S. invasion of Cambodia. In an article in *Foreign Policy*, "The Human Reality of Realpolitik," he and a colleague analyzed the process whereby American policymakers with moral sensibilities could have waged a war of such immoral consequence as the one in Vietnam. They wrote,

> The answer to that question begins with a basic intellectual approach which views foreign policy as a lifeless, bloodless set of abstractions. "Nations," "interests," "influence," "prestige"—all are disembodied and dehumanized terms which encourage easy inattention to the real people whose lives our decisions affect or even end.

Policy analysis excluded discussion of human consequences. "It simply is not *done*," the authors wrote. "Policy—good, steady policy—is made by the 'tough-minded.' To talk of suffering is to lose 'effectiveness,' almost to lose one's grip. It is seen as a sign that one's 'rational' arguments are weak."

In 1994, fifty years after the Holocaust and twenty years after America's retreat from Vietnam, it was possible to believe that the system had changed and that talk of human consequences had become admissible. Indeed, when the machetes were raised in Central Africa, the White House official primarily responsible for the shaping of U.S. foreign policy was one of the authors of that 1971 critique: Anthony Lake, President Clinton's first-term national-security adviser. The genocide in Rwanda presented Lake and the rest of the Clinton team with an opportunity to prove that "good, steady policy" could be made in the interest of saving lives.

II. The Peacekeepers

Rwanda was a test for another man as well: Romeo Dallaire, then a major general in the Canadian army who at the time of the genocide was the commander of the UN Assistance Mission in Rwanda. If ever there was a peacekeeper who believed wholeheartedly in the promise of humanitarian action, it was Dallaire. A broad-shouldered French-Canadian with deep-set sky-blue eyes, Dallaire has the thick, calloused hands of one brought up in a culture that prizes soldiering, service, and sacrifice. He saw the United Nations as the embodiment of all three.

Before his posting to Rwanda Dallaire had served as the commandant of an army brigade that sent peacekeeping battalions to Cambodia and Bosnia, but he had never seen actual combat himself. "I was like a fireman who has never been to a fire, but has dreamed for years about how he would fare when the fire came," the fifty-five-year-old Dallaire recalls. When, in the summer of 1993, he received the phone call from UN headquarters offering him the Rwanda posting, he was ecstatic. "It was answering the aim of my life," he says. "It's *all* you've been waiting for."

Dallaire was sent to command a UN force that would help to keep the peace in Rwanda, a nation the size of Vermont, which was known as "the land of a thousand hills" for its rolling terrain. Before Rwanda achieved independence from Belgium, in 1962, the Tutsi, who made up 15 percent of the populace, had enjoyed a privileged status. But independence ushered in three decades of Hutu rule, under which Tutsi were systematically discriminated against and periodically subjected to waves of killing and ethnic cleansing. In 1990 a group of armed exiles, mainly Tutsi, who had been clustered on the Ugandan border, invaded Rwanda. Over the next several years the rebels, known as the Rwandan Patriotic Front, gained ground against Hutu government forces. In 1993 Tanzania brokered peace talks, which resulted in a power-sharing agreement known as the Arusha Accords. Under its terms the Rwandan government agreed to share power with Hutu opposition parties and the Tutsi minority. UN peacekeepers would be deployed to patrol a cease-fire and assist in demilitarization and demobilization as well as to help provide a secure environment, so that exiled Tutsi could return. The hope among moderate Rwandans and Western observers was that Hutu and Tutsi would at last be able to coexist in harmony.

Hutu extremists rejected these terms and set out to terrorize Tutsi and also those Hutu politicians supportive of the peace process. In 1993 several thousand Rwandans were killed, and some 9,000 were detained. Guns, grenades, and machetes began arriving by the planeload. A pair of international commissions—one sent by the United Nations, the other by an independent collection of human-rights organizations—warned explicitly of a possible genocide.

But Dallaire knew nothing of the precariousness of the Arusha Accords. When he made a preliminary reconnaissance trip to Rwanda, in August of 1993, he was told that the country was committed to peace and that a UN presence was essential. A visit with extremists, who preferred to eradicate Tutsi rather than cede power, was not on Dallaire's itinerary. Remarkably, no UN officials in New York thought to give Dallaire copies of the alarming reports from the international investigators.

The sum total of Dallaire's intelligence data before that first trip to Rwanda consisted of one encyclopedia's summary of Rwandan history, which Major Brent Beardsley, Dallaire's executive assistant, had snatched at the last minute from his local public library. Beardsley says, "We flew to Rwanda with a Michelin road map, a copy of the Arusha agreement, and that was it. We were under the impression that the situation was quite straightforward: there was one cohesive government side and one cohesive rebel side, and they had come together to sign the peace agreement and had then requested that we come in to help them implement it."

Though Dallaire gravely underestimated the tensions brewing in Rwanda, he still felt that he would need a force of 5,000 to help the parties implement the terms of the Arusha Accords. But when his superiors warned him that the United States would never agree to pay for such a large deployment, Dallaire reluctantly trimmed his written request to 2,500. He remembers, "I was told, 'Don't ask for a brigade, because it ain't there.'"

Once he was actually posted to Rwanda, in October of 1993, Dallaire lacked not merely intelligence data and manpower but also institutional support. The small Department of Peacekeeping Operations in New York, run by the Ghanaian diplomat Kofi Annan, now the UN secretary general, was overwhelmed. Madeleine Albright, then the U.S. ambassador to the UN, recalls, "The global nine-one-one was always either busy or nobody was there." At the time of the Rwanda deployment, with a staff of a few hundred, the UN was posting 70,000 peacekeepers on seventeen missions around the world. Amid these widespread crises and logistical headaches the Rwanda mission had a very low status.

Life was not made easier for Dallaire or the UN peacekeeping office by the fact that American patience for peacekeeping was thinning. Congress owed half a billion dollars in UN dues and peacekeeping costs. It had tired of its obligation to foot a third of the bill for what had come to feel like an insatiable global appetite for mischief and an equally insatiable UN appetite for missions. The Clinton Administration had taken office better disposed toward peacekeeping than any other Administration in U.S. history. But it felt that the Department of Peacekeeping Operations needed fixing and demanded that the UN "learn to say no" to chancy or costly missions.

Every aspect of the UN Assistance Mission in Rwanda was run on a shoestring. UNAMIR (the acronym by which it was known) was equipped with hand-me-down vehicles from the UN's Cambodia mission, and only eighty of the 300 that turned up were usable. When the medical supplies ran out, in March of 1994, New York said there was no cash for resupply. Very little could be procured locally, given that Rwanda was one of Africa's poorest nations. Replacement spare parts, batteries, and even ammunition could rarely be found. Dallaire spent some 70 percent of his time battling UN logistics.

Dallaire had major problems with his personnel, as well. He commanded troops, military observers, and civilian personnel from twenty-six countries. Though multinationality is meant to be a virtue of UN missions, the diversity yielded grave discrepancies in resources. Whereas Belgian troops turned up well armed and ready to perform the tasks assigned to them, the poorer contingents showed up "bare-assed," in Dallaire's words, and demanded that the United Nations suit them up. "Since nobody else was offering to send troops, we had to take what we could get," he says. When Dallaire expressed concern, he was instructed by a senior UN official to lower his expectations. He recalls, "I was told, 'Listen, General, you are NATO-trained. This is not NATO.'" Although some 2,500 UNAMIR personnel had arrived by early April of 1994, few of the soldiers had the kit they needed to perform even basic tasks.

The signs of militarization in Rwanda were so widespread that even without much of an intelligence-gathering capacity, Dallaire was able to learn of the extremists' sinister intentions. In January of 1994 an anonymous Hutu informant, said to be high up in the inner circles of the Rwandan government, had come forward to describe the rapid arming and training of local militias. In what is now referred to as the "Dallaire fax,"

Dallaire relayed to New York the informant's claim that Hutu extremists "had been ordered to register all the Tutsi in Kigali." "He suspects it is for their extermination," Dallaire wrote. "Example he gave was that in 20 minutes his personnel could kill up to 1000 Tutsis." "Jean-Pierre," as the informant became known, had said that the militia planned first to provoke and murder a number of Belgian peacekeepers, to "thus guarantee Belgian withdrawal from Rwanda." When Dallaire notified Kofi Annan's office that UNAMIR was poised to raid Hutu arms caches, Annan's deputy forbade him to do so. Instead Dallaire was instructed to notify the Rwandan President, Juvénal Habyarimana, and the Western ambassadors of the informant's claims. Though Dallaire battled by phone with New York, and confirmed the reliability of the informant, his political masters told him plainly and consistently that the United States in particular would not support aggressive peace-keeping. (A request by the Belgians for reinforcements was also turned down.) In Washington, Dallaire's alarm was discounted. Lieutenant Colonel Tony Marley, the U.S. military liaison to the Arusha process, respected Dallaire but knew he was operating in Africa for the first time. "I thought that the neophyte meant well, but I questioned whether he knew what he was talking about," Marley recalls.

III. The Early Killings

On the evening of April 6, 1994, Romeo Dallaire was sitting on the couch in his bungalow residence in Kigali, watching CNN with Brent Beardsley. Beardsley was preparing plans for a national Sports Day that would match Tutsi rebel soldiers against Hutu government soldiers in a soccer game. Dallaire said, "You know, Brent, if the shit ever hit the fan here, none of this stuff would really matter, would it?" The next instant the phone rang. Rwandan President Habyarimana's

Mystère Falcon jet, a gift from French President François Mitterrand, had just been shot down, with Habyarimana and Burundian President Cyprien Ntaryamira aboard. Dallaire and Beardsley raced in their UN jeep to Rwandan army headquarters, where a crisis meeting was under way.

Back in Washington, Kevin Aiston, the Rwanda desk officer, knocked on the door of Deputy Assistant Secretary of State Prudence Bushnell and told her that the Presidents of Rwanda and Burundi had gone down in a plane crash. "Oh, shit," she said. "Are you sure?" In fact nobody was sure at first, but Dallaire's forces supplied confirmation within the hour. The Rwandan authorities quickly announced a curfew, and Hutu militias and government soldiers erected roadblocks around the capital.

Bushnell drafted an urgent memo to Secretary of State Warren Christopher. She was concerned about a probable outbreak of killing in both Rwanda and its neighbor Burundi. The memo read,

> If, as it appears, both Presidents have been killed, there is a strong likelihood that widespread violence could break out in either or both countries, particularly if it is confirmed that the plane was shot down. Our strategy is to appeal for calm in both countries, both through public statements and in other ways.

A few public statements proved to be virtually the only strategy that Washington would muster in the weeks ahead.

Lieutenant General Wesley Clark, who later commanded the NATO air war in Kosovo, was the director of strategic plans and policy for the Joint Chiefs of Staff at the Pentagon. On learning of the crash, Clark remembers, staff officers asked, "Is it Hutu and Tutsi or Tutu and Hutsi?" He frantically called for insight into the ethnic dimension of events in Rwanda. Unfortunately, Rwanda had never been of more than marginal concern to Washington's most influential planners.

America's best-informed Rwanda observer was not a government official but a private citizen, Alison Des Forges, a historian and a board member of Human Rights Watch, who lived in Buffalo, New York. Des Forges had been visiting Rwanda since 1963. She had received a Ph.D. from Yale in African history, specializing in Rwanda, and she could speak the Rwandan language, Kinyarwanda. Half an hour after the plane crash Des Forges got a phone call from a close friend in Kigali, the human-rights activist Monique Mujawamariya. Des Forges had been worried about Mujawamariya for weeks, because the Hutu extremist radio station, Radio Mille Collines, had branded her "a bad patriot who deserves to die." Mujawamariya had sent Human Rights Watch a chilling warning a week earlier: "For the last two weeks, all of Kigali has lived under the threat of an instantaneous, carefully prepared operation to eliminate all those who give trouble to President Habyarimana."

Now Habyarimana was dead, and Mujawamariya knew instantly that the hard-line Hutu would use the crash as a pretext to begin mass killing. "This is it," she told Des Forges on the phone. For the next twenty-four hours Des Forges called her friend's home every half hour. With each conversation Des Forges could hear the gunfire grow louder as the militia drew closer. Finally the gunmen entered Mujawamariya's home. "I don't want you to hear this," Mujawamariya said softly. "Take care of my children." She hung up the phone.

Mujawamariya's instincts were correct. Within hours of the plane crash Hutu militiamen took command of the streets of Kigali. Dallaire quickly grasped that supporters of the Arusha peace process were being targeted. His phone at UNAMIR headquarters rang constantly as Rwandans around the capital pleaded for help. Dallaire was especially concerned about Prime Minister Agathe Uwilingiyimana, a reformer who with the President's death had become the titular head of state. Just after dawn on April 7 five Ghanaian and ten Belgian peacekeepers arrived at the Prime Minister's home in order to deliver her to Radio Rwanda, so that she could broadcast an emergency appeal for calm.

Joyce Leader, the second-in-command at the U.S. embassy, lived next door to Uwilingiyimana. She spent the early hours of the morning behind the steel-barred gates of her embassy-owned house as Hutu killers hunted and dispatched their first victims. Leader's phone rang. Uwilingiyimana was on the other end. "Please hide me," she begged.

Minutes after the phone call a UN peacekeeper attempted to hike the Prime Minister over the wall separating their compounds. When Leader heard shots fired, she urged the peacekeeper to abandon the effort. "They can see you!" she shouted. Uwilingiyimana managed to slip with her husband and children into another compound, which was occupied by the UN Development Program. But the militiamen hunted them down in the yard, where the couple surrendered. There were more shots. Leader recalls, "We heard her screaming and then, suddenly, after the gunfire the screaming stopped, and we heard people cheering." Hutu gunmen in the Presidential Guard that day systematically tracked down and eliminated Rwanda's moderate leadership.

The raid on Uwilingiyimana's compound not only cost Rwanda a prominent supporter of the Arusha Accords; it also triggered the collapse of Dallaire's mission. In keeping with the plan to target the Belgians which the informant Jean-Pierre had relayed to UNAMIR in January, Hutu soldiers rounded up the peacekeepers at Uwilingiyimana's home, took them to a military camp, led the Ghanaians to safety, and then killed and savagely mutilated the ten Belgians. In Belgium the cry for either expanding UNAMIR's mandate or immediately withdrawing was prompt and loud.

In response to the initial killings by the Hutu government, Tutsi rebels of the Rwandan Patriotic Front—stationed in Kigali under the terms of the Arusha Accords—surged out of their barracks and resumed their civil war against the Hutu regime.

But under the cover of that war were early and strong indications that systematic genocide was taking place. From April 7 onward the Hutu-controlled army, the gendarmerie, and the militias worked together to wipe out Rwanda's Tutsi. Many of the early Tutsi victims found themselves specifically, not spontaneously, pursued: lists of targets had been prepared in advance, and Radio Mille Collines broadcast names, addresses, and even license-plate numbers. Killers often carried a machete in one hand and a transistor radio in the other. Tens of thousands of Tutsi fled their homes in panic and were snared and butchered at checkpoints. Little care was given to their disposal. Some were shoveled into landfills. Human flesh rotted in the sunshine. In churches bodies mingled with scattered hosts. If the killers had taken the time to tend to sanitation, it would have slowed their "sanitization" campaign.

IV. The "Last War"

The two tracks of events in Rwanda—simultaneous war and genocide—confused policymakers who had scant prior understanding of the country. Atrocities are often carried out in places that are not commonly visited, where outside expertise is limited. When country-specific knowledge is lacking, foreign governments become all the more likely to employ faulty analogies and to "fight the last war." The analogy employed by many of those who confronted the outbreak of killing in Rwanda was a peacekeeping intervention that had gone horribly wrong in Somalia.

On October 3, 1993, ten months after President Bush had sent U.S. troops to Somalia as part of what had seemed a low-risk humanitarian mission, U.S. Army Rangers and Delta special forces in Somalia attempted to seize several top advisers to the warlord Mohammed Farah Aideed. Aideed's faction had ambushed and killed two dozen Pakistani peacekeepers, and the United States was striking back. But in the firefight that ensued the Somali militia killed eighteen Americans, wounded seventy-three, and captured one Black Hawk helicopter pilot. Somali television broadcast both a video interview with the trembling, disoriented pilot and a gory procession in which the corpse of a U.S. Ranger was dragged through a Mogadishu street.

On receiving word of these events, President Clinton cut short a trip to California and convened an urgent crisis-management meeting at the White House. When an aide began recapping the situation, an angry President interrupted him. "Cut the bullshit," Clinton snapped. "Let's work this out." "Work it out" meant walk out. Republican Congressional pressure was intense. Clinton appeared on American television the next day, called off the manhunt for Aideed, temporarily reinforced the troop presence, and announced that all U.S. forces would be home within six months. The Pentagon leadership concluded that peacekeeping in Africa meant trouble and that neither the White House nor Congress would stand by it when the chips were down.

Even before the deadly blowup in Somalia the United States had resisted deploying a UN mission to Rwanda. "Anytime you mentioned peacekeeping in Africa," one U.S. official remembers, "the crucifixes and garlic would come up on every door." Having lost much of its early enthusiasm for peacekeeping and for the United Nations itself, Washington was nervous that the Rwanda mission would sour like so many others. But President Habyarimana had traveled to Washington in 1993 to offer assurances that his government was committed to carrying out the terms of the Arusha Accords. In the end, after strenuous lobbying by France (Rwanda's chief diplomatic and military patron), U.S. officials accepted the proposition that UNAMIR could be the rare "UN winner." On October 5, 1993, two days after the Somalia firefight, the United States reluctantly voted in the Security Council to authorize Dallaire's mission.

Even so, U.S. officials made it clear that Washington would give no consideration to sending U.S. troops to Rwanda. Somalia and another recent embarrassment in Haiti indicated that multilateral initiatives for humanitarian purposes would likely bring the United States all loss and no gain.

Against this backdrop, and under the leadership of Anthony Lake, the national-security adviser, the Clinton Administration accelerated the development of a formal U.S. peacekeeping doctrine. The job was given to Richard Clarke, of the National Security Council, a special assistant to the President who was known as one of the most effective bureaucrats in Washington. In an interagency process that lasted more than a year, Clarke managed the production of a presidential decision directive, PDD-25, which listed sixteen factors that policymakers needed to consider when deciding whether to support peacekeeping activities: seven factors if the United States was to vote in the UN Security Council on peace operations carried out by non-American soldiers, six additional and more stringent factors if U.S. forces were to participate in UN peacekeeping missions, and three final factors if U.S. troops were likely to engage in actual combat. In the words of Representative David Obey, of Wisconsin, the restrictive checklist tried to satisfy the American desire for "zero degree of involvement, and zero degree of risk, and zero degree of pain and confusion." The architects of the doctrine remain its strongest defenders. "Many say PDD-25 was some evil thing designed to kill peacekeeping, when in fact it was there to save peacekeeping," Clarke says. "Peacekeeping was almost dead. There was no support for it in the U.S. government, and the peacekeepers were not effective in the field." Although the directive was not publicly released until May 3, 1994, a month into the genocide, the considerations encapsulated in the doctrine and the Administration's frustration with peacekeeping greatly influenced the thinking of U.S. officials involved in shaping Rwanda policy.

V. The Peace Processors

Each of the American actors dealing with Rwanda brought particular institutional interests and biases to his or her handling of the crisis. Secretary of State Warren Christopher knew little about Africa. At one meeting with his top advisers, several weeks after the plane crash, he pulled an atlas off his shelf to help him locate the country. Belgian Foreign Minister Willie Claes recalls trying to discuss Rwanda with his American counterpart and being told, "I have other responsibilities." Officials in the State Department's Africa Bureau were, of course, better informed. Prudence Bushnell, the deputy assistant secretary, was one of them. The daughter of a diplomat, Bushnell had joined the foreign service in 1981, at the age of thirty-five. With her agile mind and sharp tongue, she had earned the attention of George Moose when she served under him at the U.S. embassy in Senegal. When Moose was named the assistant secretary of state for African affairs, in 1993, he made Bushnell his deputy. Just two weeks before the plane crash the State Department had dispatched Bushnell and a colleague to Rwanda in an effort to contain the escalating violence and to spur the stalled peace process.

Unfortunately, for all the concern of the Americans familiar with Rwanda, their diplomacy suffered from three weaknesses. First, ahead of the plane crash diplomats had repeatedly threatened to pull out UN peacekeepers in retaliation for the parties' failure to implement Arusha. These threats were of course counterproductive, because the very Hutu who opposed power-sharing wanted nothing more than a UN withdrawal. One senior U.S. official remembers, "The first response to trouble is 'Let's yank the peacekeepers.' But that is like believing that when children are misbehaving, the proper response is 'Let's send the baby-sitter home.'"

Second, before and during the massacres U.S. diplomacy revealed its natural bias toward states and toward negotiations. Because most official contact occurs between representatives of states,

U.S. officials were predisposed to trust the assurances of Rwandan officials, several of whom were plotting genocide behind the scenes. Those in the U.S. government who knew Rwanda best viewed the escalating violence with a diplomatic prejudice that left them both institutionally oriented toward the Rwandan government and reluctant to do anything to disrupt the peace process. An examination of the cable traffic from the U.S. embassy in Kigali to Washington between the signing of the Arusha agreement and the downing of the presidential plane reveals that setbacks were perceived as "dangers to the peace process" more than as "dangers to Rwandans." American criticisms were deliberately and steadfastly leveled at "both sides," though Hutu government and militia forces were usually responsible.

The U.S. ambassador in Kigali, David Rawson, proved especially vulnerable to such bias. Rawson had grown up in Burundi, where his father, an American missionary, had set up a Quaker hospital. He entered the foreign service in 1971. When, in 1993, at age fifty-two, he was given the embassy in Rwanda, his first, he could not have been more intimate with the region, the culture, or the peril. He spoke the local language— almost unprecedented for an ambassador in Central Africa. But Rawson found it difficult to imagine the Rwandans who surrounded the President as conspirators in genocide. He issued pro forma demarches over Habyarimana's obstruction of power-sharing, but the cable traffic shows that he accepted the President's assurances that he was doing all he could. The U.S. investment in the peace process gave rise to a wishful tendency to see peace "around the corner." Rawson remembers, "We were naive policy optimists, I suppose. The fact that negotiations can't work is almost not one of the options open to people who care about peace. We were looking for the hopeful signs, not the dark signs. In fact, we were looking away from the dark signs . . . One of the things I learned and should have already known is that once you launch a process, it takes on its own momentum. I had said, 'Let's try this, and then if it doesn't work, we can back away.' But bureaucracies don't allow that. Once the Washington side buys into a process, it gets pursued, almost blindly." Even after the Hutu government began exterminating Tutsi, U.S. diplomats focused most of their efforts on "re-establishing a cease-fire" and "getting Arusha back on track."

The third problematic feature of U.S. diplomacy before and during the genocide was a tendency toward blindness bred by familiarity: the few people in Washington who were paying attention to Rwanda before Habyarimana's plane was shot down were those who had been tracking Rwanda for some time and had thus come to expect a certain level of ethnic violence from the region. And because the U.S. government had done little when some 40,000 people had been killed in Hutu-Tutsi violence in Burundi in October of 1993, these officials also knew that Washington was prepared to tolerate substantial bloodshed. When the massacres began in April, some U.S. regional specialists initially suspected that Rwanda was undergoing "another flare-up" that would involve another "acceptable" (if tragic) round of ethnic murder.

Rawson had read up on genocide before his posting to Rwanda, surveying what had become a relatively extensive scholarly literature on its causes. But although he expected internecine killing, he did not anticipate the scale at which it occurred. "Nothing in Rwandan culture or history could have led a person to that forecast," he says. "Most of us thought that if a war broke out, it would be quick, that these poor people didn't have the resources, the means, to fight a sophisticated war. I couldn't have known that they would do each other in with the most economic means." George Moose agrees: "We were psychologically and imaginatively too limited."

■   ■   ■

VII. Genocide? What Genocide?

Just when did Washington know of the sinister Hutu designs on Rwanda's Tutsi? Writing in *Foreign Affairs* last year [2000], Alan Kuperman argued that President Clinton "could not have known that a nationwide genocide was under way" until about two weeks into the killing. It is true that the precise nature and extent of the slaughter was obscured by the civil war, the withdrawal of U.S. diplomatic sources, some confused press reporting, and the lies of the Rwandan government. Nonetheless, both the testimony of U.S. officials who worked the issue day to day and the declassified documents indicate that plenty was known about the killers' intentions.

A determination of genocide turns not on the numbers killed, which is always difficult to ascertain at a time of crisis, but on the perpetrators' intent: Were Hutu forces attempting to destroy Rwanda's Tutsi? The answer to this question was available early on. "By eight A.M. the morning after the plane crash we knew what was happening, that there was systematic killing of Tutsi," Joyce Leader recalls. "People were calling me and telling me who was getting killed. I knew they were going door to door." Back at the State Department she explained to her colleagues that three kinds of killing were going on: war, politically motivated murder, and genocide. Dallaire's early cables to New York likewise described the armed conflict that had resumed between rebels and government forces, and also stated plainly that savage "ethnic cleansing" of Tutsi was occurring. U.S. analysts warned that mass killings would increase. In an April 11 memo prepared for Frank Wisner, the undersecretary of defense for policy, in advance of a dinner with Henry Kissinger, a key talking point was "Unless both sides can be convinced to return to the peace process, a massive (hundreds of thousands of deaths) bloodbath will ensue."

Whatever the inevitable imperfections of U.S. intelligence early on, the reports from Rwanda were severe enough to distinguish Hutu killers from ordinary combatants in civil war. And they certainly warranted directing additional U.S. intelligence assets toward the region—to snap satellite photos of large gatherings of Rwandan civilians or of mass graves, to intercept military communications, or to infiltrate the country in person. Though there is no evidence that senior policy-makers deployed such assets, routine intelligence continued to pour in. On April 26 an unattributed intelligence memo titled "Responsibility for Massacres in Rwanda" reported that the ringleaders of the genocide, Colonel Théoneste Bagosora and his crisis committee, were determined to liquidate their opposition and exterminate the Tutsi populace. A May 9 Defense Intelligence Agency report stated plainly that the Rwandan violence was not spontaneous but was directed by the government, with lists of victims prepared well in advance. The DIA observed that an "organized parallel effort of *genocide* [was] being implemented by the army to destroy the leadership of the Tutsi community."

From April 8 onward media coverage featured eyewitness accounts describing the widespread targeting of Tutsi and the corpses piling up on Kigali's streets. American reporters relayed stories of missionaries and embassy officials who had been unable to save their Rwandan friends and neighbors from death. On April 9 a front-page *Washington Post* story quoted reports that the Rwandan employees of the major international relief agencies had been executed "in front of horrified expatriate staffers." On April 10 a *New York Times* front-page article quoted the Red Cross claim that "tens of thousands" were dead, 8,000 in Kigali alone, and that corpses were "in the houses, in the streets, everywhere." The *Post* the same day led its front-page story with a description of "a pile of corpses six feet high" outside the main hospital. On April 14 the *New York Times* reported the shooting and hacking to death of nearly 1,200 men, women,

and children in the church where they had sought refuge. On April 19 Human Rights Watch, which had excellent sources on the ground in Rwanda, estimated the number of dead at 100,000 and called for use of the term "genocide." The 100,000 figure (which proved to be a gross underestimate) was picked up immediately by the Western media, endorsed by the Red Cross, and featured on the front page of the *Washington Post*. On April 24 the *Post* reported how "the heads and limbs of victims were sorted and piled neatly, a bone-chilling order in the midst of chaos that harked back to the Holocaust." President Clinton certainly could have known that a genocide was under way, if he had wanted to know.

Even after the reality of genocide in Rwanda had become irrefutable, when bodies were shown choking the Kagera River on the nightly news, the brute fact of the slaughter failed to influence U.S. policy except in a negative way. American officials, for a variety of reasons, shunned the use of what became known as "the g-word." They felt that using it would have obliged the United States to act, under the terms of the 1948 Genocide Convention. They also believed, understandably, that it would harm U.S. credibility to name the crime and then do nothing to stop it. A discussion paper on Rwanda, prepared by an official in the Office of the Secretary of Defense and dated May 1, testifies to the nature of official thinking. Regarding issues that might be brought up at the next interagency working group, it stated,

1. Genocide Investigation: Language that calls for an international investigation of human rights abuses and possible violations of the genocide convention. *Be Careful. Legal at State was worried about this yesterday—Genocide finding could commit [the U.S. government] to actually "do something."* [Emphasis added.]

At an interagency teleconference in late April, Susan Rice, a rising star on the NSC who worked under Richard Clarke, stunned a few of the officials present when she asked, "If we use the word 'genocide' and are seen as doing nothing, what will be the effect on the November [congressional] election?" Lieutenant Colonel Tony Marley remembers the incredulity of his colleagues at the State Department. "We could believe that people would wonder that," he says, "but not that they would actually voice it." Rice does not recall the incident but concedes, "If I said it, it was completely inappropriate, as well as irrelevant."

The genocide debate in U.S. government circles began the last week of April, but it was not until May 21, six weeks after the killing began, that Secretary Christopher gave his diplomats permission to use the term "genocide"—sort of. The UN Human Rights Commission was about to meet in special session, and the U.S. representative, Geraldine Ferraro, needed guidance on whether to join a resolution stating that genocide had occurred. The stubborn U.S. stand had become untenable internationally.

The case for a label of genocide was straightforward, according to a May 18 confidential analysis prepared by the State Department's assistant secretary for intelligence and research, Toby Gati: lists of Tutsi victims' names and addresses had reportedly been prepared; Rwandan government troops and Hutu militia and youth squads were the main perpetrators; massacres were reported all over the country; humanitarian agencies were now "claiming from 200,000 to 500,000 lives" lost. Gati offered the intelligence bureau's view: "We believe 500,000 may be an exaggerated estimate, but no accurate figures are available. Systematic killings began within hours of Habyarimana's death. Most of those killed have been Tutsi civilians, including women and children." The terms of the Genocide Convention had been met. "We weren't quibbling about these numbers," Gati says. "We can never know precise figures, but our analysts had been reporting huge numbers of deaths for weeks. We were basically saying, 'A rose by any other name . . .'"

Despite this straightforward assessment, Christopher remained reluctant to speak the obvious truth. When he issued his guidance, on May 21, fully a month after Human Rights Watch had put a name to the tragedy, Christopher's instructions were hopelessly muddied.

> The delegation is authorized to agree to a resolution that states that "acts of genocide" have occurred in Rwanda or that "genocide has occurred in Rwanda." Other formulations that suggest that some, but not all of the killings in Rwanda are genocide . . . e.g. "genocide is taking place in Rwanda"—are authorized. Delegation is not authorized to agree to the characterization of any specific incident as genocide or to agree to any formulation that indicates that all killings in Rwanda are genocide.

Notably, Christopher confined permission to acknowledge full-fledged genocide to the upcoming session of the Human Rights Commission. Outside that venue State Department officials were authorized to state publicly only that *acts* of genocide had occurred.

Christine Shelly, a State Department spokesperson, had long been charged with publicly articulating the U.S. position on whether events in Rwanda counted as genocide. For two months she had avoided the term, and as her June 10 exchange with the Reuters correspondent Alan Elsner reveals, her semantic dance continued.

ELSNER: How would you describe the events taking place in Rwanda?

SHELLY: Based on the evidence we have seen from observations on the ground, we have every reason to believe that acts of genocide have occurred in Rwanda.

ELSNER: What's the difference between "acts of genocide" and "genocide"?

SHELLY: Well, I think the—as you know, there's a legal definition of this . . . clearly not all of the killings that have taken place in Rwanda are killings to which you might apply that label . . . But as to the distinctions between the words, we're trying to call what we have seen so far as best as we can; and based, again, on the evidence, we have every reason to believe that acts of genocide have occurred.

ELSNER: How many acts of genocide does it take to make genocide?

SHELLY: Alan, that's just not a question that I'm in a position to answer.

The same day, in Istanbul, Warren Christopher, by then under severe internal and external pressure, relented: "If there is any particular magic in calling it genocide, I have no hesitancy in saying that."

VIII. "Not Even a Sideshow"

Once the Americans had been evacuated, Rwanda largely dropped off the radar of most senior Clinton Administration officials. In the situation room on the seventh floor of the State Department a map of Rwanda had been hurriedly pinned to the wall in the aftermath of the plane crash, and eight banks of phones had rung off the hook. Now, with U.S. citizens safely home, the State Department chaired a daily interagency meeting, often by teleconference, designed to coordinate mid-level diplomatic and humanitarian responses. Cabinet-level officials focused on crises elsewhere. Anthony Lake recalls, "I was obsessed with Haiti and Bosnia during that period, so Rwanda was, in William Shawcross's words, a 'sideshow,' but not even a sideshow—a no-show." At the NSC the person who managed Rwanda policy was not Lake, the national-security adviser, who happened to know Africa, but Richard Clarke, who oversaw peace-keeping policy, and for whom the news from Rwanda only confirmed a deep skepticism about the viability of UN deployments. Clarke believed

that another UN failure could doom relations between Congress and the United Nations. He also sought to shield the President from congressional and public criticism. Donald Steinberg managed the Africa portfolio at the NSC and tried to look out for the dying Rwandans, but he was not an experienced infighter and, colleagues say, he "never won a single argument" with Clarke.

■ ■ ■

During the entire three months of the genocide Clinton never assembled his top policy advisers to discuss the killings. Anthony Lake likewise never gathered the "principals"—the Cabinet-level members of the foreign-policy team. Rwanda was never thought to warrant its own top-level meeting. When the subject came up, it did so along with, and subordinate to, discussions of Somalia, Haiti, and Bosnia. Whereas these crises involved U.S. personnel and stirred some public interest, Rwanda generated no sense of urgency and could safely be avoided by Clinton at no political cost. The editorial boards of the major American newspapers discouraged U.S. intervention during the genocide. They, like the Administration, lamented the killings but believed, in the words of an April 17 *Washington Post* editorial, "The United States has no recognizable national interest in taking a role, certainly not a leading role." Capitol Hill was quiet. Some in Congress were glad to be free of the expense of another flawed UN mission. Others, including a few members of the Africa subcommittees and the Congressional Black Caucus, eventually appealed tamely for the United States to play a role in ending the violence—but again, they did not dare urge U.S. involvement on the ground, and they did not kick up a public fuss. Members of Congress weren't hearing from their constituents. Pat Schroeder, of Colorado, said on April 30, "There are some groups terribly concerned about the gorillas . . . But—it sounds terrible—people just don't know what can be done about the people." Randall Robinson, of the nongovernmental organization TransAfrica, was preoccupied, staging a hunger strike to protest the U.S. repatriation of Haitian refugees. Human Rights Watch supplied exemplary intelligence and established important one-on-one contacts in the Administration, but the organization lacks a grassroots base from which to mobilize a broader segment of American society.

IX. The UN Withdrawal

When the killing began, Romeo Dallaire expected and appealed for reinforcements. Within hours of the plane crash he had cabled UN headquarters in New York: "Give me the means and I can do more." He was sending peacekeepers on rescue missions around the city, and he felt it was essential to increase the size and improve the quality of the UN's presence. But the United States opposed the idea of sending reinforcements, no matter where they were from. The fear, articulated mainly at the Pentagon but felt throughout the bureaucracy, was that what would start as a small engagement by foreign troops would end as a large and costly one by Americans. This was the lesson of Somalia, where U.S. troops had gotten into trouble in an effort to bail out the beleaguered Pakistanis. The logical outgrowth of this fear was an effort to steer clear of Rwanda entirely and be sure others did the same. Only by yanking Dallaire's entire peacekeeping force could the United States protect itself from involvement down the road.

One senior U.S. official remembers, "When the reports of the deaths of the ten Belgians came in, it was clear that it was Somalia redux, and the sense was that there would be an expectation everywhere that the U.S. would get involved. We thought leaving the peacekeepers in Rwanda and having them confront the violence would take us where we'd been before. It was a foregone conclusion that the United States wouldn't intervene and that the concept of UN peacekeeping could not be sacrificed again."

A foregone conclusion. What is most remarkable about the American response to the Rwandan genocide is not so much the absence of U.S. military action as that during the entire genocide the possibility of U.S. military intervention was never even debated. Indeed, the United States resisted intervention of any kind.

The bodies of the slain Belgian soldiers were returned to Brussels on April 14. One of the pivotal conversations in the course of the genocide took place around that time, when Willie Claes, the Belgian Foreign Minister, called the State Department to request "cover." "We are pulling out, but we don't want to be seen to be doing it alone," Claes said, asking the Americans to support a full UN withdrawal. Dallaire had not anticipated that Belgium would extract its soldiers, removing the backbone of his mission and stranding Rwandans in their hour of greatest need. "I expected the excolonial white countries would stick it out even if they took casualties," he remembers. "I thought their pride would have led them to stay to try to sort the place out. The Belgian decision caught me totally off guard. I was truly stunned."

Belgium did not want to leave ignominiously, by itself. Warren Christopher agreed to back Belgian requests for a full UN exit. Policy over the next month or so can be described simply: no U.S. military intervention, robust demands for a withdrawal of all of Dallaire's forces, and no support for a new UN mission that would challenge the killers. Belgium had the cover it needed.

On April 15 Christopher sent one of the most forceful documents to be produced in the entire three months of the genocide to Madeleine Albright at the UN—a cable instructing her to demand a full UN withdrawal. The cable, which was heavily influenced by Richard Clarke at the NSC, and which bypassed Donald Steinberg and was never seen by Anthony Lake, was unequivocal about the next steps. Saying that he had "fully" taken into account the "humanitarian reasons put forth for retention of UNAMIR elements in Rwanda," Christopher wrote that there was "insufficient justification" to retain a UN presence.

> The international community must give highest priority to full, orderly withdrawal of all UNAMIR personnel as soon as possible . . . We will oppose any effort at this time to preserve a UNAMIR presence in Rwanda . . . Our opposition to retaining a UNAMIR presence in Rwanda is firm. It is based on our conviction that the Security Council has an obligation to ensure that peacekeeping operations are viable, that they are capable of fulfilling their mandates, and that UN peacekeeping personnel are not placed or retained, knowingly, in an untenable situation.

"Once we knew the Belgians were leaving, we were left with a rump mission incapable of doing anything to help people," Clarke remembers. "They were doing nothing to stop the killings."

But Clarke underestimated the deterrent effect that Dallaire's very few peacekeepers were having. Although some soldiers hunkered down, terrified, others scoured Kigali, rescuing Tutsi, and later established defensive positions in the city, opening their doors to the fortunate Tutsi who made it through roadblocks to reach them. One Senegalese captain saved a hundred or so lives single-handedly. Some 25,000 Rwandans eventually assembled at positions manned by UNAMIR personnel. The Hutu were generally reluctant to massacre large groups of Tutsi if foreigners (armed or unarmed) were present. It did not take many UN soldiers to dissuade the Hutu from attacking. At the Hotel des Mille Collines ten peacekeepers and four UN military observers helped to protect the several hundred civilians sheltered there for the duration of the crisis. About 10,000 Rwandans gathered at the Amohoro Stadium under light UN cover. Brent Beardsley, Dallaire's executive assistant, remembers, "If there was any determined

resistance at close quarters, the government guys tended to back off." Kevin Aiston, the Rwanda desk officer at the State Department, was keeping track of Rwandan civilians under UN protection. When Prudence Bushnell told him of the U.S. decision to demand a UNAMIR withdrawal, he turned pale. "We can't," he said. Bushnell replied, "The train has already left the station."

On April 19 the Belgian Colonel Luc Marchal delivered his final salute and departed with the last of his soldiers. The Belgian withdrawal reduced Dallaire's troop strength to 2,100. More crucially, he lost his best troops. Command and control among Dallaire's remaining forces became tenuous. Dallaire soon lost every line of communication to the countryside. He had only a single satellite phone link to the outside world.

The UN Security Council now made a decision that sealed the Tutsi's fate and signaled the militia that it would have free rein. The U.S. demand for a full UN withdrawal had been opposed by some African nations, and even by Madeleine Albright; so the United States lobbied instead for a dramatic drawdown in troop strength. On April 21, amid press reports of some 100,000 dead in Rwanda, the Security Council voted to slash UNAMIR's forces to 270 men. Albright went along, publicly declaring that a "small, skeletal" operation would be left in Kigali to "show the will of the international community."

After the UN vote Clarke sent a memorandum to Lake reporting that language about "the safety and security of Rwandans under UN protection had been inserted by US/UN at the end of the day to prevent an otherwise unanimous UNSC from walking away from the at-risk Rwandans under UN protection as the peacekeepers drew down to 270." In other words, the memorandum suggested that the United States was *leading* efforts to ensure that the Rwandans under UN protection were not abandoned. The opposite was true.

Most of Dallaire's troops were evacuated by April 25. Though he was supposed to reduce the size of his force to 270, he ended up keeping 503 peacekeepers. By this time Dallaire was trying to deal with a bloody frenzy. "My force was standing knee-deep in mutilated bodies, surrounded by the guttural moans of dying people, looking into the eyes of children bleeding to death with their wounds burning in the sun and being invaded by maggots and flies," he later wrote. "I found myself walking through villages where the only sign of life was a goat, or a chicken, or a songbird, as all the people were dead, their bodies being eaten by voracious packs of wild dogs."

Dallaire had to work within narrow limits. He attempted simply to keep the positions he held and to protect the 25,000 Rwandans under UN supervision while hoping that the member states on the Security Council would change their minds and send him some help while it still mattered.

By coincidence Rwanda held one of the rotating seats on the Security Council at the time of the genocide. Neither the United States nor any other UN member state ever suggested that the representative of the genocidal government be expelled from the council. Nor did any Security Council country offer to provide safe haven to Rwandan refugees who escaped the carnage. In one instance Dallaire's forces succeeded in evacuating a group of Rwandans by plane to Kenya. The Nairobi authorities allowed the plane to land, sequestered it in a hangar, and, echoing the American decision to turn back the *S.S. St. Louis* during the Holocaust, then forced the plane to return to Rwanda. The fate of the passengers is unknown.

Throughout this period the Clinton Administration was largely silent. The closest it came to a public denunciation of the Rwandan government occurred after personal lobbying by Human Rights Watch, when Anthony Lake issued a statement calling on Rwandan military leaders by name to "do everything in their power to end the violence immediately." When I spoke with Lake six years later, and informed him that human-rights groups and U.S. officials point to this statement as the sum total of official public attempts to shame the Rwandan government in this period, he seemed stunned. "You're kidding," he said. "That's truly pathetic."

At the State Department the diplomacy was conducted privately, by telephone. Prudence Bushnell regularly set her alarm for 2:00 A.M. and phoned Rwandan government officials. She spoke several times with Augustin Bizimungu, the Rwandan military chief of staff. "These were the most bizarre phone calls," she says. "He spoke in perfectly charming French. 'Oh, it's so nice to hear from you,' he said. I told him, 'I am calling to tell you President Clinton is going to hold you accountable for the killings.' He said, 'Oh, how nice it is that your President is thinking of me.'"

X. The Pentagon "Chop"

The daily meeting of the Rwanda interagency working group was attended, either in person or by teleconference, by representatives from the various State Department bureaus, the Pentagon, the National Security Council, and the intelligence community. Any proposal that originated in the working group had to survive the Pentagon "chop." "Hard intervention," meaning U.S. military action, was obviously out of the question. But Pentagon officials routinely stymied initiatives for "soft intervention" as well.

The Pentagon discussion paper on Rwanda, referred to earlier, ran down a list of the working group's six short-term policy objectives and carped at most of them. The fear of a slippery slope was persuasive. Next to the seemingly innocuous suggestion that the United States "support the UN and others in attempts to achieve a cease-fire" the Pentagon official responded, "Need to change 'attempts' to 'political efforts'—without 'political' there is a danger of signing up to troop contributions."

The one policy move the Defense Department supported was a U.S. effort to achieve an arms embargo. But the same discussion paper acknowledged the ineffectiveness of this step:

"We do not envision it will have a significant impact on the killings because machetes, knives and other hand implements have been the most common weapons."

Dallaire never spoke to Bushnell or to Tony Marley, the U.S. military liaison to the Arusha process, during the genocide, but they all reached the same conclusions. Seeing that no troops were forthcoming, they turned their attention to measures short of full-scale deployment which might alleviate the suffering. Dallaire pleaded with New York, and Bushnell and her team recommended in Washington, that something be done to "neutralize" Radio Mille Collines.

The country best equipped to prevent the genocide planners from broadcasting murderous instructions directly to the population was the United States. Marley offered three possibilities. The United States could destroy the antenna. It could transmit "counter-broadcasts" urging perpetrators to stop the genocide. Or it could jam the hate radio station's broadcasts. This could have been done from an airborne platform such as the Air Force's Commando Solo airplane. Anthony Lake raised the matter with Secretary of Defense William Perry at the end of April. Pentagon officials considered all the proposals non-starters. On May 5 Frank Wisner, the undersecretary of defense for policy, prepared a memo for Sandy Berger, then the deputy national-security adviser. Wisner's memo testifies to the unwillingness of the U.S. government to make even financial sacrifices to diminish the killing.

We have looked at options to stop the broadcasts within the Pentagon, discussed them interagency and concluded jamming is an ineffective and expensive mechanism that will not accomplish the objective the NSC Advisor seeks.

International legal conventions complicate airborne or ground based jamming and the mountainous terrain reduces the effectiveness of either option. Commando Solo, an Air National Guard asset, is the only suitable DOD jamming platform. It costs approximately $8500 per flight hour and requires a semi-secure area of operations due to its vulnerability and limited self-protection.

I believe it would be wiser to use air to assist in Rwanda in the [food] relief effort . . .

The plane would have needed to remain in Rwandan airspace while it waited for radio transmissions to begin. "First we would have had to figure out whether it made sense to use Commando Solo," Wisner recalls. "Then we had to get it from where it was already and be sure it could be moved. Then we would have needed flight clearance from all the countries nearby. And then we would need the political go-ahead. By the time we got all this, weeks would have passed. And it was not going to solve the fundamental problem, which was one that needed to be addressed militarily." Pentagon planners understood that stopping the genocide required a military solution. Neither they nor the White House wanted any part in a military solution. Yet instead of undertaking other forms of intervention that might have at least saved some lives, they justified inaction by arguing that a military solution was required.

Whatever the limitations of radio jamming, which clearly would have been no panacea, most of the delays Wisner cites could have been avoided if senior Administration officials had followed through. But Rwanda was not their problem. Instead justifications for standing by abounded. In early May the State Department Legal Advisor's Office issued a finding against radio jamming, citing international broadcasting agreements and the American commitment to free speech. When Bushnell raised radio jamming yet again at a meeting, one Pentagon official chided her for naiveté: "Pru, radios don't kill people. *People* kill people!"

■   ■   ■

However significant and obstructionist the role of the Pentagon in April and May, Defense Department officials were stepping into a vacuum. As one U.S. official put it, "Look, nobody senior was paying any attention to this mess. And in the absence of any political leadership from the top, when you have one group that feels pretty strongly about what *shouldn't* be done, it is extremely likely they are going to end up shaping U.S. policy." Lieutenant General Wesley Clark looked to the White House for leadership. "The Pentagon is always going to be the last to want to intervene," he says. "It is up to the civilians to tell us they want to do something and we'll figure out how to do it."

■   ■   ■

XI. PDD-25 in Action

No sooner had most of Dallaire's forces been withdrawn, in late April, than a handful of nonpermanent members of the Security Council, aghast at the scale of the slaughter, pressed the major powers to send a new, beefed-up force (UNAMIR II) to Rwanda.

When Dallaire's troops had first arrived, in the fall of 1993, they had done so under a fairly traditional peacekeeping mandate known as a Chapter VI deployment—a mission that assumes a ceasefire and a desire on both sides to comply with a peace accord. The Security Council now had to decide whether it was prepared to move from peacekeeping to peace *enforcement*—that is, to a Chapter VII mission in a hostile environment. This would demand more peacekeepers with far greater resources, more-aggressive rules of engagement, and an explicit recognition that the UN soldiers were there to protect civilians.

Two proposals emerged. Dallaire submitted a plan that called for joining his remaining peacekeepers with about 5,000 well-armed soldiers he hoped could be gathered quickly by the Security Council. He wanted to secure Kigali and then fan outward to create safe havens for Rwandans who had gathered in large numbers at churches and schools and on hillsides around the country. The United States was one of the few countries that could supply the rapid airlift and logistic support needed to move reinforcements to the region. In a meeting with UN Secretary General Boutros Boutros-Ghali on May 10, Vice President Al Gore pledged U.S. help with transport.

Richard Clarke, at the NSC, and representatives of the Joint Chiefs challenged Dallaire's plan. "How do you plan to take control of the airport in Kigali so that the reinforcements will be able to land?" Clarke asked. He argued instead for an "outside-in" strategy, as opposed to Dallaire's "inside-out" approach. The U.S. proposal would have created protected zones for refugees at Rwanda's borders. It would have kept any U.S. pilots involved in airlifting the peacekeepers safely out of Rwanda. "Our proposal was the most feasible, doable thing that could have been done in the short term," Clarke insists. Dallaire's proposal, in contrast, "could not be done in the short term and could not attract peacekeepers." The U.S. plan—which was modeled on Operation Provide Comfort, for the Kurds of northern Iraq—seemed to assume that the people in need were refugees fleeing to the border, but most endangered Tutsi could not make it to the border. The most vulnerable Rwandans were those clustered together, awaiting salvation, deep inside Rwanda. Dallaire's plan would have had UN soldiers move to the Tutsi in hiding. The U.S. plan would have required civilians to move to the safe zones, negotiating murderous roadblocks on the way. "The two plans had very different objectives," Dallaire says. "My mission was to save Rwandans. Their mission was to put on a show at no risk."

America's new peacekeeping doctrine, of which Clarke was the primary architect, was unveiled on May 3, and U.S. officials applied its criteria zealously. PDD-25 did not merely circumscribe U.S.

participation in UN missions; it also limited U.S. support for other states that hoped to carry out UN missions. Before such missions could garner U.S. approval, policymakers had to answer certain questions: Were U.S. interests at stake? Was there a threat to world peace? A clear mission goal? Acceptable costs? Congressional, public, and allied support? A working cease-fire? A clear command-and-control arrangement? And, finally, what was the exit strategy?

The United States haggled at the Security Council and with the UN Department of Peacekeeping Operations for the first two weeks of May. U.S. officials pointed to the flaws in Dallaire's proposal without offering the resources that would have helped him to overcome them. On May 13 Deputy Secretary of State Strobe Talbott sent Madeleine Albright instructions on how the United States should respond to Dallaire's plan. Noting the logistic hazards of airlifting troops into the capital, Talbott wrote, "The U.S. is not prepared at this point to lift heavy equipment and troops into Kigali." The "more manageable" operation would be to create the protected zones at the border, secure humanitarian-aid deliveries, and "promot[e] restoration of a ceasefire and return to the Arusha Peace Process." Talbott acknowledged that even the minimalist American proposal contained "many unanswered questions":

> Where will the needed forces come from; how will they be transported . . . where precisely should these safe zones be created; . . . would UN forces be authorized to move out of the zones to assist affected populations not in the zones . . . will the fighting parties in Rwanda agree to this arrangement . . . what conditions would need to obtain for the operation to end successfully?

Nonetheless, Talbott concluded, "We would urge the UN to explore and refine this alternative and present the Council with a menu of at least two options in a formal report from the [Secretary General] along with cost estimates before the Security Council votes on changing UNAMIR's mandate." U.S. policymakers were asking valid questions. Dallaire's plan certainly would have required the intervening troops to take risks in an effort to reach the targeted Rwandans or to confront the Hutu militia and government forces. But the business-as-usual tone of the American inquiry did not seem appropriate to the unprecedented and utterly unconventional crisis that was under way.

On May 17, by which time most of the Tutsi victims of the genocide were already dead, the United States finally acceded to a version of Dallaire's plan. However, few African countries stepped forward to offer troops. Even if troops had been immediately available, the lethargy of the major powers would have hindered their use. Though the Administration had committed the United States to provide armored support if the African nations provided soldiers, Pentagon stalling resumed. On May 19 the UN formally requested fifty American armored personnel carriers. On May 31 the United States agreed to send the APCs from Germany to Entebbe, Uganda. But squabbles between the Pentagon and UN planners arose. Who would pay for the vehicles? Should the vehicles be tracked or wheeled? Would the UN buy them or simply lease them? And who would pay the shipping costs? Compounding the disputes was the fact that Department of Defense regulations prevented the U.S. Army from preparing the vehicles for transport until contracts had been signed. The Defense Department demanded that it be reimbursed $15 million for shipping spare parts and equipment to and from Rwanda. In mid-June the White House finally intervened. On June 19, a month after the UN request, the United States began transporting the APCs, but they were missing the radios and heavy machine guns that would be needed if UN troops came under fire. By the time the APCs arrived, the genocide was over—halted by Rwandan Patriotic Front forces under the command of the Tutsi leader, Paul Kagame.

XII. The Stories We Tell

It is not hard to conceive of how the United States might have done things differently. Ahead of the plane crash, as violence escalated, it could have agreed to Belgian pleas for UN reinforcements. Once the killing of thousands of Rwandans a day had begun, the President could have deployed U.S. troops to Rwanda. The United States could have joined Dallaire's beleaguered UNAMIR forces or, if it feared associating with shoddy UN peacekeeping, it could have intervened unilaterally with the Security Council's backing, as France eventually did in late June. The United States could also have acted without the UN's blessing, as it did five years later in Kosovo. Securing congressional support for U.S. intervention would have been extremely difficult, but by the second week of the killing Clinton could have made the case that something approximating genocide was under way, that a supreme American value was imperiled by its occurrence, and that U.S. contingents at relatively low risk could stop the extermination of a people.

Alan Kuperman wrote in *Foreign Affairs* that President Clinton was in the dark for two weeks; by the time a large U.S. force could deploy, it would not have saved "even half of the ultimate victims." The evidence indicates that the killers' intentions were known by mid-level officials and knowable by their bosses within a week of the plane crash. Any failure to fully appreciate the genocide stemmed from political, moral, and imaginative weaknesses, not informational ones. As for what force could have accomplished, Kuperman's claims are purely speculative. We cannot know how the announcement of a robust or even a limited U.S. deployment would have affected the perpetrators' behavior. It is worth noting that even Kuperman concedes that belated intervention would have saved 75,000 to 125,000—no small achievement. A more serious challenge comes from the U.S. officials who argue that no amount of

leadership from the White House would have overcome congressional opposition to sending U.S. troops to Africa. But even if that highly debatable point was true, the United States still had a variety of options. Instead of leaving it to mid-level officials to communicate with the Rwandan leadership behind the scenes, senior officials in the Administration could have taken control of the process. They could have publicly and frequently denounced the slaughter. They could have branded the crimes "genocide" at a far earlier stage. They could have called for the expulsion of the Rwandan delegation from the Security Council. On the telephone, at the UN, and on the Voice of America they could have threatened to prosecute those complicit in the genocide, naming names when possible. They could have deployed Pentagon assets to jam—even temporarily—the crucial, deadly radio broadcasts.

Instead of demanding a UN withdrawal, quibbling over costs, and coming forward (belatedly) with a plan better suited to caring for refugees than to stopping massacres, U.S. officials could have worked to make UNAMIR a force to contend with. They could have urged their Belgian allies to stay and protect Rwandan civilians. If the Belgians insisted on withdrawing, the White House could have done everything within its power to make sure that Dallaire was immediately reinforced. Senior officials could have spent U.S. political capital rallying troops from other nations and could have supplied strategic airlift and logistic support to a coalition that it had helped to create. In short, the United States could have led the world.

Why did none of these things happen? One reason is that all possible sources of pressure—U.S. allies, Congress, editorial boards, and the American people—were mute when it mattered for Rwanda. American leaders have a circular and deliberate relationship to public opinion. It is circular because public opinion is rarely if ever aroused by foreign crises, even genocidal ones, in the absence of political leadership, and yet at the same time, American leaders continually cite the absence of public support as grounds for inaction. The relationship is deliberate because American leadership is not absent in such circumstances: it was present regarding Rwanda, but devoted mainly to suppressing public outrage and thwarting UN initiatives so as to avoid acting.

Strikingly, most officials involved in shaping U.S. policy were able to define the decision not to stop genocide as ethical and moral. The Administration employed several devices to keep down enthusiasm for action and to preserve the public's sense—and, more important, its own—that U.S. policy choices were not merely politically astute but also morally acceptable. First, Administration officials exaggerated the extremity of the possible responses. Time and again U.S. leaders posed the choice as between staying out of Rwanda and "getting involved everywhere." In addition, they often presented the choice as one between doing nothing and sending in the Marines. On May 25, at the Naval Academy graduation ceremony, Clinton described America's relationship to ethnic trouble spots: "We cannot turn away from them, but our interests are not sufficiently at stake in so many of them to justify a commitment of our folks."

Second, Administration policymakers appealed to notions of the greater good. They did not simply frame U.S. policy as one contrived in order to advance the national interest or avoid U.S. casualties. Rather, they often argued against intervention from the standpoint of people committed to protecting human life. Owing to recent failures in UN peacekeeping, many humanitarian interventionists in the U.S. government were concerned about the future of America's relationship with the United Nations generally and peacekeeping specifically. They believed that the UN and humanitarianism could not afford another Somalia. Many internalized the belief that the UN had more to lose by sending reinforcements and failing than by

allowing the killings to proceed. Their chief priority, after the evacuation of the Americans, was looking after UN peacekeepers, and they justified the withdrawal of the peacekeepers on the grounds that it would ensure a future for humanitarian intervention. In other words, Dallaire's peacekeeping mission in Rwanda had to be destroyed so that peacekeeping might be saved for use elsewhere.

A third feature of the response that helped to console U.S. officials at the time was the sheer flurry of Rwanda-related activity. U.S. officials with a special concern for Rwanda took their solace from mini-victories—working on behalf of specific individuals or groups (Monique Mujawamariya; the Rwandans gathered at the hotel). Government officials involved in policy met constantly and remained "seized of the matter"; they neither appeared nor felt indifferent. Although little in the way of effective intervention emerged from midlevel meetings in Washington or New York, an abundance of memoranda and other documents did.

Finally, the almost willful delusion that what was happening in Rwanda did not amount to genocide created a nurturing ethical framework for inaction. "War" was "tragic" but created no moral imperative.

What is most frightening about this story is that it testifies to a system that in effect worked. President Clinton and his advisers had several aims. First, they wanted to avoid engagement in a conflict that posed little threat to American interests, narrowly defined. Second, they sought to appease a restless Congress by showing that they were cautious in their approach to peacekeeping. And third, they hoped to contain the political costs and avoid the moral stigma associated with allowing genocide. By and large, they achieved all three objectives. The normal operations of the foreign-policy bureaucracy and the international community permitted an illusion of continual deliberation, complex activity, and intense concern, even as Rwandans were left to die.

Robert O. Keohane

FROM *AFTER HEGEMONY*
Cooperation and Discord in the World Political Economy

Realism, Institutionalism, and Cooperation

Impressed with the difficulties of cooperation, observers have often compared world politics to a "state of war." In this conception, international politics is "a competition of units in the kind of state of nature that knows no restraints other than those which the changing necessities of the game and the shallow conveniences of the players impose" (Hoffmann, 1965, p. vii). It is anarchic in the sense that it lacks an authoritative government that can enact and enforce rules of behavior. States must rely on "the means they can generate and the arrangements they can make for themselves" (Waltz, 1979, p. 111). Conflict and war result, since each state is judge in its own cause and can use force to carry out its judgments (Waltz, 1959, p. 159). The discord that prevails is accounted for by fundamental conflicts of interest (Waltz, 1959; Tucker, 1977).

Were this portrayal of world politics correct, any cooperation that occurs would be derivative from overall patterns of conflict. Alliance cooperation would be easy to explain as a result of the operation of a balance of power, but system-wide patterns of cooperation that benefit many

From Robert O. Keohane, *After Hegemony: Cooperation and Discord in the World Political Economy* (Princeton, N.J.: Princeton University Press, 1984), Chaps. 1, 6, 7. Some of the author's notes have been omitted.

countries without being tied to an alliance system directed against an adversary would not. If international politics were a state of war, institutionalized patterns of cooperation on the basis of shared purposes should not exist except as part of a larger struggle for power. The extensive patterns of international agreement that we observe on issues as diverse as trade, financial relations, health, telecommunications, and environmental protection would be absent.

At the other extreme from these "Realists" are writers who see cooperation as essential in a world of economic interdependence, and who argue that shared economic interests create a demand for international institutions and rules (Mitrany, 1975). Such an approach, which I refer to as "Institutionalist" because of its adherents' emphasis on the functions performed by international institutions, runs the risk of being naive about power and conflict. Too often its proponents incorporate in their theories excessively optimistic assumptions about the role of ideals in world politics, or about the ability of statesmen to learn what the theorist considers the "right lessons." But sophisticated students of institutions and rules have a good deal to teach us. They view institutions not simply as formal organizations with headquarters buildings and specialized staffs, but more broadly as "recognized patterns of practice around which expectations converge" (Young, 1980, p. 337). They regard these patterns of practice as significant because they affect state behavior. Sophisticated institutionalists do not expect cooperation always to prevail, but they are aware of the malleability of interests and they argue that interdependence creates interests in cooperation.

During the first twenty years or so after World War II, these views, though very different in their intellectual origins and their broader implications about human society, made similar predictions about the world political economy, and particularly about the subject of this [discussion], the political economy of the advanced market-economy countries. Institutionalists expected successful cooperation in one field to "spill over" into others (Haas, 1958). Realists anticipated a relatively stable international economic order as a result of the dominance of the United States. Neither set of observers was surprised by what happened, although they interpreted events differently.

Institutionalists could interpret the liberal international arrangements for trade and international finance as responses to the need for policy coordination created by the fact of interdependence. These arrangements, which we will call "international regimes," contained rules, norms, principles, and decisionmaking procedures. Realists could reply that these regimes were constructed on the basis of principles espoused by the United States, and that American power was essential for their construction and maintenance. For Realists, in other words, the early postwar regimes rested on the *political hegemony* of the United States. Thus Realists and Institutionalists could both regard early postwar developments as supporting their theories.

After the mid-1960s, however, U.S. dominance in the world political economy was challenged by the economic recovery and increasing unity of Europe and by the rapid economic growth of Japan. Yet economic interdependence continued to grow, and the pace of increased U.S. involvement in the world economy even accelerated after 1970. At this point, therefore, the Institutionalist and Realist predictions began to diverge. From a strict Institutionalist standpoint, the increasing need for coordination of policy, created by interdependence, should have led to more cooperation. From a Realist perspective, by contrast, the diffusion of power should have undermined the ability of anyone to create order.

On the surface, the Realists would seem to have made the better forecast. Since the late 1960s there have been signs of decline in the extent and efficacy of efforts to cooperate in the world political economy. As American power eroded, so did international regimes. The erosion of these regimes after World War II certainly refutes a naive version of the Institutionalist faith in interdependence as a solvent of conflict and a creator of cooperation. But it does not prove that only the Realist emphasis on power as a creator of order is valid. It might be possible, after the decline of hegemonic regimes, for more symmetrical patterns of cooperation to evolve after a transitional period of discord. Indeed, the persistence of attempts at cooperation during the 1970s suggests that the decline of hegemony does not necessarily sound cooperation's death knell.

International cooperation and discord thus remain puzzling. Under what conditions can independent countries cooperate in the world political economy? In particular, can cooperation take place without hegemony and, if so, how? This [project] is designed to help us find answers to these questions. I begin with Realist insights about the role of power and the effects of hegemony. But my central arguments draw more on the Institutionalist tradition, arguing that cooperation can under some conditions develop on the basis of complementary interests, and that institutions, broadly defined, affect the patterns of cooperation that emerge.

Hegemonic leadership is unlikely to be revived in this century for the United States or any other country. Hegemonic powers have historically only emerged after world wars; during peacetime, weaker countries have tended to gain on the hegemon rather than vice versa (Gilpin, 1981). It is difficult to believe that world civilization, much less a complex international economy, would survive such a war in the nuclear age. Certainly no prosperous hegemonic power is likely to emerge from such a cataclysm. As long as a world political economy persists, therefore, its central political dilemma will be how to organize cooperation without hegemony.

■ ■ ■

A Functional Theory of International Regimes

* * * [I]nternational regimes could be created and emphasized their value for overcoming what could be called "political market failure." * * * [Following is a] detailed examination of this argument by exploring why political market failure occurs and how international regimes can help to overcome it. This investigation will help us understand both why states often comply with regime rules and why international regimes can be maintained even after the conditions that facilitated their creation have disappeared. The functional theory developed in this chapter will therefore suggest some reasons to believe that even if U.S. hegemonic leadership may have been a crucial factor in the creation of some contemporary international economic regimes, the continuation of hegemony is not necessarily essential for their continued viability.

Political Market Failure and the Coase Theorem

Like imperfect markets, world politics is characterized by institutional deficiencies that inhibit mutually advantageous cooperation. * * * [I]n this self-help system, [there are] conflicts of interest between actors. In economic terms, these conflicts

can be regarded as arising in part from the existence of externalities: actors do not bear the full costs, or receive the full benefits, of their own actions.[1] Yet in a famous article Ronald Coase (1960) argued that the presence of externalities alone does not necessarily prevent effective coordination among independent actors. Under certain conditions, declared Coase, bargaining among these actors could lead to solutions that are Pareto-optimal regardless of the rules of legal liability.

To illustrate the Coase theorem and its counter-intuitive result, suppose that soot emitted by a paint factory is deposited by the wind onto clothing hanging outdoors in the yard of an old-fashioned laundry. Assume that the damage to the laundry is greater than the $20,000 it would cost the laundry to enclose its yard and install indoor drying equipment; so if no other alternative were available, it would be worthwhile for the laundry to take these actions. Assume also, however, that it would cost the paint factory only $10,000 to eliminate its emissions of air pollutants. Social welfare would clearly be enhanced by eliminating the pollution rather than by installing indoor drying equipment, but in the absence of either governmental enforcement or bargaining, the egoistic owner of the paint factory would have no incentive to spend anything to achieve this result.

It has frequently been argued that this sort of situation requires centralized governmental authority to provide the public good of clean air. Thus if the laundry had an enforceable legal right to demand compensation, the factory owner would have an incentive to invest $10,000 in pollution control devices to avoid a $20,000 court judgment. Coase argued, however, that the pollution would be cleaned up equally efficiently even if the laundry had no such recourse. If the law, or the existence of a decentralized self-help system, gave the factory a right to pollute, the laundry owner could simply pay the factory owner a sum greater than $10,000, but less than $20,000, to install anti-soot equipment. Both parties would agree to some such bargain, since both would benefit.

In either case, the externality of pollution would be eliminated. The key difference would not be one of economic efficiency, but of distribution of benefits between the factory and the laundry. In a self-help system, the laundry would have to pay between $10,000 and $20,000 and the factory would reap a profit from its capacity to pollute. But if legal liability rules were based on "the polluter pays principle," the laundry would pay nothing and the factory would have to invest $10,000 without reaping a financial return. Coase did not dispute that rules of liability could be evaluated on grounds of fairness, but insisted that, given his assumptions, efficient arrangements could be consummated even where the rules of liability favored producers of externalities rather than their victims.

The Coase theorem has frequently been used to show the efficacy of bargaining without central authority, and it has occasionally been applied specifically to international relations (Conybeare, 1980). The principle of sovereignty in effect establishes rules of liability that put the burden of externalities on those who suffer from them. The Coase theorem could be interpreted, therefore, as predicting that problems of collective action could easily be overcome in international politics through bargaining and mutual adjustment—that is, through cooperation * * * The further inference could be drawn that the discord observed must be the result of fundamental conflicts of interest rather than problems of coordination. The Coase theorem, in other words, could be taken as minimizing the importance of [Mancur] Olson's [1965] perverse logic of collective action or of the problems of coordination emphasized by game theory. However, such a conclusion would be incorrect for two compelling sets of reasons.

In the first place, Coase specified three crucial conditions for his conclusion to hold. These were: a legal framework establishing liability for actions, presumably supported by governmental authority; perfect information; and zero transaction costs (including organization costs and the costs of making side-payments). It is absolutely clear that none of these conditions is met in world politics. World government does not exist, making property rights and rules of legal liability fragile; information is extremely costly and often held unequally by different actors; transaction costs, including costs of organization and side-payments, are often very high. Thus an *inversion* of the Coase theorem would seem more appropriate to our subject. In the absence of the conditions that Coase specified, coordination will often be thwarted by dilemmas of collective action.

Second, recent critiques of Coase's argument reinforce the conclusion that it cannot simply be applied to world politics, and suggest further interesting implications about the functions of international regimes. It has been shown on the basis of game theory that, with more than two participants, the Coase theorem cannot necessarily be demonstrated. Under certain conditions, there will be no stable solution: any coalition that forms will be inferior, for at least one of its members, to another possible coalition. The result is an infinite regress. In game-theoretic terminology, the "core" of the game is empty. When the core is empty, the assumption of zero transaction costs means that agreement is hindered rather than facilitated: "in a world of zero transaction costs, the inherent instability of all coalitions could result in endless recontracting among the firms" (Aivazian and Callen, 1981, p. 179; Veljanovski, 1982).

What do Coase and his critics together suggest about the conditions for international cooperation through bargaining? First, it appears that approximating Coase's first two conditions—that is, having a clear legal framework establishing property rights and low-cost information available in a roughly equal way to all parties—will tend to facilitate cooperative solutions. But the implications of reducing transaction costs are more complex. If transaction costs are too high, no bargains will take place; but if they are too low, under certain conditions an infinite series of unstable coalitions may form.

Inverting the Coase theorem allows us to analyze international institutions largely as responses to problems of property rights, uncertainty, and transaction costs. Without consciously designed institutions, these problems will thwart attempts to cooperate in world politics even when actors' interests are complementary. From the deficiency of the "self-help system" (even from the perspective of purely self-interested national actors) we derive a need for international regimes. Insofar as they fill this need, international regimes perform the functions of establishing patterns of legal liability, providing relatively symmetrical information, and arranging the costs of bargaining so that specific agreements can more easily be made. Regimes are developed in part because actors in world politics believe that with such arrangements they will be able to make mutually beneficial agreements that would otherwise be difficult or impossible to attain.

This is to say that the architects of regimes anticipate that the regimes will facilitate cooperation. Within the functional argument being constructed here, these expectations explain the formation of the regimes: the *anticipated effects* of the regimes account for the actions of governments that establish them. Governments believe that *ad hoc* attempts to construct particular agreements, without a regime framework, will yield inferior results compared to negotiations within the framework of regimes. Following our inversion of the Coase theorem, we can classify the reasons for this belief under the categories of legal liability (property rights), transaction costs, and problems of uncertainty. We will consider these issues in turn.

LEGAL LIABILITY

Since governments put a high value on the maintenance of their own autonomy, it is usually impossible to establish international institutions that exercise authority over states. This fact is widely recognized by officials of international organizations and their advocates in national governments as well as by scholars. It would therefore be mistaken to regard international regimes, or the organizations that constitute elements of them, as characteristically unsuccessful attempts to institutionalize centralized authority in world politics. They cannot establish patterns of legal liability that are as solid as those developed within well-ordered societies, and their architects are well aware of this limitation.

Of course, the lack of a hierarchical structure of world politics does not prevent regimes from developing bits and pieces of law (Henkin, 1979, pp. 13–22). But the principal significance of international regimes does not lie in their formal legal status, since any patterns of legal liability and property rights established in world politics are subject to being overturned by the actions of sovereign states. International regimes are more like the "quasi-agreements" that William Fellner (1949) discusses when analyzing the behavior of oligopolistic firms than they are like governments. These quasi-agreements are legally unenforceable but, like contracts, help to organize relationships in mutually beneficial ways (Lowry, 1979, p. 276). Regimes also resemble conventions: practices, regarded as common knowledge in a community, that actors conform to not because they are uniquely best, but because others conform to them as well (Hardin, 1982; Lewis, 1969; Young, 1983). What these arrangements have in common is that they are designed not to implement centralized enforcement of agreements, but rather to establish stable mutual expectations about others' patterns of behavior and to develop working relationships that will allow the parties to adapt their practices to new situations. Contracts, conventions, and quasi-agreements provide information and generate patterns of transaction costs: costs of reneging on commitments are increased, and the costs of operating within these frameworks are reduced.

Both these arrangements and international regimes are often weak and fragile. Like contracts and quasi-agreements, international regimes are frequently altered: their rules are changed, bent, or broken to meet the exigencies of the moment. They are rarely enforced automatically, and they are not self-executing. Indeed, they are often matters for negotiation and renegotiation. As [Donald] Puchala has argued, "attempts to enforce EEC regulations open political cleavages up and down the supranational-to-local continuum and spark intense politicking along the cleavage lines" (1975, p. 509).

TRANSACTION COSTS

Like oligopolistic quasi-agreements, international regimes alter the relative costs of transactions. Certain agreements are forbidden. Under the provisions of the General Agreement on Tariffs and Trade (GATT), for instance, it is not permitted to make discriminatory trade arrangements except under specific conditions. Since there is no centralized government, states can nevertheless implement such actions, but their lack of legitimacy means that such measures are likely to be costly. Under GATT rules, for instance, retaliation against such behavior is justified. By elevating injunctions to the level of principles and rules, furthermore, regimes construct linkages between issues. No longer does a specific discriminatory agreement constitute merely a particular act without general significance; on the contrary, it becomes a "violation of GATT" with serious implications for a large number of other issues. In the terms of Prisoners' Dilemma, the situation has been transformed from a single-play to an iterated game. In market-failure terms, the transaction costs of certain possible bargains have been increased, while the costs of others have been reduced. In either case, the result is the same: incentives to violate regime principles are reduced. International regimes reduce transaction costs of legitimate bargains and increase them for illegitimate ones.

International regimes also affect transaction costs in the more mundane sense of making it cheaper for governments to get together to negotiate agreements. It is more convenient to make agreements within a regime than outside of one. International economic regimes usually incorporate international organizations that provide forums for meetings and secretariats that can act as catalysts for agreement. Insofar as their principles and rules can be applied to a wide variety of particular issues, they are efficient: establishing the rules and principles at the outset makes it unnecessary to renegotiate them each time a specific question arises.

International regimes thus allow governments to take advantage of potential economics of scale. Once a regime has been established, the marginal cost of dealing with each additional issue will be lower than it would be without a regime. * * * [I]f a policy area is sufficiently dense, establishing a regime will be worthwhile. Up to a point there may even be what economists call "increasing returns to scale." In such a situation, each additional issue could be included under the regime at lower cost than the previous one. As [Paul] Samuelson notes, in modern economies, "increasing returns is the prime case of deviations from perfect competition" (1967, p. 117). In world politics, we should expect increasing returns to scale to lead to more extensive international regimes.

In view of the benefits of economies of scale, it is not surprising that specific agreements tend to be "nested" within regimes. For instance, an agreement by the United States, Japan, and the European Community in the Multilateral Trade Negotiations to reduce a particular tariff will be affected by the rules and principles of GATT—that is, by the trade regime. The trade regime, in turn, is nested within a set of other arrangements, including those for monetary relations, energy, foreign investment, aid to developing countries, and other issues, which together constitute a complex and interlinked pattern of relations among the advance market-economy countries. These, in turn, are related to military-security relations among the major states.[2]

The nesting patterns of international regimes affect transaction costs by making it easier or more difficult to link particular issues and to arrange side-payments, giving someone something on one issue in return for her help on another.[3] Clustering of issues under a regime facilitates side-payments among these issues: more potential *quids* are available for the *quo*. Without international regimes linking clusters of issues to one another, side-payments and linkages would be difficult to arrange in world politics; in the absence of a price system for the exchange of favors, institutional barriers would hinder the construction of mutually beneficial bargains.

Suppose, for instance, that each issue were handled separately from all others, by a different governmental bureau in each country. Since a side-payment or linkage always means that a government must give up something on one dimension to get something on another, there would always be a bureaucratic loser within each government. Bureaus that would lose from proposed side-payments, on issues that matter to them, would be unlikely to bear the costs of these linkages willingly on the basis of other agencies' claims that the national interest required it.

Of course, each issue is not considered separately by a different governmental department or bureau. On the contrary, issues are grouped together, in functionally organized departments such as Treasury, Commerce, and Energy (in the United States). Furthermore, how governments organize themselves to deal with foreign policy is affected by how issues are organized internationally; issues considered by different regimes are often dealt with by different bureaucracies at home. Linkages and side-payments among issues grouped in the same regime thus become easier,

since the necessary internal tradeoffs will tend to take place within rather than across bureaus; but linkages among issues falling into different regimes will remain difficult, or even become more so (since the natural linkages on those issues will be with issues within the same regime).

Insofar as issues are dealt with separately from one another on the international level, it is often hard, in simply bureaucratic terms, to arrange for them to be considered together. There are bound to be difficulties in coordinating policies of different international organizations—GATT, the IMF [International Monetary Fund], and the IEA [International Energy Agency] all have different memberships and different operating styles—in addition to the resistance that will appear to such a move within member governments. Within regimes, by contrast, side-payments are facilitated by the fact that regimes bring together negotiators to consider sets of issues that may well lie within the negotiators' bureaucratic bailiwicks at home. GATT negotiations, as well as deliberations on the international monetary system, have been characterized by extensive bargaining over side-payments and the politics of issue-linkage (Hutton, 1975). The well-known literature on "spillover" in bargaining, relating to the European Community and other integration schemes, can also be interpreted as concerned with side-payments. According to these writings, expectations that an integration arrangement can be expanded to new issue-areas permit the broadening of potential side-payments, thus facilitating agreement (Haas, 1958).

We conclude that international regimes affect the costs of transactions. The value of a potential agreement to its prospective participants will depend, in part, on how consistent it is with principles of legitimacy embodied in international regimes. Transactions that violate these principles will be costly. Regimes also affect bureaucratic costs of transactions: successful regimes organize issue-areas so that productive linkages (those that facilitate agreements consistent with the principles of the regime) are facilitated, while destructive linkages and bargains that are inconsistent with regime principles are discouraged.

UNCERTAINTY AND INFORMATION

From the perspective of market-failure theories, the informational functions of regimes are the most important of all. * * * [W]hat Akerlof [1970] called "quality uncertainty" was the crucial problem in [a] "market for lemons" example. Even in games of pure coordination with stable equilibria, this may be a problem. Conventions—commuters meeting under the clock at Grand Central Station, suburban families on a shopping trip "meeting at the car"—become important. But in simple games of coordination, severe information problems are not embedded in the structure of relationships, since actors have incentives to reveal information and their own preferences fully to one another. In these games the problem is to reach some point of agreement; but it may not matter much which of several possible points is chosen (Schelling, 1960/1978). Conventions are important and ingenuity may be required, but serious systemic impediments to the acquisition and exchange of information are lacking (Lewis, 1969; Young, 1983).

Yet as we have seen in * * * discussions of collective action and Prisoners' Dilemma, many situations—both in game theory and in world politics—are characterized by conflicts of interest as well as common interests. In such situations, actors have to worry about being deceived and double-crossed, just as the buyer of a used car has to guard against purchasing a "lemon." The literature on market failure elaborates on its most fundamental contention—that, in the absence of appropriate institutions, some mutually advantageous bargains will not be made because of uncertainty—by pointing to three particularly important sources of difficulty: *asymmetrical information; moral hazard;* and *irresponsibility.*

ASYMMETRICAL INFORMATION   Some actors may know more about a situation than others. Expecting that the resulting bargains would be unfair, "outsiders" will be reluctant to make agreements with "insiders" (Williamson, 1975, pp. 31–33). This is essentially the problem of "quality uncertainty" as discussed by Akerlof. Recall that this is a problem not merely of insufficient information, but rather of *systematically biased* patterns of information, which are recognized in advance of any agreement both by the holder of more information (the seller of the used car) and by its less well-informed prospective partner (the potential buyer of the "lemon" or "creampuff," as the case may be). Awareness that others have greater knowledge than oneself, and are therefore capable of manipulating a relationship or even engaging successful deception and double-cross, is a barrier to making agreements. When this suspicion is unfounded—that is, the agreement would be mutually benefical—it is an obstacle to improving welfare through cooperation.

This problem of asymmetrical information only appears when dishonest behavior is possible. In a society of saints, communication would be open and no one would take advantage of superior information. In our imperfect world, however, asymmetries of information are not rectified simply by communication. Not all communication reduces uncertainty, since communication may lead to asymmetrical or unfair bargaining outcomes as a result of deception. Effective communication is not measured well by the amount of talking that used-car salespersons do to customers or that governmental officials do to one another in negotiating international regimes! The information that is required in entering into an international regime is not merely information about other governments' resources and formal negotiating positions, but also accurate knowledge of their future positions. In part, this is a matter of estimating whether they will keep their commitments. As the "market for lemons" example suggests, and as we will see in more detail below, a government's reputation therefore becomes an important asset in persuading others to enter into agreements with it. International regimes help governments to assess others' reputations by providing standards of behavior against which performance can be measured, by linking these standards to specific issues, and by providing forums, often through international organizations, in which these evaluations can be made.[4] Regimes may also include international organizations whose secretariats act not only as mediators but as providers of unbiased information that is made available, more or less equally to all members. By reducing asymmetries of information through a process of upgrading the general level of available information, international regimes reduce uncertainty. Agreements based on misapprehension and deception may be avoided; mutually beneficial agreements are more likely to be made.

Regimes provide information to members, thereby reducing risks of making agreements. But the information provided by a regime may be insufficiently detailed. A government may require precise information about its prospective partners' internal evaluations of a particular situation, their intentions, the intensity of their preferences, and their willingness to adhere to an agreement even in adverse future circumstances. Governments also need to know whether other participants will follow the spirit as well as the letter of agreements, whether they will share the burden of adjustment to unexpected adverse change, and whether they are likely to seek to strengthen the regime in the future.

The significance of asymmetrical information and quality uncertainty in theories of market failure therefore calls attention to the importance not only of international regimes but also of variations in the degree of closure of different states' decisionmaking processes. Some governments maintain secrecy much more zealously than others. American officials, for example, often lament that the U.S. government leaks information "like a sieve" and claim that this openness puts the United States at a disadvantage vis-à-vis its rivals.

Surely there are disadvantages in openness. The real or apparent incoherence in policy that often accompanies it may lead the open government's partners to view it as unreliable because its top leaders, whatever their intentions, are incapable of carrying out their agreements. A cacophony of messages may render all of them uninterpretable. But some reflection on the problem of making agreements in world politics suggests that there are advantages for the open government that cannot be duplicated by countries with more tightly closed bureaucracies. Governments that cannot provide detailed and reliable information about their intentions—for instance, because their decision-making processes are closed to the outside world and their officials are prevented from developing frank informal relationships with their foreign counterparts—may be unable convincingly to persuade their potential partners of their commitment to the contemplated arrangements. Observers from other countries will be uncertain about the genuineness of officials' enthusiasm or the depth of their support for the cooperative scheme under consideration. These potential partners will therefore insist on discounting the value of prospective agreements to take account of their uncertainty. As in the "market for lemons," some potential agreements, which would be beneficial to all parties, will not be made because of "quality uncertainty"—about the quality of the closed government's commitment to the accord.[5]

MORAL HAZARD Agreements may alter incentives in such a way as to encourage less cooperative behavior. Insurance companies face this problem of "moral hazard." Property insurance, for instance, may make people less careful with their property and therefore increase the risk of loss (Arrow, 1974). The problem of moral hazard arises quite sharply in international banking. The solvency of a major country's largest banks may be essential to its financial system, or even to the stability of the entire international banking network. As a result, the country's central bank may have to intervene if one of these banks is threatened. The U.S. Federal Reserve, for instance, could hardly stand idly by while the Bank of America or Citibank became unable to meet its liabilities. Yet this responsibility creates a problem of moral hazard, since the largest banks, in effect, have automatic insurance against disastrous consequences of risky but (in the short-run at least) profitable loans. They have incentives to follow risk-seeking rather than risk-averse behavior at the expense of the central bank (Hirsch, 1977).

IRRESPONSIBILITY Some actors may be irresponsible, making commitments that they may not be able to carry out. Governments or firms may enter into agreements that they intend to keep, assuming that the environment will continue to be benign; if adversity sets in, they may be unable to keep their commitments. Banks regularly face this problem, leading them to devise standards of creditworthiness. Large governments trying to gain adherents to international agreements may face similar difficulties: countries that are enthusiastic about cooperation are likely to be those that expect to gain more, proportionately, than they contribute. This is a problem of self-selection, as discussed in the market-failure literature. For instance, if rates are not properly adjusted, people with high risks of heart attack will seek life insurance more avidly that those with longer life expectancies; people who purchased "lemons" will tend to sell them earlier on the used-car market than people with "creampuffs" (Akerlof, 1970; Arrow, 1974). In international politics, self-selection means that for certain types of activities—such as sharing research and development information—weak states (with much to gain but little to give) may have more incentive to participate than strong ones, but less incentive actually to spend funds on research and

developments.[6] Without the strong states, the enterprise as a whole will fail.

From the perspective of the outside observer, irresponsibility is an aspect of the problem of public goods and free-riding; but from the standpoint of the actor trying to determine whether to rely on a potentially irresponsible partner, it is a problem of uncertainty. Either way, informational costs and asymmetries may prevent mutually beneficial agreement.

REGIMES AND MARKET FAILURE

International regimes help states to deal with all of these problems. As the principles and rules of a regime reduce the range of expected behavior, uncertainty declines, and as information becomes more widely available, the asymmetry of its distribution is likely to lessen. Arrangements within regimes to monitor actors' behavior * * * mitigate problems of moral hazard. Linkages among particular issues within the context of regimes raise the costs of deception and irresponsibility, since the consequences of such behavior are likely to extend beyond the issue on which they are manifested. Close ties among officials involved in managing international regimes increase the ability of governments to make mutually beneficial agreements, because intergovernmental relationships characterized by ongoing communication among working-level officials, informal as well as formal, are inherently more conducive to exchange of information than are traditional relationships between closed bureaucracies. In general, regimes make it more sensible to cooperate by lowering the likelihood of being double-crossed. Whether we view this problem through the lens of game theory or that of market failure, the central conclusion is the same: international regimes can facilitate cooperation by reducing uncertainty. Like international law, broadly defined, their function is "to make human actions conform to predictable patterns so that contemplated actions can go forward with some hope of achieving a rational relationship between means and ends" (Barkun, 1968, p. 154).

Thus international regimes are useful to governments. Far from being threats to governments (in which case it would be hard to understand why they exist at all), they permit governments to attain objectives that would otherwise be unattainable. They do so in part by facilitating intergovernmental agreements. Regimes facilitate agreements by raising the anticipated costs of violating others' property rights, by altering transaction costs through the clustering of issues, and by providing reliable information to members. Regimes are relatively efficient institutions, compared with the alternative of having a myriad of unrelated agreements, since their principles, rules, and institutions create linkages among issues that give actors incentives to reach mutually beneficial agreements. They thrive in situations where states have common as well as conflicting interests on multiple, overlapping issues and where externalities are difficult but not impossible to deal with through bargaining. Where these conditions exist, international regimes can be of value to states.

We have seen that it does not follow from this argument that regimes necessarily increase global welfare. They can be used to pursue particularistic and parochial interests as well as more widely shared objectives. Nor should we conclude that all potentially valuable regimes will necessarily be instituted. * * * [E]ven regimes that promise substantial overall benefits may be difficult to invent.

■   ■   ■

Bounded Rationality and Redefinitions of Self-Interest

The perfectly rational decisionmaker * * * may face uncertainty as a result of the behavior of others, or the forces of nature, but she is assumed to make her own calculations costlessly. Yet this individual, familiar in textbooks, is not made of human flesh and blood. Even the shrewdest speculator or the most brilliant scientist faces limitations on her capacity for calculation. To imagine that all available information will be used by a decisionmaker is to exaggerate the intelligence of the human species.

Decisionmakers are in practice subject to limitations on their own cognitive abilities, quite apart from the uncertainties inherent in their environments. Herbert Simon has made this point with his usual lucidity (1982, p. 162):

> Particularly important is the distinction between those theories that locate all the conditions and constraints in the environment, outside the skin of the rational actor, and those theories that postulate important constraints arising from the limitations of the actor himself as an information processor. Theories that incorporate constraints on the information-processing capacities of the actor may be called *theories of bounded rationality.*

Actors subject to bounded rationality cannot maximize in the classical sense, because they are not capable of using all the information that is potentially available. They cannot compile exhaustive lists of alternative courses of action, ascertaining the value of each alternative and accurately judging the probability of each possible outcome (Simon, 1955/1979a, p. 10). It is crucial to emphasize that the source of their difficulties in calculation lies not merely in the complexity of the external world, but in their own cognitive limitations. In this respect, behavioral theories of bounded rationality are quite different from recent neoclassical theories, such as the theories of market failure * * *, which retain the assumption of perfect maximization:

> [In new neoclassical theories] limits and costs of information are introduced, not as psychological

characteristics of the decision maker, but as part of his technological environment. Hence, the new theories do nothing to alleviate the computational complexities facing the decision maker—do not see him coping with them by heroic approximation, simplifying and satisficing, but simply magnify and multiply them. Now he needs to compute not merely the shapes of his supply and demand curves, but in addition, the costs and benefits of computing those shapes to greater accuracy as well. Hence, to some extent, the impression that these new theories deal with the hitherto ignored phenomena of uncertainty and information transmission is illusory. (Simon, 1979b, p. 504)

In Simon's own theory, people "satisfice" rather than maximize. That is, they economize on information by searching only until they find a course of action that falls above a satisfactory level—their "aspiration level." Aspiration levels are adjusted from time to time in response to new information about the environment (Simon, 1972, p. 168). In view of people's knowledge of their own cognitive limitations, this is often a sensible strategy; it is by no means irrational and may well be the best way to make most decisions.

In ordinary life, we satisfice all the time. We economize on information by developing habits, by devising operating rules to simplify calculation in situations that repeat themselves, and by adopting general principles that we expect, in the long run, to yield satisfactory results. I do not normally calculate whether to brush my teeth in the morning, whether to hit a tennis ball directed at me with my backhand or my forehand, or whether to tell the truth when asked on the telephone whether Robert Keohane is home. On the contrary, even apart from any moral scruples I might have (for instance, about lying), I assume that my interests will be furthered better by habitually brushing my teeth, applying the rule "when in doubt, hit it with your forehand because you have a lousy backhand," and adopting the general principle of telling the truth than by calculating the costs and benefits of every alternative in each case. I do not mean to deny that I might occasionally be advantaged by pursuing a new idea at my desk rather than brushing my teeth, hitting a particular shot with my backhand, or lying to an obnoxious salesman on the telephone. If I could costlessly compute the value of each alternative, it might indeed be preferable to make the necessary calculations each time I faced a choice. But since this is not feasible, given the costs of processing information, it is in my long-run interest to eschew calculation in these situations.

Simon's analysis of bounded rationality bears some resemblance to the argument made for rule-utilitarianism in philosophy, which emphasizes the value of rules in contributing to the general happiness.[7] Rule-utilitarianism was defined by John Austin in a dictum: "Our rules would be fashioned on utility; our conduct, on our rules" (Mackie, 1977, p. 136). The rule-utilitarian adopts these rules, or "secondary principles," in John Stuart Mill's terms, in the belief that they will lead, in general, to better results than a series of *ad hoc* decisions based each time on first principles.[8] A major reason for formulating and following such rules is the limited calculating ability of human beings. In explicating his doctrine of utilitarianism, Mill therefore anticipated much of Simon's argument about bounded rationality (1861/1951, p. 30):

> Nobody argues that the art of navigation is not founded on astronomy, because sailors cannot wait to calculate the Nautical Almanack. Being rational creatures, they go to sea with it ready calculated; and all rational creatures go out upon the sea of life with their minds made up on the common questions of right and wrong, as well as on many of the far more difficult questions of wise and foolish. And this, as long as foresight is a human quality, it is to be presumed they will continue to do.

If individuals typically satisfice rather than maximize, all the more so do governments and other large organizations (Allison, 1971; Steinbruner, 1974; Snyder and Diesing, 1977). Organizational decision-making processes hardly meet the requirements of classical rationality. Organizations have multiple goals, defined in terms of aspiration levels; they search until satisfactory courses of action are found; they resort to feedback rather than systematically forecasting future conditions; and they use "standard operating procedures and rules of thumb" to make and implement decisions (Cyert and March, 1963, p. 113; March and Simon, 1958).

The behavioral theory of the firm has made it clear that satisficing does not constitute aberrant behavior that should be rectified where possible; on the contrary, it is intelligent. The leader of a large organization who demanded that the organization meet the criteria of classical rationality would herself be foolish, perhaps irrationally so. An organization whose leaders behaved in this way would become paralyzed unless their subordinates found ways to fool them into believing that impossible standards were being met. This assertion holds even more for governments than for business firms, since governments' constituencies are more varied, their goals more diverse (and frequently contradictory), and success or failure more difficult to measure. Assumptions of unbounded rationality, however dear they may be to the hearts of classical Realist theorists (Morgenthau, 1948/1966) and writers on foreign policy, are idealizations. A large, complex government would tie itself in knots by "keeping its options open," since middle-level bureaucrats would not know how to behave and the top policymakers would be overwhelmed by minor problems. The search for complete flexibility is as quixotic as looking for the Holy Grail or the fountain of youth.

If governments are viewed as constrained by bounded rationality, what are the implications for the functional argument * * * about the value of international regimes? * * * [U]nder rational-choice assumptions, international regimes are valuable to governments because they reduce transaction costs and particularly because they reduce uncertainty in the external environment. Each government is better able, with regimes in place, to predict that its counterparts will follow predictably cooperative policies. According to this theory, governments sacrifice the ability to maximize their myopic self-interest by making calculations on each issue as it arises, in return for acquiring greater certainty about others' behavior.

Under bounded rationality, the inclination of governments to join or support international regimes will be reinforced by the fact that the alternatives to regimes are less attractive than they would be if the assumptions of classical rationality were valid. Actors laboring under bounded rationality cannot calculate the costs and benefits of each alternative course of action on each issue. On the contrary, they need to simplify their own decisionmaking processes in order to function effectively at all. The rules of thumb they devise will not yield better, and will generally yield worse, results (apart from decisionmaking costs) than classically rational action—whether these rules of thumb are adopted unilaterally or as part of an international regime. Thus a comparison between the value of a unilateral rule of thumb and that of a regime rule will normally be more favorable to the regime rule than a comparison between the value of costless, perfectly rational calculation and the regime rule.

When we abandon the assumption of classical rationality, we see that it is not international regimes that deny governments the ability to make classically rational calculations. The obstacle is rather the nature of governments as large, complex organizations composed of human beings with limited problem-solving capabilities. The choice that governments actually face with respect to international regimes is not whether to adhere to regimes at the expense of maximizing utility through continuous calculation, but rather on what rules of thumb to rely. Normally, unilateral rules will fit the individual country's situation better than rules devised multi-laterally. Regime rules, however, have the advantage of constraining the actions of others. The question is whether the value of the constraints imposed on others justifies the costs of accepting regime rules in place of the rules of thumb that the country would have adopted on its own.

Thus if we accept that governments must adopt rules of thumb, the costs of adhering to international regimes appear less severe than they would be if classical rationality were a realistic possibility. Regimes merely substitute multilateral rules (presumably somewhat less congenial per se) for unilateral ones, with the advantage that other actors' behavior thereby becomes more predict-ably cooperative. International regimes neither enforce hierarchical rules on governments nor substitute their own rules for autonomous calcu-lation; instead, they provide rules of thumb in place of those that governments would otherwise adopt.

* * * [W]e can see how different our concep-tion of international regimes is from the self-help system that is often taken as revealing the essence of international politics. In a pure self-help sys-tem, each actor calculates its interests on each par-ticular issue, preserving its options until that decision has been made. The rational response to another actor's distress in such a system is to take advantage of it by driving a hard bargain, demand-ing as much as "the traffic will bear" in return for one's money, one's oil, or one's military support. Many such bargains are in fact struck in world politics, especially among adversaries; but one of the key features of international regimes is that they limit the ability of countries in a particularly strong bargaining position (however transitory) to take advantage of that situation. This limitation,

as we have stressed, is not the result of altruism but of the fact that joining a regime changes cal-culations of long-run self-interest. To a government that values its ability to make future agreements, reputation is a crucial resource; and the most important aspect of an actor's reputation in world politics is the belief of others that it will keep its future commitments even when a particular situa-tion, myopically viewed, makes it appear disad-vantageous to do so. Thus even classically rational governments will sometimes join regimes and comply with their rules. To a government seeking to economize on decisionmaking costs, the regime is also valuable for providing rules of thumb; dis-carding it would require establishing a new set of rules to guide one's bureaucracy. The convenience of rules of thumb combines with the superiority of long-run calculations of self-interest over myopic ones to reinforce adherence to rules by egoistic governments, particularly when they labor under the constraints of bounded rationality.

■   ■   ■

NOTES

1. For an elaborated version of this definition, see Davis and North (1971, p. 16).
2. For the idea of "nesting," I am indebted to Aggarwal (1981). Snidal (1981) also relies on this concept, which was used in a similar context some years ago by Barkun (1968, p. 17).
3. On linkage, see especially the work of Kenneth A. Oye (1979, 1983). See also Stein (1980) and Tollison and Willett (1979).
4. This point was suggested to me by reading Elizabeth Colson's account of how stateless societies reach consensus on the character of individuals: through discussions and gossip that allow people to "apply the standards of performance in particular roles in making an overall judgement about the total person;

this in turn allows them to predict future behavior" (1974, p. 53).

5. In 1960 Thomas Schelling made a similar argument about the problem of surprise attack. Asking how we would prove that we were not planning a surprise attack if the Russians suspected we were, he observed that "evidently it is not going to be enough just to tell the truth. . . . There has to be some way of authenticating certain facts, the facts presumably involving the disposition of forces" (p. 247). To authenticate facts requires becoming more open to external monitoring as a way of alleviating what Akerlof [1970] later called "quality uncertainty."

6. Bobrow and Kudrle found evidence of severe problems of collective goods in the IEA's energy research and development program, suggesting that "commercial interests and other national rivalries appear to have blocked extensive international cooperation" (1979, p. 170).

7. In philosophy, utilitarianism refers to an ethical theory that purports to provide generalizable principles for moral human action. Since my argument here is a positive one, seeking to explain the behavior of egoistic actors rather than to develop or criticize an ethical theory, its relationship to rule-utilitarianism in philosophy, as my colleague Susan Okin has pointed out to me, is only tangential.

8. John Mackie argues that even act-utilitarians "regularly admit the use of rules of thumb," and that whether one follows rules therefore does not distinguish act- from rule-utilitarianism (1977, p. 137). Conversely, Joseph Nye has pointed out to me that even rule-utilitarians must depart at some point from their rules for consequentialist reasons. The point here is not to draw a hard-and-fast dichotomy between the two forms of utilitarianism, but rather to point out the similarities between Mill's notion of relying on rules and Simon's conception of bounded rationality. If all utilitarians have to resort to rules of thumb to some extent, this only strengthens the point I am making about the importance of rules in affecting, but not determining, the behavior of governments. For a succinct discussion of utilitarianism in philosophy, see Urmson (1968).

BIBLIOGRAPHY

* * * *Where a date is given for an original as well as a later edition, the latter was used; page references in the text refer to it.*

Aggarwal, Vinod, 1981. Hanging by a Thread: International Regime Change in the Textile/Apparel System, 1950–1979 (Ph.D. dissertation. Stanford University).

Aivazian, Varouj A., and Jeffrey L. Callen, 1981. The Coase theorem and the empty core. *Journal of Law and Economics*, vol. 24, no. 1 (April), pp. 175–81.

Akerlof, George A., 1970. The market for "lemons." *Quarterly Journal of Economics*, vol. 84, no. 3 (August), pp. 488–500.

Allison, Graham, 1971. *Essence of Decision: Explaining the Cuban Missile Crisis* (Boston: Little, Brown).

Arrow, Kenneth J., 1974. *Essays in the Theory of Risk-Bearing* (New York: North-Holland/American Elsevier).

Barkun, Michael, 1968. *Law without Sanctions: Order in Primitive Societies and the World Community* (New Haven: Yale University Press).

Bobrow, Davis W., and Robert Kudrle, 1979. Energy R & D: in tepid pursuit of collective goods. *International Organization*, vol. 33, no. 2 (Spring), pp. 149–76.

Coase, Ronald, 1960. The problem of social cost. *Journal of Law and Economics*, vol. 3, pp. 1–44.

Colson, Elizabeth, 1974. *Tradition and Contract: The Problem of Order* (Chicago: Aldine Publishing Company).

Conybeare, John A.C., 1980. International organization and the theory of property rights. *International Organization*, vol. 34, no. 3 (Summer), pp. 307–34.

Cyert, Richard, and James G. March, 1963. *The Behavioral Theory of the Firm* (Englewood Cliffs, N.J.: Prentice-Hall).

Davis, Lance, and Douglass C. North, 1971. *Institutional Change and American Economic Growth* (Cambridge: Cambridge University Press).

Fellner, William, 1949. *Competition among the Few* (New York: Knopf).

Gilpin, Robert, 1981. *War and Change in World Politics* (Cambridge: Cambridge University Press).

Haas, Ernst B., 1958. *The Uniting of Europe* (Stanford: Stanford University Press).

Hardin, Russell, 1982. *Collective Action* (Baltimore: The Johns Hopkins University Press for Resources for the Future).

Henkin, Louis, 1979. *How Nations Behave: Law and Foreign Policy*, 2nd edition (New York: Columbia University Press for the Council on Foreign Relations).

Hirsch, Fred, 1977. The Bagehot problem. *The Manchester School*, vol. 45, no. 3 (September), pp. 241–57.

Hoffmann, Stanley, 1965. *The State of War: Essays on the Theory and Practice of International Politics* (New York: Praeger).

Hutton, Nicholas, 1975. The salience of linkage in international economic negotiations. *Journal of Common Market Studies*, vol. 13, nos. 1–2, pp. 136–60.

Krasner, Stephen D., ed., 1983. *International Regimes* (Ithaca: Cornell University Press).

Lewis, David K., 1969. *Convention: A Philosophical Study* (Cambridge: Harvard University Press).

Lowry, S. Todd. 1979. Bargain and contract theory in law and economics. In Samuels, 1979, pp. 261–82.

Mackie, J. L., 1977. *Ethics: Inventing Right and Wrong* (Harmondsworth, England: Penguin Books).

March, James G., and Herbert Simon, 1958. *Organizations* (New York: John Wiley & Sons).

Mill, John Stuart, 1861/1951. *Utilitarianism* (New York: E. P. Dutton).

Mitrany, David, 1975. *The Functional Theory of Politics* (London: St. Martin's Press for the London School of Economics and Political Science).

Morgenthau, Hans J., 1948/1966. *Politics among Nations*, 4th edition (New York: Knopf).

Olson, Mancur, 1965, *The Logic of Collective Action* (Cambridge: Harvard University Press).

Oye, Kenneth A., 1979. The domain of choice. In Oye et al., 1979, pp. 3–33.

Oye, Kenneth A., 1983 Belief Systems, Bargaining and Breakdown: International Political Economy 1929–1934 (Ph.D. dissertation, Harvard University).

Oye, Kenneth A., Donald Rothchild, and Robert J. Lieber, eds., 1979. *Eagle Entangled: U.S. Foreign Policy in a Complex World* (New York: Longman).

Puchala, Donald J., 1975. Domestic politics and regional harmonization in the European Communities. *World Politics*, vol. 27, no. 4 (July), pp. 496–520.

Samuels, Warren J., 1979. *The Economy as a System of Power* (New Brunswick, N.J.: Transaction Books).

Samuelson, Paul A., 1967. The monopolistic competition revolution. In R. E. Kuenne, ed., *Monopolistic Competition Theory* (New York: John Wiley & Sons).

Schelling, Thomas C., 1960/1980. *The Strategy of Conflict* (Cambridge: Harvard University Press).

Schelling, Thomas C., 1978. *Micromotives and Macrobehavior* (New York: W. W. Norton).

Simon, Herbert A., 1955. A behavioral model of rational choice. *Quarterly Journal of Economics*, vol. 69, no. 1 (February), pp. 99–118. Reprinted in Simon, 1979a, pp. 7–19.

Simon, Herbert A., 1972. Theories of bounded rationality. In Radner and Radner, 1972, pp. 161–76. Reprinted in Simon, 1982, pp. 408–23.

Simon, Herbert A., 1979a. *Models of Thought* (New Haven: Yale University Press).

Simon, Herbert A., 1979b. Rational decision making in business organizations. *American Economic Review*, vol. 69, no. 4 (September), pp. 493–513. Reprinted in Simon, 1982, pp. 474–94.

Simon, Herbert A., 1982. *Models of Bounded Rationality*, 2 vols. (Cambridge: MIT Press).

Snidal, Duncan, 1981. Interdependence, Regimes and International Cooperation (unpublished manuscript).

Snyder, Glenn H., and Paul Diesing, 1977. *Conflict among Nations: Bargaining, Decision making, and System Structure in International Crises* (Princeton: Princeton University Press).

Stein, Arthur A., 1980. The politics of linkage. *World Politics*, vol. 33, no. 1 (October), pp. 62–81.

Steinbruner, John D., 1974. *The Cybernetic Theory of Decision: New Dimensions of Political Analysis* (Princeton: Princeton University Press).

Tollison, Robert D., and Thomas D. Willett, 1979. An economic theory of mutually advantageous issue linkages in international negotiations. *International Organization*, vol. 33, no. 4 (Autumn), pp. 425–49.

Tucker, Robert W., 1977. *The Inequality of Nations* (New York: Basic Books).

Urmson, J. O., 1968. Utilitarianism. *International Encyclopedia of the Social Sciences* (New York: Macmillan), pp. 224–29.

Veljanovski, Cento G., 1982. The Coase theorems and the economic theory of markets and law. *Kyklos*, vol. 35, fasc. 1, pp. 53–74.

Waltz, Kenneth, 1959. *Man, the State and War* (New York: Columbia University Press).

Waltz, Kenneth, 1979. *Theory of World Politics* (Reading, Mass.: Addison-Wesley).

Williamson, Oliver, 1975. *Markets and Hierarchies: Analysis and Anti-Trust Implications* (New York: The Free Press).

Young, Oran R., 1980. International regimes: problems of concept formation. *World Politics*, vol. 32, no. 3 (April), pp. 331–56.

Young, Oran R., 1983. Regime dynamics: the rise and fall of international regimes. In Krasner, 1983, pp. 93–114.

John J. Mearsheimer

THE FALSE PROMISE OF INTERNATIONAL INSTITUTIONS

■ ■ ■

What Are Institutions?

There is no widely agreed upon definition of institutions in the international relations literature.[1] The concept is sometimes defined so broadly as to encompass all of international relations, which gives it little analytical bite.[2] For example, defining institutions as "recognized patterns of behavior or practice around which expectations converge" allows the concept to cover almost every regularized pattern of activity between states, from war to tariff bindings negotiated under the General Agreement on Tariffs and Trade (GATT), thus rendering it largely meaningless.[3] Still, it is possible to devise a useful definition that is consistent with how most institutionalist scholars employ the concept.

I define institutions as a set of rules that stipulate the ways in which states should cooperate and compete with each other.[4] They prescribe acceptable forms of state behavior, and proscribe unacceptable kinds of behavior. These rules are negotiated by states, and according to many prominent theorists, they entail the mutual acceptance of higher norms, which are "standards of behavior defined in terms of rights and obligations."[5] These rules are typically formalized in international agreements, and are usually embodied in organizations with their own personnel and budgets.[6] Although

From *International Security* 19, no. 3 (Winter 1994/95): 5–49.

rules are usually incorporated into a formal international organization, it is not the organization *per se* that compels states to obey the rules. Institutions are not a form of world government. States themselves must choose to obey the rules they created. Institutions, in short, call for the "decentralized cooperation of individual sovereign states, without any effective mechanism of command."[7]

■ ■ ■

Institutions in a Realist World

Realists * * * recognize that states sometimes operate through institutions. However, they believe that those rules reflect state calculations of self-interest based primarily on the international distribution of power. The most powerful states in the system create and shape institutions so that they can maintain their share of world power, or even increase it. In this view, institutions are essentially "arenas for acting out power relationships."[8] For realists, the causes of war and peace are mainly a function of the balance of power, and institutions largely mirror the distribution of power in the system. In short, the balance of power is the independent variable that explains war; institutions are merely an intervening variable in the process.

NATO provides a good example of realist thinking about institutions. NATO is an institution, and it certainly played a role in preventing World War III and helping the West win the Cold War. Nevertheless, NATO was basically a manifestation of the bipolar distribution of power in Europe during the Cold War, and it was that balance of power, not NATO *per se*, that provided the key to maintaining stability on the continent. NATO was essentially an American tool for managing power in the face of the Soviet threat. Now, with the collapse of the Soviet Union, realists argue that NATO must either disappear or reconstitute itself on the basis of the new distribution of power in Europe.[9] NATO cannot remain as it was during the Cold War.

■   ■   ■

Liberal Institutionalism

Liberal institutionalism does not directly address the question of whether institutions cause peace, but instead focuses on the less ambitious goal of explaining cooperation in cases where state interests are not fundamentally opposed.[10] Specifically, the theory looks at cases where states are having difficulty cooperating because they have "mixed" interests; in other words, each side has incentives both to cooperate and not to cooperate.[11] Each side can benefit from cooperation, however, which liberal institutionalists define as "goal-directed behavior that entails mutual policy adjustments so that all sides end up better off than they would otherwise be."[12] The theory is of little relevance in situations where states' interests are fundamentally conflictual and neither side thinks it has much to gain from cooperation. In these circumstances, states aim to gain advantage over each other. They think in terms of winning and losing, and this invariably leads to intense security competition, and sometimes war. But liberal institutionalism does not deal directly with these situations, and thus says little about how to resolve or even ameliorate them.

Therefore, the theory largely ignores security issues and concentrates instead on economic and, to a lesser extent, environmental issues.[13] In fact, the theory is built on the assumption that international politics can be divided into two realms—security and political economy—and that liberal institutionalism mainly applies to the latter, but not the former. * * *

■   ■   ■

According to liberal institutionalists, the principal obstacle to cooperation among states with mutual interests is the threat of cheating.[14] The famous "prisoners' dilemma," which is the analytical centerpiece of most of the liberal institutionalist literature, captures the essence of the problem that states must solve to achieve cooperation.[15] Each of two states can either cheat or cooperate with the other. Each side wants to maximize its own gain, but does not care about the size of the other side's gain; each side cares about the other side only so far as the other side's chosen strategy affects its own prospects for maximizing gain. The most attractive strategy for each state is to cheat and hope the other state pursues a cooperative strategy. In other words, a state's ideal outcome is to "sucker" the other side into thinking it is going to cooperate, and then cheat. But both sides understand this logic, and therefore both sides will try to cheat the other. Consequently, both sides will end up worse off than if they had cooperated, since mutual cheating leads to the worst possible outcome. Even though mutual cooperation is not as attractive as suckering the other side, it is certainly better than the outcome when both sides cheat.

The key to solving this dilemma is for each side to convince the other that they have a collective interest in making what appear to be short-term sacrifices (the gain that might result from successful cheating) for the sake of long-term benefits (the substantial payoff from mutual long-term cooperation). This means convincing states to accept the second-best outcome, which is mutual collaboration. The principal obstacle to reaching this cooperative outcome will be fear of getting suckered, should the other side cheat. This, in a nutshell, is the problem that institutions must solve.

To deal with this problem of "political market failure," institutions must deter cheaters and protect victims.[16] Three messages must be sent to potential cheaters: you will be caught, you will be punished immediately, and you will jeopardize future cooperative efforts. Potential victims, on the other hand, need early warning of cheating to avoid serious injury, and need the means to punish cheaters.

Liberal institutionalists do not aim to deal with cheaters and victims by changing fundamental norms of state behavior. Nor do they suggest transforming the anarchical nature of the international system. They accept the assumption that states operate in an anarchic environment and behave in a self-interested manner.[17] * * * Liberal institutionalists instead concentrate on showing how rules can work to counter the cheating problem, even while states seek to maximize their own welfare. They argue that institutions can change a state's calculations about how to maximize gains. Specifically, rules can get states to make the short-term sacrifices needed to resolve the prisoners' dilemma and thus to realize long-term gains. Institutions, in short, can produce cooperation.

Rules can ideally be employed to make four major changes in "the contractual environment."[18] First, rules can increase the number of transactions between particular states over time.[19] This *institutionalized iteration* discourages cheating in three ways. It raises the costs of cheating by creating the prospect of future gains through cooperation, thereby invoking "the shadow of the future" to deter cheating today. A state caught cheating would jeopardize its prospects of benefiting from future cooperation, since the victim would probably retaliate. In addition, iteration gives the victim the opportunity to pay back the cheater: it allows for reciprocation, the tit-for-tat strategy, which works to punish cheaters and not allow them to get away with their transgression. Finally, it rewards states that develop a reputation for faithful adherence to agreements, and punishes states that acquire a reputation for cheating.[20]

Second, rules can tie together interactions between states in different issue areas. *Issue-linkage* aims to create greater interdependence between states, who will then be reluctant to cheat in one issue area for fear that the victim—and perhaps other states as well—will retaliate in another issue area. It discourages cheating in much the same way as iteration: it raises the costs of cheating and provides a way for the victim to retaliate against the cheater.

Third, a structure of rules can increase the amount of *information* available to participants in cooperative agreements so that close monitoring is possible. Raising the level of information discourages cheating in two ways: it increases the likelihood that cheaters will be caught, and more importantly, it provides victims with early warning of cheating, thereby enabling them to take protective measures before they are badly hurt.

Fourth, rules can reduce the *transaction costs* of individual agreements.[21] When institutions perform the tasks described above, states can devote less effort to negotiating and monitoring cooperative agreements, and to hedging against possible defections. By increasing the efficiency of international cooperation, institutions make it more profitable and thus more attractive for self-interested states.

Liberal institutionalism is generally thought to be of limited utility in the security realm, because fear of cheating is considered a much greater obstacle to cooperation when military issues are at stake.[22] There is the constant threat that betrayal will result in a devastating military defeat. This threat of "swift, decisive defection" is simply not present when dealing with international economics. Given that "the costs of betrayal" are potentially much graver in the military than the economic sphere, states will be very reluctant to accept the "one step backward, two steps forward" logic which underpins the tit-for-tat strategy of conditional cooperation. One step backward in the security realm might mean destruction, in which case there will be no next step—backward or forward.[23]

* * * There is an important theoretical failing in the liberal institutionalist logic, even as it applies to economic issues. The theory is correct as far as it goes: cheating can be a serious barrier to cooperation. It ignores, however, the other major obstacle to cooperation: relative-gains concerns. As Joseph Grieco has shown, liberal institutionalists assume that states are not concerned about relative gains, but focus exclusively on absolute gains.[24] * * *

This oversight is revealed by the assumed order of preference in the prisoners' dilemma game: each state cares about how its opponent's strategy will affect its own (absolute) gains, but not about how much one side gains relative to the other. In other words, each side simply wants to get the best deal for itself, and does not pay attention to how well the other side fares in the process.[25] Nevertheless, liberal institutionalists cannot ignore relative-gains considerations, because they assume that states are self-interested actors in an anarchic system, and they recognize that military power matters to states. A theory that explicitly accepts realism's core assumptions—and liberal institutionalism does that—must confront the issue of relative gains if it hopes to develop a sound explanation for why states cooperate.

One might expect liberal institutionalist to offer the counterargument that relative-gains logic applies only to the security realm, while absolute-gains logic applies to the economic realm. Given that they are mainly concerned with explaining economic and environmental cooperation, leaving relative-gains concerns out of the theory does not matter.

There are two problems with this argument. First, if cheating were the only significant obstacle to cooperation, liberal institutionalists could argue that their theory applies to the economic, but not the military realm. In fact, they do make that argument. However, once relative-gains considerations are factored into the equation, it becomes impossible to maintain the neat dividing line between economic and military issues, mainly because military might is significantly dependent on economic might. The relative size of a state's economy has profound consequences for its standing in the international balance of military power. Therefore, relative-gains concerns must be taken into account for security reasons when looking at the economic as well as military domain. The neat dividing line that liberal institutionalists employ to specify when their theory applies has little utility when one accepts that states worry about relative gains.[26]

Second, there are non-realist (i.e., nonsecurity) logics that might explain why states worry about relative gains. Strategic trade theory, for example, provides a straightforward economic logic for why states should care about relative gains.[27] It argues that states should help their own firms gain comparative advantage over the firms of rival states, because that is the best way to insure national economic prosperity. There is also a psychological logic, which portrays individuals as caring about how well they do (or their state does) in a cooperative agreement, not for material reasons, but because it is human nature to compare one's progress with that of others.[28]

Another possible liberal institutionalist counterargument is that solving the cheating problem renders the relative-gains problem irrelevant. If states cannot cheat each other, they need not fear each other, and therefore, states would not have to worry about relative power. The problem with this argument, however, is that even if the cheating problem were solved, states would still have to worry about relative gains because gaps in gains can be translated into military advantage that can be used for coercion or aggression. And in the international system, states sometimes have conflicting interests that lead to aggression.

There is also empirical evidence that relative-gains considerations mattered during the Cold War even in economic relations among the advanced industrialized democracies in the Organization for Economic Cooperation and Development (OECD). One would not expect realist logic about relative gains to be influential in this case: the United States was a superpower with little to fear militarily from the other OECD states, and those states were unlikely to use a relative-gains advantage to threaten the United States.[29] Furthermore, the OECD states were important American allies during the Cold War, and thus the United States benefited strategically when they gained substantially in size and strength.

Nonetheless, relative gains appear to have mattered in economic relations among the advanced industrial states. Consider three prominent studies. Stephen Krasner considered efforts at cooperation in different sectors of the international communications industry. He found that states were remarkably unconcerned about cheating but deeply worried about relative gains, which led him to conclude that liberal institutionalism "is not relevant for global communications." Grieco examined American and EC efforts to implement, under the auspices of GATT, a number of agreements relating to non-tariff barriers to trade. He found that the level of success was not a function of concerns about cheating but was influenced primarily by concern about the distribution of gains. Similarly, Michael Mastanduno found that concern about relative gains, not about cheating, was an important factor in shaping American policy towards Japan in three cases: the FSX fighter aircraft, satellites, and high-definition television.[30]

I am not suggesting that relative-gains considerations make cooperation impossible; my point is simply that they can pose a serious impediment to cooperation and must therefore be taken into account when developing a theory of cooperation among states. This point is apparently now recognized by liberal institutionalists. Keohane, for example, acknowledges that he "did make a major mistake by underemphasizing distributive issues and the complexities they create for international cooperation."[31]

CAN LIBERAL INSTITUTIONALISM BE REPAIRED?

Liberal institutionalists must address two questions if they are to repair their theory. First, can institutions facilitate cooperation when states seriously care about relative gains, or do institutions only matter when states can ignore relative-gains considerations and focus instead on absolute gains? I find no evidence that liberal institutionalists believe that institutions facilitate cooperation when states care deeply about relative gains. They apparently concede that their theory only applies when relative-gains considerations matter little or hardly at all.[32] Thus the second question: when do states not worry about relative gains? The answer to this question would ultimately define the realm in which liberal institutionalism applies.

Liberal institutionalists have not addressed this important question in a systematic fashion, so any assessment of their efforts to repair the theory must be preliminary. * * *

■　■　■

PROBLEMS WITH THE EMPIRICAL RECORD

Although there is much evidence of cooperation among states, this alone does not constitute support for liberal institutionalism. What is needed is evidence of cooperation that would not have occurred in the absence of institutions because of fear of cheating, or its actual presence. But scholars have provided little evidence of cooperation of that sort, nor of cooperation failing because of cheating. Moreover, as discussed above, there is considerable evidence that states worry much about relative gains not only in security matters, but in the economic realm as well.

This dearth of empirical support for liberal institutionalism is acknowledged by proponents of that theory.[33] The empirical record is not completely blank, however, but the few historical cases that liberal institutionalists have studied provide scant support for the theory. Consider two prominent examples.

Keohane looked at the performance of the International Energy Agency (IEA) in 1974–81, a period that included the 1979 oil crisis.[34] This case does not appear to lend the theory much support. First, Keohane concedes that the IEA failed outright when put to the test in 1979: "regimeoriented efforts at cooperation do not always succeed, as the fiasco of IEA actions in 1979 illustrates."[35] He claims, however, that in 1980 the IEA had a minor success "under relatively favorable conditions" in responding to the outbreak of the Iran-Iraq War. Although he admits it is difficult to specify how much the IEA mattered in the 1980 case, he notes that "it seems clear that 'it [the IEA] leaned in the right direction'," a claim that hardly constitutes strong support for the theory.[36] Second, it does not appear from Keohane's analysis that either fear of cheating or actual cheating hindered cooperation in the 1979 case, as the theory would predict. Third, Keohane chose the IEA case precisely because it involved relations among advanced Western democracies with market economies, where the prospects for cooperation were excellent.[37] The modest impact of institutions in this case is thus all the more damning to the theory.

Lisa Martin examined the role that the European Community (EC) played during the Falklands War in helping Britain coax its reluctant allies to continue economic sanctions against Argentina after military action started.[38] She concludes that the EC helped Britain win its allies' cooperation by lowering transaction costs and facilitating issue linkage. Specifically, Britain made concessions on the EC budget and the Common Agricultural Policy (CAP); Britain's allies agreed in return to keep sanctions on Argentina.

This case, too, is less than a ringing endorsement for liberal institutionalism. First, British efforts to maintain EC sanctions against Argentina were not impeded by fears of possible cheating, which the theory identifies as the central impediment to cooperation. So this case does not present an important test of liberal institutionalism, and thus the cooperative outcome does not tell us much about the theory's explanatory power. Second, it was relatively easy for Britain and her allies to strike a deal in this case. Neither side's core interests were threatened, and neither side had to make significant sacrifices to reach an agreement. Forging an accord to continue sanctions was not a difficult undertaking. A stronger test for liberal institutionalism would require states to cooperate when doing so entailed significant costs and risks. Third, the EC was not essential to an agreement. Issues could have been linked without the EC, and although the EC may have lowered transaction costs somewhat, there is no reason to think these costs were a serious impediment to striking a deal.[39] It is noteworthy that Britain and America were able to cooperate during the Falklands War, even though the United States did not belong to the EC.

There is also evidence that directly challenges liberal institutionalism in issue areas where one would expect the theory to operate successfully. The studies discussed above by Grieco, Krasner, and Mastanduno test the institutionalist argument in a number of different political economy cases, and each finds the theory has little explanatory power. More empirical work is needed before a final judgment is rendered on the explanatory power of liberal institutionalism. Nevertheless, the evidence gathered so far is unpromising at best.

In summary, liberal institutionalism does not provide a sound basis for understanding international relations and promoting stability in the post–Cold War world. It makes modest claims about the impact of institutions, and steers clear of war and peace issues, focusing instead on the less ambitious task of explaining economic cooperation. Furthermore, the theory's causal logic is flawed, as proponents of the theory now admit. Having overlooked the relative-gains problem, they are now attempting to repair the theory, but their initial efforts are not promising. Finally, the available empirical evidence provides little support for the theory.

■　■　■　■

Conclusion

■　■　■

The attraction of institutionalist theories for both policymakers and scholars is explained, I believe, not by their intrinsic value, but by their relationship to realism, and especially to core elements of American political ideology. Realism has long been and continues to be an influential theory in the United States.[40] Leading realist thinkers such as George Kennan and Henry Kissinger, for example, occupied key policymaking positions during the Cold War. The impact of realism in the academic world is amply demonstrated in the institutionalist literature, where discussions of realism are pervasive.[41] Yet despite its influence, Americans who think seriously about foreign policy issues tend to dislike realism intensely, mainly because it clashes with their basic values. The theory stands opposed to how most Americans prefer to think about themselves and the wider world.[42]

There are four principal reasons why American elites, as well as the American public, tend to regard realism with hostility. First, realism is a pessimistic theory. It depicts a world of stark and harsh competition, and it holds out little promise of making that world more benign. Realists, as Hans Morgenthau wrote, are resigned to the fact that "there is no escape from the evil of power, regardless of what one does."[43] Such pessimism, of course, runs up against the deep-seated American belief that with time and effort, reasonable individuals can solve important social problems. Americans regard progress as both desirable and possible in politics, and they are therefore uncomfortable with realism's claim that security competition and war will persist despite our best efforts to eliminate them.[44]

Second, realism treats war as an inevitable, and indeed sometimes necessary, form of state activity. For realists, war is an extension of politics by other means. Realists are very cautious in their prescriptions about the use of force: wars should not be fought for idealistic purposes, but instead for balance-of-power reasons. Most Americans, however, tend to think of war as a hideous enterprise that should ultimately be abolished. For the time being, however, it can only justifiably be used for lofty moral goals, like "making the world safe for democracy"; it is morally incorrect to fight wars to change or preserve the balance of power. This makes the realist conception of warfare anathema to many Americans.

Third, as an analytical matter, realism does not distinguish between "good" states and "bad" states, but essentially treats them like billiard balls of varying size. In realist theory, all states are forced to seek the same goal: maximum relative power.[45] A purely realist interpretation of the Cold War, for example, allows for no meaningful difference in the motives behind American and Soviet behavior during that conflict. According to the theory, both sides must have been driven by concerns about the balance of power, and must have done what was necessary to try to achieve a favorable balance. Most Americans would recoil at such a description of the Cold War, because they believe the United States was motivated by good intentions while the Soviet Union was not.[46]

Fourth, America has a rich history of thumbing its nose at realism. For its first 140 years of existence, geography and the British navy allowed the United States to avoid serious involvement in the power politics of Europe. America had an isolationist foreign policy for most of this period, and its rhetoric explicitly emphasized the evils of entangling alliances and balancing behavior. Even as the United States finally entered its first European war in 1917, Woodrow Wilson railed against realist thinking. America has a long tradition of antirealist rhetoric, which continues to influence us today.

Given that realism is largely alien to American culture, there is a powerful demand in the United States for alternative ways of looking at the world, and especially for theories that square with basic American values. Institutionalist theories nicely meet these requirements, and that is the main source of their appeal to policymakers and scholars. Whatever else one might say about these theories, they have one undeniable advantage in the eyes of their supporters: they are not realism. Not only do institutionalist theories offer an alternative to realism, but they explicitly seek to undermine it. Moreover, institutionalists offer arguments that reflect basic American values. For example, they are optimistic about the possibility of greatly reducing, if not eliminating, security competition among states and creating a more peaceful world. They certainly do not accept the realist stricture that war is politics by other means. Institutionalists, in short, purvey a message that Americans long to hear.

There is, however, a downside for policymakers who rely on institutionalist theories: these theories do not accurately describe the world, hence policies based on them are bound to fail. The international system strongly shapes the behavior of states, limiting the amount of damage that false faith in institutional theories can cause. The constraints of the system notwithstanding, however, states still have considerable freedom of action, and their policy choices can succeed or fail in protecting American national interests and the interests of vulnerable people around the globe. The failure of the League of Nations to address German and Japanese aggression in the 1930s is a case in point. The failure of institutions to prevent or stop the war in Bosnia offers a more recent example. These cases illustrate that institutions have mattered rather little in the past; they also suggest that the false belief that institutions matter has mattered more, and has had pernicious effects. Unfortunately, misplaced reliance on institutional solutions is likely to lead to more failures in the future.

NOTES

1. Regimes and institutions are treated as synonymous concepts in this article. They are also used interchangeably in the institutionalist literature. See Robert O. Keohane, "International Institutions: Two Approaches," *International Studies Quarterly*, Vol. 32, No. 4 (December 1988), p. 384; Robert O. Keohane, *International Institutions and State Power: Essays in International Relations Theory* (Boulder, Colo.: Westview Press, 1989), pp. 3–4; and Oran R. Young, *International Cooperation: Building Regimes for Natural Resources and the Environment* (Ithaca, N.Y.: Cornell University Press, 1989), chaps. 1 and 8. The term "multilateralism" is also virtually synonymous with institutions. To quote John Ruggie, "the term 'multilateral' is an adjective that modifies the noun 'institution.' Thus, multilateralism depicts a *generic institutional form* in international relations. . . . [Specifically,] multilateralism is an institutional form which coordinates relations among three or more states on the basis of 'generalized' principles of conduct." Ruggie, "Multilateralism[: The Anatomy of an Institution]," [*International Organization*, Vol. 46, No. 3 (Summer 1992),] pp. 570–571.

2. For discussion of this point, see Arthur A. Stein, *Why Nations Cooperate: Circumstance and Choice in International Relations* (Ithaca, N.Y.: Cornell University Press, 1990), pp. 25–27. Also see Susan Strange, "*Cave! Hic Dragones:* A Critique of Regime Analysis," in Stephen D. Krasner, ed., *International Regimes*, special issue of *International Organization*, Vol. 36, No. 2 (Spring 1982), pp. 479–496.

3. Oran R. Young, "Regime Dynamics: The Rise and Fall of International Regimes," in Krasner, *International Regimes*, p. 277.

4. See Douglass C. North and Robert P. Thomas, "An Economic Theory of the Growth of the Western World," *The Economic History Review*, 2nd series, Vol. 23, No. 1 (April 1970), p. 5.

5. Krasner, *International Regimes*, p. 186. Non-realist institutions are often based on higher norms, while few, if any, realist institutions are based on norms. The dividing line between norms and rules is not sharply defined in the institutionalist literature. See Robert O. Keohane, *After Hegemony: Cooperation and Discord in the World Political Economy* (Princeton, N.J.: Princeton University Press, 1984), pp. 57–58. For example, one might argue that rules, not just norms, are concerned with rights and obligations. The key point, however, is that for many institutionalists, norms, which are core beliefs about standards of appropriate state behavior, are the foundation on which more specific rules are constructed. This distinction between norms and rules applies in a rather straightforward way in the subsequent discussion. Both collective security and critical theory challenge the realist belief that states behave in a self-interested way, and argue instead for developing norms that require states to act more altruistically. Liberal institutionalism, on the other hand, accepts the realist view that states act on the basis of self-interest, and concentrates on devising rules that facilitate cooperation among states.

6. International organizations are public agencies established through the cooperative efforts of two or more states. These administrative structures have their own budget, personnel, and buildings. John Ruggie defines them as "palpable entities with headquarters and letterheads, voting procedures, and generous pension plans." Ruggie, "Multilateralism," p. 573. Once rules are incorporated into an international organization, "they may seem almost coterminous," even though they are "distinguishable analytically." Keohane, *International Institutions and State Power*, p. 5.

7. Charles Lipson, "Is the Future of Collective Security Like the Past?" in George W. Downs, ed., *Collective Security beyond the Cold War* (Ann Arbor: University of Michigan Press), p. 114.

8. Tony Evans and Peter Wilson, "Regime Theory and the English School of International Relations: A Comparison," *Millennium: Journal of International Studies*, Vol. 21, No. 3 (Winter 1992), p. 330.

9. See Gunther Hellmann and Reinhard Wolf, "Neorealism Neoliberal Institutionalism, and the Future of NATO," *Security Studies*, Vol. 3, No. 1 (Autumn 1993), pp. 3–43.

10. Among the key liberal institutionalist works are: Robert Axelrod and Robert O. Keohane, "Achieving Cooperation under Anarchy: Strategies and Institutions," *World Politics*, Vol. 38, No. 1 (October 1985), pp. 226–254; Keohane, *After Hegemony*; Keohane, "International Institutions: Two Approaches," pp. 379–396; Keohane, *International Institutions and State Power*, chap. 1; Charles Lipson, "International Cooperation in Economic and Security Affairs," *World Politics*, Vol. 37, No. 1 (October 1984), pp. 1–23; Lisa L. Martin, "Institutions and Cooperation: Sanctions during the Falkland Islands Conflict," *International Security*, Vol. 16, No. 4 (Spring 1992), pp. 143–178; Lisa L. Martin, *Coercive Cooperation: Explaining Multilateral Economic Sanctions* (Princeton, N.J.: Princeton University Press, 1992); Kenneth A. Oye, "Explaining Cooperation under Anarchy: Hypotheses and Strategies," *World Politics,* Vol. 38, No. 1 (October 1985), pp. 1–24; and Stein, *Why Nations Cooperate.*

11. Stein, *Why Nations Cooperate*, chap. 2. Also see Keohane, *After Hegemony*, pp. 6–7, 12–13, 67–69.

12. Milner, "International Theories of Cooperation [among Nations: Strengths and Weaknesses]," [*World Politics*, Vol. 44, No. 3 (April 1992),] p. 468.

13. For examples of the theory at work in the environmental realm, see Peter M. Haas, Robert O. Keohane, and Marc A. Levy, eds., *Institutions for the Earth: Sources of Effective International Environmental Protection* (Cambridge, Mass.: MIT Press, 1993), especially chaps. 1 and 9. Some of the most important work on institutions and the environment has been done by Oran Young. See, for example, Young, *International Cooperation*. The rest of my discussion concentrates on economic, not environmental issues, for conciseness, and also because the key theoretical works in the liberal institutionalist literature focus on economic rather than environmental matters.

14. Cheating is basically a "breach of promise." Oye, "Explaining Cooperation under Anarchy," p. 1. It usually implies unobserved noncompliance, although there can be observed cheating as well. Defection is a synonym for cheating in the institutionalist literature.

15. The centrality of the prisoners' dilemma and cheating to the liberal institutionalist literature is clearly reflected in virtually all the works cited in footnote 10. As Helen Milner notes in her review essay on this literature: "The focus is primarily on the role of regimes [institutions] in solving the defection [cheating] problem." Milner, "International Theories of Cooperation," p. 475.

16. The phrase is from Keohane, *After Hegemony*, p. 85.

17. Kenneth Oye, for example, writes in the introduction to an issue of *World Politics* containing a number of liberal institutionalist essays: "Our focus is on nonaltruistic cooperation among states dwelling in international anarchy." Oye, "Explaining Cooperation under Anarchy," p. 2. Also see Keohane, "International Institutions: Two Approaches," pp. 380–381; and Keohane, *International Institutions and State Power*, p. 3.

18. Haas, Keohane, and Levy, *Institutions for the Earth*, p. 11. For general discussions of how rules work, which inform my subsequent discussion of the matter, see

Keohane, *After Hegemony*, chaps. 5–6; Martin, "Institutions and Cooperation," pp. 143–178; and Milner, "International Theories of Cooperation," pp. 474–478.

19. See Axelrod and Keohane, "Achieving Cooperation under Anarchy," pp. 248–250; Lipson, "International Cooperation," pp. 4–18.

20. Lipson, "International Cooperation," p. 5.

21. See Keohane, *After Hegemony*, pp. 89–92.

22. This point is clearly articulated in Lipson, "International Cooperation," especially pp. 12–18. The subsequent quotations in this paragraph are from ibid. Also see Axelrod and Keohane, "Achieving Cooperation under Anarchy," pp. 232–233.

23. See Roger B. Parks, "What If 'Fools Die'? A Comment on Axelrod," Letter to *American Political Science Review*, Vol. 79, No. 4 (December 1985), pp. 1173–1174.

24. See Grieco, "Anarchy and the Limits of Cooperation[: A Realist Critique of the Newest Liberal Institutionalism,]" [*International Organization*, Vol. 42, No. 3 (Summer 1988)]. Other works by Grieco bearing on the subject include: Joseph M. Grieco, "Realist Theory and the Problem of International Cooperation: Analysis with an Amended Prisoner's Dilemma Model," *Journal of Politics*, Vol. 50, No. 3 (August 1988), pp. 600–624; Grieco, *Cooperation among Nations: Europe, America, and Non-Tariff Barriers to Trade* (Ithaca, N.Y.: Cornell University Press, 1990); and Grieco, "Understanding the Problem of International Cooperation: The Limits of Neoliberal Institutionalism and the Future of Realist Theory," in Baldwin, [ed.,] *Neorealism and Neoliberalism[: The Contemporary Debate* (New York: Columbia University Press, 1993)], pp. 301–338. The telling effect of Grieco's criticism is reflected in ibid., which is essentially organized around the relative gains vs. absolute gains debate, an issue given little attention before Grieco raised it in his widely cited 1988 article. The matter was briefly discussed by two other scholars before Grieco. See Joanne Gowa, "Anarchy, Egoism, and Third Images: *The Evolution of Cooperation* and International Relations," *International Organization*, Vol.

40, No. 1 (Winter 1986), pp. 172–179; and Oran R. Young, "International Regimes: Toward a New Theory of Institutions," *World Politics*, Vol. 39, No. 1 (October 1986), pp. 118–119.

25. Lipson writes: "The Prisoner's Dilemma, in its simplest form, involves two players. Each is assumed to be a self-interested, self-reliant maximizer of his own utility, an assumption that clearly parallels the Realist conception of sovereign states in international politics." Lipson, "International Cooperation," p. 2. Realists, however, do not accept this conception of international politics and, not surprisingly, have questioned the relevance of the prisoners' dilemma (at least in its common form) for explaining much of international relations. See Gowa, "Anarchy, Egoism, and Third Images"; Grieco, "Realist Theory and the Problem of International Cooperation"; and Stephen D. Krasner, "Global Communications and National Power: Life on the Pareto Frontier," *World Politics*, Vol. 43, No. 3 (April 1991), pp. 336–366.

26. My thinking on this matter has been markedly influenced by Sean Lynn-Jones, in his June 19, 1994, correspondence with me.

27. For a short discussion of strategic trade theory, see Robert Gilpin, *The Political Economy of International Relations* (Princeton, N.J.: Princeton University Press, 1987), pp. 215–221. The most commonly cited reference on the subject is Paul R. Krugman, ed., *Strategic Trade Policy and the New International Economics* (Cambridge, Mass.: MIT Press, 1986).

28. See Robert Axelrod, *The Evolution of Cooperation* (New York: Basic Books, 1984), pp. 110–113.

29. Grieco maintains in *Cooperation among Nations* that realist logic should apply here. Robert Powell, however, points out that "in the context of negotiations between the European Community and the United States . . . it is difficult to attribute any concern for relative gains to the effects that a relative loss may have on the probability of survival." Robert Powell, "Absolute and Relative Gains in International Relations Theory," *American Political Science Review*, Vol. 85, No. 4 (December 1991), p. 1319, footnote 26. I agree with Powell. It is clear from Grieco's response to Powell that Grieco includes non-military logics like strategic trade theory in the realist tent, whereas Powell and I do not. See Grieco's contribution to "The Relative-Gains Problem for International Relations," *American Political Science Review*, Vol. 87, No. 3 (September 1993), pp. 733–735.

30. Krasner, "Global Communications and National Power," pp. 336–366; Grieco, *Cooperation among Nations*; and Michael Mastanduno, "Do Relative Gains Matter? America's Response to Japanese Industrial Policy," *International Security*, Vol. 16, No. 1 (Summer 1991), pp. 73–113. Also see Jonathan B. Tucker, "Partners and Rivals: A Model of International Collaboration in Advanced Technology," *International Organization*, Vol. 45, No. 1 (Winter 1991), pp. 83–120.

31. Keohane, "Institutional Theory and the Realist Challenge," [in Baldwin, *Neorealism and Neoliberalism*,] p. 292.

32. For example, Keohane wrote after becoming aware of Grieco's argument about relative gains: "Under specified conditions—where mutual interests are low and relative gains are therefore particularly important to states—neoliberal theory expects neorealism to explain elements of state behavior." Keohane, *International Institutions and State Power*, pp. 15–16.

33. For example, Lisa Martin writes that "scholars working in the realist tradition maintain a well-founded skepticism about the empirical impact of institutional factors on state behavior. This skepticism is grounded in a lack of studies that show precisely how and when institutions have constrained state decision-making." According to Oran Young, "One of the more surprising features of the emerging literature on regimes [institutions] is the relative absence of sustained discussions of the significance of . . . institutions, as determinants of collective outcomes at the international level." Martin, "Institutions and Cooperation," p. 144; Young, *International Cooperation*, p. 206.

34. Keohane, *After Hegemony*, chap. 10.

35. Ibid., p. 16.

36. Ibid., p. 236. A U.S. Department of Energy review of the IEA's performance in the 1980 crisis concluded

that it had "failed to fulfill its promise." Ethan B. Kapstein, *The Insecure Alliance: Energy Crises and Western Politics since 1944* (New York: Oxford University Press, 1990), p. 198.

37. Keohane, *After Hegemony*, p. 7.

38. Martin, "Institutions and Cooperation." Martin looks closely at three other cases in *Coercive Cooperation* to determine the effect of institutions on cooperation. I have concentrated on the Falklands War case, however, because it is, by her own admission, her strongest case. See ibid., p. 96.

39. Martin does not claim that agreement would not have been possible without the EC. Indeed, she appears to concede that even without the EC, Britain still could have fashioned "separate bilateral agreements with each EEC member in order to gain its cooperation, [although] this would have involved much higher transaction costs." Martin, "Institutions and Cooperation," pp. 174–175. However, transaction costs among the advanced industrial democracies are not very high in an era of rapid communications and permanent diplomatic establishments.

40. See Michael J. Smith, *Realist Thought from Weber to Kissinger* (Baton Rouge: Lousiana State University Press, 1986), chap. 1.

41. Summing up the autobiographical essays of 34 international relations scholars, Joseph Kruzel notes that "Hans Morgenthau is more frequently cited than any other name in these memoirs." Joseph Kruzel, "Reflections on the Journeys," in Joseph Kruzel and James N. Rosenau, eds., *Journeys through World Politics: Autobiographical Reflections of Thirty-four Academic Travelers* (Lexington, Mass.: Lexington Books, 1989), p. 505. Although "Morgenthau is often cited, many of the references in these pages are negative in tone. He seems to have inspired his critics even more than his supporters." Ibid.

42. See Keith L. Shimko, "Realism, Neorealism, and American Liberalism," *Review of Politics*, Vol. 54, No. 2 (Spring 1992), pp. 281–301.

43. Hans J. Morgenthau, *Scientific Man vs. Power Politics* (Chicago: University of Chicago Press, 1974), p. 201. Nevertheless, Keith Shimko convincingly argues that the shift within realism, away from Morgenthau's belief that states are motivated by an unalterable will to power, and toward Waltz's view that states are motivated by the desire for security, provides "a residual, though subdued optimism, or at least a possible basis for optimism [about international politics]. The extent to which this optimism is stressed or suppressed varies, but it is there if one wants it to be." Shimko, "Realism, Neorealism, and American Liberalism," p. 297. Realists like Stephen Van Evera, for example, point out that although states operate in a dangerous world, they can take steps to dampen security competition and minimize the danger of war. See Van Evera, *Causes of War* [Vol. II: *National Misperception and the Origins of War*, forthcoming].

44. See Reinhold Niebuhr, *The Children of Light and the Children of Darkness: A Vindication of Democracy and a Critique of Its Traditional Defense* (New York: Charles Scribner's, 1944), especially pp. 153–190. See also Samuel P. Huntington, *The Soldier and the State: The Theory and Politics of Civil-Military Relations* (New York: Vintage Books, 1964).

45. It should be emphasized that many realists have strong moral preferences and are driven by deep moral convictions. Realism is not a normative theory, however, and it provides no criteria for moral judgment. Instead, realism merely seeks to explain how the world works. Virtually all realists would prefer a world without security competition and war, but they believe that goal is unrealistic given the structure of the international system. See, for example, Robert G. Gilpin, "The Richness of the Tradition of Political Realism," in Keohane, [ed.,] *Neorealism and Its Critics*, [New York: Columbia University Press, 1986] p. 321.

46. Realism's treatment of states as billiard balls of different sizes tends to raise the hackles of comparative politics scholars, who believe that domestic political and economic factors matter greatly for explaining foreign policy behavior.

Ian Hurd

IS HUMANITARIAN INTERVENTION LEGAL?
The Rule of Law in an Incoherent World

The concept of humanitarian intervention has evolved as a subset of the laws governing the use of force and has very quickly come to occupy an institutional position alongside self-defense and Security Council authorization as a legal and legitimate reason for war. It is both widely accepted and yet still highly controversial. This article considers whether humanitarian intervention is legal under international law. This is a common question but one that produces an uncertain answer: humanitarian intervention appears to contradict the United Nations Charter, but developments in state practice since 1945 might have made it legal under certain circumstances. Those who argue for its legality cite state practice and international norms to support the view that the prohibition on war is no longer what it appears to be in the Charter. The debate suggests that humanitarian intervention is either legal or illegal depending on one's understanding of how international law is constructed, changed, and represented. Since these questions cannot be answered definitively, the uncertainty remains fundamental, and the legality of humanitarian intervention is essentially indeterminate. No amount of debate over the law or recent cases will resolve its status; it is both legal and illegal at the same time.

This article examines the implications of this finding for the idea of the rule of law in world politics. It suggests that the traditional emphasis that scholars have put on compliance with international law is misplaced; that is, the power of international law in this case comes not from its ability to differentiate rule breakers from rule followers, but rather from its ability to shape the terrain for political contestation in international relations. To the extent that state practice alters the meaning of international law, the distinction between compliance and non-compliance is unsustainable. Disputes over compliance and noncompliance are proxies for disagreements over the substantive behaviors in question, and they cannot be resolved by reference to the rules themselves. As I argue, international law should be seen as a *resource* that is used by states, rather than as a fixed standard against which we can assess behavior.

The first section of this article reviews the main elements in the legal regime on the use of force. These begin with the UN Charter, and especially Articles 2(4) and 51, but also include other treaties, such as the Genocide Convention, and other organizations, such as the African Union and NATO. Customary and treaty laws on self-defense are relevant as well. Together, these pieces help define the legal conditions under which states can use force against others. They constitute the current legal environment in which war is conducted. The second section considers how humanitarian intervention fits into this environment. It examines the evidence that humanitarian intervention is illegal and then the arguments for its legality. The former view rests on the plain language of Article 2(4) and the UN Charter as a whole, while

From *Ethics & International Affairs* 25, No.3 (Fall 2011), 293–313.

the latter position considers the behavior of states and finds that their actions have modified the black-letter law of the Charter. These two competing views cannot be reconciled, and so the third section argues that this indeterminacy is inherent in the idea of the rule of law for world politics.

It is not my goal here to argue for or against humanitarian intervention; I do not conclude that humanitarian intervention is wrong or unwise or illegitimate, or the opposites of these.[1] Rather, my aim is to show that the practice of humanitarian intervention exists in a space between legality and illegality, one where each instance of the practice can be plausibly seen as either compliance or noncompliance with international law. This article begins by trying to clarify what we know about the existing laws on humanitarian intervention. In a well-ordered world, knowing the state of the law should make it possible to assess the compliance or noncompliance of governments in particular cases. However, I conclude that the legality of humanitarian intervention *as a category* is indeterminate, and as a result the idea of compliance in particular cases is close to meaningless. Despite this, I find that the rules on humanitarian intervention are indeed consequential, but not as a yardstick for measuring compliance. What, then, is the power of law if an act can be simultaneously a violation and a compliance? The contribution that international law makes to international politics does not come at the moment where states make a choice between compliance and noncompliance. Instead, it comes in providing the resources with which states interpret, justify, and understand their behavior and the behavior of others. This is both a constraint and an opportunity for states.

The Law on the Use of Force

International law is centrally concerned with regulating war between states, and well-developed bodies of law exist on state conduct in war and the decision to use force. Both have long histories in European public international law. They originate in Christian doctrines of natural law, merge with European great power accommodations in the nineteenth century, and progress through the codification movement in the twentieth century.[2] The fundamental piece of law on the legality of the recourse to war by states is the UN Charter. It makes two contributions that are central to today's legal regime on war: it outlaws the use of force on the part of individual states, and it empowers the Security Council to make all decisions on collective measures that involve military force. Article 2(4) establishes the first element by requiring that states not use or threaten force against other states: "All members shall refrain in their international relations from the threat or use of force against the territorial integrity or political independence of any state, or in any other manner inconsistent with the Purposes of the United Nations." This is a general prohibition, set in the section of the Charter that defines the common and primary obligations of UN membership and of the organization itself, and it is often cited as the primary contribution of the UN system to international order.[3] It goes along with Article 2(3), which insists that UN members settle their interstate disputes by "peaceful means."

Article 2(4) takes away from states the legal right to use force, and Articles 24, 39, 42, and others then deliver this power to the Security Council. These sections of the Charter establish that the Council has the "primary responsibility for the maintenance of international peace and security" (Article 24) and that it can take what measures it deems necessary in that pursuit, including military action against states or other threats (Article 42). The goal of the framers of the Charter was to centralize the enforcement of international order in the hands of the great powers at the time, and to pacify the relations among other states by depriving them of independent legal channels to war. This was motivated by the understanding that the lesson of the two world wars was that state aggression must be forestalled with a forceful and collective response. Thus, intervention that is authorized by the UN Security Council is unambiguously legal, as long as it conforms to the Council's authority over "threats to international peace and security" (Article 39).[4]

In this legal environment, the principal legal justification for war by states is self-defense. States have long claimed that military force used in response to an attack by another constitutes a distinct category in law and in practice, and as a result the canon of international law generally recognizes such a right. The customary understanding of self-defense goes back as far as the field of public international law, which is to say that it was recognized by Grotius and others in seventeenth-century Europe as existing already.[5] The concept is defined as a military response to an armed attack where the response is both necessary and proportionate to the attack. In the history of the concept, it is these ideas of *necessity* and *proportionality* that generate controversy; the concept itself is not contested. Each application of the concept in practice has a productive effect that further elaborates its meaning, sometimes making it clearer and sometimes making it more complicated.[6] For instance, Israel's claim of acting in self-defense in its attack on Iraq in 1981 was widely rejected, including by the Security Council,[7] but it incidentally may have helped define the outer bounds of "necessity." The *Caroline* affair, which arose from skirmishes between the United States and Britain in 1838, provides a case in which a state's justification for its behavior has become constitutive of the categories of lawful and unlawful uses of force. The British eventually apologized for their incursion into U.S. territory, and the Americans conceded that the idea of anticipatory self-defense might exist within the concept of self-defense, but the most lasting effect of the incident was the language that it generated to judge claims of preemptive war:

that the threat must be "instant, overwhelming, and leaving no choice of means, and no moment for deliberation."[8] Michael Byers has rightly argued that prior to laws banning war, self-defense acted as a political justification rather than a legal exemption since, without laws to demarcate between legal and illegal wars, the justification of self-defense is politically useful and not legally necessary.[9]

The UN Charter as originally proposed by the United States in 1944 did not contain any reference to self-defense as a complement to the ban on war. It relied on the fact that self-defense was a widely accepted custom according to international law. What became Article 51 of the Charter was added during the 1945 San Francisco conference that founded the United Nations, and was inserted at the initiative of Latin American states, concerned that the ban on war might be interpreted to mean that they could not ask the United States to come to their aid while the Council deliberated on its response to an attack on them. The great powers did not oppose adding it, believing that it did not change the underlying customary law. The language of Article 51 reflects the peculiar status of a customary principle in a codified environment: "Nothing in the present Charter shall impair the inherent right of individual or collective self-defense if an armed attack occurs." This makes it explicit that a right to self-defense in the event of an attack exists prior to and alongside the Charter, and that Article 2(4) is immaterial to that right.[10] The international legal regime on the use of force is therefore constituted at the intersection of Articles 2(4), 39, and 51 of the UN Charter: the use of force by states against other states is prohibited by Article 2(4); the collective use of force is allowed, and is controlled entirely by the UN Security Council by Article 39, among others; and self-defense in response to an attack is defined by Article 51 as legally distinct from what is prohibited by Article 2(4).

This is the legal environment into which humanitarian intervention was presented as a justification for the use of force. It is an environment in which there are clear black-letter law prohibitions on the use or threat of force in interstate relations, and the development of humanitarianism has therefore taken place in and around that prohibition.

Is Humanitarian Intervention Legal?

In the face of these laws, can humanitarian intervention ever be legal? Recent events, from Rwanda to the Balkans to Libya and onward, have forced to the surface the tensions between humanitarianism and sovereignty, and the resulting debates have produced a set of positions on either side that are clearly identifiable.[11] Disagreements about deep points of international law, including how law changes in response to practice, how treaties are interpreted, and the meaning of compliance and noncompliance in particular cases, overlay a remarkable consensus that humanitarian intervention is an important tool for states and international organizations *whether it is legal or not*. The disagreements over how international law works, alongside a consensus in favor of the practice regardless of its legality, suggests that humanitarian intervention is likely to exacerbate the ambiguities inherent in the idea of the rule of law for sovereign states.

The Case for Illegality

The case for the illegality of humanitarian intervention rests on the plain language of the UN Charter. Article 2(4) outlaws the use of force by states and gives no suggestion that the motive behind the action matters at all. Nothing in the Charter opens the possibility that the use of force for humanitarian purposes should be understood any differently than other uses of force. Indeed, as Nikolas Sturchler reminds us, the article outlaws

both the *use* of force and the *threat* of its use, ensuring that the domain of illegality is much broader than merely cross-border military attacks.[12] The prohibition is very widely drawn, and this was no accident: the overarching purpose of the San Francisco conference was to ban war and to build an architecture in the Security Council to enforce that ban and deal with violations.[13] Bringing this idea to the present day, Ian Brownlie has said that "whilst there have been obvious changes in the political configuration of the world . . . these changes have not had any particular effects on the law." He suggests that humanitarian intervention was understood as legally defensible prior to the Charter, but became illegal in 1945:

> By the end of the nineteenth century the majority of publicists admitted that a right of humanitarian intervention (*l'intervention d'humanité*) existed. A state which had abused its sovereignty by brutal and excessively cruel treatment of those within its power, whether nationals or not, was regarded as having made itself liable to action by any state which was prepared to intervene. . . . [By 1963] few experts believed that humanitarian intervention had survived the legal regime created by the United Nations Charter.[14]

The Swedish government summarized the conventional understanding in a response to the Israeli Entebbe incident in 1976: "The Charter does not authorize any exception to this rule except for the right of self-defense and enforcement measures undertaken by the Council under Chapter VII of the Charter. This is no coincidence or oversight. Any formal exceptions permitting the use of force or of military intervention in order to achieve certain aims, however laudable, would be bound to be abused, especially by the big and strong, and to pose a threat, especially to the small and weak."[15]

The prohibition on war may be narrowed somewhat by the fact that Article 2(4) outlaws force only "against the territorial integrity or political independence" of a state. The substance of this clause has never been made clear in law or in practice, and its original intent appears to have been to expand rather than contract the scope of the ban on war.[16] It was added to the draft Charter at San Francisco by a group of small and medium-sized states that wanted to be satisfied that their independence was well protected. The argument could by made that humanitarian intervention does not involve an attack on "the territorial integrity or political independence" of its target state, and as such falls outside Article 2(4). This was essentially the argument presented by Britain to the International Court of Justice in the *Corfu Channel* case (1946–1948), claiming that its uninvited minesweeping in Albanian waters did not rise to this standard of intervention.[17] The argument failed in that case, and it has little basis in the text of the Charter or its *traveaux preparatoires*.[18]

The Charter does include references to human rights and "fundamental freedoms" for individuals, which might be read as endorsing a kind of humanitarianism. However, these do not attach to any legal commitments by the signatories, and so do not create a possibility for armed intervention in their pursuit. The famous passages of the Charter that refer to the "faith in fundamental human rights, in the dignity and worth of the human person" (Preamble) and to the "universal respect for, and observance of, human rights and fundamental freedoms" (Article 55(c)) all arise in a nonbinding context: they are goals that the UN "shall promote" or that its members are "determined" to "reaffirm." They do not create legal obligations or commitments, and they do not modify the general prohibition on the use of force. Had it been proposed in 1945 that these goals could trump the ban on war, the idea would undoubtedly have been soundly defeated by a large majority of the delegations, including all five of the Security Council's permanent-members-to-be.

A number of other international treaties subsequent to the Charter may also be relevant to this question. The Genocide Convention (1948), for instance, is sometimes understood to encourage or permit intervention against genocidal regimes, based on its Article I, which states: "The Contracting Parties confirm that genocide, whether committed in time of peace or in time of war, is a crime under international law which they undertake to prevent and punish." Here the controversy becomes whether this undertaking to prevent and punish is an authorization to use force across state boundaries or whether it refers only to the more limited set of measures described in the rest of the convention, such as prosecuting, punishing, or extraditing suspects found in one's territory. While the language of the convention can be interpreted more expansively, the limited view is the most defensible, not least because the expansive interpretation requires that a right to intervene be seen as implicit in the text. In the absence of an explicit recognition of such an important right, the more conservative reading of the law is probably appropriate.

The treaties that establish the Organization of American States (OAS) and the African Union (AU) also make possible the use of coercive collective action against their own member states, and so are sometimes read as legal pathways toward humanitarian intervention. The African Union's Constitutive Act creates a "right of the Union to intervene in a Member State pursuant to a decision of the [AU's] Assembly in respect of grave circumstances, namely: war crimes, genocide, and crimes against humanity" (Article 4(h)). This is a collective right of the Union, not an individual right of member states, and in that way it resembles the interventionary authority of the UN Security Council relative to UN member states. The AU's authority has not yet been enacted, but it does seem to establish a legal basis for humanitarian intervention among its member states. The OAS Charter does not go as far: it expressly forbids interference across borders (Article 19) while reaffirming that its members have abandoned aggressive war (Article 3(g)); but the organization is also committed to sustaining democratic governance in its members, and it has described democratic governance as inseparable from the respect for human rights.[19] There may be some possibility to combine these three elements into a right to intervene in defense of human rights or democracy, but this is doubtful. More likely, the OAS has the authority to pass judgment on the domestic governance and human rights of its members, but not to invade; its enforcement capacity is limited to suspending a misbehaving member from the organization.

For any of these treaties to modify the UN Charter's prohibition on intervention, it must overcome the further problem posed by Article 103. This clause governs conflicts between the Charter and other treaties, and it answers decisively in favor of the Charter: "In the event of a conflict between the obligations of the Members of the United Nations under the present Charter and their obligations under any other international agreement, their obligations under the present Charter shall prevail." Thus, the Charter arrogates to itself the status of constitutional law in interstate relations and nullifies contradictory laws.[20] If Article 103 is read to apply to future treaties and not just those in existence when the Charter was signed, then it appears legally impossible for a later treaty on (for instance) human rights to ease the ban on military interventions.

To a legal formalist, it is therefore clear that existing treaty law from the Charter to the present day makes no room for a legal category of humanitarian intervention. The case for the illegality of humanitarian intervention rests on the plain language of existing treaties and emphasizes the clarity of the UN Charter, as well as its near constitutional status in international politics and its universal adoption. Together, these lead to the conclusion that the purpose behind the use of force (other than self-defense) is irrelevant in law, and the effort to respond to humanitarian emergencies in states that refuse to cooperate ends up confronting the same prohibition on interstate war that was meant to stop aggression. As Byers notes, "The UN Charter provides a clear answer to these questions: in the absence of an attack, the Security Council alone can act."[21] One might follow this tradition and yet still argue in favor of a specific act of humanitarian intervention. In so doing, however, one must confront the fact that the act is illegal. The now classic example of this is the post hoc explanation that the NATO intervention in Kosovo was "illegal but legitimate."[22] Brownlie considers this to grant "a waiver of the illegality" of the act, and he opposes the claim that it provides any evidence of a change in the law itself. Thomas Franck agrees on its illegality but maintains that international justice is better served by sometimes breaking the law rather than respecting it, and that Kosovo/NATO is one such case.[23] This is a provocative position since it suggests that the idea of the rule of law is not as absolute as is usually maintained; other values might be more important than rule following.

Three Cases for Legality

To stop at the black-letter law on the use of force requires that we ignore developments in the language and practice of intervention. This may be a mistake since these changes may arguably have created a category of lawful war that encompasses humanitarianism. This is especially compelling with respect to state practice and conceptual development after 1990 or so. The case for legality rests on claims about changes in the law as a result of state behavior in the Charter era, and so is useful for examining the dynamic relationship between international law and state practice.

Two forces in international politics have repeatedly pressed humanitarian intervention onto the international legal agenda despite Article 2(4): the extension of the ideology of cosmopolitanism and human rights, which provides a moral imperative to respond to outrages against people regardless of their citizenship; and the strategic manipulation by states who see in humanitarianism a useful instrument to justify their military interventions. The second may well presume the first, since the language of humanitarianism would not be a useful tool if it did not have political resonance with deeply held beliefs about justice and obligation. But the second is also an independent force, reflecting the incentives that many actors see in adopting the language of humanitarian rescue. This contributes to its development and persistence. Both forces keep the language of humanitarianism alive in the legal discourse of states and activists, and therefore may be propelling developments in the law, though they are very different drivers for the concept and they apply, reinforce, and change it in different ways.

The case for legality can be made using three distinct arguments. All three make their case by joining together an interpretation of recent state practice with a theory of international law, but they draw on different interpretations of practice and lead to distinct implications. The first suggests that the ban on war in Article 2(4) has lost its legal force by being repeatedly violated by states in practice. There is therefore no operative international law left in that article. The second suggests that the normative environment of world politics has changed such that the rule of nonintervention has receded in the face of the progress of a norm of humanitarianism. These normative changes, it is claimed, have driven consequent changes in the formal laws and made lawful what was formerly unlawful. Finally, it is sometimes argued that the two concepts of sovereignty and humanitarian intervention are in fact complementary rather than contradictory, in the sense that sovereignty is conditional on a government respecting the obligation to protect its own people. This view argues that humanitarian intervention is lawful because the legal protections for sovereign states cease to exist if the state is engaged in the worst kinds of abuses of its citizens.

1. Desuetude and Article 2(4). The idea that Article 2(4) has lost its power due to repeated violation rests on an empirical claim about the frequency of violation and a separate conceptual claim about the legal effects of those violations. The two claims are independent of each other and each involves its own controversies. The empirical record regarding compliance with Article 2(4) was summarized by Thomas Franck in the following terms: states have "violated it, ignored it, run roughshod over it, and explained it away . . . [they] have succumbed to the temptation to settle a score, to end a dispute or to pursue their national interest through the use of force," precisely in contradiction to the rule.[24] Franck, writing in 1970, used the twenty-five-year history of post-Charter uses of force as evidence that the war practice of states had not changed much from their pre-Charter practice, and concluded: "The prohibition against the use of force in relations between states has been eroded beyond recognition."[25] Michael Glennon picked up the argument in 2001. Finding nothing in more recent history to temper Franck's pessimistic claim, he too concluded that "the upshot is that the Charter's use-of-force regime has all but collapsed. This includes, most prominently, the restraints of the general rule banning use of force among states, set out in Article 2(4)."[26]

The conceptual claim is that the legal force of Article 2(4) has been erased by this history of rule violation. It is commonly said in scholarship on international law and international politics that rules lose their force if they are frequently violated. Glennon's claim adds a formal legal element to this idea: he says "international 'rules' concerning the use of force are no longer regarded as *obligatory* by states."[27] That is, they have lost the quality that formerly gave them their legally binding character. As a formal legal process, the idea that law fails as law if it is routinely bypassed is common in domestic and international legal systems, and is known as desuetude. This is the concept that allows some outmoded laws to remain on the books despite relevant and major changes in sensibilities. In such instances, courts often refuse to enforce laws that they judge to have become irrelevant and unusable.[28] In international law, the concept is endorsed in the Vienna Convention on the Law of Treaties (1969) as one reason why a treaty might lose its force, and has appeared from time to time in opinions of the International Court of Justice, including in the *Nuclear Tests* case and the *Aegean Sea Continental Shelf* case.

If this applies in the case of Article 2(4), then the use of force by states is no longer regulated by the Charter and it is conceptually impossible for a state to be in violation of the rules. Glennon uses this line of reasoning to conclude that the United States was unconstrained in its military interventions in Afghanistan, Iraq, and elsewhere after 2001. The logic is equally applicable to uses of force for humanitarian purposes.[29] If state practice has caused the legal forms of war to become unlimited, then humanitarian intervention is no longer illegal for the same reason that all other intervention is no longer illegal: the laws have ceased to regulate it. Indeed, it follows by implication that aggression itself is also once again legal, and we have returned to the pre-1945 state of affairs, though no state has yet used this argument to justify its use of force.

2. Humanitarian Intervention as Norms-Into-Law. A very different mode of argument also maintains that the progressive development of international law now accepts humanitarian intervention as legal. This position affirms the legal force of Article 2(4), which the previous view denies, but argues that its scope has shifted as a consequence of recent practice. Like the claim on desuetude, this argument rests on an interpretation of practice joined with a theory of international law, but the practice in question comes from the statements and justifications made by states and others arguing for the legality of humanitarian intervention. Glennon and Franck reach their conclusion by arguing that

these statements are something like self-serving cheap talk, but this competing view takes them seriously as evidence that states desire that humanitarian intervention be legalized.

The key element in this argument is the claim that the law has changed through the twin mechanisms of the power of norms and the power of state practice. These powers work together to force a reinterpretation of Article 2(4) by asking that it be understood in light of "emerging normative ideas."[30] The Charter is thereby made subordinate to the normative and political environment in which it rests. It is not enough in this view to point out that a norm of humanitarian intervention exists; it must also be the case that the *law* has changed as a result.

Thomas Weiss and Ramesh Thakur, among others, make this case by invoking recent innovations in state practice.[31] These include instances in which the idea of humanitarian intervention was used by states to justify their use of force, statements by governments and others, and a reading of legal theory that shows historical strands of the concept. They point out that in 1998, Kofi Annan made the first of many claims to the effect that "state frontiers . . . should no longer be seen as watertight protection for war criminals and mass murderers."[32] This was institutionalized further through the concept of the Responsibility to Protect (RtoP), and reinforced by Annan's successor, Ban Ki-moon, on many occasions. The World Summit in 2005 included an affirmation by all states in the General Assembly of their "willingness to take timely and decisive collective action" for humanitarian purposes (though only *with* Security Council approval).[33] The Security Council explicitly endorsed the concept in Resolution 1674 in 2006, and has applied it with varying degrees of ambiguity in relation to Darfur (Resolution 1706), Somalia (1814), Libya (1973), and elsewhere.[34] The key cases of state-led humanitarian intervention include Kosovo in 1999, where NATO used humanitarian rescue to justify its bombing of Yugoslavia, and the no-fly zones of Iraq in the 1990s, designed to protect certain civilian populations from the Iraqi government. These are among the cases most often cited as evidence for the norms-into-law argument about the legality of humanitarian intervention. Each is contestable, of course, but they may form a pattern of official practice that modifies the legal regime on the use of force.

In this view, the available evidence that states are disregarding their obligations under Article 2(4) must be understood differently than Michael Glennon would have it. For Glennon (and Franck) these are violations of Article 2(4) and they suggest that states are ungoverned by international law in their use of force. For the norms-into-law approach, they are instead evidence that states have reconstituted their legal obligations around a new legal principle. According to this approach, such an intervention may not count as a "violation" at all. It is instead *constructive noncompliance*, which signals that humanitarianism is becoming legal even while Article 2(4) remains in place. Seeing international law as fluid in this way turns it into "social practice" rather than a set of fixed and external standards against which conduct can be measured.[35]

Empirically, the activist case for legalized humanitarian intervention encounters two limits. First, much of the formal support for RtoP, including the 2005 World Summit, is for the relatively easy case of intervention approved by the Security Council. This minimizes the legal innovation as well as the practical scope of the concept, because it essentially repeats what is already accepted about the Council's legal powers. More novel is the argument that humanitarianism can be legal without Council consent. Second, as Paul Williams and Alex Bellamy point out, once we include state practice as relevant to considering the law, we must also recognize the many cases where states that support RtoP in principle failed to carry it out.[36] It is unclear how to interpret these failures, since the norms-into-law case argues only the permissive case, that humanitarianism can be legal, not that it is consistently applied. And yet the practice of failing to intervene is presumably as politically powerful as the practice of intervention, and must somehow be accommodated into the argument.

3. Contingent Sovereignty. The third path to legality suggests that state sovereignty is contingent on a government providing a basic level of human rights protection to its people. This is often bundled together in a broader narrative about the responsibility to protect, but it is conceptually and legally distinct. The idea of contingent sovereignty suggests that statehood itself is legally dependent on acceptable government behavior, such that failure of a government to meet certain minimum standards nullifies its claim to noninterference. This may or may not involve a "responsibility" for outside states to intervene; but is does mean that the government in question has lost the protection entailed by sovereign statehood such that any invasion no longer involves transgressing a legal or physical boundary of nonintervention. This was neatly expressed early in the recent revolution against Muammar Qaddafi when the Italian government declared that because the Libyan state "no longer exists" its treaties with Italy ceased to have any legal content.[37] The idea of contingent sovereignty is in the end an argument about the role of international laws on sovereignty, rather than on the law on the use of force; it describes the moment at which the protections of sovereignty vanish from within. Once this happens, intervention does not count as a use of force against another *state*.

Allen Buchanan makes a related argument with respect to international recognition of secessionist movements, suggesting that the international community should assess the human rights performance of claimants to "national self-determination," so that morally defensible behavior toward one's citizens will become a necessary condition to statehood.[38] This proposal would link the institutional legal framework of sovereignty to the practice of respecting human rights and make the former conditional upon the latter. Many writers believe such a link has already been made, or has always been implicit, in the law of state sovereignty. Fernando Tesón, for example, has said that "to the extent that state sovereignty is a value, it is an instrumental not an intrinsic value. Sovereignty serves valuable human ends; and those who grossly assault them should not be allowed to shield themselves behind the sovereignty principle."[39] As early as 1992, in "An Agenda for Peace," the UN secretary-general said "the time of absolute and exclusive sovereignty, however, has passed; its theory was never matched by reality."[40] A decade later, Gareth Evans and Mohamed Sahnoun wrote of RtoP that "even the strongest supporters of state sovereignty will admit today that no state holds unlimited power to do what it wants to its own people. It is now commonly acknowledged that sovereignty implies a dual responsibility. . . . In international human rights covenants, in UN practice, and in state practice itself, sovereignty is now understood as embracing this dual responsibility."[41] Where humanitarian intervention is necessary, they suggest, sovereignty properly understood no longer exists.

All three of these views conclude that under some circumstances humanitarian intervention can be legal. The first two cases suggest that the laws on the use of force have changed since 1945 due to the behavior of states. The third suggests that the legal institution of sovereignty encompasses the possibility of legal intervention because sovereignty itself disappears at some extreme of government misbehavior. They all reconcile the tensions in the law in a way that accommodates the innovation of intervention with the traditional structures of international law and international politics: Security Council approval is not necessary; the rule of law is preserved; humanitarian and legal impulses point in the same direction.

Between Legality and Illegality

The difference between these two sets of views rests on how one understands the relation of international law to state behavior. The argument for illegality is constructed by reading the UN Charter and, after finding the answer to the question there in black-letter law, it reaches its conclusion based on the priority of state consent and treaty law over other legal resources (such as practice, custom, and so on). It suggests that state practices that contradict a piece of treaty law should be coded as "noncompliance," and that the political, moral, or transformational motives behind it are irrelevant. The law stands, independent of state behavior, even accepting that rule violation will sometimes occur. The cases for legality turn this around. They rest on the view that sustained patterns of state behavior in opposition to the rules have creative effects in international law, such that if there exists a sustained pattern of humanitarian intervention, then legalization may be taking place. This presumes that international law is a product of interstate interactions in settings beyond formal treaty negotiations. Rhetoric, recent behavior, and the apparent intentions of states are all resources for interpreting how states understand their obligations, and thus for learning what the rules are. Evidence of noncompliance with Article 2(4) is in this view a sign that states are in the process of changing the rules. Sufficient movement in this direction can come to constitute a new understanding of the law, equally binding as the *ex ante* law. This is the standard account of customary international law; and the intuition behind much of the writing on humanitarianism is that it also applies to treaty law in the Charter. This view puts practice conceptually ahead of the text of the treaty, and it puts the agency of states ahead of the constraining quality of external rules. It obviously carries its own dilemma: if legality is a function of practice rather than treaties, then in what ways are treaties constraining or even relevant?

These are deep differences, and they cannot be bridged by reference to the laws themselves. Rather, they require answering the eternal questions in the philosophy of international law about sources, foundations, and interpretation—and this is unlikely to happen. This situation suggests we should admit that international law contains both positions at once and that humanitarian intervention can be made to seem legal *or* illegal depending on one's needs. This allows us to see that both traditions have honorable pedigrees in international law. However, it also requires that we rethink what we thought we knew about the role and power of international law.

Since the contents of international law can be read to support either position, it is natural that a government will take the view that what it thinks should be done in any particular case is acceptable under international law—and will point to what it opposes as a violation of the law. Deciding in favor of one of these conclusions requires selecting the subset of evidence that supports one's favored view. This freedom to choose among interpretations of the law gives rise to a sea of self-serving claims, and to unending academic debate. Each effort to champion one side produces a predictable response from the other, and the debate has less to do with the merits of one legal interpretation than with the political needs of those making the arguments.

This is the strategic manipulation of international law, which is often taken as the opposite of the rule of law and as therefore negative. This is how Brian Tamanaha sees it in his critique of the "political" uses of law in the American context, and it is also how Michael Glennon sees it in the international context.[42] However, the humanitarian intervention case helps to show that this is wrong. Tamanaha argues against seeing the law as an instrument with which to pursue political goals. He suggests that this instrumental attitude toward the law is a threat to society because it leads to "a

Hobbesian conflict of all against all carried on within and through the legal order . . . [where] law will thus generate disputes as much as resolve them. Even when one side prevails, victory will mark only a momentary respite before the battle is resumed." The preferable alternative, he says, is to return to the model of "a few centuries ago" when "law was understood to possess a necessary content and integrity that was, in some ways, given or predetermined."[43] This noninstrumentalist attitude to law reflects the compliance model in international law, where treaties and state consent provide the integrity of predetermined rules, which stay constant despite the interpretive manipulations and rule-breaking acts of self-serving states.

What Tamanaha identifies as a problem for domestic law is in fact the normal condition of international law. The strategic manipulation of law is inherent in international law, at least with respect to the laws on the use of force and others (such as torture) where there is no international judicial body to settle disputes over the meaning of compliance. International law on self-defense, preemption, torture, and humanitarian intervention does indeed generate, as much as resolve, disputes. States invoke international law in a variety of settings to explain and justify their behavior, and to criticize and embarrass their opponents, and so the instrumental use of law is inseparable from the law itself. The political use of international law is not an aberration or a misuse of the law; it is the normal and inevitable result of striving for rules-based international politics.

Of course, it is widely accepted that international legal obligations must be interpreted in part by reference to state practice. My argument is not that this is novel, nor that it is a problem that needs to be solved. Rather, I seek to show that the ease with which we use practice to understand the content of international law works against the equally common presumption that compliance with international law has a consistent meaning.

State practice has a productive effect on the content of the law. This is evident in the progress of the concept of humanitarian intervention, which has arisen as a legal category out of the practice of states invoking the rules on the use of force in certain ways. The content of these rules is in part a function of how they have been used in the past, especially but not only the recent past. As states began to claim that Article 2(4) should not be understood as banning wars with humanitarian motives, the certainty over the meaning of the Charter eroded. Breaking international law is intrinsically linked to making international law, and both are subsets of the broad category of "using" international law. This is true for both treaties and custom, and not solely in the traditional hierarchy by which treaty trumps custom—the humanitarian intervention case shows that many states and scholars are willing to have state practice trump treaty law.

Ultimately the attempt to organize international law scholarship around the question of compliance is misplaced, at least for a significant subset of international rules. There is a growing literature that seeks to link political science and law around the empirical measurement of compliance, asking what qualities in a piece of law contribute to higher rates of compliance, or what kinds of domestic institutions correlate with higher rates of compliance, or how compliance relates to the decision to join a treaty.[44] These studies adopt an empirically oriented compliance model to studying international law, in which the causes and effects of compliance and noncompliance are the focus. Compliance is also sometimes used to try to distinguish constructivist from rationalist hypotheses about state behavior. For instance, Judith Kelley asks whether states comply with their obligations to the International Criminal Court out of an interest in material gain or out of a normative commitment, seeing the former as rationalist and the latter as normative or constructivist.[45] In all this work, it is the reasons for and effects of compliance and noncompliance that are under investigation.

The "compliance model" requires that we be able to differentiate between behavior that is compliant and behavior that is not, and in the case of humanitarian intervention this is clearly not possible. Interpretive challenges here mean that the definition of compliance is itself contested, and disputes over the meaning of the law are best understood as proxies for fights over the underlying substance of the case in question. Many areas of international law have this quality, where the parties insist on their own claims to compliance and provide legal resources that support them. Where we cannot differentiate compliance from noncompliance, the law's effect on behavior must be measured in some currency other than the rate of rule following. Robert Howse and Ruti Teitel have recently made this point, and suggest that the contribution of international law is in changing the terms and shape of the interstate bargaining that takes place in and around the rules.[46] For them, the law is a resource for states rather than a standard that distinguishes between lawful and unlawful behavior. This is supported by the humanitarian case presented here.

Despite all these ambiguities in international law, the idea of the rule of law remains powerful in international politics. States remain convinced that they should comply with rather than violate the law, and in the humanitarianism debates all sides generally represent themselves as being compliant with the rules.[47] The idea that international relations does or should take place in a rule-governed context is widely shared. This is a fundamental premise of international law both as a practice and as a scholarly field. The power of state consent is that it marks an explicit moment at which states take on commitments, and compliance is expected thereafter. While there are disagreements about whether a legal obligation provides an independent reason for compliance distinct from any other underlying reasons for action (that is, for reputation, for instrumental gain, or other logics),[48] there is very little dissent from the idea that states should comply with these obligations. Few commentators suggest that states can or should ignore their legal obligations. Those who argue against a particular obligation almost always do so in the language of compliance with some other obligation.

Conclusion

Wars begun in the pursuit of humanitarian rescue are now seen as different from wars fought for other purposes. They are now legally, politically, and conceptually separate from wars of conquest and wars of national security, even as the category of humanitarian intervention remains fiercely contested in practice. Contemporary international law can be read as either allowing or forbidding international humanitarian intervention, and the legal uncertainty around humanitarian intervention is fundamental and irresolvable. Contradictory and plausible interpretations about the legality of any act of intervention exist simultaneously, and neither can be eliminated. This does not mean that the law is unimportant; there are evident costs and benefits to states in being seen as following the rules. It means instead that law and law following should be seen as resources in the hands of states and others, deployed to influence the political context of their actions.

The debate over the legality of humanitarian intervention raises deep questions about international law. Can the statements of leaders modify the obligations contained in treaties? If states contradict established international law, does this change the law or is it a simple case of noncompliance (or can it be both)? Does the practice of humanitarian intervention (if it exists) sustain the legality of humanitarian intervention? There is no consensus over the legality of intervention, in part because there is no consensus over the sources of international law more generally. The intervention problem is inseparable from questions that have been at the heart of international law for centuries, and that we cannot expect to be answered in

order to reconcile the different views on humanitarian intervention. The legality of humanitarianism is therefore contingent on one's theory of how law works and changes. The law may well be incoherent, and it may be unable to distinguish between compliance and noncompliance, but it remains politically powerful and therefore important. The challenge for scholars is to explain how it is that the commitment to the rule of law coexists with this fundamental ambiguity.

NOTES

1. For these debates, see, e.g., Diplomatic Academy of Vienna, *The UN Security Council and the Responsibility to Protect: Policy, Process, and Practice* (Vienna: Favorita Papers 01/2010); Nicholas J. Wheeler, *Saving Strangers: Humanitarian Intervention in International Society* (New York: Oxford University Press, 2003); and J. L. Holzgrefe and Robert O. Keohane, eds., *Humanitarian Intervention: Ethical, Legal, and Political Dilemmas* (Cambridge: Cambridge University Press, 2003).

2. See James Turner Johnson, *Ideology, Reason, and the Limitation of War* (Princeton, N.J.: Princeton University Press, 1975); Ian Clark, *Legitimacy in International Society* (Oxford: Oxford University Press, 2005); and Christine D. Gray, *International Law and the Use of Force*, 3rd. ed. (Oxford: Oxford University Press, 2008).

3. See, e.g., Richard Jolly, Louis Emmerij, and Thomas G. Weiss, *UN Ideas That Changed the World* (Bloomington, Ind.: Indiana University Press, 2009).

4. Controversy over whether the Council is correctly identifying such threats is common—for instance, with respect to the Libyan sanctions in the 1990s. See B. Martenczuk, "The Security Council, the International Court and Judicial Review: What Lessons from Lockerbie?" *European Journal of International Law* 10, no. 3 (1999), pp. 517–47.

5. Gray, *International Law and the Use of Force*.

6. "Productive" here is used in the sense used by Michael N. Barnett and Raymond Duvall, eds.,

Power in Global Governance (Cambridge: Cambridge University Press, 2005).

7. United Nations Security Council Resolution 487.

8. These words first appear in a letter from Daniel Webster to Lord Ashburton, August 6, 1842; avalon. law.yale.edu/19th_century/br-1842d.asp#web2; accessed November 18, 2010.

9. Michael Byers, "Jumping the Gun," *London Review of Books* 24, no. 11 (2002), pp. 3–5.

10. See International Court of Justice, *Nicaragua* Merits, ICJ Reports, June 27, 1986, 94, para. 176.

11. See, generally, Vaughan Lowe and Antonios Tzanakopoulos, "Humanitarian Intervention," in Rüdiger Wolfrum, ed., *Max Planck Encyclopedia of Public International Law* (Oxford: Oxford University Press, 2010); Philip Alston and Euan MacDonald, eds., *Human Rights, Intervention, and the Use of Force* (New York: Oxford University Press, 2008); Martha Finnemore, *The Purpose of Intervention: Changing Beliefs about the Use of Force* (Ithaca, N.Y.: Cornell University Press, 2004); and Thomas M. Franck, *Recourse to Force: State Action Against Threats and Armed Attacks* (Cambridge: Cambridge University Press, 2002).

12. Nikolas Sturchler, *The Threat of Force in International Law* (Cambridge: Cambridge University Press, 2006).

13. Ian Hurd, *After Anarchy: Legitimacy and Power in the UN Security Council* (Princeton: Princeton University Press, 2007).

14. Ian Brownlie, " 'International Law and the Use of Force by States' Revisited," *Chinese Journal of International Law* 1, no. 1 (2002), pp. 1–19.

15. Swedish representative at the UN Security Council, cited in Gray, *International Law and the Use of Force*, pp. 32–33.

16. Bruno Simma et al., eds., *The Charter of the United Nations: A Commentary* (Oxford: Oxford University Press, 2002).

17. *Corfu Channel*, International Court of Justice, 1949.

18. Ruth B. Russell, A *History of the UN Charter: The Role of the United States* (Washington, D.C.: Brookings Institution, 1958); and Lowe and Tzanakopoulos, "Humanitarian Intervention."

19. Inter-American Democratic Charter, September 11, 2001, Lima, Peru; www.oas.org/charter/docs/resolution1_en_p4.htm.

20. Bardo Fassbender, "Rediscovering a Forgotten Constitution: Notes on the Place of the UN Charter in the International Legal Order," in Jeffrey L. Dunoff and Joel P. Trachtman, eds., *Ruling the World? Constitutionalism, International Law, and Global Governance* (Cambridge: Cambridge University Press, 2009); Kristen E. Boon, "Regime Conflicts and the UN Security Council: Applying the Law of Responsibility," *George Washington International Law Review* 42, no. 2 (2010); and Richard Burchill, "Regional Arrangements as an Expression of Diversity in the International System" (paper presented at the American Society of International Law workshop on international organizations, October 29, 2010, Washington, D.C.).

21. Byers, "Jumping the Gun."

22. Independent International Commission on Kosovo, *Kosovo Report: Conflict, International Response, Lessons Learned* (Oxford: Oxford University Press, 2000).

23. Brownlie, "International Law," p. 16; and Franck, *Recourse to Force*, See also Bruno Simma, "NATO, the UN, and the Use of Force: Legal Aspects," *European Journal of International Law* 10, no. 1 (1999); and Anthea Roberts, "Legality vs. Legitimacy: Can Uses of Force Be Illegal but Justified?" in Philip Alston and Euan MacDonald, eds., *Human Rights, Intervention, and the Use of Force* (New York: Oxford University Press, 2008).

24. Thomas M. Franck, "Who Killed Article 2(4)? Or: Changing Norms Governing the Use of Force by States," *American Journal of International Law* 64 (1970), pp. 810, 809.

25. Ibid., p. 835.

26. Michael Glennon, "The Fog of Law: Self-Defense, Inherence, and Incoherence in Article 51 of the United Nations Charter," *Harvard Journal of Law and Public Policy* 25 (2002), pp. 539–58, at 539. See also Michael Glennon, "How International Rules Die," *Georgetown Law Journal* 93 (2005), p. 939.

27. Glennon, "The Fog of Law," p. 540, emphasis added.

28. In the United States, see *Poe v. Ullman* at the U.S. Supreme Court (1961), and *Committee on Legal Ethics v. Prinz* in the West Virginia Supreme Court, 1992.

29. The argument may be logically sound, but it is empirically weak since it ignores a vast universe of state practice that contradicts it. Most state behavior upholds and reinforces the ban on war, and all of this is evidence against the argument of desuetude.

30. Michael J. Smith, "Humanitarian Intervention: An Overview of the Ethical Issues," *Ethics & International Affairs* 12 (1998), pp. 63–79, at 66.

31. Thomas G. Weiss and Ramesh Thakur, *Global Governance and the UN: An Unfinished Journey* (Bloomington, Ind.: Indiana University Press, 2010); see also the essays in Diplomatic Academy of Vienna, *The UN Security Council and the Responsibility to Protect.*

32. Kofi Annan, cited in Weiss and Thakur, *Global Governance and the UN*, p. 318.

33. "2005 World Summit Outcome: Fact Sheet"; www .un.org/summit2005/presskit/fact_sheet.pdf; accessed January 10, 2011.

34. Alex J. Bellamy, "The Responsibility to Protect—Five Years On," *Ethics & International Affairs* 24, no. 2 (Summer 2010), pp. 143–69.

35. As defined by Emanuel Adler and Vincent Pouliot, *The Practice Turn in International Theory* (Cambridge: Cambridge University Press, 2011).

36. Paul D. Williams and Alex J. Bellamy, "The Responsibility to Protect and the Crisis in Darfur," *Security Dialogue* 36, no. 1 (2005), pp. 27–47.

37. Reported in David D. Kirkpatrick and Kareen Fahim, "Libya Blames Islamic Militants and the West for Unrest," *New York Times*, February 28, 2011.

38. Allen Buchanan, *Justice, Legitimacy, and Self-Determination: Moral Foundations for International Law* (New York: Oxford University Press, 2007).

39. Fernando R. Tesón, "The Liberal Case for Humanitarian Intervention," in J. L. Holzgrefe and Robert O. Keohane, eds., *Humanitarian Intervention: Ethical, Legal, and Political Dilemmas* (Cambridge: Cambridge University Press, 2003), p. 93.

40. UN General Assembly, "An Agenda for Peace," Report of the Secretary-General, A/47/277, June 17, 1992.

41. Gareth Evans and Mohamed Sahnoun, "The Responsibility to Protect," *Foreign Affairs* 81, no. 6 (2002), pp. 99–110, at 102.

42. Brian Tamanaha, *Law as a Means to an End: Threat to the Rule of Law* (Cambridge: Cambridge University Press, 2006).

43. Ibid., pp. 1–2.

44. Harold Hongju Koh, "Why Do Nations Obey International Law?" *Yale Law Journal* 106, no. 8 (1997), pp. 2599–2659; Oona Hathaway, "Do Human Rights Treaties Make a Difference?" *Yale Law Journal* 111, no. 3 (2002), pp. 1935–2042; Judith Kelley, "Who Keeps International Commitments and Why? The International Criminal Court and Bilateral Non-Surrender Agreements," *American Political Science Review* 101, no. 3 (2007), pp. 573–89; and Emilie Hafner-Burton, Jon Pevehouse, and Jana von Stein, "Human Rights Institutions, Membership, and Compliance" (paper presented at the American Political Science Association annual meetings 2009).

45. Kelley, "Who Keeps International Commitments and Why?"

46. Robert Howse and Ruti Teitel, "Beyond Compliance: Rethinking Why International Law Matters," *Global Policy* 1, no. 2 (2010), pp. 127–36.

47. Exceptions exist, including the interesting case of the "waiver of illegality" position discussed above. This position, common on Kosovo, reveals an underlying prioritization among laws, obligations, and interests that is unconventional: proponents are suggesting that states should obey their international obligations only as long as these obligations are consistent with deeply held norms and interests and when they conflict, compliance is not required (or expected, or desired).

48. See the discussion in Jutta Brunnée and Stephen J. Toope, *Legitimacy and Legality in International Law* (Cambridge: Cambridge University Press, 2010).

Margaret E. Keck and Kathryn Sikkink

TRANSNATIONAL ADVOCACY NETWORKS IN INTERNATIONAL POLITICS

World politics at the end of the twentieth century involves, alongside states, many non-state actors that interact with each other, with states, and with international organizations. These interactions are structured in terms of networks, and transnational networks are increasingly visible in international politics. [Networks are forms of organization characterized by voluntary, reciprocal, and horizontal patterns of communication and exchange.] Some involve economic actors and firms. Some are networks of scientists and experts whose professional ties and shared causal ideas underpin their efforts to influence policy.[1] Others are networks of activists, distinguishable largely by the centrality of principled ideas or values in motivating their formation.[2] We will call these *transnational advocacy networks.* [A transnational advocacy network includes those relevant actors working internationally on an issue who are bound together by shared values, a common discourse, and dense exchanges of information and services.]

Advocacy networks are significant transnationally and domestically. By building new links among actors in civil societies, states, and international organizations, they multiply the channels of access to the international system. In such issue areas as the environment and human rights, they also make international resources available to new actors in domestic political and social struggles. By thus blurring the boundaries between a state's relations with its own nationals and the recourse both citizens and states have to the international system, advocacy networks are helping to transform the practice of national sovereignty.

■   ■   ■

Transnational advocacy networks are proliferating, and their goal is to change the behavior of states and of international organizations. Simultaneously principled and strategic actors, they "frame" issues to make them comprehensible to target audiences, to attract attention and encourage action, and to "fit" with favorable institutional venues.[3] Network actors bring new ideas, norms, and discourses into policy debates, and serve as sources of information and testimony. * * *

They also promote norm implementation, by pressuring target actors to adopt new policies, and by monitoring compliance with international standards. Insofar as is possible, they seek to maximize their influence or leverage over the target of their actions. In doing so they contribute to changing perceptions that both state and societal actors may have of their identities, interests, and preferences, to transforming their discursive positions, and ultimately to changing procedures, policies, and behavior.[4]

Networks are communicative structures. To influence discourse, procedures, and policy,

From Margaret E. Keck and Kathryn Sikkink, *Activists beyond Borders: Advocacy Networks in International Politics* (Ithaca, N.Y.: Cornell University Press, 1998), Chaps. 1, 3.

activists may engage and become part of larger policy communities that group actors working on an issue from a variety of institutional and value perspectives. Transnational advocacy networks must also be understood as political spaces, in which differently situated actors negotiate—formally or informally—the social, cultural, and political meanings of their joint enterprise.

■ ■ ■

Major actors in advocacy networks may include the following: (1) international and domestic nongovernmental research and advocacy organizations; (2) local social movements; (3) foundations; (4) the media; (5) churches, trade unions, consumer organizations, and intellectuals; (6) parts of

Table 7.1. International Nongovernmental Social Change Organizations (Categorized by the Major Issue Focus of their Work)

ISSUE AREA (N)	1953 (N = 110)	1963 (N = 141)	1973 (N = 183)	1983 (N = 348)	1993 (N = 631)
Human rights	33	38	41	79	168
	30.0%	27.0%	22.4%	22.7%	26.6%
World order	8	4	12	31	48
	7.3%	2.8%	6.6%	8.9%	7.6%
International law	14	19	25	26	26
	12.7%	13.4%	13.7%	7.4%	4.1%
Peace	11	20	14	22	59
	10.0%	14.2%	7.7%	6.3%	9.4%
Women's rights	10	14	16	25	61
	9.1%	9.9%	8.7%	7.2%	9.7%
Environment	2	5	10	26	90
	1.8%	3.5%	5.5%	7.5%	14.3%
Development	3	3	7	13	34
	2.7%	2.1%	3.8%	3.7%	5.4%
Ethnic unity/ Group rts.	10	12	18	37	29
	9.1%	8.5%	9.8%	10.6%	4.6%
Esperanto	11	18	28	41	54
	10.0%	12.8%	15.3%	11.8%	8.6%

Source: Union of International Associations, *Yearbook of International Organizations* (1953, 1963, 1973, 1983, 1993). We are indebted to Jackie Smith, University of Notre Dame, for the use of her data from 1983 and 1993, and the use of her coding form and codebook for our data collection for the period 1953–73.

regional and international intergovernmental organizations; and (7) parts of the executive and/ or parliamentary branches of governments. Not all these will be present in each advocacy network. Initial research suggests, however, that international and domestic NGOs play a central role in all advocacy networks, usually initiating actions and pressuring more powerful actors to take positions. NGOs introduce new ideas, provide information, and lobby for policy changes.

Groups in a network share values and frequently exchange information and services. The flow of information among actors in the network reveals a dense web of connections among these groups, both formal and informal. The movement of funds and services is especially notable between foundations and NGOs, and some NGOs provide services such as training for other NGOs in the same and sometimes other advocacy networks. Personnel also circulate within and among networks, as relevant players move from one to another in a version of the "revolving door."

■   ■   ■

We cannot accurately count transnational advocacy networks to measure their growth over time, but one proxy is the increase in the number of international NGOs committed to social change. Because international NGOs are key components of any advocacy network, this increase suggests broader trends in the number, size, and density of advocacy networks generally. Table 7.1 suggests that the number of international nongovernmental social change groups has increased across all issues, though to varying degrees in different issue areas. There are five times as many organizations working primarily on human rights as there were in 1950, but proportionally human rights groups have remained roughly a quarter of all such groups. Similarly, groups working on women's rights accounted for 9 percent of all groups in 1953 and in 1993. Transnational environmental organizations have

grown most dramatically in absolute and relative terms, increasing from two groups in 1953 to ninety in 1993, and from 1.8 percent of total groups in 1953 to 14.3 percent in 1993. The percentage share of groups in such issue areas as international law, peace, ethnic unity, and Esperanto, has declined.[5]

■   ■   ■

How Do Transnational Advocacy Networks Work?

Transnational advocacy networks seek influence in many of the same ways that other political groups or social movements do. Since they are not powerful in a traditional sense of the word, they must use the power of their information, ideas, and strategies to alter the information and value contexts within which states make policies. The bulk of what networks do might be termed persuasion or socialization, but neither process is devoid of conflict. Persuasion and socialization often involve not just reasoning with opponents, but also bringing pressure, arm-twisting, encouraging sanctions, and shaming. * * *

Our typology of tactics that networks use in their efforts at persuasion, socialization, and pressure includes (1) *information politics*, or the ability to quickly and credibly generate politically usable information and move it to where it will have the most impact; (2) *symbolic politics*, or the ability to call upon symbols, actions, or stories that make sense of a situation for an audience that is frequently far away;[6] (3) *leverage politics*, or the ability to call upon powerful actors to affect a situation where weaker members of a network are unlikely to have influence; and (4) *accountability politics*, or the effort to hold powerful actors to their previously stated policies or principles.

A single campaign may contain many of these elements simultaneously. For example, the human rights network disseminated information about human rights abuses in Argentina in the period 1976–83. The Mothers of the Plaza de Mayo marched in circles in the central square in Buenos Aires wearing white handkerchiefs to draw symbolic attention to the plight of their missing children. The network also tried to use both material and moral leverage against the Argentine regime, by pressuring the United States and other governments to cut off military and economic aid, and by efforts to get the UN and the Inter-American Commission on Human Rights to condemn Argentina's human rights practices. Monitoring is a variation on information politics, in which activists use information strategically to ensure accountability with public statements, existing legislation and international standards.

■   ■   ■

Network members actively seek ways to bring issues to the public agenda by framing them in innovative ways and by seeking hospitable venues. Sometimes they create issues by framing old problems in new ways; occasionally they help transform other actors' understanding of their identities and their interests. Land use rights in the Amazon, for example, took on an entirely different character and gained quite different allies viewed in a deforestation frame than they did in either social justice or regional development frames. In the 1970s and 1980s many states decided for the first time that promotion of human rights in other countries was a legitimate foreign policy goal and an authentic expression of national interest. This decision came in part from interaction with an emerging global human rights network. We argue that this represents not the victory of morality over self-interest, but a transformed understanding of national interest, possible in part because of structured interactions between state components and networks. * * *

■   ■   ■

Under What Conditions Do Advocacy Networks Have Influence?

To assess the influence of advocacy networks we must look at goal achievement at several different levels. We identify the following types or stages of network influence: (1) issue creation and agenda setting; (2) influence on discursive positions of states and international organizations; (3) influence on institutional procedures; (4) influence on policy change in "target actors" which may be states, international organizations like the World Bank, or private actors like the Nestlé Corporation; and (5) influence on state behavior.

Networks generate attention to new issues and help set agendas when they provoke media attention, debates, hearings, and meetings on issues that previously had not been a matter of public debate. Because values are the essence of advocacy networks, this stage of influence may require a modification of the "value context" in which policy debates takes place. The UN's theme years and decades, such as International Women's Decade and the Year of Indigenous Peoples, were international events promoted by networks that heightened awareness of issues.

Networks influence discursive positions when they help persuade states and international organizations to support international declarations or to change stated domestic policy positions. The role environmental networks played in shaping state positions and conference declarations at the 1992 "Earth Summit" in Rio de Janeiro is an example of this kind of impact. They may also pressure states to make more binding commitments by signing conventions and codes of conduct.

The targets of network campaigns frequently respond to demands for policy change with changes in procedures (which may affect policies in the future). The multilateral bank campaign is largely responsible for a number of changes in internal bank directives mandating greater NGO and local participation in discussions of projects. It also opened access to formerly restricted information, and led to the establishment of an independent inspection panel for World Bank projects. Procedural changes can greatly increase the opportunity for advocacy organizations to develop regular contact with other key players on an issue, and they sometimes offer the opportunity to move from outside to inside pressure strategies.

A network's activities may produce changes in policies, not only of the target states, but also of other states and/or international institutions. Explicit policy shifts seem to denote success, but even here both their causes and meanings may be elusive. We can point with some confidence to network impact where human rights network pressures have achieved cutoffs of military aid to repressive regimes, or a curtailment of repressive practices. Sometimes human rights activity even affects regime stability. But we must take care to distinguish between policy change and change in behavior; official policies regarding timber extraction in Sarawak, Malaysia, for example, may say little about how timber companies behave on the ground in the absence of enforcement.

We speak of stages of impact, and not merely types of impact, because we believe that increased attention, followed by changes in discursive positions, make governments more vulnerable to the claims that networks raise. (Discursive changes can also have a powerfully divisive effect on networks themselves, splitting insiders from outsiders, reformers from radicals.[7]) A government that claims to be protecting indigenous areas or ecological reserves is potentially more vulnerable to charges that such areas are endangered than one that makes no such claim. At that point the effort is not to make governments change their position but to hold them to their word. Meaningful policy change is thus more likely when the first three types or stages of impact have occurred.

Both issue characteristics and actor characteristics are important parts of our explanation of how networks affect political outcomes and the conditions under which networks can be effective. Issue characteristics such as salience and resonance within existing national or institutional agendas can tell us something about where networks are likely to be able to insert new ideas and discourses into policy debates. Success in influencing policy also depends on the strength and density of the network and its ability to achieve leverage. * * *

■   ■   ■

Toward a Global Civil Society?

Many other scholars now recognize that "the state does not monopolize the public sphere,"[8] and are seeking, as we are, ways to describe the sphere of international interactions under a variety of names: transnational relations, international civil society, and global civil society.[9] In these views, states no longer look unitary from the outside. Increasingly dense interactions among individuals, groups, actors from states, and international institutions appear to involve much more than representing interests on a world stage.

We contend that the advocacy network concept cannot be subsumed under notions of transnational social movements or global civil society. In particular, theorists who suggest that a global civil society will inevitably emerge from economic globalization or from revolutions in communication and transportation technologies ignore the issues of agency and political opportunity that we find central for understanding the evolution of new international institutions and relationships.

■   ■   ■

We lack convincing studies of the sustained and specific processes through which individuals and organizations create (or resist the creation of) something resembling a global civil society. Our research leads us to believe that these interactions involve much more agency than a pure diffusionist perspective suggests. Even though the implications of our findings are much broader than most political scientists would admit, the findings themselves do not yet support the strong claims about an emerging global civil society.[10] We are much more comfortable with a conception of transnational civil society as an arena of struggle, a fragmented and contested area where "the politics of transnational civil society is centrally about the way in which certain groups emerge and are legitimized (by governments, institutions, and other groups)."[11]

■ ■ ■

HUMAN RIGHTS ADVOCACY NETWORKS IN LATIN AMERICA

Argentina

Even before the military coup of March 1976, international human rights pressures had influenced the Argentine military's decision to cause political opponents to "disappear," rather than imprisoning them or executing them publicly.[12] (The technique led to the widespread use of the verb "to disappear" in a transitive sense.) The Argentine military believed they had "learned" from the international reaction to the human rights abuses after the Chilean coup. When the Chilean military executed and imprisoned large numbers of people, the ensuing uproar led to the international isolation of the regime of Augusto Pinochet. Hoping to maintain a moderate international image, the Argentine military decided to secretly kidnap, detain, and execute its victims, while denying any knowledge of their whereabouts.[13]

Although this method did initially mute the international response to the coup, Amnesty International and groups staffed by Argentine political exiles eventually were able to document and condemn the new forms of repressive practices. To counteract the rising tide of criticism, the Argentina junta invited AI for an on-site visit in 1976. In March 1977, on the first anniversary of the military coup, AI published the report on its visit, a well-documented denunciation of the abuses of the regime with emphasis on the problem of the disappeared. Amnesty estimated that the regime had taken six thousand political prisoners, most without specifying charges, and had abducted between two and ten thousand people. The report helped demonstrate that the disappearances were part of a deliberate government policy by which the military and the police kidnapped perceived opponents, took them to secret detention centers where they tortured, interrogated, and killed them, then secretly disposed of their bodies.[14] Amnesty International's denunciations of the Argentine regime were legitimized when it won the Nobel Peace Prize later that year.

Such information led the Carter administration and the French, Italian, and Swedish governments to denounce rights violations by the junta. France, Italy, and Sweden each had citizens who had been victims of Argentine repression, but their concerns extended beyond their own citizens. Although the Argentine government claimed that such attacks constituted unacceptable intervention in their internal affairs and violated Argentine sovereignty, U.S. and European officials persisted. In 1977 the U.S. government reduced the planned level of military aid for Argentina because of human rights abuses. Congress later passed a bill eliminating all military assistance to Argentina, which went into effect on 30 September 1978.[15] A number of high-level U.S. delegations met with junta members during this period to discuss human rights.

Early U.S. action on Argentina was based primarily on the human rights documentation provided by AI and other NGOs, not on information received through official channels at the embassy or the State Department.[16] For example, during a 1977 visit, Secretary of State Cyrus Vance carried a list of disappeared people prepared by human rights NGOs to present to members of the junta.[17] When Patricia Derian met with junta member Admiral Emilio Massera during a visit in 1977, she brought up the navy's use of torture. In response to Massera's denial, Derian said she had seen a rudimentary map of a secret detention center in the Navy Mechanical School, where their meeting was being held, and asked whether perhaps under their feet someone was being tortured. Among Derian's key sources of information were NGOs and especially the families of the disappeared, with whom she met frequently during her visits to Buenos Aires.[18]

Within a year of the coup, Argentine domestic human rights organizations began to develop significant external contacts. Their members traveled frequently to the United States and Europe, where they met with human rights organizations, talked to the press, and met with parliamentarians and government officials. These groups sought foreign contacts to publicize the human rights situation, to fund their activities, and to help protect themselves from further repression by their government, and they provided evidence to U.S. and European policymakers. Much of their funding came from European and U.S.-based foundations.[19]

Two key events that served to keep the case of Argentine human rights in the minds of U.S. and European policymakers reflect the impact of transnational linkages on policy. In 1979 the Argentine authorities released Jacobo Timerman, whose memoir describing his disappearance and torture by the Argentine military helped human rights organizations, members of the U.S. Jewish community, and U.S. journalists to make his case a cause célèbre in U.S. policy circles.[20] Then in 1980 the Nobel Peace Prize was awarded to an Argentine human rights activist, Adolfo Pérez Esquivel. Peace and human rights groups in the United States and Europe helped sponsor Pérez Esquivel's speaking tour to the United States exactly at the time that the OAS was considering the IACHR report on Argentina and Congress was debating the end of the arms embargo to Argentina.

The Argentine military government wanted to avoid international human rights censure. Scholars have long recognized that even authoritarian regimes depend on a combination of coercion and consent to stay in power. Without the legitimacy conferred by elections, they rely heavily on claims about their political efficancy and on nationalism.[21] Although the Argentine military mobilized nationalist rhetoric against foreign criticism, a sticking point was that Argentines, especially the groups that most supported the military regime, thought of themselves as the most European of Latin American countries. The military junta claimed to be carrying out the repression in the name of "our Western and Christian civilization."[22] But the military's intent to integrate Argentina more fully into the liberal global economic order was being jeopardized by deteriorating relations with countries most identified with that economic order, and with "Western and Christian civilization."

The junta adopted a sequence of responses to international pressures. From 1976 to 1978 the military pursued an initial strategy of denying the legitimacy of international concern over human rights in Argentina. At the same time it took actions that appear to have contradicted this strategy, such as permitting the visit of the Amnesty International mission to Argentina in 1976. The "failure" of the Amnesty visit, from the military point of view, appeared to reaffirm the junta's resistance to human rights pressures. This strategy was most obvious at the UN, where the Argentine government worked to silence international condemnation in the UN Commission on Human Rights. Ironically, the rabidly anticommunist Argentine regime found a diplomatic ally in the Soviet Union, an importer of Argentine wheat, and the two countries collaborated to block UN consideration of the Argentine human rights situation.[23] Concerned states circumvented this blockage by creating the UN Working Group on Disappearances in 1980. Human rights NGOs provided information, lobbied government delegations, and pursued joint strategies with sympathetic UN delegations.

By 1978 the Argentine government recognized that something had to be done to improve its international image in the United States and Europe, and to restore the flow of military and economic aid.[24] To these ends the junta invited the Inter-American Commission on Human Rights for an on-site visit, in exchange for a U.S. commitment to release Export-Import Bank funds and otherwise improve U.S.-Argentine relations.[25] During 1978 the human rights situation in Argentina improved significantly. [T]he practice of disappearance as a tool of state policy was curtailed only after 1978, when the government began to take the "international variable" seriously.[26]

The value of the network perspective in the Argentine case is in highlighting the fact that international pressures did not work independently, but rather in coordination with national actors. Rapid change occurred because strong domestic human rights organizations documented abuses and protested against repression, and international pressures helped protect domestic monitors and open spaces for their protest. International groups amplified both information and symbolic politics of domestic groups and projected them onto an international stage, from which they echoed back into Argentina. This classic boomerang process was executed nowhere more skillfully than in Argentina, in large part due to the courage and ability of domestic human rights organizations.

Some argue that repression stopped because the military had finally killed all the people that they thought they needed to kill. This argument disregards disagreements within the regime about the size and nature of the "enemy." International pressures affected particular factions within the military regime that had differing ideas about how much repression was "necessary." Although by the military's admission 90 percent of the *armed* opposition had been eliminated by April 1977, this did not lead to an immediate change in human rights practices.[27] By 1978 there were splits within the military about what it should do in the future. One faction was led by Admiral Massera, a right-wing populist, another by Generals Carlos Suarez Mason and Luciano Menéndez, who supported indefinite military dictatorship and unrelenting war against the left, and a third by Generals Jorge Videla and Roberto Viola, who hoped for eventual political liberalization under a military president. Over time, the Videla-Viola faction won out, and by late 1978 Videla had gained increased control over the Ministry of Foreign Affairs, previously under the influence of the navy.[28] Videla's ascendancy in the fall of 1978, combined with U.S. pressure, helps explain his ability to deliver on his promise to allow the Inter-American Commission on Human Rights visit in December.

The Argentine military government thus moved from initial refusal to accept international human rights interventions, to cosmetic cooperation with the human rights network, and eventually to concrete improvements in response to increased international pressures. Once it had invited IACHR and discovered that the commission could not be co-opted or confused, the government ended the practice of disappearance, released political prisoners, and restored some semblance of political participation. Full restoration of human rights in Argentina did not come until after the Malvinas War and the transition to democracy in 1983, but after 1980 the worst abuses had been curtailed.

In 1985, after democratization, Argentina tried the top military leaders of the juntas for human rights abuses, and a number of key network members testified: Theo Van Boven and Patricia Derian spoke about international awareness of the Argentine human rights situation, and a member of the IACHR delegation to Argentina discussed the OAS report. Clyde Snow and Eric Stover provided information about the exhumation of cadavers from mass graves. Snow's testimony, corroborated by witnesses, was a key part of the prosecutor's success in establishing that top military officers were guilty of murder.[29] A public opinion poll taken during the trials showed that 92 percent of Argentines were in favor of the trials of the military juntas.[30] The tribunal convicted five of the nine defendants, though only two—ex-president Videla, and Admiral Massera—were given life sentences. The trials were the first of their kind in Latin America, and among the very few in the world ever to try former leaders for human rights abuses during their rule. In 1990 President Carlos Menem pardoned the former officers. By the mid-1990s, however, democratic rule in Argentina was firmly entrenched, civilian authority over the military was well established, and the military had been weakened by internal disputes and severe cuts in funding.[31]

The Argentine case set important precedents for other international and regional human rights action, and shows the intricate interactions of groups and individuals within the network and the repercussions of these interactions. The story of the Grandmothers of the Plaza de Mayo is an exemplar of network interaction and unanticipated effects. The persistence of the Grandmothers helped create a new profession—what one might call "human rights forensic science." (The scientific skills existed before, but they had never been put to the service of human rights.) Once the Argentine case had demonstrated that forensic science could illuminate mass murder and lead to convictions, these skills were diffused and legitimized. Eric Stover, Clyde Snow, and the Argentine forensic anthropology team they helped create were the prime agents of international diffusion. The team later carried out exhumations and training in Chile, Bolivia, Brazil, Venezuela, and Guatemala.[32] Forensic science is being used to prosecute mass murderers in El Salvador, Honduras, Rwanda, and Bosnia. By 1996 the UN International Criminal Tribunal for the former Yugoslavia had contracted with two veterans of the Argentine forensic experiment, Stover and Dr. Robert Kirschner, to do forensic investigations for its war crimes tribunal. " 'A war crime creates a crime scene,' said Dr. Kirschner, 'That's how we treat it. We recover forensic evidence for prosecution and create a record which cannot be successfully challenged in court.' "[33]

■　■　■

Conclusions

A realist approach to international relations would have trouble attributing significance either to the network's activities or to the adoption and implementation of state human rights policies. Realism offers no convincing explanation for why relatively weak nonstate actors could affect state policy, or why states would concern themselves with the internal human rights practices of other states even when doing so interferes with the pursuit of other goals. For example, the U.S. government's pressure on Argentina on human rights led Argentina to defect from the grain embargo of the Soviet Union. Raising human rights issues with Mexico could have undermined the successful completion of the free trade agreement and cooperation with Mexico on antidrug operations. Human rights pressures have costs, even in strategically less important countries of Latin America.

In liberal versions of international relations theory, states and nonstate actors cooperate to realize joint gains or avoid mutually undesirable outcomes when they face problems they cannot resolve alone. These situations have been characterized as cooperation or coordination games with particular payoff structures.[34] But human rights issues are not easily modeled as such. Usually states can ignore the internal human rights practices of other states without incurring undesirable economic or security costs.

In the issue of human rights it is primarily principled ideas that drive change and cooperation. We cannot understand why countries, organizations, and individuals are concerned about human rights or why countries respond to human rights pressures without taking into account the role of norms and ideas in international life. Jack Donnelly has argued that such moral interests are as real as material interests, and that a sense of moral interdependence has led to the emergence of human rights regimes.[35] For human rights * * * the primary movers behind this form of principled international action are international networks.

NOTES

1. Peter Haas has called these "knowledge-based" or "epistemic communities." See Peter Haas, "Introduction: Epistemic Communities and International Policy Coordination," *Knowledge, Power and International Policy Coordination,* special issue, *International Organization* 46 (Winter 1992), pp. 1–36.

2. Ideas that specify criteria for determining whether actions are right and wrong and whether outcomes are just or unjust are shared principled beliefs or values. Beliefs about cause-effect relationships are shared casual beliefs. Judith Goldstein and Robert Keohane, eds., *Ideas and Foreign Policy: Beliefs, Institutions, and Political Change* (Ithaca: Cornell University Press, 1993), pp. 8–10.

3. David Snow and his colleagues have adapted Erving Goffman's concept of framing. We use it to mean "conscious strategic efforts by groups of people to fashion shared understandings of the world and of themselves that legitimate and motivate collective action." Definition from Doug McAdam, John D. McCarthy, and Mayer N. Zald, "Introduction," *Comparative Perspectives on Social Movements: Political Opportunities, Mobilizing Structures, and Cultural Framings,* ed. McAdam, McCarthy, and Zald (New York: Cambridge University Press, 1996), p. 6. See also Frank Baumgartner and Bryan Jones, "Agenda Dynamics and Policy Subsystems," *Journal of Politics* 53:4 (1991): 1044–74.

4. With the "constructivists" in international relations theory, we take actors and interests to be constituted in interaction. See Martha Finnemore, *National Interests in International Society* (Ithaca: Cornell University Press, 1996), who argues that "states are embedded in dense networks of transnational and international social relations that shape their perceptions of the world and their role in that world. States are *socialized* to want certain things by the international society in which they and the people in them live" (p. 2).

5. Data from a collaborative research project with Jackie G. Smith. We thank her for the use of her data from the period 1983–93, whose results are presented in Jackie G. Smith, "Characteristics of the Modern Transnational Social Movement Sector," in Jackie G. Smith, et al., eds. *Transnational Social Movements and World Politics: Solidarity beyond the State* (Syracuse: Syracuse University Press, forthcoming 1997), and for permission to use her coding form and codebook for our data collection for the period 1953–73. All

data were coded from Union of International Associations, *The Yearbook of International Organizations,* 1948–95 (published annually).

6. Alison Brysk uses the categories "information politics" and "symbolic politics" to discuss strategies of transnational actors, especially networks around Indian rights. See "Acting Globally: Indian Rights and International Politics in Latin America," in *Indigenous Peoples and Democracy in Latin America,* ed. Donna Lee Van Cott (New York: St. Martin's Press/Inter-American Dialogue, 1994), pp. 29–51; and "Hearts and Minds: Bringing Symbolic Politics Back In," *Polity* 27 (Summer 1995): 559–85.

7. We thank Jonathan Fox for reminding us of this point.

8. M. J. Peterson, "Transnational Activity, International Society, and World Politics," *Millennium* 21:3 (1992): 375–76.

9. See, for example, Ronnie Lipschutz, "Reconstructing World Politics: The Emergence of Global Civil Society," *Millennium* 21:3 (1992): 389–420; Paul Wapner, "Politics beyond the State: Environmental Activism and World Civic Politics," *World Politics* 47 (April 1995): 311–40; and the special issue of *Millennium* on social movements and world politics, 23:3 (Winter 1994).

10. Sidney Tarrow, *Power in Movement: Social Movements and Contentious Politics,* rev. ed. (Cambridge: Cambridge University Press, forthcoming 1998), Chapter 11. An earlier version appeared as "Fishnets, Internets and Catnets: Globalization and Transnational Collective Action," Instituto Juan March de Estudios e Investigaciones, Madrid: Working Papers 1996/78, March 1996; and Peterson, "Transnational Activity."

11. Andrew Hurrell and Ngaire Woods, "Globalisation and Inequality," *Millennium* 24:3 (1995), p. 468.

12. This section draws upon some material from an earlier co-authored work: Lisa L. Martin and Kathryn Sikkink, "U.S. Policy and Human Rights in Argentina and Guatemala, 1973–1980," in *Double-Edged Diplomacy: International Bargaining and Domestic Politics,* ed., Peter B. Evans, Harold K. Jacobson, and Robert D. Putnam (Berkeley: University of California Press, 1993), pp. 330–62.

13. See Emilio Mignone, *Derechos humanos y sociedad: el caso argentino* (Buenos Aires: Ediciones del Pensamiento Nacional and Centro de Estudios Legales y Sociales, 1991), p. 66; Claudio Uriarte, *Almirante Cero: Biografía No Autorizada de Emilio Eduardo Massera* (Buenos Aires: Planeta, 1992), p. 97; and Carlos H. Acuña and Catalina Smulovitz, "Adjusting the Armed Forces to Democracy: Successes, Failures, and Ambiguities in the Southern Cone," in *Constructing Democracy: Human Rights, Citizenship, and Society in Latin America*, ed. Elizabeth Jelin and Eric Hershberg (Boulder, Colo.: Westview, 1993), p. 15.

14. Amnesty International, *Report of an Amnesty International Mission to Argentina* (London: Amnesty International, 1977).

15. Congressional Research Service, Foreign Affairs and National Defense Division, *Human Rights and U.S. Foreign Assistance: Experiences and Issues in Policy Implementation (1977–1978)*, report prepared for U.S. Senate Committee on Foreign Relations, November 1979, p. 106.

16. After the 1976 coup, Argentine political exiles set up branches of the Argentine Human Rights Commission (CADHU) in Paris, Mexico, Rome, Geneva, and Washington, D.C. In October two of its members testified on human rights abuses before the U.S. House Subcommittee on Human Rights and International Organization. Iain Guest, *Behind the Disappearances: Argentina's Dirty War against Human Rights and the United Nations* (Philadelphia: University of Pennsylvania Press, 1990), pp. 66–67.

17. Interview with Robert Pastor, Wianno, Massachusetts, 28 June 1990.

18. Testimony given by Patricia Derian to the National Criminal Appeals Court in Buenos Aires during the trials of junta members. "Massera sonrió y me dijo: Sabe qué pasó con Poncio Pilatos . . . ?" *Diario del Juicio*, 18 June 1985, p. 3; Guest, *Behind the Disappearances*, pp. 161–63. Later it was confirmed that the Navy Mechanical School was one of the most

notorious secret torture and detention centers. *Nunca Más: The Report of the Argentine National Commission for the Disappeared* (New York: Farrar Straus & Giroux, 1986), pp. 79–84.

19. The Mothers of the Plaza de Mayo received grants from Dutch churches and the Norwegian Parliament, and the Ford Foundation provided funds for the Center for Legal and Social Studies (CELS) and the Grandmothers of the Plaza de Mayo.

20. Jacobo Timerman, *Prisoner without a Name, Cell without a Number* (New York: Random House, 1981).

21. See Guillermo O'Donnell, "Tensions in the Bureaucratic Authoritarian State and the Question of Democracy," in *The New Authoritarianism in Latin America*, ed. David Collier (Princeton: Princeton University Press, 1979), pp. 288, 292–94.

22. Daniel Frontalini and Maria Cristina Caiati, *El Mito de la Guerra Sucia* (Buenos Aires: Centro de Estudios Legales y Sociales, 1984), p. 24.

23. Guest, *Behind the Disappearances*, pp. 118–19, 182–83.

24. *Carta Política*, a news magazine considered to reflect the junta's views concluded in 1978 that "the principal problem facing the Argentine State has now become the international siege (*cerco internacional*)." "Cuadro de Situación," *Carta Política* 57 (August 1978): 8.

25. Interviews with Walter Mondale, Minneapolis, Minnesota, 20 June 1989, and Ricardo Yofre, Buenos Aires, 1 August 1990.

26. See Asamblea Permanente por los Derechos Humanos, *Las Cifras de la Guerra Sucia* (Buenos Aires, 1988), pp. 26–32.

27. According to a memorandum signed by General Jorge Videla, the objectives of the military government "go well beyond the simple defeat of subversion." The memorandum called for a continuation and intensification of the "general offensive against subversion," including "intense military action." "Directivo 504," 20 April 1977, in "La orden secreta de Videla," *Diario del Juicio* 28 (3 December 1985): 5–8.

28. David Rock, *Argentina, 1516–1987: From Spanish Colonization to Alfonsín* (Berkeley: University of California Press, 1985), pp. 370–71; Timerman, *Prisoner without a Name,* p. 163.

29. *Diario del Juicio* 1 (27 May 1985), and 9 (23 July 1985).

30. *Diario del Juicio* 25 (12 November 1985).

31. Acuña and Smulovitz, "Adjusting the Armed Forces to Democracy," pp. 20–21.

32. Cohen Salama, *Tumbas anónimas [informe sobre la identificación de restos de víctimas de la represión* (Buenos Aires: Catálogos Editora, 1992)], p. 275.

33. Mike O'Connor, "Harvesting Evidence in Bosnia's Killing Fields," *New York Times,* 7 April 1996, p. E3.

34. See, e.g., Arthur A. Stein, "Coordination and Collaboration: Regimes in an Anarchic World," *International Organization* 36:2 (Spring 1982): 299–324.

35. Donnelly, *Universal Human Rights [in Theory and Practice* (Ithaca: Cornell University Press, 1989)], pp. 211–12.

8   WAR AND STRIFE

Warfare and military intervention continue to be central problems of international relations. Two of the readings in this section address a core issue: the relationship between the use of force and politics. Excerpts from classic books by Carl von Clausewitz, *On War* (originally published in the 1830s), and Thomas C. Schelling, *Arms and Influence* (1966), remind us that warfare is not simply an exercise of brute force; war needs to be understood as a continuation of political bargaining. In the most influential treatise on warfare ever written, Prussian general Clausewitz reminded the generation that followed the devastating Napoleonic wars that armed conflict should not be considered a blind, all-out struggle governed by the logic of military operations. Rather, he said, the conduct of war had to be subordinated to its political objectives. These ideas resonated strongly with American strategic thinkers of Schelling's era, who worried that military plans for total nuclear war would outstrip the ability of political leaders to control them. Schelling, a Harvard professor who also advised the U.S. Air Force on its nuclear weapons strategy, explained that political bargaining and risk-taking, not military victory, lay at the heart of the use and threat of force in the nuclear era.

Like Schelling, Robert Jervis drew on mathematical game theory and theories of bargaining in his influential 1978 article on the "security dilemma," which explains how war can arise even among states that seek only to defend themselves. Like the realists, Schelling and Jervis analysts are interested in studying how states' strategies for survival can lead to tragic results. However, they go beyond the realists in examining how differences in bargaining tactics and perceptions can intensify or mitigate the struggle for security.

James D. Fearon's 1995 article, "Rationalist Explanations for War," explores the puzzle of why two rational states would ever fight a costly war rather than settle their dispute more cheaply through peaceful bargaining. He shows that three problems can hinder the achievement of bargains that would benefit both sides: first, states may have private information (such as their military capabilities) that leads the sides to make different estimates as to who would prevail in a fight; second, side A may be unable to convince side B that it would live up to their bargain in the future; third, it may be impossible to divide up the stakes that lie at the heart of the dispute.

The advent of nuclear weapons has led to a lively debate over the relationship between nuclear proliferation and international system stability. The debate has been fueled by the emergence of nuclear states in South Asia and fears over nuclearization in both Iran and North Korea. Barry R. Posen examines the policy alternatives should Iran become nuclear: preventive attacks, economic coercion, containment, and coexistence with a nuclear armed Iran. Kenneth N. Waltz takes a clear position in this debate: a nuclear Iran will lead to a more stable Middle East. Consistent with his long-time arguments on system stability, "when it comes to nuclear weapons, now as ever, more may be better."

While terrorism has long been used as a means of achieving political objectives, the attention of the international community has been drawn to this phenomenon following the September 11, 2001, attacks. Andrew H. Kydd and Barbara F. Walter explore the types of goals that terrorists seek, the strategies terrorists use to achieve those goals, the counterstrategies that can be used against terrorist tactics, and the conditions under which such strategies will or will not work.

The proliferation of terrorism and of humanitarian emergencies has reprised an old debate on when it is right to fight when states do not protect their own populations. How has the notion of humanitarian intervention evolved over time? This is discussed by Martha Finnemore in her book *The Purpose of Intervention: Changing Beliefs about the Use of Force* (2003). In this constructivist piece, Finnemore shows how changes in international system–level norms explain why states choose to intervene in the affairs of other states, even when no national interests are at stake.

Carl von Clausewitz

WAR AS AN INSTRUMENT OF POLICY

■   ■   ■

*** *War is only a part of political intercourse, therefore by no means an independent thing in itself.*

We know, certainly, that War is only called forth through the political intercourse of Governments and Nations; but in general it is supposed that such intercourse is broken off by War, and that a totally different state of things ensues, subject to no laws but its own.

We maintain, on the contrary, that War is nothing but a continuation of political intercourse, with a mixture of other means. We say mixed with other means in order thereby to maintain at the same time that this political intercourse does not cease by the War itself, is not changed into something quite different, but that, in its essence, it continues to exist, whatever may be the form of the means which it uses, and that the chief lines on which the events of the War progress, and to which they are attached, are only the general features of policy which run all through the War until peace takes place. And how can we conceive it to be otherwise? Does the cessation of diplomatic notes stop the political relations between different Nations and Governments? Is not War merely another kind of writing and language for political thoughts? It has certainly a grammar of its own, but its logic is not peculiar to itself.

Accordingly, War can never be separated from political intercourse, and if, in the consideration of the matter, this is done in any way, all the threads of the different relations are, to a certain extent, broken, and we have before us a senseless thing without an object.

This kind of idea would be indispensable even if War was perfect War, the perfectly unbridled element of hostility, for all the circumstances on which it rests, and which determine its leading features, viz. our own power, the enemy's power, Allies on both sides, the characteristics of the people and their Governments respectively, etc.—are they not of a political nature, and are they not so intimately connected with the whole political intercourse that it is impossible to separate them? But this view is doubly indispensable if we reflect that real War is no such consistent effort tending to an extreme, as it should be according to the abstract idea, but a half-and-half thing, a contradiction in itself; that, as such, it cannot follow its own laws, but must be looked upon as a part of another whole—and this whole is policy.

Policy in making use of War avoids all those rigorous conclusions which proceed from its nature; it troubles itself little about final possibilities, confining its attention to immediate probabilities. If such uncertainty in the whole action ensues therefrom, if it thereby becomes a sort of game, the policy of each Cabinet places its confidence in the belief that in this game it will surpass its neighbour in skill and sharp-sightedness.

Thus policy makes out of the all-overpowering element of War a mere instrument, changes the

From Carl von Clausewitz, *On War* (Harmondsworth: Penguin Books, 1968), Bk. 5, Chap. 6. The author's notes have been omitted.

tremendous battle-sword, which should be lifted with both hands and the whole power of the body to strike once for all, into a light handy weapon, which is even sometimes nothing more than a rapier to exchange thrusts and feints and parries.

Thus the contradictions in which man, naturally timid, becomes involved by War may be solved, if we choose to accept this as a solution.

If War belongs to policy, it will naturally take its character from thence. If policy is grand and powerful, so also will be the War, and this may be carried to the point at which War attains to *its absolute form.*

In this way of viewing the subject, therefore, we need not shut out of sight the absolute form of War, we rather keep it continually in view in the background.

Only through this kind of view War recovers unity; only by it can we see all Wars as things of *one* kind; and it is only through it that the judgement can obtain the true and perfect basis and point of view from which great plans may be traced out and determined upon.

It is true the political element does not sink deep into the details of War. Vedettes are not planted, patrols do not make their rounds from political considerations; but small as is its influence in this respect, it is great in the formation of a plan for a whole War, or a campaign, and often even for a battle.

For this reason we were in no hurry to establish this view at the commencement. While engaged with particulars, it would have given us little help, and, on the other hand, would have distracted our attention to a certain extent; in the plan of a War or campaign it is indispensable.

There is, upon the whole, nothing more important in life than to find out the right point of view from which things should be looked at and judged of, and then to keep to that point; for we can only apprehend the mass of events in their unity from *one* standpoint; and it is only the keeping to one point of view that guards us from inconsistency.

If, therefore, in drawing up a plan of a War, it is not allowable to have a two-fold or three-fold point of view, from which things may be looked at, now with the eye of a soldier, then with that of an administrator, and then again with that of a politician, etc., then the next question is, whether *policy* is necessarily paramount and everything else subordinate to it.

That policy unites in itself, and reconciles all the interests of internal administrations, even those of humanity, and whatever else are rational subjects of consideration is presupposed, for it is nothing in itself, except a mere representative and exponent of all these interests towards other States. That policy may take a false direction, and may promote unfairly the ambitious ends, the private interests, the vanity of rulers, does not concern us here; for, under no circumstances can the Art of War be regarded as its preceptor, and we can only look at policy here as the representative of the interests generally of the whole community.

The only question, therefore, is whether in framing plans for a War the political point of view should give way to the purely military (if such a point is conceivable), that is to say, should disappear altogether, or subordinate itself to it, or whether the political is to remain the ruling point of view and the military to be considered subordinate to it.

That the political point of view should end completely when War begins is only conceivable in contests which are Wars of life and death, from pure hatred: as Wars are in reality, they are, as we before said, only the expressions or manifestations of policy itself. The subordination of the political point of view to the military would be contrary to common sense, for policy has declared the War; it is the intelligent faculty, War only the instrument, and not the reverse. The subordination of the military point of view to the political is, therefore, the only thing which is possible.

If we reflect on the nature of real War, and call to mind what has been said, *that every War should* be viewed above all things according to the probability of its character, and its leading features as they are to be deduced from the political forces and proportions, and that often—indeed we may safely affirm, in our days, *almost* always—War is to be regarded as an organic whole, from which the single branches are not to be separated, in which therefore every individual activity flows into the whole, and also has its origin in the idea of this whole, then it becomes certain and palpable to us that the superior standpoint for the conduct of the War, from which its leading lines must proceed, can be no other than that of policy.

From this point of view the plans come, as it were, out of a cast; the apprehension of them and the judgement upon them become easier and more natural, our convictions respecting them gain in force, motives are more satisfying and history more intelligible.

At all events from this point of view there is no longer in the nature of things a necessary conflict between the political and military interests, and where it appears it is therefore to be regarded as imperfect knowledge only. That policy makes demands on the War which it cannot respond to, would be contrary to the supposition that it knows the instrument which it is going to use, therefore, contrary to a natural and indispensable supposition. But if policy judges correctly of the march of military events, it is entirely its affair to determine what are the events and what the direction of events most favourable to the ultimate and great end of the War.

In one word, the Art of War in its highest point of view is policy, but, no doubt, a policy which fights battles instead of writing notes.

According to this view, to leave a great military enterprise or the plan for one, to *a purely military judgement and decision* is a distinction which cannot be allowed, and is even prejudicial; indeed, it is an irrational proceeding to consult professional soldiers on the plan of a War, that they may give a

purely military opinion upon what the Cabinet ought to do; but still more absurd is the demand of Theorists that a statement of the available means of War should be laid before the General, that he may draw out a purely military plan for the War or for a campaign in accordance with those means. Experience in general also teaches us that notwithstanding the multifarious branches and scientific character of military art in the present day, still the leading outlines of a War are always determined by the Cabinet, that is, if we would use technical language, by a political not a military organ.

This is perfectly natural. None of the principal plans which are required for a War can be made without an insight into the political relations; and, in reality, when people speak, as they often do, of the prejudicial influence of policy on the conduct of a War, they say in reality something very different to what they intend. It is not this influence but the policy itself which should be found fault with. If policy is right, that is, if it succeeds in hitting the object, then it can only act with advantage on the War. If this influence of policy causes a divergence from the object, the cause is only to be looked for in a mistaken policy.

It is only when policy promises itself a wrong effect from certain military means and measures, an effect opposed to their nature, that it can exercise a prejudicial effect on War by the course it prescribes. Just as a person in a language with which he is not conversant sometimes says what he does not intend, so policy, when intending right, may often order things which do not tally with its own views.

This has happened times without end, and it shows that a certain knowledge of the nature of War is essential to the management of political intercourse.

But before going further, we must guard ourselves against a false interpretation of which this is very susceptible. We are far from holding the opinion that a War Minister smothered in official papers, a scientific engineer, or even a soldier who has been well tried in the field, would, any of them, necessarily make the best Minister of State where the Sovereign does not act for himself; or, in other words, we do not mean to say that this acquaintance with the nature of War is the principal qualification for a War Minister; elevation, superiority of mind, strength of character, these are the principal qualifications which he must possess; a knowledge of War may be supplied in one way or the other. * * *

■ ■ ■

We shall now conclude with some reflections derived from history.

In the last decade of the past century, when that remarkable change in the Art of War in Europe took place by which the best Armies found that a part of their method of War had become utterly unserviceable, and events were brought about of a magnitude far beyond what any one had any previous conception of, it certainly appeared that a false calculation of everything was to be laid to the charge of the Art of War. * * *

■ ■ ■

But is it true that the real surprise by which men's minds were seized was confined to the conduct of War, and did not rather relate to policy itself? That is: Did the ill success proceed from the influence of policy on the War, or from a wrong policy itself?

The prodigious effects of the French Revolution abroad were evidently brought about much less through new methods and views introduced by the French in the conduct of War than through the changes which it wrought in state-craft and civil administration, in the character of Governments, in the condition of the people, etc. That other Governments took a mistaken view of all these things; that they endeavoured, with their ordinary means, to hold their own against forces of a novel kind and overwhelming in strength—all that was a blunder in policy.

Would it have been possible to perceive and mend this error by a scheme for the War from a purely military point of view? Impossible. For if there had been a philosophical strategist, who merely from the nature of the hostile elements had foreseen all the consequences, and prophesied remote possibilities, still it would have been practically impossible to have turned such wisdom to account.

If policy had risen to a just appreciation of the forces which had sprung up in France, and of the new relations in the political state of Europe, it might have foreseen the consequences which must follow in respect to the great features of War, and it was only in this way that it could arrive at a correct view of the extent of the means required as well as of the best use to make of those means.

We may therefore say, that the twenty years' victories of the Revolution are chiefly to be ascribed to the erroneous policy of the Governments by which it was opposed.

It is true these errors first displayed themselves in the War, and the events of the War completely disappointed the expectations which policy entertained. But this did not take place because policy neglected to consult its military advisers. That Art of War in which the politician of the day could believe, namely, that derived from the reality of War at that time, that which belonged to the policy of the day, that familiar instrument which policy had hitherto used—*that* Art of War, I say, was naturally involved in the error of policy, and therefore could not teach it anything better. It is true that War itself underwent important alterations both in its nature and forms, which brought it nearer to its absolute form; but these changes were not brought about because the French

Government had, to a certain extent, delivered itself from the leading-strings of policy; they arose from an altered policy, produced by the French Revolution, not only in France, but over the rest of Europe as well. This policy had called forth other means and other powers, by which it became possible to conduct War with a degree of energy which could not have been thought of otherwise.

Therefore, the actual changes in the Art of War are a consequence of alterations in policy; and, so far from being an argument for the possible separation of the two, they are, on the contrary, very strong evidence of the intimacy of their connexion.

Therefore, once more: War is an instrument of policy; it must necessarily bear its character, it must measure with its scale: the conduct of War, in its great features, is therefore policy itself, which takes up the sword in place of the pen, but does not on that account cease to think according to its own laws.

Thomas C. Schelling
THE DIPLOMACY OF VIOLENCE

The usual distinction between diplomacy and force is not merely in the instruments, words or bullets, but in the relation between adversaries—in the interplay of motives and the role of communication, understandings, compromise, and restraint. Diplomacy is bargaining: it seeks outcomes that, though not ideal for either party, are better for both than some of the alternatives. In diplomacy each party somewhat controls what the other wants, and can get more by compromise, exchange, or collaboration than by taking things in his own hands and ignoring the other's wishes. The bargaining can be polite or rude, entail threats as well as offers, assume a status quo or ignore all rights and privileges, and assume mistrust rather than trust. But whether polite or impolite, constructive or aggressive, respectful or vicious, whether it occurs among friends or antagonists and whether or not there is a basis for trust and goodwill, there must be some common interest, if only in the avoidance of mutual damage, and an awareness of the need to make the other party prefer an outcome acceptable to oneself.

With enough military force a country may not need to bargain. Some things a country wants it can take, and some things it has it can keep, by sheer strength, skill and ingenuity. It can do this *forcibly*, accommodating only to opposing strength, skill, and ingenuity and without trying to appeal to an enemy's wishes. Forcibly a country can repel and expel, penetrate and occupy, seize, exterminate, disarm and disable, confine, deny access, and directly frustrate intrusion or attack. It can, that is, if it has enough strength. "Enough" depends on how much an opponent has.

There is something else, though, that force can do. It is less military, less heroic, less impersonal, and less unilateral; it is uglier, and has received less attention in Western military strategy. In addition to seizing and holding, disarming and confining, penetrating and obstructing, and all that, military force can be used *to hurt*. In addition to taking and protecting things of value it can *destroy* value. In addition to weakening an enemy militarily it can cause an enemy plain suffering.

Pain and shock, loss and grief, privation and horror are always in some degree, sometimes in terrible degree, among the results of warfare; but in traditional military science they are incidental, they are not the object. If violence can be done incidentally, though, it can also be done purposely. The power to hurt can be counted among the most impressive attributes of military force.

Hurting, unlike forcible seizure or self-defense, is not unconcerned with the interest of others. It is measured in the suffering it can cause and the victims' motivation to avoid it. Forcible action will work against weeds or floods as well as against armies, but suffering requires a victim that can feel pain or has something to lose. To inflict suffering gains nothing and saves nothing directly; it can only make people behave to avoid it. The only purpose, unless sport or revenge, must be to influence somebody's behavior, to coerce his decision or choice. To be coercive, violence has to be anticipated. And it has to be avoidable by accommodation. The power to hurt is bargaining power. To exploit it is diplomacy—vicious diplomacy, but diplomacy.

From Thomas C. Schelling, *Arms and Influence* (New Haven, Conn.: Yale University Press, 1966), Chap. 1. Some of the author's notes have been omitted.

The Contrast of Brute Force with Coercion

There is a difference between taking what you want and making someone give it to you, between fending off assault and making someone afraid to assault you, between holding what people are trying to take and making them afraid to take it, between losing what someone can forcibly take and giving it up to avoid risk or damage. It is the difference between defense and deterrence, between brute force and intimidation, between conquest and blackmail, between action and threats. It is the difference between the unilateral, "undiplomatic" recourse to strength, and coercive diplomacy based on the power to hurt.

The contrasts are several. The purely "military" or "undiplomatic" recourse to forcible action is concerned with enemy strength, not enemy interests; the coercive use of the power to hurt, though, is the very exploitation of enemy wants and fears. And brute strength is usually measured relative to enemy strength, the one directly opposing the other, while the power to hurt is typically not reduced by the enemy's power to hurt in return. Opposing strengths may cancel each other, pain and grief do not. The willingness to hurt, the credibility of a threat, and the ability to exploit the power to hurt will indeed depend on how much the adversary can hurt in return; but there is little or nothing about an adversary's pain or grief that directly reduces one's own. Two sides cannot both overcome each other with superior strength; they may both be able to hurt each other. With strength they can dispute objects of value; with sheer violence they can destroy them.

And brute force succeeds when it is used, whereas the power to hurt is most successful when held in reserve. It is the *threat* of damage, or of more damage to come, that can make someone yield or comply. It is *latent* violence that can influence someone's choice—violence that can still be withheld or inflicted, or that a victim believes can be withheld or inflicted. The threat of pain tries to structure someone's motives, while brute force tries to overcome his strength. Unhappily, the power to hurt is often communicated by some performance of it. Whether it is sheer terroristic violence to induce an irrational response, or cool premeditated violence to persuade somebody that you mean it and may do it again, it is not the pain and damage itself but its influence on somebody's behavior that matters. It is the expectation of *more* violence that gets the wanted behavior, if the power to hurt can get it at all.

To exploit a capacity for hurting and inflicting damage one needs to know what an adversary treasures and what scares him and one needs the adversary to understand what behavior of his will cause the violence to be inflicted and what will cause it to be withheld. The victim has to know what is wanted, and he may have to be assured of what is not wanted. The pain and suffering have to appear *contingent* on his behavior; it is not alone the threat that is effective—the threat of pain or loss if he fails to comply—but the corresponding assurance, possibly an implicit one, that he can avoid the pain or loss if he does comply. The prospect of certain death may stun him, but it gives him no choice.

Coercion by threat of damage also requires that our interests and our opponent's not be absolutely opposed. If his pain were our greatest delight and our satisfaction his greatest woe, we would just proceed to hurt and to frustrate each other. It is when his pain gives us little or no satisfaction compared with what he can do for us, and the action or inaction that satisfies us costs him less than the pain we can cause, that there is room for coercion. Coercion requires finding a bargain, arranging for him to be better off doing what we want—worse off not doing what we want—when he takes the threatened penalty into account.

It is this capacity for pure damage, pure violence, that is usually associated with the most vicious labor disputes, with racial disorders, with civil uprisings and their suppression, with racketeering. It is also the power to hurt rather than brute force that we use in dealing with criminals; we hurt them afterward, or threaten to, for their misdeeds rather than protect ourselves with cordons of electric wires, masonry walls, and armed guards. Jail, of course, can be either forcible restraint or threatened privation; if the object is to keep criminals out of mischief by confinement, success is measured by how many of them are gotten behind bars, but if the object is to *threaten* privation, success will be measured by how few have to be put behind bars and success then depends on the subject's understanding of the consequences. Pure damage is what a car threatens when it tries to hog the road or to keep its rightful share, or to go first through an intersection. A tank or a bulldozer can force its way regardless of others' wishes; the rest of us have to threaten damage, usually mutual damage, hoping the other driver values his car or his limbs enough to give way, hoping he sees us, and hoping he is in control of his own car. The threat of pure damage will not work against an unmanned vehicle.

This difference between coercion and brute force is as often in the intent as in the instrument. To hunt down Comanches and to exterminate them was brute force; to raid their villages to make them behave was coercive diplomacy, based on the power to hurt. The pain and loss to the Indians might have looked much the same one way as the other; the difference was one of purpose and effect. If Indians were killed because they were in the way, or somebody wanted their land, or the authorities despaired of making them behave and could not confine them and decided to exterminate them, that was pure unilateral force. If *some* Indians were killed to make *other* Indians behave, that was coercive violence—or intended to be, whether or not it was effective. The Germans at Verdun perceived themselves to be chewing up hundreds of thousands of French soldiers in a gruesome "meat-grinder." If the purpose was to eliminate a military obstacle—the French infantryman, viewed as a military "asset" rather than as a warm human being—the offensive at Verdun was a unilateral exercise of military force. If instead the object was to make the loss of young men—not of impersonal "effectives," but of sons, husbands, fathers, and the pride of French manhood—so anguishing as to be unendurable, to make surrender a welcome relief and to spoil the foretaste of an Allied victory, then it was an exercise in coercion, in applied violence, intended to offer relief upon accommodation. And of course, since any use of force tends to be brutal, thoughtless, vengeful, or plain obstinate, the motives themselves can be mixed and confused. The fact that heroism and brutality can be either coercive diplomacy or a contest in pure strength does not promise that the distinction will be made, and the strategies enlightened by the distinction, every time some vicious enterprise gets launched.

The contrast between brute force and coercion is illustrated by two alternative strategies attributed to Genghis Khan. Early in his career he pursued the war creed of the Mongols: the vanquished can never be the friends of the victors, their death is necessary for the victor's safety. This was the unilateral extermination of a menace or a liability. The turning point of his career, according to Lynn Montross, came later when he discovered how to use his power to hurt for diplomatic ends. "The great Khan, who was not inhibited by the usual mercies, conceived the plan of forcing captives—women, children, aged fathers, favorite sons—to march ahead of his army as the first potential victims of resistance."[1] Live captives have often proved more valuable than enemy dead; and the technique discovered by the Khan in his maturity remains contemporary. North Koreans and Chinese were reported to have quartered prisoners of war near strategic targets to inhibit bombing attacks by United Nations aircraft. Hostages represent the power to hurt in its purest form.

Coercive Violence in Warfare

This distinction between the power to hurt and the power to seize or hold forcibly is important in modern war, both big war and little war, hypothetical war and real war. For many years the Greeks and the Turks on Cyprus could hurt each other indefinitely but neither could quite take or hold forcibly what they wanted or protect themselves from violence by physical means. The Jews in Palestine could not expel the British in the late 1940s but they could cause pain and fear and frustration through terrorism, and eventually influence somebody's decision. The brutal war in Algeria was more a contest in pure violence than in military strength; the question was who would first find the pain and degradation unendurable. The French troops preferred—indeed they continually tried—to make it a contest of strength, to pit military force against the nationalists' capacity for terror, to exterminate or disable the nationalists and to screen off the nationalists from the victims of their violence. But because in civil war terrorists commonly have access to victims by sheer physical propinquity, the victims and their properties could not be forcibly defended and in the end the French troops themselves resorted, unsuccessfully, to a war of pain.

Nobody believes that the Russians can take Hawaii from us, or New York, or Chicago, but nobody doubts that they might destroy people and buildings in Hawaii, Chicago, or New York. Whether the Russians can conquer West Germany in any meaningful sense is questionable; whether they can hurt it terribly is not doubted. That the United States can destroy a large part of Russia is universally taken for granted; that the United States can keep from being badly hurt, even devastated, in return, or can keep Western Europe from being devastated while itself destroying Russia, is at best arguable; and it is virtually out of the question that we could conquer Russia territorially and use its economic assets unless it were by threatening disaster and inducing compliance. It is the power to hurt, not military strength in the traditional sense, that inheres in our most impressive military capabilities at the present time [1966]. We have a Department of *Defense* but emphasize *retaliation*—"to return evil for evil" (synonyms: requital, reprisal, revenge, vengeance, retribution). And it is pain and violence, not force in the traditional sense, that inheres also in some of the least impressive military capabilities of the present time—the plastic bomb, the terrorist's bullet, the burnt crops, and the tortured farmer.

War appears to be, or threatens to be, not so much a contest of strength as one of endurance, nerve, obstinacy, and pain. It appears to be, and threatens to be, not so much a contest of military strength as a bargaining process—dirty, extortionate, and often quite reluctant bargaining on one side or both—nevertheless a bargaining process.

The difference cannot quite be expressed as one between the *use* of force and the *threat* of force. The actions involved in forcible accomplishment, on the one hand, and in fulfilling a threat, on the other, can be quite different. Sometimes the most effective direct action inflicts enough cost or pain on the enemy to serve as a threat, sometimes not. The United States threatens the Soviet Union with virtual destruction of its society in the event of a surprise attack on the United States; a hundred million deaths are awesome as pure damage, but they are useless in stopping the Soviet attack—especially if the threat is to do it all afterward anyway. So it is worth while to keep the concepts distinct—to distinguish forcible action from the threat of pain—recognizing that some actions serve as both a means of forcible accomplishment and a means of inflicting pure damage, some do not. Hostages tend to entail almost pure pain and damage, as do all forms of reprisal after the fact. Some modes of self-defense may exact so little in blood or treasure as to entail negligible violence;

and some forcible actions entail so much violence that their threat can be effective by itself.

The power to hurt, though it can usually accomplish nothing directly, is potentially more versatile than a straightforward capacity for forcible accomplishment. By force alone we cannot even lead a horse to water—we have to drag him—much less make him drink. Any affirmative action, any collaboration, almost anything but physical exclusion, expulsion, or extermination, requires that an opponent or a victim *do* something, even if only to stop or get out. The threat of pain and damage may make him want to do it, and anything he can do is potentially susceptible to inducement. Brute force can only accomplish what requires no collaboration. The principle is illustrated by a technique of unarmed combat: one can disable a man by various stunning, fracturing, or killing blows, but to take him to jail one has to exploit the man's own efforts. "Come-along" holds are those that threaten pain or disablement, giving relief as long as the victim complies, giving him the option of using his own legs to get to jail.

We have to keep in mind, though, that what is pure pain, or the threat of it, at one level of decision can be equivalent to brute force at another level. Churchill was worried, during the early bombing raids on London in 1940, that Londoners might panic. Against people the bombs were pure violence, to induce their undisciplined evasion; to Churchill and the government, the bombs were a cause of inefficiency, whether they spoiled transport and made people late to work or scared people and made them afraid to work. Churchill's decisions were not going to be coerced by the fear of a few casualties. Similarly on the battlefield: tactics that frighten soldiers so that they run, duck their heads, or lay down their arms and surrender represent coercion based on the power to hurt; to the top command, which is frustrated but not coerced, such tactics are part of the contest in military discipline and strength.

The fact that violence—pure pain and damage—can be used or threatened to coerce and to deter, to intimidate and to blackmail, to demoralize and to paralyze, in a conscious process of dirty bargaining, does not by any means imply that violence is not often wanton and meaningless or, even when purposive, in danger of getting out of hand. Ancient wars were often quite "total" for the loser, the men being put to death, the women sold as slaves, the boys castrated, the cattle slaughtered, and the buildings leveled, for the sake of revenge, justice, personal gain, or merely custom. If an enemy bombs a city, by design or by carelessness, we usually bomb his if we can. In the excitement and fatigue of warfare, revenge is one of the few satisfactions that can be savored; and justice can often be construed to demand the enemy's punishment, even if it is delivered with more enthusiasm than justice requires. When Jerusalem fell to the Crusaders in 1099 the ensuing slaughter was one of the bloodiest in military chronicles. "The men of the West literally waded in gore, their march to the church of the Holy Sepulcher being gruesomely likened to 'treading out the wine press'. . . .," reports Montross (p. 138), who observes that these excesses usually came at the climax of the capture of a fortified post or city. "For long the assailants have endured more punishment than they were able to inflict; then once the walls are breached, pent up emotions find an outlet in murder, rape and plunder, which discipline is powerless to prevent." The same occurred when Tyre fell to Alexander after a painful siege, and the phenomenon was not unknown on Pacific islands in the Second World War. Pure violence, like fire, can be harnessed to a purpose; that does not mean that behind every holocaust is a shrewd intention successfully fulfilled.

But if the occurrence of violence does not always bespeak a shrewd purpose, the absence of pain and destruction is no sign that violence was idle. Violence is most purposive and most successful when it is threatened and not used. Successful threats are those that do not have to be carried out. By European standards, Denmark was virtually unharmed in the Second World War; it was violence that made the Danes submit. Withheld violence—successfully threatened violence—can look clean, even merciful. The fact that a kidnap victim is returned unharmed, against receipt of ample ransom, does not make kidnapping a nonviolent enterprise. * * *

■   ■   ■

The Strategic Role of Pain and Damage

Pure violence, nonmilitary violence, appears most conspicuously in relations between unequal countries, where there is no substantial military challenge and the outcome of military engagement is not in question. Hitler could make his threats contemptuously and brutally against Austria; he could make them, if he wished, in a more refined way against Denmark. It is noteworthy that it was Hitler, not his generals, who used this kind of language; proud military establishments do not like to think of themselves as extortionists. Their favorite job is to deliver victory, to dispose of opposing military force and to leave most of the civilian violence to politics and diplomacy. But if there is no room for doubt how a contest in strength will come out, it may be possible to bypass the military stage altogether and to proceed at once to the coercive bargaining.

A typical confrontation of unequal forces occurs at the *end* of a war, between victor and vanquished. Where Austria was vulnerable before a shot was fired, France was vulnerable after its military shield had collapsed in 1940. Surrender negotiations are the place where the threat of civil violence can come to the fore. Surrender negotiations are often so one-sided, or the potential violence so unmistakable, that bargaining succeeds and the violence remains in reserve. But the fact that most of the actual damage was done during

the military stage of the war, prior to victory and defeat, does not mean that violence was idle in the aftermath, only that it was latent and the threat of it successful.

Indeed, victory is often but a prerequisite to the exploitation of the power to hurt. When Xenophon was fighting in Asia Minor under Persian leadership, it took military strength to disperse enemy soldiers and occupy their lands; but land was not what the victor wanted, nor was victory for its own sake.

> Next day the Persian leader burned the villages to the ground, not leaving a single house standing, so as to strike terror into the other tribes to show them what would happen if they did not give in. . . . He sent some of the prisoners into the hills and told them to say that if the inhabitants did not come down and settle in their houses to submit to him, he would burn up their villages too and destroy their crops, and they would die of hunger.[2]

Military victory was but the *price of admission*. The payoff depended upon the successful threat of violence.

■   ■   ■

The Nuclear Contribution to Terror and Violence

Man has, it is said, for the first time in history enough military power to eliminate his species from the earth, weapons against which there is no conceivable defense. War has become, it is said, so destructive and terrible that it ceases to be an instrument of national power. "For the first time in human history," says Max Lerner in a book whose title, *The Age of Overkill*, conveys the point, "men have bottled up a power . . . which they have thus far not dared to use."[3] And Soviet military authorities, whose party dislikes having to accommodate an entire theory of history to a single technological event, have had to reexamine a set of principles that had been given the embarrassing name of "permanently operating factors" in warfare. Indeed, our era is epitomized by words like "the first time in human history," and by the abdication of what was "permanent."

For dramatic impact these statements are splendid. Some of them display a tendency, not at all necessary, to belittle the catastrophe of earlier wars. They may exaggerate the historical novelty of deterrence and the balance of terror. More important, they do not help to identify just what is new about war when so much destructive energy can be packed in warheads at a price that permits advanced countries to have them in large numbers. Nuclear warheads are incomparably more devastating than anything packaged before. What does that imply about war?

It is not true that for the first time in history man has the capability to destroy a large fraction, even the major part, of the human race. Japan was defenseless by August 1945. With a combination of bombing and blockade, eventually invasion, and if necessary the deliberate spread of disease, the United States could probably have exterminated the population of the Japanese islands without nuclear weapons. It would have been a gruesome, expensive, and mortifying campaign; it would have taken time and demanded persistence. But we had the economic and technical capacity to do it; and, together with the Russians or without them, we could have done the same in many populous parts of the world. Against defenseless people there is not much that nuclear weapons can do that cannot be done with an ice pick. And it would not have strained our Gross National Product to do it with ice picks.

It is a grisly thing to talk about. We did not do it and it is not imaginable that we would have done it. We had no reason; if we had had a reason, we would not have the persistence of purpose, once the fury of war had been dissipated in victory and we had taken on the task of executioner. If we and our enemies might do such a thing to each other now, and to others as well, it is not because nuclear weapons have for the first time made it feasible.

■　■　■

* * * In the past it has usually been the victors who could do what they pleased to the enemy. War has often been "total war" for the loser. With deadly monotony the Persians, Greeks, or Romans "put to death all men of military age, and sold the women and children into slavery," leaving the defeated territory nothing but its name until new settlers arrived sometime later. But the defeated could not do the same to their victors. The boys could be castrated and sold only after the war had been won, and only on the side that lost it. The power to hurt could be brought to bear only after military strength had achieved victory. The same sequence characterized the great wars of this century; for reasons of technology and geography, military force has usually had to penetrate, to exhaust, or to collapse opposing military force—to achieve military victory—before it could be brought to bear on the enemy nation itself. The Allies in World War I could not inflict coercive pain and suffering directly on the Germans in a decisive way until they could defeat the German army; and the Germans could not coerce the French people with bayonets unless they first beat the Allied troops that stood in their way. With two-dimensional warfare, there is a tendency for troops to confront each other, shielding their own lands while attempting to press into each other's. Small penetrations could not do major damage to the people; large penetrations were so destructive of military organization that they usually ended the military phase of the war.

Nuclear weapons make it possible to do monstrous violence to the enemy without first achieving victory. With nuclear weapons and today's means of delivery, one expects to penetrate an enemy homeland without first collapsing his military force. What nuclear weapons have done, or appear to do, is to promote this kind of warfare to first place. Nuclear weapons threaten to make war less military, and are responsible for the lowered status of "military victory" at the present time. *Victory is no longer a prerequisite for hurting the enemy.* And it is no assurance against being terribly hurt. One need not wait until he has won the war before inflicting "unendurable" damages on his enemy. One need not wait until he has lost the war. There was a time when the assurance of victory—false or genuine assurance—could make national leaders not just willing but sometimes enthusiastic about war. Not now.

Not only *can* nuclear weapons hurt the enemy before the war has been won, and perhaps hurt decisively enough to make the military engagement academic, but it is widely assumed that in a major war that is *all* they can do. Major war is often discussed as though it would be only a contest in national destruction. If this is indeed the case—if the destruction of cities and their populations has become, with nuclear weapons, the primary object in an all-out war—the sequence of war has been reversed. Instead of destroying enemy forces as a prelude to imposing one's will on the enemy nation, one would have to destroy the nation as a means or a prelude to destroying the enemy forces. If one cannot disable enemy forces without virtually destroying the country, the victor does not even have the option of sparing the conquered nation. He has already destroyed it. Even with blockade and strategic bombing it could be supposed that a country would be defeated before it was destroyed, or would elect surrender before annihilation had gone far. In the Civil War it could be hoped that the South would become too weak to fight before it became too weak to survive. For "all-out" war, nuclear weapons threaten to reverse this sequence.

So nuclear weapons do make a difference, marking an epoch in warfare. The difference is not just in the amount of destruction that can be accomplished but in the role of destruction and in the decision process. Nuclear weapons can change the speed of events, the control of events, the sequence of events, the relation of victor to vanquished, and the relation of homeland to fighting front. Deterrence rests today on the threat of pain and extinction, not just on the threat of military defeat. We may argue about the wisdom of announcing "unconditional surrender" as an aim in the last major war, but seem to expect "unconditional destruction" as a matter of course in another one.

Something like the same destruction always *could* be done. With nuclear weapons there is an expectation that it *would* be done. It is not "overkill" that is new; the American army surely had enough 30 caliber bullets to kill everybody in the world in 1945, or if it did not it could have bought them without any strain. What is new is plain "kill"—the idea that major war might be just a contest in the killing of countries, or not even a contest but just two parallel exercises in devastation.

That is the difference nuclear weapons make. At least they *may* make that difference. They also may not. If the weapons themselves are vulnerable to attack, or the machines that carry them, a successful surprise might eliminate the opponent's means of retribution. That an enormous explosion can be packaged in a single bomb does not by itself guarantee that the victor will receive deadly punishment. Two gunfighters facing each other in a Western town had an unquestioned capacity to kill one another; that did not guarantee that both would die in a gunfight—only the slower of the two. Less deadly weapons, permitting an injured one to shoot back before he died, might have been more conducive to a restraining balance of terror, or of caution. The very efficiency of nuclear weapons could make them ideal for starting war, if they can suddenly eliminate the enemy's capability to shoot back.

And there is a contrary possibility: that nuclear weapons are not vulnerable to attack and prove not to be terribly effective against each other, posing no need to shoot them quickly for fear they will be destroyed before they are launched, and with no task available but the systematic destruction of the enemy country and no necessary reason to do it fast rather than slowly. Imagine that nuclear destruction *had* to go slowly—that the bombs could be dropped only one per day. The prospect would look very different, something like the most terroristic guerilla warfare on a massive scale. It happens that nuclear war does not have to go slowly; but it may also not have to go speedily. The mere existence of nuclear weapons does not itself determine that everything must go off in a blinding flash, any more than that it must go slowly. Nuclear weapons do not simplify things quite that much.

■   ■   ■

War no longer looks like just a contest of strength. War and the brink of war are more a contest of nerve and risk-taking, of pain and endurance. Small wars embody the threat of a larger war; they are not just military engagements but "crisis diplomacy." The threat of war has always been somewhere underneath international diplomacy, but for Americans it is now much nearer the surface.

Like the threat of a strike in industrial relations, the threat of divorce in a family dispute, or the threat of bolting the party at a political convention, the threat of violence continuously circumscribes international politics. Neither strength nor goodwill procures immunity.

Military strategy can no longer be thought of, as it could for some countries in some eras, as the science of military victory. It is now equally, if not more, the art of coercion, of intimidation and deterrence. The instruments of war are more punitive than acquisitive. Military strategy, whether we like it or not, has become the diplomacy of violence.

NOTES

1. Lynn Montross, *War Through the Ages* (3d ed. New York, Harper and Brothers, 1960), p. 146.
2. Xenophon, *The Persian Expedition*, Rex Warner, transl. (Baltimore, Penguin Books, 1949), p. 272. "The 'rational' goal of the threat of violence," says H. L. Nieburg, "is an accommodation of interests, not the provocation of actual violence. Similarly the 'rational' goal of actual violence is demonstration of the will and capability of action, establishing a measure of the credibility of future threats, not the exhaustion of that capability in unlimited conflict." "Uses of Violence," *Journal of Conflict Resolution, 7* (1963), 44.
3. New York, Simon and Schuster, 1962, p. 47.

Robert Jervis

COOPERATION UNDER THE SECURITY DILEMMA

I. Anarchy and the Security Dilemma

The lack of an international sovereign not only permits wars to occur, but also makes it difficult for states that are satisfied with the status quo to arrive at goals that they recognize as being in their common interest. Because there are no institutions or authorities that can make and enforce international laws, the policies of cooperation that will bring mutual rewards if others cooperate may bring disaster if they do not. Because states are aware of this, anarchy encourages behavior that leaves all concerned worse off than they could be, even in the extreme case in which all states would like to freeze the status quo. This is true of the men in Rousseau's "Stag Hunt." If they cooperate to trap the stag, they will all eat well. But if one person defects to chase a rabbit—which he likes less than stag—none of the others will get anything. Thus, all actors have the same preference order, and there is a solution that gives each his first choice: (1) cooperate and trap the stag (the international analogue being cooperation and disarmament); (2) chase a rabbit while others remain at their posts (maintain a high level of arms while others are disarmed); (3) all chase rabbits (arms competition and high risk of war); and (4) stay at the original position while another chases a rabbit (being disarmed while others are armed). Unless

From *World Politics* 30, no. 2 (Jan. 1978), 167–214. Some of the author's notes have been omitted.

each person thinks that the others will cooperate, he himself will not. And why might he fear that any other person would do something that would sacrifice his own first choice? The other might not understand the situation, or might not be able to control his impulses if he saw a rabbit, or might fear that some other member of the group is unreliable. If the person voices any of these suspicions, others are more likely to fear that he will defect, thus making them more likely to defect, thus making it more rational for him to defect. Of course in this simple case—and in many that are more realistic—there are a number of arrangements that could permit cooperation. But the main point remains: although actors may know that they seek a common goal, they may not be able to reach it.

Even when there is a solution that is everyone's first choice, the international case is characterized by three difficulties not present in the Stag Hunt. First, to the incentives to defect given above must be added the potent fear that even if the other state now supports the status quo, it may become dissatisfied later. No matter how much decision makers are committed to the status quo, they cannot bind themselves and their successors to the same path. Minds can be changed, new leaders can come to power, values can shift, new opportunities and dangers can arise.

The second problem arises from a possible solution. In order to protect their possessions, states often seek to control resources or land outside their own territory. Countries that are not self-sufficient must try to assure that the necessary supplies will continue to flow in wartime. This was part of the explanation for Japan's drive into China and Southeast Asia before World War II. If there were an international authority that could guarantee access, this motive for control would disappear. But since there is not, even a state that would prefer the status quo to increasing its area of control may pursue the latter policy.

When there are believed to be tight linkages between domestic and foreign policy or between the domestic politics of two states, the quest for security may drive states to interfere pre-emptively in the domestic politics of others in order to provide an ideological buffer zone. * * *

More frequently, the concern is with direct attack. In order to protect themselves, states seek to control, or at least to neutralize, areas on their borders. But attempts to establish buffer zones can alarm others who have stakes there, who fear that undesirable precedents will be set, or who believe that their own vulnerability will be increased. When buffers are sought in areas empty of great powers, expansion tends to feed on itself in order to protect what is acquired. * * *

Though this process is most clearly visible when it involves territorial expansion, it often operates with the increase of less tangible power and influence. The expansion of power usually brings with it an expansion of responsibilities and commitments; to meet them, still greater power is required. The state will take many positions that are subject to challenge. It will be involved with a wide range of controversial issues unrelated to its core values. And retreats that would be seen as normal if made by a small power would be taken as an index of weakness inviting predation if made by a large one.

The third problem present in international politics but not in the Stag Hunt is the security dilemma: many of the means by which a state tries to increase its security decrease the security of others. In domestic society, there are several ways to increase the safety of one's person and property without endangering others. One can move to a safer neighborhood, put bars on the windows, avoid dark streets, and keep a distance from suspicious-looking characters. Of course these measures are not convenient, cheap, or certain of success. But no one save criminals need be alarmed if a person takes them. In international politics, however, one state's gain in security often inadvertently threatens others. In explaining British policy on naval disarmament in the interwar period to the Japanese, Ramsey MacDonald said that "Nobody wanted Japan to be insecure."[1] But the problem was not with British desires, but with the consequences of her policy. In earlier periods, too, Britain had needed a navy large enough to keep the shipping lanes open. But such a navy could not avoid being a menace to any other state with a coast that could be raided, trade that could be interdicted, or colonies that could be isolated. When Germany started building a powerful navy before World War I, Britain objected that it could only be an offensive weapon aimed at her. As Sir Edward Grey, the Foreign Secretary, put it to King Edward VII: "If the German Fleet ever becomes superior to ours, the German Army can conquer this country. There is no corresponding risk of this kind to Germany; for however superior our Fleet was, no naval victory could bring us any nearer to Berlin." The English position was half correct: Germany's navy was an anti-British instrument. But the British often overlooked what the Germans knew full well: "in every quarrel with England, German colonies and trade were . . . hostages for England to take." Thus, whether she intended it or not, the British Navy constituted an important instrument of coercion.[2]

II. What Makes Cooperation More Likely?

Given this gloomy picture, the obvious question is, why are we not all dead? Or, to put it less

Figure 8.1. Stag Hunt and Prisoner's Dilemma

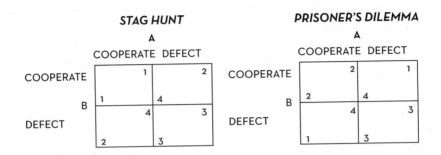

The Costs of Being Exploited (CD)

starkly, what kinds of variables ameliorate the impact of anarchy and the security dilemma? The working of several can be seen in terms of the Stag Hunt or repeated plays of the Prisoner's Dilemma.[3] The Prisoner's Dilemma differs from the Stag Hunt in that there is no solution that is in the best interests of all the participants; there are offensive as well as defensive incentives to defect from the coalition with the others; and, if the game is to be played only once, the only rational response is to defect [Figure 8.1]. But if the game is repeated indefinitely, the latter characteristic no longer holds and we can analyze the game in terms similar to those applied to the Stag Hunt. It would be in the interest of each actor to have others deprived of the power to defect; each would be willing to sacrifice this ability if others were similarly restrained. But if the others are not, then it is in the actor's interest to retain the power to defect.[4] The game theory matrices for these two situations are given below, with the numbers in the boxes being the order of the actor's preferences.

We can see the logical possibilities by rephrasing our question: "Given either of the above situations, what makes it more or less likely that the players will cooperate and arrive at CC?" The chances of achieving this outcome will be increased by: (1) anything that increases incentives to cooperate by increasing the gains of mutual cooperation (CC) and/or decreasing the costs the actor will pay if he cooperates and the other does not (CD); (2) anything that decreases the incentives for defecting by decreasing the gains of taking advantage of the other (DC) and/or increasing the costs of mutual noncooperation (DD); (3) anything that increases each side's expectation that the other will cooperate.[5]

The Costs of Being Exploited (CD)

The fear of being exploited (that is, the cost of CD) most strongly drives the security dilemma; one of the main reasons why international life is not more nasty, brutish, and short is that states are not as vulnerable as men are in a state of nature. People are easy to kill, but as Adam Smith replied to a friend who feared that the Napoleonic Wars would ruin England, "Sir, there is a great deal of ruin in a nation."[6] The easier it is to destroy a state, the greater the reason for it either to join a larger and more secure unit, or else to be especially suspicious of others, to require a large army, and, if conditions are favorable, to attack at the slightest provocation rather than wait to be attacked. If the failure to eat that day—be it venison or rabbit—means that he will starve, a person is likely to defect in the Stag Hunt even if he really likes venison and has a high level of trust in his colleagues. (Defection is especially likely if the others are also starving or if they know that he is.) By contrast, if the costs of CD are lower, if people are well-fed or states are resilient, they can afford to take a more relaxed view of threats.

A relatively low cost of CD has the effect of transforming the game from one in which both players make their choices simultaneously to one in which an actor can make his choice after the other has moved. He will not have to defect out of fear that the other will, but can wait to see what the other will do. States that can afford to be cheated in a bargain or that cannot be destroyed by a surprise attack can more easily trust others and need not act at the first, and ambiguous, sign of menace. Because they have a margin of time and error, they need not match, or more than match, any others' arms in peacetime. They can mobilize in the prewar period or even at the start of the war itself, and still survive. For example, those who opposed a crash program to develop the H-bomb felt that the U.S. margin of safety was large enough so that even if Russia managed to gain a lead in the race, America would not be endangered. The program's advocates disagreed: "If we let the Russians get the super first, catastrophe becomes all but certain."[7]

When the costs of CD are tolerable, not only is security easier to attain but, what is even more important here, the relatively low level of arms and relatively passive foreign policy that a status-quo power will be able to adopt are less likely to threaten others. Thus it is easier for status-quo states to act on their common interests if they are hard to conquer. All other things being equal, a world of small states will feel the effects of anarchy much more than a world of large ones. Defensible borders, large size, and protection against sudden attack not only aid the state, but facilitate cooperation that can benefit all states.

Of course, if one state gains invulnerability by being more powerful than most others, the problem will remain because its security provides a base from which it can exploit others. When the price a state will pay for DD is low, it leaves others with few hostages for its good behavior. Others who are more vulnerable will grow apprehensive, which will lead them to acquire more arms and will reduce the chances of cooperation. The best situation is one in which a state will not suffer greatly if others exploit it, for example, by cheating on an arms control agreement (that is, the costs of CD are low); but it will pay a high long-run price if cooperation with the others breaks down—for example, if agreements cease functioning or if there is a long war (that is, the costs of DD are high). The state's invulnerability is then mostly passive; it provides some protection, but it cannot be used to menace others. As we will discuss below, this situation is approximated when it is easier for states to defend themselves than to attack others, or when mutual deterrence obtains because neither side can protect itself.

The differences between highly vulnerable and less vulnerable states are illustrated by the contrasting policies of Britain and Austria after the Napoleonic Wars. Britain's geographic isolation and political stability allowed her to take a fairly relaxed view of disturbances on the Continent. Minor wars and small changes in territory or in the distribution of power did not affect her vital interests. An adversary who was out to overthrow the system could be stopped after he had made his intentions clear. And revolutions within other states were no menace, since they would not set off unrest within England. Austria, surrounded by strong powers, was not so fortunate; her policy had to be more closely attuned to all conflicts. By the time an aggressor-state had clearly shown its colors, Austria would be gravely threatened. And foreign revolutions, be they democratic or nationalistic, would encourage groups in Austria to upset the existing order. So it is not surprising that Metternich propounded the doctrine summarized earlier, which defended Austria's right to interfere in the internal affairs of others, and that British leaders rejected this view. Similarly, Austria wanted the Congress system to be a relatively tight one, regulating most disputes. The British favored a less centralized system. In other words, in order to protect herself, Austria had either to threaten or to harm others, whereas Britain did not. For Austria and her neighbors the security dilemma was acute; for Britain it was not.

The ultimate cost of CD is of course loss of sovereignty. This cost can vary from situation to situation. The lower it is (for instance, because the two states have compatible ideologies, are similar ethnically, have a common culture, or because the citizens of the losing state expect economic benefits), the less the impact of the security dilemma; the greater the costs, the greater the impact of the dilemma. Here is another reason why extreme differences in values and ideologies exacerbate international conflict.

■ ■ ■

SUBJECTIVE SECURITY DEMANDS

Decision makers act in terms of the vulnerability they feel, which can differ from the actual situation; we must therefore examine the decision makers' subjective security requirements. Two dimensions are involved. First, even if they agree about the objective situation, people can differ about how much security they desire—or, to put it more precisely, about the price they are willing to pay to gain increments of security. The more states value their security above all else (that is, see a prohibitively high cost in CD), the more they are likely to be sensitive to even minimal threats, and to demand high levels of arms. And if arms are positively valued because of pressures from a military-industrial complex, it will be especially hard for status-quo powers to cooperate. By contrast, the security dilemma will not operate as strongly when pressing domestic concerns increase the opportunity

costs of armaments. In this case, the net advantage of exploiting the other (DC) will be less, and the costs of arms races (that is, one aspect of DD) will be greater; therefore the state will behave as though it were relatively invulnerable.

The second aspect of subjective security is the perception of threat (that is, the estimate of whether the other will cooperate). A state that is predisposed to see either a specific other state as an adversary, or others in general as a menace, will react more strongly and more quickly than a state that sees its environment as benign. Indeed, when a state believes that another not only is not likely to be an adversary, but has sufficient interests in common with it to be an ally, then it will actually welcome an increase in the other's power.

■ ■ ■

Geography, Commitments, Beliefs, and Security through Expansion

* * * Situations vary in the ease or difficulty with which all states can simultaneously achieve a high degree of security. The influence of military technology on this variable is the subject of the next section. Here we want to treat the impact of beliefs, geography, and commitments (many of which can be considered to be modifications of geography, since they bind states to defend areas outside their homelands). In the crowded continent of Europe, security requirements were hard to mesh. Being surrounded by powerful states, Germany's problem—or the problem created by Germany—was always great and was even worse when her relations with both France and Russia were bad, such as before World War I. In that case, even a status-quo Germany, if she could not change the political situation, would almost have been forced to adopt something like the Schlieffen Plan. Because she could not hold off both of her enemies, she had to be prepared to

defeat one quickly and then deal with the other in a more leisurely fashion. If France or Russia stayed out of a war between the other state and Germany, they would allow Germany to dominate the Continent (even if that was not Germany's aim). They therefore had to deny Germany this ability, thus making Germany less secure. Although Germany's arrogant and erratic behavior, coupled with the desire for an unreasonably high level of security (which amounted to the desire to escape from her geographic plight), compounded the problem, even wise German statesmen would have been hard put to gain a high degree of security without alarming their neighbors.

■　■　■

III. Offense, Defense, and the Security Dilemma

Another approach starts with the central point of the security dilemma—that an increase in one state's security decreases the security of others—and examines the conditions under which this proposition holds. Two crucial variables are involved: whether defensive weapons and policies can be distinguished from offensive ones, and whether the defense or the offense has the advantage. The definitions are not always clear, and many cases are difficult to judge, but these two variables shed a great deal of light on the question of whether status-quo powers will adopt compatible security policies. All the variables discussed so far leave the heart of the problem untouched. But when defensive weapons differ from offensive ones, it is possible for a state to make itself more secure without making others less secure. And when the defense has the advantage over the offense, a large increase in one state's security only slightly decreases the security of the others, and status-quo powers can all enjoy a high level of security and largely escape from the state of nature.

Offense-Defense Balance

When we say that the offense has the advantage, we simply mean that it is easier to destroy the other's army and take its territory than it is to defend one's own. When the defense has the advantage, it is easier to protect and to hold than it is to move forward, destroy, and take. If effective defenses can be erected quickly, an attacker may be able to keep territory he has taken in an initial victory. Thus, the dominance of the defense made it very hard for Britain and France to push Germany out of France in World War I. But when superior defenses are difficult for an aggressor to improvise on the battlefield and must be constructed during peacetime, they provide no direct assistance to him.

The security dilemma is at its most vicious when commitments, strategy, or technology dictate that the only route to security lies through expansion. Status-quo powers must then act like aggressors; the fact that they would gladly agree to forego the opportunity for expansion in return for guarantees for their security has no implications for their behavior. Even if expansion is not sought as a goal in itself, there will be quick and drastic changes in the distribution of territory and influence. Conversely, when the defense has the advantage, status-quo states can make themselves more secure without gravely endangering others.[8] Indeed, if the defense has enough of an advantage and if the states are of roughly equal size, not only will the security dilemma cease to inhibit status-quo states from cooperating, but aggression will be next to impossible, thus rendering international anarchy relatively unimportant. If states cannot conquer each other, then the lack of sovereignty, although it presents problems of collective goods in a number of areas, no longer forces states to devote their primary attention to self-preservation. Although, if force were not usable, there would be fewer restraints on the use of nonmilitary instruments, these are rarely powerful enough to threaten the vital interests of a major state.

Two questions of the offense-defense balance can be separated. First, does the state have to spend more or less than one dollar on defensive forces to offset each dollar spent by the other side on forces that could be used to attack? If the state has one dollar to spend on increasing its security, should it put it into offensive or defensive forces? Second, with a given inventory of forces, is it better to attack or to defend? Is there an incentive to strike first or to absorb the other's blow? These two aspects are often linked: if each dollar spent on offense can overcome each dollar spent on defense, and if both sides have the same defense budgets, then both are likely to build offensive forces and find it attractive to attack rather than to wait for the adversary to strike.

These aspects affect the security dilemma in different ways. The first has its greatest impact on arms races. If the defense has the advantage, and if the status-quo powers have reasonable subjective security requirements, they can probably avoid an arms race. Although an increase in one side's arms and security will still decrease the other's security, the former's increase will be larger than the latter's decrease. So if one side increases its arms, the other can bring its security back up to its previous level by adding a smaller amount to its forces. And if the first side reacts to this change, its increase will also be smaller than the stimulus that produced it. Thus a stable equilibrium will be reached. Shifting from dynamics to statics, each side can be quite secure with forces roughly equal to those of the other. Indeed, if the defense is much more potent than the offense, each side can be willing to have forces much smaller than the other's, and can be indifferent to a wide range of the other's defense policies.

The second aspect—whether it is better to attack or to defend—influences short-run stability. When the offense has the advantage, a state's reaction to international tension will increase the chances of war. The incentives for pre-emption and the "reciprocal fear of surprise attack" in this situation have been made clear by analyses of the dangers that exist when two countries have first-strike capabilities.[9] There is no way for the state to increase its security without menacing, or even attacking, the other. Even Bismarck, who once called preventive war "committing suicide from fear of death," said that "no government, if it regards war as inevitable even if it does not want it, would be so foolish as to leave to the enemy the choice of time and occasion and to wait for the moment which is most convenient for the enemy."[10] In another arena, the same dilemma applies to the policeman in a dark alley confronting a suspected criminal who appears to be holding a weapon. Though racism may indeed be present, the security dilemma can account for many of the tragic shootings of innocent people in the ghettos.

Beliefs about the course of a war in which the offense has the advantage further deepen the security dilemma. When there are incentives to strike first, a successful attack will usually so weaken the other side that victory will be relatively quick, bloodless, and decisive. It is in these periods when conquest is possible and attractive that states consolidate power internally—for instance, by destroying the feudal barons—and expand externally. There are several consequences that decrease the chance of cooperation among status-quo states. First, war will be profitable for the winner. The costs will be low and the benefits high. Of course, losers will suffer; the fear of losing could induce states to try to form stable cooperative arrangements, but the temptation of victory will make this particularly difficult. Second, because wars are expected to be both frequent and short, there will be incentives for high levels of arms, and quick and strong reaction to the other's increases in arms. The state cannot afford to wait until there is unambiguous evidence that the other is building new weapons. Even large states that have faith in their economic strength cannot wait, because the war will be over before their products can reach the army. Third, when wars are quick, states will have to recruit allies in advance.[11] Without the opportunity for bargaining and re-alignments during the opening stages of hostilities, peacetime diplomacy loses a degree of the fluidity that facilitates balance-of-power policies. Because alliances must be secured during peacetime, the international system is more likely to become bipolar. It is hard to say whether war therefore becomes more or less likely, but this bipolarity increases tension between the two camps and makes it harder for status-quo states to gain the benefits of cooperation. Fourth, if wars are frequent, statesmen's perceptual thresholds will be adjusted accordingly and they will be quick to perceive ambiguous evidence as indicating that others are aggressive. Thus, there will be more cases of status-quo powers arming against each other in the incorrect belief that the other is hostile.

When the defense has the advantage, all the foregoing is reversed. The state that fears attack does not pre-empt—since that would be a wasteful use of its military resources—but rather prepares to receive an attack. Doing so does not decrease the security of others, and several states can do it simultaneously; the situation will therefore be stable, and status-quo powers will be able to cooperate. * * *

More is involved than short-run dynamics. When the defense is dominant, wars are likely to become stalemates and can be won only at enormous cost. Relatively small and weak states can hold off larger and stronger ones, or can deter attack by raising the costs of conquest to an unacceptable level. States then approach equality in what they can do to each other. Like the .45-caliber pistol in the American West, fortifications were the "great equalizer" in some periods. Changes in the status quo are less frequent and cooperation is more common wherever the security dilemma is thereby reduced.

Many of these arguments can be illustrated by the major powers' policies in the periods preceding the two world wars. Bismarck's wars surprised statesmen by showing that the offense had the advantage, and by being quick, relatively cheap, and quite decisive. Falling into a common error, observers projected this pattern into the future. The resulting expectations had several effects. First, states sought semi-permanent allies. In the early stages of the Franco-Prussian War, Napoleon III had thought that there would be plenty of time to recruit Austria to his side. Now, others were not going to repeat this mistake. Second, defense budgets were high and reacted quite sharply to increases on the other side. * * * Third, most decision makers thought that the next European war would not cost much blood and treasure.[12] That is one reason why war was generally seen as inevitable and why mass opinion was so bellicose. Fourth, once war seemed likely, there were strong pressures to pre-empt. Both sides believed that whoever moved first could penetrate the other deep enough to disrupt mobilization and thus gain an insurmountable advantage. (There was no such belief about the use of naval forces. Although Churchill made an ill-advised speech saying that if German ships "do not come out and fight in time of war they will be dug out like rats in a hole,"[13] everyone knew that submarines, mines, and coastal fortifications made this impossible. So at the start of the war each navy prepared to defend itself rather than attack, and the short-run destabilizing forces that launched the armies toward each other did not operate.)[14] Furthermore, each side knew that the other saw the situation the same way, thus increasing the perceived danger that the other would attack, and giving each added reasons to precipitate a war if conditions seemed favorable. In the long and the short run, there were thus both offensive and defensive incentives to strike. This situation casts light on the common question about German motives in 1914: "Did Germany unleash the war deliberately to become a world power or did she support Austria merely to defend a weakening ally," thereby protecting her own position?[15] To some extent, this question is misleading. Because of the perceived advantage of the offense, war was seen as the best route both to gaining expansion and to avoiding drastic loss of influence. There seemed to be no way for Germany merely to retain and safeguard her existing position.

Of course the war showed these beliefs to have been wrong on all points. Trenches and machine guns gave the defense an overwhelming advantage. The fighting became deadlocked and produced horrendous casualties. It made no sense for the combatants to bleed themselves to death. If they had known the power of the defense beforehand, they would have rushed for their own trenches rather than for the enemy's territory. Each side could have done this without increasing the other's incentives to strike. War might have broken out anyway, * * * but at least the pressures of time and the fear of allowing the other to get the first blow would not have contributed to this end. And, had both sides known the costs of the war, they would have negotiated much more seriously. The obvious question is why the states did not seek a negotiated settlement as soon as the shape of the war became clear. Schlieffen had said that if his plan failed, peace should be sought.[16] The answer is complex, uncertain, and largely outside of the scope of our concerns. But part of the reason was the hope and sometimes the expectation that breakthroughs could be made and the dominance of the offensive restored. Without that hope, the political and psychological pressures to fight to a decisive victory might have been overcome.

The politics of the interwar period were shaped by the memories of the previous conflict and the belief that any future war would resemble it. Political and military lessons reinforced each other in ameliorating the security dilemma. Because it was believed that the First World War had been a mistake that could have been avoided by skillful conciliation, both Britain and, to a lesser extent, France were highly sensitive to the possibility that interwar Germany was not a real threat to peace,

and alert to the danger that reacting quickly and strongly to her arms could create unnecessary conflict. And because Britain and France expected the defense to continue to dominate, they concluded that it was safe to adopt a more relaxed and non-threatening military posture.[17] Britain also felt less need to maintain tight alliance bonds. The Allies' military posture then constituted only a slight danger to Germany; had the latter been content with the status quo, it would have been easy for both sides to have felt secure behind their lines of fortifications. Of course the Germans were not content, so it is not surprising that they devoted their money and attention to finding ways out of a defense-dominated stalemate. *Blitzkrieg* tactics were necessary if they were to use force to change the status quo.

The initial stages of the war on the Western Front also contrasted with the First World War. Only with the new air arm were there any incentives to strike first, and these forces were too weak to carry out the grandiose plans that had been both dreamed and feared. The armies, still the main instrument, rushed to defensive positions. Perhaps the allies could have successfully attacked while the Germans were occupied in Poland.[18] But belief in the defense was so great that this was never seriously contemplated. Three months after the start of the war, the French Prime Minister summed up the view held by almost everyone but Hitler: on the Western Front there is "deadlock. Two Forces of equal strength and the one that attacks seeing such enormous casualties that it cannot move without endangering the continuation of the war or of the aftermath."[19] The Allies were caught in a dilemma they never fully recognized, let alone solved. On the one hand, they had very high war aims; although unconditional surrender had not yet been adopted, the British had decided from the start that the removal of Hitler was a necessary condition for peace.[20] On the other hand, there were no realistic plans or instruments for allowing the Allies to impose their will on the other side. The British Chief of the Imperial General Staff noted, "The French have no intention of carrying out an offensive for years, if at all"; the British were only slightly bolder.[21] So the Allies looked to a long war that would wear the Germans down, cause civilian suffering through shortages, and eventually undermine Hitler. There was little analysis to support this view—and indeed it probably was not supportable—but as long as the defense was dominant and the numbers on each side relatively equal, what else could the Allies do?

To summarize, the security dilemma was much less powerful after World War I than it had been before. In the later period, the expected power of the defense allowed status-quo states to pursue compatible security policies and avoid arms races. Furthermore, high tension and fear of war did not set off short-run dynamics by which each state, trying to increase its security, inadvertently acted to make war more likely. The expected high costs of war, however, led the Allies to believe that no sane German leader would run the risks entailed in an attempt to dominate the Continent, and discouraged them from risking war themselves.

TECHNOLOGY AND GEOGRAPHY

Technology and geography are the two main factors that determine whether the offense or the defense has the advantage. As Brodie notes, "On the tactical level, as a rule, few physical factors favor the attacker but many favor the defender. The defender usually has the advantage of cover. He characteristically fires from behind some form of shelter while his opponent crosses open ground."[22] Anything that increases the amount of ground the attacker has to cross, or impedes his progress across it, or makes him more vulnerable while crossing, increases the advantage accruing to the defense. When states are separated by barriers that produce these effects, the security dilemma is eased, since both can have forces adequate for defense without being able to attack. * * *

Oceans, large rivers, and mountain ranges serve the same function as buffer zones. Being hard to cross, they allow defense against superior numbers. The defender has merely to stay on his side of the barrier and so can utilize all the men he can bring up to it. The attacker's men, however, can cross only a few at a time, and they are very vulnerable when doing so. If all states were self-sufficient islands, anarchy would be much less of a problem. A small investment in shore defenses and a small army would be sufficient to repel invasion. Only very weak states would be vulnerable, and only very large ones could menace others. As noted above, the United States, and to a lesser extent Great Britain, have partly been able to escape from the state of nature because their geographical positions approximated this ideal.

Although geography cannot be changed to conform to borders, borders can and do change to conform to geography. Borders across which an attack is easy tend to be unstable. States living within them are likely to expand or be absorbed. Frequent wars are almost inevitable since attacking will often seem the best way to protect what one has. This process will stop, or at least slow down, when the state's borders reach—by expansion or contraction—a line of natural obstacles. Security without attack will then be possible. Furthermore, these lines constitute salient solutions to bargaining problems and, to the extent that they are barriers to migration, are likely to divide ethnic groups, thereby raising the costs and lowering the incentives for conquest.

Attachment to one's state and its land reinforce one quasi-geographical aid to the defense. Conquest usually becomes more difficult the deeper the attacker pushes into the other's territory. Nationalism spurs the defenders to fight harder; advancing not only lengthens the attacker's supply lines, but takes him through unfamiliar and often devastated lands that require troops for garrison duty. These stabilizing dynamics will not operate, however, if the defender's war materiel is situated near its borders, or if the people do not care about their state, but only about being on the winning side. * * *

■   ■   ■

The other major determinant of the offense-defense balance is technology. When weapons are highly vulnerable, they must be employed before they are attacked. Others can remain quite invulnerable in their bases. The former characteristics are embodied in unprotected missiles and many kinds of bombers. (It should be noted that it is not vulnerability *per se* that is crucial, but the location of the vulnerability. Bombers and missiles that are easy to destroy only after having been launched toward their targets do not create destabilizing dynamics.) Incentives to strike first are usually absent for naval forces that are threatened by a naval attack. Like missiles in hardened silos, they are usually well protected when in their bases. Both sides can then simultaneously be prepared to defend themselves successfully.

In ground warfare under some conditions, forts, trenches, and small groups of men in prepared positions can hold off large numbers of attackers. * * *

■   ■   ■

Concerning nuclear weapons, it is generally agreed that defense is impossible—a triumph not of the offense, but of deterrence. Attack makes no sense, not because it can be beaten off, but because the attacker will be destroyed in turn. In terms of the questions under consideration here, the result is the equivalent of the primacy of the defense. First, security is relatively cheap. Less than one percent of the G.N.P. is devoted to deterring a direct attack on the United States; most of it is spent on acquiring redundant systems to provide a lot of insurance against the worst conceivable contingencies. Second, both sides can simultaneously gain security in

the form of second-strike capability. Third, and related to the foregoing, second-strike capability can be maintained in the face of wide variations in the other side's military posture. There is no purely military reason why each side has to react quickly and strongly to the other's increases in arms. Any spending that the other devotes to trying to achieve first-strike capability can be neutralized by the state's spending much smaller sums on protecting its second-strike capability. Fourth, there are no incentives to strike first in a crisis.

■   ■   ■

Offense-Defense Differentiation

The other major variable that affects how strongly the security dilemma operates is whether weapons and policies that protect the state also provide the capability for attack. If they do not, the basic postulate of the security dilemma no longer applies. A state can increase its own security without decreasing that of others. The advantage of the defense can only ameliorate the security dilemma. A differentiation between offensive and defensive stances comes close to abolishing it. Such differentiation does not mean, however, that all security problems will be abolished. If the offense has the advantage, conquest and aggression will still be possible. And if the offense's advantage is great enough, status-quo powers may find it too expensive to protect themselves by defensive forces and decide to procure offensive weapons even though this will menace others. Furthermore, states will still have to worry that even if the other's military posture shows that it is peaceful now, it may develop aggressive intentions in the future.

Assuming that the defense is at least as potent as the offense, the differentiation between them allows status-quo states to behave in ways that are clearly different from those of aggressors. Three beneficial consequences follow. First, status-quo powers can identify each other, thus laying the foundations for cooperation. Conflicts growing out of the mistaken belief that the other side is expansionist will be less frequent. Second, status-quo states will obtain advance warning when others plan aggression. Before a state can attack, it has to develop and deploy offensive weapons. If procurement of these weapons cannot be disguised and takes a fair amount of time, as it almost always does, a status-quo state will have the time to take countermeasures. It need not maintain a high level of defensive arms as long as its potential adversaries are adopting a peaceful posture. * * *

■   ■   ■

* * * [I]f all states support the status quo, an obvious arms control agreement is a ban on weapons that are useful for attacking. As President Roosevelt put it in his message to the Geneva Disarmament Conference in 1933: "If all nations will agree wholly to eliminate from possession and use the weapons which make possible a successful attack, defenses automatically will become impregnable, and the frontiers and independence of every nation will become secure."[23] The fact that such treaties have been rare * * * shows either that states are not always willing to guarantee the security of others, or that it is hard to distinguish offensive from defensive weapons.

■   ■   ■

IV. Four Worlds

The two variables we have been discussing—whether the offense or the defense has the advantage, and whether offensive postures can be distinguished from defensive ones—can be combined to yield four possible worlds.

The first world is the worst for status-quo states. There is no way to get security without menacing others, and security through defense is terribly difficult to obtain. Because offensive and defensive postures are the same, status-quo states acquire the same kind of arms that are sought by aggressors. And because the offense has the advantage over the defense, attacking is the best route to protecting what you have; status-quo states will therefore behave like aggressors. The situation will be unstable. Arms races are likely. Incentives to strike first will turn crises into wars. Decisive victories and conquests will be common. States will grow and shrink rapidly, and it will be hard for any state to maintain its size and influence without trying to increase them. Cooperation among status-quo powers will be extremely hard to achieve.

There are no cases that totally fit this picture, but it bears more than a passing resemblance to Europe before World War I. Britain and Germany, although in many respects natural allies, ended up as enemies. Of course much of the explanation lies in Germany's ill-chosen policy. And from the perspective of our theory, the powers' ability to avoid war in a series of earlier crises cannot be easily explained. Nevertheless, much of the behavior in this period was the product of technology and beliefs that magnified the security dilemma. Decision makers thought that the offense had a big advantage and saw little difference between offensive and defensive military postures. The era was characterized by arms races. And once war seemed likely, mobilization races created powerful incentives to strike first.

In the nuclear era, the first world would be one in which each side relied on vulnerable weapons that were aimed at similar forces and each side understood the situation. In this case, the incentives to strike first would be very high—so high that status-quo powers as well as aggressors would be sorely tempted to pre-empt. And since the forces could be used to change the status quo as well as to preserve it, there would be no way for both sides to increase their security simultaneously. Now the familiar logic of deterrence leads both sides to see the dangers in this world.

Figure 8.2. The Security Dilemma

	Offense Has the Advantage	Defense Has the Advantage
Offensive Posture Not Distinguishable from Defensive One	1 Doubly dangerous.	2 Security dilemma, but security requirements may be compatible.
Offensive Posture Distinguishable from Defensive One	3 No security dilemma, but aggression possible. Status-quo states can follow different policy than aggressors. Warning given.	4 Doubly stable.

Indeed, the new understanding of this situation was one reason why vulnerable bombers and missiles were replaced. Ironically, the 1950s would have been more hazardous if the decision makers had been aware of the dangers of their posture and had therefore felt greater pressure to strike first. This situation could be recreated if both sides were to rely on MIRVed ICBMs.

In the second world, the security dilemma operates because offensive and defensive postures cannot be distinguished; but it does not operate as strongly as in the first world because the defense has the advantage, and so an increment in one side's strength increases its security more than it decreases the other's. So, if both sides have reasonable subjective security requirements, are of roughly equal power, and the variables discussed earlier are favorable, it is quite likely that status-quo states can adopt compatible security policies. * * *

This world is the one that comes closest to matching most periods in history. Attacking is usually harder than defending because of the strength of fortifications and obstacles. But purely defensive postures are rarely possible because fortifications are usually supplemented by armies and mobile guns which can support an attack. In the nuclear era, this world would be one in which both sides relied on relatively invulnerable ICBMs and believed that limited nuclear war was impossible. * * *

In the third world there may be no security dilemma, but there are security problems. Because states can procure defensive systems that do not threaten others, the dilemma need not operate. But because the offense has the advantage, aggression is possible, and perhaps easy. If the offense has enough of an advantage, even a status-quo state may take the initiative rather than risk being attacked and defeated. If the offense has less of an advantage, stability and cooperation are likely because the status-quo states will procure defensive forces. They need not react to others who are similarly armed, but can wait for the warning they would receive if others started to deploy offensive weapons. But each state will have to watch the others carefully, and there is room for false suspicions.

The costliness of the defense and the allure of the offense can lead to unnecessary mistrust, hostility, and war, unless some of the variables discussed earlier are operating to restrain defection.

■ ■ ■

The fourth world is doubly safe. The differentiation between offensive and defensive systems permits a way out of the security dilemma; the advantage of the defense disposes of the problems discussed in the previous paragraphs. There is no reason for a status-quo power to be tempted to procure offensive forces, and aggressors give notice of their intentions by the posture they adopt. Indeed, if the advantage of the defense is great enough, there are no security problems. The loss of the ultimate form of the power to alter the status quo would allow greater scope for the exercise of nonmilitary means and probably would tend to freeze the distribution of values.

■ ■ ■

NOTES

1. Quoted in Gerald Wheeler, *Prelude to Pearl Harbor* (Columbia: University of Missouri Press 1963), 167.

2. Quoted in Leonard Wainstein, "The Dreadnought Gap," in Robert Art and Kenneth Waltz, eds., *The Use of Force* (Boston: Little, Brown 1971), 155. * * *

3. In another article, Jervis says: "International politics sometimes resembles what is called a Prisoner's Dilemma (PD). In this scenario, two men have been caught red-handed committing a minor crime. The district attorney knows that they are also guilty of a much more serious offense. He tells each of them separately that if he confesses and squeals on his buddy, he will go free and the former colleague will go to jail for thirty years. If both of them refuse to give any information, they will be prosecuted for the minor crime and be jailed for thirty days; if they both squeal, plea-bargaining will get them ten years. In

other words, as long as each criminal cares only about himself, he will confess to the more serious crime no matter what he thinks his colleague will do. If he confesses and his buddy does not, he will get the best possible outcome (freedom); if he confesses and his buddy also does so, the outcome will not be good (ten years in jail), but it will be better than keeping silent and going to jail for thirty years. Since both can see this, both will confess. Paradoxically, if they had both been irrational and kept quiet, they would have gone to jail for only a month." (Robert Jervis, "A Political Science Perspective on the Balance of Power and the Concert," *American Historical Review* 97, no. 3 (June 1992): 720.)

4. Experimental evidence for this proposition is summarized in James Tedeschi, Barry Schlenker, and Thomas Bonoma, *Conflict, Power, and Games* (Chicago: Aldine 1973), 135–41.

5. The results of Prisoner's Dilemma games played in the labouratory support this argument. See Anatol Rapoport and Albert Chammah, *Prisoner's Dilemma* (Ann Arbor: University of Michigan Press 1965), 33–50. Also see Robert Axelrod, *Conflict of Interest* (Chicago: Markham 1970), 60–70.

6. Quoted in Bernard Brodie, *Strategy in the Missile Age* (Princeton: Princeton University Press 1959), 6.

7. Herbert York, *The Advisors: Oppenheimer, Teller, and the Superbomb* (San Francisco: Freemar, 1976), 56–60.

8. Thus, when Wolfers [*Discord and Collaboration* (Baltimore: Johns Hopkins Press 1962),] 126, argues that a status-quo state that settles for rough equality of power with its adversary, rather than seeking preponderance, may be able to convince the other to reciprocate by showing that it wants only to protect itself, not menace the other, he assumes that the defense has an advantage.

9. Schelling, [*The Strategy of Conflict* (New York: Oxford University Press 1963),] chap. 9.

10. Quoted in Fritz Fischer, *War of Illusions* (New York: Norton 1975), 377, 461.

11. George Quester, *Offense and Defense in the International System* (New York: John Wiley 1977), 105–06;

Sontag [*European Diplomatic History, 1871–1932* (New York: Appleton-Century-Crofts 1933)], 4–5.

12. Some were not so optimistic. Gray's remark is well-known: "The lamps are going out all over Europe; we shall not see them lit again in our life-time." The German Prime Minister, Bethmann Hollweg, also feared the consequences of the war. But the controlling view was that it would certainly pay for the winner.

13. Quoted in Martin Gilbert, *Winston S. Churchill,* III, *The Challenge of War, 1914–1916* (Boston: Houghton Mifflin 1971), 84.

14. Quester (fn. 33), 98–99. Robert Art, *The Influence of Foreign Policy on Seapower,* II (Beverly Hills: Sage Professional Papers in International Studies Series, 1973), 14–18, 26–28.

15. Konrad Jarausch, "The Illusion of Limited War: Chancellor Bethmann Hollweg's Calculated Risk, July 1914," *Central European History,* II (March 1969), 50.

16. Brodie (fn. 6), 58.

17. President Roosevelt and the American delegates to the League of Nations Disarmament Conference maintained that the tank and mobile heavy artillery had re-established the dominance of the offensive, thus making disarmament more urgent (Boggs, [*Attempts to Define and. Limit "Aggressive" Armament in Diplomacy and Strategy* (Columbia: University of Missouri Studies, XVI, No. 1, 1941)], pp. 31, 108), but this was a minority position and may not even have been believed by the Americans. The reduced prestige and influence of the military, and the high pressures to cut government spending throughout this period also contributed to the lowering of defense budgets.

18. Jon Kimche, *The Unfought Battle* (New York: Stein 1968); Nicholas William Bethell, *The War Hitler Won: The Fall of Poland, September 1939* (New York: Holt 1972); Alan Alexandroff and Richard Rosecrance, "Deterrence in 1939," *World Politics,* XXIX (April 1977), 404–24.

19. Roderick Macleod and Denis Kelly, eds., *Time Unguarded: The Ironside Diaries, 1937–1940* (New York: McKay 1962), 173.

20. For a short time, as France was falling, the British Cabinet did discuss reaching a negotiated peace with Hitler. The official history ignores this, but it is covered in P.M.H. Bell, *A Certain Eventuality* (Farnborough, England: Saxon House 1974), 40–48.

21. Macleod and Kelly (fn. 19), 174. In flat contradiction to common sense and almost everything they believed about modern warfare, the Allies planned an expedition to Scandinavia to cut the supply of iron ore to Germany and to aid Finland against the Russians. But the dominant mood was the one described above.

22. Brodie (fn. 6), 179.

23. Quoted in Merze Tate, *The United States and Armaments* (Cambridge: Harvard University Press 1948), 108.

James D. Fearon

RATIONALIST EXPLANATIONS FOR WAR

The central puzzle about war, and also the main reason we study it, is that wars are costly but nonetheless wars recur. Scholars have attempted to resolve the puzzle with three types of argument. First, one can argue that people (and state leaders in particular) are sometimes or always irrational. They are subject to biases and pathologies that lead them to neglect the costs of war or to misunderstand how their actions will produce it. Second, one can argue that the leaders who order war enjoy its benefits but do not pay the costs, which are suffered by soldiers and citizens. Third, one can argue that even rational leaders who consider the risks and costs of war may end up fighting nonetheless.

This article focuses on arguments of the third sort, which I will call rationalist explanations.[1] Rationalist explanations abound in the literature on international conflict, assuming a great variety of specific forms. Moreover, for at least two reasons many scholars have given rationalist explanations a certain pride of place. First, historians and political scientists who have studied the origins of particular wars often have concluded that war can be a rational alternative for leaders who are acting in their states' interest—they find that the expected benefits of war sometimes outweigh the expected costs, however unfortunate this may be. Second,

the dominant paradigm in international relations theory, neorealism, is thought to advance or even to depend on rationalist arguments about the causes of war. Indeed, if no rationalist explanation for war is theoretically or empirically tenable, then neither is neorealism. The causes of war would then lie in the defects of human nature or particular states rather than in the international system, as argued by neorealists. What I refer to here as "rationalist explanations for war" could just as well be called "neorealist explanations."[2]

This article attempts to provide a clear statement of what a rationalist explanation for war is and to characterize the full set of rationalist explanations that are both theoretically coherent and empirically plausible. It should be obvious that this theoretical exercise must take place prior to testing rationalist explanations against alternatives—we cannot perform such tests unless we know what a rationalist explanation really is. Arguably, the exercise is also foundational for neorealism. Despite its prominence, neorealist theory lacks a clearly stated and fully conceived explanation for war. As I will argue below, it is not enough to say that under anarchy nothing stops states from using force, or that anarchy forces states to rely on self-help, which engenders mutual suspicion and (through spirals or the security dilemma) armed conflict. Neither do diverse references to miscalculation, deterrence failure because of inadequate forces or incredible threats, preventive and preemptive considerations, or free-riding in alliances amount to theoretically coherent rationalist explanations for war.

From *International Organization* 49, no. 3 (Summer 1995), 379–410. Bracketed editorial insertions are the author's and three asterisks (***) are used to mark places where technical material has been omitted. Some notes and a technical appendix have been omitted.

My main argument is that on close inspection none of the principal rationalist arguments advanced in the literature holds up as an explanation because none addresses or adequately resolves the central puzzle, namely, that war is costly and risky, so rational states should have incentives to locate negotiated settlements that all would prefer to the gamble of war. The common flaw of the standard rationalist arguments is that they fail either to address or to explain adequately what prevents leaders from reaching *ex ante* (prewar) bargains that would avoid the costs and risks of fighting. A coherent rationalist explanation for war must do more than give reasons why armed conflict might appear an attractive option to a rational leader under some circumstances—it must show why states are unable to locate an alternative outcome that both would prefer to a fight.

To summarize what follows, the article will consider five rationalist arguments accepted as tenable in the literature on the causes of war. Discussed at length below, these arguments are given the following labels: (1) anarchy; (2) expected benefits greater than expected costs; (3) rational preventive war; (4) rational miscalculation due to lack of information; and (5) rational miscalculation or disagreement about relative power. I argue that the first three arguments simply do not address the question of what prevents state leaders from bargaining to a settlement that would avoid the costs of fighting. The fourth and fifth arguments do address the question, holding that rational leaders may miss a superior negotiated settlement when lack of information leads them to miscalculate relative power or resolve. However, as typically stated, neither argument explains what prevents rational leaders from using diplomacy or other forms of communication to avoid such costly miscalculations.

If these standard arguments do not resolve the puzzle on rationalist terms, what does? I propose that there are three defensible answers, which take the form of general mechanisms, or causal logics,

that operate in a variety of more specific international contexts.[3] In the first mechanism, rational leaders may be unable to locate a mutually preferable negotiated settlement due to *private information* about relative capabilities or resolve and *incentives to misrepresent* such information. Leaders know things about their military capabilities and willingness to fight that other states do not know, and in bargaining situations they can have incentives to misrepresent such private information in order to gain a better deal. I show that given these incentives, communication may not allow rational leaders to clarify relative power or resolve without generating a real risk of war. This is not simply a matter of miscalculation due to poor information but rather of specific strategic dynamics that result from the combination of asymmetric information and incentives to dissemble.

Second, rationally led states may be unable to arrange a settlement that both would prefer to war due to *commitment problems,* situations in which mutually preferable bargains are unattainable because one or more states would have an incentive to renege on the terms. While anarchy (understood as the absence of an authority capable of policing agreements) is routinely cited as a cause of war in the literature, it is difficult to find explanations for exactly why the inability to make commitments should imply that war will sometimes occur. That is, what are the specific, empirically identifiable mechanisms by which the inability to commit makes it impossible for states to strike deals that would avoid the costs of war? I identify three such specific mechanisms, arguing in particular that preventive war between rational states stems from a commitment problem rather than from differential power growth per se.

The third sort of rationalist explanation I find less compelling than the first two, although it is logically tenable. States might be unable to locate a peaceful settlement both prefer due to *issue indivisibilities.* Perhaps some issues, by their very natures, simply will not admit compromise.

Though neither example is wholly convincing, issues that might exhibit indivisibility include abortion in domestic politics and the problem of which prince sits on the throne of, say, Spain, in eighteenth- or nineteenth-century international politics. Issue indivisibility could in principle make war rational for the obvious reason that if the issue allows only a finite number of resolutions, it might be that none falls within the range that both prefer to fighting. However, the issues over which states bargain typically are complex and multidimensional; side-payments or linkages with other issues typically are possible; and in principle states could alternate or randomize among a fixed number of possible solutions to a dispute. War-prone international issues may often be *effectively* indivisible, but the cause of this indivisibility lies in domestic political and other mechanisms rather than in the nature of the issues themselves.

In the first section of the article I discuss the puzzle posed by the fact that war is costly. Using a simple formalization of the bargaining problem faced by states in conflict, I show that under very broad conditions bargains will exist that genuinely rational states would prefer to a risky and costly fight. The second section argues that rational miscalculations of relative power and resolve must be due to private information and then considers how war may result from the combination of private information and incentives to misrepresent that information in bargaining. In the third section, I discuss commitment problems as the second class of defensible rationalist explanations for war. Throughout, I specify theoretical arguments with simple game-theoretic representations and assess plausibility with historical examples.

Before beginning, I should make it clear that I am not presenting either commitment problems or private information and incentives to misrepresent as wholly novel explanations for war that are proposed here for the first time. The literature on

the causes of war is massive, and these ideas, mixed with myriad others, can be found in it in various guises. The main theoretical task facing students of war is not to add to the already long list of arguments and conjectures but instead to take apart and reassemble these diverse arguments into a coherent theory fit for guiding empirical research. Toward this end, I am arguing that when one looks carefully at the problem of explaining how war could occur between genuinely rational, unitary states, one finds that there are really only two ways to do it. The diverse rationalist or neorealist explanations commonly found in the literature fail for two reasons. First, many do not even address the relevant question–what prevents states from locating a bargain both sides would prefer to a fight? They do not address the question because it is widely but incorrectly assumed that rational states can face a situation of deadlock, wherein no agreements exist that both sides would prefer to a war.[4] Second, the rationalist arguments that do address the question—such as (4) and (5) above—do not go far enough in answering it. When fully developed, they prove to be one of the two major mechanisms developed here, namely, either a commitment problem or a problem arising from private information and incentives to misrepresent. These two mechanisms, I will argue, provide the foundations for a rationalist or neorealist theory of war.

The Puzzle

Most historians and political scientists who study war dismiss as naive the view that all wars must be unwanted because they entail destruction and suffering. Instead, most agree that while a few wars may have been unwanted by the leaders who brought them about—World War I is sometimes given as an example—many or perhaps most wars were simply wanted. The leaders involved viewed war as a costly but worthwhile gamble.[5]

Moreover, many scholars believe that wanted wars are easily explained from a rationalist perspective. Wanted wars are thought to be Pareto-efficient—they occur when no negotiated settlements exist that both sides would prefer to the gamble of military conflict. Conventional wisdom holds that while this situation may be tragic, it is entirely possible between states led by rational leaders who consider the costs and risks of fighting. Unwanted wars, which take place despite the existence of settlements both sides preferred to conflict, are thought to pose more of a puzzle, but one that is resolvable and also fairly rare.

The conventional distinction between wanted and unwanted wars misunderstands the puzzle posed by war. The reason is that the standard conception does not distinguish between two types of efficiency—*ex ante* and *ex post*. As long as both sides suffer some costs for fighting, then war is always inefficient *ex post*—both sides would have been better off if they could have achieved the same final resolution without suffering the costs (or by paying lower costs). This is true even if the costs of fighting are small, or if one or both sides viewed the potential benefits as greater than the costs, since there are still costs. Unless states enjoy the activity of fighting for its own sake, as a consumption good, then war is inefficient *ex post*.

From a rationalist perspective, the central puzzle about war is precisely this *ex post* inefficiency. Before fighting, both sides know that war will entail some costs, and even if they expect offsetting benefits they still have an incentive to avoid the costs. The central question, then, is what prevents states in a dispute from reaching an *ex ante* agreement that avoids the costs they know will be paid *ex post* if they go to war? Giving a rationalist explanation for war amounts to answering this question.

Three of the most common and widely employed rationalist arguments in the literature do not directly address or answer the question. These are arguments from anarchy, preventive war, and positive expected utility.

Anarchy

Since Kenneth Waltz's influential *Man, the State, and War*, the anarchical nature of the international realm is routinely cited as a root cause of or explanation for the recurrence of war. Waltz argued that under anarchy, without a supranational authority to make and enforce law, "war occurs because there is nothing to prevent it. . . . Among states as among men there is no automatic adjustment of interests. In the absence of a supreme authority there is then the constant possibility that conflicts will be settled by force."[6]

The argument focuses our attention on a fundamental difference between domestic and international politics. Within a well-ordered state, organized violence as a strategy is ruled out—or at least made very dangerous—by the potential reprisals of a central government. In international relations, by contrast, no agency exists that can credibly threaten reprisal for the use of force to settle disputes.[7] The claim is that without such a credible threat, war will sometimes appear the best option for states that have conflicting interests.

While I do not doubt that the condition of anarchy accounts for major differences between domestic and international politics, and that anarchy encourages both fear of and opportunities for military conflict, the standard framing of the argument is not enough to explain why wars occur and recur. Under anarchy, nothing stops states from using force if they wish. But if using force is a costly option regardless of the outcome, then why is it ever employed? How exactly does the lack of a central authority prevent states from negotiating agreements both sides would prefer to fighting? As it is typically stated, the argument that anarchy provides a rationalist explanation for war does not address this question and so does not solve the problem posed by war's *ex post* inefficiency.

Neither, it should be added, do related arguments invoking the security dilemma, the fact that under anarchy one state's efforts to make itself more secure can have the undesired but unavoidable effect of making another state less secure.[8] By itself this fact says nothing about the availability or feasibility of peaceful bargains that would avoid the costs of war. More elaborate arguments are required, and those that are typically given do not envision bargaining and do not address the puzzle of costs. Consider, for instance, a spiral scenario in which an insecure state increases its arms, rendering another so insecure that it decides to attack. If the first state anticipated the reaction producing war, then by itself this is a deadlock argument; I argue against these below. If the first state did not anticipate war and did not want it, then the problem would seem to be miscalculation rather than anarchy, and we need to know why signaling and bargaining could not have solved it. As Robert Jervis has argued, anarchy and the security dilemma may well foster arms races and territorial competition.[9] But with the exception of occasional references to the preemptive war problem, the standard security dilemma arguments do not explicitly address the question of why the inability to make commitments should necessarily make for war between rational states.[10]

Below I will argue that anarchy is indeed implicated as a cause of specific sorts of military conflict (e.g., preventive and preemptive war and in some cases war over strategic territory). In contrast to the standard arguments, however, showing how anarchy figures in a coherent rationalist explanation entails describing the specific mechanism by which states' inability to write enforceable contracts makes peaceful bargains both sides would prefer unattainable.

Preventive War

It frequently is argued that if a declining power expects it might be attacked by a rising power in the future, then a preventive war in the present

may be rational. Typically, however, preventive war arguments do not consider whether the rising and declining powers could construct a bargain, perhaps across time, that would leave both sides better off than a costly and risky preventive war would.[11] The incentives for such a deal surely exist. The rising state should not want to be attacked while it is relatively weak, so what stops it from offering concessions in the present and the future that would make the declining state prefer not to attack? Also, if war is inefficient and bargains both sides prefer to a fight will exist, why should the declining power rationally fear being attacked in the future? The standard argument supposes that an anticipated shift in the balance of power can by itself be enough to make war rational, but this is not so.

Positive Expected Utility

Perhaps the most common informal rationalist explanation found in the literature is that war may occur when two states each estimate that the expected benefits of fighting outweigh the expected costs. As Bruce Bueno de Mesquita argued in an influential formalization of this claim, war can be rational if both sides have positive expected utility for fighting; that is, if the expected utility of war (expected benefits less costs) is greater than the expected utility of remaining at peace.[12]

Informal versions of the expected utility argument typically fail to address the question of how or under what conditions it can be possible for two states both to prefer the costly gamble of war to any negotiated settlement. Formal versions have tended to avoid the question by making various restrictive and sometimes nonrationalist assumptions. To support these claims, I need to be more precise about the expected utility argument.

When Will There Exist Bargains Both Sides Prefer to War?

This section considers the question of whether and when two rationally led states could both prefer war to any negotiated settlement.

Consider two states, A and B, who have preferences over a set of issues represented by the interval $X = [0, 1]$. State A prefers issue resolutions closer to 1, while B prefers outcomes closer to 0. For concreteness we might think of x as representing the proportion of all territory between A and B that is controlled by A. [Thus, a point X in the interval represents the situation where state A controls all the territory from ϕ to X, while state B controls all the territory from X to 1.][13]

In order to say whether the set X contains negotiated settlements that both sides would prefer to conflict, it must be possible to say how the states evaluate the military option versus those outcomes. Almost all analysts of war have stressed that war is a gamble whose outcome may be determined by random or otherwise unforeseeable events.[14] As Bueno de Mesquita argued, this makes expected utility a natural candidate.[15] Suppose that if the states fight a war, state A prevails with probability $p \in [0, 1]$, and that the winner gets to choose its favorite outcome in the issue space. * * * [Thus, A's expected utility for war is $p - c$, since A gets all the territory, which is worth 1, with probability p, loses everything with probability $1 - p$, and pays a cost for fighting c_A in either event.] Similarly, state B's expected utility for war will be $1 - p - c_B$. Since we are considering rationalist theories for war, we assume that c_A and c_B are both positive. War is thus represented as a costly lottery.[16]

We can now answer the question posed above. The following result is easily demonstrated: given the assumptions stated in the last two paragraphs, there always exists a set of negotiated settlements that both sides prefer to fighting. * * *

[For example, in the special case where each state's value for an additional increment of territory is constant, the two states will both prefer any division of territory in the range from $p - c_A$ to $p + c_B$ over fighting a war. This interval represents the bargaining range, with $p - c_A$ and $p + c_B$ as the reservation levels that delimit it. This case of "risk neutral" states is depicted in Figure 8.3.]

This simple but important result is worth belaboring with some intuition. Suppose that two people (or states) are bargaining over the division of $100—if they can agree on a split they can keep what they agree to. However, in contrast to the usual economic scenarios, in this international relations example the players also have an outside option.[17] For a price of $20, they can go to war, in which case each player has a 50-percent chance of winning the whole $100. This implies that the expected value of the war option is $30 ($0.5 \cdot 100 + 0.5 \cdot 0 - 20$) for each side, so that if the players are risk-neutral, then neither should be willing to accept less than $30 in the bargaining. But notice that there is still a range of peaceful, bargained outcomes from ($31, $69) to ($69, $31) that make both sides strictly better off than the war option. Risk aversion will tend to increase the range yet further; indeed, even if the leaders pay no costs for war, a set of agreements both sides prefer to a fight will still exist provided both are risk-averse over the issues. In effect, the costs and risks of fighting open up a "wedge" of bargained solutions that risk-neutral or risk-averse states will prefer to the gamble of conflict. The existence of this *ex ante* bargaining range derives from the fact that war is inefficient *ex post*.

Three substantive assumptions are needed for the result, none of which seems particularly strong. First, the states know that there is some true probability p that one state would win in a military contest. As discussed below, it could be that the states have conflicting estimates of the likelihood of victory, and if both sides are optimistic about their chances this can obscure the bargaining

Figure 8.3. The Bargaining Range

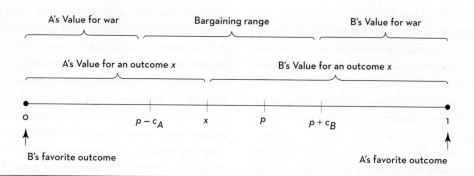

range. But even if the states have private and conflicting estimates of what would happen in a war, if they are rational, they should know that there can be only one true probability that one or the other will prevail (perhaps different from their own estimate). Thus rational states should know that there must in fact exist a set of agreements all prefer to a fight.

Second, it is assumed that the states are risk-averse or risk-neutral over the issues. Because risk attitude is defined relative to an underlying metric (such as money in economics), the substantive meaning of this assumption depends on the bargaining context. Loosely, it says that the states prefer a fifty-fifty split or share of whatever is at issue (in whatever metric it comes, if any) to a fifty-fifty chance at all or nothing, where this refers to the value of winning or losing a war. In effect, the assumption means that leaders do not like gambling when the downside risk is losing at war, which seems plausible given the presumption that state leaders normally wish to retain territory and power. A risk-acceptant leader is analogous to a compulsive gambler—willing to accept a sequence of gambles that has the expected outcome of eliminating the state and regime. Even if we admitted such a leader as rational, it seems doubtful that many have held such preferences (Hitler being a possible exception).

Finally, it was assumed that a continuous range of peaceful settlements (from 0 to 1) exists. In other words, the issues in dispute are perfectly divisible, so that there are always feasible bargains between the states' reservation levels $p - c_A$ and $p + c_B$. This third assumption immediately suggests a tenable rationalist explanation for war. Perhaps something about the nature of some international issues, such as which successor will sit on a throne, does not admit finely graded divisions and compromise. If so, then small costs for fighting and bad luck may make for rational war over such issues.

But we would immediately like to know what about the nature of an issue makes it impossible to divide up. On more thought, this seems empirically implausible. In the first place, most issues states negotiate over are quite complex—they have many dimensions of concern and allow many possible settlements. Second, if states can simply pay each other sums of money or goods (which they can, in principle), or make linkages with other issues, then this should have the effect of making any issues in dispute perfectly divisible. Before the age of nationalism, princes often bought, sold, and partitioned land.[18] In the nineteenth century the United States purchased the Louisiana Territory from France, and Alaska from Russia, and as late as 1898 President McKinley explored the possibility of buying Cuba from Spain in order to avoid a war over it.[19] Third, if something about the nature of an issue means that it can be settled in only, say, two ways, then some sort of random allocation or alternation between the two resolutions could in principle serve to create intermediate bargains. Mafia dons, for example, apparently have avoided costly internal wars by using lotteries to allocate construction contracts among families.[20]

In practice, creating intermediate settlements with cash, with linkages to other issues, or with randomization or alternation often seems difficult or impossible for states engaged in a dispute. For example, the immediate issue that gave rise to the Franco–Prussian war was a dispute over which prince would take the Spanish throne. It doubtless occurred to no one to propose that the two candidates alternate year by year, or three years for the Hapsburg and one for the Hohenzollern, or whatever. In this case as in many others, the issue could in principle have been made more continuous and was not for other reasons—here, alternating kings would have violated so many conventions and norms as to have been domestically unworkable. To give a more realistic example, nineteenth- and twentieth-century leaders cannot divide up and trade territory in international negotiations as easily as could rulers in the seventeenth and eighteenth centuries, due in part to domestic political consequences of the rise of nationalism; contrast, for example, the Congress of Vienna with the negotiations following World War I.

So in principle the indivisibility of the issues that are the subject of international bargaining can provide a coherent rationalist explanation for war. However, the real question in such cases is what prevents leaders from creating intermediate settlements, and the answer is likely to be other mechanisms (often domestic political) rather than the nature of the issues themselves.[21] Both the intrinsic complexity and richness of most matters over which states negotiate and the availability of linkages and side-payments suggest that intermediate bargains typically will exist.

It is thus not sufficient to say that positive expected utility by itself supplies a coherent or compelling rationalist explanation for war. Provided that the issues in dispute are sufficiently divisible, or that side-payments are possible, there should exist a set of negotiated agreements that have greater utility for both sides than the gamble of war does. The reason is that the *ex post* inefficiency of war opens up an *ex ante* bargaining range.

So, to explain how war could occur between rationally led states, we need to answer the following question. Given the existence of an *ex ante* bargaining range, why might states fail either to locate or to agree on an outcome in this range, so avoiding the costs and risks of war?

War Due to Private Information and Incentives to Misrepresent

Two commonly employed rationalist explanations in the literature directly address the preceding question. Both turn on the claim that war can be and often is the product of rational miscalculation. One explanation holds that a state's leaders may rationally overestimate their chance of military victory against an adversary, so producing a disagreement about relative power that only war can resolve. The other argues that rationally led states may lack information about an adversary's willingness to fight over some interest and so may challenge in the mistaken belief that war will not follow.

In this section I argue that while these ideas point toward a tenable rationalist explanation for war, neither goes far enough and neither works by itself. Both neglect the fact that states can in principle communicate with each other and so avoid a costly miscalculation of relative power or will. The cause of war cannot be simply lack of information, but whatever it is that prevents its disclosure. I argue that the fact that states have incentives to misrepresent their positions is crucial here, explaining on rationalist terms why diplomacy may not allow rational states to clarify disagreements about relative power or to avoid the miscalculation of resolve.

The mainstream international relations literature recognizes the existence of both private information and incentives to misrepresent, but typically views them as background conditions to be taken for granted rather than as key elements of an explanation of how rationally led states might end up at war. For example, Jack Levy's impressive review of the literature on the causes of war contains nothing on the role of incentives to misrepresent and discusses private information largely in the context of misperceptions of other states' intentions (which are linked to psychological biases). This is an accurate reflection of where these factors stand in the mainstream literature.[22]

Disagreements about Relative Power

Geoffrey Blainey's well-known and often-cited argument is that "wars usually begin when two nations disagree on their relative strength."[23] It is easy to see how a disagreement about relative strength—understood as conflicting estimates of the likelihood of military victory—can eliminate any *ex ante* bargaining range. Recall the example given above, where two states bargain over the division of $100, and each has the outside option of going to war. If each expects that it surely would prevail at war, then each side's expected value for the war option is $80 $(1 \cdot 100 + 0 \cdot 0 - 20)$. So given these expectations, neither side will accept less than $80 in the bargaining, implying that no negotiated outcome is mutually preferred to war. More generally, suppose that state A expects to win with probability p, state B expects to win

with probability r, and p and r sum to greater than one. Such conflicting expectations will certainly shrink and could eliminate any *ex ante* bargaining range.

But how could rationally led states have conflicting expectations about the likely outcome of military conflict? In the extreme case, how could both sides rationally expect to win? The literature barely addresses this question in explicit terms. Blainey, whom the literature views as advancing a rationalist explanation for war, in fact explains disagreements about relative power as a consequence of human *ir*rationality. He says that mutual optimism about victory in war is the product of "moods which cannot be grounded in fact" and which "permeate what appear to be rational assessments of the relative military strength of two contending powers." Mutual optimism is said to result from a "process by which nations evade reality," which hardly sounds like a rationalist explanation.[24]

Conflicting expectations about the likely outcome of military conflict may be explained in three ways. First, as Blainey suggests, emotional commitments could irrationally bias leaders' military estimates. They might, for instance, come to believe nationalist rhetoric holding that their soldiers are more courageous and spirited than those of the adversary.[25] Second, the world is a very complex place, and for this reason military analysts in different states could reach different conclusions about the likely impact of different technologies, doctrines, and tactics on the expected course of battle. Third, state leaders might have private information about militarily relevant factors—military capabilities, strategy, and tactics; the population's willingness to prosecute a long war; or third-state intentions. If a state has superior (and so private) information about any such factor, then its estimate of the probable course of battle may differ from that of an adversary.

Under a strict but standard definition of rationality, only the third explanation qualifies as an account of how rationally led states could have conflicting estimates of the probability of winning in war. As argued by John Harsanyi, if two rational agents have the same information about an uncertain event, then they should have the same beliefs about its likely outcome.[26] The claim is that given identical information, truly rational agents should reason to the same conclusions about the probability of one uncertain outcome or another. Conflicting estimates should occur only if the agents have different (and so necessarily private) information.[27]

It follows that the second explanation for disagreements about relative power listed above—the complexity of the world—is not a rationalist account. Instead, it is an account that explains conflicting military estimates as a consequence of bounded rationality. In this view, leaders or military analysts with the same information about military technology, strategy, political will, etc., might reason to different conclusions about the likely course of a war because of differential ability to cope with complexity of the problem. This is entirely plausible, but it is a bounded rationality explanation rather than a fully rationalist one.[28]

The rationalist account of how disagreements about the probability of winning might arise also seems empirically plausible. States certainly have private information about factors affecting the likely course of battle—for example, they jealously guard military secrets and often have superior information about what an ally will or will not fight for. Nonetheless, while private information about militarily relevant capabilities provides a first step, it does not provide a coherent rationalist explanation for war. The problem is that even if leaders have such private information, they should understand that their own estimates based on this information are suspect because they do not know the other side's private information. In principle, both sides could gain by sharing information, which would yield a consensus military estimate (absent bounded rationality). And, as shown above, doing so could not help but reveal bargains that both would prefer to a fight.[29]

So the question of how rationally led states can disagree about relative power devolves to the question of what prevents states from sharing private information about factors that might affect the course of battle. Before turning to this question, I will consider the second common explanation for how a rational miscalculation may produce war.

War Due to the Miscalculation of an Opponent's Willingness to Fight

Many wars have been given the following so-called rationalist explanation: state A transgressed some interest of state B in the erroneous belief that B would not fight a war over the matter. Though rationally led, state A lacked information about B's willingness to fight and simply happened to guess wrong, causing a war. Thus, some say that Germany miscalculated Russian and/or British willingness to fight in 1914; Hitler miscalculated Britain and France's willingness to resist his drive to the east; Japanese leaders in 1941 miscalculated U.S. willingness to fight a long war over control in the South Pacific; North Korea miscalculated U.S. willingness to defend South Korea; the United States miscalculated China's willingness to defend North Korea; and so on. In each case, the argument would hold that lack of information led a more-or-less rational actor to guess wrong about the extent of the bargaining range.

Blainey has argued that if states agree on relative power they are very unlikely to go to war against each other.[30] It is worth pointing out that in the preceding argument, war can occur despite complete agreement on relative power across states. To show how and for later use, I will introduce a simple model of international bargaining. As in the empirical examples just mentioned, in the model one state unilaterally chooses some revision of the status quo. The second state can then either acquiesce to the revision or can go to war to reverse it.

Formally, suppose there is a status quo resolution of the issues, [represented as number q between 0 and 1,] and that state A has the opportunity to chose any outcome x [between 0 and 1], presenting state B with a fait accompli. On observing what state A did (which might be nothing, i.e., $x = q$), state B can choose whether to go to war or to acquiesce to A's revision of the status quo.

If neither state has any private information, so that all payoffs are common knowledge, state A does best to push the outcome just up to B's reservation level $p + c_B$, which makes B just willing to acquiesce rather than go to war. With complete information, then, the states avoid the inefficient outcome of war.[31] On the other hand, if state B has private information about either its capabilities (which affect p) or its value for the issues at stake relative to the costs of conflict (c_B), then state A may not know whether a particular "demand" x will yield war or peace. Lacking this information, state A faces a trade-off in deciding whether and how much territory to "grab": The larger the grab, the greater the risk of war, but the better off A will be if state B acquiesces.

Suppose, for example, that A and B share a common estimate of p—they agree about relative power—but that A is unsure about B's costs for fighting. Under very broad conditions, if A cannot learn B's private information and if A's own costs are not too large, then state A's optimal grab produces a positive chance of war. Intuitively, if A is not too fearful of the costs of war relative to what might be gained in bargaining, it will run some risk of war in hopes of gaining on the ground. So Blainey's suggestion that a disagreement about relative power is necessary for war is incorrect—all that is necessary is that the states in dispute be unable to locate or agree on some outcome in the bargaining range. Since the bargaining range is determined not just by relative power but also by states' values for the issues at stake relative to the costs of fighting, uncertainty about the latter can (and apparently does) produce war.

Once again, it is entirely plausible that state leaders have private information about their value for various international interests relative to their costs of fighting over them.[32] Thus it seems we have a second tenable rationalist explanation for war, again based on the concept of private information. But as in the case of disagreements about relative power, the explanation fails as given because it does not explain why states cannot avoid miscalculating a potential opponent's willingness to fight. In the model, why cannot state A simply ask state B whether it would fight rather than acquiesce to a particular demand? To give a concrete example, why did German leaders in 1914 not simply ask their British and Russian counterparts what they would do if Austria were to attack Serbia? If they could have done so and if the answers could have been believed, the Germans might not have miscalculated concerning Russian and, more importantly, British willingness to fight. In consequence they might have avoided the horrendous costs of World War I.

To recap, I have argued that in a rationalist framework, disagreements about relative power and uncertainty about a potential opponent's willingness to fight must have the same source: leaders' private information about factors affecting the likely course of a war or their resolve to fight over specific interests. In order to avoid war's *ex post* inefficiency, leaders have incentives to share any such private information, which would have the effect of revealing peaceful settlements that lie within the bargaining range. So, to explain how war could occur between states led by rational leaders who consider the costs of fighting, we need to explain what would prevent them from sharing such private information.

Incentives to Misrepresent in Bargaining

Prewar bargaining may fail to locate an outcome in the bargaining range because of strategic incentives to withhold or misrepresent private information. While states have an incentive to avoid the costs of war, they also wish to obtain a favorable resolution of the issues. This latter desire can give them an incentive to exaggerate their true willingness or capability to fight, if by doing so they might deter future challenges or persuade the other side to make concessions. States can also have an incentive to conceal their capabilities or resolve, if they are concerned that revelation would make them militarily (and hence politically) vulnerable or would reduce the chances for a successful first strike. Similarly, states may conceal their true willingness to fight in order to avoid appearing as the aggressor.

Combined with the fact of private information, these various incentives to misrepresent can explain why even rational leaders may be unable to avoid the miscalculations of relative will and power that can cause war. This section first considers why this is so theoretically and then discusses two empirical examples.

A drawback of the simple bargaining model given above was that state B had no opportunity to try to communicate its willingness to fight to state A. It is easy to imagine that if communication were possible—say, if B could announce what interests in X it considered vital enough to fight over—this might at least lower the chance of war by miscalculation. To check this, we give state B an initial opportunity to make a foreign policy announcement f, which can be any statement about its foreign policy or what it considers to be vital or peripheral interests. (Assume as before that A is uncertain about B's capabilities or costs for fighting.)

If the announcement itself has no effect on either side's payoffs, then it can be shown that in any equilibrium in which state A does not choose randomly among demands, A will make the same demand regardless of what state B says, and the *ex ante* risk of war will remain the same as in the game without communication by state B. To gain an intuition for these results, suppose that A conditioned its behavior on f, grabbing more or less depending on what B announced. Then regardless of B's true willingness to fight, B does best to make the announcement that leads to the smallest grab by A—that is, B has an incentive to misrepresent its actual willingness to resist. But then A learns nothing from the announcement.[33]

This conclusion is slightly altered if the leaders of B can render the announcement f costly to make.[34] In practice, five common methods include building weapons, mobilizing troops, signing alliance treaties, supporting troops in a foreign land, and creating domestic political costs that would be paid if the announcement proves false. Of course, signaling by means of domestic political audience costs lies outside a purely unitary rational-actor framework, since this presumes a state run by an agent on behalf of a principal (the "audience") rather than a unitary state with a perfectly secure leadership. In the latter case, leaders may be able to make foreign policy announcements credible only by engaging an international reputation, taking financially costly mobilization measures, or bearing the costs and risks of limited military engagements.[35]

Even when the signal is costly, however, this will not in general completely eliminate all risk of war by miscalculation—indeed, it may even increase it. The reason concerns the nature of the signals that states have incentives to send. To be genuinely informative about a state's actual willingness or ability to fight, a signal must be costly in such a way that a state with lesser resolve or capability might not wish to send it. Actions that generate a real risk of war—for example, troop mobilizations that engage a leadership's reputation before international or domestic audiences—can easily satisfy this constraint, since states with high resolve are less fearful of taking them. In other words, a rational state may choose to run a real risk of (inefficient) war in order to signal that it will fight if not given a good deal in bargaining.[36]

The July crisis of World War I provides several examples of how incentives to misrepresent can make miscalculations of resolve hard to dispel. Soon after German leaders secretly endorsed Austrian plans to crush Serbia, they received both direct and indirect verbal indications from St. Petersburg that Russia would fight rather than acquiesce.[37] For example, on 21 July, the Russian Foreign Minister told the German ambassador that "Russia would not be able to tolerate Austria-Hungary's using threatening language to Serbia or taking military measures."[38] Such verbal statements had little effect on German leaders' beliefs, however, since they knew Russian leaders had a strategic incentive to misrepresent. On 18 July in a cable explaining Berlin's policy to Ambassador Lichnowsky in London, Secretary of State Jagow wrote that "there is certain to be some blustering in St. Petersburg."[39] Similarly, when on 26 July Lichnowsky began to report that Britain might join with France and Russia in the event of war, German Chancellor Bethmann Hollweg told his personal assistant of the "danger that France and England will commit their support to Russia in order not to alienate it, perhaps without really believing that for us mobilization means war, thinking of it as a bluff which they answer with a counterbluff."[40]

At the same time, the Chancellor had an incentive to misrepresent the strength and nature of German support for Austria's plans. Bethmann correctly anticipated that revealing this information would make Germany appear the aggressor, which might undermine Social Democratic support for his policies in Germany as well as turn British public opinion more solidly against his state.[41] This incentive led the Chancellor to avoid making direct or pointed inquiries about England's attitude in case of war. The incentive also led him to pretend to go along with the British Foreign Secretary's proposals for a conference to mediate the dispute.[42] In consequence, Lord Grey may not have grasped the need for a stronger warning to Germany until fairly late in the crisis (on 29 July), by which time diplomatic and military actions had made backing off more difficult for both Austria and Germany.

In July 1914, incentives to misrepresent private information fostered and supported miscalculations of willingness to fight. Miscalculations of relative power can arise from this same source. On the one hand, states at times have an incentive to exaggerate their capabilities in an attempt to do better in bargaining. On the other hand, they can also have the well-known incentive to withhold information about capabilities and strategy. Presumably because of the strongly zero-sum aspect of military engagements, a state that has superior knowledge of an adversary's war plans may do better in war and thus in prewar bargaining—hence, states rarely publicize war plans. While the theoretical logic has not been worked out, it seems plausible that states' incentives to conceal information about capabilities and strategy could help explain some disagreements about relative power.

The 1904 war between Japan and Russia serves to illustrate this scenario. On the eve of the war, Russian leaders believed that their military could almost certainly defeat Japan.[43] In this conviction they differed little from the view of most European observers. By contrast, at the imperial council of 4 February that decided for war, the Japanese chief of staff estimated a fifty-fifty chance of prevailing, if their attack began immediately.[44] Thus Japanese and Russian leaders disagreed about relative power—their estimates of the likelihood of victory summed to greater than 1.

Moreover, historical accounts implicate this disagreement as a major cause of the war: Russia's refusal to compromise despite repeated offers by the Japanese was motivated in large measure by their belief that Japan would not dare attack them. The Japanese Cabinet finally decided for war after the Tsar and his advisers failed to make any real compromises over Korea or Manchuria in a series of proposals exchanged in 1903. The Tsar and his top advisers were hardly eager to fight, not because they expected to lose but because they saw an Asian war as a costly diversion of resources to the wrong theater.[45] Nonetheless, they refused to make concessions from what they viewed as a position of great military strength. They believed that Japan would have to settle for less, given its relative military weakness.[46]

The disagreement arose in substantial part from Japanese private information about their military capabilities and how they compared with Russia's. A far superior intelligence service had provided the Japanese military with a clear picture of Russian strengths and weaknesses in Northeast Asia and enabled them to develop an effective offensive strategy. According to John Albert White, due to this intelligence "the Japanese government apparently faced the war with a far more accurate conception of their task than their enemy had."[47] In addition, compared with the Russians or indeed with any European power, Japanese leaders had much better knowledge of the fighting ability of the relatively untested Japanese army and of the effect of the reforms, training, and capital development of the previous decade.[48]

If by communicating this private information the Japanese could have led the Russians to see that their chances of victory were smaller than expected, they might have done so. Almost all historians who have carefully examined the case agree that the Japanese government was not bent on war for its own sake—they were willing to compromise if the Russians would as well.[49] However, it was unthinkable for the Japanese to reveal such information or convince the Russians even if they did. In the first place, the Japanese could not simply make announcements about the quality of their forces, since the Russians would have had no reason to believe them. Second, explaining how they planned to win a war might seriously compromise any such attempt by changing the likelihood that they would win; there is a trade-off between revealing information about resolve or capabilities to influence bargaining and reducing the advantages of a first strike.

In sum, the combination of private information about relative power or will and the strategic incentive to misrepresent these afford a tenable rationalist explanation for war. While states always have incentives to locate a peaceful bargain cheaper than war, they also always have incentives to do well in the bargaining. Given the fact of private information about capabilities or resolve, these incentives mean that states cannot always use quiet diplomatic conversations to discover mutually preferable settlements. It may be that the only way to surmount this barrier to communication is to take actions that produce a real risk of inefficient war.

This general mechanism operates in at least two other empirically important ways to produce conflict in specific circumstances. First, private information about the costs of fighting or the value leaders place on international interests can give them an incentive to cultivate a reputation for having lower costs or more far-flung vital interests than they actually do. If cutting a deal in one dispute would lead other states to conclude the leader's costs for using force are high, then the leader might choose a costly war rather than suffer the depredations that might follow from making concessions. The U.S. interventions in Korea and Vietnam are sometimes explained in these terms, and states surely have worried about such inferences drawn by other states for a long time.[50] The same logic operates when a small state or group (for example, Finland or the Chechens) chooses to fight a losing war against a larger one (for example, the Soviet Union or Russia) in order to develop a reputation for being hard to subjugate. In both cases, states employ war itself as a costly signal of privately known and otherwise unverifiable information about willingness to fight.

Second, since incentives to misrepresent military strength can undermine diplomatic signaling, states may be forced to use war as a credible means to reveal private information about their military capabilities. Thus, a rising state may seek out armed conflict in order to demonstrate that it is more powerful than others realize, while a state in apparent decline may fight in hope of revealing that its capabilities remain better than most believe. In both instances, the inefficient outcome of war derives from the fact that states have private information about their capabilities and a strategic incentive to misrepresent it to other states.

War as a Consequence of Commitment Problems

This section considers a second and quite different rationalist mechanism by which war may occur even though the states in dispute share the same assessment of the bargaining range. Even if private information and incentives to misrepresent it do not tempt states into a risky process of discovery or foster costly investments in reputation, states may be unable to settle on an efficient bargained outcome when for structural reasons they cannot trust each other to uphold the deal.

In this class of explanations, the structural condition of anarchy reemerges as a major factor, although for nonstandard reasons. In the conventional argument, anarchy matters because no hegemonic power exists to threaten states with "jail" if they use force. Without this threat, states become suspicious and worried about other states' intentions; they engage in self-help by building weapons; and somehow uncertainty-plus-weapons leads them ultimately to attack each other (the security dilemma or spiral model). Below, I show that anarchy does indeed matter but for more specific reasons and in more specific contexts. Anarchy matters when an unfortunate combination of state preferences and opportunities for action imply that one or both sides in a dispute have incentives to renege on peaceful bargains which, if they were enforceable, would be mutually preferred to war. I will consider three such unfortunate situations that can claim some empirical plausibility.

It should be stressed that in standard security dilemma and spiral model arguments the suspicions and lack of trust engendered by anarchy are understood to originate either from states' inability to observe each other's motivations (that is, from private information about greed or desire for conquest) or from the knowledge that motivations can change.[51] By contrast, in the arguments given below, states have no private information and motivations never change; thus states understand each other's motivations perfectly. This is not to argue that private information about the value a leadership places on expansion is unimportant in international politics—it surely is. Indeed, private information about motivation and various incentives to misrepresent it might exacerbate any of the three specific commitment problems discussed below. However, when they do so this is a matter of an interaction between informational and commitment problems rather than of anarchy per se. Our first task should be to isolate and specify the mechanisms by which anarchy itself might cause war.

Preemptive War and Offensive Advantages

Consider the problem faced by two gunslingers with the following preferences. Each would most prefer to kill the other by stealth, facing no risk of retaliation, but each prefers that both live in peace to a gunfight in which each risks death. There is a bargain here that both sides prefer to "war"—namely, that each leaves the other alone—but without the enforcement capabilities of a third party, such as an effective sheriff, they may not be able to attain it. Given their preferences, neither person can credibly commit not to defect from the bargain by trying to shoot the other in the back. Note that no matter how far the shadow of the future extends, iteration (or repeat play) will not make cooperation possible in strategic situations of this sort. Because being the "sucker" here may mean being permanently eliminated, strategies of conditional cooperation such as tit-for-tat are infeasible.[52] Thus, if we can find a plausible analogy in international relations, this example might afford a coherent rationalist explanation for war.

Preemptive war scenarios provide the analogy. If geography or military technology happened to create large first-strike or offensive advantages, then states might face the same problem as the gunslingers. To demonstrate this theoretically, I consider how offensive advantages affect the bargaining range between two states engaged in a dispute.

There are at least three ways of interpreting offensive advantages in a formal context. First, an offensive advantage might mean that a state's odds of winning are better if it attacks rather than defends. Second, an offensive advantage might mean that the costs of fighting are lower for an attacking state than for a defending state. It can be shown that no commitment problem operates in this second case, although lowering the costs of war for attackers does narrow the de facto bargaining range. Third, offensive advantages might mean that military technology and doctrine increase the variance of battlefield outcomes. That is, technology and doctrine might make total victory or total defeat more likely, while rendering stalemate and small territorial changes less likely. In this case, offensive advantages can actually reduce the expected utility of war for both sides, thus increasing the bargaining range and perhaps making war less rather than more likely. Intuitively, if states care most of all about security (understood as survival), then offensive advantages make war less safe by increasing the risk of total defeat.[53]

A commitment problem of the sort faced by the gunslingers arises only under the first interpretation, in which "offensive advantage" refers to an increase in a state's military prospects if it attacks rather than defends. To demonstrate this, let p_f be the probability that state A wins a war if A attacks; p_s the probability that A wins if A strikes second or defends; and p the chance that A wins if both states mobilize and attack at the same time. Thus, an offensive advantage exists when $p_f > p > p_s$.

Since states can always choose to attack if they wish, a peaceful resolution of the issues is feasible only if neither side has an incentive to defect unilaterally by attacking. * * * [It is easy to show that there will exist stable outcomes both sides prefer to conflict only if there is a de facto bargaining range represented by issue resolutions between $p_f - c_A$ and $p_s + c_B$. One end of the range is determined by A's value for attacking with a first strike advantage, and the other by B's.]

Notice that as p_f increases above p, and p_s decreases below it, this interval shrinks and may even disappear. Thus, first-strike advantages narrow the de facto bargaining range, while second-strike (or defensive) advantages increase it. The reason is that when first-strike advantages are large, both states must be given more from the peacetime bargain in order to allay the greater temptation of unilateral attack.

In the extreme case, [if the first-strike advantage is sufficiently large relative to the total costs of fighting,] no self-enforcing peaceful outcomes exist [$p_f - c_A$ is greater than $p_s + c_B$]. This does not mean that no bargains exist that both sides would prefer to war. Since by definition both states cannot enjoy the advantage of going first, agreements that both sides prefer to fighting are always available in principle. The problem is that under anarchy, large enough first-strike incentives (relative to cost-benefit ratios) can make all of these agreements unenforceable and incredible as bargains.

Does this prisoners' dilemma logic provide an empirically plausible explanation for war? Though I lack the space to develop the point, I would argue that first-strike and offensive advantages probably are an important factor making war more likely in a few cases, but not because they make mobilization and attack a dominant strategy, as in the extreme case above. In the pure preemptive war scenario leaders reason as follows: "The first-strike advantage is so great that regardless of how we resolve any diplomatic issues between us, one side will always want to attack the other in an effort to gain the (huge) advantage of going first." But even in July 1914, a case in which European leaders apparently held extreme views about the advantage of striking first, we do not find leaders thinking in these terms.[54] It would be rather surprising if they did, since they had all lived at peace but with the same military technology prior to July 1914. Moreover, in the crisis itself military first-strike advantages did not become a concern until quite late, and right to the end competed with significant political (and so strategic) disadvantages to striking first.[55]

Rather than completely eliminating enforceable bargains and so causing war, it seems more plausible that first-strike and offensive advantages exacerbate other causes of war by narrowing the bargaining range. If for whatever reason the issues in dispute are hard to divide up, then war will be more likely the smaller the set of enforceable agreements both sides prefer to a fight. Alternatively, the problems posed by private information and incentives to misrepresent may be more intractable when the de facto bargaining range is small.[56] For example, in 1914 large perceived first-strike advantages meant that relatively few costly signals of intent were sufficient to commit both sides to war (chiefly, for Germany/Austria and Russia). Had leaders thought defense had the advantage, the set of enforceable agreements both would have preferred would have been larger, and this may have made costly signaling less likely to have destroyed the bargaining range.

I should note that scholars have sometimes portrayed the preemptive war problem differently, assuming that neither state would want to attack unilaterally but that each would want to attack if the other was expected to also. This is a coordination problem known as "stag hunt" that would seem easily resolved by communication. At any rate, it seems farfetched to think that small numbers of states (typically dyads) would have trouble reaching the efficient solution here, if coordination were really the only problem.[57]

Preventive War as a Commitment Problem

Empirically, preventive motivations seem more prevalent and important than preemptive concerns. In his diplomatic history of Europe from 1848 to 1918, A.J.P. Taylor argued that "every war between the Great Powers [in this period] started as a preventive war, not a war of conquest."[58] In this subsection I argue that within a rationalist framework, preventive war is properly understood as arising from a commitment problem occasioned by anarchy and briefly discuss some empirical implications of this view.[59]

The theoretical framework used above is readily adapted for an analysis of the preventive war problem. Whatever their details, preventive war arguments are necessarily dynamic—they picture state leaders who think about what may happen in the future. So, we must modify the bargaining model to make it dynamic as well. Suppose state A will have the opportunity to choose the resolution of the issues in each of an infinite number of successive periods. For periods $t = 1, 2, \ldots$, state A can attempt a fait accompli to revise the status quo, choosing a demand x_t. On seeing the demand x_t, state B can either acquiesce or go to war, which state A is assumed to win with probability p_t. * * *

This model extends the one-period bargaining game considered above to an infinite-horizon case in which military power can vary over time. An important observation about the multiperiod model is that war remains a strictly inefficient outcome. It is straightforward to show that there will always exist peaceful settlements in X such that both states would prefer to see one of these settlements implemented in every period from t forward rather than go to war.[60]

The strategic dilemma is that without some third party capable of guaranteeing agreements, state A may not be able to commit itself to future foreign policy behavior that makes B prefer not to attack at some point. Consider the simple case in which A's chance of winning a war begins at p_1 and then will increase to $p_2 > p_1$ in the next period, where it will remain for all subsequent periods. Under anarchy, state A cannot commit itself not to exploit the greater bargaining leverage it will have starting in the second period. * * * [At that time, A will choose a resolution of the issues that makes state B just willing to acquiesce, given the new distribution of military power. This means that in the first period, when state B is still relatively strong, B is choosing between going to war and acquiescing to A's first period demand, which gives it some value today plus the issue equivalent of fighting a war at a disadvantage in the next period. The most state A could possibly do for B in the first period would be to cede B's most preferred outcome ($x_1 = 0$). However, if the change in relative military power is large enough, this concession can still be too small to make accepting it worthwhile for state B. B may prefer to "lock in" what it gets from war when it is relatively strong, to one period of concessions followed by a significantly worse deal when it is militarily weaker. In sum,] if B's expected decline in military power is too large relative to B's costs for war, then state A's inability to commit to restrain its foreign policy demands after it gains power makes preventive attack rational for state B.[61] Note also that A's commitment problem meshes with a parallel problem facing B. If B could commit to fight in the second period rather than accept the rising state's increased demands, then B's bargaining power would not fall in the second period, so that preventive war would be unnecessary in the first.

Several points about this rationalist analysis of preventive war are worth stressing. First, preventive war occurs here despite (and in fact partially because of) the states' agreement about relative power. Preventive war is thus another area where Blainey's argument misleads. Second, contrary to the standard formulation, the declining state attacks not because it fears being attacked in the future but because it fears the peace it will have to accept after the rival has grown stronger. To illustrate, even if Iraq had moved from Kuwait to the conquest of Saudi Arabia, invasion of the United States would not have followed. Instead, the war for Kuwait aimed to prevent the development of an oil hegemon that would have had considerable bargaining leverage due to U.S. reliance on oil.[62]

Third, while preventive war arises here from states' inability to trust each other to keep to a bargain, the lack of trust is not due to states' uncertainty about present or future motivations, as in typical security-dilemma and spiral-model accounts. In my argument, states understand each other's motivations perfectly well—there is no private information—and they further understand that each would like to avoid the costs of war—they are not ineluctably greedy. Lack of trust arises here from the situation, a structure of preferences and opportunities, that gives one party an incentive to renege. For example, regardless of expectations about Saddam Hussein's future motivation or intentions, one could predict with some confidence that decreased competition among sellers of oil would have led to higher prices. My claim is not that uncertainty about intentions is unimportant in such situations—it surely is—but that commitment and informational problems are distinct mechanisms and that a rationalist preventive war argument turns crucially on a commitment problem.

Finally, the commitment problem behind preventive war may be undermined if the determinants of military power can reliably be transferred between states. In the model, the rising state can actually have an incentive to transfer away or otherwise limit the sources of its new strength, since by doing so it may avoid being attacked. While such transfers might seem implausible from a realist perspective, the practice of "compensation" in classical balance-of-power politics may be understood in exactly these terms: states that gained territory by war or other means were expected to (and sometimes did) allow compensating gains in order to reduce the incentive for preventive war against them.[63]

Preventive motivations figured in the origins of World War I and are useful to illustrate these points. One of the reasons that German leaders were willing to run serious risks of global conflict in 1914 was that they feared the consequences of further growth of Russian military power, which appeared to them to be on a dangerous upward trajectory.[64] Even if the increase in Russian power had not led Russia to attack Austria and Germany at some point in the future—war still being a costly option—greater Russian power would have allowed St. Petersburg to pursue a more aggressive foreign policy in the Balkans and the Near East, where Austria and Russia had conflicting interests. Austrian and German leaders greatly feared the consequences of such a (pro-Slav) Russian foreign policy for the domestic stability of the Austro-Hungarian Empire, thus giving them incentives for a preventive attack on Russia.[65]

By the argument made above, the states should in principle have had incentives to cut a multiperiod deal both sides would have preferred to preventive war. For example, fearing preventive attack by Austria and Germany, Russian leaders might have wished to have committed themselves not to push so hard in the Balkans as to endanger the Dual Monarchy. But such a deal would be so obviously unenforceable as to not be worth proposing.

Leaving aside the serious monitoring difficulties, once Russia had become stronger militarily, Austria would have no choice but to acquiesce to a somewhat more aggressive Russian policy in the Balkans. And so Russia would be drawn to pursue it, regardless of its overall motivation or desire for conquest of Austria-Hungary.

While German leaders in July 1914 were willing to accept a very serious risk that Russia might go to war in support of Serbia, they seem to have hoped at the start of the crisis that Russia would accept the Austrian demarche.[66] Thus, it is hard to argue that the preventive logic itself produced the war. Rather, as is probably true for other cases in which these concerns appear, the preventive logic may have made war more likely in combination with other causes, such as private information, by making Berlin much more willing to risk war.[67] How preventive concerns impinge on international bargaining with private information is an important topic for future research.

Commitment, Strategic Territory, and the Problem of Appeasement

The objects over which states bargain frequently are themselves sources of military power. Territory is the most important example, since it may provide economic resources that can be used for the military or be strategically located, meaning that its control greatly increases a state's chances for successful attack or defense. Territory is probably also the main issue over which states fight wars.[68]

In international bargaining on issues with this property, a commitment problem can operate that makes mutually preferable negotiated solutions unattainable. The problem is similar to that underlying preventive war. Here, both sides might prefer some package of territorial concessions to a fight, but if the territory in question is strategically vital or economically important, its transfer could radically increase one side's future bargaining leverage (think of the Golan Heights). In principle, one state might prefer war to the status quo but be unable to commit not to exploit the large increase in bargaining leverage it would gain from limited territorial concessions. Thus the other state might prefer war to limited concessions (appeasement), so it might appear that the issues in dispute were indivisible. But the underlying cause of war in this instance is not indivisibility per se but rather the inability of states to make credible commitments under anarchy.[69]

As an example, the 1939 Winter War between Finland and the Soviet Union followed on the refusal of the Finnish government to cede some tiny islands in the Gulf of Finland that Stalin seems to have viewed as necessary for the defense of Leningrad in the event of a European war. One of the main reasons the Finns were so reluctant to grant these concessions was that they believed they could not trust Stalin not to use these advantages to pressure Finland for more in the future. So it is possible that Stalin's inability to commit himself not to attempt to carry out in Finland the program he had just applied in the Baltic states may have led or contributed to a costly war both sides clearly wished to avoid.[70]

Conclusion

The article has developed two major claims. First, under broad conditions the fact that fighting is costly and risky implies that there should exist negotiated agreements that rationally led states in dispute would prefer to war. This claim runs directly counter to the conventional view that rational states can and often do face a situation of deadlock, in which war occurs because no mutually preferable bargain exists.

Second, essentially two mechanisms, or causal logics, explain why rationally led states are sometimes unable to locate or agree on such a bargain:

(1) the combination of private information about resolve or capability and incentives to misrepresent these, and (2) states' inability, in specific circumstances, to commit to uphold a deal. Historical examples were intended to suggest that both mechanisms can claim empirical relevance.

I conclude by anticipating two criticisms. First, I am not saying that explanations for war based on irrationality or "pathological" domestic politics are less empirically relevant. Doubtless they are important, but we cannot say how so or in what measure if we have not clearly specified the causal mechanisms making for war in the "ideal" case of rational unitary states. In fact, a better understanding of what the assumption of rationality really implies for explaining war may actually raise our estimate of the importance of particular irrational and second-image factors.

For example, once the distinction is made clear, bounded rationality may appear a more important cause of disagreements about relative power than private information about military capabilities. If private information about capabilities was often a major factor influencing the odds of victory, then we would expect rational leaders to update their war estimates during international crises; a tough bargaining stand by an adversary would signal that the adversary was militarily stronger than expected. Diplomatic records should then contain evidence of leaders reasoning as follows: "The fact that the other side is not backing down means that we are probably less likely to win at war than we initially thought." I do not know of a single clear instance of this sort of updating in any international crisis, even though updating about an opponent's resolve, or willingness to fight, is very common.

Second, one might argue that since both anarchy and private information plus incentives to misrepresent are constant features of international politics, neither can explain why states fail to strike a bargain preferable to war in one instance but not another. This argument is correct. But the task of specifying the causal mechanisms that explain the occurrence of war must precede the identification of factors that lead the mechanisms to produce one outcome rather than another in particular settings. That is, specific models in which commitment or information problems operate allow one to analyze how different variables (such as power shifts and cost-benefit ratios in the preventive war model) make for war in some cases rather than others.

This is the sense in which these two general mechanisms provide the foundations for a coherent rationalist or neorealist theory of war. A neorealist explanation for war shows how war could occur given the assumption of rational and unitary ("billiard ball") states, the assumption made throughout this article. Consider any particular factor argued in the literature to be a cause of war under this assumption—for example, a failure to balance power, offensive advantages, multipolarity, or shifts in relative power. My claim is that showing how any such factor could cause war between rational states requires showing how the factor can occasion an unresolvable commitment or information problem in specific empirical circumstances. Short of this, the central puzzle posed by war, its costs, has not been addressed.

NOTES

1. Of course, arguments of the second sort may and often do presume rational behavior by individual leaders; that is, war may be rational for civilian or military leaders if they will enjoy various benefits of war without suffering costs imposed on the population. While I believe that "second-image" mechanisms of this sort are very important empirically, I do not explore them here. A more accurate label for the subject of the article might be "rational unitary-actor explanations," but this is cumbersome.

2. For the founding work of neorealism, see Kenneth Waltz, *Theory of International Politics* (Reading, Mass.: Addison-Wesley, 1979). For examples of theorizing along these lines, see Robert Jervis, "Cooperation Under the Security Dilemma," *World Politics* 30

(January 1978), pp. 167–214; Stephen Walt, *The Origins of Alliances* (Ithaca, N.Y.: Cornell University Press, 1987); John J. Mearsheimer, "Back to the Future: Instability in Europe After the Cold War," *International Security* 15 (Summer 1990), pp. 5–56; and Charles Glaser, "Realists as Optimists: Cooperation as Self-Help," *International Security* 19 (Winter 1994/95), pp. 50–90.

3. The sense of "mechanism" is similar to that proposed by Elster, although somewhat broader. See Jon Elster, *Political Psychology* (Cambridge: Cambridge University Press, 1993), pp. 1–7; and Jon Elster, *Nuts and Bolts for the Social Sciences* (Cambridge: Cambridge University Press, 1989), chap. 1.

4. For an influential example of this common assumption see Glenn Snyder and Paul Diesing, *Conflict among Nations* (Princeton, N.J.: Princeton University Press, 1977).

5. See, for examples, Geoffry Blainey, *The Causes of War* (New York: Free Press, 1973); Michael Howard, *The Causes of Wars* (Cambridge, Mass.: Harvard University Press, 1983), especially chap. 1; and Arthur Stein, *Why Nations Cooperate: Circumstance and Choice in International Relations* (Ithaca, N.Y.: Cornell University Press, 1990), pp. 60–64. Even the case of World War I is contested; an important historical school argues that this was a wanted war. See Fritz Fisher, *Germany's Aims in the First World War* (New York: Norton, 1967).

6. The quotation is drawn from Kenneth Waltz, *Man, the State, and War: A Theoretical Analysis* (New York: Columbia University Press, 1959), p. 188.

7. For a careful analysis and critique of this standard argument on the difference between the international and domestic arenas, see R. Harrison Wagner, "The Causes of Peace," in Roy A. Licklider, ed., *Stopping the Killing: How Civil Wars End* (New York: New York University Press, 1993), pp. 235–68 and especially pp. 251–57.

8. See John H. Herz, "Idealist Internationalism and the Security Dilemma," *World Politics* 2 (January 1950), pp. 157–80; and Jervis, "Cooperation Under the Security Dilemma." Anarchy is implicated in the

security dilemma externality by the following logic: but for anarchy, states could commit to use weapons only for nonthreatening, defensive purposes.

9. Jervis, "Cooperation under the Security Dilemma."

10. For an analysis of the security dilemma that takes into account signaling, see Andrew Kydd, "The Security Dilemma, Game Theory, and World War I," paper presented at the annual meeting of the American Political Science Association, Washington, D.C., 2–5 September 1993.

11. The most developed exception I know of is found in Stephen Van Evera, "Causes of War," Ph.D. diss., University of California, Berkeley, 1984, pp. 61–64.

12. See Bruce Bueno de Mesquita, *The War Trap* (New Haven, Conn.: Yale University Press, 1981), and "The War Trap Revisited: A Revised Expected Utility Model," *American Political Science Review* 79 (March 1985), pp. 157–76. For a generalization that introduces the idea of a bargaining range, see James D. Morrow, "A Continuous-Outcome Expected Utility Theory of War," *Journal of Conflict Resolution* 29 (September 1985), pp. 473–502. Informal versions of the expected utility argument are everywhere. For example, Waltz's statement that "A state will use force to attain its goals if, after assessing the prospects for success, it values those goals more than it values the pleasures of peace" appears in different ways in a great many works on war. See Waltz, *Man, the State, and War,* p. 60.

13. Let the states' utilities for the outcome $x \in X$ be $u_A(x)$ and $u_B(1-x)$, and assume for now that $u_A(\cdot)$ and $u_B(\cdot)$ are continuous, increasing, and weakly concave (that is, risk-neutral or risk-averse). Without losing any generality, we can set $u_i(1)=1$ and $u_i(0)=0$ for both states ($i=A, B$).

14. See, for classic examples, Thucydides, *The Peloponnesian War* (New York: Modern Library, 1951), pp. 45 and 48; and Carl von Clausewitz, *On War* (Princeton, N.J.: Princeton University Press, 1984), p. 85.

15. Bueno de Mesquita, *The War Trap.*

16. Note that in this formulation the terms c_A and c_B capture not only the states' values for the costs of war but also the value they place on winning or losing on the issues at stake. That is, c_A reflects state A's costs for war relative to any possible benefits. For example, if the two states see little to gain from winning a war against each other, then c_A and c_B would be large even if neither side expected to suffer much damage in a war.

17. On the theory of bargaining with outside options, see Martin J. Osborne and Ariel Rubinstein, *Bargaining and Markets* (New York: Academic Press, 1990), chap. 3; Motty Perry, "An Example of Price Formation in Bilateral Situations," *Econometrica* 50 (March 1986), pp. 313–21; and Robert Powell, "Bargaining in the Shadow of Power" (University of California, Berkeley, 1993, mimeographed). See also the analyses in R. Harrison Wagner, "Peace, War, and the Balance of Power," *American Political Science Review* 88 (September 1994), pp. 593–607; and Wagner, "The Causes of Peace."

18. See, for example, Evan Luard, *War in International Society* (New Haven, Conn.: Yale University Press, 1992), p. 191. Schroeder notes that "patronage, bribes, and corruption" were "a major element" of eighteenth-century international relations. See Paul Schroeder, *The Transformation of European Politics, 1763–1848* (Oxford: Oxford University Press, 1994), p. 579.

19. On Cuba, see Ernest May, *Imperial Democracy* (New York: Harper and Row, 1961), pp. 149–50. On the Louisiana Purchase, military threats raised in the U.S. Senate apparently made Napoleon more eager to negotiate the sale. See E. Wilson Lyon, *Louisiana in French Diplomacy* (Norman: University of Oklahoma Press, 1934), pp. 179 and 214ff.

20. Diego Gambetta, *The Sicilian Mafia: The Business of Private Protection* (Cambridge, Mass.: Harvard University Press, 1993), p. 214.

21. In one of the only articles on this problem, Morrow proposes a private information explanation for states' failures to link issues in many disputes. See James D. Morrow, "Signaling Difficulties with Linkage in Crisis Bargaining," *International Studies Quarterly* 36 (June 1992), pp. 153–72.

22. See Jack Levy, "The Causes of War: A Review of Theories and Evidence," in Philip E. Tetlock et al.,

eds., *Behavior, Society, and Nuclear War,* vol. 1 (Oxford: Oxford University Press, 1989), pp. 209–333. Recent work using limited-information game theory to analyze crisis bargaining places the strategic consequences of private information at the center of the analysis. See, for examples, Bruce Bueno de Mesquita and David Lalman, *War and Reason* (New Haven, Conn.: Yale University Press, 1992); James D. Fearon, "Domestic Political Audiences and the Escalation of International Disputes," *American Political Science Review* 88 (September 1994), pp. 577–92; James D. Morrow, "Capabilities, Uncertainty, and Resolve: A Limited Information Model of Crisis Bargaining," *American Journal of Political Science* 33 (November 1989), pp. 941–72; Barry Nalebuff, "Brinksmanship and Nuclear Deterrence: The Neutrality of Escalation," *Conflict Management and Peace Science* 9 (Spring 1986), pp. 19–30; and Robert Powell, *Nuclear Deterrence Theory: The Problem of Credibility* (Cambridge: Cambridge University Press, 1990).

23. Blainey, *The Causes of War,* p. 246.

24. Ibid., p. 54. Blainey also blames patriotic and nationalistic fervor, leaders' (irrational) tendency to surround themselves with yes-men, and crowd psychology.

25. See Ralph K. White, *Nobody Wanted War: Misperception in Vietnam and Other Wars* (New York: Doubleday/Anchor), chap. 7; Blainey, *The Causes of War,* p. 54; and Richard Ned Lebow, *Between Peace and War: The Nature of International Crises* (Baltimore, Md.: Johns Hopkins University Press, 1981), p. 247.

26. John C. Harsanyi, "Games with Incomplete Information Played by 'Bayesian' Players, Part III," *Management Science* 14 (March 1968), pp. 486–502.

27. Aumann observed an interesting implication of this doctrine: genuinely rational agents cannot "agree to disagree," in the sense that it cannot be commonly known that they are rational and that they hold different estimates of the likelihood of some uncertain event. See Robert Aumann, "Agreeing to Disagree," *The Annals of Statistics* 4 (November 1976), pp. 1236–39. Emerson Niou, Peter Ordeshook, and Gregory Rose note that this implies that rational states cannot agree to disagree about the probability that one or the other would win in a war in *The Balance of Power: Stability in the International System* (Cambridge: Cambridge University Press, 1989), p. 59.

28. On bounded rationality, see Herbert A. Simon, "A Behavioral Model of Rational Choice," *Quarterly Journal of Economics* 69 (February 1955), pp. 99–118.

29. This analysis runs exactly parallel to work in law and economics on pretrial bargaining in legal disputes. Early studies explained costly litigation as resulting from divergent expectations about the likely trial outcome, while in more recent work such expectations derive from private information about the strength of one's case. For a review and references, see Robert D. Cooter and Daniel L. Rubinfeld, "Economic Analysis of Legal Disputes and Their Resolution," *Journal of Economic Literature* 27 (September 1989), pp. 1067–97.

30. Blainey, *The Causes of War.*

31. This take-it-or-leave-it model of international bargaining is proposed and analyzed under conditions of both complete and incomplete information in James D. Fearon, "Threats to Use Force: The Role of Costly Signals in International Crises," Ph.D. diss., University of California, Berkeley, 1992, chap. 1. Similar results for more elaborate bargaining structures are given in my own work in progress. See James D. Fearon, "Game-Theoretic Models of International Bargaining: An Overview," University of Chicago, 1995. Powell has analyzed an alternative model in which both sides must agree if the status quo is to be revised. See Powell, "Bargaining in the Shadow of Power."

32. For examples and discussion on this point, see Fearon, "Threats to Use Force," chap. 3.

33. * * * Cheap talk announcements can affect outcomes in some bargaining contexts. For an example from economics, see Joseph Farrell and Robert Gibbons, "Cheap Talk Can Matter in Bargaining," *Journal of Economic Theory* 48 (June 1989), pp. 221–37. These authors show how cheap talk might credibly signal a

willingness to negotiate seriously that then affects subsequent terms of trade. For an example from international relations, see James D. Morrow, "Modeling the Forms of International Cooperation: Distribution Versus Information," *International Organization* 48 (Summer 1994), pp. 387–423.

34. The conclusion is likewise altered if the possibility of repeated interactions in sufficiently similar contexts is great enough that reputation building can be supported.

35. On signaling costs in crises and audience costs in particular, see Fearon, "Threats to Use Force," and "Domestic Political Audiences and the Escalation of International Disputes." For an excellent analysis of international signaling in general, see Robert Jervis, *The Logic of Images in International Relations* (Princeton, N.J.: Princeton University Press, 1970).

36. For developed models that make this point, see James Fearon, "Deterrence and the Spiral Model: The Role of Costly Signals in Crisis Bargaining," paper presented at the annual meeting of the American Political Science Association, 30 August–2 September 1990, San Francisco, Calif.; Fearon, "Domestic Political Audiences and the Escalation of International Disputes"; Morrow, "Capabilities, Uncertainty, and Resolve"; Nalebuff, "Brinkmanship and Nuclear Deterrence"; and Powell, *Nuclear Deterrence Theory*.

37. Luigi Albertini, *The Origins of the War of 1914,* vol. 2 (London: Oxford University Press, 1953), pp. 183–87.

38. Ibid., p. 187.

39. Ibid., p. 158. For the full text of the cable, see Karl Kautsky, comp., *German Documents Relating to the Outbreak of the World War* (New York: Oxford University Press, 1924), doc. no. 71, p. 130.

40. Konrad Jarausch, "The Illusion of Limited War: Chancellor Bethmann Hollweg's Calculated Risk," *Central European History* 2 (March 1969), pp. 48–76. The quotation is drawn from p. 65.

41. See L. C. F. Turner, *Origins of the First World War* (New York: Norton, 1970), p. 101; and Jarausch, "The Illusion of Limited War," p. 63. Trachtenberg writes that "one of Bethmann's basic goals was for

Germany to avoid coming across as the aggressor." See Marc Trachtenberg, *History and Strategy* (Princeton, N.J.: Princeton University Press, 1991), p. 90.

42. Albertini concludes that "on the evening of the 27th all the Chancellor sought to do was to throw dust in the eyes of Grey and lead him to believe that Berlin was seriously trying to avert a conflict, that if war broke out it would be Russia's fault and that England could therefore remain neutral." See Albertini, *The Origins of the War of 1914,* vol. 1, pp. 444–45. See also Turner, *Origins of the First World War,* p. 99.

43. See J. A. White, *The Diplomacy of the Russo–Japanese War* (Princeton, N.J.: Princeton University Press, 1964), pp. 142–43; and Ian Nish, *The Origins of the Russo–Japanese War* (London: Longman, 1985), pp. 241–42.

44. J. N. Westwood, *Russia against Japan, 1904–5: A New Look at the Russo–Japanese War* (Albany: State University of New York Press, 1986), p. 22. Estimates varied within the Japanese leadership, but with the exception of junior-level officers, few seem to have been highly confident of victory. For example, as the decision for war was taken the Japanese navy requested a two-week delay to allow it to even the odds at sea. See Nish, *The Origins of the Russo–Japanese War,* pp. 197–200 and 206–7.

45. See, for example, David Walder, *The Short Victorious War: The Russo–Japanese Conflict, 1904–5* (London: Hutchinson, 1973), pp. 53–56; and Nish, *The Origins of the Russo–Japanese War,* p. 253.

46. See White, *The Diplomacy of the Russo–Japanese War,* chaps. 6–8; Nish, *The Origins of the Russo–Japanese War,* p. 241; and Lebow, *Between Peace and War,* pp. 244–46.

47. White, *The Diplomacy of the Russo–Japanese War,* p. 139. Nish writes that "many Russians certainly took a view of [the Japanese military] which was derisory in comparison with themselves. It may be that this derived from a deliberate policy of secrecy and concealment which the Japanese army applied because of the historic coolness between the two countries." See Nish, *The Origins of the Russo–Japanese War,* p. 241.

48. The British were the major exception, who as recent allies of Japan had better knowledge of its capabilities and level of organization. See Nish, *The Origins of the Russo–Japanese War*, p. 241.

49. See, for example, William Langer, "The Origins of the Russo–Japanese War," in Carl Schorske and Elizabeth Schorske, eds., *Explorations in Crisis* (Cambridge, Mass.: Harvard University Press, 1969), p. 44.

50. For some examples, see Fearon, "Threats to Use Force," chap. 3. For a formal version of reputational dynamics due to private information, see Barry Nalebuff, "Rational Deterrence in an Imperfect World," *World Politics* 43 (April 1991), pp. 313–35.

51. See, for examples, Robert Jervis, *Perception and Misperception in International Politics* (Princeton, N.J.: Princeton University Press, 1976), pp. 62–67; Barry Posen, *The Sources of Military Doctrine* (Ithaca, N.Y.: Cornell University Press, 1984), pp. 16–17; and Charles Glaser, "The Political Consequences of Military Strategy," *World Politics* 44 (July 1992), p. 506.

52. For dynamic game models that demonstrate this, see Robert Powell, "Absolute and Relative Gains in International Relations Theory," *American Political Science Review* 85 (December 1991), pp. 1303–20; and James D. Fearon, "Cooperation and Bargaining Under Anarchy," (University of Chicago, 1994, mimeographed). On tit-for-tat and the impact of the shadow of the future, see Robert Axelrod, *The Evolution of Cooperation* (New York: Basic Books, 1984); and Kenneth Oye, ed., *Cooperation under Anarchy* (Princeton, N.J.: Princeton University Press, 1986).

53. This argument about military variance runs counter to the usual hypothesis that offensive advantages foster war. For a discussion and an empirical assessment, see James D. Fearon, "Offensive Advantages and War since 1648," paper presented at the annual meeting of the International Studies Association, 21–25 February 1995. On the offense–defense balance and war, see Jervis, "Cooperation under the Security Dilemma"; and Van Evera, "Causes of War," chap. 3.

54. For the argument about leaders' views on first-strike advantages in 1914, see Stephen Van Evera, "The Cult of the Offensive and the Origins of the First World War," *International Security* 9 (Summer 1984), pp. 58–107.

55. See, for example, Trachtenberg, *History and Strategy*, p. 90.

56. This is suggested by results in Roger Myerson and Mark Satterthwaite, "Efficient Mechanisms for Bilateral Trading," *Journal of Economic Theory* 29 (April 1983), pp. 265–81.

57. Schelling suggested that efficient coordination in stag hunt-like preemption problems might be prevented by a rational dynamic of "reciprocal fear of surprise attack." See Thomas Schelling, *The Strategy of Conflict* (Cambridge, Mass.: Harvard University Press, 1960), chap. 9. Powell has argued that no such dynamic exists between rational adversaries. See Robert Powell, "Crisis Stability in the Nuclear Age," *American Political Science Review* 83 (March 1989), pp. 61–76.

58. Taylor, *The Struggle for Mastery in Europe, 1848–1918* (London: Oxford University Press, 1954), p. 166. Carr held a similar view: "The most serious wars are fought in order to make one's own country militarily stronger or, more often, to prevent another country from becoming militarily stronger." See E. H. Carr, *The Twenty Years' Crisis, 1919–1939* (New York: Harper and Row, 1964), pp. 111–12.

59. To my knowledge, Van Evera is the only scholar whose treatment of preventive war analyzes at some length how issues of credible commitment intervene. The issue is raised by both Snyder and Levy. See Van Evera, "Causes of War," pp. 62–64; Jack Snyder, "Perceptions of the Security Dilemma in 1914," in Robert Jervis, Richard Ned Lebow, and Janice Gross Stein, eds., *Psychology and Deterrence* (Baltimore, Md.: Johns Hopkins University Press, 1985), p. 160; and Jack Levy, "Declining Power and the Preventive Motivation for War," *World Politics* 40 (October 1987), p. 96.

60. If the states go to war in period t, expected payoffs from period t on are $(p_t/(1-\delta)) - c_A$ for state A and $((1-p_t)/(1-\delta)) - c_B$ for state B where δ is the time discount factor that both states apply to payoffs to be received in the next period.

61. The formal condition for preventive war is δ
$p_2 - p_1 > c_B (1 - \delta)^2$.

62. According to Hiro, President Bush's main concern at the first National Security Council meeting following the invasion of Kuwait was the potential increase in Iraq's economic leverage and its likely influence on an "already gloomy" U.S. economy. See Dilip Hiro, *Desert Shield to Desert Storm: The Second Gulf War* (London: Harper-Collins, 1992), p. 108.

63. On compensation, see Edward V. Gulick, *Europe's Classical Balance of Power* (New York: Norton, 1955), pp. 70–72; and Paul W. Schroeder, *The Transformation of European Politics, 1763–1848*, pp. 6–7.

64. See Trachtenberg, *History and Strategy*, pp. 56–59; Albertini, *The Origins of the War of 1914*, vol. 2, pp. 129–30; Turner, *Origins of the First World War*, chap. 4; James Joll, *The Origins of the First World War* (London: Longman, 1984), p. 87; and Van Evera, "The Cult of the Offensive and the Origins of the First World War," pp. 79–85.

65. Samuel Williamson, "The Origins of World War I," *Journal of Interdisciplinary History* (Spring 1988), pp. 795–818 and pp. 797–805 in particular; and D. C. B. Lieven, *Russia and the Origins of the First World War* (New York: St. Martins, 1983), pp. 38–49.

66. Jack S. Levy, "Preferences, Constraints, and Choices in July 1914," *International Security* 15 (Winter 1990/91), pp. 234–36.

67. Levy argues that preventive considerations are rarely themselves sufficient to cause war. See Levy, "Declining Power and the Preventive Motivation for War."

68. See, for example, Kalevi J. Holsti, *Peace and War: Armed Conflicts and International Order 1648–1989* (Cambridge: Cambridge University Press, 1991); and John Vasquez, *The War Puzzle* (Cambridge: Cambridge University Press, 1993).

69. The argument is formalized in work in progress by the author, where it is shown that the conditions under which war will occur are restrictive: the states must be unable to continuously adjust the odds of victory by dividing up and trading the land. In other words, the smallest feasible territorial transfer must produce a discontinuously large change in a state's military chances for war to be possible. See also Wagner, "Peace, War, and the Balance of Power," p. 598, on this commitment problem.

70. See Max Jakobson, *The Diplomacy of the Winter War: An Account of the Russo-Finnish Conflict, 1939–1940* (Cambridge, Mass.: Harvard University Press, 1961), pp. 135–39; and Van Evera, "Causes of War," p. 63. Private information and incentives to misrepresent also caused problems in the bargaining here. See Fearon, "Threats to Use Force," chap. 3.

Barry R. Posen

A NUCLEAR-ARMED IRAN
A Difficult but Not Impossible Policy Problem

Introduction

Iran's nuclear energy research and development efforts seem on course to achieve an ability to produce highly enriched uranium, the key element of a nuclear weapon. While the capability itself would not be a violation of the Nuclear Non-Proliferation Treaty (NPT) if it were under the full scope safeguards of the International Atomic Energy Agency (IAEA), Iran's deceptive behavior in the development of this technology, as well as the flimsy economic arguments Iran has used to justify this capability, have produced broad international opposition to the program. Many reasonably fear that Iran's actual purpose is to produce nuclear weapons, though there is no definite proof that it has decided to do so. It should be acknowledged that Iran could insist on its right to enrich uranium for power reactors, but refrain from producing nuclear weapons. France, Germany, and the United Kingdom, acting under the auspices of the European Union, and with the support of the United States, have negotiated intensively with Iran since 2003 to discourage further Iranian nuclear enrichment progress; the United Nations Security Council demanded that Iran suspend enrichment and implement other important arms control measures with Resolution 1696 in July 2006. Nevertheless diplomacy has thus far been

unsuccessful, and there is no guarantee of future success.

If negotiations fail, interested powers such as the United States, the European Union, and Iran's neighbors will face three alternatives: (1) they could move from diplomacy to economic and political coercion; (2) one or more states (most probably the United States or Israel) could launch a preventive attack to erode or destroy the Iranian nuclear program; or (3) these powers could develop strategies of containment and deterrence to coexist with a nuclear-armed Iran—if Iran achieves weapons capability.

The primary purpose of this [discussion] is to address the third option—to spell out a strategy of containment and deterrence and show how it could work. I systematically review the standard objections to this strategy, and explain why they are misplaced. Summarizing the other options, I then argue that a containment and deterrence strategy is more likely to achieve U.S. strategic goals, and do so at lower risks and costs. Finally, I briefly review the proliferation risks that would arise from an Iranian nuclear program, and argue that these risks can be reduced by a deterrence and containment strategy. That said, containment of a nuclear-armed Iran is not the preferred outcome. It would be better if diplomacy were to succeed. Thus, one implication of this analysis is that the United States and its allies should review their current diplomatic approach to Iran and try to devise a more promising political strategy.

Barry R. Posen, "A Nuclear-Armed Iran: A Difficult but Not Impossible Policy Problem" (New York: Century Foundation, 2006).

For many reasons, it would be better if Iran had neither nuclear weapons, nor the enabling technologies that would permit it to build nuclear weapons:

- Neither nuclear energy nor nuclear weapons are risk-free technologies—new civil and military nuclear powers run the risks of any novice. These include environmental problems, equipment failures, and unsafe or insecure weapons storage.
- It is natural for the nonnuclear states in the region to fear a nuclear Iran. These fears may cause countermeasures that are fraught with danger—including national nuclear energy or weapons programs of their own—which also would run "novice" risks.
- As other states try to acquire nuclear weapons, they may inadvertently threaten each other, setting off new security competitions.
- Iran and any of its neighbors that chose to deploy nuclear weapons may have problems developing a secure basing method, which could tempt them to adopt "hair trigger," day-to-day alert postures, which in turn could raise the risks of accidental war or preemptive war.
- Iran may be emboldened by its possession of nuclear weapons, and could threaten the security of regional or distant powers.

These are all valid concerns, which should make even Iran wary of nuclear weaponry. These risks have prompted the international diplomatic efforts to induce Iran to refrain from the enrichment of uranium (or the reprocessing of plutonium). If these efforts fail, however, concerned states will need to choose from the three remaining alternative policies—nonmilitary coercion mainly through sanctions, preventive military strikes, or containment and deterrence.

Economic Coercion

Though economic coercion should be attempted if the current round of diplomacy fails, this seems unlikely to work unless it is combined with a new set of incentives. First, it is improbable that a particularly strong international sanctions regime can be organized against Iran. Russia, China, and even many European states fear that the initiation of a strong sanctions policy, blessed by the UN, is the first step on the road to war. Sanctions may not change Iranian behavior, but they will have further committed the international community to do something about Iran's program. Some states also will oppose a strong sanctions policy because they profit from their relationships with Iran, due to its energy resources, or expect to profit even more if they help shield Iran from stern measures. Finally, given tight oil markets and high prices, most states would not support a sanctions regime that embargoed the export of Iranian oil.[1]

Second, though Iran is not a wealthy country, it has a relatively well-rounded economy. Aside from its obvious strengths in oil and gas production, Iran is endowed with abundant raw materials and agricultural land, and has a moderately well developed industrial sector. If a sanctions regime did not close off Iran's oil exports, it seems very likely that, with its own endowments and the cash it raises from energy exports, it could weather any plausible sanctions regime.[2]

If the threat of international economic sanctions were accompanied by more focused diplomacy, it might find more support and be more credible. In particular, the United States would need to assure Iran that it has abandoned any hopes to overthrow the current regime. Some have suggested a "grand bargain" in which the United States would offer Iran a security guarantee, an end to sanctions, and the normalization of diplomatic relations, in exchange for major concessions on Iran's nuclear program and an end to support for terrorism.[3] Such a negotiating offer might reduce the concerns of fence sitters such as Russia and China, who fear that the ultimate U.S. objective is regime change, and that the United States intends to leverage ineffective sanctions into an argument for war. The offer of a grand bargain also would put Iran in a difficult position, insofar as declining the offer would be tantamount to admitting its ambitions to produce a nuclear weapon. Moreover, if such a negotiating gambit fails, and the United States turns to a strategy of containment, states in the region will be even more likely to want U.S. assistance, and will more easily be able to portray a strengthened relationship with the United States as an essential counter to Iranian ambitions.

Preventive Military Action

A military attack on Iran's nuclear infrastructure could set back the program, but probably not prevent its recovery, unless the attack were somehow to topple the Iranian government and bring a very different ruling group to power. A military strike carries significant political and military risks. If time bought by setting back the Iranian program through military strikes would be used to good effect—that is, if in the interim other disputes in which Iran is directly or indirectly involved were solved, or if Iran became a liberal-democratic mirror-image of a Western democracy—a preventive attack might look attractive. But there is no reason to believe that this will be the case, and the reverse is more probable. Small or large attacks on Iran will inject energy into Persian nationalism, strengthen the regime's argument that the West is a threat, and leave Iran with a grudge that it may express by deepening or initiating relationships with other states and groups hostile to U.S. purposes. Even regional states with something to fear from a nuclear armed Iran probably would not welcome a preventive attack, simply because the region is already so roiled with violence, much of it attributed to mistaken U.S. policies.

Published assessments of possible attacks on Iran's nuclear infrastructure necessarily involve some speculation. There are nuclear facilities that we have good public information about, but there is likely a great deal of information that is known by Western intelligence agencies that has not leaked into the public domain, and more information in Iran that has not leaked to anyone. Poor intelligence alone is one factor that might hinder the success of these operations. That said, three types of attack, of increasing strength, have been suggested.

First, some have considered very limited attacks on what seem to be critical nodes in a nuclear weapons production chain—especially Iran's plants at Isfahan to produce uranium hexafluoride gas and its facilities at Natanz to process this gas through centrifuges in order to enrich its fissionable material content. One careful analysis suggests that even Israeli fighter-bombers, armed with precision guided weapons Israel is known to possess, could destroy these facilities, presuming that they could refuel from aerial tankers en route, and fly over Jordan and Iraq, or Saudi Arabia, or Turkey.[4] For the United States, destroying these facilities would be a trivial matter. That said, the rest of the Iranian nuclear research and development effort would survive, and it seems likely that failing a change of government, Iran would persevere, and do so in a way that leaves the program less vulnerable. One might believe that a limited attack, however, would produce a relatively modest Iranian military response.

Second, some have suggested that one should try for maximum damage to the entire Iranian nuclear program. A recent analysis suggests that an attack on the Iranian nuclear infrastructure would involve four hundred aim points. The Pentagon's own intelligence would produce an even bigger target set. The United States easily could strike four hundred aim points with precision guided munitions in a single night.[5] Though no one could guarantee that this would be the end of

Iran's program, it seems likely that the setback would be far greater than the limited attack on two critical nodes. An Iranian regime might determine that an attack of this size needed to be answered with a forceful response. The regime would look weak regionally, and domestically, if it simply accepted such an attack without a response. The regime reasonably could fear that failure to respond simply would invite further attacks, because the United States would doubt Iran's capability and will. Insofar as the United States has made plain that it wants to overthrow the Iranian regime, it is unlikely that Iran would view such a large attack as the final move.

Finally, precisely because civilian and military strategists in the Bush administration seem to have accepted the preceding logic, rumors have surfaced of even larger attack plans. To the target list associated with Iran's nuclear infrastructure, would be added an array of conventional targets—including naval bases, airfields, surface-to-air missile sites, surface-to-surface missiles sites, and so on. During the first three nights of the 1991 Gulf War, coalition aircraft struck nearly three thousand targets of this kind.[6] Such attacks would have the purpose of forestalling an Iranian military retaliation against countries as close as Kuwait and as distant as Israel, U.S. forces in the region including those in Iraq, and oil tanker routes. Attacks of this size may also have the purpose of weakening the Iranian regime, though the precise mechanism is unclear, insofar as attacks of this kind have typically strengthened rather than weakened national cohesion and public support of governments, at least in the first instance. Though such an attack may succeed in reducing Iran's retaliatory options, it is implausible that it can reduce them to zero. U.S. forces in Iraq, and their line of communication, which runs through Shia populated areas where Iran has considerable influence, are quite vulnerable to tactical rocket and commando attacks that U.S. air strikes probably cannot prevent.[7] Beyond these significant immediate local costs, the United States attack will

become a significant factor in future Iranian politics, discrediting any political faction that seems remotely associated with the United States or its purposes, and providing a potent political/ideological rationale for violence against the United States and its friends for many years to come.

Given that the odds of nonmilitary coercion achieving a success seem low, and the possible costs of a significant, if partly successful, large military operation seem high, it is reasonable to consider the remaining alternative systematically—containment and deterrence of a nuclear-armed Iran.

"Grand Strategy"—Iran and the United States

Before considering the consequences of a nuclear-armed Iran for both the stability of the Middle East and Persian Gulf region and the security interests of the United States, one ought to consider the objectives that an Iranian nuclear force might be meant to serve. This requires some speculation about Iran's own "grand strategy."

Given that Iran is the most populous and economically developed state in the Persian Gulf area, a realist expects it to have ambitions to expand its power and influence in the region. Indeed, it is reasonable to expect that revolutionary Iran, like Iran under the Shah, has pretensions to regional hegemony. This is a general prediction, however, and much depends on what this means to Iran. For example, though many analysts do believe Iran has hegemonic ambitions, they usually couch this in cultural and political terms, not military terms.[8] Iran is active in expanding its influence, especially among Shia Arab populations in Iraq, in the Gulf region, and in Lebanon. Though Iran does have some disputes about islands, water rights, waterways, and coastal zones, according to the Central Intelligence Agency it has no major territorial claims beyond its borders.[9] The

United States is no doubt perceived as an obstacle to Iran's regional ambitions. Iran surely would like to reduce the United States presence in the Gulf region, especially since the Bush administration adopted regime change in Iran as an objective.

Iran uses military force with some calculation, to increase the costs to others who might obstruct its goals, rather than to remove obstacles directly. Iran is not shy about using military assistance to nonstate actors as a way to discomfit those it defines as enemies, such as the United States and Israel. Iran sees some interest in maintaining a plausible capability to disrupt the flow of oil from the Persian Gulf, by leveraging its own limited naval capacity and its geographic control of one side of the narrow Strait of Hormuz to create a threat to Western economies. This threat is probably dissuasive—a retaliatory capability, as Iran cannot disrupt the flow of oil out of the Gulf without losing its own ability to export, which is vital to its economy. On the whole, Iran seems deliberate, unafraid to use violence in limited ways, but cautious as it tries to increase its influence and reduce that of others. The main exception to this description is its inflammatory rhetoric about Israel. I hypothesize, however, that much of this rhetoric is instrumental. Iran faces a major obstacle in expanding its influence—it is a Persian state amidst Arabs, and a Shia state amidst Sunnis. These differences are important and cause most Arab regimes to mistrust Iran. Iran may be using the struggle with Israel to submerge these differences in the face of a common enemy, and so legitimate itself among those not affectively inclined to follow its leadership, and weak enough to fear its power.

The United States pursues an ambitious interrelated complex of economic, security, and political objectives in the Persian Gulf. At this moment, political and security goals loom largest. President [George W.] Bush wishes to transform the politics of the region and bring liberal democracy to the regional states, including Iran. The president identifies the absence of democracy in the region as a cause of terrorism, and terrorism as a danger to the United States. Hence political transformation is a security goal. The president also believes that the West cannot wait for transformation to end terror, so he pursues terrorists, and real and suspected state sponsors, with conventional military power—and is waging two wars to do so. Finally, the president believes that the United States must ensure that hostile powers, which Iran is deemed to be, do not get their hands on weapons of mass destruction, because the president and his allies do not agree with the analysis I advance below.

The United States also has more traditional economic interests in the Gulf, which also are connected to security interests. Much of the world's internationally traded oil comes from the Gulf, so the United States is interested in the free flow of oil from the region. It also wishes to ensure that the oil resources not come under the control of hostile powers that might use it as a coercive lever. And finally, the United States wants to assure that the earnings from oil exports not end up in mischievous hands. These concerns generate a broad security agenda—including the defense of oil routes, the prevention of the conquest of any oil state by another, and watchful oversight of the internal politics of certain countries to ensure that dangerous elements not come to power. U.S. strategists may also believe that U.S. hegemony in the Gulf region gives them some leverage over oil exports, and thus increases U.S. power in other parts of the world. For all these reasons, the United States must maintain a very large military presence, and remain the predominant military power in the Gulf region.

This brief assessment of Iranian and U.S. goals suggests that these two powers are destined to be in an intensely competitive relationship. Each has cards to play in this competition. Iran knows the region well, has an excellent geographic position, and may be able to find support in Shiite Arab populations in neighboring countries. Though economically and militarily weak compared to the United States, it is the strongest power in the Gulf, and has proven itself capable of mobilizing very large ground forces. The United States has a giant economy and the world's most advanced military. The United States also has two potential political advantages. Historically, most states consider large proximate land powers such as Iran to be more dangerous to them than distant sea powers such as the United States. And, Iran—an Islamic country, with potential Shia domestic allies in many [G]ulf states—poses a more credible threat of domestic destabilization than does the U.S. rhetoric of democratization. However powerful and assertive the United States may be, neighboring Iran poses at least as great a threat—and perhaps a greater threat. Hence, despite the present diplomatic ill effects of its mistakes in Iraq, over time the United States is likely to prove the more attractive ally to most states in the region.

Nuclear weapons would make Iran a somewhat more powerful state, which could allow it to pursue certain interests with greater vigor. Fear of Iranian nuclear weapons may cause other states in the region to want their own nuclear weapons, which may in turn cause still others to want nuclear weapons. This would not only be a problem in its own terms, it could further damage the Nuclear Non-Proliferation Treaty and the institutions that sustain it. The ability of the United States and its allies and friends outside and inside the region to contain and deter Iran will affect whether or not significant nuclear proliferation occurs in the region, so I turn first to the likely U.S. and regional responses to a nuclear Iran.

Nuclear-Armed Iran's Four Threats

Reviewing the debate over Iranian nuclear weapons, one can find four different strategic fears of a nuclear-armed Iran: (1) Iran could be emboldened by the possession of a deterrent force and its foreign policy thus would become more adventurous and more violent; (2) Iran could directly threaten others with nuclear attack unless certain demands were met; (3) Iran could give nuclear weapons to nonstate actors; and (4) Iran simply could attack Israel with nuclear weapons—heedless of the inevitable Israeli nuclear retaliation.

A More Adventurous Iran

During the recent fighting between Israel and Hezbollah, President Bush averred that the event would have been much more dangerous had Iran possessed nuclear weapons, but he did not explain why. His implication was that Iran would have been more inclined to involve itself directly in the crisis. The argument would be that Iran's leadership would shelter behind its nuclear deterrent. Great powers would be afraid to attack Iran directly, especially to invade Iran, if they faced the risk of nuclear escalation. So Iran would be free to do anything from meddling in the internal affairs of other countries to invading them with conventional forces, because it could control its costs. This concern is quite reasonable; Iran's leaders might have this idea, but how much different would the situation be than it is today?

Iran already dabbles in subversion and terror. Its leaders do not seem too concerned about invasion, and overthrow, and with good reason. Iran's population is some 70 million, and its land area is roughly three times the size of France. The United States, with the most capable army in the world, is having a difficult time controlling five of Iraq's eighteen provinces, and perhaps 12 million of its 26.8 million people. Iran is surely concerned about other retaliatory responses, including air attacks and even embargos. This is why Iran is somewhat careful to limit its activities and cover its tracks. It might perceive itself to be more secure from retaliatory air attack with a nuclear deterrent, but Israel's nuclear deterrent did not save it from rocket attack in the recent fighting in Lebanon. And from what is known about U.S. Cold War military planning for war against the Soviet Union, and for that matter possible conflict with China today, large nuclear retaliatory forces do not deter the United States from planning large scale conventional air operations against nuclear-armed countries.

Iran's leaders might also perceive that actual conventional attacks on its neighbors would carry less risk than in the past, due to possession of a nuclear deterrent. But counterattacks on its homeland is only one cost of such a gambit. Iran's conventional military offensive capability is not very great, and it would take enormous investments to improve them much. U.S. military spending is currently nearly three times Iran's total GDP, and ninety times Iran's defense effort.[10] Saudi Arabia might be able to defend itself without U.S. help, but we know from the 1991 Iraqi invasion of Kuwait that the kingdom and the United States have cooperated to assure that U.S. reinforcements can reach Saudi Arabia very quickly. Though tiny countries such as Kuwait and the Gulf sheikdoms cannot hope to defend themselves against Iran on their own, reinforcement with high-technology U.S. military forces would assure that Iran's offensive forces could not conquer these countries, and there again preparations have already been made to enable rapid U.S. reinforcement. And, for the foreseeable future, it seems very likely that considerable U.S. forces will be based in the Gulf states and the adjacent waters. Even if Iran's leaders somehow feel safe at home, the forces they dispatch abroad would surely be destroyed, and they likely understand this very well as they have had a box seat at two U.S. conventional wars in the region, and seen much of their own surface fleet sunk by the United States.

Direct Threats from Iran

A second possible use of Iran's nuclear weapons is bald nuclear coercion—especially against nonnuclear neighbors. Nuclear coercion, even against the weak, has certain risks, so it is hard to guess what Iranian interest would be worth such a gambit. In a drive for Gulf hegemony, Iran might demand that those of its neighbors who are close to the United States should weaken these ties—throw out U.S. forces, deny them ports of call and landing rights, destroy prepositioned equipment sites, and cease importing U.S. weapons. Less plausibly, Iran might demand that other oil producing states agree with its own views at any given time about how much oil to pump, or what to charge for it, though this does not seem worth a nuclear crisis. It is worth noting that, since the end of World War II, no nuclear power has found a way to use nuclear threats to achieve offensive strategic objectives.

These gambits are unlikely to work, and the United States and its allies can act to forestall them. During the Cold War, the United States offered the protection of its nuclear deterrent forces to many allies who did not possess nuclear weapons—every NATO member state except Britain and France. The United States promised that if NATO were to be attacked by the Soviet Union with nuclear weapons, it would respond. Indeed, NATO strategy called for the employment of nuclear weapons in the event of a successful Soviet conventional invasion of NATO states. The United States made this commitment in spite of virtual nuclear parity with the Soviet Union. The United States risked annihilation to secure its interests in Europe.

The United States has, at least since the late 1970s, perceived itself through Democratic and Republican administrations to have a very strong interest in the security of Persian Gulf countries. It is likely that the United States would offer the

Gulf Arab countries a nuclear "guarantee." Given that U.S. strategic nuclear forces today are vastly more powerful than anything Iran is likely to be able to deploy, the United States runs less risk in offering such an assurance than it did during the Cold War, and Iran would face very grave risks if it challenged them. Indeed, given U.S. nuclear advantages, Iran would be running the risk of a preemptive U.S. nuclear strike against Iranian forces, in the event that it began to alert these forces to add credibility to its threat. Put bluntly, to be a nuclear-armed state is to be a nuclear target.

Would a state such as Saudi Arabia be willing to count on the U.S. nuclear guarantee? Would it be willing to stand up to an Iranian threat, and risk the possibility that Iran might not be deterred? This is impossible to know. But, Saudi Arabia would know one thing: if it succumbed to Iran's blandishments once, and severed its connections to the United States, it essentially would become a satellite of Iran, and there would be no end to Iran's demands.

Iran and Nonstate Actors

Since the September 11, 2001, attacks on the United States, many have been concerned that nuclear weapons could fall into the hands of terrorists. One way this could occur, it is feared, would be for a state with a weapons program to give or sell one to a terrorist group. Such action seems unlikely in the case of Iran, or any state, because it serves no strategic purpose, invites retaliation, and cannot be controlled. It is perhaps the most self-destructive thing that any nation-state can do.

What strategic purpose, other than pure destruction, could such an action serve? A single nuclear weapon exploded in the United States, or any other state, would be a truly horrible event. But it would not destroy the existence of that state, or destroy its political power. And it would enrage that state, and no doubt cause extraordinary efforts to discover, and punish, the source of the attack.

If the weapon is tracked back to the source, the source country will be blamed. It will be blamed not only by the victim, but by other states, terrified by the implications of the action. The victim surely will try to punish the supplier, and it is likely that this punishment would involve nuclear strikes. Iran or any other nuclear weapons provider might hope to avoid detection, but they could only hope—they could not count on it. The characteristics of the explosion may provide some indications of the origin of the weapon.[11] Moreover, once the explosion occurs, intelligence collected and either ignored or misunderstood prior to the event will be reviewed in light of the event, and may have new meaning. Additionally, there are not all that many potential sources of a nuclear weapon—wherever an explosion occurs one can be sure that intelligence would quickly focus on nuclear problem states such as North Korea, Iran, and Pakistan. Indeed, these states are so likely to end up in the spotlight for a terrorist use of a nuclear weapon, they probably have an interest in stopping *any* conspiracies of this kind that they discover.

Once a weapon is supplied to the nonstate actor, the supplying state has no guarantee that it will be used for the original agreed purpose. The nonstate actor may have promised to attack Israel, but instead may attack France, or the United States. Alternatively, that actor may simply be a middleman, and sell or trade the device to someone else. The risks cannot be controlled by the supplying state.

Iran and Israel

It is occasionally suggested that Iran in particular, because of its leaders' undisguised hatred for the state of Israel, and quite open assertions that the Middle East would be better off if Israel disappeared, might act to make their fantasies a reality. Iran could use its future nuclear weapons to annihilate the state of Israel, unconcerned about Israeli nuclear retaliation because Iran is a large country that would somehow survive a nuclear exchange with Israel, while Israel is a small country that would be entirely destroyed.

A few fission weapons would horribly damage the state of Israel, and a few fusion weapons would surely destroy it. But neither kind of attack could reliably shield Iran from a devastating response. Israel has had years to work on developing and shielding its nuclear deterrent. It is generally attributed with as many as 200 fission warheads, deliverable by several different methods, including Intermediate Range Ballistic Missile[s].[12] Were Iran to proceed with a weapons program, Israel would surely improve its own capabilities. Though Iran's population is large, and much of it is dispersed, about a quarter of Iranians (over fifteen million people) live in eight cities conservatively within range of Israel's Jericho II missile.[13] Much of Iran's economic capacity is also concentrated in these cities.[14] Nuclear attacks on these cities, plus some oil industry targets, would destroy Iran as a functioning society and prevent its recovery. There is little in the behavior of the leaders of revolutionary Iran that suggests they would see this as a good trade.

A premise of the foregoing fears is that Iran is led by religious fanatics, who might be more interested in the next world than this one. The current president of Iran, Mahmoud Ahmadinejad, has made statements that have caused observers to doubt his risk aversion and his grasp on reality. It is important to note, however, that in Iran's governing structure, the president does not have much influence over security policy. This belongs to the Supreme Leader Ayatollah Khamenei. Though its implications are much disputed, he has issued a *fatwa* against the development, production, stockpiling, and use of nuclear weapons.[15] This suggests awareness that nuclear weapons are particularly destructive and terrible. Iran's religious leaders have in the past shown themselves sensitive to costs. The founder of Iran's revolution, Ayatollah Khomeini, ceased the war with Iraq in the 1980s when he determined that the costs were too great.[16] By modern standards these costs were high, perhaps half a million dead. But those casualties pale against the casualties of a nuclear exchange with Israel. And Iran's suffering in a nuclear exchange with Israel would pale against its likely suffering in an exchange with the United States.

Mahmoud Ahmadinejad is nevertheless a worrying figure. He has denied that the Jewish Holocaust is a proven fact. He has said, or implied, that Israel should disappear from the map of the Middle East. In the first instance he denies a horror for world Jewry. In the second, he promises a new horror for the Jews, and given Israel's nuclear capabilities, a horror for Iranians as well if his own country were involved. What we cannot know is whether these observations are offered to produce a certain emotional effect, or whether he understands the implications of his utterances and believes and accepts them. Fortunately, few predict that Iran can acquire nuclear weapons soon, which gives time to assess and monitor Ahmadinejad's actual strategic influence in Iran, and to discredit him in Iran and in the wider world by regularly pointing out the very grave risks that his ideas hold for his country. Iranians will have a chance to reconsider this man's leadership abilities. He came in with a vote; he can go out the same way. The time in office of Iranian presidents is fixed in any case— limited to two four-year terms.

Other Issues Resulting from a Nuclear-Armed Iran

A final set of concerns about a nuclear-armed Iran arise not from what Iran would or would not do from the point of view of considered strategy, but from a mixed bag of concerns about inadequate Iranian resources, organizational incompetence, and political decentralization. These concerns are not trivial, but even those who raise them do not advocate preventive war to avoid them, which helps put the risks in context.[17]

The first problem is the risk that, due to their relative poverty and inexperience, new nuclear states, such as Iran, will be unable or unwilling to develop the secure retaliatory forces necessary for a stable deterrent relationship. Iran's nuclear force could be small, vulnerable to attack, and lacking secure command and control. Such a force could attract preemption by a neighbor. Or, fearing preemption by a neighbor, Iran could adopt "hair-trigger" alert postures, or due to poor command and control, a fearful Iran might in a crisis inadvertently launch a nuclear weapon. These are all valid concerns, but many of these problems would be in Iran's hands to solve.

Precisely because even a single nuclear explosion is so destructive, Iran does not need a particularly large nuclear force to deter nuclear attacks by other nuclear states. If Iran's secondary purpose is to discourage further any effort to conquer Iran and change the government, then the state attempting to do that will inevitably present lucrative proximate targets for Iranian nuclear weapons. To deter its neighbors, or invaders, Iran does not need particularly long-ranged survivable systems—short-range mobile missiles should be sufficient and these are the easiest to hide.

Iran's most reasonable strategy is to disperse and hide its small force as best it can, and keep it quiet so that foreign intelligence means cannot attack it. This means eschewing dangerous alert postures, first-strike doctrines, and the like. Dispersal, secrecy, stealth, and communications security are the means to to survival, though they may present some command and control issues, and some nuclear security issues. There is no reason in principle, however, why a state such as Iran cannot use multiple-key arrangements to ensure against the unauthorized launch of its weapons.

Analysts of nuclear weapons organizations, however, fairly point to the fact that states do not always base their nuclear weapons in reasonable ways. And they do not necessarily confine their objectives to basic deterrence. Iran may decide that it wants a first-strike capability versus its neighbors, such as Israel. Such a dream is probably unachievable, but Iran might attempt to develop such a capability. This would set up an unstable strategic relationship between the two countries, and any crises would include an element of great risk, as one or the other became tempted to preempt. In the U.S.-Soviet case, these problems ultimately lead the two sides to ensure that some piece of their nuclear forces would likely survive an exchange to visit a horrible retaliation, and thus deter the other's first-strike temptations. These risks also led them to become quite cautious in their political competition, but there were hair-raising episodes along the way, and there is no reason to rule out similar events in the case of Iran.

On the other hand, it is virtually impossible for Iran to achieve a first-strike capability versus the United States. Any risks that Iran took in its basing mode and alert posture to get ready for a first strike against Israel could easily make it more vulnerable to a first strike from the United States. Spending its nuclear forces on Israel would leave Iran politically and militarily vulnerable to a huge U.S. retaliation. By striking first, it would have legitimated a U.S. nuclear attack, while simultaneously weakening its own deterrent with the weapons it had expended. The United States is the greater threat to Iran because it is much more powerful than Israel, and has actual strategic objectives in the Gulf. It is strategically reasonable for Iran to focus its deterrent energies on the United States, which it can only influence with a secure retaliatory force, capable of threatening U.S. forces and interests in the region.

A final potential problem in Iran is the apparent decentralization of power in the country. Iran essentially has two military organizations: the "professional" military, and the Revolutionary Guard Corps. The latter is ideologically motivated, secretive, and involved in assisting armed groups abroad in Iraq and Lebanon. Many fear that the latter would end up in control of the weapons, or at least with considerable access to them. Given the nature of this organization, some of its members might be willing to do things that the higher political authorities in the state would not choose to do. They might give the weapons away, or use them without authorization. It is impossible to know whether this would occur in Iran. The Revolutionary Guards are generally considered to be very loyal to the Supreme Leader, the ultimate political authority.[18] This should work against renegade behavior. Iran is dedicating considerable national resources to nuclear energy, and if it pursued its current path through to a complete weapons program, it will have devoted many more resources. It is likely, though not guaranteed, that Iran's leaders will take care to put the weapons under the control of people they trust to obey their orders. All states having relations with Iran have an interest in this matter. Nuclear powers must make clear to Iran that its nuclear weapons would be a state responsibility. It will not matter to others whether an Iranian nuclear weapon was employed or exported by "rogue" elements within the state. Even nonnuclear powers can convey this message to Iran, letting Iran know that such an excuse would not win Iran any diplomatic cover. Iran must also be carefully watched for signs of sloppy control practices, and if they appear, other states must make these practices a primary issue in their relations with Iran.

Regional Nuclear Proliferation and Risks to the Non-Proliferation Treaty

States in range of Iran's nuclear weapons will reasonably wish to take measures to protect themselves against nuclear coercion and nuclear attack. Iran's neighbors have three policy options to ensure themselves against a nuclear-armed Iran. They can choose to appease Iran comprehensively; they can find a nuclear guarantor; they can build their own nuclear weapons. Though elements of these three policies could be combined, one will tend to dominate.

Most countries will decline to appease Iran, if they have another plausible option, because most nation-states enjoy their autonomy and do not wish to give it up. Comprehensive appeasement is the road to ruin; one set of concessions to a demanding Iran could easily lead to another, until the state in question loses the ability to recover any shred of sovereignty. Comprehensive appeasement will likely only prove preferable to states facing a disastrous war, or disastrous defeat, with no hope of survival. Historically, this sort of behavior is generally only found among the very weak, and typically when they lack any other option.

The most important choice is whether states will seek their own nuclear weapons, or seek the protection of another nuclear power, if that protection is offered. That said, only a few states in the Middle East and Persian Gulf have the resources to attempt their own autonomous nuclear weapons programs. I have argued above that the United States likely would offer protection to regional states in order to protect its interests in the Persian Gulf from Iran. It also may offer such protection in order to forestall a spasm of nuclear proliferation in the region. The policies of the United States, and to a lesser extent the principal European states and the European Union, will be the most decisive determinant of whether or not Iran's nuclear programs are emulated.

At this time, and for the foreseeable future, four regional powers can be considered candidate nuclear competitors with Iran: Israel (already a nuclear-armed state), Egypt, Saudi Arabia, and Turkey.

Israel depends on the United States for its advanced conventional weaponry, but it is unwilling to count on any state for its immediate defense. Israel has had a nuclear weapons program for a very long time, though it declines to discuss the matter publicly. Open sources estimate a stockpile of two hundred weapons. Israel is believed to be able to deliver weapons by ballistic missile and by aircraft, and perhaps by submarine launched cruise missile. It seems to have taken care to produce a secure second-strike capability. In the face of an open Iranian program, Israel may be tempted to go public with its own program.

Though Iran is quite vulnerable to nuclear attack today, Israel might intensify its preparations to ensure that Iran understands just how dangerous nuclear threats toward Israel would be. Not many Israeli nuclear weapons would need to survive an attempted Iranian first strike to ruin Iran forever. Open improvements in Israeli nuclear capabilities, especially if accompanied by extensive public rhetoric, would likely raise security and prestige concerns among its neighbors. The United States would be wise to urge Israel to refrain from strong nuclear declarations, unless Iran's own public declarations about its nuclear capability demand a response.

Egypt would be concerned for reasons of both prestige and security if Iran was to become a nuclear weapons state, and Israel was to become an open nuclear power. Egypt at one time had an active nuclear energy research program, and there was concern that it could become a nuclear weapons [state]. It has the technological and scientific expertise and has recently announced a new civilian nuclear energy program.[19] Absent active U.S. diplomacy, and strategic guarantees, Egypt probably would follow suit in developing nuclear weapons. Egypt faces a number of barriers, however. First, it is highly dependent on the United States for conventional weaponry. The United States surely would suspend this relationship if Egypt decided to pursue nuclear weapons. This would be quite unsettling to Egypt's internal politics. Second, Egypt is a poor country; foreign economic assistance would also dry up if Egypt decided to go nuclear. Third, given that Israel is already a nuclear weapons state, and Iran is well ahead of Egypt, Egypt would go through a period of both conventional and nuclear vulnerability as it attempted to produce nuclear weapons. Egypt could choose to accept all these risks and costs, but it seems more plausible that the United States and the European Union could find a package of assurances and incentives that would be acceptable to Egypt.

Saudi Arabia would face similar, though stronger temptations, than Egypt. Saudi Arabia is arguably the other "great power" of the Persian Gulf region, and thus a natural competitor with Iran. With the demise of Iraq, it is the undisputed leader of the Arab states in the Gulf, and thus a rival to an Iran trying to expand its sphere of influence. Due to their proximity, Iran and Saudi Arabia are vulnerable to one another's conventional military power. Saudi Arabia likely views itself as the protector of Sunni Arabs from Shia Arabs, and from Shia Iran.

Saudi Arabia does not, however, have a developed nuclear science and technology effort. And it does not have the other industrial capabilities needed to support a nuclear weapons program and associated delivery systems. Saudi Arabia would thus take quite a long time to develop its own nuclear forces, and like Egypt, would be vulnerable in the interval. They would have to rely on an external guarantee, and the guarantor probably would not want to be a party to any nuclear program. With its wealth, however, it cannot be ruled out that the Saudis would simply try to buy nuclear weapons. They would need more than a few to compete with an Iranian program, and they would need delivery systems. Pakistan seems the only possible source, but it is under a great deal of scrutiny. Pakistan would face enormous pressure not to transfer complete weapons to another party. Finally, Saudi Arabia does have good reason to believe that outsiders are committed to its security. The United States and other great powers have extensive economic and military interests in maintaining Saudi security. The United States has demonstrated its commitment in many ways, including war. The Saudis are accustomed to security cooperation with the United States. A U.S. guarantee likely would prove the most attractive option for Saudi Arabia.

Turkey also will be concerned, for security and prestige reasons, about a nuclear weapons capability in neighboring Iran. Turkey's economic, scientific, and engineering capabilities probably make it more capable of going nuclear than either Egypt or Saudi Arabia. Turkey's calculation will be affected by other political interests, however. Turkey is a member of NATO, a nuclear alliance, and thus already enjoys a nuclear guarantee by the United States. Dozens of tactical nuclear weapons are based in Turkey, and some of Turkey's aircraft are wired to deliver these weapons, which could be turned over to them under circumstances determined by the United States, and based on long-standing procedures agreed within NATO. This relationship would be jeopardized were Turkey to embark on its own independent nuclear weapons program. Turkey also aspires to membership in the European Union. Though the Europeans have been only moderately encouraging, it seems likely that the EU would discourage an independent Turkish nuclear effort. Conversely, it seems possible that the EU might become more accommodating of Turkey's effort to join the EU if that helped discourage a Turkish nuclear program.

In sum, a nuclear Iran creates risks of additional nuclear proliferation in the Persian Gulf and Middle East regions. At the same time, these risks will be affected by the U.S. response. If the United States behaves consistent with its past interpretation of its regional interests and global interests, then it can mute the incentives of three of the four states in question to acquire nuclear weapons. This is not a sure thing, of course, and the United States will need to show leadership and sagacity. That said, it looks as if the kinds of policies recommended in this paper in the event of an Iranian nuclear weapons capability are similar to what the United States, its allies, and other Asian powers are doing in response to the North Korean nuclear weapons test. The United States and its allies have demonstrated their solidarity; North Korea has been warned not to export its nuclear weapons; and the United Nations has instituted a sanctions regime, which effectively legalizes searches of North Korean ships, planes, trucks, and railroad cars for nuclear contraband.

If Iran ultimately does get nuclear weapons, this will surely further damage the NPT. Insofar as Iran will have launched and developed its program under the cover of the NPT, member states will lose confidence that the system actually protects them in any way. Many member states with the capacity to build their own nuclear weapons will want to move themselves closer to an ability to do so in the event that any of their neighbors defect from the treaty. They will want to be months rather than years away from their own nuclear weapons. If some do this, then all may wish to do so. Thus the warning time that the treaty mechanisms provide to other members that regions are turning dangerous—warning that could be used for preventive diplomacy—will be shortened. If actual widespread and rapid proliferation then occurs in the Persian Gulf and Middle East, then the treaty obviously will have suffered a major failure.

Alternatively, Iran's weapons success will cause some member states of the NPT to demand even more aggressively than they already do that the entire treaty be renegotiated, with much stricter constraints on the technologies that nonnuclear weapon member states can pursue. This is a double-edged sword, because the nonnuclear weapon states will want a reopened negotiation to place further limits on the existing nuclear weapons states. This will make for a tense, and perhaps fruitless, negotiation. Foresight about all these difficulties will, however, provide an extra incentive for the advanced countries to discourage regional nuclear emulation of Iran.

Conclusion

A nuclear-armed Iran is not a trivial problem—for its neighbors or the United States. Indeed, Iran itself would be entering a difficult new period in its history. It would be better by far for Iran to forgo those technology development initiatives that would allow it to make a decision to become a nuclear weapons state. But current diplomatic efforts may fail, and the question arises as to whether preventive war dominates a strategy of containment and deterrence. This choice can only be considered if a strategy of containment is elucidated, and its odds of success assessed. Should Iran become a nuclear power, both the immediate strategic risks and the proliferation risks can be addressed with a reinvigorated commitment of U.S. power to stability and security in the Persian Gulf and the Middle East. Such a commitment is reasonable given U.S. strategic interests in the region. The United States should seek the help of outside partners in Europe and elsewhere in making this commitment. The United States can and should make it clear to Iran that the overt or covert use of its nuclear weapons, for blackmail or for war, would put Iran in the gravest danger of nuclear retaliation. The United States should similarly explain to regional actors why it is willing to make this commitment. Both the United States and regional actors may wish to reinforce this commitment with security agreements and some visible military preparations. At the same time, it will be necessary for the United States to forgo any future efforts to replace the Iranian regime. This would run nuclear risks that neither the United States, nor other great powers, nor regional powers will wish to run.

The strategy of deterrence and containment has worked for the United States before; there is no reason why it cannot work again. Relative to Iran, the United States and its likely allies have vastly superior material capabilities, a far more favorable situation than the in Cold War. In a confrontation with the United States, Iran would run risks of complete destruction, and it cannot threaten the United States with comparable damage.

Bismarck said of preventive war that it was like committing suicide out of fear of death. A preventive war versus Iran might not be suicidal, but it will definitely hurt. The United States and its allies have many military and diplomatic cards to play to manage the dangers posed by a nuclear-armed Iran. That said, a replay of the Cold War competition in the Persian Gulf is not a happy outcome. Though I think it is preferable to preventive war, far better would be a diplomatic solution. Since it is unlikely that economic pressure alone will bring diplomatic success, it would be wise to offer Iran a package of incentives more consistent with its apparent concerns than has been offered thus far. If Iran were to decline such an offer, this clarification of its purposes would assist the ultimate diplomacy of containment and deterrence.

NOTES

1. Jeffrey J. Schott, Institute for International Economics, "Economic Sanctions, Oil, and Iran," Testimony before the Joint Economic Committee, U.S. Congress, Hearing on "Energy and the Iranian Economy," July 25, 2006, available online at http://www.iie.com/publications/papers/paper.cfm?ResearchID=649.

2. Lionel Beehner, "What Sanctions Mean for Iran's Economy," Council on Foreign Relations Background Paper, May 2006, available online at http://www.cfr.org/publication/10590/what_sanctions_mean_for_irans_economy.html?

3. Flynt Leverett, "The Race for Iran," *New York Times*, June 20, 2006.

4. Austin Long and Whitney Raas, "Osirak Redux? Assessing Israeli Capabilities to Destroy Iranian Nuclear Facilities," April 2006, SSP Working Paper, available online at http://web.mit.edu/ssp/Publications/working_papers/wp_06-1.pdf.

5. For example, two hundred fighter bombers could easily deliver four hundred precision guided weapons against four hundred aim points. Given the U.S. naval and air presence in the Persian Gulf, this rather limited attack could probably be launched with little reinforcement.

6. Thomas A. Keaney and Eliot A. Cohen, *Gulf War Air Power Survey Summary Report* (Washington, D.C.: Government Printing Office, 1993), Figure 5, "Coalition Air Strikes by Day Against Iraqi Target Sets," p. 13 (numbers estimated from graph).

7. The recent Israeli experience in Lebanon is relevant. Neither the Israeli Air Force nor the powerful counterbattery attacks of the Israeli Army's artillery could prevent Hezbollah from launching a hundred or more artillery rockets into northern Israel almost every night. Given the length of the Iran/Iraq border, it seems likely that Iran could infiltrate small units into Iraq to raid bases and truck convoys. At this moment, Iran likely has agents in Southern Iraq, and has sufficiently strong relationships with Shiite militias that some of these militias might assist Iran. Finally, Iran's intelligence on the location and strength of coalition forces is likely very good. It would not be surprising if Iran had precise coordinates for many of these potential targets, and spotters close to these targets, both of which would improve the performance of its otherwise inaccurate long range artillery rockets.

8. Robert Lowe and Claire Spencer, eds., *Iran, Its Neighbors and the Regional Crises, A Middle East Programme Report* (London: Royal Institute of International Affairs, 2006), pp. 6, 8–12; See also Vali Nasr, "When the Shiites Rise," *Foreign Affairs* 85 (July/August 2006): 58–74, esp. 66–68. Ray Takeyh, "A Profile in Defiance, Being Mahmoud Admadinejad," *National Interest*, no. 83 (Spring 2006): pp. 16–21 makes the point that the new Iranian president and his coterie of Iraq war veterans seem more religious, more nationalistic, and more confrontational than others in the Iranian political elite, but that they are only one faction.

9. *The World Factbook*, U.S. Central Intelligence Agency, available online at https://www.cia.gov/cia/publications/factbook/geos/ir.html, accessed Sept[ember] 25, 2006.

10. *The Military Balance 2006* (London: International Institute for Strategic Studies, and Routledge, 2006), pp. 18, 187.

11. William Dunlop and Harold Smith, "Who Did It? Using International Forensics to Detect and Deter Nuclear Terrorism," *Arms Control Today*, October 2006, available online at http://www.armscontrol.org/act/2006_10/CVRForensics.asp, accessed October 29, 2006.

12. *The Military Balance 2006*, p. 191.

13. For population concentrations see, "World Urbanization Prospects: The 2005 Revision Population Database," "Iran," U.N. Population Division, available online at http://esa.un.org/unup, accessed 23 September 2006. Jericho II range estimates by Austin Long.

14. Perhaps a third of Iranian manufacturing industry is concentrated in or near Tehran, Karaj, and Isfahan alone. See "Table 7.9, Manufacturing Establishments by Legal Status and Ostan: 1381," Statistical Centre of Iran, available online at http://www.sci.org.ir/portal/faces/public/sci_en/sci_en.selecteddata/sci_en.yearbookdata, accessed September 29, 2006.

15. Mark Fitzpatrick, "Assessing Iran's Nuclear Program," *Survival* 48, no. 3 (Autumn 2006): 13.

16. Graham E. Fuller, "War and Revolution in Iran," *Current History* (February 1989): 81–100. "In basic terms, Khomeini faced a stark choice between pursuing an increasingly unattainable revolutionary victory

over Iraq and the survival of the Islamic Revolution itself" (p. 81).

17. Scott D. Sagan, "How to Keep the Bomb from Iran," *Foreign Affairs* 85 (September/October 2006): 45–59. Sagan raises many of the concerns outlined here. These concerns lead him to advise a focused diplomatic effort to discourage Iran from proceeding with its enrichment program. He explicitly concludes, however, that preventive war is not an appropriate answer to the Iranian program. Implicitly, therefore, he accepts that however problematical a nuclear Iran might be, these risks do not exceed those associated with a preventive war.

18. Jim Walsh, "Iran and the Nuclear Issue: Negotiated Settlement or Escalation?" Testimony before the Subcommittee on Federal Financial Management, Government Information and International Security, Committee on Homeland Security and Governmental Affairs, United States Senate, July 20, 2006, Washington, D.C.

19. For an excellent review of the nuclear potential of Egypt, Turkey, and Saudi Arabia, see Wyn Q. Bowen and Joanna Kidd, "The Nuclear Capabilities and Ambitions of Iran's Neighbors," in *Getting Ready for a Nuclear-Ready Iran*, Henry Sokolski and Patrick Clawson, eds. (Carlyle Barracks, Penn.: U.S. Army War College, Strategic Studies Institute, 2005), pp. 51–88, available online at www.strategicstudiesinstitute.army.mil/. See also William Wallis and Roula Khalaf, "Speculation after Egypt Revives Nuclear Plans," *Financial Times*, September 25, 2006, available online at http://www.ft.com/cms/s/6e01b312 -4cba-11db-b03c-0000779e2340.html, accessed October 29, 2006.

Kenneth N. Waltz

WHY IRAN SHOULD GET THE BOMB
Nuclear Balancing Would Mean Stability

The past several months have witnessed a heated debate over the best way for the United States and Israel to respond to Iran's nuclear activities. As the argument has raged, the United States has tightened its already robust sanctions regime against the Islamic Republic, and the European Union announced in January that it will begin an embargo on Iranian oil on July 1. Although the United States, the EU, and Iran have recently returned to the negotiating table, a palpable sense of crisis still looms.

It should not. Most U.S., European, and Israeli commentators and policymakers warn that a nuclear-armed Iran would be the worst possible outcome of the current standoff. In fact, it would probably be the best possible result: the one most likely to restore stability to the Middle East.

Power Begs to Be Balanced

The crisis over Iran's nuclear program could end in three different ways. First, diplomacy coupled with serious sanctions could convince Iran to abandon its pursuit of a nuclear weapon. But this outcome is unlikely: the historical record indicates that a country bent on acquiring nuclear weapons can rarely be dissuaded from doing so. Punishing a state through economic sanctions does not inexorably derail its nuclear program. Take North Korea, which succeeded in building its weapons despite countless rounds of sanctions and UN Security Council resolutions. If Tehran determines that its security depends on possessing nuclear weapons, sanctions are unlikely to change its mind. In fact, adding still more sanctions now could make Iran feel even more vulnerable, giving it still more reason to seek the protection of the ultimate deterrent.

The second possible outcome is that Iran stops short of testing a nuclear weapon but develops a breakout capability, the capacity to build and test one quite quickly. Iran would not be the first country to acquire a sophisticated nuclear program without building an actual bomb. Japan, for instance, maintains a vast civilian nuclear infrastructure. Experts believe that it could produce a nuclear weapon on short notice.

Such a breakout capability might satisfy the domestic political needs of Iran's rulers by assuring hard-liners that they can enjoy all the benefits of having a bomb (such as greater security) without the downsides (such as international isolation and condemnation). The problem is that a breakout capability might not work as intended.

The United States and its European allies are primarily concerned with weaponization, so they might accept a scenario in which Iran stops short of a nuclear weapon. Israel, however, has made it clear that it views a significant Iranian enrichment capacity alone as an unacceptable threat. It is possible, then, that a verifiable commitment

From *Foreign Affairs* 91, no. 4 (July/August 2012), 2–5.

from Iran to stop short of a weapon could appease major Western powers but leave the Israelis unsatisfied. Israel would be less intimidated by a virtual nuclear weapon than it would be by an actual one and therefore would likely continue its risky efforts at subverting Iran's nuclear program through sabotage and assassination—which could lead Iran to conclude that a breakout capability is an insufficient deterrent, after all, and that only weaponization can provide it with the security it seeks.

The third possible outcome of the standoff is that Iran continues its current course and publicly goes nuclear by testing a weapon. U.S. and Israeli officials have declared that outcome unacceptable, arguing that a nuclear Iran is a uniquely terrifying prospect, even an existential threat. Such language is typical of major powers, which have historically gotten riled up whenever another country has begun to develop a nuclear weapon of its own. Yet so far, every time another country has managed to shoulder its way into the nuclear club, the other members have always changed tack and decided to live with it. In fact, by reducing imbalances in military power, new nuclear states generally produce more regional and international stability, not less.

Israel's regional nuclear monopoly, which has proved remarkably durable for the past four decades, has long fueled instability in the Middle East. In no other region of the world does a lone, unchecked nuclear state exist. It is Israel's nuclear arsenal, not Iran's desire for one, that has contributed most to the current crisis. Power, after all, begs to be balanced. What is surprising about the Israeli case is that it has taken so long for a potential balancer to emerge.

Of course, it is easy to understand why Israel wants to remain the sole nuclear power in the region and why it is willing to use force to secure that status. In 1981, Israel bombed Iraq to prevent a challenge to its nuclear monopoly. It did the same to Syria in 2007 and is now considering similar action against Iran. But the very acts that have allowed Israel to maintain its nuclear edge in the short term have prolonged an imbalance that is unsustainable in the long term. Israel's proven ability to strike potential nuclear rivals with impunity has inevitably made its enemies anxious to develop the means to prevent Israel from doing so again. In this way, the current tensions are best viewed not as the early stages of a relatively recent Iranian nuclear crisis but rather as the final stages of a decades-long Middle East nuclear crisis that will end only when a balance of military power is restored.

Unfounded Fears

One reason the danger of a nuclear Iran has been grossly exaggerated is that the debate surrounding it has been distorted by misplaced worries and fundamental misunderstandings of how states generally behave in the international system. The first prominent concern, which undergirds many others, is that the Iranian regime is innately irrational. Despite a widespread belief to the contrary, Iranian policy is made not by "mad mullahs" but by perfectly sane ayatollahs who want to survive just like any other leaders. Although Iran's leaders indulge in inflammatory and hateful rhetoric, they show no propensity for self-destruction. It would be a grave error for policymakers in the United States and Israel to assume otherwise.

Yet that is precisely what many U.S. and Israeli officials and analysts have done. Portraying Iran as irrational has allowed them to argue that the logic of nuclear deterrence does not apply to the Islamic Republic. If Iran acquired a nuclear weapon, they warn, it would not hesitate to use it in a first strike against Israel, even though doing so would invite massive retaliation and risk destroying everything the Iranian regime holds dear.

Although it is impossible to be certain of Iranian intentions, it is far more likely that if Iran desires nuclear weapons, it is for the purpose of providing for its own security, not to improve its offensive capabilities (or destroy itself). Iran may be intransigent at the negotiating table and defiant in the face of sanctions, but it still acts to secure its own preservation. Iran's leaders did not, for example, attempt to close the Strait of Hormuz despite issuing blustery warnings that they might do so after the EU announced its planned oil embargo in January. The Iranian regime clearly concluded that it did not want to provoke what would surely have been a swift and devastating American response to such a move.

Nevertheless, even some observers and policymakers who accept that the Iranian regime is rational still worry that a nuclear weapon would embolden it, providing Tehran with a shield that would allow it to act more aggressively and increase its support for terrorism. Some analysts even fear that Iran would directly provide terrorists with nuclear arms. The problem with these concerns is that they contradict the record of every other nuclear weapons state going back to 1945. History shows that when countries acquire the bomb, they feel increasingly vulnerable and become acutely aware that their nuclear weapons make them a potential target in the eyes of major powers. This awareness discourages nuclear states from bold and aggressive action. Maoist China, for example, became much less bellicose after acquiring nuclear weapons in 1964, and India and Pakistan have both become more cautious since going nuclear. There is little reason to believe Iran would break this mold.

As for the risk of a handoff to terrorists, no country could transfer nuclear weapons without running a high risk of being found out. U.S. surveillance capabilities would pose a serious obstacle, as would the United States' impressive and growing ability to identify the source of fissile material. Moreover, countries can never entirely control or even predict the behavior of the terrorist groups they sponsor. Once a country such as Iran acquires a nuclear capability, it will have every reason to maintain full control over its arsenal. After all, building a bomb is costly and dangerous. It would make little sense to transfer the product of that investment to parties that cannot be trusted or managed.

Another oft-touted worry is that if Iran obtains the bomb, other states in the region will follow suit, leading to a nuclear arms race in the Middle East. But the nuclear age is now almost 70 years old, and so far, fears of proliferation have proved to be unfounded. Properly defined, the term "proliferation" means a rapid and uncontrolled spread. Nothing like that has occurred; in fact, since 1970, there has been a marked slowdown in the emergence of nuclear states. There is no reason to expect that this pattern will change now. Should Iran become the second Middle Eastern nuclear power since 1945, it would hardly signal the start of a landslide. When Israel acquired the bomb in the 1960s, it was at war with many of its neighbors. Its nuclear arms were a much bigger threat to the Arab world than Iran's program is today. If an atomic Israel did not trigger an arms race then, there is no reason a nuclear Iran should now.

Rest Assured

In 1991, the historical rivals India and Pakistan signed a treaty agreeing not to target each other's nuclear facilities. They realized that far more worrisome than their adversary's nuclear deterrent was the instability produced by challenges to it. Since then, even in the face of high tensions and risky provocations, the two countries have kept the peace. Israel and Iran would do well to consider this precedent. If Iran goes nuclear, Israel and Iran will deter each other, as nuclear powers always have. There has never been a full-scale war between two nuclear-armed states. Once Iran crosses the nuclear threshold, deterrence will apply, even if the Iranian arsenal is relatively small. No other country in the region will have an incentive to acquire its own nuclear capability, and the current crisis will finally dissipate, leading to a Middle East that is more stable than it is today.

For that reason, the United States and its allies need not take such pains to prevent the Iranians from developing a nuclear weapon. Diplomacy between Iran and the major powers should continue, because open lines of communication will make the Western countries feel better able to live with a nuclear Iran. But the current sanctions on Iran can be dropped: they primarily harm ordinary Iranians, with little purpose.

Most important, policymakers and citizens in the Arab world, Europe, Israel, and the United States should take comfort from the fact that history has shown that where nuclear capabilities emerge, so, too, does stability. When it comes to nuclear weapons, now as ever, more may be better.

Andrew H. Kydd and Barbara F. Walter

THE STRATEGIES OF TERRORISM

Terrorism often works. Extremist organizations such as al-Qaida, Hamas, and the Tamil Tigers engage in terrorism because it frequently delivers the desired response. The October 1983 suicide attack against the U.S. Marine barracks in Beirut, for example, convinced the United States to withdraw its soldiers from Lebanon.[1] The United States pulled its soldiers out of Saudi Arabia two years after the terrorist attacks of September 11, 2001, even though the U.S. military had been building up its forces in that country for more than a decade.[2] The Philippines recalled its troops from Iraq nearly a month early after a Filipino truck driver was kidnapped by Iraqi extremists.[3] In fact, terrorism has been so successful that between 1980 and 2003, half of all suicide terrorist campaigns were closely followed by substantial concessions by the target governments.[4] Hijacking planes, blowing up buses, and kidnapping individuals may seem irrational and incoherent to outside observers, but these tactics can be surprisingly effective in achieving a terrorist group's political aims.

Despite the salience of terrorism today, scholars and policymakers are only beginning to understand how and why it works. Much has been written on the origins of terror, the motivations of terrorists, and counterterror responses, but little has appeared on the strategies terrorist organizations employ and the conditions under which these strategies succeed or fail. Alan Krueger, David Laitin, Jitka Maleckova, and Alberto Abadie, for example, have traced the effects of poverty, education, and political freedom on terrorist recruitment.[5] Jessica Stern has examined the grievances that give rise to terrorism and the networks, money, and operations that allow terrorist organizations to thrive.[6] What is lacking, however, is a clear understanding of the larger strategic games terrorists are playing and the ways in which state responses help or hinder them.

Effective counterstrategies cannot be designed without first understanding the strategic logic that drives terrorist violence. Terrorism works not simply because it instills fear in target populations, but because it causes governments and individuals to respond in ways that aid the terrorists' cause. The Irish Republican Army (IRA) bombed pubs, parks, and shopping districts in London because its leadership believed that such acts would convince Britain to relinquish Northern Ireland. In targeting the World Trade Center and the Pentagon on September 11, al-Qaida hoped to raise the costs for the United States of supporting Israel, Saudi Arabia, and other Arab regimes, and to provoke the United States into a military response designed to mobilize Muslims around the world. That so many targeted governments respond in the way that terrorist organizations intend underscores the need for understanding the reasoning behind this type of violence.

In this article we seek answers to four questions. First, what types of goals do terrorists seek to achieve? Second, what strategies do they pursue to achieve these goals? Third, why do these strategies work in some cases but not in others? And fourth, given these strategies, what are the targeted governments' best responses to prevent terrorism and protect their countries from future attacks?

From *International Security* 31, no. 1 (Summer 2006), 49–80.

The core of our argument is that terrorist violence is a form of costly signaling. Terrorists are too weak to impose their will directly by force of arms. They are sometimes strong enough, however, to persuade audiences to do as they wish by altering the audience's beliefs about such matters as the terrorist's ability to impose costs and their degree of commitment to their cause. Given the conflict of interest between terrorists and their targets, ordinary communication or "cheap talk" is insufficient to change minds or influence behavior. If al-Qaida had informed the United States on September 10, 2001, that it would kill 3,000 Americans unless the United States withdrew from Saudi Arabia, the threat might have sparked concern, but it would not have had the same impact as the attacks that followed. Because it is hard for weak actors to make credible threats, terrorists are forced to display publicly just how far they are willing to go to obtain their desired results.

There are five principal strategic logics of costly signaling at work in terrorist campaigns: (1) attrition, (2) intimidation, (3) provocation, (4) spoiling, and (5) outbidding. In an attrition strategy, terrorists seek to persuade the enemy that the terrorists are strong enough to impose considerable costs if the enemy continues a particular policy. Terrorists using intimidation try to convince the population that the terrorists are strong enough to punish disobedience and that the government is too weak to stop them, so that people behave as the terrorists wish. A provocation strategy is an attempt to induce the enemy to respond to terrorism with indiscriminate violence, which radicalizes the population and moves them to support the terrorists. Spoilers attack in an effort to persuade the enemy that moderates on the terrorists' side are weak and untrustworthy, thus undermining attempts to reach a peace settlement. Groups engaged in outbidding use violence to convince the public that the terrorists have greater resolve to fight the enemy than rival groups, and therefore are worthy of support. Understanding these five distinct strategic logics is crucial not only for understanding terrorism but also for designing effective antiterror policies.[7]

The article is divided into two main sections. The first discusses the goals terrorists pursue and examines the forty-two groups currently on the U.S. State Department's list of foreign terrorist organizations (FTOs).[8] The second section develops the costly signaling approach to terrorism, analyzes the five strategies that terrorists use to achieve their goals, discusses the conditions in which each of these strategies is likely to be successful, and draws out the implications for the best counterterror responses.

The Goals of Terrorism

For years the press has portrayed terrorists as crazy extremists who commit indiscriminate acts of violence, without any larger goal beyond revenge or a desire to produce fear in an enemy population. This characterization derives some support from statements made by terrorists themselves. For example, a young Hamas suicide bomber whose bomb failed to detonate said, "I know that there are other ways to do jihad. But this one is sweet—the sweetest. All martyrdom operations, if done for Allah's sake, hurt less than a gnat's bite!"[9] Volunteers for a suicide mission may have a variety of motives—obtaining rewards in the afterlife, avenging a family member killed by the enemy, or simply collecting financial rewards for their descendants. By contrast, the goals driving terrorist organizations are usually political objectives, and it is these goals that determine whether and how terrorist campaigns will be launched.

We define "terrorism" as the use of violence against civilians by nonstate actors to attain political goals.[10] These goals can be conceptualized in a variety of ways. Individuals and groups often have hierarchies of objectives, where broader goals lead to more proximate objectives, which then become

Table 8.1. Foreign Terrorist Organizations and their Goals

NAME	ULTIMATE GOALS	RC	TC	PC	SC	SQM
Abu Nidal Organization	Destroy Israel; establish Palestinian state	X	X			
Abu Sayyaf Group	Secede from Philippines		X			
Al-Aqsa Martyrs' Brigade	Destroy Israel; establish Palestinian state	X	X			
Ansar al-Islam	Evict United States from Iraq; establish Islamic state	X		X		
Armed Islamic Group	Establish Islamic state in Algeria	X				
Asbat al-Ansar	Establish Islamic state in Lebanon	X				
Aum Shinrikyo	Seize power in Japan; hasten the Apocalypse	X	X			
Basque Fatherland and Liberty (ETA)	Secede from Spain		X			
Communist Party of the Philippines/New People's Army	Establish Communist state in Philippines	X				
Continuity Irish Republican Army	Evict Britain from Northern Ireland; unite with Eire		X			
Al-Gama'a al-Islamiyya (Islamic Group)	Establish Islamic state in Egypt	X				
Hamas (Islamic Resistance Movement)	Destroy Israel; establish Palestinian Islamic state	X	X			
Harakat ul-Mujahidin	Evict India from Kashmir; unite with Pakistan		X			
Hezbollah (Party of God)	Originally: evict Israel from Lebanon; now: destroy Israel and establish Palestinian Islamic state	X	X			
Islamic Jihad Group	Establish Islamic state in Uzbekistan; reduce U.S. influence	X		X		
Islamic Movement of Uzbekistan	Establish Islamic state in Uzbekistan	X				
Jaish-e-Mohammed (Army of Mohammed)	Evict India from Kashmir; unite with Pakistan	X	X			

(continued)

Table 8.1. Foreign Terrorist Organizations and their Goals (Continued)

NAME	ULTIMATE GOALS	RC	TC	PC	SC	SQM
Jemaah Islamiya	Establish Islamic state in Indonesia	X				
Al-Jihad (Egyptian Islamic Jihad)	Establish Islamic state in Egypt	X				
Kahane Chai (Kach)	Expand Israel		X			
Kongra-Gel (formerly Kurdistan Workers' Party)	Secede from Turkey		X			
Lashkar-e Tayyiba (Army of the Righteous)	Evict India from Kashmir; unite with Pakistan		X			
Lashkar i Jhangvi	Establish Islamic state in Pakistan	X				
Liberation Tigers of Tamil Eelam	Secede from Sri Lanka		X			
Libyan Islamic Fighting Group	Establish Islamic state in Libya	X				
Moroccan Islamic Combatant Group	Establish Islamic state in Morocco	X				
Mujahedin-e Khalq Organization	Overthrow Iranian government	X				
National Liberation Army	Establish Marxist government in Colombia	X				
Palestine Liberation Front	Destroy Israel; establish Palestinian state	X	X			
Palestinian Islamic Jihad	Destroy Israel; establish Palestinian state	X	X			
Popular Front for the Liberation of Palestine	Destroy Israel; establish Palestinian state	X	X			
Popular Front for the Liberation of Palestine—General Command	Destroy Israel; establish Palestinian state	X	X			
Al-Qaida	Establish Islamic states in Middle East; destroy Israel; reduce U.S. influence	X	X	X		
Al-Qaida in Iraq (Zarqawi group)	Evict United States from Iraq; establish Islamic state	X		X		
Real Irish Republican Army	Evict Britain from Northern Ireland; unite with Eire		X			

		RC	TC	PC	SC	SQM
Revolutionary Armed Forces of Colombia	Establish Marxist state in Colombia	X				
Revolutionary Nuclei (formerly Revolutionary People's Struggle)	Establish Marxist state in Greece	X				
Revolutionary Organization 7 November	Establish Marxist state in Greece	X				
Revolutionary People's Liberation Party/Front	Establish Marxist state in Turkey	X				
Salafist Group for Call and Combat	Establish Islamic state in Algeria	X				
Shining Path (Sendero Luminoso)	Establish Marxist state in Peru	X				
United Self-Defense Forces of Colombia	Preserve Colombian state					X
Total		31	19	4	0	1

NOTE: RC: regime change; TC: territorial change; PC: policy change; SC: social control; and SQM: status quo maintenance. Coding of goals is the authors'.

SOURCE: Office of Counterterrorism, U.S. Department of State, "Foreign Terrorist Organizations," fact sheet, October 11, 2005.

specific goals in more tactical analyses.[11] For the sake of simplicity, we adopt the common distinction between goals (or ultimate desires) and strategies (or plans of action to attain the goals).

Although the ultimate goals of terrorists have varied over time, five have had enduring importance: regime change, territorial change, policy change, social control, and status quo maintenance. Regime change is the overthrow of a government and its replacement with one led by the terrorists or at least one more to their liking.[12] Most Marxist groups, including the Shining Path (Sendero Luminoso) in Peru have sought this goal. Territorial change is taking territory away from a state either to establish a new state (as the Tamil Tigers seek to do in Tamil areas of Sri Lanka) or to join another state (as Lashkar-e Tayyiba would like to do by incorporating Indian Kashmir into Pakistan). Policy change is a broader category of lesser demands, such as al-Qaida's demand that the United States drop its support for Israel and corrupt Arab regimes such as Saudi Arabia. Social control constrains the behavior of individuals, rather than the state. In the United States, the Ku Klux Klan sought the continued oppression of African Americans after the Civil War. More recently, antiabortion groups have sought to kill doctors who perform abortions to deter other doctors from providing this service. Finally, status quo maintenance is the support of an existing regime or a territorial arrangement against political groups that seek to change it. Many right-wing paramilitary organizations in Latin America, such as the United Self-Defense Force of Colombia, have sought this goal.[13] Protestant paramilitary groups in Northern Ireland supported maintenance of the territorial status quo (Northern Ireland as British territory) against IRA demands that the territory be transferred to Ireland.[14]

Some organizations hold multiple goals and may view one as facilitating another. For instance, by seeking to weaken U.S. support for Arab regimes (which would represent a policy change by the United States), al-Qaida is working toward the overthrow of those regimes (or regime change). As another example, Hamas aims to drive Israel out of the occupied territories (territorial change) and then to overthrow it (regime change).

A cross section of terrorist organizations listed in Table 8.1 illustrates the range of goals and their relative frequency. Of the forty-two groups currently designated as FTOs by the U.S. State Department, thirty-one seek regime change, nineteen seek territorial change, four seek policy change, and one seeks to maintain the status quo.[15] The list is neither exhaustive nor representative of all terrorist groups, and it does not reflect the frequency of goals in the universe of cases. None of the FTOs appear to pursue social control, but some domestic groups, which are by definition not on the list, are more interested in this goal.[16] What Table 8.1 reveals, however, is the instrumental nature of terrorist violence and some of the more popular political objectives being sought.

The Strategies of Terrorist Violence

To achieve their long-term objectives, terrorists pursue a variety of strategies. Scholars have suggested a number of typologies of terrorist strategies and tactics over the years. In a pathbreaking early analysis of terrorism, Thomas Thornton offered five proximate objectives: morale building, advertising, disorientation (of the target population), elimination of opposing forces, and provocation.[17] Martha Crenshaw also identifies advertising and provocation as proximate objectives, along with weakening the government, enforcing obedience in the population, and outbidding.[18] David Fromkin argues that provocation is *the* strategy of terrorism.[19] Edward Price writes that terrorists must delegitimize the regime and impose costs on occupying forces, and he identifies kidnapping, assassination, advertising, and provocation as tactics.[20] Although these analyses are helpful in identifying strategies of terrorism, they fail to derive them from a coherent framework, spell out their logic in detail, and consider best responses to them.

A fruitful starting point for a theory of terrorist strategies is the literature on uncertainty, conflict, and costly signaling. Uncertainty has long been understood to be a cause of conflict. Geoffrey Blainey argued that wars begin when states disagree about their relative power, and they end when states agree again.[21] James Fearon and other theorists built upon this insight and showed that uncertainty about a state's willingness to fight can cause conflict.[22] If states are unsure what other states will fight for, they may demand too much in negotiations and end up in conflict. This uncertainty could reflect a disagreement about power, as Blainey understood, or a disagreement over resolve, willpower, or the intensity of preferences over the issue. The United States and North Vietnam did not disagree over their relative power, but the United States fatally underestimated North Vietnamese determination to achieve victory.

Uncertainty about trustworthiness or moderation of preferences can also cause conflict. Thomas Hobbes argued that if individuals mistrust each other, they have an incentive to initiate an attack rather than risk being attacked by surprise.[23] John Herz, Robert Jervis, and others have developed this concept in the international relations context under the heading of the security dilemma and the spiral model.[24] States are often uncertain about each other's ultimate ambitions, intentions, and preferences. Because of this, anything that increases one side's belief that the other is deceitful, expansionist, risk acceptant, or hostile increases incentives to fight rather than cooperate.

If uncertainty about power, resolve, and trustworthiness can lead to violence, then communication on these topics is the key to preventing (or instigating) conflict. The problem is that simple verbal statements are often not credible, because actors frequently have incentives to lie and bluff. If by saying "We're resolved," the North Vietnamese could have persuaded the United States to abandon the South in 1965, then North Vietnam would have had every incentive to say so even if it was not that resolute. In reality, they had to fight a long and costly war to prove their point. Similarly, when Mikhail Gorbachev wanted to reassure the West and end the Cold War, verbal declarations of innocent intentions were insufficient, because previous Soviet leaders had made similar statements. Instead, real arms reductions, such as the 1987 Intermediate-Range Nuclear Forces Treaty, were necessary for Western opinion to change.

Because talk is cheap, states and terrorists who wish to influence the behavior of an adversary must resort to costly signals.[25] Costly signals are actions so costly that bluffers and liars are unwilling to take them.[26] In international crises, mobilizing forces or drawing a very public line in the sand are examples of strategies that less resolved actors might find too costly to take.[27] War itself, or the willingness to endure it, can serve as a forceful signal of resolve and provide believable information about power and capabilities.[28] Costly signals separate the wheat from the chaff and allow honest communication, although sometimes at a terrible price.

To obtain their political goals, terrorists need to provide credible information to the audiences whose behavior they hope to influence. Terrorists play to two key audiences: governments whose policies they wish to influence and individuals on the terrorists' own side whose support or obedience they seek to gain.[29] The targeted governments are central because they can grant concessions over policy or territory that the terrorists are seeking. The terrorists' domestic audience is also important, because they can provide resources to the terrorist group and must obey its edicts on social or political issues.

Figure 8.4 shows how the three subjects of uncertainty (power, resolve, and trustworthiness)

Figure 8.4. Strategies of Terrorist Violence

		Target of Persuasion	
		Enemy	Own Population
	Power	attrition	intimidation
Subject of Uncertainty	Resolve		outbidding
	Trustworthiness	spoiling	provocation

combine with the two targets of persuasion (the enemy government and the domestic population) to yield a family of five signaling strategies. These strategies form a theoretically cohesive set that we believe represents most of the commonly used strategies in important terrorist campaigns around the world today.[30] A terrorist organization can of course pursue more than one strategy at a time. The September 11 terrorist attacks, for example, were probably part of both an attrition strategy and a provocation strategy. By targeting the heart of the United States' financial district, al-Qaida may have been attempting to increase the cost of the U.S. policy of stationing soldiers in Saudi Arabia. But by targeting prominent symbols of American economic and military power, al-Qaida may also have been trying to goad the United States into an extreme military response that would serve al-Qaida's larger goal of radicalizing the world's Muslim population. The challenge for policymakers in targeted countries is to calibrate their responses in ways that do not further any of the terrorists' goals.

Below we analyze the five terrorist strategies in greater detail, discuss the conditions under which each is likely to succeed, and relate these conditions to the appropriate counterterrorism strategies.

Attrition: A Battle of Wills

The most important task for any terrorist group is to persuade the enemy that the group is strong and resolute enough to inflict serious costs, so that the enemy yields to the terrorists' demands.[31] The attrition strategy is designed to accomplish this task.[32] In an attrition campaign, the greater the costs a terrorist organization is able to inflict, the more credible its threat to inflict future costs, and the more likely the target is to grant concessions. During the last years of the British Empire, the Greeks in Cyprus, Jews in Palestine, and Arabs in Aden used a war of attrition strategy against their colonizer. By targeting Britain with terrorist attacks, they eventually convinced the political leadership that maintaining control over these territories would not be worth the cost in British lives.[33] Attacks by Hezbollah and Hamas against Israel, particularly during the second intifada, also appear to be guided by this strategy. In a letter written in the early 1990s to the leadership of Hamas, the organization's master bomb maker, Yahya Ayyash, said, "We paid a high price when we used only sling-shots and stones. We need to exert more pressure, make the cost of the occupation that much more expensive in human lives, that much more unbearable."[34]

Robert Pape presents the most thorough exposition of terrorism as a war of attrition in his analysis of suicide bombing.[35] Based on a data set of all suicide attacks from 1980 to 2003 (315 in total), Pape argues that suicide terrorism is employed by weak actors for whom peaceful tactics have failed and conventional military tactics are infeasible because of the imbalance of power. The strategy is to inflict costs on the enemy until it withdraws its occupying forces: the greater the costs inflicted, the more likely the enemy is to withdraw. Pape asserts that terrorists began to recognize the effectiveness of suicide terrorism with the 1983 Hezbollah attack against U.S. Marines in Beirut that killed 241 people. Since then, suicide terrorism has been employed in nationalist struggles around the world.

CONDITIONS FAVORABLE TO ATTRITION

A war of attrition strategy is more effective against some targets than others. Three variables are likely to figure in the outcome: the state's level of interest in the issue under dispute, the constraints on its ability to retaliate, and its sensitivity to the costs of violence.

The first variable, the state's degree of interest in the disputed issue, is fundamental. States with only peripheral interests at stake often capitulate to terrorist demands; states with more important interests at stake rarely do. The United States withdrew from Lebanon following the bombing of the marine barracks because it had only a marginal interest in maintaining stability and preventing Syrian domination of that country. In that case, the costs of the attack clearly outweighed the U.S. interests at stake. Similarly, Israel withdrew from southern Lebanon in 2000 because the costs of the occupation outstripped Israel's desire to maintain a buffer zone in that region. In contrast, the United States responded to the September 11 attacks by launching offensive wars in Afghanistan and Iraq rather than withdrawing U.S. troops from the region, as al-Qaida demanded (though U.S. troops did ultimately leave Saudi Arabia for Iraq). Similarly, Israel is unlikely to withdraw from East Jerusalem, much less allow itself to become an Islamic state as Hamas has demanded.

The second variable, constraints on retaliation, affects the costs paid by the terrorists for pursuing a war of attrition. Terrorist organizations almost always are weaker than the governments they target and, as a result, are vulnerable to government retaliation. The more constrained the government is in its use of force, the less costly an attrition strategy is, and the longer the terrorists can hold out in the hopes of achieving their goal. For instance, the Israelis have the military means to commit genocide against the Palestinian people or to expel them to surrounding Arab countries. Israel, however, depends for its long-term survival on close ties with Europe and the United States. Western support for Israel would plummet in response to an Israeli strategy designed to inflict mass casualties, making such a strategy prohibitively costly. This constraint makes a war of attrition strategy less costly (and more attractive) for the Palestinians.

Democracies may be more constrained in their ability to retaliate than authoritarian regimes. Pape finds that suicide bombers target democracies exclusively and argues that this is in part because of constraints on their ability to strike back.[36] Capable authoritarian regimes are able to gather more information on their populations than democracies and can more easily round up suspected terrorists and target those sympathetic to them. They are also less constrained by human rights considerations in their interrogation and retaliation practices.[37]

The ease with which a terrorist organization can be targeted also influences a country's ability to retaliate forcefully. Terrorist organizations such as al-Qaida that are widely dispersed, difficult to identify, or otherwise hard to target are at an advantage in a war of attrition because their enemies will have difficulty delivering punishment. Israel has, through superior intelligence gathering, been able to assassinate top members of Hamas's leadership at will, including its founder and spiritual leader, Sheik Ahmed Yassin, as well as his successor, Abdel Aziz Rantisi. The United States, by contrast, has been unable to locate Osama bin Laden and his top deputy, Ayman al-Zawahiri.

The third variable is a target's cost tolerance. Governments that are able to absorb heavier costs and hold out longer are less inviting targets for an attrition strategy. Terrorist organizations are likely to gauge a target's cost tolerance based on at least two factors: the target's regime type and the target's past behavior toward other terrorists. Regime type is important because democracies may be less able to tolerate the painful effects of terrorism than non-democracies. Citizens of democracies, their fears stoked by media reports and warnings of continued vulnerability, are more likely to demand an end to the attacks. In more authoritarian states, the government exerts more control over the media and can disregard public opinion to a greater extent. The Russian government's heavy-handed response to hostage situations, for example, suggests a higher tolerance for casualties than a more fully democratic government would have. Additionally, because terrorist organizations operate more freely in democracies and politicians must interact with the public to maintain political support, terrorists have an easier time targeting prominent individuals for assassination. Of four leaders assassinated by terrorists in the past quarter century—Indira Gandhi, Rajiv Gandhi, Yitzak Rabin, and Anwar Sadat—three were leaders of democracies.

Among democratic states, sensitivity to costs may vary with the party in power. When more dovish parties are in charge, the target may be perceived to have lower cost tolerances than if a more hawkish party were at the helm. The dove-hawk dimension may correlate with the left-right dimension in domestic politics, leading left-wing parties to be more likely to grant terrorist demands. This traditional divide between peace and security has characterized Israeli politics for years. Labor Party Prime Minister Ehud Barak was elected on a platform of withdrawing Israeli forces from Lebanon and making peace with the Palestinians; in contrast, Likud Party Prime Minister Ariel Sharon was elected on a platform of meeting terrorists with military force. Hoping for greater concessions, terrorists may preferentially attack dovish parties.

The number of prior concessions made to other terrorists is also likely to influence perceptions of the target's cost tolerance. Governments that have already yielded to terrorist demands are more likely to experience additional terrorist attacks. Evidence abounds that terrorists explicitly consider the prior behavior of states and are encouraged by signs of weakness. Israel's precipitous withdrawal from southern Lebanon in May 2000 convinced Hamas that the Israeli leadership's resolve was weakening and encouraged Hamas leaders to initiate the second intifada in September 2000.[38] Israelis fear the same inference will be drawn from their withdrawal from Gaza. A Hamas leader interviewed in October 2005 declared, "When we took up arms and launched [the second intifada], we succeeded in less than five years to force the Israelis to withdraw from the Gaza Strip. This fulfilled everyone's dream. I think we have to benefit from this experience by applying it accordingly to the West Bank and other occupied areas."[39] The past behavior of a targeted government, therefore, also provides important information to terrorist groups about its likely future behavior and the success of this particular strategy.

Perhaps the most important example of a terrorist group pursuing an attrition strategy is al-Qaida's war with the United States. In a November 2004 broadcast, bin Laden boasted, "We gained experience in guerilla and attritional warfare in our struggle against the great oppressive superpower, Russia, in which we and the mujahidin ground it down for ten years until it went bankrupt, and decided to withdraw in defeat. . . . We are continuing to make America bleed to the point of bankruptcy."[40] Al-Qaida's goal—policy change—is well suited to an attrition strategy. Bin Laden has frequently argued that the United States lacks the resolve to fight a long attritional war, as in his February 1996 declaration of jihad:

> Where was this false courage of yours when the explosion in Beirut took place in 1983 A.D.? You were transformed into scattered bits and pieces; 241 soldiers were killed, most of them Marines. And where was this courage of yours when two explosions made you leave Aden in less than twenty-four hours!
>
> But your most disgraceful case was in Somalia; where, after vigorous propaganda about the power of the U.S. and its post–cold war leadership of the new world order, you moved tens of thousands of international forces, including twenty-eight thousand American soldiers, into Somalia. However, when tens of your soldiers were killed in minor battles and one American pilot was dragged in the streets of Mogadishu, you left the area in disappointment, humiliation, and defeat, carrying your dead with you. Clinton appeared in front of the whole world threatening and promising revenge, but these threats were merely a preparation for withdrawal. You had been disgraced by Allah and you withdrew; the extent of your impotence and weaknesses became very clear.[41]

Although difficult to prove, it also appears that bin Laden believed that he and his organization would be hard to target with counterattacks, making a war of attrition strategy even more appealing. In 2001 the Taliban was on the verge of eliminating armed resistance in northern Afghanistan; and, as a landlocked country, Afghanistan must have seemed relatively invulnerable to a U.S. invasion. The United States had bombed al-Qaida camps before to no effect. Even if the United States invaded, Afghanistan was both costly and difficult to conquer, as the Soviets discovered in the 1980s. In the end, of course, the Taliban would have been well advised to insist that the September 11 attacks be delayed until the Northern Alliance was defeated, but the latter's dramatic success with U.S. help was perhaps difficult to anticipate.

BEST RESPONSES TO ATTRITION

There are at least five counterstrategies available to a state engaged in a war of attrition. First, the targeted government can concede inessential issues in exchange for peace, a strategy that we believe is frequently pursued though rarely admitted.[42] In some cases, the terrorists will genuinely care more about the disputed issue and be willing to outlast the target. In such cases, concessions are likely to be the state's best response. Other potential challengers, however, may perceive this response as a sign of weakness, which could lead them to launch their own attacks. To reduce the damage to its reputation, the target can vigorously fight other wars of attrition over issues it cares more deeply about, thus signaling a willingness to bear costs if the matter is of sufficient consequence.

Second, where the issue under dispute is important enough to the targeted state that it does not want to grant any concessions, the government may engage in targeted retaliation. Retaliation can target the leadership of the terrorist group, its followers, their assets, and other objects of value. Care must be taken, however, that the retaliation is precisely targeted, because the terrorist organization could simultaneously be pursuing a strategy of provocation. A harsh, indiscriminate response might make a war of attrition more costly for the terrorists, but it would also harm innocent civilians who might then serve as willing recruits for the terrorists. The Israeli policy of assassination of terrorist leaders is shaped by this concern.

Third, a state can harden likely targets to minimize the costs the terrorist organization can inflict. If targeted governments can prevent most attacks from being executed, a war of attrition strategy will not be able to inflict the costs necessary to convince the target to concede. The wall separating Israel from the West Bank and Gaza is a large-scale example of this counterstrategy. The United States has been less successful in hardening its own valuable targets, such as nuclear and chemical plants and the container shipping system, despite the creation of the Department of Homeland Security.[43] Protecting these types of targets is essential if one seeks to deter additional attacks and discourage the use of attrition.

Fourth, states should seek to deny terrorists access to the most destructive weapons, especially nuclear and biological ones. Any weapon that can inflict enormous costs will be particularly attractive to terrorists pursuing a war of attrition. The greater the destruction, the higher the likelihood that the target will concede increasingly consequential issues. Particular attention should be placed on securing Russian stockpiles of fissile material and on halting the spread of uranium enrichment technology to Iran and North Korea. No other country has as much material under so little government control as Russia, and Iran and North Korea are vital because of the links both countries have to terrorist organizations.[44]

Finally, states can strive to minimize the psychological costs of terrorism and the tendency people have to overreact. John Mueller has noted that the risks associated with terrorism are actually quite small; for the average U.S. citizen, the likelihood of being a victim of a terrorist attack is about the same as that of being struck by light[n]ing.[45] Government public education programs should therefore be careful not to overstate the threat, for this plays into the hands of the terrorists. If Americans become convinced that terrorism, while a deadly problem, is no more of a health risk than drunk driving, smoking, or obesity, then al-Qaida's attrition strategy will be undercut. What the United States should seek to avoid are any unnecessary costs associated with wasteful and misguided counterterror programs. The more costs the United States inflicts on itself in the name of counterterrorism policies of dubious utility, the more likely a war of attrition strategy is to succeed.

Intimidation: The Reign of Terror

Intimidation is akin to the strategy of deterrence, preventing some undesired behavior by means of threats and costly signals.[46] It is most frequently used when terrorist organizations wish to overthrow a government in power or gain social control over a given population. It works by demonstrating that the terrorists have the power to punish whoever disobeys them, and that the government is powerless to stop them.

Terrorists are often in competition with the government for the support of the population. Terrorists who wish to bring down a government must somehow convince the government's defenders that continued backing of the government will be costly. One way to do this is to provide clear evidence that the terrorist organization can kill those individuals who continue to sustain the regime. By targeting the government's more visible agents and supporters, such as mayors, police, prosecutors, and pro-regime citizens, terrorist organizations demonstrate that they have the ability to hurt their opponents and that the government is too weak to punish the terrorists or protect future victims.

Terrorists can also use an intimidation strategy to gain greater social control over a population. Terrorists may turn to this strategy in situations where a government has consistently refused to implement a policy a terrorist group favors and where efforts to change the state's policy appear futile. In this case, terrorists use intimidation to impose the desired policy directly on the population, gaining compliance through selective violence and the threat of future reprisals. In the United States, antiabortion activists have bombed clinics to prevent individuals from performing or seeking abortions, and in the 1960s racist groups burned churches to deter African Americans from claiming their civil rights. In Afghanistan, the Taliban beheaded the principal of a girls school to deter others from providing education for girls.[47]

An intimidation strategy can encompass a range of actions—from assassinations of individuals in positions of power to car bombings of police recruits, such as those carried out by the Zarqawi group in Iraq. It can also include massacres of civilians who have cooperated with the government or rival groups, such as the 1957 massacre at Melouza by the National Liberation Front during the Algerian war for independence.[48] This strategy was taken to an extreme by the Armed Islamic Group in Algeria's civil war of the 1990s. In that war, Islamist guerrillas massacred thousands of people suspected of switching their allegiance to the government. Massacres were especially common in villages that had once been under firm rebel control but that the army was attempting to retake and clear of rebels. Stathis Kalyvas argues that these conditions pose extreme dilemmas for the local inhabitants, who usually wish to support whoever will provide security, but are often left exposed when the government begins to retake an area but has not established effective control.[49]

CONDITIONS FAVORABLE TO INTIMIDATION

When the goal is regime change, weak states and rough terrain are two factors that facilitate intimidation. James Fearon and David Laitin argue that civil wars are likely to erupt and continue where the government is weak and the territory is large and difficult to traverse. These conditions allow small insurgent groups to carve out portions of a country as a base for challenging the central government.[50] Intimidation is likely to be used against civilians on the fault lines between rebel and government control to deter individuals from supporting the government.

When the goal is social control, weak states again facilitate intimidation. When the justice system is too feeble to effectively prosecute crimes associated with intimidation, people will either live in fear or seek protection from non-state actors such as local militias or gangs. Penetration of the justice system by sympathizers of a terrorist group also facilitates an intimidation strategy, because police and courts will be reluctant to prosecute crimes and may even be complicit in them.

BEST RESPONSES TO INTIMIDATION

When the terrorist goal is regime change, the best response to intimidation is to retake territory from the rebels in discrete chunks and in a decisive fashion. Ambiguity about who is in charge should be minimized, even if this means temporarily ceding some areas to the rebels to concentrate resources on selected sections of territory. This response is embodied in the "clear-and-hold strategy" that U.S. forces are employing in Iraq. The 2005 National Strategy for Victory in Iraq specifically identifies intimidation as the "strategy of our enemies."[51] The proper response, as Secretary of State Condoleezza Rice stated in October 2005, "is to clear, hold, and build: clear areas from insurgent control, hold them securely, and build durable national Iraqi institutions."[52] If rebels control their own zone and have no access to the government zone, they will have no incentive to kill the civilians they control and no ability to kill the civilians the government controls. In this situation, there is no uncertainty about who is in control;

the information that would be provided by intimidation is already known. The U.S. military developed the clear-and-hold strategy during the final years of U.S. involvement in Vietnam. A principal strategy of the Vietcong was intimidation—to prevent collaboration with the government and build up control in the countryside. In the early years of the war, the United States responded with search and destroy missions, essentially an attrition strategy. Given that the insurgents were not pursuing an attrition strategy, and were not particularly vulnerable to one, this initial counterstrategy was a mistake. Clear-and-hold was the more appropriate response because it limited the Vietcong's access to potential targets and thus undercut its strategy.[53]

Clear-and-hold has its limitations. It is usually impossible to completely deny terrorists entry into the government-controlled zones. In 2002 Chechen terrorists were able to hold a theater audience of 912 people hostage in the heart of Moscow, and 130 were killed in the operation to retake the building. The Shining Path frequently struck in Lima, far from its mountain strongholds. In such situations, a more effective counterstrategy would be to invest in protecting the targets of attacks. In most states, most of the time, the majority of state agents do not need to worry about their physical security, because no one wants to harm them. However, certain state agents, such as prosecutors of organized crime, are more accustomed to danger, and procedures have been developed to protect them. These procedures should be applied to election workers, rural officials and police, community activists, and any individual who plays a visible role in the support and functioning of the embattled government.

When the terrorist goal is social control, the best response is strengthening law enforcement. This may require more resources to enable the government to effectively investigate and prosecute crimes. More controversial, it may mean using national agencies such as the Federal Bureau of Investigation to bypass local officials who are sympathetic to the terrorist group and investigating law enforcement agencies to purge such sympathizers if they obstruct justice. The state can also offer additional protection to potential targets and increase penalties for violence against them. For instance, the 1994 federal Freedom of Access to Clinic Entrances Act, passed in the wake of the 1993 killing of a doctor at an abortion clinic in Florida, prohibits any violence designed to prevent people from entering such clinics.

Provocation: Lighting the Fuse

A provocation strategy is often used in pursuit of regime change and territorial change, the most popular goals of the FTOs listed by the State Department. It is designed to persuade the domestic audience that the target of attacks is evil and untrustworthy and must be vigorously resisted.

Terrorist organizations seeking to replace a regime face a significant challenge: they are usually much more hostile to the regime than a majority of the state's citizens. Al-Qaida may wish to topple the House of Saud, but if a majority of citizens do not support this goal, al-Qaida is unlikely to achieve it. Similarly, if most Tamils are satisfied living in a united Sri Lanka, the Tamil Tigers' drive for independence will fail. To succeed, therefore, a terrorist organization must first convince moderate citizens that their government needs to be replaced or that independence from the central government is the only acceptable outcome.

Provocation helps shift citizen support away from the incumbent regime. In a provocation strategy, terrorists seek to goad the target government into a military response that harms civilians within the terrorist organization's home territory.[54] The aim is to convince them that the government is so evil that the radical goals of the terrorists are justified and support for their organization is warranted.[55] This is what the Basque Fatherland and

Liberty group (ETA) sought to do in Spain. For years, Madrid responded to ETA attacks with repressive measures against the Basque community, mobilizing many of its members against the government even if they did not condone those attacks. As one expert on this conflict writes, "Nothing radicalizes a people faster than the unleashing of undisciplined security forces on its towns and villages."[56]

David Lake argues that moderates are radicalized because government attacks provide important information about the type of leadership in power and its willingness to negotiate with more moderate elements.[57] Ethan Bueno de Mesquita and Eric Dickson develop this idea and show that if the government has the ability to carry out a discriminating response to terrorism but chooses an undiscriminating one, it reveals itself to be unconcerned with the welfare of the country's citizens. Provocation, therefore, is a way for terrorists to force an enemy government to reveal information about itself that then helps the organization recruit additional members.[58]

CONDITIONS FAVORABLE TO PROVOCATION

Constraints on retaliation and regime type are again important in determining when provocation is successful. For provocation to work, the government must be capable of middling levels of brutality. A government willing and able to commit genocide makes a bad target for provocation, as the response will destroy the constituency the terrorists represent. At the opposite pole, a government so committed to human rights and the rule of law that it is incapable of inflicting indiscriminate punishment also makes a bad target, because it cannot be provoked. Such a government might be an attractive target for an attrition strategy if it is not very good at stopping attacks, but provocation will be ineffective.

What explains why a government would choose a less discriminating counterstrategy over a more

precise one? In some instances, a large-scale military response will enhance the security of a country rather than detract from it. If the target government is able to eliminate the leadership of a terrorist organization and its operatives, terrorism is likely to cease or be greatly reduced even if collateral damage radicalizes moderates to some extent. A large-scale military response may also enhance the security of a country, despite radicalizing some moderates, if it deters additional attacks from other terrorist groups that may be considering a war of attrition. Target governments may calculate that the negative consequences of a provocation strategy are acceptable under these conditions.

Domestic political considerations are also likely to influence the type of response that the leadership of a target state chooses. Democracies may be more susceptible to provocation than nondemocracies. Populations that have suffered from terrorist violence will naturally want their government to take action to stop terrorism. Unfortunately, many of the more discriminating tools of counterterrorism, such as infiltrating terrorist cells, sharing intelligence with other countries, and arresting individuals, are not visible to the publics these actions serve to protect. Bueno de Mesquita has argued that democratic leaders may have to employ the more public and less discriminating counterterror strategies to prove that their government is taking sufficient action against terrorists, even if these steps are provocative.[59] Pressure for a provocative counterresponse may also be particularly acute for more hard-line administrations whose constituents may demand greater action.[60] Counterstrategies, therefore, are influenced in part by the political system from which they emerge.

The United States in September 2001 was ripe for provocation, and al-Qaida appears to have understood this. The new administration of George W. Bush was known to be hawkish in its foreign policy and in its attitude toward the use of military power. In a November 2004 videotape, bin Laden bragged that al-Qaida found it "easy for us to provoke this administration."[61] The strategy appears to be working. A 2004 Pew survey found that international trust in the United States had declined significantly in response to the invasion of Iraq.[62] Similarly, a 2004 report by the International Institute for Strategic Studies found that al-Qaida's recruitment and fundraising efforts had been given a major boost by the U.S. invasion of Iraq.[63] In the words of Shibley Telhami, "What we're seeing now is a disturbing sympathy with al-Qaida coupled with resentment toward the United States."[64] The Bush administration's eagerness to overthrow Saddam Hussein, a desire that predated the September 11 attacks, has, in the words of bin Laden, "contributed to these remarkable results for al-Qaida."[65]

BEST RESPONSES TO PROVOCATION

The best response to provocation is a discriminating strategy that inflicts as little collateral damage as possible. Countries should seek out and destroy the terrorists and their immediate backers to reduce the likelihood of future terror attacks, but they must carefully isolate these targets from the general population, which may or may not be sympathetic to the terrorists.[66] This type of discriminating response will require superior intelligence capabilities. In this regard, the United States' efforts to invest in information-gathering abilities in response to September 11 have been underwhelming. Even the most basic steps, such as developing a deeper pool of expertise in the regional languages, have been slow in coming.[67] This stands in contrast to U.S. behavior during the Cold War, when the government sponsored research centers at top universities to analyze every aspect of the Soviet economic, military, and political system. The weakness of the U.S. intelligence apparatus has been most clearly revealed in the inability of the United States to eliminate bin Laden and al-Zawahiri, and in the United States' decision to invade Iraq.[68] Faulty U.S. intelligence

has simultaneously protected al-Qaida leaders from death and led to the destruction of thousands of Muslim civilians—exactly the response al-Qaida was likely seeking.

Spoiling: Sabotaging the Peace

The goal of a spoiling strategy is to ensure that peace overtures between moderate leaders on the terrorists' side and the target government do not succeed.[69] It works by playing on the mistrust between these two groups and succeeds when one or both parties fail to sign or implement a settlement. It is often employed when the ultimate objective is territorial change.

Terrorists resort to a spoiling strategy when relations between two enemies are improving and a peace agreement threatens the terrorists' more far-reaching goals. Peace agreements alarm terrorists because they understand that moderate citizens are less likely to support ongoing violence once a compromise agreement between more moderate groups has been reached. Thus, Iranian radicals kidnapped fifty-two Americans in Tehran in 1979 not because relations between the United States and Iran were becoming more belligerent, but because three days earlier Iran's relatively moderate prime minister, Mehdi Bazargan, met with the U.S. national security adviser, Zbigniew Brzezinski, and the two were photographed shaking hands. From the perspective of the radicals, a real danger of reconciliation existed between the two countries, and violence was used to prevent this.[70] A similar problem has hampered Arab-Israeli peace negotiations, as well as talks between Protestants and Catholics in Northern Ireland.

A spoiling strategy works by persuading the enemy that moderates on the terrorists' side cannot be trusted to abide by a peace deal. Whenever two sides negotiate a peace agreement, there is uncertainty about whether the deal is self-enforcing. Each side fears that even if it honors its commitments, the other side may not, catapulting it back to war on disadvantageous terms. Some Israelis, for example, feared that if Israel returned an additional 13 percent of the West Bank to the Palestinians, as mandated by the 1998 Wye accord, the Palestinian Authority would relaunch its struggle from an improved territorial base. Extremists understand that moderates look for signs that their former enemy will violate an agreement and that targeting these moderates with violence will heighten their fears that they will be exploited. Thus terrorist attacks are designed to persuade a targeted group that the seemingly moderate opposition with whom it negotiated an agreement will not or cannot stop terrorism, and hence cannot be trusted to honor an agreement.

Terrorist acts are particularly effective during peace negotiations because opposing parties are naturally distrustful of each other's motives and have limited sources of information about each other's intentions. Thus, even if moderate leaders are willing to aggressively suppress extremists on their side, terrorists know that isolated violence might still convince the target to reject the deal. A reason for this is that the targeted group may not be able to readily observe the extent of the crackdown and must base its judgments primarily on whether terrorism occurs or not. Even a sincere effort at self-policing, therefore, will not necessarily convince the targeted group to proceed with a settlement if a terrorist attack occurs.

CONDITIONS FAVORABLE TO SPOILING

Terrorists pursuing a spoiling strategy are likely to be more successful when the enemy perceives moderates on their side to be strong and therefore more capable of halting terrorism.[71] When an attack occurs, the target cannot be sure whether moderates on the other side can suppress their own extremists but choose not to, or are weak and lack the ability to stop them. Israelis, for example, frequently questioned whether Yasser Arafat was simply unable to stop terrorist attacks against Israel or was unwilling to do so. The weaker the moderates are perceived to be, the less impact a terrorist attack will have on the other side's trust, and the less likely such an attack is to convince them to abandon a peace agreement.

The Israeli-Palestinian conflict, and in particular the Oslo peace process, has been plagued by spoilers. On the Palestinian side, Hamas's violent attacks coincided with the ratification and implementation of accords—occasions when increased mistrust could thwart progress toward peace. Hamas also stepped up its attacks prior to Israeli elections in 1996 and 2001, in which Labor was the incumbent party, in an effort to persuade Israeli voters to cast their votes for the less cooperative and less trusting hard-line Likud Party.[72] Terrorism was especially effective after Arafat's 1996 electoral victory, when it became clear to the Israelis that Arafat was, at the time, a popular and powerful leader within the Palestinian community.[73] This in turn suggested to the Israelis that Arafat was capable of cracking down aggressively on terrorist violence but was unwilling to do so, a sign that he could not be trusted to keep the peace.

BEST RESPONSES TO SPOILING

When mutual trust is high, a peace settlement can be implemented despite ongoing terrorist acts and the potential vulnerabilities the agreement can create. Trust, however, is rarely high after long conflicts, which is why spoilers can strike with a reasonable chance that their attack will be successful. Strategies that build trust and reduce vulnerability are, therefore, the best response to spoiling.

Vulnerabilities emerge in peace processes in two ways. Symmetric vulnerabilities occur during the implementation of a deal because both sides must lower their guard. The Israelis, for example, have had to relax controls over the occupied territories, and the Palestinians were obligated to disarm militant groups. Such symmetric vulnerabilities can be eased by third-party monitoring and verification of the peace implementation process. Monitoring can help reduce uncertainty regarding the behavior of the parties. Even better, third-party enforcement of the deal can make reneging more costly, increasing confidence in the deal and its ultimate success.[74]

Vulnerabilities can also be longer term and asymmetric. In any peace deal between Israel and the Palestinians, the ability of the Palestinians to harm Israel will inevitably grow as Palestinians build their own state and acquire greater military capabilities. This change in the balance of power can make it difficult for the side that will see an increase in its power to credibly commit not to take advantage of this increase later on. This commitment problem can cause conflicts to be prolonged even though there are possible peace agreements that both sides would prefer to war.[75]

The problem of shifting power can be addressed in at least three ways. First, agreements themselves can be crafted in ways that limit the post-treaty shift in power. Power-sharing agreements such as that between the Liberals and Conservatives to create a single shared presidency in Colombia in 1957 are one example of this. Allowing the defeated side to retain some military capabilities, as Confederate officers were allowed to do after the surrender at Appomattox, is another example.[76] Second, peace settlements can require the side about to be advantaged to send a costly signal of its honorable intentions, such as providing constitutional protections of minority rights. An example is the Constitutional Law on National Minorities passed in Croatia in 2002, which protects the right of minorities to obtain an education in their own language. Finally, parties can credibly commit to an agreement by participating in international institutions that insist on the protection of minority rights. A government that is willing to join the European Union effectively constrains itself from exploiting a minority group because of the high costs to that government of being ejected from the group.

Outbidding: Zealots versus Sellouts

Outbidding arises when two key conditions hold: two or more domestic parties are competing for leadership of their side, and the general population is uncertain about which of the groups best represents their interests.[77] The competition between Hamas and Fatah is a classic case where two groups vie for the support of the Palestinian citizens and where the average Palestinian is uncertain about which side he or she ought to back.

If citizens had full information about the preferences of the competing groups, an outbidding strategy would be unnecessary and ineffective; citizens would simply support the group that best aligned with their own interests. In reality, however, citizens cannot be sure if the group competing for power truly represents their preferences. The group could be a strong and resolute defender of the cause (zealots) or weak and ineffective stooges of the enemy (sellouts). If citizens support zealots, they get a strong champion but with some risk that they will be dragged into a confrontation with the enemy that they end up losing. If citizens support sellouts, they get peace but at the price of accepting a worse outcome than might have been achieved with additional armed struggle. Groups competing for power have an incentive to signal that they are zealots rather than sellouts. Terrorist attacks can serve this function by signaling that a group has the will to continue the armed struggle despite its costs.

Three reasons help to explain why groups are likely to be rewarded for being more militant rather than less. First, in bargaining contexts, it is often useful to be represented by an agent who is more hard-line than oneself. Hard-line agents will reject deals that one would accept, which will force the adversary to make a better offer than one would get by representing oneself in the negotiations.[78] Palestinians might therefore prefer Hamas as a negotiating agent with Israel because it has a reputation for resolve and will reject inferior deals.

Second, uncertainty may also exist about the type of adversary the population and its competing groups are facing. If the population believes there is some chance that their adversary is untrustworthy (unwilling to compromise under any condition), then they know that conflict may be inevitable, in which case being represented by zealots may be advantageous.[79]

A third factor that may favor outbidding is that office-holding itself may produce incentives to sell out. Here, the problem lies with the benefits groups receive once in office (i.e., income and power). Citizens fear that their leaders, once in office, may betray important principles and decide to settle with the enemy on unfavorable terms. They know that holding office skews one's preferences toward selling out, but they remain unsure about which of their leaders is most likely to give in. Terrorist organizations exploit this uncertainty by using violence to signal their commitment to a cause. Being perceived as more extreme than the median voter works to the terrorists' benefit because it balances out the "tempering effect" of being in office.

An interesting aspect of the outbidding strategy is that the enemy is only tangentially related to the strategic interaction. In fact, an attack motivated by outbidding may not even be designed to achieve any goal related to the enemy, such as inducing a concession or scuttling a peace treaty. The process is almost entirely concerned with the signal it sends to domestic audiences uncertain about their own leadership and its commitment to a cause. As such, outbidding provides a potential explanation for terrorist attacks that continue even when they seem unable to produce any real results.

CONDITIONS FAVORABLE TO OUTBIDDING

Outbidding will be favored when multiple groups are competing for the allegiance of a similar demographic base of support. In Peru, the 1970s saw the development of a number of leftist groups seeking to represent the poor and indigenous population. When the military turned over power to an elected government in 1980, the Shining Path took up an armed struggle to distinguish itself from groups that chose to pursue electoral politics.[80] It also embarked on an assassination campaign designed to weaken rival leftist groups and intimidate their followers. When organizations encounter less competition for the support of their main constituents, outbidding will be less appealing.

BEST RESPONSES TO OUTBIDDING

One solution to the problem of outbidding would be to eliminate the struggle for power by encouraging competing groups to consolidate into a unified opposition. If competition among resistance groups is eliminated, the incentive for outbidding also disappears. The downside of this counterstrategy is that a unified opposition may be stronger than a divided one. United oppositions, however, can make peace and deliver, whereas divided ones may face greater structural disincentives to do so.

An alternative strategy for the government to pursue in the face of outbidding is to validate the strategy chosen by nonviolent groups by granting them concessions and attempting to satisfy the demands of their constituents. If outbidding can be shown to yield poor results in comparison to playing within the system, groups may be persuaded to abandon the strategy. As in the case of the Shining Path, this may require providing physical protection to competing groups in case the outbidder turns to intimidation in its competition with less violent rivals. In general, any steps that can be taken to make the non-outbidding groups seem successful (e.g., channeling resources and government services to their constituents) will also help undermine the outbidders. The high turnout in the December 2005 Iraqi election in Sunni-dominated regions may indicate that outbidding is beginning to fail in the communities most strongly opposed to the new political system.[81]

Conclusion

Terrorist violence is a form of costly signaling by which terrorists attempt to influence the beliefs of their enemy and the population they represent or wish to control. They use violence to signal their strength and resolve in an effort to produce concessions from their enemy and obedience and support from their followers. They also attack both to sow mistrust between moderates who might want to make peace and to provoke a reaction that makes the enemy appear barbarous and untrustworthy.

In this article, we have laid out the five main goals terrorist organizations seek and the five most important terrorist strategies, and we have outlined when they are likely to be tried and what the best counterstrategies might look like. What becomes clear in this brief analysis is that a deeper study of each of the five strategies is needed to reveal the nuanced ways in which terrorism works, and to refine responses to it. We conclude by highlighting two variables that will be important in any such analysis, and by a final reflection on counterterror policies that are strategically independent or not predicated on the specific strategy being used.

The first variable is information. It has long been a truism that the central front in counterinsurgency warfare is the information front. The same is true in terrorism. Costly signaling is pointless in the absence of uncertainty on the part of the recipient of the signal. Attrition is designed to convince the target that the costs of maintaining a policy are not worth the gains; if the target already knew this, it would have ceded the issue without an attack being launched. Provocation is designed to goad the target into retaliating indiscriminately (because it lacks information to discriminate), which will persuade the population that the target is malevolent (because it is uncertain of the target's intentions). The other strategies are similarly predicated on uncertainty, intelligence, learning, and communication. Thus, it bears emphasizing that the problem of terrorism is not a problem of applying force per se, but one of acquiring intelligence and affecting beliefs. With the right information, the proper application of force is comparatively straightforward. The struggle against terrorism is, therefore, not usefully guided by the metaphor of a "war on terrorism" any more than policies designed to alleviate poverty are usefully guided by the metaphor of a "war on poverty" or narcotics policy by a "war on drugs." The struggle against terrorism can more usefully be thought of as a struggle to collect and disseminate reliable information in environments fraught with uncertainty.

The second important variable is regime type. Democracies have been the sole targets of attritional suicide bombing campaigns, whereas authoritarian regimes such as those in Algeria routinely face campaigns by rebel groups pursuing an intimidation strategy. Democracies also seem to be more susceptible to attrition and provocation strategies. This type of variation cries out for deeper analysis of the strengths and weakness of different regime types in the face of different terrorist strategies. Our analysis suggests that democracies are more likely to be sensitive to the costs of terrorist attacks, to grant concessions to terrorists so as to limit future attacks, to be constrained in their ability to pursue a lengthy attritional campaign against an organization, but also to be under greater pressure to "do something." This does not mean that all democracies will behave incorrectly in the face of terrorist attacks all the time. Democratic regimes may possess certain structural features, however, that make them attractive targets for terrorism.

Finally, we realize that our discussion is only a beginning and that further elaboration of each of the strategies and their corresponding counter-strategies awaits future research. We also understand that not all counterterrorism policies are predicated on the specific strategy terrorists pursue. Our analysis is at the middling level of strategic interaction. At the tactical level are all the tools of intelligence gathering and target defense that make sense no matter what the terrorist's strategy is. At the higher level are the primary sources of terrorism such as poverty, education, international conflict, and chauvinistic indoctrination that enable terrorist organizations to operate and survive in the first place. Our aim in this article has been to try to understand why these organizations choose certain forms of violence, and how this violence serves their larger purposes. The United States has the ability to reduce the likelihood of additional attacks on its territory and citizens. But it will be much more successful if it first understands the goals terrorists are seeking and the underlying strategic logic by which a plane flying into a skyscraper might deliver the desired response.

NOTES

1. Thomas L. Friedman, "Marines Complete Beirut Pullback: Moslems Move In," *New York Times*, February 27, 2004.

2. Don Van Natta Jr., "The Struggle for Iraq: Last American Combat Troops Quit Saudi Arabia," *New York Times*, September 22, 2003.

3. James Glanz, "Hostage Is Freed after Philippine Troops Are Withdrawn from Iraq," *New York Times*, July 21, 2004.

4. Robert A. Pape, *Dying to Win: The Strategic Logic of Suicide Terrorism* (New York: Random House, 2005), p. 65.

5. Alan B. Krueger and David D. Laitin, "Kto Kogo? A Cross-Country Study of the Origins and Targets of Terrorism," Princeton University and Stanford University, 2003; Alan B. Krueger and Jitka Maleckova, "Education, Poverty, and Terrorism: Is There a Causal Connection?" *Journal of Economic Perspectives*, Vol. 17,

No. 4 (November 2003), pp. 119–144; and Alberto Abadie, "Poverty, Political Freedom, and the Roots of Terrorism," Faculty Research Working Papers Series, RWP04-043 (Cambridge, Mass.: John F. Kennedy School of Government, Harvard University, 2004).

6. Jessica Stern, *Terror in the Name of God: Why Religious Militants Kill* (New York: Ecco-HarperCollins, 2003).

7. Of course, terrorists will also be seeking best responses to government responses. A pair of strategies that are best responses to each other constitutes a Nash equilibrium, the fundamental prediction tool of game theory.

8. Office of Counterterrorism, U.S. Department of State, "Foreign Terrorist Organizations," fact sheet, October 11, 2005, http://www.state.gov/s/ct/rls/fs/3719.htm.

9. Quoted in Nasra Hassan, "An Arsenal of Believers: Talking to the 'Human Bombs,'" *New Yorker*, November 19, 2001, p. 37.

10. For discussion of differing definitions of terrorism, see Alex P. Schmid and Albert J. Jongman, *Political Terrorism: A New Guide to Actors, Authors, Concepts, Data Bases, Theories, and Literature* (New Brunswick, N.J.: Transaction, 1988), pp. 1–38. We do not focus on state terrorism because states face very different opportunities and constraints in their use of violence, and we do not believe the two cases are similar enough to be profitably analyzed together.

11. For the distinction between goals and strategies, see David A. Lake and Robert Powell, eds., *Strategic Choice and International Relations* (Princeton, N.J.: Princeton University Press, 1999), especially chap. 1.

12. On revolutionary terrorism, see Martha Crenshaw Hutchinson, "The Concept of Revolutionary Terrorism," *Journal of Conflict Resolution*, Vol. 16, No. 3 (September 1972), pp. 383–396; Martha Crenshaw Hutchinson, *Revolutionary Terrorism: The FLN in Algeria, 1954–1962* (Stanford, Calif.: Hoover Institution Press, 1978); and H. Edward Price Jr., "The Strategy and Tactics of Revolutionary Terrorism," *Comparative Studies in Society and History*, Vol. 19, No. 1 (January 1977), pp. 52–66.

13. This group has recently surrendered its weapons.

14. Some analysts argue that many terrorist organizations have degenerated into little more than self-perpetuating businesses that primarily seek to enhance their own power and wealth, and only articulate political goals for rhetorical purposes. See, for example, Stern, *Terror in the Name of God*, pp. 235–236. This suggests that power and wealth should be considered goals in their own right. All organizations, however, seek power and wealth to further their political objectives, and these are better viewed as instrumental in nature.

15. A difficult coding issue arises in determining when a group is a nonstate actor engaged in status quo maintenance and when it is simply a covert agent of the state. Some death squads were linked to elements in the armed forces, yet were not necessarily responsive to the chief executive of the country. Others were tied to right-wing parties and are more clearly nonstate, unless that party is the party in power. See Bruce D. Campbell and Arthur D. Brenner, eds., *Death Squads in Global Perspective: Murder with Deniability* (New York: Palgrave Macmillan, 2002).

16. The Taliban, which is not listed, does pursue social control; and the Israeli group Kach, which seeks to maintain the subordinate status of Palestinians in Israel and eventually to expel them, may also be considered to seek it. The Memorial Institute for the Prevention of Terrorism maintains a database of terrorist organizations that includes more than forty groups based in the United States. Some of these can be considered to seek social control, such as the Army of God, which targets doctors who provide abortions. See http://www.tkb.org.

17. Thomas Perry Thornton, "Terror as a Weapon of Political Agitation," in Harry Eckstein, ed., *Internal War: Problems and Approaches* (London: Free Press of Glencoe, 1964), p. 87.

18. Martha Crenshaw, "The Causes of Terrorism," *Comparative Politics*, Vol. 13, No. 4 (July 1981), pp. 379–399.

19. David Fromkin, "The Strategy of Terrorism," *Foreign Affairs*, Vol. 53, No. 4 (July 1975), pp. 683–698.

20. Price, "The Strategy and Tactics of Revolutionary Terrorism," pp. 54–58. Other related discussions include Paul Wilkinson, "The Strategic Implications of Terrorism," in M.L. Sondhi, ed., *Terrorism and Political Violence: A Sourcebook* (New Delhi: Haranand Publications, 2000); Paul Wilkinson, *Terrorism and the Liberal State* (New York: New York University Press, 1986), pp. 110–118; and Schmid and Jongman, *Political Terrorism*, pp. 50–59.

21. Geoffrey Blainey, *The Causes of War*, 3d ed. (New York: Free Press, 1988), p. 122.

22. James D. Fearon, "Rationalist Explanations for War," *International Organization*, Vol. 49, No. 3 (Summer 1995), pp. 379–414; and Robert Powell, "Bargaining Theory and International Conflict," *Annual Review of Political Science*, Vol. 5 (June 2002), pp. 1–30.

23. Thomas Hobbes, *Leviathan* (New York: Penguin, [1651] 1968), pp. 184.

24. John H. Herz, "Idealist Internationalism and the Security Dilemma," *World Politics*, Vol. 2, No. 2 (January 1950), pp. 157–180; Robert Jervis, *Perception and Misperception in International Politics* (Princeton, N.J.: Princeton University Press, 1976); Robert Jervis, "Cooperation under the Security Dilemma," *World Politics*, Vol. 30, No. 2 (January 1978), pp. 167–214; and Charles L. Glaser, "The Security Dilemma Revisited," *World Politics*, Vol. 50, No. 1 (October 1997), pp. 171–202.

25. Andrew H. Kydd, *Trust and Mistrust in International Relations* (Princeton, N.J.: Princeton University Press, 2005).

26. John G. Riley, "Silver Signals: Twenty-five Years of Screening and Signaling," *Journal of Economic Literature*, Vol. 39, No. 2 (June 2001), pp. 432–478.

27. James D. Fearon, "Signaling Foreign Policy Interests: Tying Hands vs. Sunk Costs," *Journal of Conflict Resolution*, Vol. 41, No. 1 (February 1977), pp. 68–90.

28. Dan Reiter, "Exploring the Bargaining Model of War," *Perspectives on Politics*, Vol. 1, No. 1 (March 2003), pp. 27–43; and Robert Powell, "Bargaining and Learning While Fighting," *American Journal of Political Science*, Vol. 48, No. 2 (April 2004), pp. 344–361.

29. Rival terrorist or moderate groups are also important, but terrorism is not often used to signal such groups. Sometimes rival groups are targeted in an effort to eliminate them, but this violence is usually thought of as internecine warfare rather than terrorism. The targeted government may also be divided into multiple actors, but these divisions are not crucial for a broad understanding of terrorist strategies.

30. This list is not exhaustive. In particular, it omits two strategies that have received attention in the literature: advertising and retaliation. Advertising may play a role in the beginning of some conflicts, but it does not sustain long-term campaigns of terrorist violence. Retaliation is a motivation for some terrorists, but terrorism would continue even if the state did not strike at terrorists, because terrorism is designed to achieve some goal, not just avenge counterterrorist attacks.

31. Per Baltzer Overgaard, "The Scale of Terrorist Attacks as a Signal of Resources," *Journal of Conflict Resolution*, Vol. 38, No. 3 (September 1994), pp. 452–478; and Harvey E. Lapan and Todd Sandler, "Terrorism and Signaling," *European Journal of Political Economy*, Vol. 9, No. 3 (August 1993), pp. 383–398.

32. J. Maynard Smith, "The Theory of Games and Evolution in Animal Conflicts," *Journal of Theoretical Biology*, Vol. 47 (1974), pp. 209–211; John J. Mearsheimer, *Conventional Deterrence* (Ithaca, N.Y.: Cornell University Press, 1983), pp. 33–35; and James D. Fearon, "Bargaining, Enforcement, and International Cooperation," *International Organization*, Vol. 52, No. 2 (Spring 1998), pp. 269–305.

33. Bernard Lewis, "The Revolt of Islam," *New Yorker*, November 19, 2001, p. 61.

34. Quoted in Hassan, "An Arsenal of Believers," p. 38.

35. Robert A. Pape, "The Strategic Logic of Suicide Terrorism," *American Political Science Review,* Vol. 97, No. 3 (August 2003), pp. 343–361; and Pape, *Dying to Win.*

36. Pape, *Dying to Win*, p. 44. Krueger and Laitin also find that targets of terrorism tend to be democratic. See Krueger and Laitin, "Kto Kogo?"

37. The U.S. program of extraordinary rendition, for example, is an effort to evade the restrictions usually faced by democracies by outsourcing the dirty work.

38. Debate Goes On Over Lebanon Withdrawal, *Haaretz*, May 23, 2001; and Daoud Kuttab, "The Lebanon Lesson," *Jerusalem Post*, May 25, 2000.

39. Interview with Mahmoud Khalid al-Zahar, *Al Jazeera*, October 22, 2005.

40. Osama bin Laden, *Messages to the World: The Statements of Osama bin Laden*, trans. James Howarth, ed. Bruce Lawrence (London: Verso, 2005), pp. 241–242.

41. Osama bin Laden, "Declaration of War against the Americans Occupying the Land of the Two Holy Places," *Al-Quds Al-Arabi*, August 1996, http://www.pbs.org/newshour/terrorism/international/fatwa_1996.html.

42. Peter C. Sederberg, "Conciliation as Counter-terrorist Strategy," *Journal of Peace Research*, Vol. 32, No. 3 (August 1995), pp. 295–312.

43. Stephen Flynn, *America the Vulnerable: How Our Government Is Failing to Protect Us from Terrorism* (New York: HarperCollins, 2004).

44. Graham T. Allison, Owen R. Coté Jr., Richard A. Falkenrath, and Steven E. Miller, *Avoiding Nuclear Anarchy: Containing the Threat of Loose Russian Nuclear Weapons and Fissile Material* (Cambridge, Mass.: MIT Press, 1996); and Graham Allison, *Nuclear Terrorism: The Ultimate Preventable Catastrophe* (New York: Times Books, 2004).

45. John Mueller, "Six Rather Unusual Propositions about Terrorism," *Terrorism and Political Violence*, Vol. 17, No. 4 (Winter 2005), pp. 487–505.

46. The literature on deterrence is vast. See, for example, Thomas C. Schelling, *Arms and Influence* (New Haven, Conn.: Yale University Press, 1966); and Christopher H. Achen and Duncan Snidal, "Rational Deterrence Theory and Comparative Case Studies," *World Politics*, Vol. 41, No. 2 (January 1989), pp. 143–169.

47. Noor Khan, "Militants Behead Afghan Principal for Educating Girls," *Boston Globe*, January 5, 2006.

48. Crenshaw Hutchinson, "The Concept of Revolutionary Terrorism," p. 390.

49. Stathis N. Kalyvas, "Wanton and Senseless? The Logic of Massacres in Algeria," *Rationality and Society*, Vol. 11, No. 3 (August 1999), pp. 243–285.

50. James D. Fearon and David D. Laitin, "Ethnicity, Insurgency, and Civil War," *American Political Science Review*, Vol. 97, No. 1 (February 2003), pp. 75–90.

51. United States National Security Council, *National Strategy for Victory in Iraq* (Washington, D.C.: White House, November 2005), p. 7.

52. Secretary of State Condoleezza Rice, "Iraq and U.S. Policy," testimony before the U.S. Senate Committee on Foreign Relations, October 19, 2005, 109th Cong., 1st sess., http://www.foreign.senate.gov/testimony/2005/RiceTestimony051019.pdf.

53. See Lewis Sorley, *A Better War: The Unexamined Victories and the Final Tragedy of America's Last Years in Vietnam* (New York: Harcourt, 1999). This thesis is not without controversy. See Matt Steinglass, "Vietnam and Victory," *Boston Globe*, December 18, 2005.

54. Fromkin, "The Strategy of Terrorism."

55. Crenshaw, "The Causes of Terrorism," p. 387; and Price, "The Strategy and Tactics of Revolutionary Terrorism," p. 58.

56. Paddy Woodworth, "Why Do They Kill? The Basque Conflict in Spain," *World Policy Journal,* Vol. 18, No. 1 (Spring 2001), p. 7.

57. David A. Lake, "Rational Extremism: Understanding Terrorism in the Twenty-first Century," *Dialog-IO*, Vol. 56, No. 2 (Spring 2002), pp. 15–29.

58. Ethan Bueno de Mesquita and Eric S. Dickson, "The Propaganda of the Deed: Terrorism, Counterterrorism, and Mobilization," Washington University and New York University, 2005. Bueno de Mesquita and Dickson also argue that government violence lowers economic prosperity, which favors extremists in their competition with moderates.

59. Ethan Bueno de Mesquita, "Politics and the Suboptimal Provision of Counterterror," *International Organization* [Vol. 61, No. 1 (Winter 2007), pp. 9–36].

60. On the other hand, more dovish regimes might feel political pressure to take strong visible actions, whereas a regime with hawkish credentials could credibly claim that it was pursuing effective but nonvisible tactics. For a similar logic, see Kenneth A. Schultz, "The Politics of Risking Peace: Do Hawks or Doves Deliver the Olive Branch?" *International Organization*, Vol. 59, No. 1 (Winter 2005), pp. 1–38.

61. Bin Laden, *Messages to the World*, pp. 241–242.

62. Pew Research Center for the People and the Press, Pew Global Attitudes Project: Nine-Nation Survey, "A Year after the Iraq War: Mistrust of America in Europe Ever Higher, Muslim Anger Persists," March 16, 2004.

63. See International Institute for Strategic Studies, *Strategic Survey, 2003/4: An Evaluation and Forecast of World Affairs* (London: Routledge, 2005).

64. Quoted in Dafna Linzer, "Poll Shows Growing Arab Rancor at U.S.," *Washington Post*, July 23, 2004.

65. Bob Woodward, *Plan of Attack* (New York: Simon and Schuster, 2004), pp. 21–23; and bin Laden, *Messages to the World*, pp. 241–242.

66. A program of economic and social assistance to these more moderate elements would provide counterevidence that the target is not malicious or evil as the terrorist organizations had claimed.

67. Farah Stockman, "Tomorrow's Homework: Reading, Writing, and Arabic," *Boston Globe*, January 6, 2006.

68. For an analysis of obstacles to innovation in U.S. intelligence agencies, see Amy B. Zegart, "September 11 and the Adaptation Failure of U.S. Intelligence Agencies," *International Security,* Vol. 29, No. 4 (Spring 2005), pp. 78–111.

69. Stephen John Stedman, "Spoiler Problems in Peace Processes," *International Security*, Vol. 22, No. 2 (Fall 1997), pp. 5–53.

70. Lewis, "The Revolt of Islam," p. 54.

71. Andrew H. Kydd and Barbara F. Walter, "Sabotaging the Peace: The Politics of Extremist Violence," *International Organization*, Vol. 56, No. 2 (Spring 2002), pp. 263–296.

72. Claude Berrebi and Esteban F. Klor, "On Terrorism and Electoral Outcomes: Theory and Evidence from the Israeli-Palestinian Conflict," Princeton University and Hebrew University of Jerusalem, 2004.

73. Kydd and Walter, "Sabotaging the Peace," pp. 279–289.

74. Barbara F. Walter, *Committing to Peace: The Successful Settlement of Civil Wars* (Princeton, N.J.: Princeton University Press, 2002); and Holger Schmidt, "When (and Why) Do Brokers Have to Be Honest? Impartiality and Third-Party Support for Peace Implementation after Civil Wars, 1945–1999," Georgetown University, 2004.

75. Fearon, "Rationalist Explanations for War"; James D. Fearon, "Commitment Problems and the Spread of Ethnic Conflict," in David A. Lake and Donald Rothchild, eds., *The International Spread of Ethnic Conflict: Fear, Diffusion, and Escalation* (Princeton, N.J.: Princeton University Press, 1998); and Robert Powell, "The Inefficient Use of Power: Costly Conflict with Complete Information," *American Political Science Review*, Vol. 98, No. 2 (May 2004), pp. 231–241.

76. As part of the terms of surrender, Confederate officers were allowed to keep their sidearms and personal property (including their horses) and return home.

77. For the most extensive treatment of terrorism and outbidding, see Mia Bloom, *Dying to Kill: The Allure of Suicide Terrorism* (New York: Columbia University Press, 2005). See also Stuart J. Kaufman, "Spiraling to Ethnic War: Elites, Masses, and Moscow in Moldova's Civil War," *International Security*, Vol. 21, No. 2 (Fall 1996), pp. 108–138.

78. Abhinay Muthoo, *Bargaining Theory with Applications* (Cambridge: Cambridge University Press, 1999), p. 230.

79. Rui J.P. de Figueiredo Jr. and Barry R. Weingast, "The Rationality of Fear: Political Opportunism and Ethnic Conflict," in Barbara F. Walter and Jack Snyder, eds., *Civil Wars, Insecurity, and Intervention* (New York: Columbia University Press, 1999), pp. 261–302.

80. James Ron, "Ideology in Context: Explaining Sendero Luminoso's Tactical Escalation," *Journal of Peace Research*, Vol. 38, No. 5 (September 2001), p. 582.

81. Dexter Filkins, "Iraqis, Including Sunnis, Vote in Large Numbers on Calm Day," *New York Times*, December 16, 2005.

Martha Finnemore

CHANGING NORMS OF HUMANITARIAN INTERVENTION

Since the end of the cold war states have increasingly come under pressure to intervene militarily and, in fact, *have* intervened militarily to protect citizens other than their own from humanitarian disasters. Recent efforts by NATO to protect Albanian Kosovars in Yugoslavia from ethnic cleansing, efforts to alleviate starvation and establish some kind of political order in Somalia, endeavors to enforce protected areas for Kurds and no-fly zones over Shiites in Iraq, and the huge UN military effort to disarm parties and rebuild a state in Cambodia are all instances of military action whose primary goal is not territorial or strategic but humanitarian.

Realist and neoliberal theories do not provide good explanations for this behavior. The interests these theories impute to states are geostrategic or economic or both, yet many or most of these interventions occur in states of negligible geostrategic or economic importance to the intervenors. Thus no obvious national interest is at stake for the states bearing the burden of the military intervention in most if not all these cases. Somalia is, perhaps, the clearest example of military action undertaken in a state of little or no strategic or economic importance to the principal intervenor. Similarly, in Cambodia, the states that played central roles in the UN military action were, with the exception of China, not states that had any obvious geostrategic interests

there by 1989; China, which did have a geostrategic interest, bore little of the burden of intervening. Realism and neoliberalism offer powerful explanations of the Persian Gulf War but have little to say about the extension of that war to Kurdish and Shiite protection through the enforcement of UN Resolution 688. The United States, France, and Britain have been allowing abuse of the Kurds for centuries. Why they should start caring about them now is not clear.

The recent pattern of humanitarian interventions raises the issue of what interests intervening states could possibly be pursuing. In most of these cases, the intervention targets are insignificant by any usual measure of geostrategic or economic interest. Why, then, do states intervene? This [discussion] argues that the pattern of intervention cannot be understood apart from the changing normative context in which it occurs. Normative context is important because it shapes conceptions of interest and gives purpose and meaning to action. It shapes the rights and duties states believe they have toward one another, and it shapes the goals they value, the means they believe are effective and legitimate to obtain those goals, and the political costs and benefits attached to different choices.

*** I examine the role of humanitarian norms in shaping patterns of humanitarian military intervention over the past 180 years and the ways those norms have changed over time creating new patterns of intervention behavior. Three factors, in particular, have changed. Who is human has changed,

From Martha Finnemore, *The Purpose of Intervention: Changing Beliefs about the Use of Force* (Ithaca, N.Y., and London: Cornell University Press, 2003), Chap. 3.

that is, who can successfully claim humanitarian protection from strong states has changed. In the nineteenth century, only white Christians received protection; mistreatment of other groups did not evoke the same concern. By the end of the twentieth century, however, most of the protected populations were non-white, non-Christian groups. How we intervene has changed. Humanitarian intervention now must be multilateral in order to be acceptable and legitimate. Since 1945 states have consistently rejected attempts to justify unilateral interventions as "humanitarian"; in the nineteenth century, however, they were accepted. Our military goals and definitions of "success" have also changed. Powerful states in the nineteenth century could simply install a government they liked as a result of these operations. Today we can only install a process, namely, elections. Given that elections often do not produce humane and just leaders (despite occasional attempts to manipulate them to do so), this may not be a particularly functional change, but it is a necessary one in the current international normative context.

By "humanitarian intervention" I mean deploying military force across borders for the purpose of protecting foreign nationals from man-made violence. Interventions to protect foreign nationals from natural disasters are excluded from the analysis. I am interested in the changing purpose of force, and, in such cases, militaries are not using force but are deployed in a completely consensual manner for their logistical and technical capabilities. Similarly interventions to protect a state's *own* nationals from abuse are excluded in this analysis. Although international legal scholars once categorized such interventions as humanitarian, these do not present the same intellectual puzzles about interests since protecting one's own nationals is clearly connected to conventional understandings of national interest.[1]

The analysis proceeds in five parts. The first shows that realist and neoliberal approaches to international politics do not provide good explanations of humanitarian intervention as a practice, much less how they have changed over time, because the interests they emphasize do not seem to correlate with these interventions. A more inductive approach that attends to the role of normative and ethical understandings can remedy this by allowing us to problematize interests and the way they change. In the second section I demonstrate that change has, indeed, occurred by examining humanitarian intervention practices in the nineteenth century and inducing a sketch of the norms governing behavior in that period from both the military actions taken and the way leaders spoke of them. Among the findings is the sharply circumscribed understanding of who was "human" and could successfully claim protection from powerful states. The third section traces the expansion of this definition of "humanity" by examining efforts to abolish slavery, the slave trade, and colonization. Although these were not the only arenas in which people fought to expand the West's definition of "humanity," they were important ones that involved military coercion, and thus they provide insight into intermediate stages in the evolution of links between humanitarian claims and military action. The fourth section briefly reviews humanitarian intervention as a state practice since 1945, paying particular attention to non-cases, that is, cases where humanitarian action could or should have been claimed but was not. These cases suggest that sovereignty and self-determination norms trumped humanitarian claims during the cold war, a relationship that no longer holds with consistency. They further suggest that unilateral intervention, even for humanitarian purposes, is normatively suspect in contemporary politics and that states will work hard to construct multilateral coalitions for this purpose. [I conclude] by comparing the goals or end states sought by intervenors in the nineteenth century versus the twentieth and [argue] that contemporary intervention norms contain powerful contradictions that make "success" difficult to achieve, not for material or logistical reasons but for normative ones.

Understanding Humanitarian Action

Humanitarian intervention looks odd from conventional perspectives on international politics because it does not conform to the conceptions of interest that they specify. Realists would expect to see some geostrategic or political advantage to be gained by intervening states. Neoliberals might emphasize economic or trade advantages for intervenors. These are hard to find in most post-1989 cases. The 1992–93 U.S. action in Somalia was a clear case of intervention without obvious interests. Economically Somalia was insignificant to the United States. Security interests are also hard to find. The United States had voluntarily given up its base at Berbera in Somalia, because advances in communications and aircraft technology made it obsolete for the communications and refueling purposes it once served. Further, the U.S. intervention in that country was not carried out in a way that would have furthered strategic interests. If the United States truly had had designs on Somalia, it should have welcomed the role of disarming the clans. It did not. The United States resisted UN pressure to "pacify" the country as part of its mission. In fact, U.S. officials were clearly and consistently interested not in controlling any part of Somalia but in getting out of the country as soon as possible—sooner, indeed, than the UN would have liked. That some administration officials opposed the Somalia intervention on precisely the grounds that no vital U.S. interest was involved underscores the realists' problem.

The massive intervention under UN auspices to reconstruct Cambodia in the early 1990s presented similar anomalies. Like Somalia, Cambodia was economically insignificant to the intervenors and, with the cold war ended, was strategically significant to none of the five powers on the Security Council except China, which bore very little of the intervention burden. Indeed, U.S. involvement appears to have been motivated by domestic opposition to the return of the Khmers Rouges on moral grounds—another anomaly for these approaches—rather than by geopolitical or economic interests. Kosovo and Bosnia touched the security interests of the major intervenor, the United States, only derivatively in that those states are in Europe. However, events in these places did not prompt intervention from major European powers, whose interests would presumably be much more involved, despite much U.S. urging. These targets are outside the NATO alliance and hence trigger none of that alliance's security guarantees; in both cases, moreover, intervention served no strong domestic constituency and was militarily and politically risky.

Liberals of a more classical and Kantian type might argue that these interventions were motivated by an interest in promoting democracy and liberal values. After all, the UN's political blueprint for reconstructing these states after intervention has occurred is a liberal one. However, these arguments run afoul of the evidence. The United States consistently refused to take on the state building and democratization mission in Somalia, which liberal arguments would have expected to have been at the heart of U.S. efforts. Similarly the UN stopped short of authorizing an overthrow of Saddam Hussein in Iraq in 1991, even when this was militarily possible and was supported by many in the U.S. armed forces. The United Nations, NATO, and especially the United States have emphasized the humanitarian rather than democratizing nature of these interventions, both rhetorically and in their actions on the ground.

None of these realist or liberal approaches provides an answer to the question: "What interests are intervening states pursuing?" A generous interpretation would conclude that realism and liberalism simply are not helpful in understanding these interventions, since the specification of interests is outside their analysis. To the extent that these approaches *do* specify interests, however, those specifications appear wrong in these cases.

The failure of these approaches leads me to adopt another method of analysis. Lacking any good alternative explanation that casts doubt on them, I take the intervenors' humanitarian claims seriously and try to untangle what, exactly, they mean by "humanitarian intervention," what makes those claims compelling to states, and what constraints exist on this kind of behavior. When intervenors claim humanitarian motives, I want to know what it means to them to be "humanitarian"— what action does that entail (or not entail). I want to know what kinds of claims prompt a humanitarian intervention (and what claims do not). I want to know the extent to which and the ways in which "humanitarianism" competes with (or complements) other kinds of incentives states might have to intervene (or not to intervene). This last point is important. Although there have been a rash of interventions since 1989 that look particularly altruistic, all interventions are prompted by a mixture of motivations in some way. Even if the principal decision maker had only one consideration in mind (which is unlikely), the vast number of people involved in these operations, often people from different intervening states, bring different motivations to bear on the intervention as it unfolds. Humanitarian motivations will interact differently with other state goals, depending on how humanitarian action is defined and what other kinds of goals states have. These definitions may change over time. For example, antidemocratic human rights abusers have now been defined as threats to international peace and security, which might explain why many more humanitarian interventions were undertaken in the 1990s than in any previous ten-year period.[2]

The empirical evidence presented here consistently points to the interwoven and interdependent character of norms that influence international behavior. Humanitarianism—its influence and definition—is bound up in other normative changes, particularly sovereignty norms and human rights norms. Mutually reinforcing and consistent norms appear to strengthen one another; success in one area (such as abolishing slavery) strengthens and legitimates new claims in logically and morally related norms (such as human rights and humanitarian intervention). The relationship identified here between slavery, sovereignty, and humanitarian intervention suggests the importance of viewing norms not as individual "things" floating atomistically in some international social space but rather as part of a highly structured social context. It may make more sense to think of a fabric of interlocking and interwoven norms rather than to think of individual norms concerning a specific issue, as current scholarship, my own included, has been inclined to do. Change in one set of norms may open possibilities for, and even logically or ethically require changes in, other norms and practices. Without attending to these relationships, we will miss the larger picture.[3]

Humanitarian Intervention in the Nineteenth Century

Before the twentieth century virtually all instances of military intervention to protect people other than the intervenor's own nationals involved protection of Christians from the Ottoman Turks.[4] In at least four instances during the nineteenth century European states used humanitarian claims to influence Balkan policy in ways that would have required states to use force—the Greek War for Independence (1821–27); in Syria/Lebanon (1860–61); during the Bulgarian agitation of 1876–78; and in response to the Armenian massacres

(1894–1917). Although not all these instances led to a full-scale military intervention, the claims made and their effects on policy in the other cases shed light on the evolution and influence of humanitarian claims during this period. I give a brief account of each incident below, highlighting commonalities and change.

GREEK WAR FOR INDEPENDENCE (1821–27)

Russia took an immediate interest in the Greek insurrection and threatened to use force against the Turks as early as the first year of the war. In part its motivations were geostrategic; Russia had been pursuing a general strategy of weakening the Ottomans and consolidating control in the Balkans for years. But the justifications Russia offered were largely humanitarian. Russia had long seen itself as the defender of Orthodox Christians under Turkish rule. Atrocities, such as the wholesale massacres of Christians and sale of women into slavery, coupled with the Sultan's order to seize the Venerable Patriarch of the Orthodox Church after mass on Easter morning, hang him and three Archbishops, and then have the bodies thrown into the Bosphorus, formed the centerpiece of Russia's complaints against the Turks and the justification of its threats of force.[5]

Other European powers, with the exception of France, opposed intervention largely because they were concerned that weakening Turkey would strengthen Russia.[6] However, although the governments of Europe seemed little affected by these atrocities, significant segments of their publics were. A Philhellenic movement had spread throughout Europe, especially in the more democratic societies of Britain, France, and parts of Germany. The movement drew on two popular sentiments: the European identification with the classical Hellenic tradition and the appeal of Christians oppressed by the Infidel. Philhellenic aid societies in Western Europe sent large sums of money and even volunteers, including Lord Byron, to Greece during the war. Indeed, it was a British Captain Hastings who commanded the Greek flotilla that destroyed a Turkish squadron off Salona and provoked the decisive battle at Navarino.[7] Russian threats of unilateral action against the Sultan eventually forced the British to become involved, and in 1827 the two powers, together with Charles X of France in his capacity as "Most Christian King," sent an armada that roundly defeated Ibrahim at Navarino in October 1827.

It would be hard to argue that humanitarian considerations were the only reason to intervene in this case; geostrategic factors were also very important. However, humanitarian disasters were the catalyst for intervention, galvanizing decision makers and powerful domestic elites. Humanitarianism also provided the public justification for intervention, and the episode is revealing about humanitarian intervention norms in several ways. First, it illustrates the circumscribed definition of who was "human" in the nineteenth-century conception. Massacring Christians was a humanitarian disaster; massacring Muslims was not. There were plenty of atrocities on both sides in this conflict. Many of the massacres of Christians by Ottomans were in response to previous massacres of Muslims at Morea and elsewhere in April 1821. For example, Greek Christians massacred approximately eight thousand Turkish Muslims in the town of Tripolitza in 1821. In all, about twenty thousand Muslims were massacred during the war in Greece without causing concern among the Great Powers. Since, under the law of the Ottoman Empire, the Christian Patriarch of Constantinople was responsible for the good behavior of his flock, his execution was viewed justified on grounds of these atrocities against Muslims.[8] The European Powers, however, were impressed only by the murder of Christians and less troubled about the fact that the initial atrocities of the war were committed by the Christian insurgents (admittedly after years of harsh Ottoman rule). The initial Christian uprising at Morea "might well have been allowed to burn itself out 'beyond the pale of civilization'"; it was only the wide-scale and very visible atrocities against Christians that put the events on the agenda of major powers.[9]

Second, intervening states, particularly Russia and France, placed humanitarian factors together with religious considerations at the center for their continued calls for intervention and application of force. As will be seen in other nineteenth-century cases, religion was important in both motivating humanitarian action and defining who is human. Notions about Christian charity supported general humanitarian impulses, but specific religious identifications had the effect of privileging certain people over others. In this case Christians were privileged over Muslims. Elsewhere, as later in Armenia and Bulgaria, denominational differences within Christianity appear important both in motivating action and in restraining it.

Third, the intervention was multilateral. The reasons in this case were largely geostrategic (restraining Russia from temptation to use this intervention for other purposes), but, as subsequent discussion will show, multilateralism as a characteristic of legitimate intervention becomes increasingly important.

Fourth, mass publics were involved. Not only did public opinion influence policy making in a diffuse way, but publics were organized trans-nationally in ways that strongly foreshadow humanitarian activity by nongovernmental orga-nizations (NGOs) in the late twentieth century. Philhellenism was a more diffuse movement than the bureaucratized NGOs we have now, but the individual Philhellenic societies communicated across national borders and these groups were able to supply both military and financial aid directly to partisans on the ground, bypassing their governments.

LEBANON/SYRIA (1860–61)

In May 1860 conflict between Druze and Maronite populations broke out in what is now Lebanon but at the time was Syria under Ottoman rule. Initial rioting became wholesale massacre of Maronite populations, first by the Druze and later by Otto-man troops. The conflict sparked outrage in the French popular press. As early as 1250, Louis IX signed a charter with the Maronite Christians in the Levant guaranteeing protection as if they were French subjects and, in effect, making them part of the French nation. Since then, France had styled itself as the "protector" of Latin Christians in the Levant. Napoleon III thus eagerly sup-ported military intervention in the region at least in part to placate "outraged Catholic opinion" at home. Russia was also eager to intervene, and Britain became involved in the intervention to prevent France and Russia from using the incident to expand.[10]

On August 3, 1860, the six Great Powers (Aus-tria, France, Britain, Prussia, Russia, and Turkey) signed a protocol authorizing the dispatch of twelve thousand European troops to the region to aid the Sultan in stopping violence and establishing order. A letter from the French foreign minister, Thouve-nal, to the French ambassador in Turkey stressed that "the object of the mission is to assist stopping, by prompt and energetic measures, the effusion of blood, and [to put] an end to the outrages com-mitted against Christians, which cannot remain unpunished." The protocol further emphasized the lack of strategic and political ambitions of the Powers acting in this matter.[11]

France supplied half of the twelve thousand troops immediately and dispatched them in August 1860. The other states sent token warships and high-ranking officers but no ground troops, which meant that, in the end, the six thousand French troops were the sum total of the interven-tion force. The French forces received high marks for their humanitarian conduct while in the region, putting a stop to the fighting and helping villagers to rebuild homes and farms. They left when agreement was reached among the Powers for Christian representation in the government of the region.[12]

This case repeats many of the features of the Greek intervention. Again, saving Christians was central to the justification for intervention. Public opinion seems to have some impact, this time on the vigor with which Napoleon pursued an interventionist policy. The multilateral character of the intervention was different, however, in that there was multilateral consultation and agreement on the intervention plan but execution was essentially unilateral.

THE BULGARIAN AGITATION (1876–78)

In May 1876 Ottoman troops massacred unarmed and poorly organized agitators in Bulgaria. A British government investigation put the number killed at twelve thousand with fifty-nine villages destroyed and an entire church full of people set ablaze after they had already surrendered to Ottoman soldiers. The investigation confirmed that Ottoman soldiers and officers were promoted and decorated rather than punished for these actions.[13] Accounts of the atrocities gathered by American missionaries and sent to British reporters began appearing in British newspapers in mid-June. The reports inflamed public opinion, and protest meetings were organized throughout the country, particularly in the North where W. T. Stead and his paper, the *Northern Echo*, were a focus of agitation.[14]

The result was a split in British politics. Prime Minister Disraeli publicly refused to change British policy of support for Turkey over the matter, stating that British material interests outweighed the lives of Bulgarians.[15] However, Lord Derby, the Conservative foreign secretary, telegraphed Constantinople that "any renewal of the outrages

would be more fatal to the Porte than the loss of a battle."[16] More important, former prime minister Gladstone came out of retirement to oppose Disraeli on the issue, making the Bulgarian atrocities the centerpiece of his anti-Disraeli campaign.[17] Although Gladstone found a great deal of support in various public circles, he did not have similar success in government. The issue barely affected British policy. Disraeli was forced to carry out the investigation mentioned above, and did offer proposals for internal Ottoman reforms to protect minorities—proposals Russia rejected as being too timid.[18]

Russia was the only state to intervene in the wake of the Bulgarian massacres. The treaty that ended the Crimean War was supposed to protect Christians under Ottoman rule. Russia justified her threats of force on the basis of Turkey's violation of these humanitarian guarantees. In March 1877 the Great Powers issued a protocol reiterating demands for the protection of Christians in the Ottoman Empire guaranteed in the 1856 treaty ending the Crimean War. After Constantinople rejected the protocol, Russia sent in troops in April 1877. Russia easily defeated the Ottoman troops and signed the Treaty of San Stefano, which created a large independent Bulgarian state—an arrangement that was drastically revised by the Congress of Berlin.

As in the previous cases, saving Christians was an essential feature of this incident, and Gladstone and Russia's justifications for action were framed in this way. However, military action in this case was not multilateral; Russia intervened unilaterally and, although other powers worried about Russian opportunism and how Russian actions might alter the strategic balance in the region, none said that the intervention was illegitimate or unacceptable because it was unilateral. Public opinion and the media, in particular, were powerful influences on the politics of this episode. Transnational groups, mostly church and missionary groups, were a major source of information for publics in powerful states about the atrocities being committed. These groups actively worked to get information out of Bulgaria and into the hands of sympathetic media outlets in a conscious attempt to arouse public opinion and influence policy in ways that resemble current NGO activist tactics. Although public opinion was not able to change British policy in this case, it was able to make adherence to that policy much more difficult for Disraeli in domestic terms.

ARMENIA (1894–1917)

The Armenian case offers some interesting insights into the scope of Christianity requiring defense by European powers in the last century. Unlike the Orthodox Christians in Greece and Bulgaria and the Maronites in Syria, the Armenian Christians had no European champion. The Armenian Church was not in communion with the Orthodox Church, hence Armenian appeals had never resonated in Russia; the Armenians were not portrayed as "brothers" to the Russians as were the Bulgarians and other Orthodox Slavs. Similarly, no non-Orthodox European state had ever offered protection nor did they have historical ties as the French did with the Maronites. Thus many of the reasons to intervene in other cases were lacking in the Armenian case.

That the Armenians were Christians, albeit of a different kind, does seem to have had some influence on policy. The Treaty of Berlin explicitly bound the Sultan to carry out internal political reforms to protect Armenians, but the nature, timing, and monitoring of these provisions were left vague and were never enforced. The Congress of Berlin ignored an Armenian petition for an arrangement similar to that set up in Lebanon following the Maronite massacres (a Christian governor under Ottoman rule). Gladstone took up the matter in 1880 when he returned to power but dropped it when Bismarck voiced opposition.[19]

The wave of massacres against Armenians beginning in 1894 was far worse than any of the other atrocities examined here in terms of both the number killed or the brutality of their executions. Nine hundred people were killed and twenty-four villages burned in the Sassum massacres in August 1894. After this the intensity increased. Between fifty thousand and seventy thousand were killed in 1895. In 1896 the massacres moved into Constantinople where, on August 28–29, six thousand Armenians were killed in the capital.[20]

These events were well known and highly publicized in Europe.[21] Gladstone came out of retirement yet again to denounce the Ottomans and called Abd-ul-Hamid the "Great Assassin." French writers denounced him as "the Red Sultan." The European powers demanded an inquiry, which produced extensive documentation of "horrors unutterable, unspeakable, unimaginable by the mind of man" for European governments and the press.[22] Public opinion pressed for intervention, and both Britain and France used humanitarian justifications to threaten force. However, neither acted. Germany by this time was a force to be reckoned with, and the Kaiser was courting Turkey. Russia was nervous about nationalist aspirations in the Balkans generally and had no special affection for the Armenians, as noted above. Their combined opposition made the price of intervention higher than either the British or French were willing to pay.[23]

These four episodes are suggestive in several ways. They make it very clear that humanitarian intervention is not new in the twentieth century. The role played by what we now call "transnational civil society" or NGOs is also not new. There certainly were far fewer of these organizations and the networks of ties were much thinner, but they did exist and have influence even 180 years ago.

These episodes also say something about the relationship of humanitarian goals to other foreign-policy goals in the period. Humanitarian action was never taken when it jeopardized other articulated goals or interests of a state. Humanitarians were sometimes able to mount considerable pressure on policy makers to act contrary to stated geostrategic interests, as in the case of Disraeli and the Bulgarian agitation, but they never succeeded. Humanitarian claims did succeed, however, in creating new interests and new reasons for states to act where none had existed. Without the massacre of Maronites in Syria, France would almost certainly not have intervened. It is less clear whether there would have been intervention in the Greek War for Independence or in Bulgaria without humanitarian justifications for such interventions. Russia certainly had other reasons to intervene in both cases, but Russia was also the state that identified most with the Orthodox Christians being massacred. Whether the humanitarian claims from fellow Orthodox Christians alone would have been sufficient for intervention without any geostrategic issues at stake is impossible to know. The role of humanitarian claims in these cases thus seems to be constitutive and permissive rather than determinative. Humanitarian appeals created interests where none previously existed and provided legitimate justifications for intervention that otherwise might not have been taken; however, they certainly did not require intervention or override alliance commitments or realpolitik understandings of national security and foreign policy making.

Humanitarian intervention in the nineteenth century could be implemented in a variety of ways. Action could be multilateral, as in the case of Greek independence, unilateral, as when Russia intervened in Bulgaria, or some mixture of the two, as in Lebanon/Syria where intervention was planned by several states but execution was unilateral. As shown below, this variety of forms for intervention changes over time. Specifically the unilateral option for either the planning or execution of humanitarian intervention appears to have disappeared in the twentieth century, and multilateral options have become more elaborate and institutionalized.

Finally, and perhaps most significant, intervenors found reasons to identify with the victims of humanitarian disasters in some important and exclusive way. The minimal rationale for such identification was that the victims to be protected by intervention were Christians; there were no instances of European powers considering intervention to protect non-Christians. Pogroms against Jews did not provoke intervention. Neither did Russian massacres of Turks in Central Asia in the 1860s.[24] Neither did mass killings in China during the Taiping Rebellion against the Manchus.[25] Neither did mass killings by colonial rulers in their colonies.[26] Neither did massacres of Native Americans in the United States. Often a more specific identification or social tie existed between intervenor and intervened, as between the Orthodox Slav Russians and the Orthodox Slav Bulgarians. In fact, as the Armenian case suggests, the lack of an intense identification may contribute to inaction.

Over time, these exclusive modes of identification changed in European powers. People in Western states began to identify with non-Western populations during the twentieth century with profound political consequences, among them a greater tendency to undertake humanitarian intervention. Longer-standing identifications with Caucasians and Christians continue to be strong. That non-Christians and non-whites are now sometimes protected does not mean that their claims are equally effective as those of Christians and whites. But that their claims are entertained at all, and that these people are sometimes protected, is new. It is not the fact of humanitarian behavior that has changed but its focus. The task at hand is to explain how extending and deepening this identification to other groups changed humanitarian intervention.

The Expansion of "Humanity" and Sovereignty

The expansion of "humanity" between the nineteenth and late twentieth centuries drives much of the change we see in humanitarian intervention behavior, both directly and indirectly. It does this directly by creating identification with and legitimating normative demands by people who previously were invisible in the politics of the West. It contributes to change indirectly through the role it plays in promoting and legitimating new norms of sovereignty, specifically anticolonialism and self-determination. These changes in understandings about humanity and sovereignty obviously do much more than change humanitarian intervention. They alter the purpose of force broadly in world politics, changing the way people think about legitimate and effective uses of state coercion in a variety of areas. Understandings that shape social purpose do not exist, after all, in a vacuum. Social purpose is formed by a dense web of social understandings that are logically and ethically interrelated and, at least to some degree, mutually supporting. Thus changes in one strand of this web tend to have wide effects, causing other kinds of understandings to adjust. Social psychological mechanisms, such as cognitive dissonance, contribute to this process, but so, too, do institutional processes. People who are confronted with the fact that they hold contradictory views will try to adjust their beliefs to alleviate dissonance between them. Similarly lawyers and judges recognize "logical coherence" as a powerful standard for arbitrating between competing normative claims within the law; norms that no longer "fit" within the larger normative fabric of understandings are likely to be rejected in judicial processes and lose the support of associated social institutions.[27]

Like humanitarian intervention, slavery and colonialism were two large-scale activities in which state force intersected with humanitarian claims in the nineteenth century. In many ways slavery was the conceptual opposite of humanitarian intervention: It involved the use of state force to deny and suppress claims about humanitarian need rather than to provide protection. The effort to stamp out the slave trade raises cross-border humanitarian issues that reveal the limits in when states would use force and provides an interesting comparison with our intervention cases. Colonialism connects views about humanity with understandings about legitimate sovereignty and political organization. Colonialism was justified initially, in part, as a humane form of rule. The West was bringing the benefits of civilization to those in need. Decolonization involved turning this understanding of "humane" politics on its head, and the sovereignty norms that emerged from that struggle are extremely important to the subsequent practices of humanitarian intervention. If, indeed, changes in understandings about "humanity" have broad, interrelated effects, we should expect to see these transformed understandings reshaping states' policies and their use of force in dealing with colonialism.

ABOLITION OF SLAVERY AND THE SLAVE TRADE

The abolition of slavery and the slave trade in the nineteenth century were essential to the universalization of "humanity." European states generally accepted and legalized both slavery and the slave trade in the seventeenth and eighteenth centuries, but by the nineteenth century these same states proclaimed these practices "repugnant to the principles of humanity and universal morality."[28] Human beings previously viewed as beyond the edge of humanity—as being property—came to be viewed as human, and with that status came certain, albeit minimal, privileges and protections. For example, states did use military force to suppress the slave trade. Britain was particularly active in this regard and succeeded in having the slave trade labeled as piracy, thus enabling Britain to seize and board ships sailing under non-British flags that were suspected of carrying contraband slaves.[29]

Although in some ways this is an important case of a state using force to promote humanitarian ends, the fashion in which the British framed and justified their actions also speaks to the limits of humanitarian claims in the early to mid-nineteenth century. First, the British limited their military action to abolishing the *trade* in slaves, not slavery itself. No military intervention was undertaken on behalf of endangered Africans in slavery as it had been on behalf of endangered white Christians. Further, although the British public and many political figures contributed to a climate of international opinion that viewed slavery with increasing distaste, the abolition of slavery as a domestic institution of property rights was accomplished in each state where it had previously been legal without other states intervening militarily.[30] Moreover, the British government's strategy for ending the slave trade was to label such trafficking as piracy, which in turn meant the slaves were "contraband," that is, still property. The British justified their actions on the basis of Maritime Rights governing commerce. The practices of slavery and slaveholding themselves did not provoke the same reaction as Ottoman abuse of Christians. This may be because the perpetrators of the humanitarian violations were "civilized" Christian nations (as opposed to the infidel Turks).[31] Another reason was probably that the targets of these humanitarian violations were black Africans, not "fellow [i.e., white] Christians" or "brother Slavs." Thus it appears that by the 1830s black Africans had become sufficiently "human" that enslaving them was illegal inside Europe, but enslaving them outside Europe was only distasteful. One could keep them enslaved if one kept them at home, within domestic borders. Abuse of Africans did not merit military intervention inside another state.

Slavery itself was thus never the cause of military intervention, and, although trade in slaves did provoke some military action, it was limited in both scope and justification. The abolition of slavery was accomplished in most of the world through either domestic mechanisms (sometimes violent ones, as in the United States) or through the transnational advocacy networks that have been described elsewhere or by both these means.[32] Once accomplished, however, the equality norms that defeated slavery norms fed back into later decisions about humanitarian intervention in interesting ways. For example, accusations of racism aimed at Western states that had provided much more attention and aid to Bosnia than Somalia in the early 1990s were important factors in mobilizing support for the intervention in Somalia, particularly from the U.S. government.[33]

COLONIZATION, DECOLONIZATION, AND SELF-DETERMINATION

Justifications for both colonization and decolonization offer additional lenses through which to examine changing understandings of who is "human" and how these understandings shape uses of force. Both processes—colonization and its undoing—were justified, at least in part, in humanitarian terms. However, the understanding of what constituted humanity was different in the two episodes in ways that bear on the current investigation of humanitarian intervention norms.

The vast economic literature on colonization often overlooks the strong moral dimension that many of the colonizers perceived and articulated. Colonization was a crusade. It would bring the benefits of civilization to the "dark" reaches of the earth. It was a sacred trust, the white man's burden, and was mandated by God that these Europeans venture out to parts of the globe unknown to them, bringing what they understood to be a better way of life to the inhabitants there. Colonization for the missionaries and those driven by social conscience was a humanitarian undertaking of huge proportions and, consequently, of huge significance.

Colonialism's humanitarian mission was of a particular kind, however. The mission of colonialism was to "civilize" the non-European world—to bring the "benefits" of European social, political, economic, and cultural arrangements to Asia, Africa, and the Americas. Until these peoples were "civilized" they remained savages, barbarians, less than human. Thus, in a critical sense, the core of the colonial humanitarian mission was to *create* humanity where none had previously existed. Non-Europeans became human in European eyes by becoming Christian, by adopting European-style structures of property rights, by embracing European-style territorial political arrangements, by entering the growing European-based international economy.[34]

Decolonization also had strong humanitarian justifications.[35] By the mid-twentieth century normative understandings about humanity had shifted. Humanity was no longer something one could create by bringing civilization to savages. Rather, humanity was inherent in individual human beings. It had become universalized and was not culturally dependent as it was in earlier centuries. Asians and Africans were now viewed as having human "rights," and among these was the right to determine their own political future—the right to self-determination.

Like other major normative changes, the rise of human rights norms and decolonization are part of a larger, interrelated set of changes in the international normative web. Norms do not just evolve; they coevolve. Those studying norm change generally, and decolonization and slavery specifically, have noted several features of this coevolutionary process. The first, as indicated above, comes from international legal scholars who have emphasized the power of logical coherence in creating legitimacy in normative structures.[36] Norms that fit logically with other powerful norms are more

likely to become persuasive and to shape behavior. Thus changes in core normative structures (in this case, changes toward recognition of human equality within Europe) provided an ethical platform from which activists could work for normative changes elsewhere in society and a way to frame their appeals that would be powerful. Mutually reinforcing and logically consistent norms appear to be harder to attack and to have an advantage in the normative contestations that occur in social life. In this sense, logic internal to norms themselves shapes their development and, consequently, shapes social change.

Applied to decolonization, the argument would be that the spread of these decolonization norms is the result, at least to some extent, of their "fit" within the logical structure of other powerful preexisting European norms. As liberal beliefs about the "natural" rights of man spread and gained power within Europe, they influenced Europe's relationship with non-European peoples in important ways. The egalitarian social movements sweeping the European West in the eighteenth and nineteenth centuries were justified with universal truths about the nature and equality of human beings. These notions were then exported to the non-European world as part of the civilizing mission of colonialism. Once people begin to believe, at least in principle, in human equality, there is no logical limit to the expansion of human rights and self-determination.[37]

The logical expansion of these arguments fueled attacks on both slavery and colonization. Slavery, more blatantly a violation of these emerging European norms, came under attack first. Demands for decolonization came more slowly and had to contend with the counter claims for the beneficial humanitarian effects of European rule. However, logic alone could not dismantle these institutions. In both cases former slaves and Western-educated colonial elites were instrumental in change. Having been "civilized" and Europeanized, they were able to use Europe's own norms against these institutions. These people undermined the social legitimacy of both slave holders and colonizers simply by being exemplars of "human" non-Europeans who could read, write, worship, work, and function in Western society. Their simple existence undercut the legitimacy of slavery and colonialism within a European framework of proclaimed human equality.

Another feature that channels contemporary normative coevolution is the rational-legal structure in which it is embedded. Increasingly since the nineteenth century international normative understandings have been codified in international law, international regimes, and the mandates of formal international organizations. To the extent that legal processes operate, the logical coherence processes described above will be amplified, since law requires explicit demonstrations of such logical fit to support its claims. International organizations, too, can amplify the power of new normative claims if these are enshrined in their mandates, structure, or operating procedures. For example, the United Nations played a significant role in the decolonization process and the consolidation of anticolonialism norms. Self-determination norms are proclaimed in the UN Charter, but the organization also contained Trusteeship machinery and one-state-one-vote voting structures that gave majority power to the weak, often formerly colonized states, all of which contributed to an international legal, organizational, and normative environment that made colonial practices increasingly illegitimate and difficult to carry out.[38]

Humanitarian Intervention since 1945

Unlike humanitarian intervention practices in the nineteenth century, virtually all the instances in which claims of humanitarian intervention have been made in the post-1945 period concern military action on behalf of non-Christians, non-Europeans, or both. Cambodia, Somalia, Bosnian Muslims, Kurds in Iraq, Albanian Muslims in Kosovo all fit this pattern. The "humanity" worth protecting has widened as a result of the normative changes described above. However, humanitarian intervention practices have also become more limited in a different dimension: Intervening states often shied away from humanitarian claims during the cold war when they could have made them. One would think that states would claim the moral high ground in their military actions whenever it was at all credible, and strong humanitarian claims were certainly credible in at least three cases: India's intervention in East Pakistan in the wake of massacres by Pakistani troops; Tanzania's intervention in Uganda toppling the Idi Amin regime; and Vietnam's intervention in Cambodia ousting the Khmers Rouges. Amin and Pol Pot were two of the most notorious killers in a century full of infamous brutal leaders. If states could use humanitarian claims anywhere, it should have been in these cases, yet they did not. In fact, India initially claimed humanitarian justifications on the floor of the United Nations but quickly retracted them, expunging statements from the UN record. Why?

The argument here is that this reluctance stems not from norms about what is "humanitarian" but from norms about legitimate intervention. Although the scope of who qualifies as human has widened enormously and the range of humanitarian activities that states routinely undertake has expanded, norms about intervention have also changed, albeit less drastically. Humanitarian military intervention now must be *multilateral* to be legitimate; without multilateralism, claims of humanitarian motivation and justification are suspect.[39] As we saw in the nineteenth century, multilateralism is not new; it has often characterized humanitarian military action. However, states in the nineteenth century still invoked and accepted humanitarian justifications even when intervention was unilateral (for example, Russia in Bulgaria during the 1870s, and, in part, France in Lebanon). That did not happen in the twentieth century nor has it happened in the twenty-first century. Without multilateralism, states will not and apparently cannot successfully claim humanitarian justification.[40]

The move to multilateralism is not obviously dictated by the functional demands of intervention or military effectiveness. Certainly multilateralism had (and has) important advantages for states. It increases the transparency of each state's actions to others and so reassures states that opportunities for adventurism and expansion will not be used. It can be a way of sharing costs and thus be cheaper for states than unilateral action. However, multilateralism carries with it significant costs of its own. Cooperation and coordination problems involved in such action, an issue political scientists have examined in detail, can make it difficult to sustain multilateral action.[41] Perhaps more important, multilateral action requires the sacrifice of power and control over the intervention. Further, it may seriously compromise the military effectiveness of those operations, as recent debates over command and control in UN military operations suggest.

There are no obvious efficiency reasons for states to prefer either multilateral or unilateral intervention to achieve humanitarian ends. Each type of intervention has advantages and disadvantages. The choice depends, in large part, on perceptions about the political acceptability and political costs of each, which, in turn, depend on the normative context. As is discussed below, multilateralism in the present day has become institutionalized in ways that make unilateral intervention, particularly intervention not justified as self-defense, unacceptably costly, not in material terms but in social and political terms. A brief examination of these "non-cases" of humanitarian intervention and the way that states debated and justified these actions provides some insight into the normative fabric of contemporary intervention

and the limitations these impose on humanitarian action.

UNILATERAL INTERVENTIONS IN HUMANITARIAN DISASTERS[42]

a. India in East Pakistan (1971). Pakistan had been under military rule by West Pakistani officials since partition. When the first free elections were held in November 1970, the Awami League won 167 out of 169 parliamentary seats reserved for East Pakistan in the National Assembly. The Awami League had not urged political independence for the East during the elections but did run on a list of demands concerning one-man-one-vote political representation and increased economic autonomy for the East. The government in the West viewed the Awami League's electoral victory as a threat. In the wake of these electoral results, the government in Islamabad decided to postpone the convening of the new National Assembly indefinitely, and in March 1971 the West Pakistani army started killing unarmed civilians indiscriminately, raping women, burning homes, and looting or destroying property. At least one million people were killed, and millions more fled across the border into India.[43] Following months of tension, border incidents, and increased pressure from the influx of refugees, India sent troops into East Pakistan. After twelve days the Pakistani army surrendered at Dacca, and the new state of Bangladesh was established.

As in many of the nineteenth-century cases, the intervenor here had an array of geopolitical interests. Humanitarian concerns were not the only reason, or even, perhaps, the most important reason, to intervene. However, this is a case in which intervention could be justified in humanitarian terms, and initially the Indian representatives in both the General Assembly and the Security Council did articulate such a justification.[44] These arguments were widely rejected by other states, including many with no particular interest in politics on the subcontinent. States as diverse as Argentina, Tunisia, China, Saudi Arabia, and the United States all responded to India's claims by arguing that principles of sovereignty and noninterference should take precedence and that India had no right to meddle in what they all viewed as an "internal matter." In response to this rejection of its claims, India retracted its humanitarian justifications, choosing instead to rely on self-defense to defend its actions.[45]

b. Tanzania in Uganda (1979). This episode began as a straightforward territorial dispute. In the autumn of 1978 Ugandan troops invaded and occupied the Kagera salient—territory between the Uganda-Tanzania border and the Kagera River in Tanzania.[46] On November 1 Amin announced annexation of the territory. Nyerere considered the annexation tantamount to an act of war and, on November 15, launched an offensive from the south bank of the Kagera River. Amin, fearing defeat, offered to withdraw from the occupied territories if Nyerere would promise to cease support for Ugandan dissidents and agree not to attempt to overthrow his government. Nyerere refused and made explicit his intention to help dissidents topple the Amin regime. In January 1979 Tanzanian troops crossed into Uganda, and, by April, these troops, joined by some Ugandan rebel groups, had occupied Kampala and installed a new government headed by Yusef Lule.

As in the previous case, there were nonhumanitarian reasons to intervene; but if territorial issues were the only concern, the Tanzanians could have stopped at the border, having evicted Ugandan forces, or pushed them back into Uganda short of Kampala. The explicit statement of intent to topple the regime seems out of proportion to the low-level territorial squabble. However, humanitarian considerations clearly compounded other motives in this case. Tesón makes a strong case that Nyerere's intense dislike of Amin's regime and its abusive practices influenced the scale of the response. Nyerere had already publicly called Amin a murderer

and refused to sit with him on the Authority of the East African Community.[47] Tesón also presents strong evidence that the lack of support or material help for Uganda in this intervention from the UN, the Organization of African Unity (OAU), or any state besides Libya suggests tacit international acceptance of what otherwise would have been universally condemned as international aggression because of the human rights record of the target state.[48]

Despite evidence of humanitarian motivations, Tanzania never claimed humanitarian justification. In fact, Tanzania went out of its way to disclaim responsibility for the felicitous humanitarian outcome of its actions. It claimed only that it was acting in response to Amin's invasion and that its actions just happened to coincide with a revolt against Amin inside Uganda. When Sudan and Nigeria criticized Tanzania for interfering in another state's internal affairs in violation of the OAU charter, it was the new Ugandan regime that invoked humanitarian justifications for Tanzania's actions. The regime criticized the critics, arguing that members of the OAU should not "hide behind the formula of non-intervention when human rights are blatantly being violated."[49]

c. Vietnam in Cambodia (1979). In 1975 the Chinese-backed Khmers Rouges took power in Cambodia and launched a policy of internal "purification" entailing the atrocities and genocide now made famous by the 1984 movie *The Killing Fields.* This regime, under the leadership of Pol Pot, was also aggressively anti-Vietnamese and engaged in a number of border incursions during the late 1970s. Determined to end this border activity, the Vietnamese and an anti–Pol Pot army of exiled Cambodians invaded the country in December 1978, succeeded in routing the Khmers Rouges by January 1979, and installed a sympathetic government under the name People's Republic of Kampuchea (PRK).

Again, humanitarian considerations may not have been central to Vietnam's decision to intervene, but humanitarian justifications would seem to have offered some political cover to the internationally unpopular Vietnamese regime. However, like Tanzania, the Vietnamese made no appeal to humanitarian justifications. Instead, they argued that they were only helping the Cambodian people to achieve self-determination against the neo-colonial regime of Pol Pot, which had been "the product of the hegemonistic and expansionist policy of the Peking authorities."[50] Even if Vietnam *had* offered humanitarian justifications for intervention, indications are that other states would have rejected them. A number of states mentioned Pol Pot's appalling human rights violations in their condemnations of Vietnam's action but said, nonetheless, that these violations did not entitle Vietnam to intervene. During the UN debate no state spoke in favor of the right to unilateral humanitarian intervention, and several states (Greece, the Netherlands, Yugoslavia, and India) that had previously supported humanitarian intervention arguments in the UN voted for the resolution condemning Vietnam's intervention.[51]

MULTILATERAL INTERVENTION IN HUMANITARIAN DISASTERS

To be legitimate in contemporary politics, humanitarian intervention must be multilateral. The cold war made such multilateral efforts politically difficult to orchestrate, but, since 1989, several large-scale interventions have been carried out claiming humanitarian justifications as their raison d'être. All have been multilateral. Most visible among these have been the following:

- the U.S., British, and French efforts to protect Kurdish and Shiite populations inside Iraq following the Gulf War;
- the United Nations Transitional Authority in Cambodia (UNTAC) mission to end civil war and to reestablish a democratic political order in Cambodia;

- the large-scale U.S. and UN effort to end starvation and to construct a democratic state in Somalia;
- deployment of UN and NATO troops to protect civilian, especially Muslim, populations primarily from Serbian forces in Bosnia;
- NATO's campaign to stop the ethnic cleansing of Albanian Muslims in the province of Kosovo, Yugoslavia.

Although these efforts have attracted varying amounts of criticism concerning their effectiveness, their legitimacy has received little or no criticism. Further, and unlike their nineteenth-century counterparts, all have been organized through standing international organizations—most often the United Nations. Indeed, the UN Charter has provided the normative framework in which much of the normative contestation over intervention practices has occurred since 1945. Specifically, the Charter enshrines two principles that at times conflict. On the one hand, Article 2 preserves states' sovereign rights as the organizing principle of the international system. The corollary is a near-absolute rule of nonintervention. On the other hand, Article 1 of the Charter emphasizes human rights and justice as a fundamental mission of the United Nations, and subsequent UN actions (among them, the adoption of the Universal Declaration of Human Rights) have strengthened this claim. Gross humanitarian abuses by states against their own citizens, like those discussed [here,] bring these two central principles into conflict.

In this struggle between principles, the balance seems to have shifted since the end of the cold war, and humanitarian claims now frequently trump sovereignty claims. States still may not respond to humanitarian appeals, but they do not hesitate because they think such intervention will be denounced internationally as illegitimate. A brief look at the "non-case" of Rwanda illustrates this. Contemporary humanitarian intervention norms do more than just "allow" intervention. The

Genocide Convention actually makes action mandatory. Signatories must stop genocide, defined as "acts committed with intent to destroy, in whole or in part, a national, ethnical, racial or religious group."[52] Although the failure of the West to respond to the Rwandan genocide in 1994 shows that humanitarian claims must compete with other interests states have as they weigh the decision to use force, the episode also reveals something about the normative terrain on which these interventions are debated. In contrast to the cold war cases, no significant constituency was claiming that intervention in Rwanda for humanitarian purposes would have been illegitimate or an illegal breach of sovereignty. States did not fear the kind of response India received when it intervened in East Pakistan. France, the one state to intervene (briefly and with multilateral authorization) was criticized not because the intervention was illegitimate but because its actions aided the *génocidaires* rather than the victims.[53] States understood very well that legally and ethically this case required intervention, and because they did not want to intervene for other reasons, they had to work hard to suppress information and to avoid the word "genocide" in order to sidestep their obligations.[54] When the killing was (conveniently) over, the American president, Bill Clinton, actually went to Rwanda and apologized for his administration's inaction. While the Rwandan case can be viewed pessimistically as a case where ethics were ignored and states did what was convenient, it also reveals that states understood and publicly acknowledged a set of obligations that certainly did not exist in the nineteenth century and probably not during most of the cold war. States understood that they had not just a right but a duty to intervene in this case. That the Americans apologized substantiates this.[55]

In addition to a shift in normative burdens to act, intervention norms now place strict requirements on the ways humanitarian intervention can be carried out. Humanitarian intervention must be multilateral when it occurs. It must be organized under multilateral, preferably UN, auspices or with explicit multilateral consent. Further, it must be implemented with a multilateral force if at all possible. Specifically the intervention force should contain troops from "disinterested" states, usually middle-level powers outside the region of conflict—another dimension of multilateralism not found in nineteenth-century practice.

Contemporary multilateralism thus differs from the multilateral action of the nineteenth century. The latter was what John Ruggie might call "quantitative" multilateralism and only thinly so.[56] Nineteenth-century multilateralism was strategic. States intervened together to keep an eye on one another and to discourage adventurism or exploitation of the situation for nonhumanitarian gains. Multilateralism was driven by shared fears and perceived threats, not by shared norms and principles. States did not even coordinate and collaborate extensively to achieve their goals. Military deployments in the nineteenth century may have been contemporaneous, but they were largely separate; there was virtually no joint planning or coordination of operations. This follows logically from the nature of multilateralism, since strategic surveillance of one's partners is not a shared goal but a private one.

Recent interventions exhibit much more of what Ruggie calls the "qualitative dimension" of multilateralism. They are organized according to, and in defense of, "generalized principles" of international responsibility and the use of military force, many of which are codified in the UN Charter, in UN Declarations, and in the UN's standard operating procedures. These principles emphasize international responsibilities for ensuring human rights and justice, and dictate appropriate procedures for intervening such as the necessity of obtaining Security Council authorization for action. They also require that intervening forces be composed not just of troops of more than one state but of troops from disinterested states other than Great Powers—not a feature of nineteenth-century action.

Contemporary multilateralism is deeply political and normative, not just strategic. It is shaped by shared notions about when use of force is legitimate and appropriate. Contemporary legitimacy criteria for use of force, in turn, derive from these shared principles, articulated most often through the UN, about consultation and coordination with other states before acting and about multinational composition of forces. U.S. interventions in Somalia and Haiti were not multilateral because the United States needed the involvement of other states for military or strategic reasons. The United States was capable of supplying the forces necessary and, in fact, did supply the lion's share. No other Great Power was particularly worried about U.S. opportunism in these areas so none joined the action for surveillance reasons. These interventions were multilateral for political and normative reasons. To be legitimate and politically acceptable, the United States needed UN authorization and international participation for these operations. Whereas Russia, France, and Britain tolerated one another's presence in operations to save Christians from the infidel Turk, the United States had to beg other states to join it for a humanitarian operation in Haiti.

Multilateral norms create political benefits for conformance and costs for nonconforming action. They create, in part, the structure of incentives states face. Realists or neoliberal institutionalists might argue that in the contemporary world multilateral behavior is efficient and unproblematically self-interested because multilateralism helps to generate political support for intervention both domestically and internationally. However, this argument only begs the question: *Why* is multilateralism necessary to generate political support? It was not necessary in the nineteenth century.

Indeed, multilateralism, as currently practiced, was inconceivable in the nineteenth century. As discussed earlier, nothing about the logic of multilateralism itself makes it clearly superior to unilateral action. Each action has advantages and costs to states, and the costs of multilateral intervention have become abundantly clear in recent UN operations. One testament to the power of these multilateral norms is that states adhere to them even when they know that doing so compromises the effectiveness of the mission. Criticisms of the UN's ineffectiveness for military operations are widespread. That UN involvement continues to be a central feature of these operations, despite the UN's apparent lack of military competence, underscores the power of multilateral norms.[57]

Multilateralism legitimizes action by signaling broad support for the actor's goals. Intervenors use it to demonstrate that their purpose in intervening is not merely self-serving and particularistic but is joined in some way to community interests that other states share.[58] Making this demonstration is often vital in mustering international support for an intervention, as India discovered, and can be crucial in generating domestic support as well. Conversely, failure to intervene multilaterally creates political costs. Other states and domestic constituencies both start to question the aims and motives of intervenors when others will not join and international organizations will not bless an operation. These benefits and costs flow not from material features of the intervention but from the expectations that states and people in contemporary politics share about what constitutes legitimate uses of force. Perceptions of illegitimacy may eventually have material consequences for intervenors, but the motivations for imposing those costs are normative.

Both realist and neoliberal analyses fail to ask where incentives come from. They also fail to ask where interests come from. A century ago the plight of non-white, non-Christians was not an "interest" of Western states, certainly not one that could prompt the deployment of troops. Similarly, a century ago, states saw no interest in multilateral authorization, coordination, and use of troops from "disinterested" states. The argument here is that these interests and incentives have been constituted socially through state practice and the evolution of shared norms through which states act.

Conclusion

Humanitarian intervention practices are not new. They have, however, changed over time in some systemic and important ways. First, the definition of who qualifies as human and is therefore deserving of humanitarian protection by foreign governments has changed. Whereas in the nineteenth century European Christians were the sole focus of humanitarian intervention, this focus has been expanded and universalized such that by the late twentieth century all human beings were treated as equally deserving in the international normative discourse. In fact, states are very sensitive to charges that they are "normatively backward" and still privately harbor distinctions. When Boutros-Ghali, shortly after becoming Secretary-General, charged that powerful states were attending to disasters in white, European Bosnia at the expense of non-white, African Somalia, the United States and other states became defensive, refocused attention, and ultimately launched a full-scale intervention in Somalia before acting in Bosnia.

Second, although humanitarian intervention in the nineteenth century was frequently multilateral, it was not necessarily so. Russia, for example, claimed humanitarian justifications for its intervention in Bulgaria in the 1870s; France was similarly allowed to intervene unilaterally, with no companion force to guard against adventurism. Other states did not contest, much less reject, these claims despite the fact that Russia, at least, had nonhumanitarian motives for intervening. They did, however, reject similar claims by India in the twentieth century. By the twentieth century, not only did multilateralism appear to be necessary to claim humanitarian justifications but sanction by the United Nations or some other formal organization was required. The United States, Britain, and France, for example, went out of their way to find authority in UN resolutions for their protection of Kurds in Iraq.

These changes have not taken place in isolation. Changes in humanitarian intervention behavior are intimately connected with other sweeping changes in the normative fabric that have taken place over the past two centuries. Who counts as human has changed, not just for intervention but in all arenas of social life—slavery, colonialism, but also political participation generally at all levels and in most parts of the world. Similarly multilateralism norms are by no means specific to, or even most consequential for, intervention behavior. As Ruggie and his colleagues have amply documented, these norms pervade virtually all aspects of interstate politics, particularly among the most powerful Western states (which are also the most likely and most capable intervenors).[59] The related proliferation of formal institutions and the ever-expanding use of these rational-legal authority structures to coordinate and implement international decision making are also generalized phenomena. These trends have clear and specific impacts on contemporary humanitarian interventions but are also present and powerful in a wide variety of areas of world politics.[60] These interconnections should not surprise us. Indeed, they are to be expected given both the social psychological and institutional mechanisms at work to resolve normative paradoxes and the ways that these extend normative changes to logically and ethically related areas of social life. Changes as fundamental as the ones examined here, namely, changes in who is human and in the multilateral and rational-legal structure of politics, are logically connected to a vast range of political activity and appear again in other cases of intervention. * * *

NOTES

1. Scholars of international law have increasingly made the distinction I make here and have reserved the term "humanitarian intervention" for military protection of foreign citizens, as I do, in order to follow changing state practice. See Anthony Clark Arend and Robert J. Beck, *International Law and the Use of Force: Beyond the UN Charter Paradigm* (New York: Routledge, 1993), esp. chap. 8; and Fernando Tesón, *Humanitarian Intervention: An Inquiry into Law and Morality* (Dobbs Ferry, N.Y.: Transnational, 1988).

2. For more on the way that respect for human rights has become an integral part of contemporary definitions of "security" and how this was accomplished, most visibly at the UN in the 1970s during the anti-apartheid movement, see Audie Klotz, "Norms Reconstituting Interests: Global Racial Equality and U.S. Sanctions against South Africa," *International Organization* 49, no. 3 (summer 1995): 451–78; Michael Barnett, "Bringing in the New World Order: Liberalism, Legitimacy, and the United Nations," *World Politics* (July 1997): 526–51; and Michael Barnett and Martha Finnemore, "The Politics, Power, and Pathologies of International Organizations," *International Organization* 53, no. 4 (1999): 699–732.

3. That the regimes literature, which brought norms back into the study of international politics in the 1980s, defined norms in issue-specific terms probably influenced this orientation in the scholarship. Arguments about interrelationships between norms and the nature of an overarching social normative structure have been made by sociological institutionalists, legal scholars, and, to a lesser extent, scholars of the English school like Gerrit Gong in his discussion of standards of "civilisation" (Gerrit Gong, *The Standard of "Civilisation" in International Society* [Oxford: Clarendon, 1984]). See the discussion of the content of the world polity in George Thomas, John Meyer, Francisco Ramirez and John Boli, eds., *Institutional Structure: Constituting State, Society, and the Individual* (Newbury Park, Calif.: Sage, 1987), esp. chap. 1; John Boli and George M. Thomas, eds., *Constructing World Culture: International Nongovernmental Organizations since 1875* (Stanford: Stanford University Press, 1999), esp. chaps. 1–2 and the conclusion. On the kinds of norm relationships that contribute to legitimacy and fairness, see Thomas M. Franck, *The Power of Legitimacy among Nations* (New York: Oxford University Press, 1990); Thomas M. Franck, *Fairness in International Law and Institutions* (New York: Oxford University Press, 1995); and Gong, *The Standard of "Civilisation."*

4. Intervention in the Boxer Rebellion in China (1898–1900) is an interesting related case. I omit it from the analysis here because the primary goal of intervenors was to protect their own nationals, not the Chinese. But the intervention did have the happy result of protecting a large number of mostly Christian Chinese from slaughter.

5. J. A. R. Marriott, *The Eastern Question: An Historical Study in European Diplomacy* (Oxford: Clarendon, 1917), 183–85. Atrocities continued through the more than five years of the conflict and fueled the Russian claims. Perhaps the most sensational of these were the atrocities Egyptian troops committed under Ibrahim when they arrived to quell the Greek insurrection in 1825 for the Sultan (to whom they were vassals). Egyptian troops began a process of wholesale extermination of the Greek populace, apparently aimed at recolonization of the area by Muslims. This fresh round of horrors was cited by European powers for their final press toward a solution.

6. France had a long-standing protective arrangement with eastern Christians, as described below, and had consistently favored armed intervention (*Cambridge Modern History*, 10:193).

7. William St. Clair, *That Greece Might Still Be Free* (London: Oxford University Press, 1972), 81; C. W. Crawley, *The Question of Greek Independence* (New York: Fertig, 1973), 1; *Cambridge Modern History*, 10:180, 196. In addition to St. Clair, two other sources on the Philhellenic movement are Douglas Dakin, *British and American Philhellenes during the War of Greek Independence, 1821–1833* (Thessaloniki, 1955); and Theophilus C. Prousis, *Russian Society and*

the Greek Revolution (DeKalb: Northern Illinois University Press, 1994).

8. Eric Carlton, *Massacres: An Historical Perspective* (Aldershot, Hants., England: Scolar, 1994), 82. Marriott, *The Eastern Question*, 183; *Cambridge Modern History*, 10:178–83.

9. *Cambridge Modern History*, 10:178–79.

10. R. W. Seton-Watson, *Britain in Europe, 1789 to 1914* (New York: Macmillan, 1937), 419–21; Marc Trachtenberg, "Intervention in Historical Perspective," in *Emerging Norms of Justified Intervention*, ed. Laura W. Reed and Carl Kaysen (Cambridge, Mass.: American Academy of Arts and Sciences, 1993), 23.

11. Louis B. Sohn and Thomas Buergenthal, *International Protection of Human Rights* (Indianapolis: Bobbs-Merrill, 1973), 156–60.

12. A. L. Tiwabi, *A Modern History of Syria* (London: Macmillan, 1969), 131; Seton-Watson, *Britain in Europe*, 421.

13. Mason Whiting Tyler, *The European Powers and the Near East, 1875–1908* (Minneapolis: University of Minnesota Press, 1925), 66 n.; Seton-Watson, *Britain in Europe*, 519–20; Marriott, *The Eastern Question*, 291–92; *Cambridge Modern History*, 12:384.

14. Seton-Watson, *Britain in Europe*, 519.

15. Mercia Macdermott, *A History of Bulgaria, 1393–1885* (New York: Praeger, 1962), 280.

16. *Cambridge Modern History*, 12:384.

17. Tyler, *European Powers and the Near East*, 70. Gladstone even published a pamphlet on the subject, *The Bulgarian Horrors and the Question of the East*, which sold more than two hundred thousand copies. Seton-Watson, *Britain in Europe*, 519; Marriott, *The Eastern Question*, 293.

18. Macdermott, *History of Bulgaria*, 277; Tyler, *European Powers and the Near East*, 21.

19. *Cambridge Modern History*, 12:415–17; Marriott, *The Eastern Question*, 349–51.

20. Of course, these events late in the nineteenth century were only the tip of the iceberg. More than a million Armenians were killed by Turks during World War I, but the war environment obviates discussions of military intervention.

21. Indeed, there were many firsthand European accounts of the Constantinople massacres since execution gangs even forced their way into the houses of foreigners to execute Armenian servants (*Cambridge Modern History*, 12:417).

22. The quotation is from Lord Rosebery as cited in *Cambridge History of British Foreign Policy*, 3:234.

23. *Cambridge Modern History*, 12:417–18; Sohn and Buergenthal, *International Protection of Human Rights*, 181.

24. For more on this topic, see Stanford J. Shaw and Ezel Kural Shaw, *History of the Ottoman Empire and Modern Turkey*, vol. 2, *Reform, Revolution, and Republic: The Rise of Modern Turkey* (Cambridge: Cambridge University Press, 1977).

25. Christopher Hibbert, *The Dragon Wakes: China and the West, 1793–1911* (Newton Abbot, Devon, England: Reader's Union, 1971). Hibbert estimates that the three-day massacre in Nanking alone killed more than one hundred thousand people (*The Dragon Wakes*, 303).

26. In one of the more egregious incidents of this kind the Germans killed sixty-five thousand indigenous inhabitants of German Southwest Africa (Namibia) in 1904. See Barbara Harff, "The Etiology of Genocides," in *Genocide and the Modern Age: Etiology and Case Studies of Mass Death*, ed. Isidor Wallimann and Michael N. Dobkowski (New York: Greenwood, 1987), 46, 56.

27. For more social psychological underpinnings, see Alice Eagly and Shelly Chaiken, *The Psychology of Attitudes* (Fort Worth, Tex.: Harcourt Brace Jovanovich, 1993). For more on logical coherence in law, see Franck, *The Power of Legitimacy*, esp. chap. 10.

28. Quotation comes from the Eight Power Declaration concerning the Universal Abolition of the Trade in Negroes, signed February 8, 1815, by Britain, France, Spain, Sweden, Austria, Prussia, Russia, and Portugal; quoted in Leslie Bethell, *The Abolition of the Brazilian Slave Trade* (Cambridge: Cambridge University Press, 1970), 14.

29. Bethell, *Abolition of the Brazilian Slave Trade*, chap. 1. In 1850 Britain went so far as to fire on and board

ships in Brazilian ports to enforce anti-slave-trafficking treaties (Bethell, *Abolition of the Brazilian Slave Trade,* 329–31). One might argue that such action was a violation of sovereignty and thus qualifies as military intervention, but, if so, they were interventions of a very peripheral kind. Note, too, that British public opinion on abolition of the slave trade was not uniform. See Chaim D. Kaufmann and Robert A. Pape, "Explaining Costly International Moral Action: Britain's Sixty-Year Campaign against the Atlantic Slave Trade," *International Organization* 53, no. 4 (1999): 631–68.

30. The United States is a possible exception. One could argue that the North intervened militarily in the South to abolish slavery. Such an argument would presume that (a) there were always two separate states such that the North's action could be understood as "intervention," rather than civil war, and (b) that abolishing slavery rather than maintaining the Union was the primary reason for the North's initial action. Both assumptions are open to serious question. (The Emancipation Proclamation was not signed until 1863 when the war was already half over.) Thus, although the case is suggestive of the growing power of a broader conception of "humanity," I do not treat it in this analysis.

31. For an extended treatment of the importance of the categories "civilized" and "barbarian" on state behavior in the nineteenth century, see Gong, *The Standard of "Civilisation."*

32. Margaret Keck and Kathryn Sikkink, *Activists beyond Borders* (Ithaca, N.Y.: Cornell University Press, 1998), chap. 2; James Lee Ray, "The Abolition of Slavery and the End of International War," *International Organization* 43, no. 3 (1989): 405–39.

33. See Boutros-Ghali's comment in the July 22, 1992, Security Council meeting. Rep. Howard Wolpe made a similar comment in the House Africa Subcommittee hearings on June 23, 1992, about double standards in policy toward Bosnia and Somalia. The black caucus became galvanized around this "double standard" issue and became a powerful lobbying force in the administration, and its influence was felt by General Colin Powell, then chairman of the Joint Chiefs of Staff, among others. For details of the U.S. decision-making process on Somalia, see John G. Sommer, *Hope Restored? Humanitarian Aid in Somalia, 1990–1994* (Washington, D.C.: Refugee Policy Group, 1994). For a discussion of Boutros-Ghali and Wolpe, see Sommer, *Hope Restored?* 22 n. 63; for a discussion of Powell, see 30 n. 100.

34. Gerrit Gong provides a much more extensive discussion of what "civilization" meant to Europeans from an international legal perspective. See Gong, *The Standard of "Civilisation."* Uday Mehta investigates the philosophical underpinnings of colonialism in Lockean liberalism and the strategies aimed at the systematic political exclusion of culturally dissimilar colonized peoples by liberals professing universal freedom and rights. One of these strategies was civilizational infantilization; treating peoples in India, for example, like children allowed liberals to exclude them from political participation and, at the same time, justified extensive tutelage in European social conventions in the name of civilizing them and preparing them for liberal political life (Uday S. Mehta, "Liberal Strategies of Exclusion," *Politics and Society* 18 [1990]: 427–54).

Of necessity this very abbreviated picture of colonialism obscures the enormous variety in European views of what they were doing. Some social reformers and missionaries no doubt had far more generous notions of the "humanity" of the non-Europeans they came in contact with and treated them with respect. For more racist participants in the colonialist project, no amount of Christian piety or Europeanization would ever raise these non-Europeans to a level of humanity comparable to that of Europeans. My goal in this sketch is to emphasize the effort to create humanity, so that readers will see the connections with decolonization.

35. To reiterate, I am making no claims about the causes of decolonization. These causes were obviously complex and have been treated extensively in the vast literature on the subject. I argue only that humanitarian norms were central in the justification for decolonization.

36. For an excellent exposition, see Franck, *The Power of Legitimacy*, esp. chap. 10.

37. Neta Crawford, "Decolonization as an International Norm: The Evolution of Practices, Arguments, and Beliefs," in *Emerging Norms of Justified Intervention*, ed. Laura Reed and Carl Kaysen (Cambridge, Mass.: American Academy of Arts and Sciences, 1993), 37–61 at 53; Neta Crawford, *Argument and Change in World Politics: Ethics, Decolonization, and Humanitarian Intervention* (New York: Cambridge University Press, 2002). David Lumsdaine makes a similar point about the expanding internal logic of domestic welfare arguments that led to the creation of the foreign aid regime in his *Moral Vision in International Politics: The Foreign Aid Regime, 1949–1989* (Princeton, N.J.: Princeton University Press, 1993).

38. Crawford, "Decolonization as an International Norm," 37–61; Crawford, *Argument and Change in World Politics;* Michael Barnett, "The United Nations and the Politics of Peace: From Juridical Sovereignty to Empirical Sovereignty," *Global Governance* 1 (1995): 79–97.

39. Other authors have noted a similar trend in related areas. David Lumsdaine discusses the role of multilateral versus bilateral giving of foreign aid in his *Moral Vision in International Politics.*

40. An interesting exception that proves the rule is the U.S. claim of humanitarian justifications for its intervention in Grenada. First, the human beings to be protected by the intervention were not Grenadians but U.S. nationals. Protecting one's own nationals can still be construed as protecting national interests and is therefore not anomalous or of interest analytically in the way that state action to protect nationals of *other* states is. Second, the humanitarian justification offered by the United States was widely rejected in the international community, which underscores the point made here that states are generally suspicious of unilateral humanitarian intervention. See the discussion in Tesón, *Humanitarian Intervention*, 188–200; and Arend and Beck, *International Law and the Use of Force*, 126–28.

The apparent illegitimacy of unilateral humanitarian intervention is probably related to two broad issues that cannot be treated adequately in this limited space, namely, the expansion of multilateralism as a practice and the strengthening of juridical sovereignty norms, especially among weak states. On multilateralism, see John Ruggie, ed., *Multilateralism Matters* (New York: Columbia University Press, 1993). Concerning the strengthening of sovereignty norms among weak states, see Stephen D. Krasner, *Structural Conflict* (Berkeley: University of California Press, 1985). For an empirical demonstration of the increased robustness of sovereign statehood as a political form in the periphery, see David Strang, "Anomaly and Commonplace in European Political Expansion: Realist and Institutional Accounts," *International Organization* 45, no. 2 (spring 1991): 143–62.

41. Significantly, those who are more optimistic about solving these problems and about the utility of multilateral action rely on norms and shared social purpose to overcome these problems. Norms are an essential part both of regimes and multilateralism in the two touchstone volumes on these topics. See Stephen D. Krasner, ed., *International Regimes* (Ithaca, N.Y.: Cornell University Press, 1983); and Ruggie, *Multilateralism Matters.*

42. These synopses are drawn, in large part, from Tesón, *Humanitarian Intervention*, chap. 8; Michael Akehurst, "Humanitarian Intervention," in *Intervention in World Politics,* ed. Hedley Bull (Oxford: Clarendon, 1984), 95–118; and Arend and Beck, *International Law and the Use of Force*, chap. 8.

43. Estimates of the number of refugees vary wildly. The Pakistani government put the number at two million; the Indian government claimed ten million. Independent estimates have ranged from five to nine million. See Tesón, *Humanitarian Intervention*, 182, including n. 163 for discussion.

44. See ibid., 186 n. 187, for the text of a General Assembly speech by the Indian representative articulating this justification. See also Akehurst, "Humanitarian Intervention," 96.

45. Akehurst concludes that India actually had prior statements concerning humanitarian justifications deleted from the Official Record of the UN ("Humanitarian Intervention," 96–97).

46. Amin attempted to justify this move by claiming that Tanzania had previously invaded Ugandan territory.

47. Tesón, *Humanitarian Intervention*, 164.

48. Ibid., 164–67.

49. As quoted in Akehurst, "Humanitarian Intervention," 99.

50. As quoted ibid., 97 n. 17.

51. One reason for the virtual absence of humanitarian arguments in this case, compared to the Tanzanian case, may have been the way the intervention was conducted. Tanzania exerted much less control over the kind of regime that replaced Amin, making the subsequent Ugandan regime's defense of Tanzania's actions as "liberation" less implausible than were Vietnam's claims that it, too, was helping to liberate Cambodia by installing a puppet regime that answered to Hanoi.

52. The definition in Article 2 of the 1948 Genocide Convention lists the following specific acts as included in the term "genocide": "(a) Killing members of the group; (b) Causing serious bodily or mental harm to members of the group; (c) Deliberately inflicting on the group conditions of life calculated to bring about its physical destruction in whole or in part; (d) Imposing measures intended to prevent births within the group; (e) Forcibly transferring children of the group to another group" (Convention on the prevention and punishment of the crime of genocide, Adopted by Resolution 260 (III) A of the United Nations General Assembly on December 9, 1948. Available at http://www.unhchr.ch/html/menu3/b/p_genoci.htm).

53. For particularly damning accounts, see Philip Gourevitch, *We Wish to Inform You That Tomorrow We Will Be Killed with Our Families* (New York: Farrar, Straus and Giroux, 1998), chap. 11; and Samantha Power, *"A Problem from Hell": America and the Age of Genocide* (New York: Basic Books, 2002), chap. 10.

54. The suppression of a cable from the United Nations Assistance Mission in Rwanda (UNAMIR) commander in Kigali, Dallaire, to his superiors at the Department of Peace Operations in New York (then run by Kofi Annan) was a scandal when it was uncovered. See Gourevitch, *We Wish to Inform You*; Michael Barnett, *Eyewitness to a Genocide: The United Nations and Rwanda* (Ithaca, N.Y.: Cornell University Press, 2002); Michael Barnett, "The UN Security Council, Indifference, and Genocide and Rwanda," *Cultural Anthropology* 12, no. 4 (1997): 551–78; *Frontline* documentary, "The Triumph of Evil," and accompanying website at www.pbs.org/wgbh/pages/shows/frontline/evil. The U.S. administration's attempts to avoid "the G word" would have been comical if they did not have such tragic effects. See the *Frontline* documentary, "The Triumph of Evil," and interviews with James Woods and Tony Marley at www.pbs.org/wgbh/pages/shows/frontline/evil.

55. Samantha Power would probably be unimpressed with this change. She argues that the United States has known about virtually every genocide in the twentieth century and never acted to stop any of them. I do not dispute her claim; rather, we are investigating a different question. Power wants to know why the United States has not acted to stop genocide; I want to know why the United States has done any humanitarian intervention at all. See Power, *"A Problem from Hell."*

56. John G. Ruggie, "Multilateralism: The Anatomy of an Institution," in Ruggie, *Multilateralism Matters*, 6. Ruggie's edited volume provides an excellent analysis of the sources and power of multilateral norms generally.

57. Contemporary multilateralism is not, therefore, "better" or more efficient and effective than the nineteenth-century brand. I contend only that it is different. This difference in multilateralism poses a particular challenge to neoliberal institutionalists. These scholars have sophisticated arguments about why international cooperation should be robust and why it might vary across issue areas. They cannot, however, explain these qualitative changes in multilateralism, nor can they explain changes in the

amount of multilateral activity over time without appealing to exogenous variables (like changes in markets or technology).

58. For a more generalized argument about the ways international organizations enjoy legitimacy of action because they are able to present themselves as guardians of community interests as opposed to self-seeking states, see Michael N. Barnett and Martha Finnemore, *The Power and Pathologies of International Organizations* (Ithaca, N.Y.: Cornell University Press, forthcoming).

59. Ruggie, *Multilateralism Matters*.

60. Barnett and Finnemore, "The Politics, Power, and Pathologies of International Organizations"; Barnett and Finnemore, *The Power and Pathologies of International Organizations*.

INTERNATIONAL POLITICAL ECONOMY

9

Economic issues are critical to understanding international relations in the twenty-first century. In the first selection here, a classic from *U.S. Power and the Multinational Corporation* (1975), Robert Gilpin concisely discusses the relationship between economics and politics. He examines the three basic conceptions of political economy (liberalism, radicalism, and mercantilism), comparing their perspectives on the nature of economic relations; their theories of change; and how they characterize the relationship between economics and politics. In the next selection, Erik Gartzke also sees a relationship between economics and politics. The benefits of economic liberalism or capitalism lead to a more peaceful world, he argues. Free markets reduce the prospect of war as competition moves to the economic realm and resorting to war becomes unprofitable; in short, there is a capitalist peace.

International economic institutions play a key role in the globalized liberal economy of the twenty-first century. Helen V. Milner examines the impact of these institutions—the International Monetary Fund, the World Bank, and the World Trade Organization—on developing countries. Finding that some states have developed while others have not, she explores explanations for these differences. All economic governance institutions confronted an unparalleled situation beginning in the global economic crisis of 2008. Writing four years later, Daniel Drezner provides empirical evidence that the governance system worked, in that it responded to the crisis in an effective way.

One of the more contentious debates in the era of economic globalization has been over the relationship between growth and equity. Or, as Lloyd Gruber asks, "Can we really have it all?" Gruber examines the key theoretical links between trade and growth, on the one hand, and trade and inequality, on the other. But researchers need to do better, he says, examining the long-run effects of "the free trade bandwagon" on redistribution.

Another important issue in globalization is tackled by Yotam Margalit: why do individuals fear globalization? Cross-national surveys show that less-educated, lower skilled people, irrespective of their country's position in the global economy, are more opposed to trade openness, even though some would actually benefit. Using a variety of research methodologies, Margalit finds that individuals fear not so much the economic consequences as the social and cultural consequences of globalization.

Petroleum-exporting states would be expected to show particularly strong growth rates from globalization in an era of high demand for their product. Michael L. Ross, in a chapter from his book *How Petroleum Wealth Shapes the Development of Nations* (2012), finds that petroleum-rich countries have made substantial progress. But why have these states not done better? Ross examines contending explanations— lack of democracy, civil war, lack of opportunities for women, poor government policies, and failed government institutions. He concludes that petro-states do not uniformly have poor institutions, but those institutions are confronted by the particularly difficult task of managing volume and volatility of revenues.

Robert Gilpin
THE NATURE
OF POLITICAL ECONOMY

The international corporations have evidently declared ideological war on the "antiquated" nation state.... The charge that materialism, modernization and internationalism is the new liberal creed of corporate capitalism is a valid one. The implication is clear: the nation state as a political unit of democratic decision-making must, in the interest of "progress," yield control to the new mercantile mini-powers.[1]

While the structure of the multinational corporation is a modern concept, designed to meet the requirements of a modern age, the nation state is a very old-fashioned idea and badly adapted to serve the needs of our present complex world.[2]

These two statements—the first by Kari Levitt, a Canadian nationalist, the second by George Ball, a former United States undersecretary of state—express a dominant theme of contemporary writings on international relations. International society, we are told, is increasingly rent between its economic and its political organization. On the one hand, powerful economic and technological forces are creating a highly interdependent world economy, thus diminishing the traditional significance of national boundaries. On the other hand, the nation-state continues to command men's loyalties and to be the basic unit of political decision making. As one writer has put the issue, "The conflict of our era is between ethnocentric nationalism and geocentric technology."[3]

Ball and Levitt represent two contending positions with respect to this conflict. Whereas Ball advocates the diminution of the power of the nation-state in order to give full rein to the productive potentialities of the multinational corporation, Levitt argues for a powerful nationalism which could counterbalance American corporate domination. What appears to one as the logical and desirable consequence of economic rationality seems to the other to be an effort on the part of American imperialism to eliminate all contending centers of power.

Although the advent of the multinational corporation has put the question of the relationship between economics and politics in a new guise, it is an old issue. In the nineteenth century, for example, it was this issue that divided classical liberals like John Stuart Mill from economic nationalists, represented by Georg Friedrich List. Whereas the former gave primacy in the organization of society to economics and the production of wealth, the latter emphasized the political determination of economic relations. As this issue is central both to the contemporary debate on the multinational corporation and to the argument of this study, this chapter analyzes the three major treatments of the relationship between economics and politics—that is, the three major ideologies of political economy.

From Robert Gilpin, *U.S. Power and the Multinational Corporation* (New York: Basic Books, 1975), Chap. 1.

The Meaning of Political Economy

The argument of this study is that the relationship between economics and politics, at least in the modern world, is a reciprocal one. On the one hand, politics largely determines the framework of economic activity and channels it in directions intended to serve the interests of dominant groups; the exercise of power in all its forms is a major determinant of the nature of an economic system. On the other hand, the economic process itself tends to redistribute power and wealth; it transforms the power relationships among groups. This in turn leads to a transformation of the political system, thereby giving rise to a new structure of economic relationships. Thus, the dynamics of international relations in the modern world is largely a function of the reciprocal interaction between economics and politics.

First of all, what do I mean by "politics" or "economics"? Charles Kindleberger speaks of economics and politics as two different methods of allocating scarce resources: the first through a market mechanism, the latter through a budget.[4] Robert Keohane and Joseph Nye, in an excellent analysis of international political economy, define economics and politics in terms of two levels of analysis: those of structure and of process.[5] Politics is the domain "having to do with the establishment of an order of relations, a structure. . . ."[6] Economics deals with "short-term allocative behavior (i.e., holding institutions, fundamental assumptions, and expectations constant). . . ."[7] Like Kindleberger's definition, however, this definition tends to isolate economic and political phenomena except under certain conditions, which Keohane and Nye define as the "politicization" of the economic system. Neither formulation comes to terms adequately with the dynamic and intimate nature of the relationship between the two.

In this study, the issue of the relationship between economics and politics translates into that between wealth and power. According to this statement of the problem, economics takes as its province the creation and distribution of wealth; politics is the realm of power. I shall examine their relationship from several ideological perspectives, including my own. But what is wealth? What is power?

In response to the question, What is wealth?, an economist-colleague responded, "What do you want, my thirty-second or thirty-volume answer?" Basic concepts are elusive in economics, as in any field of inquiry. No unchallengeable definitions are possible. Ask a physicist for his definition of the nature of space, time, and matter, and you will not get a very satisfying response. What you will get is an *operational* definition, one which is usable: it permits the physicist to build an intellectual edifice whose foundations would crumble under the scrutiny of the philosopher.

Similarly, the concept of wealth, upon which the science of economics ultimately rests, cannot be clarified in a definitive way. Paul Samuelson, in his textbook, doesn't even try, though he provides a clue in his definition of economics as "the study of how men and society *choose* . . . to employ *scarce* productive resources . . . to produce various commodities . . . and distribute them for consumption."[8] Following this lead, we can say that wealth is anything (capital, land, or labor) that can generate future income; it is composed of physical assets and human capital (including embodied knowledge).

The basic concept of political science is power. Most political scientists would not stop here; they would include in the definition of political science the purpose for which power is used, whether this be the advancement of the public welfare or the domination of one group over another. In any case, few would dissent from the following statement of Harold Lasswell and Abraham Kaplan:

The concept of power is perhaps the most fundamental in the whole of political science:

the political process is the shaping, distribution, and exercise of power (in a wider sense, of all the deference values, or of influence in general.)[9]

Power as such is not the sole or even the principal goal of state behavior. Other goals or values constitute the objectives pursued by nation-states: welfare, security, prestige. But power in its several forms (military, economic, psychological) is ultimately the necessary means to achieve these goals. For this reason, nation-states are intensely jealous of and sensitive to their relative power position. The distribution of power is important because it profoundly affects the ability of states to achieve what they perceive to be their interests.

The nature of power, however, is even more elusive than that of wealth. The number and variety of definitions should be an embarrassment to political scientists. Unfortunately, this study cannot bring the intradisciplinary squabble to an end. Rather, it adopts the definition used by Hans Morgenthau in his influential *Politics among Nations*: "man's control over the minds and actions of other men."[10] Thus, power, like wealth, is the capacity to produce certain results.

Unlike wealth, however, power can not be quantified; indeed, it cannot be overemphasized that power has an important psychological dimension. Perceptions of power relations are of critical importance; as a consequence, a fundamental task of statesmen is to manipulate the perceptions of other statesmen regarding the distribution of power. Moreover, power is relative to a specific situation or set of circumstances; there is no single hierarchy of power in international relations. Power may take many forms—military, economic, or psychological—though, in the final analysis, force is the ultimate form of power. Finally, the inability to predict the behavior of others or the outcome of events is of great significance. Uncertainty regarding the distribution of power and the ability of the statesmen to control events plays an important role in international relations. Ultimately, the determination of the distribution of power can be made only in retrospect as a consequence of war. It is precisely for this reason that war has had, unfortunately, such a central place in the history of international relations. In short, power is an elusive concept indeed upon which to erect a science of politics.

■   ■   ■

The distinction * * * between economics as the science of wealth and politics as the science of power is essentially an analytical one. In the real world, wealth and power are ultimately joined. This, in fact, is the basic rationale for a political economy of international relations. But in order to develop the argument of this study, wealth and power will be treated, at least for the moment, as analytically distinct.

To provide a perspective on the nature of political economy, the next section of the chapter will discuss the three prevailing conceptions of political economy: liberalism, Marxism, and mercantilism. Liberalism regards politics and economics as relatively separable and autonomous spheres of activities; I associate most professional economists as well as many other academics, businessmen, and American officials with this outlook. Marxism refers to the radical critique of capitalism identified with Karl Marx and his contemporary disciples; according to this conception, economics determines politics and political structure. Mercantilism is a more questionable term because of its historical association with the desire of nation-states for a trade surplus and for treasure (money). One must distinguish, however, between the specific form mercantilism took in the seventeenth and eighteenth centuries and the general outlook of mercantilistic thought. The essence of the mercantilistic perspective, whether it is labeled economic nationalism, protectionism, or the doctrine of the German Historical School, is the subservience of the economy to the state and its interests—interests that range from matters of domestic welfare to those of international security. It is this more general meaning of mercantilism that is implied by the use of the term in this study.

■ ■ ■

Three Conceptions of Political Economy

The three prevailing conceptions of political economy differ on many points. Several critical differences will be examined in this brief comparison. (See Table 9.1.)

The Nature of Economic Relations

The basic assumption of liberalism is that the nature of international economic relations is essentially harmonious. Herein lay the great intellectual innovation of Adam Smith. Disputing his mercantilist predecessors, Smith argued that international economic relations could be made a positive-sum game; that is to say, everyone could gain, and no one need lose, from a proper ordering of economic relations, albeit the distribution of these gains may not be equal. Following Smith, liberalism assumes that there is a basic harmony between true national interest and cosmopolitan economic interest. Thus, a prominent member of this school of thought has written, in response to a radical critique, that the economic efficiency of the sterling standard in the nineteenth century and that of the dollar standard in the twentieth century serve "the cosmopolitan interest in a national form."[11] Although Great Britain and the United States gained the most from the international role of their respective currencies, everyone else gained as well.

Liberals argue that, given this underlying identity of national and cosmopolitan interests in a free market, the state should not interfere with economic transactions across national boundaries.

Table 9.1. Comparison of the Three Conceptions of Political Economy

	LIBERALISM	MARXISM	MERCANTILISM
Nature of economic relations	Harmonious	Conflictual	Conflictual
Nature of the actors	Households and firms	Economic classes	Nation-states
Goal of economic activity	Maximization of global welfare	Maximization of class interests	Maximization of national interest
Relationship between economics and politics	Economics should determine politics	Economics does determine politics	Politics determines economics
Theory of change	Dynamic equilibrium	Tendency toward disequilibrium	Shifts in the distribution of power

Through free exchange of commodities, removal of restrictions on the flow of investment, and an international division of labor, everyone will benefit in the long run as a result of a more efficient utilization of the world's scarce resources. The national interest is therefore best served, liberals maintain, by a generous and cooperative attitude regarding economic relations with other countries. In essence, the pursuit of self-interest in a free, competitive economy achieves the greatest good for the greatest number in international no less than in the national society.

Both mercantilists and Marxists, on the other hand, begin with the premise that the essence of economic relations is conflictual. There is no underlying harmony; indeed, one group's gain is another's loss. Thus, in the language of game theory, whereas liberals regard economic relations as a nonzero-sum game, Marxists and mercantilists view economic relations as essentially a zero-sum game.

The Goal of Economic Activity

For the liberal, the goal of economic activity is the optimum or efficient use of the world's scarce resources and the maximization of world welfare. While most liberals refuse to make value judgments regarding income distribution, Marxists and mercantilists stress the distributive effects of economic relations. For the Marxist the distribution of wealth among social classess is central; for the mercantilist it is the distribution of employment, industry, and military power among nation-states that is most significant Thus, the goal of economic (and political) activity for both Marxists and mercantilists is the redistribution of wealth and power.

The State and Public Policy

These three perspectives differ decisively in their views regarding the nature of the economic actors. In Marxist analysis, the basic actors in both domestic and international relations are economic classes; the interests of the dominant class determine the foreign policy of the state. For mercantilists, the real actors in international economic relations are nation-states; national interest determines foreign policy. National interest may at times be influenced by the peculiar economic interests of classes, elites, or other subgroups of the society; but factors of geography, external configurations of power, and the exigencies of national survival are primary in determining foreign policy. Thus, whereas liberals speak of world welfare and Marxists of class interests, mercantilists recognize only the interests of particular nation-states.

Although liberal economists such as David Ricardo and Joseph Schumpeter recognized the importance of class conflict and neoclassical liberals analyze economic growth and policy in terms of national economies, the liberal emphasis is on the individual consumer, firm, or entrepreneur. The liberal ideal is summarized in the view of Harry Johnson that the nation-state has no meaning as an economic entity.[12]

Underlying these contrasting views are differing conceptions of the nature of the state and public policy. For liberals, the state represents an aggregation of private interests: public policy is but the outcome of a pluralistic struggle among interest groups. Marxists, on the other hand, regard the state as simply the "executive committee of the ruling class," and public policy reflects its interests. Mercantilists, however, regard the state as an organic unit in its own right: the whole is greater than the sum of its parts. Public policy, therefore, embodies the national interest or Rousseau's "general will" as conceived by the political élite.

The Relationship between Economics and Politics; Theories of Change

Liberalism, Marxism, and mercantilism also have differing views on the relationship between economics and politics. And their differences on this issue are directly relevant to their contrasting theories of international political change.

Although the liberal ideal is the separation of economics from politics in the interest of maximizing world welfare, the fulfillment of this ideal would have important political implications. The classical statement of these implications was that of Adam Smith in *The Wealth of Nations*.[13] Economic growth, Smith argued, is primarily a function of the extent of the division of labor, which in turn is dependent upon the scale of the market. Thus he attacked the barriers erected by feudal principalities and mercantilistic states against the exchange of goods and the enlargement of markets. If men were to multiply their wealth, Smith argued, the contradiction between political organization and economic rationality had to be resolved in favor of the latter. That is, the pursuit of wealth should determine the nature of the political order.

Subsequently, from nineteenth-century economic liberals to twentieth-century writers on economic integration, there has existed "the dream . . . of a great republic of world commerce, in which national boundaries would cease to have any great economic importance and the web of trade would bind all the people of the world in the prosperity of peace."[14] For liberals the long-term trend is toward world integration, wherein functions, authority, and loyalties will be transferred from "smaller units to larger ones; from states to federalism; from federalism to supranational unions and from these to superstates."[15] The logic of economic and technological development, it is argued, has set mankind on an inexorable course toward global political unification and world peace.

In Marxism, the concept of the contradiction between economic and political relations was enacted into historical law. Whereas classical liberals—although Smith less than others—held that the requirements of economic rationality *ought* to determine political relations, the Marxist position was that the mode of production does in fact determine the superstructure of political relations. Therefore, it is argued, history can be understood as the product of the dialectical process—the contradiction between the evolving techniques of production and the resistant sociopolitical system.

Although Marx and Engels wrote remarkably little on international economics, Engels, in his famous polemic, *Anti-Duhring*, explicitly considers whether economics or politics is primary in determining the structure of international relations.[16] E. K. Duhring, a minor figure in the German Historical School, had argued, in contradiction to Marxism, that property and market relations resulted less from the economic logic of capitalism than from extraeconomic political factors: "The basis of the exploitation of man by man was an historical act of force which created an exploitative economic system for the benefit of the stronger man or class."[17] Since Engels, in his attack on Duhring, used the example of the unification of Germany through the Zollverein or customs union of 1833, his analysis is directly relevant to this discussion of the relationship between economics and political organization.

Engels argued that when contradictions arise between economic and political structures, political power adapts itself to the changes in the balance of economic forces; politics yields to the dictates of economic development. Thus, in the case of nineteenth-century Germany, the requirements of industrial production had become incompatible with its feudal, politically fragmented structure. "Though political reaction was victorious in 1815 and again in 1848," he argued, "it was unable to prevent the growth of large-scale industry in Germany and the growing participation of German commerce in the world market."[18] In summary, Engels wrote, "German unity had become an economic necessity."[19]

In the view of both Smith and Engels, the nation-state represented a progressive stage in human development, because it enlarged the political realm of economic activity. In each successive economic epoch, advances in technology and an increasing scale of production necessitate an enlargement of political organization. Because the city-state and feudalism restricted the scale of production and the division of labor made possible by the Industrial Revolution, they prevented the efficient utilization of resources and were, therefore, superseded by larger political units. Smith considered this to be a desirable objective; for Engels it was an historical necessity. Thus, in the opinion of liberals, the establishment of the Zollverein was a movement toward maximizing world economic welfare;[20] for Marxists it was the unavoidable triumph of the German industrialists over the feudal aristocracy.

Mercantilist writers from Alexander Hamilton to Frederich List to Charles de Gaulle, on the other hand, have emphasized the primacy of politics; politics, in this view, determines economic organization. Whereas Marxists and liberals have pointed to the production of wealth as the basic determinant of social and political organization, the mercantilists of the German Historical School, for example, stressed the primacy of national security, industrial development, and national sentiment in international political and economic dynamics.

In response to Engels's interpretation of the unification of Germany, mercantilists would no doubt agree with Jacob Viner that "Prussia engineered the customs union primarily for political reasons, in order to gain hegemony or at least influence over the lesser German states. It was largely in order to make certain that the hegemony should be Prussian and not Austrian that Prussia continually opposed Austrian entry into the Union, either openly or by pressing for a customs union tariff lower than highly protectionist Austria could stomach."[21] In pursuit of this strategic interest, it was "Prussian might, rather than a common zeal for political unification arising out of economic partnership, (that) . . . played the major role."[22]

In contrast to Marxism, neither liberalism nor mercantilism has a developed theory of dynamics. The basic assumption of orthodox economic analysis (liberalism) is the tendency toward equilibrium; liberalism takes for granted the existing social order and given institutions. Change is assumed to be gradual and adaptive—a continuous process of dynamic equilibrium. There is no necessary connection between such political phenomena as war and revolution and the evolution of the economic system, although they would not deny that misguided statesmen can blunder into war over economic issues or that revolutions are conflicts over the distribution of wealth; but neither is inevitably linked to the evolution of the productive system. As for mercantilism, it sees change as taking place owing to shifts in the balance of power; yet, mercantilist writers such as members of the German Historical School and contemporary political realists have not developed a systematic theory of how this shift occurs.

On the other hand, dynamics is central to Marxism; indeed Marxism is essentially a theory of social *change*. It emphasizes the tendency toward *dis*equilibrium owing to changes in the means of production, and the consequent effects on the everpresent class conflict. When these tendencies can no longer be contained, the sociopolitical system breaks down through violent upheaval. Thus war and revolution are seen as an integral part of the economic process. Politics and economics are intimately joined.

Why an International Economy?

From these differences among the three ideologies, one can get a sense of their respective explanations for the existence and functioning of the international economy.

An interdependent world economy constitutes the normal state of affairs for most liberal economists. Responding to technological advances in transportation and communications, the scope of the market mechanism, according to this analysis, continuously expands. Thus, despite temporary setbacks, the long-term trend is toward global economic integration. The functioning of the international economy is determined primarily by considerations of efficiency. The role of the dollar as the basis of the international monetary system, for example, is explained by the preference for it among traders and nations as the vehicle of international commerce.[23] The system is maintained by the mutuality of the benefits provided by trade, monetary arrangements, and investment.

A second view—one shared by Marxists and mercantilists alike—is that every interdependent international economy is essentially an imperial or hierarchical system. The imperial or hegemonic power organizes trade, monetary, and investment relations in order to advance its own economic and political interests. In the absence of the economic and especially the political influence of the hegemonic power, the system would fragment into autarkic economies or regional blocs. Whereas for liberalism maintenance of harmonious international market relations is the norm, for Marxism and mercantilism conflicts of class or national interests are the norm.

■   ■   ■

NOTES

1. Kari Levitt, "The Hinterland Economy," *Canadian Forum* 50 (July–August 1970): 163.

2. George W. Ball, "The Promise of the Multinational Corporation," *Fortune*, June 1, 1967, p. 80.

3. Sidney Rolfe, "Updating Adam Smith," *Interplay* (November 1968): 15.

4. Charles Kindleberger, *Power and Money: The Economics of International Politics and the Politics of International Economics* (New York: Basic Books, 1970), p. 5.

5. Robert Keohane and Joseph Nye, "World Politics and the International Economic System," in *The Future of the International Economic Order: An Agenda for Research*, ed. C. Fred Bergsten (Lexington, Mass.: D. C. Heath, 1973), p. 116.

6. Ibid.

7. Ibid., p. 117.

8. Paul Samuelson, *Economics: An Introductory Analysis* (New York: McGraw-Hill, 1967), p. 5.

9. Harold Lasswell and Abraham Kaplan, *Power and Society: A Framework for Political Inquiry* (New Haven: Yale University Press, 1950), p. 75.

10. Hans Morgenthau, *Politics among Nations* (New York: Alfred A. Knopf), p. 26. For a more complex but essentially identical view, see Robert Dahl, *Modern Political Analysis* (Englewood Cliffs, N.J.: Prentice-Hall, 1963).

11. Kindleberger, *Power and Money*, p. 227.

12. For Johnson's critique of economic nationalism, see Harry Johnson, ed., *Economic Nationalism in Old and New States* (Chicago: University of Chicago Press, 1967).

13. Adam Smith, *The Wealth of Nations* (New York: Modem Library, 1937).

14. J. B. Condliffe, *The Commerce of Nations* (New York: W. W. Norton, 1950), p. 136.

15. Amitai Etzioni, "The Dialectics of Supranational Unification" in *International Political Communities* (New York: Doubleday, 1966), p. 147.

16. The relevant sections appear in Ernst Wangerman, ed., *The Role of Force in History: A Study of Bismarck's Policy of Blood and Iron*, trans. Jack Cohen (New York: International Publishers, 1968).

17. Ibid., p. 12.

18. Ibid., p. 13.

19. Ibid., p. 14.

20. Gustav Stopler, *The German Economy* (New York: Harcourt, Brace and World, 1967), p. 11.

21. Jacob Viner, *The Customs Union Issue*, Studies in the Administration of International Law and Organization, no. 10 (New York: Carnegie Endowment for International Peace, 1950), pp. 98–99.

22. Ibid., p. 101.

23. Richard Cooper, "Eurodollars, Reserve Dollars, and Asymmetrics in the International Monetary System," *Journal of International Economics* 2 (September 1972): 325–44.

Erik Gartzke

CAPITALIST PEACE OR DEMOCRATIC PEACE?

With war in the Middle East and the prospect of terrorist attacks at sites ranging from major airports to the local shopping mall, it may be appropriate to remind ourselves that much of the world is experiencing an extended period of peace. Indeed, developed countries have not fought each other since the Second World War. This peace is unusual because powerful nations are historically the most conflict-prone.

Since before the time of Thucydides, states have used wealth to acquire more territory and to dominate the affairs of their neighbours. Understanding the reasons that the powerful countries of today are less prone to dispute than their predecessors is critical to maintaining the peace and to extending its benefits more broadly.

Policies predicated on inaccurate associations between democracy and peace, for example, seem destined to create as many problems as they solve. Classical liberal theory provides two streams of explanation for peace, one focusing on the forms and practices of government, the other on free markets and private property. The former, seen most particularly in the writings of Immanuel Kant, has received extensive attention from students of international politics in the last decade. Kant was wrong when he claimed that republics are less warlike than other forms of government. Instead, researchers have found that democracies are less likely to fight each other, while being no less ready to use force generally. This "democratic peace" has

been further proscribed by the discovery that developing democracies are just as war-prone as developing dictatorships.

Liberal political economy offers no such contradiction. Scholars such as Montesquieu, Adam Smith, Richard Cobden, Norman Angell and Richard Rosecrance have long speculated that free markets have the potential to free states from the looming prospect of recurrent warfare. Capitalism encourages co-operation among states by creating conditions that make war unappealing or unnecessary. Free markets create another venue to competition among countries, often containing minor conflicts below the level of military force. The transformation of commerce made possible by economic freedom also leads to a transformation in international affairs. Conquest becomes expensive and unprofitable. Wealth in modern economies is much harder to "steal" through force than was the case among agricultural and early industrial societies.

This "capitalist peace" has been slow to reach fruition but the tools and evidence are now in place to establish a firmer connection between economic freedom and reductions in conflict. I have used the Index of Economic Freedom developed by Gwartney and Lawson and multivariate statistical analysis to show that free markets appear to encourage peace. I have also evaluated several other factors often thought to influence whether states fight. Economic freedom is one of the rare factors that generally discourages conflict among nations. Democracy is desirable for many reasons but policies that encourage, or even seek

From *Institute of Public Affairs Review* 57, no. 4 (Dec. 2005), 13–16.

to impose, representative government are unlikely to contribute directly to international peace.

Free markets, and not democracy, have a general impact on the propensity of states to resort to military violence. At best, democracy may reduce conflict only among advanced industrialized economies. Developing countries do not benefit from a democratic peace. Especially in regions dominated by autocratic governments, the introduction of democracy can have little immediate impact on international co-operation.

Students of international political economy have long argued that global markets promote global amity. Mill, for example, claimed that "It is commerce which is rapidly rendering war obsolete, by strengthening and multiplying the personal interests which are in natural opposition to it." The problem, of course, is that Mill was wrong. Numerous wars and smaller conflicts stand between the present and the pristine optimism of nineteenth-century liberal political economists.

What did they miss? What did they understand correctly? What evidence is there that their basic vision contains insights of lasting validity?

The Capitalist Peace: An Evolving Explanation

The intellectual liberal tradition of economic peace beginning with Montesquieu, Mill, Adam Smith and others, and progressing through Richard Cobden, Norman Angell and Richard Rosecrance suggests a variety of ways in which capitalism can encourage peace.

Perhaps the most general explanation is that economic interdependence creates something of mutual value to countries, which then leaves states loath to fight for fear of destroying economic benefits that they prize. While this is not implausible, the explanation depends on the supposition that items of mutual value do not themselves spark or facilitate conflict.

Thomas Schelling tells a story of two mountain climbers tied together by a rope that in effect creates one common destiny. Schelling shows how something of mutual value can be used strategically to manipulate a counterpart; states that share economic linkages can in fact use the economic linkages to play a game of chicken: the more valuable the linkages, the more effective and telling is the game.

If a state is reluctant to endanger the benefits of prosperous economic ties, it does not follow that peace will ensue. Other countries must be tempted to view a reluctance to fight as a vulnerability. To ensure peace, all possible participants must be unwilling to play the game of chicken or, indeed, to use military force.

Students of international relations traditionally looked to motive and opportunity (capability) to explain war. However, as murder-mystery novels and the game of Clue® make clear, these conditions are seldom sufficient. Individuals, groups, and countries often disagree, but usually entities with different interests find that they can negotiate bargains that avoid more costly or flamboyant behavior.

Economic freedom is important to peace for at least two reasons. First, free markets act as a sounding board for political activity. Actions that frighten markets discourage investment, drive down economic conditions domestically, and thus are likely to be avoided by local leaders. The use of force abroad is often associated with a decline in domestic investment and with outflows of capital.

To the degree that leaders are willing to make foreign policy statements that scare capital markets, and to the extent that free monetary policies are in place that make it difficult for the government to interfere with capital flows, the international community may be able to infer a leader's true resolve. Knowing what an opponent is willing to do makes it possible to bargain more effectively, so

Figure 9.1. *Effect of Economic Freedom on Militarized Interstate Disputes*

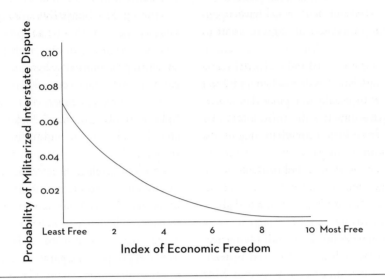

Figure 9.2. *Effect of Democracy on Militarized Interstate Disputes*

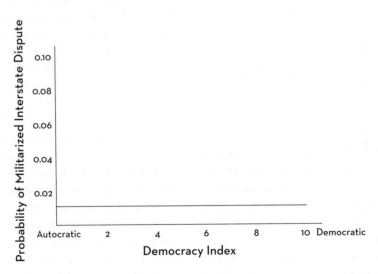

Source: Full details for Figures 9.1 and 9.2 are available in the *Economic Freedom of the World Index 2005*, available at http://www.ipa.org.au.

that resorting to violence to obtain what one side needs is less often necessary. Autonomous global markets create a venue through which leaders can establish credibility without needing to escalate to military force.

Second, economies based on intellectual and financial capital are less dependent upon, and less interested in, occupying foreign territory. Historically, wealth was a function of arable acres. Big countries with lots of land were rich countries. Within these societies, wealth was achieved by sidling up to the sovereign; being a friend of the king meant land, which meant power. Indeed, maintaining one's economic position was equivalent to being involved in politics.

Modern societies do not work this way. Wealth is not primarily derived from agriculture. Instead, money is made or maintained through innovative ideas and entrepreneurial spirit. Commodity prices and labour costs in developed economies have consistently trended in opposite directions. Armies of occupation are expensive and the proceeds of resource theft made possible by conquest are increasingly marginal.

The Future of Capitalist Peace

With the foregoing in mind, it is possible to speculate about the evolution of international relations. Some implications are promising and some are not. Countries with free and prosperous economies have a good chance of maintaining and even deepening the peace that has characterized the latter half of the twentieth century. The shift toward post-industrial production has already occurred in these countries, bringing with it a reduction in the utility for war. Free-market capitalism also seems entrenched. However, maintaining the existing commercial and financial systems across relatively open borders is an ongoing concern. Protectionism

can return, as it has in the past. The United States, in particular, needs to continue its leadership role in promoting global capitalism. Changes in the nature of production that discourage prosperous countries from wars of conquest may be reversed or degraded by subsequent technological, social, military, or environmental change.

At present, developed countries field effective fighting forces but find the labour-intensive activity of policing and administering conquered territory difficult and unprofitable. Developing countries can more effectively benefit from conquest, but these countries are often unable to maintain or deploy military forces capable of winning wars. Saddam Hussein wanted Kuwait but could not keep it. The United States and its coalition allies could take Kuwait but did not want it, at least not as real estate. If resource theft again becomes expedient, as was generally the case in the past, then we will again see wealthy nations conquer and take.

Yet, even with rising oil prices, it pays to remember that crude oil remains much cheaper by volume than the bottled water guzzled by thirsty armies of occupation. The Pentagon estimated recently that the life-cycle cost of a soldier exceeds US$4 million. In any event, lowering the cost of occupation is only half the profit equation. Information economies will remain poor targets for territorial aggrandizement and expansion of the global information economy promotes peace.

The situation is less rosy for developing countries. While the major economic powers may have lost interest in conquest, there remains occasional enthusiasm for using force to redirect the policies or politics of developing countries. Wars will continue as long as states differ in their views about the conduct of international affairs. Warfare among developing nations will remain unaffected by the capitalist peace as long as the economies of many developing countries remain fettered by governmental control.

Similarly, economic development is required to shift emphasis from land, labour and other traditional inputs to production and toward intellectual and financial capital, inputs that are less easily acquired through force. A problem will arise as increasing wealth and domestic political stability provide developing countries with the resources to project power beyond their nominal borders. Much of Africa and South America is partitioned according to the whims of long-dead European diplomats and existing borders do not reflect historic or current ethnic, linguistic or cultural boundaries. Economic development may literally provide the ammunition for rising conflict in the developing world. To avoid development creating a tinderbox of the southern hemisphere, it is necessary that increasing prosperity coincide with a relative decline in the value for territory and with growing dependence on global capital. The advantage of late-industrializing countries is that they may skip the most dangerous stages of industrialization.

For instance, the "outsourcing" of services, telemarketing and software industries, while vexing to many in the developed world, helps to create economies in the developing world that are less inclined toward war. The Indo-Pakistani conflict has regularly erupted in warfare, but leaders in both countries have recently come to accept that their more open economies suffer greatly from active hostilities. The growing dependence on international capital and the declining value of disputed territory relative to technological innovation means that the impetus to make peace has increased and the value of war has declined. On Cyprus, three decades of tense peace are gradually being replaced by the recognition that access to the knowledge economies of Europe is much more

critical to prosperity than possession of orchards and pastures.

Given finite resources, the attentions of developed nations are best directed at reinforcing and propagating the free-market principles and practices that lead to peace over much of the northern hemisphere. The United States, in particular, has used its status as hegemon to champion capitalism and to encourage economic development.

In short, to achieve the goals of peace and freedom, the developed countries of the world must sponsor the extension of capitalist institutions and practices.

Conclusion

Adam Smith had the great insight two centuries ago that self-interest, unfettered by bureaucratic guidance or constraints, served the common good better than state control. Market forces act as an "invisible hand" freeing the productive potential of human populations. Today, there is increasing evidence that an invisible hand also acts on the foreign policies of nations. Global markets offer an alternative to the revelatory mechanism of warfare, while prosperity makes some forms of aggression unprofitable.

The search for world peace has long been consumed with the need for selflessness, though altruism appears to have achieved little pacific impact in practice. Instead, it is a by-product of self-interest that has been found to yield yet another virtuous social effect. The flowering of economic freedom, what some have derisively labeled "greed," has begun to dampen the fires of war that to many seemed perennial and inherent, a product of civilization itself.

Helen V. Milner

GLOBALIZATION, DEVELOPMENT, AND INTERNATIONAL INSTITUTIONS
Normative and Positive Perspectives

Introduction

At the conclusion of World War II, several international institutions were created to manage the world economy and prevent another Great Depression. These institutions include the International Monetary Fund (IMF), the International Bank for Reconstruction and Development (now called the World Bank), and the General Agreement on Tariffs and Trade (GATT), which was expanded and institutionalized into the World Trade Organization (WTO) in 1995. These institutions have not only persisted for over five decades, but they have also expanded their mandates, changed their missions, and increased their membership. They have, however, become highly contested. As Stiglitz notes, "International bureaucrats—the faceless symbols of the world economic order—are under attack everywhere. . . . Virtually every major meeting of the International Monetary Fund, the World Bank and the World Trade Organization is now the scene of conflict and turmoil."[1]

Their critics come from both the left and right wings of the political spectrum. Anti-globalization forces from the left see them as instruments for the domination of the developing countries by both the rich countries or the forces of international capitalism. Critics from the right view these institutions as usurping the role of the market and easing pressures on developing states to adopt efficient, market-promoting policies. These debates often occur in a highly ideological and polemical fashion; they would benefit from being more informed by social science. By reviewing some of the recent social science literature, this essay addresses three questions: what has been the impact of these institutions on the developing countries, why have they had this impact, and what should be their role in the development process.

Conventional wisdom in international and comparative political economy has held that international institutions, like the IMF, World Bank, and WTO (and its predecessor, the GATT), have been largely beneficial for the countries in them. These institutions, it is claimed, constrain the behavior of the most powerful countries and provide information and monitoring capacities that enable states to cooperate.[2] All states involved are better off with these institutions than otherwise. Recently, however, evidence has mounted that these institutions may not be so beneficial for the developing countries.

Discerning the impact of these institutions requires that one address difficult counterfactual

From *Perspectives on Politics* 3, no. 4 (Dec. 2005), 833–854.
Some of the author's notes have been omitted.

questions.[3] Would the developing countries have been better off if these institutions had not existed? Would resources for aid and crisis management have been as plentiful or more so if they had not existed? Would globalization have occurred as fast and extensively, or even faster and deeper, if these international institutions had not been present? Counterfactuals cannot be answered directly because they presume a situation which did not occur and rely on speculation about what this hypothetical world would have been like.[4] Researchers can only make indirect counterfactual speculations. First, longitudinal comparison asks whether a developing country performed as well before it joined the institution (or participated in its programs) as after it did so. This enables the researcher to hold constant many characteristics of the country that do not change over time. Second, cross-sectional comparison asks if countries belonging to the institution (or participating in its programs) fare better or worse than those countries who do not. These comparisons are usually not enough. Part of the problem of knowing what the "right" counterfactual is depends on why countries join. Selection bias arises if the countries are joining or participating for nonrandom reasons which are not held constant. If countries choose to participate only under certain conditions, then the counterfactual experiment must correct for this or its results are likely to be biased. Because selection bias can arise from both observed and unobserved factors, correcting for selection effects is not straightforward. Little of the research on these international institutions addresses all of these methodological issues.

Assessing the impact of these institutions involves addressing this counterfactual. But recent normative scholarship claims that answering this counterfactual is not enough for assessing their role. It proposes different standards for evaluation and raises the contentious question of what standard one should use to assess the responsibility of

these institutions for the developing countries. This debate involves the extent of moral obligations that the rich countries and the institutions they created have regarding the poor countries, ranging from a limited "duty of assistance" to a cosmopolitan striving for equality. Combining normative and empirical scholarship may be unusual, but it may be fruitful. As Beitz claims, "reflection about reform of global governance is well advanced in other venues, both academic and political, almost never with the benefit of the moral clarity that might be contributed by an articulate philosophical conception of global political justice."[5]

■ ■ ■

The Role of the International Economic Institutions

The roles of the three main institutions have changed over time; in addition, their membership has become nearly universal. All of these institutions were created by the victors in World War II and were intended to help them avoid another global depression. Part of the problem for these institutions lies in their legacy. They were designed to help the developed countries create a cooperative and stable world economy in a nonglobalized world.

The IMF was established to support the fixed exchange rate system created at the Bretton Woods Conference in 1944; its role was to aid countries that were experiencing difficulties in maintaining their fixed exchange rate by providing them with short term loans. It was a lender of last resort and a provider of funds in crisis, enabling countries to avoid competitive devaluations. Ensuring a stable international monetary system to promote trade and growth was its central mission. From an initial membership of 29 countries, it has become almost universal with 184 members.

With the collapse of the Bretton Woods fixed exchange rate system in the early 1970s, this role changed. The IMF dealt less with the developed countries and more with the developing ones. It provided long and short term loans at below-market interest rates for countries in all sorts of economic difficulty, making it less distinct from the World Bank. It began attaching increasing numbers of conditions to those loans ("conditionality"), negotiating with countries to make major changes in their domestic policies and institutions. Promoting economic growth as well as resolving specific crises became its mission, which meant that ever more countries became involved in these so-called structural adjustment programs. Indeed, as Vreeland notes, in 2000 alone the IMF had programs with sixty countries, or more than one-third of the developing world. These changes made the IMF more similar to the World Bank.

Formed after World War II, the Bank concentrated mostly on reconstruction and later on development; in 1960, with the formation of the International Development Association (IDA), the Bank moved further toward economic development programs.[6] Many countries over the years have received both IMF and World Bank loans, often simultaneously.[7] The World Bank also gives interest-free loans and grants (similar to foreign aid) to the poorest developing countries. This aid has been heavily used in Africa; indeed, in 2003, 51 percent of it went to sub-Saharan Africa. This overlap of missions, proliferation of adjustment loans, and expansion of conditionality are central issues today.

The WTO's central mission has been to promote trade liberalization by fostering negotiations among countries to reciprocally lower their trade barriers and providing information about countries' trade policies. Membership in the GATT/WTO has grown importantly over the years, from a mere 23 in 1947 to 146 countries in 2003.[8] Like the IMF and World Bank, the GATT was originally a negotiating forum for the developed countries; its impact on the developing countries has grown slowly over time. The liberalization of trade policy has become an accepted doctrine for most developing countries; barriers in the developing world have fallen significantly since 1980.[9] In addition, the WTO's mission has increasingly involved the connections between domestic policies and trade barriers. With significant lowering of tariffs and quotas, many domestic policies such as intellectual property laws, environmental policy, domestic subsidies, and tax laws, are now seen to affect trade flows and hence to reside within the WTO's jurisdiction. As with conditionality in the monetary domain, the attack on trade barriers has increasingly brought this international institution into contact with domestic politics.

The GATT/WTO system has sponsored numerous trade negotiation rounds over the past fifty years. The most recently concluded negotiations, called the Uruguay Round, ended in late 1994 with the debut of the WTO and accords lowering trade barriers and extending agreements into other areas such as intellectual property and foreign investment. This system relies on reciprocity, attempting to balance countries' gains and losses. The WTO is now conducting the new Doha Round of trade negotiations, which is intended to address the problems of the developing countries more directly.

The Experience of the Developing Countries

Debate over these institutions has arisen from the seeming lack of progress in the developing world. Except for the World Bank, the original and primary mission of these institutions was not promoting growth in the developing world. Nevertheless, since the change in their roles from the 1970s onward, they have increasingly been judged by their impact on the poor. Fairly or not, the question has been whether these institutions have fostered development.[10]

Each of these institutions has promoted the adoption of market-friendly policies, and part of the reaction against them has been connected to these policies. "The widespread recourse of indebted developing countries to structural adjustment loans from the Bretton Woods institutions in the aftermath of the debt crisis of the early 1980s played a pivotal role in the redefinition of trade and industrialization strategies. Prominent among the conditions attached to these loans was the liberalization of policies towards trade and FDI (foreign direct investment). This was in line with the rising influence of pro-market economic doctrines during this period. Under these structural adjustment programs, there was a significant increase in the number of cases of trade and investment liberalization in many developing countries."[11]

But concerns abound over whether trade and capital market liberalization, privatization, deregulation, austerity, and the other elements of the so-called Washington Consensus that these institutions advocated promote development in poor countries. If one looks solely at the economic side, progress has been mixed in many developing countries. As Easterly concludes, "there was much lending, little adjustment, and little growth in the 1980s and 1990s" in the developing world.[12] Annual per capita growth for the developing countries averaged 0 percent for the years from 1980 to 1998, whereas from 1960–1979 their growth had averaged about 2.5 percent annually.[13] Poverty remains very high, with roughly 20 percent of the world's population living on less than a dollar a day and more than 45 percent on less than two dollars a day.[14] Because of these conditions, some 18 million people a year die of easily preventable causes, many

of them children.[15] A sizable number of these countries were worse off economically in 2000 than they were in the 1980. World Bank data indicate, for instance, that per capita income was lower in 1999 in at least nine countries (for which we have data) than in 1960: Haiti, Nicaragua, Central African Republic, Chad, Ghana, Madagascar, Niger, Rwanda, and Zambia.[16] From 1980 to 2002, twenty countries experienced a decrease in their human development indexes, which include more than just economic growth.[17]

Since 1980 the world's poorest countries have done worse economically than the richest.[18] In the 1980s the high income countries of the Organisation for Economic Co-operation and Development (OECD) grew at 2.5 percent annually and in the 1990s at 1.8 percent; the developing countries grew at 0.7 percent and 1.7 percent, respectively.[19] Moreover, if one excludes East Asia where the growth was extraordinary (5.6 percent in the 1980s and 6.4 percent in the 1990s), the developing countries grew much more slowly than the developed ones. Thus, they have been falling further behind the rich countries, increasing the gap between the two. As Lant Pritchett has shown, over the period 1820 to 1992 the divergence in incomes between the world's rich and poor has grown enormously.[20] In 1820 the richest country had three times the income that the poorest did; in the early 1990s this number was thirty.[21] Much of this divergence is due to the rich countries' rapid growth.[22]

Economic crises among the developing countries have also proliferated after the 1970s. In addition, the debt problems of many developing countries have increased. "Total debt of developing countries increased until 1999 and then stabilized at about $3 trillion as of last year [that is, 2003]. Furthermore, while debt has declined as a proportion of GDP, it remains high at some 40 percent, and the ratio of debt to exports at 113 percent. More importantly, the net resource transfer—the resources available for use after paying interest—has been negative in recent years for all regions. These magnitudes suggest that it is difficult to consider current levels of debt sustainable and helping growth."[23]

The performance of the developing countries has not been uniformly poor, however. From 1960 to 2000, life expectancy increased from 46 to 63 years in the developing world. Child mortality rates were halved in the same period, as were illiteracy rates.[24] Poverty as a percentage of the developing countries' populations has declined recently.[25] Including China, where the declines have been enormous, the percentage of people in the developing countries living on the poverty threshold of $1 a day has fallen from over 28 percent in 1990 to below 22 percent in 2000.[26] The percentage living on $2 a day in the developing world also fell from 61 percent to 54 percent in this period.[27] Unfortunately, the absolute numbers of the desperately poor have not fallen much, if at all, because of high growth population rates.[28]

The developing countries have also upgraded their role in the world economy. They now are producers and exporters of manufactures and not primarily of primary products. In 2000, about 64 percent of low and middle income countries' exports were manufactures, while only 10 percent were agriculture, and their share of world trade in manufactures rose over this period from 9 percent to 26 percent.[29] Especially in East and South Asia, the developing economies have become tightly integrated into the world production and trading system led by multinational corporations. This increase in the value-added and the diversification of developing countries' production and trade has been a boon for many.

This mixed record of economic outcomes has raised questions about the impact of these international economic institutions. But one must pose the counterfactual to assess their impact: would the performance of these countries have been better, the same, or even worse had these institutions not existed?

Theories about the Functions and Benefits of International Institutions

Many international relations scholars have argued that countries should benefit from these institutions. States rationally decide to join them; therefore, they join only if the net benefits are greater than those offered by staying out of the organization. Membership is voluntary. The net utility derived from joining could be negative, but less negative than that incurred by remaining outside the institution. As Gruber has argued, if the most powerful states define the alternatives open to the developing countries and set up multilateral institutions, the developing countries can be better off by joining them than staying outside, but worse off than if the institutions never existed.[30] The rush lately by all countries to join these institutions suggests that developing countries have found them to be more beneficial than the alternative of staying out, but it does not moot the question of whether they would be better of without any of these multilateral institutions in the first place. Four reasons are often theorized for the existence of these institutions: (1) constraining the great powers, (2) providing information and reducing transaction costs, (3) facilitating reciprocity, and (4) promoting reform in domestic politics.

Constraining the Great Powers

International institutions may exert a constraint on the underlying anarchy of the international system. They make the use of force and power by states to achieve their goals less likely; the rules, norms, and procedures established by these institutions replace to some extent the pursuit of national interest by power. Most importantly, as Ikenberry claims, they help to harness the behavior of the most powerful states.[31] By creating and complying with these institutions, the Great Powers, or hegemon, can reassure other states that they will not take advantage of them. The strongest bind themselves to a set of norms and rules that the other states voluntarily agree to accept.

Evidence for this effect is mixed. As the WTO points out, "trade is likely to expand and be more profitable under conditions of certainty and security as to the terms of market access and the rules of trade—precommitment around a set of rules also diminishes the role of power and size in determining outcomes."[32] This motivation is important in trade where countries with large markets, and hence market power, can use this to obtain more favorable trading arrangements in bilateral negotiations with smaller countries.

Nevertheless, critics maintain that developing countries have not gained much from the GATT trade rounds; most of the gains have gone to developed countries. Some scholars even allege that the trade rounds have allowed the developed countries to exploit the developing ones by engaging them in unfair agreements. As Stiglitz says, "previous rounds of trade negotiations [in the GATT/WTO] had protected the interests of the advanced industrial countries—or more accurately, special interests within those countries—without concomitant benefits for the lesser developed countries."[33] The unbalanced outcome of the recent Uruguay trade round is an important issue. "Several computable general equilibrium models have shown that the Uruguay Round results disproportionately benefit developed country gross domestic products (GDPs) compared to developing countries, and that some developing countries would actually suffer a net GDP loss from the Uruguay Round—at least in the short run."[34]

Developing countries have raised concerns about the equity of the outcome of this and other rounds. "With hindsight, many developing country governments perceived the outcome of the Uruguay Round to have been unbalanced. For most developing countries (some did gain), the crux of the unfavourable deal was the limited market access concessions they obtained from developed countries in exchange for the high costs they now realize they incurred in binding themselves to the new multilateral trade rules."[35] Others note that asymmetric outcomes are an intrinsic part of the GATT/WTO bargaining process. "[Trade] rounds have been concluded through power-based bargaining that has yielded asymmetrical contracts favoring the interests of powerful states. The agenda-setting process (the formulation of proposals that are difficult to amend), which takes place between launch and conclusion, has been dominated by powerful states; the extent of that domination has depended upon the extent to which powerful countries have planned to use their power to conclude the round."[36]

The counterfactual one must pose is the following: without the GATT or WTO would the developing countries be better off if they had to negotiate bilaterally with the large, rich countries? Multilateralism seems well suited to giving the developing countries a better outcome than would such bilateral negotiations.[37] "Multilateralism ensures transparency, and provides protection—however inadequate—against the asymmetries of power and influence in the international community."[38] It may not only place some constraints on the behavior of the large, developed countries, but it may also encourage developing countries to realize their common interests and counterbalance the rich countries. By giving them more political voice than otherwise, institutions like the WTO may enhance their capacity to influence outcomes.

Evidence of the constraining power of the IMF or World Bank is less apparent. Decisions in the IMF and World Bank are taken by weighted voting, with the rich countries—and especially the United States—having the lion's share of votes. Since the end of the fixed exchange rate system in the early 1970s, these institutions have basically collected funds from the developed countries and private capital markets to give to the developing ones under increasing conditions. Conditionality has been designed by these institutions with the tacit support of the developed countries, and it has been negotiated with the poor ones. Since the late 1970s few, if any, developed countries have not been subject to IMF programs; only the developing world has. Article IV of the IMF charter requires surveillance of all members and discussion of the problems in their fiscal and monetary policies, but since the late 1970s, de facto this has not applied to the developed countries.[39] The IMF has remarked on its own inefficacy: "Nowhere is the difficulty of conducting surveillance more apparent than in the relations between the IMF and the major industrial countries. Effective oversight over the policies of the largest countries is obviously essential if surveillance is to be uniform and symmetric across the membership, but progress in achieving that goal has been slow and hesitant."[40] It is difficult to argue that the IMF and World Bank constrain the exercise of power by the developed countries. Indeed, these multilateral institutions may enhance the capacity of the rich countries to collectively enforce their will on the poor countries, as Rodrik argues.[41]

Does their existence change the behavior of the rich? Without the two institutions, would the developed countries lend or donate as much as they do now? Does multilateral lending and aid substitute for or complement bilateral giving? Would the least well-off and the most politically insignificant countries be left to fend for themselves if they ran into economic crises, should the World Bank and IMF not exist? And would the terms of any aid or loans given bilaterally be worse for these countries than they are now? Evidence exists that bilateral aid tends to be more oriented toward the political and economic interests of donors than is multilateral aid.[42] Some critics of the IMF and World Bank claim that countries would experience fewer crises since they would be

more attentive to their financial situation in the absence of the moral hazard presented by the existence of these multilateral organizations.[43] Others scholars have demonstrated that the distribution of aid and loans even with these institutions is weighted toward the economically better off and the politically more important developing countries.[44] For instance, Stone shows that in lending to the transition countries the IMF gave more and imposed lighter conditions on those states with stronger political ties to the United States.[45] Further, he shows how this political process undermines the credibility of the IMF's position and induces the recipient countries to ignore its conditionality. His research, however, does not really address the question of whether the IMF's presence affected the overall amount of lending or the allocation of those loans, relative to a situation where the Fund did not exist. These counterfactuals are essential for addressing questions about these multilateral institutions, but they are difficult to assess.

Providing Information and Reducing Transaction Costs

Following New Institutionalism theories, some argue that a major reason for these institutions is the lowering of transaction costs and the provision of information to facilitate multilateral cooperation in an anarchic world. As Keohane writes, international institutions "facilitate agreements by raising the anticipated costs of violating others' property rights, by altering transaction costs through clustering of issues, and by providing reliable information to members. [They] are relatively efficient institutions, compared to the alternative of having a myriad of unrelated agreements, since their principles, rules, and institutions create linkages among issues that give actors incentives to reach mutually beneficial agreements."[46] For him, international institutions also reduce uncertainty by monitoring the member states' behavior and allowing decentralized enforcement through reciprocity strategies.[47]

Scholars such as Anne Krueger have suggested just such an informational role for the IMF and World Bank.[48] Surveying and reporting on the policy behavior of member countries, providing information about the likelihood of crises, and being a repository of expert information are key roles for these institutions. The Meltzer Commission also emphasizes this role, and the most severe critics on the right imply that the IMF and World Bank should give up all roles except monitoring and providing expert information to member states. Others have noted the expertise role of the IFIs. "The World Bank is widely recognized to have exercised power over development policies far greater than its budget, as a percentage of North/South aid flows, would suggest because of the expertise it houses. . . . This expertise, coupled with its claim to "neutrality" and its "apolitical" technocratic decision-making style, have given the World Bank an authoritative voice with which it has successfully dictated the content, direction, and scope of global development over the past fifty years."[49]

The WTO has also been seen as an information-provision institution. It monitors and reports on the compliance of states with the commitments they have made to each other. This task reassures other member countries and domestic publics about the behavior of their political leaders, making cooperation more likely and sustainable.[50]

Informational arguments suggest that all states gain from participation in such institutions.[51] This mutual gain explains the voluntary participation of states in these multilateral forums. The expectation would be that developing countries join largely for these informational benefits, but there remains the issue of who provides what information for whose benefit. Are the developing countries providing more information than otherwise? Are the principal beneficiaries private investors in the developing countries or in the developed world, other domestic groups, or the institutions themselves? Do the IMF and World Bank provide developing countries with useful information about other members or with expertise that would otherwise be unavailable? These empirical questions have not been examined much.

One central complaint against the IMF and World Bank is that the policy advice they give (especially the "Washington Consensus" advice) has been unhelpful, if not detrimental, since it failed to take into account the circumstances of the developing countries.[52] The claim is that the policy expertise given (or imposed via conditionality) has not been beneficial. For instance, Stiglitz, Bhagwati, and others have all criticized the IMF for pushing the developing countries into opening their capital markets.[53] They have argued that little, if any, economic evidence or theory supports this, the consequences have been negative for most countries, and the main beneficiaries have been private investors in the developed world. As Stiglitz writes, "the [main] problem is that the IMF (and sometimes the other international economic organizations) presents as received doctrines propositions and policy recommendations for which there is not widespread agreement; indeed, in the case of capital market liberalization, there was scant evidence in support and a massive amount of evidence against."[54] Even the advice to open their economies to trade has not been unquestioned. Economic analysis shows that the impact of trade openness on economic growth can be positive but also insignificant.[55]

Easterly's book is also an indictment of the economic policy prescriptions of the Bank and Fund. Each chapter shows how the prevailing wisdom guiding economic policy prescriptions in the IFIs has either been proven wrong or never been attempted to be proven right or wrong. As he concludes, "in part II, we saw that the search for a magic formula to turn poverty into prosperity failed . . . Growth failed to respond to any of these formulas . . ."[56]

Vreeland's book supports these claims about the failed policy advice of the IMF. His research shows that IMF programs lower economic growth and redistribute income away from the most needy; the impact of conditionality is to retard development. As he concludes, this result means that either the IMF's policy prescriptions are incorrect or economic growth and poverty reduction are not the goals of the IMF. Stone's findings counter these; he shows that IMF programs do reduce inflation and return greater macroeconomic stability but only when they are not interfered with by political factors. Thus, even the informational value of the international institutions has been questioned.

Facilitating Reciprocity

International institutions facilitate reciprocity strategies among countries in an anarchic environment. Cooperation in anarchy relies on reciprocity, but more cooperation can be sustained if it need not require simultaneous and perfectly balanced exchanges. "International regimes can be thought of in part as arrangements that facilitate nonsimultaneous exchange."[57] Bagwell and Staiger have developed the most rigorous claims about the importance of reciprocity for the international trading system.[58] If countries are sizable economic actors in world markets, then they can use trade policy to manipulate their terms of trade and gain advantages over their trading partners. If these big countries set trade policy unilaterally, they will arrive at an inefficient outcome, sacrificing the gains to be had from mutual trade liberalization. Reciprocity enhanced by the WTO's rules and monitoring can provide a context in which these big countries can achieve more efficient, cooperative outcomes. The main function of international institutions is to make reciprocity credible and feasible.

In the case of the large, rich countries in world trade this motivation seems apparent. The United States, European Union and Japan have used the GATT/WTO to enforce reciprocity strategies and lower their trade barriers. However, there is little evidence that this reciprocity has extended to the developing world. Many developing countries did not join the WTO until recently; most of the developing country members did not reciprocally liberalize their trade in the trade rounds.

In the period until the launch of the Uruguay Round and the formation of the WTO, only the industrial countries were meaningful participants in multilateral trade negotiations. They bargained amongst themselves to reduce trade barriers, while developing countries were largely out of this process and had few obligations to liberalize. The latter availed themselves of the benefits of industrial country liberalization, courtesy of the Most Favored Nation (MFN) principle, but that defined pretty much the limits of their contribution to or benefits from the General Agreement on Tariffs and Trade (GATT). Industrial countries were content with this arrangement, in part because it alleviated the pressure on them to liberalize sensitive sectors such as agriculture and clothing, but perhaps more importantly because the markets of developing countries were not at that stage sufficiently attractive.[59]

This situation is not unexpected. Theories about the value of reciprocity in trade depend on the assumption that the country is a large trader (that is, it can affect prices); for most developing countries, this is not a realistic assumption.[60] "Countries with small markets are just not attractive enough for larger trading partners to engage in meaningful reciprocity negotiations."[61] The 100 largest developing countries (excluding the transition economies) accounted for 29 percent of total world exports in 2003; the United States alone accounted for 10 percent, the EU (excluding intra-EU trade) for 15 percent and Japan for 6.5 percent.[62]

In addition, many of the developing countries received preferential access to developed countries' markets, as noted above. Ironically, this access has reduced their interest in reciprocal multilateral liberalization since it simply reduces their preference margins.[63] "The problem with granting preferential access in goods trade as the payoff to small and poor countries is that it is counterproductive and even perverse. Although preferential access does provide rents in the short run, the empirical evidence suggests that preferences do not provide a basis for sustaining long-run growth.[64] In addition, preferences create an incentive for recipients to have more protectionist regimes.[65] For most of the developing world then, ensuring reciprocity has not been a main function of the trade regime.[66]

Facilitating Reform in Domestic Politics

Some scholars have speculated that joining an international institution and publicly agreeing to abide by its rules, norms, and practices has important domestic political consequences. It can help domestic leaders to alter policies at home that they otherwise would not be able to do. It can help them lock in "good" policies (that is, ones that enhance general welfare) and resist pressures by special interests to adopt "bad" policies (that is, ones that benefit special interests only). Or it can help domestic leaders to activate interest groups to counterbalance other groups' pressures and thus introduce different policies than otherwise.

Several logics exist to support these claims. For some, once leaders join an institution it becomes hard for them to violate its practices since leaders who do so tarnish their international reputations and are less capable of making new agreements; their publics lose from this and are more likely to evict the leader, making noncompliance more costly than otherwise.[67] Others argue that domestic publics receive signals from the monitoring of international institutions and that when the institution sounds a violation alarm, some domestic groups hear this and know their leaders are probably giving in to special interests and become more likely to vote them out of office.[68] For others the key is that achieving cooperative agreements with other countries brings advantages for some domestic groups that otherwise would not be involved in a change of policy; once their interests are engaged through the multilateral process, they can become strong proponents for policy change at home.[69]

Evidence for this binding effect is not extensive in the trade area. Mattoo and Subramanian, for instance, show that the poorest countries (roughly a third of all countries) have not used the WTO to make commitments. "For a vast majority of the poor and small countries, both the proportion of [tariff] bindings in the industrial sector is small and the wedge between actual and committed tariffs is large, indicating that countries have given themselves a large margin of flexibility to reverse their trade policies without facing adverse consequences in the WTO."[70]

Moreover, as others have noted, many of the developing countries chose to liberalize their trade regimes unilaterally.[71] That is, they decided to open their markets before joining the WTO; membership in the WTO was not necessary for them to liberalize. Once they liberalized, however, membership then became more important; it helped to prevent the raising of trade barriers.

The domestic political consequences of IMF and World Bank membership may be important but little research addresses this directly. Vreeland notes that countries underwent IMF programs out of choice as much as necessity. Governments were using the IMF to produce changes in policies that they desired, but unfortunately, these changes did not produce economic growth or poverty reduction. His analysis demonstrates that the programs were used instead to promote the welfare of capital owners, who tend to be the richest groups in developing countries and thus may have further hurt developing countries. Stone's analysis also shows that compliance with the IMF has been variable, and that, especially for important borrowers, domestic binding or compliance has been low. In sum, we do not know what the overall domestic effect of IMF and World Bank membership on countries has been.

Four Sources of the Problems with International Institutions

If the WTO, IMF, and World Bank do not provide the benefits for developing countries that scholars predict they might, what could explain this? Four claims have been advanced. Some argue that these institutions have minimal impact. Others argue that they are captured by either the powerful rich countries or by private producers and investors and so do not focus on the interests of the poor countries. Finally, the problems may lie with the internal organization and dynamics of the institutions themselves and the failure of the member countries to monitor their behavior.

1. NO IMPACT It may be that these institutions had little or no impact on the developing countries. Their fate could be far more sensitive to other forces, such as globalization and domestic politics.

Because of technological innovation, reduced communications and transportation costs, and policy changes, the developing countries have been increasingly exposed to the world economy.[72] But the capacity of the IMF and World Bank has not grown proportionately, and thus, they are less able to help, especially at times of crisis. "The IFIs seek to fulfill their role of technical and financial support, but the relative size of their financing remains low. They constitute only about 19 per cent

of total debt outstanding by developing countries, and only 13 per cent among middle-income countries."[73] The developing countries have thus experienced increasing globalization while the IFIs capacity has not kept up with the rising demand for funds.

The debate over the impact of globalization on the developing countries is too vast to join here, but suffice it to say that many scholars have argued that globalization is having a large effect on such countries (whether it is positive or negative is much debated).[74] Globalization, however, is not disconnected from the WTO, World Bank, and IMF. These institutions were intended to help manage the process of integrating the developing economies into the world one. Nevertheless, the larger point is that globalization may have done more to affect these countries than these international institutions.

Others have attributed the outcomes of the developing countries to their own domestic problems. Political instability, corruption, civil war, lack of the rule of law, and authoritarianism are viewed as the bigger sources of their problems. Recent research touting the importance of domestic political institutions supports this line of argument. Without institutions that protect private property rights for broad segments of the population, growth is unlikely.[75] In this view, reforming domestic institutions is a first priority to promote sustained growth.[76] To the extent that the international institutions have advanced such institutional reform, they have helped the developing world. To the degree they have permitted developing nations to avoid or postpone such domestic change, they have hurt their prospects for development. From this perspective, it is essential not to attribute too much impact to the three international economic institutions. Much as realists in international relations maintain, these institutions may be more epiphenomenal; whatever impact they have, if any, is derived from their role in some larger political or economic structure.

2. CAPTURE BY THE POWERFUL DEVELOPED COUNTRIES For many scholars, Realists and others, these institutions were created by and for the interests of the large, rich countries. They were established at American initiative during its hegemony following World War II. American and European dominance in these organizations has been sealed by their sizable market power and their de facto control over the institutions' operations. Serving the interests of the advanced industrial nations has meant either that the interests of the poor countries were at best neglected and at worst damaged. "There are thus serious problems with the current structure and processes of global governance. Foremost among these is the vast inequality in the power and capacity of different nation states. At the root of this is the inequality in the economic power of different nations. The industrialized countries have far higher per capita incomes, which translates into economic clout in negotiations to shape global governance. They are the source of much-needed markets, foreign investments, financial capital, and technology. The ownership and control of these vital assets gives them immense economic power. This creates a built-in tendency for the process of global governance to be in the interests of powerful players, especially in rich nations."[77] In this view, the international institutions have not helped much since they are oriented to promote the interests of the developed countries.

This bias operates in a number of ways in each organization. World Bank aid has been questioned. It has been heavily used in sub-Saharan Africa, but this region has done least well. Scholars have argued that this aid has been used to prop up authoritarian governments and to continue with failed policies longer than they otherwise could have.[78] The link between the amount of aid a country received and its growth rate remains disputed; many find that aid alone has no significant impact on economic growth.[79] But aid flows have not been allocated to the neediest countries. Studies show that donor interests, both economic and foreign policy ones, often dictate which countries receive what aid, and when.[80] Countries with poor governments and policies may for other reasons receive large allocations of aid; the priorities of rich donors may undermine the developmental impact of aid.

According to other scholars, policy recommendations the developing countries were given reflected the experiences and interests of the rich countries. Trade liberalization promoted by the WTO and IMF occurred too quickly and without (enough) concern for finding alternative means for the poor countries to fund their budgets and develop social safety nets. For others, the problem is more how the agenda is set and how negotiating power is distributed. In the WTO, Steinberg shows the enormous power of the rich countries. "The secretariat's bias in favor of great powers has been largely a result of who staffs it and the shadow of power under which it works. From its founding until 1999, every GATT and WTO Director-General was from Canada, Europe, or the United States, and most of the senior staff of the GATT/WTO secretariat have been nationals of powerful countries. Secretariat officials' . . . actions have usually been heavily influenced or even suggested by representatives of the most powerful states. For example . . . the package of proposals that became the basis for the final stages of negotiation in the Uruguay Round . . . was largely a collection of proposals prepared by and developed and negotiated between the EC and the United States."[81]

IMF and World Bank conditionality programs mandating capital market liberalization, privatization and governmental austerity programs often ran aground because the developing countries did not have the financial or legal institutions to support such policies. These policies might work in the context of the developed world where these institutions existed. An example of this is Russia, which Stiglitz and Stone discuss in detail. They show that American government officials pushed the IMF to loan and continue loaning large sums to Russia, that the IMF promoted policy changes that the Russian political economy could not handle, and finally that American pressure undercut the ability of the IMF to induce Russia to reform. "The officials who applied Washington Consensus policies failed to appreciate the social context of the transition economies";[82] privatization in the absence of a legal framework of corporate governance only helped cause economic and political problems. Stone, who presents a more optimistic picture of the IMF largely because his central focus is on reducing inflation and not increasing growth or equality, shows that American influence on the IMF is pervasive and pernicious. In the Russian case, for instance, he claims that the IMF made some mistakes (for example, in advising capital market liberalization in 1996, which was pushed by the Americans) but that most of the problems came not from IMF advice but from Russia's failure to listen to the IMF. American pressure on the IMF and support for Russia were largely to blame for this outcome; Russian politicians knew that the IMF would never carry out their threats since the United States would never let them. Stone's identification of the credibility problems that big country interference with the IMF engenders is a novel and subtle mechanism for rich country influence on the developing world.

Pressure from the rich countries has been seen as causing the international institutions at times to provide unhelpful advice as well as to shift the agenda and negotiating outcomes away from those favorable to the developing world. Bhagwati notes that "the rush to abandon controls on capital flows . . . was hardly a consequence of finance ministers and other policy makers in the developing countries suddenly acknowledging the folly of their ways. It reflected instead external pressures . . . from both the IMF and the U.S. Treasury."[83] Thacker shows that the United States exerts a great deal of influence over which countries get IMF loans.[84] Countries voting similarly to the United States in the United Nations do better at the IMF. The literature on foreign aid also suggests that a country's relationship to powerful sponsors makes a difference. Countries tend to get more aid from all sources the more ties they have to powerful, rich countries, especially the once-colonial powers. Loans, aid, and advice may respond to the pressures of the most powerful developed countries, while trade agreements may promote the agendas and interests of these rich countries, but are these effects more or less likely when multilateral institutions exist than when these relations must be negotiated bilaterally?

3. CAPTURE BY PRIVATE PRODUCERS AND INVESTORS

Some have argued that the mission of the WTO, IMF, and World Bank have been increasingly dominated by the interests of private producers and investors.[85] Sometimes their influence over these institutions operates through the power of the United States and European governments, and other times it operates independently or even at cross purposes from the developed countries' interests. The impression given is that these commercial and financial interests have hijacked the agenda of these institutions and have turned them into enforcers of open access to the markets of the poor countries. Furthermore, globalization has increased the influence of these private actors. "The governance structure of the global financial system has also been transformed. As private financial flows have come to dwarf official flows, the role and influence of private actors such as banks, hedge funds, equity funds and rating agencies has increased substantially. As a result, these private financial agencies now exert tremendous power over the economic policies of developing countries, especially the emerging market economies."[86]

Stiglitz claims that "financial interests have dominated the thinking at the IMF, [and] commercial interests have had an equally dominant role at the WTO."[87] Even Bhagwati, who holds one of the most positive views about globalization, indicts the "Wall Street-U.S. Treasury complex" for many of the undesirable policies promoted by the international institutions and resultant problems they created for the developing countries.[88] Is there strong evidence for this? One area that many scholars have pointed to is the WTO's promotion of trade-related aspects of intellectual property rights (TRIPs), especially in drugs and pharmaceuticals. As Bhagwati claims, "the multinationals have, through their interest-driven lobbying, helped set the rules in the world trading, intellectual property, aid and other regimes that are occasionally harmful to the interest of the poor countries."[89] He notes that a key example of this harmful effect has been in intellectual property protection where "the pharmaceutical and software companies muscled their way into the WTO and turned it into a royalty-collection agency because the WTO can apply trade sanctions."[90] He goes on to describe how the industries lobbied to get their views onto the American trade policy agenda and then used the United States government to force this onto the WTO and the developing countries.[91]

The impact of private actors seems most well-documented in the case of the IMF. Gould's research, for example, shows that the number and nature of conditionality in the IMF have responded increasingly to private investors. Their influence has grown because such investors play such a prominent role in international financing. As she claims,

> many of the controversial changes in the terms of Fund conditionality agreements reflect the interests and preferences of supplementary financiers. The Fund often provides only a fraction of the amount of financing that a borrowing country needs in order to balance its payments that year and implement the Fund's recommended program. Both the Fund and the borrower rely (often explicitly) on outside financing to supplement the Fund's financing. This reliance gives the supplementary financiers some leverage over the design of Fund programs. The supplementary financiers, in turn, want to influence the design of Fund programs because these programs help them ensure that borrowers are using their financing in the ways they prefer.[92]

Perhaps international economic institutions like the IMF, World Bank, and WTO are a means for private actors to affect policies in the developing countries, particularly when globalization is high. Scholars "have pointed out that liberal international regimes improve the bargaining power of private investors vis-à-vis governments and other groups in society."[93] Again, the counterfactual deserves consideration: would the developing countries have been more or less subject to the pressure of private capital if these institutions had not existed?

4. INTERNAL DYSFUNCTIONS AND FAILURE OF ACCOUNTABILITY

Some scholars have been sensitive to the internal dynamics of the institutions themselves. They claim these organizations have developed their own internal logics, which may not serve the interests of the poor (or rich) countries. Effective control over them by either the advanced industrial countries or the developing ones may be difficult; long chains of delegation allow them much slack and make adequate monitoring of their behavior costly.[94] Principal-agent models suggest such outcomes are especially likely when multiple principals (that is, countries) try to control a single agent (that is, the institution); in these situations, the ability of the bureaucracy to play off different countries' interests and to avoid monitoring is maximized. Unlike the previous explanations that treated international institutions as mere servants of either powerful states or private producers and investors, this claim gives the organizations broad independence and wide latitude for autonomous action.

Vaubel has been one of the foremost proponents of this view.[95] He produces evidence showing that bureaucratic incentives within the IMF and other international institutions lead to policies and practices inappropriate for their stated purposes. Concerns over career advancement and budget size induce actors within these agencies to focus on making loans and giving aid, but not on monitoring the results. Giving more loans and aid is always preferred to giving fewer, and recipients know this and use it to extract more. "If both institutions [that is, the IMF and World Bank] are left to themselves, they will likely revert to internal bureaucratic politics determining loans. The act of making loans will be rewarded rather than the act of helping the poor in each country."[96]

As noted by Barnett and Finnemore, the IR literature has tended to take a benign view of international organizations, viewing them as instruments for facilitating cooperation and making efficient agreements.[97] But "IOs often produce undesirable and even self-defeating outcomes repeatedly, without punishment much less dismantlement . . . In this view, decisions are not made after a rational decision process but rather through a competitive bargaining process over turf, budgets, and staff that may benefit parts of the organization at the expense of overall goals."[98] For instance, they point to the case of the World Bank: "Many scholars and journalists, and even the current head of the World Bank, have noticed that the bank has accumulated a rather distinctive record of 'failures' but continues to operate with the same criteria and has shown a marked lack of interest in evaluating the effectiveness of its own projects."[99] A series of internal problems could be responsible thus for the performance of these institutions vis-à-vis the developing countries.

These four problems are not exclusive or exhaustive. Enumerating them is important. Figuring out which problems affect which institutions seems important and understudied. Moreover, the type of reform desired depends on the problem. For example, Stone recommends further insulation of the IMF from the pressures of the donors, especially the United States. He wants the IMF to be more like an independent central bank. Insulation is desirable if the main problem is that they are too easily pressured by the rich countries or by private investors. Stiglitz, among others, however, has the opposite view. He thinks they should be more transparent and open to developing-country influence. Studies of bureaucracy in general see insulation as necessary, if undesirable, outside influences are strong and leaders are tempted to yield to them; but they see insulation as the problem itself if the bureaucracy's unaccountability and standard operating procedures are the failings. If the IMF's problem results mainly from its own internal organization and logic, then further insulation is only going to worsen the problem. Without further systematic evidence about the sources of these institutions' main problems in delivering benefits, to the developing countries, reform proposals may do more harm than good.

In sum, today's international economic institutions seem to be falling short of the goals that theories expect of them, and the reasons seem numerous. The current state of our knowledge does not warrant advocating the abolition of these international institutions, however. They appear to provide some benefits to the poor countries over the most likely counterfactual scenarios. But they probably could be reformed to provide even greater benefits.

■　　■　　■

Conclusions: What Is to Be Done?

What do we know about the impact of the major international economic institutions, the IMF, World Bank, and the WTO, on the developing countries? Have these institutions improved the lives of the poor in these countries? Have they made the developing countries better off than they would have been in the absence of these global institutions? Is this counterfactual the appropriate standard to evaluate them by? What is the moral obligation of the rich countries and their international institutions to the poor ones? Should the institutions be reformed to better fulfill their "duty of assistance" to the poor? Or is a better standard for their evaluation one that asks whether the institutions could be reformed at low cost to the rich countries so that they would provide more benefits to the poor ones? How do normative and positive analyses together shed light on these institutions?

In terms of the four major functions that theories of international institutions identify, these three global institutions seem to have failed to live up to the expectations of these theories in their impact on the developing countries. They have had a difficult time constraining the large, developed countries; most of the time these countries have bargained hard to maximize their advantage vis-à-vis the developing nations. Perhaps they have left the developing countries better off than if they had to negotiate bilaterally for access to trade, aid, and loans, but it seems as if these institutions could have bargained less hard with the developing countries at little cost to themselves or the developed countries and thus provided more benefits for the poor.

The IMF, World Bank, and WTO have certainly helped provide monitoring and information. But the monitoring and information provision have been asymmetric; it is the developing countries that are monitored and provide more information than otherwise. This action, however, may make the developed countries and private investors more likely to trade with, invest in, and provide loans to the poor countries, but the terms of these agreements have often imposed multiple and powerful conditions on the developing countries that may have impeded their growth.

Facilitating reciprocity has been a central function attributed to international institutions. For these three organizations, reciprocity vis-à-vis the developing world has not been a central mission; trade agreements have often been very asymmetric and the aid and lending programs are one way. Finally, the ability to alter domestic politics by creating support or locking it in for reform has been less studied, but seems to clearly have had an impact. The impact of the international institutions on the developing countries and their domestic situation has been powerful but not always benign.

The difficulties faced by the international institutions in providing benefits for the developing countries have arisen from at least four sources. It may be the case that globalization has simply overwhelmed these institutions and that their impact is minor compared to other factors, especially with a large and open world economy, and it is likely that domestic weaknesses account for part of their poor performance. But their problems may also lie in the pressures exerted by the large, developed countries and private producers and investors. Both of these groups have shaped the functioning of the WTO, IMF, and World Bank. The powerful, rich countries have bargained hard within these institutions to advance their own interests. Private producers and investors have directly and indirectly affected the performance of the institutions through their central role in the world economy. All of these institutions were established to support and facilitate private trade and capital flows, not to supplant them. Finally, one cannot overlook the claim that part of the problems arises from the internal organization and procedures of the institutions themselves. Making loans and imposing conditions may be more important for career advancement than measuring the impact of these activities on the developing nations.

Positive, empirical research asks the question of whether the developing world would have been better or worse off with the presence of these international institutions than without them. The evidence suggests that even though problems abound with the institutions, one cannot rule out the counterfactual: without these institutions many developing countries could be worse off as they faced bilateral negotiations with the most powerful countries. Thus, advocating their abolition is premature.

Nevertheless, one has to ask if this question is the right one. Arguments from one stream of moral philosophers imply that it is not. Cosmopolitan versions of global distributive justice see this question as insufficient. They propose one ask whether these institutions could be reformed at low cost to the wealthy countries to provide more benefits to the poor. Are these institutions the best feasible ones that could help the developing countries without imposing large costs on the developed ones?

By many accounts, the answer is negative. A number of feasible and low cost reforms could be enacted that would render these institutions much more helpful to the poor at limited cost to the rich. Pogge makes such a case for the WTO.[100] By the standards posed in global distributive justice arguments, reforming the international institutions is imperative. Interestingly, normative and positive analyses sometimes agree; some international economists such as Bhagwati and Stiglitz propose similar reforms.

In addition to policy implications, several ramifications for future research arise from the arguments surveyed here. Pogge's point about the "nationalist" research agenda in the field is salient. His prescription that we include more international factors in research on the sources of poverty and economic and political development is not unfamiliar and seems a worthy one. Including global factors and their interactions with domestic ones in comparative studies is an important step that cannot be emphasized enough.

The field would benefit from more research on the actual effects of international institutions, rather than debates about whether they are autonomous agents. More empirical research on the ways in which these institutions function and on the forces that prevent them from functioning as our theories predict is essential. This is particularly the case vis-à-vis the developing countries, many of whom do not have the capacity to evaluate the impact of these institutions on their fortunes. "Identifying who gains and who loses from existing policies is important both to determine the need for policy change and to build support for such change. For example, documenting how specific OECD policies hurt the poor both at home and in developing countries can have a powerful effect on mobilizing support for welfare improving reforms. . . . Building coalitions with NGOs and other groups that care about development is vital in generating the political momentum that is needed to improve access in sensitive sectors and improve the rules of the game in the WTO."[101] Generating greater academic knowledge thus may contribute vastly to producing better policy and outcomes, which may be a moral imperative given the grave problems of the developing countries.

NOTES

1. Stiglitz 2002, 3.
2. For example, Keohane 1984; Ikenberry 2001.
3. Counterfactuals are defined as "subjunctive conditionals in which the antecedent is known . . . to be false" (Tetlock and Belkin 1996, 4). A critical issue is how can one know what would have happened if the antecedent was false, that is, if factor X, which was present, had not been present. This problem of cotenability, identified by Elster (1978) early on, remains crucial: counterfactuals require connecting principles that sustain but do not require the conditional claim,

and these connecting principles must specify all else that would have to be true for the false conditional claim to have been true.

4. Tetlock and Belkin 1996.

5. Beitz 2005, 26.

6. In fiscal 2003, IBRD provided loans totaling $11.2 billion in support of 99 projects in 37 countries. In 2003, the grant arm of the Bank, the International Development Association (IDA), provided $7.3 billion in financing for 141 projects in 55 low-income countries (World Bank *Annual Report* 2004).

7. In the fourteen years between 1980 and 1994, Ghana received nineteen adjustment loans from the IMF and World Bank; Argentina, fifteen; Peru, eight; and Zambia, twelve (Easterly 2001a, 104–5).

8. WTO, World Trade Report 2003.

9. Studies show that WTO membership by developing countries has had little, if any, impact on the level of either their trade flows or their trade barriers (Rose 2002; Rose 2004; Milner with Kubota 2005; Subramanian and Wei 2003; Özden and Reinhardt 2002; Özden and Reinhardt 2004). Many developing countries were members of the GATT but retained very high trade barriers.

10. Defining development itself is an issue. Sen (2000) provides an excellent discussion and a rationale for a broad conception.

11. International Labor Organization 2004, 33.

12. Easterly 2001a, 102–3.

13. Easterly 2001b; Easterly 2001a, 101.

14. Chen and Ravaillon 2005, table 2.

15. Pogge 2002, 2.

16. This data from World Bank WDI 2003 is measured in 1995 $ using the chain method. Using constant dollar purchasing power parity data from the World Bank, the number of countries whose GNP per capita was lower in 2000 than in 1975 rises to 37, most in Africa, then Latin America and the Middle East. Even this calculation is likely to understate the problem; the worst off countries are most likely not to have any data, for example, Afghanistan, North Korea, Yemen, and Somalia.

17. UNDP 2004, 132.

18. Easterly 2001a, 60.

19. World Bank 2004, 43.

20. Pritchett 1997.

21. Easterly 2001a, 62.

22. The debate over whether inequality is falling or rising is too extensive to reproduce here. The answer depends on how it is measured (for example, Sala-i-Martin 2002a and Sala-i-Martin 2002b).

23. Loser 2004, 2.

24. UNDP 2004, 129.

25. Pogge and Reddy (2005) dispute these poverty figures, claiming they understate absolute poverty greatly.

26. World Bank 2004, 46. Even excluding China, this ratio fell from 27 percent to 23 percent. China joined the IMF and World Bank in 1980 and used their facilities often for the first fifteen years or so. It acceded to the WTO in 2003.

27. World Bank 2004, 46.

28. See Aisbett (2005) for a discussion of different interpretations of the data on globalization and poverty.

29. World Bank 2004, 40.

30. Gruber 2000.

31. Ikenberry 2001.

32. WTO 2003, xviii.

33. Stiglitz 2002, 61.

34. Steinberg 2002, 366.

35. ILO 2004, 33.

36. Steinberg 2002, 341.

37. If the large countries compete for access to the small countries' markets in a bilateral system, the small may find advantages. The recent Mercosur negotiations with the EU for a PTA have had an impact on the US position in its negotiations with the Mercosur countries for the Free Trade Area of the Americas.

38. ILO 2004, 6.

39. It is not clear that the IMF would tolerate some of the recurrent practices of the developed countries; many have run persistent government budget and current account deficits of a magnitude that the IMF condemns in the developing countries.

40. Boughton 2001, 135–36.

41. Rodrik 1996.

42. For example, Maizels and Nissanke 1984; Lumsdaine 1993; Milner 2004.

43. For example, Meltzer 2000. Moral hazard is a situation in which doing something for someone changes their incentives to help themselves. The common example is home insurance; when owners have insurance that fully replaces their house, they may be less attentive to making sure it does not burn down.

44. For example, Alesina and Dollar 2000.

45. Stone 2002.

46. Keohane 1984, 97.

47. These arguments tend to overlook the distributional effects of institutions, and to focus on the mutual gains from cooperation within the institution. See Martin and Simmons 1998.

48. Krueger 1998.

49. Barnett and Finnemore 1999, 709–10.

50. For example, Mansfield, Milner and Rosendorff 2002; Milner, Rosendorff and Mansfield, 2004.

51. Keohane is ambivalent, arguing throughout much of the book that membership is voluntary and rational, meaning members should be better off than otherwise if they join and remain. But in his final chapter, he notes that these institutions reflect the interests of the rich countries, and that while the poor countries gain from them, they might gain more if they were reformed (1984, 256).

52. "Many critics of the IMF's handling of the Asian financial crises have argued that the IMF inappropriately applied a standardized formula of budget cuts plus high interest rates to combat rapid currency depreciation without appreciating the unique and local causes of this depreciation. These governments were not profligate spenders, and austerity policies did little to reassure investors, yet the IMF prescribed roughly the same remedy that it had in Latin America. The result, by the IMF's later admission, was to make matters worse" (Barnett and Finnemore 1999, 721).

53. Stiglitz 2002, chap. 3; Bhagwati 2004, 204.

54. Stiglitz 2002, 220.

55. For example, Sachs and Warner 1995; Frankel and Romer 1999; Rodriguez and Rodrik 2001; UNCTAD 2004.

56. Stiglitz 2002, 143.

57. Keohane 1984, 129.

58. Bagwell and Staiger 2002.

59. Mattoo and Subramanian 2004, 6.

60. Mattoo and Subramanian (2004) survey 62 small and poor countries, which account for about one-third of the world's total countries but they individually account for less than 0.05 percent of world trade, and collectively for only 1.1 percent of global trade. China is the only developing country that has a significant share of the world market; its share of world exports has risen from less than 1 percent in 1980 to 6 percent in 2003.

61. Mattoo and Subramanian 2004, 11.

62. WTO, International Trade Statistics, 2004.

63. Mattoo and Subramanian 2004, 19.

64. Romalis 2003.

65. Özden and Reinhardt 2004.

66. The IMF and World Bank do not seem to play much of a role in enforcing reciprocity. As noted before, they obtain their funds and mandates from the developed countries and do their lending and aid giving in the developing world. The symmetric treatment of rich and poor countries is not evident.

67. E.g., McGillivray and Smith 2000.

68. For example, Mansfield, Milner and Rosendorff 2002.

69. For example, Gilligan 1997; Bailey, Goldstein and Weingast 1997.

70. Mattoo and Subramanian 2004, 11.

71. For example, Milner with Kubota 2005.

72. Their trade dependence has grown significantly from approximately 50 percent in 1960 to over 80 percent in 2000, or nearly a 60 percent increase, for the about 80 developing countries accounting for more than 70 percent of world population.

73. UNCTAD, Ext Debt #24, 2004, 2.

74. For example, Rodrik 1997; Kaufman and Segura-Ubiergo 2001; Adsera and Boix 2002; Mosley 2003.

75. For example, Acemoglu, Johnson, and Robinson 2001; Acemoglu, Johnson, and Robinson 2002; Rodrik, Subramanian, and Trebbi 2002; Easterly and Levine 2002.

76. For example, Acemoglu, Johnson, and Robinson 2001; Acemoglu, Johnson, and Robinson 2002; Rodrik, Subramanian, and Trebbi 2002; Easterly and Levine 2002. The causes of differential growth may lie in international politics. The way in which the great powers colonized the developing countries centuries ago is strongly related to their growth prospect now. It is not easy to disentangle domestic and international factors.

77. ILO, 2004, 76.

78. For example, Bueno de Mesquita and Root 2002; Van de Walle 2001.

79. For example, Burnside and Dollar 2000; Easterly 2003.

80. For example, Schraeder et al. 1998; McKinlay and Little 1977; McKinlay and Little 1978; Alesina and Dollar 2000.

81. Steinberg 2002, 356.

82. Stiglitz 2002, 160.

83. Bhagwati 2004, 204.

84. Thacker 1999.

85. The articles of agreement of the IBRD and the IMF give as one of their main purposes the promotion of private foreign investment in the developing countries. So it is not a surprise that the two institutions are susceptible to pressures from private investors.

86. ILO 2004, 35.

87. Stiglitz 2002, 216.

88. Bhagwati 2004, 205.

89. Bhagwati 2004, 182.

90. Bhagwati 2004, 182.

91. Chaudhuri, Goldberg, and Jia (2003) show in a sophisticated counterfactual analysis that in a key segment of the pharmaceuticals market in India, the losses to Indian consumers are far greater than the increased profits of foreign producers from the introduction of TRIPs.

92. Gould 2004, ch8, p. 1. For Gould, supplementary financiers are both public and private actors.

93. Keohane 1984, 253.

94. For example, Vreeland 2003, 157.

95. Vaubel 1986; Vaubel 1996.

96. Easterly 2001a, 290.

97. Barnett and Finnemore 1999, 701.

98. Barnett and Finnemore 1999, 701, 717.

99. Barnett and Finnemore 1999, 723.

100. Pogge 2002, 162.

101. Hoekman 2002, 26.

REFERENCES

Acemoglu, Daron, Simon Johnson, and James Robinson. 2001. The colonial origins of comparative development: An empirical investigation. *American Economic Review* 91 (5): 1369–1401.

Acemoglu, Daron, Simon Johnson, and James Robinson. 2002. Reversal of fortune: Geography and institutions in the making of the modern world income distribution. *Quarterly Journal of Economics* 117 (4): 1231–94.

Adsera, Alicia, and Carles Boix. 2002. Trade, democracy and the size of the public sector: The political underpinnings of openness. *International Organization* 56 (2): 229–62.

Aisbett, Emma. 2005. Why are the critics so convinced that globalization is bad for the poor? *National Bureau of Economic Research Working Paper* 11066.

Alesina, Alberto, and David Dollar. 2000. Who gives foreign aid to whom and why? *Journal of Economic Growth* 5(1): 33–63.

Bagwell, Kyle, and Robert W. Staiger. 2002. *The economics of the world trading system.* Cambridge: MIT Press.

Bailey, Michael A., Judith Goldstein, Barry R. Weingast. 1997. The institutional roots of American trade policy: Politics, coalitions, and international trade. *World Politics* 49(3): 309–338.

Barnett, Michael N., and Martha Finnemore. 1999. The politics, power, and pathologies of international organizations. *International Organization* 53 (4): 699–732.

Barry, Brian M. 1995. *Justice as impartiality.* Oxford: Oxford University Press.

Beitz, Charles R. 1979. *Political theory and international relations.* Princeton: Princeton University Press.

———. 1999. International liberalism and distributive justice: A survey of recent thought. *World Politics* 51(2): 269–96.

———. 2000. Rawls's law of peoples. *Ethics* 110(4): 669–696.

———. 2005. Cosmopolitanism and global justice. *The Journal of Ethics* 9 (1–2): 11–27.

Bhagwati, Jagdish. 2004. *In defense of globalization.* New York: Oxford University Press.

Bird, Graham, and Dane Rowlands. 2001. IMF Lending: How is it affected by economic, political and institutional factors? *Policy Reform* 4 (3): 243–70.

Blake, Michael. 2001. Distributive justice, state coercion and autonomy. *Philosophy and Public Affairs* 30 (3): 257–95.

Boughton, James M. 2001. *Silent revolution: The International Monetary Fund 1979–1989.* Washington, DC: IMF.

Buchanan, Allen. 2000. Rawls's law of peoples: Rules for a vanished Westphalian world. *Ethics* 110 (4): 697–721.

Bueno de Mesquita, Bruce, and Hilton Root, eds. 2002. *Governing for prosperity.* New Haven: Yale University Press.

Burnside, Craig, and David Dollar. 2000. Aid, policies and growth. *American Economic Review* 90(4): 847–68.

Caney, Simon. 2001. International distributive justice. *Political Studies* 49 (4): 974–97.

Chaudhuri, Shubham, Pinelopi Goldberg, and Panle Jia. 2003. Estimating the effects of global patent protection for pharmaceuticals: A case study of fluoroquinolones in India. Unpublished manuscript.

Chen, Shaohua, and Martin Ravaillon. 2005. How have the world's poorest fared since the early 1980s? World Bank Staff Paper 3341.

Cullity, Garrett. 1994. International aid and the scope of kindness. *Ethics* 105 (1): 99–127.

Elster, Jon. 1978. *Logic and society: Contradictions and possible worlds.* New York: John Wiley.

Easterly, William. 2001a. *The elusive quest for growth: Economists' adventures and misadventures in the tropics.* Cambridge: MIT Press.

———. 2001b. The lost decades: Developing countries' stagnation in spite of policy reform, 1980–1998. *Journal of Economic Growth* 6 (2): 135–57.

———. 2003. Can foreign aid buy growth? *Journal of Economic Perspectives* 17 (3): 23–48.

Easterly, William, and Ross Levine. 2002. Tropics, germs and crops: How endowments influence economic development. National Bureau of Economic Research Working Paper 9106.

Frankel, Jeffrey A., and David Romer. 1999. Does trade cause growth? *American Economic Review* 89 (3): 379–99.

Gilligan, Michael J. 1997. *Empowering exporters.* Ann Arbor, MI: University of Michigan Press.

Gould, Erica R. 2004. Money talks: The International Monetary Fund, conditionality and supplementary financiers. Unpublished manuscript.

Grant, Ruth W., and Robert O. Keohane. 2005. Accountability and abuses of power in world politics. *American Political Science Review* 99 (1): 29–43.

Gruber, Lloyd. 2000. *Ruling the world: Power politics and the rise of supranational institutions.* Princeton: Princeton University Press.

Hoekman, Bernard. 2002. Economic development and the WTO after Doha. World Bank Policy Research Working Paper 2851.

Ikenberry, G. John. 2001. *After victory: Institutions, strategic restraint, and the rebuilding of order after major wars.* Princeton: Princeton University Press.

International Labor Organization. 2004. *A fair globalization: Creating opportunities for all.* Geneva: International Labor Office.

Kaufman, Robert R., and Alex Segura-Ubiergo. 2001. Globalization, domestic politics, and social spending in Latin America: A time-series cross-section analysis, 1973–97. *World Politics* 53 (4): 553–87.

Keohane, Robert O. 1984. *After hegemony: Cooperation and discord in the world political economy.* Princeton: Princeton University Press.

Krueger, Anne O. 1998. Whither the World Bank and the IMF? *Journal of Economic Literature* 36 (4): 1983–2020.

Kuper, Andrews. 2004. *Democracy beyond borders: Justice and representation in global institutions.* New York: Oxford University Press.

Loser, Claudio M. 2004. External debt sustainability: Guidelines for low- and middle-income countries. G-24 Discussion Paper Series 26. Geneva.

Lumsdaine, David Halloran. 1993. *Moral vision in international politics: The foreign aid regime, 1949–1989.* Princeton: Princeton University Press.

Macedo, Stephen. 2004. What self-governing peoples owe to one another: Universalism, diversity and the law of peoples. *Fordham Law Review* 72 (5): 1721–38.

Maizels, Alfred, and Machiko K. Nissanke. 1984. Motivations for aid to developing countries. *World Development* 12 (9): 879–900.

Mansfield, Edward D., Helen V. Milner, and B. Peter Rosendorff. 2002. Why democracies cooperate more: Electoral control and international trade agreements. *International Organization* 56 (3): 477–514.

Martin, Lisa, and Beth Simmons. 1998. Theories and empirical studies of international institutions. *International Organization* 52 (4): 729–57.

Mattoo, Aaditya, and Arvind Subramanian. 2004. The WTO and the poorest countries: The stark reality. IMF Working Paper 04/81.

McGillivray, Fiona, and Alastair Smith. 2000. Trust and cooperation through agent specific punishments. *International Organization* 54 (4): 809–24.

McKinlay, Robert D, and Richard Little. 1977. A foreign policy model of US bilateral aid allocation. *World Politics* 30 (1): 58–86.

———. 1978. A foreign policy model of the distribution of British bilateral aid, 1960–70. *British Journal of Political Science* 8 (3): 313–31.

Meltzer, Alan. 2000. Report of the international financial institutions advisory commission. Meltzer Commission. Washington, DC.

Milner, Helen V. 1998. Rationalizing politics: The emerging synthesis of international, American, and comparative politics. *International Organization* 52 (4): 759–86.

———. 2004. Why multilateralism? Foreign aid and domestic principal-agent problems. Unpublished manuscript.

Milner, Helen V., with Keiko Kubota. 2005. Why the move to free trade? Democracy and trade policy in the developing countries, 1970–1999. *International Organization* 59 (1): 107–43.

Milner, Helen V., B. Peter Rosendorff, and Edward Mansfield. 2004. International trade and domestic politics: The domestic sources of international trade agreements and organizations. *The impact of international law on international cooperation.* Eyal Benvenisti and Moshe Hirsch, eds. Cambridge, UK: Cambridge University Press.

Mosley, Layna. 2003. *Global capital and national governments.* New York: Cambridge University Press.

Nagel, Thomas. 2005. The problem of global justice. *Philosophy and Public Affairs.* 33 (2): 113–47.

Özden, Çaglar, and Eric Reinhardt. 2002. The perversity of preferences: GSP and developing countries trade policies, 1976–2000. World Bank Working Papers 2955.

Özden, Çaglar, and Eric Reinhardt. 2004. First do no harm: The effect of trade preferences on developing country exports. World Bank Research Paper.

Pogge, Thomas W. 2002. *World poverty and human rights.* Cambridge, UK: Polity.

Pogge, Thomans, and Sanjay Reddy. 2005. How *not* to count the poor. Forthcoming in *Measuring global poverty,* Sudhir Anand and Joseph Stiglitz, eds. Oxford: Oxford University Press.

Pritchett, Lant. 1997. Divergence, big time. *Journal of Economic Perspectives* 11 (3): 3–17.

Rawls, John. 1999. *The law of peoples; with, The idea of public reason revisited.* Cambridge: Harvard University Press.

Risse, Mathias. 2004a. Does the global order harm the poor? Unpublished manuscript, Harvard University, John F. Kennedy School of Government.

———. 2004b. What we owe to the global poor. *Journal of Ethics* 9 (1/2): 81–117.

Rodriguez, Francisco, and Dani Rodrik. 2001. Trade policy and economic growth: A skeptic's guide to the cross-national evidence. *NBER macroeconomics annual 2000.* Ben S. Bernancke and Kenneth Rogoff. Cambridge: MIT Press for NBER: 261–325.

Rodrik, Dani. 1996. Why is there multilateral lending? In *Annual World Bank conference on development economics, 1995,* ed. Michael Bruno and Boris Pleeskovic, 167–93. Washington, DC: International Monetary Fund.

———. 1997. *Has globalization gone too far?* Washington, DC: Institute for International Economics.

———. 2000. Development strategies for the next century. Paper prepared for the conference on "Developing Economies in the Twenty-First Century," Ciba, Japan, January 26–27. http://ksghome.harvard.edu/~.drodrik.academic.ksg/.

Rodrik, Dani, Arvind Subramanian, and Francesco Trebbi. 2002. Institutions rule: The primacy of institutions over geography and integration in economic development. National Bureau of Economic Research Working Paper 9305.

Romalis, John. 2003. Would rich country trade preferences help poor countries grow? Evidence from the generalized system of preferences. Manuscript. http://gsbwww.uchicago.edu/fac/john.romalis/research/.

Rose, Andrew K. 2002. Do WTO members have a more liberal trade policy? National Bureau of Economic Research Working Paper 9347.

———. 2004. Do we really know that the WTO increases trade? *American Economic Review* 94(1): 98–114.

Sachs, Jeffrey, and Andrew Warner. 1995. Economic reform and the process of global integration. *Brookings Papers on Economic Activity* (1): 1–118.

Sala-i-Martin, Xavier. 2002a. The world distribution of income (estimated from individual country distributions). NBER working paper #8933.

———. 2002b. The disturbing "rise" of global income inequality. NBER Working Paper 8904.

Schraeder, Peter J., Stephen W. Hook, and Bruce Taylor. 1998. Clarifying the foreign aid puzzle: A comparison of American, Japanese, French and Swedish aid flows. *World Politics* 50 (2): 294–323.

Sen, Amartya. 2000. *Development as freedom.* New York: Alfred A. Knopf.

Singer, Peter. 1972. Famine, affluence, and morality. *Philosophy & Public Affairs* 1 (3): 229–243.

———. 2002. *One world: The ethics of globalization.* New Haven: Yale University Press.

Steinberg, Richard. 2002. In the shadow of law or power? Consensus-based bargaining and outcomes in the in

the GATT/WTO. *International Organization* 56 (2): 339–74.

Stiglitz, Joseph E. 2002. *Globalization and its discontents.* New York: W. W. Norton.

Stone, Randall W. 2002. *Lending credibility: The International Monetary Fund and the post-communist transition.* Princeton: Princeton University Press.

Subramanian, Arvind, and Shang-Jin Wei. 2003. The WTO promotes trade, strongly but unevenly. National Bureau of Economic Research Working Paper 10024.

Tetlock, Philip E., and Aaron Belkin, eds. 1996. *Counterfactual thought experiments in world politics: Logical, methodological, and psychological perspectives.* Princeton: Princeton University Press.

Thacker, Strom Cronan. 1999. The high politics of IMF lending. *World Politics* 52 (1): 38–75.

United Nations Conference on Trade and Development (UNCTAD). 2004. *Trade and poverty.* Geneva: UNCTAD.

UNDP. 2004. *Human development report 2004.* New York: UNDP.

Van de Walle, Nicolas. 2001. *African economies and the politics of permanent crisis, 1979–1999.* New York: Cambridge University Press.

Vaubel, Roland. 1986. A public choice approach to international organization. *Public Choice* 51 (1): 39–57.

———. 1996. Bureaucracy at the IMF and the World Bank: A comparison of the evidence. *World Economy* 19 (2): 195–210.

Vreeland, James Raymond. 2003. *The IMF and economic development.* New York: Cambridge University.

World Bank. 2002. *World development indicators.* Washington, DC: World Bank.

———. 2003. *Annual report 2003.* Washington, DC: World Bank.

———. 2004. *Annual report 2004.* Washington, DC: World Bank.

———. 2004. *Global economic prospects.* Washington, DC: World Bank.

World Trade Organization. 2003. *World trade report 2003.* Geneva: World Trade Organization.

———. 2004. *International trade statistics.* Geneva: World Trade Organization.

Daniel W. Drezner

THE IRONY OF GLOBAL ECONOMIC GOVERNANCE
The System Worked

Introduction

The 2008 financial crisis posed the biggest challenge to the global economy since the Great Depression and provided a severe "stress test" for global economic governance. A review of economic outcomes, policy outputs, and institutional resilience reveals that these regimes performed well during the acute phase of the crisis, ensuring the continuation of an open global economy. Even though some policy outcomes have been less than optimal, international institutions and frameworks performed contrary to expectations. Simply put, the system worked.

During the first ten months of the Great Recession, global stock market capitalization plummeted lower as a percentage of its precrisis level than during the first ten months of the Great Depression.[1] Housing prices in the United States declined more than twice as much as they did during the Great Depression.[2] The global decline in asset values led to aggregate losses of $27 trillion in 2008—a half-year's worth of global economic output.[3] Global unemployment increased by an estimated fourteen million people in 2008 alone.[4] Nearly four years after the crisis, concerns about systemic risk still continue.[5]

The demand for global economic governance structures to perform effectively is at its greatest

during crises. An open global economy lessens the stagnation that comes from a financial crisis, preventing a downturn from metastasizing into another Great Depression. One of the primary purposes of multilateral economic institutions is to provide global public goods—such as keeping barriers to cross-border exchange low. Even if states are the primary actors in world politics, they rely on a bevy of acronym-laden institutions—the International Monetary Fund (IMF), World Trade Organization (WTO), Bank for International Settlements (BIS), and Group of Twenty (G20)—to coordinate action on the global scale. International institutions can be the policymaker's pacifier. In an anarchic world, these structures reduce uncertainty for all participating actors. When they function well, they facilitate communication and foster shared understanding between policy principals. When they function poorly, a lack of trust and a surfeit of uncertainty stymies responsible authorities from cooperating.

Since the Great Recession began, there has been no shortage of scorn for the state of global economic governance among pundits and scholars.[6] Nevertheless, a closer look at the global response to the financial crisis reveals a more optimistic picture. Despite initial shocks that were more severe than the 1929 financial crisis, national policy elites and multilateral economic institutions responded quickly and robustly. Whether one looks at economic outcomes, policy outputs, or institutional resilience, global economic

Working Paper, Council on Foreign Relations, International Institutions and Global Governance Program (Oct. 2012).

governance structures have either reinforced or improved upon the status quo since the collapse of the subprime mortgage bubble. To be sure, there remain areas where governance has either faltered or failed, but on the whole, the global regime worked.

How Does Global Economic Governance Work?

Debates about whether global governance works or not usually do not suffer from an abundance of data. More typically, critics of the current system tend to rely on a few stylized facts that are meant to suggest general dysfunction. In recent years, the three events most commonly cited are:[7]

- *The collapse of the Doha round.* Just before the financial crisis hit its acute phase, last-gasp efforts to the Doha round of WTO negotiations stalled out. Subsequent G20 pledges to abstain from protectionism and complete the Doha round of world trade talks have been as common as they have been toothless. Within the first six months of the financial crisis, seventeen of the twenty countries had violated that pledge, implementing a combined forty-seven measures to restrict trade at the expense of other countries.[8] The current status of the Doha round is so moribund that the Bush administration's last U.S. trade representative advocated abandoning the effort.[9]
- *The breakdown of macroeconomic policy consensus at the 2010 Toronto G20 summit.* Prior to the Toronto summit, there was a rough consensus among the G20 in favor of government stimulus to keep the global economy afloat. The United States went into that summit to argue for more expansionary monetary and fiscal policy, but came out of it with no consensus. Other countries embraced austerity

policies instead. In the subsequent eighteen months, numerous G20 members accused each other of starting a currency war.
- *The escalation of Europe's sovereign debt crisis.* As an increasing number of eurozone economies have found their fiscal fortunes collapsing, European institutions have appeared powerless to stop the spreading financial contagion. If the European Union, the single most powerful regional institution in existence, cannot cope with this crisis, why should we expect global governance structures to do better with bigger problems?

These facts are true, but they are not the whole truth. To ascertain the effectiveness of global economic governance after the 2008 financial crisis, it is useful to look at three different levels of analysis. First, what do the policy outcomes look like? How have global output, trade, and other capital flows responded since the start of the Great Recession? Second, what do the policy outputs look like? Have important international institutions provided policies that experts would consider significant and useful in response to the global financial crisis? Finally, have these governance structures demonstrated institutional resiliency and flexibility? A common complaint prior to 2008 was that these institutions had not adapted to the shifting distribution of power. Have these structures maintained their relevance and authority? Have they responded to the shifts in the distribution of power to ensure that the powerful actors continue to buy into existing arrangements?

Policy Outcomes

In looking at outcomes, the obvious question is how well the global economy has recovered from the 2008 crisis, The current literature on economic downturns suggests two factors that impose significant barriers to a strong recovery from the

Great Recession: it was triggered by a financial crisis and it was global in scope. Whether measuring output, per capita income, or employment, financial crashes trigger downturns that last longer and have far weaker recoveries than standard business cycle downturns.[10] Furthermore, the global nature of the crisis makes it extremely difficult for countries to export their way out of the problem. Countries that have experienced severe banking crises since World War II have usually done so when the global economy was largely unaffected. That was not the case for the Great Recession.

The global economy has rebounded much better than during the Great Depression. Economists Barry Eichengreen and Kevin O'Rourke have compiled data to compare global economic performance from the start of the crises (see Figures 9.3 and 9.4).[11] Two facts stand out in their comparisons. First, the percentage drop in global industrial output and world trade levels at the start of the 2008 financial crisis was more precipitous than the falloffs following the October 1929 stock market crash. The drop in industrial output was greater in 2008 nine months into the crisis than it was eighty years earlier after the same amount of time. The drop in trade flows was more than twice as large. Second, the post-2008 rebound has been far more robust. Four years after the onset of the Great Recession, global industrial output is 10 percent higher than when the recession began. In contrast, four years after the 1929 stock market crash, industrial output was at only two-thirds of precrisis levels.

A similar story can be told with aggregate economic growth. According to World Bank figures, global economic output rebounded in 2010 with 2.3 percent growth, followed up in 2011 with 4.2 percent growth. The global growth rate in 2011 was 44 percent higher than the average of the

Figure 9.3. World Industrial Production: Great Depression vs. Great Recession

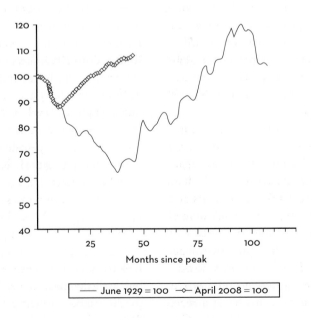

Months since peak

— June 1929 = 100 ◇ April 2008 = 100

Source: Eichengreen and O'Rourke, "A tale of two depressions redux"

Figure 9.4. World Trade Volumes: *Great Depression vs. Great Recession*

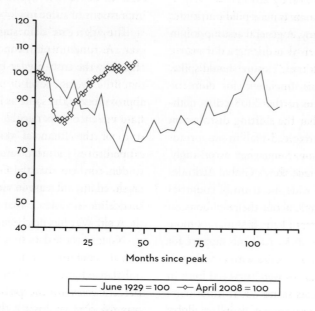

Months since peak

— June 1929 = 100   —◇— April 2008 = 100

Source: Eichengreen and O'Rourke, "A tale of two depressions redux"

previous decade. Even more intriguing, the growth continued to be poverty reducing.[12] The World Bank's latest figures suggest that despite the 2008 financial crisis, extreme poverty continued to decline across all the major regions of the globe. And the developing world achieved its first Millennium Development Goal of halving the 1990 levels of extreme poverty.[13]

An important reason for the quick return to positive economic growth is that cross-border flows did not dry up after the 2008 crisis. Again, compared to the Great Depression, trade flows have rebounded extremely well.[14] Four years after the 1929 stock market crash, trade flows were off by 25 percent compared to precrisis levels. Current trade flows, in contrast, are more than 5 percent higher than in 2008. Even compared to other postwar recessions, the current period has seen robust cross-border exchange. Indeed, as a report from CFR's Maurice R. Greenberg Center for Geoeconomic Studies concluded in May 2012, "The

growth in world trade since the start of the [current] recovery exceeds even the best of the prior postwar experiences."[15]

Other cross-border flows have also rebounded from 2008–2009 lows. Global foreign direct investment (FDI) has returned to robust levels. FDI inflows rose by 17 percent in 2011 alone. This put annual FDI levels at $1.5 trillion, surpassing the three-year precrisis average, though still approximately 25 percent below the 2007 peak. More generally, global foreign investment assets reached $96 trillion, a 5 percent increase from precrisis highs. Remittances from migrant workers have become an increasingly important revenue stream to the developing world—and the 2008 financial crisis did not dampen that income stream. Cross-border remittances to developing countries quickly rebounded to precrisis levels and then rose to an estimated all-time high of $372 billion in 2011, with growth rates in 2011 that exceeded those in 2010. Total cross-border remittances were more than $501 billion last year, and are estimated to reach $615 billion by 2014.[16]

Another salient outcome is mass public attitudes about the global economy. A general assumption in public opinion research is that during a downturn, demand for greater economic closure should spike, as individuals scapegoat foreigners for domestic woes. The global nature of the 2008 crisis, combined with anxiety about the shifting distribution of power, should have triggered a fall in support for an open global economy. Somewhat surprisingly, however, the reverse is true. Pew's Global Attitudes Project has surveyed a wide spectrum of countries since 2002, asking people about their opinions on both international trade and the free market more generally.[17] The results show resilient support for expanding trade and business ties with other countries. Twenty-four countries were surveyed both in 2007 and at least one year after 2008, including a majority of the G20 economies. Overall, eighteen of those twenty-four countries showed equal or greater support for trade in 2009 than two years earlier. By 2011, twenty of twenty-four countries showed greater or equal support for trade compared to 2007. Indeed, between 2007 and 2012, the unweighted average support for more trade in these countries increased from 78.5 percent to 83.6 percent. Contrary to expectation, there has been no mass public rejection of the open global economy. Indeed, public support for the open trading system has strengthened, despite softening public support for free-market economics more generally.[18]

The final outcome addresses a dog that hasn't barked: the effect of the Great Recession on cross-border conflict and violence. During the initial stages of the crisis, multiple analysts asserted that the financial crisis would lead states to increase their use of force as a tool for staying in power.[19] Whether through greater internal repression, diversionary wars, arms races, or a ratcheting up of great power conflict, there were genuine concerns that the global economic downturn would lead to an increase in conflict. Violence in the Middle East, border disputes in the South China Sea, and even the disruptions of the Occupy movement fuel impressions of surge in global public disorder.

The aggregate data suggests otherwise, however. A fundamental conclusion from a recent report by the Institute for Economics and Peace is that "the average level of peacefulness in 2012 is approximately the same as it was in 2007."[20] Interstate violence in particular has declined since the start of the financial crisis—as have military expenditures in most sampled countries. Other studies confirm that the Great Recession has not triggered any increase in violent conflict; the secular decline in violence that started with the end of the Cold War has not been reversed.[21]

None of these data suggest that the global economy is operating swimmingly. Growth remains unbalanced and fragile, and has clearly slowed in 2012. Transnational capital flows remain depressed compared to precrisis levels—primarily due to a drying up of cross-border interbank lending in Europe. Currency volatility remains an ongoing concern. Compared to the aftermath of other postwar recessions, growth in output, investment, and employment in the developed world have all lagged behind. But the Great Recession is not like other postwar recessions in either scope or kind; expecting a standard V-shaped recovery was unreasonable. One financial analyst characterizes the current global economy as in a state of "contained depression."[22] The operative word is contained, however. Given the severity, reach, and depth of the 2008 financial crisis, the proper comparison is with the Great Depression. And by that standard, the outcome variables look impressive.

Policy Outputs

It could be that the global economy has experienced a moderate bounce back in spite rather than because of the global policy response. Economists like Paul Krugman and Joseph Stiglitz have been particularly scornful of policymakers and central bankers.[23] In assessing policy outputs, Charles Kindleberger provided the classic definition of what should be done to stabilize the global economy during a severe financial crisis: "(a) maintaining a relatively open market for distress goods; (b) providing countercyclical long-term lending; and (c) discounting in crisis."[24] Serious concerns were voiced in late 2008 and early 2009 about the inability of anyone to provide these kinds of public goods, threatening a repeat of the trade protectionism and beggar-thy-neighbor policies of the 1930s.[25]

By Kindleberger's criteria, however, public goods provision has been quite robust since 2008. On the surface, the open market for distressed goods seemed under threat. The death of the Doha round, the rise of G20 protectionism after the fall 2008 summit, and the explosion of anti-dumping cases that occurred at the onset of the financial crisis suggested that markets were drifting toward closure.

According to the WTO's data, anti-dumping initiations surged by 30 percent in 2008 alone. This surge quickly receded, however. Figure 9.5 shows that by 2011, antidumping initiations had declined dramatically to precrisis levels. Indeed, these cases have fallen to their lowest levels since the WTO's founding in 1995. Both countervailing duty complaints and safeguards initiations have also fallen to precrisis levels.

Some post-2008 measures aren't captured in these traditional metrics of nontariff barriers, but similar results hold. Most of those implemented measures were concentrated in countries that already possessed higher barriers to global economic integration, such as Russia and Argentina. Even including these additional measures, the combined effect of protectionist actions for the first year after the peak of the financial crisis affected less than 0.8 percent of global trade.[26] Furthermore, the use of these protectionist measures declined additionally in 2010 to

Figure 9.5. Trade Restrictions, 2006–2011

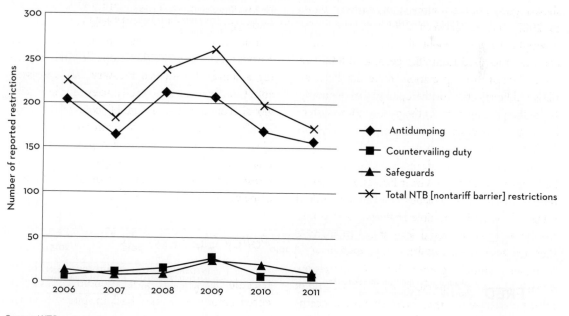

Source: WTO

Number of reported restrictions

◆ Antidumping
■ Countervailing duty
▲ Safeguards
✕ Total NTB [nontariff barrier] restrictions

Source: WTO

cover only 0.2 percent of global trade. Protectionist actions rose again in 2012, but again, the effect of these measures remains modest.[27] The quick turn-around and growth in trade levels show that these measures have not seriously impeded market access.[28] In part, accelerated steps toward trade liberalization at the bilateral and regional levels have blunted the effect of these protectionist actions.

Proponents of trade liberalization embrace the bicycle theory—the belief that unless multilateral trade liberalization moves forward, the entire global trade regime will collapse because of a lack of forward momentum. The past four years suggest that there are limits to that rule of thumb. Recent surveys of global business leaders reveal that concerns about protectionism have stayed at a low level.[29] At a minimum, the bicycle of world trade is still coasting forward at high speed.

From the earliest stages of the financial crisis, there was also concerted and coordinated action among central banks to ensure both discounting and countercyclical lending. The central banks of the major economics began cutting interest rates slowly after the fall of 2007. By the fall of 2008 they were cutting rates ruthlessly and in a coordinated fashion, as Figure 9.6 indicates. According to BIS estimates, global real interest rates fell from an average of 3 percent prior to the crisis to zero in 2012—in the advanced industrialized economies, the real interest rate was effectively negative.[30] At present, the highest interest rate among the major advanced economies is 0.75 percent, offered by the European Central Bank. Not content with lowering interest rates, most of the major central banks also expanded other credit facilities and engaged in more creative forms of quantitative easing. Between

Figure 9.6. Major Policy Interest Rates, 2007–2012

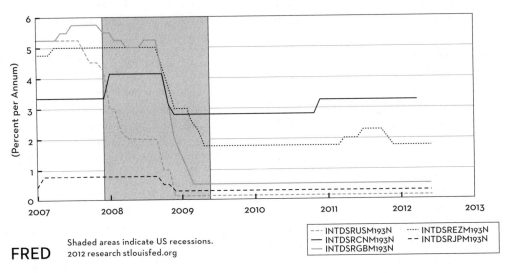

Interest Rates, Discount Rate for United States (INTDSRUSM193N), Interest Rates, Discount Rate for Euro Area (INTDSREZM193N), Interest Rates, Discount Rate for China (INTDSRCNM193N), Interest Rates, Discount Rate for Japan (INTDSRJPM193N), Interest Rates, Discount Rate for United Kingdom (INTDSRGBM193N)

FRED Shaded areas indicate US recessions.
2012 research stlouisfed.org

--- INTDSRUSM193N   ····· INTDSREZM193N
—— INTDSRCNM193N   – – INTDSRJPM193N
—— INTDSRGBM193N

Source: St. Louis Federal Reserve Bank

2007 and 2012, the balance sheets of the central banks in the advanced industrialized economies more than doubled. BIS acknowledged in its 2012 annual report that "decisive action by central banks during the global financial crisis was probably crucial in preventing a repeat of the experiences of the Great Depression."[31]

Central banks and finance ministries also took coordinated action during the fall of 2008 to try to ensure cross-border lending as to avert currency and solvency crises. In October of that year, the Group of Seven (G7) economies plus Switzerland agreed to unlimited currency swaps in order to ensure liquidity would be maintained in the system. The United States then extended its currency-swap facility to Brazil, Singapore, Mexico, and South Korea. The European Central Bank expanded its swap arrangements for euros with Hungary, Denmark, and Poland. China, Japan, South Korea, and the Association of Southeast Asian Nations (ASEAN) economics broadened the Chang Mai Initiative into an $80 billion swap arrangement to ensure liquidity. The IMF created the Short-Term Liquidity Facility designed to "establish quick-disbursing financing for countries with strong economic policies that are facing temporary liquidity problems."[32] The fund also negotiated emergency financing for Hungary, Pakistan, Iceland, and Ukraine.

Over the longer term, the great powers bulked up the resources of the international financial institutions to provide for further countercyclical lending. In 2009 the G20 agreed to triple the IMF's reserves to $750 billion. In 2012, in response to the worsening European sovereign debt crisis, G20 countries combined to pledge more than $430 billion in additional resources. The World Bank's International Development Association (IDA), which offers up the most concessionary form of lending, also increased its resources. The sixteenth IDA replenishment was a record $49.3 billion—an 18 percent increase of IDA resources from three years earlier. By Kindleberger's criteria, global economic governance worked reasonably well in response to the 2008 financial crisis.

To be sure, there exist global public goods that go beyond Kindleberger's criteria. Macroeconomic policy coordination would be an additional area of possible cooperation, as would coordinating and clarifying cross-border financial regulations. Again, however, the international system acted in these areas after 2008. Between late 2007 and the June 2010 G20 Toronto summit, the major economies agreed on the need for aggressive and expansionary fiscal and monetary policies in the wake of the financial crisis. Even reluctant contributors like Germany—whose finance minister blasted the "crass Keynesianism" of these policies in December 2008—eventually bowed to pressure from economists and G20 peers. Indeed, in 2009, Germany enacted the third-largest fiscal stimulus in the world.[33]

Progress has also been made on regulatory coordination in finance and investment rules. There were developments in two areas in particular: banking regulation and investor protectionism. In the former area, international regulators have significantly revised the Basel core banking principles. At the November 2010 Seoul summit, the G20 approved the Basel III banking standards. Basel III took only two years to negotiate—an extraordinarily brief period given that the Basel II standards took more than six years to hammer out. The new rules, scheduled to be phased in over the rest of this decade, increase the amount of reserve capital banks need to keep on hand and add additional countercyclical capital buffers to prevent financial institutions from engaging in pro-cyclical lending.

Financial sector scholars have debated whether Basel III is a sufficient upgrade in regulatory stringency and whether it will be implemented too slowly or not at all. There is consensus, however, on two points. First, Basel III clearly represents an upgrade over the Basel II standards in preventing bank failures.[34] Second, the dampening effects of the new standards on economic growth are negligible. Furthermore, these standards were approved despite fierce resistance from the global banking industry. In November 2011 the Financial Stability Board designated global systemically important banks that will be required to keep additional capital on hand, and it plans to identify global systemically important nonfinancial institutions by the end of 2012.[35]

Progress was also made in investor protectionism against state-owned enterprises and funds. The rise of sovereign wealth funds prior to 2008 had precipitated a ratcheting up of restrictions to cross-border investment by state-owned enterprises and funds. The Organization of Economic Cooperation and Development (OECD) articulated its own guidelines for recipient countries but warned that unless these funds demonstrated greater transparency, barriers to investment would likely rise even further. In September 2008 an IMF-brokered process approved a set of Generally Accepted Principles and Practices (GAPP) for sovereign wealth funds. These voluntary guidelines—also called the Santiago Principles—consisted of twenty-four guidelines addressing the legal and institutional frameworks, governance issues, and risk management of these funds. Contemporaneous press reports characterized the new rules as "a rare triumph for IMF financial diplomacy."[36] The expert consensus among financial analysts, regulators, and academics was that these principles—if fully implemented—address most recipient country concerns.[37] Since the IMF approved the Santiago Principles, furthermore, investor protectionism has declined.[38]

Institutional Resilience and Flexibility

The degree of institutional resiliency and flexibility at the global level has been rather remarkable. Once the acute phase of the 2008 financial crisis began, the G20 quickly supplanted the G7 and Group of Eight (G8) as the focal point for global economic governance. At the September 2009 G20 summit in Pittsburgh, the member countries explicitly avowed that they had "designated the G20 to be the premier forum for our international economic cooperation."[39] This move addressed the worsening problem of the G8's waning power and relevancy—a problem of which G8 members were painfully aware.[40] The G20 grouping comprises 85 percent of global economic output, 80 percent of global trade, and 66 percent of global population. The G20 is not perfectly inclusive, and it has a somewhat idiosyncratic membership at the margins, but it is a far more legitimate and representative body than the G8.[41] As Geoffrey Garrett puts it, "the G20 is globally representative yet small enough to make consensual decision-making feasible."[42] As a club of great powers, consensus within the G20 should lead to effective policy coordination across a wide range of issues.[43]

To be sure, having the capacity to be an effective body and actually *being* effective are two different things. The perception is that the G20's political momentum stalled out years ago after countries disagreed on macroeconomic imbalances and the virtues of austerity. The reality is a bit more complex. According to the University of Toronto's G20 Information Centre, compliance with G20 commitments actually increased over time. They measured G20 adherence to "chosen priority commitments." Measured on a per country average, G20 members have steadily improved since the 61.5 percent compliance rate for the April 2009 London Summit commitments, rising all the way to 77 percent for the November 2011 Cannes Summit.[44]

An obvious rejoinder is that this kind of assessment inflates compliance because the pledges made at these summits are increasingly modest.[45] It could be that the G20 has simply scaled back its ambitions—even in its "priority commitments"—making compliance easier. There are examples, however, of great powers using the G20 as a means of blunting domestic pressures for greater protectionism—at precisely the moment when the group was thought to be losing its momentum. For example, the G20 has served as a useful mechanism to defuse tensions concerning China's undervalued currency. In response to congressional pressure for more robust action, in April 2010 Treasury secretary Timothy Geithner cited the G20 meetings as "the best avenue for advancing U. S. interests" on China's manipulation of its exchange rate.[46] In June of that year, President Barack Obama sent a letter to his G20 colleagues stressing the importance of "market-determined exchange rates." Three days after the president's letter was sent, the People's Bank of China announced that it would "enhance the RMB exchange rate flexibility." For the next two years, the renminbi nominally appreciated at a rate of 5 percent a year—more so if one factors in the differences in national inflation rates.[47]

Other important financial bodies also strengthened their membership and authority as a response to the 2008 crisis. In March 2009, the Basel Committee on Banking Supervision expanded its membership from thirteen advanced industrialized states to twenty-seven countries by adding the developing country members of the G20. The Financial Stability Forum was renamed the Financial Stability Board in April 2009, was given greater responsibilities for regulatory coordination, and similarly expanded to include the developing country members of the G20 in its membership. During this period the Committee of the Global Financial System also grew in size from thirteen countries to twenty-two members, adding Brazil, China, and India, among others. The Financial Action Task Force on money laundering has added China, India, and South Korea to its grouping over the past five years. Prior to 2008, the G7 countries dominated most of these financial standard-setting agencies.[48] In terms of membership, that is no longer the case.

The International Monetary Fund and World Bank have also changed after the financial crisis, though on the surface that might not appear to be the case. The implicit compact in which a

European is given the IMF managing director slot and an American the World Bank presidency has continued over the past two years. Despite the scandals that engulfed Dominique Strauss-Kahn in 2011 and Paul Wolfowitz five years earlier, former French finance minister Christine Lagarde replaced Strauss-Kahn in 2011 and American Jim Yong Kim became the new World Bank president in 2012.

Beneath the surface, however, the bank and the fund have witnessed significant evolution. Power within the IMF is based on quota size, calculated using a complex formula of economic variables. Prior to 2007, the allotment of quotas in the IMF bore little resemblance to the distribution of economic power. This has changed. The most significant step has been two rounds of quota reform in the IMF, the first enacted in 2008 and the second to be completed by the end of this year. The explicit goal of the quota reform was to expand the voting power of advanced developing economies to better reflect the distribution of economic power. Once completed, China will possess the third-largest voting share in the fund and all four of the BRIC (Brazil, Russia, India, and China) economies will be among the ten largest shareholders in the IMF.[49] The World Bank Group underwent a parallel set of reforms. Between 2008 and 2010, the voting power of developing and transition economies within the main World Bank institution (the International Bank for Reconstruction and Development) had been increased by 4.59 percentage points, and China became the third-largest voting member. The International Finance Corporation (IFC) approved an even larger shift of 6.09 percentage points. More important, the bank's development committee agreed that bank and IFC shareholding would be reviewed every five years beginning in 2015, routinizing the process.[50]

While the appointments of Lagarde and Kim might seem retrograde, they came with political bargaining that reflected the greater influence of the advanced developing countries. In both cases, the nominee had to woo developing countries to secure political support in advance of voting. The appointment of Chinese national Min Zhu to be a deputy managing director of the IMF at the same time that Lagarde took over shows a shift in the distribution of senior-level appointments toward the advanced developing economies.

The content of the bank and fund policies has also shifted to better reflect developing country concerns. In a staff paper, the IMF acknowledged that "capital controls may be useful in addressing both macroeconomic and financial stability concerns in the face of inflow surges," a shift from the Washington consensus.[51] As for the bank, Kim's appointment to the presidency in 2012 highlights the shift in priorities. Trained as a doctor and an anthropologist, Kim's entire career has focused entirely on health policy until now. This suggests that the bank will use a more capacious notion of development going forward.

The trade and investment regimes have displayed somewhat less resiliency than global financial governance—but these regimes have not withered on the vine either. The multilateral trade regime in particular would appear to have suffered the most from the Great Recession. The collapse of the Doha round was a severe blow to the World Trade Organization. Nevertheless, the WTO as an institution has endured. Indeed, it has expanded its reach in several ways. Geographically, the WTO finally secured the accession of the Russian Federation, the last G20 nonmember, after a slow-motion, fifteen-year negotiation process. The WTO's dispute settlement mechanism helped contain the spread of protectionist measures that the Great Recession triggered. There is no evidence that compliance with these rulings has waned since 2008; the available evidence suggests that the WTO's dispute settlement arm is still playing a valuable role.[52] The WTO's Government Procurement Agreement (GPA) helped blunt the most blatant parts of the "Buy American" provisions of the 2009 fiscal stimulus, thereby preventing a cascade of fiscal protectionism. Although the GPA is only plurilateral, China is now negotiating to join the agreement. The United States, European Union, and China are also accelerating talks on a services liberalization agreement that would encompass most of the OECD economies as well as developing countries.

In truth, the Doha round had lost its momentum long before the 2007–2008 financial crisis, and it was effectively moribund before the Great Recession started. What is interesting to note is that the enthusiasm for greater trade liberalization has not lost its momentum, but rather found a new outlet: the explosion of regional and bilateral free trade agreements (FTAs). The traditional expectation that an economic downturn would dampen enthusiasm for greater openness has not been borne out by the data on FTAs. In the four years prior to the collapse of Lehman Brothers, fifty-one FTAs were reported to the World Trade Organization. In the four years since Lehman, fifty-eight free trade agreements have been registered.[53] A transpacific partnership and a transatlantic free trade zone are at preliminary stages of negotiation as well. To be sure, not all of these FTAs were created equal. Some of them have greater coverage of goods than others. Some of them might promote more trade diversion than trade creation. Nevertheless, the patterned growth of these FTAs mirrors how they spread in the late nineteenth century.[54] Although these FTAs do not possess the "most-favored nation" provision that accelerated trade liberalization in the nineteenth century, the political economy of trade diversion still generates competitive incentives for a growth in FTAs, thereby leading to a similar outcome.[55] Through their own shared understandings and dispute settlement mechanisms, they act as an additional brake on protectionist policies.[56]

There is no multilateral investment regime to display resiliency. Instead, investment is governed by a network of bilateral investment treaties

Figure 9.7. Annual Count of Bilateral Investment Treaties, 1960–2011

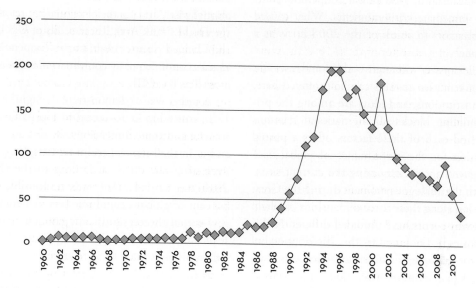

Source: UNCTAD

(BITs). Compared to the data on free trade agreements, it would appear that the pace of BITs has slowed since 2008. According to United Nations Conference on Trade and Development (UNCTAD) data, an annual average of seventy-eight BITs were completed in the three years prior to 2008; only an average of sixty-one per annum were negotiated in the three years after 2008. That indicates a slowdown. A look at the series over the longer term, however, reveals that this slowdown is not surprising. As Figure 9.7 shows, the peak of BIT negotiations took place in the decade after the end of the Cold War. From 1992 to 2001, an annual average of 160 BITs were negotiated. After 2001, however, the number of negotiated BITs declined, following a standard diffusion pattern. Based on that kind of pattern of diffusion, the past three years have seen expected levels of BIT growth.

Why Has the System Worked?

Global economic governance did what was necessary during the Great Recession—but why did the system work? The precrisis observations about sclerotic international institutions and waning American power did not seem off the mark. How did these actors manage to produce the necessary policy outputs and reforms to stave off systemic collapse? The most commonly provided answer is that the shared sense of crisis spurred the major economies into joint action. The crisis mentality did not lead to sustained cooperation during the Great Depression, however. Significant postwar economic downturns—such as the end of the Bretton Woods regime, the oil shocks of the 1970s, and the failure of the European Exchange

Rate Mechanism in the early 1990s—also failed to spur meaningful great power cooperation during the immediate crisis moments. What caused powerful actors to think of the 2008 crisis as a shared one?

A fuller answer will require additional research, but some tentative answers can be proffered here. Power, institutions, and ideas are among the primary building blocks of international relations theory, and each of these factors offers a partial explanation for the performance of global economic governance. Comparing the current situation with the analogous moment during the Great Depression along these three dimensions can help explain why events have unfolded differently this time around. Looking at the distribution of power, for example, the interwar period was truly a moment of great power transition. At the start of the Great Depression, the United Kingdom's lack of financial muscle badly hampered its leadership efforts. Even as it was trying to maintain the gold standard, Great Britain possessed only 4 percent of the world's gold reserves.[57]

In contrast, U.S. power and leadership during the recent crisis turned out to be more robust than expected. This was particularly true in the financial realm. Despite occasional grumblings among the BRICs, the U.S. dollar's hegemony as the world's reserve currency remains unchallenged, giving the United States the financial power that the United Kingdom lacked eight decades ago. Capital surplus countries—such as China— exaggerated the leverage they could obtain from holding large amounts of dollar-denominated reserves.[58] They rapidly discovered that U.S. dollar hegemony bound their interests to the United States on financial issues. While domestic politics might have prevented a more robust U.S. policy response, partisan gridlock did not prevent the United States from pursuing emergency rescue packages (via the 2008 Troubled Assets Relief Program), expansionary fiscal policy (via the 2009 American Recovery and Reinvestment Act),

expansionary monetary policy (via interest rate cuts, two rounds of quantitative easing, and Operation Twist), and financial regulatory reform (via the Dodd-Frank Act). These deeds of U.S. leadership helped secure multilateral cooperation on macroeconomic policy coordination for two years, as well as Basel III.

Another way to demonstrate the significance of U.S. leadership is to compare and contrast the finance and trade dimensions. As just noted, U.S. power in the financial realm remained significant even after the crisis; according to the IMF, in 2010 the United States was responsible for 25 percent of global capital markets. American policy outputs were significant enough to display leadership on these issues. The picture looks very different on trade. U.S. relative power on this issue had faded: U.S. imports as a share of total world imports declined from 18.1 percent of total imports in 2001 to 12.3 percent a decade later. U.S. policy on this issue was inert.[59] The executive branch's trade promotion authority expired, and legislative demands for protectionism spiked. Not surprisingly, the global policy response on trade has been somewhat more muted than on finance.

Despite weaker U.S. power and leadership, the global trade regime has remained resilient— particularly when compared to the 1930s. This highlights another significant factor: the thicker institutional environment. There were very few multilateral economic institutions of relevance during the Great Depression. No multilateral trade regime existed, and international financial structures remained nascent. The last major effort to rewrite the global rules—the 1933 London Monetary and Economic Conference—ended in acrimony.[60] Newly inaugurated president Franklin D. Roosevelt unilaterally took the United States off the gold standard, signaling an end to any attempt at multilateral cooperation.

In contrast, the current institutional environment is much thicker, with status-quo policies focused on promoting greater economic openness. A panoply of preexisting informal and formal regimes was able to supply needed services during a time of global economic crisis. At a minimum, institutions like the G20 functioned as useful focal points for the major economies to coordinate policy responses. International institutions like the Bank of International Settlements further provided crucial expertise to rewrite the global rules of the game. Even if the Doha round petered out, the WTO's dispute settlement mechanism remained in place to coordinate and adjudicate monitoring and enforcement. Furthermore, the status-quo preference for each element of these regimes was to promote greater cross-border exchange within the rule of law. It is easier for international institutions to reinforce existing global economic norms than to devise new ones. Even if these structures were operating on autopilot, they had already been pointed in the right direction.

The final difference between the interwar era and the current day is the state of economic ideas. As the Great Depression worsened during the decade of the 1930s, there was no expert consensus about the best way to resuscitate the economy. Prominent economists like John Maynard Keynes, who had been staunch advocates of free trade a decade earlier, reversed themselves as the depression worsened. There was no agreement on the proper macroeconomic policy response to the downturn, nor was there any agreement about how to fix the broken gold standard.

There has also been a rethinking of causal beliefs after the 2008 financial crisis, but this rethink has been much less severe. Former Federal Reserve chairman Alan Greenspan made headlines when he admitted that his faith in the intellectual edifice of self-correcting markets had collapsed. As previously noted, the IMF has reversed course on the utility of temporary capital controls. Though the Washington consensus might be fraying, it has not been dissolved or replaced by a "Beijing consensus"—indeed,

it is far from clear that a Beijing consensus actually exists.[61] Postcrisis surveys of leading economists suggest that a powerful consensus remains on several essential international policy dimensions. For example, the University of Chicago has run an economic experts panel for the past few years. The survey results show a strong consensus on the virtues of freer trade and a rejection of returning to the gold standard to regulate international exchange rates. On the other hand, there is much less consensus on monetary policy and the benefits of further quantitative easing.[62] This absence of agreement reflects a much greater policy debate on the subject, helping to explain why macroeconomic policy coordination has been less robust.

Why the Misperception?

Why is there such a profound gap between perceptions and reality in evaluating the performance of multilateral economic institutions? The simplest explanation is that the core economies—the advanced industrialized democracies—have not rebounded as vigorously as expected. Two trends have marked most postwar global business cycles: economies rebound as vigorously as they drop, and the advanced industrialized states suffer less than the economic periphery. Neither of these trends has held during the Great Recession. As previously noted, the recovery from a financial crisis tends to be longer and slower than standard business-cycle recessions. After the 2008 financial crisis, the recovery has been particularly weak in the advanced industrialized economies. According to the Economist Intelligence Unit, the OECD economies have averaged GDP growth of 0.5 percent between 2008 and 2012. The non-OECD economies have averaged 5.2 percent during the same period. A weak economy feeds perceptions of institutional breakdown. The 2012 Edelman Trust Barometer reflects this phenomenon; contrary to traditional numbers, trust of elite institutions is significantly higher among developing countries than in the developed democracies.[63] Since most analyses of global governance structures have been anchored in the developed world, it is not surprising that this literature suffers from a pessimistic bias.

Pessimism about current economic conditions in the developed world might also be causing analysts to conflate poor domestic and regional governance with poor global governance. The primary causes for domestic economic weakness in the United States, Europe, and Japan are not global in origin—and neither are the best policy responses, Japan's current economic woes are a function of two decades of slack economic growth combined with the aftereffects of the Fukushima disaster. American economic misfortunes have little to do with either the global economy or global economic governance. Indeed, the United States has benefited from the current state of international affairs through lower borrowing costs and higher exports. Domestic political deadlock and uncertainty, on the other hand, have contributed to the anemic U.S. recovery. Already, concerns about the coming fiscal cliff have dampened economic activity.[64] Eroding policy consensus within the Federal Reserve has not helped either. Without more expansionary fiscal and monetary policies, it will take even longer for the necessary private-sector deleveraging to play itself out.

Europe's situation is more complex. To be sure, the Great Recession was the trigger for the eurozone's sovereign debt crisis. The international response to the crisis has been that of a modest supporting role. The IMF has proffered both its technical expertise and financial support in excess of $100 billion to Greece, Portugal, and Ireland. The United States and other major economies have offered to reopen swap lines with the European Central Bank to ensure liquidity. European and national policy responses to the crisis, however, have badly exacerbated the economic situation. Greece's reckless pre-crisis levels of government spending and borrowing made that economy a ripe target for market pessimism. The initial European bailout package for Greece was woefully inadequate, allowing the crisis to fester. The austerity policies advocated in some quarters have not panned out as expected. The European Central Bank's decision to prematurely raise interest rates in early 2010 helped stall out the nascent recovery on the continent. On the fiscal side of the equation, austerity-related policies have led to a double-dip recession in Great Britain, higher borrowing costs in Spain and Italy, and continued uncertainty about the future of the euro. Europe's fiscal and monetary policies have been less expansionary than in the United States. This, in turn, has prevented any appreciable private-sector deleveraging in Europe, thereby guaranteeing a longer downturn before any sustained recovery is possible.[65]

The IMF has come under criticism for failing to exert more influence over the eurozone crisis. One official recently resigned, blasting the fund for its European bias and the consensus culture that keeps it from criticizing countries in the middle of lending programs. There are two counterpoints to this argument, however. First, the IMF *has* been critical at various moments during the eurozone crisis. Fund staff issued warnings about the health of the European banks in August 2011, and IMF managing director Lagarde called explicitly for debt sharing among the eurozone in June 2012.[66] The first criticism received significant pushback from the European Central Bank and eurozone governments, and Germany ignored the second criticism. This leads to the second point: it is highly unlikely that national governments would feel compelled to respond to IMF criticism in the absence of a market response. The fund must walk a tightrope between transparent criticism and setting off market panic. This is hardly an ideal vantage point for strong-arming governments with sizable IMF quotas.

A final reason for misperception about global economic governance is exaggerated nostalgia for the past eras of global economic governance. The presumption in much of the commentary on the current global political economy is that both governance structures and hegemonic leadership were better and stronger in the past. Much of this commentary evokes the 1940s, when the creation of the Bretton Woods institutions, backstopped by the United States, ushered in a new era of global governance. The contrast between U.S. leadership then and now seems stark.

This comparison elides some inconvenient facts, however. The late 1940s were indeed the acme of American hegemonic leadership. Even during that peak, however, the United States failed to ratify the Havana Charter that would have created an International Trade Organization with wider scope than the current WTO. With the Marshall Plan, the United States decided to act outside the purview of Bretton Woods institutions, weakening their influence. After the late forties, American leadership and global financial governance experienced as many misses as hits. The logic of the Bretton Woods system rested on an economic contradiction that became known as the Triffin dilemma. Extravagant macroeconomic policies in the United States, combined with a growing reluctance to accommodate the U.S. position, eroded that global financial order. As the logical contradictions of the Bretton Woods regime became more evident, existing policy coordination mechanisms failed to correct the problem. By 1971, when the United States unilaterally decided to close the gold window, all of the major economies had chosen to ameliorate domestic interests rather than coordinate action at the global level.[67] In ending Bretton Woods, the United States also undercut the IMF's original purpose for existence.

Post-Bretton Woods global economic governance was equally haphazard. An increase in anti-dumping, countervailing duties, and non-tariff barriers weakened the rules of the global trading system over the next two decades. Neither the United States nor any global governance structure was able to prevent the Organization of the Petroleum Exporting Countries (OPEC) from raising energy prices from 1973 to 1986.[68] Exchange rates and macroeconomic policy coordination devolved from the IMF to the G7. A predictable cycle emerged: other G7 countries would pressure the United States to scale back its fiscal deficits. In turn, the United States would pressure Japan and West Germany to expand their domestic consumption in order to act as locomotives of growth. Not surprisingly, the most common outcome on the macroeconomic front was a stalemate.[69]

Even perceived successes in macroeconomic policy coordination have had mixed results. The 1985 Plaza Accord helped depreciate the value of the dollar while allowing the yen to rise in value, but it was also the beginning of an unsustainable asset bubble in Japan. In Europe, the creation of the euro would seem to count as an example of successful coordination. The Growth and Stability Pact that was attached to the creation of the common European currency, however, was less successful. Within a year of the euro's birth, five of the eleven member countries were not in compliance; by 2005, the three largest countries in the eurozone were ignoring the pact.[70] Regardless of the distribution of power or the robustness of international institutions, the history of macroeconomic policy coordination is not a distinguished one.[71]

None of this is to deny that global economic governance was useful and stabilizing at various points after 1945. Rather, it is to observe that even during the heyday of American hegemony, the ability of global economic governance to solve ongoing global economic problems was limited.[72] The original point of Kindleberger's analysis of the Great Depression was to discuss what needed to be done during a global economic crisis. By that standard, the post-2008 performance of vital institutions has been far better than extant commentary suggests. Expecting more than an effective crisis response might be unrealistic.

Conclusion

Five years ago, there were rampant fears that waning American power would paralyze global economic regimes. The crisis of the Great Recession exacerbated those fears even further. A review of policy outcomes, policy outputs, and institutional resilience shows a different picture. Global trade and investment levels have recovered from the plunge that occurred in late 2008. A mélange of international coordination mechanisms facilitated the provision of policy outputs from 2008 onward. Existing global governance structures, particularly in finance, have revamped themselves to accommodate shifts in the distribution of power. The World Economic Forum's survey of global experts shows rising confidence in global governance and global cooperation.[73] The evidence suggests that global governance structures adapted and responded to the 2008 financial crisis in a robust fashion. They passed the stress test. The picture presented here is at odds with prevailing conventional wisdom on this subject.

This does not mean that global economic governance will continue to function effectively going forward. It is worth remembering that there were genuine efforts to provide global public goods in 1929 as well, but they eventually fizzled out. The failure of the major economies to assist Austria after the Credit Anstalt bank crashed in 1931 led to a cascade of bank failures across Europe and the United States. The collapse of the 1933 London conference guaranteed an ongoing absence of policy coordination for the next several years.

The start of the Great Depression was bad. International policy coordination failures made it worse. Such a scenario could play out again. There is no shortage of latent or ongoing crises that could lead to a serious breakdown in global economic governance. The IMF's reluctance to take more critical actions to address the curozone crisis have already prompted one angry resignation letter from an IMF staffer. The summer 2012 drought in the midwestern United States could trigger another spike in food prices. The heated protectionist rhetoric of the 2012 presidential campaign in the United States, or the nationalist rhetoric accompanying China's 2012 leadership transition, could spark a Sino-American trade war. If global economic growth continues to be mediocre, the surprising effectiveness of global economic governance could peter out. Incipient signs of backsliding in the WTO and G20 might mushroom into a true "G-Zero" world.[74]

It is equally possible, however, that a renewed crisis would trigger a renewed surge in policy coordination. As scholar G. John Ikenberry has observed, "the complex interdependence that is unleashed in an open and loosely rule-based order generates some expanding realms of exchange and investment that result in a growing array of firms, interest groups and other sorts of political stakeholders who seek to preserve the stability and openness of the system."[75] The post-2008 economic order has remained open, entrenching these interests even more across the globe. Despite uncertain times, the open economic system that has been in operation since 1945 does not appear to be closing anytime soon.

NOTES

1. Barry Eichengreen and Kevin O'Rourke, "A tale of two depressions," VoxEU.org, March 8, 2010, http://www.voxeu.org/index.php?q=node/3421.

2. Carmen Reinhart and Kenneth Rogoff, *This Time Is Different: Eight Centuries of Financial Folly* (Princeton: Princeton University Press, 2009), p. 226.

3. Charles Roxburgh, Susan Lund, and John Piotrowski, *Mapping global capital markets 2011*, McKinsey Global Institute, August 2011. An Asian Development Bank report also estimates the 2008 decline in asset values to have been twice as large. See Claudio Loser, "Global Financial Turmoil and

Emerging Market Economies," *Asian Development Bank*, March 2009, p. 7.

4. *The Financial and Economic Crisis: A Decent Work Response* (Geneva: International Labour Organization, 2009), p. v.

5. See, for example, the *Financial Times-Economist* Business Barometer, August 2012.

6. See, for example, Richard Samans, Klaus Schwab, and Mark Malloch-Brown, "Running the World, After the Crash," *Foreign Policy* 184 (January/February 2011), pp. 80–83. See also Lee Howell, "The Failure of Governance in a Hyperconnected World," *New York Times*, January 10, 2012.

7. These are by no means the only facts mentioned when talking about the perceived failure of global economic governance. Other examples include the PBOC chairman's March 2009 call for a "super-sovereign currency" to replace the dollar, the failure of the Copenhagen climate change summit in December 2009, and the continuation of the norm whereby a European heads the IMF and an American helms the World Bank. Quite often haplessuess at the United Nations is also cited as evidence of the failure of global governance more generally.

8. Elisa Gamberoni and Richard Newfarmer, "Trade Protection: Incipient but Worrisome Trends," World Bank Trade Note No. 37, March 2, 2009.

9. Susan Schwab, "After Doha," *Foreign Affairs*, vol. 90, May/June 2011.

10. Carmen Reinhart and Kenneth Rogoff, "The Aftermath of Financial Crises," in Reinhart and Rogoff, *This Time Is Different: Eight Centuries of Financial Folly* (Princeton: Princeton University Press, 2009); Claessens, Kose, and Terrones, "Financial Cycles: What? How? When?" IMF Working Paper 11/76, April 2011; Carmen Reinhart and Vincent Reinhart, "After the Fall," NBER Working Paper No. 16334, September 2010; Barry Eichengreen, "Crisis and Growth in the Advanced Economies: What We Know, What We Don't Know, and What We Can Learn from the 1930s," *Comparative Economic Studies* 53 (March 2011), pp. 383–406.

11. Eichengreen and O'Rourke, "A tale of two depressions"; Eichengreen and O'Rourke, "A tale of two depressions redux," VoxEU.org, March 6, 2012, http://www.voxeu.org/article/tale-two-depressions-redux.

12. *World Development Indicators*, World Bank, July 9, 2012.

13. Ibid. See also Shaochua Chen and Martin Rayallion, "An update to the World Bank's Estimate of consumption poverty in the developing world," March 1, 2012; Annie Lowrey, "Dire Poverty Falls Despite Global Slump, Report Finds," *New York Times*, March 6, 2012.

14. Data in this paragraph comes from Eichengreen and O'Rourke, "A tale of two depressions redux."

15. Dinah Walker, "Quarterly Update: The Economic Recovery in Historical Context," Council on Foreign Relations, August 13, 2012.

16. For FDI data, see the OECD/UNCTAD report "Seventh report on G20 investment measures," July 2012. For foreign investment assets, sec Roxburgh, Lund, and Piotrowski, *Mapping Global Capital Markets 2011*, p. 31. For remittance flows, see Dilip Ratha and Ani Silwal, "Remittances flows in 2011: An Update," *Migration and Development Brief* 18, World Bank, April 23, 2012.

17. See data gathered by the Pew Global Attitudes Project, Pew Research Center, 2012, http://www.pewglobal.org/database/?indicator=16&survey=13&response=Good&20thing&mode=table.

18. On the latter, see data gathered by the Pew Global Attitudes Project, Pew Research Center, 2012, http://www.pewglobal.org/database/?indicator=18&survey=12&response=Agree&mode=table.

19. See, for example, Paul Rogers, "The Tipping Point?" Oxford Research Group, November 2008; Joshua Kurlantzick, "The World is Bumpy," *New Republic*, July 15, 2009; Rogers Brubaker, "Economic Crisis, Nationalism, and Politicized Ethnicity," in Craig Calhoun and Georgi Derlugian, eds., *The Deepening Crisis: Governance Challenges After Neoliberalism* (New York: New York University Press, 2011), p. 93.

20. Institute for Economics and Peace, *Global Peace Index 2012*, June 2012, p. 37.

21. See, for example, the Human Security Report Project, *Human Security Report 2009/2010: The Causes of Peace and the Shrinking Costs of War* (New York: Oxford University Press, 2010).

22. David Levy, "The Contained Depression," Jerome Levy Forecasting Center, April 2012.

23. Paul Krugman, *End This Depression Now!* (New York: W.W. Norton, 2012); Joseph Stiglitz, *The Price of Inequality* (New York: W.W. Norton, 2012).

24. Kindleberger, *The World In Depression*, 292.

25. "The Return of Economic Nationalism," *Economist*, February 5, 2009; Kurlantzick, "The World is Bumpy"; Michael Sesit, "Smoot-Hawley's Ghost Appears as Economy Tanks," *Bloomberg News*, February 19, 2009; Rawi Abdelal and Adam Segal, "Yes, Globalization Passed Its Peak," ForeignAffairs.com, March 17, 2009.

26. Uri Dadush, Shimelse Ali, and Rachel Esplin Odell, "Is Protectionism Dying?" Carnegie Papers in International Economics, May 2011. Furthermore, while these measures are undeniably restrictive in nature, a case can be made that they represent a form of "efficient protectionism": small and symbolic measures that mollify protectionist constituencies in exchange for preserving and strengthening the overall level of economic openness. See C. Fred Bergsten, "A Renaissance for U.S. Trade Policy?" *Foreign Affairs*, vol. 81, November/December 2002.

27. See Simon Evenett, "Débacle," VoxEU.org, June 14, 2012. As a counter, however, see also Chad Bown, "Import Protection Update," VoxEU.org. August 18, 2012.

28. Dadush, Ali, and Odell, "Is Protectionism Dying?"; Matthieu Bussiere, Emilia Perez-Barreiro, Roland Straub, and Daria Taglioni, "Protectionist Responses to the Crisis: Global Trends and Implications," *World Economy*, vol. 34, May 2011.

29. Between May 2011 and August 2012, a maximum of 13 percent of business executives cited trade protectionism as a serious concern. See the *Financial Times-Economist* Business Barometer, http://www.ft

.com/intl/cms/s/0/2648032c-c78d-11eI-8686 -00144feab49a.html#axzz23kj5DEaP.

30. Bank of International Settlements, *82nd Annual Report*, June 24, 2012, p. 39.

31. Ibid., p. 41.

32. "IMF Creates Short-Term Liquidity Facility for Market-Access Countries," IMF Press Release No. 08/262, October 29, 2008.

33. Eswar Prasad and Isaac Sorkin, "Assessing the G-20 Stimulus Plans: A Deeper Look," Brookings Institution, March 2009.

34. Adrian Blundell-Wignall and Paul Atkinson, "Thinking Beyond Basel III: Necessary Solutions for Capital and Liquidity," *OECD Journal: Financial Market Trends*, vol. 1, 2010; Nicolas Verou, "Financial Reform after the Crisis: An Early Assessment," Peterson Institute for International Economics Working Paper 12–2, January 2012.

35. It should be noted that some scholars have questioned whether the FSB has the capability and flexibility to impose more rigorous standards on the global financial system. See Stephany Griffith-Jones, Eric Helleiner, and Ngaire Woods, eds., *The Financial Stability Board: An Effective Fourth Pillar of Global Economic Governance?* (Waterloo: Centre for International Governance Innovation, June 2010).

36. Bob Davis, "Foreign Funds Agree to Set of Guiding Principles," *Wall Street Journal*, September 3, 2008.

37. *Minding the GAPP: Sovereign wealth, transparency and the "Santiago Principles,"* Deloitte Touche Tohmatsu, October 2008; Edward Truman, "Making the World Safe for Sovereign Wealth Funds," *Real Time Economic Issues Watch*, October 14, 2008; Cohen and DeLong, *The End of Influence*, p. 89.

38. OECD/UNCTAD, "Seventh Report on G20 investment measures."

39. "G20 to become main economic forum," al-Jazeera, September 28, 2009, http://www.aljazeera.com/news/americas/2009/09/20099252124936203.html.

40. Mark Sobel and Louellen Stedman, "The Evolution of the G-7 and Economic Policy Coordination," U.S. Treasury Department Occasional Paper No. 3, July

2006; Drezner, "The New New World Order," *Foreign Affairs*, vol. 86, March/April 2007.

41. The G20 also has no treaty status or permanent secretariat, but there are theoretical arguments in favor of this informal status. See, for example, Charles Lipson, "Why are some international agreements informal?" *International Organization*, vol. 45, September 1991.

42. Geoffrey Garrett, "G2 in G20: China, the United States, and the World after the Global Financial Crisis," *Global Policy*, vol. 1, January 2010, p. 29.

43. Daniel W. Drezner, *All Politics is Global: Explaining International Regulatory Regimes* (Princeton: Princeton University Press, 2007).

44. *2011 Cannes G20 Summit Final Compliance Report*, G20 Information Centre, p. 12.

45. George Downs, David Rocke, and Peter Barsoom, "Is the Good News About Compliance Good News About Cooperation?" *International Organization*, vol. 50, June 1996.

46. "Geithner Statement on Delay of Report on China Currency Policies," Real Time Economics, *Wall Street Journal*, April 3, 2010, http://blogs.wsj.com/economics/2010/04/03/geithner-statement-on-delay-of-report-on-china-currency-policies/.

47. David Leonhardt, "As U.S. Currency Rises, U.S. Keeps Up the Pressure," *New York Times*, February 15, 2012. It should be noted, however, that the yuan has depreciated against the dollar for much of 2012.

48. Daniel W. Drezner, "Club Standards and International Finance," in Daniel W. Drezner, *All Politics Is Global*.

49. For more on IMF quota reform, see "IMF Quotas," International Monetary Fund, August 24, 2012.

50. "World Bank Group Reform: An Update," World Bank Group Development Committee, September 30, 2010.

51. Jonathan D. Ostry, Atish R. Ghosh, Karl Habermeier, Marcos Chamon, Mahvash S. Qureshi, and Dennis B.S. Reinhardt, "Capital Inflows: The Role of Controls," IMF Staff Position Note SPN/10/04, International Monetary Fund, February 19, 2010.

52. Alan Beattie, "Decommission the weapons of trade warfare," *Financial Times*, August 8, 2012.

53. "Regional Trade Agreements Information System," World Trade Organization, August 27, 2012, http://rtais.wto.org/UI/PublicPreDefRepByElF.aspx.

54. David Lazer, "The Free Trade Epidemic of the 1860s and Other Outbreaks of Economic Discrimination," *World Politics*, vol. 51, July 1999.

55. See Daniel W. Drezner, *U.S. Trade Strategy: Free Versus Fair?* (New York: Council on Foreign Relations Press, 2006), pp. 71–92, for more on this dynamic.

56. Dadush et al, "Is Protectionism Dying?" pp. 8–9.

57. Jeffry Frieden, "The established order collapses," in Jeffry Frieden, *Global Capitalism: Its Fall and Rise in the Twentieth Century* (New York: W.W. Norton, 2006); Liquat Ahamed, *Lords of Finance: The Bankers Who Broke The World* (New York Penguin, 2009).

58. The arguments in this paragraph draw from Daniel W. Drezner, "Bad Debts: Assessing China's Financial Influence in Great Power Politics," *International Security*, vol. 34, Fall 2009; and Daniel W. Drezner, "Will Currency Follow the Flag?" *International Relations of the Asia-Pacific*, vol. 10, September 2010.

59. Data from WTO: http://stat.wto.org/StatisticalProgram/WSDBStatProgramHome.aspx, accessed August 2012.

60. Herbert Feis, *1933: Characters in Crisis* (Boston: Little Brown and Company, 1966).

61. Matt Ferchen, "Whose China Model is it Anyway? The contentious search for consensus," *Review of International Political Economy*, forthcoming.

62. On the gold standard and free trade, see "Gold Standard," IGM Forum, University of Chicago Booth School of Business, January 12, 2012; and "Free Trade," IGM Forum, University of Chicago Booth School of Business, March 13, 2012. On monetary policy, see "Monetary Policy," IGM Forum, University of Chicago Booth School of Business, September 29, 2011. For further evidence of the absence of consensus on monetary policy, compare Martin Wolf, "We still have that sinking feeling," *Financial Times*, July 10, 2012, with Mohamed El-Erian, "Central Bankers Can't Save the World," *Bloomberg View*, August 2, 2012. See also Joe Weisenthal, "The Biggest Tragedy in Economics," *Business Insider*, September 7, 2012.

63. Data from the Edelman Trust Barometer can be accessed at http://trust.edelman.com/trust-download/global-results/.

64. Nelson D. Schwartz, "Fearing an Impasse in Congress, Industry Cuts Spending," *New York Times*, August 5, 2012.

65. Reinhart and Rogoff, *This Time Is Different*; Charles Roxburgh, Susan Lund, Toos Daruvala, James Manyika, Richard Dobbs, Ramon Forn, and Karen Croxson, *Debt and Deleveraging: Uneven Progress on the Path to Growth*, McKinsey Global Institute, January 2012.

66. Alan Beattie and Chris Giles, "IMF and curozone clash over estimates," *Financial Times*, August 31, 2011; James Kanter, "IMF Urges Europe's Strongest to Shoulder Burdens of Currency Bloc," *New York Times*, June 21, 2012.

67. Joanne Gowa, *Closing the Gold Window: Domestic Politics and the End of Bretton Woods* (Ithaca: Cornell University Press, 1984).

68. Robert Keohane, "Theory of Hegemonic Stability and Changes in International Economic Regimes, 1967–1977," in Ole Holsti, Randolph Siverson, and Alexander George, eds., *Change in the International System* (Boulder: Westview Press, 1980), pp. 131–62.

69. Robert Putnam and Nicholas Bayne, *Hanging Together: Cooperation and Conflict in the Seven-Power Summits* (Cambridge: Harvard University Press, 1987); David M. Andrews, ed., *International Monetary Power* (Ithaca: Cornell University Press, 2005).

70. Kathryn Dominguez, "The European Central Bank, the Euro, and Global Financial Markets," *Journal of Economic Perspectives*, vol. 20, Fall 2006.

71. Thomas Willett, "Developments in the Political Economy of Policy Coordination," *Open Economies Review*, vol. 10, May 1999.

72. This parallels the recent argument by Robert Kagan that people exaggerate the effectiveness of American hegemony in the past as well. Robert Kagan, *The World America Made* (New York: Knopf, 2012).

73. "Global Confidence Index," World Economic Forum, August 22, 2012, http://www.weforum.org/content/pages/global-confidence-index.

74. Ian Bremmer and Nouriel Roubini, "A G-Zero World," *Foreign Affairs*, vol. 90, March/April 2011; Ian Bremmer, *Every Nation for Itself* (New York: Portfolio/Penguin, 2012).

75. G. John Ikenberry, *Liberal Leviathan* (Princeton: Princeton University Press, 2011), p. 340.

Lloyd Gruber

GLOBALISATION WITH GROWTH AND EQUITY
Can We Really Have It All?

Before the 1980s, students of economic and political development spent a great deal of time worrying about the fundamental trade-off between growth and equity: governments could deliver one or the other, but asking for both was asking too much. Over the course of the 1980s and 1990s, however, this view—the conventional wisdom of previous decades—began to be challenged. Rather than treating the growth/equity trade-off as an inescapable feature of capitalist development, the literature now emphasised the *absence* of such a trade-off.[1] One had only to look at Sweden, where growth and equity were fused in a near-perfect harmony, to see there was nothing necessary or inevitable about it. For comparative scholars, then, the question was why some political economies (such as Sweden's) were able to overcome the trade-off while others weren't. Stripped to its essence, the answer given by this body of work was simple: equitable growth was a product of good institutions. And Sweden, with its highly organised labour markets, had some of the world's best.

Shifting the focus to the developing world, this article questions whether it is still realistic to expect developing countries—even those possessing "good institutions"—to navigate their way to the high-growth/low-inequality equilibria enjoyed by Sweden and its Scandinavian neighbours throughout much of the postwar period. The new institutionalism's fundamental premise is certainly

correct: institutions do matter. At the same time, however, it is important to remember that Sweden's distinctive labour market institutions existed within a larger context, as indeed did all of its institutions, political as well as economic. That context was globalisation. And so it remains: if anything, the gale force winds of globalisation are likely to become more powerful over time, not less. Nor, in this respect, is Sweden in any way exceptional. As time goes on, the developing world's prospects for growth and equality are likely to be heavily conditioned, if not determined, by global forces. We may not yet have reached the point where the effects of globalisation matter more than the domestic-institutional effects on which the development literature has been focusing since the 1980s, but we are certainly moving in that direction—and moving fast.

Looking ahead, this article explains how this new openness to international market forces could end up reactivating the growth/equity trade-off that so preoccupied earlier comparative scholars. I begin by revisiting the conventional wisdom on growth. While much of the past decade's economic literature on trade and growth has focused on empirical issues, sections two and three return to the relationship's underlying theoretical logic. Or logics plural, for contributors to this vast body of literature advance more than one. After delineating the core ideas behind three of these logics, I explain why none of their causal pathways is as conceptually airtight as today's globalisation

From *Third World Quarterly* 32, no. 4 (2011), 629–652.

enthusiasts would have us believe. Just as the empirics of the trade-growth relationship remain a matter of dispute, so too, even today, are the links between trade and growth open to serious *theoretical* debate.

After bringing these theoretical controversies to the surface, I set them aside in sections four and five in order to focus on the equity side of the growth/equity trade-off. Even if trade is conducive to economic growth, it may not be conducive to equity. In section four I draw on recent scholarly work to explain why inequality could rise along with trade even in the labour-abundant countries that make up much of the developing world. Section five then moves beyond the trade literature's separate growth and equity debates to suggest what new insights might be generated by conjoining the two. All things equal, growth and development are mutually reinforcing; they go hand in hand. But when inequality is rising, all things are *not* equal, and it would not be surprising to find low-earning households at the bottom tail of a fast-growing developing country's earnings distribution suffering a decline in their living standards, whether objectively (in absolute terms) or "merely" subjectively (as households perceive their material situations to be deteriorating relative to those of other households in their communities or the nation as a whole).

An inequality-induced rise in redistribution could go a long way towards alleviating these disparities, of course, at least in theory. In practice, however, the elites of developing societies may not be especially keen to transfer their wealth to the less privileged. Indeed, the extent to which rising inequality could reduce, rather than increase, these elites' enthusiasm for progressive redistribution is precisely the sort of trade-off "re-activating" question that section five suggests deserves closer scrutiny. And yet, as fundamentally political as they are, questions about trade's impact on the functioning of domestic redistributive mechanisms and institutions have not to date been at the forefront of development research within political science.[2] After fleshing out this point in section six, I use the article's concluding section to lay out a broader research agenda as well as to suggest some narrower, more concrete points of empirical entry into it.

From Trade to Growth: Theoretical Foundations

Does the expansion of markets from the domestic to the international sphere promote long-run economic prosperity? The standard answer is that it does: international trade, though not the only source of economic growth, is surely an important one. And as global trade increases, its independent contribution to long-run prosperity is likely to rise as well—independent, that is, in the sense of being exogenous to other (purely domestic) sources of prosperity.

As depicted in Figure 9.8, the underlying causal logic is extraordinarily simple, almost absurdly so. But then simple means parsimonious, and parsimonious theories are the building blocks of scientific progress. Look beneath the surface, however, and the theoretical waters quickly become cloudy. Take the link between trade and growth. As theoretical propositions go, it is hard to get more basic. But what is the theoretical basis for this link, exactly? Perhaps that first boldface plus sign in the figure would better be represented by a giant question mark.

Although the language I am using here is playful, the conceptual uncertainties at issue are both real and serious. It may well be true that trade stimulates growth, as does globalisation more generally, but it is not enough for empirically oriented economists and econometricians to observe this pattern in data. Beyond the econometrics, we would also like to explain *why* openness and growth are correlated. And therein, often submerged in a sea of

Figure 9.8. Trade and Welfare: The Washington Consensus

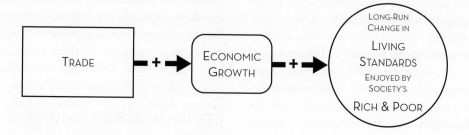

empirical work, lies real controversy, for economic theory offers not one explanation for the link but three.

The first is comparative advantage. Inasmuch as globalisation's impact on growth is positive, it could be that trade discourages countries from producing goods and services that other countries could produce more efficiently were they to specialise in producing them. By the logic that David Ricardo famously clarified in 1817—and that Paul Samuelson would later describe as the most beautiful idea in economics—the elimination of trade barriers encourages just this sort of specialisation: it encourages each country to concentrate on producing whatever commodities it is best at producing. So far, so good—except that the logic of comparative advantage may not be correct. Did Ricardo make a mistake? It is possible that he did, though I want to put off discussing that possibility for a few moments to concentrate on a different (potential) problem: perhaps the principle of comparative advantage, though as logically sound today as it was when Ricardo devised it in the 1800s, simply no longer applies.

Recently—over just the past 15 years or so— two *other* logics have come to dominate economic discussion of the trade-to-growth nexus. To be fair, those who embrace these alternative explanations for globalisation's positive growth effects do not dispute that the static gains envisaged by Samuelson, Heckscher and Ohlin, and other proponents of Ricardo's theoretical framework are real. These gains do exist in their view, as in Ricardo's; trade allows capital-abundant countries to shift production into capital-intensive sectors and labour-abundant countries to shift into labour-intensive sectors and, as a result of these trade-facilitated reallocations, improves the efficiency of the world economy as a whole. Each country produces more with less, and is thereby made richer. It's just that the magnitude of these reallocative riches—their causal weight in the global growth equation—has been diminishing over time (or so it is argued) while other trade-related gains, "dynamic" gains impossible to subsume within the static comparative-advantage framework, have been growing.

Which brings us to the second logic. Here it is competition that explains trade's positive impact on prosperity rather than (or in addition to) comparative advantage. As markets expand—first domestically and then, with globalisation, internationally—so, too, do the competitive pressures bearing down on individual producers. Faced with this pressure, firms innovate and, through that innovation, increase their overall productivity. Either that or they get driven out.

The argument here may not be as elegant as Ricardo's but, like the Spanish Inquisition, it is ruthlessly efficient. More openness means more competition, and more competition propels the search for new technologies and more efficient ways of doing business. And the search never stops. Globalisation is not a one-time-only source of productivity gains but a continuous source. Its impact on growth is dynamic.

This second logic thus differs markedly from the static arguments of Ricardo or Heckscher and Ohlin. It also subsumes a couple of other arguments sometimes advanced for—or against—globalisation. In the simplest version of the competition story, trade fuels innovation by spreading fear. If I don't build a better mousetrap, someone else will—if not my neighbour then someone in another mice-ridden part of the world with which my country now trades—and my business will go *out* of business. But trade can also fuel innovation in a more circuitous fashion, not just by spreading fear but by spreading new ideas, new techniques, even new ways of thinking. And how does it do this? The most direct way is through the sorts of exchanges and "technology transfers" that occur when multinational corporations from one country set up shop in another.[3] Yet however it occurs, whether directly and deliberately or indirectly and fortuitously, this cross-border transmission of ideas is part of a larger competitive dynamic. And in most versions of the story—and certainly the bestselling ones—it is good for growth.

The first logic may be the most beautiful and the second the simplest, but it is for developing the third that Nobel prizes are currently being awarded. The origins of the idea date back to the mid-1980s when a group of trade economists reared on Ricardo (and Heckscher, Ohlin, etc) looked out at the world and observed that, contrary to Ricardo's vision of countries trading on their differences, the vast bulk of global trade occurred among countries with virtually identical factor endowments. Industrialised countries, which at that time accounted for more than three-quarters of total world trade, were abundant in precisely the same factor—capital—and when they engaged in trade, it was to exchange very

similar types of (capital-intensive) goods, not wine for cloth but Airbus for Boeing and BMW for Lexus. This preponderance of *intra*- rather than *inter*-industry trade required an explanation, and Paul Krugman, who, along with Elhanan Helpman, was to emerge as the third logic's chief logician, provided one.[4] If all that intra-industry trade was happening, Krugman reasoned, it must be because the lowering of barriers to intra-industry trade was efficient. But *why* was it efficient?

Krugman's great insight was to see that the global expansion of markets, in addition to permitting each country to exploit its distinctive comparative advantage, also made it possible for firms in countries possessing the same comparative advantage to scale up production for a larger market. What these firms exploit is not their country's comparative advantage so much as the lower costs associated with large-scale manufacturing: the larger the market, the longer the production runs these firms can afford to run, and with longer production runs come lower prices. Everyone gains. And, once again, these gains are dynamic, limited only by the size of the world market. Like the Energizer batteries it manufactures, the Energizer Corporation's production runs—and the price reductions they make possible—keep going and going. And going.[5]

Trade and Growth Today: The Opposite of Consensus

As I hope the previous section's brief discussion has made clear, the economist's engine-room contains at least three powerful machines: comparative advantage, competition and new trade theory. As to which engine's underlying causal mechanism most accurately depicts trade's positive impact on long-run economic growth—or whether they work best when they work together—there is to date nothing resembling a consensus, either in Washington or anywhere else. What we see, instead, are continuing dialogues and debates. International economists have their theoretical engines running, but it is still unclear, even after the new trade theory's recent surge, whose causal mechanism will go furthest.

There is, of course, yet another possibility. Perhaps *none* of the three mechanisms adequately explains trade's positive impact. And indeed, each is open to challenge, with some economists—even mainstream scholars such as Dani Rodrik and, as far as capital mobility is concerned, Jagdish Bhagwati and Barry Eichengreen—harbouring such deep reservations about the current wave of globalisation that a three-car collision (or its theoretical equivalent) cannot yet be ruled out.

Trade's long-term distributional consequences, to which I will turn below, are the focus of some of these reservations, but not all. In addition, the reservationists (a better term than sceptics) within the economics profession worry that the internationalisation of markets, even with all it has going for it, could end up stifling rather than stimulating aggregate growth. As globalisation proceeds, the aggregate pie may well get bigger—but it could also shrink.

Take comparative advantage and that question I posed about it earlier: is the reasoning underlying Ricardo's famous logic entirely, well, logical? If things worked the way the argument says they should, developing countries would specialise in the low-skill-intensive industries in which, being labour-abundant, they held a comparative advantage. As they did so, however, resources would move out of these economies' most technologically innovative economic sectors, the very sectors on which developing countries' longer-run growth arguably depends. While the industrialised North would get to specialise in skill-intensive industries characterised by increasing returns, the developing countries of the South would focus on agriculture and the extractive industries that, while closer to

their areas of comparative advantage initially, afford little scope for productive improvements down the road.[6] Just as one can always build a better mousetrap, one can also build a better computer mouse. But as for pumping oil and mining copper—or, one might add, picking tomatoes or coffee beans—once you've mastered the basics, it is hard to go much further. The basics are pretty much all there is.

To be fair to Ricardo, the conclusion reached by those who embrace this line of criticism, which is really an amalgam of comparative advantage and the other two (more dynamic) logics, is not that globalisation undermines growth in developing countries, let alone that it prevents growth. Empirically, of course, some of these countries have been able to escape their comparative-advantage straitjackets and, whether for institutional reasons, cultural reasons, or just plain luck, move expeditiously through the process that Marx termed "primitive accumulation." Reinvesting the profits they earned by exporting low-wage manufactured goods to the voracious consumers of wealthier economies, businesses in South Korea and Taiwan—and today, it would appear, in countries such as China and Vietnam—have risen rapidly up the value chain.[7] But even if these Korean and Taiwanese businesses had not risen anywhere, the Korean and Taiwanese people would still be more prosperous (according to logic number 1) than if their leaders had never opened up their countries' domestic markets. The prosperity gains they enjoy thanks to trade may be static or even, over time, diminishing, but they are gains nonetheless. If there is a concern here, then, it is for reasons having more to do with what Ricardo's logic implies about the North-South growth differential than with growth, or its absence, *per se.*[8]

But enough about Ricardo. What about the second logic? As markets expand, do they really become more competitive? As it happens, that too is an open question. Consider the old infant-industry argument against opening domestic markets to external competition. Politically, the argument was naïve in the extreme: protectionist barriers, once in place, are exceedingly difficult to remove, and woe betide any government that tries. Economically, however, the logic underpinning the argument may not have been so crazy. As Rodrik has pointed out, the idea of releasing a country's fledgling home-grown industries into the world of the grown-ups is only a sensible (growth-stimulating) idea if those industries are prepared.[9]

Ideally, of course, the owners of a country's infant industries would already have become accustomed to working within the regulatory framework of the global marketplace by the time their governments had released their firms, and the people they employ would already have cultivated the necessary work habits. At the same time, public sector officials would have provided both groups—the employers and the employees—with social safety nets, established clear property rights, and taken whatever other steps were needed to nurture their economy's infants into adulthood. In the real world, however, this ideal level of preparedness may not always be achieved, and thrusting unprepared businesses into an intensely competitive global environment could be a big mistake. If too many of a country's once-thriving domestic firms succumb to international pressures, the long-run impact of globalisation's gale of creative destruction could end up slowing an economy's rate of expansion rather than accelerating it. And there is nothing naïve about that.

As for new trade theory—that's logic number 3—the idea that trade increases market size and allows firms to exploit scale economies is hard to criticise. Less clear, however, are the long-run consequences of that exploitation for global, or even national, prosperity.[10] As a thought experiment, imagine a world in which every country gets to enjoy a global monopoly in a particular niche or sector. China could be the world's one and only producer of buttons (to take Paul Collier's favourite example), while US firms thoroughly dominated the world market in, say, aeroplanes. Each country—not just China or the US—would act as a global monopolist, and as long as its firms kept their prices low enough to deter entry, each would reap enormous profits.

While it makes for a nice story, this is not at all what the structure of today's world economy actually looks like. Few countries enjoy 100 percent market share in any product category. Nor does it appear that we are headed inexorably in that direction—that it is simply a matter of time before each country acquires a monopoly of its own. Nor, finally, is there any *theoretical* reason to assume globalisation's long-run equilibrium will resemble this growth-maximising ideal. A more theoretically plausible scenario is that some countries will capture global monopolies (or near-monopolies) in certain sectors, that others won't, and that, thanks to trade, the first group of countries will enjoy high growth while the economies of the second group exhibit low or even negative growth.

To be clear, all the countries in the second group would prefer to be in the first. It is just that breaking into the big leagues is not easy, even in the long run. As for why it is so difficult, new trade theory offers several different answers.[11] Of these, the most worrisome is the tendency for countries with one well established niche to attract others. In the economics literature the virtuous-cycle aspects of this process are attributed, not surprisingly, to economic forces. Most important are the positive economic externalities that spill over from each country's quasi-monopolistic firms. Facing little competition, these firms are highly profitable, and their shareholders benefit. But other firms in their vicinity also benefit, including firms that may not have existed when their economy's first world market leader was initially created. These other firms have the luxury of piggy-backing on the externalities generated by the prime mover. By the time the newcomers arrive on the scene, an infrastructure has already been put in place, and a skilled workforce too—which is why the newcomers are attracted to the scene in the first instance and, indeed, what makes it a scene. And as more and more newcomers arrive, they begin producing externalities of their own, and what started out as a scene becomes the blockbuster motion picture that has everyone talking.

As this process takes on a life of its own, the rich (firms) get richer, and the countries in which they are located get richer too. That is the good news: hubs agglomerate. The bad news is that *other* countries—though their diversified, hub-free economies may once have been healthy—could see investment in their own economies dry up and their growth rates decline. Having missed out on the agglomerating-hub business when it first got going, they are now too far from the action.

Nor is it obvious what they could do to get any closer. Putting money into education might help, but it is hard to build good schools in a recessionary climate. What's more, they would need to be *really* good schools, since the "spokes" would be starting at a big disadvantage. And while the spoke economy's consumers might pay lower prices for the commodities they imported from countries located closer to the action, these imports, even if they cost less, would still cost something. Where would the spoke's consumers get the earnings to pay for them? It is hard to see, just as it is hard to see where their governments would find the tax revenues to pay for new schools. With growth in the doldrums all bets would be off.

Rather than a consensus position, then, the simple globalisation-causes-growth conjecture that inspired the Washington Consensus is just that: a conjecture. There may well be a "bottom line" eventually. Until then, however, economists will be burrowing, slowly but productively, down toward it.

Trade and Inequality: Another Open Question

Not that growth is, or should be, the only relevant consideration. There are, in fact, two separate bottom lines for which economists have organised search parties. While one team is investigating whether open policies are capable of increasing the overall size of a society's economic pie, a second is asking whether the slices of that pie are likely to be divided any more equally after societies have globalised than before.

All economies—even those closed to international trade and investment—reward certain individuals more than others. The second question at issue here is not just whether globalisation creates winners and losers but whether it does so in ways that systematically widen the gap between the two groups' respective economic fortunes. The nexus between openness and economic growth may lie at the centre of the Washington Consensus, but as even Adam Smith appreciated—and as Amartya Sen has spent much of his career reminding his fellow economists—income growth isn't everything.

Enter, or (more precisely) re-enter, the Heckscher-Ohlin trade model. Recall this model's main prediction: driven by the inexorable logic of comparative advantage, countries will respond to new trade opportunities by specialising in whatever product lines make most intensive use of their abundant factors. All economies become more productive as a result of this process, and all get richer. But again, these are aggregate effects. What about trade's *distributional* consequences? In 1941 Wolfgang Stolper and Paul Samuelson wrote a justifiably celebrated paper drawing out the Heckscher-Ohlin framework's distributive implications.[12] As countries are encouraged (by trade) to exploit their abundant factors, the people fortunate enough to own those factors will enjoy increased demand for their productive assets, they argued, while the demand for—and hence the returns to—each country's scarce factors will fall.

That's fall with a capital F, for the returns accruing to the scarce factors in any long-run Heckscher-Ohlin equilibrium would be lower not only in relative terms but, as Stolper and Samuelson took pains to show, in absolute terms as well. Absent any government redistribution, trade would leave holders of these factors materially worse off than they had been in the protectionist status quo.[13]

From an egalitarian perspective, of course, this is not necessarily a bad thing. In developing countries, the people whose material interests would be most threatened by trade in this model would be 'capitalists', including those who earned their market incomes by exploiting their prior investments in human capital. And compared with unskilled labourers, small-holding farmers, and other trade-advantaged owners of the developing world's abundant factors, these people are rich. As comparative advantage works its magic on global trade patterns, we should not be surprised to discover the initial (typically very large) gap between the market returns of a developing country's richest and poorest inhabitants disappearing.[14]

But that is only in the developing world. The Stolper-Samuelson extension to the Heckscher-Ohlin model would famously predict the opposite dynamic in the capital-abundant countries of the industrialised world. As these countries move more aggressively into capital-intensive production—and just as aggressively out of lower paying low-tech sectors producing goods and services more efficiently imported from developing countries—their earnings distributions should be becoming more, not less, dispersed. Here then, as even some of globalisation's most ardent champions concede, the expansion of trade would be throwing fuel on the fires of market-generated inequality. And although the evidence is by no means conclusive, a large number of studies do suggest that openness to trade and the greater mobility of capital have

been having precisely that effect: just as Heckscher and Ohlin (and Stolper and Samuelson) would have predicted, they are accentuating disparities in the OECD's pre-existing distribution of market earnings.[15]

On the other hand, no one claims that globalisation has been the only motivating force behind these trends, nor that its impact on inequality, inasmuch as the elimination of trade barriers and opening of financial markets have been driving the action, is *necessarily* consistent with the Heckscher-Ohlin model.[16] But to say that something else is going on—which is almost certainly the case—just begs the question of what it is.

For proponents of new trade theory, that something is an altogether different causal mechanism, a trade-related dynamic even more powerful than the one analysed by Ricardo, Heckscher and Ohlin, Stolper and Samuelson and, until the new trade theory came along, virtually everyone else. More powerful, but also—from an egalitarian perspective—more problematic.

Recall new trade theory's strikingly different vision of global trade's long-run equilibrium. Remember all those clusters of economic activity discussed earlier, the ones that existed alongside swaths of economic wasteland? Let us leave the wastelands aside for now and simply assume that every country possesses at least one globally competitive economic sector. So long as barriers to entry are high and there aren't too many firms bidding down the profits accruing to any one firm in that sector, each of these firms should be able to act as a quasi-monopolist, generating 'excess returns' for its owners. Such high returns would in turn make possible the paying out of high wages. Workers fortunate enough to be employed by their country's global powerhouses would win, other workers would lose and, at a first approximation, domestic earnings would become increasingly skewed in all countries, developed and developing alike.

This picture of the long-run inequality dynamic is not just different from Stolper and

Samuelson's. It is also, in some ways, even more frightening.[17] Must things turn out this way? Perhaps not. Ideally—taking once again the progressive-egalitarian's point of view—each country would be able to shift its entire workforce into its winner-take-all industry or sector. In practice, however, its ability to pull off this manoeuvre could be highly circumscribed by at least two less-than-ideal realities. The first has to do with the size of the market. While it would be nice to think that everyone in the United States could be employed by Boeing Inc and everyone in China by Button Inc, even global markets, as vast as they are, have their limits. How many passenger jets or buttons does the world really want?

The second constraint takes us from the global arena down to the factory floor. If we stay with the assumptions I have just been making about each country's quasi-monopolistic market structure, there seems little question that the firms operating in those countries' dominant sectors would benefit from globalisation. But firms are collections of people (among other things) and some of those people—the stockholders, for instance—are likely to walk away with considerably more money in their pockets than others get to put in theirs. While the owners of a profitable firm always have the option of paying higher wages, their willingness to pursue that option (and thereby ensure that the entire firm really does benefit) is a variable.

Egalitarians, then, have a major problem on their hands. For as globalisation advances, the owners of monopolistic firms are likely to see their market returns rise—assuming this chain of logic is correct—while the workers they hire, though employed in a world-class firm, could see theirs fall. Over time the wage-share variable could thus end up varying in but one direction: downwards.

The chain of logic here is actually more general, going well beyond the new trade theory's claims about agglomeration dynamics and their impact on an economy's earnings distribution. Globalisation, according to this more general line of argument, makes it easier for employers—all employers, not just those operating within their countries' agglomerating sectors—to reduce the wages they pay out without fear of disrupting business as usual. Why? Because the workers to whom those wages are paid know that, were they to protest, their employers could move their operations abroad and hire substitute workers at a lower price. Globalisation makes that option possible today in a way that, in earlier times, it never was. And even where outsourcing is infeasible, globalisation can still operate in ways that weaken the bargaining power of employees. Employers may not always be able to move production overseas, but if, by raising the wage bill, they would expose the firms they run to increased globalisation-facilitated international competition, they can still drive a hard bargain with their employees. An employer's threat to go out of business if its workers stand firm may have all the credibility the employer needs to get what it wants.

This is the globalisation-fuelled race to the bottom that led Dani Rodrik to question whether things may have "gone too far."[18] To be sure, not every economist agrees with Rodrik's logic here; nor do some political scientists.[19] But if globalisation does create the kinds of bargaining asymmetries that Rodrik's argument suggests it must, the holes in which workers find themselves could get deeper as globalisation proceeds—and the earnings gap even wider.

Suffice it to say that the globalisation debate within economics is much less settled than either the Washington Consensus or its much-heralded successor, the Post-Washington Consensus, makes it appear. Rather than a single causal logic, economics offers up many, each spotlighting a different causal mechanism and each mechanism implying, if not a different set of conclusions, then a different way of getting to the same conclusion. And that's just the theoretical debate. The empirical task of bringing all these pathways and the controversies surrounding them to the data—and

Figure 9.9. Trade and Welfare: A Broader Perspective

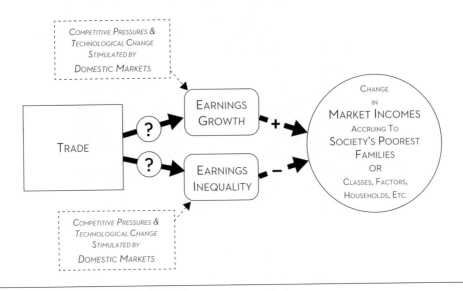

to the extent some pathways look more promising than others, weighing the independent impact of the international factors on which they focus—has really only just begun (see Figure 9.9).

Growth Versus Equity

The point that efficiency and equity can come into conflict is a familiar one (see note 1). Usually, however, the authors who invoke that point do so in the interests of refuting it. Any government that tries to stimulate economic growth by aggressively pursuing market-oriented policies is unlikely to escape such a trade-off in the early stages of reform, of course, as some members of society—those lacking assets and skills valued by the marketplace—see their market earnings decline. That is but a short-run effect, however, and, as the saying goes, you can't make an omelette without breaking eggs. Wait long enough and each society's broken eggs will eventually find their way to new jobs. And as the initial market-losers repair themselves, their earnings will begin to rise until, at some point, the gap that had once stood between their earnings and the returns of the initial market-winners stops expanding and begins to shrink.

One variant of this no-trade-off scenario is depicted in the top panel of Figure 9.10. Here, globalisation—if that is assumed to be the motor driving the process from the "before" on the left to the "after" on the right—lifts the long-run market incomes of well-off households by the same percentage as it lifts the earnings of poorer ones. What's not to like? And if the growth in incomes generated by globalisation is pro-poor, with incomes rising even faster at the bottom of the wage and earnings distribution than at the top, the Rawlsian case for globalisation looks even stronger (see Case 2 in the figure).

But how are we to assess the outcome depicted in the figure's bottom panel? Here, as in Cases 1 and 2, the society's average income rises, a happy development that for the purposes of argument we are attributing to globalisation. But while we could extol the virtues of globalisation as an engine of

Figure 9.10. Do Divided Societies Face a Trade-off Between Growth and Equity?

Case 1: Even Growth

Rapid growth with no change in the poor's share of society's total earnings ⇒ Equal percentage gains for all, rich and poor alike

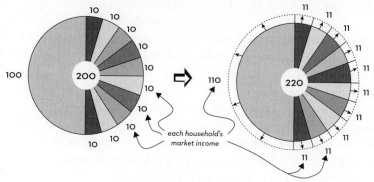

each household's market income

Case 2: Pro-Poor Growth

Growth now concentrated on lower-income households ⇒ Gains enjoyed by the society's 10 disadvantaged households exceed those accruing to its one 'elite' household (though higher-income households may also benefit)

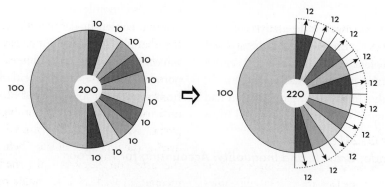

Case 3: Zero-Sum Growth

Rapid growth as above, though the poorest 10 households now see their share of the society's total earnings decline ⇒ Relative losses for lower-income households, with absolute losses also possible

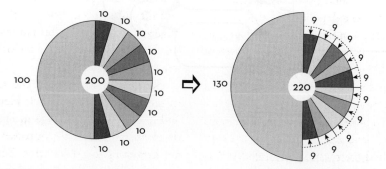

growth, we would also have to be concerned about its impact on inequality. Just as the before-and-after comparison depicted in Case 3 fails the Rawlsian test, so too would globalisation or, for that matter, any "engine" responsible for moving the society from its high-quality before to a lower-quality after.

Though stylised, this Case 3 scenario nicely illustrates the broader point I am trying to make here. It is fine for economists to examine globalisation's growth and inequality effects separately. That is surely the place to start. But when it comes to assessing globalisation's overall economic desirability—to evaluating whether, on balance, the policy intervention it represents is a smart move or an irresponsible one—how these two effects combine also matters. And yet it is precisely this combination that, I would suggest, has been missing from the economic debate thus far (see Figure 9.11).

Or, to be more precise, it is the analysis of *combinations* that has been missing, for the stylised combinations depicted above in Cases 1, 2, and 3 hardly exhaust the possibilities. Recall Case 3, where the growth stimulated by globalisation had lifted the earnings of the average household (thus

boosting the society's per capita income) but depressed the earnings of bottom-end households. Now suppose that the disadvantaged households at the bottom tail of the earnings distribution, rather than having to endure an absolute globalisation-induced decline in their market incomes, had suffered "only" a relative decline. Suppose, in other words, that the right-hand side of the pie depicted in Figure 9.10, rather than shrinking as the society moved away from the before-globalisation status quo, stayed the same size or even, perhaps, expanded, albeit by less than that of the large slice accruing to the 'elite' household whose income is displayed on the left. Would we now regard globalisation as a win-win proposition?

The question does not lend itself to a consensus answer. In part, that is because it introduces difficult moral and philosophical issues beyond the realm of economics as it is ordinarily conceived.[20] Another consensus-defying aspect of the question is the implicit weighting it assigns to inequality's subjective dimension. Absolutes are not unimportant, of course, but particularly as one moves from societies at low levels of economic development, where those at the bottom are just getting

Figure 9.11. Trade, Growth, and Inequality: Accounting for the Poor

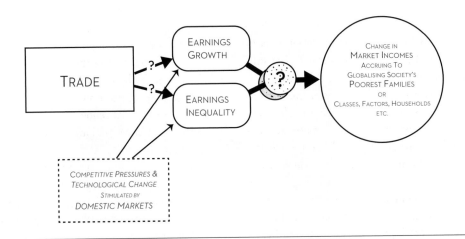

Figure 9.12. Growth and Redistribution: A Worst-case Scenario

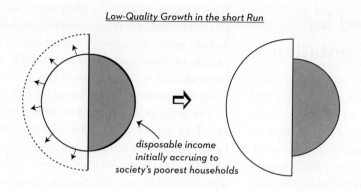

Low-Quality Growth in the short Run

disposable income
initially accruing to
society's poorest households

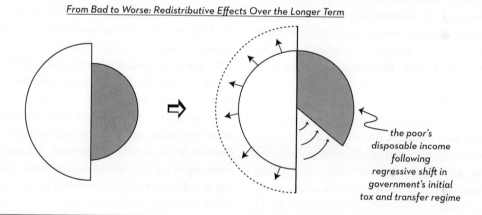

From Bad to Worse: Redistributive Effects Over the Longer Term

the poor's
disposable income
following
regressive shift in
government's initial
tox and transfer regime

---

by, to advanced industrialised economies, where subsistence is no longer as tenuous, relative considerations would surely also have to figure into one's "ultimate" standard-of-living calculus.[21]

And there is also, finally, the *political* dimension: rising trade-induced inequality could drag down more objective indicators of material well-being as well—by impeding good governance and the protection of property rights, for instance. Continuing with this line of analysis, one might worry that, in countries characterised by high inequality, the better-off would have fewer incentives to support improvements in the delivery of healthcare, primary education and other publicly provided services. The rich, in opting out of the public system, could end up depressing the objective living standards enjoyed by households located further down the earnings spectrum even if the market incomes accruing to those households had been rising.[22] In this way, trade liberalisation's impact on life expectancy, infant mortality, and other objective indicators of well-being—an impact that might have been positive in a less inegalitarian society—could turn negative, depressed by globalisation-induced inequities and their redistribution-suppressing spillovers (see Figure 9.12).

Globalisation and Political Science: The Need for Theoretical Reorientation

Are governments doing their poorest citizens a favour when they dismantle barriers to trade and allow markets to expand? Or do their liberalising policies—by reducing support for the provision of public goods—end up worsening these citizens' material situations, not just during the short-run transition to the new market equilibrium, but over the longer term as well? Just as the discipline of economics is intensely engaged in an as-yet-unresolved debate about trade's long-run impact on economic growth and development, one might have thought that political scientists would be equally engaged in similar bottom-line questions about globalisation's long-term impact on *political* growth and development.

In truth, however, most political scientists—inasmuch as their research focuses on globalisation—are interested in an altogether different set of issues. Rather than examining trade and capital mobility's long-run domestic political consequences, the theoretical core of political science's globalisation-centred International Political Economy (IPE) literature asks two questions.

One concerns the institutional underpinnings of this globalising process, and of international co-operation more generally. Globalisation has been accompanied by the creation of all sorts of new, or newly reinvigorated, regional and multilateral arrangements. The European Central Bank, the North American Free Trade Agreement, the World Trade Organization, the G-7—it is a long list and, like the G-7 (now G-20), it is expanding all the time. Why do all these institutions exist? What purposes do they serve? Instead of a single answer, the IPE literature offers a range of views on the "how" of globalisation.

The same is true for the IPE literature's second question, namely why the process is occurring at all. To the extent that the process has been driven by political forces—as it surely has, at least as much as by exogenous technological developments—how exactly do those forces operate? For IPE scholars engaged in this second line of inquiry, disentangling and prioritising the causes of globalisation has been the main objective, as well as the major source of productive conflict. On one side, very broadly speaking, are those who see globalisation as the happy culmination of dozens, if not hundreds, of prior interstate negotiations and bargains. When countries liberalise reciprocally—by entering into co-operative agreements with their partners or, better still, establishing a fully fledged multilateral institution to solidify these arrangements—they get all the gains from trade *plus* whatever added benefits their partners had agreed to provide them in return for their letting them in on the deal.

And yet, the promise of all these gains notwithstanding, these sorts of co-operative deals can be quite difficult to pull off in practice. For attached to those gains are the risks of opportunism, that is, of being exploited by one's partners after a new agreement has taken effect. These risks may loom larger in periods of geopolitical uncertainty, when today's friends could easily turn out to be tomorrow's enemies. But even when the security environment is relatively stable, the riskiness of international transactions is never far from the minds of policy makers. So why, then, have we recently been seeing so much co-operative deal making?

For contributors on this first side of the "why globalisation?" debate, it is a credit to government officials—and also, perhaps, to their policy-making teams' training in the new institutional economics. Yes, proponents of this line of argument concede, the types of co-operation that undergird globalisation are risky and collective action problems are pervasive. But over time, by studying past successes and failures and paying particular attention to the potential role and design of international institutions, policy makers are learning how to solve these problems. They are figuring it out.[23]

So much for that side of the debate. The other side sees power, and go-it-alone power in particular, as the driving force behind globalisation.[24] If the governments of powerful countries think that their constituents are benefiting from globalisation, the bandwagon will keep rolling, in this view; and if not, the forces of globalisation will stop or (at a minimum) slow down. As for governing elites in other countries, whether or not *they* think globalisation is beneficial is, from a power-politics perspective, irrelevant. When looked at through their eyes, the game they are being asked to play—and which, given the alternatives, it would be irrational for them not to play—may appear more zero-sum than positive-sum. Although they end up co-operating with the powerful pro-globalisation coalition, they do so unhappily, for the collective action problem their participation has helped solve was never actually a problem, at least not for them; it was their coalition partners' problem. Only *after* the weaker states have opened their markets do their own problems begin.

As trivial as it may seem, the point here is fundamental: the process of international economic integration can create large numbers of short-term losers without necessarily causing that process to collapse. Why not? Because the countries whose political leaders do not lose may be in a position to 'go it alone'. Assuming this is the case—that certain nations would benefit from an open market regime even if they were to be its only members—the regime itself becomes a *fait accompli*, leaving other nations to choose between what their leaders may view as a bad option (voluntarily opening their markets to foreign trade and investment) and an even worse alternative (opting out of those markets and incurring the economic and political costs of exclusion). Under these circumstances, the anti-globalisation countries would be foolish

to choose the second option. But if they are better off choosing the first, it is only because a third alternative—returning to the days when all countries restricted access to their domestic markets—is now outside their choice sets. Their pro-globalisation neighbours have removed it.

That said, the globalisation losers in this scenario are political actors. They are states or, more precisely, the parties and individuals responsible for conducting their country's foreign policy and, in that capacity, for deciding whether or not to cooperate with their counterparts in other countries. Out of necessity, these actors tend to be concerned with the effects of their actions in the near term. But as for the long run—and as for the poor—these considerations barely register in their thinking, and for perfectly understandable, if not exactly good, reasons.

Although it zeroes in on the losers' side of the story, then, this second body of IPE scholarship allows for the possibility that go-it-alone power, the status-quo-shifting capability enjoyed by globalisation's prime movers, is a force for long-term good—everyone's good, not just that of the wealthy or the powerful. Nor, of course, do those on the first side of the causes-of-globalisation debate take issue with this rather sanguine rendering of globalisation's long-run story, emphasising as they do the positive-sum possibilities of global interdependence. In the end, therefore, the no-trade-off "you can have it all" view of trade emerges from these political science debates wholly intact. For on that point—and perhaps only that point—there was never much of a fight.

Moving Ahead by Stepping Back

As we have just seen, most studies of globalisation written by political scientists examine the phenomenon's economic and political origins and ask, in effect, how we've managed to come as far as we have. In contrast, my analysis in this article has fast-forwarded directly to the end, to a culmination of previous globalising trends that is still many years, if not decades, away, and asked: did we really want to go there?

Absent a major reassessment by the United States and the member states of the EU, this culmination may come sooner than we think. Indeed, if there is to be any 'rethinking' of globalisation, there could be no better occasion for it than the present moment, a period in which globalisation's US and European prime movers are struggling mightily to reignite their economies. As the saying goes, every crisis is an opportunity waiting to be discovered.

Even in the midst of a severe global depression, however, this most fundamental of all globalisation questions—should we stay or should we go?—has received relatively little systematic attention. If globalisation is going out, it's with a whimper too quiet to register in any serious scholar's analytical headphones.

It is true that the late 2000s have seen the emergence of something approaching a consensus on the need for tightening the regulation of financial flows, both internationally, in the upward delegation of formerly domestic powers to the IMF and other supranational bodies, and domestically, in the form of new restrictions and, where necessary, new legislation. Interestingly, though, that near-universal shift in opinion has been limited to finance. On this point, hardly anyone—not even regulatory enthusiast Paul Krugman—has suggested a more radical reconsideration of globalisation writ large.[25]

What is surprising here is not that policy makers have been reluctant to reconsider the longer-term consequences of their trade policies; it is the reluctance of *academics* that raises questions. National politicians have their hands full at the moment, after all, and given the constraints imposed by the electoral calendar, they are rarely much interested in debating the long-term effects of their policies anyway. Social scientists do not have such pressing matters to attend to, however, and analysing the long-run consequences of governments' policy choices is one of the "matters" that most excites them—except, it would appear, when those choices involve globalisation.

That's an exaggeration, of course, but as a broad characterisation of the international relations literature discussed in the previous section, I think the basic point stands. In economics, by contrast, trade's welfare consequences are today the subject of heated scholarly disagreements, as they have been at least since the days of Adam Smith. This is very much to the discipline's credit. And yet, as highlighted above in the article's third and fourth sections, the more recent economics literature has tended to compartmentalise these disputes into two stand-alone debates—one on trade's long-run growth effects, a second on its long-run consequences for inequality—when simple logic suggests the two sets of disagreements ought to be conjoined into a single, broader debate.

The purpose of my last figure is simply to underscore this need for broadening academic inquiry into the long-run effects of today's free trade bandwagon, both within and, more importantly, across each discipline's distinct compartments (see Figure 9.13). While broader arguments are not always more insightful or productive, this particular case is one where a little broadening could, it seems to me, go a long way. Drawing more economists and political scientists into the debate would be a useful first step in that direction. To achieve real progress, however, we will need to alter—and, specifically, to widen—the debate itself: the disciplinary walls behind which scholarly inquiry into globalisation's long-run welfare consequences has been confined until now (the work of a few renegades such as Dani Rodrik and Robert Wade excepted) will need to be dismantled. It is to these twin tasks, this back-to-basics refocusing and cross-disciplinary widening,

Figure 9.13. Opening Up the Debate on Openness: Big Questions for Future Research

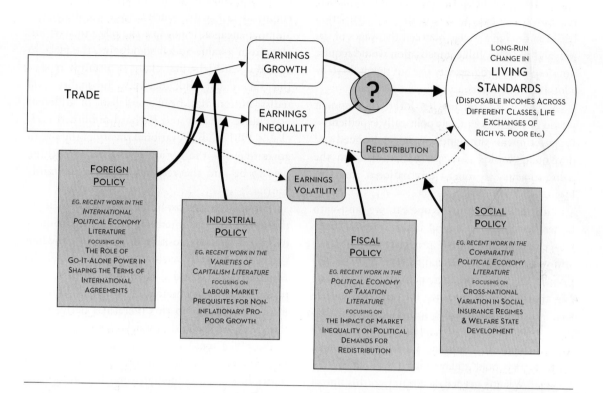

that contributors to the globalisation literature must now turn.

What would this mean in practice? To take just one of the four "open boxes" depicted at the bottom of Figure 9.13—the one labelled Fiscal Policy—it would mean digging deeper into the conceptual holes that riddle much of the existing work on inequality's long-run welfare consequences. Only rarely do analysts pay careful attention to the income bases of the inequality measures they employ in their research; sometimes these indicators are derived from data on earnings, and sometimes they are derived from data on disposable income. Although the two may be related, globalisation's first-order effect is likely to be on earnings. If researchers from the World Bank find no association between a country's openness to trade and its level of inequality, it could be that they are using an inequality measure derived from disposable income.[26] Openness might well be driving up *earnings* inequality; it's just that these countries' governments are taking corrective action—through increased redistribution—to ensure that their economies' globalisation-fuelled earnings asymmetries do not get translated into disposable-income asymmetries, with the "ultimate" living standards of households at the bottom deteriorating in either relative or, worse yet, absolute terms.

Except that an empirical analysis I have undertaken elsewhere shows that governments have *not* been taking corrective (progressive) action.[27] Nor will they, if earnings inequality keeps rising. In that event the results of my econometric analysis suggest that we should be expecting less, not more, effort on the redistributive front, precisely when more effort would be needed. And as President Obama's current predicament underscores, even "more effort" may not be enough, for inasmuch as globalisation has been driving a wedge between the wages of the rich and the poor, full compensation would require not simply that progressivity rise but that it do so by a lot! Is that too much to ask?

Maybe it is. And maybe, for that reason, it would be wise—not merely politically expedient—for governments throughout today's advanced and developing worlds to begin retreating from the commitments to open international markets forged by their predecessors.[28]

Or maybe not. Already one can see (and with better data and more careful analysis, we are likely to see more clearly) that progressivity does not always decline with inequality. There are exceptions to the rule. And does such a rule even exist? My analysis found evidence for one—an inverse rule, with redistribution responding inversely to prior inequality—but the robustness of my findings are open to question, and the parameters, even if they hold today, may not hold in the future.[29] What is needed, according to this line of analysis, is more time and, from social democrats and progressives, more patience. Governments will be pressed into action eventually, the argument runs, but first the poor's material prospects will need to deteriorate further (yes, even further). It's the omelette analogy: governments won't stir their redistributive whisks until globalisation has broken the requisite number of eggs.

But what about all those cracked eggs? Could any omelette ever be large and tasty enough to justify their sacrifice? And what if our kitchen's chefs-of-state fail to deliver that omelette, or *any* omelette? What if, midway through the recipe, a new team of chefs takes over, one accustomed to preparing haute cuisine dishes for a more refined, upper-class clientele?

The point of asking these (admittedly silly) questions is to highlight the need—a serious need—for new *theoretical* work on redistribution.

One could argue that there are already plenty of theoretical models in the literature, and that the empirical task with which a number of scholars are now engaged is not just the place to start but also, from a value-added standpoint, the place to end. But while the first claim is certainly true—the theoretical link between inequality and redistribution has been modelled in different ways since Meltzer and Richard published their classic 1981 study "A rational theory of the size of government"—the notion that there is nothing new to be said theoretically is just as certainly untrue.[30]

For one thing, most of the theorists working in this area have been interested in isolating inequality's impact on the position of a country's median voter. The simplest versions—those found in the Alesina/Rodrik and Milanovic papers, for instance, whose theoretical insights (like those of most contributors to this literature) derive from the Meltzer/Richard model—have inequality pushing the median to the left. In what sense, however, does the median voter vote? The United States has not one median voter but many: one for the executive branch, where the median's position is chosen by the president, the sole "decider," another for the 435-member House of Representatives, a third for the Senate, a fourth for the Supreme Court, another 50 where matters of state policy are concerned, and hundreds more when it comes to public schooling, where each local district has the final say. It is not as if these medians ever get together to select a single "national" median.

There is, in any event, an altogether different (and so far, it has to be said, less well developed) line of theory that does not start from the preferences of the median voter or, for that matter, any voter. The question that animates this alternative perspective is whether economic inequality might be contributing to political inequality by empowering—not just enriching—the wealthy at the expense of the middle classes and the poor. As the rich get richer, they can afford to put more of their already greater material resources to use in trying to "capture" the policy-making process. But they do not just try; in this alternative theory the rich invariably succeed. And as they take charge, those at the bottom find themselves unable to get their redistributive preferences translated into policy even when they make up a majority in the district's, the state's, or even the whole country's electorate. Instead, redistribution either declines or, if it increases, it does so by an amount less than would be necessary to fully compensate the poor.[31]

Given the combination of high stakes and high (theoretical) uncertainty, the task of filling in our existing theories of redistribution should be seen as an integral part of the larger progressive research strategy I am advocating here. How would we expect inequality and redistribution to interact in a theoretical world where politicians and voters always behave rationally? What in *that* world would the dynamic look like? The answer isn't obvious. And with the global economy in crisis, it's time to find out.

NOTES

1. Arthur Okun's work offers the clearest statement of the earlier view. See especially A Okun, *Equality and Efficiency: The Big Tradeoff*, Washington, DC: Brookings Institution, 1975. While Okun's view has been challenged over the years by numerous scholars, the critiques levelled by Adam Przeworski and Michael Wallerstein were among the earliest and most forceful. See, for example, A Przeworski & M Wallerstein, 'Democratic capitalism at the crossroads', *Democracy*, 2, 1982, pp 52–68. The Przeworski-Wallerstein critiques also proved influential, filtering as they did into policy debates of the time. See R Kuttner, *The Economic Illusion: False Choices between Prosperity and Social Justice*, Boston, MA: Houghton Mifflin, 1984.

2. Two noteworthy exceptions are RR Kaufman & A Segura-Ubiergo, 'Globalization, domestic politics, and social spending in Latin America', *World Politics*, 53(4), 2001, pp 553–587; and N Rudra, 'Globalization and the decline of the welfare slate in less-developed countries', *International Organization*, 56(2), 2002, pp 411–445.

3. Another means of transmission, only slightly less direct, is through the process of emulation. Here the new technology is not transferred so much as stolen or, less pejoratively, borrowed from its originators in other countries. See A Gerschenkron, *Economic Backwardness in Historical Perspective*, Cambridge, MA: Belknap, 1962; and RH Wade, *Governing the Market*, Princeton, NJ: Princeton University Press, 2003.

4. See E Helpman & P Krugman, *Market Structure and Foreign Trade: Increasing Returns, Imperfect Competition, and the International Economy*, Cambridge, MA: MIT Press, 1985; and Helpman & Krugman, *Trade Policy and Market Structure*, Cambridge, MA: MIT Press, 1989.

5. The rationale for opening global capital markets has a similar 'new trade' flavour. The larger the pool of investment capital, the easier it is for investors to spread risk. And with lower risks and greater diversification come lower interest rates and less chance of productive investments going unfunded. (A large pool of cheap capital could also encourage unproductive investments, of course, as a handful of forward-thinking economists—chiefly Nouriel Roubini and Robert Shiller—were cautioning well before the subprime mortgage crisis of 2008 made it an obvious point.)

6. While the concern here is with developing economies becoming trapped in low-spill-over industries, the idea that having a comparative advantage in resource-intensive activities can impede a country's economic progress also has a monetary dimension. On the political economy of so-called Dutch Disease, see, among others, M Ross, 'The political economy of the resource curse', *World Politics*, 51, 1999, pp 297–322.

7. See, for example, Wade, *Governing the Market*; and A Kohli, *State-Directed Development*, Cambridge: Cambridge University Press, 2004.

8. Not that a large North-South divide, or the possibility that globalisation may be working systematically

to widen it, isn't itself a cause for concern. See, for example, RH Wade, 'Globalization, poverty, and inequality', in J Ravenhill (ed), *Global Political Economy*, Oxford: Oxford University Press, 2005.

9. See, for instance, D Rodrik, 'Getting interventions right: how South Korea and Taiwan grew rich', *Economic Policy*, 20, 1995, pp 55–107.

10. The notion that these consequences are invariably positive, and that globalisation is therefore 'good for growth', is certainly not the view of Paul Krugman, for instance, who, mere moments after having helped formulate the new-trade logic in his work with Elhanan Helpman (see note 4), began calling attention to its potentially *negative* growth implications in P Krugman (ed), *Strategic Trade Policy and the New International Economics*, Cambridge, MA: MIT Press, 1986. See also P Krugman & AJ Venables, 'Globalization and the inequality of nations', *Quarterly Journal of Economics*, 110(4), 1995, pp 857–880.

11. In addition to the works by Helpman and Krugman cited above, the discussion here draws on, among others, G Grossman & E Helpman, *Innovation and Growth in the Global Economy*, Cambridge, MA: MIT Press, 1991; RC Feenstra, 'Integration of trade and disintegration of production in the global economy', *Journal of Economic Perspectives*, 12(4), 1998, pp 31–50; and D Trefler & SC Zhu, 'Trade and inequality in developing countries: a general equilibrium analysis', *Journal of International Economics*, 65, 2005, pp 21–48. Although these economists start from different methodological premises, their conclusions about global capitalism and its hard-wired inegalitarian tendencies are strikingly similar to those reached by dependency theorists decades earlier. See, for example, AG Frank, *Capitalism and Underdevelopment in Latin America*, London: Penguin Books, 1971.

12. W Stolper & P Samuelson, 'Protection and real wages', *Review of Economic Studies*, 9(1), 1941, pp 58–73.

13. In theory, governments can always top up the market incomes of individuals who find themselves at the bottom of an increasing earnings gap. Then, too, redistribution can also fall. Both possibilities are theoretically equivalent, though—as I elaborate in my concluding section—their theoretical implications deserve closer scrutiny than they have received thus far. For present purposes the point to emphasise is simply that most economic theorising about globalisation, from H-O to S-S and even H-K (Helpman-Krugman), is concerned with the impact of trade and capital liberalisation on market earnings—or, as here, earnings inequality—rather than on *post*-market disposable incomes.

14. At least at first: if we waited long enough, the gap would reappear, only now—thanks to globalisation—with the (initially) rich and the (initially) poor having changed places in the earnings distribution. Though consistent with the Stolper-Samuelson logic, however, this possibility has received little attention in the trade-and-inequality literature to date, thanks, I suspect, to questions about whether globalisation's long run could ever be long enough to permit such a fundamental role reversal to take place.

15. Exhibit A is the much-lamented 'financialisation' of the OECD economies, a process that has accompanied the removal of their barriers to trade and capital over the past 20 years. It is only natural (so the Heckscher-Ohlin story would go) that the industrialised world has concentrated on its comparative advantage in capital-intensive production, including the skill-intensive work of managing investments and providing financial services. Nor should it come as any surprise that, as the OECD specialised in its comparative advantage, holders of these economies' abundant factor—capital—enjoyed staggering increases, both absolute and relative, in their assets' market returns.

16. Taking the second point, the correspondence between the H-O model's predicted dynamics for industrialised countries and the empirical reality could simply be a fluke. Perhaps these dynamics, although they exist, are overwhelmed by some other non-H-O, but still globalisation-related, set of forces. It is also possible that the H-O framework just needs to be refined or the concept of 'factor' broadened to

include aspects of the institutional environment in which firms operate. On this last point, see N Nunn, 'Relationship-specificity, incomplete contracts, and the pattern of trade'. *Quarterly Journal of Economics*, 122(2), 2007, pp 569–600.

17. See E Helpman, O Itskhoki & S Redding, *Wages, Unemployment and Inequality with Heterogeneous Firms and Workers*, Centre for Economic Performance Working Paper, London School of Economics, 2008, for a recent argument along these lines. Although I do not address it here, the resulting inequality would have an important spatial component, with the cities and regions containing each country's global monopolist growing rapidly, high rents and all, while other parts of the country stagnate.

18. Although he emphasises the substituting-workers threat far more than the going-out-of-business threat, Rodrik provides a particularly lucid account of the underlying logic. See esp D Rodrik, *Has Globalization Gone Too Far?*, Washington, DC: Institute for International Economics, 1997, pp 16–19.

19. Nor do some political scientists. See D Vogel, *Trading Up: Consumer and Environmental Regulation in a Global Economy*, Cambridge, MA: Harvard University Press, 1997; and L Gruber, *Ruling the World: Power Politics and the Rise of Supranational Institutions*, Princeton, NJ: Princeton University Press, 2000.

20. But see A Sen, *Development as Freedom*, New York: Knopf, 1999; and Sen, *The Idea of Justice*, Cambridge, MA: Harvard University Press, 2009. At issue here is not just inequality and economic deprivation but the neglect of human rights more generally. On this point, see I Khan, *The Unheard Truth: Poverty and Human Rights*, New York: WW Norton, 2009.

21. RG Wilkinson & K Pickett, *The Spirit Level: Why Greater Equality Makes Societies Stronger*, London: Bloomsbury, 2009. See also AE Clark, N Kristensen & N Westergard-Nielsen, 'Economic satisfaction and income rank in small neighbourhoods', *Journal of the European Economic Association*, 7(2–3), 2009, pp 519–527.

22. For further investigation of these points, see L Gruber & S Kosack, 'The tertiary tilt: education, inequality, and the politics of development', paper presented at the Annual Meetings of the American Political Science Association, Washington, DC, 2010.

23. While the literature here is vast, Robert O Keohane's work is surety the place to start. See esp Keohane *After Hegemony*, Princeton, NJ: Princeton University Press, 2005; and Keohane, 'Governance in a partially globalized world', *American Political Science Review*, 95(1), 2001, pp 1–13.

24. Gruber, *Ruling the World*; and Gruber, 'Power politics and the free trade bandwagon', *Comparative Political Studies*, 34(7), 2001, pp 703–741. See also SD Krasner, 'State power and the structure of international trade', *World Politics*, 28(3), 1976, pp 317–347; and T Moe, 'Power and political institutions', *Perspective on Politics*, 3(2), 2005, pp 215–233.

25. The implication here is that globalisation is a choice and, as such, could be un-chosen if, out of concern for the future, today's policy makers ever wanted to change course. For a different view, see TL Friedman, *The World is Flat*, New York: Farrar, Straus, and Giroux, 2005.

26. Cf D Dollar & A Kraay, 'Spreading the wealth', *Foreign Affairs*, 82(1), 2002, pp 120–133.

27. L Gruber, 'The interdependence tradeoff: does International integration inhibit domestic integration?', paper presented at the Annual Meetings of the American Political Science Association, Boston, MA, 2008.

28. Not that such a retreat would have to take us all the way back to the pre-globalisation *status quo ante*. That would be impossible. As noted earlier, however, it would also be a mistake to assume that globalisation in its current form is here to stay. It is precisely because globalisation differs from the 'truly' exogenous variables in the economists' earnings equations—technological change leading the list of usual suspects—that it merits special attention.

29. And speaking of the future, one can legitimately ask whether the surging earnings inequality we have recently been seeing will prove to be a self-limiting, hence transitory, phenomenon. This is possible, but

so, too, is the opposite extreme: countries could find their domestic earnings gaps widening at an accelerating rate. With China's entry into global markets, the labour-scarce economies of the North have been administered a powerful new earnings depressant. It is a drug whose effects are unlikely to wear off in the near future, whatever aggressive steps President Obama might take to lift the spirits and, more importantly, the bargaining power of organised labour in the US. A better—though (in my view) still tenuous—case for optimism lies on the redistribution side, as I elaborate here.

30. AH Meltzer & SF Richard, 'A rational theory of the size of government', *Journal of Political Economy*, 89(5), 1981, pp 914–927. More recent 'classics' include A Alesina & D Rodrik, 'Distributive politics and economic growth', *Quarterly Journal of Economics*, 109(2), 1994, pp 465–490; B Milanovic, 'The median-voter hypothesis, income inequality, and income redistribution: an empirical test with the required data', *European Journal of Political Economy*, 16, 2000, pp 367–410; L Kenworthy & J Pontusson, 'Rising inequality and the politics of redistribution in affluent countries', *Perspectives on Politics*, 3(3), 2005, pp 449–471; and T Besley, *Principled Agents? The Political Economy of Good Government*, Oxford: Oxford University Press, 2007.

31. See, for example, P Krugman, *The Conscience of a Liberal*, New York: WW Norton, 2007; T Frank, *The Wrecking Crew: How Conservatives Rule*, New York: Metropolitan Books, 2008; and L Bartels, *Unequal Democracy: The Political Economy of the New Gilded Age*, Princeton, NJ: Princeton University Press, 2008.

Yotam Margalit

LOST IN GLOBALIZATION
International Economic Integration and the Sources of Popular Discontent

The liberalization of national economies and their opening up to international trade in recent decades have produced substantial gains for many, but have also generated deep discontent among many others (Rodrik 1997; Stiglitz 2002). Politicians in various countries have taken note of this discontentment and routinely attempt to seize upon it to shore up political support: condemnations of job losses due to offshoring, attacks on the unfair practices of foreign trading partners, and calls for protectionist trade policies can all be seen in this light. Notably, this phenomenon is not limited to a specific country or region. Anti-openness appeals are often embraced by a wide array of political parties and candidates, ranging from the recent wave of leftist populists in Latin America, through postcommunist parties in Eastern Europe, to the far right in Western Europe.[1] Yet despite the fact that disaffection with economic globalization is a politically salient issue, not much is known about the constituencies that feel harmed by economic openness.[2] What characterizes the individuals that view themselves as losing out from their country's integration into the global economy? What specific aspects of economic openness cause them to view it as harmful?

Popular opposition to economic globalization has commonly been attributed to its impact on people's earning capacity. Much of the scholarly focus has thus been on exploring the association

between individuals' labor market standing, measured either by their sector of employment or by the factor of production they own (for example, skill level), and their attitudes on trade liberalization. Yet while arguments based on changes in the labor market offer some important insights into people's attitudes toward economic openness, the explanatory power of these arguments has been shown to be quite limited. First, analyses of survey data find only a weak association between the exposure of people's employment sector to foreign competition and their attitudes on trade policy (for example, Scheve and Slaughter 2001). Furthermore, survey data consistently reveals a pattern that is at odds also with the second, factor-based explanation, Whereas the classic Stolper-Samuelson theorem suggests that lower-skilled individuals should be more (less) opposed to trade openness than skilled individuals in advanced (developing) economies, cross-national data show that less-educated (and presumably lower-skilled) individuals are consistently more opposed to trade openness than their higher-educated counterparts, regardless of their country's relative factor endowment and position in the global economy (for example, Baker 2003; Beaulieu, Bennaroch, and Gaisford 2004). This "education puzzle" suggests that an explanation based on a factor-based model is insufficient by itself for explaining variation in mass attitudes on trade openness.[3]

In examining similar survey data on individual attitudes, various scholars also point to the correlation between opposition to trade openness and

From *International Studies Quarterly* 56, no. 3 (Sept. 2012), 484–500.

nationalist-chauvinist attitudes (O'Rourke and Sinnott 2001; Mayda and Rodrik 2005) or ethnocentrism (Mansfield and Mutz 2009). These studies advance the debate by suggesting that attitudes on trade openness may be influenced also by non-economic concerns. However, these observational studies do not deal with the crucial question of whether there is a causal link between non-economic sentiments and attitudes on trade openness, nor do those studies attempt to explore the direction in which causality runs. It could be, for example, that the adverse material effects of openness to international trade underlie *both* the opposition to trade liberalization and the emergence of chauvinist-nationalist views, rather than the latter causing the former. Yet if non-economic sentiments are not a cause of support for trade protectionism, then the correlation these scholars find is irrelevant for explaining the sources of popular opposition to trade openness. Without a theoretical account to explain this empirical association between non-economic sentiments and views on trade openness, as well as a research design that can test for a causal relationship, the nature of this association remains an unresolved question.

This paper builds on and extends the literature by putting forward and testing an argument about the sources of people's perception that international economic integration is harmful. I contend that many individuals fear not only the oft-cited material consequences of trade liberalization, but also what they perceive to be its social and cultural consequences. They view the material effects of trade liberalization as part of a broader "package" of openness, which also includes processes such as growing exposure to foreign influences, westernization, and shifting moral codes. Anxiety about this broader set of changes that people intuitively perceive as byproducts of economic openness underlies some of the opposition to trade liberalization. Furthermore, I argue that anxiety about the perceived social and cultural consequences of

economic integration helps explain why less-educated individuals are consistently more opposed to economic integration than those more educated, even in countries where a factor-based model would predict otherwise.

I use data from two cross-national surveys and an experiment to test this "openness package" argument. The cross-national data reveal a strong empirical relationship between people's views about social-cultural aspects of openness and their views about the impact of international trade. The survey experiment, designed to illuminate the causal nature of this relationship, demonstrates that a heightening of cultural concerns intensifies people's view of trade liberalization as harmful. Importantly, this effect is found to be strong only among less-educated individuals, a finding that helps account for the "education puzzle" noted above. I also test other mechanisms for explaining people's perceptions of being harmed by economic integration, such as labor market effects and concerns about *relative* economic change. The analysis shows that even when accounting for the effect of these alternative mechanisms, social-cultural factors have major explanatory power.

In sum, this article makes three contributions. First, it develops an argument and presents data about the important role of the perceived social-cultural consequences of openness as a source of popular discontentment with international economic integration. The empirical analysis compares the explanatory strength of the argument to a broad set of alternative explanations, including some that have not been explored before. Second, the article presents experimental results that offer the first evidence of a causal link between cultural concerns and opposition to trade liberalization. Finally, the article goes some way toward resolving a key empirical puzzle in the literature, namely the finding that less-educated individuals are more trade protectionist than highly educated members of their country, regardless of their country's relative position in the global economy.

The rest of the paper proceeds as follows. Next, I review the main insights in the literature regarding the winners and losers from trade openness. I then discuss the limitations of existing approaches and lay out the paper's argument. The subsequent sections present the results of the analysis of observational cross-national data, followed by experimental evidence from the U.S. The final section outlines the argument's broader implications and concludes.

Sources of Opposition to Economic Globalization

Interest in understanding of the underpinnings of mass attitudes toward economic globalization has spawned a substantial literature on the determinants of individual preferences on trade policy. The literature has focused primarily on the distributive consequences of trade as the source of those preferences. According to the classic Heckscher-Ohlin (H-O) model and the Stolper-Samuelson theorem built on it, trade brings a country to export goods whose production is intensive in its abundant factor while importing goods that are intensive in their relatively scarce factor. This logic implies that the losers from trade openness are the unskilled laborers in skill-abundant countries and the skilled laborers in skill-scarce countries.[4] Indeed, several studies have found evidence that among more skilled individuals (typically measured by their level of education), support for free trade is lower in economies that are relatively skill-scarce than in economies that are skill-abundant (for example, Beaulieu et al. 2004; Baker 2005). However, as noted earlier, these studies also find that even in the skill-scarce countries, less-educated individuals are substantially more opposed to trade openness than the higher educated individuals.[5] For example, in a study of 15 skill-scarce Latin American economies, Beaulieu et al. (2004) find that educated individuals are more supportive of trade than the less educated in *all* 15 countries.[6] This finding poses a challenge to the central prediction of the H-O model and has led scholars to suggest that education, perhaps through the content of the curricula, has an independent effect on the way people assess the benefits of open markets (Hainmueller and Hiscox 2006).

Others have posited that due to the immobility of certain factors of production, the key cleavage along which support and opposition to trade lies in the short ran is the industry in which individuals are employed. This specific factors approach, often referred to as the Ricardo–Viner (R–V) model, suggests that the losers from trade openness are first and foremost those working in import-sensitive industries (Magee 1978; Irwin 1996). While certainly a plausible explanation, empirical analyses find that industry affiliation is an inconsistent or weak predictor of individual attitudes on trade (for example, Scheve and Slaughter 2001; Hays, Ehrlich, and Peinhardt 2005; Mansfield and Mutz 2009).

Material-based discontentment with economic openness could also be the result of subjective notions about one's *relative* economic standing in society, a mechanism explored in the "economics of happiness" literature (for example, Blanchflower and Oswald 1999; Easterlin 2001). Indeed, individuals living in recently liberalized developing economies often perceive their personal situation to be worse off than in the pre-liberalization period, despite experiencing real income gains following the transition (Graham and Pettinato 2002). The key explanation the authors offer for this apparent dissonance is that those dissatisfied individuals are comparing themselves to others in society who have fared better than they have, leading to what the authors describe as the "frustrated achievers" phenomenon. In the context of this paper, the argument suggests that opposition to trade openness may be driven by discontentment about changes in one's relative standing in society, rather than by losses in absolute terms.

Other analyses of trade attitudes also incorporate controls that proxy for non-economic sentiments

(O'Rourke and Sinnott 2001; Mayda and Rodrik 2005; Mansfield and Mutz 2009). These studies find a strong association between individuals' views on trade openness and nationalist-chauvinist or ethnocentric inclinations.[7] These associations hold even when controlling for a range of other individual-level characteristics. Yet as noted, the nature of the correlation between ideological factors and people's preferences on trade policy is ambiguous for a number of reasons. First, it could be that the correlation is spurious and does not represent any causal link in people's minds. Second, it could also be that the adverse economic effects of international trade underlie both people's nationalist views and their opposition to trade openness, rather than the former causing the latter. Given that trade openness tends to be beneficial for countries at the aggregate (that is, national) level, it is not a priori obvious why holders of nationalist sentiments should oppose trade openness.[8] In other words, to make the claim that non-economic concerns are shaping attitudes on trade openness (in this case, nationalism–chauvinism causing protectionist sentiments), both a clearer theoretical elaboration of this association is needed and an empirical strategy to test it. This is the task to which I now turn.

The Openness "Package"

International economic integration is a unique economic phenomenon in that it has not only material effects but also wide-reaching cultural and social consequences. Increases in trade (particularly of cultural goods and services), migration of labor, foreign direct investment, and the growing presence of foreign multinationals are all changes that have unambiguous social and cultural aspects. Indeed, much of the voluminous literature on globalization is dedicated to analyzing these non-economic aspects, emphasizing a range of processes that globalization brings about. These include the growing exposure to foreign influences and changing domestic value orientations (for example, Giddens 2000; Inglehart 2000), a shift from a collectivist toward a more individualistic society (Beck 1992; Triandis 1995), and growing Western and American economic and cultural dominance (Ritzer 2000; Beck 2006).

Yet despite the recognition that global integration is a multidimensional phenomenon with significant social and cultural consequences, the debate over the determinants of popular support for openness to trade has predominantly centered on the economic dimension, focusing on the impact of trade liberalization on people's labor market standing and consumption opportunities. The key question is whether this view is justified: In forming attitudes about the impact of trade openness on their well-being, do individuals disentangle the broad and complex effects of "openness" and separately assess the material effects of trade?

I argue that many individuals do not. Instead, they perceive international trade as having the oft-cited economic impacts, but also associate it with substantial social and cultural consequences. People view the material effects of trade as only one component of a broader "package" of openness that includes processes such as those discussed in the literature mentioned above, be it the increasing exposure to foreign influences, a shift towards a less traditionalist society, or growing American cultural dominance. I conjecture that people's deep apprehension about these social-cultural processes translates also into a negative view of the broader openness "package," accounting for some of the discontentment with trade liberalization and economic integration more broadly.[9]

An Illustrative Example

It is probably safe to say that individuals do not perceive *all* economic phenomena to have significant social and cultural implications. To illustrate why economic integration is different in this respect, let us briefly consider the case of trade in cultural goods and services, which nicely illustrates some of the characteristics of the social-cultural dimension on which my argument rests.[10]

Since 1980, the size of the cultural and creative industries has grown almost threefold and in 2002 accounted for more than 7% of the world's GDP.[11] Between the years 1994–2002, the period covered by the latest UNESCO report, absolute *levels* of exports and imports in cultural goods were highest in the advanced economies, but *growth* in the imports of cultural goods was fastest in the low-income and lower-middle-income economies, increasing at an astounding average annual rate of 26.7% and 12.4%, respectively.[12]

Overall, the United States has been the largest exporter of cultural goods and services combined,[13] dominating the export markets for core cultural goods both to developing and to advanced economies.[14] For example, a country like Brazil imports approximately 30% of its cultural goods from the United States while it imports only 14% from all other Latin American countries combined.[15] Similarly, in 2003, South Africa imported only a fraction of its core cultural goods from other African countries, while the United States and the United Kingdom alone accounted for half its imports.

Importantly, American dominance can be seen also in its trading relations with other *advanced* economies. Exports of American films, for example, have grown from representing 35% of box office revenue in continental Europe in the mid-1960s to above 80% by 2000.[16] And in the broadcasting content domain, the EU countries sustained a trade deficit with the United States that was almost 15 times the value of their exports to North America.[17] Notably, these imbalances have taken place despite European legislation explicitly designed to protect local cultural production.

This example of trade in cultural goods and services suggests that individuals may associate trade liberalization with more than "just" its distributive consequences.[18] This expectation indeed finds grounding in a growing body of public opinion research which shows that people's attitudes on a range of phenomena associated with international integration fuse both economic and social-cultural concerns. For example, various studies offer evidence that attitudes toward immigrants and immigration policy are largely driven by individuals' cultural values and beliefs, not just by fears about the fiscal or labor market consequences of immigration (Citrin, Green, Muste, and Wong 1997; Sniderman, Hagendoorn, and Prior 2004; Hainmueller and Hiscox 2007, 2010). Similarly, in examining support and opposition to EU integration, several studies find that people's stances are better accounted for by measures of cultural anxieties than by demographic or occupational characteristics (De Master and Le Roy 2000; McLaren 2002). These studies support the notion that non-economic concerns are important factors in shaping people's view of economic integration as harmful.

Empirical Implications

People's views on the impact of their country opening up economically represent considerations on a number of dimensions, be it the impact of economic openness on the availability and the variety of products on the shelves, the quality of available jobs, or the changing price levels of goods. The social-cultural consequences that my argument emphasizes are also important outcomes that people associate with international economic integration but certainly not the only ones. It is thus likely that attitudes on economic integration vary temporally as a function of how salient each of these different dimensions of openness is in people's minds at a given point of time: In periods when the negative social-cultural aspects of openness are made more salient (for example, due to controversies in the news or public statements by politicians), apprehension about economic integration is likely to increase.[19]

Yet the degree to which concerns along the various dimensions shape the public's views on economic integration is likely to vary not only as a function of the relative *salience* of each dimension at a given moment in time, but also as a function of the prevalence of each set of concerns across different segments of society. One key source of variation in people's degree of concern with the cultural dimension of openness is likely to be their level of education, since multiple studies find a strong negative association between educational attainment and measures of out-group bias and intolerance of other cultures (for example, Bobo and Licari 1989; Coenders and Scheepers 2003). Less-educated individuals are also found to exhibit stronger feelings of in-group superiority along lines of ethnicity, race, or nation (Wagner and Zick 1995). Scholars attribute such findings not only to cognitive and personal development, but also to the role of education in exposing individuals to foreign cultures and by creating more cosmopolitan social networks (Vogt 1997; Chandler and Tsai 2001). These findings thus suggest that the argument advanced here could also, at least partially, account for the "education puzzle" described earlier: If one were to find that cultural concerns about openness are not only more prevalent among individuals with a lower level of education, but are also causally related to a negative view of international economic openness, this would help explain the consistent empirical association observed between lower education and greater opposition to trade liberalization.

In sum, the argument developed here has three key observable implications, which can be specified as distinct hypotheses:

Hypothesis 1: *Individuals apprehensive about social and cultural openness are more likely to view trade liberalization as harmful, controlling for other socioeconomic characteristics.*

If this relationship between social-cultural anxieties and attitudes on trade openness is causally interlinked (and not merely a correlation), opposition to trade liberalization should be greater when the social-cultural threat is more salient. This implies that:

Hypothesis 2: *An increase in the salience of negative social-cultural issues associated with openness should lead to greater hostility toward free trade.*

And finally, as noted earlier, if social-cultural concerns about openness are more prevalent among less-educated individuals, the implication would be that:

Hypothesis 3: *An increase in the salience of social-cultural processes associated with openness should have, on average, a greater negative effect on the way less-educated individuals perceive the impact of trade liberalization than on the views of highly educated individuals.*

In the empirical sections that follow, I present tests for each of the three propositions.

Data and Empirical Approach

The data discussed in this section and used in the subsequent analysis are based on the *Pew Global Attitudes Project*, a data set comprised of 40 national surveys carried out in five continents in 2002 (Pew 2003).[20] In the online appendix, I present the results of an additional analysis that relies on a different cross-national data set, the *International Social Survey Program* (ISSP) from 2003. By testing the implications of the theory on two different data sets, one can draw greater confidence that the findings are not driven by artifacts in the design of a specific survey such as ordering effects or question framing.[21]

The Pew survey is well suited for this research since it includes questions on both economic and cultural aspects of globalization. Having both sets of questions is crucial for testing the paper's argument. The dependent variable used in the analysis is based on respondents' answers to the following question (henceforth referred to as the "main question"):

Now thinking about you and your family—do you think the growing trade and business ties between our country and other countries are very good, somewhat good, somewhat bad, or very bad for you and your family?

I categorize the self-perceived *Losers* as those respondents who answered the main question as either "somewhat bad" or "very bad"; conversely, *Gainers* are those who answered "somewhat good" or "very good."

To test the argument that people's sense of personal harm from economic integration is driven in part by apprehension about the social-cultural changes they associate with openness, I use factor analysis to construct a measure of cultural threat based on responses to a set of seven survey items listed in Table 9.2. These items deal with some of the most common non-economic issues mentioned in the context of international integration: exposure to foreign influences, the spread of American ideas, changes to the traditional way of life, and the import of cultural goods ("foreign TV and movies"). A principle factor analysis shows the seven survey items load on a single dimension.[22] I then construct the *cultural threat* variable as a weighted sum of the responses to the seven items and standardize it with a mean of zero and a standard deviation of one.[23] Table 9.2 reports the scoring coefficient weights of each item used in constructing the *cultural threat* measure.

The survey items capture a somewhat narrow aspect of the range of issues associated with globalization and ignore other relevant issues, in particular people's attitudes on immigration. While the issue of immigration is an important and ubiquitous aspect in the globalization debate, I intentionally exclude direct questions about immigration

Table 9.2. Factor Analysis of Items Dealing With Cultural and Social Change

SURVEY ITEM	WEIGHT
Our traditional way of life is getting lost (/remains strong)	0.072
Our way of life needs to be protected against foreign influence	0.044
Having the opportunity to watch movies and TV and listen to music from different parts of the world is a good (/bad) thing	0.159
I like (/I do not like) the pace of modern life	0.111
Consumerism and Commercialism are a threat (/not a threat) to our culture	0.095
It's good (/bad) that American ideas and customs are spreading here	0.214
I like (/dislike) American music, movies, and television	0.307

Source: Author's calculations using data from PEW Global Altitudes Survey (2003).

since the responses to these questions may be interpreted as representing economic concerns about labor market threat rather than individuals' views on social and cultural issues (Mayda 2006; Malhotra, Margalit, and Mo 2010). By limiting the constructed factor to these seven items that focus more directly on cultural aspects of openness, the analysis provides a clearer and more exacting test of the paper's argument.[24]

To test the hypothesis derived from the Heckscher-Ohlin model (henceforth H–O), I use educational attainment as a proxy for respondents' skill level.[25] The factor endowment argument holds that an individual that completed their high school education in a skill-scarce country, such as Bolivia, has a very different standing in the local labor market than a high school graduate in a skill-abundant country, such as Germany. To account for the differential effect of skill on people's attitudes as a function of their standing in the labor market, I again follow the standard approach in the literature and include an interaction term of individual skill and the country's skill endowment. Measurement of a country's skill endowment is problematic due to lack of comparable cross-national data. I therefore use the natural log of a country's per capita GDP as a proxy for a country's skill abundance. The interaction term of skill and skill abundance is represented with the $Education \times GDP$ per capita variable.[26] In addition, as another set of controls, I include in the model a set of dummy variables for respondents' employment status. The categories include full-time employees, part-time employees, self-employed, pensioners, and individuals not in the labor market (for example, homemakers).

As an additional measure for testing the role of labor market concerns as the source of attitudes on economic integration, I also generate a variable based on people's *subjective view* of change in the labor market over the past 5 years, and whether they attribute the change to globalization or not. The variable is constructed from two questions:

First, the survey asked whether the "availability of good paying jobs" has changed over the past 5 years for better, worse, or not at all. The follow-up question asked whether they attribute this change "largely to the world becoming more connected" or "mostly to other reasons." I use the responses to the two questions to generate a variable that ranges from one (job situation improved, largely because of globalization) to seven (job situation worsened, largely because of globalization).[27]

To assess the empirical strength of the hypothesis that people's *relative* position in society affects their subjective perceptions of gain and loss, one would ideally need a good panel data set that tracks changes in people's economic well-being as well as their attitudes on economic globalization over time. Since such measures are not available, I examine the explanatory power of two different indicators that proxy for relative position. The first is centered on earnings, comparing whether an absolute measure of real income or a measure of relative income is a stronger predictor of perceived loss from economic openness. Since a $30,000 annual household income places an individual in the third income quintile in a country like Germany, but in the top income quintile in a country like India, the question of interest is whether, when pooling observations from all countries together, attitudes on trade openness are better predicted by one's absolute income or measures of relative income.

The variable *Income* denotes the absolute household earning of each respondent. To control for differences across countries in the cost of living, I convert the reported incomes from the local currency into US dollars at the date of the survey, standardize the incomes as annual earnings, and adjust for purchasing power parity. The income figure is then logged. I also calculate the *Relative Income* variable as the income quintile into which the respondent falls within their own country.

A second test of the logic of relative change is based on a measure of respondents' self-reported level of well-being. Respondents were asked to rate both their current situation and their situation 5 years ago on a 10-step "ladder of life" ranging from 1 to 10 (from the worst to the best "possible life for you"). I use these two measures to generate two different variables: *Current State* denotes the answer to the question about the respondent's current standing; the variable *5-year Change* is calculated by subtracting the current well-being from the (retrospective) well-being reported for 5 years ago. These two measures enable us to test whether (i) the self-perceived losers from economic globalization are simply "gripers," that is, individuals who are unhappy about life in general and (ii) whether a sense of relative change in well-being is associated with perceived harm from trade openness.

In addition to the variables described above, I control for gender, since women are consistently found to be more apprehensive about free trade, possibly due to child-rearing considerations that affect their prospects in the labor market (Burgoon and Hiscox 2003). Finally, I also control for respondents' age, since older people may find it more difficult to adjust to new skill requirements in the labor market and thus view economic integration as more detrimental.

Results

In order to examine the sources of people's perception of being harmed by economic globalization, it is useful to begin by examining the variation in such perceptions across countries with different levels of economic openness and development. Figure 9.14 provides a rough indication of the variation in the size of the group of self-perceived losers in a range of countries. The size of the group varies significantly across the different countries, as less than six percent of the respondents in the United Kingdom, but close to 20% in Bolivia, believe that economic openness is harmful to their families.[28]

Figure 9.14. Self-Perceived Losers from International Economic Integration, by Country

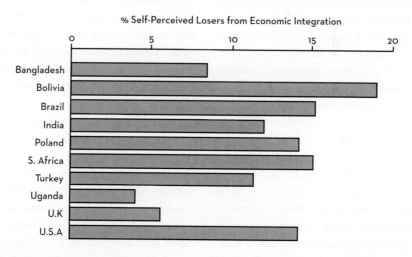

Note: Self-perceived "losers" are defined as those that described the effect of growing trade and business ties with other countries as "somewhat bad" or "very bad" for their families.

Source: PEW Global Attitudes Project, 2003

Figure 9.15. Cultural Threat Perceptions, by Education and Views on Economic Integration

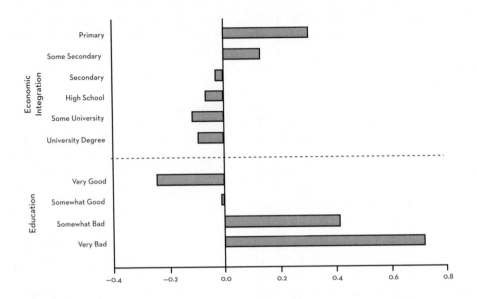

Note: In both charts, the mean level of cultural threat is measured along the x-axis. The groupings in the bottom panel of the chart (that is, below the dotted line) are based on respondents' perception of how economic openness integrate their family. Respondents in the upper panel are grouped by level of education.

An intuitive explanation for this variation might be the varying types of shocks that different economies have undergone as a result of integration into world markets: Countries more exposed to trade and capital flows may have experienced deeper changes and therefore may have a larger constituency of self-perceived losers. The data, however, do not support this conjecture. The correlation between trade openness and perceptions of the effect of economic integration is low ($r=.07$).[29] Similarly, the correlation between a country's GDP and respondents' attitudes is also low ($r=.1$). There seems to be a limited empirical relationship between macroeconomic indicators of development or trade openness and the extent of perceived gains or losses from economic integration. This leaves the open question of what *does* account for the observed variation in people's perceptions, and what are the characteristics of the self-perceived losers?

To address these questions, I proceed by examining the relationship between cultural concerns and the sense of being harmed by international economic integration. The lower panel in Figure 9.15 compares the mean levels of the *cultural threat* measure among groups that differ with respect to how they perceive the impact of economic integration on their families. As the figure demonstrates, cultural threat is much greater among those that view economic integration as harmful than among those that view it as beneficial. Moreover, since the measure of cultural threat is standardized, one can see that the rate of cultural threat is below average among those who feel that they are gaining from economic integration, but above average among the self-perceived losers. In fact, among those who feel most harmed by economic integration, the average rate of cultural threat is within the top

Table 9.3. Predictors of Perceived Loss from International Economic Integration

	(1)	(2)	(3)	(4)	(5)
Education	-0.013 (0.002)**	-0.013 (0.002)**	-0.010 (0.002)**	0.035 (0.016)*	0.037 (0.016)*
Cultural Threat			0.058 (0.003)**	0.057 (0.003)**	0.057 (0.003)**
Real Income (USD, ppp)	-0.013 (0.003)**	-0.012 (0.003)**	-0.009 (0.003)**	-0.007 (0.003)**	-0.007 (0.003)**
Age	0.0007 (0.0002)**	0.0006 (0.0002)**	-0.0002 (0.0002)	-0.0003 (0.0002)	-0.0003 (0.0002)
Female	0.003 (0.005)	0.003 (0.005)	0 (0.005)	0.002 (0.005)	0.002 (0.005)
Part-time Employee	0.020 (0.011)†	0.022 (0.011)*	0.020 (0.01)†	0.020 (0.01)†	0.019 (0.01)†
Pensioner	0.024 (0.012)*	0.025 (0.012)*	0.014 (0.011)	0.012 (0.011)	0.012 (0.011)
Self-employed	-0.008 (0.008)	-0.008 (0.008)	-0.009 (0.007)	-0.008 (0.007)	-0.009 (0.007)
Unemployed	0.014 (0.011)	0.012 (0.011)	0.011 (0.01)	0.007 (0.01)	0.008 (0.01)
Not in Labor Force	0.015 (0.007)*	0.017 (0.007)*	0.015 (0.007)*	0.015 (0.007)*	0.015 (0.007)*
Job Situation		0.011 (0.001)**	0.008 (0.001)**	0.008 (0.001)**	0.008 (0.001)**
Edu × GDPpc(logged)				-0.005 (0.002)**	-0.005 (0.002)**
Current State				-0.005 (0.001)**	-0.005 (0.001)**
Five-year Change				0.0003 (0.001)	0.0005 (0.001)
Relative Income					-0.007 (0.002)**
Pseudo Log-likelihood	-7993.13	-7911.56	-7568.47	-7548.5	-7543.03
Pseudo R^2	.13	.136	.173	.175	.176
N	23,797	23,705	23,705	23,705	23,705

Notes: The coefficients of the probit analysis are estimated marginal effects ($\partial F/\partial x k$), that is, the marginal effect on $Pr(y=1)$ given a unit increase in the value of the relevant (continuous) regressor (xk), holding all other regressors at their respective sample means. Each model includes a full set of country dummies (coefficients not reported).
† Significant at 10%; * Significant at 5%; ** Significant at 1%.

quartile of the distribution on the *cultural threat* variable. The differences between each of the four groups are highly significant in statistical terms ($p < .01$).

The upper panel of Figure 9.15 examines the mean rates of cultural threat among groups with different education levels. Again, a clear pattern emerges whereby cultural anxieties are much greater among less-educated individuals. As noted, this pattern is consistent with a large literature that documents the relationship between education level and cultural attitudes.

Next, we introduce additional controls into the analysis. Table 9.3 presents the results of the multivariate regression estimates in which the dependent variable is a binary measure based on the Main Question that takes the value "1" if the respondent perceives their family to be harmed by economic integration and zero otherwise. For ease of interpretation, the reported results are the estimated marginal effects.[30] Column (1) shows that self-perceived loss is associated with lower levels of education, lower income, older age, unemployment, not participating in the labor market, or being employed in a part-time job. Women are also more likely to view themselves as worse off from trade openness, though the effect is not well specified.

The results also indicate that *cultural threat* is strongly associated with self-perceived loss: The magnitude of the effect is large and statistically significant under all the different specifications. As columns (3–5) demonstrate, individuals that are more anxious about social-cultural changes are much more likely to believe that economic integration is making them worse off. Also notable is the fact that inclusion of the *cultural threat* measure in the model consistently decreases the magnitude of the *education* variable, reduces the significance of the *pensioner* variable, and reverses the sign associated with *age*. These changes suggest that at least some of the negative attitudes among less-educated and older individuals toward trade openness can be accounted for by concerns regarding social and cultural change.

Holding all variables in column (4) at their means, a change from a respondent being culturally "secure" (associated with responses in the bottom 10th percentile on the *cultural threat* variable) to one that is culturally threatened (at the 90th percentile level) increases the likelihood of the respondent perceiving herself as worse off from economic integration almost fivefold (from 4.3% to 20.4%). Holding all other variables at their means, a positive change of one standard deviation in the *cultural threat* measure increases the likelihood of the respondent perceiving trade as having an adverse effect by six percentage points. In comparison, a downward change of one standard deviation in the income variable increases the same probability by slightly less than a single percentage point. In other words, the association between cultural threat and views on international trade is substantial both in an absolute and a relative sense.[31]

How well does the cultural threat argument perform compared to the other explanations? Hypotheses centered on the labor market as the source of attitudes on trade policy receive mixed results. On the one hand, and as noted above, some of the variables pertaining to people's labor market standing are indeed associated with people's attitudes (in particular, part-time employment and not being in the labor market). Moreover, *Job Situation*, the subjective measure of people's perceptions of globalization's impact on the labor market, is significant in all specifications. An individual who thinks that globalization has had a detrimental effect on the overall availability of well-paying jobs is substantially more likely to hold negative views about the impact of economic integration on their own well-being than someone who thinks that globalization has improved the offerings in the labor market (11.8% versus 7.1%).

Furthermore, the findings are consistent with the expectation of the H–O logic, as the sign on the coefficient for the interaction term *Education × GDP* per capita is negative and statistically significant (column 4). This relationship implies that for a given level of skill (as measured by educational attainment), a respondent in a skill-abundant country is less likely to view herself as worse off from trade openness than someone with an equivalent skill in a skill-scarce country. Conversely, unskilled laborers are less likely to view economic integration favorably in economies that are more skill abundant.[32]

However, even when accounting for this cross-national pattern, individuals with lower levels of education are more disposed to feel harmed by economic integration than their highly educated counterparts irrespective of the country's position in the global economy. This is the case when restricting the analysis to the more advanced economies (those with per capita GDP over $15,000) or to the least developed ones (those with per capita GDP below $2,000): In both settings, the coefficient associated with education is negative. These findings mirror the results of previous studies that have documented this education effect and point to the limits of using the H_2O model to explain people's views on trade openness.[33] Notably, the results hold in a range of robustness tests, including estimations that use unweighted data, exclude imputed observations, or use an altogether different data set.[34]

Next, I test the hypothesis that people's relative standing in the labor market is a key factor in explaining attitudes on trade openness. Table 9.3 compares the explanatory strength of measures of respondents' absolute and relative income. Column (4) uses the log of respondents' absolute income in US dollars (adjusted for purchasing power parity), and column (5) replaces this measure with the income quintile of the respondent. As the table shows, the overall fit of the models using either of the measures is almost identical, suggesting that neither of the measures has substantially stronger explanatory power. In substantive terms, holding all other variables at their means, a change from being located at the top income quintile to the bottom income quintile is associated with a three-percentage point increase in the likelihood of a respondent perceiving economic globalization as harmful to their family's well-being.

A second measure of relative change is constructed by differencing respondents' reported subjective well-being at the present time with the same assessment of their well-being 5 years earlier. Although the results show a negative correlation between people's sense of well-being and their propensity to view economic integration as harmful, there does not seem to be a significant relationship between the perceived *change* in people's standing (from 5 years ago) and self-perceived loss from economic integration. The estimated effect of *5-year change* is miniscule, and the standard error is large. In sum, the two tests of the importance of relative standing, both across subjects (in terms of income) and within subjects (in terms of changes in an individual's well-being over time) do not indicate that concerns about relative standing are a major factor explaining negative views of economic integration.

Notably, the set of findings presented in Table 9.3 and discussed above are not driven by a specific country or geographical region. Table 9.4 presents results from two separate estimations for different geographic regions, one estimation with and the other without the *cultural threat* variable. The estimation of both models includes the same control variables used in column (1) of Table 9.3 (coefficients for the controls are not reported). The results make two points evident: First, the effect of the *cultural threat* variable is positive, statistically significant, and substantively large in all geographic regions. Furthermore, in all regions, the model that includes the *cultural threat* predictor is shown to have substantially greater explanatory power than the model without the predictor. In some regions (for example, Western Democracies, Asia), a model that controls for respondents' views on cultural openness explains almost three times more of the variation than the nested model without the *cultural threat* control. Second, the size of the effect associated with education consistently decreases, in some cases quite substantially, once respondents' level of cultural threat is included in the estimation. This suggests that while education has an independent effect on perceptions about the impact of economic globalization—perhaps as a proxy for skill attainment, perhaps by education increasing sophistication about the gains from trade—this effect is smaller once we account for individuals' cultural concerns. In the next section, I present an experiment that further explores this relationship between cultural concerns, education level, and views on economic openness.[35]

Survey Experiment

The analysis of the cross-national data reveals a strong empirical association between people's views on cultural openness and their perceptions of how economic integration affects them. Yet such analysis cannot ascertain whether a causal relationship exists, nor reveal the direction of causality. Establishing whether cultural concerns generate opposition to international trade is meaningful since if the correlation is spurious, or if the causal process, operates only in the reverse direction, then cultural concerns are irrelevant for explaining the opposition to trade openness.

To address this issue, I carried out a randomized survey experiment on a national sample of US respondents. As before, the hypothesis underlying the experiment holds that people's view on the impact of international trade is influenced by their concerns about social and cultural changes that they associate with growing economic openness. If the two are unrelated in people's minds, then a prime that increases the prominence of such social-cultural concerns is expected to have no effect on people's assessments of the impact of international trade. Yet if the cultural prime is found to exert a discernable impact on people's views on trade liberalization, this would suggest that the cultural issues that individuals associate with openness do indeed influence their assessments of international trade.[36]

Such a priming experiment, it should be noted, assumes that people's views on the merits of international trade vary over time as a function of the extent to which they think of, and worry about, the social-cultural aspects of openness in a given period. Otherwise, exposure to primes that make the social-cultural aspects more prominent would have no impact on people's assessment of trade.

By collecting demographic data on the respondents, this experimental design also enables us to examine whether there are systematic differences in the way educated and less-educated individuals respond to the priming of cultural issues. The expectation is that if more of the less-educated individuals are anxious about the social-cultural aspects of openness, then exposure to the cultural prime would have a greater negative impact on their support for trade liberalization than on the highly educated. If such a systematic difference exists, it could provide at least a partial explanation for the "education puzzle" reported earlier.

Finally, to provide another yardstick for assessing the impact of cultural issues on people's thinking about economic integration, I test the effect of another priming treatment that triggers an altogether different set of associations. Since it could be that people view free trade positively (or negatively) because they generally support minimal government intervention, I prompt one treatment group with a "libertarian" prime. In the next section, I describe the design of the experiment, followed by a presentation of the results.

Experimental Design

The survey experiment fielded by the online polling firm YouGov/Polimetrix, Inc., in August 2006 included 1,455 American respondents and was carried out as follows: Respondents were randomly assigned into either a control or one of two treatment groups. The first treatment group was exposed to a "cultural" prime and the other treatment group

Table 9.4. Education, Cultural Threat, and Perceived Loss from International Economic Integration, by Region

	Western Democracies		Eastern Europe		Asia		Middle East & North Africa		Sub-Saharan Africa		Latin America	
	(1)	(2)	(1)	(2)	(1)	(2)	(1)	(2)	(1)	(2)	(1)	(2)
Education	-0.019	-0.017	-0.022	-0.018	-0.010	-0.009	-0.023	-0.021	-0.007	-0.004	-0.013	-0.010
	(0.005)**	(0.004)**	(0.007)**	(0.006)**	(0.005)*	(0.005)*	(0.008)**	(0.008)**	(0.004)†	(0.004)	(0.004)**	(0.004)*
Cultural Threat		0.050		0.072		0.049		0.119		0.042		0.067
		(0.006)**		(0.006)**		(0.007)**		(0.012)**		(0.004)**		(0.006)**
Pseudo R²	.037	.089	.076	.152	.03	.074	.117	.156	.246	.272	.073	.113
N	2,893	2,893	2,580	2,580	5,466	5,466	2,369	2,369	5,932	5,932	4,836	4,836

Notes: The coefficients of the probit analysis are estimated marginal effects (∂F/∂xk), that is, the marginal effect on Pr (y = 1) given a unit increase in the value of the relevant (continuous) regressor (xk), holding all other regressors at their respective sample means. All regressions include country's fixed effects and controls for income, age, gender, part-time employee, pensioner, self-employed, unemployed, and not in labor force (coefficients not reported).

† Significant at 10%; * Significant at 5%; ** Significant at 1%.

to a "libertarian" prime. Participants in each of the groups were asked a set of four initial questions that differed in their content. The cultural prime treatment consisted of a set of questions about social and cultural issues such as their perceptions of changes in Americans' traditional way of life or whether the US anthem should be allowed to be sung in schools in a language other than English. The libertarian treatment consisted of questions relating to respondents' views on the optimal role of government. Finally, respondents in the control group were prompted with a set of "filler" questions about their preferences on outdoor activities.[37] Following this set of initial questions, *all three* groups were asked the exact same question about their view on the impact of economic integration: "Do you think that growing trade and business ties of the United States with other countries have made the average American better or worse off?"[38]

Conducting the experiment with American subjects poses a hard test for the argument, since concerns in other countries about foreign cultural influences are often considered to be at least partially due to apprehension about "Americanization" and a consequent concern about the loss of local traditions. In the United States, a key exporter of culture rather than an importer, concerns regarding cultural exposure are therefore likely to be of smaller magnitude than in most other countries. Results found in the United States may thus be regarded as measuring a lower bound of the phenomenon discussed here.

Experiment Results

The results of the experiment are reported in Figure 9.16. The figure shows that respondents exposed to the cultural prime offered more negative assessments of the impact of economic integration than individuals exposed to the libertarian prime or those in the control group. However, the cultural prime is shown to have had a significant effect only on the attitudes of less-educated respondents (measured here as those with no college education). Following exposure to the cultural prime, less-educated respondents held more negative views on the effect of economic integration than those in the control group. The mean response rate was 3.37 versus 3.0, respectively, a difference of 14% along the five-point rating scale (the difference is significant at the $p < .03$ level).[39] To interpret this difference in more substantive terms, consider the following: While 44% of respondents in the control group described economic integration as harmful, the corresponding figure among those exposed to the cultural prime rose to 54%.[40] Notably, there was no treatment effect among respondents exposed to the libertarian questions; their views were not different from those in the control group. And again, the treatments had no effect on the attitudes of highly educated individuals.

To test whether the results were driven by any other confounding variables for which the random assignment of respondents did not account, I examine the results also in a multivariate regression. Table 9.5 reports the results of the analysis. As before, the dependent variable is respondents' views on the impact of economic integration measured on a five-point scale. Results reported in column (1) confirm that the cultural prime did not have a statistically significant effect on the population at large. However, column (2) shows that exposure to the cultural prime did cause less-educated individuals to assess the impact of economic integration more negatively. The interaction term of education and the cultural prime is negative and highly significant in statistical terms ($p < .05$), in line with H3. Furthermore, as column (3) confirms, these results hold also when controlling for other possible confounding factors.

One interpretation of this finding is that the views on trade liberalization of less-educated individuals were more negatively affected by the cultural prime than the views of the highly educated because apprehension about cultural openness is more prevalent among the less educated. Indeed,

Figure 9.16. Experimental Treatment, Education Level, and Perception of Economic Integration as Harmful

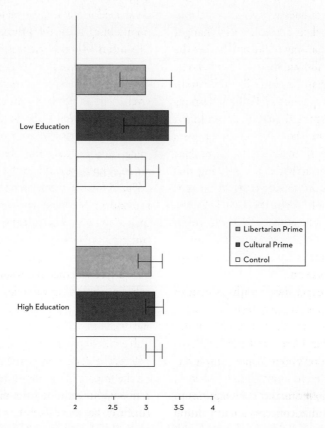

Note: The x-axis denotes the mean response to the question about the perceived Impact of economic integration on the average American. Possible answers: (1) "very good"; (2) "somewhat good"; (3) "neither good nor bad"; (4) "somewhat bad"; (5) "very bad". Each bar represents the mean response of a different treatment group. The difference of means among less-educated individuals between the cultural prime and the control group is highly significant ($p < .003$); differences between other experimental groups are not statistically significant.

this contention is supported by the data, which shows that 51.6% of the less-educated held culturally "protectionist" views on all the questions used to construct the cultural prime, while among highly educated individuals the corresponding figure was only 41.8% (difference significant at $p < .05$). Yet an alternative explanation may be that the effect of the prime on individuals with lower education was stronger not because of their cultural sensitivities but simply because they are more susceptible to priming. This experiment cannot definitively rule

this explanation out; however, it should be noted that the literature on priming offers no evidence to suggest that less-educated individuals are systematically more susceptible to primes (in fact, a number of experimental studies find the opposite relationship).[41] Furthermore, the experiment shows that the less educated were unaffected by the libertarian prime, a finding that indicates that the specific content of the prime (and not simply education level) determines whether or not individuals' responses are affected by the prime.

Table 9.5. Experimental Treatment, Education, and Attitudes on Economic Integration

	(1)	(2)	(3)
Cultural Prime	0.071 (0.062)	0.666 (0.296)**	0.704 (0.296)**
Libertarian Prime	−0.016 (0.077)	0.128 (0.364)	0.106 (0.365)
Education		0.123 (0.1)	0.13 (0.101)
Cultural Prime x Education		−0.328 (0.159)**	−0.351 (0.16)**
Libertarian Prime x Education		−0.08 (0.197)	−0.069 (0.197)
Female			0.225 (0.056)***
Age			0.001 (0.002)
Pseudo R^2	.000	.006	.011
N	1,455	1,455	1,455

Note: Dependent variable is respondents' attitude on the impact of economic integration, ranging from (1) very good to (5) very bad. Standard errors in parentheses. Reported entries obtained from estimating in an ordered probit model.

* Significant at 10%; ** Significant at 5%; *** Significant at 1%.

In sum, the results offer further evidence in support of the hypothesis that concerns about cultural and social change that individuals associate with openness influence their views on international economic integration. Importantly, this link between the economic and cultural aspects of openness is shown to be pronounced among less educated individuals. This result is in line with the finding that educated individuals are on average more positively disposed toward economic integration than less-educated individuals, regardless of the skill abundance of the country in which they live. Hainmueller and Hiscox (2006) documented this pattern and hypothesized that the education effect on support for trade may have to do with greater exposure to economic curricula. The experimental findings presented here suggest that lower-educated individuals may, at least in part, be more apprehensive about economic integration for a different reason, namely that they are more likely to associate economic integration with a set of social and cultural consequences that they view as harmful.[42]

Conclusion

This article argues that people's assessments of the impact of international economic integration are partly shaped by the social and cultural changes that they associate with growing economic openness. Individuals apprehensive about these social-cultural consequences are more disposed to view economic integration as harmful. The analysis demonstrates that the empirical association between social-cultural views and attitudes on economic integration holds across geographical regions, countries that differ in terms of their level of economic development, and different sets of cross-national survey data. Furthermore, the study offers the first test of a causal relationship between attitudes on cultural change and opposition to economic openness, providing further evidence in support of the article's argument. While other explanations proposed in the literature, such as those centered on employment effects (Scheve and Slaughter 2001; Mayda and Rodrik 2005) or on people's concerns about relative economic standing (Graham and Pettinato 2002) are also shown to have explanatory power, the size of the variation accounted for by the measure of social-cultural threat indicates that this is a major factor explaining popular apprehension about international economic integration.

These findings suggest that in thinking about the political manifestations of discontentment with globalization, the anti-openness political "camp" should be seen as encompassing individuals with highly divergent concerns and beliefs. Some oppose economic integration because it exposes them to the risks of lower income, job insecurity, and unemployment. Others, however, oppose economic integration because it is seen as part of a broader process of change that affects some of the things they care most deeply about, be it the values and ideas that their children are exposed to, the traditions respected in their society, or their national and cultural identity. Studying the opposition to trade liberalization and economic globalization more broadly as driven merely by its distributive consequences is therefore a framework that is too narrow and which leaves out much of what is politically significant about the phenomenon in question.

The evidence put forward here contributes to the growing literature on the impact of economic globalization on domestic political competition (for example, Mughan and Lacy 2002; Meunier 2004; Kriesi et al. 2006; Walter 2010; Margalit 2011). It suggests that in studying the electoral repercussions of globalization, future research should examine how political parties use anti-openness messages to appeal to voters' discontentment with international integration. The findings also offer insight as to why political parties with diverse agendas such as the People's Party (SVP) in Switzerland, "Self-defense" in Poland, or Rafael Correa's Alianza PAIS in Ecuador do not only aim their anti-openness message at the labor market effects of economic integration. Instead, they also incorporate traditionalist, nationalist, or even religious appeals that offer a sense of protection on the social-cultural dimensions of economic integration. A promising avenue for future research would be to explore whether this phenomenon is a result of political entrepreneurs exploiting the connection voters are making intuitively between the economic and the social-cultural aspects of openness, or whether the politicians themselves are those making this connection salient to voters.

Finally, the findings presented here also speak to the ongoing debate regarding the policies needed to sustain popular support for open markets. Scholars often note that although international trade can have sharp distributive consequences with clear winners and losers, the *aggregate* gains from trade imply that the surplus can be used to compensate the losers and assuage their opposition to trade liberalization. This is the rationale underlying calls for expanding public funding for active labor market programs that provide wage insurance and retraining services for workers hurt by trade, such as the TAA program in the United States and similar programs in Western Europe (Marcal 2001; Davidson, Matusz, and Nelson 2007). Others cast doubt on the ability of such programs to effectively assuage the losers' discontentment and call instead for a substantial redistribution of income (Scheve and Slaughter 2007). The evidence presented here suggests that while such measures could help alleviate some of the opposition toward economic globalization, they are likely to have only a limited effect; substantial opposition among the constituencies that feel socially and culturally discomfitted by growing openness is likely to remain strong.

NOTES

1. On the Western European case, see Swank and Betz (2003); Kriesi, Grande, Lachat, Dolezal, Bornschier, and Frey (2006). On the effects of globalization on Eastern European politics and the appeal of postcommunist parties, see the edited volume of Bozóki and Ishiyama 2002, particularly chapter 17. See the *Economist*, "The Return of Populism," 12 April 2006, for a discussion of the sources of populist success in Latin America.

2. Throughout the article, I use the terms "economic globalization," "economic integration," and "economic openness" interchangeably.

3. While economic globalization also includes other aspects such as foreign direct investment and capital flows, the empirical section of this paper focuses on people's views on trade openness.

4. In an interesting theoretical elaboration, Baker (2005) argues that the distributive consequences of trade openness on individuals as consumers, not just as laborers, is also consistent with the H-O logic.

5. The one exception is Mayda and Rodrik's finding that in Thailand, a developing economy, less-educated individuals were more pro-trade than educated.

6. The difference between the mean attitudes of the skilled and unskilled was statistically significant in eight of the cases.

7. O'Rourke and Sinnott divide nationalist sentiments into two separate categories: patriotic and chauvinistic sentiments. They define their measure of patriotism as capturing a "preference and sense of superiority of one's own country" and chauvinism as an exclusive sense of nationality of the "my country right or wrong" variety. Both measures are found to be strongly correlated with preferences for trade protectionism. Mayda and Rodrik (2005) use the same survey data and categorize similar survey items under one label as capturing nationalist sentiments.

8. See Krugman and Obstfeld (1994) for a review of the basic theoretical argument why trade openness is welfare enhancing at the aggregate level. See Sachs and Warner (1995) and Wacziarg and Welch (2003) for empirical evidence on the positive relationship between trade liberalization and growth (but also see Rodriguez and Rodrik (2000) for a more skeptical view of the evidence).

9. The argument does not imply that all individuals threatened by the social-cultural aspects of openness necessarily view economic integration as harmful, but suggests that there is a substantial group of individuals for which this is the case. In line with Prospect Theory's notion that losses loom larger than gains (Kahneman and Tversky 1979). It is likely that individuals whom openness has made better off in one dimension (economic or cultural) and worse off in the other will tend to focus on the adverse effect of the openness process. In other words, only a few individuals harmed by economic integration will support it because they approve of its cultural consequences.

10. To be clear, trade in cultural goods does not comprise the sole source of change underlying the perception that globalization has a social-cultural dimension. Nonetheless, this case is a useful illustration of the logic underlying the argument that people perceive economic integration as part of a broader openness "package."

11. UNESCO Institute for Statistics 2005, p. 9.

12. Ibid, p.69, Table 111–3.

13. The US exports $7 billion in cultural good and services; the second largest exporter is the U.K. ($1.5 billion).

14. Core cultural goods are defined as goods with an explicit cultural content.

15. The figures are based on the UN COMtrade DESA/UNSD data, 2004, and reported in UNESCO Institute for Statistics 2005, p. 34.

16. See Putnam (1998, p. 266). See Cowen (2002) for an analysis of this trend (pp. 74–83).

17. Data are based on the ETS/European Audiovisual Observatory, 2002, and reported in UNESCO Institute for Statistics (2005, p. 48).

18. Importantly, the relevant empirical question here is not whether individuals are correct in attributing

these social–cultural consequences to economic integration, but whether or not this is how people perceive the consequences of economic integration.

19. For example, during the debate over the GATT agreement, French Minister of Culture Jacques Toubon described his opposition as a fight for the "survival of [French] culture" and for the French "way of life." ("GATT et culture: Laisser respirer nos âmesl", *Le Monde*, 1 October 1993). Similarly, then-president Francois Mitterrand stated: "What is at issue is the cultural identity of nations, the right of each people to its own culture, the freedom to create and choose one's images. . . . A society that relinquishes to others its means of representation, is an enslaved society" (McMahon 1995).

20. The original data set includes 44 countries. However, in several countries, a set of important questions necessary for the analysis was not asked. The analyses thus exclude Egypt, Vietnam, China, and Uzbekistan. Approximately 91% of the respondents answered the question on the effects of trade openness on themselves and their family. To avoid losing additional observations, missing observations were imputed for several independent variables, most notably education (6.4% of the observations). Substantive results were unchanged when conducting the analyses with and without the imputed observations. See appendix 1 for a complete list of the countries included in the study.

21. To reduce clutter and avoid confusion regarding the measurement of the variables used in the two analyses, I defer the results from the analysis of the ISSP survey to the online appendix.

22. The first (and only) retained dimension has an elgen value of 1.43. The next dimension has an eigen value of 0.37.

23. The weights of each item in constructing the index are obtained using a varlmax-rolated matrix and are provided on the right column of the table. For a test of robustness, I re-ran all the analyses reported in the subsequent sections using a factor analysis after dropping any one of items from the seven-item list. The results are substantively similar indicating that no single survey item is responsible for the obtained

results. I also re-estimated the models after dropping the questions pertaining to US influence, since these may be construed as measuring anti-Americanism rather than a social–cultural concern. Once again, the substantive results all hold, and both the magnitude and the statistical significance of the *cultural threat* variable remain high.

24. The Pew survey also includes two items about immigration: One asking about the perceived influence of immigrants on the "way things are going in [survey country]" (q15) and the other asking respondents to rate the degree to which they view immigration as "a problem" (q35). Inclusion of respondents' answers to these two questions in the factor analysis shows them to load on the same dimension as the other seven items and further strengthens the results reported in Table 9.3. Both the marginal effect associated with this alternative cultural threat measure and the overall fit of the model increase. However, to minimize the possible "contamination" of the cultural threat measure by questions that may be construed as capturing an economic concern, I err on the side of caution and exclude these two questions from the reported analysis.

25. This is a highly imperfect measure, albeit a commonly used one in the literature on trade preferences (for example, Scheve and Slaughter 2001; Mayda and Rodrik 2005).

26. I do not include a separate control for GDP per capita due to the inclusion of country fixed effects.

27. See appendix I for more detail on the coding of the variable.

28. For clarity of presentation, the graph includes only a sample of the countries in the survey.

29. Attitudes on trade at the national level are calculated as the mean score of the respondents to the Main Question (higher values mean greater apprehension about the effects of trade). Trade openness is calculated as the sum of a country's exports and imports as percentage of its GDP. When excluding Kenya and Jordan, two outliers with over 45% of respondents saying trade openness is harmful to them, the correlation between trade openness and attitudes on trade is somewhat higher ($r = .17$).

30. In substantive terms, this measure denotes the marginal effect on the probability of a respondent viewing herself as harmed by economic globalization given a one-unit increase in the value of the predictor variable, while holding all other variables at their sample means. I also estimated a set of ordered probit models using a dependent variable measured along a four-point scale instead of a dichotomous measure. The results remain substantively and statistically very similar.

31. As noted, I also estimated the same specifications using an alternative measure of cultural threat that includes also attitudes on immigration. Re-estimating the benchmark specification in column (4), the marginal effect associated with this alternative measure of *cultural threat* increases to 6.0%, and the overall fit of the model increases from 0.175 to 0.181.

32. I also estimated a logistic mixed-effect hierarchical model that accounts for the inclusion of a country-level variable in the model (GDP per capita). The substantive results are almost unchanged: The interaction of education and country income remains negative ($\beta_{Educ} \times$ GDP $= -0.052$, $p = .004$), and the *cultural threat* variable remains positive and highly significant ($\beta_{cultural\ threat} = 0.62$, $p < .001$).

33. For example, Hainmueller and Hiscox 2006; Beaulieu et al. 2004.

34. See the online appendix for full results of a second set of tests with different cross-national data.

35. Interestingly, the magnitude of the *cultural threat* variable varies across regions and is, for example, almost three times larger in the Middle East and North Africa than in Asia. One of course should *not* interpret this finding as if cultural threat is itself three times larger in the Middle East and North Africa than in Asia but rather that the association between cultural threat and negative attitudes on the impact of economic openness is substantially larger in the former region than in the latter. Explaining this variation as well as identifying the exact sources of people's sense of cultural threat are challenges beyond the scope of this paper, but certainly merit further study.

36. To make the logic underlying this contention clearer, let us consider the hypothesis that one of the factors shaping opposition to immigration is people's perception that immigration leads to higher rates of crime. If people do not associate immigration with crime, then priming individuals with information that makes the issue of crime more salient in people's minds should not affect their attitudes on immigration (assuming that there is no other pathway by which individuals make the connection between crime and immigration). Yet if immigrants are associated in people's minds with crime, then the prime is likely to strengthen respondents' anti-immigrant sentiment.

37. See appendix 2 for the complete question protocol.

38. The five-point scale ranged from (1) "A lot better off" to (5) "A lot worse off." The cross-national survey and the experimental study do not me the exact same question wording: While the Pew survey asked respondents about trade's impact on them personally, the experimental question gauges respondents' views on trade's Impact on the average American. Other research, however, suggests that the results would be similar if the two dependent variable questions were the same. For example, Sears and Funk (1990) find that people typically rely on collective-level information rather than personal experiences in formulating policy views. More pertinently, Mansfield and Mutz (2009) find that people's assessments of trade openness represent socio-tropic considerations, that is, trade views are closely tied to how individuals perceive trade openness to affect the broader population.

39. See Table 9.7 for full results and *t*-statistics.

40. As before, respondents are coded as viewing economic integration as harmful if they describe it as "somewhat bad" or "very bad."

41. For example, see Petty and Wegener 1991; Petty 2001; Schwarz, Bless, and Bohner 1991; Kuo and Margalit forthcoming.

42. Hainmueller and Hiscox (2000) report that including predictors associated with nationalist attachments in an analysis of ISSP data from 1995 had no substantial effect on decreasing the magnitude of the education measure as a predictor of trade attitudes. The actual site of the effect is not reported. The Online Appendix reports a similar test using the ISSP data from a latter wave (2003).

Once a measure of cultural threat is included in the regression, the magnitude associated with the education variable decreases by almost 30%. Note that this change is comparable in size to the effect found when using the Pew Data (columns (2) and (3) In Table 9.3).

REFERENCES

Baker, Andy. (2003) Why Is Trade Reform So Popular in Latin America? A Consumption-Based Theory of Trade Policy Preferences. *World Politics* 55 (3): 423–455.

Baker, Andy. (2005) Who Wants to Globalize? Consumer Tastes and Labor Markets in a Theory of Trade Policy Beliefs. *American Journal of Political Science* 49 (4): 924–938.

Beaulieu, Eugene, Michael Bennaroch, and Jim Gaisford. (2004) *Intra-Industry Trade Liberalization, Wage Inequality and Trade Policy Preferences.* Mimeograph: University of Calgary.

Beck, Ulrich. (1992) *Risk Society: Towards a New Modernity.* London: Sage Publications.

Beck, Ulrich. (2006) *The Cosmopolitan Vision.* Cambridge, UK: Polity.

Blanchflower, David G., and Andrew J. Oswald. (1999) *Well-being, Insecurity and the Decline of American Job Satisfaction.* Working paper, Hanover, NH: Dartmouth College.

Bobo, Lawrence, and Frederick C. Licari. (1989) Education and Political Tolerance: Testing the Effects of Cognitive Sophistication and Target Group Affect. *Public Opinion Quarterly* 53: 285–303.

Bozóki, Andres, and John T. Ishiyama. Eds. (2002) *The Communist Successor Parties of Central and Eastern Europe.* Armonk, NY: M. E. Sharpe.

Burgoon, Brian, and Michael Hiscox. (2003) The Mysterious Case of Female Protectionism: Gender Bias in the Attitudes and Politics of International Trade. Paper Presented at the Annual Meeting of the American Political Science Association, Chicago.

Chandler, Charles R., and Yung-Mei Tsai. (2001) Social Factors Influencing Immigration Attitudes: An Analysis of Data from the General Social Survey. *Social Science Journal* 38 (2): 177–188.

Citrin, Jack, Donald P. Green, Christopher Muste, and Cara Wong. (1997) Public Opinion toward Immigration Reform: The Role of Economic Motivations. *Journal of Politics* 59 (3): 858–881.

Coenders, Marcel, and Peer Scheepers. (2003) The Effect of Education on Nationalism and Ethnic Exclusionism: An International Comparison. *Political Psychology* 24: 313–341.

Cowen, Tyler. (2002) *Creative Destruction.* Princeton, NJ: Princeton University Press.

Davidson, Carl, Steven J. Matusz, and Douglas R. Nelson, (2007) Can Compensation Save Free Trade? *Journal of International Economics* 71 (8): 167–186.

De Master, Sara, and Michael K. Le Roy. (2000) Xenophobia and the European Union. *Comparative Politics* 32 (4): 419–436.

Easterlin, Richard A. (2001) Income and Happiness: Towards a Unified Theory. *The Economic Journal* 111: 465–484.

Giddens, Anthony. (2000) *Runaway World: How Globalization Is Reshaping Our Lives.* New York: Routledge.

Graham, Carol, and Stefano Pettinato. (2002) Frustrated Achievers: Winners, Losers and Subjective Well-Being in New Market Economies. *The Journal of Development Studies* 38 (4): 100–140.

Hainmueller, Jens, and Michael Hiscox. (2006) Learning to Love Globalization: The Effects of Education on Individual Attitudes toward International Trade. *International Organization* 60 (2): 469–498.

Hainmueller, Jens, and Michael Hiscox. (2007) Educated Preferences: Explaining Individual Attitudes toward Immigration in Europe. *International Organization* 61 (2): 399–442.

Hainmueller, Jens, and Michael Hiscox. (2010) Attitude Towards Highly Skilled and Low Skilled Immigration: Evidence from a Survey Experiment. *American Political Science Review* 104 (1): 61–84.

Hays, Jude C., Sean D. Enrlich, and Clint Peinhardt. (2005) Government Spending and Public Support for Trade in the OECD: An Empirical Test of the Embedded Liberalism Thesis. *International Organization* 59: 473–494.

Inglehart, Roland. (2000) Globalization and Postmodern Values. *Washington Quarterly* 23 (1): 215–228.

Irwin, Douglass A. (1996) Industry or Class Cleavages Over Trade Policy? Evidence from the British General Election of 1923. In *The Political Economy of Trade Policy: Papers in Honor of Jagdish Bhagwati*, edited by R. G. Feenstra, G. M. Grossman, and D. A. Irwin. Cambridge, MA: MIT Press.

Kahneman, Daniel, and Amos Tversky. (1979) Prospect Theory—Analysis of Decision Under Risk. *Econometrica* 47 (2): 263–291.

Kriesi, Hanspeter, Edgar Grande, Roman Laghat, Martin Dolezal, Simon Bornschier, and Timotheos Frey. (2006) Globalization and the Transformation of the National Political Space: Six European Countries Compared. *European Journal of Political Research* 45 (6): 921–956.

Krugman, Paul R., and Maurice Obstfeld. (1994) *International Economics,* 3rd edition. New York: Harper-Collins.

Kuo, Alex, and Yotam Margalit. Measuring Individual Identity: An Experimental Approach. *Comparative Politics.* Forthcoming.

Magee, Stephen P. Ed. (1978). *Three Simple Tests of the Stolper-Samuelson Theorem. Issues in International Economics.* London: Oriel.

Malhotra, Neil, Yotam Margalit, and Cecilia H. Mo. (2010) Economic Explanations for Opposition to Immigration: Distinguishing Between Prevalence and Magnitude. Paper presented at the Annual Meeting of the American Political Science Association, Washington, DC, August.

Mansfield, Edward, and Diana Mutz. (2009) Support for Free Trade: Self-Interest, Sociotropic Politics, and Out Group Anxiety. *International Organization* 63 (2): 423–457.

Marcal, Leah E. (2001) Does Trade Adjustment Assistance Help Trade-Displaced Workers? *Contemporary Economic Policy* 19 (1): 59–72.

Margalit, Yotam. (2011) Costly Jobs: Trade-Related Layoffs, Government Compensation and Voting in U.S. Presidential Elections. *American Political Science Review* 105 (1): 166–188.

Mayda, Anna M. (2006) Who Is Against Immigration? A Cross-Country Investigation of Attitudes Towards Immigrants. *Review of Economics and Statistics* 88 (3): 510–530.

Mayda, Anna M., and Dani Rodrik. (2005) Why Are Some People (and Countries) More Protectionist Than Others? *European Economic Review* 49 (6): 1393–1430.

McLaren, Lauren M. (2002) Public Support for the European Union: Cost/Benefit Analysis or Perceived Cultural Threat. *Journal of Politics* 64 (2): 551–566.

McMahon, Darrin. (1995) *Echoes of a Recent Past; Contemporary French Anti-Americanism in Historical and Cultural Perspective.* International Security Studies at Yale University.

Meunier, Sophie. (2004) Globalization and Europe-anization: A Challenge to French Politics. *French Politics* 2: 125–150.

Mughan, Anthony, and Dean Lacy. (2002) Economic Performance, Job Insecurity and Electoral Choice. *British Journal of Political Science* 32: 513–533.

O'Rourke, Kevin H., and Richard Sinnott. (2001) What Determines Attitudes Towards Protection? Some Cross-Country Evidence. Paper read at the Brookings Trade Forum.

Petty, Richard E. (2001) Subtle Influences on Judgment and Behavior: Who Is Most Susceptible? In *Social Influence: Direct and Indirect Processes*, edited by J. Forgas, and K. Williams. Philadelphia, PA: Psychology Press.

Petty, Richard E., and Duane T. Wegener. (1991) Thought Systems, Argument Quality, and Persuasion. In *The Content, Structure, and Operation of Thought Systems*, edited by Robert S. Wyer Jr. and Thomas Srull. Hillsdale, NJ: Lawrence Erlbaum Associates, Inc. Publishers.

Pew Research Center. (2003) The Pew Global Attitudes Project. Available at http://people-press.org/pgap/.

Pottnam, David, with Neil Watson. (1998) *Movies and Money.* New York: Alfred A. Knopf.

Ritzer, George. (2000) *The McDonaldization of Society.* Thousand Oaks, CA: Pine Forge Press.

Rodríguez, Francisco, and Dani Rodrik. (2000) Trade Policy and Economic Growth: A Skeptic's Guide to the

Cross-National Evidence. In *NBER Macroeconomics Annual 2000*, edited by Ben Bernanke and Kenneth Rogoff. Cambridge, MA: MIT Press.

Rodrik, Dani. (1997) *Has Globalization Gone Too Far?* Washington, DC: Institute for International Economics.

Sachs, Jeffrey D., and Andrew Warner. (1995) Economic Reform and the Process of Global Integration. *Brookings Papers on Economic Activity* 1: 1–118.

Scheve, Kenneth F., and Matthew J. Slaughter. (2001) What Determines Individual Trade-Policy Preferences? *Journal of International Economics* 54 (2): 267–292.

Soueve, Kenneth F., and Matthew J. Slaughter. (2007) A New Deal for Globalization. *Foreign Affairs* 86 (4): 34–47.

Schwarz, Norbert, Herbert Bless, and Gerd Bohner. (1991) Mood and Persuasion: Affective States Influence the Processing of Persuasive Communications. In *Advances in Experimental Social Psychology*, edited by M. P. Zanna. San Diego, CA: Academic Press.

Sears, David O., and Carolyn L. Funk. (1990) Self-Interest in Americans' Political Opinions. In *Beyond Self-Interest*, edited by Jane J. Mansbridge. Chicago: University of Chicago Press.

Sniderman, Paul M., Louk Hagendoorn, and Markus Prior. (2004) Predispositional Factors and Situational Triggers: Exclusionary Reactions to Immigrant Minorities. *American Political Science Review* 98: 35–50.

Stiglitz, Joseph E. (2002) *Globalization and its Discontents*, 1st edition. New York: Norton.

Swank, Duane, and Hans-Georg Betz. (2003) Globalization, the Welfare State and Right-Wing Populism in Western Europe. *Socio-Economic Review* 1: 215–245.

Triandis, Harry C. (1995) Individualism & Collectivism. *New Directions in Social Psychology*. Boulder: Westview Press.

UNESCO Institute for Statistics. (2005) International Flows of Selected Goods and Services, 1994–2003: Defining and Capturing the Flows of Global Cultural Trade. Available at hltp://unesdoc.unesco.org/images/0014/001428/142812e.pdf.

Vogt, W. Paul (1997) *Tolerance & Education: Learning to Live with Diversity and Difference.* London: Sage.

Wacziarg, Romain, and Karen Horn Welch. (2008) Trade Liberalization and Growth: New Evidence. *World Bank Economic Review* 22: 187–131.

Wagner, Ulrich, and Andreas Zick. (1995) The Relation of Formal Education to Ethnic Prejudice: Its Reliability, Validity and Explanation. *European Journal of Social Psychology* 25: 41–56.

Walter, Stefanie. (2010) Globalization and the Welfare State: Testing the Microfoundations of the Compensation Hypothesis. *International Studies Quarterly* 54 (2): 403–426.

Appendix 1: Measurement of Control Variables

Education

Variable is coded based on the highest level of education attained by the respondent. The categories are 1. No formal education; 2. Completed primary education; 3. Some secondary education; 4. Completed high school; 5. Some university or college education; and 6. Completed university or college degree.

Income

The variable is coded based on responses to the question: "Here is a list of incomes. Which of these does your household fall into counting all wages, salaries, pensions, and other incomes that come in? Just give the letter of the group your household falls into, before taxes and other deductions." In each country, the responses were a set of ranges. To generate a specific dollar figure, I assigned each of the respondents the middle point within that range (that is, if a respondent earns in the range of $2,500-$3,000 US dollars, the respondent's income was calculated as $2,750). The income of respondents in the bottom income category (between $0 and $X) was calculated as 80% of the upper bound (that is, as 0.8 * $X). The income of the top category, which was often "above X dollars," was calculated as 25% above the category's lower bound (that is, 1.25 * $X).

Job Situation

The variable is coded based on responses to two questions: (i) "Has each of the following gotten better or worse over the last 5 years in our country: The availability of good-paying jobs?" (1. Better; 2. Worse; 3. Has not changed; 4. Don't know) and (ii) "Do you think this change in the availability of good-paying jobs is largely because of the way the world has become more connected or mostly for other reasons?" (1. Largely because world more connected; 2. Mostly other reasons; 3. DK.) The *Job Situation* variable is coded as follows (the first number in the parentheses corresponds to respondents' answer to the first question; the second number to the second question): 1. (1,1); 2. (1,3); 3. (1,2); 4, (3 or 4 in Q1); 5. (3,2); 6. (3,3); 7. (3,1).

Current State

The variable is coded on a 1–10 scale, based on the response to the following question: Here is a ladder representing the "ladder of life." Let's suppose the top of the ladder represents the best possible life for you, and the bottom the worst possible life for you. On which step of the ladder do you feel you personally stand at the present time?

Five-year Change

Deducting *current state* from the response to the follow-up question: On which step would you say you stood 5 years ago?

Countries included in the PEW Global Attitudes survey and covered in the analysis: Angola, Argentina, Bangladesh, Bolivia, Brazil, Bulgaria, Canada, Czech Republic, France, Germany, Ghana, Great Britain, Guatemala, Honduras, India, Indonesia, Italy, Ivory Coast, Japan, Jordan, Kenya, Lebanon, Mali, Mexico, Nigeria, Pakistan, Peru, Philippines, Poland, Russia, Senegal, Slovak Republic, South Africa, South Korea, Tanzania, Turkey, Uganda, Ukraine, Venezuela, and the USA.

Appendix 2: Experimental Treatments

Listed below are the questions used as the opening questions in each experimental treatments. These questions were followed by the dependent variable on the effects of trade and economic openness.

Questions to the Control Group

In a typical week, how often do you do physical exercise (for example, jogging, hiking)?

    1. Five times or more; 2. 3–4 times; 3. 1–2 times; 4. Hardly ever.

Do you like doing outdoor activities (such as hiking, biking, climbing)?

    1. Very much like; 2. Somewhat like; 3. Somewhat dislike; 4. Strongly dislike.

Of the following sporting activities, which do you like best?

    1. Jogging; 2. Playing team sports; 3. Hiking; 4. Working out in the gym; 5. None of the above.

Over the last 2 years, how often have you visited any of the national parks?

    1. Five times or more; 2. 1–4 times; 3. Did not visit any national parks.

Cultural Prime Questions

There has recently been a debate about whether the US National anthem, the Star Spangled Banner, should be sung in some schools in Spanish and not in English. Some people think that singing the National anthem in another language hurts our culture. What do you think?

"The Star Spangled Banner should be sung only in English (or in any language)".

In some countries, homosexual (gay) couples are legally allowed to many and are recognized by the law in exactly the same way as a married heterosexual (straight) couple. There is now a growing debate within the United States about whether similar legislation should be enacted. Do you favor or oppose allowing gay marriages in the United States? (1. Strongly favor—5. Strongly oppose).

Do you agree or disagree with the following statement: "Our traditional way of life is getting lost".

(1. Strongly agree—5. Strongly disagree).

Do you agree or disagree with the following statement: "These days American culture is increasingly threatened". (1. Strongly agree—5. Strongly disagree).

Table 9.6. Descriptive Statistics Pew Global Attitudes Data

VARIABLE	MEAN	SD	MIN	MAX
Age	37.904	14.882	18	97
Cultural Threat	-0.024	0.984	-2.038	2.244
Current State	5.552	2.165	0	10
Edu x GDPpc(log)	30.191	13.682	6.326	61.594
Education	3.564	1.491	1	6
Female	0.478	0.500	0	1
Five-year Change	0.035	2.532	-10	10
Income (quintile)	2.617	1.475	1	5
Job Situation	4.528	1.984	1	7
Loss from Econ. Integration	0.126	0.332	0	1
Not in Labor Force	0.307	0.461	0	1
Part-time Employee	0.078	0.268	0	1
Pensioner	0.091	0.287	0	1
Real Income (log)	8.699	1.439	0	11.736
Self-employed	0.156	0.363	0	1
Unemployed	0.071	0.256	0	1

N=23,705

Table 9.7. Perception of Economic Integration as Harmful, by Exposure to Treatment and Education Level

TREATMENT	EDUCATION: LOW			EDUCATION: HIGH		
	MEAN	T-STAT	N	MEAN	T-STAT	N
Control	3.0		137	3.12		561
Cultural prime	3.37	2.2**	89	3.13	0.15	413
Libertarian prime	3.04	0.2	48	3.08	0.34	207

Notes: Mean score denotes the average view of respondents on the effect of economic openness rated on a 1 (very good) to 5 (very bad) scale. The t statistic is obtained from a t-test comparing the treatment and control group.

Table 9.8. Descriptive Statistics: Survey Experiment

	CULTURAL PRIME		LIBERTARIAN PRIME		CONTROL		FULL SAMPLE			
	MEAN	SD	MEAN	SD	MEAN	SD	MEAN	SD	MIN	MAX
Econ. Integration	3.17	1.25	3.07	1.28	3.09	1.27	3.09	1.27	1	5
Education	1.82	0.33	1.81	0.39	1.80	0.40	1.80	0.40	1	2
Female	1.51	1.50	1.53	1.50	1.51	1.50	1.51	1.50	1	2
Age	49.60	15.12	49.35	15.43	51.15	15.23	51.15	15.23	18	90
N	502		235		698		1,455			

Libertarian Prime Questions

We would now like to ask you a few questions about issues discussed in the news. For each of the following statements, please select the answer that best describes your view:

"The current level of taxation in the United States is too low" (1. Strongly agree—5. Strongly disagree).

"Governments tend to be wasteful" (1. Strongly agree—5. Strongly disagree).

"To accommodate the growing numbers of convicted felons, the federal government should build more prisons" (1. Strongly agree—5. Strongly disagree).

"Freedom is having a government that doesn't interfere in my life" (1. Strongly agree—5. Strongly disagree).

Michael L. Ross

OIL, ECONOMIC GROWTH, AND POLITICAL INSTITUTIONS

Hectic prosperity is followed all too swiftly by complete collapse.

—PAUL FRANKEL, "ESSENTIALS OF PETROLEUM, 1946"

In the 1950s and 1960s, most social scientists believed that natural resource wealth was good for economic growth: the mineral-rich states of Africa seemed to have a promising future but the mineral-poor states of East Asia would probably face great hardships. Yet by the mid-1990s, the opposite seemed to be true: the resource-poor states of East Asia had enjoyed decades of strong growth, while most of Africa's resource-rich states were development failures. The oil-rich Middle Eastern states—which until the mid-1970s, had enjoyed spectacular growth—spent most of the 1980s and early 1990s losing ground. By 2005, at least half of the OPEC countries were poorer than they had been thirty years earlier. Economists began to argue that natural resource wealth in general, and oil wealth in particular, could paradoxically reduce economic growth in the developing world by triggering "corruption, weak governance, rent-seeking, [and] plunder."[1]

Much of this conventional wisdom is mistaken: oil does not typically lead to slower economic growth, bureaucratic ineffectiveness, unusually high levels of corruption, or unusually low levels of human development. Economic growth in the oil states has been erratic, but neither faster nor slower than economic growth in other states. The real

mystery is why the oil states have had normal growth rates, when they should have had faster than normal economic growth, given their enormous natural wealth.

Did the Oil States Have Slow Economic Growth?

Many influential studies contend that oil wealth is an *economic* curse: the more oil that countries extract, the slower their economic growth.[2] Most studies focus on the period between 1970 and 1990, when the oil-producing states were indeed economically troubled. But if we look over a longer period, we see that economic growth in the oil states has not been unusually slow, although, it has been unusually volatile.

Table 9.9 summarizes the per capita growth rates of both the oil and non-oil states between 1960 and 2006. Over the whole period, the oil-producing states grew at about the same rate as other countries; in the developing world, their growth rates were virtually identical—just over 1.5 percent a year.

But if we divide these forty-seven years into three shorter periods, we find a surprising pattern: the oil-producing states had alternating spells of exceptionally fast and exceptionally slow economic growth. From 1960 to 1973, the oil producers grew faster than other countries; from 1974 to 1989, they

From Michael L. Ross, *The Oil Curse: How Petroleum Wealth Shapes the Development of Nations* (Princeton: Princeton University Press, 2012), 189–221.

Table 9.9. Annual Economic Growth per Capita, 1960–2006

	NON-OIL PRODUCERS	OIL PRODUCERS	DIFFERENCE
All countries			
1960–2006	1.76	1.67	−0.09
1960–73	2.77	45	1.72***
1974–89	1.14	0.22	−0.93***
1990–2006	1.45	2.04	0.59**
Developing countries only			
1960–2006	1.56	1.54	−0.02
1960–73	2.34	4.67	2.33***
1974–89	0.97	−0.38	−1.35***
1990–2006	1.42	2.24	0.82***

*significant at 10%, in a one-tailed t-test
**significant at 5%
***significant at 1%
Source: Calculated from data collected in Maddison 2009

grew more slowly; and from 1990 to 2006, they once again grew more quickly. If we leave out the advanced industrialized countries, the gap between the oil states and everyone else—in both good times and bad—becomes even wider.

We can also look at the standard deviation of these growth rates, to see how much they typically fluctuated from year to year. Among all countries in the world, the standard deviation of growth was about 40 percent higher for oil producers than for non-oil producers. Among the developing countries, it was more than 60 percent higher for the oil producers.

Another way to explore the economic effects of oil is to track the year-by-year economic fortunes of the developing world's major oil producers—the thirteen countries that produced on average at least a thousand dollars per capita in oil and gas

during the 1970s and 1980s, and whose fortunes were hence most closely bound to their petroleum assets (see Figure 9.17).[3] In 1950, these states were already about six times richer than other developing countries. Over the next two decades, the gap between these states and the rest of the developing world grew larger, reaching a peak at the time of the first oil shock in 1973–74. Yet from 1974 to 1989, their per capita incomes dropped by an average of 47 percent; by 1990, four of them (Iraq, Kuwait, Qatar, and the United Arab Emirates) were poorer than they had been in 1950, when measured by income per capita.

This was partly because their economies were closely tied to global trends in oil prices. Figure 9.18 once again shows the average per capita incomes of these thirteen countries from 1950 to 2006, but now juxtaposes them with the price of oil (all figures

Figure 9.17. Incomes of the Leading Oil Producers, 1950-2006

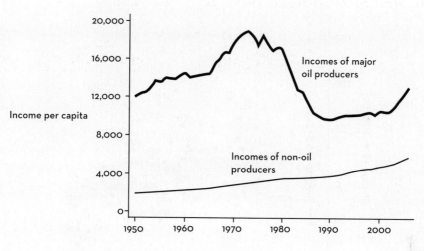

Notes: The dark line shows the mean income per capita of the thirteen-largest oil and gas producers in the 1960s, 1970s, and 1980s, outside of North America and Europe: Algeria, Bahrain, Gabon, Iran, Iraq, Kuwait, Libya, Oman, Qatar, Saudi Arabia, Trinidad, the United Arab Emirates, and Venezuela. Brunei produced a comparable amount of oil, but there are no reliable data on its growth record. The light line includes all other developing states. Incomes are measured in constant 2007 dollars.

SOURCE: Calculated from data in Maddison 2009

Figure 9.18. Incomes of the Leading Oil Producers and Oil Prices, 1950-2006

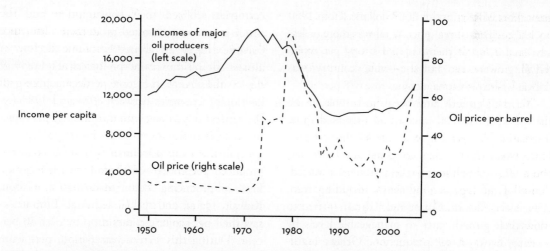

Notes: The solid line shows the mean income per capita of the thirteen-largest oil and gas producers in the 1960s, 1970s, and 1980s outside of North America and Europe. The broken line shows the price of a barrel of oil in constant 2007 dollars.

SOURCES: Calculated from data in Maddison 2009; BP 2010

Figure 9.19. Changes in Income per Capita, 1974–1989

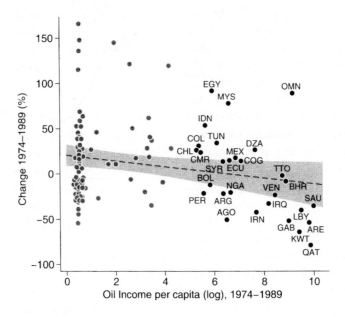

Notes: The vertical axis indicates the percentage change in each country's per capita income from 1974 to 1989. The figure includes all developing countries.

Source: Calculated from data in Maddison 2009

are calibrated in constant 2007 dollars). From 1950 to 1973, while the real price of oil was more or less unchanged, all of them enjoyed strong per capita GDP growth; the fastest-growing country was Libya, where per capita incomes rose 678 percent.

Yet their growth rates began to tumble in the 1970s, when the real price of oil increased more than ninefold. Almost all of the leading oil producers had trouble managing the windfalls that they received, although their strategies varied. Some of the biggest producers—including Iran, Venezuela, Kuwait, Qatar, and Bahrain—tried to slow their growth rates to manageable levels by cutting back on oil production. Others maintained or boosted production to fund ambitious development programs.

Between 1980 and 1986, the real price of oil dropped by more than two-thirds, as Western

countries reduced their consumption and the Saudi government boosted production. The price collapse led to an abrupt economic decline in almost all of the major producers. Figure 9.19 depicts the change in income per capita among all developing countries between 1974 and 1989 (on the vertical axis), along with their average per capita income from oil and gas (on the horizontal axis). In general, the more petroleum that these countries produced, the greater was the fall in their incomes. Five oil-producing countries—Angola, Gabon, Kuwait, Qatar, and the United Arab Emirates—saw their per capita incomes drop by over 50 percent. During this sixteen-year period, petroleum *was* an economic curse: the more that countries produced, the larger their economic decline.

Not all of the oil states suffered. The two most economically successful oil-producing states during the 1974–89 slump were Oman and Malaysia, whose per capita incomes rose 89 and 78 percent, respectively. In Figure 9.19, they are the countries closest to the upper-right corner, combining high oil incomes with high economic growth. Why did Oman and Malaysia do so well?

Government leadership was an important factor. The Malaysian government, in particular, deserves credit for building a well-diversified economy and a strong manufacturing sector, thanks to both skillful industrial policies and an oil endowment that was too small to cause serious problems from the Dutch Disease.[4]

But Oman and Malaysia had another advantage: they were able to compensate for the 1980–86 collapse in oil prices by increasing their production (see Figures 9.20 and 9.21). Their strong economic records were at least partly due to good fortune, since new oil reserves gave each nation the capacity to boost production while prices were falling. This was only possible because they were not members of OPEC and thus able to ignore OPEC policies. While OPEC producers tried to limit or restrain their production to reverse the fall in world prices, from 1980 to 1989 Oman and Malaysia were free to increase production by 130 and 110 percent, respectively.

Among the OPEC states, the best performer between 1974 and 1989 was Indonesia, which grew by 54 percent. Several studies have attributed Indonesia's relatively strong record to its wiser policies, including the more deliberate pace of its windfall spending, larger investments in its agricultural sector, and its strict policy of maintaining a balanced budget and convertible currency.[5]

All of these factors mattered. But it is crucial to remember that on a per capita basis, Indonesia produced less oil and gas than any other OPEC state. In 1980, its peak year, it earned $333 per capita in oil and gas income—less than half the oil income of the next-largest producer, Ecuador, and about 1 percent of Saudi Arabia's. Since Indonesia did not enjoy the same windfalls as its OPEC

brethren in the 1970s, it suffered less from plummeting oil prices in the 1980s. Indonesia was less cursed because it had less oil.

Despite the strong records of these three states, the 1974–89 period was a disaster for most oil producers, and led many economists to conclude that natural resource wealth in general, and petroleum in particular, was an economic blight. The term resource curse—first used in print by economic geographer Richard Auty in 1993—made its way into popular use to describe the paradoxical ailments of resource-rich countries.[6] Most of these studies were shortsighted, however. The seminal analysis of Jeffrey Sachs and Andrew Warner, for example, concluded that resource abundance was a curse, but only examined the dismal period from 1971 to 1989. Many later studies of the resource curse covered roughly the same period and came to the same conclusion.

Yet after hitting bottom around 1989, the oil states once again did relatively well. Oil-producing countries grew about 40 percent faster than the rest of the world from 1990 to 2006. Outside of Europe and North America, they grew more than 55 percent faster than other countries. When averaged over the whole 1960–2006 period, the oil and nonoil states had virtually identical growth records.

What has set the oil states apart over the last half century is not less economic growth but more economic volatility. If not for the miserable years between 1974 and 1989, the petroleum states would have significantly outperformed the nonpetroleum ones, especially in the developing world.

This suggests that on average, petroleum has not been an economic curse—even for developing countries—in the strict sense of the term: oil did not make states poorer than they would be otherwise. If oil really was an economic curse, the countries with the greatest per capita oil wealth—like Saudi Arabia, Libya, Venezuela, and Gabon—should be among the world's poorest countries. They are in fact much richer than neighboring countries with little or no oil.

Figure 9.20. Oil Production in Oman and World Oil Prices, 1960–2006

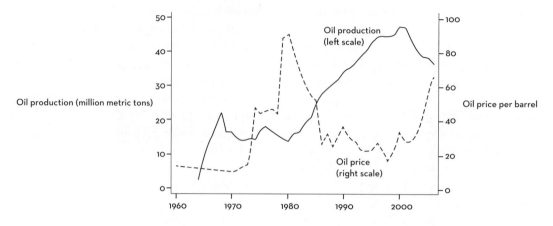

Notes: Oil production (solid line) is measured in million metric tons. Oil prices (broken line) are in constant 2007 dollars.

Sources: US Geological Survey n.d.; BP 2010

Figure 9.21. Oil Production in Malaysia and World Oil Prices, 1960–2006

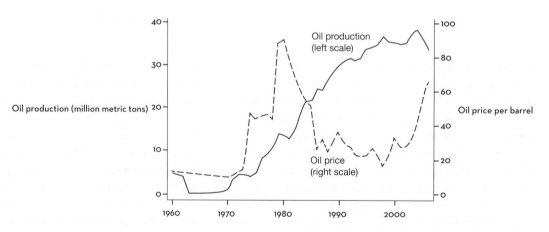

Notes: Oil production (solid line) is measured in million metric tons. Oil prices (broken line) are in constant 2007 dollars.

Sources: US Geological Survey n.d.; BP 2010

Figure 9.22. Changes in Child Mortality, 1970–2003

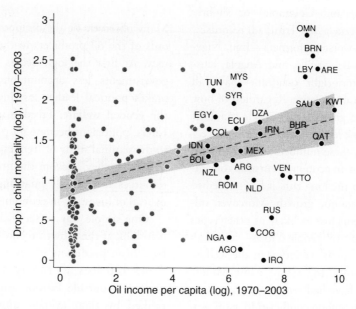

Notes: The numbers on the vertical axis indicate how much a country's child mortality rate dropped from 1970 to 2003; higher numbers indicate a larger drop. Rather than measure the absolute change in child mortality rates—since countries with lower initial rates would necessarily show smaller improvements—it measures changes in the natural log of child mortality rates.

Source: Calculated from data in World Bank n.d.

Of course, a country's growth rate may not tell us much about the population's well-being. Perhaps the growth produced by extracting oil does little to alleviate poverty or improve people's lives. A better measure might be a country's child mortality rate, which can explain a lot about the living conditions of people in the lower-income brackets, including their access to clean water, sanitation, maternal and neonatal health care, nutrition, and education. Data on child mortality is available for most countries in the world since about 1970.

Figure 9.22 plots all countries according to how much oil and gas they produced, and how much their child mortality rates changed, between 1970 and 2003.[7] There are three notable patterns. First, at a global level more oil is associated with faster improvements in child health. This was not just a product of faster economic growth: even when income growth is controlled for, countries with more oil *on average* made better progress.

Second, there was great variation in the performances of the oil rich states, which was roughly correlated with their region. The global association between oil and improvements in child mortality was driven entirely by the strong records of the Middle Eastern countries in the upper-right-hand corner of Figure 9.22—notably Oman, the United Arab Emirates, and Libya, and to a lesser extent, Saudi Arabia, Kuwait, Bahrain, Algeria, and Iran.[8] If these states are removed from the picture, the salutary effects of petroleum wealth disappear.

The African oil producers—Angola, Nigeria, and Congo-Brazzaville—are at the other extreme, showing almost no gains in human welfare despite their oil wealth. The countries of Latin America fall in the middle, with average (Ecuador, Mexico, Argentina, Bolivia, and Colombia) or slightly below average (Venezuela and Trinidad) records.[9]

Finally, the five-worst performers—Iraq, Nigeria, Russia, Congo-Brazzaville, and Angola, clustered in the bottom-right quadrant—have all suffered from endemic violence. Regardless of how it affects economic growth, oil wealth can hurt social welfare when it leads to large-scale violence.

Taken together, these numbers suggest that oil wealth has not been an economic curse as conventionally defined: in the long run, it has not led to atypically slow economic growth. Moreover, oil-funded growth seems just as likely as other types of growth to improve people's lives—although there has been enormous variation in the welfare gains of the oil-producing states. Most Middle Eastern producers have had remarkably fast gains in child health. But among conflict-ridden oil producers, especially in Africa, there have been few, if any, improvements.

The Puzzle of "Normal" Growth

Even if oil wealth has not been harmful, many oil producers seem to have a milder form of the resource curse: they are not as well off as they should be, given their geologic wealth. If the oil states grew at the same overall pace as the non-oil ones, it means that they gained no advantage from their remarkable subsoil assets. This implies something went wrong: basic economic theory tells us that countries with more capital—and hence more money to invest in their people and infrastructure—should grow more quickly. Oil windfalls are a kind of capital, and should have produced high levels of investment-fueled growth. Why were the growth rates of the oil-producing countries average, when they should have been above average?

Democracy

Many observers tie the disappointing growth records of the oil producers to their lack of democracy. At first the logic seems sound: oil makes governments less accountable, which in turn makes political leaders less inclined to promote the general welfare. Freed from the scrutiny of voters, politicians become shortsighted; according to the seminal study of "rentier states" by Hussein Mahdavy, they "devote the greater part of their resources to jealously guarding the status quo," instead of investing in economic development.[10]

One simple way to see if democracy matters is to look at the growth records of countries that have been producing oil over many years. * * * Table 9.10 lists all twenty-eight long-term oil producers outside Europe and North America, ranked by their average annual growth rates between 1960 (or if they became independent after 1960, the first year of their independence) and 2006. It also lists the fraction of this period in which they had democratic governments and ongoing civil wars. These figures range from zero (no years of democracy and no years with civil war) to one (democracy every year and civil war every year). For comparison, it also lists the average numbers for all countries outside the OECD.

Only four of these twenty-eight countries have been democratic for more than half of the time since 1960 (Trinidad, Argentina, Ecuador, and Venezuela). Of these four, one is among the top-ten performers (Trinidad), one is among the bottom ten (Venezuela), and the other two are in the middle. Four other countries had briefer spells of democracy (Mexico, Romania, Nigeria, and the Republic of Congo), but all are clustered in the middle. There is no clear growth advantage to having a democratic government. Some autocrats ruin their country's economies, but others make smart investments in long-term growth.

What is true for the oil states is true more generally for the rest of the world. Most cross-country studies find little evidence that democracy helps economic growth, although there is no consensus.[11] Some analysts argue that whether or not democracy boosts growth, it improves the welfare of the average citizen.[12] Unfortunately, these studies rely on incomplete data sets that overlook the records of well-run autocracies. Once these are accounted for, the "democratic advantage" grows weaker or disappears altogether.[13] In theory, democratic governments should be more attentive to the welfare needs of their citizens; in practice, democracies often fail to deliver.

This does not mean democracy is worthless. It provides people with greater opportunities, greater dignity, and greater freedom to live the lives they choose. And the concluding chapter argues that transparency and accountability can help countries escape some of the *political* ailments caused by oil wealth. But historically, democracies have not done much better than nondemocracies at turning their oil wealth into sustainable economic growth.

Civil War

If oil leads to more frequent civil wars, and civil wars are economically damaging, perhaps violent insurgencies explain why oil producers have failed to grow more quickly.

In a handful of countries this is painfully true. Algeria, Angola, Congo-Brazzaville, Iran, Iraq, Nigeria, and Russia have all suffered from devastating conflicts (both civil and international) that drained them of resources that might have otherwise boosted their growth.

Still, civil wars are much rarer than the disappointingly normal growth records of most oil states. Look again at Table 9.10. Among the ten countries with the worst records, only two (Russia and Iraq) had significant periods of civil war. Among the ten countries with the best records, four (Malaysia, Iran, Azerbaijan, and Syria) had

significant episodes of armed conflict, yet still managed to post higher-than-average growth. Armed conflict can explain a limited number of catastrophes, but it tells us surprisingly little about the economic performance of most oil-rich states.

Women and Population Growth

A more powerful explanation for slower-than-expected growth is that petroleum wealth tends to choke off opportunities for women. * * * One consequence is that women in oil-rich countries have unusually high fertility rates, which leads to faster population growth and slower per capita economic growth. If their populations grew more slowly, the oil-producing countries would have grown more quickly.

Sociologists have long observed that when women take jobs outside the home, they tend to have fewer children.[14] This is one reason why population growth is slower in rich countries than in poor ones. In more advanced economies, women have more opportunities to earn their own incomes, and the better their opportunities in the workforce, the later they marry and the fewer children they choose to have. Since women in oil-rich states have fewer chances to work outside the home, they typically marry when they are younger and have more children than they otherwise might.

Keeping women out of the labor force also boosts population growth through a second route: by encouraging excessive immigration. When the demand for workers exceeds the number of working-age male citizens, countries have two choices: they can hire more women, or import male workers from abroad. * * * Many oil-rich countries, particularly in the Middle East and North Africa, have taken the second route—bringing in foreign workers instead of employing their own female citizens.

The combination of high fertility and high immigration leads to unusually fast population growth. In countries whose economic growth is

Table 9.10. Economic Growth Among Long-Term Oil Producers, 1960–2006

These are the twenty-eight countries outside North America and Europe that have consistently produced significant quantities of oil or gas since 1960, or if they became independent after 1960, since their first year of independence. They are ranked by their annual per capita growth rate. Also shown is the fraction of this period that they had democratic governments and ongoing civil wars. For comparison, it also lists the average figures for all non-OECD countries.

	COUNTRY	ANNUAL GROWTH	DEMOCRACY	CIVIL WARS
1	Oman	5.56	0	0.09
2	Malaysia	4.13	0	0.17
3	Iran	2.85	0	0.51
4	Azerbaijan	2.79	0	0.11
5	Trinidad	2.61	1	0.02
6	Syria	2.36	0	0.11
7	Kazakhstan	2.26	0	0
8	Mexico	2.03	0.15	0.04
9	Saudi Arabia	1.98	0	0.02
10	Bahrain	1.93	0	0
11	Romania	1.89	0.36	0.02
	Non-OECD average	*1.56*	*0.31*	*0.16*
12	Libya	1.54	0	0
13	Nigeria	1.45	0.38	0.13
14	Argentina	1.35	0.68	0.13
15	Algeria	1.34	0	0.34
16	Ecuador	1.17	0.62	0
17	Congo Republic	1.09	0.17	0.13
18	Angola	0.58	0	0.62
19	Uzbekistan	0.51	0	0.04
20	Russia/USSR	0.35	0	0.3
21	Gabon	0.22	0	0.02
22	Turkmenistan	0.15	0	0
23	Venezuela	0.11	1	0.04
24	Brunei	−0.48	0	0
25	UAE	−0.64	0	0
26	Kuwait	−0.86	0	0
27	Iraq	−1.03	0	0.79
28	Qatar	−1.51	0	0

Sources: Calculated from economic data in Maddison 2009; democracy data in Cheibub, Gandhi, and Vreeland 2010; conflict data in Gleditsch et al. 2002

fueled by manufacturing, population growth falls quickly. In countries whose growth comes from selling oil, population growth rates fall more slowly or not at all. This is not only true in the Persian Gulf but also in North Africa (Libya and Algeria), Africa (Gabon and the Republic of Congo), and Latin America (Venezuela and Trinidad).[15]

This pattern has far-reaching economic consequences, since in an economy based on oil exports, the faster a country's population growth is, the slower the growth of its income per capita. Keeping women out of the workforce has led to slower per capita economic growth in the oil states.

Once we control for the effects of population growth, the economic performance of the oil states improves sharply.[16] One simple way to do this is by looking at a country's total GDP growth instead of its per capita GDP growth. For example, in Kuwait, the per capita GDP dropped from about $28,900 in 1950 to just $13,200 in 2006—a fall of more than 50 percent—which looks disastrous. But this was only because a 760 percent rise in Kuwait's total GDP was outpaced by an equally astounding 1660 percent leap in its total population. If its population grew at a more normal rate—closer to the rate of non-oil developing countries over the same period—its per capita growth would have been a lot more impressive.

Table 9.11 is similar to Table 9.9, but compares countries by the growth of their total GDP, rather than their per capita GDP. There are some striking differences between the two tables. In Table 9.9, there is no statistically significant difference between the oil and non-oil states in the growth of their

Table 9.11. Annual Economic Growth, 1960–2006

This table displays the annual growth in the *total* GDP, while Table 9.9 shows the annual growth in *per capita* GDP.

	NON-OIL PRODUCERS	OIL PRODUCERS	DIFFERENCE
All countries			
1960–2006	3.72	4.05	0.33**
1960–73	5.06	8.21	3.15***
1974–89	3.25	2.83	−0.42*
1990–2006	3.02	3.81	0.79***
Developing countries only			
1960–2006	3.97	4.63	0.66***
1960–73	4.96	9.07	4.11***
1974–89	3.43	2.95	−0.48*
1990–2006	3.58	4.62	1.05***

*significant at 10%, in a one-tailed t-test
**significant at 5%
***significant at 1%

Source: Calculated from data collected in Maddison 2009

Figure 9.23. Annual Growth in Total GDP, 1960–2006

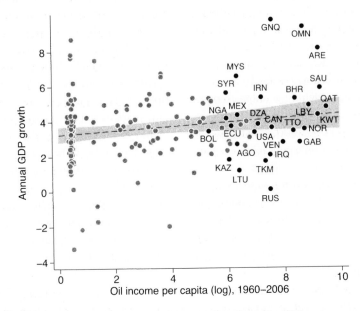

Note: These numbers show the average annual GDP growth rate in all countries from 1960 to 2006.

Source: Calculated from data in Maddison 2009

GDP per capita over the full 1960–2006 period. But Table 9.11 shows that the oil states recorded significantly higher growth in their total GDP than the non-oil states did over the same period.

When measured by total income growth, the performance of the oil states also improves in each of the three periods: the oil states outpaced the non-oil states by a wider margin when times were good (1960–73 and 1990–2006), and fell behind by a smaller margin when times were bad (1974–89).

We can see the same overall pattern in a scatterplot. Figure 9.23 compares all countries from 1960 to 2006 according to their total GDP growth and oil income: countries with more oil had significantly faster growth. The most obvious outlier is Russia, whose economy was decimated by the Soviet collapse. If not for oil's damaging effects on women's work, the petroleum-rich countries would have outperformed the non-oil states, improving the lives of women and men alike.

The Volatility Problem

The second impediment to faster growth is inappropriate government policies—particularly policies that fail to offset the volatility of oil revenues.

* * * Oil revenues have been volatile, especially since the early 1970s. This volatility can hurt economic growth by creating uncertainty about the future, which in turn discourages private-sector investment.[17] Volatility is more harmful for low-income states than high-income ones, partly because their financial markets are less sophisticated and hence less able to help investors hedge against risks.[18] In commodity-exporting developing states, volatility in the terms of trade has historically kept investors away, causing these countries to fall further behind the United States and Europe.[19] One recent study found that natural resource exports typically have a positive direct effect on growth,

but a larger, indirect, negative effect due to the economic volatility that they create.[20]

Yet economic volatility alone cannot be blamed for slow growth: volatility in the oil states is driven by fluctuations in the government's resource revenues, and governments have—at least in theory—the ability to smooth out these fluctuations. If benevolent accountants instead of politicians ran oil-rich governments, their economies would be a lot steadier. The failure of oil-funded governments to stabilize their economies is one of the central puzzles of the resource curse.

The basic method for smoothing out volatility has been known since biblical times, when the Egyptian pharaoh—following Joseph's advice—saved a fraction of his kingdom's grain during seven years of prosperity to carry his people through seven years of famine. In economic language, the pharaoh had adopted *countercyclical policies*—policies to set aside a fraction of the surplus during a boom, and draw down this surplus during a bust.

For countries that depend on exhaustible resources like petroleum, the careful use of this surplus is unusually important. * * * The depletion of oil reserves can lead to a decline in government revenues. To counteract the economic slowdown that this would otherwise cause, governments can invest a fraction of their resource revenues in more sustainable assets, like the nation's physical capital (infrastructure), human capital (education), or even financial assets abroad. An oil-producing country that follows this strategy can compensate for the loss of its natural assets by accumulating other types of assets—in effect, trading wealth below the ground for wealth above the ground. But if it merely consumes its oil wealth instead of investing it, future generations will suffer when the oil runs out.

This principle—that when countries rely on nonrenewable resources, they should invest a certain fraction of their revenues in more sustainable forms of wealth—is known as the Hartwick rule.[21] Countries that follow the Hartwick rule can grow richer over time, even as they deplete their natural capital. They should also have more diversified economies, as their natural capital is transformed into other types of capital.

Fortunately, these two government tasks—smoothing out volatile revenues, and investing them in sustainable assets—go hand in hand.[22] Investment is critical, but it cannot be done all at once. Economies have a limited ability to absorb new investments, which are typically constrained by diminishing returns. For instance, if a government tries to build too much infrastructure too quickly, it will lead to poor planning, lax oversight, and shoddy construction at inflated prices. When governments receive large windfalls, economists advise them to only make domestic investments that yield a sufficiently high rate of return and save any remaining funds for countercyclical use.[23]

Virtually all oil-rich governments acknowledge the importance of countercyclical fiscal policies, yet they rarely have success in implementing them.

According to several major studies, many of the largest oil producers in the 1970s and 1980s failed to implement countercyclical fiscal policies, and squandered a large fraction of their windfalls. Alan Gelb's sweeping analysis of Algeria, Ecuador, Iran, Nigeria, Trinidad, and Venezuela found that over the course of the 1973–74 and 1978–79 oil shocks, spending rose faster than revenues in five of the six states—all of them except tiny Trinidad.[24] Auty's study of an overlapping group of oil exporters (Nigeria, Indonesia, Trinidad, and Venezuela) confirmed that all of their governments had performed dismally.[25]

Sometimes politicians acknowledge that managing large revenue windfalls is difficult. In the mid-1970s, Mexican president José López Portillo cautioned his compatriots, "The capacity for monetary digestion is like that of a human body. You can't eat more than you can digest or you become ill. It's the same way with the economy."[26] But governments rarely exercise this restraint; instead, they effectively let the size of their reserves determine the size of their national budgets. Indeed,

López Portillo helped boost Mexico's oil production almost fourfold between 1972 and 1980, at the same time that prices were soaring; the result was a sudden glut of revenues that led to Mexico's economic crisis in 1982.

Did the oil states learn from their policy mistakes in the 1970s and 1980s? At first glance, the answer seems to be "yes." Since the early 1990s, many oil producers have established special funds to help them manage their resource revenues for either countercyclical use, investments to offset future depletion, or both. A closer inspection, though, shows that these funds have been surprisingly ineffective. Many governments violate their own rules about depositing money into or withdrawing money from their resource funds; others devise loopholes that undermine their fund's effectiveness. Two recent studies by the IMF—which generally favors the establishment of these funds—found no discernible evidence that they helped governments improve their fiscal performance.[27] A third IMF study of eight African oil producers found that even under highly favorable assumptions, their governments had adopted policies that were fiscally unsustainable.[28]

A recent World Bank study also found that many of the petroleum states have not made large enough investments to satisfy the Hartwick rule. They have used their oil revenues for consumption instead, losing an opportunity to raise incomes and diversify their economies. If Nigeria and Gabon had followed the Hartwick rule between 1970 and 2005, they would be about three times wealthier than they are now; Venezuela and Trinidad would be about two and a half times richer.[29]

The overrapid spending of resource windfalls is not a new problem, nor is it confined to oil. One striking historical example is nineteenth-century Peru, which was the world's leading supplier of guano (dried seabird excrement)—at the time, a valuable commercial fertilizer. From 1840 to 1879, a handful of tiny islands off the Peruvian coast provided the world with virtually its only supply of guano. The guano was easy to extract: it was shoveled off cliffs and tossed into wooden chutes, where it slid directly into the holds of waiting ships. Labor costs were low, because the workforce was made up of slaves, prisoners, army deserters, and Chinese "coolies" imported under slavelike conditions.[30]

Thanks to its near monopoly on global supplies and appallingly low labor costs, the guano boom gave the Peruvian government enormous windfalls. Between 1846 and 1873, government revenues jumped five-fold, yet over the same period, government expenditures rose eightfold, producing unsustainable foreign debts. In 1876, with guano supplies close to exhaustion, the Peruvian government declared bankruptcy.[31]

Explaining Failed Policies

If the Old Testament's pharaoh was able to build up resources during the fat years to use during the lean ones, why can't today's oil producers?

One possible answer is that government institutions are themselves damaged by oil revenues. If oil makes governments less effective, it could impair their ability to maintain countercyclical policies—a bit like the doctor who is so weakened by disease, they cannot properly treat their patients.

There are several ways this could occur. Revenue volatility could shorten the government's planning horizon, which would subvert major investment projects. Since revenue fluctuations produce fluctuations in government budgets, projects that take many years to implement—such as major improvements in the country's health, education, or physical infrastructure—stand a high risk of being suspended or canceled when revenues drop. Government officials who anticipate this problem may cope by avoiding long-term programs altogether and spending their funds quickly before they disappear.

Another possible culprit is what might be called "bureaucratic overstretch," meaning that a government's revenues expand more quickly than its capacity to efficiently manage them. Most governments worry about having too little money, not too much. But resource-rich countries sometimes receive windfalls that overwhelm their bureaucratic capacity, amplifying the danger that they will be poorly used.[32]

During the early days of his rule, Ibn Saud, the founding monarch of Saudi Arabia, could carry the entire national treasury in his camel's saddlebags. After prospectors discovered oil in 1938, Saud's government was flooded with tens of millions—and soon billions—of dollars in oil revenues, which it had little capacity to manage.[33] The tumultuous expansion of the Saudi state in the 1950s led to administrative chaos. According to Steffen Hertog,

> As far as institutions mattered, their day-to-day operations were often carried out rather autonomously, with ministries run as personal fiefdoms. The administrative sprawl and personalized

nature of authority meant that coordination between agencies was largely lacking, with different institutions often producing directly contradictory decisions and jurisdictions remaining unclear. As early as 1952, six different entities were supposed to be in charge of economic planning.[34]

Many scholars make a more ambitious claim: that petroleum wealth leads to "bad institutions," making governments weaker, more corrupt, less competent, and less able to maintain wise fiscal policies. Kiren Aziz Chaudhry asserts that oil rents impair the development of an effective state bureaucracy, which leaves states "weak" and unable to develop sound economic policies.[35] Terry Lynn Karl maintained in her influential book *The Paradox of Plenty* that revenue from petroleum diminishes the state's authority by causing a "rentier psychology," bouts of "petromania," and "multiplying the opportunities for both public authorities and private interests to engage in rent-seeking."[36] Timothy Besley and Torsten Persson develop a formal model in which resource

Table 9.12. Perceived Government Quality, 1996–2006

Higher numbers indicate better government quality—meaning greater effectiveness and better control of corruption. Country scores for government effectiveness range from −2.16 to 2.22; scores for corruption control range from −1.76 to 2.53.

	NON-OIL PRODUCERS	OIL PRODUCERS	DIFFERENCE
Level of government effectiveness, 2006	−0.120	0.007	0.0127
Level of corruption control, 2006	−0.132	−0.026	0.107
Change in government effectiveness, 1996–2006	−0.003	−0.077	−0.073
Change in corruption control, 1996–2006	−0.037	0.022	0.059

*significant at 10%, in a one-tailed t-test
**significant at 5%
***significant at 1%
Source: Calculated from data in Kaufman and Kraay 2008

Figure 9.24. Changes in Control of Corruption, 1996–2006

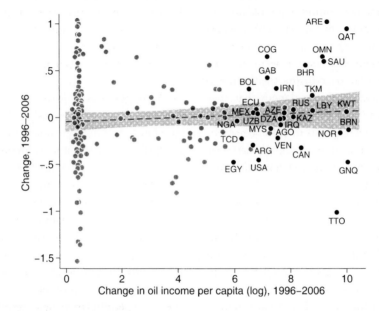

Notes: The numbers show the change in each country's corruption control score from 1996 to 2006. Higher numbers suggest greater improvements in the control of corruption. The horizontal axis shows the absolute change in each country's oil income per capita (log) over the same period.

Source: Calculated from data on corruption control in Kaufman and Kraay 2008.11

rents discourage politicians from investing in the state's bureaucratic capacity, leaving it weak and unable to foster private-sector growth.[37] Scores of other studies make similar arguments.[38]

These contentions might be right, but they are deceptively hard to verify. Social scientists do a terrible job of defining and measuring "institutions," which makes these claims difficult to falsify. To the extent these arguments can be tested, they do not fit well with the evidence.

If extracting oil were bad for government institutions, we should see a negative correlation between a country's oil income and the quality of its government. Since we typically lack measures of a government's actual performance, social scientists often rely on measures of a government's *perceived* performance. The World Bank has compiled the most carefully assembled measures, based on data from commercial risk-rating agencies, NGOs, and multilateral aid agencies. Higher numbers indicate better outcomes, such as greater "government effectiveness" and better "control of corruption."[39]

In Table 9.12, the first row compares the perceived government effectiveness of oil and non-oil states in 2006. The oil-producing states have slightly *better* scores, although the differences are not statistically significant. The second row compares their control of corruption scores. Again, the oil states have better scores, but not significantly so.

We can also look at *changes in* rather than *levels of* government quality. Some theories suggest that a government's quality is harmed by changes in its oil income—that is, by a boom in oil revenues—as opposed to its level of oil income.[40] Looking at changes is also a simple way to control for fixed factors that might be also affecting government quality, and masking the true impact of petroleum.

Row 3 shows how government effectiveness scores changed from 1996 to 2006—a time when virtually all hydrocarbon producers were enjoying large revenue increases from surging prices. While government effectiveness declined in the oil states relative to the non-oil ones, the differences were again not statistically significant. Row 4 demonstrates that the corruption scores of the oil states improved slightly more than the non-oil states, but not significantly so.

Figure 9.24 offers a closer look at changes in countries' corruption scores from 1996 to 2006, compared to changes in their oil income. The fitted line slopes slightly upward—countries with more oil became slightly less corrupt—but country performances varied widely. Five states on the Arabian Peninsula improved their ability to control corruption (Saudi Arabia, the United Arab Emirates, Qatar, Oman, and Bahrain), as did some of the African producers (the Republic of Congo and Gabon). Corruption grew worse in other oil-producing states, in both the developing world (Trinidad, Equatorial Guinea, and Venezuela) and the developed one (Norway, Canada, Netherlands, and the United States). There is little prima facie evidence that oil revenues tend to hurt government quality.

Two Fallacies

If having more oil does not damage the quality of government institutions in any clear-cut way, why do so many intelligent studies—often based on data-crunching exercises—claim otherwise?

Many researchers are led astray by two fallacies. The first might be called the Beverly Hillbillies fallacy. In case you missed it, the *Beverly Hillbillies* was a popular television comedy in the 1960s that featured a lovable but unsophisticated family, the Clampetts, from the Ozarks who suddenly become rich when they strike oil. After the Clampetts move into a fancy mansion in Beverly Hills, they clash comically with their snooty, self-absorbed neighbors.

Here is where the fallacy comes in. The Clampetts' sudden windfall made them just as wealthy as their neighbors, but since they were raised in poverty, they lack their neighbors' fancy educations and upper-class manners.[41] A statistical analysis of families in their neighborhood would show that those with oil wealth (i.e., the Clampetts) were less educated than those without; observers might mistakenly infer that oil wealth causes families to become less educated. But oil wealth did not make the Clampetts uneducated or unsophisticated. It made them wealthier—lifting them into a new, more educated peer group—without affecting their education or manners. Comparing the Clampetts to their new Beverly Hills neighbors makes their oil windfall look like a curse. But compared to a more realistic peer group—like their longtime Ozark neighbors—their education and manners are probably quite typical.

Many studies of oil and institutional quality made a similar mistake by implicitly comparing newly enriched oil countries to a new peer group of middle- and high-income states, whose institutions have developed over many years. This makes the nouveau riche oil states look institutionally stunted.

For example, Figure 9.25 shows that richer countries tend to have more effective governments. There is a strong correlation between a country's per capita income (on the horizontal axis) and the perceived effectiveness of its government (on the vertical axis). Similar patterns have been found in scores of academic studies that link a country's income and the effectiveness of its government: higher incomes tend to make governments more effective, and more effective governments tend to make their countries richer.[42] This is a bit like the two-way correlation between income and education in Beverly Hills (and everywhere else): richer

Figure 9.25. Incomes and Perceived Government Effectiveness, 2005

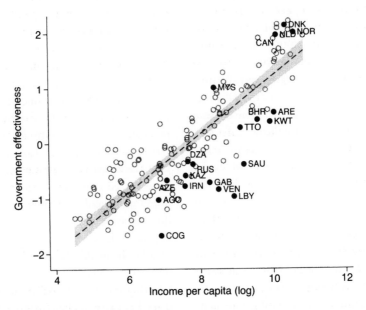

Notes: The vertical axis shows government effectiveness scores, with high numbers indicating greater effectiveness. The solid dots are oil-producing countries, and the hollow dots are non-oil countries.

Source: Data on perceived government effectiveness are taken from Kaufman and Kraay 2008

families can afford higher levels of education, and more educated people tend to earn higher incomes.

Notice the position of countries that produce at least a thousand dollars per person in oil income—marked with three-letter country abbreviations. Most of them lie below the fitted line, suggesting they have unusually ineffective governments for countries at their income levels. If we control for a country's income, we could easily conclude that producing oil tends to diminish the effectiveness of governments.

There is a more benign interpretation, however: perhaps oil raised their incomes, but without influencing the effectiveness of their governments. A spike in global oil prices, or the exploitation of a new oil reserve, could make a country richer without either helping or hurting the quality of its government—just as finding oil raised the Clampetts' income without affecting their education

levels. If this occurred, we would observe no direct correlation between a country's oil income and the quality of its government—yet oil would still appear to be correlated with low government quality *when we control for a country's income,* since compared to countries with similar incomes, government quality in the oil producers would be anomalously low. Just because oil quickly lifts a country's income without producing an equally fast increase in the effectiveness of its government does not mean that oil has *harmed* the government—only that it has not helped it in the way scholars had naively assumed.[43]

Scholars might also be misled by the fallacy of unobserved burdens. Imagine a middle-aged professor walking briskly uphill toward a lecture hall, trailed by his much slower teaching assistant. Observers might infer that the professor is in better shape than their teaching assistant. But the teaching assistant's backpack holds the professor's heavy laptop, a projector, and five textbooks. The professor's own backpack is empty except for a piece of chalk. The two individuals are equally fit, but a heavier load slows down the teaching assistant. Yet because people cannot observe the differences in their respective burdens, they erroneously conclude that the professor is more fit.

When looking at government effectiveness, scholars often make the same mistake: we infer that low-performing governments must have "weak institutions," without considering variations in the difficulties of their tasks. We forget to look in the backpack.

When oil-funded governments handle their revenues poorly, observers often blame it on the government's institutional weakness. This assumes that managing volatile resource revenues is no more burdensome than managing a much smoother flow of tax receipts. But maybe enacting consistent countercyclical policies is more onerous than we realize. Perhaps the problem is not that the oil states have exceptionally weak institutions and need normal ones; perhaps they already have normal institutions, but need exceptionally strong ones.

Even countries without resource wealth, whose revenues are much steadier, have trouble maintaining countercyclical fiscal policies. Many studies find that fiscal policies in the developing world, in both oil and non-oil states, tend to be procyclical instead of countercyclical. Having unstable oil revenues makes countercyclical policies even harder to sustain.[44]

The Mystery of Policy Failure

Why do governments find countercyclical policies so difficult to sustain? Let us return to our basic model of oil politics, which features a ruler who wants to remain in power, citizens who want to

improve their welfare, and oil revenues flowing to the government. * * * The ruler faces constant pressure from citizens to spend more money and improve their welfare. To implement countercyclical fiscal policies, a ruler must make an intertemporal trade-off—displeasing citizens today in order to make them better off in the future.

Scholars recognize four sets of factors that can affect the likelihood of these trade-offs—factors that can affect democracies and dictatorships, wise and foolish leaders, and rich and poor states alike. Unfortunately, these studies underscore how difficult it can be to make these trade-offs, even if they make citizens better off in the long run.

Uncertainty among Rulers

One factor is a ruler's beliefs about how long they will remain in office. Imagine an oil-producing government headed by a wise leader who wants to adopt countercyclical fiscal policies. If these policies are to be effective, they must be maintained in future years, so that any surpluses accrued during a boom are available during a bust. But our leader cannot bind their successors to the course they want to set; policies and institutions established by today's government can be dissolved by future ones. Recognizing that the money they place in reserve might be lost to patronage and corruption by a less responsible successor, a wise ruler might prefer to use it right away on projects that they think have more merit. The more that they believe they will soon lose power, the stronger the ruler's incentive to spend the money quickly.

Similarly, a greedy ruler will also be affected by their expectations about the length of their time in office. Imagine a leader whose fiscal decisions are driven entirely by their desire for power and personal wealth, and who wants to use the windfall solely for patronage and corruption. And assume that there are diminishing marginal returns to patronage and corruption, meaning that the ruler would be better off dispensing favors over several years, rather than all at once. If the ruler believes that they will soon be replaced, they lose any incentive to hold back a budget surplus for future use.

These examples suggest that political leaders who are more secure in office will be more likely to restrain spending during economic booms; leaders who are less secure will exercise less restraint.[45] This does not necessarily mean that authoritarian governments should have better fiscal policies than democratic ones. Much can be done to give democratic leaders longer time horizons and encourage greater restraint.[46] In *The Federalist*, Alexander Hamilton used this argument to explain the advantages of having a president who could stand for reelection:

> An avaricious man, who might happen to fill the office (of president), looking forward to the time when he must at all events yield up the emoluments he enjoyed, would feel a propensity, not easy to be resisted by such a man, to make the best use of the opportunity he enjoyed while it lasted, and might not scruple to have recourse to the most corrupt expedients to make the harvest as abundant as it was transitory; though the same man, probably, with a different prospect before him, might content himself with the regular perquisites of his situation, and might even be unwilling to risk the consequences of an abuse of his opportunities. . . . But with the prospect before him of approaching an inevitable annihilation, his avarice would be likely to get the victory over his caution, his vanity, or his ambition.[47]

More recently, Macartan Humphreys and Martin Sandbu have shown that when a resource-rich government is subject to more checks and balances, it is less likely to overspend any surpluses.[48] Alberto Alesina, Filipe Campante, and Guido Tabellini maintain that among democracies, the critical factor is corruption: democracies in the developing world with greater corruption have worse fiscal policies than democracies with less corruption.[49]

The Selection of Rulers

The way that leaders are chosen can also make a difference. Suppose that our model country is a democracy, and the government receives a large oil windfall on the eve of an election. Voters must choose between a wise candidate who wants to restrain spending and a greedy candidate who wants to spend the windfall right away. To compete for votes, each candidate must raise campaign funds, and the one who raises more money is more likely to win. To raise these funds, each makes promises of future patronage to their supporters.

Under these simple conditions, the candidate who is more willing to spend the government's resources on patronage will gain an advantage over their opponent, since they are able to promise government benefits to a larger number of voting blocs. Even in countries with no patronage, candidates who make more generous promises to the electorate—for new roads, schools, and jobs—can have an edge over opponents who promise less. The same dynamic can occur in authoritarian countries. Michael Herb explains that in some Middle Eastern monarchies, would-be crown princes must bribe other family members with promises of oil money and cabinet appointments to rise toward the throne.[50] Resource-rich countries sometimes face a problem of *adverse selection*: rivals who promise less restraint may end up replacing leaders who favor more fiscal restraint.[51]

The problem of adverse selection can be illustrated by one of the largest corruption scandals in US history—the Teapot Dome scandal, which shook the administration of President Warren Harding in the early 1920s.[52] Among the world's major oil producers, the United States is an anomaly: most of its onshore oil reserves are privately owned and regulated by states, not by the national government. But in 1920, the most valuable untapped oil fields in the country—perhaps in the world—were located on land owned by and under the jurisdiction of the national government. The Teapot Dome field in Wyoming along with several smaller fields in California had been set aside for the exclusive use of the US Navy in times of national emergency. Even though these fields were worth several billion dollars (in today's money), the Wilson administration, in office from 1913 to early 1921, resisted pressure from oil company lobbyists to release them for commercial use.

The Republican Party was heavily favored to win the 1921 general election, and many candidates vied for the nomination. Harding, an obscure senator from Ohio with no special policy agenda beyond "a return to normalcy," was one of the less inspired candidates.[53] A count of party delegates on the eve of the nominating convention showed Harding running a distant sixth. The *Wall Street Journal* gave him an eight-to-one shot at the nomination, while the sportswriter Ring Lardner put his odds at two hundred to one.

As the Republican convention began, several wealthy oil executives approached the leading candidates and offered them large donations in exchange for future access to the navy's oil fields. Most refused, but Harding—whose campaign was desperately short of money—readily agreed to the bargain. With sudden access to several million dollars, Harding was able to purchase the support of enough delegates to capture the nomination. After receiving further infusions of cash from eager oil executives, he won the general election in a landslide. On taking office, Harding appointed Albert Fall, the favored candidate of his oil industry backers, to the post of interior secretary. Fall soon granted extremely valuable no-bid leases for the navy's oil fields to Harding's backers. Harding's willingness to sell off government assets as patronage, instead of saving them for future use in an emergency, helped him triumph in the election.

The Role of Citizens

The preferences of the citizens are also important, especially in democracies. If the citizens are well informed and understand the benefits of countercyclical policies, the ruler should find it easier to exercise fiscal restraint.

But even if the electorate is well informed, under some conditions citizens might nonetheless push for faster spending. If the population is sharply divided into competing factions—perhaps along ethnic, regional, or class lines—supporters of the current government may favor the immediate distribution of any windfalls, out of fear that a future government will favor a rival faction and exclude them from the spoils.[54] Even if they are not divided, voters are also less likely to favor restraint when they perceive the government as corrupt or incompetent, since they fear that an unspent surplus will be squandered or embezzled rather than saved for future use.[55]

Of course, this is not an irrational fear. Many governments *do* squander their windfalls. Inefficient windfall use can hence become a self-fulfilling prophecy: because the public believes any surplus will be misspent, the government may be forced to disburse it right away—even if doing so causes the very misspending that citizens anticipate. But prudent windfall use—accompanied by sufficient transparency—might also create a positive feedback loop: when citizens believe their government will save and invest a windfall responsibly, they may become more patient about receiving the resulting benefits.

The Role of Credit Markets

Governments bear much of the blame for overrapid spending, yet credit markets also play a role.

There is a common saying that banks will loan you an umbrella when the sun is shining, but ask for it back when it rains. The adage reflects the ironic way that credit markets work: bankers only finance customers who are better off—even though they are less in need—because they are more likely to pay their loans back.

The same pattern holds at a global level when the borrowers are governments: when a government's revenues go up, so does its ability to borrow money. Unfortunately, this means that governments find it easier to borrow money during good economic times and harder to borrow during bad times—fostering procyclical fiscal policies.[56]

The backward logic of credit markets aggravated the economic problems of many oil-producing states in the 1980s. When their oil revenues soared in the 1970s, so did their creditworthiness. Since the value of their exports was growing quickly, international banks believed that these governments would be able to service the debts of large loans, and offered them to the governments on generous terms. A 2008 study by Irfan Nooruddin found that between 1970 and 2000, the more oil that countries produced, the higher their debt burden.

Sometimes it makes economic sense for oil-producing governments to borrow money. Years may pass between the day that a valuable oil field is discovered and the day it begins to yield significant revenues for the government. If the government borrows money against future production, it can expand at a smoother and more manageable pace, and its people can enjoy the benefits of oil wealth sooner. In poor countries, where the need for food, education, and health services is urgent, loans against future revenues can save lives.

But governments should not borrow more than they can pay back, and the ability of oil-dependent governments to repay their loans depends heavily on the future price of oil. In the late 1970s, bankers and government officials believed that the underlying conditions that were producing record oil prices would continue indefinitely, and hence that oil-producing governments would have enough revenues to service large loans.

When the price of oil collapsed after 1980, the governments of eight major petroleum exporters—Mexico, Venezuela, Nigeria, Gabon, the Republic of Congo, Trinidad, Algeria, and Ecuador—became crippled by debt; all were forced to turn to the IMF for help.[57] The availability of easy credit helped these governments accelerate public spending when prices were high, with loans that had to be repaid when prices were low—making their economies more volatile, not less.

In theory, democracy might help restrain government borrowing, since taxpayers might be more worried than their political leaders about their country's long-term financial health. Nooruddin's study, however, found the reverse: democratic oil producers have had worse debt problems than nondemocratic oil producers.[58] Once again, democracy is less helpful for the economy than we might hope.

The study of oil and economic growth is strewn with misconceptions. Many books and articles claim that oil wealth leads to weak state institutions, slower economic growth, and a decline in human development. Yet these studies typically focus on the troubled 1970–90 period and fall prey to some common fallacies.

Amore careful look at the data suggests that the oil states have grown at about the same rate as other countries—indicating that oil has not typically been harmful, but has also not created the economic boost that we might expect. Collier aptly describes the economic troubles of the oil producers as "predominantly a missed opportunity."[59]

One reason for these missed opportunities has been the failure of many oil states to provide good jobs for women, which would slow the growth of their populations. A second reason has been their failure to maintain appropriate fiscal policies—not because the oil producers have abnormally weak institutions, but because offsetting the volatility of oil revenues is abnormally difficult. These policies failures, though, are not caused by atypically bad or weak government institutions. Most oil states seem to have relatively normal institutions. The problem is that the oil states need exceptionally strong ones to cope with the volume and volatility of their revenues.

NOTES

1. Sala-i-Martin and Subramanian 2003, 4.
2. The seminal paper on this topic was by economists Jeffrey Sachs and Andrew Warner (1995). Building on earlier work by Alan Gelb and his colleagues (1988) and Richard Auty (1990), Sachs and Warner looked at the growth rates of ninety-seven countries, and found that countries that were more dependent on natural resource exports in 1971 had abnormally slow growth rates over the next 18 years. The correlation remained significant even after the authors controlled for a wide range of growth-related variables. For important contributions to this debate, see also Manzano and Rigobon 2007; Sala-i-Martin and Subramanian 2003; Papyrakis and Gerlagh 2004; Robinson, Torvik, and Verdier 2006; Melhum, Moene, and Torvik 2006; Collier and Goderis 2009. Recent skeptics include Brunnschweiler and Bulte 2008; Alexeev and Conrad 2009. For reviews of this literature, see Ross 1999; Stevens and Dietsche 2008; Wick and Bulte 2009; Frankel 2010.
3. In the 1960s, 1970s, and 1980s, the developing world's thirteen-largest petroleum producers on a per capita basis were: Algeria, Bahrain, Gabon, Iran, Iraq, Kuwait, Libya, Oman, Qatar, Saudi Arabia, Trinidad, the United Arab Emirates, and Venezuela. Brunei produced a comparable amount of oil, but there are no reliable data on its growth record. To understand the trajectory of the oil-rich states in the developing world, this is a better group of countries to look at than OPEC, since OPEC excludes some oil-rich countries (like Bahrain, Oman, and Trinidad), but includes more modestly endowed ones (such as Ecuador, Indonesia, and Nigeria).
4. Abidin 2001.
5. See Bevan, Collier, and Gunning 1999; Lewis 2007. Andrew Rosser (2007) points to broader, structural factors that affected Indonesia's success, including the cold war and Indonesia's position in the global economy.
6. Although Auty may have been the first scholar to use "resource curse" in print, he does not claim to have coined the term. He notes that others used it informally before he placed it in the subtitle of his 1993 book.
7. I have reversed the scale on the y-axis so that higher numbers indicate better outcomes—in this case, faster reductions in child mortality.
8. The only non-Middle Eastern country to reach the upper-right corner was tiny Brunei. Interestingly, Brunei is similar to oil-rich Persian Gulf countries like Kuwait and Qatar: it is small, overwhelmingly Muslim, and ruled by a traditional monarch.
9. This variation in outcomes underscores the value of studies that try to explain variations in the trajectories of the oil states. See Melhum, Moene, and Torvik 2006; Smith 2007.
10. Mahdavy 1970, 442.
11. Barro 1997; Tavares and Wacziarg 2001; Gerring, Thacker, and Alfaro 2005.
12. Halperin, Siegle, and Weinstein 2005; Bueno de Mesquita et al. 2003; Lake and Baum 2001.
13. Ross 2006b.
14. See, for example, Brewster and Rindfuss 2000.
15. Notice that a country's oil production does not seem to have an *absolute* effect on its fertility rate: more petroleum is not directly correlated with higher fertility and faster population growth. The impact of petroleum only emerges when we control for a country's income. Yet this does not seem to be just a Beverly Hillbillies effect (which I explain later): even after generations of higher incomes, fertility rates in the oil-rich states remain anomalously high. For more on this issue, see Jamal et al. 2010.
16. Anca Cotet and Kevin Tsui (2010) report a similar finding—that oil rents lead to higher fertility rates, faaster population growth, and hence slower per capita growth.
17. Ramey and Ramey 1995; Acemoglu et al. 2003.
18. Loayza et al. 2007.
19. Blattman, Hwang, and Williamson 2007.
20. van der Ploeg and Poelhekke 2009.

21. Hartwick 1977.

22. Even though these two tasks are distinct, I lump them together for the purposes of this discussion.

23. See, for example, Humphreys, Sachs, and Stiglitz 2007; Collier et al. 2009; Gelb and Grasman 2010.

24. Gelb and Associates 1988.

25. Auty 1990.

26. Quoted in Yergin 1991, 667.

27. IMF 2007; Davis et al. 2003.

28. York and Zhan 2009.

29. Hamilton, Ruta, and Tajibaeva 2005.

30. Conditions were so onerous that scarcely a day passed without an attempted suicide among the workers. To solve a labor shortage in 1862, contractors kidnapped about one thousand Easter Island natives—about a third of the island's population. Although the French and British governments eventually forced the Peruvian government to return the Easter Islanders in 1863, only fifteen survived the ordeal and returned home alive.

31. This account is based on Levin 1960; Hunt 1985.

32. Government bodies that manage the booming resource sector are especially vulnerable to bureaucratic overstretch. Since they have authority over resources that have suddenly grown valuable, governments can be plagued by what I called "rent seizing" in an earlier book. Rent seizing occurs when politicians sweep aside institutional constraints to gain control of how a valuable resource is allocated and regulated—giving them the power to use it for patronage or corruption (Ross 2001b).

Madagascar provides a recent example. Until 2005, the government allocated mining rights in an arm's-length manner, through an agency designed to prevent political interference and promote transparency. But the system began to break down in 2006 in the face of rising mineral prices. The power to allocate permits was transferred from the formerly independent Mining Cadastre Office to political appointees who disregarded Madagascar's Mining Code, abandoned measures like competitive bidding that had fostered transparency, and instead distributed licenses through an opaque, discretionary, and almost certainly corrupt process (Kaiser 2010).

33. Yergin 1991.

34. Hertog 2007, 546.

35. Chaudhry 1989.

36. Karl 1997, 57, 67, 15.

37. Besley and Persson 2010.

38. See also Mahdavy 1970; Leite and Weidmann 1999; Isham et al. 2005; Bulte, Damania, and Deacon 2005. For an excellent review of these arguments, see Wick and Bulte 2009.

39. Kaufman and Kraay 2008. Unfortunately, expert opinions about corruption seem to be poor predictors of actual corruption. See, for example, Olken 2009; Razafindrakoto and Roubaud 2010.

40. Tornell and Lane 1999.

41. The Clampetts liked to boast that the most educated member of their family, Jethro Bodine, successfully completed sixth grade.

42. See, for example, La Porta et al. 1999; Adsera, Boix, and Payne 2003.

43. The Beverly Hillbillies fallacy could also be seen as a kind of post-treatment bias: oil seems to be negatively correlated with institutional quality once we control for income, but since oil affects income, the inclusion of income in the model produces a biased estimate of oil's true impact. Michael Alexeev and Robert Conrad (2009) make a similar point in their statistical analysis of oil and institutions, showing that once the impact of oil on income is properly accounted for, oil is no longer correlated with a reduction in institutional quality. Xavier Sala-i-Martin and Arvind Subramanian (2003) also make this argument, but Alexeev and Conrad assert that their econometric remedy is inadequate. Michael Herb (2005) suggests that a similar problem creates the false appearance that oil hinders democracy, Alexeev and Conrad, however, find that oil is still associated with less democracy after accounting for the effect of oil on income.

44. Catão and Sutton 2002; Manasse 2006; Talvi and Végh 2005; Alesina, Campante, and Tabellini 2008; Ilzetzki and Végh 2008. Some studies of oil and institutions make a third mistake: they argue that oil is detrimental to state strength, but measure state strength as the amount of taxes collected by the government. See,

for example, Chaudhry 1997; Thies 2010; Besley and Persson 2010. * * * Oil revenues necessarily reduce a government's reliance on tax revenues by increasing its nontax revenues. Just because an oil-rich country collects less tax revenue does not ipso facto demonstrate that its government is weak or ineffective.

45. Herschman 2009. For a discussion of the factors that influence a politician's time horizon and hence their preferred spending rate, see Levi 1988. Macartan Humphreys and Martin Sandbu (2007) use a formal model to explore, in far greater detail, conditions that may affect the likelihood of restraint.

46. Alesina, Campante, and Tabellini 2008.

47. Hamilton, Madison, and Jay [1788] 2000, no. 72.

48. Humphreys and Sandbu 2007.

49. Alesina, Campante, and Tabellini 2008.

50. Herb 1999.

51. For a more carefully developed look at this dynamic, see Collier and Hoeffler 2009.

52. The following account is drawn from McCartney 2008.

53. According to William McAdoo, secretary of the treasury under Woodrow Wilson, "[Harding's] speeches left the impression of an army of pompous phrases moving over a landscape in search of an idea. Sometimes these meandering words would actually capture a straggling thought and bear it off triumphantly, a prisoner in their midst, until it died of servitude and overwork." Quoted in McCartney 2008, 43.

54. Humphreys and Sandbu 2007.

55. Alesina, Campante, and Tabellini 2008.

56. Catão and Sutton 2002; Kaminsky, Reinhart, and Végh 2004.

57. After the first oil shock in 1975, even Indonesia, which managed its modest windfall more prudently, was troubled by an explosion of debt (Bresnan 1993).

58. Nooruddin 2008.

59. Collier 2010, 44.

REFERENCES

Abidin, Mahani Zainal. 2001. "Competitive Industrialization with Natural Resource Abundance: Malaysia." In *Resource Abundance and Economic Development*, edited by Richard M. Auty, 147–64. Oxford: Oxford University Press.

Acemoglu, Daron, Simon Johnson, James A. Robinson, and Yunyong Thaicharoen. 2003. "Institutional Causes, Macroeconomic Symptoms: Volatility, Crises, and Growth." *Journal of Monetary Economics* 50 (1): 49–123.

Adsera, Alicia, Carles Boix, and Mark Payne. 2003. "Are You Being Served? Political Accountability and Quality of Government." *Journal of Law, Economics, and Organization* 19 (2): 445–90.

Alesina, Alberto, Filipe Campante, and Guido Tabellini. 2008. "Why Is Fiscal Policy Often Procyclical?" *Journal of the European Economic Association* 6 (5): 1006–36.

Alexeev, Michael, and Robert Conrad. 2009. "The Elusive Curse of Oil." *Review of Economics and Statistics* 91 (3): 586–98.

Auty, Richard M. 1990. *Resource-Based Industrialization: Sowing the Oil in Eight Developing Countries.* Oxford: Claredon Press.

Barro, Robert J. 1997. *Determinants of Economic Growth: A Cross-country Empirical Study.* Cambridge, MA: MIT Press.

Besley, Timothy, and Torsten Persson. 2010. "State Capacity, Conflict, and Development." *Econometrica* 78 (1): 1–34.

Bevan, David L., Paul Collier, and Jan Willem Gunning. 1999. *Nigeria and Indonesia.* New York: Oxford University Press.

Blattman, Christopher, Jason Hwang, and Jeffrey Williamson. 2007. "Winners and Losers in the Commodity Lottery: The Impact of Terms of Trade Growth and Volatility in the Periphery, 1870–1939." *Journal of Development Economics* 82 (1): 156–79.

BP. 2010. "BP Statistical Review of World Energy." London: British Petroleum.

Bresnan, John. 1993. *Managing Indonesia: The Modern Political Economy.* New York: Columbia University Press.

Brewster, Karin, and Ronald Rindfuss. 2000. "Fertility and Women's Employment in Industrialized Nations." *Annual Review of Sociology* 26:271–96.

Brunnschweiler, Christa, and Erwin Bulte. 2008. "The Resource Curse Revisited and Revised: A Tale of Paradoxes and Red Herrings." *Journal of Environmental Economics and Management* 55 (3): 248–64.

Bueno de Mesquita, Bruce, Alastair Smith, Randolph M. Siverson, and James D. Morrow. 2003. *The Logic of Political Survival.* Cambridge, MA: MIT Press.

Bulte, Erwin, Richard Damania, and Robert T. Deacon. 2005. "Resource Intensity, Institutions, and Development." *World Development* 33 (7): 1029–44.

Catão, Luis, and Bennett Sutton. 2002. "Sovereign Defaults." Washington, DC: International Monetary Fund.

Chaudhry, Kiren Aziz. 1989. "The Price of Wealth: Business and State in Labor Remittance and Oil Economies." *International Organization* 43 (1): 101–45.

———. 1997. *The Price of Wealth: Economies and Institutions in the Middle East.* Ithaca, NY: Cornell University Press.

Cheibub, José Antonio, Jennifer Gandhi, and James R. Vreeland. 2010. "Democracy and Dictatorship Revisited." *Public Choice* 143 (1–2): 1–35.

Collier, Paul. 2010. *The Plundered Planet.* New York: Oxford University Press.

Collier, Paul, and Benedikt Goderis. 2009. "Commodity Prices, Growth, and the Natural Resource Curse: Reconciling a Conundrum." Unpublished paper, Center for the Study of African Economies, Oxford.

Collier. 2009. "Testing the Neocon Agenda: Democracy in Resource-Rich Societies." *European Economic Review* 53 (3): 293–308.

Collier, Paul, Frederick van der Ploeg, Michael Spence, and Anthony Venables. 2009. "Managing Resource Revenues in Developing Economies." Oxcarre Research Papers. Oxford: Oxford: Department of Economics, Oxford University.

Cotet, Anca, and Kevin K. Tsui. 2010. "Resource Curse or Malthusian Trap? Evidence from Oil Discoveries and Extractions." Unpublished paper, Muncie, IN.

Davis, Jeffrey, Rolando Ossowski, James Daniel, and Steven Barnett. 2003. "Stabilization and Savings Funds for Nonrenewable Resources: Experience and Fiscal Policy Implications." In *Fiscal Policy Formulation and Implementation in Oil-Producing Countries,* edited by Jeffrey Davis, Rolando Ossowski, and Annalisa Fedelino, 273–315. Washington, DC: International Monetary Fund.

Frankel, Jeffrey A. 2010. "The Natural Resource Curse: A Survey." NBER Working Paper. Cambridge, MA: National Bureau of Economic Research.

Gelb, Alan, and Associates. 1988. *Oil Windfalls Blessing or Curse?* New York: Oxford University Press.

Gelb, Alan, and Sina Grasman. 2010. "How Should Oil Exporters Spend Their Rents?" Working Paper. Washington, DC: Center for Global Development.

Gerring, John, Strom C. Thacker, and Rodrigo Alfaro. 2005. "Democracy and Human Development." Unpublished paper, Boston University.

Gleditsch, Nils Petter, Peter Wallensteen, Mikael Eriksson, Margareta Sollenberg, and Harvard Strand. 2002. "Armed Conflict, 1946–2001: A New Dataset." *Journal of Peace Research* 39 (5): 615–37.

Halperin, Morton H., Joseph T. Siegle, and Michael W. Weinstein. 2005. *The Democracy Advantage.* New York: Routledge.

Hamilton, Alexander, James Madison, and John Jay. [1788] 2000. *The Federalist Papers.* New York: Signet.

Hamilton, Kirk, Giovanni Ruta, and Liaila Tajibaeva. 2005. "Capital Accumulation and Resource Depletion: A Hartwick Rule Counterfactual." World Bank Policy Research Working Papers. Washington, DC: World Bank.

Hartwick, John M. 1977. "Intergenerational Equity and the Investing of Rents from Exhaustible Resources." *American Economic Review* 67 (5): 972–74.

Heilbrunn, John. 2005. "Oil and Water? Elite Politicians and Corruption in France." *Comparative Politics* 37 (3): 277–96.

Herb, Michael. 1999. *All in the Family: Absolutism, Revolution, and Democracy in the Middle East.* Albany: State University of New York Press.

Herschman, Andrea. 2009. "The Politics of Oil Wealth Management: Lessons from the Caspian and Beyond." Unpublished paper, University of California at Los Angeles.

Hertog, Steffen. 2007. "Shaping the Saudi State: Human Agency's Shifting Role in Rentier-State Formation." *International Journal of Middle East Studies* 39:539–63.

Humphreys, Macartan, Jeffrey Sachs, and Joseph E. Stiglitz. 2007. *Escaping the Resource Curse.* New York: Columbia University Press.

Humphreys, Macartan, and Martin E. Sandbu. 2007. "The Political Economy of Natural Resource Funds." In *Escaping the Resource Curse,* edited by Macartan Humphreys, Jeffrey Sachs and Joseph E. Stiglitz, 194–234. New York: Columbia University Press, 2007.

Hunt, Shane J. 1985. "Growth and Guano in Nineteenth-Century Peru." In *The Latin American Economies,* edited by Roberto Cortes Conde and Shane J. Hunt, 255–318. New York: Holmes and Meier.

Ilzetzki, Ethan, and Carlos A. Végh. 2008. "Procyclical Fiscal Policy in Developing Countries: Truth or Fiction?" Unpublished paper.

International Monetary Fund. 2007. "Russian Federation: 2007 Article IV Consultation." Washington, DC: International Monetary Fund.

Isham, Jonathan, Michael Woolcock, Lant Pritchett, and Gwen Busby. 2005. "The Varieties of the Rentier Experience: How Natural Resource Export Structures Affect the Political Economy of Growth." *World Bank Economic Review* 19 (2): 141–74.

Jamal, Amaney, Irfan Nooruddin, Michael L. Ross, and Michael Hoffman. 2010. "Fertility and Economic Development in the Muslim World." Unpublished paper, Princeton University, Princeton, NJ.

Kaiser, Kai. 2010. *Rents to Riches.* Washington, DC: World Bank. Kalyvas, Stathis. 2007. "Civil Wars." In *Handbook of Political Science,* edited by Susan Stokes and Carles Boix, 416–34. New York: Oxford University Press.

Kaminsky, Graciela, Carmen Reinhart, and Carlos A. Végh. 2004. "When It Rains, It Pours: Procyclical Capital Flows and Macroeconomic Policies." *NBER Macroeconomics Annual* 19:11–53.

Karl, Terry Lynn. 1997. *The Paradox of Plenty: Oil Booms and Petro-States.* Berkeley: University of California Press.

Kaufmann, Daniel, and Aart Kraay. 2008. "Governance Indicators: Where Are We, Where Should We Be Going?" *World Bank Research Observer* 23 (1): 1–30.

La Porta, Rafael, Florencio Lopez-de-Silanes, Andrei Shleifer, and Robert W. Vishny. 1999. "The Quality of Government." *Journal of Law, Economics, and Organization* 15 (1): 222–79.

Lake, David A., and Matthew Baum. 2001. "The Invisible Hand of Democracy: Political Control and the Provision of Public Services." *Comparative Political Studies* 34 (6): 587–621.

Leite, Carlos, and Jens Weidmann. 1999. "Does Mother Nature Corrupt? Natural Resources, Corruption, and Economic Growth." IMF Working Paper. Washington, DC: International Monetary Fund.

Levi, Margaret. 1988. *Of Rule and Revenue.* Berkeley: University of California Press.

Levin, Jonathan V. 1960. *The Export Economies: Their Pattern of Development in Historical Perspective.* Cambridge, MA: Harvard University Press.

Lewis, Peter. 2007. *Growing Apart: Oil, Politics, and Economic Change in Indonesia and Nigeria.* Ann Arbor: University of Michigan Press.

Loayza, Norman V., Romain Ranciere, Luis Serven, and Jaume Ventura. 2007. "Macroeconomic Volatility and Welfare in Developing Countries: An Introduction." *World Bank Economic Review* 21 (3): 343–57.

Maddison, Angus. 2009. "Historical Statistics of the World Economy, 1–2008." Unpublished paper, Groeningen, Netherlands.

Mahdavy, Hussein. 1970. "The Patterns and Problems of Economic Development in Rentier States: The Case of Iran." In *Studies in Economic History of the Middle East,* edited by M. A. Cook, 428–67. London: Oxford University Press.

Manasse, Paolo. 2006. "Procyclical Fiscal Policy: Shocks, Rules, and Institutions—a View from Mars." Washington, DC: International Monetary Fund.

Manzano, Osmel, and Roberto Rigobon. 2007. "Resource Curse or Debt Overhang?" In *Natural Resources: Neither Curse nor Destiny,* edited by Daniel Lederman and William F. Maloney, 41–70. Washington, DC: World Bank.

McCartney, Laton. 2008. *The Teapot Dome Scandal.* New York: Random House.

Melhum, Halvor, Karl Moene, and Ragnar Torvik. 2006. "Institutions and the Resource Curse." *Economic Journal* 116 (1): 1–20.

Olken, Benjamin. 2009. "Corruption Perceptions vs. Corruption Reality." *Journal of Public Economics* 93 (7–8): 950–64.

Papyrakis, Elissaios, and Reyer Gerlagh. 2004. "The Resource Curse Hypothesis and Its Transmission Channels." *Journal of Comparative Economics* 32 (1): 181–93.

Ramey, Garey, and Valerie Ramey. 1995. "Cross-country Evidence on the Link between Volatility and Growth." *American Economic Review* 85 (5): 1138–51.

Razafindrakoto, Mireille, and Francois Roubaud. 2010. "Are International Databases on Corruption Reliable? A Comparison of Expert Opinion Surveys and Household Surveys in sub-Saharan Africa." *World Development* 38 (8): 1057–69.

Robinson, James A., Ragnar Torvik, and Thierry Verdier. 2006. "Political Foundations of the Resource Curse." *Journal of Development Economics* 79 (2): 447–68.

Ross, Michael L. 1999. "The Political Economy of the Resource Curse." *World Politics* 51 (2): 297–322.

———. 2001b. *Timber Booms and Institutional Breakdown in Southeast Asia.* New York: Cambridge University Press.

———. 2006b. "Is Democracy Good for the Poor?" *American Journal of Political Science* 50 (4): 860–74.

Rosser, Andrew. 2007. "Escaping the Resource Curse: The Case of Indonesia." *Journal of Contemporary Asia* 37 (1): 38–58.

Sachs, Jeffrey D., and Andrew M. Warner. 1995. "Natural Resource Abundance and Economic Growth." Development Discussion Paper 517a. Cambridge, MA: Harvard Institute for International Development.

Sala-i-Martin, Xavier, and Arvind Subramanian. 2003. "Addressing the Natural Resource Curse: An Illustration from Nigeria." IMF Working Paper. Washington, DC: International Monetary Fund.

Smith, Benjamin. 2007. *Hard Times in the Land of Plenty.* Ithaca, NY: Cornell University Press.

Stevens, Paul, and Evelyn Dietsche. 2008. "Resource Curse: An Analysis of Causes, Experiences, and Possible Ways Forward." *Energy Policy* 36 (1): 56–65.

Talvi, Ernesto, and Carlos A. Végh. 2005. "Tax Base Variability and Procyclical Fiscal Policy in Developing Countries." *Journal of Development Economics* 78(1): 156–90.

Tavares, José, and Romain Wacziarg. 2001. "How Democracy Affects Growth." *European Economic Review* 45:1341–78.

Thies, Cameron G. 2010. "Of Rulers, Rebels, and Revenue: State Capacity, Civil War Onset, and Primary Commodities." *Journal of Peace Research* 47 (3): 321–32.

Tornell, Aaron, and Philip R. Lane. 1999. "The Voracity Effect." *American Economic Review* 89 (1): 22–46.

US Geological Survey. n.d. *Minerals Yearbook.* Washington, DC: US Department of the Interior.

van der Ploeg, Frederick, and Steven Phoelhekke. 2009. "Volatility and the Natural Resource Curse." Oxcarre Research Papers. Oxford: Oxford: Department of Economics, Oxford University.

Wick, Katharina, and Erwin Bulte. 2009. "The Curse of Natural Resources." *Annual Review of Resource Economics* 1:139–56.

World Bank. n.d. "World Development Indicators." Available at http://data.worldbank.org/.

Yergin, Daniel. 1991. *The Prize: The Epic Quest for Oil, Money, and Power.* New York: Simon and Schuster.

York, Robert, and Zaijin Zhan. 2009. "Fiscal Vulnerability and Sustainability in Oil-Producing sub-Saharan African Countries." IMF Working Paper. Washington, DC: International Monetary Fund.

10 HUMAN RIGHTS

For generations, the idea of human rights has been contested. Which rights should be included? Which are excluded? How are rights determined in a culturally diverse world? Amartya Sen develops the argument that human rights need to be viewed as entitlements to capability—the opportunity to have freedom. Eschewing the idea of a fixed listing of capabilities, Sen suggests a process of public reasoning to arrive at an understanding of capability.

In a chapter from *Universal Human Rights in Theory and Practice* (2nd ed., 2003), Jack Donnelly probes whether there can be universal human rights. At the level of concepts, he sees an extensive consensus on a limited set of obligations defined in the Universal Declaration of Human Rights. But, he suggests, the ways these rights are implemented may vary, thus offering logical explanations for the persistence of arguments that rights should vary by culture.

As a result of increasing demand at the international level for rights protection, states have ratified many human rights treaties, but does that adherence lead to a change in state behavior? Emilie M. Hafner-Burton and Kiyoteru Tsutsui have examined this critical empirical question in a series of articles. Their previous research shows that democracies do change behavior if civil society actors take up the cause of human rights. In this selection, the authors examine the difficult case—do repressive governments in countries where change is most needed alter their behavior when they sign rights treaties? Drawing on ratification of the International Covenant on Civil and Political Rights and the International Convention Against Torture, the authors find that international human rights treaties had no effect on state behavior, a disappointing finding for those advocating international human rights.

Amartya Sen

HUMAN RIGHTS AND CAPABILITIES

Introduction

The moral appeal of human rights has been used for varying purposes, from resisting torture and arbitrary incarceration to demanding the end of hunger and of medical neglect. There is hardly any country in the world—from China, South Africa and Egypt to Mexico, Britain and the United States—in which arguments involving human rights have not been raised in one context or another in contemporary political debates.

However, despite the tremendous appeal of the idea of human rights, it is also seen by many as being intellectually frail—lacking in foundation and perhaps even in coherence and cogency. The remarkable co-existence of stirring appeal and deep conceptual scepticism is not new. The American Declaration of Independence took it to be 'self-evident' that everyone is "endowed by their Creator with certain inalienable rights", and 13 years later, in 1789, the French declaration of 'the rights of man' asserted that "men are born and remain free and equal in rights". But it did not take Jeremy Bentham long to insist, in *Anarchical Fallacies*, written during 1791–1792, that "natural rights is simple nonsense: natural and imprescriptible rights [an American phrase], rhetorical nonsense, nonsense upon stilts" (Bentham, 1792/1843, p. 501). That division remains very alive today, and there are many who see the idea of human rights as no more than "bawling upon paper" (to use another of Bentham's barbed descriptions).

From *Journal of Human Development* 6, no. 2 (July 2005), 151–166.

The concepts of human rights and human capabilities have something of a common motivation, but they differ in many distinct ways. It is useful to ask whether considering the two concepts together—capabilities and human rights—can help the understanding of each. I will divide the exercise into four specific questions. First, can human rights be seen as entitlements to certain basic capabilities, and will this be a good way of thinking about human rights? Second, can the capability perspective provide a comprehensive coverage of the content of human rights? Third, since human rights need specificity, does the use of the capability perspective for elucidating human rights require a full articulation of the list of capabilities? And finally, how can we go about ascertaining the content of human rights and of basic capabilities when our values are supposed to be quite divergent, especially across borders of nationality and community? Can we have anything like a universalist approach to these ideas, in a world where cultures differ and practical preoccupations are also diverse?

Human Rights as Entitlements to Capabilities

It is possible to argue that human rights are best seen as rights to certain specific freedoms, and that the correlate obligation to consider the associated duties must also be centred around what others can do to safeguard and expand these freedoms. Since capabilities can be seen, broadly, as freedoms of particular kinds, this would seem to establish a basic connection between the two categories of ideas.

We run, however, into an immediate difficulty here. I have argued elsewhere that 'opportunity' and 'process' are two aspects of freedom that require distinction, with the importance of each deserving specific acknowledgement.[1] While the opportunity aspect of freedoms would seem to belong to the same kind of territory as capabilities, it is not at all clear that the same can be said about the process aspect of freedom.

An example can bring out the *separate* (although not necessarily independent) relevance of both *substantive opportunities* and *freedom of processes*. Consider a woman, let us call her Natasha, who decides that she would like to go out in the evening. To take care of some considerations that are not central to the issues involved here (but which could make the discussion more complex), it is assumed that there are no particular safety risks involved in her going out, and that she has critically reflected on this decision and judged that going out would be the sensible—indeed the ideal—thing to do.

Now consider the threat of a violation of this freedom if some authoritarian guardians of society decide that she must not go out ('it is most unseemly'), and if they force her, in one way or another, to stay indoors. To see that there are two distinct issues involved in this one violation, consider an alternative case in which the authoritarian bosses decide that she must—absolutely *must*—go out ('you are expelled for the evening—just obey'). There is clearly a violation of freedom even here though Natasha is being forced to do exactly what she would have chosen to do anyway, and this is readily seen when we compare the two alternatives 'choosing freely to go out' and 'being forced to go out'. The latter involves an immediate violation of the *process aspect* of Natasha's freedom, since an action is being forced on her (even though it is an action she would have freely chosen also).

The opportunity aspect may also be affected, since a plausible accounting of opportunities can include having options and it can *inter alia* include valuing free choice. However, the violation of the opportunity aspect would be more substantial and manifest if she were not only forced to do something chosen by another, but in fact forced to do something she would not otherwise choose to do. The comparison between 'being forced to go out' (when she would have gone out anyway, if free) and, say, 'being forced to polish the shoes of others at home' (not her favourite way of spending time, I should explain) brings out this contrast, which is primarily one of the opportunity aspect, rather than the process aspect. In the incarceration of Natasha, we can see two different ways in which she is losing her freedom: first, she is being forced to do something, with no freedom of choice (a violation of her process freedom); and second, what Natasha is being obliged to do is not something she would choose to do, if she had any plausible alternative (a violation of her substantive opportunity to do what she would like to do).[2]

It is important to recognise that both processes and opportunities can figure powerfully in the content of human rights. A denial of 'due process' in being, say, sentenced without a proper trial can be an infringement of human rights (no matter what the outcome of the fair trial might be), and so can be the denial of opportunity of medical treatment, or the opportunity of living without the danger of being assaulted (going beyond the exact process through which these opportunities are made real).

The idea of 'capability' (i.e. the opportunity to achieve valuable combinations of human functionings—what a person is able to do or be) can be very helpful in understanding the opportunity aspect of freedom and human rights.[3] Indeed, even though the concept of opportunity is often invoked, it does require considerable elaboration, and capability can help in this elucidation. For example, seeing opportunity in terms of capability allows us to distinguish appropriately between (i) whether a person is actually able to do things she would value *doing*, and (ii) whether she possesses the *means or instruments or permissions* to pursue what she would like to do (her actual ability to do that pursuing may depend on many contingent circumstances). By shifting attention, in particular, towards the former, the capability-based approach resists an overconcentration on means (such as incomes and primary goods) that can be found in some theories of justice (e.g. in the Rawlsian Difference Principle). The capability approach can help to identify the possibility that two persons can have very different substantial opportunities even when they have exactly the same set of means: for example, a disabled person can do far less than an able-bodied person can, with exactly the same income and other 'primary goods'. The disabled person cannot, thus, be judged to be equally advantaged—with the same opportunities—as the person without any physical handicap but with the same set of means or instruments (such as income and wealth and other primary goods and resources).

The capability perspective allows us to take into account the parametric variability in the relation between the means, on the one hand, and the actual opportunities, on the other.[4] Differences in the capability to function can arise even with the same set of personal means (such as primary goods) for a variety of reasons, such as: (1) *physical or mental heterogeneities among persons* (related, for example, to disability, or proneness to illness); (2) *variations in non-personal resources* (such as the nature of public health care, or societal cohesion and the helpfulness of the community); (3) *environmental diversities* (such as climatic conditions, or varying threats from epidemic diseases or from local crime); or (4) *different relative positions vis-à-vis others* (well illustrated by Adam Smith's discussion, in the *Wealth of Nations*, of the fact that the clothing and other resources one needs "to appear in public without shame" depends on what other people standardly wear, which in turn could be more expensive in rich societies than in poorer ones).

I should, however, note here that there has been some serious criticism of describing these substantive opportunities (such as the capability to live one kind of a life or another) as 'freedoms', and it has been argued that this makes the idea of freedom too inclusive. For example, in her illuminating and sympathetic critique of my *Development as Freedom*, Susan Okin has presented arguments to suggest that I tend "to overextend the concept of freedom".[5] She has argued: "It is hard to conceive of some human functionings, or the fulfilment of some needs and wants, such as good health and nourishment, as freedoms without stretching the term until it seems to refer to everything that is of central value to human beings" (Okin, 2003, p. 292).

There is, certainly, considerable scope for argument on how extensively the term freedom should be used. But the particular example considered in Okin's counter-argument reflects a misinterpretation. There is no suggestion whatever that a functioning (e.g. being in good health or being well nourished) should be seen as freedom of any kind, such as capability. Rather, capability concentrates on the *opportunity* to be able to have combinations of functionings (including, in this case, the opportunity to be well-nourished), and the person is free to make use of this opportunity or not. A capability reflects the alternative combinations of functionings from which the person can choose one combination. It is, therefore, not being suggested at all that being well-nourished is to be seen as a freedom. The term freedom, in the form of capability, is used here to refer to the extent to which the person is free to choose particular levels of functionings (such as being well-nourished), and that is not the same thing as what the person actually decides to choose. During India's struggle for independence from the Raj, Mahatma Gandhi famously did not use that opportunity to be well fed when he chose to fast, as a protest against the policies of the Raj. In terms of the actual functioning of being well-nourished, the fasting Gandhi did not differ from a starving famine victim, but the freedoms and opportunities they respectively had were quite different.

Indeed, the *freedom to have* any particular thing can be substantially distinguished from actually *having* that thing. What a person is free to have—not just what he actually has—is relevant, I have argued, to a theory of justice.[6] A theory of rights also has reason to be involved with substantive freedoms.

Many of the terrible deprivations in the world have arisen from a lack of freedom to escape destitution. Even though indolence and inactivity had been classic themes in the old literature on poverty, people have starved and suffered because of a lack of alternative possibilities. It is the connection of poverty with unfreedom that led Marx to argue passionately for the need to replace "the domination of circumstances and chance over individuals by the domination of individuals over chance and circumstances".[7]

The importance of freedom can be brought out also by considering other types of issues that are also central to human rights. Consider the freedom of immigrants to retain their ancestral cultural customs and lifestyles. This complex subject cannot be adequately assessed without distinguishing between *doing* something and being free to do that thing. A strong argument can be constructed in favour of an immigrant's having the freedom to retain her ancestral lifestyle, but this must not be seen as an argument in favour of her pursuing that ancestral lifestyle whether she herself chooses that pursuit or not. The central issue, in this argument, is the person's freedom to choose how she should live—including the *opportunity* to pursue ancestral customs—and it cannot be turned into an argument for that person specifically pursuing those customs in particular, irrespective of the alternatives she has.[8] The importance of capability—reflecting opportunities—is central to this distinction.

The Process Aspect of Freedom and Information Pluralism

In the discussion so far I have been concentrating on what the capability perspective can do for a theory of justice or of human rights, but I would now like to turn to what it *cannot* do. While the idea of capability has considerable merit in the assessment of the opportunity aspect of freedom, it cannot possibly deal adequately with the process aspect of freedom, since capabilities are characteristics of individual advantages, and they fall short of telling us enough about the fairness or equity of the processes involved, or about the freedom of citizens to invoke and utilise procedures that are equitable.

The contrast of perspectives can be brought out with many different types of illustrations; let me choose a rather harsh example. It is, by now, fairly well established that, given symmetric care, women tend to live longer than men. If one were concerned only with capabilities (and nothing else), and in particular with equality of the capability to live long, it would have been possible to construct an argument for giving men more medical attention than women to counteract the natural masculine handicap. But giving women less medical attention than men for the same health problems would clearly violate an important requirement of process equity, and it seems reasonable to argue, in cases of this kind, that demands of equity in process freedom could sensibly override a single-minded concentration on the opportunity aspect of freedom (and on the requirements of capability equality in particular). While it is important to emphasise the relevance of the capability perspective in judging people's substantive opportunities (particularly in comparison with alternative approaches that focus on incomes, or primary goods, or resources), that point does not, in any way, go against seeing the relevance also of the process aspect of freedom in a theory of human rights—or, for that matter, in a theory of justice.

In this context, I should comment briefly also on a misinterpretation of the general relevance of the capability perspective in a theory of justice. A theory of justice—or more generally an adequate theory of normative social choice—has to be alive both to the fairness of the processes involved and to the equity and efficiency of the substantive opportunities that people can enjoy.[9] In dealing with the latter, capability can indeed provide a very helpful perspective, in comparison with, say, the Rawlsian concentration on 'primary goods'. But capability can hardly serve as the sole informational basis for the *other* considerations, related to processes, that must also be accommodated in normative social choice theory.

Consider the different components of Rawls's (1971) theory of justice. Rawls's 'first principle' of justice involves the priority of liberty, and the first part of the 'second principle' involves process fairness, through demanding that 'positions and offices be open to all.' The force and cogency of these Rawlsian concerns (underlying his first principle and the first part of the second principle) can neither be ignored nor be adequately addressed through relying only on the informational base of capabilities. We may not agree with Rawls's own way of dealing with these issues, but these issues have to be addressed, and they cannot be sensibly addressed within the substantive boundaries of capability accounting.

On the other hand, the capability perspective comes into its own in dealing with the *remainder* of the second principle; namely, 'the Difference Principle'—a principle that is particularly concerned with the distribution of advantages that different people enjoy (a consideration that Rawls tried to capture, I believe inadequately, within the confines of the accounting of 'primary goods'). The territory that Rawls reserved for primary goods, as used in his Difference Principle, would

indeed, I argue, be better served by the capability perspective. That does not, however, obliterate in any way the relevance of the rest of the territory of justice (related to the first principle and the first part of the second principle), in which process considerations, including liberty and procedural equity, figure.

A similar plurality of informational base has to be invoked in dealing with the multiplicity of considerations that underlie a theory of human rights. Capabilities and the opportunity aspect of freedom, important as they are, have to be supplemented by considerations of fair processes and the lack of violation of people's right to invoke and utilise them.

Listing Capabilities

I turn now to the controversial question of the listing of capabilities. In its application, the capability approach allows considerable variations in application. Martha Nussbaum has discussed powerfully the advantages of identifying an overarching 'list of capabilities', with given priorities. My own reluctance to join the search for such a canonical list arises partly from my difficulty in seeing how the exact lists and weights would be chosen without appropriate specification of the context of their use (which could vary), but also from a disinclination to accept any substantive diminution of the domain of public reasoning. The framework of capabilities helps, in my judgement, to clarify and illuminate the subject matter of public reasoning, which can involve epistemic issues (including claims of objective importance) as well as ethical and political ones. It cannot, I would argue, sensibly aim at displacing the need for continued public reasoning.

Indeed, I would submit that one of the uses of the capability perspective is to bring out the need for transparent valuational scrutiny of individual advantages and adversities, since the different *functionings* have to be assessed and weighted in relation to each other, and the opportunities of having different *combinations* of functionings also have to be evaluated.[10] The richness of the capability perspective broadly interpreted, thus, includes its insistence on the need for open valuational scrutiny for making social judgements, and in this sense it fits in well with the importance of public reasoning. This openness of transparent valuation contrasts with burying the evaluative exercise in some mechanical—and valuationally opaque—convention (e.g. by taking market-evaluated income to be the invariable standard of individual advantage, thereby giving implicit normative priority to institutionally determined market prices).

The problem is not with listing important capabilities, but with insisting on one pre-determined canonical list of capabilities, chosen by theorists without any general social discussion or public reasoning. To have such a fixed list, emanating entirely from pure theory, is to deny the possibility of fruitful public participation on what should be included and why.

I have, of course, discussed various lists of capabilities that would seem to demand attention in theories of justice and more generally in social assessment, such as the freedom to be well nourished, to live disease-free lives, to be able to move around, to be educated, to participate in public life, and so on. Indeed, right from my first writings on using the capability perspective (for example, the 1979 Tanner Lecture 'Equality of what?'; Sen, 1980), I have tried to discuss the relevance of specific capabilities that are important in a particular exercise. The 1979 Tanner lecture went into the relevance of "the ability to move about" (I discussed why disabilities can be a central concern in a way that an income-centred approach may not be able to grasp), along with other basic capabilities, such as "the ability to meet one's nutritional requirements, the wherewithal to be clothed and sheltered, the power to participate in the social life of the community". The contrast between lists of capabilities and commodities was a central concern in

Commodities and Capabilities (Sen, 1985a). The relevance of many capabilities that are often neglected were discussed in my second set of Tanner Lectures, given at Cambridge University under the title *The Standard of Living* (Hawthorn, 1987).

My scepticism is about fixing a cemented list of capabilities that is seen as being absolutely complete (nothing could be added to it) and totally fixed (it could not respond to public reasoning and to the formation of social values). I am a great believer in theory, and certainly accept that a good theory of evaluation and assessment has to bring out the relevance of what we are free to do and free to be (the capabilities in general), as opposed to the material goods we have and the commodities we can command. But I must also argue that pure theory cannot 'freeze' a list of capabilities for all societies for all time to come, irrespective of what the citizens come to understand and value. That would be not only a denial of the reach of democracy, but also a misunderstanding of what pure theory can do, completely divorced from the particular social reality that any particular society faces.

Along with the exercise of listing the relevant capabilities, there is also the problem of determining the relative weights and importance of the different capabilities included in the relevant list. Even with a given list, the question of valuation cannot be avoided. There is sometimes a temptation not only to have one fixed list, but also to have the elements of the list ordered in a lexicographic way. But this can hardly work. For example, the ability to be well-nourished cannot in general be put invariably *above* or *below* the ability to be well-sheltered (with the implication that the tiniest improvement of the higher ranked capability will always count as more important than a large change in the lower ranked one). The judgement must take into account the extent to which the different abilities are being realised or violated. Also, the weighting must be contingent on circumstances. We may have to give priority to the ability to be well-nourished when people are dying of hunger in their homes, whereas the freedom to be sheltered may rightly receive more weight when people are in general well-fed, but lack shelter and protection from the elements.

Some of the basic capabilities (with which my 1979 Tanner Lecture was particularly concerned) will no doubt figure in every list of relevant capabilities in every society. But the exact list to be used will have to take note of the purpose of the exercise. There is often good sense in narrowing the coverage of capabilities for a specific purpose. Jean Drèze and I have tried to invoke such lists of elementary capabilities in dealing with 'hunger and public action', and in a different context, in dealing with India's economic and social achievements and failures (Drèze and Sen, 1989, 2002). I see Martha Nussbaum's powerful use of a given list of capabilities for some minimal rights against deprivation as being extremely useful, in the same practical way. For another practical purpose, we may need quite a different list.

For example, when my friend Mahbub ul Haq asked me, in 1989, to work with him on indicators of human development, and in particular to help develop a general index for global assessment and critique, it was clear to me that we were Involved in a particular exercise of specific relevance. So the 'Human Development Index' was based on a very minimal listing of capabilities, with a particular focus on getting at a minimally basic quality of life, calculable from available statistics, in a way that the Gross National Product or Gross Domestic Product failed to capture (United Nations Development Programme, 1990). Lists of capabilities have to be used for various purposes, and so long as we understand what we are doing (and, in particular, that we are getting a list for a particular reason, related to assessment, evaluation, or critique), we do not put ourselves against other lists that may be relevant or useful for other purposes.

All this has to be contrasted with insisting on one 'final list of capabilities that matter'. To decide that some capability will not figure in the list of relevant capabilities at all amounts to putting a zero weight on that capability for every exercise, no matter what the exercise is concerned with, and no matter what the social conditions are. This could be very dogmatic, for many distinct reasons.

First, we use capabilities for different purposes. What we focus on cannot be independent of what we are doing and why (e.g. whether we are evaluating poverty, specifying certain basic human rights, getting a rough and ready measure of human development, and so on).

Second, social conditions and the priorities that they suggest may vary. For example, given the nature of poverty in India as well as the nature of available technology, it was not unreasonable in 1947 (when India became independent) to concentrate on elementary education, basic health, and so on, and to not worry too much about whether everyone can effectively communicate across the country and beyond. However, with the development of the internet and its wide-ranging applications, and the advance made in information technology (not least in India), access to the web and the freedom of general communication has become a very important capability that is of interest and relevance to all Indians.

Third, even with given social conditions, public discussion and reasoning can lead to a better understanding of the role, reach and the significance of particular capabilities. For example, one of the many contributions of feminist economics has precisely been to bring out the importance of certain freedoms that were not recognised very clearly—or at all—earlier on; for example, freedom from the imposition of fixed and time-honoured family roles, or immunity from implicit derogation through the rhetoric of social communication.

To insist on a 'fixed forever' list of capabilities would deny the possibility of progress in social understanding, and also go against the productive role of public discussion, social agitation, and open debates. I have nothing against the listing of capabilities (and take part in that activity often enough), but I have to stand up against any proposal of a grand mausoleum to one fixed and final list of capabilities.

Public Reasoning, Cultural Diversity and Universality

I turn now to the final question. If the listing of capabilities must be subject to the test of public reasoning, how can we proceed in a world of differing values and disparate cultures? How can we judge the acceptability of claims to human rights and to relevant capabilities, and assess the challenges they may face? How would such a disputation—or a defence—proceed? I would argue that, like the assessment of other ethical claims, there must be some test of open and informed scrutiny, and it is to such a scrutiny that we have to look in order to proceed to a disavowal or an affirmation. The status that these ethical claims have must be ultimately dependent on their survivability in unobstructed discussion. In this sense, the viability of human rights is linked with what John Rawls has called 'public reasoning' and its role in 'ethical objectivity'.[11]

Indeed, the role of public reasoning in the formulation and vindication of human rights is extremely important to understand. Any general plausibility that these ethical claims—or their denials—have is, on this theory, dependent on their ability to survive and flourish when they encounter unobstructed discussion and scrutiny (along with adequately wide informational availability). The force of a claim for a human right would be seriously undermined if it were possible to show that they are unlikely to survive open public scrutiny. But contrary to a commonly offered reason for scepticism and rejection, the case for human rights cannot be discarded simply by pointing to the possibility that in politically and socially repressive regimes, which do not allow open public discussion, many of these human rights are not taken seriously at all.

Open critical scrutiny is essential for dismissal as well as for defence. The fact that monitoring of violations of human rights and the procedure of 'naming and shaming' can be so effective (at least, in putting the violators on the defensive) is some indication of the wide reach of public reasoning when information becomes available and ethical arguments are allowed rather than suppressed.

It is, however, important not to keep the domain of public reasoning confined to a given society only, especially in the case of human rights, in view of the inescapably universalist nature of these rights. This is in contrast with Rawls's inclination, particularly in his later works, to limit such public confrontation within the boundaries of each particular nation (or each 'people', as Rawls calls this regional collectivity), for determining what would be just, at least in domestic affairs.[12] We can demand, on the contrary, that the discussion has to include, even for domestic justice (if only to avoid parochial prejudices and to examine a broader range of counter-arguments), views also from 'a certain distance'. The necessity of this was powerfully identified by Adam Smith:

> We can never survey our own sentiments and motives, we can never form any judgment concerning them; unless we remove ourselves, as it were, from our own natural station, and endeavour to view them as at a certain distance from us. But we can do this in no other way than by endeavouring to view them with the eyes of other people, or as other people are likely to view them.[13]

Questions are often raised about whether distant people can, in fact, provide useful scrutiny of local issues, given what are taken to be 'uncrossable' barriers of culture. One of Edmund Burke's criticisms of the French declaration of the 'rights of man' and its universalist spirit was concerned with disputing the acceptability of that notion in other cultures. Burke argued that "the liberties and the restrictions vary with times and circumstances, and admit of infinite modifications, that cannot be settled upon any abstract rule".[14] The belief that the universality that is meant to underlie the notion of human rights is profoundly mistaken has, for this reason, found expression in many other writings as well.

A belief in uncrossable barriers between the values of different cultures has surfaced and resurfaced repeatedly over the centuries, and they are forcefully articulated today. The claim of magnificent uniqueness—and often of superiority—has sometimes come from critics of 'Western values', varying from champions of regional ethics (well illustrated by the fuss in the 1990s about the peerless excellence of 'Asian values'), or religious or cultural separatists (with or without being accompanied by fundamentalism of one kind or another). Sometimes, however, the claim of uniqueness has come from Western particularists. A good example is Samuel Huntington's (1996) insistence that the "West was West long before it was modern", and his claim that "a sense of individualism and a tradition of individual rights and liberties" are "unique among civilized societies". Similarly, no less a historian of ideas than Gertrude Himmelfarb has argued that ideas of 'justice', 'right', 'reason' and 'love of humanity' are "predominantly, perhaps even uniquely, Western values" (1996, pp. 74–75).

I have discussed these diagnoses elsewhere (for example Sen, 1999). Contrary to cultural stereotypes, the histories of different countries in the world have shown considerable variations over time as well as between different groups within the same country. When, in the twelfth century, the Jewish philosopher Maimonedes had to flee an intolerant Europe and its Inquisitions to try to safeguard his human right to stick to his own religious beliefs and practice, he sought shelter in Emperor Saladin's Egypt (via Fez and Palestine),

and found an honoured position in the court of this Muslim emperor. Several hundred years later, when, in Agra, the Moghal emperor of India, Akbar, was arguing—and legislating—on the government's duty to uphold the right to religious freedom of all citizens, the European Inquisitions were still going on, and Giordano Bruno was burnt at the stake in Rome, in 1600.

In his autobiography, *Long Walk to Freedom*, Nelson Mandela (1994, p. 21) describes how he learned about democracy and individual rights, as a young boy, by seeing the proceedings of the local meetings held in the regent's house in Mqhekezweni:

> Everyone who wanted to speak did so. It was democracy in its purest form. There may have been a hierarchy of importance among the speakers, but everyone was heard, chief and subject, warrior and medicine man, shopkeeper and farmer, landowner and laborer.

Not only are the differences on the subject of freedoms and rights that actually exist between different societies often much exaggerated, but also there is, typically, little note taken of substantial variations *within* each local culture—over time and even at a point of time (in particular, right now). What are taken to be 'foreign' criticisms often correspond to internal criticisms from non-mainstream groups.[15] If, say, Iranian dissidents are imprisoned by an authoritarian regime precisely because of their heterodoxy, any suggestion that they should be seen as 'ambassadors of Western values' rather than as 'Iranian dissidents' would only add serious insult to manifest injury. Being culturally non-partisan requires respecting the participation of people from any corner of the earth, which is not the same thing as accepting the prevailing priorities, especially among dominant groups in particular societies, when information is extremely restricted and discussions and disagreements are not permitted.

Scrutiny from a 'distance' may have something to offer in the assessment of practices as different from each other as the stoning of adulterous women In the Taliban's Afghanistan and the abounding use of capital punishment (sometimes with mass jubilation) in parts of the United States. This is the kind of issue that made Smith insist that "the eyes of the rest of mankind" must be invoked to understand whether "a punishment appears equitable".[16] Ultimately, the discipline of critical moral scrutiny requires, among other things, "endeavouring to view [our sentiments and beliefs] with the eyes of other people, or as other people are likely to view them" (*The Theory of Moral Sentiments*, III, 1, 2; in Smith, 1976, p. 110).

Intellectual interactions across the borders can be as important in rich societies as they are in poorer ones. The point to note here is not so much whether we are *allowed* to chat across borders and to make cross-boundary scrutiny, but that the discipline of critical assessment of moral sentiments—no matter how locally established they are—*requires* that we view our practices *inter alia* from a certain distance.

Both the understanding of human rights and of the adequacy of a list of basic capabilities, I would argue, are intimately linked with the reach of public discussion—between persons and across borders. The viability and universality of human rights and of an acceptable specification of capabilities are dependent on their ability to survive open critical scrutiny in public reasoning.

Conclusions

To conclude, the two concepts—human rights and capabilities—go well with each other, so long as we do not try to subsume either entirely within the other. There are many human rights for which the capability perspective has much to offer. However, human rights to important process freedoms cannot be adequately analysed within the capability approach.

Furthermore, both human rights and capabilities have to depend on the process of public reasoning, which neither can lose without serious impoverishment of its respective intellectual content. The methodology of public scrutiny draws on Rawlsian understanding of 'objectivity' in ethics, but the impartiality that is needed cannot be confined within the borders of a nation. We have to go much beyond Rawls for that reason, just as we also have to go beyond the enlightenment provided by his use of 'primary goods', and invoke, in that context, the more articulate framework of capabilities. The need for extension does not, of course, reduce our debt to John Rawls. Neither human rights nor capabilities would have been easy to understand without his pioneering departures.

NOTES

1. See Sen (2002a), particularly the Arrow Lectures ('Freedom and Social Choice') included there (essays 20–22).
2. An investigation of more complex features of the opportunity aspect and the process aspect of freedoms can be found in the Arrow Lectures ('Freedom and Social Choice') In Sen (2002a, essays 20–22).
3. On the concept of capability, see Sen (1980, 1985a, 1985b), Nussbaum and Sen (1993), and Nussbaum (2000). See also the related theories of substantial opportunities developed by Arneson (1989), Cohen (1989), and Roemer (1996), among other contributions.
4. The relevance of such parametric variability for a theory of justice is discussed in Sen (1990).
5. See Okin (2003, p. 293). On related issues see also Joshua Cohen (1994, especially pp. 278–280), and G. A. Cohen (1995, especially pp. 120–125).
6. See Sen (1980, 1985a, 1985b). In contrast, G. A. Cohen has presented arguments in favour of focusing on achieved functionings—related to his concept of 'midfare'—rather than on capability (see Cohen, 1989, 1993).
7. See Marx (1845–1846/1977, p. 190).

8. There is a substantial difference between: (1) valuing multiculturalism because of the way—and to the extent that—it enhances the freedoms of the people involved to choose to live as they would like (and have reason to like); and (2) valuing cultural diversity *per se*, which focuses on the descriptive characteristics of a social pattern, rather than on the freedoms of the people involved. The contrast receives investigation in the *Human Development Report 2004* (United Nations Development Programme, 2004).

9. On the plurality of concerns that include processes as well as opportunities, which is inescapably involved in normative social choice (including theories of justice), see Sen (1970, 1985b). Since I have often encountered the diagnosis that I propound a "capability-based theory of justice", I should make it clear that this could be true only in the very limited sense of naming something according to one *principal* part of it (comparable with, say, using England for Britain). It is only one part of the informational base of a theory of justice that the capability perspective can expect to fill.

10. I cannot emphasise adequately how important I believe it is to understand that the need for an explicit valuational exercise is an advantage, rather than a limitation, of the capability approach, because valuational decisions have to be explicitly discussed, rather than being derived from some mechanical formula that is used, without scrutiny and assessment. For arguments *against* my position on this issue, see Beitz (1986) and Williams (1987). My own position is more fully discussed in Sen (1999, 2004).

11. See Rawls (1971, 1993, especially pp. 110–113).

12. See particularly John Rawls (1999). See also Rawls's formulation of the original position in *Political Liberalism* (Rawls, 1993, p. 12): "I assume that the basic structure is that of a closed society: that is, we are to regard it as self-contained and as having no relations with other societies. . . . That a society is closed is a considerable abstraction, justified only because it enables us to focus on certain main questions free from distracting details."

13. See Smith (1759/1790, III, 1, 2). Smith (1976, p. 110). I have tried to discuss and extend the Smithian perspective on moral reasoning in Sen (2002b).

14. Quoted In Lukes (1997, p. 238).

15. On this see Nussbaum and Sen (1988).

16. Smith (1978/1982, p. 104).

REFERENCES

Arneson, R. (1989) 'Equality and Equal Opportunity for Welfare', *Philosophical Studies*, 56, pp. 77–93.

Beitz, C. (1986) 'Amartya Sen's resources, values and development', *Economics and Philosophy*, 2, pp. 282–290.

Bentham, J. (1792) *Anarchical Fallacies; Being an Examination of the Declaration of Rights Issued during the French Revolution* [Republished in J. Bowring (Ed.) (1843) *The Works of Jeremy Bentham*, volume II, William Talt, Edinburgh].

Cohen, G.A. (1989) 'On the currency of egalitarian Justice', *Ethics*, 99, pp. 906–944.

Cohen, G.A. (1993) 'Equality of what? On welfare, resources and capabilities', in M. Nussbaum and A. Sen (Eds.), *The Quality of Life*, Clarendon Press, Oxford.

Cohen, G.A. (1995) 'Review: Amartya Sen's unequal world', *The New Left Review*, January, pp. 117–129.

Cohen, J. (1994) 'Review of Sen's *Inequality Reexamined*', *Journal of Philosophy*, 92, pp. 275–288.

Drèze, J. and Sen, A. (1989) *Hunger and Public Action*, Clarendon Press, Oxford.

Drèze, J. and Sen, A. (2002) *India: Participation and Development*, Oxford University Press, Delhi.

Hawthorn, G. (Ed.) (1987) *Amartya Sen et al, The Standard of Living*, Cambridge University Press, Cambridge.

Himmelfarb, G. (1996) 'The illusions of cosmopolitanism', in M. Nussbaum with respondents (Ed.), *For Love of Country*, Beacon Press, Boston.

Huntington, S. (1996) *The Clash of Civilizations and the Remaking of World Order*, Simon and Schuster, New York.

Lukes, S. (1997) 'Five fabies about human rights', in M. Ishay (Ed.), *The Human Rights Reader*, Routledge, London.

Mandela, N. (1994) *Long Walk to Freedom*, Little, Brown & Co., Boston.

Marx, K. (1845–1846) *The German Ideology*, with F. Engels [Republished in D. McLellan (Ed.) (1977) *Karl Marx: Selected Writings*, Oxford University Press, Oxford].

Nussbaum, M. (2000) *Women and Human Development: The Capabilities Approach*, Cambridge University Press, Cambridge.

Nussbaum, M. and Sen, A. (1988) 'Internal criticism and Indian rationalist traditions', in M. Krausz (Ed.), *Relativism: Interpretation and Confrontation*, University of Notre Dame Press, Notre Dame.

Nussbaum, M. and Sen, A. (Eds) (1993) *The Quality of Life*, Clarendon Press, Oxford.

Okin, S. (2003) 'Poverty, Well-being and gender: what counts, who's heard?', *Philosophy and Public Affairs*, 31, pp. 280–316.

Rawls, J. (1971) *A Theory of Justice*, Harvard University Press, Cambridge, MA.

Rawls, J. (1993) *Political Liberalism*, Columbia University Press, New York.

Rawls, J. (1999) *The Law of Peoples*, Harvard University Press, Cambridge, MA.

Roemer, J.E. (1996) *Theories of Distributive Justice*, Harvard University Press, Cambridge, MA.

Sen, A. (1970) *Collective Choice and Social Welfare*, Holden-Day, San Francisco [Republished by North-Holland, Amsterdam].

Sen, A. (1980) 'Equality of what?', in S. McMurrin (Ed.), *Tanner Lectures on Human Values*, volume I, Cambridge University Press, Cambridge: University of Utah Press, Cambridge.

Sen, A. (1985a) *Commodities and Capabilities*, North-Holland, Amsterdam.

Sen, A. (1985b) 'Well-being, agency and freedom: the Dewey Lectures 1984', *Journal of Philosophy*, 82, pp. 169–221.

Sen, A. (1985/1987) *The Standard of Living*, Tanner Lectures, Cambridge University Press, Cambridge.

Sen, A. (1990) 'Justice: means versus freedoms', *Philosophy and Public Affairs*, 19, pp. 111–121.

Sen, A. (1999) *Development as Freedom*, Knopf, New York: Oxford University Press, New York.

Sen, A. (2002a) *Rationality and Freedom*, Harvard University Press, Cambridge, MA.

Sen, A. (2002b) 'Open and closed impartiality', *The Journal of Philosophy*, 99, pp. 445–469.

Sen, A. (2004) 'Elements of a theory of human rights', *Philosophy and Public Affairs*, 32(4), pp. 315–356.

Smith, A. (1759/1790/1976) *The Theory of Moral Sentiments*, revised edition 1790 [Republished by Clarendon Press, Oxford].

Smith, A. (1776/1979) *An Inquiry into the Nature and Causes of the Wealth of Nations*, Clarendon Press, Oxford [Reprinted by Liberty Press, 1981].

Smith, A. (1978/1982) in R.L. Meek, D.D. Raphael and P.G. Stein (Eds.), *Lectures on Jurisprudence*, Clarendon Press, Oxford [Reprinted by Liberty Press, Indianapolis].

United Nations Development Programme (1990) *Human Development Report 1990*, Oxford University Press, Oxford.

United Nations Development Programme (2004) *Human Development Report 2004*, Oxford University Press, Oxford.

Williams, B. (1987) 'The standard of living: interests and capabilities', in G. Hawthorn (Ed.), *Amartya Sen et al, The Standard of Living*, Cambridge University Press, Cambridge.

Jack Donnelly

HUMAN RIGHTS AND CULTURAL RELATIVISM

Cultural relativity is an undeniable fact; moral rules and social institutions evidence astonishing cultural and historical variability. The doctrine of cultural relativism holds that some such variations cannot be legitimately criticized by outsiders. I argue, instead, for a fundamentally universalistic approach to internationally recognized human rights.

In most recent discussions of cultures or civilizations[1]—whether they are seen as clashing, converging, or conversing—the emphasis has been on differences, especially differences between the West and the rest. From a broad cross-cultural or intercivilizational perspective, however, the most striking fact about human rights in the contemporary world is the extensive overlapping consensus on the Universal Declaration of Human Rights. * * * Real conflicts do indeed exist over a few internationally recognized human rights. There are numerous variations in interpretations and modes of implementing internationally recognized human rights. Nonetheless, I argue that culture[2] poses only a modest challenge to the contemporary normative universality of human rights.

1. Defining Cultural Relativism

When internal and external judgments of a practice diverge, cultural relativists give priority to the internal judgments of a society. In its most extreme form, what we can call *radical cultural relativism* holds that culture is the sole source of the validity of a moral right or rule.[3] *Radical universalism*, by contrast, would hold that culture is irrelevant to the (universal) validity, of moral rights and rules. The body of the continuum defined by these end points can be roughly divided into what we can call strong and weak cultural relativism.

Strong cultural relativism holds that culture is the principal source of the validity of a right or rule. At its furthest extreme, strong cultural relativism accepts a few basic rights with virtually universal application but allows such a wide range of variation that two entirely justifiable sets of rights might overlap only slightly.

Weak cultural relativism, which might also be called strong universalism, considers culture a secondary source of the validity of a right or rule. Universality is initially presumed, but the relativity of human nature, communities, and rules checks potential excesses of universalism. At its furthest extreme, weak cultural relativism recognizes a comprehensive set of prima facie universal human rights but allows limited local variations.

We can also distinguish a qualitative dimension to relativist claims. Legitimate cultural divergences from international human rights norms might be advocated concerning the *substance* of lists of human rights, the *interpretation* of particular rights, and the *form* in which those rights are implemented. * * * I will defend a weak cultural relativist (strong universalist) position that permits devia-

From *Universal Human Rights in Theory and Practice* (Ithaca: Cornell University Press, 2003), Chap. 6, 89–106.

tions from international human rights norms primarily at the level of form or implementation.

2. Relativity and Universality: A Necessary Tension

Beyond the obvious dangers of moral imperialism, radical universalism requires a rigid hierarchical ordering of the multiple moral communities to which we belong. The radical universalist would give absolute priority to the demands of the cosmopolitan moral community over other ("lower") communities. Such a complete denial of national and subnational ethical autonomy, however, is rare and implausible. There is no compelling moral reason why peoples cannot accept, say, the nation-state, as a major locus of extrafamilial moral and political commitments. And at least certain choices of a variety of moral communities demand respect from outsiders—not uncritical acceptance, let alone emulation, but, in some cases at least, tolerance.

But if human rights are based in human nature, on the fact that one is a human being, how can human rights be relative in any fundamental way? The simple answer is that human nature is itself relative. * * * There is a sense in which this is true even biologically. For example, if marriage partners are chosen on the basis of cultural preferences for certain physical attributes, the gene pool in a community may be altered. More important, culture can significantly influence the presence and expression of many aspects of human nature by encouraging or discouraging the development or perpetuation of certain personality traits and types. Whether we stress the "unalterable" core or the variability around it—and however we judge their relative size and importance—"human nature," the realized nature of real human beings, is as much a social project as a natural given.

But if human nature were infinitely variable, or if all moral values were determined solely by culture (as radical cultural relativism holds), there could be no human rights (rights that one has "simply as a human being") because the concept "human being" would have no specificity or moral significance. As we saw in the case of Hindu India, * * * some societies have not even recognized "human being" as a descriptive category. The very names of many cultures mean simply "the people" (e.g., Hopi, Arapahoe), and their origin myths define them as separate from outsiders, who are somehow "not-human."

Such views, however, are almost universally rejected in the contemporary world. For example, chattel slavery and caste-based legal and political systems, which implicitly deny the existence of a morally significant common humanity, are almost universally condemned, even in the most rigid class societies.

The radical relativist response that consensus is morally irrelevant is logically impeccable. But many people do believe that such consensus strengthens a rule, and most think that it increases the justifiability of certain sorts of international action. In effect, a moral analogue to customary international law seems to operate. If a practice is nearly universal and generally perceived as obligatory, it is required of all members of the community. Even a weak cosmopolitan moral community imposes substantive limitations on the range of permissible moral variation.

Notice, however, that I contend only that there are a few cross-culturally valid moral *values*. This still leaves open, the possibility of a radical cultural relativist denial of human *rights*. Plausible arguments can be (and have been) advanced to justify alternative mechanisms to guarantee human dignity. But few states today attempt such an argument. In all regions of the world, a strong commitment to human *rights* is almost universally proclaimed. Even where practice throws that commitment into question, such a widespread rhetorical "fashion" must have some substantive basis.

That basis * * * lies in the hazards to human dignity posed by modern markets and states. The political power of traditional rulers usually was substantially limited by customs and laws that were entirely independent of human rights. The relative technological and administrative weakness of traditional political institutions further restrained abuses of power. In such a world, inalienable entitlements of individuals held against state and society might plausibly be held to be superfluous (because dignity was guaranteed by alternative mechanisms), if not positively dangerous to important and well-established values and practices.

Such a world, however, exists today only in a relatively small number of isolated areas. The modern state, even in the Third World, not only has been freed from many of the moral constraints of custom but also has a far greater administrative and technological reach. It thus represents a serious threat to basic human dignity, whether that dignity is defined in "traditional" or "modern" terms. In such circumstances, human rights seem necessary rather than optional. Radical or unrestricted relativism thus is as inappropriate as radical universalism.[4] Some kind of intermediate position is required.

3. Internal Versus External Judgments

Respect for autonomous moral communities would seem to demand a certain deference to a society's internal evaluations of its practices, but to commit ourselves to acting on the basis of the moral judgments of others would abrogate our own moral responsibilities. The choice between internal and external evaluations is a moral one, and whatever choice we make will be problematic.

Where internal and external judgments conflict, assessing the relative importance attached to those judgments may be a reasonable place to start in seeking to resolve them. Figure 10.1 offers a simple typology.

Case 1—morally unimportant both externally and internally—is uninteresting. Whether or not one maintains one's initial external condemnation is of little intrinsic interest to anyone. Case 2—externally unimportant, internally very important—is probably best handled by refusing to press the negative external judgment. To press a negative external judgment that one feels is relatively unimportant when the issue is of great importance internally usually will be, at best insensitive. By the same token, Case 3—externally very important, internally unimportant—presents the best occasion to press an external judgment (with some tact).

Case 4, in which the practice is of great moral importance to both sides, is the most difficult to handle, but even here we may have good reasons to press a negative external judgment. Consider, for example, slavery. Most people today would agree that no matter how ancient and well established the practice may be, to turn one's back on the enslavement of human beings in the name of cultural relativity would reflect moral obtuseness, not sensitivity. Human sacrifice, trial by ordeal, extrajudicial execution, and female infanticide are other cultural practices that are (in my view rightly) condemned by almost all external observers today.

Underlying such judgments is the inherent universality of basic moral precepts, at least as we understand morality in the West. We simply do not believe that our moral precepts are for us and us alone. This is most evident in Kant's deontological universalism. But it is no less true of the principle of utility. And, of course, human rights are also inherently universal.

In any case, our moral precepts are *our* moral precepts. As such, they demand our obedience. To abandon them simply because others reject them

Figure 10.1. Type Conflicts over Culturally Relative Practices

		Internal judgment of practice	
		Morally unimportant	Morally very important
External judgment of practice	Morally unimportant	Case 1	Case 2
	Morally very important	Case 3	Case 4

is to fail to give proper weight to our own moral beliefs (at least where they involve central moral precepts such as the equality of all human beings and the protection of innocents).

Finally, no matter how firmly someone else, or even a whole culture, believes differently, at some point—slavery and untouchability come to mind—we simply must say that those contrary beliefs are wrong. Negative external judgments may be problematic. In some cases, however, they are not merely permissible but demanded.

4. Concepts, Interpretations, Implementations

In evaluating arguments of cultural relativism, we must distinguish between variations in substance, interpretation, and form. Even very weak cultural relativists—that is, strong universalists—are likely to allow considerable variation in the form in which rights are implemented. For example, whether free legal assistance is required by the right to equal protection of the laws usually will best be viewed as largely beyond the legitimate reach of universal standards. Important differences between strong and weak relativists are likely to

arise, however, at the levels of interpretation and, especially, substance.

A. Substance or Concept

The Universal Declaration generally formulates rights at the level of what I will call the *concept,* an abstract, general statement of an orienting value. "Everyone has the right to work, to free choice of employment, to just and favorable conditions of work and to protection against unemployment" (Art. 23). *Only* at this level do I claim that there is a consensus on the rights of the Universal Declaration, and at this level, most appeals to cultural relativism fail.

It is difficult to imagine arguments against recognizing the rights of Articles 3–12, which include life, liberty, and security of the person; the guarantee of legal personality, equality before the law, and privacy, and protections against slavery, arbitrary arrest, detention, or exile, and inhuman or degrading treatment. These are so clearly connected to basic requirements of human dignity, and are stated in sufficiently general terms, that virtually every morally defensible contemporary form of social organization must recognize them (although perhaps not necessarily as inalienable rights). I am even tempted to say that conceptions of human nature or society that are incompatible with such rights are almost by definition indefensible in contemporary international society.

Civil rights such as freedom of conscience, speech, and association may be a bit more relative. Because they assume the existence and positive evaluation of relatively autonomous individuals, they may be of questionable applicability in strong, thriving traditional communities. In such communities, however, they would rarely be at issue. If traditional practices truly are based on and protect culturally accepted conceptions of human dignity, then members of such a community will not have the desire or the need to claim such rights. In the more typical contemporary case, however, in which relatively autonomous individuals face modern states, it is hard for me to imagine a defensible conception of human dignity that does not include almost all of these rights. A similar argument can be made for the economic and social rights of the Universal Declaration.

In twenty years of working with issues of cultural relativism, I have developed a simple test that I pose to skeptical audiences. Which rights in the Universal Declaration, I ask, does your society or culture reject? Rarely has a single full right (other than the right to private property) been rejected. Never has it been suggested to me that as many as four should be eliminated.

Typical was the experience I had in Iran in early 2001, where I posed this question to three different audiences. In each case, discussion moved quickly to freedom of religion, and in particular atheism and apostasy by Muslims (which the Universal Declaration permits but Iran prohibits).[5] Given the continuing repression of Iranian Bahais—although, for the moment at least, the apparent end to executions—this was quite a sensitive issue. Even here, though, the challenge was not to the principle, or even the right, of freedom of religion (which almost all Muslims support) but to competing "Western" and "Muslim" conceptions of its limits.

And we must remember that *every* society places some limits on religious liberty. In the United States, for example, recent court cases have dealt with forced medical treatment for the children of Christian Scientists, live animal sacrifice by practitioners of santaria, and the rights of Jehovah's Witnesses to evangelize at private residences.

We must be careful, however, not to read too much into this consensus at the level of the concept, which may obscure important disagreements concerning definitions and implicit limitations. Consider Article 5 of the Universal Declaration: "No one shall be subjected to torture or to cruel, inhuman or degrading treatment or punishment." The real controversy comes over definitions of terms such as "cruel." Is the death penalty cruel, inhuman, or degrading? Most European states consider it to be. The United States does not. We must recognize and address such differences without overstating their importance or misrepresenting their character.

Implicit limits on rights may also pose challenges to universalist arguments. Most of the rights in the Universal Declaration are formulated in categorical terms. For example, Article 19 begins: "Everyone has the right to freedom of opinion and expression." To use the hackneyed American example, this does not mean that one can scream "Fire!" in a crowded theater. All rights have limits.[6] But if these limits differ widely and systematically across civilizations, the resulting differences in human rights practices might indeed be considerable.

Are there systematic differences in definitions of terms across civilizations? Do cultures differ systematically in the standard limits they put on the exercises of rights? And if these differences are systematic, how significant are they? I have suggested that the answers to these questions are largely negative. For reasons of space—as well as the fact that such negative arguments cannot be conclusively established—I leave this claim as a challenge. Critics may refute my argument with several well-chosen examples of substantial cultural variation either at the level of concepts or in systematic variations at the level of interpretation that undermine the apparent conceptual consensus. So far, at least, I have not encountered anyone capable of presenting such, a pattern of contradictory evidence, except in the case of small and relatively isolated communities.[7]

B. Interpretations

What ought to count, for example, as adequate protection against unemployment? Does it mean a guaranteed job, or is it enough to provide compensation to those who are unemployed? Both seem to me plausible interpretations. Some such variations in interpreting rights seem not merely defensible but desirable, and even necessary.

Particular human rights are like "essentially contested concepts," in which there is a substantial but rather general consensus on basic meaning coupled with no less important, systematic, and apparently irresolvable conflicts of interpretations (Gallie 1968). In such circumstances, culture provides one plausible and defensible mechanism for selecting interpretations (and forms).

We should also note that the Universal Declaration lists some rights that are best viewed as interpretations. For example, the right of free and full consent of intending spouses reflects an interpretation of marriage over which legitimate controversy is possible. Notice, however, that the right (as stated in Sec. 2 of Art. 16) is subordinate to the right to marry and to found a family (over which, at this highest level of generality, there is little international dispute). Furthermore, some traditional customs, such as bride price, provide alternative protections for women that address at least some of the underlying concerns that gave rise to the norm of free and full consent.

I would suggest, however, that defensible variations in interpretations are likely to be relatively modest in number. And not all "interpretations" are equally plausible or defensible. They are

interpretations not free associations or arbitrary, let alone self-interested, stipulations. The meaning of, for example, "the right to political participation" is controversial, but an election in which a people were allowed to choose an absolute dictator for life ("one man, one vote, once," as a West African quip put it) is simply indefensible.

We must also note that considerable divergences in interpretation exist not only between but also *within* cultures or civilizations. Consider, for example, differences within the West between Europe and the United States on the death penalty and the welfare state. Japan and Vietnam have rather different interpretations of the rights to freedom of speech and association, despite being East Asians.

Even where there are variations between two cultures, we still need to ask whether culture in fact is the source of cause of these differences. I doubt that we are actually saying much of interest or importance when we talk of, say, Japan as Asian. Consider the common claim that Asian societies are communitarian and consensual and Western societies are individualistic and competitive. What exactly is this supposed to explain, or even refer to, in any particular Asian or Western country? Dutch or Norwegian politics is at least as consensual as Thai politics. The Dutch welfare state is in its own way as caring and paternalistic as the most traditional of Japanese employers. Such examples, which are easily multiplied, suggest that even where variations in practice exist, culture does much less explanatory work than most relativists suggest—or at least that the "culture" in question is more local or national rather than regional or a matter of civilization.

C. Implementation or Form

Just as concepts need to be interpreted, interpretations need to be implemented in law and political practice. To continue with the example of the right to work, what rate of unemployment compensation should be provided, for how long, in what circumstances? The range of actual and defensible variation here is considerable—although limited by the governing concept and interpretation.

Even a number of rights in the International Human Rights Covenants involve specifications at the level of form. For example, Article 10(2)(b) of the International Covenant on Civil and Political Rights requires the segregation of juvenile defendants. In some cultures the very notion of a juvenile criminal defendant (or a penitentiary system) does not exist Although there are good reasons to suggest such rules, to demand them in the face of strong reasoned opposition seems to me to make little sense—so long as the underlying objectives are realized in some other fashion.

Differences in implementations, however, often seem to have little to do with culture. And even where they do, it is not obvious that cultural differences deserve more (or less) respect than differing implementations attributable to other causes (e.g., levels of economic development or unique national historical experiences).

I stress this three-level scheme to avoid a common misconception. My argument is for universality only at the level of the concept. The Universal Declaration insists that all states share a limited but important range of obligations. It is, in its own words, "a common standard of achievement for all peoples and all nations." The ways in which these rights are implemented, however, so long as they fall within the range of variation consistent with the overarching concept, are matters of legitimate variation. * * *

This is particularly important because most of the "hot button" issues in recent discussions have occurred at the level of implementation. For example, debates about pornography are about the limits—interpretation or implementation—of freedom of expression. Most Western countries permit the graphic depiction of virtually any sex act (so long as it does not involve and is not shown to children). Many others countries punish those who produce, distribute, or consume such material. This dispute, however, does not suggest a rejection of human rights, the idea of personal autonomy, or even the right to freedom of speech.

We should also note that controversy over pornography rages internally in many countries. Every country criminalizes some forms of pornography, and most countries—Taliban Afghanistan being the exception that proves the rule—permit some depictions of sexual behavior or the display of erotic images that another country has within living memory banned as pornographic. Wherever one draws the line, it leaves intact both the basic internationally recognized human right to freedom of speech and the underlying value of personal autonomy.

D. Universality within Diversity

There are at least three ways in which rights that vary in form and interpretation can still be plausibly described as "universal." First, and most important, there may be an overlapping consensus * * * on the substance of the list, despite diversity in interpretations and implementations. Second, even where there are differences at the level of snhstanre or concept, a large common core may exist with relatively few differences "around the edges." Third, even where substantial substantive disagreements occur, we might still be justified in speaking of universal rights if there are strong statistical regularities and the outliers are few and clearly overshadowed by the central tendency.

In contemporary international society, I think that we can say that there are few far outliers (e.g., North Korea) at least at the level of agreed-on concepts. I would admit that overlapping conceptual consensus often is thin. Nonetheless, I think that we can fairly (although not without controversy) say that variations at the level of concepts are infrequent. Somewhat more contentious is the claim that I would also advance that the range of diversity in standard interpretations is modest and poses relatively few serious international political disputes.

We do not face an either-or choice between cultural relativism and universal human rights. Rather, we need to recognize both the universality of human rights and their particularity and thus accept a certain *limited* relativity, especially with respect to forms of implementation. We must take seriously the initially paradoxical idea of the relative universality of internationally recognized human rights.[8]

5. Explaining the Persistence of Culturalist Arguments

If my argument for relative universality is even close to correct, how can we explain the persistence of foundational appeals to culture? If we could explain this puzzle, both for the relativist arguments * * * and for the claims about human rights in traditional societies, * * * the plausibility of a universalist perspective would be enhanced. At least six explanations come to mind.

First, it is surprisingly common for even otherwise sophisticated individuals to take the particular institutions associated with the realization of a right in their country or culture to be essential to that right. Americans, in particular, seem to have unusually great difficulty in realizing that the way we do things here is not necessarily what international human rights norms require.

Second, narrow-minded and ham-handed (Western, and especially American) international human rights policies and statements exacerbate these confusions. Consider Michael Fay, an American teenager who vandalized hundreds of thousands of dollars worth of property in Singapore. When he was sentenced to be publicly caned,

there was a furor in the United States. President Clinton argued, with apparently genuine indignation, that it was abominable to cane someone, but he failed to find it even notable that in his own country people are being fried in the electric chair. If this indeed is what universalism means—and I hasten to repeat that it is not—then of course relativism looks far more attractive.

The legacy of colonialism provides a third important explanation for the popularity of relativist arguments. African, Asian, and Muslim (as well as Latin American) leaders and citizens have vivid, sometimes personal, recollections of their sufferings under colonial masters. Even when the statements and actions of great powers stay within the range of the overlapping consensus on the Universal Declaration, there is understandable (although not necessarily justifiable) sensitivity to external pressure. (Compare the sensitivity of the United States to external criticism even in the absence of such a historical legacy.) When international pressures exceed the bounds of the overlapping consensus, that sensitivity often becomes (justifiably) very intense.

Fourth, arguments of relativism are often rooted in a desire to express and foster national, regional, cultural, or civilizational pride. It is no coincidence that the "Asian values" debate * * * took off in the wake of the Asian economic miracle and dramatically subsided after the 1977 financial crisis.

The belief that such arguments have instrumental efficacy in promoting internationally recognized human rights is a fifth important reason. For example, Daniel Bell plausibly argues that building human rights implementation strategies on local traditions (1) is "more likely to lead to long term commitment to human rights"; (2) "may shed light on the groups most likely to bring about desirable social and political change"; (3) "allows the human rights activist to draw on the most compelling justifications"; (4) "may shed light on the appropriate attitude to be employed by human rights activists"; and (5) "may also make one more sensitive to the possibility of alternative" mechanisms for protecting rights (1996: 657–659). I would insist only that we be clear that this is a practical, not a theoretical, argument; that we operate with a plausible theory of culture and an accurate understanding of the culture in question; and that we not assume that culture trumps international norms. "To realize greater social justice on an international scale, activists and intellectuals must take culture seriously, but not in the totalizing, undifferentiated way in which some leaders of non-Western nations have used it as a trump card" (L. Bell 2001: 21).

This leads to the sixth, and perhaps the most important, explanation for the prevalence of culturalist arguments, namely, that they are used by vicious elites as a way to attempt to deflect attention from their repressive policies. And well-meaning Westerners with a well-developed sense of the legacy of Western colonialism indirectly support such arguments when they shy away from criticizing arguments advanced by non-Westerners even when they are empirically inaccurate or morally absurd.

6. Culture and Politics

So far I have proceeded, in line with the standard assumption of cultural relativists, by treating "cultures" as homogenous, static, all-encompassing, and voluntarily accepted "things," the substance of which can be relatively easily and uncontroversially determined. None of these assumptions is defensible.

A. Identifying a "Culture"

Cultures are anything but homogenous. In fact, differences *within* civilizations often are as striking and as important as those between civilizations. "The Western tradition," for example, includes both Caligula and Marcus Aurelius, Francis of Assisi and Torquemada, Leopold II of Belgium and Albert Schweitzer, Jesus and Hitler—and just about everything in between.

We thus face a difficult problem even in determining what is to count as evidence for a claim of the form "civilization *x* holds belief *y*." Political authorities are but one (very problematic) source of evidence of the views and practices of a civilization. Nor can we rely on authoritative texts. For example, the Christian Bible has significantly shaped Western civilization. But even when particular practices do not diverge from what one might expect from reading this "foundational" text and setting aside the fact that such expectations change with time, place, and reader—few Western practices are adequately explained in terms of, let alone reducible to, those texts.[9]

Even the long-established practice of leading states may diverge significantly from the norms and values of the civilization of which they are a part. The United States, for example, is in many ways a very *atypical* Western country in its approach to economic and social rights. In characterizing and comparing civilizations, we must not mistake some particular expressions, however characteristic, for the whole. For example, Christianity and secularism are arguably equally important to modern Western civilization. And the balance between secular and religious forces, values, and orientations varies dramatically with time, place, and issue in "the West."

Such cautions are especially important because culturalist arguments regularly rely on appeals to a distant past, such as the precolonial African village, Native American tribes, and traditional Islamic societies. The traditional culture advanced to justify cultural relativism far too often no longer exists—if it ever did in the idealized form in which it is typically presented. In the Third World today we usually see not the persistence of "traditional" culture in the face of "modern" intrusions, or even the development of syncretic cultures and values, but rather disruptive "Westernization," rapid cultural change, or people enthusiastically embracing "modern" practices and values.[10] And the modern nation-states and contemporary nationalist regimes that have replaced traditional communities and practices cannot be judged by standards of a bygone era.

We must also be careful to distinguish "civilization" or "culture" from religion and politics. The United States is a state, a political entity, not a civilization. Islam is not a civilization but a religion, or, as many believers would put it, a true and comprehensive way of life that transcends culture or civilization. An "Islamic civilization"—centered on Mecca and running, say, from the Maghreb to the Indus—does not include all Muslims, or even all majority Muslim countries. The broader Muslim world, running from Dakar to Jakarta, may be an international political unit of growing interest or importance, but it certainly is not a culture or civilization. And tens of millions of Muslims live outside of even this community.

B. The Politics of Cultural Relativism

Cultures are not merely diverse but are contested. In fact, contemporary anthropologists increasingly depict "cultures" not as "things" but as sites of contestation. "Rather than simply a domain of sharing and commonality, culture figures here more as a site of difference and contestation, simultaneously ground and stake of a rich field of cultural-political practices" (Gupta and Ferguson 1997: 5).

> Culture is usually viewed by the new cultural theorists as contested—a social context in which power struggles are constantly waged over the meaning and control of what Pierre Bourdieu has called "symbolic capital" as well as over more overtly material forms of wealth and power. In short, culture is not a given, but rather a congeries of ways of thinking, believing, and acting that are constantly in the state of

being produced; it is contingent and always unstable, especially as the forces of "modernity" have barreled down upon most people throughout the world over the course of the twentieth century. (Bell, Nathan, and Peleg 2001: 11)

> All forms of cultural relativism fundamentally fail to recognize culture as an ongoing historic and institutional process where the existence of a given custom does not mean that the custom is either adaptive, optimal, or consented to by a majority of its adherents. Culture is far more effectively characterized as an ongoing adaptation to a changing environment rather than as a static superorganic entity. In a changing environment, cultural practices routinely outlive their usefulness, and cultural values change either through internal dialogue within the cultural group or through cross-cultural influences. (Zechenter 1997: 332–333)

"Culture" is constructed through selective appropriations from a diverse and contested past and present. Those appropriations are rarely neutral in process, intent, or consequences. Cultural relativist arguments thus regularly obscure often troubling realities of power and politics.

Arguments of cultural relativism are far too often made by (or on behalf of) economic and political elites that have long since left traditional culture behind. Even when this represents an admirable effort to retain or recapture cherished traditional values, it is at least ironic to see "Westernized" elites warning against the values and practices they have adopted. There is also more than a hint of a troubling, even tragic, paternalism. For example, "villagization" in Tanzania, which was supposed to reflect traditional African conceptions, was accomplished only by force, against the strong opposition of much of the population.

Even such troubling sincerity is unfortunately rare. Government officials denounce the corrosive individualism of Western values—while they line their pockets with the proceeds of massive corruption, drive imported luxury automobiles, and plan European or American vacations. Leaders sing the praises of traditional communities—while they wield arbitrary power antithetical to traditional values, pursue development policies that systematically undermine traditional communities, and replace traditional leaders with corrupt cronies and party hacks. Rigged elections, military dictatorships, and malnutrition caused by government incentives to produce cash crops rather than food are just a few of the widespread abuses of internationally recognized human rights that do not express, but rather infringe, indigenous cultural values.

In traditional cultures—at least the kinds of traditional cultures that might justify deviations from international human rights standards—people are not victims of the arbitrary decisions of rulers whose principal claim to power is their control of modern instruments of force and administration. Traditional customs and practices usually provide each person with a place in society and a certain amount of dignity and protection. Furthermore, rulers and ruled (and rich and poor) usually are linked by reciprocal bonds. The human rights violations of most Third World regimes are as antithetical to such cultural traditions as they are to "Western" human rights conceptions.

Relativist arguments became particularly perverse when they support a small elite that has arrogated to itself the "right" to speak for "its" culture or civilization, and then imposes its own self-interested views and practices on the broader society—invoking cultural relativism abroad while ruthlessly trampling on local customs. Consider, for example, Suharto and his cronies in Indonesia, who sought to cloak their version of modern state-based repression and crony capitalism in the aura of traditional culture. In Zaire, President Mobutu created the practice of *salongo*, a form of communal labor with a supposedly traditional basis, which was in fact essentially a revival of the colonial, practice of corvee labor (Callaghy 1980: 490). Macias Nguema of Equatorial Guinea, perhaps the most vicious ruler independent black Africa has seen, called himself "Grand Master of Popular Education, Science, and Traditional Culture," a title that might be comical were the situation not so tragic.

7. Dialogue over Real Differences

The above discussion is intentionally one-sided. I have drawn attention to commonalities and minimized (real) differences. But even if I am correct about the extent of those differences, we must not confuse overlapping consensus with homogeneity.

Furthermore, the fact that differences are *relatively* minor, in the context of the full body of internationally recognized human rights, does not mean that they are unimportant, especially at the level of day-to-day polities. Question about such issues as capital and corporal punishment, the limits of religious liberty, and the dimensions of gender equality merit intensive discussions both within and between states and civilizations.

Should traditional notions of "family values" and gender roles be emphasized in the interest of children and society, or should families be conceived in more individualistic and egalitarian terms? What is the proper balance between rewarding individual economic initiative and redistributive taxation in the interest of social harmony and support for disadvantaged individuals and groups? At what point should the words or behaviors of deviant or dissident individuals be forced to give way the interests or desires of society?

Questions such as these, which in my terminology involve conflicting interpretations, involve vital issues of political controversy in virtually all societies. In discussing them we must often walk the difficult line between respect for the other and respect for one's own values. * * * Here I want to consider a relatively easy case—slavery—in an unconventional way.

Suppose that in contemporary Saudi Arabia a group were to emerge arguing that because slavery was accepted in the early Muslim world it should be reinstituted in contemporary Saudi Arabia. I am certain that almost all Saudis, from the most learned clerics to the most ordinary citizens, would reject this view. But how should these individuals be dealt with?

Dialogue seems to me the appropriate route, so long as they do not attempt to *practice* slavery. Those in the majority who would remonstrate these individuals for their despicable views have, I think, an obligation to use precisely such forceful moral terms. Nonetheless, freedom of belief and speech requires the majority to tolerate these views, in the minimal sense of not imposing legal liabilities on those who hold or express them. Should they attempt to practice slavery, however, the force of the law is appropriately applied to suppress and punish this practice. Condemnation by outsiders also seems appropriate, although so long as the problem is restricted to expressions of beliefs only in Saudi Arabia there probably will be few occasions for such condemnations.

But suppose that the unthinkable were to occur and the practice of slavery were reintroduced in Saudi Arabia—not, let us imagine, as a matter of law, but rather through the state refusing to prosecute slave-holders. Here we run up against the state system and the fact that international human rights law gives states near total discretion to implement internationally recognized human rights within their own territories.

One might argue that slavery is legally prohibited as a matter of *jus cogens*, general principles of law, and customary (as well as treaty) law. But coercive international enforcement is extraordinarily contentious and without much legal precedent. Outsiders, however, remain bound by their own moral principles (as well as by international human rights norms) to condemn such practices in the strongest possible terms. And foreign states would be entirely justified in putting whatever pressure, short of force, they could mobilize on Saudi Arabia to halt the practice.

This hypothetical example illustrates the fact that *some* cultural practices, rather than deserve our respect, demand our condemnation. It also indicates, though, that some beliefs, however despicable, demand our toleration—because freedom of opinion and belief is an internationally recognized human right. So long as one stays within the limits of internationally recognized human rights, one is entitled to at least a limited and grudging toleration and the personal space that comes with that. But such individuals are *owed* nothing more.

Many cases, however, are not so easy. This is especially true where cultures are undergoing substantial or unusually rapid transformation. In much of the Third World we regularly face the problem of "modem" individuals or groups who reject traditional practices. Should we give priority to the idea of community self-determination and permit the enforcement of customary practices against modern "deviants" even if this violates "universal" human rights? Or should individual self-determination prevail, thus sanctioning claims of universal human rights against traditional society?

In discussing women's rights in Africa, Rhoda Howard suggests an attractive and widely applicable compromise strategy (1984: 66–68). On a combination of practical and moral grounds, she argues against an outright ban on such practices as child betrothal and widow inheritance, but she also argues strongly for national legislation that permits women (and the families of female children) to "opt out" of traditional practices. This would permit individuals and families to, in effect, choose the terms on which they participate in the cultures that are of value to their lives. Unless we think of culture as an oppressive external force, this seems entirely appropriate.

Conflicting practices, however, may sometimes be irreconcilable. For example, a right to private ownership of the means of production is incompatible with the maintenance of a village society in which families hold only rights of use to communally owned land. Allowing individuals to opt out and fully own their land would destroy the traditional system. Even such conflicts, however, may sometimes be resolved, or at least minimized, by the physical or legal separation of adherents of old and new values, particularly with practices that are not material to the maintenance or integrity of either culture.

Nevertheless, a choice must sometimes be made, at least by default, between irreconcilable practices. Such cases take us out of the realm in which useful general guidelines are possible. Fortunately, though, they are the exception rather than the rule—although no easier for that fact to deal with when they do arise.

It would be dangerous either to deny differences between civilizations where they do exist or to exaggerate their extent or practical importance. Whatever the situation in other issue areas, in the case of human rights, for all the undeniable differences, it is the similarities across civilizations that are more striking and important Whatever our differences, now or in the past, all contemporary civilizations are linked by the growing recognition of the Universal Declaration as, in its own words, "a common standard of achievement for all peoples and all nations." Or, as I prefer to put it, human rights are relatively universal.

NOTES

1. Civilizations seems to be emerging as the term of choice in UN-based discussions. 2001 was designated the United Nations Year of Dialogue Among Civilizations. For a sampling of Unesco sources, see http://www.unesco.org/dialogue2001/en/culturer.htm. I use "culture" and "civilization" more or less interchangeably, although I think that a useful convention would be to treat civilizations as larger or broader: for example, French culture but Western civilization.

2. * * * I begin by taking at face value the common understanding of culture as static, unitary, and integral. * * *

3. I am concerned here only with cultural relativist views as they apply to human rights, although my argument probably has applicability to other relativist claims.

4. We can also note that radical relativism is descriptively inaccurate. Few people anywhere believe that their moral beliefs rest on nothing more than tradition. The radical relativist insistence that they do offers an implausible (and unattractive) account of the nature and meaning of morality.

5. Gender equality, perhaps surprisingly, did not come up (although these were elite, English-speaking audiences, and Iran has, self-consciously, made considerable progress on women's rights issues in recent years). But even when it does, dispute usually focuses on the meaning of nondiscrimination or on particular practices, such as equal rights in marriage.

6. Logically, there can be at most one absolute right (unless we implausibly assume that rights never conflict with one another).

7. The general similarity of regional human rights instruments underscores this argument. Even the African Charter of Human and Peoples' Rights, the most heterodox regional treaty, differs largely at the level of interpretation and, in substance or concept, by addition (of peoples' rights) rather than by subtraction.

8. Coming at a similar perspective from the other end of the spectrum, Richard Wilson notes that human rights, and struggles over their implementation, "are embedded in local normative orders and yet are caught within webs of power and meaning which extend beyond the local" (1997: 23). Andrew Nathan has recently described this orientation as "tempered universalism" (2001).

9. To cite one example of misplaced textualism, Roger Ames (1997) manages to devote an entire article to

"the conversation on Chinese human rights" that manages to make only a few passing, exceedingly delicate, mentions of events since 1949. China and its culture would seem to have been unaffected by such forces as decades of brutal party dictatorship or the impact of both socialism and capitalism on land tenure and residence patterns. In fact, although he cites a number of passages from Confucius, Ames does not even attempt to show how traditional Confucian ideas express themselves in contemporary Chinese human rights debates.

10. None of this should be surprising when we compare the legal, political, and cultural practices of the contemporary West with those of, ancient Athens, medieval Paris, Renaissance Florence, or even Victorian London.

REFERENCES

Ames, Roger. 1997. "Continuing the Conversation on Chinese Human Rights." *Ethics and International Affairs* 11: 177–205.

Bell, Daniel A. 1996. "The East Asian Challenge to Human Rights: Reflections on an East-West Dialogue." *Human Rights Quarterly* 18 (August): 641–667.

Bell, Lynda, Andrew J. Nathan, and Ilan Peleg. 2001. "Introduction: Culture and Human Rights." In *Negotiating Culture and Human Rights.* Edited by Lynda Bell, Andrew J. Nathan, and Ilan Peleg. New York: Columbia University Press.

Bell, Lynda S. 2001. "Who Produces Asian Identity? Discourses, Discrimination, and Chinese Peasant Women in the Quest for Human Rights." In *Negotiating Culture and Human Rights.* Edited by Lynda Bell, Andrew J. Nathan, and Ilan Peleg. New York: Columbia University Press.

Gallie, W. B. 1968. "Essentially Contested Concepts." In *Philosophy and the Historical Understanding.* New York: Schocken Books.

Gupta, Akhil, and James Ferguson. 1997. "Culture, Power, Place: Ethnography at the End of an Era." In *Culture, Power, Place: Explorations in Critical Anthropology.* Edited by Akhil Gupta and James Ferguson. Durham: Duke University Press.

Howard, Rhoda E. 1984. "Women's Rights in English-Speaking Sub-Saharan Africa." In *Human Rights and Development in Africa.* Edited by Claude E. Welch Jr. and Ronald I. Meltzer. Albany: State University of New York Press.

Kant, Immanuel. 1983. *Prepetual Peace and Other Essays.* Translated by Ted Humphrey. Indianapolis: Hackett.

Nathan. 2001. "Universalism: A Particularistic Account." In *Negotiating Culture and Human Rights.* Edited by Lynda Bell, Andrew J. Nathan, and Ilan Peleg. New York: Columbia University Press.

Wilson, Richard. 1997. "Introduction." In *Human Rights, Culture and Context: Anthropological Perspectives.* Edited by Richard Wilson. London: Pluto Press.

Zechenter, Elizabeth M. 1997. "In the Name of Cultural Relativism and the Abuse of the Individual." *Journal of Anthropological Research* 53 (Fall): 319–347.

Emilie M. Hafner-Burton and Kiyoteru Tsutsui

JUSTICE LOST!

The Failure of International Human Rights Law To Matter Where Needed Most

Introduction

By almost any measure, nearly half of the world's governments today are repressive, systematically abusing human beings living within their borders.[1] Many scholars and policymakers have been working to bring these governments to justice as they attempt to identify which human rights policies hold repressors accountable for their actions and stop future abuses (Koh, 2002). Among their tools are international human rights laws, designed in the aftermath of severe atrocities during World War II to prevent future repression. Human rights scholars and advocates have long been hopeful about the prospects for reform. While a few quantitative scholars have culled new evidence suggesting that laws often do not work very well (Hathaway, 2002; Hafner-Burton, 2005), others show hope for reforms on the margins, in democratizing (Simmons, 2006) or already democratic states (Neumayer, 2005). Our concern in this article is with the efficacy of these laws to reform those actors most in need of improvement: repressive states whose governments violate or allow violation of human rights within their borders. Are human rights laws really hopeless to bring about reforms, even marginal, among the worst abusers?

Despite recent skepticism, scholars of international relations, law, and sociology have long argued that laws can make a difference, and hope for improvement is common (Landman, 2005; see Hafner-Burton & Ron, 2006). Many politicians and nongovernmental activists also believe that human rights laws initiate processes and dialogues that involve learning over time and, through learning, the eventual change in belief about rational or appropriate actions (Abbott & Snidal, 2000). They provide rules and organizational structures that constrain national sovereignty, serving as justification and a forum for action that can shape governments' political interests and belief about appropriate actions (Chayes & Chayes, 1998; Franck, 1988; Lutz & Sikkink, 2000). And persuasive accounts argue that governments ratify human rights treaties, not always as symbolic acts, but also as expressions of preference for reform (Simmons, 2006). By almost all such accounts, if human rights laws matter for political reform, they will take time to be of importance, as belief change and capacity-building for implementation are unlikely to be easy or immediate and may well happen in fits and starts (Chayes & Chayes, 1993).

Theories of compliance, however, are to some extent divorced from research. Current findings largely emphasize that treaties work in some cases—democracies. But these studies largely ignore the dynamics of compliance. This is troubling because the human rights regime was created precisely to stop outbreaks of extreme violence among the world's worst abusers, and its

From *Journal of Peace Research* 44, no.4 (July 2007), 407–425.

founders knew this process would take time. Perhaps researchers are finding that treaties matter most on the margins because studies are not taking the dynamics of compliance seriously. Maybe repressive autocrats simply need more time to come under the sway of international laws and build capacity than other, more democratic, states.

Consider first what we know about effectiveness. In the face of widespread confidence that laws matter, Hathaway's (2002) path-breaking article shook scholarly faith in human rights treaties, arguing that they do little to ensure better behaviors. Since this provocative study, other scholars have been notably more optimistic. Simmons (2006) argues that international legal commitments do matter; they have their most important consequences for states that have experienced democratic accountability and refuse to allow their governments to turn back. Hafner-Burton & Tsutsui (2005) demonstrate that linkage to international civil society often encourages reform in cases where international law alone is unsuccessful. Neumayer (2005) extends both arguments to show that commitment to international law often does improve respect for human rights, primarily for states with democratically accountable governments or strong civil society. The optimism, however, is narrow in scope, as current scholarship implies that human rights laws matter least among governments that were the primary targets of the legal regime—terribly repressive, autocratic states without internal advocates for reform.

Consider next what we know about the dynamics of treaty compliance. Conformity with international law is a domestic political process. Implementing human rights laws requires not only the political will at home, but also the political capacity. Both probably will be hardest to build in repressive non-democracies, and conformity with international human rights laws will

almost certainly take longer to stick in these cases. The burgeoning empirical literature on human rights compliance has yet to effectively consider whether treaty effectiveness fluctuates over time. For instance, Neumayer (2005) and Keith (1999) consider whether several global and regional human rights treaties make a difference in human rights behaviors *the very same year* as ratification. Not surprisingly, they find no direct empirical relationship. Hafner-Burton (2005) examines whether any of the core UN human rights laws encourage protection of people from political terror *one year after* ratification and also finds no significant association. All unreservedly overlook basic theoretical arguments suggesting that soft laws generally take time to be successfully implemented, and that human rights laws in particular are likely to be effective only after substantial learning and capacity-building have taken place-features of international human rights law that 'may be seen as an extreme case of the time lag between undertaking and performance' (Chayes & Chayes, 1998: 16).

Other empirical research acknowledges that 'human rights treaties, if they have effects on country practices, do so relatively slowly' (Hathaway, 2002: 1990). To consider these dynamics, both Hathaway (2002) and Hafner-Burton & Tsutsui (2005) analyze the relationship between the *duration in years* since ratification of the core UN human rights laws and compliance behavior. In so doing, they test the proposition that, as the years go on, human rights laws should be more and more effective in producing results. They find no evidence. Yet neither study is a good test of dynamic theories of international law. Treaties may certainly take time to influence behaviors, but, in the realm of human rights, it is unlikely that learning or capacity-building takes place at a steady or uniform pace over time. Compliance with international human rights laws, if it takes place at all, may well happen sporadically and in fits and starts. If so, these duration variables are a weak test of important theories on the matter.

Does this methodological problem explain the discouraging results about compliance? Maybe human rights laws do protect the people most in danger of violations, but only in fits and starts and only long after ratification, when leaders' minds can be swayed and national capacities for reform built. Perhaps democracy is not the only answer.

In the following pages, we advance four propositions about repressive governments' compliance with international human rights law. First, advocates are correct: an impressive cascade of norms has taken place in the realm of international justice. Governments, *including repressive ones*, easily and frequently make legal commitments to international human rights treaties, subscribing to recognized norms of protection and creating opportunities for socialization, learning, and capacity-building processes necessary for lasting reforms. Second, the problem is not only methodological; treaty commitments to the pursuit of justice have no clear or independent effects on most very repressive states' behaviors, either immediately or, more importantly, long into the future. Either most repressive governments have failed to learn that the protection of human rights is essential or they lack the capacity necessary to implement policies of protection. As a result, recent statistical confidence about the treaty regime implies a broader problem—that the regime is actually failing in countries where reform is most urgently needed and that more time for learning and capacity-building is unlikely alone to solve the problem. Third, recent findings that treaty effectiveness is conditional on democracy and civil society do not explain the behavior of the world's serious repressors. Fourth, most realistic institutional reforms are unlikely to help much; so far, deeper delegation of legal authority to the international regime does not make reforms much more likely, even over time.

The Good News about Treaty Commitment

Significant thought has been given to explaining why governments commonly belong to the international human rights legal regime (Cole, 2005; Goodliffe & Hawkins, 2005; Vreeland, 2007; Wotipka & Tsutsui, 2001). We build on these insights with a focused attention to the behaviors of those states arguably most in need of reform, where repression is severe and individuals experience considerable brutality.

Human rights laws are abundant. Among them, the International Covenant on Civil and Political Rights (CCPR) and the International Convention against Torture and Other Cruel, Inhuman, or Degrading Treatment or Punishment (CAT) are commonly distinguished among treaties as the most successful and important, outlawing the most severe kinds of violations (Hathaway, 2002). They are certainly among the most studied. Each treaty articulates an impressive array of obligations for governments to follow, including precise details as to what behaviors are and are not appropriate. Authority to monitor implementation is modestly delegated to two independent committees; the Human Rights Committee for the CCPR and the Committee against Torture for the CAT; governments can choose to recognize or reject the jurisdiction of both committees and to implement or ignore their recommendations.[2]

In the following section, we aim to demonstrate a remarkable fact. No matter how we measure repression of personal integrity rights, repressive states that allow murder, torture, kidnapping, and other cruel, inhuman, or degrading treatment or punishment of people just as commonly belong to the CCPR and the CAT outlawing these behaviors as governments that protect human rights reasonably well. Figure 10.2 presents evidence that has been systematically culled from our data from 1976, the year the CCPR came into force, to the last year of observation, 2003.

We begin by defining what we mean by a repressive state, *repressor*, and how we identify them. Because we are concerned with two particular treaties, the CCPR and the CAT, we consider repression of the human rights enshrined in both: the rights to personal integrity. We examine annual data published by Amnesty International (AI), although we have run all analyses in this article on an alternative measure collected by the Bureau of Democracy, Human Rights, and Labor at the US State Department (SD) as a robustness check; any discrepancies are reported in the footnotes. We combine data collected across three samples by Poe & Tate (1994), Gibney & Dalton (1996), and Hafner-Burton (2005) to create a single measure with observations on 182 states from 1976 to 2003.[3] Following Gastil (1980), we define repression, *repression*$_{it}$, as an ordinal variable ranging across five levels of behavior:

1. countries are under secure rule of law, political imprisonment and torture are rare, and political murders are extremely rare;
2. imprisonment for nonviolent political activities is limited, torture and beating are exceptional, and political murder is rare;
3. political imprisonment is extensive, execution and political murders may be common, and detention for political views is acceptable;
4. the practices of level 3 are expanded to a larger segment of the population, murders and disappearances are common, but terror affects primarily those who interest themselves in political practice or ideas;
5. levels of terror are population-wide and decisionmakers do not limit the means by which they pursue private or ideological goals.

In order to identify repressor states, we consider any state that achieves a score of 3 or higher *at the time of treaty ratification* to be unquestionably repressive, employing political torture and terror. We call this state a repressor, *repressor*$_{it}$ and code them dichotomously for efficiency.[4] We consider states that achieve a score of 1 or 2 to be reasonably protective by contrast, because acts of repression, if they are observed, are extremely rare.[5]

Using this common definition for *repressor*$_{it}$ to identify our population of violating states, we consider the extent to which these states belong to the human rights legal regime, ratifying the CCPR or the CAT into national law. We accordingly estimate Model 1:

$$treaty\ commitment_{it} = \alpha + \beta_1\ repressor_i + \beta_2\ polity_{it} + \beta_3\ regime\ durability_{it} + \beta_4\ GDPpc_{it} + \beta_5\ trade_{it} + \beta_6\ civil\ war_{it} + \beta_7\ war_{it} + \beta_8\ population_{it} + \beta_9\ North\ America_{it} + \beta_{10}\ Europe_{it} + \beta_{11}\ Africa_{it} + \beta_{12}\ Middle\ East_{it} + \beta_{13}\ Asia_{it} + \delta_i + m_{it} \quad (1)$$

Our dependent variable, *treaty commitment*$_{it}$, is a binary variable coded 0 if a state i in year t has made no formal commitment to either the CCPR or the CAT by ratifying, acceding, or succeeding to the treaties, and 1 if that state has committed to either or both treaties. Our aim in Model 1 is to determine whether states that are observably repressive at the time of ratification are any more or less likely to belong to human rights laws than those that are reasonably protective, having already institutionalized the norms to which they make commitments. To pursue this aim systematically, we control for a variety of other motivations considered relevant in state decisions on treaty membership (Cole, 2005; Goodliffe & Hawkins, 2005; Hathaway, 2002; Moravcsik, 1995).[6]

Polity$_{it}$ measures domestic regime characteristics. The well-known variable, which takes on values ranging from 10 (most democratic) to −10 (most autocratic), is measured as an index of five primary institutional features: the competitiveness of chief executive selection, the openness of that process to social groups, the level of institutional constraints placed on the chief executive's

Figure 10.2. The Predicted Probability of Treaty Commitment, 1976–2003: Repressors Versus Protectors

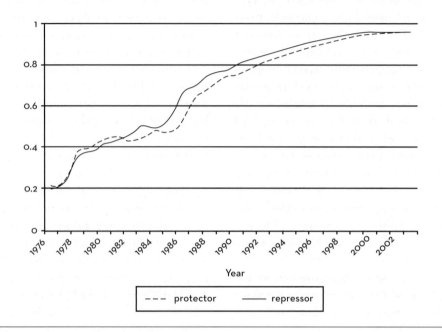

decisionmaking authority, the competitiveness of political participation, and the degree to which binding rules govern political participation.[7] *Regime durability*$_{it}$ counts the number of years since a state has undergone a structural regime transition. This variable is commonplace in the literature, and we control for it accordingly. A transition is defined as a movement on the Polity IV scale of three points or more.

To control for economic factors that scholars believe may influence treaty commitment, we employ several standard variables. Gross domestic product per capita in constant US dollars, *pcGDP*$_{it}$, controls for the effect of economic development. *Trade*$_{it}$ controls for the sum of a state's total exports and imports of goods and services measured as a share of gross domestic product. Both measures are collected by the World Bank and logged to reduce the skew of their distributions.

To control for political conditions where violence is openly sanctioned by the state, we control for *civil war*$_{it}$ and *war*$_{it}$. Both are dichotomous variables equaling 1 if a country is at war and 0 otherwise.[8] Finally, we control for regional effects by including dummy variables indicating whether a state is a part of America, Europe, Africa, the Middle East, or Asia, and for a state's total *population*$_{it}$, logged. δ_i are fixed effects for time that de-trend correlations within states across time (although not within time across states, which is equal to zero by assumption), and m_{it} is a stochastic term.

Figure 10.2 plots predicted probabilities that repressors (*repressor*$_i$ = 1) and protectors (*repressor*$_i$ = 0) will make commitments to either treaty (Long, 1997).[9] The y-axis reports probabilities calculated at the mean of all variables in the model. In order to explore ratification propensity over time, the x-axis reports the year in which the prediction was calculated—for example, in 1976, a repressive state had a 0.2 probability of joining the regime, and so forth.[10] The figure indicates two systematic features of the commitment process. First, there is nothing about using torture or otherwise repressing rights to personal integrity that prevents a government from making commitments to international laws to abolish repression, Repressors are just as likely to commit to the human rights legal regime as protectors; this information includes consideration of all political behaviors controlled for in Equation (1). Second, ratification has become nearly ubiquitous over time; the probability that either a protector or repressor had made a commitment to the human rights regime in 1976—the year the CCPR went into force—was about 0.02; by 2003, this probability was almost 1.[11]

Evidence clearly shows that governments that torture and terrorize their people commonly pledge commitment to human rights laws, obligating themselves and their future leaders to implement norms protecting all human beings.[12] For pundits expecting that human rights regimes make a difference, this observation should be good news. Such commitments may initiate learning, socialization, and persuasive compliance dynamics that, over time, can encourage reform. But do these acts of commitment actually help to protect the people most in need of protection? We consider this question in the following section.

The Bad News about Compliance

Many scholars are hopeful that, when states make commitments to international legal norms, governments will act accordingly (Chayes & Chayes, 1998; Finnemore, 1996; Goodman & Jinks, 2003; Henkin, 1979; Koh, 1996–97; Mitchell, 1993). Some believe that repressive leaders commonly adopt human rights laws instrumentally as a means to gain related benefits, but that instrumental adaptation can, over time, lead to processes of moral consciousness-raising, argumentation, persuasion, institutionalization, and even habituation (Risse, Ropp & Sikkink, 1999). These processes can, in turn, create the conditions for behavioral change, as governments stop committing or supporting acts of repression and build capacity both to protect human rights and to punish those who violate them.

Others argue that governments join human rights laws when they are committed to their fundamental goals in the first place, even when belonging is costly (Hathaway, 2003, 2005; Simmons, 2006). Indeed, states are regularly observed to comply with international law without any enforcement, a likely artifact of state selection into legal regimes that require only modest changes in behavior (Downs, Rocke & Barsoom, 1996).[13] Still others suggest that international human rights laws reform repressive states through acculturation—a general process by which actors adopt the beliefs and behavioral patterns of surrounding cultures through mimicry or assimilation (Goodman & Jinks, 2003; Powell & DiMaggio, 1991; Scott, Meyer & Boli, 1994). All of these theories are plausible; however, they suggest that any observable compliance behavior will likely take time, as beliefs do not change overnight, and building physical and legal infrastructures to support human rights can be costly and time consuming. Maybe human rights treaties do matter for the world's repressive autocrats, but they simply require more time to have an effect.

We are skeptical that international human rights laws in general, and the CCPR and the CAT in particular, directly or regularly encourage most repressive states to substantially reform, to value or protect human beings' fundamental rights to life, liberty, and justice, even over time. To a handful of skeptics who see international laws generally as cheap talk, this is not news; to many scholars of international law, international relations, and sociology, as well as to the founders of the human rights regime and the nongovernmental organizations who support their cause, this claim is worrisome. Our concerns are manifold, but we emphasize four in particular (Hafner-Burton, 2005).

First, we share the view that governments are strategic actors that make commitments to human rights treaties for deliberate and self-interested reasons. Understanding compliance dynamics accordingly obliges us to know something about the process of commitment—whether and why repressive states join treaties in the first place which almost certainly helps to explain whether treaties themselves make a difference. Violators, we believe, by and large do not join human rights laws in such great numbers because they are committed to reforms or because treaties require only modest changes in behavior. On the contrary, the CCPR and the CAT require major reforms and oblige governments with no interest or capacity to comply with these laws to regularly commit anyway, knowing that neither treaty can successfully enforce the norms they are designed to protect. It is our belief that repressive states commonly belong to the human rights regime because they gain certain political advantages from membership but all the while can get away with murder. Most governments joining the international human rights legal regime accordingly are not open to new ways of behaving, thus making learning, socialization, and persuasion improbable.

Second, we are skeptical that repressive states, once they join the treaty regime, will come to internalize the legal norms to which they subscribe over time, through active processes of socialization or learning. We do not believe that socialization and learning are impossible or undesirable. Rather, we believe there are strong reasons to be skeptical that either method of belief change is likely to take place or provide strong incentives to change most repressive actors' behaviors most of the time, no

matter how much time passes after ratification. Socialization and learning require changing actors' preferences for repression, and these preferences are likely to be highly valued by repressive states, whose leaders accumulate power and wealth through terror. Socialization and learning are also likely to be slow-acting forms of influence, taking place over a very long time horizon, but confronting resistance to beliefs that are often sticky and resistant to change (Anderson, 1989; Slusher & Anderson, 1996). In those rare instances when socialization and learning do take place, newly persuaded leaders may not be consistent across time, as new rulers may come to power and new opponent groups may form with preferences for repression. Moreover, socialization and learning require repeated access to target repressors and many of these actors are likely to be marginalized from participation in human rights institutions, remaining isolated from active processes of norm inculcation (Hafner-Burton & Tsutsui, 2005).[14]

Third, we are most skeptical that repressive states, facing degrees of cognitive and social pressures to conform, adopt human rights reforms through processes of acculturation alone.[15] We do not argue that acculturation processes, like socialization and learning, are irrelevant to all political choices. They may certainly inform states' identities, preferences, and interests in important ways (Meyer et al., 1997). However, we emphasize that repressive states are characterized by leaders that employ or condone repression purposively and strategically; acts of terror are accordingly seldom accidental or random, and they often bring high rewards for those that use them. Reforms are usually deliberate and costly, often requiring leaders in power to give up certain authorities and privileges they have become accustomed to enjoying. Improvements in protection of human rights do not, as a result, happen tacitly or through simple processes of mimicry without some convincing motivation. Repressive leaders can certainly reform, but they are unlikely by any stretch of the imagination to give up repression simply because their neighbors have.

Finally, even when leaders decide to reform their human rights practices, they may not succeed in changing the government's or non-state actors' actual practices quickly. Building the legal and physical infrastructure to protect human rights and to punish violations is a costly process that requires not only conviction on behalf of a government's leaders, but also substantial resources and expertise that are often lacking in violating states suffering from legacies of repression. Leaders seeking reform commonly face serious resistance from other elites who have vested interests in continuing repression, or from lower-level officials who have grown accustomed to the organizational culture of repression, which can delay or paralyze leaders' efforts to improve the practices (Ron, 2000).

Do terribly repressive states reform when they belong to human rights treaties over a long period of time? How much time does it take to internalize the human rights norms to which they make commitments? We are encouraged that many common and important responses suggest that legal commitments matter; that repressive states can and do reform; and that reform, if it does not happen right away, can take place over time, as norms become more and more internalized and as civil society actors use international laws as a recourse for lobbying. Our arguments, however, have led us to mainly expect the contrary. We advance three hypotheses: (1) that repressive states' legal commitments to the human rights regime do not typically promote reforms; (2) that this gap between commitment and practice will often persist over time, as norms of justice rarely become institutionalized through processes of international law alone; and (3) that most feasible reforms to the legal regime will probably not solve this problem. The following section explores the merits of our conjectures.

Evidence

We begin with a general replication of previous studies by estimating Model 2 predicting *repression*$_{it}$ behavior (from 1 to 5 on our ordinal scale) to evaluate the impact of treaty ratification after one year. We use Hafner-Burton (2005) as our base model.[16]

$$repression_{it} = \alpha + \beta_1\, CAT_{it-1} + \beta_2\, CCPR_{it-1} + \\ \beta_3\, GDPpc_{it-1} + \beta_4\, trade_{it-1} + \beta_5\, population_{it-1} + \\ \beta_6\, polity_{it-1} + \beta_7\, regime\ durability_{it-1} + \\ \beta_8\, civil\ war_{it-1} + \beta_9\, war_{it-1} + \delta_i + m_{it} \quad (2)$$

We first consider all states in our sample[17] in order to replicate existing studies and control for standard economic and political factors thought to influence repression. Column 1 of Table 10.1 summarizes our ordered logit estimates appropriate to the structure of the dependent variable and reports Huber–White standard errors appropriate to the nature of our data. We include δ_i in order to de-trend correlations within states across time, as the data by nature suffer from autocorrelation.[18] Our findings confirm that state commitment to either treaty does not increase the likelihood of reform. Governments more often than not commit to protect norms of human rights but do not follow through on those commitments.

Columns 2 and 3 of Table 10.1 summarize our replication of previous findings that treaty effects are conditional on democracy and civil society; we accordingly introduce interaction terms between treaties and *polity*$_{it-1}$ and *civil society*$_{it-1}$, which we measure as the number of nongovernmental organizations registered in each state according to the Union of International Associations.[19] Consistent with Hafner-Burton & Tsutsui (2005), Neumayer (2005), and Simmons (2006), we find that human rights treaties, specifically the CCPR, are most effective when ratified by states with democratic systems of government or strong civil society

Table 10.1 Ordered Logic Estimates of State Repression, 1976–2003

Variables	ALL STATES			STATES REPRESSIVE AT THE TIME OF RATIFICATION		
	(1) Base model	(2) Democracy	(3) Civil society	(1) Base model	(2) Democracy	(3) Civil society
CAT_{it-1}	−0.008	0.064	0.100	−0.019	0.007	0.508
	(0.211)	(0.207)	(0.284)	(0.238)	(0.232)*	(0.449)
$CCPR_{it-1}$	0.019	−0.048	0.909**	0.181	0.023	0.565
	(0.227)	(0.221)	(0.302)	(0.250)	(0.268)	(0.396)
$CAT_{it-1} \times polity_{it-1}$		−0.002			−0.005	
		(0.023)			(0.031)	
$CCPR_{it-1} \times polity_{it-1}$		−0.073*			−0.046	
		(0.028)			(0.029)	
$CAT_{it-1} \times$ civil society$_{it-1}$			2.00E-04			−7.37E-04
			(3.00E-04)			(6.47E-04)
$CCPR_{it-1} \times$ civil society$_{it-1}$			−0.002***			−1.16E-03+
			(4.55E-04)			(6.11E-04)
Civil society$_{it-1}$			8.83E-04			0.002*
			(6.46E-04)			(8.82E-04)
GDPpc$_{it-1}$	−0.217*	−0.202*	−0.115	0.119	0.122	0.091
	(0.092)	(0.092)	(0.119)	(0.118)	(0.118)	(0.137)
Trade$_{it-1}$	−0.632**	−0.670**	−0.731**	−0.941***	−0.941***	−1.038***
	(0.208)	(0.206)	(0.213)	(0.242)	(0.245)	(0.262)
Population$_{it-1}$	0.403***	0.386***	0.384***	0.278***	0.266	0.115
	(0.069)	(0.071)	(0.102)	(0.085)	(0.086)**	(0.130)

Polity$_{it-1}$	−0.089***	−0.047*	−0.091***	−0.028	0.008	−0.030
	(0.017)	(0.023)	(0.020)	(0.023)	(0.025)	(0.027)
Regime durability$_{it-1}$	−0.021***	−0.021***	−0.022***	0.002	0.003	0.004
	(0.005)	(0.005)	(0.005)	(0.011)	(0.010)	(0.011)
Civil war$_{it-1}$	1.717***	1.699***	1.714***	1.636***	1.649***	1.726***
	(0.348)	(0.334)	(0.324)	(0.312)	(0.320)	(0.326)
War$_{it-1}$	1.185*	1.108*	1.322***	0.169	0.003	−0.231
	(0.528)	(0.436)	(0.330)	(0.573)	(0.669)	(0.855)
N	3,345	3,345	2,764	1,998	1,998	1,642
Chi2	249.22***	266.87***	310.55***	187.38***	218.6***	165.14***
Log likelihood	−4,033.17	−4,006.65	−3,259.92	−2,561.64	−2,556.75	−2,095.47

Notes: + $p \leq 0.1$; * $p \leq 0.05$; ** $p \leq 0.01$; *** $p \leq 0.001$. Numbers in parentheses are Huber–White standard errors.

advocates. We now use these replications as our base for hypothesis testing.

In order to test our first hypothesis, we consider whether states that were repressive *at the time they ratified* the CAT or the CCPR have reformed one year after commitment (*repressor$_i$*), improving their human rights practices.[20] We accordingly re-estimate Equation (2), observing only states that were repressive at the time of treaty ratification. Column 4 of Table 10.1 reports our findings, Repressors that accept legal norms to protect human beings, ratifying either the CAT or the CCPR, are not likely, with any degree of confidence, to reform their practices after their commitments (Hafner-Burton & Tsutsui, 2005). Moreover, when we test whether this hypothesis is conditional on democracy and civil society, as previous research assumes, we find that neither treaty is effective even when they are ratified by repressive states on the more democratic end of the spectrum or by repressive states with strong civil society; previous research, it seems, has located a set of conditional effects that matter least for those states that need reform the most.[21] Moreover, we see some evidence to suggest that, among repressors, the more democratic states that ratify the CAT are actually likely to have worse practices. Estimates also suggest to us that states that have higher per capita incomes and trade, are free from civil war, and are governed by democratic institutions are more likely to respect human rights—findings consistent with many studies before ours (Henderson, 1991; Poe, Tate & Keith, 1999; Richards, Gelleny & Sacko, 2001).[22] Repressor states, it seems, are keen to join the treaty regime but not equally enthusiastic to implement those commitments, at least not right away, although the regime could be working to keep them from worse brutality. Yet, as we have mentioned, core theories of compliance suggest that implementation is likely to happen only oversome unknown but potentially considerable period of time, and the path to reform may

be a bumpy (rather than an upward trending) one.

Our next concern, correspondingly, is to test our second hypothesis to determine whether repressive states that have ratified either treaty put reforms into practice over time. Socialization toward internalization of these norms, as well as the capacity to implement reforms, may simply take time for many governments not accustomed to protecting human rights or without the proper resources. Moreover, this dynamic process may not be steadily increasing. In order to test our second hypothesis, we run the same base model (Column 4 of Table 10.1) 14 more times, now replacing CAT_{it-1} and $CCPR_{it-1}$ with lags from 2 to 15 years.[23] For the purpose of efficiency, we have chosen to illustrate our tests graphically by plotting our coefficients of substantive interest and their confidence intervals at 95%; all results are available in the replication file.

The solid black lines in Figures 10.3 and 10.4 plot the coefficients on CAT_{it-1} and $CCPR_{it-1}$ across each lag model, controlling for all the variables in Equation (2) and considering only states repressive at the time of treaty ratification. The dotted lines represent their confidence intervals at 95%. Both figures unquestionably show that point estimates may fall anywhere within the confidence intervals which contain zero. Simply put, neither treaty has a systematic effect on repressive states' behaviors even a decade and a half after commitment.

We investigate our findings further in Figure 10.5 by offering predicted probabilities to better clarify what these coefficients mean substantively. In particular, we are concerned with understanding whether a state guilty of the most radical forms of violations (*repression$_{it}$* = 5) at the time it ratified the CAT or the CCPR is more likely to reform as the years go by. This figure provides insight on two questions: what is the probability that an average violent repressor[24] will reform

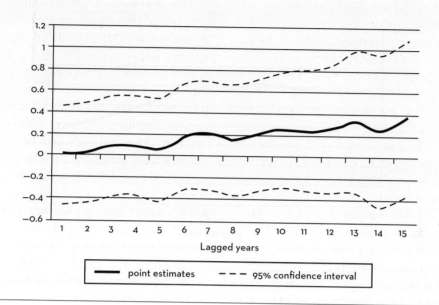

Figure 10.3. *Point Estimates of the Effects over Time of CAT Ratification on Human Rights Reform: For Governments Repressive at the Time of Ratification, 15-Year Duration*

human rights after joining various human rights treaties and after various years of commitment?[25]

In our previous graphs, the black lines represented point estimates. In Figure 10.5, the lines represent predicted probabilities calculated from the point estimates (Column 4 in Table 10.1) that an extreme repressor has undertaken *any* notable human rights reforms at the time of our observation. We consider any movement toward categories 4, 3, 2, or 1 on *repression*$_{it}$ to indicate reform, a very liberal interpretation of improvement. Our predictions indicate that, without any global legal commitments to protect human rights norms, the world's most violent repressors are likely to undertake reforms about 50% of the time; this is about the same chance that they will reform after they have ratified either human rights treaty.[26] International law, it seems, does not increase the chance of reform at all in most terribly repressive

states, although it may prevent slippage into worse violations.

All told, this information suggests that human rights treaties are least effective in making improvements in precisely those states that need them the most and for which they were originally designed—the world's worst abusers. It is not clear whether the results are due to a selection effect or the weak achievements of the treaties themselves, and it is possible that treaties are actually working a little by preventing represents from abusing even more. Yet, if repressive governments are being socialized by or learning from the human rights legal regime to believe something new about human rights norms, either they are mostly learning the wrong message, that repression in the face of commitment to international law is acceptable behavior, or socialization to new beliefs is weak in the face of leaders' political incapacity to reform.

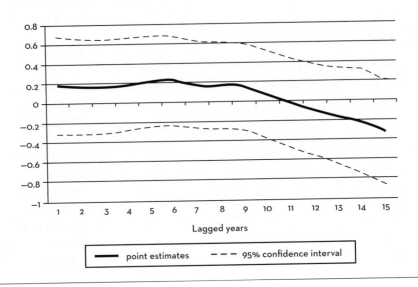

Figure 10.4. Point Estimates of the Effects over Time of CCPR Ratification on Human Rights Reform: For Governments Repressive at the Time of Ratification, 15-Year Duration

Figure 10.5. Predicted Probabilities that the World's Most Repressive States Will Reform Human Rights over 15 Years

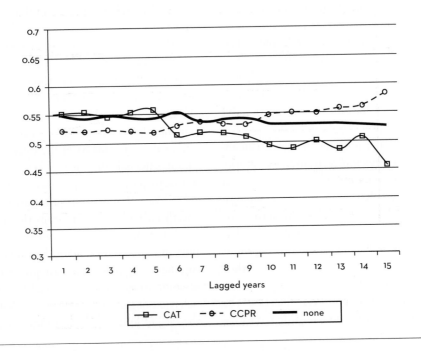

And these roadblocks to better human rights practices appear persistent over time.

Delegation of Authority

If commitments to the CAT and the CCPR provide little in the way of motivations for most repressive governments to reform their human rights behaviors in accordance with lawful norms, many of our critics, especially in the legal and policy communities, believe laws providing for greater delegation can help. Indeed, the Protocol was explicitly designed to improve on and add to existing enforcement mechanisms. One such law is already available, the first Optional Protocol to the International Covenant on Civil and Political Rights (CCPR OP).

By itself, the CCPR's monitoring capacity is very limited. Governments that belong to the CCPR pledge only to submit reports to the Human Rights Committee (commonly referred to as the Committee) evaluating the measures they have adopted in support of treaty norms.[27] Without further consent from governments, however, the Committee only has the authority to study the reports, submitted by governments under scrutiny for violations, ask questions of government representatives, and respond with general comments. A law with moderately greater delegation, however, is available.

When a state adopts the CCPR OP, that government makes an additional commitment to recognize the competence of the Committee. Authority has been delegated to the Committee to entertain complaints made against a state by

Figure 10.6. Point Estimates of the Effects over Time of CCPR OP Ratification on Human Rights Reform for Governments Repressive at the Time of Ratification, 15-Year Duration

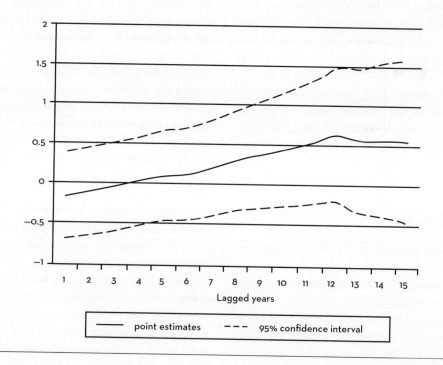

individual victims of a violation of any of the rights protected by the treaty.[28] The Optional Protocol is certainly not hard law, but it does delegate greater external competences for oversight and intervention and, therefore, places more substantial constraints on governments' authority to violate the norms to which they commit. Are repressive states that commit to the CCPR OP, a harder form of international law, any more likely to reform?

We again seek to economize and present our results graphically rather than in table format. Figure 10.6 plots coefficients to interpret our findings. We calculate these coefficients from our core model, Equation (2), on the sample of repressor states with the addition of a new variable, $CCPROP_{it-1 \ldots N}$, where N equals 1–15 lagged years.[29] As before, we run 15 separate models, one for each lag year, and we plot the results only of our variable of substantive interest.[30] We find that the likelihood of reform after deeper commitment to human rights treaty law, ratifying the CCPR Optional Protocol, is indistinguishable from zero. Simply put, delegating more authority for monitoring the implementation of human rights by providing victims with an official forum to articulate the injustices they have suffered does not seem to matter for implementation—a result that may also be explained by the selection process. Repressive states that join simply are not listening, or, if they are, they lack the resources or political will to take action.

Conclusion

Much human rights research is dedicated to showing the ways in which international institutions, including human rights treaties, can make a difference, even inside horribly repressive regimes. Recent statistical studies qualify this belief, showing the ways that treaties matter but only under some circumstances. They raise an important question: can human rights laws help in the most severe cases of abuse? Is the problem that the world's worst repressors might need more time to come under the sway of international law, to build capacity to implement reforms, and to change the minds of their perpetrators?

Our findings add to recent statistical findings, which discover some hope for effect among a small group of states. We identify systematic limitations to the human rights legal regime for precisely those states that need the most oversight—there in severe crisis. Is it enough that the human rights regime can help only a small number of states and a small percentage of the world's population, leaving behind those who are worst abused? How can we build and support a better international regime that, after decades of binding commitments and various institutional reforms to boost compliance, is still not making a noticeable difference in so many cases?

Evidence shows that international laws are working in some democratic states with an active civil society. But we are confronted with overwhelming evidence that these cases of influence are not applicable to the world's most repressive states; that, more often than not, repressive governments that formally commit to international treaties protecting our most basic human rights never come close to reform; that socialization, persuasion, and learning, if they are taking place over time, are not teaching the right messages to the governments that need the most help or are weak in the face of incapacity to implement; and that, in the few instances where new ways of acting are indeed being learned, leaders are not effectively implementing those ideas to better protect people. Moreover, the democratic scope conditions are even narrower than previously thought.

These findings raise important questions. If commitment to international law appears to have no direct effect on reform for the world's worst abusers, either because the treaties are too weak to do much good or the abusive states most open to reform are selecting not to join them, why are so many governments, organizations, and human rights advocates concerned with ratification? Why do the United States and the European Union make commitments to human rights laws a core principle of foreign policy, trade, and aid? Why do human rights organizations spend so many resources mobilizing campaigns for membership? Why does the UN do the same? What is driving the selection process? If treaties do not matter where they need to, why do states and advocates push them so fiercely? What other purposes and interests are treaties serving? And what other tools can help the worst abusers reform?

NOTES

1. In 2003, 81 of 168 states in the Amnesty International report, 88 of 176 states in the US State Department report, and 81 of 188 states in the Freedom House report were observed to commit significant acts of repression.

2. Complete details of the treaties' provisions are available from http://www.unhchr.ch/html/menu3/b/a_ccpr.htm and http://www.unhchr.ch/html/menu3/b/h_cat39.htm (accessed 10 December 2005).

3. For details of the data, see Appendix (http://www.prio.no/jpr/datasets).

4. We have run sensitivity analyses to ensure that our dichotomous coding is appropriate. In these analyses, we coded states that received a score of 3 in a given year as a *moderate repressor$_i$*, 4 a *severe repressor$_i$* and 5 an *extreme repressor$_i$* Analyses using *moderate, severe,* or *extreme repressor$_i$* in the place of *repressor$_i$* produce consistent results.

5. A complete list of repressor states is available in the replication file.

6. For detailed justifications of each control variable, see the sources cited.

7. See online Appendix for details on the data.

8. For a detailed explanation of the data, see online Appendix.

9. All other results, including the coefficients and standard errors from which these probabilities are calculated, are available in the replication file.

10. Confidence intervals are not reported around the predictions for visual clarity. However, they are available in the data replication file and indicate that there is no statistical difference between repressors and protectors in their likelihood of treaty ratification, regardless of the year in which we compute the prediction.

11. Although there are some slight variations in samples and reports between AI and SD, results are generally consistent across both human rights-reporting sources.

12. The data replication file provides further information about spatial and institutional variation in ratification behaviors. We consider six major world regions and discover (using predictions) that repressive states that make legal commitments to the human rights treaty regime are distributed around the world fairly equally, coming from every major region except Asia. Surprisingly, repressors ruled by democratic and autocratic governments are equally likely to have ratified one treaty, although democracies are slightly more likely to have ratified both.

13. This finding is nicely articulated in the case of human rights by Moravcsik (1995), who shows that European human rights regimes are likely to have little effect on those states that are not already disposed toward transformation, namely newly developing states.

14. Owing to the lack of substantive penalties in the CCPR and the CAT, repressive governments can choose to ignore deadlines for their country reports or submit falsified reports, hence avoiding good-faith participation in the treaty mechanisms, which could trigger some form of socialization.

15. We distinguish between socialization and acculturation in terms of the degree of agency at work. Socialization takes place with purposive actors making decisions to change policies, while acculturation is guided more by imitation in the face of uncertainty.

16. The model and control variables are very similar to those employed by other major studies of repression, including Poe & Tate (1994), Keith (1999), Hathaway (2002), Hafner-Burton &Tsutsui (2005), and Neumayer (2005). See these studies for detailed discussions and justifications of these variables.

17. Please see online Appendix for a discussion of the impact of missing data on our analyses.

18. An alternative procedure for addressing autocorrelation is to include a lagged dependent variable. However, there is substantial debate as to whether this practice is appropriate or necessary, as the method risks bias in the estimations. Fixed time effects are a suitable alternative, and we include them here on this basis. However, we estimate a model with a lagged dependent variable as a robust check and find no substantive difference in the estimates; the lag is positive and significant, but all other variables remain consistent with the results reported in Table 10.1 Results ate reported in the replication file. We therefore do not include the lagged variable in the remainder of our analyses.

19. We do not include $civil\ society_{it-1}$ into the base model, because several hundred observations are missing; we later include the variable as a robustness check on our results.

20. Consistent with our earlier analyses, we again define this population as any state for which $repression_i = 1$ at the time of ratification.

21. Of the states observed in this sample, 20% are repressors with democratic systems of government; 47% are repressors with above average links to civil society.

22. Although our primary concern is not to explain variation in effect of human rights treaties on protectors versus repressors, it is worth noting that comparing results for repressors and protectors shows interesting variations. For instance, protectors with higher GDP per capita and greater regime stability are more likely to improve their human tights practices, white these effects disappear among repressors. Also, ratification of the CCPR has a modest positive impact on practice, as does Polity. Conversely, trade can improve practice among repressors, but the effect does not stand among protectors. Equally interesting is the finding that population pressure and civil war have worsening effects on practice in both repressors and protectors.

23. We have chosen a period of 15 years in order to cover the period of time observed in our sample between the entry into force of the CAT (1987) and the last year of our data observation (2003). Lags allow us to observe new information about compliance to assess the 'bumpiness' of the path, although they have costs and are not an ideal form of dynamic modeling.

24. We define average by custom as the mean of all variables in Equation (2), excluding the dependent variable, $repression_{it-1}$ and our variables of substantive interest, $CAT_{it-1...N}$ and $CCPR_{it-1...N}$.

25. Figures 4B and 4C, available in the data replication file, plot the same findings for less extreme forms of violations, $repression_{it} = 4$ and $repression_{it} = 3$. Findings are relatively consistent and so not reported here.

26. Although the probabilities for reform after 15 years of CAT and CCPR ratification are slightly lower and higher, respectively, than for no commitment to treaties, these estimates fall within 95% confidence intervals and are accordingly indistinguishable from each other. Confidence intervals for all predications are not shown here for sake of visual clarity but are available in our replication data.

27. Participating governments must submit these reports within one year of the entry into force of the CCPR or whenever the Committee makes a request. The Secretary-General of the United Nations, after consultation with the Committee, may circulate the reports to specialized UN agencies. Article 40 of the CCPR and subsequent Committee resolutions describe this procedure in greater detail.

28. Article 2 of the Optional Protocol stipulates that individuals who claim that any of their rights enumerated in the Covenant have been violated and who have exhausted all available domestic remedies

may submit a written communication to the Committee for consideration.

29. Over 50% of states that have ratified the CCPR Optional Protocol were repressors.

30. For example, in our first model, we rerun Equation (2) results, presented in Column 2 of Table 10.1 however, we add one new variable, $CCPROP_{it-1}$. In our second model, we rerun the same equation, now adding $CCPROP_{it-1}$, and so on.

REFERENCES

Abbott, Kenneth W. & Duncan Snidal, 2000. 'Hard and Soft Law in International Governance', *International Organization* 54(3): 421–456.

Anderson, Craig A., 1989. 'Causal Reasoning and Belief Perseverance', in D. W. Schumann, ed., *Proceedings of the Society for Consumer Psychology*. Knoxville, TN: University of Tennessee (115–120).

Chayes, Abram & Antonia Handler Chayes, 1993. 'On Compliance', *International Organization* 47(2): 175–205.

Chayes, Abram & Antonia Handler Chayes, 1998. *The New Sovereignty: Compliance with International Regulatory Agreements*. Cambridge, MA: Harvard University Press.

Cleveland, Sarah H., 2001. 'Norm Internalization and U.S. Economic Sanctions', *Yale Journal of International Law* 26(1): 1–102.

Cole, Wade M., 2005. 'Sovereignty Relinquished? Explaining Commitment to the International Human Rights Covenants, 1966–1999', *American Sociological Review* 70(3): 472–495.

Downs, George W.; David M. Rocke & Peter N. Barsoom, 1996. 'Is the Good News About Compliance Good News About Cooperation?', *International Organization* 50(3): 379–406.

Finnemore, Martha, 1996. 'Norms, Culture, and World Politics: Insights from Sociology's Institutionalism', *International Organization* 50(2): 325–347.

Finnemore, Martha & Kathryn Sikkink, 1998. 'International Norm Dynamics and Political Change', *International Organization* 52(4): 887–917.

Franck, Thomas M., 1988. 'Legitimacy in the International System', *American Journal of International Law* 82(4): 705–758.

Gastil, Raymond, 1980. *Freedom in the World: Political Rights and Civil Liberties, 1980*. New Brunswick, NJ: Transaction.

Gibney, Mark & Matthew Dalton, 1996. 'The Political Terror Scale', in Stuart S. Nagel & David Louis Cingranelli, eds, *Human Rights and Developing Country*. Greenwich, CT: JAI.

Gibney, Mark; Vanessa Dalton & Marc Vockell, 1992. 'USA Refugee Policy: A Human Rights Analysis Update', *Journal of Refugee Studies* 5(1): 33–46.

Goodliffe, Jay & Darren Hawkins, 2005. 'Explaining Commitment: States and the Convention Against Torture', *Journal of Politics* 68(2): 358–371.

Goodman, Ryan & Derek Jinks, 2003. 'Measuring the Effects of Human Rights Treaties', *European Journal of International Law* 14(1): 171–183.

Hafner-Burton, Emilie M., 2005. 'Trading Human Rights: How Preferential Trade Arrangements Influence Government Repression', *International Organization* 59(3): 593–629.

Hafner-Burton, Emilie & James Ron, 2006. 'Seeing Double: Human Rights Through Qualitative and Quantitative Eyes', unpublished manuscript (http://www. princeton.edu/~ehafher/).

Hafner-Burton, Emilie & Kiyoteru Tsutsui, 2005. 'Human Rights in a Globalizing World: The Paradox of Empty Promises', *American Journal of Sociology* 110(5): 1373–1411.

Hathaway, Oona A., 2002. 'Do Human Rights Treaties Make a Difference?', *Yale Law Journal* 111(8): 1935–2042.

Hathaway, Oona A., 2003. 'The Cost of Commitment', *Stanford Law Review* 55 (May): 1821–1862.

Hathaway, Oona A., 2005. 'The Promise and Limits of the International Law of Torture', in Oona A. Hathaway & H. H. Koh, eds, *Foundations of International Law and Politics*. New York: Foundation (228–237).

Henderson, Conway W., 1991. 'Conditions Affecting the Use of Political Repression', *Journal of Conflict Resolution* 35(1): 120–142.

Henkin, Louis, 1979. *How Nations Behave: Law and Foreign Policy.* New York: Columbia University Press.

Jaggcrs, Keith & Ted Robert Gurr, 1995. 'Tracking Democracy's Third Wave with the Polity III Data', *Journal of Peace Research* 32(4): 469–482.

Keith, Linda Camp, 1999. 'The United Nations International Covenant on Civil and Political Rights: Does It Make a Difference in Human Rights Behavior?', *Journal of Peace Research* 36(1): 95–118.

Keohane, Robert O.; Andrew Moravcsik & Anne-Marie Slaughter, 2001. 'Legalized Dispute Resolution: Interstate and Transnational', *International Organization* 54(3): 457–488.

Koh, Harold Hongju, 1996–97. 'Why Do Nations Obey International Law', *Yale Law Journal* 106(8): 2599–2659.

Koh, Harold Hongju, 2002. 'A United States Human Rights Policy for the 21st Century', *Saint Louis University Law Journal* 46(2): 293–344.

Landman, Todd, 2005. *Protecting Human Rights: A Comparative Study.* Washington, DC: Georgetown University Press.

Long, J. Scott, 1997. *Regression Models for Categorical and Limited Dependent Variables.* Thousand Oaks, CA: Sage.

Lutz, Ellen L. & Kathryn Sikkink, 2000. 'International Human Rights Law and Practice in Latin America', *International Organization* 54(3): 633–659.

Mearsheimer, John, 1994/1995. 'The False Promise of International Institutions', *International Security* 19(3): 5–49.

Meyer, John W.; John Boli, George M. Thomas & Francisco O. Ramirez, 1997. 'World Society and the Nation-State', *American Journal of Sociology* 103(1): 144–181.

Mitchell, Ronald D., 1993. 'Compliance Theory: A Synthesis', *Review of European Community and International Environmental Law* 2(4): 327–334.

Moravcsik, Andrew, 1995. 'Explaining International Human Rights Regimes: Liberal Theory and Western Europe', *European Journal of International Relations* 1(2): 157–189.

Moravcsik, Andrew, 2000. 'The Origins of Human Rights Regimes: Democratic Delegation in Postwar Europe', *International Organization* 54(2): 217–252.

Neumayer, Eric, 2005. 'Do International Human Rights Treaties Improve Respect for Human Rights?', *Journal of Conflict Resolution* 49(6): 925–953.

Poe, Steven C. & C. Neal Tate, 1994. 'Repression of Human Rights to Personal Integrity in the 1980s: A Global Analysis', *American Political Science Review* 88(4): 853–872.

Poe, Steven C.; C. Neal Tate & Linda Camp Keith, 1999. 'Repression of the Human Right to Personal Integrity Revisited: A Global Cross-National Study Covering the Years 1976–1993', *International Studies Quarterly* 43(2): 291–313.

Powell, Walter W. & Paul J. DiMaggio, eds, 1991. *The New Institutionalism in Organizational Analysis.* Chicago, IL: University of Chicago Press.

Richards, David L.; Ronald D. Gelleny & David H. Sacko, 2001. 'Money With a Mean Streak? Foreign Economic Penetration and Government Respect for Human Rights in Developing Countries', *International Studies Quarterly* 45(2): 219–239.

Risse, Thomas; Stephen C. Ropp & Kathryn Sikkink, eds, 1999. *The Power of Human Rights: International Norms and Domestic Change.* New York: Cambridge University Press.

Ron, James, 2000. 'Savage Restraint: Israel, Palestine and the Dialectics of Legal Repression', *Social Problems* 47(4): 445–472.

Scott, W. Richard; John W. Meyer & John Boli, 1994. *Institutional Environments and Organizations: Structural Complexity and Individualism.* Thousand Oaks, CA: Sage.

Simmons, Beth, 2006. 'Complying with the Law: The Case of International Human Rights Treaties', unpublished manuscript, Harvard University.

Slusher, Morgan P. & Craig A. Anderson, 1996. 'Using Causal Persuasive Arguments To Change Beliefs and Teach New Information: The Mediating Role of Explanation Availability and Evaluation Bias in the Acceptance of Knowledge', *Journal of Educational Psychology* 88(1): 110–122.

Strange, Susan, 1982. 'Cave Hic Dragones! A Critique of Regime Analysis', *International Organization* 36(2): 479–496.

Vreeland, James Raymond, 2007. 'Political Institutions and Human Rights: Why Dictatorships Enter Into the United Nations Convention Against Torture', *International Organization*.

Waltz, Kenneth N., 1979. *Theory of International Politics*. New York: McGraw-Hill.

Wotipka, Christine Min & Kiyoteru Tsutsui, 2001. 'Global Human Rights and State Sovereignty: Nation-States' Ratification of International Human Rights Treaties, 1965–1999', presented at the annual meetings of the American Sociological Association, Anaheim, CA, 18–21 August.

TRANSNATIONAL ISSUES

11

Arising out of the interconnectedness of globalization, transnational concerns have become part of the global agenda. Such concerns include the environment, pollution, population, health, and international crime. For many transnational issues, the rights and responsibilities of the individual, the state, and the international community may be incompatible or even diverge. Do the rights of the individual take precedence over the right of the community in the use of land and natural resources? Does a couple have the right of unlimited procreation when resources are limited? In his pathbreaking 1968 article, Garrett Hardin posits in unequivocal terms that the pursuit of individual interests may not necessarily lead to the common good. Strategies to address that "tragedy" are delineated in stark, yet profound, ways.

Nobel Prize winner Elinor Ostrom, drawing on decades of in-depth studies of local institutions and the environment, examines solutions to common pool resource problems in fisheries, forests, and water systems. Contrary to those advocating one management strategy—privatization, government takeover, or community takeover—she suggests that one size does not fit all. Multi-level governance solutions can percolate up from those most affected.

Of various environmental issues, none is as global or as controversial as climate change, pitting economic versus environmental forces. Robert O. Keohane and David G. Victor see many different cooperation problems within the climate change issue, demanding a variety of structures and approaches. Rather than an integrated Kyoto-style regulatory system, the authors call for a complex of systems which forge rules according to different conditions.

Health is another transnational issue. While much attention at the global level has been paid to communicable diseases like HIV/AIDS, polio, and avian flu, Thomas J. Bollyky brings our attention to preventable and treatable noncommunicable diseases. One of the ironic trends of our time is that as countries develop, communicable diseases may decline, but noncommunicable diseases may increase. The good news is that there are low-cost solutions to address those health issues.

Garrett Hardin

THE TRAGEDY OF THE COMMONS

The population problem has no technical solution; it requires a fundamental extension in morality.

At the end of a thoughtful article on the future of nuclear war, Wiesner and York[1] concluded that: "Both sides in the arms race are . . . confronted by the dilemma of steadily increasing military power and steadily decreasing national security. *It is our considered professional judgment that this dilemma has no technical solution.* If the great powers continue to look for solutions in the area of science and technology only, the result will be to worsen the situation."

I would like to focus your attention not on the subject of the article (national security in a nuclear world) but on the kind of conclusion they reached, namely that there is no technical solution to the problem. An implicit and almost universal assumption of discussions published in professional and semipopular scientific journals is that the problem under discussion has a technical solution. A technical solution may be defined as one that requires a change only in the techniques of the natural sciences, demanding little or nothing in the way of change in human values or ideas of morality.

In our day (though not in earlier times) technical solutions are always welcome. Because of previous failures in prophecy, it takes courage to assert that a desired technical solution is not possible. Wiesner and York exhibited this courage; publishing in a science journal, they insisted that the solution to the problem was not to be found in the natural sciences. They cautiously qualified

From *Science* 162, no. 3859 (Dec. 13, 1968), 1243–1248.

their statement with the phrase, "It is our considered professional judgment. . . ." Whether they were right or not is not the concern of the present article. Rather, the concern here is with the important concept of a class of human problems which can be called "no technical solution problems," and, more specifically, with the identification and discussion of one of these.

It is easy to show that the class is not a null class. Recall the game of tick-tack-toe. Consider the problem, "How can I win the game of tick-tack-toe?" It is well known that I cannot, if I assume (in keeping with the conventions of game theory) that my opponent understands the game perfectly. Put another way, there is no "technical solution" to the problem. I can win only by giving a radical meaning to the word "win." I can hit my opponent over the head; or I can drug him; or I can falsify the records. Every way in which I "win" involves, in some sense, an abandonment of the game, as we intuitively understand it. (I can also, of course, openly abandon the game—refuse to play it. This is what most adults do.)

The class of "No technical solution problems" has members. My thesis is that the "population problem," as conventionally conceived, is a member of this class. How it is conventionally conceived needs some comment. It is fair to say that most people who anguish over the population problem are trying to find a way to avoid the evils of overpopulation without relinquishing any of the privileges they now enjoy. They think that farming the seas or developing new strains of wheat will solve the problem—technologically. I try to show here that the solution they seek cannot be found. The population problem cannot be solved in a technical way, any more than can the problem of winning the game of tick-tack-toe.

What Shall We Maximize?

Population, as Malthus said, naturally tends to grow "geometrically," or, as we would now say, exponentially. In a finite world this means that the per capita share of the world's goods must steadily decrease. Is ours a finite world?

A fair defense can be put forward for the view that the world is infinite; or that we do not know that it is not. But, in terms of the practical problems that we must face in the next few generations with the foreseeable technology, it is clear that we will greatly increase human misery if we do not, during the immediate future, assume that the world available to the terrestrial human population is finite. "Space" is no escape.[2]

A finite world can support only a finite population; therefore, population growth must eventually equal zero. (The case of perpetual wide fluctuations above and below zero is a trivial variant that need not be discussed.) When this condition is met, what will be the situation of mankind? Specifically, can Bentham's goal of "the greatest good for the greatest number" be realized?

No—for two reasons, each sufficient by itself. The first is a theoretical one. It is not mathematically possible to maximize for two (or more) variables at the same time. This was clearly stated by von Neumann and Morgenstern,[3] but the principle is implicit in the theory of partial differential equations, dating back at least to D'Alembert (1717–1783).

The second reason springs directly from biological facts. To live, any organism must have a source of energy (for example, food). This energy is utilized for two purposes: mere maintenance and work. For man, maintenance of life requires about 1600 kilo-calories a day ("maintenance calories"). Anything that he does over and above

merely staying alive will be defined as work, and is supported by "work calories" which he takes in. Work calories are used not only for what we call work in common speech; they are also required for all forms of enjoyment, from swimming and automobile racing to playing music and writing poetry. If our goal is to maximize population it is obvious what we must do: We must make the work calories per person approach as close to zero as possible. No gourmet meals, no vacations, no sports, no music, no literature, no art. . . . I think that everyone will grant, without argument or proof, that maximizing population does not maximize goods. Bentham's goal is impossible.

In reaching this conclusion I have made the usual assumption that it is the acquisition of energy that is the problem. The appearance of atomic energy has led some to question this assumption. However, given an infinite source of energy, population growth still produces an inescapable problem. The problem of the acquisition of energy is replaced by the problem of its dissipation, as J. H. Fremlin has so wittily shown.[4] The arithmetic signs in the analysis are, as it were, reversed; but Bentham's goal is still unobtainable.

The optimum population is, then, less than the maximum. The difficulty of defining the optimum is enormous; so far as I know, no one has seriously tackled this problem. Reaching an acceptable and stable solution will surely require more than one generation of hard analytical work—and much persuasion.

We want the maximum good per person; but what is good? To one person it is wilderness, to another it is ski lodges for thousands. To one it is estuaries to nourish ducks for hunters to shoot; to another it is factory land. Comparing one good with another is, we usually say, impossible because goods are incommensurable. Incommensurables cannot be compared.

Theoretically this may be true; but in real life incommensurables *are* commensurable. Only a criterion of judgment and a system of weighting are needed. In nature the criterion is survival. Is it better for a species to be small and hide-able, or large and powerful? Natural selection commensurates the incommensurables. The compromise achieved depends on a natural weighting of the values of the variables.

Man must imitate this process. There is no doubt that in fact he already does, but unconsciously. It is when the hidden decisions are made explicit that the arguments begin. The problem for the years ahead is to work out an acceptable theory of weighting. Synergistic effects, nonlinear variation, and difficulties in discounting the future make the intellectual problem difficult, but not (in principle) insoluble.

Has any cultural group solved this practical problem at the present time, even on an intuitive level? One simple fact proves that none has: there is no prosperous population in the world today that has, and has had for some time, a growth rate of zero. Any people that has intuitively identified its optimum point will soon reach it, after which its growth rate becomes and remains zero.

Of course, a positive growth rate might be taken as evidence that a population is below its optimum. However, by any reasonable standards, the most rapidly growing populations on earth today are (in general) the most miserable. This association (which need not be invariable) casts doubt on the optimistic assumption that the positive growth rate of a population is evidence that it has yet to reach its optimum.

We can make little progress in working toward optimum poulation size until we explicitly exorcize the spirit of Adam Smith in the field of practical demography. In economic affairs, *The Wealth of Nations* (1776) popularized the "invisible hand," the idea that an individual who "intends only his own gain," is, as it were, "led by an invisible hand to promote . . . the public interest."[5] Adam Smith did not assert that this was invariably true, and perhaps neither did any of his followers. But he contributed to a dominant tendency of thought that has ever since interfered with positive action based on rational analysis, namely, the tendency to assume that decisions reached individually will, in fact, be the best decisions for an entire society. If this assumption is correct it justifies the continuance of our present policy of laissez-faire in reproduction. If it is correct we can assume that men will control their individual fecundity so as to produce the optimum population. If the assumption is not correct, we need to reexamine our individual freedoms to see which ones are defensible.

Tragedy of Freedom in a Commons

The rebuttal to the invisible hand in population control is to be found in a scenario first sketched in a little-known pamphlet[6] in 1833 by a mathematical amateur named William Forster Lloyd (1794–1852). We may well call it "the tragedy of the commons," using the word "tragedy" as the philosopher Whitehead used it[7]: "The essence of dramatic tragedy is not unhappiness. It resides in the solemnity of the remorseless working of things:" He then goes on to say, "This inevitableness of destiny can only be illustrated in terms of human life by incidents which in fact involve unhappiness. For it is only by them that the futility of escape can be made evident in the drama."

The tragedy of the commons develops in this way. Picture a pasture open to all. It is to be expected that each herdsman will try to keep as many cattle as possible on the commons. Such an arrangement may work reasonably satisfactorily for centuries because tribal wars, poaching, and disease keep the numbers of both man and beast well below the carrying capacity of the land. Finally, however, comes the day of reckoning, that is, the day when the long-desired goal of social stability becomes a reality. At this point, the inherent logic of the commons remorselessly generates tragedy.

As a rational being, each herdsman seeks to maximize his gain. Explicitly or implicitly, more or less consciously, he asks, "What is the utility *to me* of adding one more animal to my herd?" This utility has one negative and one positive component.

1) The positive component is a function of the increment of one animal. Since the herdsman receives all the proceeds from the sale of the additional animal, the positive utility is nearly +1.

2) The negative component is a function of the additional overgrazing created by one more animal. Since, however, the effects of overgrazing are shared by all the herdsmen, the negative utility for any particular decision-making herdsman is only a fraction of −1.

Adding together the component partial utilities, the rational herdsman concludes that the only sensible course for him to pursue is to add another animal to his herd. And another; and another. . . . But this is the conclusion reached by each and every rational herdsman sharing a commons. Therein is the tragedy. Each man is locked into a system that compels him to increase his herd without limit—in a world that is limited. Ruin is the destination toward which all men rush, each pursuing his own best interest in a society that believes in the freedom of the commons. Freedom in a commons brings ruin to all.

Some would say that this is a platitude. Would that it were! In a sense, it was learned thousands of years ago, but natural selection favors the forces of psychological denial.[8] The individual benefits as an individual from his ability to deny the truth even though society as a whole, of which he is a part, suffers. Education can counteract the natural tendency to do the wrong thing, but the inexorable succession of generations requires that the basis for this knowledge be constantly refreshed.

A simple incident that occurred a few years ago in Leominster, Massachusetts, shows how perishable the knowledge is. During the Christmas shopping season the parking meters downtown were covered with plastic bags that bore tags reading: "Do not open until after Christmas. Free parking courtesy of the mayor and city council." In other words, facing the prospect of an increased demand for already scarce space, the city fathers reinstituted the system of the commons. (Cynically, we suspect that they gained more votes than they lost by this retrogressive act.)

In an approximate way, the logic of the commons has been understood for a long time, perhaps since the discovery of agriculture or the invention of private property in real estate. But it is understood mostly only in special cases which are not sufficiently generalized. Even at this late date, cattlemen leasing national land on the western ranges demonstrate no more than an ambivalent understanding, in constantly pressuring federal authorities to increase the head count to the point where overgrazing produces erosion and weed-dominance. Likewise, the oceans of the world continue to suffer from the survival of the philosophy of the commons. Maritime nations still respond automatically to the shibboleth of the "freedom of the seas." Professing to believe in the "inexhaustible resources of the oceans," they bring species after species of fish and whales closer to extinction.[9]

The National Parks present another instance of the working out of the tragedy of the commons. At present, they are open to all, without limit. The parks themselves are limited in extent—there is only one Yosemite Valley—whereas population seems to grow without limit. The values that visitors seek in the parks are steadily eroded. Plainly, we must soon cease to treat the parks as commons or they will be of no value to anyone.

What shall we do? We have several options. We might sell them off as private property. We might keep them as public property, but allocate the right to enter them. The allocation might be on the basis of wealth, by the use of an auction system. It might be on the basis of merit, as defined by some agreed-upon standards. It might be by lottery. Or it might be on a first-come, first-served basis, administered to long queues. These, I think, are all the reasonable possibilities. They are all objectionable. But we must choose—or acquiesce in the destruction of the commons that we call our National Parks.

Pollution

In a reverse way, the tragedy of the commons reappears in problems of pollution. Here it is not a question of taking something out of the commons, but of putting something in—sewage, or chemical, radioactive, and heat wastes into water; noxious and dangerous fumes into the air; and distracting and unpleasant advertising signs into the line of sight. The calculations of utility are much the same as before. The rational man finds that his share of the cost of the wastes he discharges into the commons is less than the cost of purifying his wastes before releasing them. Since this is true for everyone, we are locked into a system of "fouling our own nest," so long as we behave only as independent, rational, free-enterprisers.

The tragedy of the commons as a food basket is averted by private property, or something formally like it. But the air and waters surrounding us cannot readily be fenced, and so the tragedy of the commons as a cesspool must be prevented by different means, by coercive laws or taxing devices that make it cheaper for the polluter to treat his pollutants than to discharge them untreated. We have not progressed as far with the solution of this problem as we have with the first. Indeed, our particular concept of private property, which deters us from exhausting the positive resources of the earth, favors pollution. The owner of a factory on the bank of a stream—whose property extends to the middle of the stream—often has difficulty seeing why it is not his natural right to muddy the waters flowing past his door. The law, always behind the times, requires elaborate stitching and fitting to adapt it to this newly perceived aspect of the commons.

The pollution problem is a consequence of population. It did not much matter how a lonely American frontiersman disposed of his waste. "Flowing water purifies itself every 10 miles," my grandfather used to say, and the myth was near enough to the truth when he was a boy, for there were not too many people. But as population became denser, the natural chemical and biological recycling processes became overloaded, calling for a redefinition of property rights.

How to Legislate Temperance?

Analysis of the pollution problem as a function of population density uncovers a not generally recognized principle of morality, namely: *the morality of an act is a function of the state of the system at the time it is performed.*[10] Using the commons as a cesspool does not harm the general public under frontier conditions, because there is no public; the same behavior in a metropolis is unbearable. A hundred and fifty years ago a plainsman could kill an American bison, cut out only the tongue for his dinner, and discard the rest of the animal. He was not in any important sense being wasteful. Today, with only a few thousand bison left, we would be appalled at such behavior.

In passing, it is worth noting that the morality of an act cannot be determined from a photograph. One does not know whether a man killing an elephant or setting fire to the grassland is harming others until one knows the total system in which his act appears. "One picture is worth a thousand words," said an ancient Chinese; but it may take 10,000 words to validate it. It is as tempting to ecologists as it is to reformers in general to try to persuade others by way of the photographic shortcut. But the essen[c]e of an argument cannot be photographed: it must be presented rationally—in words.

That morality is system-sensitive escaped the attention of most codifiers of ethics in the past. "Thou shalt not . . ." is the form of traditional ethical directives which make no allowance for particular circumstances. The laws of our society follow the pattern of ancient ethics, and therefore are poorly suited to governing a complex, crowded, changeable world. Our epicyclic solution is to augment statutory law with administrative law. Since it is practically impossible to spell out all the conditions under which it is safe to burn trash in the back yard or to run an automobile without smog-control, by law we delegate the details to bureaus. The result is administrative law, which is rightly feared for an ancient reason—*Quis custodiet ipsos custodes?*—"Who shall watch the watchers themselves?" John Adams said that we must have "a government of laws and not men." Bureau administrators, trying to evaluate the morality of acts in the total system, are singularly liable to corruption, producing a government by men, not laws.

Prohibition is easy to legislate (though not necessarily to enforce); but how do we legislate temperance? Experience indicates that it can be accomplished best through the mediation of administrative law. We limit possibilities unnecessarily if we suppose that the sentiment of *Quis custodiet* denies us the use of administrative law. We should rather retain the phrase as a perpetual reminder of fearful dangers we cannot avoid. The great challenge facing us now is to invent the corrective feedbacks that are needed to keep custodians honest. We must find ways to legitimate the needed authority of both the custodians and the corrective feedbacks.

Freedom to Breed Is Intolerable

The tragedy of the commons is involved in population problems in another way. In a world governed solely by the principle of "dog eat dog"—if

indeed there ever was such a world—how many children a family had would not be a matter of public concern. Parents who bred too exuberantly would leave fewer descendants, not more, because they would be unable to care adequately for their children. David Lack and others have found that such a negative feedback demonstrably controls the fecundity of birds.[11] But men are not birds, and have not acted like them for millenniums, at least.

If each human family were dependent only on its own resources; *if* the children of improvident parents starved to death; *if,* thus, overbreeding brought its own "punishment" to the germ line— *then* there would be no public interest in controlling the breeding of families. But our society is deeply committed to the welfare state,[12] and hence is confronted with another aspect of the tragedy of the commons.

In a welfare state, how shall we deal with the family, the religion, the race, or the class (or indeed any distinguishable and cohesive group) that adopts overbreeding as a policy to secure its own aggrandizement?[13] To couple the concept of freedom to breed with the belief that everyone born has an equal right to the commons is to lock the world into a tragic course of action.

Unfortunately this is just the course of action that is being pursued by the United Nations. In late 1967, some 30 nations agreed to the following[14]:

> The Universal Declaration of Human Rights describes the family as the natural and fundamental unit of society. It follows that any choice and decision with regard to the size of the family must irrevocably rest with the family itself, and cannot be made by anyone else.

It is painful to have to deny categorically the validity of this right; denying it, one feels as uncomfortable as a resident of Salem, Massachusetts, who denied the reality of witches in the 17th century. At the present time, in liberal quarters, something like a taboo acts to inhibit criticism of the United Nations. There is a feeling that the United Nations is "our last and best hope," that we shouldn't find fault with it; we shouldn't play into the hands of the archconservatives. However, let us not forget what Robert Louis Stevenson said: "The truth that is suppressed by friends is the readiest weapon of the enemy." If we love the truth we must openly deny the validity of the Universal Declaration of Human Rights, even though it is promoted by the United Nations. We should also join with Kingsley Davis[15] in attempting to get Planned Parenthood-World Population to see the error of its ways in embracing the same tragic ideal.

Conscience Is Self-Eliminating

It is a mistake to think that we can control the breeding of mankind in the long run by an appeal to conscience. Charles Galton Darwin made this point when he spoke on the centennial of the publication of his grandfather's great book. The argument is straightforward and Darwinian.

People vary. Confronted with appeals to limit breeding, some people will undoubtedly respond to the plea more than others. Those who have more children will produce a larger fraction of the next generation than those with more susceptible consciences. The difference will be accentuated, generation by generation.

In C. G. Darwin's words: "It may well be that it would take hundreds of generations for the progenitive instinct to develop in this way, but if it should do so, nature would have taken her revenge, and the variety *Homo contracipiens* would become extinct and would be replaced by the variety *Homo progenitivus*."[16]

The argument assumes that conscience or the desire for children (no matter which) is hereditary—but hereditary only in the most general formal

sense. The result will be the same whether the attitude is transmitted through germ cells, or exosomatically, to use A. J. Lotka's term. (If one denies the latter possibility as well as the former, then what's the point of education?) The argument has here been stated in the context of the population problem, but it applies equally well to any instance in which society appeals to an individual exploiting a commons to restrain himself for the general good—by means of his conscience. To make such an appeal is to set up a selective system that works toward the elimination of conscience from the race.

Pathogenic Effects of Conscience

The long-term disadvantage of an appeal to conscience should be enough to condemn it; but has serious short-term disadvantages as well. If we ask a man who is exploiting a commons to desist "in the name of conscience," what are we saying to him? What does he hear?—not only at the moment but also in the wee small hours of the night when, half asleep, he remembers not merely the words we used but also the nonverbal communication cues we gave him unawares? Sooner or later, consciously or subconsciously, he senses that he has received two communications, and that they are contradictory: (i) (intended communication) "If you don't do as we ask, we will openly condemn you for not acting like a responsible citizen"; (ii) (the unintended communication) "If you *do* behave as we ask, we will secretly condemn you for a simpleton who can be shamed into standing aside while the rest of us exploit the commons."

Everyman then is caught in what Bateson has called a "double bind." Bateson and his co-workers have made a plausible case for viewing the double bind as an important causative factor in the genesis of schizophrenia.[17] The double bind may not always be so damaging, but it always endangers the mental health of anyone to whom it is applied. "A bad conscience," said Nietzsche, "is a kind of illness."

To conjure up a conscience in others is tempting to anyone who wishes to extend his control beyond the legal limits. Leaders at the highest level succumb to this temptation. Has any President during the past generation failed to call on labor unions to moderate voluntarily their demands for higher wages, or to steel companies to honor voluntary guidelines on prices? I can recall none. The rhetoric used on such occasions is designed to produce feelings of guilt in noncooperators.

For centuries it was assumed without proof that guilt was a valuable, perhaps even an indispensable, ingredient of the civilized life. Now, in this post-Freudian world, we doubt it.

Paul Goodman speaks from the modern point of view when he says: "No good has ever come from feeling guilty, neither intelligence, policy, nor compassion. The guilty do not pay attention to the object but only to themselves, and not even to their own interests, which might make sense, but to their anxieties."[18]

One does not have to be a professional psychiatrist to see the consequences of anxiety. We in the Western world are just emerging from a dreadful two-centuries-long Dark Ages of Eros that was sustained partly by prohibition laws, but perhaps more effectively by the anxiety-generating mechanisms of education. Alex Comfort has told the story well in *The Anxiety Makers*[19]; it is not a pretty one.

Since proof is difficult, we may even concede that the results of anxiety may sometimes, from certain points of view, be desirable. The larger question we should ask is whether, as a matter of policy, we should ever encourage the use of a technique the tendency (if not the intention) of which is psychologically pathogenic. We hear much talk these days of responsible parenthood; the coupled words are incorporated into the titles of some organizations devoted to birth control. Some people have proposed massive propaganda campaigns to instill responsibility into the nation's (or the world's) breeders. But what is the meaning of the word responsibility in this context? Is it not merely a synonym for the word conscience? When we use the word responsibility in the absence of substantial sanctions are we not trying to browbeat a free man in a commons into acting against his own interest? Responsibility is a verbal counterfeit for a substantial *quid pro quo*. It is an attempt to get something for nothing.

If the word responsibility is to be used at all, I suggest that it be in the sense Charles Frankel uses it.[20] "Responsibility," says this philosopher, "is the product of definite social arrangements." Notice that Frankel calls for social arrangements—not propaganda.

Mutual Coercion Mutually Agreed Upon

The social arrangements that produce responsibility are arrangements that create coercion, of some sort. Consider bank-robbing. The man who takes money from a bank acts as if the bank were a commons. How do we prevent such action? Certainly not by trying to control his behavior solely by a verbal appeal to his sense of responsibility. Rather than rely on propaganda we follow Frankel's lead and insist that a bank is not a commons; we seek the definite social arrangements that will keep it from becoming a commons. That we thereby infringe on the freedom of would-be robbers we neither deny nor regret.

The morality of bank-robbing is particularly easy to understand because we accept complete prohibition of this activity. We are willing to say "Thou shalt not rob banks," without providing for exceptions. But temperance also can be created by coercion. Taxing is a good coercive device. To keep downtown shoppers temperate in their use of parking space we introduce parking meters for short periods, and traffic fines for longer ones. We need not actually forbid a citizen to park as long as he wants to; we need merely make it increasingly expensive for him to do so. Not prohibition, but carefully biased options are what we offer him. A Madison Avenue man might call this persuasion; I prefer the greater candor of the word coercion.

Coercion is a dirty word to most liberals now, but it need not forever be so. As with the four-letter words, its dirtiness can be cleansed away by exposure to the light, by saying it over and over without apology or embarrassment. To many, the word coercion implies arbitrary decisions of distant and irresponsible bureaucrats; but this is not a necessary part of its meaning. The only kind of coercion I recommend is mutual coercion, mutually agreed upon by the majority of the people affected.

To say that we mutually agree to coercion is not to say that we are required to enjoy it, or even to pretend we enjoy it. Who enjoys taxes? We all grumble about them. But we accept compulsory taxes because we recognize that voluntary taxes would favor the conscienceless. We institute and (grumblingly) support taxes and other coercive devices to escape the horror of the commons.

An alternative to the commons need not be perfectly just to be preferable. With real estate and other material goods, the alternative we have chosen is the institution of private property coupled with legal inheritance. Is this system perfectly just? As a genetically trained biologist I deny that it is. It seems to me that, if there are to be differences in individual inheritance, legal possession should be perfectly correlated with biological inheritance—that those who are biologically more fit to be the custodians of property and power should legally inherit more. But genetic recombination continually makes a mockery of the doctrine of "like father, like son" implicit in our laws of legal inheritance. An idiot can inherit millions, and a trust fund can keep his estate intact. We must admit that our legal system of private property plus inheritance is unjust—but we put up with it

because we are not convinced, at the moment, that anyone has invented a better system. The alternative of the commons is too horrifying to contemplate. Injustice is preferable to total ruin.

It is one of the peculiarities of the warfare between reform and the status quo that it is thoughtlessly governed by a double standard. Whenever a reform measure is proposed it is often defeated when its opponents triumphantly discover a flaw in it. As Kingsley Davis has pointed out,[21] worshippers of the status quo sometimes imply that no reform is possible without unanimous agreement, an implication contrary to historical fact. As nearly as I can make out, automatic rejection of proposed reforms is based on one of two unconscious assumptions: (i) that the status quo is perfect; or (ii) that the choice we face is between reform and no action; if the proposed reform is imperfect, we presumably should take no action at all, while we wait for a perfect proposal.

But we can never do nothing. That which we have done for thousands of years is also action. It also produces evils. Once we are aware that the status quo is action, we can then compare its discoverable advantages and disadvantages with the predicted advantages and disadvantages of the proposed reform, discounting as best we can for our lack of experience. On the basis of such a comparison, we can make a rational decision which will not involve the unworkable assumption that only perfect systems are tolerable.

Recognition of Necessity

Perhaps the simplest summary of this analysis of man's population problems is this: the commons, if justifiable at all, is justifiable only under conditions of low-population density. As the human population has increased, the commons has had to be abandoned in one aspect after another.

First we abandoned the commons in food gathering, enclosing farm land and restricting pastures and hunting and fishing areas. These restrictions are still not complete throughout the world.

Somewhat later we saw that the commons as a place for waste disposal would also have to be abandoned. Restrictions on the disposal of domestic sewage are widely accepted in the Western world; we are still struggling to close the commons to pollution by automobiles, factories, insecticide sprayers, fertilizing operations, and atomic energy installations.

In a still more embryonic state is our recognition of the evils of the commons in matters of pleasure. There is almost no restriction on the propagation of sound waves in the public medium. The shopping public is assaulted with mindless music, without its consent. Our government is paying out billions of dollars to create supersonic transport which will disturb 50,000 people for every one person who is whisked from coast to coast 3 hours faster. Advertisers muddy the airwaves of radio and television and pollute the view of travelers. We are a long way from outlawing the commons in matters of pleasure. Is this because our Puritan inheritance makes us view pleasure as something of a sin, and pain (that is, the pollution of advertising) as the sign of virtue?

Every new enclosure of the commons involves the infringement of somebody's personal liberty. Infringements made in the distant past are accepted because no contemporary complains of a loss. It is the newly proposed infringements that we vigorously oppose; cries of "rights" and "freedom" fill the air. But what does "freedom" mean? When men mutually agreed to pass laws against robbing, mankind became more free, not less so. Individuals locked into the logic of the commons are free only to bring on universal ruin; once they see the necessity of mutual coercion, they become free to pursue other goals. I believe it was Hegel who said, "Freedom is the recognition of necessity."

The most important aspect of necessity that we must now recognize, is the necessity of abandoning the commons in breeding. No technical solution can rescue us from the misery of overpopulation. Freedom to breed will bring ruin to all. At the moment, to avoid hard decisions many of us are tempted to propagandize for conscience and responsible parenthood. The temptation must be resisted, because an appeal to independently acting consciences selects for the disappearance of all conscience in the long run, and an increase in anxiety in the short.

The only way we can preserve and nurture other and more precious freedoms is by relinquishing the freedom to breed, and that very soon. "Freedom is the recognition of necessity"—and it is the role of education to reveal to all the necessity of abandoning the freedom to breed. Only so, can we put an end to this aspect of the tragedy of the commons.

NOTES

1. J. B. Wiesner and H. F. York, *Sci. Amer.* 211 (No. 4), 27 (1964).
2. G. Hardin, *J. Hered.* 50, 68 (1959); S. von Hoernor, *Science* 137, 18 (1962).
3. J. von Neumann and O. Morgenstern, *Theory of Games and Economic Behavior* (Princeton Univ. Press, Princeton, N.J., 1947), p. 11.
4. J. H. Fremlin, *New Sci.*, No. 415 (1964), p. 285.
5. A. Smith, *The Wealth of Nations* (Modern Library, New York, 1937), p. 423.
6. W. F. Lloyd, *Two Lectures on the Checks to Population* (Oxford Univ. Press, Oxford, England, 1833), reprinted (in part) in *Population, Evolution, and Birth Control*, G. Hardin, Ed. (Freeman, San Francisco, 1964), p. 37.
7. A. N. Whitehead, *Science and the Modern World* (Mentor, New York, 1948), p. 17.
8. G. Hardin, Ed. *Population, Evolution, and Birth Control* (Freeman, San Francisco, 1964), p. 56.
9. S. McVay, *Sci. Amer.* 216 (No. 8), 13 (1966).
10. J. Fletcher, *Situation Ethics* (Westminster, Philadelphia, 1966).

11. D. Lack, *The Natural Regulation of Animal Numbers* (Clarendon Press, Oxford, 1954).
12. H. Girvetz, *From Wealth to Welfare* (Stanford Univ. Press, Stanford, Calif., 1950).
13. G. Hardin, *Perspec. Biol. Med.* 6, 366 (1963).
14. U. Thant, *Int. Planned Parenthood News*, No. 168 (February 1968), p. 3.
15. K. Davis, *Science* 158, 730 (1967).
16. S. Tax, Ed., *Evolution after Darwin* (Univ. of Chicago Press, Chicago, 1960), vol. 2, p. 469.
17. G. Bateson, D. D. Jackson, J. Haley, J. Weakland, *Behav. Sci.* 1, 251 (1956).
18. P. Goodman, *New York Rev. Books* 10(8), 22 (23 May 1968).
19. A. Comfort, *The Anxiety Makers* (Nelson, London, 1967).
20. C. Frankel, *The Case for Modern Man* (Harper, New York, 1955), p. 203.
21. J. D. Roslansky, *Genetics and the Future of Man* (Appleton-Century-Crofts, New York, 1966), p. 177.

Elinor Ostrom

INSTITUTIONS AND THE ENVIRONMENT

Introduction

The first thing that an institutional theorist wants to do when given an assignment to write a chapter on 'Institutions and the Environment' is to clarify how these concepts will be defined. In everyday parlance, the terms 'institutions' and 'environment' are used casually and refer to many things. Sometimes people refer to a local prison as an institution, or to a broad practice within a society, such as 'the institution of marriage'. The 'environment' can be used to refer to the immediate area surrounding a particular setting or to the global atmosphere. Fortunately, over time, ever clearer and more useful definitions for institutions, for the diverse forms of 'the environment', and as well as for the linked levels of interaction, are being developed and used by researchers—particularly those interested in how institutions enhance or adversely affect multiple objects and processes related to ecological systems (see Aoki, 2001; North, 2005; Ostrom *et al.*, 2007).

In this chapter, the term *institutions* refers to the *rules* that humans use when interacting within a wide variety of repetitive and structured situations at multiple levels of analysis (North, 2005; Ostrom, 2005). Individuals who regularly interact use rules (or the absence of rules) designated by government authorities as relevant for situations of a particular type. They may also develop and enforce their own rules. Individuals interacting within a particular rule-structured situation linked

to a specific environment may also adopt norms regarding their behaviour given the others who are involved and their actions over time. In light of the rules, and shared norms when relevant, individuals adopt strategies leading to consequences for themselves and for others (Crawford and Ostrom, 1995). As individuals learn more about the outcome of their own and others' actions within a particular situation, they may change norms and strategies leading to better or worse outcomes for themselves and the relevant environment.

Many environmental goods are common-pool resources, which will be the focus for this article. *Common-pool resources* include resources that are sufficiently large that excluding potential beneficiaries from using them for consumptive or non-consumptive purposes is non-trivial. Each individual consumptive use (for example, harvesting a truckload of forest products or withdrawing water from an irrigation system) reduces the resource units that are available to others (Ostrom and Ostrom, 1977; Ostrom *et al.*, 1994). Without effective institutions to limit who can use diverse harvesting practices, highly valued, common-pool resources are overharvested and destroyed (FAO, 2005; Mullon *et al.*, 2005; Myers and Worm, 2003).

Modelling the Open-Access Problem

Developing formal models has been an important tool for institutional theorists for analysing why common-pool resources are overharvested and

From *Economic Affairs* 28, no. 3 (Sept. 2008), 24–31.

Figure 11.1. The Gordon Model of Fishery Bioeconomics

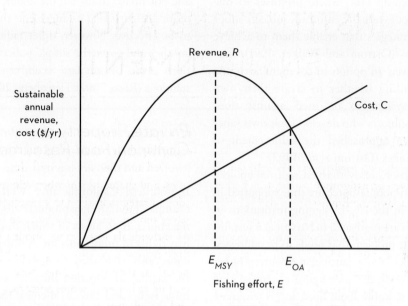

Source: Clark (2006, p. 11)

what might be done to avert their destruction. One of the earliest, most powerful and long-lasting models of a common-pool resource is the static model of a fishery published by Scott Gordon in 1954. In an open-access fishery, Gordon (and many other scholars who have drawn extensively on his work) posited that each fisher would invest effort in harvesting until they reached a bionomic equilibrium, E_{OA}, where *total* revenue equals *total* cost. The bionomic equilibrium (E_{OA} in Figure 11.1) generates a high level of rent dissipation. If fishers were to fish at a maximum sustainable yield E_{MSY}, substantial economic gains would be achieved. The problem is that each fisher still makes money at E_{MSY} and other fishers would want to enter the fishery. As long as the fishery is open to any fisher who wants to earn money, the bionomic equilibrium will persist rather than the maximum sustainable yield.

This static model has repeatedly been used to show why common-pool resources that generate highly valued resource units will be overharvested

when no effective rules limit entry or withdrawals. The power of the Gordon model comes from the clarity of its representation of why unregulated common-pool resources are overharvested. On the other hand, its simplicity is also a weakness when used for designing new institutions to overcome economic incentives to overharvest. As Colin Clark (2006, p. 15) reflects, the static, 'stick-figure' model is too simplistic for analysts to apply it as if it adequately described all common-pool resources. The presumption of many analysts has been that all one has to do is to impose rules so that harvesters face different incentives and withdraw at a maximum sustained yield.

The Gordon model has been used as the underlying theoretical model for the design of a series of laboratory experiments on behaviour related to common-pool resources. The predictions of the Gordon model regarding overharvesting are supported when subjects make anonymous decisions and cannot communicate with one another (Ostrom *et al.*, 1994). Given an opportunity to use 'cheap talk' where promises to one another are not externally enforced, subjects adopt norms and strategies that enable them to achieve higher returns (Ostrom and Walker, 1991). Further, when given an option to covenant with one another regarding whether to create their own sanctioning system to be used against non-cooperators, subjects who develop their own sanctioning system approached the achievement of optimal outcomes (Ostrom *et al.*, 1992).

The predictions of overharvesting from an *open access* common-pool resource are thus supported in the field and in the lab. Designing institutions so that harvesters are motivated to harvest at a sustainable level is the problem that needs to be addressed with knowledge about particular resources rather than just accepting the 'stick figure' as representing all one needs to know about open access resources. Unfortunately, too many reforms are presented as not much more than 'stick figures', and scholars, policy-makers and communities have had to learn the hard way about finding rules that match the complex ecologies that are involved in diverse common-pool resources.

Recommending Optimal Institutions

The widespread acceptance of the Gordon model has led policy analysts to recommend three idealised institutions to induce individual users to engage in sustainable harvesting practices. Some of the rules recommended as 'optimal' are private property (Demsetz, 1967; Raymond, 2003), government ownership (Lovejoy, 2006; Terborgh, 1999, 2000), or community control (Vermillion and Sagardoy, 1999). Multiple examples exist where moving to government ownership, private property or community control of a common-pool resource has worked

to help users achieve more efficient short-term results and potentially to sustain the resource over the long term. The particular arrangements that have proven to be effective, however, differ radically from one another and from the simple policy recommendations made by scholars recommending 'optimal' solutions (Rose, 2002; Tietenberg, 2002).

Private Property and Common-Pool Resources

In southern California after World War II, for example, groundwater producers used the California courts as an arena in which to determine who had rights to pump how much water per year. The courts also established a 'watermaster' to determine the factual information initially needed to determine rights and then to monitor the adherence of water producers to the agreements (Blomquist, 1992). In the groundwater basins that were adjudicated and rights allocated, markets for water rights emerged rapidly. Furthermore, water rights tended to be sold or leased by those who had lower marginal productivity to those with higher marginal productivity—such as water companies who needed rights to pump water to meet peak demands—and by rights holders who were exiting the resource (either by moving away, ceasing or changing their business) to users who wished to expand their access to local water sources.

After half a decade, times have changed in regard to the population of the region, local water sources and water availability in several linked aqueducts. The continuing jurisdiction of the California court system has enabled water producers to adjust the rules they had earlier negotiated to cope with disturbance and changing conditions (Blomquist and Ostrom, 2008; Steed and Blomquist, 2006). In some years, producers were authorised to take more than their assigned rights so long as they then curtailed their water production at a later time (similar to receiving a monetary loan from the bank that has to be paid back). And, in some cases, producers were authorised to take less than their assigned shares and 'bank' or store water for future withdrawal. Furthermore, the water producers have experimented with a diversity of other institutions, such as the creation of special districts to levy a substantial tax on pumped water, to pay for basin replenishment as well as monitoring and reporting on basin conditions. Thus, while privatising rights was a crucial step in reducing continued overharvesting of groundwater in Los Angeles, it was only one of a complex series of institutional changes and adaptations over time.

In relationship to fisheries, individual transferable quota (ITQ) systems are frequently recommended as the 'optimal' strategy (Raymond, 2003; Scott, 1988). Notable cases exist where establishing an ITQ system has averted a collapse of a fishery, but few of the 'successes' were immediate. All took some time adjusting various aspects after a national government agency first designed an ITQ system. Most of the successes have evolved into more complex systems relying on multiple institutional arrangements rather than being simple ITQ systems.

The British Columbia trawl fishery for groundfish, for example, had been heavily utilised since World War II (Grafton *et al.*, 2006). Early efforts to control overfishing by governmental policies included: restricting the number of fishing vehicles and the equipment that could be used, the assignment of total allowable catch (TAC) quotas, and the assignment of fishing trip quotas. Massive overharvesting led to the closing of the fishery in 1995. Within a few years, the fishery was reopened with new regulations including an annual ITQ system granted by the Federal Minister of Fisheries for each species (Clark, 2006, pp. 238–240). Thus, fishers do not 'own' the quota assigned, but some trading is allowed, and no ITQs have been taken away from assigned trawlers. In addition, all catches are recorded by onboard observers to avoid earlier problems of underreporting. Clark (2006, p. 239) observed that the ITQ system has led to profound changes:

> 'First, catch data are now reliable, allowing the scientists to perform believable TAC estimates. [This is the result of the observer programme, not of the ITQ system itself, although the latter no doubt implies a degree of acceptance and support of the observer programme.]
>
> 'Second, a decrease in fleet capacity has occurred, as both small and large vessels have sold their quotas and withdrawn front the fishery . . .
>
> 'In terms of resource conservation, discards are not only accurately quantified, but have also been significantly reduced because of the ITQ generated economic incentives against catching unwanted species.'

Thus, the ITQ system has had a positive impact on the fishery, but an effective monitoring system was also an essential aspect of the success. The importance of realistic provisions for monitoring the conformance of resource users to a property rights allocation is rarely mentioned when scholars recommend ITQ systems.

While smaller-scale inshore fishing had long existed in New Zealand's inshore waters (Johnson and Haworth, 2004), large-scale, deepwater, commercial fisheries developed later in New Zealand than in British Columbia due to heavy fishing by foreign fleets in waters surrounding New Zealand. New Zealand declared its 200-mile Exclusive Economic Zone in 1983 and the government immediately began to offer incentives to domestic, commercial fishers to encourage them to replace the foreign fleets that had been overfishing their waters. In 1986, New Zealand became one of the first countries to adopt a market-based fishery regulation when it adopted a quota management system (QMS) and allocated ITQs to a subset of domestic fisheries (Annala, 1996). The government also removed the subsidies it had established just a few years earlier.

New Zealand authorities had to make still further adjustments as they discovered that the biological models underlying the initial allocation of permanent allocation of fixed quotas needed to be adjusted over time in light of further evidence. After considerable renegotiation, commercial fishers received a revised ITQ in 1990 based on a proportion of the total catch assigned annually (Yandle and Dewees, 2003). Commercial fishers also demanded a greater role in determining quotas and other fishery policies resulting in the Fisheries Amendment Act being passed in 1999, which recognised commercial stakeholder organisations (CSOs) as 'approved service delivery organizations' that may compete for contracts to provide scientific research and other fisheries services. Furthermore, CSOs are essentially the recognised voice of the industry for the fishery they represent. In essence, the original ITQ system evolved into a 'co-management' system but one in which some major interests—such as customary Maori interests, recreational fisheries and environmental groups—are not recognised (Yandle, 2003). Furthermore, Yandle (2007) has Identified some of the 'mismatches' involved in the relationships among the property rights assigned to different groups along both temporal and spatial dimensions (Cash *et al.*, 2006). In regard to spatial mismatches, Yandle (2007) identifies overlapping or poorly defined boundaries such as those among:

> 'customary Maori fishing, aquaculture, marine reserves, and commercial fishing [that] create political or physical competition for access to marine resources, as well as frustration within the commercial fishing community, which perceives that its broad, but not exclusive, spatial rights are eaten away by the smaller but more exclusively defined spatial rights of interests such as marine reserves, customary Maori fishing, and aquaculture.'

The multiple problems of reconciling diverse interests with multiple types of property rights in a spatial domain have led to rapid legislative changes that tend to make the overall system more fragile (Yandle, 2008).

One of the most famous (or infamous, depending on the view of the reader) ITQ systems was gradually introduced in Iceland after multiple crises in Icelandic fishery stocks (Arnason, 1993). After experimenting with diverse TAC systems and considerable controversy, a uniform ITQ system was adopted in 1990 for all relevant fisheries (Eggertsson, 2005). Similar to the evolved New Zealand ITQ system, quotas are not to fixed quantities but rather to a 'share' of the annual authorised catch level set by the Icelandic government based on the recommendation of fishery experts. The Iceland ITQ system appears to have averted the collapse of many valuable species for the Iceland fishery. It has been less successful in restoring the Icelandic cod stocks, which have suffered dramatic losses throughout the North Atlantic region (Finlayson and McCay, 1998).

In his analysis of the long and conflict-ridden road to the Icelandic ITQ system, Eggertsson (2004) reflects that introducing major institutional changes is a 'subtle art' rather than a simple use of a 'one-size-fits-all' formula. Eggertsson criticises the work of fellow economists who have created a sense of 'false optimism' about how to manage complex fisheries. Simply designing a system in a top-down fashion and imposing it on the harvesters does not turn out to be as successful or adaptive as working with the users of a common-pool resource over time to develop a system that is well matched to the ecological system as well as to the practices, norms and long-term economic welfare of the participants.

Government Property and Common-Pool Resources

For some scholars, public ownership of land is the *only* way to achieve sustained conservation over time (Lovejoy, 2006; Terborgh, 1999). This has led to proposals for creating a system of government-protected areas across the world (Ghimire and Pimbert, 1997). Currently, more than 100,000 protected areas already exist and include approximately 10% of the forested areas in the world (Barber *et al.*, 2004). While considerable enthusiasm exists for creating protected areas, their performance has varied substantially.

Some positive evaluations of the effectiveness of protected areas rely on qualitative ratings by government officials and park managers at multiple sites rather than independent studies (Bruner *et al.*, 2001; Ervin, 2003). While it is important to learn what officials think about their progress, full reliance on self-assessments may introduce serious biases in the analysis (Hockings, 2003; Nepstad *et al.*, 2006). A study of forest conditions evaluated by an independent forester or ecologist for 76 government-owned protected parks as contrasted to 87 forests owned under a diversity of arrangements (private, community, government) did not find *any* statistical difference in the forest conditions between protected areas and all others (Hayes, 2006; see also Gibson *et al.*, 2005).

A large study conducted by the World Wildlife Fund (WWF) included over 200 protected areas in 27 countries. The WWF found that many protected areas lacked key financial and human resources, a sound legal basis, and did not have effective control over their boundaries (WWF, 2004). Owing to these conditions, extensive conflicts among park residents, park personnel and with local communities that surround many protected areas are frequently reported as well as illegal harvesting (Wells and Brandon, 1992). Nepstad *et al.* (2006) broadened the debate by examining several different tenure arrangements within protected areas including extractive reserves, indigenous territories and national forests in Brazil. Under conditions of intense colonisation pressures, they found that strictly protected areas are more vulnerable to deforestation and fire than indigenous reserves. These and other studies indicate the need to shift away from the presumption that creating government-owned parks and reserves is the *only* way to protect forests and biodiversity.

Carefully controlled analyses over time of remotely sensed images of deforestation levels in national parks located in the *same* country have found that some are well protected and others not. Ostrom and Nagendra (2006) provide strong evidence that the Mahananda Wildlife Sanctuary in West Bengal, India, has successfully prevented deforestation, but this success involves high administrative costs and considerable conflict with the local population. On the other hand, the Tadoba Andhari Tiger Reserve in Maharashtra, with only a modest budget, is not able to control entry into the forest and the loss of forested land is substantial. Forests within Tikal National Park in the Mayan Biosphere Reserve in Guatemala—well-financed through fees collected from tourists—are in excellent condition (Dietz *et al.*, 2006). At the same time, nearby national parks—Laguna del Tigre National Park and the Sierra del Lacondon National Park—even though they are in the same ecological zone and under the same institutional structure, are ravaged by illegal harvesting.

Community Property and Common-Pool Resources

While some scholars have been overly enthusiastic about the performance of diverse kinds of community ownership or involvement as a solution to overharvesting of common-pool resources (Western and Wright, 1994), strong involvement of a community is no more a panacea than private or governmental ownership (Campbell *et al.*, 2001; Meinzen-Dick, 2007; Nagendra, 2007). Empirical studies of common-pool resources under community control have shown that benefits are sometimes distributed in an unequal fashion among community members (Oyono *et al.*, 2005; Platteau, 2004) leading in some cases to the exclusion of the poorest members of a community (Malla, 2000).

Little evidence exists that *simply* turning common-pool resources over to local users will avoid overharvesting. Some communities manage their fisheries or forests better than others (Acheson, 2003; Andersson, 2004; Gibson *et al.*, 2000). While strong evidence exists that local communities are capable of creating robust local institutions for governing local resources sustainably (Bray and Klepeis, 2005; NRC, 2002; Ostrom, 1990, 2005), some analysts have gone overboard and proposed community-based conservation as another cure-all (Berkes, 2007). This has led some donor-funded efforts to turn control over to local residents with a simple blueprint approach (Pritchett and Woolcock, 2004), leading to little community involvement and enabling local 'elite capture' of benefits. Moreover, total 'turnover' ignores the necessity of managing common-pool resources at multiple levels, with vertical and horizontal interplay among institutions.

Community management in a variety of forms—direct ownership, government concessions, or other long-term co-management arrangements—has the capacity to be as effective or, under certain conditions, more effective than government ownership (Bray *et al.*, 2005). The debate over the effectiveness of diverse institutions needs to be extended to a larger landscape of tenure regimes than just community ownership. Various forms of co-management do assign substantial management responsibilities and access to resources in and around a resource, and a wide variety of community management types, from full ownership to community-rights concessions on public lands to private management, can be effective if they are well tailored to the particular attributes of a resource and the larger and smaller resources to which it is linked. Simple solutions do not exist for managing complex ecologies (Campbell *et al.*, 2006; McPeak *et al.*, 2006).

From Optimal Solutions to Adaptive Multi-Level Governance

A key finding from decades of in-depth studies of institutions and the environment is that the same rules that work welt in one setting are part of failed systems elsewhere! There are no 'optimal' rules that can be applied to all fisheries, all forests, or all water systems (Grafton, 2000; Ostrom, 2007). We simply must stop relying on stick-figure models alone and proposing 'one-size-fits-all' solutions, given that these solutions have themselves generated tragedies when widely applied rather than solved them.

Instead of presenting stick-figure models of resource systems, institutional theorists need to recognise what ecologists recognised long ago: the complexity of what we study and the necessity of recognising the non-linear, self-organising and dynamic aspects as well as the multiple objectives and the spatial and temporal scales involved. As the distinguished ecologist Simon Levin (1999, p. 2) has summarised:

'That is, ecosystems are complex, adaptive systems and hence, are characterized by historical dependency, complex dynamics, and multiple basins of attraction. The management of such systems presents fundamental challenges, made especially difficult by the fact that the putative controllers (humans) are essential parts of the system and, hence, essential parts of the problem . . .

'There are a number of lessons that emerge from this study and guide it. Most important is the importance of experimentation, learning and adaptation.'

Institutional economists need to recognise that deriving a simple, beautiful mathematical model is not the only goal of our analysis. Adopting more complex approaches—including flow charts, simulations, dynamic systems analysis and the specification of multiple factors—is not a sign of failure when the systems being analysed are fundamentally complex and multi-level (Wilson, 2006; Wilson *et al.*, 2007). Models are powerful tools and we need to develop them so that they can be used to capture more complex phenomena (Costanza *et al.*, 2001). We cause harm, however, by recommending one-size-fits-all institutional prescriptions based on overly simplified models of resources to solve problems of overharvesting.

Thinking About Policy Recommendations

In earlier efforts to analyse which rules worked best related to fisheries, irrigation systems and forests, we found a simply gigantic number of individual rules that were used in the field (Ostrom, 2005; Schlager, 1994; Tang, 1994). Focusing on boundary rules that define who can gain access to enter and harvest from a resource, we have identified three broad classes:

- 'Residency or Membership Rules' that specify residency or membership requirements.
- 'Personal Characteristic Rules' that require ascribed or acquired personal attributes (e.g. age, gender, education, skill test, etc.).
- 'Relationship to a Resource Rules' that specify conditions of use depending on the relationship of a user with the resources (e.g. length and continuity of use, ownership of land or other asset, acquisition of licence, etc.).

We have found empirical examples of four types of Residency or Membership Rules, nine types of Personal Characteristic Rules, and 13 Relationship to a Resource Rules. Some specific boundary rules specify more than one category (e.g. a user must be over 21, have taken a skill test, and use a specific type of technology to be an authorised user of a particular resource) (see Ostrom, 2005, Ch. 8).

It is important to note that repeated studies have not yet found *specific* rules that have a statistically positive relationship to performance in a large number of common-pool resources (Dietz *et al.*, 2006; Gibson *et al.*, 2000; NRC, 2002). On the other hand, the absence of *any* boundary rule or *any* monitoring effort to ensure that a well-defined set of authorised users are following the rules related to timing, technology and quantity of harvesting *is* consistently associated with poor performance (Ostrom and Nagendra, 2006; Ostrom *et al.*, 1994).

After reading and coding hundreds of cases that described both successful and unsuccessful private, government and community property arrangements, without finding a clear set of *specific* rules associated with long-term sustainability, I derived a set of design principles to characterise those cases of local, common-pool resources that had survived long periods of time (Ostrom, 1990). The predictive power of these design principles in helping to distinguish successful from unsuccessful cases has now been supported by multiple studies (Dayton-Johnson, 2000; Marshall, 2005; Sarkerand Itoh, 2001; Trawick, 2001; Weinstein, 2000).

To apply what we have learned to policy, we can translate the design principles into a set of questions that those involved in designing and adapting institutional arrangements for a particular resource system would need to address, Basically, any institutional arrangement for regulating a common-pool resource to achieve multiple objectives needs to help harvesters and officials address the following questions in a way that is understood by those involved and considered legitimate given the characteristics of the resource, the community involved and the larger economic and political domains:

- Who is allowed to harvest which kinds of resource units?
- What will be the timing, quantity, location and technology used for harvesting?
- Who is obligated to contribute resources to maintain the resource system itself?
- How are harvesting and maintenance activities to be monitored and enforced?
- How are conflicts over harvesting and maintenance to be resolved?
- How will cross-scale linkages be dealt with on a regular basis?
- How will risks of the unknown be taken into consideration?
- How will the rules affecting the above be changed over time with changes in the performance of the resource system, the strategies of participants and external opportunities and constraints?

Instead of presuming that one can design an optimal system in advance and then make it work, we must think about ways to analyse the structure of common-pool resources, how these change over time, and adopt a multi-level, experimental approach rather than a top-down approach to the design of effective institutions.

Experimenting with Rule Changes

We need to understand the institutional design processes involving an effort to tinker with a large number of component parts (see Jacob, 1977). Those who tinker with any tools—including rules—are trying to find combinations that work together more effectively than other combinations in a particular setting. Policy changes are experiments based on more or less informed expectations about potential outcomes and the distribution of these outcomes for participants across time and space (Campbell, 1969, 1975). Whenever individuals agree to add a rule, change a rule, or adopt someone else's proposed rule set, they are conducting a policy experiment. Moreover, the complexity of the ever-changing biophysical world combined with the complexity of rule systems means that any proposed rule change faces a non-trivial probability of error.

When rules related to common-pool resources are made by a single governing authority for an entire nation, policy-makers have to experiment simultaneously with *all* of the common-pool resources within their jurisdiction with each policy change. For very small countries with similar ecosystems, this may not be a problem. For large countries, however, rules that are appropriate in one region are rarely effective in another. And, once a change has been made and implemented, further changes will not be made rapidly. The process of experimentation will usually be slow, and information about results may be contradictory and difficult to interpret. A policy change that is based on erroneous data about one key structural variable or a false assumption about how actors will react, can lead to a major disaster (see Berkes, 2007; Brock and Carpenter, 2007). Further, as Dixit (2004) has shown, arbitrary policy changes and tax laws made by a highly centralised governance regime may result insubstantial rent seeking and graft.

In any design process where there is a substantial probability of error, having redundant teams of designers has repeatedly been shown to have considerable advantage (see Bendor, 1985; Landau, 1969, 1973; Page, 2007). Given the logic of combinatorics, it is impossible to conduct a *complete* analysis of the expected performance of all of the potential rule changes that could be made to change the incentives of resource users. Instead of developing models that generate optimal outcomes, we need to understand what level of redundancy, overlap and autonomy help to adapt rules that work for particular resources under specific social-economic conditions. And, then, we need to focus on how to enhance the robustness of these institutions to diverse disturbances that will 'hit' them over time (Anderies *et al.*, 2007; Janssen *et al.*, 2007).

REFERENCES

Acheson, I. (2003) *Capturing the Commons: Devising Institutions to Manage the Maine Lobster Industry*, Hanover, NH: University Press of New England.

Anderies, J. M., A. A. Rodriguez, M. A. Janssen and O. Cifadloz (2007) 'Panaceas, Uncertainty, and the Robust Control Framework in Sustainability Science', *PNAS*, 104, 15194–15199.

Andersson, K. P. (2004) 'Who Talks with Whom? The Role of Repeated Interactions in Decentralized Forest Governance', *World Development*, 32, 233–249.

Annala, J. H. (1996) 'New Zealand's ITQ System: Have the First Eight Years Been a Success or a Failure?', *Reviews in Fish Biology and Fisheries*, 6, 44–62.

Aoki, M. (2001) *Toward a Comparative Institutional Analysis*, Cambridge, MA: MIT Press.

Arnason, R. (1993) 'The Icelandic Individual Transferable Quota System: A Descriptive Account', *Marine Resource Economics*, 8, 201–218.

Barber, C., K. Miller and M. Boness (eds.) (2004) *Securing Protected Areas in the Face of Global Change: Issues and Strategies*, Gland, Switzerland: International Union for Conservation of Nature and Natural Resources. Available at: http://www.lucn.org/themes/wcpa/pubs/pdfs/securingpas.pdf.

Bendor, J. (1985) *Parallel Systems: Redundancy in Government*, Berkeley, CA: University of California Press.

Berkes, F. (2007) 'Community-based Conservation in a Globalized World', *PNAS*, 104, 15188–15193.

Blomquist, W. (1992) *Dividing the Waters: Governing Groundwater in Southern California*, San Francisco, CA: ICS Press.

Blomquist, W. and E. Ostrom (2008) 'Deliberation, Learning, and Institutional Change: The Evolution of Institutions in Judicial Settings', *Constitutional Political Economy* (online first).

Bray, D. B. and P. Klepeis (2005) 'Deforestation, Forest Transitions, and Institutions for Sustainability in Southeastern Mexico, 1900–2000', *Environment and History*, 11, 195–223.

Bray, D. B., L. Merino-Pérez and D. Barry (eds.) (2005) *The Community Forests of Mexico: Managing for Sustainable Landscapes*, Austin, TX: University of Texas Press.

Brock, W. A. and S. R. Carpenter (2007) 'Panaceas and Diversification of Environmental Policy', *PNAS*, 104, 15206–15211.

Bruner, A. G., R. E. Gullison, R. E. Rice and G. A. B. da Fonseca (2001) 'Effectiveness of Parks in Protecting Tropical Biodiversity', *Science*, 291, 125–128.

Campbell, B., P. Frost, J. A. Sayer, S. Vermeulen, M. Ruiz-Perez, A. Cunningham and P. Ravi (2001) 'Assessing the Performance of Natural Resource Systems', *Conservation Ecology*, 5, 2, 22 [online].

Campbell, B. M., I. J. Gordon, M, K. Luckert, L. Petheram and S. Vetter (2006) 'In Search of Optimal Stocking Regimes in Semi-arid Grazing Lands: One Size Does Not Fit All', *Ecological Economics*, 60, 75–85.

Campbell, D. T. (1969) 'Reforms as Experiments', *American Psychologist*, 24, 409–429.

Campbell, D, T. (1975) 'On the Conflicts between Biological and Social Evolution and between Psychology and Moral Tradition', *American Psychologist*, 30, 1103–1126.

Cash, D. W., W. N. Adger, F. Berkes, P. Garden, L. Lebel, P. Olsson, L. Pritchard and O. Young (2006) 'Scale and Cross-scale Dynamics: Governance and information in a Multilevel World', *Ecology and Society*, 11, 2, 8 [online].

Clark, C. (2006) *The Worldwide Crisis in Fisheries: Economic Models and Human Behavior*, Cambridge: Cambridge University Press.

Costanza, R., B. Low, E. Ostrom and J. Wilson (eds.) (2001) *Institutions, Ecosystems, and Sustainability*, New York: Lewis.

Crawford, S. E. S. and E. Ostrom (1995) 'A Grammar of Institutions', *American Political Science Review*, 89, 582–600. Revised version appears as Chapter 5 in E. Ostrom (ed.) (2005) *Understanding Institutional Diversity*, Princeton, NJ: Princeton University Press, pp. 137–174.

Dayton-Johnson, J. (2000) 'Determinants of Collective Action on the Local Commons: A Model with Evidence from Mexico', *Journal of Development Economics*, 62, 181–208.

Demsetz, H. (1967) 'Toward a Theory of Property Rights', *American Economic Review*, 57, 347–359.

Dietz, T., E. Ostrom and P. Stern (2006) 'The Struggle to Govern the Commons', in D. Kennedy (ed.) *State of the Planet 2006–2007*, Washington, DC: Island Press, pp. 126–141.

Dixit, A. K. (2004) *Lawlessness and Economics: Alternative Modes of Governance*, Princeton, NJ: Princeton University Press.

Eggertsson, T. (2004) The Subtle Art of Major Institutional Change: Introducing Property Rights in the Iceland Fisheries', In G. van Huyleborook, W. Verkeke and L. Lauwers (eds.) *Role of Institutions in Rural Policies and Agricultural Models*, Amsterdam: Elsevier, pp. 43–59.

Eggertsson, T. (2005) *Imperfect Institutions: Possibilities and Limits of Reform*, Ann Arbor, MI: University of Michigan Press.

Ervin, J. (2003) 'Rapid Assessment of Protected Area Management Effectiveness in Four Countries', *Bioscience*, 53, 833–841.

FAO (Food and Agriculture Organization) (2005) *Global forest Resources Assessment*, Rome: Food and Agriculture Organization of the United Nations.

Finlayson, A. C. and B. J. McCay (1998) 'Crossing the Threshold of Ecosystem Resilience: The Commercial Extinction of Northern Cod', in F. Berkes and C. Folke (eds.) *Linking Social and Ecological Systems: Management Practices and Social Mechanisms for Building Resilience*, New York: Cambridge University Press, pp. 311–338.

Ghimire, K. B. and M. P. Pimbert (eds.) (1997) *Social Change and Conservation: Environmental Politics and Impacts of National Parks and Protected Areas*, London: Earthscan.

Gibson, C., M. McKean and E. Ostrom (eds.) (2000) *People and Forests: Communities, Institutions, and Governance*, Cambridge, MA: MIT Press.

Gibson, C., J. Williams and E. Ostrom (2005) 'Local Enforcement and Better Forests', *World Development*, 33, 273–284.

Gordon, H. S. (1954) 'The Economic Theory of a Common Property Resource: The Fishery', *Journal of Political Economy*, 62, 124–142.

Grafton, R. Q. (2000) 'Governance of the Commons: A Role for the State', *Land Economics*, 76, 504–517.

Grafton, R. Q. *et al.* (2006) 'Incentive-based Approaches to Sustainable Fisheries', *Canadian Journal of Fisheries and Aquatic Sciences*, 63, 699–710.

Hayes, T. (2006) 'Parks, People, and Forest Protection: An Institutional Assessment of the Effectiveness of Protected Areas', *World Development*, 34, 2064–2075.

Hockings, M. (2003) 'Systems for Assessing the Effectiveness of Management In Protected Areas', *Bioscience*, 53, 823–832.

Jacob, F. (1977) 'Evolution and Tinkering', *Science*, 196, 1161–1166.

Janssen, M., J. M. Anderies and E. Ostrom (2007) 'Robustness of Social-Ecological Systems to Spatial and Temporal Variability', *Society and Natural Resources*, 20, 307–322.

Johnson, D, and J. Haworth (2004) *Hooked: The Story of the New Zealand Fishing Industry*, Christchurch, New Zealand: Hazard Press.

Landau, M. (1969) 'Redundancy, Rationality, and the Problem of Duplication and Overlap', *Public Administration Review*, 29, 346–358.

Landau, M. (1973) 'Federalism, Redundancy, and System Reliability', *Publius*, 3, 173–196.

Levin, S. A. (1999) *Fragile Dominion: Complexity and the Commons*, Reading, MA: Perseus Books.

Lovejoy, T. E. (2006) 'Protected Areas: A Prism for a Changing World', *Trends in Ecology and Evolution*, 21, 329–333.

Malla, Y. B. (2000) 'Impact of Community Forestry Policy on Rural Livelihoods and Food Security in Nepal', *Unasylva*, 51, No. 202, 37–45.

Marshall, G. (2005) *Economics for Collaborative Environmental Management: Renegotiating the Commons*, London: Earthscan.

McPeak, J., D. R. Lee and C. B. Barrett (2006) 'Introduction to a Special Section: The Dynamics of Coupled Human and Natural Systems', *Environment and Development Economics*, 11, 9–13.

Meinzen-Dick, R. (2007) 'Beyond Panaceas in Water Institutions', *PNAS*, 104, 15200–15205.

Mullon, J. W., P. Freon and P. Cury (2005) 'The Dynamics of Collapse in World Fisheries', *Fish and Fisheries*, 6, 110–120.

Myers, R. A. and B. Worm (2003) 'Rapid Worldwide Depletion of Predatory Fish Communities', *Nature*, 423, 280–283.

Nagendra, H. (2007) 'Drivers of Reforestation in Human-dominated Forests', *PNAS*, 104, 15218–15223.

Nepstad, D. *et al.* (2006) 'Inhibition of Amazon Deforestation and Fire by Parks and Indigenous Lands', *Conservation Biology*, 20, 65–73.

North, D, C. (2005) *Understanding the Process of Institutional Change*, Princeton, NJ: Princeton University Press.

NRC (National Research Council) (2002) *The Drama of the Commons*, Committee on the Human Dimensions of Global Change, E. Ostrom, T. Dietz, N. Dolšak, P. Stern, S. Stonich and E. Weber (eds.), Washington, DC: National Academy Press.

Ostrom, E. (1990) *Governing the Commons: The Evolution of Institutions for Collective Action*, New York: Cambridge University Press.

Ostrom, E. (2005) *Understanding Institutional Diversity*, Princeton, NJ: Princeton University Press.

Ostrom, E. (2007) 'A Diagnostic Approach for Going beyond Panaceas', *PNAS*, 104, 15181–15187.

Ostrom, E. and H. Nagendra (2006) 'Insights on Linking Forests, Trees, and People from the Air, on the Ground, and in the Laboratory', *PNAS*, 103, 19224–19231.

Ostrom, E. and J. Walker (1991) 'Communication in a Commons: Cooperation without External Enforcement', in T. R. Palfrey (ed.) *Laboratory Research in Political Economy*, Ann Arbor, MI: University of Michigan Press, pp. 287–322.

Ostrom, E., R. Gardner and J. Walker (1994) *Rules, Games, and Common-pool Resources*, Ann Arbor, MI: University of Michigan Press.

Ostrom, E., M. A. Janssen and J. M. Anderies (2007) 'Going beyond Panaceas', *PNAS*, 104, 15176–15178.

Ostrom, E., J. Walker and R. Gardner (1992) 'Covenants with and without a Sword: Self-governance is Possible', *American Political Science Review*, 86, 404–417.

Ostrom, V. and E. Ostrom (1977) 'Public Goods and Public Choices', in E. S. Savas (ed.) *Alternatives for Delivering Public Services: Toward Improved Performance*, Boulder, CO: Westview Press, pp. 7–49. Reprinted in M. McGinnis (ed.) (1999) *Polycentricity and Local Public Economies: Readings from the Workshop in Political Theory and Policy Analysis*, Ann Arbor, MI: University of Michigan Press, pp. 75–103.

Oyono, P. R., C. Kouna and W. Mala (2005) 'Benefits of Forests in Cameroon. Global Structure, Issues involving Access and Decision-making Hiccoughs', *Forest Policy and Economics*, 7, 357–368.

Page, S. E. (2007) *The Difference: How the Power of Diversity Creates Better Groups, Firms, Schools, and Societies*, Princeton, NJ: Princeton University Press.

Platteau, J. (2004) 'Monitoring Elite Capture in Community-driven Development', *Development and Change*, 35, 223–246.

Pritchett, L. and M. Woolcock (2004) 'Solutions when the Solution is the Problem: Arraying the Disarray in Development', *World Development*, 32, 191–212.

Raymond, L. (2003) *Private Rights in Public Resources: Equity and Property Allocation in Market-based Environmental Policy*, Washington, DC: Resources for the Future.

Rose, C. M. (2002) 'Common Property, Regulatory Property, and Environmental Protection: Comparing Community-based Management to Tradable Environmental Allowances', in Committee on the

Human Dimensions of Global Change, E. Ostrom, T. Dietz, N. Dolšak, P. Stern, S. Stonich and E. Weber (eds.) *The Drama of the Commons*, Washington, DC: National Academy Press, pp. 233–257.

Sarker, A. and T. Itoh (2001) 'Design Principles in Long-enduring Institutions of Japanese Irrigation Common-pool Resources', *Agricultural Water Management*, 48, 2, 89–102.

Schlager, E. (1994) 'Fishers' Institutional Responses to Common-pool Resource Dilemmas', in E. Ostrom, R. Gardner and J. Walker (eds.) *Rules, Games, and Common-pool Resources*, Ann Arbor, MI: University of Michigan Press, pp. 247–265.

Scott, A. (1988) 'Development of Property in the Fishery', *Marine Resource Economics*, 5, 289–331.

Steed, B. and W. Blomquist (2006) 'Responses to Ecological and Human Threats to a California Water Basin Governance System', Paper presented at the 26th Annual Meeting of the Association for Politics and the Life Sciences (APLS), Indiana University, Bloomington, 25–26 October.

Tang, S. Y. (1994) 'Institutions and Performance in Irrigation Systems', In E. Ostrom, R. Gardner and J. Walker (eds.) *Rules; Games, and Common-pool Resources*, Ann Arbor, MI: University of Michigan Press, pp. 225–245.

Terborgh, J. (1999) *Requiem for Nature*, Washington, DC: Island Press.

Terborgh, J, (2000) 'The Fate of Tropical Forests: A Matter of Stewardship', *Conservation Biology*, 14, 1358–1361.

Tietenberg, T. (2002) The Tradable Permits Approach to Protecting the Commons: What Have We Learned?', In Committee on the Human Dimensions of Global Change, E. Ostrom, T. Dietz, N. Dolšak, P. Stern, S. Stonich and E. Weber(eds.) *The Drama of the Commons*, Washington, DC: National Academy Press, pp. 197–232.

Trawick, P. (2001) 'Successfully Governing the Commons: Principles of Social Organization in an Andean Irrigation System', *Human Ecology*, 29, 1–26.

Vermillion, D. and J. Sagardoy (1999) *Transfer of Irrigation Management Services*, Rome: Food and Agriculture Organization of the United Nations.

Weinstein, M. S. (2000) 'Pieces of the Puzzle: Solutions for Community-based Fisheries Management from Native Canadians, Japanese Cooperatives, and Common Property Researchers', *Georgetown International Environmental Low Review*, 12, 375–412.

Wells, M. and K. Brandon (1992) *People and Parks: Linking Protected Area Management with Local Communities*, Washington, DC: World Bank.

Western, D. and R. M. Wright (1994) The Background to Community-based Conservation', in D. Western, R. M. Wright and S. C. Strum (eds.) *Natural Connections: Perspectives on Community-based Conservation*, Washington, DC: Island Press, pp. 1–14.

Wilson, J. (2006) 'Matching Social and Ecological Systems in Complex Ocean Fisheries', *Ecology and Society*, 11, 1, 9 [online].

Wilson, J., L. Yan and C. Wilson (2007) 'The Precursors of Governance in the Maine Lobster Fishery', *PNAS*, 104, 15212–15217.

WWF (World Wildlife Fund International) (2004) *Are Protected Areas Working? An Analysis of Forest Protected Areas by WWF*, Gland, Switzerland: World Wildlife Fund.

Yandle, T. (2003) 'The Challenge of Building Successful Stakeholder Organizations: New Zealand's Experience in Developing a Fisheries Co-management Regime', *Marine Policy*, 27, 179–192.

Yandle, T. (2007) 'Understanding the Consequences of Property Rights Mismatches: A Case Study of New Zealand's Marine Resources', *Ecology and Society*, 12, 2, 27 [online].

Yandle, T. (2008) The Promise and Perils of Building a Co-management Regime: An Institutional Assessment of New Zealand Fisheries Management between 1999 and 2005', *Marine Policy*, 32, 132–141.

Yandle, T. and C. Dewees (2003) 'Privatizing the Commons . . . Twelve Years Later: Fishers' Experiences with New Zealand's Market-based Fisheries Management', in N. Dolšak and E. Ostrom (eds.) *The Commons in the New Millennium: Challenges and Adaptations*, Cambridge, MA: MIT Press, pp. 101–127.

Robert O. Keohane and David G. Victor

THE REGIME COMPLEX FOR CLIMATE CHANGE

For two decades, governments have struggled to craft a strong, integrated, and comprehensive regulatory system for managing climate change. Instead their efforts have produced a varied array of narrowly-focused regulatory regimes—what we call the "regime complex for climate change." The elements of this regime complex are linked more or less closely to one another, sometimes conflicting, usually mutually reinforcing.[1]

This article explores the continuum between comprehensive international regulatory institutions, which are usually focused on a single integrated legal instrument, at one end of a spectrum and highly fragmented arrangements at the other. In between these two extremes are nested regimes and regime complexes, which are loosely coupled sets of specific regimes.[2] We outline an analytical framework to help to explain why regulatory efforts in different issue areas yield outcomes that vary along this spectrum. We argue that, in the case of climate change, the structural and interest diversity inherent in contemporary world politics tends to generate the formation of a regime complex rather than a comprehensive, integrated regime. For policymakers keen to make international regulation more effective, a strategy focused on managing a regime complex may allow for more effective management of climate change than large political and diplomatic investments in efforts to craft a comprehensive regime. Recent

years have seen massive global summits, such as the Copenhagen meeting organized around the goal of a single universal treaty, but our analysis suggests that more focused and decentralized activities will have a bigger impact. In settings of high uncertainty and policy flux, regime complexes are not just politically more realistic but they also offer some significant advantages such as flexibility and adaptability.

We first describe the regime complex for climate change, which has not been comprehensively designed but rather has emerged as a result of many choices—made mainly by states and their diplomatic agents—at different times and on different specific issues. These institutional arrangements constitute a textbook illustration of a regime complex and thus provide a useful illustration for building a more general theory.

We next seek to explain why efforts to regulate climate change have yielded a regime complex. We argue that climate change is actually many different cooperation problems, implying different tasks and structures. Three forces—the distribution of interests, the gains from linkages, and the management of uncertainty—help to account for the variation in institutional outcomes, from integration to fragmentation. These forces create incentives for governments and non-state actors to invest in a wide array of institutions rather than a single hierarchy. That array includes some tight couplings, especially where links between regime elements help channel resources such as money, technology, and ideas. However, most of

From *Perspectives on Politics* 9, no.1 (Mar. 2011), 7–23.

the institutional elements in that array are decentralized and marked by loose couplings and lack of hierarchy.

We then explore ways to facilitate more effective policy action on the pressing contemporary challenges of climate change. Despite some success in Cancun (December 2010) to institutionalize agreements made in Copenhagen a year earlier, efforts to create an integrated, comprehensive regime are unlikely to be successful. They risk diverting political and economic resources from narrower regulatory institutions focused on particular climate change problems. A multitude of narrower, partially linked efforts will reinforce the regime complex that is already emerging. Such a policy strategy can yield institutions that are more flexible and adaptable—a point we illustrate with examples from international emissions trading, innovation in strategies to manage forests, accommodation of border tax adjustments, and cooperation on technology policy. Although such a strategy of focusing on loosely coupled elements is promising, it is not *necessarily* superior. To improve on the elusive search for a comprehensive regime, a regime complex must meet standards of coherence, accountability, determinacy, sustainability, epistemic quality, and fairness.

The failure of efforts to develop a comprehensive, integrated climate regime reflects resistance to costly policies in rich countries, such as the United States, and in developing countries alike. It also reflects policy choices that have unwisely concentrated diplomatic efforts on crafting integrated international legal regimes. The sources of failure are deep seated, and the prevailing literature is not optimistic.[3] Although we do not disagree with this pessimistic outlook, we argue that the infeasibility of a comprehensive and integrated regime is not a reason for despair: actions can be taken to alleviate the problem and to enhance global cooperation on climate change.

International Cooperation and the Regime Complex for Climate Change

We think about the regime complex for climate change in ways that are consistent with the analytical framework that one of us helped to develop in the 1970s, and that he has since sought to elaborate.[4] International regimes with legally binding rules are formally constructed by elites who represent state interests as they conceive them. Elites face a wide array of political pressures, both domestic and international, that determine how they calculate interests and make decisions on behalf of the state. And while states remain central to the process of making and implementing international law, many other non-state actors play important roles, including nongovernmental organizations (NGOs), business enterprises, and the media. At times these groups act independently; they also form constituencies that influence the tenure and decisions of elites and thus the calculus of state interests. The interests of these constituencies are multiple and often conflicting, since the benefits and costs of action fall differently, and shift over time. The weighting of state interests in determining international outcomes, such as the design and content of international agreements, depends on the power resources, relevant to the issue area, that are available to the states involved. Power is a function of both the impact of one's own decisions on others (which depends mainly on size and economic output) and on favorable asymmetries in interdependence leading to better default (no-agreement) positions for the state.

How these constituencies organize and conceive of their interests varies over time, since perceived interests are also a function of changing information and beliefs. That is, ideas often matter.[5]

To further their interests, states build international institutions—"regimes"—to help them realize the benefits from cooperation. Such institutions help states achieve their objectives through reducing contracting costs, providing focal points, enhancing information and therefore credibility, monitoring compliance, and assisting in sanctioning deviant behavior.[6]

When states invest resources in building regulatory regimes, the outcomes can vary along a continuum. At one extreme are fully integrated institutions that impose regulation through comprehensive, hierarchical rules. At the other extreme are highly fragmented collections of institutions with no identifiable core and weak or nonexistent linkages between regime elements. In between is a wide range that includes nested (semi-hierarchical) regimes with identifiable cores and non-hierarchical but loosely coupled systems of institutions.[7] What we are calling "regime complexes" are arrangements of the loosely coupled variety located somewhere in the middle of this continuum. Regime complexes are marked by connections between the specific and relatively narrow regimes but the absence of an overall architecture or hierarchy that structures the whole set. While the term "regime complex" is not new, what has been missing is a theoretical explanation for why this institutional form prevails in some areas but not others.

Three forces could help to explain where a regime becomes situated on the continuum. One is the distribution of interests, weighted by power. We expect comprehensive regimes when the interests of all crucial powerful actors (states and non-states) are sufficiently similar, across a broad issue area, that they "demand" a singular international institution as the best way to gain the benefits of cooperation. Information and beliefs about which institutional forms suit their interests may facilitate a convergence of interests around a single regulatory regime. Strong demand by all key players around a common objective yields an integrated institution with no viable rivals. The ozone layer accords emerged in this way, with a dominant set of ideas that favored a United Nations-sponsored global treaty on the ozone layer and a strong demand from the most powerful states, firms, and NGOs to invest resources exclusively in that treaty.[8]

Of course, international regimes often come about not through deliberate decision-making at one international conference, but rather emerge as a result of "codifying informal rights and rules that have evolved over time through a process of converging expectations or tacit bargaining."[9] That is, they emerge in path-dependent, historically-shaped ways.[10] The full importance of path dependence is beyond this article, but path dependence can explain why states and non-state actors alike encourage (or tolerate) a plethora of regulatory institutions especially when their interests diverge and no unique focal points have emerged. A multiplicity of regulatory regimes offers opportunities to shop or shift forums.[11] Once many different institutions are already firmly in place and the benefits from forum shopping are apparent to at least some important states, some degree of fragmentation may be difficult to reverse.

A second force is uncertainty. When states seek to cooperate on highly complicated issues with large numbers of other actors, they may be highly uncertain about the gains they will accrue and their exposure to risks from regulation. As cooperation deepens, governments are increasingly unable to make reliable promises about exactly what they will be willing and able to implement, since large shifts in domestic policy necessarily require highly capable systems of public administration and affect important national interest groups in ways that are hard to predict with precision. In such settings, smaller groups of states often form "clubs" that are easier to manage because they are smaller. Clubs also allow members to withhold benefits from states that do not share their interests or seek to act as free riders.[12] As a result, even when the structure of a cooperation issue would seem to call for a large and broad regulatory regime, uncertainty can lead to smaller cooperative structures that vary in membership.

A third force is linkage. Many issue-areas lend themselves to linkages as a way to enlarge the scope for deal-making, which encourages integration.[13] Indeed, many institutions are designed to encourage linkages that increase the gains from cooperation and strengthen the incentive for compliance. The evolution of the General Agreement on Tariffs and Trade (GATT) and the World Trade Organization (WTO), for example, encouraged (until about a decade ago) investment in a single integrated regime because private benefits to states and to major transnational actors such as multinational enterprises from the regime were large and readily extended to all member states through the norms of most favored nation status and reciprocity. These norms made it easier for states to link many trade-related issues, and the reciprocal nature of trade encouraged such linkages as well. In other settings, institutional design may favor continued fragmentation such as when it is administratively difficult to link different regulatory arrangements.

Linkages help define the boundaries around an issue-area. Where linkages lead to deeper cooperation an issue area can expand in size, such as happened under the GATT/WTO regime, which originally focused on border tariffs and now encompasses a broader array of trade-related measures such as subsidies, government procurement, and food safety standards. In trade, linkages arose not just in the formation of new agreements, but also through the WTO's system for enforcement of trade obligations. Where cooperation focuses on an issue area that does not readily lead to integrating linkages, then the result can be a broad, thin regime or many individual regimes focused on individual areas where cooperation is possible. The issue-area of "biological diversity" has emerged in this way, with one broad treaty that has minimal impact (The Convention on Biological Diversity) and many narrower agreements (many of which predate the broad agreement) that focus on particular elements such as regulating trade in endangered species, coordinating the protection of wilderness areas, and

promoting stronger intellectual property rights on biodiversity-related innovations.[14] Weak linkages blur the boundaries around an issue-area—in the extreme leading to legal agreements, such as the Convention on Biological Diversity, that touch on so many diverse areas of possible international coordination that the agreement is unable to focus much practical policy effort on any topic.

We have identified three forces for integration or fragmentation: the diversity of interests, uncertainly, and linkages. These forces may be present, to different degrees, in any issue-area. Next we examine how those forces interact using the example of climate change. The climate change regime complex is a loosely coupled system of institutions; it has no clear hierarchy or core, yet many of its elements are linked in complementary ways. It occupies neither extreme. Instead, it is a regime complex whose elements are loosely linked to one another, between the poles of integration and fragmentation.

The Climate Change Regime Complex

The most visible efforts to create climate institutions cluster around the United Nations Framework Convention on Climate Change (UNFCCC). By design the UNFCCC is nearly universal in membership. It spawned the Kyoto protocol with the aim of being a thickening and comprehensive regime, modeled on the same process of institutional evolution that occurred in the ozone layer where a single UN-sponsored treaty system emerged as the sole, integrated regulatory system.[15] In practice, because Kyoto placed no obligations on developing countries and because the United States never ratified the agreement, its effect was narrow, thin, and in most of the world, ultimately symbolic.[16] Attempts are now under way to renegotiate and extend the Kyoto Protocol under

Figure 11.2. The Regime Complex for Managing Climate Change

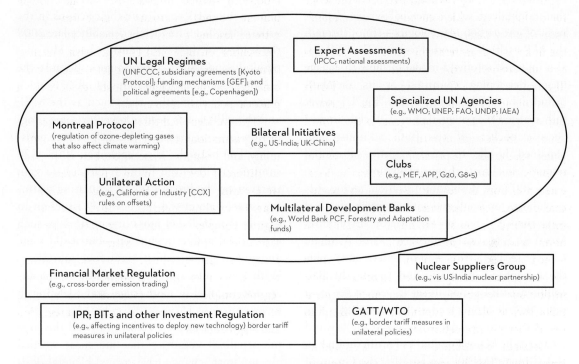

Note: Boxes show the main institutional elements and initiatives that comprise the climate change regime complex. (For a thorough recent description of many elements of the regime complex, see Michonski and Levi 2010). Elements inside the oval represent forums where substantial efforts at rule-making have occurred, focused on one or more of the tasks needed to manage the diversity of cooperation problems that arise with climate change; elements outside are areas where climate rule making is requiring additional, supporting rules.

the auspices of the UNFCCC. In adiditon, several other clusters of institutional efforts are taking shape, with none of them organized in a hierarchy. Figure 11.2 illustrates the arrangements.

Facing gridlock in the universal UN-sponsored talks, several governments have tried to create smaller clubs of key countries that could cooperate on climate change issues. Some of these efforts are *de novo*, which has required club leaders to incur the costs of organization. Others build on existing institutions, which offers the advantage of lower transaction costs but the disadvantage that membership and expectations are already largely formed. We have identified four nascent club-making efforts. We

do not expect that the climate change issue will survive as a prominent element in all of these clubs, but each club has been host to regulatory and collaborative initiatives that have attracted resources and could channel path-dependent efforts in the future.

The first, created by the United States under George W. Bush in the wake of criticism about the US decision to abandon the Kyoto treaty, is the Asia Pacific Partnership (APP). Six countries on the Asian rim agreed in 2005 to cooperate on research and deployment of new low-carbon technologies. (A seventh, Canada, joined in 2007.) APP was intended to chart an alternative path to the Kyoto process (only one of its members [Japan] was a strong advocate for Kyoto-style regulation of emissions) while also forging special relationships that might lead to commercially-viable deployment of low-carbon technologies—if not through the APP itself, then in other forums. The APP was also intended to offer a model for how to engage major developing countries, as its members included both China and India. The US never fully realized the potential of its APP club, in part because pockets of the Bush administration remained hostile to investing any substantial resources in climate change regulation.

In 2007 the Bush administration, seeing that its club was too small and without much practical consequence, created the Major Economies Meetings on Energy Security and Climate Change (MEM). This club of sixteen states plus the European Union first met before the Bali conference and aimed to set its own rules for a more flexible strategy to reduce emissions. The MEM exists to this day—reoriented slightly and renamed the Major Economies Forum on Energy and Climate (MEF).[17] In parallel, the Group of Eight (G8) club took up the climate issue, which has been relatively easy since the G8 already existed and was in perennial search of agenda items. Every G8 meeting during the last six years has included a prominent statement on climate change. Starting in 2005, several G8 meetings have also included a stepchild session where G8 leaders met with leaders from the five most pivotal developing countries (the so-called "G8+5"); climate change was always on their agenda. Among intergovernmental institutions, the G8 and EU have offered the earliest and clearest articulation for the global goal of limiting warming at 2 degrees Celsius above pre-industrial levels.

Finally, frustration with the small size of the G8 (and the irrelevance of the G8+5) created pressures for a larger, regular meeting of leaders from the most important industrialized and developing countries: the group of 20 (G20). The original G20—the Group of Twenty Finance Ministers and Central Bank Governors—was created by Canada and the United States to help finance ministers coordinate their actions in the wake of the Asian financial crisis. Since late 2008 the leaders of the G20 countries have also met regularly and issued communiqués. Because the G20 engages finance and industry officials much more readily than other clubs such as the MEF and the APP, it has been a locus for some progress on low-cost measures that help reduce emissions. For example, the September 2009 G20 summit in Pittsburgh found it difficult to gain traction on the broad issue of regulating warming gases—energy was just one of 17 issues on an agenda that included more urgent troubles such as financial market regulation—but it did forge an agreement to reduce fossil fuel subsidies.[18] With lower subsidies, fuel users will be encouraged to use fuel in more frugal ways, leading to lower emissions.

In addition to these clubs, nearly all the large industrialized countries that are most worried about climate change have created bilateral deals of various types. The UK has created a bilateral partnership with China to test advanced coal combustion technologies. Other countries, including Australia, France and the US, as well as several private firms, are also crafting bilateral deals concerning coal and nuclear power with the Chinese government and Chinese institutions such as the country's large electric utilities. The US has also forged a major partnership to give India access to fissile material and technology that had been unavailable because India was not part of the nuclear nonproliferation treaty. This arrangement, which could lead to massive reductions in India's emissions relative to the expected level, required in turn new multilateral decisions within the 45 member Nuclear Suppliers Group, as well as difficult domestic negotiations in both India and the United States.[19] Since about 2007 the UN process has included active diplomacy to improve management of forests—the so-called "reducing emissions from deforestation and degradation (REDD)" process. Those efforts have produced new agreements but not much practical benefit for forests until several major governments that are rich in forests (Brazil and Indonesia, notably) and also keen to invest in forest protection (Norway and the United States, among others) focused on practical deals for forest protection. A bilateral deal between Norway and Indonesia in 2010 signaled the first major investment under these REDD-related efforts, and many other similar bilateral and "club" arrangements on forests are taking shape at this writing. Some are following the model that Norway set with Indonesia.

While most efforts to set targets for warming emissions have focused on the UNFCCC, other regulatory treaties have a big impact on emissions of these gases. Indeed, some studies have concluded that the Montreal Protocol on the Ozone Layer has actually had a much bigger impact than the Kyoto Protocol on warming because the gases that are the chief cause of ozone depletion are also extremely potent warming agents.[20] Frustrated by lack of progress in the UNFCCC system, some governments have explored fuller use of the Montreal Protocol to cut some of the industrial gases that were invented to replace ozone-depleting substances but themselves proved to be strong warming agents. Several regional air pollution institutions may ultimately play an important role in climate change as well. Some of the pollutants they regulate mask warming—notably sulfure oxides (which cause acid rain and thus are regulated, but which also lead to sulfate particles that can make clouds brighter and thus dampen warming); international rules on the allowable sulfur content for the fuels burned by ocean-going ships are likely to increase warming by lessening this sulfate-masking effect. Increased attention is now focused on particulate pollution, which is presently regulated because it contributes to local air pollution; there is mounting evidence that sooty particulate pollution (also called "black carbon") is a big cause

of climate change.[21] Regional institutions, such as in Asia and the Arctic, are now exploring how to coordinate black carbon regulations since these particles not only cause warming but also lead to regional effects such as melting of ice packs and glaciers. (Soot is dark and thus absorbs heat when it dusts bright snow and ice.)

Existing multilateral institutions, notably the World Bank, have also been a locus of institution-building on climate change. For example, the World Bank sponsored the Prototype Carbon Fund (PCF) in the late 1990s to channel early investment into the Kyoto Protocol's Clean Development Mechanism (CDM)—the mechanism that encourages investment in low-emission technologies and practices in developing countries. The experience with PCF projects, in turn, helped speed the process of designing rules for the CDM and probably raised the quality of the subsequent CDM projects. The Bank, working with other multilateral institutions and through the Global Environment Facility (GEF), also manages the formal financial mechanisms that pay for developing country participation under the UNFCCC and the Kyoto treaty. (It plays a similar role in other multilateral environmental institutions.) In addition to these efforts, which are formally subordinate to the UNFCCC institutions, the Bank also manages several other funding windows that are formally distinct. It is organizing a large fund to invest in projects that reduce deforestation and has created a special fund to help countries adapt to the effects of climate change. Perhaps most important, the Bank has adopted an across-the-board effort to bring climate change concerns into its main lending and granting activities, thus creating much larger leverage on the money that flows into agriculture, power plants, infrastructure, and other investments that cause or are affected by the changing climate.[22]

Beyond these efforts at formal international coordination, a number of unilateral initiatives are intended to encourage changes in behavior in other jurisdictions. For example, frustration at the slow progress of US federal legislation has led at least two sub-units within the United States to adopt their own limits on emissions—California (under AB32 and other legislation) and the northeastern states (under the Regional Greenhouse Gas Initiative, or RGGI). Both those sub-national systems include emission trading schemes with "docking" provisions for international trading, which would allow these states to set rules that created valuable private goods (emission credits) that firms could generate in other countries.[23] In addition to these unilateral actions by governments, regulatory efforts led by civil society organizations are emerging. NGOs have organized to build awareness and to focus on practical solutions for controlling emissions. Many firms have adopted their own regulatory programs and have also created coalitions to press for regulatory action. Among the examples is the US Climate Action Partnership (US-CAP), an alliance of firms and NGOs.

So far, we have focused on efforts to coordinate regulation of emissions. In addition, there is growing attention to the need to adapt to a changing climate. Funding for adaptation has come partly from a small tax on CDM transactions and mainly from government budgets; efforts to build larger adaptation funds have faltered, in part due to the inability to link this funding need to a large, reliable source of resources. Governments promised at Copenhagen in December 2009 and again in Cancun a year later to expand vastly funding for adaptation. Very poor, vulnerable countries have become increasingly well organized to demand help with adaptation since they see climate change as inevitable.

There is also a small but growing investment into technologies, known as "geoengineering," that might crudely offset warming in case the climate started changing quickly in catastrophic ways. A wide array of international institutions is now considering whether and how to govern geoengineering. Where such technologies involve manipulation of the oceans, the London Dumping Convention has already been involved. Where they affect biological diversity, the Convention on Biological Diversity is exploring regulatory options (including a formal decision in November 2010 aimed at discouraging geoengineering research). Where they influence the ozone layer, the Montreal Protocol on the Ozone Layer might play a role. Wholly new international agreements might emerge in this area in the future.

International cooperation has also focused on such other tasks as improving shared knowledge about the science of climate change. The most prominent of these efforts are organized under the intergovernmental Panel on Climate Change (IPCC) that sponsors in-depth scientific reviews. IPCC also entertains requests, which come at arm's length from other institutions such as the UNFCCC, to provide technical information such as the reporting procedures for emissions inventories. In parallel with the multilateral IPCC process, several governments have undertaken their own assessments—often looking expansively not just at impacts at home but also around the world.

International cooperation on climate change has been under way for decades, yet there remains no central core to the emerging regulatory arrangements on climate change. Instead, what we observe is an array of regulatory elements that is only partially organized hierarchically. Some are attached to existing narrow and deep regimes—such as bilateral initiatives that are making it easier for India to obtain fissile material, or the efforts to mainstream climate change issues within the existing robust World Bank system for lending and grants. Others involve nascent institutions such as the emerging markets for carbon offsets and trading, which in some cases have not progressed beyond initial modest efforts (e.g., the RGGI market), while others are becoming deep quickly (e.g., the EU's emission trading scheme). These efforts are akin to the Cambrian explosion—a wide array of diverse institutional forms emerges, and through selection and accident a few are chosen. The outcome of these efforts is at neither extreme in the continuum on institutional forms—it is neither integrated nor fully fragmented. Instead, loosely coupled arrangements among institutions are linked in a variety of ways—in which the UNFCCC process is particularly important but is not unrivalled—that together form a regime complex. In the next section, we aim to explain this outcome.

Toward Explaining the Regime Complex for Climate Change

The three generic forces discussed above help explain variation in the integration or fragmentation of international institutions. The *distribution of interests* helps explain why no single institution has emerged. Originally, differences between the EU and US mostly explained the lack of agreement on the Kyoto system. Today, major developing countries also have their own ideas about regulatory institutions, which has led to even more dispersion in institutional preferences. *Uncertainty* has made most governments wary about making costly commitments to global institutions when they are unsure of the benefits and whether other countries will make and honor promises to implement comparable efforts. And across most of the cooperation problems in climate change, governments are still struggling to find productive *linkages*, although in a few areas those linkages are tight and deep, such as the links between emission trading systems and compensation.

These three generic forces interact with two specific attributes of the climate change problem. First, a dispersed institutional outcome is due to *problem diversity:* the specific cooperation problems inherent in the challenge of "climate change" are enormously varied. Climate change is actually many distinct problems—each with its own attributes, administrative challenges, and distinctive political constituencies.[24] The diversity of problems is, in turn, associated with parallel diverse patterns of interests, power, information and beliefs. We see at least four distinct cooperation problems under the broad banner of "climate change":

1. The hardest and most central problem is *coordination of emission regulations.*
2. Another problem is *compensation*—such as financial transfers—for countries that are unwilling or unable to adopt emission controls. For example, essentially all developing countries at the Kyoto talks were unwilling to agree on measures limiting emissions in the absence of payments through mechanisms such as the CDM.
3. A third problem is *coordinating efforts* to brace for a changing climate, principally through adaptation, but possibly with geoengineering. With geoengineering, action by one or a few actors may be too tempting and needs to be prevented, which makes the cooperation challenge the opposite of collective action to control emissions. That is, the challenge in geoengineering is how to make it *more difficult* rather than easier to act.[25]
4. The final cooperation problem is *coordination of common scientific assessments* to increase the public good of shared knowledge about the causes and consequences of climate change. (International cooperation is also required to promote and coordinate investments in new technologies, which also have public good characteristics. Most carbon-related technologies are traded in a global marketplace and, thus, the well-known market failures leading to under-investment in research and development are increasingly global in scope.)

Put differently, there is no single "climate change" problem but an array of different cooperation games, each with their own incentives to free ride. Each of these individual cooperation problems is linked, to different degrees, to the others.

A second reason for dispersion of efforts is rooted in the severe *political difficulties* that confront any serious program for controlling emissions, which is the first and most important area for international cooperation. Deep cuts in emissions ultimately require global cooperation because the main warming pollutants are costly to regulate and influence economic competitiveness. Deep cuts require governments to adopt regulations that will influence the behavior of millions of firms and many more households—a particular challenge in countries that have weak, fragmented, or corrupt systems of public administration. And the benefits from these efforts are both uncertain and arise far in the future, while the costs are immediate.

We can now offer a tentative account of why the problem of climate change is likely neither to yield an integrated, comprehensive regime nor to be fully fragmented.

From a functional standpoint, the specific international cooperation problems involved in managing climate change are so varied that a single institutional response is exceptionally difficult to organize and sustain. Indeed, the diversity of problems is typically accompanied by a diversity of interests, power, information, and beliefs. Where contracting around these individual cooperation problems is coupled to other institutional arrangements, it is prohibitively complicated to arrange all couplings *ex ante* into a single comprehensive regime. No single country has the power to impose a solution on all others.

Not only are climate issues diverse; they are characterized by high uncertainty, interests, power, information and beliefs are changing quickly. This is evident in the rapid rise of China and India as large emitters as well as in shifting beliefs about the dangers of climate change in popular and scientific discourse. Such rapid changes alter the institutional forms that important countries favor and are willing to accept. As we argued above in general terms, such uncertainties make governments reluctant to enter into comprehensive agreements that make substantial policy demands.

Strategic considerations involving decisions about linkages also push toward an outcome that is fragmented, yet includes many loose couplings. On the one hand, the diversity of interests promotes tendencies toward fragmentation. Specific regimes are often anchored on private goods supplied to a small number of actors whose interests are similar to each other but dissimilar to other actors. These interests are also interdependent because, for example, regulatory decisions affect economic competition. Members of this "club" will then seek to maintain these arrangements for their own benefit. The benefits of a comprehensive regime may not seem sufficient to justify the bargaining efforts and concessions that would be required. On the other hand, a fully fragmented response is unlikely to satisfy the interests of the leading states, which make the largest investments in building institutions and which expect first-mover advantages. They will seek hierarchies or, failing that, linkages among issues that create politically-sustainable arrangements that are consistent with their interests. So the net result on climate change is a set of clubs that are linked in multiple ways.

Some examples help illustrate how linkages can arise between different regulatory elements and lead to a regime complex, rather than a fully fragmented set of institutions. States that seek deep cuts in emissions must find ways to compensate more reluctant nations that are also formidable economic competitors. The scale of resources being demanded is far beyond what most donor governments would accept—for example, the "Copenhagen Accord" that outlines the main points of agreement from the Copenhagen conference calls for $100 billion annually in new financial flows from industrialized to developing countries by

2020, a number comparable with the sum of all official foreign aid.[26] Faced with the infeasibility of organizing these large, new flows as direct government-to-government transfers, instead governments that have the strongest interest in an effective climate change regime are linking the compensation regime to emission control regulations that create carbon markets. The mechanisms employed already include the CDM and are likely to encompass various other offset schemes, including new offset systems focused on forests and land use. Efforts to promote greater innovation in low-emission technologies also benefit from links to carbon markets since the linkages create a price on emissions and a source of funding. Similarly, important linkages have emerged between the system for providing information about climate dangers and emission control efforts. The "Bali Roadmap" that set the agenda for the two years of diplomatic talks leading to the Copenhagen conference, for example, explicitly used the IPCC's findings about "safe" levels of warming gases in outlining the countries that must participate in efforts to control emissions.

These three forces—the dispersed distribution of power-weighted interests, uncertainty, and linkages—help to explain the loosely coupled nature of the regime complex for climate change.

In other areas of international relations, a diversity of cooperation problems has not always led to fragmented institutions or a regime complex—for example, the trade issue area has come to span a highly diverse array of types of international cooperation largely within a unified legal framework under the GATT/WTO. But that outcome in trade reflected two realities: that the scope of trade talks began with a focus on narrower issues (mainly tariffs) and the nature of trade readily led to strong linkages. The expansion of the Issue-area today called "trade" from tariffs to a wide variety of trade barriers took almost half a century. By contrast, climate change diplomacy has engaged a broad array of topics from the outset and is still early in its evolution—the first formal diplomatic talks on climate change were only two decades ago. Problem diversity in climate change magnifies the three forces identified earlier as causes of fragmentation: it generates more complicated and shifting distributions of interests; it increases uncertainty; and it makes it harder to forge reliable linkages.

Path-dependence and organizational practices have also reinforced this pattern. Different countries and sectors have become interested in serious action on climate change at different times. When the timing of action varies, the leaders construct partial institutions that suit their purposes and their interests. Once they have done so, they are likely to resist changing these arrangements fundamentally, since it is costly to change organizational structures and state leaders are likely to engage in satisficing behavior so as long as the regime complex performs essential functions passably well.[27]

For example, Europe has been much more committed to the Kyoto process than most other industrialized countries, including notably the United States. The EU has invested heavily in the construction of international regulatory regimes for climate change that are based on legally binding targets and timetables as well as international emissions trading. In turn, the EU has crafted its own policies at home to align with that international approach. For the EU, different approaches are now more difficult to envision and implement—even as other countries find that they favor other regulatory schemes not anchored in binding targets and timetables. It may therefore be easier to build parallel club-oriented regimes as part of a regime complex than to try to re-open negotiations to achieve a comprehensive, integrated regime. Indeed, the final compromise reached at the Copenhagen conference explicitly creates legal flexibility so that some nations can continue the formal legal mechanisms such as extensions of the Kyoto Protocol while others (notably the United States and probably China, along with some other large developing countries) adopt different approaches. Such dispersion is likely to continue as more countries with diverse interests and capabilities—the developing countries—become seriously engaged in regulation in different ways and at different points in time.

Implications for Policy

The emergence of a climate change regime complex, rather than an integrated, comprehensive climate change regime, does not necessarily provide reasons to despair. On the contrary, policy-makers who seek more effective limitation on the magnitude of climate change can use regime complexes to their advantage. The high likelihood of loosely coupled outcomes suggests that countries most committed to doing something about global warming should rethink the strategy that has dominated most of their efforts so far: the unwavering investment in massive, integrated legal instruments and global summits such as witnessed in Copenhagen.

One potential advantage of regime complexes lies in the ability to fix and avoid the faults of integrated regulatory systems that are already apparent in the UNFCCC and the Kyoto Protocol. It is difficult to design effective regulatory systems in the context of a multiplicity of cooperation problems, a broad and shifting distribution of interests, extreme uncertainty about which measures governments are willing and able to implement, and ambiguity about how to craft viable linkages. When diplomats attempt to craft integrated agreements to span those many problems the outcome is likely to be unwieldy. And once established, the difficulty of renegotiation with so many distinct cooperation problems, interests, uncertainties, and linkages will lead participants to cling to existing institutions, which take on monopoly characteristics. Heroic efforts then concentrate on the monopoly; rival efforts, even when they could be more effective, are pilloried as distractions. For example, the broad coalition of developing countries—the so-called Group of 77 ("G77") and China—lambasted attempts to work in small groups and outside the UNFCCC process during the run-up to the Copenhagen conference, despite mounting evidence that universal negotiations were making little progress.[28]

The dysfunctions of the UNFCCC monopoly are especially evident in two areas. First, perhaps the most important aspect of the Kyoto Protocol is its system for encouraging low-emission investments in developing countries—the Clean Development Mechanism (CDM). Over the long term, engagement with developing countries is essential since it is mathematically impossible to reach deep cuts in world emissions of warming gases without these countries' participation.[29] The main compensation mechanism for enticing the participation of developing countries has been linkage to emission credit markets through the CDM. Yet studies suggest that a large fraction—perhaps half or even more—of the CDM credits issued do not represent bona fide reductions in emissions due to poor administration.[30] Despite this realization, it is proving very difficult to fix the CDM due to the complex and highly politicized nature of decision-making within its UN-based administrative system and the Kyoto Protocol. Moreover, the governments that have the greatest ability to push for changes in CDM administration also face strong pressures to ensure there is an even larger supply of credits, which makes compliance with the Kyoto targets easier, rather than higher quality credits.[31] The CDM monopoly has effectively excluded offsets in some areas (e.g., carbon storage and nuclear power) while favoring offsets in areas that may be less cost-effective, such as small, rural renewable energy projects. Since these rules create path dependence, such offsets rules are likely to be transposed into a new comprehensive regime, with the result the carbon equivalent of Gresham's law. Instead of a monopoly, if governments create other kinds of offset systems they could learn more about which kinds of systems work best. Competition between offsets schemes, if well designed, could reverse the perverse incentives that have plagued the CDM.

Secondly, the UNFCCC/Kyoto arrangements for linking national trading systems have encountered difficulties. The Kyoto architects envisioned that national emission control systems could be linked together to form an international trading system. In practice, the rules for "docking" have proven to be inflexible and do not encourage much additional effort by governments. More flexible docking rules would allow a wider array of countries to sell allowances into established carbon markets, conditional on setting country-wide or sectoral caps, and would therefore broaden the scope of carbon trading systems.[32] Yet it has proved difficult for countries to change their status under the UNFCCC/Kyoto system in ways that would expand the scope of effective emission controls. Kazakhstan has sought for over a decade to join Annex I of the Kyoto Protocol so it can participate more fully in carbon markets; but It has not been permitted to do so.[33] In this situation, a voluntary action that would contribute to the objective of the Kyoto Protocol is prohibited by procedural barriers and veto-points built into that agreement.

While institutional monopolies have dysfunctions, a regime complex can also be too fragmented. Components may conflict with one another in ways that yield gridlock rather than innovation; the lack of hierarchy among specific regimes can create critical veto points; through forum-shopping there could in principle be a "race to the bottom." Our argument is not that regime complexes are absolutely better than other institutional forms. Rather, we argue that actual international cooperation is unlikely to be integrated and comprehensive. An integrated regime might be attractive as the most legitimate institutional form, but efforts to craft such a regime face enormous political and organizational barriers. The result of efforts to tilt at such a system, as in climate change, will be gridlock and only weak substantive commitments. A more loosely coupled system is inevitable.

If governments and non-state actors that seek more effective management of climate change behave strategically, they can use the fragmented institutions to their advantage. Specifically, regime complexes—that is, loosely coupled sets of specific regimes—offer two distinct advantages: flexibility across issues and adaptability over time.

FLEXIBILITY ACROSS ISSUES Without a requirement that all rules be bound within a common institution, it may be possible to adapt rules to distinctively different conditions on different issues, or for different coalitions of actors. Different states can sign on to different sets of agreements, making it more likely that they would adhere to some constraints on greenhouse gas emissions. One variant of such a flexible approach involves proposals popular with Australia, the US, and several other governments (including key developing countries) during the negotiations leading to the Copenhagen conference that states construct "schedules" of their proposed climate change actions, rather than acceding to a common set of targets and timetables.[34] This approach is similar to the flexibility afforded when large governments engage in complex negotiations to accede to the WTO; each country's particular accession deal is tailored to its circumstances.[35] This approach was tried early in the climate change process under the heading of "pledge and review," but that idea lost favor when no government made the effort to flesh out how the concept would work in practice, and the governments and interest groups most keen on emission controls—notably in the EU governments and NGOs—favored simpler targets and timetables for emissions.[36] At Copenhagen when governments could not agree on a comprehensive regulatory system the Institutional form that remained agreeable was this more flexible system of schedules.[37] At this writing, about five-dozen countries have offered their policy schedules and negotiations are under way to find places where those policy promises can lead to more effective international cooperation. Serious international cooperation is emerging "bottom up" because integrated "top down" institutions have been too difficult to craft.

ADAPTABILITY OVER TIME Regime complexes may also have higher adaptability over time. Changes in different issue areas, or within the domestic politics of different countries, are likely to occur at different rates. Governments may make promises for policy coordination in international negotiations that prove unexpectedly difficult or impossible to implement at home; as one country adjusts its national efforts, other governments, too, may need to make alterations. In contrast with integrated, tightly coupled monopoly institutions, regime complexes may be able to adapt more readily—especially when adaptation requires complex changes in norms and behavior. Loose coupling may also be advantaged when the best strategy for institutional adaptation is unclear and thus many diverse efforts should be tried and the more effective ones selected through experience. Applied to climate change, this benefit is probably particularly important for engaging developing countries that are wary about obligations that could become too onerous too quickly, but the particular fears vary with each country and its circumstances.

These advantages of greater flexibility and adaptability stem, in part, from decision-making structures. In global institutions that are designed for legitimacy, such as the UN, decisions are made through universal voting rules that also often yield inaction. The UNFCCC has never adopted formal procedures for voting because the decision to adopt those procedures required unanimous consent and oil-exporting countries (a group generally abhorrent to policies that would cut consumption of carbon fuels) refused to agree. (Today, 15 years after the UNFCCC entered into force, the institution still works with provisional rules of procedure and takes all significant decisions by consensus.) Leaders are needed to incur the cost of organizing an effective response to problems in managing common pool resources, yet those few leaders who are willing and able to commit adequate resources may refuse to make the effort unless they can capture a large share of the benefits. Clubs with private decision-making rather than universal access help leaders avoid institutional outcomes that are thin and lack ambition because they must attract the consent of too many other countries with diverging interests.

Variation in Regime Complexes: Criteria for Assessment

We now turn briefly from our positive analysis to a normative commentary. As we have noted above, our argument about regime complexes does not imply that such a complex will solve climate change problems in an efficient or timely manner. We also do not assume that the advantages of a regime complex, which we have identified, will outweigh their liabilities. On the contrary, dispersed institutions can also be associated with chaos, a proliferation of veto points, and gridlock that deters policy makers and private investors from devoting resources to the climate change problem. And even if these pitfalls are avoided, the transaction costs of regime complexes may be higher than for integrated regimes with a single legal form and set of administrative rules.[38] Proposals for specific elements that would further fragment cooperation on climate change—such as new clubs or invitations for other institutions to take up topics that could help manage climate change—should therefore be carefully analyzed to see whether they would enhance the overall performance of the regime complex. Whether the proliferation of different forums working on the climate issue—such as the G20, the MEF, various bilateral technology and investment partnerships, and private sector and NGO initiatives—is an asset or liability depends on their content and how these efforts are coupled.

Normative assessments or proposals for new institutional arrangements should be made on the basis of carefully considered evaluative criteria. We propose six such criteria, each of which defines a dimension of variation running from dysfunctional to functional. Regime complexes toward the positive end of each of the six dimensions are likely to be normatively more justifiable than complexes that score lower on these dimensions.

1. *Coherence.* The various specific regimes of a climate change regime complex could be compatible and mutually reinforcing; they could be incompatible and mutually harmful; or they could be somewhere between these extremes. A regime whose components are compatible and mutually reinforcing is coherent. Where compatibilities exist they encourage linkages that make it easier to channel resources from one element of the regime complex to another—such as from a national emission-trading program to an international scheme to protect forests or compensate developing countries.

2. *Accountability.* The elements of the regime complex should be accountable to relevant audiences, including not just slates but nongovernmental organizations and publics. Accountability means that "some actors have the right to hold other actors to a set of standards, to judge whether they have fulfilled their responsibilities in light of these standards, and to impose sanctions if they determine that these responsibilities have not been met."[39] Accountability helps create legitimacy (which may be in shorter supply in the absence of a single unified regime) and can also help create shared information that lowers uncertainty.

3. *Determinacy.* A climate change regime complex should be determinate in the sense that the rules have "a readily ascertainable normative content."[40] Determinacy is important both to enhance compliance and to reduce uncertainty in general. It can also help build confidence that despite a broad and shifting distribution of interests, important actors are making efforts to coordinate policy and manage the climate problem. Where rules are determinate it will be easier for governments and firms to invest resources in putting those rules into practice—for example, by building low-carbon energy systems—and once in practice those rules can more readily encourage others to make similar investments.

4. *Sustainability.* Sustainable regimes have components that reinforce one another and may also build in redundancy, to withstand shocks. Sustainable regimes are superior since they reduce uncertainty, in this case about future rules. Most of the policies and investments needed to reduce emissions and to adapt to climate change are very long-lived; governments and private firms especially are unlikely to make them without confidence that the regulatory system is durable.

5. *Epistemic quality.* Like comprehensive regimes, regime complexes can vary in epistemic quality, particularly in the consistency between their rules and scientific knowledge. Epistemic quality is important for legitimacy as well as effectiveness.[41]

6. *Fairness.* Since multilateral institutions always reflect disparities of power and interests, they never perfectly reflect abstract normative standards of fairness, and should not be evaluated on the basis of whether they achieve this utopian objective. But they should provide benefits widely, and not discriminate against states that are willing to cooperate.

In general, conflicts of interests and values and asymmetries of power that are endemic in world politics mean that one cannot expect international institutions to rate well on the basis of these normative criteria. Even taking that reality into account, however, the climate change regime complex of 1997–2010, dominated by the institutions established by the Kyoto Protocol, does not get high rankings on these six criteria. The division of countries under Kyoto into industrialized ("Annex I") and developing ("non-Annex I") countries implied a regime of low coherence and accountability in which the absence of binding rules for some states was of questionable fairness, reduced incentives for others to accept such rules, and made it impossible to hold many states accountable for their actions. The Kyoto treaty and its parent, the UNFCCC, contain no credible compliance mechanisms and (unlike the WTO) no mandatory dispute-settlement institutions, which reduce their determinacy. The dissatisfaction of the United States and other large emitters (and therefore powerful players) such as China threaten its sustainability. The difficulty of changing the rules in light of new information and interests has limited the epistemic quality of the regime complex. In light of these defects, it is not surprising that the Kyoto system, itself, has lacked much real impact on the climate problem. Developing countries joined because membership required little effort; many rich countries were reluctant to make and keep commitments to it except where those commitments largely aligned with what those countries were already willing to implement.

Specific Implications for Policy

Finally, we draw several implications for policy. We focus on actions that leading governments, NGOs, and firms could pursue in efforts to make a regime complex more effective.

First, a regime complex could favor more strategic use of international emission trading. Trading has become the policy instrument of choice for nearly all governments that are implementing the most demanding policies. Well-designed trading systems could be very important because they leverage large amounts of capital and because some of that capital could flow to developing countries through "offsets" such as the CDM. The CDM, for all its flaws, has already generated emission credits worth perhaps ten times the value of classic government-to-government funding.

Attempts to create an Integrated UNFCCC/Kyoto regime have yielded only one set of accounting procedures and offsets rules to govern which kinds of international trades get formal credit (i.e., the CDM). A more competitive system, with a multitude of rules, would be more effective. Governments in industrialized countries that are most interested in controlling emissions could set their own offset rules—tighter than the CDM—and open trading windows to any other country with equally strict (or stricter) offset policies. Rules requiring buyers to be liable for the quality of the credits they purchase would create additional incentives for quality, as well as new pricing mechanisms so that markets could assess and reward the highest quality trading—making it much easier for investors in projects that yield bona fide reductions in emissions to earn a reliable return. A diversity of offsets rules would yield a much wider array of real experience that could inform future efforts to create common rules and common "floor" standards. Within a regime complex there would be many different trading systems with different prices, trading rules, and transaction volumes.[42] International offsets could become the arbitrage points that link those trading systems. Market pricing that reflects quality would make the climate change regime complex more accountable, and by allowing fungibility through the pricing mechanism coherence can be maintained even as many different arrangements are tested.

Second, a loosely coupled system could create special opportunities for innovation around offsets for land use and forestry. Land use is a large source of warming emissions and also potentially a very low cost way to absorb extra emissions from the atmosphere. However, in Kyoto these issues were so controversial that governments could not agree to allow much investment in land use and forestry projects—the forested nations, especially, feared intrusion on their national policies. Now that the CDM has demonstrated that capital flows through offsets are credible, those same nations—notably Brazil and Indonesia—have reversed course and favor special offsets rules for forestry and land use. We welcome that shift and the development of so-called "REDD+" rules that will encourage countries rich in forests to protect and plant. We caution, though, that at this stage the best rules are still unclear and there are (as with offsets generally) advantages to encouraging a diversity of approaches. Getting serious about land use change will improve the epistemic quality of cooperation on climate change since these are major, largely unregulated, sources of emissions. And since many of these emissions come from especially poor countries, this also offers an opportunity to improve the fairness of the climate change regime complex.

Third, a regime complex, in contrast with efforts to build a single integrated regime, could more readily manage conflicts and synergies that arise at the joints between climate change and other areas of international cooperation, which would lead to more coherent and determinate regulatory arrangements, Raustiala and Victor hypothesized that much of the institutional innovation in regime complexes would arise at the joints between regime elements.[43] In climate change, one of the most pressing issues at the joints is accommodating border tax adjustments (BTAs). Many analysts are wary of such schemes and other trade measures because they fear that BTAs could lead to trade discrimination that, in turn, will undermine successful cooperation in other areas, notably the WTO and other trade liberalization agreements. We share some of that concern, but we note that border tariffs make it possible to create private goods, thus increasing incentives for countries to dock into a carbon

trading system to avoid Imposition of BTAs. Furthermore, BTAs could be politically important in countries that were considering establishing and maintaining carbon trading systems, by providing assurances that regulatory efforts at home will not erode investment and jobs. Hence from a political perspective—both international and domestic—BTAs are attractive instruments. Yet BTAs are only feasible within a regime complex since opposition to such policies by developing countries assures that any formal effort to negotiate BTAs as part of an integrated, comprehensive climate regime would be vetoed.

Properly designed border tax adjustments could be consistent with obligations in other institutions, notably the WTO.[44] To do so, legal scholars suggest they must meet three conditions: (1) a close connection between the means employed and essential climate change policy; (2) non-discriminatory application, so that the measure does not serve as "a disguised restriction on international trade"; and (3) respect for administrative due process, as has been required on other issues by the WTO Appellate Body. We suggest that policy-makers within the most active climate clubs devise rules for BTAs that are consistent with these guidelines, in an effort to avoid conflict with WTO rules. We suggest that the WTO itself help prepare the ground rather than waiting for this issue to arise through formal disputes. The inclusion of BTAs is an example of a nascent coupling that could exist between efforts to manage climate change and the large, integrated institutions that govern trade.

Finally, a regime complex offers the flexibility for cooperation on other topics, such as investments in research and development, that could complement the central task of cutting emissions. Under the UNFCCC/Kyoto Process there have been some halting efforts to promote technological innovation, but these efforts have not had any practical effect on national technology policies. Smaller clubs of leading governments could agree to coordinate and amplify their policies aimed at advancing innovation in low-emission technologies. While the incentive to craft and coordinate technology policies in the UNFCCC/Kyoto system is weak, within a club the benefits would be more visible as would the potential for creating private goods such as intellectual property and revenues from exclusive markets for low emission technology.[45]

Success in the formation of innovation clubs would eventually make most aspects of the climate change problem easier to solve and politically more sustainable. Successful innovation of inexpensive low-emission technologies will lower the cost of emission controls. Indeed, the central cause of success in the ozone layer regime was the appearance of new technologies at very low (sometimes essentially zero) cost. Difficult problems in managing common pool resources are made much easier when low-cost technologies blunt the incentives to defect and when new technologies offer many local benefits (e.g., improved energy security and lower local pollution). Furthermore, the emergence of a belief system around the prospects of "clean tech" revolutions and green jobs could also help mobilize new interest groups that favor effective climate policy. But this belief system will only be sustainable, and worthwhile in the long run, if it is seen as realistic and a reliable source of private benefits.[46]

As a practical matter, keener interest in technology would require the leading innovators to coordinate much larger national investments in innovation. While new knowledge is a global public good, systems of innovation are organized at the national and sectoral levels. The good news is that an innovation club should be relatively easy to organize since only six countries account for about 85% of all research and development investment.[47] The bad news is that spending on energy technology has not even recovered to the levels seen in the early 1980s. Spending is now rising, but some of that new money is linked to economic stimulus programs that are coming to an end. A new technology

strategy is needed that would include both coordination of national investment levels and sharing of experiences about the best organization for innovation and implementation.[48]

Even though a coherent, effective, and legitimate comprehensive regime seems politically unattainable, the UNFCCC would still have an important role to play in a climate regime complex. But within a regime complex the UNFCCC is only one component, albeit a major one.

The Framework Convention could be used as an umbrella under which many different efforts proceed. It would supply functions that are best provided on a universal basis, such as standards for reporting on emissions, providing a forum for negotiating broad decisions, and perhaps instructing technical bodies (e.g., the IPCC) to gather and assess information. It could perhaps become a means to ensure that the various components of a regime complex are coherent and mutually supportive, although so far very little of the political investment in the UNFCCC has been mobilized around this umbrella function. However, there are dangers lurking in every monopoly, and countries that are most keen to slow global warming could make it clear that if the Framework Convention does not provide this useful umbrella role, there are other institutional options available.

Overtime, the UNFCCC might evolve into a deeper institution and perhaps the core of an integrated regulatory system. The array of "club" efforts underway presently could perhaps come to be governed by common rules—akin, perhaps, to most favored nation status and reciprocity in the GATT/WTO system, which have helped ensure that particular club deals crafted on trade are generalized to a larger number of countries. But we caution against policy efforts that would move too quickly in that direction. Managing common-pool resources is unlike the more reciprocal task of reducing barriers to trade in goods and services. Since it is especially difficult to internalize the benefits from actions on common-pool resources, the exclusivity that comes from clubs is a particularly important incentive for first movers to invest in building institutions.

Conclusion

The international institutions that regulate issues related to climate change are diverse in membership and content. They have been created at different times, and by different groups of countries. They have been crafted in a context of diverse interests, high uncertainty, and shifting linkages. They are not integrated, comprehensive, or arranged in a clear hierarchy. They form a loosely-linked regime complex rather than a single international regime.

The infeasibility of a strong comprehensive regime makes climate change a very difficult international problem to manage. And surely it would be better if the domestic political systems around the world were generating a strong demand for action in ways that were potentially consistent with one another. Indeed, there is reason to be pessimistic about whether global emissions can be reduced in time to prevent very damaging climate change.[49] Yet we argue for making the best of this situation rather than continuing to pursue the elusive goal of a comprehensive, integrated regime—a goal that is both unattainable and distracts policymakers from more effective strategies. We have suggested that regime complexes have some distinctive advantages over integrated, comprehensive regimes. They should be viewed not as ideal constructions but outcomes that emerge from real-world political, organizational, and informational constraints. Regime complexes can be much more flexible and adaptable than integrated-comprehensive regimes. Indeed, the Clean Development Mechanism and the Kyoto "docking" rules illustrate the counterproductive rigidities that are often built into comprehensive regimes.

Whether loosely-linked climate regimes will be more effective than efforts to craft a single integrated regime depends in part on how well they meet the six criteria we have put forward: coherence, accountability, determinacy, sustainability, epistemic quality, and fairness. More generally, an effective climate change regime complex would generate positive feedback: incentives for a "race to the top." In a well-functioning regime complex, efforts by one set of countries to take stronger action would generate imitation by others, rather than actions designed to "free-ride" on others commitments.[50] Although a comprehensive global trading system is unlikely, much emissions reduction could be achieved through a linked set of national and regional trading systems, in which offsets would help generate incentives for laggards to raise their own standards in order to benefit from these financial flows. A loosely-linked regime complex could allow for experimental innovation with respect to land use forest offsets, as in present initiatives to reduce deforestation. It could also enable border tax adjustments to be used in selected situations, and to be linked to the broader benefits of WTO membership. Finally, technology innovation clubs could use private incentives to leverage research and investments that would make limiting emissions more feasible and less costly.

In such a regime complex, the UNFCCC would continue to play an umbrella role and provide the framework for a number of essential functions, including serving as a legal setting, providing information, and constituting a forum for negotiations. Over time, if convergence in policy preferences took place and if a large number of reinforcing linkages were to appear, the UNFCCC could yet evolve into an integrated and comprehensive policy regime. At the present juncture, however, both political reality and the need for flexibility and diversity suggest that it is preferable to work for a loosely linked but effective regime complex for climate change.

NOTES

1. Raustiala and Victor 2004, 295. Our paper had been written, titled and submitted for publication before we saw a similarly-titled working paper of the Council on Foreign Relations (Michonski and Levi 2010). That paper is quite different from ours; it is a useful policy-oriented survey of international institutions that are relevant to climate change.

2. Alter and Meunler 2009. For an additional perspective on the causes of integration or fragmentation, with application to climate change, see Biermann et al. 2009. A similar line of thinking—focused on explaining the allocation and fragmentation of governance decisions—is in the literature on "multi-level governance," such as notably Hooghe and Marks 2003. And on nested regimes see, for example, Aggarwal 1998.

3. Although this paper is focused on the international regime complex, we recognize that international efforts of all types face severe barriers in the form of domestic politics.

4. Keohane and Nye 1977.

5. Goldstein and Keohane 1993; O'Neill 1999.

6. Keohane 1984.

7. For more on the different species of regime complexes, see Alter and Meunier 2009 and the symposium they introduce.

8. Parson 2003.

9. Young 1997, 10.

10. Pierson 2000.

11. Braithwaite and Drahos 2000, 29. See also Busch 2007.

12. Keohane and Nye 2001; Kahler and Lake 2003. On club goods and uncertainty, see Cornes and Sandler 1996. The club argument can also be extended to relationships among sub-units of governments, which can form governmental networks. See Slaughter 2004. There is less analysis of clubs in the study of international environmental cooperation, but on this point see, for example, the study of the Arctic regime by Young and Osherenko 1993. Applied to climate change, see Victor in press.

13. Alter and Meunier 2009.

14. Raustiala and Victor 2004.

15. Victor forthcoming.

16. For an early discussion, see Victor 2001.

17. Lesage, Van de Graaf, and Westphal 2010, 140–143.

18. "The Pittsburgh Summit: Key Accomplishments," http://www.piltsburghsummit.gov/resources/129665.htm (accessed 1 October 2010).

19. For details on the potential reductions from a wide array of Indian policy initiatives, including this one, see Ral and Victor 2009.

20. Velders et al. 2007.

21. See Ramanathan and Carmichael 2008, among many other papers by Ramanathan and colleagues.

22. See, e.g., World Bank 2008 and World Bank Independent Evaluation Group 2009.

23. At time of writing, the California system (see section 96400 in California Air Resources Board 2009) seems more robust. The RGGI is struggling to remain relevant because it has oversupplied emission credits and its auctions now yield extremely low prices.

24. We will focus on the many different international cooperation problems. However, in many other respects "climate change" is not a single problem to be "solved" but a lens through which many scientific, cultural and political disagreements refract. For more on that, see Hulme 2009.

25. We use the term "geoengineering" loosely here. There are many forms, but the type of geoengineering that is most relevant is known as "solar radiation management"—for example, making the atmosphere more reflective to cool the planet quickly. Victor et al. 2009.

26. UNFCCC 2009.

27. Simon 1959.

28. Ibrahim 2009.

29. Clarke et al. 2009.

30. Schneider 2007; Wara and Victor 2008; Wara 2009.

31. Governments that are the largest buyers of CDM credits and thus in the strongest position to reform the system also have the highest compliance costs—for example the EU and Japan. Thus firms in those countries are especially keen to keep a large supply of CDM credits because that is the

only way they can be sure to comply without costs exploding.

32. Petsonk 2009; Wagner et al. 2009; Grubb et al. 2010; Stavins, Jaffe, and Ranson 2009.

33. Petsonk 2009.

34. The Minister for Climate Change and Water of Australia, Penny Wong, made this argument in a speech at New York University, September 21, 2009.

35. E.g., Michalopoulos 2002.

36. Victor 2009.

37. UNFCCC 2009.

38. We are indebted for this point to Liliana Andonova.

39. Grant and Keohane 2005, 29.

40. Franck 1990, 52.

41. Buchanan and Keohane 2006, 424–433.

42. Victor, House, and Joy 2005. Biermann et al. 2009 are more skeptical of non-integrated regimes out of fear that a multiplicity of institutions will create conflicting rules, although they have not looked in-depth at particular rules, nor at the example of emission trading.

43. Raustiala and Victor 2004.

44. WTO-UNEP 2009. See also Hufbauer, Charnovitz, and Kim 2009.

45. Victor, in press, ch. 5.

46. We are mindful that the widespread belief that spending on green technology will yield jobs and economic growth is still to be proven. For a skeptical view, see Kahn 2009. Moreover, while green jobs will surely appear, many of them will occur in the global economy where it is difficult to concentrate in the jurisdictions that are first movers.

47. This list includes the United States, Japan, China, and a few European countries. China is on the list today and is rising rapidly; a decade ago, it was a bit player in innovation.

48. Measuring research and development effort is difficult, and there are no reliable data on the world effort in energy. For total world spending on all forms of research and development, see OECD 2008, which ranks the top spenders at US, Japan. China, Germany, France and the UK. (If the EU is summed as a whole then it ranks second behind the US). On the research and development problem in energy, see Dooley 1998

among others. For a seminal warning about pork in large energy demonstration projects see, Cohen and Noll 1991.

49. See National Research Council 2010.

50. We are indebted to Scott Barrett and Marc Levy for making this point, in different terms, at a seminar at Columbia University, September 29, 2010.

REFERENCES

Aggarwal, V. K., ed. 1998. Institutional Designs for a Complex World: Bargaining, Linkages, and Nesting. Ithaca, NY: Cornell University Press.

Alter, Karen J., and Meunier, Sophie. 2009. "The Politics of International Regime Complexity—Symposium." Perspectives on Politics 7(1): 13–24.

Biermann, Frank, Pattberg, Philipp, van Asselt, Harro, and Zelli, Fariborz. 2009. "The Fragmentation of Global Governance Architectures: A Framework for Analysis." Global Environmental Politics 9(4): 14–40.

Braithwaite, John, and Drahos, Peter. 2000. Global Business Regulation. Cambridge: Cambridge University Press.

Buchanan, Allen, and Keohane, Robert O. 2006. "The Legitimacy of Global Governance Institutions." Ethics and International Affairs 20(4): 405–37.

Busch, Marc L. 2007. "Overlapping Institutions, Forum Shopping, and Dispute Settlement in International Trade." International Organization 61(4): 735–61.

California Air Resources Board. 2009. Preliminary Draft Regulation for a California Cap-and-Trade Program, November 24. www.arb.ca.gov/cc/capandtrade/meetings/121409/pdr.pdf.

Clarke, Leon, Edmonds, Jae, Krey, Volker, Richels, Richard, Rose, Steven, and Tavoni, Massimo. 2009. "International Climate Policy Architectures: Overview of the EMF 22 International Scenarios." Energy Economics 31 (2): S64–81.

Cohen, Linda R., and Noll, Roger. 1991. The Technology Pork Barrel. Washington, DC: Brookings Institution.

Cornes, Richard, and Sandler, Todd. 1996. The Theory of Externalities, Public Goods, and Club Goods. 2d ed. New York: Cambridge University Press.

Dooley, James J. 1998. "Unintended Consequences: Energy R&D in a Deregulated Energy Market." Energy Policy 26(7): 547–55.

Franck, Thomas. 1990. The Power of Legitimacy among Nations. New York: Oxford University Press.

Goldstein, Judith, and Keohane, Robert O., eds. 1993. Ideas and Foreign Policy: Beliefs, Institutions, and Political Change, Ithaca: Cornell University Press.

Grant, Ruth W., and Keohane, Robert O. 2005. "Accountability and Abuses of Power in World Politics." American Political Science Review 99(1): 29–43.

Grubb, Michael, Lalng, Tim, Counsell, Thomas, and Willan, Catherine. 2010. "Global Carbon Mechanisms: Lessons and Implications." Climatic Change, January 16.

Hooghe, Liesbet, and Marks, Gary. 2003. "Unraveling the Central State, but How? Types of Multi-level Governance." American Political Science Review 97(2): 233–43.

Hufbauer, Gary C., Charnovitz, Steve, and Kim, Jisun. 2009. Global Warming and the World Trading System. Washington, DC: Peterson Institute for International Economics.

Hulme, Mike. 2009. Why We Disagree about Climate Change. New York: Cambridge University Press.

Ibrahim, Ibrahim Mirghani. 2009. "Statement on Behalf of the Group of 77 and China by H.E. Ambassador Ibrahim Mirghani Ibrahim, Head of Delegation to the Republic of Sudan, at the Closing Plenary of the Resumed Ninth Session of the Ad Hoc Working Group under the Kyoto Protocol (AWG-KP 9)." November 6, Barcelona, Spain, www.g77.org/statement/2009.html.

Kahler, Miles, and Lake, David A. 2003. Governance in a Global Economy: Political Authority in Transition. Princeton: Princeton University Press.

Kahn, Matthew. 2009. "Think Again: The Green Economy." Foreign Policy (May/June).

Keohane, Robert O. 1984. After Hegemony: Cooperation and Discord in the World Political Economy. Princeton: Princeton University Press.

Keohane, Robert O., and Nye, Joseph S. Jr. 2001 [1977]. Power and Interdependence. 3d ed. New York: Addison Wesley Longman.

Keohane, Robert O., and Nye, Joseph S. Jr. 2001. "The Club Model of Multilateral Cooperation and Problems of Democratic Legitimacy." In Efficiency, Equity, Legitimacy: The Multilateral Trading System at the Millennium, ed. Porter, Roger, Sauvé, Pierre, Subramanian, Arvind, and Zampetti, Americo Beviglia. Washington, DC: Brookings Institution.

Lesage, Dries, Van de Graaf, Thijs, and Westphal, Kersten. 2010. Global Energy Governance in a Multipolar World. Farnham, Surrey (UK): Ashgate Publishing.

Michalopoulos, Constantine. 2002. "WTO Accession." In Development, Trade and the WTO: A Handbook, ed. Hoekman, Bernard M., Maltoo, Aaditya, and English, Philip. Washington, DC: The World Bank.

Michonski, Katherine E., and Levi, Michael A. 2010. The Regime Complex for Global Climate Change. New York: Council on Foreign Relations.

National Research Council. 2010. "America's Climate Choices: Report." In Advancing the Science of Climate Change and Limiting the Magnitude of Future Climate Change. Washington: The National Academies Press.

O'Neill, Barry. 1999. Honor, Symbols, and War. Ann Arbor: University of Michigan Press.

Organization for Economic Cooperation and Development (OECD). 2008. Main Science and Technology Indicators 2008/2. Paris: OECD.

Parson, Edward A. 2003. Protecting the Ozone Layer: Science and Strategy. New York: Oxford University Press.

Petsonk, Annie. 2009. "Docking Stations: Designing a More Open Legal and Policy Architecture for a Post-2012 Framework to Combat Climate Change." Duke Journal of Comparative and International Law 19(3): 433–66.

Pierson, Paul. 2000. "Increasing Returns, Path Dependence, and the Study of Politics." American Political Science Review 94(2): 251–67.

Ral, Varun, and Victor, David G. 2009. "Climate Change and the Energy Challenge: A Pragmatic Approach for India." Economic and Political Weekly 44(31): 78–85.

Ramanathan, V., and Carmichael, G. 2008. "Global and Regional Climate Changes due to Black Carbon." Nature Geoscience 1:221–7.

Raustiala, Kal, and Victor, David. 2004. "The Regime Complex for Plant Genetic Resources." International Organization 58(2): 277–310.

Schneider, Lambert. 2007. "Is the CDM Fulfilling its Environmental and Sustainable Development Objectives? An Evaluation of the CDM and Options for Improvement." Öko-Institut report prepared for the WWF. Berlin: Öko-Institut. www3.oeko.de/oekodoc/622/2007-162-en.pdf.

Simon, Herbert A. 1959. "Theories of Decision-Making in Economics and Behavioral Science." American Economic Review 49(3): 253–83.

Slaughter, Anne-Marie. 2004. A New World Order. Princeton: Princeton University Press.

Stavins, Robert, Jaffe, Judson, and Ranson, Matthew. 2009. "Linking Tradable Permit Systems: A Key Element of Emerging International Climate Policy Architecture." Ecology Law Quarterly 36(4): 789–808.

United Nations Framework Convention on Climate Change (UNFCCC). 2009. "Decision 2/CP.15: Copenhagen Accord." Report of the Conference of the Parties on its Fifteenth Session, Copenhagen, December 7–19. FCCC/CP/2009/11/Add.1. http://unfccc.int/resource/docs/2009/cop15/eng/11a01.pdf.

Velders, Guus J.M., Andersen, Stephen O., Daniel, John S., Fahey, David W., and McFarland, Mack. 2007. "The Importance of the Montreal Protocol in Protecting Climate." Proceedings of the National Academy of Sciences 104(12): 4814–19.

Victor, David G. 2001. Collapse of the Kyoto Protocol and the Struggle to Slow Global Warming. Princeton: Princeton University Press.

Victor, David G. 2009. "Plan B for Copenhagen." Nature 461(7262): 342–4.

Victor, David G. in press. Global Warming Gridlock: Creating More Effective Strategies for Protecting the Planet. Cambridge: Cambridge University Press.

Victor, David G., House, Joshua C., and Joy, Sarah. 2005. "A Madisonian Approach to Climate Policy." Science 309(5742): 1820–1.

Victor, David G., Morgan, M. Granger, Apt, Jay, Steinbruner, John, and Ricke, Katherine. 2009. "The Geoengineering Option: A Last Resort Against Global Warming?" Foreign Affairs 88(2): 64–76.

Wagner, Gernot, Keohane, Nathaniel, Petsonk, Annie, and Wang, James. 2009. "Docking into a Global Carbon Market: Clean Investment Budgets to Finance Low-Carbon Economic Development." In The Economics and Politics of Climate Change, ed. Helm, Dieter and Hepburn, Cameron. New York: Oxford University Press.

Wara, Michael. 2009. "Methods of Cost Containment in a Greenhouse Gas Emissions Trading Program." Testimony to U.S. Senate Committee on Energy and Natural Resources, September 15. http://energy.senate.gov/public/_files/WaraTestimony091509.pdf.

Wara, Michael W., and Victor, David G. 2008. A Realistic Policy on International Carbon Offsets. Working Paper 74. Stanford: Program on Energy and Sustainable Development, Stanford University.

World Bank. 2008. Development and Climate Change: A Strategic Framework for the World Bank Group. Washington, DC: The World Bank.

World Bank Independent Evaluation Group. 2009. Climate Change and the World Bank Group. Phase I: An Evaluation of World Bank Win-Win Energy Policy Reforms. Washington, DC: The World Bank.

World Trade Organization and United Nations Environmental Program. 2009. Trade and Climate Change: WTO-UNEP Report. Geneva: WTO.

Young, Oran R. 1997. Global Governance: Drawing Insights from the Environmental Experience. Cambridge, MA: MIT Press.

Young, Oran R., and Osherenko, Gail, eds. 1993. Polar Politics: Creating International Environmental Regimes. Ithaca, NY: Cornell University Press.

Thomas J. Bollyky

DEVELOPING SYMPTOMS
Noncommunicable Diseases Go Global

When most people in developed countries think of the biggest health challenges confronting the developing world, they envision a small boy in a rural, dusty village beset by an exotic parasite or bacterial blight. But increasingly, that image is wrong. Instead, it is the working-age woman living in an urban slum, suffering from diabetes, cervical cancer, or stroke—noncommunicable diseases (NCDS) that once confronted wealthy nations alone.

NCDS in developing countries are occurring more rapidly, arising in younger people, and leading to far worse health outcomes than ever seen in developed countries. This epidemic results from persistent poverty, unprecedented urbanization, and freer trade in emerging-market nations, which have not yet established the health and regulatory systems needed to treat and prevent NCDS. According to the World Economic Forum's 2010 Global Risks report, these diseases pose a greater threat to global economic development than fiscal crises, natural disasters, corruption, or infectious disease.

The international community has done little to help. Most donors remain focused on the battle against infectious diseases, reluctant to divert their funds. A recent UN General Assembly meeting devoted to NCDS produced few concrete measures. With the global economy still in decline and funding scarce, the chances of new effective cooperation seem smaller than ever.

Collective action on NCDS need not wait for UN endorsement, economic recovery, or a reallocation of money away from campaigns against

infectious diseases. The international community can make progress now by addressing those NCDS that are especially prevalent among poor people in developing countries and by helping their governments combat those diseases. For this effort to succeed, the United States must lead the way. In doing so, it can help curtail avoidable sickness and death and set the precedent for action on other emerging global health challenges that share the same origins and devastating consequences for the world's poor as the NCD crisis.

The Disease Divide

The NCD problem in developing countries is far worse than it has ever been in the developed world. NCDS in emerging-market nations are arising in young working-age populations at higher rates and with more detrimental outcomes than in wealthy states. According to the World Health Organization (WHO), 80 percent of deaths from NCDS now occur in low- and middle-income countries, up from 40 percent in 1990. People with NCDS in middle-income countries are more than twice as likely to die before age 60 as those in high-income nations, and people in low-income countries are four times as likely to do so.

NCDS that are preventable or treatable in developed countries are often death sentences in the developing world. Whereas cervical cancer can largely be prevented in developed countries thanks to the human papillomavirus vaccine, in sub-Saharan Africa and South Asia, it is the leading cause of death from cancer among women.

m Foreign Affairs 91, no. 3 (May/June 2012), 134–144.

The mortality rate in China from stroke is four to six times as high as in France, Japan, or the United States. Ninety percent of children with leukemia in high-income countries can be cured, but 90 percent of those with that disease in the world's 25 poorest countries die from it. By 2030, NCDS will be the leading cause of death and disability in every region of the world.

The rise of NCDS has devastating social and economic consequences for developing countries. The frequent onset of these diseases among younger populations consumes scarce health-care resources, saps labor from the work force and hinders economic development, and makes it harder for governments to address other threats, such as infectious diseases. On the household level, NCDS consume budgets and rob families of their primary wage earners. A recent report by Harvard University and the World Economic Forum projects that over the next two decades, NCDS will inflict $14 trillion in economic losses on the developing world.

Living Dangerously

The reasons for the exploding NCD crisis in developing countries begin, paradoxically, with increased life expectancy. The greater availability of effective medical technologies, such as vaccines, and the improved diffusion of good public health practices, such as hand washing and breastfeeding, has sharply lowered child mortality across the globe. The vast majority of the world's newborns are now immunized against diseases such as measles, polio, and yellow fever, and the widespread use of oral rehydration salts has made cholera deaths increasingly rare. According to the World Bank, infant mortality decreased by half between 1960 and 2005 in 80 percent of the countries for which there are data, and global average life expectancy increased from 31 years in 1900 to almost 67 years by 2009.

Extending lives is, of course, a good thing. But the problem is that although life expectancies for the poor have increased in low- and middle-income countries, they have done so without the gains in personal wealth and better health systems that accompanied the rise in longevity in most developed countries. With the significant exception of China, the poor have not benefited from the recent economic growth in developing countries. Since 1981, the number of people worldwide living on less than $1.25 per day—1.1 billion—has remained roughly the same, and more than two-thirds of those people now live in middle-income countries. Meanwhile, health-care spending, although slowly expanding in Latin America, the Middle East, and parts of Asia, remains incredibly low; the state of Connecticut allocates more to it than the 38 low-income countries in sub-Saharan Africa combined. With such little public support, the poor in developing nations often cannot afford preventive or chronic care, increasing the odds of disability and death from diabetes, cancer, and other NCDS that people contract after their adolescent years.

The nearly nonexistent regulation of tobacco, alcohol, and processed food products in many developing countries compounds the challenges of rampant poverty and inadequate health care by increasing the likelihood that poor people will develop NCDS. These nations fear that increased taxes on unhealthy products will damage their economies and lead to public discontent. Regulators face strident opposition from tobacco, food, and beverage producers, which are sometimes partly or fully owned by the government in question. In many developing countries, patient-advocacy groups hardly exist. Civil litigation, which played a critical role in improving tobacco control and education in the United States, is far less common and successful in the developing world. And inadequate labeling and regulation of ingredients hurt the poor most, since they have neither the opportunity to educate themselves about health risks nor the money to buy healthier food.

Meanwhile, freer trade and the increased global integration of tobacco, food, and beverage markets are overwhelming the little public health infrastructure that does exist in many developing countries. With stagnating sales in high-income nations, multinational companies now target low- and middle-income countries, launching sophisticated advertising campaigns to drive growth. Tobacco companies, in particular, use billboards, cartoon characters, music sponsorships, and other methods now prohibited in most of the developed world to entice women, who used to be less likely to smoke than men. These tactics have raised tobacco sales across Asia, eastern Europe, and Latin America and are expected to do so in Africa. In more than 60 percent of the countries surveyed in a 2008 study by the WHO and the U.S. Centers for Disease Control and Prevention, girls now smoke just as often as boys.

Unprecedented rates of urbanization in developing countries have exacerbated these challenges. In 1950, over 70 percent of the world's population lived in towns and villages; by 2008, a majority had moved to cities. Most of this urbanization has occurred in emerging-market nations, where cities have little public health infrastructure. The result has been slums—90 percent of which are in developing countries and which house nearly one billion people. The inhabitants of these densely packed areas, faced with pollution outdoors and the burning of fuels indoors, are more susceptible to cardiovascular and respiratory diseases. Slum dwellers are more likely to buy tobacco products and cheap processed foods and less likely to have access to adequate nutrition or public health education.

The Right Prescription

Despite the enormity of the NCD epidemic devastating the poor in developing countries. It is possible to slow and reverse it. The measures necessary to prevent NCDS in healthy people are well known, and affordable medicines exist for improving care for those already living with these diseases. Treatments for NCDS, such as insulin and asthma inhalers, are no longer under patent and would do much to reduce avoidable disability and death if made more widely available. The World Bank estimates that developing countries could lower their projected rates of disability and death from NCDS by half by raising taxes on and restricting the marketing of tobacco and alcohol, reducing salt and trans fats in foods, and using beta-blockers, aspirin, and other low-cost interventions to control hypertension.

The international community can help developing countries build the capacity necessary to implement these policies. To begin with, the WHO and its member countries should attempt to reach a firm consensus on the prevention and treatment strategies needed to address the NCDS particularly striking the poor in developing nations. Next, based on those strategies, they should design a practical package of programs that emerging-market countries can implement even in low-infrastructure settings. This might involve, for instance, determining the minimum level of taxes and the scope of marketing restrictions needed to diminish unhealthy alcohol consumption. Experienced health and tax officials from the developed world should then work with their counterparts in the developing world to build their capacity to carry out these protocols.

Modest levels of aid from philanthropic foundations, donor governments, and multilateral development banks would enable low-income countries to pilot and launch these efforts. Developed countries should establish a program to monitor these NCD control measures, publishing the results to hold governments accountable for their implementation.

Collectively Stalled

The international community has long known of the NCD crisis plaguing the developing world. The WHO first called attention to the problem in 1996, when it issued a landmark report that contradicted long-standing views of NCDS as diseases of affluence, reporting that they would soon dwarf the burden of infectious diseases in developing countries and pose severe challenges to their health-care systems. Over the next decade, the WHO concluded an international treaty on tobacco control, produced numerous strategy papers on NCD prevention and treatment, and launched a department dedicated to addressing NCDS on a global level.

Yet despite these efforts, the WHO attracted little international support for action against NCDS. Global health donors and institutions remained preoccupied with containing infectious diseases and improving maternal and child health. According to a 2010 report by the Center for Global Development, between 2004 and 2008, 70 percent of total funding for NCDS came from just three sources, by far the largest of which was the WHO itself. That same report found that in 2007, programs devoted to NCDS received less than three percent of the nearly $22 billion spent on global health.

To place NCDS firmly on the international agenda, a group of concerned countries and nongovernmental organizations (NGOS) successfully lobbied to hold a high-level meeting on NCDS at the UN General Assembly in September 2011. Organizers agreed that the meeting would address the challenges of NCDS worldwide but focus on cancer, diabetes, cardiovascular disease, and respiratory Illnesses, in part because those diseases share four major risk factors: tobacco use, alcohol use, physical inactivity, and an unhealthy diet. The WHO produced a set of strategies to reduce these factors, estimating that it would cost approximately $11.4 billion per year to fund them in developing countries. Expectations for the meeting were high. The only other UN General Assembly meetings on health have concerned HIV/AIDS, and they helped motivate donors to spend billions of dollars on lifesaving drugs for the developing world.

Yet optimism faded before the meeting had even begun. NGOS fought over the lack of focus on other major NCDS, such as mental illnesses. The donors that have dominated the international responses to infectious diseases, such as the Bill and Melinda Gates Foundation, argued that the meeting could distract from existing global health initiatives and divert their funding. Advance negotiations among UN member countries became bogged down in disagreements over whether to agree to NCD reduction targets and mandatory measures to contain these diseases worldwide; the tobacco, food, beverage, and pharmaceutical industries lobbied heavily against such regulations. And although 130 countries, 30 heads of state, and hundreds of NGOS came to advocate for action on a bewildering array of diseases, when the conference opened, the streets outside the UN were empty of the masses of supporters and patients that had characterized the UN high-level meetings on HIV/AIDS.

The commitments that emerged from the meeting were largely rhetorical. The resulting political declaration recognized the "epidemic proportions" of NCDS and noted that countries can prevent them with cost-efficient public health measures, but it did not mandate specific methods nor even argue for their adoption. It endorsed private-sector partnerships and the sharing of technical assistance between developed and developing countries, but it failed to designate anyone to organize or fund such initiatives. The most concrete action mandated was to shift the responsibility for NCDS back to the WHO, charging it with generating voluntary disease- and risk-reduction targets, since nations could not agree on mandatory policies, and asking UN members to "consider" these targets in developing their national NCD plans. The WHO recently announced that it would probably not be able to get its 194 member countries to agree on these voluntary targets until at least May 2013.

In the end, the UN meeting helped mobilize the NGO community and broaden public recognition of the human and economic loll of NCDS worldwide. Several governments, of their own volition, introduced new regulations on trans fats and dietary salt. Numerous corporations, such as PepsiCo, announced that they would launch voluntary initiatives to make their products healthier and donate funds to improve the treatment of NCDS. Even so, frustrated supporters demanded a more comprehensive meeting to address the social and economic causes of NCDS worldwide. Critics cited these modest results as proof that amid the global financial troubles and corporate lobbying, collective action on NCDS is impossible.

All at Once and None at All

Yet the notion that a weak global economy and a conspiracy of industrial lobbyists prevented progress at the UN meeting is wrong. As currently pursued, international efforts on NCDS would also fail to generate support in a good economy—as they have since the WHO first reported the emerging epidemic of NCDS. The effectiveness of corporate lobbying at the UN meeting was a symptom of poorly conceived collective action on NCDS, not its cause.

Collective efforts against NCDS have failed because of the disparate nature of these diseases and the decision to try to address them on a global level. In addition to cancer, diabetes, cardiovascular disease, and respiratory illnesses, NCDS include a wide array of conditions, such as skin diseases, congenital anomalies, mental disorders, rheumatoid arthritis, and dental decay. These diseases are not all chronic, related to unhealthy habits, or even noncommunicable. As a class, NCDS have little in common other than being the diseases that become more prevalent as a population reduces the plagues and parasites that kill children and adolescents. NCDS are, in short, the diseases of those with longer lives.

Trying to address these diseases as a single class and on a global level has both broadened opposition and diffused support for effective action. On one hand, addressing NCDS as a single category has united a wide array of otherwise disconnected industries, from agriculture to pharmaceutical companies and restaurants, against global targets to reduce NCDS and their risk factors. On the other hand, it has made it difficult to mobilize states and sufferers of NCDS worldwide around a specific and meaningful policy agenda. And when NCDS are presented as imposing the same challenges in developed and developing countries alike, policymakers and potential donors are apt to conclude that they cannot be solved by international action and are simply the natural consequence of economic development.

To move forward, the international community should focus on the NCDS and risk factors especially prevalent among the developing-country poor and on the particular needs of their governments to address them. This targeted approach would build stronger international support for concrete action while minimizing the number of potential opponents.

Tobacco offers a good place to start. According to the WHO, tobacco use already kills more people annually than HIV/AIDS, tuberculosis, and malaria combined. In the coming decades, it is projected to debilitate and kill hundreds of millions more, largely in low- and middle-income countries. Tobacco use is the only leading risk factor common to all the major groups of NCDS: cancer, diabetes, cardiovascular illness, and respiratory dysfunction. By increasing support for tobacco control in developing countries, the international community could help reduce one of the most significant threats to global health today.

Fortunately, a platform for combating tobacco use already exists: the WHO Framework Convention on Tobacco Control (FCTC), a binding treaty with 173 member states that mandates taxes, advertising, and other measures to lower demand for tobacco products. The WHO, in partnership with Bloomberg Philanthropies, developed a package of evidence-based strategies, called MPOWER, to turn the broad mandates of the FCTC into practical programs that developing-country governments can implement. Together with the Centers for Disease Control and Prevention, the WHO tracks global tobacco use and the implementation of the FCTC and publishes the results. The Campaign for Tobacco-Free Kids works with local media and civil society to hold governments accountable for enforcing the recommendations put forth by MPOWER.

These programs are making progress, but they are limited by a lack of funding and technical capacity within developing countries, as well as fierce industry opposition. Outside the handful of developing countries that receive support from Bloomberg Philanthropies and the Gates Foundation, tobacco control in developing countries remains woefully underfunded. A low-cost way to extend anti-tobacco programs to other developing countries is for the international community to integrate these programs into existing global health initiatives on tuberculosis and maternal and child health. Countries with experience in regulating and taxing tobacco, such as the United States, should help build those capacities in developing countries. Developed countries must also stop trying to reduce tobacco tariffs and protect tobacco-related investments in their trade agreements with low-income nations. With these measures, developed countries can support the world's poorest countries in their efforts to make sustainable progress against tobacco use.

Meanwhile, international initiatives to reduce the intake of alcohol, trans fats, and salt should focus for the time being on existing programs and partnerships with suppliers and retailers designed to make their beverages and food healthier. These voluntary measures may not replace the need for taxes and regulations in these areas, but they could promote progress until the capacity and popular support for such programs grow. When that time comes, the improvements made in country-level regulatory and taxation systems for tobacco control could be extended to address alcohol, trans fats, salt, and other NCD risk factors. Integrating the monitoring of alcohol and unhealthy food consumption into the existing international tobacco-surveillance system would also offer a cost-effective means of collecting evidence on the implementation of the initiatives in these areas.

Yet prevention measures alone cannot solve the NCD problem. Expanding existing international vaccine-procurement mechanisms to include essential medicines for NCDS would help developing countries obtain the supplies necessary to meet the needs of their citizens. More donor support is required for product-development partnerships, such as the international organization PATH, which is working to adapt existing medical technologies for NCDS for use by low-income countries.

Finally, the international community should not forget the poorest countries, where the consumption of unhealthy products is low and tobacco-prevention programs would offer only limited benefits to those suffering from cancer, diabetes, and other NCDS. International NCD efforts should aid these countries by supporting the expansion of existing treatment programs, such as those established in Africa by the U.S. President's Emergency Plan for AIDS Relief and Partners in Health, to encompass the treatment of NCDS.

From Village to Slum

Global health needs are changing. The NCD crisis in developing countries represents one part of a set of growing health challenges, from food safety and environmental pollution to road safely and substandard medicines, now replacing infectious diseases as the major causes of premature disability and death worldwide. These other challenges share similar origins as NCDS—freer trade, unprecedented urbanization, and limited local government capacity—and likewise have devastating consequences for the world's poor.

Whether targeting NCDS one by one or approaching them comprehensively, the international community will depend on the United States to lead. To make progress, Washington will need to demonstrate a sustained commitment to reducing the avoidable disability and deaths that result from persistent poverty and unequal access to effective prevention and treatment programs. The same commitment motivated U.S. initiatives on infectious diseases and maternal and child health, and should do so again with regard to NCDS. U.S. engagement can help catalyze international action not only against the current wave of diseases sweeping across developing countries but also against these other emerging health problems.

Washington has dedicated past global health initiatives to delivering food, drugs, and other health technologies to the world's poor. In doing so, it has been able to achieve progress even in countries with dysfunctional governments. But it cannot enforce the regulations on smoke-free public places, food and drug safety, urban sanitation, and road traffic that are now needed in such settings. Accordingly, the fundamental challenge in this new era of global health is not necessarily new medicine but better governance.

To meet this challenge, the United States will need to recalibrate its approach to global health. The Centers for Disease Control and Prevention, the U.S. Food and Drug Administration, and other U.S. regulatory and technical agencies must have more resources and a greater mandate to support the efforts of their developing-country counterparts. The contributions of U.S. diplomatic and aid agencies, such as the State Department and the U.S. Agency for International Development, will remain important, but they will be limited to funding pilot programs and creating the international consensus that can give the governments of emerging-market nations courage in the face of industry opposition. Closer collaboration between U.S. trade and regulatory officials on international standards could make it easier for developing countries to adopt strict tobacco, food, and drug regulations that would facilitate both commerce and public health. The United States should coordinate its efforts with the WHO and regional entitles such as the Pan American Health Organization, which convene states with similar cultures, economic circumstances, and demographic challenges. With these low-cost measures, the United States can extend the same lifesaving support that it has provided to the little boy in a rural, dusty village to the working-age woman living in an urban slum.

CREDITS

Bollyky, Thomas J.: "Developing Symptoms: Non-communicable Diseases Go Global," from *Foreign Affairs* (May/June 2012), Volume 91, Issue 3, pp. 134–144. Reprinted by permission of *Foreign Affairs*. Copyright © 2012 by the Council on Foreign Relations, Inc.

Clausewitz, Carl von.: "War as an Instrument of Policy," from ON WAR (Routledge 1962; Penguin 1968) p. 402–410. © 1968 Penguin Group. Reprinted by permission.

Donnelly, Jack: "Chapter 6: Human Rights and Cultural Relativism," from Universal Human Rights in Theory and Practice, 2nd edition. Copyright © 2002 by Cornell University. Used by permission of the publisher, Cornell University Press.

Doyle, Michael W.: "Liberalism and World Politics," from *American Political Science Review*, Vol. 80, no. 4 (Dec. 1986): 1151–1169. Copyright © 1986 by American Political Science Association. Reprinted with the permission of Cambridge University Press.

Drezner, Daniel W.: "The Irony of Global Economic Governance: The System Worked," from the Council on Foreign Relations' International Institutions and Global Governance Program. Copyright © 2012 by the Council of Foreign Relations Press. Reprinted with permission.

Escribà-Folch, Abel and Joseph Wright: "Dealing with Tyranny: International Sanctions and the Survival of Authoritarian Rulers," from *International Studies Quarterly*, June 2010, Volume 54, Issue 2, pp. 335–359. Reprinted with permission.

Fearon, James D.: "Rationalist Explanations for War," *International Organization*, 49:3 (Summer, 1995), pp. 379–414. © 1995 by the IO Foundation and the Massachusetts Institute of Technology. Reprinted by permission.

Finnemore, Martha: From THE PURPOSE OF INTERVENTION: CHANGING BELIEFS ABOUT THE USE OF FORCE. Chapter 3: "Changing Norms of Humanitarian Intervention," 2003. pp. 52–84. Reprinted by permission of Columbia University Press. "Legitimacy, Hypocrisy, and the Social Structure of Unipolarity: Why Being a Unipole Isn't All It's Cracked Up to Be" from *World Politics* (January 2009) Pages 58–85 (Volume 61, Issue 1), pp. 58–85. Reprinted with permission.

Fortna, Virginia Page: From DOES PEACEING WORK? SHAPING BELLIGERENTS' CHOICES AFTER CIVIL WAR (Princeton: Princeton Univ. Press, 2008), pp. 1–4, 172–179. Reprinted by permission of Princeton University Press.

Fukuyama, Francis: "The Future of History," *Foreign Affairs*, Vol. 91, No. 1, Jan/Feb. 2012, pp. 53–61. Reprinted by permission of *Foreign Affairs* Copyright © 2012 by the Council on Foreign Relations, Inc.

Gartzke, Erik: "Capitalist Peace or Democratic Peace," from *Institute of Public Affairs Review*, Volume 57, Issue 4, pp. 13–16. Reprinted with permission of the Institute of Public Affairs.

Gilpin, Robert: "The Nature of Political Economy," from U.S. POWER AND THE MULTINATIONAL CORPORATION: THE POLITICAL ECONOMY OF FOREIGN DIRECT INVESTMENT, pp. 20–33. Copyright © 1975 by Basic Books, Inc. Reprinted by permission of Basic Books, a member of Perseus Books Group.

Gruber, Lloyd: "Globalisation with Growth and Equity: Can We Really Have it All?" from *Third World Quarterly* (2011), Volume 32, No. 4, pp. 629–652. Reprinted with permission.

Hall, Todd H.: "We Will Not Swallow This Bitter Fruit: Theorizing a Diplomacy of Anger," from *Security Studies*, Oct. – Dec. 2011, Volume 20, Issue 4, pp. 521–555. Reprinted with permission.

Hafner-Burton, Emilie E. and Kiyoteru Tsutsui: "Justice Lost! The Failure of International Human Rights Law to Matter Where Needed Most," from *Journal of Peace Research* (July 2007), Volume 44, No. 4, pp. 407–425. Reprinted by permission of Sage Publications UK.

Hardin, Garrett: From "The Tragedy of the Commons," *Science* 162 (Dec, 13, 1968), 1243–1248. Reprinted with permission from AAAS.

Huntington, Samuel: "The Clash of Civilization." Reprinted by permission of *Foreign Affairs* (Summer 1993). Copyright © 1993 by the Council on Foreign Relations, Inc.

Hurd, Ian: "Is Humanitarian Intervention Legal? The Rule of Law in an Incoherent World," from *Ethics and International Affairs*, Fall 2011, Volume 25, Issue 3, pp. 293–313. Reprinted with permission.

Ikenberry, G. John, Michael Mastanduno, William C. Wohlforth: "Unipolarity, State Behavior and Systemic Consequences." From *World Politics* 61, no. 1 (Jan. 2009): 1–27. Reprinted by permission of Cambridge University Press.

Jervis, Robert. "Hypotheses on Misperception." From *World Politics* 20, no. 3 (April 1968): 454–479. Reprinted by permission of Cambridge University Press. "Cooperation under the Security Dilemma." From *World Politics* 30, no. 2 (Jan. 1978): 167–214. Copyright © 1978. Reprinted by permission of Cambridge University Press.

Keck, Margaret E. and Sikkink, Kathryn: "Transnational Advocacy Networks in International Politics." From ACTIVISTS BEYOND BORDERS: ADVOCACY NETWORKS IN INTERNATIONAL POLITICS, pp. 1–3, 9–11, 16–18, 25–26, 32–34, 104–110, 119–120. Copyright © 1998 by Cornell University. Used by permission of the publisher, Cornell University Press.

Kennan, George: "The Sources of Soviet Conduct." Reprinted by permission of *Foreign Affairs* (July 1947). Copyright © 1947 by the Council on Foreign Relations, Inc.

Keohane, Robert O.: From AFTER HEGEMONY: COOPERATION AND DISCORD IN THE WORLD POLITICAL ECONOMY (Princeton: Princeton Univ. Press, 1984), pp. 7–10, 85–98, 111–16. Reprinted by permission of Princeton University Press. "The Regime Complex for Climate Change," by Robert O. Keohane and David G. Victor from *Perspectives on Politics* (March 2011), Volume 9, Issue 1, pp. 7–23. Reprinted by permission of Cambridge University Press.

Krasner, Stephen D.: "Sharing Sovereignty: New Institutions for Collapsed and Failing States", *International Security*, 29:2 (Fall, 2004), pp. 85–120. © 2004 by the President and Fellows of Harvard College and the Massachusetts Institute of Technology. Reprinted by permission.

Kydd, Andrew and Barbara Walter.: "The Strategies of Terrorism," *International Security*, 31:1 (Summer, 2006), pp. 49–80. © 2006 by the President and Fellows of Harvard College and the Massachusetts Institute of Technology. Reprinted by permission.

Margalit, Yotam: "Lost in Globalization: International Economic Integration and the Sources of Popular Discontent," from *International Studies Quarterly* (September 2012), Volume 56, Issue 3, pp. 484–500. Reprinted with permission.

Mearsheimer, John: "Anarchy and the Struggle for Power," from TRAGEDY OF GREAT POWER POLITICS by John Mearsheimer. Copyright © 2001 by John J. Mearsheimer. Used by permission of W.W. Norton & Company, Inc. "The False Promise of International Institutions", *International Security*, 19:3 (Winter, 1994), pp. 5–49. © 1995 by the President and Fellows of Harvard College and the Massachusetts Institute of Technology. Reprinted by permission.